Lecture Notes in Artificial Intelligence 2557

Subseries of Lecture Notes in Computer Science
Edited by J. G. Carbonell and J. Siekmann

Lecture Notes in Computer Science

Edited by G. Goos, J. Hartmanis, and J. van Leeuwen

Springer

Berlin
Heidelberg
New York
Barcelona
Hong Kong
London
Milan
Paris
Tokyo

Bob McKay   John Slaney (Eds.)

AI 2002: Advances in Artificial Intelligence

15th Australian Joint Conference on Artificial Intelligence
Canberra, Australia, December 2-6, 2002
Proceedings

 Springer

Series Editors

Jaime G. Carbonell, Carnegie Mellon University, Pittsburgh, PA, USA
Jörg Siekmann, University of Saarland, Saarbrücken, Germany

Volume Editors

Bob McKay
University of New South Wales
Australian Defence Force Academy
Canberra ACT 2600, Australia
E-mail: rim@cs.adfa.edu.au

John Slaney
Australian National University
Computer Science Laboratory, RSISE Building
Canberra ACT 0200, Australia
E-mail: jks@discus.anu.edu.au

Cataloging-in-Publication Data applied for

A catalog record for this book is available from the Library of Congress.

Bibliographic information published by Die Deutsche Bibliothek
Die Deutsche Bibliothek lists this publication in the Deutsche Nationalbibliografie;
detailed bibliographic data is available in the Internet at <http://dnb.ddb.de>.

CR Subject Classification (1998): I.2, F.1, F.4.1, H.3, H.2.8

ISSN 0302-9743
ISBN 3-540-00197-2 Springer-Verlag Berlin Heidelberg New York

Springer-Verlag Berlin Heidelberg New York
a member of BertelsmannSpringer Science+Business Media GmbH

http://www.springer.de

© Springer-Verlag Berlin Heidelberg 2002
Printed in Germany

Typesetting: Camera-ready by author, data conversion by PTP-Berlin, Stefan Sossna e.K.
Printed on acid-free paper   SPIN: 10871770   06/3142   5 4 3 2 1 0

Preface

AI 2002 is the 15th in the series of annual conferences on artificial intelligence held in Australia. This conference is the major forum for the presentation of artificial intelligence research in Australia, encompassing all aspects of that broad field. It has traditionally attracted significant international participation, as was again the case in 2002.

The current volume is based on the proceedings of AI 2002. Full length versions of all submitted papers were refereed by an international program committee, each paper receiving at least two independent reviews. As a result, 62 papers were selected for oral presentation in the conference, and 12 more for poster presentation, out of 117 submissions. One-page abstracts of the posters are published in this volume, along with the full papers selected for oral presentation.

In addition to the scientific track represented here, the conference featured a program of tutorials and workshops, and plenary talks by five invited speakers: Peter van Beek (University of Waterloo, Canada), Eric Bonabeau (Icosystem Corporation, USA), Ming Li (University of California at Santa Barbara), Bernhard Nebel (Albert-Ludwigs-Universität Freiburg, Germany) and Zoltan Somogyi (University of Melbourne, Australia). It was colocated with a number of related events: an AI Applications Symposium, the 6th Australia-Japan Joint Workshop on Intelligent and Evolutionary Systems, the Australasian Workshop on Computational Logic (AWCL), and the annual conference of the Australasian Association for Logic (AAL).

AI 2002 was presented by the Australian National University, the University of Canberra, and the University of New South Wales through the Australian Defence Force Academy. In addition to those institutions, we wish to thank the many people whose contribution made the conference possible, starting with the Program Committee and panel of reviewers who produced over 200 reviews of papers under time constraints. We also wish to thank our colleagues on the Conference Committee chaired by John Lloyd, and especially the Organizing Chair, Hussein Abbass.

Finally, this work is partially sponsored by the Department of the Navy Grant N62649-02-1-0009 issued by US FISC YOKOSUKA. The United States Government has a royalty-free license throughout the world in all copyrightable material contained herein.

December 2002

Robert I. McKay
John Slaney

Conference Officials

Committee Chairs

General Chair	John Lloyd (Australian National University)
Advisory Co-chairs	Charles Newton (University of New South Wales) and Michael Wagner (University of Canberra)
Organizing Chair	Hussein Abbass (University of New South Wales)
Technical Co-chairs	Bob McKay (University of New South Wales) and John Slaney (ANU)
AI Symposium Chair	Eric Tsui (CSC, Computer Sciences Corporation, Australia)
Special Events and Workshops Chair	Ruhul Sarker (University of New South Wales)
Tutorials Chair	Masoud Mohammadian (UC)
Publicity Chair	Rohan Baxter (CSIRO, Commonwealth Scientific & Industrial Research Organization)
Sponsorship Chair	Daryl Essam (University of New South Wales)

Program Committee

Hussein Abbass: Australian Defence Force Academy
Leila Alem: CSIRO
Mark Bedau: Reed University, USA
Alan Blair: University of Melbourne
Michael Brooks: University of Adelaide
Rod Brooks: Massachusetts Institute of Technology, USA
Robert Dale: Macquarie University
Paul Darwen: University of Queensland
Tom Gedeon: Murdoch University
John Gero: University of Sydney
David Green: Charles Sturt University
Jong-Hwan Kim: Korea Advanced Institute of Science and Technology
Van Le: University of Canberra
John Lloyd: Australian National University
Kim Marriott: Monash University
Bob McKay: Australian Defence Force Academy
Masoud Mohammadian: University of Canberra
Ann Nicholson: Monash University
Mehmet Orgun: Macquarie University
Morri Pagnucco: University of New South Wales

Marcus Randall: Bond University
Ruhul Sarker: Australian Defence Force Academy
Ken Satoh: National Institute of Informatics, Japan
Abdul Sattar: Griffith University
Joaquin Sitte: Queensland University of Technology
John Slaney: Australian National University
Sylvie Thiébaux: Australian National University
Paolo Traverso: IRST, Trento, Italy
Eric Tsui: CSC
Michael Wagner: University of Canberra
Toby Walsh: University College Cork, Ireland
Geoff Webb: Deakin University
Graham Williams: CSIRO
Maryanne Williams: Newcastle University
Alex Zelinsky: Australian National University
Chengqi Zhang: Deakin University
Ingrid Zukerman: Monash University

Other Referees

David Albrecht
Paolo Avesani
Stuart Bain
Michael Barlow
Marco Benedetti
Piergiorgio Bertoli
Lawrie Brown
Antonio Cerone
Samir Chopra
Frantz Clermont
Philippe Codognet
Enrico Giunchiglia
Guido Governatori

Victor Jauregui
Charles Kemp
Robert Kowalski
Padmanabhan Krishnan
Rex Kwok
Yuefeng Li
Chunsheng Li
Lee Mansfield
Bernd Meyer
Naoyuki Nide
Vineet Padmanabhan
Andrew Paplinski
Torsten Seemann

Luciano Serafini
Steve Sugden
John Thornton
Satoshi Tojo
Rodney Topor
Biao Wang
Yingying Wen
Akihiro Yamamoto
Ying Yang
Xin Yao
Shichao Zhang
Zili Zhang

Table of Contents

Agents

Intelligent Systems

Bayesian Reasoning and Classification

Evolutionary Algorithms

Neural Networks I

Reinforcement Learning

Constraints and Scheduling

Neural Net Applications I

Learning Theory II

Satisfiability Reasoning

Neural Net Applications II

Machine Learning Applications

Fuzzy Reasoning

Neural Networks II and CBR

Abstracts of Posters

A Controlled Language to Assist Conversion of Use Case Descriptions into Concept Lattices

Debbie Richards, Kathrin Boettger, and Oscar Aguilera

Department of Computing,
Centre for Language Technology,
Division of Information and Communication Sciences,
Macquarie University, Sydney, Australia
{richards}@ics.mq.edu.au

Abstract. System requirements are often incomplete and riddled with contradictions leading to failed projects. Formal methods have been offered to minimise these problems. However the use of such techniques requires highly trained specialists and results in a process that users have little involvement with. We have developed a *viewpoint development* approach, known as RECOCASE, to capture requirements from multiple viewpoints directly from the users which are automatically modelled to identify and reconcile differences between stakeholder requirements. The requirements are captured as use case descriptions in natural language according to current popular practice in object-oriented system development. We use LinkGrammar on the use case sentences to output flat logical forms which we translate into crosstables and generate concept lattices using Formal Concept Analysis. To improve the output of our natural language process we have designed a controlled language to constrain the grammar and style. In this paper we introduce our natural language approach and describe and justify a controlled language we have developed to assist natural language translation.

1 Introducing the Viewpoint Development Approach

System requirements are often incomplete and riddled with contradictions leading to failed projects. Formal methods have been offered to minimise these problems, however the use of such techniques requires highly trained specialists and results in a process that users have little involvement with. We have developed a *viewpoint development* approach, known as RECOCASE, to capture and RECOncile requirements from multiple viewpoints directly from the users. The key distinguishing feature of our approach is the use of *concept lattices* to assist the identification and reconciliation of requirements from multiple viewpoints. In our approach the requirements are captured as use case descriptions (Jacobson 1992) in natural language according to current popular practice in object-oriented system development. Formal concept analysis (FCA) provides a way of discovering, organising and visualising concepts from data. The use of an extensional and intensional definition of concepts offered by FCA is seen to be particularly

R.I. McKay and J. Slaney (Eds.): AI 2002, LNAI 2557, pp. 1–11, 2002.

useful for conflict identification. Our work concerns taking multiple use case descriptions in natural language (requirements data) and applying FCA to assist merging of viewpoints.

We have recently conducted evaluations of the comprehensibility of the line diagram (a visualisation of the concept lattice) as a way of analysing and comparing use case descriptions. Our study involved 201 second year analysis and design students who answered questions using line diagrams OR the original textual descriptions. Five different line diagrams were considered, four of which included multiple viewpoints in the one diagram. Our findings show that the line diagram could be learnt by 58% of our subjects after a 5 minute introduction, questions were 20-80% more likely to be correct when using the line diagram as opposed to textual sentences and that 61% of students preferred using the line diagram over sentences to answer the questions. In all cases answering the questions using the diagrams was 1.5 to 9.9 times faster than using sentences. With such promising results we are encouraged to pursue this line of research. However the feasability of our approach relies on a number of things including providing an easy (preferably automatic) way of tranforming use case descriptions into a format that could be used by FCA and which develops comprehensible concept lattices. In the next section we give an overview of our approach to natural language processing. In section 3 we review some of the problems concerning natural language and how a controlled language can reduce the problems. In Section 4 we offer our controlled language and our motivations for it. A summary of the work is given in the final section.

2   The Natural Language Process

Formal Concept Analysis is a mathematical approach to data analysis (Wille 1982, 1992). *FCA* is used for data analysis tasks to find, structure and display relationships between concepts, which consist of sets of objects and the sets of attributes they share. Thus this method helps in understanding a given domain and in building a domain model for it. To build these models we begin with a *formal context*. A *formal context* is a triple (G, M, I). G is a set of objects, M a set of attributes and I a binary relation $I \subseteq G \times M$ between objects and attributes. If $m \epsilon M$ is an attribute of $g \epsilon G$ then $(g, m) \epsilon I$ is valid.

A *formal concept* (A,B) of the *formal context* (G, M, I) is defined as a pair of objects $A \subseteq G$ and attributes $B \subseteq M$ with $B := \{m \epsilon M | \forall g \epsilon A : (g, m) \epsilon I\}$ and $A := \{g \epsilon G | \forall m \epsilon B : (g, m) \epsilon I\}$. A natural *subconcept / superconcept* relationship $\leq$ of *formal concepts* can be defined as $(A_1, B_1) \leq (A_2, B_2) \Leftrightarrow A_1 \subseteq A_2$ or $(A_1, B_1) \leq (A_2, B_2) \Leftrightarrow B_2 \subseteq B_1$. Thus a *formal concept* $C_1 = (A_1, B_1)$ is a *subconcept* of the *formal concept* $C_2 = (A_2, B_2)$ if A_1 is a subset of A_2 or B_1 is a superset of B_2. C_2 is called *superconcept* of *formal concept* C_1.

A *concept lattice* is an algebraic structure with certain infimum and supremum operations. The set of concepts and their relations can be visualised as a line diagram. It allows the investigation and interpretation of relationships between *concepts*, objects and attributes. The nodes of the graph represent the *concepts* Two *concepts* C_1 and C_2 are connected if $C_1 \leq C_2$ and if there is no *concept* C_3 with $C_1 \leq C_3 \leq C_2$. Although it is a directed acyclic graph the edges are not provided with arrowheads. Instead the convention holds that the *superconcept* always appears above its *subconcepts*. The top element of the graph is the *concept* (G, G') and the bottom element the *concept* (M', M). To find all attributes belonging to an object, one starts with the node which represents the object, and follows all paths to the top element. In this way one also finds all *superconcepts* of a *concept*. To find all *subconcepts* of a *concept* one follow all paths to the bottom element.

Our use of FCA to display and compare use case descriptions is novel and requires some special preprocessing of the data. First of all we must resolve what is an object in our data and what are the attribtutes. Although words and morphemes are the smallest meaningful units in language, humans mostly communicate in phrases and sentences with each other (Fromkin, 1996). Therefore this approach considers each sentence as an object. Finding attributes is not so easy. One option is to create one attribute for each predicate representing a word of the sentence. However the resulting *concept lattice* would not be readable in most cases. To produce a more meaningful visualisation we need to break the sentence into word phrases. We achieve this by passing the use case descriptions entered by the viewpoint owners into RECOCASE-tool to the ExtrAns System. ExtrAns uses LinkGrammar to return all alternative syntactic dependencies between the words of a sentence. The syntactic structure consists of a set of labelled links connecting pairs of words. To find a syntactic structure LinkGrammar uses a dictionary containing the linking requirements of words. The words of a syntactic structure are connected in such a way, that the links satisfy the linking requirements for each word of the sentence (satisfaction), that the links do not cross (planarity) and that all words form a connected graph (connectivity) (Sleater and Temperly, 1991). The FLFs output by ExtrAns are processed by RECOCASE-logic to produce a *formal context*, as the one shown in Table 1 for the following 3 sentences:

1. 'The customer inserts the card in the ATM.'
2. 'The ATM checks if the card is valid.'
3. 'The ATM gives a prompt for the code to the customer.'

where an attribute is created for each predicate of the FLFs. The *concept lattice* for Table 1 is given in Figure 1.

In this section we have given an introduction to how our approach transforms natural language sentences into concept lattices. We now explore some of the motivation for handling natural language, why we suggest a controlled language and the constraints of our controlled language.

3   Natural, Formal, and Controlled Language

Natural language is often used to describe system requirements, however natural language is inherently ambiguous and complex in syntax and semantics. A term is ambiguous, if there exists more than one interpretation. One can distinguish

Table 1. Crosstable for sentences 1-3

	1	2	3	4	5	6	7	8	9	10
s1	x	x	x	x						
s2					x	x	x			
s3					x			x	x	x

Table 2. Columns for crosstable in Table 1

1 customer	5 ATM	9 prompt for code
2 insert	6 check	10 to customer
3 card of customer	7 if valid card	
4 in ATM	8 give	

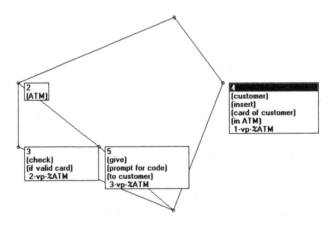

Fig. 1. Representation of sentences in RECOCASE

between *lexical ambiguity* and *structural ambiguity*. A sentence can be ambiguous because of *lexical ambiguity* if the sentence contains one or more ambiguous words e.g. *homonyms*. *Homonyms* are different words that are either pronouned the same, or spelt the same, or both. Since this approach considers written English, homonyms which are pronounced the same but not spelt the same are not of interest. *Structural ambiguity* can occur if two ore more meanings of a sentence are not the result of *lexical ambiguity* but of two or more structures which underly the same sentence. For example the sentence 'The ATM customer inserts the ATM card with a PIN number.' is ambiguous because of *structural ambiguity*. Figure 2 shows two possible sentence structure trees of this sentence. A ordinary sentence (*S*) is always subdivided into a noun phrase (*NP*) and a verb phrase (*VP*). A noun phrase always contains a noun (*N*) and sometimes a determiner (*Det*) and a prepositional phrase (*PPs*) which consist of a preposition (*P*) and a noun phrase. A verb phrase always contains a verb (*V*) and sometimes a noun phrase and a prepositional phrase. Thus the prepositional phrase 'with a PIN number' can be associated with the verb 'insert' and means 'together with the PIN number' (see figure 2 -A-). Another interpretation exists with 'the ATM card has a PIN number' (see figure 2 -B-) where the prepositional phrase 'with a PIN number' is part of the noun phrase 'the ATM card with a PIN number'. There are more rules of the english language but not relevant for this example (see Fromkin et al. 1996). Thus the syntactic structure of a sentence is important to its meaning.

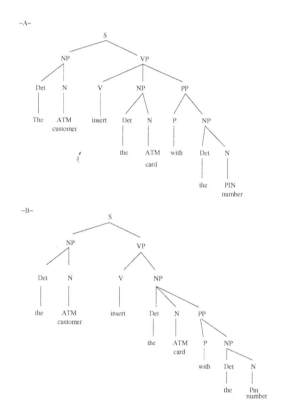

Fig. 2. Syntactic Structures of the Sentence 'The ATM customer inserts the ATM card with a PIN number.'

Sentences which have the same meaning are called *paraphrases*. The use of *synonyms*, which are words which sound different but have the same meaning, can create *lexical paraphrase*. There are many dictionaries of synomyns. But there are no perfect *synonyms* since no two words ever have exactly the same meaning (Fromkin 1996). A word is *polysemous* if it has several closely related but slightly different meanings. A word can share one of its meanings with another word, which can be seen as a kind of *partial synonymy*. So it is possible that two or more words have the same meaning when applied to a certain domain but not in connection with all domains (e.g. 'mature' and 'ripe' applied to the domain fruit). People also use *antonyms*, which are words that are opposite in meaning. For this approach *complementary pairs* (e.g. alive and dead) are of interest because the negative of one word of a *complementary pair* is synonymous with the other (e.g. not alive and dead). Also of interest are *relational opposites* (e.g. give and receive). *relational opposites* display symmetry in their meaning (e.g. if X gives Y to Z, then Z receives Y from X). *Complementary pairs* and *Relational opposites* can thus be used to describe one thing in another way.

Another important fact is that people describe things at varying levels of detail. Some people describe things in great detail, some people write at a more abstract level. For example people use *hyponyms* and *hypernyms*. A *hyponym* is a word which is more specific than another word. A word which is more general than another word is called *hypernym*. The difficulty of finding *homonyms*, *synonyms*, *hyponyms* and *hypernyms* is based on the fact that the sense of a word usually depends on its enviroment. In our case the enviroment is a requirements specification for a particular project.

An alternative to *natural language* is to use a *formal specification language*. A *formal language* consists of variables $(v_0, v_1, \ldots)$, logic symbols $(\neg, \forall, \ldots)$, parentheses $((,))$, comma, constant symbols, function symbols and predicate symbols. For instance programming languages are *formal languages*. One problem of using *formal languages* is that not all stakeholders understand this language. This can lead to the fact, that documents written in *formal language* can not be accepted as a contract for the software system (Schwitter and Fuchs, 1996) or if the specification would be accepted, the specification might not reflect the real needs of the stakeholder and thus the developed system can not satisfy the stakeholder needs. To solve this problem Schwitter and Fuchs (1996) proposed to restrict *natural language* to a controlled subset with a well-defined syntax and semantics.

Huijsen (1998) defines *controlled language* as follows: "A *controlled language* is an explicitly defined restriction of a *natural language* that specifies constraints on lexicon, grammar and style." A *controlled language* aims to reduce ambiguity, redundancy, size and complexity. Using a *controlled language* makes computational text processing more reliable (Huijsen 1998). Thus a *controlled language* is developed as a reduced *natural language* to take advantage of the benefits and avoid the disadvantages of *formal languages*. That means that the *controlled language* can still be read as natural text. *Controlled language* should be expressive enough to allow natural usage. But on the other hand the language should be designed in such a way, that the language can be processed accurately and efficiently by the computer. *Controlled language* is based on a certain sentence structure. Sentences which are written in this principle structure can be combined by constructors (e.g. negation, if-then, and, or) to powerful phrases (Schwitter and Fuchs, 1996). Controlled or simplified English is already used in various applications. It is used for technical documentation (AECMA 1995), for knowledge-based machine translation in the KANT system (Mitamura and Nyberg 1995) and as a data based query language (Androutsopoulos 1995).

3.1 Controlled Language

The controlled language designed for the approach using FCA restricts the grammar and the style. The vocabulary is restricted only on a low level. We provide a justification for each rule motivated by our desire to produce a model of the use case descriptions as a *concept lattice*.

Words:

[W1] The viewpoint author should consistently use the same word when referring to the same thing and avoid the use of synonyms, hyponyms and hypernyms.
Why: To reduce the number of nodes of the *concept lattice* and assist reconciliation.

[W2] If it is possible to use several words then the viewpoint author should use the shortest and simplest word.
Why: To reduce the length of labels of the *concept lattice*.

[W3] The viewpoint author should not use personal pronouns (e.g. he, she, it) and possessive pronouns (his, her, its, hers).
Why: Pronouns are notoriously difficult to resolve since the search space for the correct noun might be very deep.

[W4] The viewpoint author should not use modal verbs (e.g. might, could, should).
Why: Modal verbs express doubt.

[W5] The viewpoint author should not use symbols, semicolons, dashes and colons.
Why: RECOCASE is using tools for natural language processing that can not process these characters.

[W6] The viewpoint author should not write slang.
Why: They are often not contained in dictionaries.

[W7] The viewpoint author should not use symbols (e.g. #) and abbreviations instead of words (e.g number) and phrases.
Why: They are often not contained in dictionaries.

[W8] The viewpoint author should write 'do not' instead of 'don't', 'does not' instead of 'doesn't', 'has not' instead of 'hasn't' and 'have not' instead of 'haven't'.
Why: RECOCASE is using tools for natural language processing that can not process sentences containing these structures.

Sentences:

[S1] The viewpoint author should not write using the functional requirements style, which are generally stated in terms of what the system shall do ('The system shall ... '). The viewpoint author should write scenario text. Thus each sentence should describe an action or a state.
Action:

[S2] An action should be described in one grammatical form - a simple action in which one *actor* either accomplishes a task or passes information to another *actor*.
A simple sentence has the general structure: sentence: <subject> <predicate> predicate: <predicator> <complement(s)>
A sentence should contain one subject, one verb and depending on the verb zero (intransitive verbs), one (transitive verbs) or two (ditransitive verbs) complements.

[S3] The subject should be the system or an actor.
Why: To make the structure and content of concepts consistent.

[S4] The subject should trigger the action. The subject should not be the object of the action.
Why: To make the structure and content of concepts consistent.
Example: YES: The system ejects the card to the customer. NO: The customer gets the card from the system.

[S5] The verb should describe the action.
Why: To make the structure and content of concepts consistent.
Example: YES: The ATM checks the card. ...NO: The ATM checking of the card ...

[S6] The viewpoint author should use active voice instead of passive voice.
Why: It is important to know who triggers the action.

[S7] The viewpoint author should use the present tense format of the verbs.
Why: It helps in writing scenario text as a sequence of simple sentences.

State:

[S8] A state can describe a state of an object, a result of an action or a condition before or until an action can be performed (see F6 and F7).

[S9] The viewpoint author should avoid the use of negations.
Why: It is important to know what the system or the actors can do and what the user expects, not what they can not do or what they do not expect.

[S10] The viewpoint author should avoid the use of adverbs.
Why: Adverbs often express non-functional requirements not functional requirements (e.g. quickly, easily). Adverbs often add only inexact information, which are not useful for developing a software system.

[S11] The viewpoint author should use prepositional phrases to modify a verb. The viewpoint author should avoid the use of relative clauses, which should be used to modify a noun.
Why: A prepositional phrase can sometimes be associated with the verb or with a noun. The human can often use information from the context to decide which interpretation is meant. But it is difficult to use the computer to do this. Another reason is to standardize the *concept lattice.*

[S12] Use quotation marks to mark messages and captions.
Why: It assists in the analysis of the sentence structure.

[S13] All sentences should end with a full stop.
Why: For sentence segmentation.

[S14] The viewpoint author should use a noun with the determiner 'a' or 'the'.
Why: It assists recognition of nouns.

[S15] The viewpoint author should use the phrase structure 'of' instead of the genitive form.
Why: RECOCASE is using tools for natural language processing that can not process sentences containing these structures.
Example: YES: the card of the customer NO: the customer's card

Flow of actions and states:

[F1] The viewpoint author should describe the flow of actions and states sequentially and should not use flash backs and forward references.
Why: To make the structure and content of concepts consistent.

[F2] The flow of actions should be event-response oriented.
Why: To not forget any action.

[F3] The viewpoint author should describe only one action per sentence and thus the author should not write composite sentences of actions like the following sentence structures and combinations of them:

[action_1] then [action_2]

[action_2] after [action_1]   or   after [action_1] [action_2]

[action_1] before [action_2]   or   before [action_2] [action_1]

[action_1], [action_2], . . . and [action_n]

[action_1], [action_2], . . . or [action_n]

Why: To make the structure and content of concepts consistent.

[F4] The viewpoint author should use the following sentence structures to describe actions which happen simultaneously:

[action_1] meanwhile [action_2]

[action_1], [action_2], . . . and [action_n] at the same time.

[F5] The viewpoint author should use the following sentence structures to describe that the ordering is not important:

[action_1], [action_2], . . . and [action_n] in any temporal order.

[F6] The viewpoint author should use the following sentence structures to describe a iteration of actions:

repeat [number] until [states]

[action_1], [action_2], . . . and [action_n]

repeat while [states]

[action_1], [action_2], . . . and [action_n]

Alternative flow of actions:

[F7] The viewpoint author should use logical operators to make the dependence between clause and phrasal structures explicit. The viewpoint author should avoid sentence structures with 'unless', 'otherwise', 'if not' and 'else'. To express that an action is performed only under a certain condition the viewpoint author should use the following sentence structure. If [states] then [action].

Why: RECOCASE is using tools for natural language processing. These tools are still not able to process sentences containing these structures.

[F8] The viewpoint author should avoid the use of coordinations by 'and' or 'or'.

Why: For the sake of simplicity and clarity.

4   Tool Support to Assist Controlled Language Compliance

Many of the constraints included in our controlled language can be automatically detected and in some cases corrected. In this section we review some ways in which the RECOCASE-tool can suppport the user in following the controlled language. The following are suggestions addressing the enforcement of the guidelines. The particular guideline being adressed is given as the heading.

[**W1**] A possibility to improve viewpoint descriptions for the translation into *concept lattices* is to find 'synonyms', 'hyponyms' and 'hypernyms'. By doing this concepts can be made more similiar which increases the readability of a *concept lattice*. Only small improvements might be achieved by using a dictionary valid for all domains like 'Wordnet' since there are no perfect synonyms because no two words never have exactly the same meaning (Fromkin 1996, p.131).

[**W3-W5**] The output of LinkGrammar's word segmentizer can be used to check if phrases like personal pronouns (e.g. he, she, it), possessive pronouns (his, her, its, hers) modal auxiliaries (e.g. can, shall), semicolons, dashes and colons are not used according to [W3-W5].

[**W6-W7**] For the word segmentizer of LinkGrammar unknown words are marked as keywords. Reasons could be that the spelling is incorrect or the word is not held in the dictionary of LinkGrammar (e.g. slang and abbreviations). In the last case there exists the possibility to extend the dictionary or to choose another word to ensure that the outcome of further steps of language processing is correct.

[**S2**] LinkGrammar can separate the sentence into noun and verb phrases. This can be used to transpose composed sentences into simple sentences according to [S2].

[**S3**] The linkage type 'S' of the syntactic structure connects subject nouns to the finite verbs. By using this it is possible to check guideline [S3], if the subject is the system or an *actor*.

[**S6**] Extrans can be used to check if viewpoints contain imperative sentences or passive sentences, which do not define an *agent*. If the FLF of a sentence provides the predicate 'hearer' then the sentence might be a imperative sentence. The predicate 'anonym_object' refers to a passive sentence, which do not define an agent. In both cases the *viewpoint agent* could be asked to change the sentences. For example the FLF of the sentence 'The card is checked' contains the predicate 'anonym_object'. The *viewpoint agent* should change the sentence to 'The ATM checks the card.'.

5   Conclusion and Future Work

The RECOCASE viewpoint development approach pivots around the analysis and reconciliation of multiple viewpoints for a use case description. We have not presented our reconciliation strategies, group process or our CASE tool. In this paper we have focused on the early phases in our process model which translates natural language sentences into a concept lattice. To reduce the various problems with natural language processing such as structural and semantic ambiguity we have suggested a controlled language particularly designed for improving the comprehensibility of the sentences when viewed as a line diagram. The evaluations we have performed already indicate that the concept lattice structure can assist identification of shared concepts and inconsistencies.

The study mentioned in Section 1 with included evaluation of the guidelines. The Plain English guidelines we provided to participant is given in Appendix A. 97 of the 201 students were given the guidelines to assist use case authoring. Our results show 40/79 felt confident using the guidelines, 25/79 were neutral and 14/79 lacked confidence. 52/79 found the guidelines helpful, 18/79 were neutral and 27/79 did not find the guidelines helpful. Another 18 students had the guidelines but did not fill in the comments section. We measured if having the guidelines affected whether subjects were more likely to conform to the fourteen points in our guidelines. We found that subjects with guidelines were more likely to use the same word to refer to the same thing and avoid use of pronouns, modal verbs, adverbs, conjunctions and disjunctions. We will be performing comparisons of our results with the guideline evaluations conducted by Cox (2001). We are about to conduct usability testing of our group process and extensive comparative evaluation of our approach and tool with other formal requirements, natural language and group decision techniques.

References

1. The European Association of Aerospace Industries (AECMA): *AECMA Simplified english*, AECMA-Document: PSC-85-16598, A Guide for the Preparation of Aircraft Maintenance Documentation in the International Aerospace Maintenance Language, Issue 1, September 1995
2. Androutsopoulos, I., Ritchie, G. D. and Thanisch, P.: *Natural Language Interfaces to Databases - An Introduction*, Journal of Natural Language Engineering, vol.1, no.1, Cambridge University Press, 1995
3. Cox, K., (2001) *Experimental Material*, http://dec/bournemouth.ac.uk/staff/kcox/UCwriting.htm, 2001
4. Fromkin, V., Rodman, R., Collins, P. and Blair, D., (1996) *An introduction to language*, 3th edition, Harcourt Brace & Company, Australia
5. Jacobson, I., (1992) *Object-Oriented Software Engineering*, Addison-Wesley
6. Huijsen W. O. (1998) *Controlled Language - An Introduction*, Proceedings of the second international Workshop on Controlled Language Applications.
7. Melcuk, I., (1988) *Dependency Syntax: Theory and Practice*, State Uni. of NY Press
8. Mitamura, T. and Nyberg, E. H.: *Controlled English for Knowledge-Based MT: Experience with the KANT System*, Center for Machine Translation, Carnegie Mellon University, Pittsburgh, 1995
9. Sleator, D. D. and Temperley, D., (1991) *Parsing English with a Link Grammar*, Technical Report CMU-CS-91-196, Carnegie Mellon University, School of Computer Science, Pittsburgh, PA
10. Wille, R., (1982) *Restructing Lattice Theory: An Approach Based on Hierarchies of Concepts*, Ordered Sets, D. Reichel, Dordrecht, pp. 445–470
11. Wille, R., (1992) *Concept Lattices and Conceptual Knowledge*, Computers and Mathematics with Applications, 23, pp. 493–522

Appendix A – Plain English General Guidelines (Abbreviated and Reordered for Space)

- Use words in a consistent way. Avoid the use of synonyms, hyponyms and hypernyms.
- Do not use personal pronouns (e.g. he, she, it). Do not use possessive pronouns (e.g. his).
- Do not use modal verbs (e.g. may-might, can-could, shall-should).
- Use prepositional phrases to modify the verb (e.g The boy saw with a telescope the girl).
- Use a relative clause to modify a noun (e.g. The boy saw the girl who had a telescope).
- Do not write functional requirements (e.g. NOT ''The system shall ...'), instead of writing scenario text.   • Each sentence should describe an action or a state.
- Describe the flow of actions and states sequentially. Do not use flash backs and forward references.   • Use the phrase 'of' instead of the genitive form.
- The flow of actions should be event-response oriented, that is, consider what the user does and how the system responds.   • Avoid the use of coordinations by 'and' or 'or'.
- A sentence should contain one subject, one verb and depending on the verb zero (intransitive verbs such as sit, come, lie), one (transitive verbs) or two (ditransitive verbs) complements (called objects).   • Use a noun together with the determiner 'a' or 'the'.
- Write actions in the active voice NOT the passive voice (e.g the borrower returns the book, NOT the book is returned by the borrower).   • Use verbs in present tense.
- The subject should be the system or an actor.   • The subject should trigger the action.
- The verb (not a noun) should describe the action.   • Do not use negations.
- Do not use semicolons, dashes and colons.   • Avoid the use of adverbs (e.g. quickly).
- Use quotation marks to mark messages and captions. • All sentences should end with a full stop.
- Describe an action in one grammatical form - a simple action in which one actor either accomplishes a task or passes information to another actor.

Preferred Document Classification for a Highly Inflectional/Derivational Language

Kyongho Min[1], William H. Wilson[2], and Yoo-Jin Moon[3]

[1]School of Information Technology, Auckland University of Technology,
Private Bag 92006, Auckland, 1020, New Zealand
kyongho.min@aut.ac.nz
[2] School of Computer Science and Engineering,
University of New South Wales, Sydney, Australia
billw@cse.unsw.edu.au
[3] Dept of Management Information Systems,
Hankook University of Foreign Studies, Yongin, Korea
yjmoon@hufs.ac.kr

Astract. This paper describes methods of document classification for a highly inflectional/derivational language that forms monolithic compound noun terms, like Dutch and Korean. The system is composed of three phases: (1) a Korean morphological analyzer called HAM (Kang, 1993), (2) an application of compound noun phrase analysis to the result of HAM analysis and extraction of terms whose syntactic categories are noun, name (proper noun), verb, and adjective, and (3) an effective document classification algorithm based on *preferred class score* heuristics. This paper focuses on the comparison of document classification methods including a simple heuristic method, and preferred class score heuristics employing two factors namely *ICF* (inverted class frequency) and *IDF* (inverted document frequency) with/without term frequency weight. In addition this paper describes a simple classification approach without a learning algorithm rather than a vector space model with a complex training and classification algorithm such as cosine similarity measurement. The experimental results show 95.7% correct classifications of 720 training data and 63.8%–71.3% of randomly chosen 80 testing data through various methods.

1 Introduction

Information on the world wide web is growing very fast and the role of search engines is becoming more important. The search engine can be improved by two methods: an effective indexing scheme for task document contents and an efficient ranking system to pinpoint precise and necessary information for users rather than to show massive amount of retrieved documents [13]. Both methods would be greatly improved by accurate document class information.

This paper focuses on the implementation of effective document classification systems for Korean newspaper articles, based on:

R.I. McKay and J. Slaney (Eds.): AI 2002, LNAI 2557, pp. 12–23, 2002.
© Springer-Verlag Berlin Heidelberg 2002

(a) HAM – Hangul Analyser of Morphology [11],

(b) a compound noun term analyser based on a longest substring algorithm [9] employing an agenda-based chart parsing technique,

(c) extraction of document classification features based on syntactic information such as entity terms (e.g. noun and names), verb, and adjective, and

(d) a *preferred-class-scored* document classification algorithm without a training process but with two classification factors namely ICF (inverted class frequency) and IDF (inverted document frequency),

rather than complex and time consuming classification methods and training processes such as the vector space method of [10]. The term, *preferred class score*, means that each term used in classification process has its preferred score for a specific class on the basis of classification algorithms. The algorithm proceeds by computing a number of scores, as using these to decide a preferred class. Thus we refer to the algorithm and the scores using the label "preferred class score" (PCS).

Many researchers have studied efficient text classification algorithms. The methods employed have included vector space classification for a medical document filtering system[1] with an IDF factor and cosine similarity measurement [16]; Okapi's *tf* score [1]; a supervised learning algorithm based on neural network back propagation with an ICF factor and X-square (X^2) algorithm to extract class features for Korean documents [8]; a rule-based disjunctive production method based on term frequencies and boolean combinations of co-occurrence terms[2] [2]; a context sensitive rule-based Boolean method considering a word's position in the context [5]; semantic classification based on conceptual models after processing documents syntactically (e.g. Lingsoft's *Nptool* is applied by [3] [4]; rule-based classification features based on important words extracted, called field association words, that are constructed hierarchically, rather than being based on all terms except for stop words [7]. Comparisons of various classification algorithms have been performed [5], [10], [14], [18]. When extracting class features, most systems have used direct terms in the testing and training data except for stop words or low frequency words (i.e. removal of words with less than 3 occurrences in the class features).

Li and Jain [14] tested four common classification algorithms (i.e. naive Bayes, Nearest neighbour based on TF-IDF, Decision tree, and a subspace method). Yang and Liu [18] studied five different classification algorithms, based on support vector machine (SVM), k-Nearest neighbour, backpropagation-trained feedforward networks, Linear Least-squares Fit, and Naive Bayes. Joachims [10] compared the performance of three distinct classification algorithms: a naive Bayes algorithm, Rocchio's TF-IDF heuristics, and a probabilistic analysis of TF-IDF heuristics.

---

[1] Their testing data belonged to one of 15 classes, and the classification accuracy difference between top performing classes (average 87%) and low performing classes (average 57%) was 30%.

[2] For example, if a document includes the words such as "wheat" and "farm", then the document is classified as *wheat* class on the basis of a set of disjunctive production rules.

These previous researchers have studied the effects of the following factors for document classification: the number of features, the rareness of class documents, a term's frequency in a testing document, the rule-based Boolean combination of the terms for the class feature sets, various learning algorithms to extract best class feature sets, and different similarity measurement methods based on an ICF and IDF. In addition previous studies have shown that the performance of various classification methods has not been consistent because of different training techniques and testing environment employed. This paper focuses on a simple and effective classification algorithm, the application of various numbers of feature sets, and the pure comparison of classification methods employing an ICF/IDF without any learning and training algorithms.

Our methods classify a document to one of 8 topic areas (e.g. domestic news, economy, world news, information and science, culture and life, political news, sports, and entertainment), using a compound noun term analyser and a heuristic document classification algorithm, and will be described in the next section. In section 3, our experimental results with documents from an online Korean newspaper_will be discussed and section 4 describes problems and possible further improvements of the current approach, followed by conclusions in section 5.

2   Methods of Document Classification

This section describes the method of document classification in three phases: morphological analysis based on the HAM (Hangul Analysis Module [11] system, a term extraction method and analysis of compound noun terms, and document classification algorithms based on *Preferred Class Score* (*PCS*).

2.1 Morphological Analysis of Words

Korean is a highly inflected language requiring very complex computation for Korean NLP. In addition, the analysis of Korean morphology is very difficult for many reasons. First, each syllable (i.e. morpheme) in a word can have different meaning when used by itself. For example, *"bank"* – a financial institution – is "은행" in Korean, and the word is composed of two syllables ("은", "행"). If the word is treated as a compound noun term, then it would be analysed as "silver row" in English (*"silver"* for "은" and *"row"* for "행"). Second, Korean has no capital letters to enable one to distinguish a proper noun from other nouns. Third, Korean is highly inflectional and derivational. In the case of verb inflections, there are different forms of inflections with aspects, modals, and mixed together (e.g. imperative, passive, etc.).

HAM for Linux [12] was employed for efficient and effective Korean morphological analysis because the HAM system has been continually enhanced since 1993 [11]. HAM reads a Korean text file and returns the multiple morphological analyses of each word in the text.

After morphological analysis of each document using the HAM system, the ambiguities of each word were manually removed to choose the best morphological analysis and extract terms from documents. The ambiguities of a word range from 1 to 4, in our data set, which includes 17470 distinct words.

2.2 Compound Noun Phrase Analysis

The Korean morphology analyzer HAM focused on the analysis of inflectional and derivational morphemes with affix analysis [12]. However, HAM does not analyse compound noun terms into nominal terms. Korean compound noun terms, like Dutch, do not have a word boundary symbol such as the space used in English, and some compound terms resulted from a segmentation error. Even though the conceptual importance of each noun term in a compound noun term may depend on its meaning in the text, we analysed the compound noun term to use each noun term as a class feature, rather than use the compound noun term itself.

To extract the correct class features of noun terms, the compound noun terms are processed by a longest substring algorithm [9] incorporated with an agenda-based chart parsing technique [6] to handle many ambiguities that arise because each single syllable in a Korean word would be meaningful by itself.

The compound noun analyser selects one analysis from the alternatives on the basis of a penalty scheme. Each substring found has its penalty score that computes the number of remaining bytes left behind after processing the substring. This scheme prefers longer substrings to shorter substrings.

For example, the compound noun term ("a Korean bank" in English) or a proper noun ("The Bank of Korea" in English) "한국은행" has positional indexes: e.g. $_0$ 한 $_1$ 국 $_2$ 은 $_3$ 행 $_4$. The first substring "한" ("deep grievance" in English) as a noun covers 2 bytes with 6 bytes left behind for substring processing. At each position, the compound noun analyser searches for all legal substrings (i.e. noun words) rightward until the end of the string. " 한국" (e.g. 'Korea' in English) from 0 to 2 is the next legal substring; " 한국은" from 0 to 3 is not a legal substring, and so on – the analyser continues to find legal substrings until the end of the substring. Thus the legal nominal substrings are extracted from the leftmost position to the end of the string by moving the starting position right by a syllable at a time.

At this stage, the compound noun analyser computes the penalty score of each substring found. For example, the nominal substring " 한" has a penalty score of 6. Another substring " 한국" has a penalty score of 4. Thus, the penalty scheme considers the amount of substring (expressed in bytes) left behind for substring analysis.

After the compound noun analysis, all legal substrings extracted are used to find the best analysis of the compound noun term by a chart parsing technique. An agenda-based chart parsing technique tries to find all possible parse trees covering an input sentence [6]. This technique is applied to get the best analysis of the Korean compound noun term. At each position within a string, there are corresponding agenda items such as legal nominal strings. This chart parsing technique produces the best combination of nominal terms with the least penalty score. If there are multiple analyses with the same penalty score and the same number of combinations, then the system has no further choice criteria.

After morphological and compound noun analysis, the class feature sets are extracted from the training data. The class feature sets are composed of the roots of nominals, proper names, verbal, and adjectival terms, rather than direct terms, and excluding stop words. The words whose syntactic categories are adverbs, case-markers, and affixes are not considered for class features, and the remaining words are treated as unknown words, which might be numbers, alphanumeric words, and compound words with Korean and English parts, in either order.

2.3 Preferred Class Score Classification

We tried six preferred class score algorithms and rated them for effectiveness and simplicity. When computing a class score for a term in the document, no probability or similarity measurement is used in the classification process. Only each term's class score is considered on the basis of a simple voting score, ICF, or IDF logarithm to decide which class is to be preferred. Three basic algorithms are implemented, for performance comparison, along with variants that use weighting by term frequency within the document.

The algorithm descriptions use the following symbols:
T_{ik} = Term i extracted from a document D_k.
C_j = Class j from a set of pre-defined classes
$Df(T_{ik})$ = the frequency of term T_i in test document D_k.
$Tf(T)$ = the frequency of term T collected from the total documents.
$Cf(T_{ij})$ = the frequency of a term T_i in the class C_j feature set.

One&Only Algorithm

This algorithm classifies documents by a simple voting scheme. When the system applies the voting scheme to each term T_{ik} in test document D_k, the frequency of term T_i in each class feature set, e.g. $C_1, C_2, ..., C_n$, where n = 8 in this paper, is retrieved to decide the class with a maximum frequency for term T_{ik}. If the frequency of term T_i in class C_j feature set, $Cf(T_{ij})$, is highest among other class feature sets, then the preferred class score 1 is allocated to class C_j and other classes, $C_1, C_2, ... C_{j-1}, C_{j+1}, ... C_n$, have 0 of the preferred class score for term T_{ik}. For example, term T_i in document D_k has the following frequencies in the class feature sets: $Cf(T_{i1}) = 25$, $Cf(T_{i2}) = 45$, $Cf(T_{i3}) = 85$, $Cf(T_{i4}) = 33$. The preferred class score for class C_3 is 1 and other classes are allocated 0 as their preferred class score.

After summation of each class's score over all terms in the document, the class with the maximum score is chosen for the class of the document. The preferred class score, $\Pi\Sigma\Sigma(T_iX_\Psi)$, of document D_k is the sum of preferred class scores, $\Pi\Sigma\Sigma(\Delta_kX_\Psi)$, of each term T_{ik} in document D_k.

Let document D_k have extracted terms $\{T_{1k}, T_{2k}, T_{3k}, \ldots T_{nk}\}$ with frequencies of each class $Cf(T_{ij})$.

$$\text{if } Cf(T_{ij}) = M\alpha\xi\{Cf(T_{ij})\},$$

Then $\Pi X \Sigma(T_i X_\Psi)$ *Otherwise*

$$(1)$$

Here $M\alpha\xi\{Cf(T_{ij})\} = Max_{j=1}^{m}\{Cf(T_{i1}), Cf(T_{i2}), \ldots Cf(T_{im})\}$.

After computing and summing up each term's $PCS(T_iC_j)$ in document D_k, the class with maximum $PCS(D_kC_j)$ is chosen for the class of the tested document.

$$\Pi X \Sigma(\Delta_K X_\Psi) = Max\left\{\sum_{i=1}^{i=n}\sum_{j=1}^{m} PCS(T_iC_j)\right\} \tag{2}$$

The second algorithm (One&Only Filter1 in table 2) employs filtering heuristics based on the total frequency of a term $(Tf(T))$. If the frequency $Tf(T)$ is less than 8 (i.e. total classes – 86.7% of total terms of the training data, see table 1), then the classification process discards the term from classification features and reduces the number of class feature sets. This weighting scheme uses the remaining 13.3% of terms as class features for document classification (see section 3.1). Thus the changed equation (3) is

$$\Pi X \Sigma(T_i X_\Psi) = \begin{cases} 1, & \text{if } Cf(T_{ij}) = M\alpha\xi\{Cf(T_{ij})\} \text{ and iff } Tf(T_i) > 7 \\ 0, & \text{Otherwise} \end{cases} \tag{3}$$

Preferred Class Score Based on Inverted Document or Class Frequency
These algorithms are based on either Inverted Document Frequency (IDF) or Inverted Class Frequency (ICF) [10], [8]. They compute similarity between a tested document and training data. The document classification algorithm employing ICF is based on $tf * log(N/cf)$ where tf is the term frequency in the document and N is the number of classes. As the cf (i.e. the class frequency of the term) becomes smaller, the logarithm of the term increases (e.g. cf = N, then log(N/cf) = 0). In this algorithm, the term's qualification as a class feature depends on the term's sparseness through class feature sets (i.e. documents classified for the training data). For example, if term T_1 has 1 for its inverted class frequency and term T_2 has 7 for its inverted class frequency, then the logarithm of T_1, log(8/1), is greater than that of T_2, log(8/7), where N is 8. The occurrence of term T_1 is sparser than term T_2 through classes. However, if a term occurs through all classes (i.e cf = N), then the difference of the term's frequencies in each class feature set is not considered, even though the term would be a significant class feature. In terms of the class frequency data in section 3.1, two percent of the terms in

the class feature set had log(N/cf) = 0, in the domain of this system, and so did not affect classification process.

Instead of computation of similarities being used for training data and for testing data, the preferred class score method is employed. The class of a testing document is the class with maximum PCS based on ICF or IDF logarithm functions. If the sum of the $\Pi\Sigma X$ ($\Delta_\kappa X_1$) score of class C_l is greater than the other class's $\Pi\Sigma X$ ($\Delta_\kappa X_{1...\mu}$) scores for the testing document, then the document's class is Class C_l. For $\Pi X\Sigma I X\Phi$ ($\Delta_\kappa X_\phi$), N is the total number of classes (i.e. 8 in this paper) and for $\Pi X\Sigma I\Delta\Phi$ ($\Delta_\kappa X_\phi$), N is the total number of training documents (i.e. 720 in this paper).

$$\Pi X\Sigma I X\Phi\,(\Delta_\kappa X_\phi)= Max\left\{\sum_{i=1}^{i=n}\sum_{j=1}^{m} Cf(T_{ij})*\log(N\,/\,ICf(T_i))\right\} \quad (4)$$

If the inverted document frequency (IDF) is applied, then the classification score is

$$\Pi X\Sigma I\Delta\Phi\,(\Delta_\kappa X_\phi) = Max\left\{\sum_{i=1}^{i=n}\sum_{j=1}^{m} Cf(T_{ij})*\log(N\,/\,IDf(T_i))\right\} \quad (5)$$

Thus, the preferred class score is used in the classification algorithms rather than, for example, complex cosine similarity computation. However, these algorithms do not consider the positive local information in each testing document, such as the frequency of each term. The following two algorithms weigh the positive local information so that more frequently occurring terms are preferred for classification. Both IDF and ICF logarithm functions are weighted by a term frequency obtained from the testing document. For *Weighted PCSICF* and *PCSIDF* algorithms, the term frequency of each document ($Df(T_{ik})$) is applied to the *PCSICF* and *PCSIDF* algorithms.

$$\Phi\epsilon\iota\gamma\eta\tau\epsilon\delta\quad \Pi X\Sigma I X\Phi(\Delta_\kappa X_\phi)= Max\left\{\sum_{i=1}^{n}\sum_{j=1}^{m} Df(T_{ik})*Cf(T_{ij})*\log(N/ICf(T_i))\right\} \quad (6)$$

$$\Phi\epsilon\iota\gamma\eta\tau\epsilon\delta\quad \Pi X\Sigma I\Delta\Phi(\Delta_\kappa X_\phi)= Max\left\{\sum_{i=1}^{n}\sum_{j=1}^{m} Df(T_{ik})*Cf(T_{ij})*\log(N/IDf(T_i))\right\} \quad (7)$$

The classification algorithms evaluate relationships involving three things: (a) each term's distributions through classes and training documents, (b) each term's weight in a test document, and (c) the number of class features used for classification process based on each term's preferred class score.

3   Experimental Results

The experimental results show that the simple voting classification algorithm performs well for the data, collected from a Korean online newspaper. The system is implemented in Perl5.0 on a Linux platform.

3.1 Data Collection and Extraction of Class Feature Sets

The training data (i.e. data used for extracting the class feature sets) and testing data were collected from one of the major Korean daily newspapers from 01/08/2000 to 31/08/2000. From 8 topic classes, 100 news articles for each topic were collected for training and testing the systems that we implemented. The class of each article is based on the classification given by the newspaper. Thus it would be possible for other human experts to classify some articles into difference classes. The eight classes are domestic news (DSO), economy (DEC), world news (DIN), information and science (DIS), culture and life (DCL), political news (DPO), sports (DSP), and entertainment (DST). In this paper, some words were not considered as either feature sets or terms for a document. For example, alphanumeric words such as combination of Korean/English and numbers, and words combined with Korean and English (vice versa) were not used as class features (i.e. total 17470 features) for document classification. In this case, the words (7.6% of the data) are classified as unknown words.

From each class, 10 articles were selected randomly for the performance tests with the various algorithms and the remainder were used for extraction of class feature sets. Table 1 shows the term frequency ratios obtained from all the words occurring in the 720 training articles and that 86.6% of the class feature sets have less than 8 occurrences in the training documents.

Table 1. Term Frequency Ratios

Term Frequency	1	2	3	4	5	6	7	8	9	10	> 10
Training Data (%)	51.2	14.7	8.2	4.9	3.3	2.4	1.9	1.5	1.0	1.0	9.8

The inverted class frequencies ($ICF(T_j)$) of all terms in the training sets are as follows: terms occurring in 1 class only are 10349 (59%), 2 classes 2892 (17%), 3 classes 1517 (9%), 4 classes 877 (5%), 5 classes 581 (3%), 6 classes 442 (3%), 7 classes 378 (2%), and 8 classes 434 (2%). Thus the algorithms based on the inverted class frequency do not use 2% of class features for classification.

The class feature of DCL has large overlaps with other class features, including DST > DIS > DSO. The largest overlap between class feature sets is DCL and DST (2522 overlapping features, 14% of total feature sets) and the next largest overlap is between DCL and DIS (2235 features, 12.8% of total feature sets). Three class feature sets are overlapped with other class feature sets more than the average, namely they are DCL > DIS > DST in order. The least overlapping class feature set on average through classes is DSP (1223 features, 7.0% of total feature sets).

The class feature sets were collected from a small number of training data and this resulted in about 8.2% of terms in the testing documents being unclassified. If these terms were classified as some class feature sets, then the classification performance would be different.

3.2 Result of Document Classification

In terms of the precision ratio of document classification with 80 sample texts (8 document categories and each class has 10 sample texts), the best performance was obtained by *PCS(ICF)* weighted with a term frequency in a document. This algorithm correctly classified 71.3% of testing documents. The simplest algorithm, One&Only, performs 5.3% worse than the best algorithm. Compared to algorithms not employing local document information (term frequency in a testing document), the algorithms weighted by term frequency perform classification better by 1.3%–5.3%. The One&Only algorithm successfully classified the training data on average 95.7%. Through classes, DSP shows the best classification ratio and DST shows the worst classification ratio.

Table 2. Correct Classification Results (precision ratio (%))

Algorithm	DCL	DEC	DIN	DIS	DPO	DSO	DSP	DST	Average
Training data with One&Only	100.0	94.4	94.4	90.0	96.7	95.6	100.0	94.4	95.7
One&Only	80.0	60.0	50.0	50.0	90.0	70.0	100.0	30.0	66.0
PCS(ICF)	60.0	60.0	40.0	60.0	80.0	60.0	100.0	60.0	65.0
PCS(IDF)	60.0	60.0	40.0	50.0	100.0	70.0	100.0	60.0	67.5
Weighted PCS(ICF)	60.0	70.0	60.0	70.0	90.0	70.0	100.0	50.0	71.3
Weighted PCS(IDF)	60.0	60.0	50.0	60.0	100.0	80.0	100.0	40.0	68.8
One&Only Filter1	80.0	60.0	40.0	50.0	100.0	60.0	100.0	20.0	63.8
Average	66.7	61.7	46.7	56.7	93.3	68.3	100.0	43.3	67.1

Table 2 shows 1.0–1.5 percent difference between the One&Only algorithm and the *PCS(ICF)* algorithm and the *PCS(IDF)* algorithm. The simple technique, One&Only, shows good performance compared to other classification algorithms. When the number of class feature sets was reduced to 13.3% of all the class feature sets to classify the test documents (One&Only Filter1 algorithm), the classification performance was worse by 2.2%, compared to One&Only. This result shows that the classification of a document does not depend greatly on the number of class features.

The *PCS(ICF)* algorithm depends greatly on log(N/ICF), even though there would be a distinct difference in the term frequency in the case where ICF is equal to N. If the ICF becomes lower, then the value becomes higher. The One&Only algorithm can compensate for this lack of distinct frequency difference when a class feature's *ICF* value is equal to N (i.e. log(N/ICF) = 0). When the algorithms are not weighted by term frequency in the testing document, *PCS(IDF)* performs 2.5% better than *PCS(ICF)*. However, if both algorithms are weighted by the term frequency, weighted *PCS(ICF)* performs 2.5% better than weighted *PCS(IDF)*. Thus the local document information greatly influences the performance of *PCS(ICF)* but not that of *PCS(IDF)*.

Table 3. Correct Classification Results (recall ratio (%))

Algorithm	DCL	DEC	DIN	DIS	DPO	DSO	DSP	DST	Average
Training data with One&Only	94.7	95.5	98.8	94.2	90.6	94.5	97.8	100.0	95.8
One&Only	36.4	100.0	83.3	83.3	69.2	53.8	100.0	75.0	75.1
PCS(ICF)	50.0	75.0	66.7	60.0	61.5	66.7	90.9	66.7	67.2
PCS(IDF)	46.2	100.0	100.0	71.4	62.5	53.8	90.9	60.0	73.1
Weighted PCS(ICF)	46.2	100.0	100.0	58.3	75.0	70.0	90.9	55.6	74.5
Weighted PCS(IDF)	42.9	100.0	100.0	75.0	66.7	61.5	90.9	50.0	73.4
One&Only Filter1	36.4	85.7	80.0	83.3	64.3	58.3	90.0	75.0	71.6
Average	43.0	93.5	88.3	71.9	66.5	60.7	92.3	63.7	72.5

Table 3 shows the recall ratio of 6 algorithms. The recall ratio is computed as (the number of correct classifications/the total number of classifications). Through classes, DEC and DSP shows the best recall ratio and DCL shows the worst recall ratio. The simplest algorithm, One&Only, shows the best performance of the 6 algorithms. When algorithms are weighted by the term frequency in a document, the performance was improved by 0.3%–7.3%. Not surprisingly *PCS(ICF)* was greatly affected by this local information but not *PCS(IDF)*.

4   Further Improvement

In this paper, the simple classification algorithm One&Only shows good performance in comparison to the algorithms based on both *ICF* and *IDF* factors. However, the class feature sets do not include, on average, 8.2% terms in the testing document. In the future, the class feature sets extracted from more extensive training data would improve classification algorithm performance.

The morphological analyser and compound noun analyser are required to improve disambiguation between noun and proper noun (e.g. "현대" (the present) vs "현대" (Hyundai enterpreneur)) because Korean is not a case-sensitive language. In addition, a Korean NP parser rather than a compound noun analysis would improve the accuracy of the extraction of class feature set by using syntactic categories, such as adjective, affix, cardinal, and dependent noun. The compound noun analysis would be improved to handle the bilingual terms and the alphanumerical terms.

If the system cannot provide class feature sets from training data enough to cover all terms in the documents classified, there would be unknown terms that do not belong to any class feature sets. If the number of unknown terms is large, then this will affect the classification results. In this case, a thesaurus or Korean Noun/VerbNet [15] would be one possible solution.

5   Conclusion

Document classification based on statistical methods will contribute to the efficiency and effectiveness of information search and information filtering. However, previous techniques have employed complex training and classification algorithms. This paper describes a parsimonious document classification algorithm without a complex learning process, pure comparisons of both ICF and IDF factors for document classification algorithms, and an efficient method of Korean compound noun analysis. When analysing Korean compound noun terms, an agenda-based chart parsing technique was applied to longest substring extraction, with a heuristic penalty score system.

The method described in this paper extracted the root forms of words of four categories (e.g. are noun, verb, proper noun (i.e. name) and adjective) for class features and classification, after applying morphological analysis to the document rather than the use of direct terms excluding stop words and low frequency words.

The performance of the simple classification algorithm, One&Only, was satisfactory, compared to complex algorithms based on *ICF* and *IDF*, on the basis of complexity of classification and training processes. The One&Only algorithm correctly classifies 66% of the testing documents. *PCS(ICF)* weighted by term frequencies in the testing document resulted in 71.6% success rate of correct classification. When the algorithm is weighted by term frequency in documents, *ICF(PCS)* was greatly affected but not *IDF(PCS)*. The overlapping rate between class feature sets affects classification results and the class with the least overlapping class features showed the best classification result.

Acknowledgement. We greatly appreciate the permission of Prof. Kang, S. from Kookmin University, to use the Linux version of his Korean Morphology Analysis, HAM. His application contributes to the implementation of document classification system in this paper.

References

1. Allan, J., Leuski, A., Swan, R., Byrd, D.: Evaluating combinations of ranked lists and visualizations of inter-document similarity. Information Processing and Management. 37 (2001) 435–458
2. Apte, C., Demerau, F., Weiss M.: Automated Learning of Decision Rules for Text Categorization. ACM Transactions on Information Systems. 12(3) (1994) 233–251
3. Arppe A.: Term Extraction from Unrestricted Text. http://www.lingsoft.fi/doc/nptool/ term- extraction. (1995)
4. Brasethvik, T., Gulla J.: Natural Language Analysis for Semantic Document Modeling. Data & Knowledge Engineering. 38 (2001) 45–62
5. Cohen, W., Singer, Y.: Context-Sensitive Learning Methods for Text Categorization, ACM Transactions on Information Systems, 7(2) (1999) 141–173
6. Earley, J.: An Efficient Context-Free Parsing Algorithm. CACM. 13(2) (1970) 94–102
7. Fuketa, M., Lee, S., Tsuji, T., Okada, M., Aoe, J.: A Document Classification Method by Using Field Association Words. Information Science. 126 (2000) 57–70
8. Han, K., Sun, B., Han, S., Rim, K.: A Study on Development of Automatic Categorization System for Internet Documents. KIPS Journal. 7(9) (2000) 2867–2875
9. Hirshberg, D.S.: Algorithms for the Longest Common Subsequence Problem. The Journal of ACM. 24(4) (1977) 664–675
10. Joachims, T.: A Probabilistic Analysis of the Rocchio Algorithm with TFIDF for Text Categorization. Proceedings of International Conference of Machine Learning (CIML97). (1997) 143–151
11. Kang, S.: Korean Morphological Analysis Using Syllable Information and Multi-word Unit Information. Ph.D thesis. Seoul National University (1993)
12. Kang, S.: Korean Morphological Analysis Program for Linux OS, http://nlp.kookmin.ac.kr. (2001)
13. Lewis, D., Jones, K.S.: Natural Language Processing for Information Retrieval. Communication of the ACM. 39(1) (1996) 92–101
14. Li, Y., Jain, A.: Classification of Text Documents. The Computer Journal. 41(8) (1998) 537–546
15. Moon, Y., Min, K.: (2000). Verifying Appropriateness of the Semantic Networks and Integration for the Selectional Restriction Relation. Proceedings of the 2000 MIS/OA International Conference. Seoul Korea (2000) 535–539
16. Mostafa, J., Lam, W.: Automatic classification using supervised learning in a medical document filtering application. Information Processing and Management. 36 (2000) 415–444
17. Salton, G., Singhal, A., Mitra, M., Buckley C.: Automatic Text Structuring and Summarization. Information Processing and Management. 33(2) (1997) 193–207
18. Yang, Y., Liu, X.: A Re-examination of Text Categorization Methods. Proceedings of ACM SIGIR Conference on Research and Development Retrieval. (1999) 42–49

Experiments in Query Paraphrasing for Information Retrieval

Ingrid Zukerman[1], Bhavani Raskutti[2], and Yingying Wen[1]

[1] School of Computer Science and Software Engineering
Monash University, Clayton, VICTORIA 3800, AUSTRALIA
{ingrid,ywen}@csse.monash.edu.au
[2] Telstra Research Laboratories
770 Blackburn Road, Clayton, VICTORIA 3168, AUSTRALIA
Bhavani.Raskutti@team.telstra.com

Abstract. We investigate the effect of paraphrase generation on document retrieval performance. Specifically, we describe experiments where three information sources are used to generate lexical paraphrases of queries posed to the Internet. These information sources are: WordNet, a Webster-based thesaurus, and a combination of Webster and WordNet. Corpus-based information and word-similarity information are then used to rank the paraphrases. We evaluated our mechanism using 404 queries whose answers reside in the LA Times subset of the TREC-9 corpus. Our experiments show that query paraphrasing improves retrieval performance, and that performance is influenced both by the number of paraphrases generated for a query and by their quality. Specifically, the best performance was obtained using WordNet, which improves document recall by 14% and increases the number of questions that can be answered by 8%.

1 Introduction

In recent years, we have witnessed the development of a large number of domain-specific retrieval systems that are accessed by a large and diverse user base, e.g., company FAQs and help systems. Consequently, the vocabulary of the queries posed by the users is often different from the vocabulary within particular Internet resources, leading to retrieval failure. In this paper, we investigate the effect of lexical paraphrases, which replace the content words of the queries, on document retrieval performance. Specifically, we describe experiments where three information sources are used to generate lexical paraphrases: WordNet [1], a thesaurus automatically constructed on the basis of the Webster on-line dictionary, and a combination of the Webster-based thesaurus and WordNet. These information sources together with part-of-speech information are used to propose words that may be used to replace the original words in a query. We then build candidate paraphrases from combinations of these replacement words. The resultant paraphrases are scored using word co-occurrence information obtained from a corpus and word-similarity scores obtained from the Webster-based thesaurus, and the highest scoring paraphrases are retained.

R.I. McKay and J. Slaney (Eds.): AI 2002, LNAI 2557, pp. 24–35, 2002.
© Springer-Verlag Berlin Heidelberg 2002

Our evaluation assessed the quality of the generated paraphrases, as well as the effect of query paraphrasing on document retrieval performance. Both assessments were based on paraphrases of 404 queries whose answers reside in the LA Times subset of the TREC-9 corpus. The three information sources yielded paraphrases of different quality according to our taggers (with the Webster-WordNet combination yielding the best paraphrases, and the Webster-based thesaurus yielding the worst). However, these differences did not transfer to document retrieval performance, where the best performance was obtained using WordNet alone. This information source yielded a 14% improvement in document recall, and an 8% improvement in the number of queries that can be answered with the retrieved documents (Section 6).

In the next section we describe related research. In Section 3, we discuss the resources used by our mechanism. The paraphrase generation and document retrieval processes are described in Section 4. Section 5 presents sample paraphrases, followed by our evaluation and concluding remarks.

2   Related Research

The vocabulary mis-match between user queries and indexed documents is often addressed through query expansion. Two common techniques for query expansion are *blind relevance feedback* [2,3] and *word sense disambiguation (WSD)* [4,5,6,7]. Blind relevance feedback consists of retrieving a small number of documents using a query given by a user, and then constructing an expanded query that includes content words that appear frequently in these documents. This expanded query is used to retrieve a new set of documents. WSD often precedes query expansion to avoid retrieving irrelevant information. Mihalcea and Moldovan [4] and Lytinen *et al.* [5] used a machine readable thesaurus, specifically WordNet [1], to obtain the sense of a word, while Schütze and Pedersen [6] and Lin [7] used a corpus-based approach where they automatically constructed a thesaurus on the basis of contextual information. Harabagiu *et al.* [8] offer a different form of query expansion, where they use WordNet to propose synonyms for the words in a query, and apply heuristics to select which words to paraphrase. The improvements in retrieval performance reported by Mitra *et al.* [3] are comparable to those reported here (note that these researchers consider precision, while we consider recall). The results obtained by Schütze and Pedersen and by Lytinen *et al.* are encouraging. However, experimental results reported in [9,10] indicate that the improvement in IR performance due to WSD is restricted to short queries, and that IR performance is very sensitive to disambiguation errors.

Our approach to document retrieval differs from the above approaches in that the expansion of a query takes the form of alternative lexical paraphrases. The expectation is that these paraphrases will also be useful when performing answer extraction in the next stage of this project. Like Harabagiu *et al.* [8], we obtain from an on-line resource alternative words to those in the original query. However, our method for the generation of these alternatives [11] differs from theirs. In addition, in this research we focus on the comparison of the retrieval performance obtained using three information sources for the generation of lexical paraphrases: WordNet, a thesaurus automatically constructed on the basis of the Webster on-line dictionary, and a combination of the Webster-based thesaurus and WordNet.

3   Resources

Our system uses syntactic, semantic and statistical information for paraphrase generation. Syntactic information for each query was obtained from Brill's part-of-speech (PoS) tagger [12]. Two types of semantic information were obtained: (1) different types of synonyms for the words in a query were obtained from WordNet [1], and (2) words whose dictionary definition is similar to that of the words in a query were obtained from the Webster on-line dictionary (http://www.dict.org). The calculation of the similarity scores between the dictionary words is described in Section 4.4. The corpus used for information retrieval and for the collection of statistical information was the LA Times portion of the NIST Text Research Collection (//trec.nist.gov). This corpus was small enough to satisfy our disk space limitations, and sufficiently large to yield statistically significant results (131,896 documents). Full-text indexing was performed for the documents in the LA Times collection, using lemmas (rather than words). The lemmas for the words in the LA Times collection were also obtained from WordNet [1].

The statistical information and the word-similarity scores obtained from the Webster dictionary were used to assign a score to the paraphrases generated for a query (Section 4.4). The statistical information was stored in a lemma dictionary (202,485 lemmas) and a lemma-pair dictionary (37,341,156 lemma-pairs). The lemma dictionary associates with each lemma the number of times it appears in the corpus. The lemma-pair dictionary associates with each lemma-pair the number of times it appears in a five-word window in the corpus (not counting stop words and closed-class words). Lemma-pairs which appear only once constitute 64% of the pairs, and were omitted from our dictionary owing to disk space limitations.

4   Procedure

The procedure for paraphrasing a query consists of the following steps:

1. Tokenize, tag and lemmatize the query.
2. Generate replacement lemmas for each content lemma in the query (stop words are ignored).
3. Propose paraphrases for the query using different combinations of replacement lemmas, compute a score for each paraphrase, and rank the paraphrases according to their score. The lemmatized query plus the 19 top paraphrases are retained.

Documents are then retrieved for the query and its paraphrases.

4.1   Tagging and Lemmatizing the Queries

We used the part-of-speech (PoS) of a word to constrain the number of replacement words generated for it. Brill's tagger incorrectly tagged 16% of the queries, which were then manually corrected. After tagging, each query was lemmatized (using WordNet). This was done since the index used for document retrieval is lemma-based.

4.2 Proposing Replacements for Each Word

We investigated three information sources for proposing replacements for the content words in a query: WordNet, an automatically-built thesaurus based on the Webster dictionary, and a combination of Webster and WordNet. WordNet is a knowledge-intensive, hand-built, lexical repository, which provides a baseline against which we can compare the performance obtained using an automatically constructed thesaurus. The hybrid Webster+WordNet combination enables us to assess the relative contribution of each of these resources to the system's performance.

WordNet. The following types of WordNet synonyms were generated for each content lemma in a query: synonyms, attributes, pertainyms and seealsos [1].[1] For example, according to WordNet, a synonym for "high" is "steep", an attribute is "height", and a seealso is "tall"; a pertainym for "chinese" is "China".

Webster. A thesaurus based on the Webster dictionary was automatically constructed using the vector-space model. To this effect, we built a vector from the content lemmas in the definition of each word in the dictionary (excluding stop words). The weight of each content lemma in the vector was determined using a variant of the TFIDF measure (Term Frequency Inverse Document Frequency) [13]. We then applied the cosine measure to determine the similarity between the vector corresponding to each word in the dictionary and the vectors corresponding to the other words. The words that were most similar to the word under consideration were retained, together with their cosine similarity measure.

Our use of the Webster dictionary differs from the corpus-based approaches for automatic thesaurus construction described in Section 2 [6,7] in that these approaches build similarity lists based on the context where the words are used. In contrast, our similarity lists are built based on dictionary definitions of the words. Also, it is worth noting that the context-based approach requires a larger corpus than the dictionary-based approach.

Webster+WordNet. We used additional WordNet options, including hypernyms and hyponyms, when generating replacement lemmas for the content lemmas in a query. We then employed the similarity list obtained from the Webster-based thesaurus to filter the candidates proposed by WordNet.[2] If a lemma was absent from the Webster-based thesaurus, then only its WordNet synonyms were considered. The expectation was that this approach would yield the best of both worlds, by combining the different perspectives afforded by these resources.

4.3 Paraphrasing Queries

Query paraphrases were generated by an iterative process which considers each content lemma in a query in turn, and proposes a replacement lemma from those collected from

---

[1] In preliminary experiments we also generated hypernyms and hyponyms. However, this increased exponentially the number alternative paraphrases.

[2] This filtering process curbs the combinatorial explosion which took place when using hypernyms and hyponyms in the WordNet-only experiment.

our information sources (Section 4.2). Queries which do not have sufficient context are not paraphrased. These are queries where all the words except one are stop words or closed-class words.

4.4 Computing Paraphrase Scores

The score of a paraphrase depends on two factors: (1) how common are the lemma combinations in the paraphrase, and (2) how similar is the paraphrase to the original query. The paraphrases generated using only WordNet were scored using the first factor (since WordNet does not maintain word similarity scores), while the paraphrases generated using the Webster-based thesaurus were scored using both factors.

Probability of lemma combinations. Ideally, this score would be represented by $\Pr(l_1, \ldots, l_n)$, where n is the number of lemmas in the paraphrase. However, in the absence of sufficient information to compute this joint probability, approximations based on conditional probabilities are often used, e.g.,

$$\Pr(l_1, \ldots, l_n) \simeq \Pr(l_n | l_{n-1}) \times \ldots \times \Pr(l_2 | l_1) \times \Pr(l_1)$$

Unfortunately, this approximation yielded poor paraphrases in preliminary trials. We postulate that this is due to two reasons: (1) it takes into account the interaction between a lemma l_i and only one other lemma (without considering the rest of the lemmas in the query), and (2) relatively infrequent lemma combinations involving one frequent lemma are penalized (which is correct for conditional probabilities). For instance, if l_j appears 10 times in the corpus and l_i-l_j appears 4 times, $P(l_i | l_j) = 0.4\alpha$ (where α is a normalizing constant). In contrast, if l'_j appears 200 times in the corpus and l'_i-l'_j appears 30 times, $P(l'_i | l'_j) = 0.15\alpha$. However, l'_i-l'_j is a more frequent lemma combination, and should contribute a higher score to the paraphrase.

To address these problems, we propose using the joint probability of a pair of lemmas instead of their conditional probability. In the above example, this yields $P(l_i, l_j) = 4\beta$ and $P(l'_i, l'_j) = 30\beta$ (where β is a normalizing constant). These probabilities reflect more accurately the goodness of paraphrases containing these lemma-pairs. The resulting approximation of the probability of a paraphrase composed of lemmas $l_1, \ldots, l_n$ is as follows:

$$\Pr(l_1, \ldots, l_n) \simeq \prod_{i=1}^{n} \prod_{j=i+1}^{n} \Pr(l_i, l_j) \tag{1}$$

$\Pr(l_i, l_j)$ is obtained directly from the lemma-pair frequencies, yielding

$$\Pr(l_1, \ldots, l_n) \simeq \prod_{i=1}^{n} \prod_{j=i+1}^{n} \beta \times \mathrm{freq}(l_i, l_j)$$

where β is a normalizing constant.[3] Since this constant is not informative with respect to the relative scores of the paraphrases for a particular query, we drop it from consideration, and use only the frequencies to calculate the score of a paraphrase. Thus, our frequency-based scoring function is

$$\mathcal{PF}(l_1, \ldots, l_n) = \prod_{i=1}^{n} \prod_{j=i+1}^{n} \mathrm{freq}(l_i, l_j) \tag{2}$$

---

[3] $\beta = \dfrac{1}{\text{\# of lemma-pairs}^{n(n-1)/2}} = \dfrac{1}{37{,}341{,}156^{n(n-1)/2}}$.

Similarity between a paraphrase and the original query. This score is the average of the similarity score between each lemma in the paraphrase and the corresponding lemma in the original query. Given the original query composed of content lemmas $\{ol_1, \ldots, ol_n\}$, and a paraphrase $\{l_1, \ldots, l_n\}$, such that the similarity score between l_i and ol_i is $sim(l_i, ol_i)$ (obtained using the cosine similarity measure as described in Section 4.2), the similarity score of the paraphrase is

$$\mathcal{SIM}(l_1, \ldots, l_n) = \frac{1}{n} \sum_{i=1}^{n} sim(l_i, ol_i) \tag{3}$$

Thus, the score of a paraphrase is

$$\mathcal{PS}(l_1, \ldots, l_n) = \mathcal{PF}(l_1, \ldots, l_n) \times \mathcal{SIM}(l_1, \ldots, l_n) \tag{4}$$

4.5 Retrieving Documents for Each Query

Our retrieval process differs from the standard one in that for each query Q, we adjust the scores of the retrieved documents according to the scores of the paraphrases of Q (obtained from Equation 4). Our retrieval process consists of the following steps:

1. For each paraphrase P_i of Q ($i = 0, \ldots, \#\_para\_Q$), where P_0 is the lemmatized query:
   a) Extract the content lemmas from P_i: $l_{i,1}, \ldots l_{i,N}$, where N is the number of content lemmas in paraphrase P_i.
   b) For each lemma, compute a score for the retrieved documents using the TFIDF measure. Let $tfidf(D_k, l_{i,j})$ be the score of document D_k retrieved for lemma $l_{i,j}$ ($j = 1, \ldots, N$). When a document D_k is retrieved by more than one lemma in a paraphrase P_i, its TFIDF scores are added, yielding the score $\sum_{j=1}^{N} tfidf(D_k, l_{i,j})$. This score indicates how well D_k matches the lemmas in paraphrase P_i. In order to take into account the plausibility of P_i, this score is multiplied by $\mathcal{PS}(P_i)$ – the score of P_i obtained from Equation 4. This yields $\mathcal{DS}_{k,i}$, the score of document D_k for paraphrase P_i.

$$\mathcal{DS}_{k,i} = \mathcal{PS}(P_i) \times \sum_{j=1}^{N} tfidf(D_k, l_{i,j}) \tag{5}$$

2. For each document D_k, add the scores from each paraphrase (Equation 5), yielding

$$\mathcal{DS}_k = \sum_{i=1}^{\#\_para\_Q} \mathcal{PS}(P_i) \times \sum_{j=1}^{N} tfidf(D_k, l_{i,j}) \tag{6}$$

An outcome of this method is that lemmas which appear in several paraphrases receive a higher weight. This indirectly identifies the important words in a query, which positively affects retrieval performance (Section 6.2).

This approach combines the paraphrase scoring factors into a single score, separating the paraphrase-scoring process from the document retrieval process. In the future, we propose to investigate an alternative approach which combines the lemma similarity scores obtained from the Webster-based thesaurus with the TFIDF scores obtained from

Table 1. Sample query paraphrases: WordNet, Webster, Webster+WordNet

Who is the Greek God of the Sea ?		
WordNet	*Webster*	*Webster+WordNet*
who be the greek god of the sea ?	*who be the greek god of the sea ?*	*who be the greek god of the sea ?*
who be the greek god of the ocean ?	who be the greek god of the profound ?	who be the greek god of the ocean ?
who be the greek god of the sea ?	who be the greek god of the swell ?	who be the greek divinity of the sea ?
who be the greece deity of the sea ?	who be the greek god of the surf ?	who be the grecian god of the sea ?
who be the greece divinity of the sea ?	who be the greek god of the terra ?	who be the hellenic god of the sea ?
who be the greece immortal of the sea ?	who be the greek god of the wae ?	who be the grecian god of the ocean ?
who be the greece idol of the sea ?	who be the greek god of the salina ?	who be the hellenic god of the ocean ?
who be the greek deity of the sea ?	who be the greek god of the seacoast ?	who be the greek divinity of the ocean ?
who be the greek divinity of the sea ?	who be the greek god of the apogee ?	who be the grecian divinity of the sea ?
who be the greek immortal of the sea ?	who be the greek god of the river ?	who be the grecian divinity of the ocean ?
who be the greek idol of the sea ?	who be the greek god of the surge ?	who be the hellenic divinity of the sea ?
Who invented television ?		
WordNet	*Webster*	*Webster+WordNet*
who invent television ?	*who invent television ?*	*who invent television ?*
who manufacture television ?	who plan television ?	who invent tv ?
who manufacture video ?	who learn television ?	who forge tv ?
who manufacture tv ?	who smith television ?	who invent video ?
who invent tv ?	who imagine television ?	who invent telly ?
who devise television ?	who occur television ?	who forge television ?
who forge tv ?	who frame television ?	who forge video ?
who invent video ?	who investigate television ?	who forge telly ?
who invent telly ?	who plot television ?	who fabricate television ?
who contrive television ?	who consult television ?	who fabricate tv ?
who contrive tv ?	who fabric television ?	who fabricate video ?

the document retrieval process. In this approach, the TFIDF scores will be weighted by the similarity scores, yielding the following equation instead of Equation 5 (recall that the 0-th paraphrase is the lemmatized query)

$$\mathcal{DS}_{k,i} = \mathcal{PF}(P_i) \times \sum_{j=1}^{N} sim(l_{i,j}, l_{0,j}) \times \textit{tfidf}(D_k, l_{i,j}) \qquad (7)$$

5   Sample Results

Table 1 shows the top 10 paraphrases (in ranked order of their score) generated by our system for two sample queries using the three information sources (the lemmatized query is listed first and shown in italics). These examples illustrate the combined effect of contextual information and the lemmas suggested by WordNet, the Webster-based thesaurus, and both resources in combination. The first query shows that the paraphrases obtained using WordNet (with and without the Webster-based thesaurus) are more felic-itous than those obtained with the Webster-based thesaurus alone. This outcome may be attributed to the generally appropriate synonyms returned by WordNet for the lemmas in this query, while the replacement of "sea" with "terra" and "saline" suggested by the Webster-based thesaurus is inappropriate. The second query yields a mixed paraphras-ing performance for all information sources. The problematic paraphrases are generated because our corpus-based information supports WordNet's suggestion of "video" as a synonym for "television"[4], and WordNet's and Webster's suggestions of replacement

---

[4] The word "television" does not appear in the Webster on-line dictionary (published in 1913). Hence, it was paraphrased using only WordNet synonyms in the combined experiment.

lemmas for "invent" (e.g., "manufacture", "fabricate", "plot"), which are inappropriate in the context of the question.

6   Evaluation

The performance of our system was evaluated along two dimensions: subjective and task-oriented. Our subjective evaluation sought to assess the quality of the paraphrases generated using the three information sources. The task-oriented evaluation determined whether paraphrases improved retrieval performance. We used the TREC-9 judgments to identify documents in the LA Times collection which contain answers to the TREC-9 queries. From a total of 131,896 documents, there were 1211 documents which had correct judgments for 404 of the 693 TREC-9 queries. These 404 queries were used for both types of evaluation.

6.1   Subjective Evaluation

Two people outside the research team inspected the paraphrases generated using Word-Net. This allowed us to calculate a Kappa statistic for inter-tagger agreement [14], which was 51%, indicating that opinions regarding the appropriateness of a paraphrase differ substantially. One of the taggers also assessed the paraphrases obtained using the Webster-based thesaurus and the Webster+WordNet combination. The paraphrases were tagged as Right/Wrong, and Common/Uncommon (only for Right tags). A paraphrase was tagged Right if it conveyed the same meaning as the original sentence. A Right paraphrase was tagged Uncommon if the tagger thought it had unusual words.

WordNet. One of our taggers considered 36.5% of our paraphrases correct, while the other tagged as correct only 29.5% of the paraphrases (the first tagger was retained for the other two experiments). The main difference between the taggers was in the level of accuracy they demanded from the paraphrases. For instance, one tagger accepted using "epithet" as a synonym of the noun "name", while the other rejected this usage. The taggers also differed in their assessment for the Common/Uncommon dimension. The first tagger considered 73% of the correct paraphrases to be Common, while the second tagger considered 65% to be Common. This variation, which is consistent with the variation in Right/Wrong assessments, may be attributed to differences in the taggers' tolerance.

Webster. The paraphrases generated by this information source were considered quite inappropriate by our tagger, who judged correct only 9% of the paraphrases. Of these, the vast majority (89%) were considered Common.

Webster+WordNet. This information source generated the best paraphrases, with 44.3% of the paraphrases judged Right by the tagger, and 85.6% of the Right paraphrases considered to be Common.

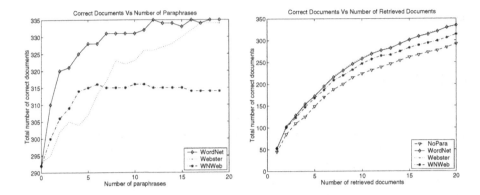

Fig. 1. Effect of information source on document recall: WordNet, Webster-based thesaurus, and Webster+WordNet

6.2   Task-Based Evaluation

The performance of our system was evaluated by comparing the documents retrieved using the three information sources with the judgments for the 404 TREC-9 queries which had answers within the LA Times collection.

For each run, we submitted to the retrieval engine increasing sets of paraphrases as follows: first the lemmatized query alone (Set 0), next the query plus 1 paraphrase (Set 1), then the query plus 2 paraphrases (Set 2), and so on, up to a maximum of 19 paraphrases (Set 19). For each submission, we varied the number of documents returned by the retrieval engine from 1 to 20 documents.

We consider two measures of retrieval performance: (1) *document recall*, and (2) *number of queries answered*. We use document recall because in a question answering application we want to maximize the chances of finding the answer to a user's query. The hope is that returning a large number of documents that contain this answer (measured by recall) will be helpful during the answer extraction phase of this project, e.g., by using a clustering mechanism [15]. However, recall alone is not sufficient to evaluate the performance of our system, as even with a high overall document recall, it is possible that we are retrieving many documents for relatively few queries, and leaving many queries unanswered. We therefore consider a second measure, viz the number of queries answered, which counts the number of queries for which the system has retrieved at least one document that contains the answer to the query.

Document Recall. Figure 1(a) depicts the number of correct documents retrieved (for 20 retrieved documents) for each of the three information sources (WordNet, Webster and Webster+WordNet) as a function of the number of paraphrases in a set (from 0 to 19). In order to compare queries that had different numbers of paraphrases, whenever the maximum number of paraphrases for a query was less than 19, the results obtained for this maximum number were replicated for the paraphrase sets of higher cardinality. For instance, if only 6 paraphrases were generated for a query, the number of correct documents retrieved for the 6 paraphrases was replicated for Sets 7 to 19.

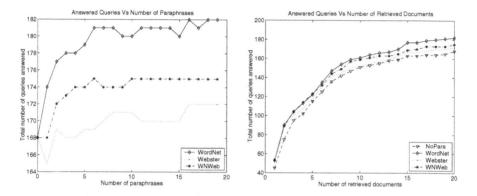

Fig. 2. Effect of information source on number of queries answered: WordNet, Webster-based thesaurus, and Webster+WordNet

When only the lemmatized query was submitted for retrieval (0 paraphrases), 292 correct documents were retrieved. For WordNet and Webster+WordNet (designated WN-Web in Figures 1 and 2), this number increases dramatically for the first few paraphrases and eventually levels out. The leveling-out point occurs earlier for the Webster+WordNet combination than for WordNet alone, since the combined information source generates the smallest number of paraphrases (5.2 paraphrases per query, compared to 9.4 paraphrases per query for WordNet, and 13.9 for Webster). However, the retrieval performance for WordNet is significantly better than that obtained with Webster+WordNet. The retrieval performance for the Webster-based thesaurus differs from the performance for the other two information sources in that it improves steadily as more paraphrases are generated, reaching a maximum of 334 correct documents retrieved for 18 paraphrases (compared to 335 correct documents retrieved when using WordNet).

Figure 1(b) depicts the number of correct documents retrieved (for 19 paraphrases or maximum paraphrases) for the three information sources as a function of the number of documents retrieved (from 1 to 20). As for Figure 1(a), paraphrasing is shown to improve recall performance for all information sources. Specifically, the recall performance obtained for the Webster-based thesaurus is similar to that obtained for WordNet, while the recall for the combined Webster+WordNet resource is worse. In addition, as expected, recall performance improves as more documents are retrieved.

As shown by our subjective evaluation, the Webster+WordNet combination yields significantly better and fewer paraphrases than the other information sources. Surprisingly however, this effect did not transfer to the retrieval process, since WordNet alone performed significantly better than the Webster+WordNet combination, and Webster alone performed significantly better than the combined information source when a large number of paraphrases was used for document retrieval. These results indicate that document recall is mainly influenced by the average number of paraphrases per query, which may be used to overcome the effect of paraphrases of low quality.

Number of Queries Answered. Figure 2(a) depicts the number of queries for which the retrieved documents contain answers (for 20 retrieved documents) for each of the three information sources (WordNet, Webster and Webster+WordNet) as a function of the number of paraphrases in a set (from 0 to 19). As for document recall, WordNet exhibits the best performance, improving the number of answered queries from 169 (without paraphrasing) to 182. The combined Webster+WordNet combination also increases the number of answered queries, but to a lesser extent. In contrast, the Webster-based the-saurus alone initially reduces the number of answered queries, and achieves only a small improvement in performance when a large number of paraphrases is used for document retrieval. This indicates that the recall performance of the Webster-based thesaurus is due to an increase in the number of relevant documents retrieved for queries that already had answer-documents without being paraphrased. In the future, we will investigate a paraphrasing technique which leverages the strengths of each information source by combining WordNet-based retrieval with Webster-based retrieval using a union-like op-erator, rather than an intersection or filtering operator.

Figure 2(b) depicts the number of answered queries (for 19 paraphrases or maximum paraphrases) for the three information sources as a function of the number of documents retrieved (from 1 to 20). As for Figure 2(a), maximum paraphrasing is shown to improve the number of questions answered for the all the information sources. In addition, as expected, the number of questions answered increases as more documents are retrieved.

7   Conclusion

We have offered a mechanism for the generation of lexical paraphrases of queries posed to an Internet resource, and have compared the performance of this mechanism when using three lexical information sources: WordNet, a Webster-based thesaurus, and Webster+WordNet. Statistical information, obtained from a corpus, and word-similarity scores, obtained from the Webster-based thesaurus, were used to rank the paraphrases. Our results show that: (1) query paraphrasing improves document retrieval performance, (2) document recall is mainly influenced by the average number of paraphrases generated for a query, and (3) question-answering performance is influenced both by the average number of paraphrases and their quality. The information source that gave the best perfor-mance overall (WordNet) generated a moderate number of medium quality paraphrases per query (compared to Webster, which yielded many poor quality paraphrases per query, and Webster+WordNet, which generated a few high quality paraphrases per query).

References

1. Miller, G., Beckwith, R., Fellbaum, C., Gross, D., Miller, K.: Introduction to WordNet: An on-line lexical database. Journal of Lexicography **3** (1990) 235–244
2. Buckley, C., Salton, G., Allan, J., Singhal, A.: Automatic query expansion using SMART. In Harman, D., ed.: The Third Text REtrieval Conference (TREC3). National Institute of Standards and Technology Special Publication (1995)
3. Mitra, M., Singhal, A., Buckley, C.: Improving automatic query expansion. In: SIGIR'98 – Proceedings of the 21th ACM International Conference on Research and Development in Information Retrieval, Melbourne, Australia (1998) 206–214

4. Mihalcea, R., Moldovan, D.: A method for word sense disambiguation of unrestricted text. In: ACL99 – Proceedings of the 37th Annual Meeting of the Association for Computational Linguistics, Baltimore, Maryland (1999)
5. Lytinen, S., Tomuro, N., Repede, T.: The use of WordNet sense tagging in FAQfinder. In: Proceedings of the AAAI00 Workshop on AI and Web Search, Austin, Texas (2000)
6. Schütze, H., Pedersen, J.O.: Information retrieval based on word senses. In: Proceedings of the Fourth Annual Symposium on Document Analysis and Information Retrieval, Las Vegas, Nevada (1995) 161–175
7. Lin, D.: Automatic retrieval and clustering of similar words. In: COLING-ACL'98 – Proceedings of the International Conference on Computational Linguistics and the Annual Meeting of the Association for Computational Linguistics, Montreal, Canada (1998) 768–774
8. Harabagiu, S., Moldovan, D., Pasca, M., Mihalcea, R., Surdeanu, M., Bunescu, R., Girju, R., Rus, V., Morarescu, P.: The role of lexico-semantic feedback in open domain textual question-answering. In: ACL01 – Proceedings of the 39th Annual Meeting of the Association for Computational Linguistics, Toulouse, France (2001) 274–281
9. Sanderson, M.: Word sense disambiguation and information retrieval. In: SIGIR'94 – Proceedings of the 17th ACM International Conference on Research and Development in Information Retrieval, Dublin, Ireland (1994) 142–151
10. Gonzalo, J., Verdejo, F., Chugur, I., Cigarran, J.: Indexing with WordNet synsets can improve text retrieval. In: Proceedings of the COLING-ACL'98 Workshop on Usage of WordNet in Natural Language Processing Systems, Montreal, Canada (1998) 38–44
11. Zukerman, I., Raskutti, B.: Lexical query paraphrasing for document retrieval. In: COLING'02 – Proceedings of the International Conference on Computational Linguistics, Taipei, Taiwan (2002) 1177-1183
12. Brill, E.: A simple rule-based part of speech tagger. In: ANLP-92 – Proceedings of the Third Conference on Applied Natural Language Processing, Trento, IT (1992) 152–155
13. Salton, G., McGill, M.: An Introduction to Modern Information Retrieval. McGraw Hill (1983)
14. Carletta, J.: Assessing agreement on classification tasks: The Kappa statistic. Computational Linguistics **22** (1996) 249–254
15. Kwok, C.C., Etzioni, O., Weld, D.S.: Scaling question answering to the web. In: WWW10 – Proceedings of the Tenth International World Wide Web Conference, Hong Kong (2001) 150–161

Dynamic Decision-Making in Logic Programming and Game Theory

Marina De Vos and Dirk Vermeir

[1] Dept of Computer Science
University of Bath
mdv@cs.bath.ac.uk
[2] Dept. of Computer Science
Vrije Universiteit Brussel, VUB
dvermeir@vub.ac.be

Abstract. We present a framework for decision making with circumstance-dependent preferences and decisions. This formalism, called Ordered Choice Logic Programming, allows decisions that comprise multiple alternatives, which become available only when a choice between them is forced. The skeptical semantics is based on answer sets for which we provide a fixpoint characterization and a bottom-up algorithm. OCLPs can be used to represent and extend game theory concepts. We demonstrate that OCLPs allow an elegant translation of finite extensive games with perfect information such that the c-answer sets correspond to the Nash equilibria of the game. These equilibria are not player-deterministic, in the sense that a single player, given the other players' actions, could rationally leave an equilibrium state by changing her action profile. Therefor cautious Nash equilibria are introduced as the answer sets of the transformed game.

1 Introduction

Preferences or order among defaults and alternatives for a decision play an important role in knowledge representation and non-monotonic reasoning. In case of conflict, humans tend to prefer a default or alternative that corresponds to more reliable, more complete, more preferred or more specific information. In recent years, several proposals for the explicit representation of preference in logic programming formalisms have been put forward: [LV90,AAP+98] are just two examples.

Working with preferences/order has applications in various domains, e.g. law, object orientation, model based diagnosis or configuration tasks. In this paper we present a formalism that enables reasoning about decisions involving multiple alternatives that are dependent on the situation. The dynamics of our formalism is demonstrated by the following example.

Example 1. This year, the choice for a holiday destination has been reduced to a city trip to London or a fortnight stay in either Spain or Cuba. A weekend London is rather short and Cuba is expensive. With a larger budget however, we could have both a holiday in Cuba and a trip to London. Given these considerations, there are two possible outcomes: we have a small budget and we should opt for Spain, or with a larger budget, we can combine Cuba and London.

R.I. McKay and J. Slaney (Eds.): AI 2002, LNAI 2557, pp. 36–47, 2002.
© Springer-Verlag Berlin Heidelberg 2002

In both situations we have that Cuba, Spain and London are alternatives for the choice of a travel destination since to have no summer vacation is not an option. In the first outcome, we simply take the best possible alternative: Spain. Otherwise, we have good reason to take more than one alternative. So we take both Cuba and London.

To allow this kind of reasoning we need two mechanisms: one to set the conditional decisions and one to allow circumstance-dependent preferences for the possible alternatives of the decisions. As argued in [DVV99], choice logic programs are an intuitive tool for representing decision-problems, as the semantics ensures that exactly one alternative is chosen when the condition for the decision is met. For the preferences, we use a multi-alternative generalization of the ideas behind ordered logic programming[LV90]. Our formalism, called Ordered Choice Logic Programming (OCLP), combines the best of these formalisms by defining a strict partial order among choice logic programs, called components. Each component inherits the rules from less specific components. The normal semantics is used until a conflict arises; then the more specific alternative is decided upon. We equip our OCLPs with an answer set semantics to obtain the rational solutions for the represented decision-problem. A fixpoint characterization and an efficient algorithm for our semantics will be provided. Furthermore we demonstrate that a logic program or a choice logic program can be elegantly transformed to a negation-free OCLP such that the stable models of the former are obtained as the answer sets of the latter.

Although ordered choice logic programming can add new viewpoints to the above mentioned application domains, we will focus on a novel application in Game Theory. In [DVV00], it was shown that an extensive game with perfect information can be transformed into an OCLP such that the c-answer sets of the latter correspond to the Nash equilibria of the former. Although these equilibria are very useful for predicting the outcome of a game, it is possible that a player, given the other players' actions, still has a rational choice between multiple outcomes. To overcome this, we introduce cautious Nash equilibria as the answer sets of the transformed programs.

2   Choice Logic Programming

A *Choice Logic Program* [DVV99], CLP for short, is a finite set of rules of the form $A \leftarrow B$ where A and B are finite sets of ground atoms. Intuitively, atoms in A are assumed to be mutually exclusive while B is read as a conjunction (note that A may be empty, i.e. constraints are allowed). The set A is called the head of the rule r, denoted H_r, while B is its body, denoted B_r. In examples, we often use "$\oplus$" to denote exclusive or, while "," is used to denote conjunction.

The *Herbrand base* of a CLP P, denoted $\mathcal{B}_P$, is the set of all atoms that appear in P. An *interpretation* is a consistent[1] subset of $\mathcal{B}_P \cup \neg \mathcal{B}_P$. For an interpretation I, we use I^+ to denote its positive part, i.e. $I^+ = I \cap \mathcal{B}_P$. Similarly, we use I^- to denote the negative part of I, i.e. $I^- = \neg(I \cap \neg \mathcal{B}_P)$. An atom a is *true* (resp. *false*) w.r.t. to an interpretation I for a CLP P if $a \in I^+$ (resp. $a \in I^-$). An interpretation is *total* iff $I^+ \cup I^- = \mathcal{B}_P$. The set of all interpretations is denoted $\mathcal{I}_P$. The positive complement of an interpretation I, denoted $\bar{I}$, equals $\mathcal{B}_P \setminus I^+$.

---

[1] A set A is consistent iff $A \cap \neg A = \emptyset$.

A rule r in a CLP is said to be *applicable* w.r.t. an interpretation I when $B_r \subseteq I$. Since we are modeling choice, we have that r is *applied* when r is applicable and $|H_r \cap I| = 1^2$. A *model* is defined in the usual way as a total interpretation that makes every applicable rule applied. A model M is said to be *minimal* if there does not exist a model N such that $N^+ \subset M^+$. For choice logic programs, the stable model[3] and the minimal model semantics coincides.

3   Ordered Choice Logic Programming

An ordered choice logic program [DVV00] is a collection of choice logic programs, called components, each representing a portion of information. The relevance or preciseness of each component with respect to the other components is expressed by a strict pointed partial order[4].

Definition 1. *An **Ordered Choice Logic Program**, or OCLP, is a pair $\langle \mathcal{C}, \prec \rangle$ where $\mathcal{C}$ is a finite set of choice logic programs, called **components**, and "$\prec$" is a strict pointed partial order on $\mathcal{C}$.*

For two components $C_1, C_2 \in \mathcal{C}$, $C_1 \prec C_2$ implies that C_2 contains more general information than C_1. Throughout the examples, we will often represent an OCLP P by means of a directed acyclic graph (dag) in which the nodes represent the components and the arcs the $\prec$-relation.

Example 2. The decision problem from the introduction (Example 1) can easily be written as the OCLP in Figure 1.

For an OCLP P, we introduce P^* as the CLP that contains all the rules that appear in one of the components of the OCLP. Each rule $r \in P^*$ is assumed to be labeled by the component it was taken from and we use $c(r)$ to retrieve this component.

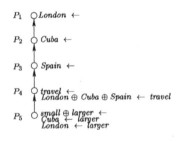

P_1 London ←

P_2 Cuba ←

P_3 Spain ←

P_4 travel ←
        London ⊕ Cuba ⊕ Spain ← travel

P_5 small ⊕ larger ←
        Cuba ← larger
        London ← larger

Fig. 1. The OCLP of Example 2

Having P^*, we can define an interpretation for an OCLP as an interpretation of the underlying P^*, leaving the definitions for an applicable and applied rule unchanged.

Example 3. The sets $I = \{ Cuba, small, \neg Spain, \neg travel \}$, $J = \{ travel, Cuba, small, \neg London, \neg Spain, \neg larger \}$, $K = \{ travel, Spain, small, \neg larger, \neg London, \neg Cuba \}$ and $L = \{ travel, larger, London, Spain, Cuba, \neg small \}$ are all interpretations for the OCLP of Example 2. The interpretation I makes the rule $small \oplus larger \leftarrow$ applied while the rule $London \leftarrow$ is applicable but not applied. While J, K and L are total, I is not.

---

[2] For a a set X, we use $|X|$ do denote its cardinality.

[3] [DVV99] for detailed information.

[4] A relation R on a set A is a strict partial order iff R is anti-reflexive, anti-symmetric and transitive. R is pointed if there is an element $a \in A$ such that aRb for all $b \in A$.

A decision involves a choice between several alternatives, as indicated by so-called *choice rules*, i.e. rules with multiple head atoms. To determine which atoms are alternatives for each other, we also need to take into account the preference order: an atom a is an *alternative* for an atom b in a component C if there is an applicable choice rule present in a component at least as preferred as C, such that a and b appear together in the head.

Definition 2. *Let $P = \langle \mathcal{C}, \prec \rangle$ be an OCLP, I an interpretation and let $C \in \mathcal{C}$. The set of **alternatives in** C for an atom $a \in \mathcal{B}_{P^*}$ w.r.t. I, denoted $\Omega_C^I(a)$, is defined as[5]:*

$$\Omega_C^I(a) = \{b \mid \exists r \in P^* \cdot c(r) \preccurlyeq C \wedge B_r \subseteq I \wedge a, b \in H_r \text{ with } a \neq b\}.$$

As long as we do not encounter any conflict, we can adapt the usual ordered logic semantics [LV90] where defeat among rules is used to select a more preferred alternative. But what happens if two alternatives are equally preferred? In this paper, we adopt a cautious approach[6] where a rule r is only defeated if there are more preferred rules suggesting alternatives for each atom in H_r.

Definition 3. *Let I be an interpretation for an OCLP P. A rule $r \in P^*$ is **defeated w.r.t.** I iff $\forall a \in H_r \cdot \exists r' \in P^* \cdot c(r') \prec c(r) \wedge B_{r'} \subseteq I \wedge H_{r'} \subseteq \Omega_{c(r)}^I(a)$.*

The reason for requiring that the head of a defeater contains only alternatives makes sure that the defeater is operational in the same context as the defeated rule.

Example 4. Reconsider the interpretations from Example 3. The alternatives for $Cuba$ in P_2 w.r.t. J are $\Omega_{P_2}^J(Cuba) = \{Spain, London\}$. W.r.t. I we obtain $\Omega_{P_2}^I(Cuba) = \emptyset$, since the choice rule in P_3 is not applicable. When we take P_5 instead of P_2, we obtain, w.r.t. J: $\Omega_{P_5}^J(Cuba) = \emptyset$.

The rule $London \leftarrow$ is defeated w.r.t. J by the rule $Cuba \leftarrow$. The rule $London \oplus Cuba \oplus Spain \leftarrow$ is defeated w.r.t. L by the two rules in P_5.

Definition 4. *Let P be an OCLP. A total interpretation I is a **model** iff every rule in P^* is either not applicable, applied or defeated w.r.t. I. A model M is called **minimal** iff M is minimal according to set inclusion.*

Example 5. In Example 3, only K and L are models. Model L is not minimal because of the model $Z = \{travel, larger, Cuba, London, \neg Spain, \neg small\}$. The minimal models K and Z correspond to the intuitive outcomes of the problem.

4 The Answer Set Semantics

4.1 Definition

The simple minimal semantics presented above does not always yield intuitive outcomes, as demonstrated by the program below.

---

[5] $\preccurlyeq$ is the reflexive closure of $\prec$.
[6] A credulous approach to this program can be found in [DVV00].

Example 6. Consider the program $P = \langle \{c_1, c_2, c_3\}, \prec \rangle$ where $c_1 = \{a \leftarrow\}$, $c_2 = \{b \leftarrow\}$, $c_3 = \{a \oplus b \leftarrow c\}$ and $c_3 \prec c_2 \prec c_1$. The minimal models are $\{a, b\}$, where no choice between a and b is forced, and $\{c, b\}$. The latter is not intuitive due to the gratuitous assumption of c.

We introduce the so-called answer set semantics which, while preserving minimality, prevents unnatural models such as the one from Example 6.

Definition 5. *Let M be a total interpretation for an OCLP P. The **Gelfond-Lifschitz transformation** for P w.r.t. M, denoted P^M, is the choice logic program obtained from P^* by removing all defeated rules. M is called an **answer set** for P iff M is a stable model for P^M.*

4.2   Fixpoint Characterization

Although negation is not explicitly present in an ordered choice logic program, it does appear implicitly. Taking a decision implies that you select one alternative to be true while the others need to be falsified. To group all atoms that may be considered false, we extend the notion of unfounded set for choice logic programs[DVV99] to handle preference. In order to do so, the notion of indefeasible rules is introduced to guarantee that a rule will not be defeated if one extends the current interpretation.

Definition 6. *Let I be an interpretation for an OCLP P. A rule r from P is said to be **indefeasible** w.r.t. I iff r is not defeated w.r.t. any interpretation J such that $I \subseteq J$. A set $X \subseteq \mathcal{B}_{P^*}$ is called an **unfounded set** w.r.t. I iff for each $a \in X$ one of the following conditions is satisfied:*

1. *$\exists r \equiv (a \oplus A \leftarrow B) \in P^* \cdot B \subseteq I \wedge A \cap I \neq \emptyset \wedge r$ is indefeasible w.r.t. I; or*
2. *$\exists \leftarrow B, a \cdot B \subseteq I$; or*
3. *$\forall r \in P^*$ where $a \in H_r$, one of the following conditions holds:*
    a) *$B_r \cap \neg I \neq \emptyset$; or*
    b) *$B_r \cap X \neq \emptyset$; or*
    c) *r is defeated w.r.t. I; or*
    d) *$(H_r \setminus \{a\}) \cap I \neq \emptyset$; or*
    e) *$H_r \cap B_r \neq \emptyset$.*

*The set of all unfounded sets for P w.r.t. I is denoted $\mathcal{U}_P(I)$. The **greatest unfounded set** for P w.r.t. I, denoted $\mathcal{GUS}_P(I)$, is the union of all unfounded sets for P w.r.t. I. I is said to be **unfounded-free** iff $I \cap \mathcal{GUS}_P(I) = \emptyset$.*

Condition (1) above expresses that the choice is exclusive (r cannot be defeated, so $|H_r \cap I|$ has to be 1 in order for I to be or become a model) and thus alternatives to the actual choice are to be considered false. Condition (2) implies that any atom that would cause a constraint to be violated must be considered false. Condition (3) generalizes the definition in [DVV99] where we have added conditions c) and d). The latter is a weaker version of condition (1). In case condition (3) is satisfied, we know that there is no reason to consider a true.

It is easy to verify that $\mathcal{GUS}_P(I)$ is itself an unfounded set for P w.r.t. I and that the $\mathcal{GUS}_P$-operator is monotonic.

The greatest unfounded set is a useful tool for the detection of models and answer sets, as demonstrated by the following theorem.

Theorem 1. *Let M be a model for an OCLP P. Then $M^- \in \mathcal{U}_P(M)$. Moreover, M is an answer set iff M is unfounded-free, i.e. $M \cap \mathcal{GUS}_P(M) = \emptyset$, which is itself equivalent to $\mathcal{GUS}_P(M) = M^-$.*

While the $\mathcal{GUS}_P$-operator yields false atoms, the next operator produces atoms that must be true in any model extension of its argument. Combined with $\mathcal{GUS}_P$, we obtain an operator that gives an indication on how to change an interpretation in order to extend it to a model.

Definition 7. *The **immediate consequence operator** $\mathcal{T}_P : 2^{\mathcal{B}_{P^*} \cup \neg \mathcal{B}_{P^*}} \to 2^{\mathcal{B}_{P^*}}$, where P be an OCLP, is defined by $\mathcal{T}_P(I) = \{a \in \mathcal{B}_{P^*} \mid \exists A \oplus a \leftarrow B \in P^* \cdot A \subseteq \neg I \wedge B \subseteq I \wedge r \text{ is indefeasible w.r.t. } I\}$.*
The operator $\mathcal{W}_P : \mathcal{I}_P \to 2^{\mathcal{B}_{P^*} \cup \neg \mathcal{B}_{P^*}}$ is defined by $\mathcal{W}_P(I) = \mathcal{T}_P(I) \cup \neg \mathcal{GUS}_P(I)$.

Theorem 2. *Let P be an OCLP. A total interpretation $M \in \mathcal{I}_P$ is an answer set iff M is a fixpoint of $\mathcal{W}_P$.*

The least fixpoint $\mathcal{W}_P^\omega$ of $\mathcal{W}_P$, if it exists[7], can be regarded as the "kernel" of any answer set (e.g $\mathcal{W}_P^\omega$ is a subset of every answer set). If $\mathcal{W}_P^\omega$ does not not exist, we know that the program does not have an answer set. If $\mathcal{W}_P^\omega$ is total, it must be the unique answer set of P

4.3   Algorithm

For $\mathcal{W}_P$ to be useful in the computation of answer sets, we need a way to compute greatest unfounded set. The best way of dealing with this is providing a fixpoint-operator. This operator, given a program, an interpretation and a set of atoms, should maintain those atoms that can belong to an unfounded set w.r.t. the given interpretation. By repeating this process, starting from the Herbrand base, one automatically obtains the greatest unfounded set. Doing this, we immmediately have a tool to verify unfounded-freeness of an interpretation. The operator taking care of this is called the $\mathcal{R}_{P,I}$-operator. The selection of atoms from the input is identical to verifying whether the input would be an unfounded set, with this difference that instead of having a yes/no answer the operator returns those atoms in the set fulfilling the conditions.

If $\mathcal{W}_P^\omega$ is total, it is the unique answer set. Otherwise, a mechanism is required to proceed from $\mathcal{W}_P^\omega$ toward an answer set. Since $\mathcal{W}_P^\omega \cup \neg \overline{\mathcal{W}_P^\omega}$ cannot be a model, we know that there must exist an applicable rule which is not defeated and not yet applied. In this case we have to choose which of the head elements we will assume to be true; the others will then be assumed false. The combination of such literals is called a choice set. The collection of all these choice sets w.r.t. an interpretation I is denoted $\mathcal{C}_P(I)$. Thus we can go from $\mathcal{W}_P^\omega$ to any answer set by simply adding choice sets until there are no more

---

[7] The fixpoint may not exists because $\mathcal{W}_P^n(I)$ can become inconsistent, i.e outside of the domain of $\mathcal{W}_P$, for some $n > 0$.

Procedure *Compute-Answer*(I_n:SetOfLiterals);   (* I_n always consistent *)
var X, I'_n, I_{n+1} : SetOfLiterals;
begin

      if $\mathcal{C}_P(I_n) = \emptyset$ (* no choices available *)
      then if $\mathcal{R}^{\omega}_{P,I_n \cup \neg \overline{I_n}}(I_n^+) = \emptyset$ (* and unfounded-free *)
             output "$I_n \cup \neg \overline{I_n}$ is an answer set of P";
         end-if;
      else for each $X \in \mathcal{C}_P(I_n)$ **do**   (* branch over all choice sets *)
             $I_{n+1} := I_n \cup X$;   (* Assume the truth of a choice set *)
             repeat   (* add atoms by means of the $\mathcal{T}_P$-operator *)
                $I'_n := I_{n+1}$;
                $I_{n+1} := \mathcal{T}_P(I_n) \cup I_n$;
             until $I_{n+1} = I'_n$ or $I_{n+1} \cap \neg I_{n+1} \neq \emptyset$;
             if $I_{n+1} \cap \neg I_{n+1} = \emptyset$ (* I_{n+1} is consistent *)
             then *Compute-Answer*(I_{n+1});
             end-if;
        end-for;
        end-if;
end-procedure;

var I, J : SetOfLiterals;
      G : SetOfAtoms;
begin (*Main *)
      $I := \emptyset$;
      repeat   (* Computation of $\mathcal{W}_P^{\omega}$ if it exists *)
         $J := I$;
         $G := \mathcal{GUS}_P(J)$;   (* by means of $\mathcal{R}^{\omega}_{P,J}(\mathcal{B}_{P^*})$ *)
         if $G \cap J \neq \emptyset$ (* J not unfounded-free *)
         then exit
         end-if;
         $I := \mathcal{T}_P(J) \cup \neg G$;   (* $= \mathcal{W}_P(J)$ *)
      until $I = J$;
      if $I^+ \cup I^- = \mathcal{B}_{P^*}$
      then output "I is the unique answer set for P";
      else *Compute-Answer*(I)
      end-if;
end.

Fig. 2. The Algorithm for the computation of answer sets.

choice sets available. There is no telling which choice sets should be taken, so we need to branch over all of them. To prevent too much wild guessing, we will use a combination of applying choice sets and the immediate consequence operator. Because it is possible that a wrong choice is made, we also need some consistency testing along the way and an unfounded-freeness test of the final interpretation made total by adding the negation of any remaining undecided atoms. An answer set is found if an interpretation survives all the tests. The algorithm is depicted in Fig. 2.

    For a finite OCLP this program halts in a finite amount of time returning the answer sets.

5 Logic Programming in OCLP

In [DVV99] it was shown that choice logic programs can represent semi-negative logic programs However, the stable models of the logic program did not exactly match with the stable models of the CLP: an extra condition, namely rationality, was required. Generalizing to OCLP, we do obtain a full one-to-one correspondence.

We can take it even a step further to the answer set semantics of general logic programs[8].

Definition 8. *Let P be a general semi-negative logic program. The corresponding OCLP P_L is defined by $\langle \{C, R, N\}, C \prec R \prec N \rangle$ with*

$$N = \{a^\neg \leftarrow \ \mid a \in \mathcal{B}_P\} \ ,$$
$$R = \{a \leftarrow B, C^\neg \in R \mid r : a \leftarrow B, \neg C \in P\} \cup$$
$$\{a^\neg \leftarrow B, C^\neg \in R \mid r : \neg a \leftarrow B, \neg C\} \cup$$
$$\{ \leftarrow B, C^\neg \in R \mid r : \ \leftarrow B, \neg C\} \ ,$$
$$C = \{a \oplus a^\neg \leftarrow a \mid a \in \mathcal{B}_P\} \ ,$$

where, for $a \in \mathcal{B}_P$, $a^\neg$ is a fresh atom representing $\neg a$.

Intuitively, the choice rules in C force a choice between a and $\neg a$ while the rules in N encode "negation by default" and the rules in R ensure consistency.

Theorem 3. *Let P be a general logic program. Then, $M \subseteq \mathcal{B}_P$ is an answer set of P iff S is an answer set for P_L with[9]. $S^+ = M^+ \cup (\mathcal{B}_P \setminus M)^\neg$.*

The proof of this theorem relies on the choice rules to be of the form $a \oplus a^\neg \leftarrow a$. The next example demonstrates that this is indeed essential.

Example 7. Consider the very simple logic program P: *vacation $\leftarrow$ vacation* .
Obviously, we obtain $\emptyset$ as the only answer set of this program. When we apply the transformation of Definition 8, we obtain a OCLP P_L with a single answer set M with $M^+ = \{vacation^\neg\}$. Suppose we would use choice rules with empty body. Then the program P_L would produce two answer sets: M and N with $N^+ = \{vacation\}$.

6 Extensive Games with Perfect Information

An extensive game[OR96] is a detailed description of a sequential structure representing the decision problems encountered by agents (called *players*) in strategic decision making (agents are capable of reasoning about their actions in a rational manner). The agents in the game are perfectly informed of all events that previously occurred. Thus, they can decide upon their action(s) using information about the actions which have already taken place. This is done by means of passing *histories* of previous actions to the deciding agents. *Terminal histories* are obtained when all the agents/players have

---

[8] Programs that also allow negation-as-failure in the head of their rules [Lif00]
[9] For a set $X \in \mathcal{B}_P$, $X^\neg = \{a^\neg \mid a \in X\}$.

made their decision(s). Players have a preference for certain outcomes over others. Often, preferences are indirectly modeled using the concept of *payoff* where players are assumed to prefer outcomes where they receive a higher payoff.

Summarizing, an extensive game with perfect information is a 4-tuple $\langle N, H, P, (\geq_i)_{i \in N} \rangle$, containing the players N of the game, the histories H, where each history is a sequence of actions, a player function $P : H \to N$ telling who's turn it is after a certain history and a preference relation $\leq_i$ for each player i over the set of terminal histories. We will use $A(h)$ to denoted the set of actions a player can choose from after an non-terminal history h.

For the examples, we use a more convenient tree representation: each path starting at the root represents a history. The terminal histories are the paths ending in the leafs. The numbers next to the nodes represent the players while the labels on the arcs represent actions. The numbers below the terminal histories are payoffs representing the players' preferences (the first number is the payoff of the first player, the second number is the payoff of the second player).

A *strategy* of a player in an extensive game is a plan that specifies the actions chosen by the player for every history after which it is her turn to move. A *strategy profile* contains a strategy for each player.

The first solution concept for an extensive game with perfect information ignores the sequential structure of the game; it treats the strategies as choices that are made once and for all before the actual game starts. A strategy profile is a *Nash equilibrium* if no player can unilaterally improve upon her choice. Put in another way, given the other players' strategies, the strategy stated for the player is the best she can do.

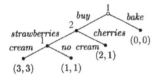

Fig. 3. The cake game of Example 8

Example 8. The game in Fig. 3 models an individuals' predicament in the following situation: two ladies have decided that they wanted fruit cake for dessert. There are two possibilities: they either bake a cake or they buy one. At the bakery shop one can choose strawberry and cherry cake. For strawberry cake there is the possibility to have whipped cream on top or not. They agree that the first lady will decide on how to get the cake and, if necessary, whether a topping is wanted or not. The second lady will be picking the type of fruit cake. This game has two Nash equilibria:

$$\{\{buy, cream\}, \{strawberries\}\} \text{ and} \{\{buy, no\_cream\}, \{cherries\}\} \text{ .}$$

In [DVV00], it was shown that OCLPs an be used to represent this type of game in order to obtain the equilibria. However, the correspondence relies on a more credulous notion of defeating, which we reproduce below.

Definition 9. *Let I be an interpretation for a OCLP P. A rule $r \in P^*$ is **c-defeated** w.r.t. I iff $\forall a \in H_r \cdot \exists r' \in P^* \cdot c(r) \not\prec c(r') \land r'$ is applied w.r.t. $I \land H_{r'} \subseteq \Omega^I_{c(r)}(a)$.*

The difference with ordinary defeat is that we here allow that c-defeaters come from the same or an unrelated component. However in return we demand that this c-defeater is applied instead of just applicable.

The definitions for *c-models* and *c-answer sets* are the same (see Definition 4 and Definition 5) as the definitions for ordinary models and answer sets except that c-defeating is used instead of defeating. The credulous semantics can be used to obtain a game's Nash equilibria.

Definition 10. *Let* $\langle N, H, P, (\geq_i)_{i \in N} \rangle$ *be a extensive game with perfect information. The corresponding OCLP* P_n *can be constructed in the following way:*

1. $\mathcal{C} = \{C^t\} \cup \{C_u \mid \exists i \in N, h \in Z \cdot u = U_i(h)\}$;
2. $C^t \prec C_u$ *for all* $C_u \in \mathcal{C}$;
3. $\forall C_u, C_w \in \mathcal{C} \cdot C_u \prec C_w$ *iff* $u > w$;
4. $\forall h \in (H \setminus Z) \cdot (A(h) \leftarrow) \in C^t$;
5. $\forall h = h_1 a h_2 \in Z \cdot a \leftarrow B \in C_u$ *with* $B = \{b \in [h]^{10} \mid h = h_3 b h_4, P(h_3) \neq P(h_1)\}$ *and* $u = U_{P(h_1)}(h)$.

The set of components consists of a component containing all the decisions that need to be considered and a component for each payoff. The order among the components follows the expected payoff (higher payoffs correspond to more specific components) with the decision component at the bottom of the hierarchy (the most specific component). Since Nash equilibria do not take into account the sequential structure of the game, players have to decide upon their strategy before starting the game, leaving them to reason about both past and future. This is reflected in the rules: each rule in a payoff component is made out of a terminal history (path from top to bottom in the tree) where the head represents the action taken when considering the past and future created by the other players according to this history. The component of the rule corresponds with the payoff the deciding player would receive in case the history was carried out.

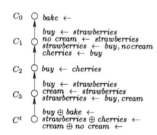

Fig. 4. P_n of Example 4

Theorem 4. *Let* $G = \langle N, H, P, (\geq_i)_{i \in N} \rangle$ *be a finite extensive game with perfect information and let* P_n *be its corresponding OCLP. Then,* s^* *is a Nash equilibrium for* G *iff* s^* *is a c-answer set for* P_n.

Example 9. Fig 4 depicts the corresponding OCLP P_n of the game in Example 8. This program has two c-answer sets corresponding to the Nash equilibria of the game.

When rational players engage in a game they will always choose strategy profiles that belong to a Nash equilibrium. A deterministic game would be a game for which the outcome was already known from the start. An example of such a game is the Prisoner's Dilemma. Real determinism can only exist when there is a single Nash equilibrium. Demanding that every game should have only one logical outcome would be unrealistic.

However, we feel that having multiple outcomes should be a strategic decision of many players and not just a single player. In other words, it should not

---

[10] We use $[h]$ to denote the set of actions appearing in a sequence h.

be possible for a single player, given the other players' actions, to deviate rationally from the envisioned outcome. We call this *player-determinism*. The equilibrium $\{\{buy, no\_cream\}, cherries\}$ of Example 8 makes the game not player-deterministic. Given the actions of the first player, e.g. $\{buy, no\_cream\}$, the second player can still rationally decide between *strawberries* and *cherries*. Both actions would yield her a payoff of 1. So, the first player cannot be certain that she will receive the payoff of Nash equilibrium.

To characterize such situations, we introduce cautious Nash equilibria as the (skeptical) answer sets of the corresponding program.

Definition 11. *Let* $G = \langle N, H, P, (\geq_i)_{i \in N} \rangle$ *be a finite extensive game with perfect information and let* P_n *be its corresponding OCLP. A strategy profile* s^* *is a **cautious Nash equilibrium** iff* s^* *is an answer set for* P_n.

Example 10. Consider the extensive game from Example 8. This program has one cautious Nash equilibrium: $M = \{\{buy, cream\}, \{strawberries\}\}$.

Theorem 5. *Let* $\langle N, H, P, (\geq_i)_{i \in N} \rangle$ *be an extensive game with perfect information. Then, every cautious Nash equilibrium for this game is also a Nash equilibrium.*

Cautious Nash equilibria have some interesting properties that distinguish them from normal Nash equilibria. E.g. two cautious Nash equilibria cannot have the same strategies for all but one player unless the same outcome is reached.

7   Relationship with Other Approaches

7.1   OCLP and Game Theory

In the previous section we not only demonstrated that OCLP can be used to retrieve game theoretic notions but that they also allow to extend game theory. Besides defining new equilibria, OCLPs are capable to represent more complex games more easily: variables, depending on the their unification different decisions need to be made and external information influencing the game's outcome are just two examples. Perhaps even more important is the ability for a player to take more than one action as demonstrated by the Travel OCLP of the introduction (Examples 1 and 2). If we just consider the first three components (P_1, P_2 and P_3), we see the representation extensive game with a single player (the person who wants to go on vacation). In this case the equilibrium would be $\{spain\}$ which corresponds to the situation with a smaller budget. With a larger budget, you will be able to afford more than one vacation. In game theory this is simply not possible: every player is forced to take a single action.

7.2   Preferences/Order

Over the years various logic (programming) formalisms have been introduced to deal with the notions of preference, order and updates. Most of these systems can be divided into two groups: the ones that uses the mechanism of preference to filter out unwanted models and the once that incorporate preference into their model semantics from the start. Examples of the former are: [SI96] with a preference on atoms and [BE99] to obtain the most preferred answer sets. Our OCLPs can found in the latter group. Other examples of such formalisms are: [Bre96] with preferences being part of rules, [BLR98] and [LV90] which use a similar defeating strategy as us for respectively disjunctive logic programs and extended logic programs. The main difference between our systems is the way alternatives are defined. In previous systems alternatives are fixed as an atoms and its (classical) negation. An other example is the dynamic logic programming of [AAP+98]. A stable model of such a dynamic logic program is a stable model of the generalized program obtained by removing the rejected rules. The definition of a rejected rule corresponds to our definition of a defeated rule when a and $\neg a$ are considered alternatives. Since the stable model semantics and the answer set semantics coincide for generalized logic programs. it is not hard to see that Definition 8, with some minor changes, can used to retrieve the stable models of the dynamic logic program. The only thing we need to do is to replace the component R by the P_is of the dynamic logic program $\bigoplus\{P_i : i \in S\}$ and to replace every occurrence of $\neg a$ by $a^\neg$.

References

[AAP+98] José Júlio Alferes, Leite J. A., Luís Moniz Pereira, Halina Przymusinska, and Teodor C. Przymusinski. Dynamic logic programming. In Cohn et al. [CSS98], pages 98–111.

[BE99]   Gerhard Brewka and Thomas Eiter. Preferred answer sets for extended logic programs. *Artificial Intelligence*, 109(1-2):297–356, April 1999.

[BLR98]   Francesco Buccafurri, Nicola Leone, and Pasquale Rullo. Disjunctive ordered logic: Semantics and expressiveness. In Cohn et al. [CSS98], pages 418–431.

[Bre96]   Gerhard Brewka. Well-Founded Semantics for Extended Logic Programs with Dynamic Preferences. *Journal of Artificial Intelligence Research*, 4:19–36, 1996.

[CSS98]   Anthony G. Cohn, Lenhard K. Schubert, and Stuart C. Shapiro, editors. *Proceedings of the Sixth International Conference on Principles of Knowledge Representation and Reasoning*, 1998. Morgan Kaufmann.

[DVV99]   Marina De Vos and Dirk Vermeir. On the Role of Negation in Choice Logic Programs. In Michael Gelfond, Nicola Leone, and Gerald Pfeifer, editors, *Logic Programming and Non-Monotonic Reasoning Conference (LPNMR'99)*, volume 1730 of *LNAI*, pages 236–246, 1999. Springer Verlag.

[DVV00]   Marina De Vos and Dirk Vermeir. A Logic for Modelling Decision Making with Dynamic Preferences. In *Proceedings of the Logic in Artificial Intelligence (Jelia2000) workshop*, number 1999 in *LNAI*, pages 391–406, 2000. Springer Verlag.

[Lif00]   Vladimir Lifschitz. Answer set programming and plan generation. *Journal of Artificial Intelligence*, page to appear, 2000.

[LV90]   Els Laenens and Dirk Vermeir. A Fixpoint Semantics of Ordered Logic, *Journal of Logic and Computation*, 1(2), pp. 159–185, 1990.

[OR96]   Martin J. Osborne and Ariel Rubinstein. *A Course in Game Theory*. The MIT Press, Cambridge, Massachusets, London, England, third edition, 1996.

[SI96]   Chiaki Sakama and Katsumi Inoue. Representing Priorities in Logic Programs. In Michael Maher, editor, *Proceedings of the 1996 Joint International Conference and Symposium on Logic Programming*, pages 82–96, 1996. MIT Press.

On a Linear Representation Theory for Quantitative Belief Change

Akira Fusaoka

Department of Computer Science, Ritsumeikan University
Nojihigashi, Kusatsu-city, SIGA, 525-8577, JAPAN
`fusaoka@cs.ritsumei.ac.jp`

Abstract. In this paper, we present a method to deal with the quantitative belief change based on the linear algebra. Since an epistemic state of agent is represented by a set of the subjective probability, which she conceived for each possible world, we can regard this epistemic state as a point of vector space which spanned by the basis of possible worlds. The knowledge which causes the belief change is treated as a matrix on this vector space. The observation of new fact about the current world is characterized as a projection matrix. On the other hand, the knowledge that some action changes the world is represented as a basis transformation matrix. In this framework, we present a unified method of belief change both for propositional and probabilistic knowledge so that the logical or probabilistic reasoning is reduced to the matrix calculation.

1 Introduction

In this paper, we propose a method to deal with dynamics of the quantitative belief change based on a linear algebra, aiming at to present an easy calculation method for the belief revision. We represent an epistemic state of an agent by a vector of the subjective probability which she holds for each possible world. Namely, we consider that a set of the epistemic state constitutes a vector space spanned by the basis of possible worlds, and also we regard the knowledge that causes the belief change as an operator which transforms the current state to another. We treat the knowledge represented by the linear operator, namely matrix. This means that the new state after belief change can be constituted by superposion of the components of the old state. Therefore, the new state after an agent learns A at the state u, which is usually denoted by $u \circ A$, is given by Au. Especially, we use two types of matrices: the diagonal projection for the observation and the basis transformation matrix for the action. In terms of these matrices, we characterize the quantitative belief revision, the belief update and the conditionals.

We introduce the linear formulation for the belief change from the following reasons.

1. We construct the belief revision from two basic operations : conditioning and imaging. As we discuss later, the imaging is essentially a linear transformation of the probability distribution so that it can be effectively treated with

R.I. McKay and J. Slaney (Eds.): AI 2002, LNAI 2557, pp. 48–59, 2002.
© Springer-Verlag Berlin Heidelberg 2002

a matrix. The conditioning is a belief change in accordance with Bayesian principle. It is also linear if we use it with the normalization of vectors.

2. The language of the propositional logic is inadequate to represent the information which an agent receives from her environment for the same formula often causes the different belief revision. The matrix representation of knowledge allows the broader class of knowledge. Especially, we focus on the projective matrix which allows the description of the many types of knowledge with the revision method.

3. Since the logical or probabilistic reasoning in the belief change can be reduced to the matrix calculation in our linear framework, we can present a simple calculation method to deal with the belief change.

The belief change has been studied intensively in the fields of AI and philosophy. Gärdenfores and his colleagues define the belief revision and give the characterization in the form of the postulate (AGM-Theory) [1]. The belief revision is a simple belief change caused by the static knowledge about the real world. If the new knowledge φ is consistent with the current epistemic state, φ is just added by cutting off the $\neg\varphi$-worlds from the epistemic state (this transaction is called belief expansion, especially). On the other hand, if φ conflicts to the current epistemic state, a part of her old beliefs must be deleted because they are incorrect. Katsuno and Mendelzon present another belief change called the belief update. The belief update is the revision of the epistemic state forced by the change of the world [10]. They also give the characterization for both belief update and belief revision in the basis of the possible worlds semantics (KM-Theory) [9]. In both AGM and KM-theory, the belief set is used as an epistemic state. However, the conditional sentence "if φ then ψ" requires yet another belief change which is essentially different from the belief revision and the belief update due to the conditional preservation. Namely, when "if φ then ψ" is learned in the epistemic state s, the subsequent belief change by φ must accept ψ even if φ is not known in s. In much of recent works, the ranking of belief is introduced into the belief set in order to deal with the conditionals. The ranking function is the similar notion of the probability of the belief.

In this paper, we use a set of the possible world and its probability as the agent's epistemic attitude. In the probabilistic theory, there are two basic methods of belief change: conditioning and imaging [12]. The conditioning is the method based on the Bayesian conditional probability. Namely, the probability $p'(e)$ for a possible world e after an agent learns φ is given by $p(e \mid \varphi)$, where $p(e)$ is the probability of e before she knows φ. We can regarded the conditioning as the belief change associated with the observation. On the other hand, we deal with the belief update with the imaging rather than conditioning. The imaging is the method introduced by Lewis to characterize the conditionals [12]. The imaging on φ constitutes the new epistemic states by shifting the original probability of each $\neg\varphi$-world e over to the φ-worlds $e', e'', \cdots$, where $e', e'', \cdots$ are assumed to be the most resemble world to e. The imaging is considered to be the thought experiment by the minimal action which makes φ true.

The conditionals "if φ then ψ" requires the more complicated treatments than the update, if φ is not known at the current state. Namely, the $\neg\varphi$-worlds are hypothetically shifted to the $varphi$-worlds as the first step (we consider that the possible world itself is shifted instead of its probability). And then ψ is verified by the conditioning so that the probability of each world is adjusted. These two steps are similar to the update. However, the current state is hypothetical because the actual world is unchanged. Therefore, the current state must be pulled back to the original state in the third step. This is done by the inverse action of the first stage. We call this process a general imaging.

We give an intuitive explanation for the proposed method by using the simple example.

Example 1. The three-prisoner paradox. Three prisoners A,B,C have been tried and wait for the sentences. They know that one of them will be declared guilty and others are not guilty. The prisoner A believes that the guard knows who will be condemned. He requests to the guard to pass the letter to one of other prisoners who is not guilty. The guard returns back and tells him that he passed the letter to B and B is not guilty. How does the belief state of A change after this event?

Let G_A, G_B, G_C be the propositions that A, B, C is guilty, respectively, and let S_B, S_C denote the propositions that B, C is selected. We have 6 possible worlds $W = \{e_1 = \{G_A S_B\}, e_2 = \{G_A S_C\}, e_3 = \{G_B S_B\}, e_4 = \{G_B S_C\}, e_5 = \{G_C S_B\}, e_6 = \{G_C S_C\}\}$. The epistemic state of the prisoner A is represented by (u, v) where **B:** $u = (x_1, x_2, ..., x_6)$ and **C:** $v = (y_1, y_2, ..., y_6)$.

1. At the initial situation, A's epistemic state (u_0, v_0) is
   $u_0 = (\frac{1}{6}, \frac{1}{6}, \frac{1}{6}, \frac{1}{6}, \frac{1}{6}, \frac{1}{6})$ and $v_0 = (1, 1, 1, 1, 1, 1)$.

2. The knowledge that the guard knows who is guilty and he will pass the letter to the prisoner to be released is represented by the sentence:
   $K_1 =$ if G_B then S_C and if G_C then S_B
   This sentence is a conditional rather than a logical implication because it is not only the knowledge about the current real world but the general belief which holds even in the other worlds. Therefore, the prisoner A considers that the value of **Cf** which he holds for the possible world $e_3(G_B S_B)$ must be moved to the world $e_4(G_B S_C)$. Similarly, the value of e_6 is moved to the world e_5. We can treat this belief change (imaging) by the following matrix

$$K_1 = \begin{pmatrix} 1 & 0 & 0 & 0 & 0 & 0 \\ 0 & 1 & 0 & 0 & 0 & 0 \\ 0 & 0 & 1 & 0 & 1 & 0 \\ 0 & 0 & 0 & 1 & 0 & 1 \\ 0 & 0 & 0 & 0 & 0 & 0 \\ 0 & 0 & 0 & 0 & 0 & 0 \end{pmatrix}$$

When the prisoner A believes K_1, his state changes to $u_1 = K_1 u_0$. namely,
$u_1 = (\frac{1}{6}, \frac{1}{6}, 0, \frac{1}{3}, \frac{1}{3}, 0)$
In addition to the update of **Cf**, the kripke structure **Ks** must be

changed to $v_1 = (1,1,1,1,0,0)$. This is given by the conditioning on $(G_B \supset S_C) \wedge (G_C \supset S_B)$. This operator is represented by the matrix

$$K_1' = \begin{pmatrix} 1 & 0 & 0 & 0 & 0 & 0 \\ 0 & 1 & 0 & 0 & 0 & 0 \\ 0 & 0 & 1 & 0 & 0 & 0 \\ 0 & 0 & 0 & 1 & 0 & 0 \\ 0 & 0 & 0 & 0 & 0 & 0 \\ 0 & 0 & 0 & 0 & 0 & 0 \end{pmatrix}$$

Namely. $v_1 = K_1' v_0$

3. the information "the guard selects B and B is not guilty" is described by the usual propositional formula

$$\neg G_B \wedge S_B$$

This is the knowledge about the real worlds so that we can treat this belief change (an expansion) by the conditinalizing on $\neg G_B \wedge S_B$, which is given by the following matrix

$$K_2 = \begin{pmatrix} 1 & 0 & 0 & 0 & 0 & 0 \\ 0 & 0 & 0 & 0 & 0 & 0 \\ 0 & 0 & 0 & 0 & 0 & 0 \\ 0 & 0 & 0 & 0 & 0 & 0 \\ 0 & 0 & 0 & 0 & 1 & 0 \\ 0 & 0 & 0 & 0 & 0 & 0 \end{pmatrix}$$

The kripke structure is unchanged because K_2 is the knowledge about the real world.

Therefore, the A'epistemic state u_3 after this information is $K_2 u_2 = (\frac{1}{6}, 0, 0, 0, \frac{1}{3}, 0)$. By the normalization, we have $u_3 = (\frac{1}{3}, 0, 0, 0, \frac{2}{3}, 0)$
Namely, the probability of G_A is unchanged but that of G_C is increased twice.

On the contrary, if the prisoner A believes that the guard has no knowledge about who will be condemned, A has the different result.
In this case, $u_1 = u_0$ so that the final state u_3 is $(\frac{1}{6}, 0, 0, 0, \frac{1}{6}, 0)$. By the normalization, we have
$u_3 = (\frac{1}{2}, 0, 0, 0, \frac{1}{2}, 0)$
Namely, the probability for G_A is increased to $\frac{1}{2}$.

2   A Space of Epistemic States

2.1   An Epistemic State

Let $\mathcal{L}$ be a prepositional language. Throughout this paper, we treat the sentence of $\mathcal{L}$

Definition 1. Possible world. Let $\{e_1, e_2, \cdots, e_n\}$ be a set of possible worlds. We write $e_i \models \varphi$ if a sentence φ is true in e_i, namely e_i is φ-world.

Definition 2. Epistemic space. Let W be a vector space spanned by the basis $\{e_1, e_2, \cdots, e_n\}$. Any point $u \in W$ is a superposition of the basis, that is $u = \alpha_1 e_1 + \alpha_2 e_2 + \cdots + \alpha_n e_n$, which we denote by $u = (\alpha_1, \alpha_2, \cdots, \alpha_n)$ where $0 \leq \alpha_i \leq 1$ and $\sum_{i=1}^{n} \alpha_i = 1$. Intuitively, α_i means the subjective probability for the possible world e_i, namely the strength of the belief that e_i actually coincides with the real world.

For any $u = (\alpha_1, \alpha_2, \cdots, \alpha_n)$, $u \models \varphi$ if and only if $e_i \models \varphi$ for $\alpha_i \neq 0$. We define the formula $f(u)$ associated with u by

$$f(u) = \bigvee \varphi \text{ where } u \models \varphi$$

For any sentence φ, the strength of belief for a sentence φ at a vector u is given by

$$prob(\varphi, u) = \Sigma_{i;e_i \models \varphi} u_i$$

Note that $prob(\varphi, u) = 1$ if and only if $u \models \varphi$. The vectors u, v are said to be qualitatively equivalent if and only if $f(u) = f(v)$. We denote by $u \approx v$. The quantitative belief change of u is always accompanied with the qualitative one which is defined from this relation.

Definition 3. Epistemic space. We define the epistemic state of an agent as a vector $u \in W$.

Definition 4. Normalization. A vector u is a provability distribution so that it must be normalized. We denote the normalization of u by $<u>$, namely,

$$<u>_i = \frac{u_i}{u_1 + u_2 + \cdots + u_n}$$

Definition 5. Action. An action is a mapping from W to W. When an action is performed at some world e_i, it is transferred to the other worlds. We assume that action is non-deterministic, so that e_i is transferred to the linear combination $a_{1i} e_1 + a_{2i} e_2 + \cdots + a_{ni} e_n$ where a_{ji} is the probability of transfer from e_i to e_j. Therefore, $\Sigma a_{ji} = 1$, that is the matrix $A = (a_{ij}$ is a stochastic matrix. If A is regular, we can regard this transaction as the basis transformation.

2.2   Knowledge Operator

In this paper, we treat the following types of knowledge operator of which content is given by a propositional formula. Because the difference in these types is based upon the temporal modality of the knowledge rather than its content, we use the modal operator G to represent the knowledge.

1. Belief expansion: the propositional formula φ that is consistent with the agent's state. Usually the knowledge φ gives a description of the current state of the real world.
2. Belief revision: the propositional formula φ which conflicts to the agent's state.
3. Belief update: The formula $\boldsymbol{F}\varphi$. This operator intuitively means that some event changes the real world and φ holds in the result. The $\boldsymbol{F}$ can be regarded as a " sometime" operator which causes the time promotion in the world.
4. Conditionals: we treat a conditional "if φ then ψ" with the formula $\boldsymbol{F}^{-1}\boldsymbol{F}(\varphi \supset \psi)$.
   When the agent receives the conditional statement, she imagines the hypothetical space such that $prob(\psi \mid \varphi)$ is sufficiently close to 1 because the probability of the conditional is given by the conditional probability. This thought experiment is corresponding to $\boldsymbol{F}(\varphi \supset \psi)$. And then it must be pulled back to the original state. So that the formula $\boldsymbol{F}^{-1}\boldsymbol{F}(\varphi \supset \psi)$ correspond to the conditional.

2.3 Projection

Since the epistemic state is unchanged if the given information is already known, the knowledge operator must be represented by the projection matrix which satisfies the condition $P^2 = P$.

Definition 6. Knowledge operator. Let P be a $n \times n$ matrix. P is called a knowledge operator if P is a projection, namely $P^2 = P$.

When an agent knows the information P at the state u, her state is transferred to Pu. Because $P(Pu) = Pu$, the eigenvalue of the knowledge operator is 1 and the result state is the eigenvector of P. Namely, when an agent knows P, her epistemic state is dropped into the eigenstate of P.

Let $S(P) = \{Px \mid x \in W\}$ and $Ker(P) = \{y \mid Py = 0 \text{ for } y \in W\}$. Note that W is separated to two subspace $S(P)$ and $Ker(P)$ by a projection P, that is, $W = S(P) \oplus Ker(P)$. Also, there is a projection P such that $S(P) = U$ for every subspace U.

$S(P)$ is a set of states in which knowledge P is known. On the other hand, $Ker(P)$ is a set of states in which knowledge P is believed to be false. The projection $E - P$ generates a subspace $Ker(P)$ so that $E - P$ is regarded as a negation of P, where E is the unit matrix. We represent a negation $E - P$ by $\bar{P}$.

Also we can introduce the AND, OR operations of projections formally. Namely, AND $P1 \cap P2$ is defined by $S(P1 \cap P2) = S(P1) \cap S(P2)$ and OR $P1 \cup P2$ is given by the condition that $S(P1 \cup P2)$ is the largest subspace such that $S(P) \subseteq S(P1) \cup S(P2)$. However, these logical operations $\bar{P}, P1 \cap P2, P1 \cup P2$ does not necessarily form the propositional logic (generally, it is a quantum logic).

The following theorem is known for the projection.

Theorem 1. For any projection P, there exists a regular matrix T such that $P = T^{-1}\Delta T$, where Δ is a diagonal projection, namely a diagonal matrix of whose elements are 0 or 1.

Definition 4. Knowledge class. For any regular matrix T, a set of projection K_T is defined as $K_T = \{P \mid P = T^{-1}\Delta T$ for some diagonal projection $\Delta\}$.
Each class K_T constitutes a propositional logic by the operations $\bar{P}, P1 \cap P2, P1 \cup P2$.

Theorem 2.

(1) For any $A, B \in K_T, AB = BA$.
(2) the logical operations restricted in K_T are simplified.
 $\bar{A} = E - A$
 $A \cap B = AB$
 $A \cup B = A + B - AB$
 K_T constitutes a propositional logic with these operations.

We omit the proof of this theorem but it is straightforward.

This theorem means that for any regular matrix T, there exists a knowledge class K_T and the logical reasoning is possible in each class. Note that it is not necessarily $AB = BA$ if A, B belong to the different classes. $AB \neq BA$ means that it is impossible to know A and B simultaneously.

3   Conditioning and Imaging

We can characterize the conditioning and the imaging in the terms of the knowledge class.

3.1   Conditioning

The conditioning is the belief change in accordance with Bayes' rule.

Theorem 3. For each propositional formula φ, a diagonal projection Δ_φ such that
$\Delta_\varphi(ii) = 1$ if $e_i \models \varphi$ else $\Delta_\varphi(ii) = 0$, $\Delta_\varphi(ij) = 0$ if $i \neq j$
is a knowledge operator corresponding to the conditioning on φ.
Namely, the operator for the conditioning is an element of K_E.
  Proof
    Let $u = (x_1, x_2, \cdots, x_n)$ and $v = \Delta_\varphi = (y_1, y_2, \cdots, y_n)$. We show that $prob(e_i, v) = prob(e_i \mid \varphi, u)$ for each i.
Clearly, if $\Delta_\varphi(ii) = 1$ then $y_i = x_i$ else $y_i = 0$. By the normalization, $< \Delta_\varphi u >= (\frac{y_1}{y}, \cdots, \frac{y_n}{y})$ where $y = \Sigma_{i=1}^n y_i = prob(\varphi, v)$. Therefore,

$$\frac{y_i}{y} = \frac{prob(e_i \wedge \varphi, u)}{prob(\varphi, u)} = prob(e_i \mid \varphi, u)$$

The logical operations in K_E can be identified with those of the original propositional language $\mathcal{L}$. Namely,

$$\Delta_{\neg\varphi} = \bar{\Delta}_{\varphi} = E - \Delta_{\varphi}$$
$$\Delta_{\varphi\wedge\psi} = \Delta_{\varphi} \cap \Delta_{\psi} = \Delta_{\varphi}\Delta_{\psi}$$
$$\Delta_{\varphi\vee\psi} = \Delta_{\varphi} \vee \Delta_{\psi} = \Delta_{\varphi} + \Delta_{\psi} - \Delta_{\varphi}\Delta_{\psi}$$

3.2 Imaging

The imaging on φ is the thought process of an agent such that the probability of each $\neg\varphi$-world is moved over to the φ-worlds. The $\neg\varphi$-worlds retain none of their original probability and the shares of the probability are added to the original probability for each φ-world. The shift amount from e_i to e_j is generally depending on φ. Therefore, the imaging operator M_{φ} is given by

$$M_{\varphi} = \Delta_{\varphi} + \Gamma\varphi$$

where Γ_{φ} is a shift matrix which satisfies $\gamma_{ii} = 0$, and $\gamma_{ij} = 0$ if $e_i \models \neg\varphi$ or $e_j \models \varphi$ so that $\Delta_{\varphi}\Gamma_{\varphi} = \Gamma_{\varphi}, \Gamma_{\varphi}\Delta_{\varphi} = 0$. From this property, the imaging matrix is a projection Namely, $M_{\varphi}^2 = M_{\varphi}$. In fact, M_{φ} is an element of the class K_T for the regular matrix $T = \Delta_{\varphi} + \Gamma_{\varphi} - \Delta_{\neg\varphi}$. T satisfies $T^{-1} = T$ and also $M_{\varphi} = T\Delta_{\varphi}T = \Delta_{\varphi}T$. Conversely, this relation gives the characterization for the imaging matrix.

Theorem 4. For any regular matrix T such that $T^2 = E$ and $T\Delta_{\varphi}T = \Delta_{\varphi}T$, $\Delta_{\varphi}T$ is an imaging matrix.

Proof By applying Δ_{φ} to the both sides of $T\Delta_{\varphi}T = \Delta_{\varphi}T$, we have the projection condition $\Delta_{\varphi}T\Delta_{\varphi}T = \Delta_{\varphi}T$. Moreover, applying T to the both sides of this equation, $\Delta_{\varphi}T\Delta_{\varphi}T^2 = \Delta_{\varphi}T^2$. From $T^2 = E$, we have $\Delta_{\varphi}T\Delta_{\varphi} = \Delta_{\varphi}$. Let $\Gamma\varphi = \Delta_{\varphi}T\Delta_{\neg\varphi}$. $\Gamma\varphi$ is a shift matrix because $\Delta_{\varphi}\Gamma_{\varphi} = \Gamma_{\varphi}, \Gamma_{\varphi}\Delta_{\varphi} = 0$. Therefore, $M_{\varphi} = \Delta_{\varphi} + \Gamma\varphi = \Delta_{\varphi}T\Delta_{\varphi} + \Delta_{\varphi}T\Delta_{\neg\varphi} = \Delta_{\varphi}T$.

Intuitively, this theorem means that an imaging on φ is a thought experiment of observing φ after changing the world by T. Note that T gives the minimal change of the world in the meaning that each possible world moves to the similar worlds.

In many revision methods of probabilistic distribution, however, a property called logical coherence is required which means that if we imagine on φ and then image $\varphi \wedge \psi$, we should obtain the same result as if we imagine on $\varphi \wedge \psi$ in only one step. Namely, the logical coherence is the requirement for the successive imaging such that

$$M_{\varphi\wedge\psi}M_{\varphi} = M_{\varphi\wedge\psi}$$

We can obtain the coherent imaging operator by iterating the simplest imaging which distributes the probability of one possible world to the other worlds. Let $D = (d_{ij})$ is $N \times N$ matrix of which element d_{ij} means the rate of distribution from e_i to e_j when the probability of only e_i is distributed. Intuitively, D corresponds to the degree of resemblance between any two possible worlds e_i and e_j, so that we assume $d_{ij} = d_{ji} \geq 0, d_{ii} = 0$. The coherent imaging operator M_φ is defined by using D, although we omit the precise calculation.

Theorem 5. For any sentence *varphi* and the matrix D, the coherent imaging operator on φ is given by

$$M_\varphi = \Delta_\varphi + \Gamma_\varphi, \text{where}$$

$$\Gamma_\varphi = \Delta_\varphi D \Delta_{\neg\varphi}(E - \Delta_{\neg\varphi} D \Delta_{\neg\varphi})^{-1}$$

We slightly extend the imaging operator.

Definition 7. The imaging on φ under ψ means the process which moves the probability of $\neg\varphi \wedge \psi$-worlds over to $\varphi \wedge \psi$-worlds while $\neg\psi$-worlds are unchanged. Namely,

$$M_{\varphi,\psi} = \Delta_\varphi + \Delta_{\varphi\wedge\psi}\Gamma_\varphi\Delta_{\neg\varphi\wedge\psi}$$

4 Belief Change

4.1 Belief Revision

When the knowledge φ is consistent with the epistemic state u, the new state is given by the conditioning on φ. On contrary, if $prob(\varphi, u) = 0$ then the all nonzero values of u must be reset to 0 and at least one of φ-world must have nonzero probability. Although there have been a lot of revision methods concerning how to determine the probability of the φ-world, the belief revision defined by AGM postulates is the most standard.[1]. The probabilistic version of this revision is nonlinear but we can treat it by the imaging based on the Pearl's ε-theory

Let H be a $N \times N$ regular matrix such that $H_{ij} = \varepsilon^{\rho_{ij}}$ where ρ_{ij} is a distance from e_i to e_j, where ε is defined to be a very small number, namely an infinitesimal.

The revision matrix R_φ is given by

$$R_\varphi = \Delta_\varphi + \Delta_\varphi H \Delta_{\neg\varphi}$$

Example 2. The book and magazine. [10] Suppose b means the book is on the floor, and m means the magazine is on the floor. The agent believes that $(\neg b \wedge m) \vee (b \wedge \neg m)$. Let consider two situations: (1) the agent receives the knowledge $\varphi = (b \wedge m) \vee (\neg b \wedge \neg m)$ contrary to her current belief. (2) the agent receives the knowledge $\psi = b$.

The epistemic space W is given by $W = \{e_1 = \{b \wedge m\}, e_2 = \{\neg b \wedge m\}, e_1 = \{b \wedge \neg m\}, e_1 = \{\neg b \wedge \neg m\}\}$. The initial state is $u_0 = (0, \alpha, 1 - \alpha, 0)$. We use the distance of two worlds that is measured by the number of propositional letter on which they differ.

(1) The revision matrix R_φ is given by

$$R_\varphi = \begin{pmatrix} 1 & \varepsilon & \varepsilon & 0 \\ 0 & 0 & 0 & 0 \\ 0 & 0 & 0 & 0 \\ 0 & \varepsilon & \varepsilon & 1 \end{pmatrix}$$

The agent's new state is given by
$R_\varphi u_0 = (\epsilon, 0, 0, \epsilon$
Although this state is apparently close to 0, it gives the new state by the normalization.

$$u_1 = < R_\varphi u_0 > = (\frac{1}{2}, 0, 0, \frac{1}{2})$$

(2) The belief revision operator gives the correct answer even for the belief expansion. The revision by ψ is

$$R_\psi = \begin{pmatrix} 1 & \varepsilon & \varepsilon & \varepsilon^2 \\ 0 & 0 & 0 & 0 \\ \varepsilon & \varepsilon^2 & 1 & \varepsilon \\ 0 & 0 & 0 & 0 \end{pmatrix}$$

$R_\psi u_0 = (\epsilon, 0, \epsilon^2 \alpha + \beta, 0)$ By normalization, $< R_\psi u_0 > = (0, 0, 1, 0) = < \Delta_\psi u_0 >$.
   The linear belief revision R_φ satisfies the probabilistic version of AGM postulates for the belief revision. Namely, for any $u \neq 0$,

1. $prob(\varphi, R_\varphi) = 1$
2. if $\varphi \equiv \psi$ then $R_\varphi = R_\psi$
3. if $R_\varphi \neq O$(zero matrix) then $R_\varphi u \neq 0$
4. if $\Delta_\varphi u \neq 0$ then $R_\varphi u = \Delta_\varphi u$
5. if $prob(\psi, R_\varphi u) \neq 0$ then $\Delta_\psi R_\varphi u = R_{\varphi \wedge \psi} u$

Proof We give a proof for the last postulate. The others are obvious.
$R_{\varphi \wedge \psi} = \Delta_{\varphi \wedge \psi} \{E + H\Delta_{\neg \varphi \vee \neg \psi}\}$
$= \Delta_\psi \Delta_\varphi \{E + H\Delta_{\neg \varphi} + H\Delta_{\neg \psi \wedge \varphi}\}$
$if \Delta_\varphi u = 0$ then $\Delta_{\neg \psi \wedge \varphi} u = 0$.
So that $R_{\varphi \wedge \psi} = \Delta_\psi \Delta_\varphi \{E + H\Delta_{\neg \varphi}\} = \Delta_\psi R_\varphi$.
if $\Delta_\varphi u \neq 0$ then $H\Delta_{\neg \varphi} u$ and $\Delta_{\neg \psi \wedge \varphi} u$ are infinitesimal
so that $R_{\varphi \wedge \psi} = \Delta_\psi \Delta_\varphi = \Delta_\psi R_\varphi$

4.2   Belief Update

When the knowledge $F\varphi$ is received at the state u, the agent considers that φ becomes to be true after some unknown change of the world, so that she imagines that a set of φ-worlds are acquired by the minimal change of the world. This thought process can be implemented by the imaging on φ. Namely, the belief update by $F\varphi$ at the state u is given by $M_\varphi u$.
   By virtue of the logical coherence of imaging, the iteration $F(\varphi \wedge \psi)F\varphi u$ is equivalent to $F(\varphi \wedge \psi)u$. However, the iteration of the belief revision by ψ after

updating u by φ is not reduced to the belief update of the state u by $\varphi \wedge \psi$ unless $u \models \varphi \supset \psi$, because the imaging on ψ is necessary if ψ is not known at u. We have a weak version of the iteration $\psi F \varphi \approx F(\varphi \wedge \psi)$. This property is one of the KM-postulates for the belief update. All other postulates also hold in this weak form.

4.3   Conditionals

Roughly speaking, a conditional sentence *if φ then ψ* has two different interpretations : the indicative conditionals and the subjunctive conditionals.

1. the indicative conditionals:
   The indicative conditionals are equivalent to the logical implication $\varphi \supset \psi$. We assume that $\varphi \supset \psi$ is the factual knowledge about the real world. The belief change caused by this knowledge is treated with the belief revision $R_{\varphi \supset \psi}$.
2. the subjunctive conditionals:
   The subjunctive conditionals has the meaning that for every φ-world e_i, there exists the possible world e_j closest to e_i such that $e_j \models \psi$. We represent the subjunctive conditional by $FG(\varphi \supset \psi)$. Therefore, the belief change by this knowledge at the state (u, v) is given $(M_{\psi, \varphi} u, R_{\varphi \supset \psi} v)$.

5   Non-linguistic Knowledge

5.1   Probabilistic Knowledge

When a probabilistic knowledge *the probability of φ is ρ where $0 < \rho < 1$* is learned at the epistemic state (u, v), the revised probability distribution u' is given by Bayesian principle (Jeffery's rule). Namely,

$$u' = \rho < \Delta_\varphi u > +(1 - \rho) < \Delta_{\neg \varphi} u >$$

5.2   Action Operator

When the agent receives the information about the action, she is considered to simulate the action in every possible world. We assume that the action is nondeterministic, each possible world is transferred to a linear combination of the possible worlds. In this thought experiment, the probability of the original epistemic state is distributed in the similar way to the imaging. Namely, we can treat this transaction via the basis transformation matrix.

6   Concluding Remarks

There have been few works about the belief revision from the standpoint of the space of knowledge states and its operators. But it seems to be necessary if we assume the continuous attitude for the knowledge state. In this paper, we present a linear framework for the belief change and characterize some kinds of belief change such as belief expansion, imaging and knowledge of action based on the matrix theory.

Much more remains for future works. For example, the knowledge in the form of conditionals must be examined in the linear framework. Moreover, we need a method to deal with the multi-agent knowledge space and the knowledge about other's knowledge.

References

1. Alchourròn, C.E., P. Gärdenfors and D. Makinson (1985). On the logic of theory change: Partial meet functions for contraction and revision. *J.Symbolic Logic* 50:510–530.
2. Boutilier, C. (1998). Unified model of qualitative belief change: a dynamical system perspective. *Artificial Intelligence* 98:281–316.
3. Darwiche, A. and J. Pearl (1997). On the logic of iterated belief revision. *Artificial Intelligence* 89:1–29.
4. Dubois, D. and H. Prade (1992). Belief Change and Possibility Theory. In P.Gärdenfors (ed.)*Belief Revision*, Cambridge Univ. Press, pp. 142–182.
5. Engesser, K. and D.M. Gabbay (2002).Quantum logic, Hilbert space, revision theory. *Artificial Intelligence* 136:61–100.
6. Friedman, N. and J.Y.Halpern (1996). Belief revision: a critique. In *Proc. 6th Inter.Conf.on Principles of Knowledge Representation and reasoning*, pp. 421–431.
7. Gärdenfors, P. (1988). *Knowledge in flux*. MIT Press.
8. Goldszmidt, M. and J. Pearl (1996) Qualitative probabilities for default reasoning, belief revision and causal modeling. *Artificial Intelligence* 84:57–112.
9. Katsuno, H. and A Mendelzon (1991). Propositional knowledge base revision and minimal change. *Artificial Intelligence* 52:263–294.
10. Katsuno, H. and A Mendelzon (1991). On the difference between updating a knowledge base and revising it. In *Proc. 2nd Inter.Conf.on Principles of Knowledge Representation and reasoning*, pp. 383–394,1991.
11. Kern-Isberner, G. (2001). *Conditionals in nonmonotonic reasoning and belief revision*. Lecture notes in artificial intelligence LNAI 2087. Springer-Verlag.
12. Lewis, D.K. (1976). Probabilities of conditionals and conditional probabilities. *The Philosophical Review* 85:297–315.
13. Smith, L. (1984). *Linear algebra*. Springer-Verlag.
14. Voorbraak, F. (1999). Probabilistic Belief Change: Expansion, Conditioning and Constraining. In *Proc. 15th Inter.Conf.on Uncertainty in Artificial Intelligence*, pp. 655–662.

Trust in Secure Communication Systems – The Concept, Representations, and Reasoning Techniques

Chuchang Liu and Maris A. Ozols

Information Networks Division
Defence Science and Technology Organisation
PO Box 1500, Edinburgh, SA 5111, Australia
{Chuchang.Liu,Maris.Ozols}@dsto.defence.gov.au

Abstract. The purpose of communication is the exchange of information among agents. Whether an agent believes a message passed by others to be reliable depends on trust which the agent would put in the system supporting secure communications required. Indeed, every security system depends on trust, in one form or another, among agents of the system. Different forms of trust exist to address different types of problems and mitigate risk in certain conditions. This paper discusses the concept of trust in general, and intends to investigate modelling methodologies for describing and reasoning about trust and agent beliefs.

1 Introduction

We can view the purpose of communication as the exchange of information among agents. Whether an agent believes a received message to be reliable depends on trust which the agent puts in the system supporting the communications. Trust is thus essential to communication channels. As we see, new information technology services are increasingly being applied in our daily life for e-commerce, web-based access to information, and interpersonal interactions via email rather than voice or face-to-face, etc., many of which require trust and security. Different forms of trust exist to address different types of problems and mitigate risk for different situations.

Although the importance of trust in communications has been recognised [5], researchers and system developers still face the most essential problems about trust, such as what trust is, how to classify trust in secure communications, what kind of trust may be involved in a system etc. [4,7,8,11]. There are no generally agreed techniques or tools that can be used for the specification of, and reasoning about, trust and agent beliefs [7]. Therefore, studies focusing on theoretical aspects to provide general methodologies for modelling trust in communication system are highly desirable. Once a solid theoretical foundation for building trustworthy systems is established, it could guide system developers towards the design of security architectures, and help users to understand and

R.I. McKay and J. Slaney (Eds.): AI 2002, LNAI 2557, pp. 60–70, 2002.

analyse properties of the security achitecture for achieving the security goals required.

This paper discusses the concept of trust, and investigates modelling methodologies that can be generally used for describing and reasoning about trust in secure communication systems. The rest of the paper is organized as follows. In Section 2, based on an analysis of existing definitions about trust, we give our definition of trust. Section 3 discusses representations of beliefs and trust. Section 4 presents a simple trust model for secure communications; and Section 5 introduces several reasoning techniques that can be applied for deriving agent beliefs in a given system. The final section concludes with a short discussion on possible future work.

2   Definition of Trust

The notion of trust is fundamental for understanding the interactions between agents [6,13,15]. Agents can be human beings, machines, organizations, and other entities. It is hard to give a definition of trust as it is overly complex and appears to be attributed many different meanings depending on where and how it is used. There is no consensus in the literature as to what trust is, although there have been a number of definitions of trust proposed for addressing some specific aspects related to authentication, authorisation, and e-commerce *etc*. We list the following definitions as examples:

- Kini and Choobineh [11] define: *Trust in a system is a belief that is influenced by the individual's opinion about critical system features.* In their view, trust is a belief that affects one's attitude, trust in a system is an individuals beliefs in competence, dependability, and security of the system under conditions of risk.
- In a survey of trust in Intenet services, Grandison and Sloman [7] give the following definition: *Trust is the firm belief in the competence of an entity to act dependably, securely and reliably with a specified context.*
- Dimitrakos [4] gives a formal definition of trust in e-commerce as follows: *Trust of a party A in a party B for a service X is the measurable belief of A in that B behaves dependably for a specified period within a specified context.*
- Jones [9] defines trust as *the property of a business relationship, such that reliance can be placed on the business partners and the business transaction developed with them.*

In these definitions, different attributes – reliability, dependability, security, competence *etc* are considered. Perhaps, it is right that we have to consider these attributes depending on the environment where trust is being specified. As we metioned before, security systems depend on trust among agents of the system, different forms of trust exist to address different types of problems. Therefore, defining trust as a belief related to an environment is perhaps suitable for modelling agent beliefs in some specific situations. However, there may still be some confusions arising by such definitions.

Let us consider such a scenario: In a critical system, only legal users are allowed to access the database DB, and DB trusts an authentication server, AS, and asks AS to check the identity of each user who wants to query it. Assume that a user A sends a message to say "I am a legal user of DB" for getting into DB. After checking A's identity, AS reports to DB that the message sent by A is true, then DB may believe that A is a legal user. DB's belief is obviously influenced by AS's opinion. However, we cannot say such a belief expresses DS's trust in A. In fact, DS only trusts AS and it therefore believes what AS says; DS does not trust users, so it asks AS to check the identity of each user. What we can say is that the belief of DB ("A is a legal user") is obtained based on the trust of DB in AS (indicating DB would accept the opinion of AS). This indicates that trust and belief are different notions. Therefore, we argue that, for developing a formal approach to the description of, and reasoning about, trust and beliefs, we have to distinguish the notion of trust from that of belief.

The Macquarie Concise Dictionary [3] gives the meaning of *trust* (as a noun), which contains:

> 1. *reliance on the integrity, justice, etc., of a person, or on some quality or attribute of a thing, ... 4. one on whom or that on which one relies. 5. the state of being relied on, or the state of one to whom something is entrusted. ... 7. the condition of being confided to another's care ...*

In contrast, this dictionary defines *belief* as "*that which is believed, an accepted opinion*", therefore, "an agent A has belief in X" means that A will accept X to be true. From these explanations in the dictionary, it is not difficult to see the conceptual difference between the words "trust" and "belief".

Based on these basic meanings of trust, and considering the specific use of trust in secure digital communications, we give a definition of trust as follows:

Definition 1 *Agent A has* trust *in agent B (or simply, A trusts B), whenever A is likely to believe what B says on a specific topic. We call such a relation a* trust relation *from A to B. Trust of a system is the union of all trust relations between agents within the system.*

For example, assume that in the Sales group Alice is John's supervisor, and that "John trusts Alice" is in fact that Alice and John are situated in a supervision relationship, which means that John will believe Alice's statements on sales matters, due to her competence and responsibility as supervisor. Obviously, in this view, John's trust in Alice is not just a belief, but due to the existing trust, John may obtain new beliefs from Alice's instructions.

Trust may influence beliefs. John trusts Alice, so he believes the information sent by Alice this morning which says that X is not reliable, although earlier he believed X to be reliable. Without Alice's information "John trusts Alice" is still true if there is no change to the situation. That is, without this belief, John's trust in Alice still exists. In this view, we do not think that defining trust as a kind of belief is appropriate for modelling trust and agent beliefs. Perhaps, it is better to see trust as the base of beliefs or meta-belief, from which agent beliefs may be derived. It seems that our defintion is closer to the one of Jones [9], where trust is defined as the property of business relationship and agent beliefs could therefore be obtained based on the property.

3   Representations of Belief and Trust

Beliefs are facts, such as "Alice believes that Bob has the key k", "John believes that Bob does not have the key k", "Bob believes that message M is reliable", "Mary believes that for all agent A, if A is a member of the group, A has read the file doc", and "Alice believes that Bob believes that message M is reliable" etc. Such facts can naturally be expressed by introduction of modal operators to express agent beliefs. We introduce the modal operator $\mathbf{B}_A$ to mean "A believes", $\mathbf{B}_A(\varphi)$ is therefore read as "Agent A believes formula φ (to be true)". Thus, the above beliefs can formally be written as:

$\mathbf{B}_{alice}\ has(bob, k)$,
$\mathbf{B}_{john}\ \neg has(bob, k)$,
$\mathbf{B}_{bob}\ reliable(M)$,
$\mathbf{B}_{mary}\ (\forall A(is\_group\_member(A) \rightarrow has\_read(A, doc)))$, and
$\mathbf{B}_{alice}(\mathbf{B}_{bob}\ reliable(M))$.

Note that beliefs are related to agents, so the formal representation of an agent's belief starts with a modal operator subscribed with the particular agent's name.

In a logical framework, reasoning about agent beliefs is a process in which one starts from some assumptions (assumed beliefs) to derive a (new) belief. Formally, let Γ be a set of beliefs (formulae), φ a formula expressing an agent's belief, then the process deriving φ from Γ or a proof for $\Gamma \vdash \varphi$ will not only contain applications of ordinary logical axioms and inference rules, but also depends on the trust of agents. Therefore, how to formalize trust is an important issue for reasoning about agent beliefs.

Trust is not just a belief, it represents the agent's confidence in the behavior of other agents it relies on. An agent's belief may be derived from its own confidence in what other agents say. According to the definition of trust given above, trust of a system defines a set of trust relations among the agents of the system. Based on the relation set, we may obtain some rules that can be applied to derive agent beliefs.

Let τ be a system and Ω the set of agents. Assume that $\mathcal{R}$ is the set of trust relations over Ω defined as $(A, B) \in \mathcal{R}$ if and only if A trusts B. Thus, for the given system the trust relation (A, B) may determine, for example, the following rule:

$B\ says\ \varphi \Longrightarrow \mathbf{B}_A(\varphi)$,

called the *trust rule* and read as "from B says φ infer A believes φ (to be true)".

Recall the example given in Section 2, we have that DB trusts AS. Thus, by the above rule, from a fact that AS says that A is legal user, we may obtain a belief that DB believes "A is legal user". Note that this belief does not mean that DB should trust agent A, although it may allow A to access itself based on this belief.

Instead, we clearly distinguished "trust" from "belief" by employing different representation forms:

- Beliefs are facts that are represented as formulae starting with a modal operator, and
- Trust in a given system is specified as a set of rules, which may be viewed as meta-beliefs of agents but not beliefs. A rule has the form of "$\varphi_1, \ldots, \varphi_n \Longrightarrow \psi$", where $\varphi_1, \ldots, \varphi_n, \psi$ are formulae, and is read as "from $\varphi_1, \ldots, \varphi_n$ infer ψ". The rules are applied for reasoning about beliefs.

In specifying trust in systems, different trust forms may be adopted for different systems. In some systems, one may give the following rule as the interpretation for the trust relation (A, B):

$$B \text{ says } \varphi \Longrightarrow \mathbf{B}_A(\mathbf{B}_B(\varphi)),$$

called the *honesty rule*, which means that agents believe that an honest agent, say B, believes what B itself says. We may also combine the two rules above and give the following interpretations for the trust relation (A, B) in a system:

$$B \text{ says } \varphi \Longrightarrow \mathbf{B}_A(\varphi), \text{ and}$$
$$B \text{ says } \varphi \Longrightarrow \mathbf{B}_A(\mathbf{B}_B(\varphi)).$$

Further examples will be given late. We give some basic charateristic properties of trust relationships as follows:

- No global trust exists in a secure communication environment. In other words, there are no agents who can be trusted by all others. This is obvious in distributed systems. Trust depends on the agent (observer): two different agents will not necessarily equally trust some received information. For instance, we cannot require that an agent C believes the information provided by an agent A although other agent, e.g. B, has accepted this information as true.
- Trust is not static. The trust of an agent can be changed dynamically. For example, for two weeks agent A trusts agent B, but this morning A found that B lied to him, so A no longer trusts B.
- There is no full trust. A's full trust in B would mean that A believes everything B says. However, in most cases this is impossible – an agent cannot believe all statements provided by another agent. We choose a limited trust model, where "agent A trusts agent B" means that A will only trust B on some topics.
- Trusting relations may lack the properties of transitivity and symmetry. That is, we cannot derive the conclusion "A_1 trusts A_3" from "A_1 trusts A_2" and "A_2 trusts A_3", and cannot assert that we should have "B trusts A" from "A trusts B". With a representation of trust, it is easy to capture this property.

Here we only listed four basic properties of trust. For more discussion about such kinds of properties, we refer the reader to Dimitrakos [4].

The reader may have noted that, from a particular trust rule such as B *says* $\varphi \implies \mathbf{B}_A(\varphi)$, it seems that the agent A will believe anything that B says, and this conflicts with the third property above. However, we need to note that such rules are given for a specific system that is defined in a certain specific domain and all formulae φ are particularly given on the specific domain. A full version of the logic may capture these domains of trust, but we do not do so in this paper. Therefore, actually the agent A only believes those statements provided by B on the specific domain.

4   A Simple Trust Model for Secure Communications

We view a communication environment to be a large complex system consisting of a collection of agents that interact in the system. The objective of communication is the interchange of information between a source and its destination. In secure communications, a very basic problem we may encounter is whether a message sent by an agent is reliably received by other agents. Agents should gain their beliefs regarding whether messages they received are reliable based on their trust.

In a simple trust model, we assume that, in a secure communication system, an agent does not trust any other agents but only the security mechanisms (as a special agent) in the system whose trustworthiness has been verified based on required evaluation criteria. In other words, beliefs of agents can only be obtained based on their trust in the security mechanisms of the system.

A system may or may not be equipped with security mechanisms, and security mechanisms may be simple or complex. In the special case where there is the empty set of security mechanisms for the system, agents will have no beliefs regarding the messages they received, since they have no trust. In any other case, some security mechanisms are provided. Therefore, for reasoning about agent beliefs for a secure communication system, according to the simple trust model, the key is to obtain the rules specifying the trust in the system, i.e., to specify the trust that agents put in the security mechanisms of the system.

For example, assume that, in a given system, cryptographic protocols are applied for authentication purposes, then we may have the following rules to specify the trust in the system (see [2,14]):

$\mathbf{B}_A$ *share_key*(A, B, K), *received*$(A, \{X\}_K, B) \implies \mathbf{B}_A$ *said*(B, X).
$\mathbf{B}_A$ *owner_of_pub_key*(B, K), *sees*$(A, \{X\}_{K^{-1}}) \implies \mathbf{B}_A$ *said*(B, X).

where $\{X\}_K$ represents the message X encrypted under the key K, and, for a public key K, K^{-1} is the private key corresponding to K. The first rule states that, from the facts that agent A believes K to be the shared key with agent B and A received a message $\{X\}_K$ from B, one may derive the conclusion that A believes that B once said X. The second rule is about public key, indicating that from the facts that agent A believes B to be the owner of the public key K

and A sees the message $\{X\}_{K^{-1}}$, one may obtain the conclusion that A believes that B once said X.

In summary, to reason about beliefs of agents, we have to use those assumptions that describe agents' trust in security mechanisms (or trusted agents) of the system. According to the method proposed in [12], all these assumptions can be encapsulated in a notion of trust and represented as a set of rules (axioms) contained in a trust theory for the system under an appropriate logical framework. Thus, the trust theory will provide a basis for reasoning about agent beliefs in the system.

5   Reasoning Techniques

For reasoning about trust, we need to develop an appropriate logical framework. In general, one can expect the logic used for modeling trust to be rich enough to represent interactions among agents of a given system, actions agents may take, temporal constraints, and assertions relating to duty and obligation as ethical concepts etc. Reasoning about trust is in fact reasoning about agent beliefs. Therefore the logic should possesses the ability to represent beliefs. A belief represents a disposition of an agent on a proposition, so a logic of express propositional dispositions should be able to express the required relations between believers and attitudes. Classical first-order logic cannot handle such relations well. The modal logic approach is able to enhance propositional and first-order logics with modal operators to represent agent beliefs.

Following a general methodology for building trust theories for reasoning about trust [12], let $\mathcal{AX}$ be an axiomatic system of a logical language, which consists of a set of axioms and a set of rules of inference. Consider a given communication system τ. We will treat a rule specifying trust in the system as a proper axiom, called the trust axiom. That is, the (trust) rules discussed in the previous sections will be represented by axioms. Concretely, a rule $\varphi_1, \ldots, \varphi_n \Longrightarrow \psi$ will be replaced by the axiom $\varphi_1 \wedge \ldots \wedge \varphi_n \to \psi$. Thus, if $\mathcal{T}^{(\tau)}$ is the set of axioms specifying trust in the system τ, then

$$\mathcal{AX} \cup \mathcal{T}^{(\tau)}$$

will form a trust theory for the system.

The reader may note that there are still some problems when we perform a reasoning process based on a modal logical framework although, as we mentioned above, modal logics are especially suitable to represent agent beliefs. Consider an example given below. Assume that the set of rules specifying trust in a given system τ, $\mathcal{T}^{(\tau)}$, contains the following rules (axioms):

R1. *john says* $\varphi \to \mathbf{B}_{alice}(\varphi)$
R2. *bob says* $\varphi \to \mathbf{B}_{alice}(\varphi)$

where φ can be arbitrary formula. According to the discussion we made before, these rules specify such a fact that the agent Alice trusts the agent John as well as the agent Bob. That is, the agent Alice believes what John says as well as what Bob says. If, in some case, John says that C is a valid certificate while Bob say that C is not valid, then what belief on C may Alice have? Formally, the question is: if we have the facts that

P1. *john says valid(C)*
P2. *bob says* $(\neg valid(C))$

then what belief of Alice may be derived? We may have a reasoning process as follows:

(1)	*john says valid(C)*	(assumption)
(2)	*bob says* $(\neg valid(C))$	(assumption)
(3)	*john says valid(C)* $\rightarrow \mathbf{B}_{alice}(valid(C))$	(rule R1)
(4)	*bob says* $(\neg valid(C)) \rightarrow \mathbf{B}_{alice}(\neg valid(C))$	(rule R2)
(5)	$\mathbf{B}_{alice}(valid(C))$	(from (1) and (3))
(6)	$\mathbf{B}_{alice}(\neg valid(C))$	(from (2) and (4))
(7)	$\mathbf{B}_{alice}(valid(C)) \wedge \mathbf{B}_{alice}(\neg valid(C))$	(from (5) and (6))

The last formula is obviously inconsistent to one's ordinary view - nobody intentionally believes that the same thing is true and is not true; it is also inconsistent in any logic, say TML [12], containing the modal axiom $\mathbf{B}_A(\neg \varphi) \rightarrow \neg(\mathbf{B}_A \varphi)$.

Given soundness of $\mathcal{AX}$, undesirable inconsistencies can still be added through the specific trust axioms. This problem can be addressed by modification to rule application in the reasoning process. In the following, we introduce several new reasoning techniques to the logical framework, and expect them to be useful for solving this problem.

1. Defeasible reasoning. We introduce a superiority relation to the set $\mathcal{T}^{(\tau)}$ based on the levels of an agent's trust. That is, if agent A trusts B_1 more than it trusts B_2, then the rule "B_1 *says* $\varphi \rightarrow \mathbf{B}_A(\varphi)$" is superior to the rule "B_2 *says* $\varphi \rightarrow \mathbf{B}_A(\varphi)$". Formally, we have: Let $\mathcal{R} = \{r_1, \ldots, r_n\}$ be a set of rules. A superiority relation on $\mathcal{R}$ is any asymmetric binary relation, denoted by $>$, on $\mathcal{R}$. That is, for any $1 \leq i, j \leq n$, if $r_i > r_j$, then not $r_j > r_i$. We read $r_i > r_j$ as the rule r_i is superior to the rule r_j.

We do not give a formal discussion on the proof techniques in defeasible logic, and refer the reader to Antoniou and Billington [1].

Here we simply adopt the above example to show how the defeasible reasoning technique can solve the problems of inconsistency. We assume that a superiority relation to $\mathcal{T}^{(\tau)}$ have been defined and we have R1>R2. This means that, in the reasoning process, we may have an idea that the result by application of R1 may be better than the one by application of R2. Concretely, if the resulted formula by application of R1 is φ while the resulted formula by application of R2 is $\neg\varphi$, then φ should be regarded as more reliable than $\neg\varphi$ since Alice trusts John more than she trusts Bob. Therefore, φ is derived from the reasoning process. Thus, we have the following deductions, which avoids inconsistent conclusions:

(1)	*john says valid(C)*	(assumption)
(2)	*bob says (¬valid(C))*	(assumption)
(3)	*john says valid(C)* → $\mathbf{B}_{alice}(valid(C))$	(rule R1)
(4)	*bob says (¬valid(C))* → $\mathbf{B}_{alice}(\neg valid(C))$	(rule R2)
(5)	$\mathbf{B}_{alice}(valid(C))$ (from (1) & (3), (2) & (4), and the relation R1>R2)	

Inversely, if we have R2>R1, then the fifth formula should be $\mathbf{B}_{alice}(\neg valid(C))$ in the above reasoning process.

Note that, if by R1 we have φ, by R2 we have ψ, and ψ and φ are not contradictory, then use of the superiority relation does not raise a need to choose one formula from φ and ψ. For example, the following deductions are possible and correct:

(1)	*john says valid(C)*	(assumption)
(2)	*bob says (is_reliable(X))*	(assumption)
(3)	*john says valid(C)* → $\mathbf{B}_{alice}(valid(C))$	(rule R1)
(4)	*bob says (is_reliable(X))* → $\mathbf{B}_{alice}(is\_reliable(X))$	(rule R2)
(5)	$\mathbf{B}_{alice}(valid(C))$	(from (1) and (3))
(6)	$\mathbf{B}_{alice}(is\_reliable(X))$	(from (2)and (4))

From this reasoning process, we obtain two beliefs of Alice: she believes that C is valid, and believes that X is reliable.

2. Reasoning about trust with safety principle. An agent may derive its own belief on a particular statement based on the beliefs of those agents it trusts by a specific principle, called the *safety principle* and stated as follow:

– If an agent believes that all agents whom it trusts believe a statement, then it can believe that statement.

Formally, let $TR_A = \{B_1, \ldots, B_n\}$ be the set of all agents whom the agent A trusts, and φ be a formula (statement). Suppose that, in A's beliefs, each member of TR_A has its own opinion on φ, i.e., for all $i, 1 \le i \le n$, $\mathbf{B}_{B_i}\varphi$ or $\mathbf{B}_{B_i}\neg\varphi$ but not both. The question is: If agent A believes all these beliefs, then what belief on φ may A have? The safety principle gives an answer to a particular case: if A believes that all $B_i(i = 1, \ldots, n)$ believe φ, then A can believe φ. Thus, we may add the following rule to $\mathcal{T}^{(\tau)}$:

$$\mathbf{B}_A(\mathbf{B}_{B_1}\varphi) \wedge \ldots \wedge \mathbf{B}_A(\mathbf{B}_{B_n}\varphi) \to \mathbf{B}_A\varphi.$$

Therefore, if $\mathbf{B}_A(\mathbf{B}_{B_1}\varphi), \ldots, \mathbf{B}_A(\mathbf{B}_{B_n}\varphi)$ have been proved from a set of formulae, Γ, then $\mathbf{B}_A\varphi$ can be derived, we thus have $\Gamma \vdash \mathbf{B}_A\varphi$.

The rule to represent a safety principle can be used for describing trust involved in those systems for which multiple authentications are required for security purposes.

3. Manage uncertainty based on the Opinion Model. Jøsang proposed a subjective logic (SL) [10] that is based on a trust model with uncertainty, called the *Opinion Model*. This logic is developed for mapping concerning propositions rather than the truth of them. It is subjective because the value taken by the opinion is independent of the truth of the position. In such a model, each agent has an opinion about each particular proposition. An opinion is made up of three values: *belief*, *disbelief* and *ignorance*, denoted by b, d, and i, respectively, which satisfy the following relation:

$$b + d + i = 1$$

That is, for any proposition p, there is an opinion, denoted by $w_p = \{b_p, d_p, i_p\}$, that an agent has about the proposition.

The opinion model can be used to solve the problem of an agent having a difficulty in determining what it should believe about a statement when other agents it trusts have inconsistent beliefs on this statement.

Let $\mathcal{AX} \cup \mathcal{T}^{(\tau)}$ be the trust theory for a system τ under a chosen logical framework (not necessarily the logic SL). Assume that $TR_A = \{B_1, \ldots, B_n\}$ is the set of all agents whom the agent A trusts, and φ be a formula. If A knows (believes) what opinion on φ each member of TR_A has: some of them definitely believe φ, some of them definitely believe $\neg\varphi$, i.e., do not believe φ, the others have no idea on φ. Concretely, suppose that there are r B's, for which we have $\mathbf{B}_A(\mathbf{B}_{B_i}\varphi)$, s B's, for which we have $\mathbf{B}_A(\mathbf{B}_{B_i}(\neg\varphi))$, and k B's who have no idea on φ, where $r + s + k = n$. Then we say that agent A believes that the opinion of TR_A on φ is $\{r/n, s/n, k/n\}$.

To the system τ, we suggest that there is a decision rule for agents. The rule allows an agent to determine what decision (on a particular statement) it can make based on the opinion of those agents it trusts. For example, we may have a decision rule as follows:

- Let TR_A be the set of all agents whom the agent A trusts. Suppose A believes that $\{b, d, i\}$ is the opinion of TR_A on a statement φ, then, if $i \geq 0.5$, A ignores φ; otherwise if $b > d$ A accepts φ as true, or if $b \leq d$ A accepts $\neg\varphi$ as true.

Note that different systems may use different decision rules as different systems may have different security requirements.

6 Conclusion

We have discussed the concept of trust and given a formal definition for trust that can avoid the confusions arising from unclear definitions with the notion of trust. We have also investigated modeling methodologies for specifying, and reasoning about, trust in secure communication systems. In particular, addressing the problems that may appear in the reasoning process, three reasoning techniques suitable for reasoning about trust have been proposed.

Continuing the discussion of the general methodology to build a theory for reasoning about trust in a security system, the future work would focus on reasoning techniques – further elaborating the technique proposed in this paper, and developing new techniques, such as the technique based on the game theory, probability reasoning and so on.

References

1. G. Antoniou and D. Billington. Relating defeasible and default logic. In *AI2001: Advances in Artificial Intelligence*, Lecture Notes in Artificial Intelligence, Vol. 2256, pages 13–24. Springer-Verlag, 2001.
2. M. Burrows, M. Abadi, and R. M. Needham. A logic of authentication. *ACM Transactions on Computer Systems*, 8(1):18–36, 1990.
3. Arthur Delbridge and J. R. L. Bernard, editors. *The Macquarie Concise Dictionary*. The Macquarie Library, 1988.
4. Theo Dimitrakos. System models, e-risks and e-trust. towards bridging the gap? Available from http://www.bitd.clrc.ac.uk/PersonPublications/26853, 2001.
5. N.M. Frank and L. Peters. Building trust: the importance of both task and social precursors. In *Proceedings of the International Conference on Engineering and Technology Management: Pioneering New Technologies – Management Issues and Challenges in the Third Millennium*, 1998.
6. E. Gerck. Overview of Certificate Systems: X.509, CA, PGP and SKIP. Available from http://mcg.org.br/.
7. T. Grandison and M. Sloman. A survey of trust in internet applications. *IEEE Communications Surveys and Tutorials*, Fourth Quarter, 2000. Available from http://www.comsoc.org/pubs/surveys/.
8. Andrew J.I. Jones. On the concept of trust. *Decision Support Systems*, 33:225–232, 2002.
9. S. Jones. TRUST-EC: requirements for trust and confidence in E-commerce. European Commission, Joint Research Centre, 1999.
10. A. Jøsang. An algebra for assessing trust in certification chains. In *Proceedings of the Network and Distributed Systems Security (NDSS'99) Symposium*. The Internet Society, 1999.
11. A. Kini and J. Choobineh. Trust in electronic commerce: Definition and theoretical consideration. In *Proceedings of the 31st International Conference on System Sciences*, Hawaii, 1998.
12. C. Liu. Logical foundations for reasoning about trust in secure digital communication. In *AI2001: Advances in Artificial Intelligence*, Lecture Notes in Artificial Intelligence, Vol. 2256, pages 333–344. Springer-Verlag, 2001.
13. C. Liu, M. A. Ozols, and T. Cant. An axiomatic basis for reasoning about trust in PKIs. In *Proceedings of the 6th Australasian Conference on Information Security and Privacy (ACISP 2001)*, volume 2119 of *Lecture Notes in Computer Science*, pages 274–291. Springer, 2001.
14. P. F. Syverson and P. C. van Oorschot. On unifying some cryptographic protocol logics. In *Proceedings of the IEEE Society Symposium on Research in Security and Privacy*, pages 234–248, Oakland, CA USA, 1994. IEEE Computer Society Press.
15. R. Yahalom, B. Klein, and Th. Beth. Trust relationships in security systems – A distributed authentication prespective. In *Proceedings of the 1993 IEEE Computer Society Symposium on research in Security and Privacy*, pages 151–164, 1993.

Foundations for a Formalism of Nearness

Jane Brennan and Eric Martin

The University of New South Wales
School of Computer Science and Engineering
Artificial Intelligence Group
Sydney NSW 2052
Australia
{jbrennan|emartin}@cse.unsw.edu.au
Fax: +61 2 9385-4936
Phone: +61 2 9385-6906|6936

Abstract. Reasoning about your spatial environment can be a challenging task, especially when you are a robot trying to rely solely on quantitative measures. With nearness being such a vague concept, a qualitative representation is an obvious choice offering a wider range of possible values.

This paper introduces a qualitative representation for spatial proximity that accounts for absolute binary nearness relations. The formalism is based on the notion of perceived points, called sites, in a point based universe. Proximity concepts are determined by the parameters of distance between two sites and weight of each of those sites. These parameters were drawn from the concept of Generalised Voronoi Diagrams.

Cognitively useful models and interpretations of our formalism are shown in both a navigation and a natural language context.

1 Introduction

Reasoning about your spatial environment can be a challenging task, especially when you are a robot trying to rely solely on quantitative measures. Imprecise or incomplete sensory information is a fact of life, which is however handled exceptionally well by humans. It comes therefore as no surprise that the qualitative aspects of human reasoning have been of great interest to the many fields that need to utilise spatial cognition. In this paper, we will focus on one particular aspect of spatial knowledge and reasoning, the notion of proximity or the notion of closeness as perceived by a cognitive agent. A note on terminology, proximity of space is often also referred to as *nearness* [11][1] and will be used interchangeably in this paper.

Many previously devised formalisms either stipulate the notion of nearness by using natural language expressions such as "near" or "close", or use ternary relative nearness relations such as van Benthem's logic of space discussed in section 2. The aim of this work is to provide a formalism that can qualitatively

---

[1] "nearness, n.2"

R.I. McKay and J. Slaney (Eds.): AI 2002, LNAI 2557, pp. 71–82, 2002.

account for absolute binary proximity relations and is based on as few parameters as possible in a universe as general as possible. The formalism draws on the idea of Power Diagrams as discussed in section 3.1. The formalism ultimately aims at describing both concepts of proximity valid for any value of the parameters and the scope of each concept for specific values of the parameters. In this paper, we are focusing on the former, leaving the latter to further research.

We will give a short review of some of the work relevant to our formalism in section 2. Section 3 discusses the concept of nearness in the context of Power Diagrams or Generalised Voronoi Diagrams. The foundations for a formalism based on these parameters are introduced in subsection 3.3. The formalism is then discussed in the context of different concepts of nearness in a navigational model in subsection 3.4 and in a natural language model in section 4. As for the navigational context, the ordered set of proximity concepts defined in section 3 is applied to a navigation example. In the natural language context, the formalism is applied to a given set of spatial expressions, thus deriving a model. Section 5 provides a conclusion and a summary of further work.

2   Previous Research

With nearness being such a vague concept[2], a qualitative representation is an obvious choice offering a wider range of possible values. Generally, some distance measure is devised to determine the grade of proximity[3]. With nearness sought to be qualitatively described, a qualitative representation for distance is also a natural choice.

The use of distance as the main determiner for nearness is supported by the results of Gahegan's [5] experiments conducted to identify influencing factors of proximity. While there were several influences, distance appeared to be the most dominant one. The other factors however cannot be neglected completely, if one wants to derive at a cognitively useful theory and the theory presented in this paper leaves room for all possible factors by incorporating a generic weight (see section 3 for more detail). Gahegan [6] also proposed to the usage of Voronoi diagrams, however, the idea was not elaborated formally.

Studying the research conducted in the area of spatial reasoning and spatial knowledge representation during the last decade, it seems that one of the very influential works was the Region Connection Calculus ([12],[13]).

The Region Connection Calculus (RCC) was devised to provide an easily usable subset of topological relations between spatial regions. It is based on the notion of connectedness i.e., regions are either connected, which then provides different degrees of connectedness, or they are discrete. However, RCC does not account for different degrees of proximity or nearness, because discreteness can not be graded. Randell [14], in order to overcome this shortcoming, uses van Benthem's [3] logic of space to account for nearness. Van Benthem suggested, as an extension to his logic of time, a logic of space that uses comparative distances

---

[2] see Worboy's discussion on vagueness [17] p. 635
[3] i.e., the distance between the objects in question is taken as an indicator for the nearness status

to describe proximity. These comparative distances are represented as ternary relations. For example, using van Benthem's logic, the nearness relation between some of the objects shown in Figure 1, can be described as "b is nearer to a than c" and "b is as near to a as d".

This is no doubt a very powerful representation, however, it does not account for absolute binary proximity relations such as "a is close to b". In computational geometry, the notion of nearness is dealt with by weighted Voronoi Diagrams where, in a point based plane, the area of influence of some distinct points or centres stretches out some radius determined by the weight of the generator points defining all the points covered by this influence as near. Ordinary Vornoi Diagrams assume that all distinct points have the same weight and a Voronoi Region for each of these points is defined, thereby ensuring that every point in the plane falls into the region of one of those centres. Power Diagrams combine both types of information. While this paper mainly focuses on the

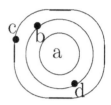

Fig. 1. Ternary Nearness Relations

information of the influence areas, the Voronoi Region information is very useful in certain contexts and will therefore be considered for later use.

3   A Formalism to Account for Nearness

Many approaches to representing spatial proximity are implicit in their nature accounting for specific spatial situations or settings only. The ultimate aim for this framework is to provide a more explicit description. Thus covering a much wider range of problems relating to spatial and possibly even non-spatial proximity. The following encompasses the foundations for the formalism, elaborating on some aspects of spatial proximity concepts.

3.1   Power Diagrams and Their Treatment of Nearness

Voronoi Diagrams are the special and simpler case of Generalised Voronoi Diagrams (or Power Diagrams) where all sites have the same weight.

Choosing a canonical set S of distinct points in the plane (commonly called sites), regions are assigned to every site p by assigning every point to p's region that is not further from p than from any other site q. Regions that share a boundary or edge (i.e., the points of that boundary have the same distance from p and q) are called spatial neighbours. The resulting plane divided into regions like that is called a Voronoi diagram. Voronoi diagrams provide very useful tools by transforming distances into a network of topological relations. [4] Mathematically a Voronoi diagram can be described as:

$$vo(p) = \{x \in \mathbb{R}^2 \mid D(x,p) \le D(x,q) \; \forall q \in S\}$$

The Voronoi Diagram described above can also be referred to as Ordinary Voronoi Diagram (OVD).

74	J. Brennan and E. Martin

In the context of this paper, sites represent spatial entities, which are perceived as important to the current spatial scene by the cognitive agent. For example, looking at a map, these entities could be obvious map features such as cities. In the following, sites will always be referred to as p, q, r, while x, y, z will denote any point in the universe. Power Diagrams incorporate the impact every site has on its surroundings[4] determined by a weight assigned to the site while maintaining the information provided by Voronoi Regions[5]. As mentioned before, the specific case of every site in the diagram having exactly the same weight results in the Ordinary Voronoi Diagram (OVD) as described above.

The weight of sites in Power Diagrams represents the influencing factors of spatial proximity. It is a generic measure leaving room for application dependent factors influencing nearness perception. In the example of residential areas[6], a set of shops might have a very small influence[7] due to its functionality implying *the closer the better*, but a toxic waste dump would have a very big influence[8] due to its potential negative effects on its surroundings, implying *the further away the better*.

Aurenhammer[2] approaches the problem of site weighting by replacing the distance D by $D^2(x, p) - \omega(p)$ with $\omega(p)$ being the weight of p. Note that the above formula is not very well defined, because it also accounts for $D(p, x)$ which would require $\omega(x)$, which in this context is not available.

When incorporating the weight, the edge of a particular site is shifted depending on the weight of the two neighbouring sites without disconnecting any regions that had previously been connected by a Voronoi Edge. It should be noted that connection also includes overlapping and inclusion. Gavrilova [7] discusses an algorithm to construct Power Diagrams from Voronoi Diagrams. In her approach, the power circle of site p is also described as a circle with p at its centre and a radius of $\sqrt{\omega(p)}$. If the power circles of two neighbouring sites p and q intersect, their chordal is their new shared edge. If they do not intersect, the existing edge is shifted by $\Delta(p, q) = \frac{\omega(p) - \omega(q)}{2 * D(p,q)}$.

While all of the information encoded in a Power Diagram is considered important, for the purpose of this paper only the area of influence is used.

Gärdenfors and Williams [9] suggested the usage of RCC relations and Voronoi Tessellation in conceptual spaces. However, it remains unclear how the concepts are placed in the metric space, which is a necessity for generating the Voronoi Diagrams. Very interesting is however, their suggestion of using both, the Voronoi Edges and the weighted site information to reason about the nearness of concepts.

We will now move on to a formal theory dealing in great detail with the notion of nearness in topology, thus providing a tool to go beyond the limiting concept of discreteness by allowing differentiation between near and not near.

---

[4] i.e. the area of influence

[5] adjusted according to the weights of neighbouring sites

[6] This example is taken from Guesgen[8].

[7] i.e. small weight

[8] i.e. very big weight

3.2   Proximity Spaces

Proximity spaces deal with the notion of nearness in a very formal way, accouting for its pure mathematics origin.

In this theory, which was widely discussed in the 1950s (e.g. [15]), the notion of nearness is defined between points or sets in a topological space. Proximity spaces thoroughly consider the implications of proximity to topological and uniform spaces.

Let $(\mathcal{U}, D)$ be a pseudo-metric space (discussed in more detail in section 3.3). Given two sets A and B in $\mathcal{U}$, we say that A is near B iff $D(A, B)$, which is defined as $\inf\{D(a, b) : a \in A, b \in B\}$, is equal to zero[9]. Hence two sets are close if they share a closure point[10]. Moreover identifying a point p with $\{p\}$, a point and a set are near iff the point belongs to the closure of the set. Also note that when $(\mathcal{U}, D)$ is actually a metric space, two points are close iff they are the same.

Extending the above, we can say that the set P is called a proximity space, if for any two of its subsets closeness can be evaluated by the following properties:

1. If set A is close to B, then B is close to A.
2. The union of the sets A and B is close to C iff at least one of the sets A or B is close to C.
3. Each point x in P is close to itself.
4. For any two sets A and B which are far from each other there exist sets C and D, $C \cup D = P$, such that A is far from C and B is far from D.

From the definition of proximity spaces, we can conclude that for any two sets A and B generated from the sites in the universe, if $A \cap B \neq 0$ then A and B are close to each other. A and B represent the influence areas of their generating sites. This leads us to our principle definition of nearness.

3.3   Formalism of Nearness

The foundations of our formalism are based on the notion of *pseudo-distance*.

Pseudo-Distance and Pseudo-Equality

Recall the definition of pseudo-distance[11]: A function $D : \mathcal{U}^2 \to \mathbb{R}_+$ is a pseudo-distance iff:

(P1) $\forall x \in \mathcal{U}$, $D(x, x) = 0$
(P2) $\forall x, y \in \mathcal{U}$, $D(x, y) = D(y, x)$
(P3) $\forall x, y, z \in \mathcal{U}$, $D(x, z) \leq D(x, y) + D(y, z)$

Note that the above definition also allows for $x \neq y$ if $D(x, y) = 0$

Notation: $x =_D y \leftrightarrow D(x, y) = 0$ describes pseudo-equality defined by D; $=_D$ is the equivalence relation over $\mathcal{U}$ accounting for the metric space equivalence relation $x = y$ and also for the fact of x being as close as possible to y i.e., being intuitively next to each other, so close that they are almost indistinguishable however not equal in the traditional sense.

---

[9] Since D is a pseudo-distance, two distinct points p and q can be such that $D(p, q) = 0$; in this case, p and q are said to be asymptotically the same.

[10] A closure point of a set A can also be described as a member of the skin of A.

[11] i.e. distance in pseudo-metric space

Dense Pseudo-Metric Spaces

It is assumed that there exists infinitely many individuals representing material spatial entities. Through an abstraction process, assumed to be performed by the cognitive agent, the universe of discourse $\mathcal{U}$ is an infinite and *dense* pseudo-metric space. Density is defined as follows.

Definition 1. $(\mathcal{U}, D)$ *is said to be dense just in case for all* $p, q \in \mathcal{U}$ *and* $\Gamma_1, \Gamma_2 > 0$, *if* $D(p, q) < \Gamma_1 + \Gamma_2$ *then* $\{x \in \mathcal{U} \mid D(p, x) < \Gamma_1\} \cap \{x \in \mathcal{U} \mid D(x, q) < \Gamma_2\} \neq \emptyset$.

Weights and Power Circles

Every site p has a weight $\omega(p)$ associated with it, retained from the abstracted "real world" entity. The weight is therefore an abstraction to code quantitative and qualitative properties of sites considered important by a cognitive agent such as the factors previously discussed in conjunction with Gahegan's work. The interpretation of the weights is restricted to physical constraints such as an agent's vision ability or the danger impact of a falling tree. Therefore the weight of every site is a combination of the object's physical properties and what the agent perceives of it in the context of the current situation or the task to be performed by the agent. The mental or cognitive ability of the agent itself in terms of spatial reasoning is added as part of newly defined nearness concepts. The weight of a site is always greater than zero, because every point has to be at least in its own area of influence:

(P4) $\omega(p) > 0$.

The introduction of qualitative measures for the weight in terms of fuzzy sets is left for later papers. This paper will focus on foundations of the formalism itself, as space restrictions do not allow for a full exposition of fuzzy weight sets.

The area of influence of a site p is a function of the weight $\omega(p)$; for the nearness formalism it is described as the set of points in the area of influence, including p.

Definition 2 (Power). $Power_D^\omega(p) = \{x \in \mathcal{U} \mid D(x, p) \leq \omega(p)\}$

When the context permits, we will write $Power(p)$ instead of $Power_D^\omega(p)$. Note that although the square root of the weight is used in the Voronoi definition of Power Diagrams, only the weight itself is used in the above power circle definition. The user can define the weight appropriately if the square root or in fact any other function on the weight is required. It is however essential to use the same function ω consistently.

Let us now consider nearness for some specific distances and weights. We will examine the effects of some distance and weight on the power circle itself. They are basic examples, but are worth mentioning here.

Equality of two points: For any point x and site p, let $D_0(x, p) = 0$ if $x = p$ and $D_0(x, p) = 1$ otherwise. We can then conclude by the definition of power:
   It holds for any $\omega(p) < 1$ that for all sites p, $Power_{D_0}^\omega = \{p\}$
   It holds for any $\omega(p) \geq 1$ that for all sites p, $Power_{D_0}^\omega = \mathcal{U}$.

Pseudo-Equality: For any point x and site p, let $D_1(x, p) = 0$ if $x =_D p$ and $D_1(x, p) = 1$ otherwise. We can then conclude by the definition of power: It holds for any $\omega(p) < 1$ that for all sites p, $Power^{\omega}_{D_1} = \{x \in \mathcal{U} \mid x =_D p\}$. It holds for any $\omega(p) \geq 1$ that for all sites p, $Power^{\omega}_{D_1} = \mathcal{U}$.

Definition 3 (Nearness). *The relation $Near(p, q)$ between two sites p and q holds iff $Power(p) \cap Power(q) \neq \emptyset$.*

Nearness is defined as reflexive and symmetric relation, because every site is in the proximity of itself and both sites are within the vicinity of each other.
(P5) $Near(p, q) \leftrightarrow Near(q, p)$
(P6) $Near(p, p)$

Weight and distance are the parameters of nearness. Nearness can be considered in two different dimensions. One is a discrete dimension, in which D and ω can have any value, however the constraints defined on their behaviour will result in different discrete concepts of *Near*. The second dimension considers D and ω as specific and continuous parameters, which can be applied to any concept, therefore allowing "fine-tuning" of the specific concepts of *Near* in the other dimension, showing the scope of every concept for particular D and ω.

Figure 2 shows this principle with the *Concepts*-axis representing the first dimension and the *Parameters*-axis representing the second dimension. The dotted line shows that for any given specific distance D and weight ω, each concept has a certain restricted scope. Note that this scope might cover the entire universe for certain values of D and ω and certain concepts. For the purpose of this paper, we will mainly be focusing on the concepts themselves and leave an extensive consideration of specific values of D and ω for future work.

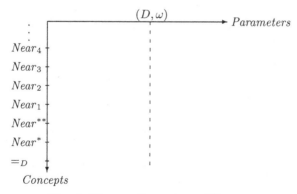

Fig. 2. The two dimensions of Nearness

As can be seen in Figure 2, we are also aiming at introducing an ordering amongst the given concepts i.e., $Near^*_i < Near^*_{i+1}$. The ordering however requires all the concepts to be placed in the same branch of a conceptual lattice. Subsection 3.4 will extend on this idea by supplying such a set of concepts in the context of a navigational setting.

The following properties of nearness hold for any distance D and weight ω.

Equality of Sites

Equality of sites i.e., the distance between sites being zero, is not very interesting, but is included for completeness.

Proposition 1. *The equivalence relation defined by $=$ is a refinement of the equivalence relation defined by $=_D$.*

Proof. By (P1). Note that this property of nearness is also a more specific concept of nearness.

External Connectedness of Sites

The reader familiar with the Region Connection Calculus (RCC) [13] will notice that this particular case is identical with the relation $EC(x,y)$ in RCC. $EC(x,y)$ is valid for regions and holds if two regions are externally connected i.e., have at least one common point. This was extended by Asher and Vieu [1] to assume the regions to have only closure points in common when they are externally connected. That way, the relation can also account for real world objects considered to touch each other without sharing any of their matter. In this formalism, we are restricted to points and therefore resort to pseudo-metric space, where two points can be as close as possible to each other without being identical, when the distance between them is zero.

Proposition 2. *For all $p, q \in \mathcal{U}$, if $p =_D q$ then $Near(p,q)$.*

Proof. Let p and q be such that $p =_D q$. By the definition of Power, $p \in Power(q)$ and $q \in Power(p)$. We conclude with the definition of Near.

Inclusion of at Least One Site

Proposition 3. *For all $p, q \in \mathcal{U}$, if $D(p,q) \leq sub(\omega(p), \omega(q))$ then $Near(p,q)$.*

Proof. If $D(p,q) \leq \omega(p)$ then by Definition 2, $q \in Power(p)$. q is also element of $Power(q)$. Therefore $Power(p)$ and $Power(q)$ have at least the point q in common. The case of $D(p,q) \leq \omega(q)$ is analogous.

Inclusion of Both Sites

Proposition 4. *Suppose that $\mathcal{U}$ is dense. For all $p, q \in \mathcal{U}$, if $D(p,q) < \omega(p) + \omega(q)$ then $Near(p,q)$.*

Proof. By the choice of $\mathcal{U}$, if $D(p,q) < D(x,p) + D(x,q)$ then $Power(p) \cap Power(q) \neq \emptyset$. Hence $Near(p,q)$.

Corollary 1. *If $\mathcal{U} = \mathbb{R}^n$ i.e., Euclidean Space, then $D(p,q) \leq \omega(p) + \omega(q) \Rightarrow Near(p,q)$.*

3.4   Concepts of Nearness in Navigation

We will now discuss specific concepts of nearness as refinements and generalisations of *Near* as given in definition 3.

Generalisations of *Near*

Let us consider the following example in which the distinct points in the space are now a distinct set of trees in a forest; the agent is a bushwalker trying to navigate from one tree to an unknown point in the forest and back to the initial position. In this context, the weight assigned to every tree could be the distance how far the agent can see standing against the tree. Another aspect that needs to be added is the reasoning abilities of this agent during navigation. An agent with rather bad navigating skills might only feel comfortable to walk to the next tree he or she can see and back to the one he or she started from. For a better navigator, he or she might feel comfortable to navigate along a couple of these "near" trees and back. Thus, given that the total distance is not very far and hard to cover, considering the first and the last tree actually being near to each other. The following definition gives this kind of concept, being a generalisation of *Near* as given in definition 3.

Definition 4. *Let $i > 0$ given. For any two sites p and q: $Near_i(p,q)$ holds iff there exists $r_0, ..., r_i$ with $r_0 = p$, $r_i = q$ and for all $j < i$, $Power(r_j) \cap Power(r_{j+1}) \neq \emptyset$.*

These concepts of nearness are shown in Figure 2 as $Near_1$ and upwards, with $Near_1$ representing the general concept of *Near* of definition 3. A clear ordering occurs for these concepts such that: $Near_i < Near_{i+1}$.

Refinements of *Near*

Let us now look at a bushwalker, who might only consider trees near if at least one of them is in sight of the other. This situation could occur if the agent is, for example, at a smaller tree from which he or she can see a tall tree in the distance but not vice versa.

Definition 5. *For all $p,q \in \mathcal{U}$, $Near^{**}(p,q)$ holds iff $p \in Power(q)$ or $q \in Power(p)$.*

Another agent might only consider trees near each other, if he or she can see either tree positioned at the other.

Definition 6. *For all $p,q \in \mathcal{U}$, $Near^*(p,q)$ holds iff $p \in Power(q)$ and $q \in Power(p)$.*

The concept of pseudo-equality is stated in proposition 2 and would, in this context, refer to a bushwalker only feeling comfortable to walk to another tree virtually next to the tree he or she is positioned at. Indeed a rather bad navigator.

3.5   Enriching the Formalism

In order to enrich the formalism to gain more expressive power for reasoning, we will now add the notion of one site being in between two others.

Definition 7 (*Between(r, p, q)*). *For all $p,q,r \in \mathcal{U}$, if $D(p,q) = D(p,r) + D(r,q)$ then r is said to be between p and q.*

The additional condition $min\{\omega(p), \omega(q)\} \leq \omega(r)$ needs to be imposed on the *Between*-relation to ensure compatibility of *Near* w.r.t. the *Between*-relation. Indeed, if p is near q; and r is between p and q then we want r to be near both p and q, which is guaranteed by the additional condition.

4   A Natural Language Example

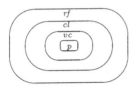

Fig. 3. Influence Areas

The following section describes an informal approach to representing spatial prepositions. Then we will move on to a model of nearness as represented in natural language that complies with the properties stated in the previous section.

Kettani et al. [10] suggested a grading of closeness in terms of influence areas. In the context of a model to generate natural language route descriptions, considering topology, orientation and distance between objects, the notion of *influence area* was used to assign qualitative distances of proximity to the individual objects in the existing cognitive map. The notion of influence area itself describes an imaginary area surrounding objects perceived in the environment in order to grade proximity, generally reflected in natural language by words such as *very close, close* and *relative far*. Influence areas are described as a portion of space surrounding an object such that the influence area has an interior and an exterior border having the same shape as the object. The length of an imaginary perpendicular line crossing the influence area from one point on the interior border to another point on the exterior border is called the width of this influence area. While this width is a subjective measure of a person's perception, Kettani et al. [10] used simple Euclidean geometry to calculate the width of the influence area of objects in their cognitive maps so as to make practical use of their ideas in the navigating system.

The formalism discussed in section 3 can be used to provide a more general model for the influence areas suggested by Kettani et al. and possibly even account for gradings finer than natural language, similar to the concept definitions in section 3.5. When D and ω are left unspecified, $Near(p,q)$ is the more abstract notion. It is often useful to restrict D and ω to satisfy some conditions or even to take a particular value, in which $Near(p,q)$ becomes more specific or fully determined respectively. We claim that if $Near^+(p,q)$ is any "reasonable" interpretation of p and q being intuitively near each other then $Near^+(p,q) \to Near(p,q)$. In the following model different $Near^+(p,q)$ are considered. The intuitions behind this framework are the same as in Kettani et al.'s model. It should be noted that while Kettani et al.'s approach is not symmetric for reasons discussed later, our framework can still be applied to their model in most contexts. We will now define the spatial prepositions as used in Kettani et al. using a subjective choice of behaviour of the nearness formalism and its properties.

very close: $vc(p,q) \equiv_{def} p =_D q$.
Note that by Proposition 2 if $vc(p,q)$ then $Near(p,q)$.
close: $cl(p,q) \equiv_{def} D(p,q) \leq max\{\omega(p), \omega(q)\}$
Note that by Proposition 3 if $cl(p,q)$ then $Near(p,q)$.
relative far: $rf(p,q) \equiv_{def} D(p,q) \leq \omega(p) + \omega(q)$
Note that by Proposition 4 extended by Corollary 1 if $rf(p,q)$ then $Near(p,q)$.

While symmetric nearness can go a long way in describing proximity between two objects, its superconcept of asymmetric nearness is often required in spatial natural language. The following subsection gives a short exposition of non-symmetric nearness relations and their definition.

4.1 The Superset of Asymmetric Nearness

For example if "the bicycle is near the church", we cannot necessarily conclude that "the church is near the bicycle". This kind of effect has been extensively researched cross-linguistically and is apparent as the division of objects into reference object and object to be localised. Objects are categorised by criteria such as their size or mobility. For an extensive discussion on this subject see Talmy [16].

The following definition of asymmetric nearness accounts for this fact.

Definition 8 (Asymmetric Nearness). *We say that site p is near site q, if p is in the power circle of q: $Near\_as(p, q) \leftrightarrow p \in Power(q)$*

5 Conclusions and Outlook

This paper introduces a qualitative representation for spatial proximity based on the notion of perceived points i.e., sites in a point based universe. Proximity concepts are determined by the parameters of distance between two sites and the weight of each of those sites. These parameters were drawn from the concept of Generalised Voronoi Diagrams.

It was shown that an ordered set of proximity concepts can be derived for a navigation example. The application of the existing formalism to spatial natural language expressions in order to derive a model from the formalism was also presented. Thus showing cognitively useful models and interpretations of the existing formalism.

The aim for future work is to extend the conceptual ordering to the superset of asymmetric nearness relations in order to account for asymmetric perception as displayed by natural spatial language. This will enable the development of the formalism into a more general framework, which will provide an explicit representation for spatial proximity and also elaborate on the scope of concepts within the context of specific values of distances D and weights ω. While this paper focuses on spatial proximity, we also find it desirable to provide a future formalism that is a valid representation for any kind of proximity.

References

1. N. Asher and L. Vieu: Towards a Geometry of Common Sense: A Semantics and a Complete Axiomatization of Mereotopology; In *IJCAI'95–Proceedings Volume 1*, pp. 846–852, 1995.
2. F. Aurenhammer: Voronoi Diagrams – A Survey of a Fundamental Geometric Data Structure; In *ACM Computer Survey*, Vol. 23, No. 3, September 1991.

3. J.F.A.K. van Benthem: The logic of time – a model theoretic investigation into the varieties of temporal ontology and temporal discourse; Kluwer Academic Publishing, Dordrecht, 1991.

4. G. Edwards and B. Moulin: Toward the Simulation of Spatial Mental Images Using the Voronoi Model, In *Representation and Processing of Spatial Expressions*, P. Olivier and K.-P. Gapp (eds), pp. 163–184, Lawrence Erlbaum Associates, 1998.

5. M. Gahegan: Proximity Operators for Qualitative Spatial Reasoning; In *Spatial Information Theory – A Theoretical Basis for GIS*, A.U. Frank, W. Kuhn (eds), LNCS 988, Springer Verlag, Berlin, 1995.

6. M. Gahegan, I. Lee: Data structures and algorithms to support interactive spatial analysis using dynamic Voronoi diagrams; In *Computers, Environment and Urban Systems*, 24(2000), pp. 509-537, Elsevier Science Ltd.

7. M. Gavrilova and J. Rokne: An efficient algorithm for construction of the power diagram from the Voronoi diagram in the plane; In *International Journal of Computer Mathematics*, **61**(1-2), pp. 49–61, Overseas Publisher Association, 1996.

8. H.W. Guesgen and J. Albrecht: Imprecise reasoning in geographic information systems; In *Fuzzy Sets and Systems*, Vol. 113(2000), pp. 121–131, Elsevier Science Ltd.

9. P. Gärdenfors and M.-A. Williams: Reasoning about Categories in Conceptual Spaces; In *Proceedings of Seventeenth International Joint Conference on Artificial Intelligence*, Morgan Kaufmann, pp. 385–392, 2001.

10. D. Kettani and B. Moulin: A spatial model based on the notion of spatial conceptual map and of object's influence areas; In *Spatial Information Theory – Cognitive and Computational Foundations of Geographic Information Science*, C. Freksa, D.M. Mark (eds), LNCS 1661, pp. 401—416, Springer Verlag, Berlin, 1999.

11. Oxford English Dictionary, J. A. Simpson and E. S. C. Weiner (eds), Oxford: Clarendon Press, OED Online – Oxford University Press, (1989).

12. D.A. Randell: Analysing the Familiar – Reasoning about space and time in the everyday world; *PhD Thesis*, University of Warwick, UK, 1991.

13. D. A. Randell, Z. Cui and A. G. Cohn: A Spatial Logic Based on Regions and Connection; In *Proc. 3rd Int. Conf. on Knowledge Representation and Reasoning*, 165–176, Morgan Kaufmann, San Mateo, 1992.

14. D.A. Randell: From Images to Bodies - Modelling and Exploiting Spatial Occlusion and Motion Parallax ; In *Proceedings of Seventeenth International Joint Conference on Artificial Intelligence*, Morgan Kaufmann, pp. 57–63, 2001.

15. Ju. M. Smirnov: On Proximity Spaces; In *Matematicheskii Sbornik N.S.*, Vol. 31, No. 73, pp. 543-574 (in Russian),(English translation in *AMS Translation Service* 2, **38**, 5–35), 1952.

16. L. Talmy: How Language Structures Space; In *Spatial Orientation – Theory, Research, and Application*, H.L. Pick (jr.), L.P. Acredolo (eds), Plenum Press, New York and London, 1983.

17. M.F. Worboys: Nearness relations in environmental space; In *International Journal of Geographical Information Science*, Vol.15, No.7, pp. 633–651, 2001.

Semantic Selection for Resolution in Clause Graphs

Seungyeob Choi and Manfred Kerber*

School of Computer Science
The University of Birmingham
Birmingham B15 2TT, England
{S.Choi, M.Kerber}@cs.bham.ac.uk

Abstract. In this contribution we present a variant of a resolution theorem prover which selects resolution steps based on the proportion of models a newly generated clause satisfies compared to all models given in a reference class. This reference class is generated from a subset of the initial clause set. Since the empty clause does not satisfy any models, preference is given to such clauses which satisfy few models only. Because computing the number of models is computationally expensive on the one hand, but will remain almost unchanged after the application of one single resolution step on the other hand, we adapt Kowalski's connection graph method to store the number of models at each link.

1   Introduction

Resolution [16] is probably the best developed approach to automated theorem proving, in which the problem is transformed into a clausal form and a proof is searched for on this clause level. Many powerful systems have been built on this paradigm, e.g. MKRP [6], OTTER [11], SPASS [20], and VAMPIRE [15]. On the one hand, these systems show remarkable performance on many problems in particular application areas. Recently a variant of OTTER successfully solved the Robbins problem [12] that had remained as an open problem for several decades. On the other hand, since these methods depend largely on blind search, exponential explosion is unavoidable. The key technique consists of efficiently searching through a big search space and making good heuristic choices.

Semantic information seems, to a large extent, to be used as a form of heuristic knowledge in human problem solving. Therefore it is natural to think that automated theorem provers can also benefit from the use of semantic information. Some work has been done to integrate semantic information into resolution theorem proving. Slaney et al. [19,7] developed the SCOTT-system which combines the model generator FINDER [18] and the resolution theorem prover OTTER. To speak in a simplified way, SCOTT extends the set of support strategy by the introduction of a semantic satisfiability check, which is based on iterated model

---

* The second author likes to thank Norman Foo and the Knowledge Systems Group at the AI Department of the University of New South Wales for their hospitality.

R.I. McKay and J. Slaney (Eds.): AI 2002, LNAI 2557, pp. 83–94, 2002.

generation. It could be shown that this approach makes a significant improvement for some examples. Plaisted et al. [4,14] implemented a theorem prover using *hyper-linking* techniques [10] with the concept of semantic guidance.

The connection graph proof procedure was first introduced by Kowalski [9]. The main idea is to explicitly represent all resolution possibilities as links in a graph between literals, where the links store not only the applicability but additionally the most general unifier for the application. MKRP is a big theorem proving system which was built in the 1970's and 1980's based on the connection graph method. For a recent overview on the clause graph procedure see [17]. Independently of open theoretical questions like completeness investigated by Eisinger [5] the method has not attracted much attention in more recent resolution theorem provers since the computational overhead to explicitly represent the unifiers in a graph does not pay off. Other techniques like indexing are more important for efficiency. In other words the graph is used to store information which can be more cheaply computed from first principles. In particular, the heuristic choice on which link to resolve only marginally makes use of the links.

The approach presented here can be seen as an attempt to use the connection graph in resolution theorem proving in a more promising way, namely heuristic guidance is provided by the number of models of clauses. First a number of models is generated from the given theory, then a clause graph is constructed out of the set of all clauses, and finally a proof is searched for by heuristic selection of the links. The heuristic selects a link that is most promising in the sense that it has a minimal number of models which fulfil its offspring. Our prototype implementation is built using KEIM [8]. Note that an adaptation of the semantic guidance presented in this paper can be applied to clause selection in other resolution theorem provers as well. We chose the clause graph as it provides a convenient data structure to store the relevant information.

2   The Clause Graph Procedure

The clause graph represents the set of clauses as a graph in which each node corresponds to a literal. The graph consists of one or more groups of literals and each group is a clause. Two complementary unifiable literals are connected by a link which indicates the unification possibility between the literals.

Suppose we have a clause set $\{\neg P(a), P(x) \vee \neg Q(x) \vee R(x), Q(a) \vee \neg R(y)\}$, the set has 3 clauses and 6 literals. Since $\neg P(a)$ and $P(x)$ can be resolved by a common unifier, they are linked together.

We select one of the links in the graph, apply the resolution rule, remove the link, create the new clause which may inherit literals from both ancestors, and insert the new links for this new clause. The new links are a subset of the links of the parent clauses. For instance from the graph in Fig. 1 we obtain by resolving on the rightmost link between $R(x)$ and $\neg R(y)$ the clause graph (unifiers not displayed) in Fig. 2.

Since the link resolved upon is deleted, the clause graph now contains two *pure* literals, $R(x)$ and $\neg R(y)$, which have no links to others. The clauses con-

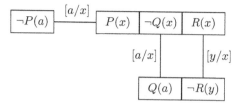

Fig. 1. Example of an initial clause graph

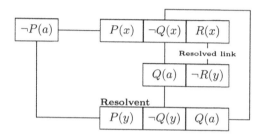

Fig. 2. Clause graph after one step

taining pure literals can be removed from the clause graph, since they cannot have the empty clause as their successor. When a clause is removed, all links connected to the clause are also removed as no links can exist without nodes. The removal of a link may produce a further pure literal in the clause connected to the opposite end, which can also be removed. In fact, an application of a resolution step can cause a chain reaction of reductions, which in extreme cases can lead to the collapse of the whole graph, showing that the original problem was satisfiable. This is the case for the graph in Fig. 2.

3   Model Generation and Semantically Guided Resolution

The semantics of a set of first-order formulas is represented by a pair $\mathcal{M} = (\mathcal{D}, \mathcal{I})$, consisting of a domain and an interpretation. The domain $\mathcal{D}$ is a nonempty set of objects, and the interpretation $\mathcal{I}$ is a mapping from the terms of the language to values in the domain, and formulas are mapped to truth values. We say $\mathcal{M}$ is a model of a formula (or formula set) if the formula is (or all formulas in the formula set are) evaluated to true.

Assume we have a first-order problem given by a formula set Γ and formula φ for which we want to show that φ follows from Γ (i.e., $\Gamma \models \varphi$). Furthermore we assume that the formula set Γ is consistent, that is, that it has models. In resolution theorem proving φ is negated and it is proved that $\Gamma \cup \{\neg\varphi\}$ is unsatisfiable, that is, has no model.

For our procedure we make the assumption – as in set of support – that the background theory Γ is consistent. Hence it has a model. Furthermore the method as described below makes use of the assumption that there are *finite* models for Γ since we make use of a model generator which generates finite models (If no finite models are found, the method reduces to the standard connection graph method). This is, however, an assumption that can be relaxed if we proceed to a model generator which can generate infinite models. Anyway, we think that the class of problems, for which finite models are sufficient, is rich enough that it deserves investigation.

Slaney's FINDER system [18] is a model generator which fixes the domain to a specific number of objects and then performs an exhaustive search in the space of functions and constants which can be satisfied in that domain. We use FINDER as a model generator to generate a set of models $\mathcal{M} = \{\mathfrak{m}_1, \mathfrak{m}_2, \ldots, \mathfrak{m}_n\}$ from a formula set $\Gamma = \{\varphi_1, \varphi_2, \ldots, \varphi_m\}$.

FINDER generates models with a fixed cardinality of the domain $\mathcal{D}$. It is possible to give lower and upper bounds for the cardinality of $\mathcal{D}$. We may either take all models found in a certain bound or limit the result to a certain number of models we are interested in. We have experimented which number of models should be considered best. In our experiments, as described in section 7, we use a cardinality of the reference set of models $\mathcal{M}$ between 40 and 100.

4   The Clause Graph with Semantic Guidance

Let Γ be a set of assumptions and φ be the conclusion, such that $\Gamma \models \varphi$, and let Γ^* and $\{\neg\varphi\}^*$ be the sets of clauses obtained from normalisation of Γ and $\{\neg\varphi\}$, respectively. The resolution procedure searches for a contradiction (an empty clause) from $\Gamma^* \cup \{\neg\varphi\}^*$. The finite model set $\mathcal{M} = \{\mathfrak{m}_1, \mathfrak{m}_2, \ldots, \mathfrak{m}_n \mid \mathfrak{m}_i \models \Gamma^*\}$ is generated from the assumptions Γ^* with the interpretation domain fixed to a finite set of objects.[1] Let $\mathcal{C}$ be the corresponding initial clause set.

$$\mathcal{C} = \Gamma^* \cup \{\neg\varphi\}^*$$

We use $\mathcal{I}^\mathfrak{m}$ to denote the interpretation of a clause C ($C \in \mathcal{C}$) using a model $\mathfrak{m}$.

$$\mathcal{I}^\mathfrak{m} : C \rightsquigarrow \{T, F\}$$

$\mathcal{M}^C$ is a subset of $\mathcal{M}$ such that $\mathcal{M}^C = \{\mathfrak{m}_i \mid \mathcal{I}^{\mathfrak{m}_i} : C \to T, \mathfrak{m}_i \in \mathcal{M}\}$. Suppose two clauses C_1 and C_2 ($C_1, C_2 \in \mathcal{C}$) have literals unifiable with each other. Let C' be the new clause as a result of the application of resolution on C_1, C_2. A link σ is defined as $\sigma = (C_1, C_2, C', |\mathcal{M}^{C'}|)$, a set consisting of the references to two parents clauses, the resolvent, and the number of models in which the resolvent is evaluated to true. The clause graph $\mathcal{G} = (\mathcal{C}, \mathcal{L})$ consists of a set of clauses $\mathcal{C}$ and a set of links $\mathcal{L}$ for all unifiable pairs of literals.

In the set of links $\mathcal{L} = \{\sigma_1, \sigma_2, \ldots, \sigma_n\}$, we choose a σ_{min} with the least number of models $|\mathcal{M}^{C'}|$. The resolvent C' is added to the clause set, σ_{min} is removed from the link set, and all links connected to C_1 or C_2 are potentially copied with substitutions $[C'/C_1]$ and $[C'/C_2]$ applied.

$$\mathcal{C}_{new} \leftarrow \mathcal{C} \cup \{C'(\sigma_{min})\}$$

---

[1] Note that the models have to interpret any additional symbols in φ^* as well.

$$\mathcal{L}_{new} \leftarrow (\mathcal{L} - \sigma_{min}) \cup \{\sigma \mid \sigma_{C_1}, \sigma_{C_2}, [C'/C_1], [C'/C_2]\}$$

$$\mathcal{G} \leftarrow (\mathcal{C}_{new}, \mathcal{L}_{new})$$

In summary, our procedure is as follows. If we want to show $\Gamma \models \varphi$ with φ as theorem from which we generate the set of support, we first generate a set of models from Γ^* with a model generator, concretely FINDER. The next steps are to construct a clause graph from the set of clauses of $\Gamma^* \cup \{\neg\varphi\}^*$, applying resolution rules to all connected literals in the graph, producing resolvents, evaluating these in the set of models and counting the number of models in which each resolvent is true. We use the links in the clause graph to store the number of models in order not to have to recompute them in each cycle.[2] The selection of the link on which the next step is to be performed follows a heuristic which is based on the number of models in which the resolvent is true.[3]

The procedure in pseudo code is displayed in Fig. 3. An abstract view of the

```
INPUT:  Γ*      ;;; hypotheses
        φ*      ;;; conclusion
M := GenerateModels(Γ*);
G := ConstructGraph(Γ* ∪ {¬φ}*);
FOR EVERY L a link in G let
     N := number of models of L in M and insert Label(L,N);
REPEAT
     Select(L,G);
     Res := Resolve(L);
     Insert(Res,G);
     FOR EVERY L is a link connected to Res let
          N := number of models of L in M and insert Label(L,N);
     Simplify
UNTIL empty clause derived OR G empty
```

Fig. 3. Pseudo code for the semantic clause graph procedure

data flow can be found as a flow chart in Fig. 4. The following is an abstract description of the whole system. The most important parts are the model generator, the initialising procedure, and the selection procedure. The model generator

---

[2] Just to store the numbers does not make use of the full potential of the connection graph method. In a variant, it would be possible to store the names of the models in each link. This would improve the performance, since better use can be made of the inheritance mechanism. Only those models of the resolvent of the parent link have to be checked and are potentially inherited. Furthermore, the total number of models could be reduced by taking into the reference set only pairwise non-isomorphic models.

[3] We have also experimented with a variant in which the selection makes a probabilistic choice with a bias towards heuristically promising links, in order to obtain probabilistic completeness. We have no space to describe this here.

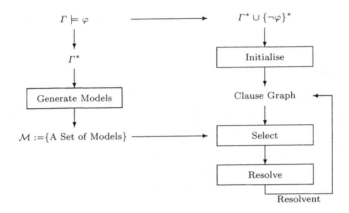

Fig. 4. Proving procedure flowchart

takes the input theory and generates models of it. The initialising procedure builds the initial clause graph with literal nodes and links; it calculates semantic plausibility for all links and stores them in the links. The selection procedure chooses the links on which to operate next.

5   An Example Problem

As an example, let us look at the problem to show that from "orthogonal is symmetric" follows that "parallel is also symmetric" (P stands for parallel and Q for orthogonal):

$$\{\forall x \forall y (P(x,y) \leftrightarrow \exists z(Q(x,z) \wedge Q(z,y))),$$
$$\forall x \forall y (Q(x,y) \rightarrow Q(y,x))\}$$
$$\models \forall x \forall y (P(x,y) \rightarrow P(y,x))$$

To prove the consequence relation by resolution we assume the first set $\Gamma = \{(\forall x \forall y (P(x,y) \leftrightarrow \exists z(Q(x,z) \wedge Q(z,y)))) \wedge (\forall x \forall y (Q(x,y) \rightarrow Q(y,x)))\}$ and negate the second part $\varphi = \forall x \forall y (P(x,y) \rightarrow P(y,x))$. By normalisation we get:

$$\Gamma^* : \quad \{\neg P(x,y) \vee Q(x,f(x,y)),$$
$$\neg P(x,y) \vee Q(f(x,y),y),$$
$$P(x,y) \vee \neg Q(x,z) \vee \neg Q(z,y),$$
$$\neg Q(x,y) \vee Q(y,x)\}$$
$$\{\neg \varphi\}^* : \quad \{P(a,b),$$
$$\neg P(b,a)\}$$

If we fix the cardinality to 2, FINDER selects an interpretation domain to $\mathcal{D} = \{0,1\}$ and generates models in Table 1 from Γ^*. The number of models generated from Γ is 240. The procedure is now set up to count for each possible step in the

Table 1. Models generated by FINDER

Models	m_1	m_2	m_3	m_4	m_5	m_6	m_7	m_8	$\cdots$	m_{100}	m_{101}	m_{102}	$\cdots$	m_{239}	m_{240}
$P(0,0)$	F	F	F	F	F	F	F	F	$\cdots$	T	T	T	$\cdots$	T	T
$P(0,1)$	F	F	F	F	F	F	F	F	$\cdots$	F	F	F	$\cdots$	T	T
$P(1,0)$	F	F	F	F	F	F	F	F	$\cdots$	F	F	F	$\cdots$	T	T
$P(1,1)$	F	F	F	F	F	F	F	F	$\cdots$	T	T	T	$\cdots$	T	T
$Q(0,0)$	F	F	F	F	F	F	F	F	$\cdots$	F	F	F	$\cdots$	T	T
$Q(0,1)$	F	F	F	F	F	F	F	F	$\cdots$	T	T	T	$\cdots$	T	T
$Q(1,0)$	F	F	F	F	F	F	F	F	$\cdots$	T	T	T	$\cdots$	T	T
$Q(1,1)$	F	F	F	F	F	F	F	F	$\cdots$	F	F	F	$\cdots$	T	T
$f(0,0)$	0	0	0	0	1	1	1	1	$\cdots$	1	1	1	$\cdots$	1	1
$f(0,1)$	0	0	0	0	0	0	0	0	$\cdots$	0	1	1	$\cdots$	1	1
$f(1,0)$	0	0	0	0	0	0	0	0	$\cdots$	0	0	0	$\cdots$	1	1
$f(1,1)$	0	0	0	0	0	0	0	0	$\cdots$	0	0	0	$\cdots$	1	1
a	0	0	1	1	0	0	1	1	$\cdots$	1	0	0	$\cdots$	1	1
b	0	1	0	1	0	1	0	1	$\cdots$	1	0	1	$\cdots$	0	1

calculus (resolution, factorisation) how many interpretations in $\mathcal{M}$ are models of the resulting clause. Fig. 5 shows the clause graph labelled with semantic information and three links (Link-1, Link-2, Link-3) have fewer models than others do.

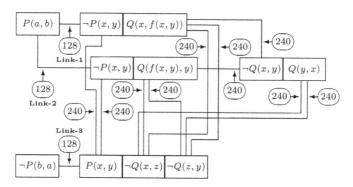

Fig. 5. Initial clause graph

As shown in Fig. 6 the application of resolution to Link-1, Link-2 and Link-3 give rise to Resolvent-1, Resolvent-2, and Resolvent-3, respectively. Those resolvents inherit links from their parents. While the number of models of each link needs to be recalculated, this is computationally not too expensive compared to other forms of heuristics. Furthermore as remarked in footnote 2 the approach can be refined to minimise this by making stronger usage of the inheritance. All the models of an inherited link must be a subset of the model set of the original

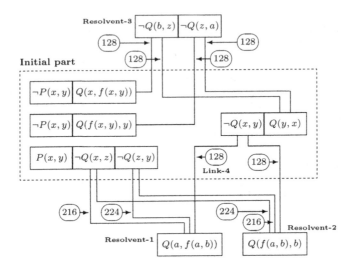

Fig. 6. Clause graph after 3 steps

link of the parent clause, which makes recalculation even easier. In Fig. 6, the model numbers of the inherited links are 128, 216 and 224. If there is more than one link with the same minimal number of models, the one that has been created first is selected. Two clauses $P(a, b)$ and $\neg P(b, a)$ now have pure literals and are removed from the graph.

In Fig. 6, there are three new resolvents and ten new links. We display only the number of models for the ten newly generated links. Six of the links have 128 models, two have 216, and two have 224. So far the smallest number is still 128, and Link-4 is selected because it was the one created first. When we resolve on Link-4, five new links are created. One of them has only 112 models which is the smallest so far. We select it and apply resolution. The new resolvent also has a link with 112 models and it should be selected again. After selecting it and making another new resolvent, three new links are made and they have 128, 112, and 0 models, respectively. The link of 0 models is between the clauses $\neg Q(f(a,b), b)$ and $Q(f(a,b), b)$ and produces the empty clause as a result of a resolution step.

6   Considerations into the Class of Reference Models

Although the semantic guidance results in a smaller search space, it may be expensive to maintain the full set of original models and check every link with respect to all models, of which there are often thousands or more, even with the domain cardinality fixed to 2. Hence it is advisable to keep the reference set manageable in order to make the approach practically feasible.

Table 2 shows the number of models and the number of steps for the example taken from section 5. The second column shows the factor of n which indicates that every nth model is taken from the original model class in order to form a reference set. One interesting feature is that the models do not provide good

Table 2. Reduced set of reference models

Models	Factor	Steps
240	1	6
120	2	6
80	3	6
60	4	Time out
48	5	6
40	6	6
30	8	Time out
24	10	8
20	12	11
15	16	Time out
12	20	Time out
10	24	Time out

heuristics if the factor is 4, 8 or 16. In this particular example, as we have seen in the table of models, the assumption and conclusion have two Skolem constants a and b. The interpretations of these constants are the same in every 4th model if the domain $\mathcal{D}$ is fixed to $\{0, 1\}$, which means that if we take every nth model where n is $4i$ (i integer), both a and b are always interpreted as 1. In the experiments we avoided non-informative subsets of the reference models by choosing the factor to be an odd prime number, such as 7, 11, 13, 17, 19, etc. or by making a random selection.

So far all model sets used in our examples were generated with the domain cardinality fixed to 2. Typically, a bigger cardinality makes each model more informative, and models of cardinality 2 cannot be considered as representative for all finite models. However, as our experiments show, even the class of two element models often bears useful semantic information from which good heuristics for our purpose can be derived. While it is easy to use models with larger cardinality in our approach and to choose randomly a feasible set from all models, the model generation takes typically much longer for higher cardinalities. In the example above, with a cardinality of 3, the number of models is 939078, and with 4 even 4194304. In the following we fix the domain cardinality for our experiments to 2.

7 Experiments on Pelletier Examples

We have tested our semantic clause graph theorem prover (SCG) with full predicate logic problems from Pelletier's examples [13]. Table 3 shows how many steps

Table 3. Experiments on Pelletier examples

Problem	Sos Steps	SCG Original Models	SCG Original Steps	SCG Reduced Models	SCG Reduced Steps	OTTER Steps
Par/Orth	82	240	6	40	6	17
Pelletier 35	0	4096	0	40	0	0
Pelletier 36	4	592	7	53	7	11
Pelletier 37	3	664320	Time out	67	3	3
Pelletier 38	Time out	4194304	Time out	81	Time out	Time out
Pelletier 39*	5	32	0	32	0	2
Pelletier 40*	Time out	128	10	42	14	48
Pelletier 41*	9	18	2	18	2	2
Pelletier 42*	Time out	128	6	42	6	17
Pelletier 43*	Time out	640	101	91	101	138
Pelletier 44	8	2336	16	75	18	10
Pelletier 45	Time out	181760	Time out	86	Time out	28
Pelletier 46	Time out	29968	Time out	80	Time out	52
Pelletier 47	Time out	–	–	–	–	Time out

Sos, SCG: The number of steps the semantic clause graph procedure takes.
OTTER: The number of clauses OTTER generates.
*: The semantic clause graph takes fewer steps than the set of support.
–: means that the model generation itself took longer than 12 hours.

the prover takes to prove each example[4]. Par/Orth is the parallelity and orthogonality problem presented in section 5, and Problem 35-47 are all examples of full predicate logic without identity and functions from Pelletier's problem set [13]. The left most column is the number of steps our set of support strategy prover (Sos) takes to prove the problem. The prover is also based on the same clause graph but, instead of semantic guidance, it makes use of the set of support strategy [21]. The next four columns show the numbers of models in both the original and reduced set and the numbers of steps it takes to prove the problem with the model set. The proof found in step 0 means that it was found during the construction of the initial graph. The number n of models in the reduced sets is taken so that it should be in the range of 40 to 100, which seems to be a good choice. When the prover does not produce the result in a reasonable amount of time (in our experiments 12 hours on a SunE420R with four 450MHz processors), the step is rated as time out.

---

[4] Since SCG uses a different algorithm from OTTER, we apply different measurements – the number of clauses generated and added to the set of support in OTTER, and the number of clauses selected and added to the clause graph in SCG. In SCG, we use a step to denote a resolution step which includes selecting a pair of clauses, resolving them, adding the resolvent into the clause set (or the clause graph in SCG), and updating the set (or the graph in SCG). In OTTER the number of steps is measured by the number of clauses generated.

Although in some examples like Problem 36 and 44 the semantic clause graph prover needs more steps because the problems are relatively easy and the proof may be found in the first several steps by chance with the set of support strategy, in other examples like Problem 39, 40, 41, 42 and 43 the semantic information provides good heuristics for guiding the search. It significantly reduces the number of steps required to search for the proof over the set of support approach.

The right most column is the number of clauses that OTTER generates. Please note that our implementation is only a prototype and wants to show the potential of the approach. On the one hand, the current implementation is based on the Lisp extension KEIM [8] and is not a very fast system. Furthermore, semantic guidance is the only search control it has, while OTTER employs a variety of sophisticated search control mechanisms. On the other hand, each link in SCG already contains a resolvent rather than a unifier. For this reason, a comparison of the run time behaviour of the systems would not be informative. In order to make a fair comparison with the OTTER prover, it would be necessary to integrate the approach directly in OTTER.

8 Conclusion and Future Work

We have described the semantic clause graph prover and presented experimental results. Our approach differs from other semantically guided provers in that it generates models only once at the beginning and uses them during the rest of the procedure, while other semantic approaches like SCOTT [19] generate models not only from the initial clauses but also from new ones. This is an advantage of our approach since in general model generation is computationally much more expensive than checking. Of course, we lose SCOTT's advantage to have a model set which intimately reflects the current state of the proof search.

The performance of semantically guided resolution depends to a great degree on the availability of good models. Our experiments which make use of two-element models show that even there valuable heuristic information can be obtained. To which degree other model classes, like non-isomorphic models, are more promising or not has to be studied for different example classes. Semantic guidance seems to be a standard technique humans use when searching for proofs. Rather than generating models from scratch, they often use *typical examples*. It remains an open question whether and to which extent this is necessary in our context. It may also be important to use infinite models as investigated by Caferra and Peltier [2].

The semantic clause graph prover can be extended by adding a pre-processor of semantic refinements of assumption clauses [3]. The idea is to use models to guide the search, not as in other approaches that backwardly guide the search for an empty clause between the assumptions and the negated conclusion, but forwardly rewrite the assumptions to a form that is semantically closer to the conclusion. Once the potential of semantic guidance is better understood, the heuristic information can be used alongside other types of heuristic information, which constitutes the strength of up-to-date systems.

References

1. A. Bundy, editor. *Proceedings of the 12th CADE*, LNAI 814. Springer-Verlag, 1994.
2. R. Caferra and N. Peltier. Disinference rules, model building and abduction. In E. Orłowska, editor, *Logic at Work: Essays Dedicated to the Memory of Helena Rasiowa*, chapter 20, pages 331–353. Physica-Verlag, 1999.
3. S. Choi. Towards semantic goal-directed forward reasoning in resolution. In D. Scott, editor, *Proceedings of the AIMSA'2002*, LNAI 2443, pages 243–252, 2002.
4. H. Chu and D.A. Plaisted. Semantically guided first-order theorem proving using hyper-linking. In Bundy [1], pages 192–206.
5. N. Eisinger. *Completeness, Confluence, and Related Properties of Clause Graph Resolution*. Research Notes in Artificial Intelligence. Pitman, London, 1991.
6. N. Eisinger and H.J. Ohlbach. The Markgraf Karl Refutation Procedure (MKRP). In J. Siekmann, editor, *Proceedings of the 8th CADE*, LNAI 230, pages 681–682. Springer-Verlag, 1986.
7. K. Hodgson and J. Slaney. Development of a semantically guided theorem prover. In Goré et al. *Proceedings of the IJCAR 2001*, LNAI 2083, pages 443–447. Springer-Verlag, 2001.
8. X. Huang, M. Kerber, M. Kohlhase, E. Melis, D. Nesmith, J. Richts, and J. Siekmann. KEIM: A toolkit for automated deduction. In Bundy [1], pages 807–810.
9. R. Kowalski. A proof procedure using connection graphs. *Journal of the Association for Computing Machinery*, 22(4):572–595, 1975.
10. S.J. Lee and D.A. Plaisted. Eliminating duplication with the hyper-linking strategy. *Journal of Automated Reasoning*, 9(1):25–42, 1992.
11. W. McCune. *OTTER 3.0 Reference Manual and Guide*. Mathematics and Computer Science Division, Argonne National Laboratory, Argonne, Illinois, USA, 1994.
12. W. McCune. Solution of the Robbins problem. *Journal of Automated Reasoning*, 19:263–276, 1997.
13. F.J. Pelletier. Seventy-five problems for testing automatic theorem provers. *Journal of Automated Reasoning*, 2(2):191–216, 1986.
14. D.A. Plaisted and Y. Zhu. Ordered semantic hyper-linking. *Journal of Automated Reasoning*, 25(3):167–217, 2000.
15. A. Riazanov and A. Voronkov. Vampire 1.1. In Goré et al. *Proceedings of the IJCAR 2001*, LNAI 2083, pages 376–380. Springer-Verlag, 2001.
16. J.A. Robinson. A machine-oriented logic based on the resolution principle. *Journal of the Association for Computing Machinery*, 12(1):23–41, 1965.
17. J. Siekmann and G. Wrightson. An open research problem: Strong completeness of R. Kowalski's connection graph proof procedure. *Logic Journal of the IGPL*, 10(1):85–103, 2002.
18. J. Slaney. FINDER: Finite Domain Enumerator. In Bundy [1], pages 798–801.
19. J. Slaney, E. Lusk, and W. McCune. SCOTT: Semantically Constrained Otter. In Bundy [1], pages 764–768.
20. C. Weidenbach, B. Gaede, and G. Rock. SPASS & FLOTTER, Version 0.42. In M. A. McRobbie and J. K. Slaney, editors, *Proceedings of the 13th CADE*, LNAI 1104, pages 141–145. Springer-Verlag, 1996.
21. L. Wos, G.A. Robinson, and D.F. Carson. Efficiency and completeness of the set of support strategy in theorem proving. *Journal of the Association for Computing Machinery*, 12(4):536–541, 1965.

Machine-Checking the Timed Interval Calculus

Jeremy E. Dawson* and Rajeev Goré**

Department of Computer Science and Automated Reasoning Group
Australian National University, Canberra ACT 0200, Australia
{jeremy,rpg}@discus.anu.edu.au

Abstract. We describe how we used the interactive theorem prover
Isabelle to formalise and check the laws of the Timed Interval Calculus
(TIC). We also describe some important corrections to, clarifications of,
and flaws in these laws, found as a result of our work.

Keywords. Reasoning about time, automated reasoning, theorem proving

1 Introduction

Reasoning about time plays a fundamental role in artificial intelligence and computer science. Various approaches have been taken to formalise such reasoning.
A logic-based approach leads to propositional temporal logics [5] while a more
direct approach leads to various calculi for reasoning about time explicitly [1,
13,4]. The logical approaches have an in-built rigour due to soundness and completeness results with respect to rigorous semantics. The direct methods are
more intuitive and easier to use for practitioners who are not always well-versed
with formal logic. Nevertheless, the logical consistency of such direct methods
is paramount for applications. For example, the Timed Interval Calculus (TIC)
has been used in the formal development of a real-time system [10].

Following Fidge et al. [4], Wabenhorst [12] gives a rigorous semantics for
the TIC in terms of our usual set-theoretic understanding of time, points and
intervals. He states 18 "laws" designed to enable convenient proofs about the
TIC, and gives proofs of some important theorems about the TIC. We used the
proof assistant Isabelle to formalise and check the logical rigour of these laws
with respect to their semantics. It might seem that the validity of the laws (and,
even more so, many of our lemmas) is intuitively obvious. However, the "devil is
in the detail", and rigorous formalisations such as ours have often exposed bugs,
even in refereed publications. Indeed, we found problems with the laws given in
[4] and [12], once again showing the worth of machine-checked proofs.

Various authors have already formalised another interval calculus called the
Duration Calculus [13]. Heilmann's [6] proof assistant Isabelle/DC is built using
Isabelle and SVC (Stanford Validity Checker), while Skakkebæk's [11] PC/DC
(Proof Checker for Duration Calculus) is built upon PVS.

---

* Supported by an Australian Research Council Large Grant
** Supported by an Australian Research Council QEII Fellowship

However, we know of only one other attempt to formalise the TIC. In [2], Cerone describes an implementation of the TIC in the theorem prover Ergo. This work differs from ours in the following important respects. Cerone provides an extensive axiomatisation of the time domain, whereas we use the theory of the reals provided with Isabelle/HOL. In respect of concatenation, our work is based on the definition given by Wabenhorst, from which we proved more powerful results which were more convenient to use. Cerone assumes more powerful axioms, which are not proved to be derivable from Wabenhorst's formulation. If, therefore, they were in fact not derivable from Wabenhorst's formulation, this would not become apparent from the work in [2]. In fact, Cerone's axiom I9 appears to allow concatenation of two intervals which are both open at their common endpoint, though this difference from [12] is not commented on. Cerone sets up a special syntax and many axioms relating to lifting functions and predicates over the time and interval domains, which make definition of Wabenhorst's special brackets easier. Finally, [2] deals with proofs of only 5 laws.

In the remainder of § 1 we introduce the TIC, Isabelle, and Wabenhorst's laws in some detail. In § 2 we describe our formalisation of the laws and the problems we encountered. In § 3 we conclude. The full code of our machine-implementation can be found at http://discus.anu.edu.au/~jeremy/tic/tic-files/.

1.1   The Timed Interval Calculus

The Timed Interval Calculus (TIC) is introduced by Fidge et al. [4] as a formal method for reasoning about time-dependent behaviour. As in other timed-trace formalisms, a time-dependent variable is modelled by a function from the set of real numbers. The TIC allows us to reason about (non-empty and finite) time intervals over some domain of time $\mathbb{T}$. Time intervals are represented as all time points in $\mathbb{T}$ between some start-point a and some end-point b. There are then four possible choices depending upon whether the end-points are included or excluded from this interval. For example, the notation $(a, b]$ indicates all time intervals between a and b which exclude a but include b.

The main specification format in TIC is a notation for defining the set of all time intervals in which some predicate P is everywhere true. The predicate may depend not only on the particular time point but also on the endpoints or length of the interval. The notation uses special brackets to distinguish the four possible choices for including and excluding end-points. Fidge et al. [4] give 13 laws which capture fundamental properties of time intervals defined via the TIC notation. In [12] Wabenhorst gives 18 such laws, including most of those in [4]. The correctness of these laws is the focus of our work.

1.2   Isabelle/HOL

Isabelle is an automated proof assistant [8]. Its meta-logic is an intuitionistic typed higher-order logic, sufficient to support the built-in inference steps of higher-order unification and term rewriting. Isabelle accepts inference rules of the form "from $\alpha_1, \alpha_2, \ldots, \alpha_n$, infer β" where the α_i and β are expressions of the Isabelle meta-logic, or are expressions using a new syntax, defined by the user, for some "object logic". In practice most users would build on one of the comprehensive "object logics" already supplied [9].

We use the most commonly used Isabelle object logic, Higher Order Logic (HOL), which is an Isabelle theory based on the higher-order logic of Church [3] and the HOL system of Gordon [7]. Thus it includes quantification and abstraction over higher-order functions and predicates. The HOL theory uses Isabelle's own type system and function application and abstraction: that is, object-level types and functions are identified with meta-level types and functions. Isabelle/HOL contains constructs found in functional programming languages (such as datatype and let) which greatly facilitates re-implementing a program in Isabelle/HOL, and then reasoning about it. However limitations (not found in, say, Standard ML itself) prevent defining types which are empty or which are not sets, or functions which may not terminate.

Due to space limitations, we assume that the reader has some familiarity with Isabelle and logical frameworks in general.

1.3 TIC Definitions and Laws

As stated previously, $\mathbb{T}$ is some fixed domain of time points, typically the reals (our proofs use the completeness and density of the reals). The set of all non-empty finite time intervals over this domain is $\mathbb{I}$. Following Fidge et al. [4], Wabenhorst [12] defines several symbols – the following definitions are (or are close to) his. Suppose P is some predicate, and let α be the start-point and ω be the end-point of our intervals.

Let (-P-] be the set (of *left-open-and-right-closed* intervals)

$$(-P\text{-}] \equiv \{(\alpha \ldots \omega] \mid \alpha, \omega : \mathbb{T} \wedge \alpha < \omega \wedge \forall t : (\alpha \ldots \omega] P(t, \alpha, \omega)\}$$

Thus all intervals in (-P-] are non-empty, and for every interval $I \in (-P\text{-}]$ and every $x \in I$, x satisfies P. Note that predicate P may also depend on the endpoints α and ω of the interval, whose length $\omega - \alpha$ is often abbreviated by δ.

The *left-and-right-open* intervals (-P-), the *left-closed-and-right-open* intervals [-P-) and the *left-and-right-closed* intervals [-P-] are defined similarly, though for [-P-] the non-emptiness condition is $\alpha \leq \omega$. The *right-open* intervals [(-P-) are defined by [(-P-) $\equiv$ [-P-) $\cup$ (-P-), and [(-P-], (-P-)], [-P-)] and [(-P-)] are defined correspondingly as the *right-closed, left-open, left-closed* and *left-and-right-open-or-closed* intervals respectively. In the Isabelle code [(-P-) is represented as [(-P-), and the others likewise.

To reason about adjacent intervals, Wabenhorst defines concatenation of sets of intervals. Two intervals x and y can be joined if they meet with no overlap or gap, that is, $x \cup y$ is an interval and $x \cap y = \emptyset$. Then, for sets X and Y of intervals, their concatenation $X;Y$ is obtained by joining $x \in X$ with $y \in Y$ wherever this is possible. Thus

$$X;Y \equiv \{x \cup y \mid x : X \wedge y : Y \wedge x \cup y : \mathbb{I} \wedge \forall t_1 : x \; \forall t_2 : y \; t_1 < t_2\}$$

Exceptionally, **1** is used for $\{\emptyset\}$, which may be an operand for, and is an identity of, the concatenation operator. Finally, $\overline{S}$ means $S \cup \mathbf{1}$.

A predicate P is defined to have the *finite variability property* if there exists a duration $\xi > 0$ such that $[(\neg P\text{-})]; [(\text{-}\Diamond P\text{-})]; [(\neg P\text{-})] \subseteq [(\text{-}\delta >= \xi\text{-})]$.

Wabenhorst [12] gives 18 laws for the Timed Interval Calculus, as shown in Figure 1. Fidge et al. [4] give 13 laws, most of which are included in Wabenhorst's 18 laws. The remaining two are shown in Figure 2.

A common special case for $[(\text{-}P\text{-})]$ (etc) is where predicate P takes a single argument, and does not involve the endpoints of the interval: the latter is expressed by the condition "if α, ω and δ do not occur free in P" (e.g. Law 11).

However in formalising the laws, we noticed a similar phrase in Law 10 involving arbitrary sets of intervals S, T, U. We saw this as meaningless, except in the special case where S, T, U have a form such as $[\text{-}P\text{-}]$ or $(\text{-}P\text{-})$ — see § 2.1.

2   Verification of the Laws

As can be seen from Figure 1, Wabenhorst's laws are really statements about the special notation of TIC. The semantics of this notation is its underlying meaning in terms of sets of time intervals over $\mathbb{T}$, which is stated to be the real numbers $\mathbb{R}$. To verify these laws, we must confirm that they are correct with respect to this underlying semantics, so we had to reason formally about real numbers. We used the real number libraries for Isabelle/HOL, which include theorems relating to least upper bounds and completeness and density of the reals.

The datatype `interval`, defined below, uses the two endpoints of the interval, and an indicator of whether the interval is closed or open at these endpoints:

```
datatype interval =
        CC real real | CO real real | OC real real | OO real real
```

This datatype allows (many different values representing the) empty interval, so many of our theorems include the additional condition that the interval(s) concerned are non-empty. The set of all non-empty intervals is $\mathbb{I}$, written in Isabelle as II. We wrote numerous functions for reasoning about aspects of intervals: the types and short-hand notations for some of these are shown in Figure 3. We describe many of these in what follows at appropriate places.

We found it streamlined some proofs to be able to consider each end of an interval separately. Thus we defined a datatype `bndty` to take a real bound and indicate whether an interval is open or closed at that bound, and functions `ubt` ("upper bound and type") and `lbt`, for example:

```
datatype bndty = Closed real | Open real
ubt_CC = "ubt (CC ?beg ?end) = Closed ?end" : thm
```

The function `setof` gives the actual set which an `interval` defines:

```
setof_OC = "setof (OC ?beg ?end) = {x.?beg < x & x <= ?end}" : thm
```

Law 1 (Monotonicity) If for all α, ω and δ in $\mathbb{T}$ and all $t : (\alpha \ldots \omega]$
$P(t, \alpha, \omega) \Rightarrow Q(t, \alpha, \omega)$, then $(\text{-}P\text{-}] \subseteq (\text{-}Q\text{-}]$.

Law 2 (True and false) $[(\text{-}true\text{-})] = \mathbb{I}$ and $[(\text{-}false\text{-})] = \emptyset$

Law 3 (And) $[(\text{-}P\text{-})] \cap [(\text{-}Q\text{-})] = [(\text{-}P \wedge Q\text{-})]$

Law 4 (Or) $[(\text{-}P\text{-})] \cup [(\text{-}Q\text{-})] \subseteq [(\text{-}P \vee Q\text{-})]$

Law 5 (Not) $[(\text{-}\neg P\text{-})] \subseteq \mathbb{I} \backslash [(\text{-}P\text{-})]$

Law 6 (Concatenation monotonicity) If $S \subseteq S'$ and $T \subseteq T'$ then $S; T \subseteq S'; T'$.

Law 7 (Concatenation associativity) $(S \; ; \; T) \; ; \; U = S \; ; \; (T \; ; \; U)$

Law 8 (Concatenation zero and unit) $S; \emptyset = \emptyset; S = \emptyset$ and $S; 1 = 1; S = S$.

Law 9 (Concat. union) $(S \cup T); U = (S; U) \cup (T; U)$ and $S; (T \cup U) = (S; T) \cup (S; U)$

Law 10 (Concatenate intersection) $(S \cap T); U \subseteq (S; U) \cap (T; U)$ and $U; (S \cap T) \subseteq (U; S) \cap (U; T)$ Equality holds in the first case if ω and δ are not free in S and T, and in the second case if α and δ are not free in S and T.

Law 11 (Concatenate property) If α, ω and δ do not occur free in P, then $[(\text{-}P \wedge \delta > 0\text{-})] = [(\text{-}P\text{-})]; [(\text{-}P\text{-})]$.

Law 12 (Always) If α, ω and δ are not free in P, then $[(\text{-}\Box P\text{-})] = [(\text{-}P\text{-})]$.

Law 13 (Induction on Lengths) Let $H(X)$ be a formula containing $X : \mathbb{PI} \cup 1$, but no occurrence of negation or the complement of X. Let P be a predicate for which the finite variability property holds. If
(a) $H(1)$ and
(b) $H(X) \Rightarrow H(X \cup (X; [(\text{-}P\text{-})]) \cup (X; [(\text{-}\neg P\text{-})]))$
then $H(\overline{\mathbb{I}})$.

Law 14 (Induction on Histories) Let $H(X)$ be a formula containing $X : \mathbb{PI}$, but no occurrence of negation or the complement of X. Let P be a predicate for which the finite variability property holds. If
(a) $H([(\text{-}\omega < 0\text{-})])$ and
(b) $H(X) \Rightarrow H(X \cup (X; [(\text{-}P\text{-})]) \cup (X; [(\text{-}\neg P\text{-})]))$
then $H([(\text{-}\alpha < 0\text{-})])$.

Law 15 (Ignore Prefix) Suppose that there exists $r : \mathbb{T}$ such that for all $I : [(\text{-}\alpha < r\text{-})]$, $\{I\}; S \subseteq \{I\}; T$. Then $S \subseteq T$.

Law 16 (Distribute Intersection) If α, ω and δ are not free in P, then $[(\text{-}P\text{-})] \cap (S; T) = ([(\text{-}P\text{-})] \cap S); ([(\text{-}P\text{-})] \cap T)$.

Law 17 (Endpoints) If α, ω and δ are not free in P and Q, and if P or Q is finitely variable, then
$$[(\text{-}P \vee Q\text{-})] = \overline{[(\text{-}P \vee Q\text{-})]}; ([(\text{-}P\text{-})] \cup [(\text{-}Q\text{-})]) = ([(\text{-}P\text{-})] \cup [(\text{-}Q\text{-})]); \overline{[(\text{-}P \vee Q\text{-})]}$$

Law 18 (Implicit Duration) If α, ω and δ are not free in P and Q, then
$$[(\text{-}P \wedge \delta > r\text{-})] \subseteq \overline{[(\text{-}true\text{-})]}; [(\text{-}Q\text{-})] \Leftrightarrow [(\text{-}P \wedge \delta > r\text{-})] \subseteq \overline{[(\text{-}\delta \leq r\text{-})]}; [(\text{-}Q\text{-})]$$

Fig. 1. Laws for the Timed Interval Calculus

Law 11 (Concatenate fixed intersection) If $r \geq 0$ then
$$((S \cap [(\text{-}\delta = r\text{-})]); T) \cap ((U \cap [(\text{-}\delta = r\text{-})]); V) = (S \cap U \cap [(\text{-}\delta = r\text{-})]); (T \cap V)$$
$$\& \; (S; (U \cap (\text{-}\delta = r\text{-})])) \cap (T; (V \cap (\text{-}\delta = r\text{-})])) = (S \cap T); (U \cap V \cap (\text{-}\delta = r\text{-})])$$
Similarly with $[(\text{-}\ldots\text{-})]$ and $(\text{-}\ldots\text{-})]$ replaced by $[(\text{-}\ldots\text{-}]$ and $[\text{-}\ldots\text{-})]$ respectively.

Law 13 (Concatenate duration) If α, ω and δ are not free in P, $r \geq 0$ and $s \geq 0$, where $r > 0$ or $s > 0$, then $[(\text{-}P \wedge \delta = r + s\text{-})] = [(\text{-}P \wedge \delta = r\text{-})]; [(\text{-}P \wedge \delta = s\text{-})]$

Fig. 2. Additional Laws of Fidge et al.

```
consts
  setof        :: "interval => real set"
  nonempty     :: "interval => bool"
  negint       :: "interval => interval"
  emptyint     :: "interval"
  no_aod       :: "([real] => bool) => ([real, real, real] => bool)"
  OCints       :: "([real, real, real] => bool) => interval set"  ("'(-_-]")
  cat          :: "[interval set, interval set] => interval set"
                  ("_ ;; _" [75, 76] 75)
  clp, crp     :: "interval set => bool"
  ubt          :: "interval => bndty"
  lbt          :: "interval => bndty"
  btopp, negbt :: "bndty => bndty"
  ubc          :: "bndty => real => bool"
  lbc          :: "bndty => real => bool"
  realval      :: "bndty => real"
  "--->"       :: "['a => bool, 'a => bool] => bool"       (infixr 25)
```

Fig. 3. Various Functions for Reasoning About Intervals

Lemma 1. *(i) On non-empty intervals, the function* setof *is 1-1.*
(ii) The upper and lower bounds of an interval (including their types, ie, Closed
or Open) *determine the interval.*

```
setof_cong = "[| nonempty ?int1; setof ?int1 = setof ?int2 |]
    ==> ?int1 = ?int2" : thm
bts_unique = "[| lbt ?int1 = lbt ?int2; ubt ?int1 = ubt ?int2 |]
    ==> ?int1 = ?int2" : thm
```

It was frequently convenient to use a theorem relating to the upper bound
of an interval and use the theorem relating to the upper bound of the negated
interval, rather than prove from scratch the corresponding theorem for the lower
bound. So we defined a function negint, which negates an interval, and a function negbt, which negates a bound, by, for example:

```
negint_0 = "negint (OC ?beg ?end) = CO (- ?end) (- ?beg)" : thm
negbt_Open = "negbt (Open ?x) = Open (- ?x)" : thm
```

Thus we have lemmata such as the following.

Lemma 2. *The upper bound of the negation of A is the negation of the lower*
bound of A.   ubt_neg = "ubt (negint ?A) = negbt (lbt ?A)" : thm

In discussing concatenation of intervals, we are interested in pairs (A, B) of
intervals such that (for example) ubt $A =$ Closed r and lbt $B =$ Open r since
such intervals meet with no overlap or gap at r. We therefore defined a function
btopp which "opposes" an Open bound into a Closed one, and vice versa.

```
btopp_Closed = "btopp (Closed ?x) = Open ?x" : thm
```

For a point t to lie within an interval like $(\alpha \ldots \omega]$, it must satisfy $\alpha < t$ and
$t \leq \omega$. We refer to these two conditions as the "lower (upper) bound condition".
Just as we found it convenient to consider separately the lower and upper bounds

of an interval, we found it convenient to consider separately these two conditions satisfied by points within an interval. So we defined further functions ubc and lbc (one clause of the definition is given below), and proved the lemma bnd_conds.

```
ubc_Closed = "ubc (Closed ?end) ?x = (?x <= ?end)" : thm
```

Lemma 3 (bnd_conds). *A point lies in an interval if and only if it satisfies the lower and upper bound conditions for the interval.*

```
bnd_conds = "(?x : setof ?intvl) =
   (lbc (lbt ?intvl) ?x & ubc (ubt ?intvl) ?x)" : thm
```

We then needed facilities to manipulation these conditions. Firstly a "lifted" implication --->, which provides a reflexive and anti-symmetric ordering.

```
liftimp         = "?p ---> ?q == ALL s. ?p s --> ?q s" : thm
liftimp_refl'   = "?s = ?t ==> ?s ---> ?t" : thm
liftimp_antisym = "[| ?t ---> ?s; ?s ---> ?t |] ==> ?s = ?t" : thm
```

Relation ---> is also transitive, but we do not use this. It is not generally linear, but the result ubc_linear and the others shown below were useful.

Lemma 4. (ubc_cong) *The function ubc is 1-1.*
(ubc_linear) *The relation ---> is linear on conditions of the form ubc s.*
(ubc_rel) *If x satisfies the upper bound condition for an interval, and $y \leq x$, then y satisfies the upper bound condition for the interval.*

```
ubc_cong   = "ubc ?t = ubc ?s ==> ?t = ?s" : thm
ubc_linear = "(ubc ?t ---> ubc ?s) | (ubc ?s ---> ubc ?t)" : thm
ubc_rel    = "[| ubc ?b ?x; ?y <= ?x |] ==> ubc ?b ?y" : thm
```

Several results related these functions to ones previously described, e.g.:

Lemma 5. (ubc_opp) *Let b be a bound, and b' its opposite (ie, Open instead of Closed, or vice versa). Consider b as a lower bound and b' as an upper bound. Then x is within b' if and only if x is not within b.*
(ubc_neg) *Let b be a bound, and b' its negation (eg, if b is Open z then b' is Open $(-z)$). Consider b as a lower bound and b' as an upper bound. Then x is within b' if and only if $-x$ is within b.*

```
ubc_opp = "ubc (btopp ?b) ?x = (~ lbc ?b ?x)" : thm
ubc_neg = "ubc (negbt ?b) ?x = lbc ?b (- ?x)" : thm
```

Results using properties of real numbers often required many easy lemmata and a proof by cases: e.g. ubc x ---> ubc y has four cases of which one is:

```
"(ubc (Closed ?x) ---> ubc (Open ?y)) = (?x < ?y)" : thm
```

We now give results which, though in some cases intuitively quite simple, were more difficult to prove because our mental model of an interval includes some aspects which are not part of the definition. Therefore we had to prove some results about intervals which we needed to use later. The theorem betw_char, which was quite difficult to prove, gives a characterisation of finite intervals. The result disj_alt is related to the manner in which concatenation is defined.

Lemma 6. (betw_char) *A set S is an interval if and only if it is bounded above and below and satisfies the condition that for any $x, y \in S$ and any z, if $x \leq z \leq y$ then $z \in S$.*
(disj_alt) *If I_1 and I_2 are disjoint intervals, then either every point in I_1 is less than every point in I_2, or vice versa.*

```
betw_char = "(EX intvl. setof intvl = ?S) =
((EX ub. isUb UNIV ?S ub) & (EX lb. isLb UNIV ?S lb) &
 (ALL x y z. x <= z & z <= y & x : ?S & y : ?S --> z : ?S))" : thm
disj_alt = "(setof ?I1 Int setof ?I2 = {}) =
 ((ALL t1:setof ?I1. ALL t2:setof ?I2. t1 < t2) |
  (ALL t1:setof ?I1. ALL t2:setof ?I2. t2 < t1))" : thm
```

2.1   Concatenation

Proving results about concatenation of interval sets was considerably more difficult. We defined a predicate abuts to indicate that two intervals meet exactly, so that they may be joined. The definition is abuts_def, but we found that some other characterisations of abuts were more useful. Note that ?S *<= ?x means $\forall y \in S.y \leq x$. Proving these results was surprisingly tedious and difficult.

Lemma 7. (abuts_def) *Two sets A and B abut iff the upper bound x of A is the lower bound of B, and x is in one but not both.*
(abuts_un_disj) *Two non-empty intervals A and B abut iff their union is an interval and all points in A are less than all points in B.*
(abuts_betw_char) *If A and B are intervals, and $a \in A, b \in B$, then A and B abut iff for any c such that $a \leq c \leq b$, c is in exactly one of A and B.*
(abuts_UnL) *If A, B, C are sets, $b \in B$ and $\forall a \in A.a \leq b$ then B and C abut iff $(A \cup B)$ and C abut.*

```
abuts_def = "abuts ?A ?B == EX x.
   isLub UNIV ?A x & isGlb UNIV ?B x & (x : ?A) = (x ~: ?B)" : thm
abuts_un_disj = "[| nonempty ?A; nonempty ?B |] ==>
   abuts (setof ?A) (setof ?B) =
      ((EX C. setof C = setof ?A Un setof ?B) &
       (ALL a:setof ?A. ALL b:setof ?B. a < b))" : thm
abuts_betw_char = "[| ?a : setof ?A; ?b : setof ?B; ?a <= ?b |]
   ==> abuts (setof ?A) (setof ?B) = (ALL c.
   ?a <= c & c <= ?b --> (c : setof ?A) = (c ~: setof ?B))" : thm
abuts_UnL = "[| ?b : ?B; ?A *<= ?b |] ==>
   abuts ?B ?C = abuts (?A Un ?B) ?C" : thm
```

Here Un is the set union operation in Isabelle/HOL, while Int (used later) is the set intersection operation. We use "; ;" to stand for the TIC concatenation operator ";", and define concatenation (of *sets* of intervals) by

```
cat_def = "?X ;; ?Y == {intvl.  EX x:?X.  EX y:?Y.
  setof intvl = setof x Un setof y &
    (ALL t1:setof x. ALL t2: setof y. t1 < t2)}" : thm
```

We prove an alternative characterisation cat_abuts. The easy lemma mem_cat_UN relates $\{a\}; ; \{b\}$ to $A; ; B$ where A and B are sets of intervals and a and b are intervals.

Lemma 8. (mem_cat_UN) $x \in A; B$ *if and only if there exist* $a \in A, b \in B$ *such that* $x \in \{a\}; \{b\}$.
(cat_abuts) $x \in \{a\}; \{b\}$ *if and only if* $a \cup b$ *is an interval and, if* a *and* b *are non-empty, they abut.*

```
mem_cat_UN =
  "(?x : ?A;;?B) = (EX a:?A. EX b:?B. ?x : {a};;{b})" : thm
cat_abuts = "?A ;; ?B = {intvl.  EX a:?A.  EX b:?B.
  setof intvl = setof a Un setof b &
  (nonempty a & nonempty b --> abuts (setof a) (setof b))}" : thm
```

The proof of Law 7 (Concatenate associativity) turned out to be more difficult than most of the others. Our first proof was achieved using cat_abuts, abuts_un_disj, abuts_UnL, and a corresponding result abuts_UnR.

Subsequently we found an easier approach. We used abuts_bnds to characterise when two intervals can be joined, and single_cat' to describe the result of joining them. It was straightforward but tedious to then prove single_cat3l', and the similar result single_cat3r', differing only in containing (?x :{?A} ;;({?B} ;; {?C})). Proving Law 7 was then straightforward.

Lemma 9. (abuts_bnds) *Two non-empty intervals* A *and* B *abut iff the upper bound of* A *is the opposite of the lower bound of* B.
(single_cat') *Two non-empty intervals* B *and* C *can be concatenated to form a third interval* A *iff they abut (as above) and* A, B *have the same lower bound, and* A, C *have the same upper bound.*

```
abuts_bnds = "[| nonempty ?A; nonempty ?B |]  ==>
 abuts (setof ?A) (setof ?B) = (ubt ?A = btopp (lbt ?B))" : thm
single_cat' = "[| nonempty ?B; nonempty ?C |] ==>
 (?A : {?B} ;; {?C}) = (lbt ?A = lbt ?B
    & ubt ?A = ubt ?C & ubt ?B = btopp (lbt ?C))" : thm
single_cat3l' = "[| nonempty ?A; nonempty ?B; nonempty ?C |] ==>
 (?x : {?A} ;; {?B} ;; {?C}) = (lbt ?x = lbt ?A
    & ubt ?x = ubt ?C & ubt ?A = btopp (lbt ?B)
    & ubt ?B = btopp (lbt ?C))" : thm
```

As mentioned above, Law 10 as stated was meaningless, something which we found as soon as we started to think about how we would formalise the law in Isabelle, showing the value of a detailed formalisation. We felt that the "⊆" parts were correct, but that the statement "Equality holds ... if ω and δ are not free in S and T " is not meaningful. References to ω and δ makes sense only in the context of a function P (of t, α, and ω), which arises when the forms of S and T are drawn from $[(-.-)], [(-.-], [(-.-), [-.-)], [-.-], [-.-), (-.-)], (-.-],$ and $(-.-)$.

We have therefore proved a version of Law 10 where both S and T are of the *same* form, and that form is one of $[(-.-)], [(-.-], [(-.-), [-.-)], [-.-], [-.-), (-.-)], (-.-],$ and $(-.-)$. We are currently formalising the cases in this version of Law 10 where S and T are of different forms.

Alternatively, changing Law 10 to allow S, T and U to be arbitrary avoids the question of references to α, δ and ω altogether, but letting $S = \{[1 \ldots 2]\}$, $T = \{[1 \ldots 3]\}$, $U = [(-true-)]$ gives a counter-example to this version of Law 10.

Finally, we also tried to replace Law 10 by a more complex law. We defined a predicate `clp` of a set of intervals ("Closed under taking Left Part") to mean that for $x \in S$, if y is a non-empty interval which has the same left endpoint but a lower right endpoint, then $y \in S$. Under the assumption that S and T satisfy this condition, we then proved equality of one of the clauses of Law 10 as below:

```
clp_def = "clp ?S == ALL s:?S.   ALL a:II.
 (ubc (ubt a) ---> ubc (ubt s)) & lbt s = lbt a --> a : ?S" : thm
law10ra = "[| ?S <= II; ?T <= II; clp ?S; clp ?T |] ==>
 (?S Int ?T) ;; ?U = ?S ;; ?U Int ?T ;; ?U" : thm
```

But condition `clp` is too strong: $[(-P-)]$ satisfies it, but $[(-P-]$ and $[(-P-)$ do not.

Law 11 was formulated as follows. It uses `no_aod` whose argument is a predicate P which depends only on t, not on α or ω. The % symbol is Isabelle's notation for the function abstraction operator λ.

```
law11 = "[(-%t a w. ?P t & 0 < w - a-)] =
           [(-no_aod ?P-)] ;; [(-no_aod ?P-)]" : thm
no_aod_def = "no_aod ?Q ?t ?a ?w == ?Q ?t" : thm
```

The forward direction required 4 cases (is the interval open or closed at either end) and the reverse 16 cases (using the form of each of the two intervals).

We also considered Laws 11 and 13 of [4] (see Figure 2), which concern concatenation of sets of intervals and are different from any of Wabenhorst's laws. We proved Law 11. However we found that Law 13 is wrong as it stands – it requires the stronger assumption $r > 0$ *and* $s > 0$. For if, say, $s = 0$, then the only intervals of length s are those which are closed at both ends, and yet $[(-P \wedge \delta = r + s-)]$ can contain intervals which are open at the right-hand end. We proved the law with the stronger assumption $r > 0$ and $s > 0$.

2.2   The Modality □

The modality $\diamond$ is used to express the notion of a property holding somewhere within an interval, and $[(-\diamond P-)]$ is used for the set of intervals within which P

holds somewhere. The definition uses the fact that, in that case, P will hold on a subinterval, which may be at the left- and/or right-hand end of the interval, or both, or neither. Thus $[(\text{-}\Diamond P\text{-})] \equiv$

$$([[(\text{-}true\text{-})]; ; [(\text{-}P\text{-})]; ; [(\text{-}true\text{-})] \cup [(\text{-}true\text{-})]; ; [(\text{-}P\text{-})] \cup [(\text{-}P\text{-})]; ; [(\text{-}true\text{-})] \cup [(\text{-}P\text{-})]])$$

Wabenhorst also defines $[(\text{-}\Box P\text{-})] \equiv \mathbb{I} \setminus [(\text{-}\Diamond P\text{-})]$, noting it is not generally equal to $[(\text{-}P\text{-})]$. Law 12 states that equality holds if α, ω and δ do not occur free in P, and, again, this is expressed using the function no_aod. Again, the proof involved a large number of cases, depending on whether a point not satisfying P is in the interior or either end of a larger interval, and whether that larger interval is closed or open at each endpoint.

2.3   The Remaining Laws

Laws 13, 14 and 17 involves the finite variability property, which is intended to put a lower limit on the time within which a property can change from false to true to false again. Clearly, if either P or Q has such a lower limit, then any interval within which, at each time, either P or Q holds, is a concatenation of sub-intervals within each of which either P holds or Q holds. Law 17 gives a weaker variant of this statement. It was the most difficult of the laws to prove.

   Laws 13 and 14 refer to a formula $H(X)$ containing X but "no occurrence of negation or the complement of X". In Appendix A of [12], Wabenhorst defines the language allowed for the construction of $H(\_)$. To check Laws 13 and 14, we would have to formalise this language in Isabelle/HOL and define its semantics.

   However, in attempting to prove a related result we discovered a counterexample to Law 13. Let the predicate P be defined as $\delta > 0 \land t$ is rational. Then $[(\text{-}P\text{-})] = \emptyset$ (since any non-zero interval contains rationals and irrationals), and $[(\text{-}\neg P\text{-})] = [\text{-}\delta = 0\text{-}]$. Therefore likewise $[(\text{-}\Diamond P\text{-})] = \emptyset$, and so P trivially satisfies the finite variability property. Define $H(X) \equiv X \subseteq S$, where S is the minimal set of intervals such that the conditions *(a)* and *(b)* of Law 13 are satisfied. Then, we find that $H(X)$ can hold only where all intervals in X are of length zero.

   Now such a P hardly seems "finitely variable", so there appears to be a problem with the definition of finite variability. Law 17, which also uses "finitely variable", does not suffer from this problem because the requirement "α, ω and δ are not free in P" prevents us from using such a P as a counterexample.

   Laws 15 and 16 were easy. However Law 18 was difficult: formalising the proof revealed that the cases when $r = 0$ and $r < 0$, which each require separate treatment, were overlooked in the informal proof given in the appendix of [12].

3   Conclusion and Further Work

We have demonstrated the value of formalising the Timed Interval Calculus, highlighting certain issues which need to be addressed in a formal treatment, but which were overlooked in the informal treatment. The process of formalising the TIC led to the discovery that Law 10 is incorrect as it stands, that Law 13 (and probably Law 14 likewise) is incorrect due to a problem with the definition of finite variability, that Law 13 of [4] requires stronger assumptions, and that the proof of Law 18 required a clarification. While all other laws have been verified in Isabelle, Wabenhorst's Laws 10, 13 and probably 14, require revision and present a danger to those who might use them blindly.

We are currently formalising the cases in Law 10 where S and T are of *different* forms (see § 2.1). We also need to fix the definition of "finite variability", formalise, in Isabelle, the language for expressing $H(X)$, and then check Wabenhorst's Laws 13 and 14 in Isabelle.

An interesting open question is that of completeness: is every statement true of intervals provable using (a superset of) the laws ? This does not appear to have been investigated, and might be a considerable endeavour.

Acknowledgements. We are extremely grateful to Axel Wabenhorst for his prompt clarifications, and to Brendan Mahony for bibliographic pointers.

References

1. J F Allen. Towards a theory of action and time. Artif. Intel. 23:123–154, 1984.
2. A Cerone. Axiomatisation of an Interval Calculus for Theorem Proving. In C J Fidge (Ed), CATS'00: Elect. Notes in Theor. Comp. Sci. 42, Elsevier 2001.
3. A Church. A formulation of the simple theory of types. *JSL*, 5:56–68, 1940.
4. C J Fidge, I J Hayes, A P Martin, A K Wabenhorst, A Set-Theoretic Model for Real-Time Specification and Reasoning. In J Jeuring (Ed), Proc. MPC'98, LNCS 1422:188–206, Springer, 1998.
5. R I Goldblatt, Logics of Time and Computation, CSLI Lecture Notes Number 7, Center for the Study of Language and Information, Stanford, 1987.
6. S T Heilmann, Proof Support for Duration Calculus, PhD thesis, Dept. of Inf. Tech., Tech. Univ. of Denmark, Jan. 1999. See http://www.sth.dk/sth/.
7. M J C Gordon and T F Melham. *Introduction to HOL: a Theorem Proving Environment for Higher Order Logic.* Cambridge University Press, 1993.
8. L C Paulson. *The Isabelle Reference Manual.* Comp. Lab., Univ. of Cambridge, 1999. See http://www.cl.cam.ac.uk/Research/HVG/Isabelle/docs.html
9. L C Paulson. *Isabelle's Logics.* Computer Lab. Univ. of Cambridge, 1999. See http://www.cl.cam.ac.uk/Research/HVG/Isabelle/docs.html
10. B P Mahony and C Millerchip and I J Hayes. *A boiler control system: A case study in timed refinement.* International Invitational Workshop - Design and Review of Software Controlled Safety-Related Systems, Ottawa, June, 1993.
11. J Skakkebæk, A verification assistant for a real-time logic, PhD thesis, TR 150, Dept. of Computer Science, Technical University of Denmark, 1994.
12. A Wabenhorst. Induction in the Timed Interval Calculus. Technical Report 99-36, SVRC, University of Queensland, 1999.
13. M R Hansen and Z Chaochen. Duration calculus, logical foundations. Formal Aspects of Computing, 9 (1997), 283–303.

Modeling Programs with Unstructured Control Flow for Debugging

Wolfgang Mayer and Markus Stumptner

University of South Australia
Advanced Computing Research Centre
5095 Mawson Lakes SA, Adelaide, Australia
{mayer,mst}@cs.unisa.edu.au

Abstract. Even with modern software development methodologies, the actual debugging of source code, i.e., location and identification of errors in the program when errant behavior is encountered during testing, remains a crucial part of software development. To apply model-based diagnosis techniques, which have long been state of the art in hardware diagnosis, for automatic debugging, a model of a given program must be automatically created from the source code. This work describes a model that reflects the execution semantics of the Java language, including exceptions and unstructured control flow, thereby providing unprecedented scope in the application of model-based diagnosis to programs. Besides the structural model building process, a behavioral description of some of the model components is given. Finally, impacts of the modeling decisions on the diagnostic process are considered.

1 Introduction

Debugging, i.e., detecting a faulty behavior within a program, locating the cause of the fault, and fixing the fault by means of changing the program, continues to be a crucial and challenging task in software development. Many papers have been published so far in the domain of finding faults in software, e.g., testing or formal verification [1], and locating them, e.g., program slicing [23] and automatic program debugging [19,11]. More recently model-based diagnosis [18] has been used for locating faults in software by several researchers [2,10,15]. [2] shows the relationship between automatic program debugging and the model-based approach. In [24] the author discusses the relationship between slicing and model-based debugging.

This paper extends prior research on model-based diagnosis for locating bugs in programs written in mainstream programming languages, with the language Java used as an example. The idea behind the model-based debugging approach is (1) to automatically compile a program to its logical model or to a constraint satisfaction problem, (2) to use the model together with test cases and a model-based diagnosis engine for computing the diagnosis candidates, and (3) to map the candidates back to their corresponding locations within the original program. Formally, given a set of test cases on which the program is run, a (minimal) diagnosis is defined as a (minimal) set of incorrectness assumptions $AB(C)$ on a subset $C \in \Delta$ of components $COMP$ in the program (usually statements) such that $\{AB(C)|C \in \Delta\} \cup \{\neg AB(C)|C \in COMP \setminus \Delta\} \cup SD$ is consistent [18].

R.I. McKay and J. Slaney (Eds.): AI 2002, LNAI 2557, pp. 107–118, 2002.

Here, SD is a logical theory describing the program's behavior under the assumption that components work correctly. Since the computation depends on observations in terms of test case output, unlike formal verification approaches, no separate formal specification is necessary - everything but the test cases is computed automatically from the source code. Conversely, where verification model checkers produce counterexamples, the outcome of the diagnosis process are code locations. Model-based debugging thus complements, rather than replaces verification techniques.

Diagnosis granularity is primarily determined by the choice of diagnosis components, e.g., statements, expressions, or other program entities. The crucial factor that determines discrimination, i.e., the ability to focus quickly on a particular error, is the selection of the model. In the past two categories of models developed in the Jade project were published which represent two end points of the spectrum: dependency-based [12] and value-based models [13].

The models presented in [14,17] have successfully been applied to debug Java programs. The tests consist of small to medium sized Java programs together with their faulty variants and given test cases. A comparison of the models and their effectiveness relative to each other as well as compared to a normal interactive debugger was given in [15]. Whereas these methods have been applied to large scale programs in concurrent languages [22], so far, one important factor that has held up experimentation with "off the shelf" example programs has been the omission of certain frequently used language constructs from our models, most notably exception handling. The hierarchical structure of the models renders them unsuitable for diagnosing programs which do not conform to the assumption of a "structured" control flow based purely on loop and if statements, This excludes a wide array of language features which includes structured exceptions handling constructs, recursive method calls, return statements, and jump statements. This paper addresses that issue and presents a different modeling approach, where the restrictions on program structure are relaxed in order to overcome the limitations of previous models. As a result it represents a significant step towards a model of that language that can cover arbitrary Java programs.

The new modeling algorithm is based on building a modular, multi-directional version of the classical control flow graph (CFG) [6], which represents an approximation of all possible execution paths. The nodes of this CFG represent *basic blocks* (i.e. a sequence of operations that always executes sequentially without branching), and the arcs represent the control flow between these blocks. In a following step, the CFG is enhanced by dataflow information. The variables that are used and modified by a basic block are computed and arcs between any two dataflow-dependent blocks are inserted. The basic blocks in each method are then transformed into a constraint network. The constraints are grouped in two categories that represent the semantics of the language elements (e.g. the computational statements and expressions) on one hand and flow control restrictions on the other hand (e.g., turning off alternate execution paths to the one actually taken). The constraint variables are likewise partitioned, one group representing the actual program variables accessed and modified by the code, the other group representing the control flow (i.e., the selection of which statements are executed). As a result, control and dataflow of a program can be reasoned about in a uniform framework. The representation of the program execution as a constraint system provides means for computing values in both directions: forward and backward. This is essential for ap-

```
1   class Fac {
2     static int f(int x) throws OutOfRangeException {
3       if (x < 0) throw new OutOfRangeException();
4       else if (x == 0) return 1;
5       else return x * f( x - 1 );
6     }
7     static boolean exception = false;
8     static int main() {
9       int fac = 0;
10      try {
11        fac = f(3);
12      } catch(OutOfRangeException ex) {
13        exception = true;
14      }
15      return fac;
16    }
17  }
```

Fig. 1. Example Program

plying model-based debugging approaches, which rely on an effective theorem prover generating small conflict sets.

The paper is organized as follows: In Section 2 we describe the construction of the bidirectional CFG, followed by the description of how the diagnosis model is actually constructed in Section 3. Finally, we discuss the capabilities of the model (in particular the types of errors that can be identified).

2 Modeling Unstructured Control Flow

The automatic transformation from the Java source code to the logic model used for diagnosis proceeds in three steps.

Build CFG. The program is transformed into its CFG representation. Each method is represented as a directed graph with basic blocks as nodes and all possible transitions between each nodes as arcs. In addition, nodes are included for each method's (unique) entry and (potentially multiple, since there is a separate one for every type of exception) exit points. Details about the algorithm can be found in [20]. Note that we utilize the intra-procedural version of their algorithm, as method calls are represented hierarchically. Therefore, if a called method has multiple possible exit paths, the call must be the last statement in the basic block.

Compute Dataflow Information. In this step the CFG is enhanced by dataflow information. In particular, for each basic block the variables that are used and modified are computed using an abstract interpretation approach [3]. For instance variables, the approach of [15] is followed (i.e. the instance variables are treated similarly to global variables).

Transform CFG into Constraint Representation. Each basic block of the CFG is transformed into a constraint representation improved over that of [15] by transforming each basic block separately (instead of building one large constraint network).

The transformation of a basic block can be summarized as follows: The program is decomposed into a set of primitive language elements (e.g. variable access, assignments, operators, method calls, etc.), which are ordered according to the execution semantics of the Java language. For each primitive element a constraint is generated that simulates the effects of the element in both forward and backward direction. For every assignment to a variable, a new constraint variable is generated and is subsequently used up to the point in the code where the variable is reassigned. For unnamed results of expressions an auxiliary constraint variable is created. A special placeholder component is inserted for each method call and loop statement that summarizes the effects of the method or loop. Similar to the CFG construction, these components have output connections for each exit node of the called method's (the loop's) model.

To obtain a model of the whole method, the models of the basic blocks are composed according to the control and dataflow information computed previously. The blocks are processed in the (partial-)order that is specified by the control flow graph. For each block, the block's model is added to the method's model and is connected to those constraint variables defined by already processed blocks that are used by some constraint in the block.

However, due to the nonlinear control flow, for some blocks more than one constraint variable can represent a particular program variable. Consider the program in Fig. 1. The program dependency graph for method main() is depicted in Fig. 2(a). Here, for Block D, two possible definitions of variable fac are visible (Block A and Block C). Traditionally, this problem is avoided by inserting dataflow ϕ-functions [4], which select among one of the two possible paths. A similar approach is taken here, where the ϕ functions are modeled by additional *merge* constraints, that combine the different constraint variables into a single variable that is subsequently used as input for the block.

In case of traditional dataflow analysis, inserting ϕ functions for each control flow join is sufficient, as reasoning is performed in only one direction. When reasoning in both directions, similar functions have to be introduced for control flow branches. As before, these 'inverse ϕ functions' are modeled by additional *split* constraints. A split constraint uses the current connection as input and distributes the information to its output variables (there is one for each possible path). Note that the behavior of split and merge constraints is equivalent, but operating in the opposite direction.

After all blocks have been assembled into a single model, constraint variables for all variables used by a block that are not previously defined in the method are created and are associated with the method's entry point. Similarly, all modified externally visible variables are collected and associated with each of the method's exit points.

The modeling of the control flow proceeds as follows. For each basic block b a constraint variable $ctrl(b)$ is created that represents the control flow for b given the program run ρ executed under the current test case. The domain of control variables is defined as $\{\top, \bot, ?\}$. If $ctrl(b) = \top$, b is definitely executed for ρ. If $ctrl(b) = \bot$, b is definitely not executed, and if $ctrl(b) = ?$, we do not know. Together with other constraints ensuring required properties for the control flow, this is equivalent to removing all paths that require the execution of this block from the CFG. Split and merge constraints are not associated with a control variable, as they cannot be disabled.

If the last statement s in a basic block b represents a branch statement (i.e. a conditional statement or a method call with multiple possible exit points), the model of s provides an additional output connection for each possible exit of the method. The connections correspond to the possible transitions in the CFG after s is executed. They are connected to the control variables of the following blocks that correspond to the paths taken. If s is not a branch, the value of the control variable of b would be always equal to the control variable of the following block b'. Therefore, the b' reuses the control variable associated with b.

Similar to the dataflow connections above, for blocks with multiple incoming control edges, additional constraints that merge all the incoming control connections into one variable are inserted.

To ensure the control variables accurately model the program's control flow, a further condition must be ensured: for each block, not more than one transition must be taken upon exit from the block. Further, if a block definitely is executed, the taken exit transition is also definitely executed. These conditions are ensured by adding explicit (*liveness*) constraints.

Finally, to combine the reasoning about data and control flow, each of the dataflow constraint variables v is also associated with a control variable. For variables associated with outgoing connections of a basic block b, $ctrl(b)$ is used for this. Otherwise, if v corresponds to the output of a split constraint, the control variable corresponding to the path the variable represents is selected.

Example. To illustrate the modeling process, reconsider the program from Fig. 1. The model of method main is depicted in Fig. 2(b).

Control flow at the entry point of the method is represented by constraint variable a. The call of method f() splits the control flow in two separate paths. Therefore, split components are inserted for the variables fac and exception.[1] Besides the connections representing the data flow for the two variables, the split constraints are connected to the constraint variables representing the control flow corresponding to the data connections. Note that for both the split components the value of the represented variable is not used in the non-exceptional branch and therefore the variables representing these branches are omitted. Nevertheless, the components may not be removed from the model, as they form a propagation barrier for the backward reasoning algorithm in case it is unknown which path of the branch is followed and the values are different for any two paths. The path represented by variable b represents the transition to the exception handler block. The normal return from the method is represented by c. As exactly one of these paths has to be followed if Block A can be reached, the constraint live enforces this condition. The model of Block D requires variable fac and the control flow as input connections. As there are multiple incoming arcs for both dependencies in the CFG, merge constraints have to be inserted. The constraint for variable fac is connected to the two output ports providing the values of the variable and to the control variables a and c of the corresponding blocks. Further, the output port of the merge constraint is connected to the input port of Block D, which requires the value of fac, and to D's control variable. The merge constraint for variable exception is connected in a similar way.

Optimize Model. In addition to the previous model building steps, the constraint system can be further simplified by transformations similar to those in [8]. Here, merge

---

[1] Here, knowledge about the program's structure is incorporated into the model building process. For the example it is known that, following the method call, the CFG consists of a single entry/single exit (SESE) region [8] to Block D. Therefore, only the modified variables of this SESE region are considered when generating dataflow split components. See also the *Optimize Model* section below.

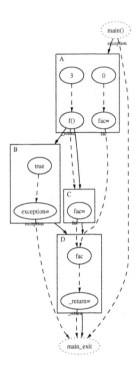

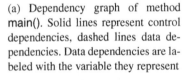

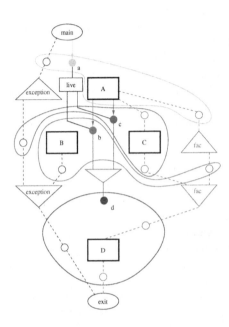

(a) Dependency graph of method main(). Solid lines represent control dependencies, dashed lines data dependencies. Data dependencies are labeled with the variable they represent

(b) Model of Method main(). For clarity, blocks are drawn without embedded constraints. Constraint variables are drawn as circles (control variables are drawn filled). Split and merge constraints are represented by triangles. The set of blocks and variables associated with a control variable are drawn as hyper-edges containing the control variable.

Fig. 2.

constraints for control flow edges can be eliminated if they merge all control flow variables contained in a Single Entry Single Exit (SESE) region (i.e. a merge constraint can be replaced by a SESE's control input connection if the constraint postdominates the region). In the example above, statements in lines 10–14 form a SESE region, which contains exactly the control variables b and c. Therefore, the merge constraint and constraint variable d are removed and all connections to d are redirected to a, which is the control variable for the entire SESE region. Figure 3 depicts the final model of method main(). Similarly, dataflow split and merge constraints may be removed if a SESE region does not modify the corresponding variables.

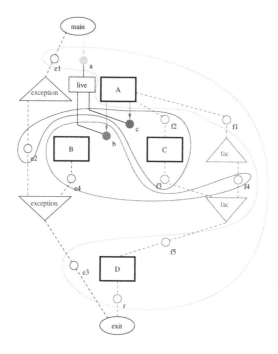

Fig. 3. Optimized Model of Method main().

3   Execution Semantics

This section briefly describes the behavior of the model components. For brevity, only essential components and differences to [15,14] are presented.

First, the bijection between program statements and model components is abandoned. This makes it possible to represent a single statement as multiple components and allows fine grained control over the model's assumptions, spanning multiple levels in the program structure. The assumptions for each constraint are grouped into a hierarchy, resembling the program structure. This provides means for making assumptions about single statements, blocks of statements, and hierarchically nested statements. In particular, the representation allows to distinguish the calling of a wrong method from a faulty implementation of the called method. Also, this representation is expected to reduce the complexity of the diagnostic process, as program structure can be exploited to speedup diagnosing (the approach is taken from [5]).

A description of the most important model components follows (C represents a constraint and $\neg AB$ denotes that the component is assumed to behave correctly):

Constants. Component representing constant literals enforce their output value to be equal to the constant k specified in the program.

$$\neg AB(C) \wedge const(C) \Rightarrow out(C) = k$$

Variable Access and Assignments are modeled by constraints propagate the value of the input variable to the output constraint variable. For assignments, the input connection represents the result of the right hand side expression. Otherwise, the connection is associated with the current value of the variable.

$$\neg AB(C) \wedge (ident(C) \vee assign(C)) \Rightarrow out(C) = in(C)$$

Operators. Constraints modeling operators compute the value for the output variable by applying the represented operator to the values provided by input variables. For binary operators the behavior is specified as follows (op_C represents the operator that is modeled by the constraint):

$$\neg AB(C) \wedge binop(C) \Rightarrow out(C) = op_C(in1(C), in2(C))$$

Method Calls. Method calls are represented as a single component with entry connections representing the union of the input connections used by each of the possibly called method's models. The output connections are formed in a similar way. In difference to the model from [15], the component modeling the method call provides output connections for the modified variables not only for a normal return from the method, but also for exceptional exits. For each of the possibly thrown exceptions the component provides output ports corresponding to the modified variables, together with a control connection representing the exceptional path.

When the method call component is executed, the model of each of the method call candidates is retrieved. The component representing the call is replaced by a switch component, which simulates the selection of the called method according to the receiver's dynamic type. The component provides output ports for each candidate, which represent the control flow activation for the method. The models of the methods are then inlined into the model of the calling method, using the control connections provided by the switch component. The input and output connections of the models are replaced by the input and output connections attached to the former method call component, eventually with the insertion of split and merge constraints as necessary.

$$\forall_{t \in Types} (\neg AB(C) \wedge call(C) \wedge type(C) = t \Rightarrow M_t(C))$$

Types denotes the set of possible types of the receiver object, $M_t(C)$ denotes the model of the method that is executed for type t (with inputs and outputs substituted with C's variables), and $type(C)$ represents the value of the input constraint variable that corresponds to the receiver's dynamic type. Note that the switch component is implicit in the rules' antecedence.

Although this representation incurs a slightly higher overhead at runtime compared to inlined method models, it is particularly useful for dealing with recursive methods, as the recursion depth need not be known when building the model. Another advantage of the hierarchical approach is the fact that it is easy to define abnormal modes for a method call. For inlined CFGs this is not easily possible in every case. Furthermore, for some programs and test cases the models may remain smaller, as methods that are not needed to derive a conflict need not be expanded.

While Loops. Components representing loops are treated similarly to method call components. In contrast to method calls, here the model of the loop (the body and the condition) is known in advance and therefore the switch component is unnecessary. When the loop is expanded (i.e. the condition evaluates to $\top$), the model of the condition and the body is inserted before the component representing the loop. If the condition evaluates to $\perp$, the loop component is removed from the model and its output connections are replaced with its input connections. Otherwise, the component remains in the model, as it is not known how many iterations the loop executes.

$$\neg AB(C) \wedge while(C) \wedge M_{cond}(C) \models \perp \Rightarrow \forall_{v \in MVars} (out_v(C) = in_v(C))$$

$cond(C)$ represents the evaluation of the condition's model using the constraint's input values, $MVars$ represents the variables modified by the loop condition or the loop body. Note that the behavior of the component is undefined for the case where the condition does not evaluate to $\top$ or $\perp$.

Dataflow Split & Merge. These components represent the dataflow ϕ functions, either in forward direction (merge), or in backward direction (split). Each component dealing with n input or output paths has connections $data_i$ (each associated with a control variable $control_i$) ($i \in [1 \dots n]$), which represent the data variables for each of the paths. Further, the variable $data_u$ (associated with $control_u$) represents the unified connections of $data_i$. The behavior of these components can be formalized as follows (assume each of the $data$ connections holds a set of values):

Let $Active$ denote the subset of indices i where $control_i(C) \neq \perp$. Then

$$dfmerge(C) \Rightarrow control_u(C) = \top \Rightarrow \forall_i (data_u(C) \subseteq data_i(C) \vee control_i(C) = \perp)$$

$$dfmerge(C) \Rightarrow control_u(C) \neq \perp \Rightarrow data_u(C) \supseteq \bigcap_{i \in Active} data_i(C)$$

The first equation states that if the unified connection definitely corresponds to an executable block, then all the values must be supplied by every data connection that can possibly be executed. The second condition covers the case where the unified connection might correspond to an executable block: in this case the unified connection must be consistent with the intersection of all other data connections.

Control merge components representing joins in control flow are modeled similarly to the previous paragraph, but no data connections are present. Each component has n input variables $control_i$ and an output variable $control_o$. The behavior is given as follows:

$$cfmerge(C) \Rightarrow control_o(C) = \bigvee_i control_i(C)$$

Liveness constraints ensure that if a statement (except the last statement of the program) is reachable then exactly one of its successors is executed. The constraint has an input variable $live_i$ for each of the statement's successor paths and is also connected to the surrounding block's liveness variable $live_p$.

$$liveness(C) \Rightarrow \left(live_p(C) = \bigvee_i live_i(C) \right) \wedge \left(\bigwedge_{i \neq j} \neg live_i(C) \vee \neg live_j(C) \right)$$

3.1   Example

To demonstrate them model's ability to effectively locate faults, reconsider the program in Fig. 1 together with a test case that specifies the value true for variable exception and 0 for the result of main(). As a first step, the values provided by the test case are inserted into the model: e3 = true, r = 0, and a = ⊤ (the entry and exit points of the method are reachable). Further, at the beginning of the diagnostic process it is assumed that all components are correct. By propagating values through the model, e4 = true and e1 = false are derived. For e3, both values are derived, which results in a conflict. Therefore, the corresponding branch of the model is eliminated by adding c = ⊥ for the associated control variable c. a = ⊤ together with ¬AB($\boxed{11}$) derive b = ⊥, which violates the liveness constraint (because of c = ⊥). Therefore, the model is found inconsistent and the conflict {¬AB($\boxed{7}$), ¬AB($\boxed{11}$)} [2] is returned. To break the conflict, either {AB($\boxed{7}$)} or {AB($\boxed{11}$)} has to be valid. Assuming {AB($\boxed{7}$)}, true is derived for e1–e4 without causing a conflict. r = 0, a = ⊤, and ¬AB($\boxed{15}$) derive 0 for f3–f5. On the other hand, a = ⊤ and ¬AB($\boxed{11}$) derive c = ⊤ and 6 for f2 and f3, resulting in a contradiction for f3 (with the value 0 derived in the previous inference). Hence, $\boxed{7}$ cannot be a diagnosis and cannot be responsible for the misbehavior. For {AB($\boxed{11}$)} values for e1–e3 are derived as in the first computation. However, b = ⊥ cannot be derived and therefore the model is consistent. As a result, {AB($\boxed{11}$)} is the only single fault diagnosis.

4   Discussion

This section provides an overview over the impact of some modeling decisions on the diagnostic process.

Conflicts. To be able to derive conflicts after a model has been found inconsistent[3], the propagation algorithm must keep track of which constraints derive which values. Alternatively, approaches similar to [9] can be applied.

For efficiency, the constraint network propagates only deltas of values, so that execution in the next propagation cycle can be focused on the newly added values. Also, method calls and loops are expanded to full models only when reasonable input values are present at their inputs (e.g. only if the receiver is known).

Faults. The model proposed herein is able to locate general functional faults, where parts of a program are faulty without assigning to wrong variables. This also includes the subclass of structural faults where a wrong variable is *used*. Faults can be detected not only in the top level method, but also in hierarchically embedded program elements. However, the model assumes the control flow graph to be fixed and therefore faults causing changes in the CFG cannot be located reliably. For example, changing the type of the exception of a throw statement may cause a changed control flow, as a different catch block may be responsible for the new type.

Dealing with structural faults is generally more difficult, as the model has to be modified dynamically during the diagnostic process. The modular modeling approach helps to avoid unnecessary re-computation, as structural changes that are not visible outside a method do not trigger a model update for the calling methods.

---

[2] Statements are identified by their line numbers.

[3] The model herein derives an inconsistency iff there is no possible and consistent path between the model's start node and its end node.

Another approach for detecting structural faults we currently incorporate into the model is to compare the dependencies of the program with the dependencies specified by assertions and design information [21,7].

Contracts. To reduce the amount of user interaction required to isolate a faulty statement, assertions may be inserted into the program (e.g. via the Java 1.4 assert statement). Assertion expressions are translated into the model. However, components representing assertions are always assumed to work correctly, i.e. there is no conventional abnormal mode for these components. Pre- and postconditions are treated similarly to assertions. Preconditions are translated into assertions and are inserted before the first statement of the method. Postconditions are converted to assertions and are inserted after each statement causing a return to the caller.

5   Conclusion

Model-based debugging carries considerable promise based on the concept of automatically deriving a diagnosis model from the program source code and using this, together with input-output test vectors, to identify faults in programs [16]. An effective model representation is a crucial step in building a framework for model-based debugging. This work represents the first time that non-structured control flow is represented in a diagnosis model. We have described the computation of the bidirectional control flow graph that permits reasoning about unstructured control flows on both directions as required for diagnostic reasoning. After optimizing the graph to remove "dead" path combinations, we have described how the code and graph are mapped into the logic-based diagnosis model. Notably, this approach omits the strict view of a component representing one statement of earlier work [15] and provides a more flexible mapping from code to model.

Since real-world programs make frequent use of constructs such as exceptions, this model represents a significant step beyond earlier models that represented Java programs for debugging, but were restricted to linear control flows. As it shares the basic model-based architectures, it can be smoothly incorporated into the implemented JADE intelligent debugging engine [15].

References

[1] Edmund M. Clarke, Orna Grumberg, and David E. Long. Model Checking and Abstraction. *ACM Transactions on Programming Languages and Systems*, 16(5):1512–1542, September 1994.

[2] Luca Console, Gerhard Friedrich, and Daniele Theseider Dupré. Model-based diagnosis meets error diagnosis in logic programs. In *Proceedings 13th International Joint Conf. on Artificial Intelligence*, pages 1494–1499, Chambery, August 1993.

[3] Patrick Cousot and Radhia Cousot. Abstract interpretation: A unified latice model for static analysis fo programs by construction of approximation of fixpoints. In *Proceedings on Principles of Programming Languages*, volume 4, Los Angeles, California, January 1977.

[4] Ron Cytron, Jeanne Ferrante, Barry K. Rosen, Mark N. Wegman, and F. Kenneth Zadeck. Efficiently computing static single assignment form and the control dependence graph. *ACM TOPLAS*, 13(4):451–490, 1991.

[5] Alexander Felfernig, Gerhard Friedrich, Dietmar Jannach, and Markus Stumptner. Consistency based diagnosis of configuration knowledge-bases. In *Proceedings of the Tenth International Workshop on Principles of Diagnosis*, Loch Awe, June 1999.

[6] Jeanne Ferrante, Karl J. Ottenstein, and Joe D. Warren. The program dependence graph and its use in optimization. *ACM Transactions on Programming Languages and Systems*, 9(3):319–349, 1987.

[7] Daniel Jackson. Aspect: Detecting Bugs with Abstract Dependences. *ACM Transactions on Software Engineering and Methodology*, 4(2):109–145, April 1995.

[8] Richard Johnson and Keshav Pingali. Dependence-based program analysis. In *SIGPLAN Conference on Programming Language Design and Implementation*, pages 78–89, 1993.

[9] Ulrich Junker. QUICKXPLAIN: Conflict detection for arbitrary constraint propagation algorithms. In *IJCAI'01 Workshop on Modelling and Solving problems with constraints*, Seattle, WA, USA, August 2001.

[10] Beat Liver. Modeling software systems for diagnosis. In *Proceedings of the Fifth International Workshop on Principles of Diagnosis*, pages 179–184, New Paltz, NY, October 1994.

[11] J. W. Lloyd. Declarative Error Diagnosis. *New Generation Computing*, 5:133–154, 1987.

[12] Cristinel Mateis, Markus Stumptner, and Franz Wotawa. Debugging of Java programs using a model-based approach. In *Proceedings of the Tenth International Workshop on Principles of Diagnosis*, Loch Awe, Scotland, 1999.

[13] Cristinel Mateis, Markus Stumptner, and Franz Wotawa. Modeling Java Programs for Diagnosis. In *Proceedings of the European Conference on Artificial Intelligence (ECAI)*, Berlin, Germany, August 2000.

[14] Cristinel Mateis, Markus Stumptner, and Franz Wotawa. A Value-Based Diagnosis Model for Java Programs. In *Proceedings of the Eleventh International Workshop on Principles of Diagnosis*, Morelia, Mexico, June 2000.

[15] Wolfgang Mayer, Markus Stumptner, Dominik Wieland, and Franz Wotawa. Can AI help to improve debugging substantially? Debugging Experiences with Value-Based Models. In F. van Harmelen, editor, *Proc. ECAI*, Amsterdam, 2002.

[16] Wolfgang Mayer, Markus Stumptner, Dominik Wieland, and Franz Wotawa. Towards an Integrated Debugging Environment. In F. van Harmelen, editor, *Proc. ECAI*, Amsterdam, 2002.

[17] Wolfgang Mayer, Markus Stumptner, and Franz Wotawa. Model-based Debugging or How to Diagnose Programs Automatically. In *Proceedings of the International Conference on Industrial and Engineering Applications of Artificial Intelligence and Expert Systems*, Springer LNAI, Cairns, Australia, June 2002.

[18] Raymond Reiter. A theory of diagnosis from first principles. *Artificial Intelligence*, 32(1):57–95, 1987.

[19] Ehud Shapiro. *Algorithmic Program Debugging*. MIT Press, Cambridge, Massachusetts, 1983.

[20] Saurabh Sinha and Mary Jean Harrold. Analysis and Testing of Programs with Exception Handling Constructs. *IEEE Transactions on Software Engineering*, 26(9), 2000.

[21] Markus Stumptner. Using design information to identify structural software faults. In *Proceedings 14th Australian Joint Conference on Artificial Intelligence*, Springer LNAI 2256, pages 473–486, Adelaide, December 2001.

[22] Markus Stumptner and Franz Wotawa. Using Model-Based Reasoning for Locating Faults in VHDL Designs. *Künstliche Intelligenz*, 14(4):62–67, 2000.

[23] Mark Weiser. Program slicing. *IEEE Transactions on Software Engineering*, 10(4):352–357, July 1984.

[24] Franz Wotawa. On the Relationship between Model-Based Debugging and Program Slicing. *Artificial Intelligence*, 135(1–2):124–143, 2002.

Message Length Formulation of Support Vector Machines for Binary Classification – A Preliminary Scheme

Lara Kornienko, David L. Dowe, and David W. Albrecht

School of Computer Science and Software Engineering,
Monash University, Clayton, Victoria, 3800, Australia
{larak,dld,dwa}@bruce.csse.monash.edu.au

Abstract. This paper presents a preliminary attempt at performing extrinsic binary classification by reformulating the Support Vector Machine (SVM) approach in a Bayesian Message Length framework. The reformulation uses the Minimum Message Length (MML) principle as a way of costing each hyperplane via a two-part message. This message defines a separating hyperplane. The length of this message is used as an objective function for a search through the hypothesis space of possible hyperplanes used to dichotomise a set of data points.
Two preliminary MML implementations are presented here, which differ in the (Bayesian) coding schemes used and the search procedures. The generalisation ability of these two reformulations on both artificial and real data sets are compared against current implementations of Support Vector Machines - namely SVM^{light}, the Lagrangian Support Vector Machine and SMOBR.
It was found that, in general, all implementations improved as the size of the data sets increased. The MML implementations tended to perform best on the inseparable data sets and the real data set. Our preliminary MML scheme showed itself to be a strong competitor against the classical SVM, despite inefficiencies in the current scheme.

Keywords. Machine Learning, Knowledge discovery and data mining

1 Introduction

This paper presents a new way of performing extrinsic binary classification by reformulating the classical Support Vector Machine (SVM) approach in a Message Length framework. Our preliminary reformulation uses the Minimum Message Length (MML) principle [19,22,20] as a way of costing each hyperplane via a two-part message.

The two-part message used by MML acts as an inference metric and has its roots in Bayesian information theory. Its purpose is essentially to find the shortest or most concise representation of a given set of data.

Due to its general fundamental nature [20], MML can be used as a metric in various applications – in particular, the classification of data using SVMs. SVMs

R.I. McKay and J. Slaney (Eds.): AI 2002, LNAI 2557, pp. 119–130, 2002.

have a basis in statistical learning theory – which was first introduced by Vapnik [17] and have since been developed as a classification technique. In order to find the hyperplane which best separates a set of data points, the classical SVM solves a quadratic optimisation problem. The aim of this paper is to combine the two techniques, thus developing a new classification system where MML is used as the objective function in the search for a separating hyperplane.

The performance of such a preliminary reformulation is compared against that of three classical Support Vector Machines, namely Joachims's SVM^{light} [9], Mangasarian and Musicant's Lagrangian Support Vector Machine [13] and Marcelo Barros de Almeida's SMOBR [1]. The data sets used to test the performance of these SVMs were varied in size and degree of noise to reveal any strengths and weaknesses of the implementations.

Section 2 gives a brief review of SVM theory, which is followed by a description of the MML principle in section 3. Section 4 gives details of the preliminary reformulation itself and section 5 presents some preliminary results. A section discussing possible extensions and applications concludes the paper.

2   Support Vector Machines for Binary Classification

Support Vector Machines have been recognised in a wide variety of areas, such as face identification [15], bioinformatics [4] and database marketing [2] as being powerful and flexible tools for classification. This paper will investigate linear SVMs for binary classification.

The general binary classification problem deals with a set of training data $X = \{x_1, ..., x_N\} \subseteq \Re^n$ (Euclidean n-space), and their corresponding labels $Y = \{y_1, ..., y_N\} \subseteq \{-1, 1\}$. The problem is to find a decision function $f : \Re^n \to \{-1, 1\}$ that predicts the label of new, previously unseen data points to minimise the probability of misclassification. A linear SVM is the decision function $f(\mathbf{x}) = \text{sign}((\mathbf{w} \cdot \mathbf{x}) - b)$ where $\mathbf{w}$ and b define the hyperplane $\mathbf{w} \cdot \mathbf{x} = b$ and

$$\text{sign}(z) = \begin{cases} 1 & \text{if } z > 0 \\ -1 & \text{otherwise} \end{cases}$$

To find the *optimal* SVM, one needs to find the $\mathbf{w} = (w_1, \ldots, w_n)$ and b which are solutions of the following problem:

$$\min \frac{1}{2} \sum_{k=1}^{n} w_k^2 + \sum_{k=1}^{N} \phi(\xi_k), \quad y_i(\mathbf{w} \cdot \mathbf{x_i} - b) \geq 1 - \xi_i, \quad \xi_i \geq 0,$$

for every $i = 1, \ldots, N$; where ϕ is a penalty function discussed below.

The criterion which is being minimised consists of two terms. The reciprocal, $2/\sum_{k=1}^{n} w_k^2$, of the first term is called the margin, and in the case when the data is separable (i.e. all the data labelled +1 lie on one side of a hyperplane and all data labelled −1 lie on the other), it is the distance between closest points of the opposing classes. Whenever the data is not separable, the second term is required. This term represents the penalty for misclassification, and the penalty function

ϕ, in this term is generally of the form $\phi(\xi) = C\xi^r$, where $r \geq 1$ and C is a given constant. In this paper we compare our results against three SVM methods: Joachims's SVM^{light} which uses $r = 1$, Mangasarian & Musicant's Lagrangian Support Vector Machine , which uses $r = 2$ and SMOBR, an implementation of Platt's Sequential Minimal Optimisation (SMO) algorithm [16], which uses $r = 1$. Default parameter values have been used in all cases.

3   Minimum Message Length Learning

Minimum Message Length (MML) is a Bayesian inference technique based on information theory. The MML principle involves the minimisation of the length of a two-part message in order to find the optimal representation of some data. The structure of this two-part message is typically [19,22,20]:

(code for **Hypothesis**) (code for **Data**| **Hypothesis**)

where the Hypothesis is a model chosen from a (continuous or discrete) hypothesis space and the Data is encoded given the chosen Hypothesis.

MML aims to find the most economical encoding of the data. The shortest message length will result from a choice of hypothesis that is complex enough to convey sufficient information about the data, without being so complex that generalisation to new data points is poor. It can also be used in a wide number of applications since it is invariant under 1-to-1 re-parameterisation for n-dimensional estimation problems [20].

As an example, in [18], MML and various other model selection methods were used to estimate a series of polynomials. It was found that of the five tested, MML consistently provided the best predictive curve. Applications include segmentation of ordered data [7], and decision trees [23] and many others [20].

4   Formulating SVMs in an MML Framework

The classical SVM can be presented in a message length framework by expressing the physical position of the hyperplane and the encoding of the data in terms of a two-part message. The length of this message is then minimised to find the MML hyperplane.

Two preliminary methods of costing the hyperplane are presented in this paper, **MML$_{\mathbf{NU}}^{\mathbf{WT}}$** and **MML$_{\mathbf{SR}}^{\mathbf{WT}}$**, and in each of these cases, in case of highly inseparable data, there was an option as to whether the placement of a hyperplane was mandatory. In general the form of the message used to cost each hyperplane is:

Part I: {physical position of hyperplane + class distributions}

+

Part II: {class for each point}

In the situation where no hyperplane is placed, the message is only made up of the cost of a single binomial distribution. That is, the cost of the physical position of the hyperplane in the first part of the message is omitted.

4.1 Physical Position of the Hypothesis

The component 'physical position of hypothesis' in the first part of the message is the encoding of the direction and offset of the hyperplane which separates the classes.

The Hyperplane's Direction

Due to the fact that an infinite number of directions and offsets can be considered, a preliminary but efficient coding scheme to deal with this was devised.

The direction of the hyperplane is defined by a perpendicular weight vector, $\mathbf{w}$. For search purposes, $\mathbf{w}$ was imagined to be a unit vector passing through the origin. The co-ordinates of the tip of $\mathbf{w}$ lie on the surface (a circle in Euclidean 2-space, $\Re^2$; a sphere in Euclidean 3-space, $\Re^3$) defines the direction of $\mathbf{w}$.

To iterate over all directions, the surface was successively partitioned into regions (initially there are $2^{dimension-1}$ regions) and the midpoints of such regions used to define new directions. The number of vertices that define each region is equal to the dimension, n, of the space. So, in $\Re^2$, there might be two points on the circle which define the vertices and the corresponding direction would be found by taking the point on that circle that is midway between the vertices. For example, these initial vertices on the circle in $\Re^2$ are the points on the circumference corresponding to the angular co-ordinates 0, $\frac{\pi}{2}$ and π.

Alternatively one could imagine the x-y axes in a Cartesian plane. The midpoint of the first region (where x and y are both positive) is the level 0 direction corresponding to the polar co-ordinate $\frac{\pi}{4}$. The midpoint of the second region (where x is negative and y is positive) corresponds to the polar coordinate $\frac{3\pi}{4}$. In $\Re^3$, a spherical surface is used. This must be broken up into (spherical) triangular regions and a new direction given by the midpoint of a particular (spherical) triangle. The initial coordinates can be defined by the point of intersection of the x, y and z axes in a 3-dimensional Cartesian plane with the sphere's surface.

The process of partitioning can be done an infinite number of times, each level of partition resulting in more directions ($dimension^{level} \times 2^{dimension-1}$) and smaller regions. A probability can be associated with each direction based on how many new regions are defined at that level of partitioning. This could be transformed into a message length by taking the $-\log_2$ of the probability.

The probability sequence used in this paper is the Wallace Tree sequence [23, 10]. This sequence is a code for strict binary trees. It is related to the Catalan numbers, where the number of strict binary trees with n nodes is the mth Catalan number, $C_m = \frac{(2m!)}{m!(m+1)!}$, where $m = (n-1)/2$. The probability of an n-bit code word, and hence of the encoding of a strict binary tree of n nodes, is 2^{-n}, and the sum of these probabilities is $\sum_{m=0}^{\infty} C_m . 2^{-(2m+1)} = 1$.

Now let $s_0 = 1, s_m = \sum_{i=0}^{m} C_i$. In the context of assigning probabilities to hyperplane directions, for each of the C_m levels between level $s_{m-1} + 1$ and level s_m, the sum of probabilities of the directions on each level is $2^{-(2m+1)}$. In particular, the first level (i.e. level = 0) of directions are assigned a probability such that the sum of the probabilities of the directions on that level is $1/2$, the second level's direction probabilities sum to $1/8$, the third and fourth level probabilities sum to $1/32$ each.

A second probability sequence was also implemented [10], but not included in this paper. It corresponds to a non-uniform code, assigning a probability of $1/2$ to the first level of directions (level $= 0$), $1/4$ to the second level, $1/8$ to the third, $1/2^{n+1}$ to the nth. It was noticed that by using this non-uniform code as opposed to the Wallace Tree code had little effect on the final Kullback-Leibler distance mean and standard deviation. Indeed, the hyperplanes chosen in both cases were often identical. However, because the Wallace Tree (WT) code is universal and its code length sequence increases far less rapidly than that of the non-uniform code, we only use the WT code for encoding the hyperplane direction.

The Hyperplane's Offset

Once a hyperplane direction is defined and encoded as above, all data points are projected onto the line whose direction vector is $\mathbf{w}$ to find an appropriate offset. This means that regardless of the dimension of the space, finding the offset - as below - is always reduced to one-dimension.

Two methods for encoding the offset were investigated. Together with the rest of the coding scheme, the first method will be called $\mathbf{MML_{NU}^{WT}}$ and the second method will be called $\mathbf{MML_{SR}^{WT}}$. The first method uses a data-independent partitioning of the unit vector $\mathbf{w}$ using a non-uniform code (similar to the discrete coding sequence for the circle). The second method places a hyperplane mid-way between each pair of data points using a uniform continuous prior distribution - and also takes the distance between the two current points into account by using a quantity called the Separation Ratio. These will be discussed shortly.

These two methods of encoding the offset via a data-independent partitioning of $\mathbf{w}$ with a non-uniform code involve taking the current $\mathbf{w}$, projecting the data points onto a line through the origin in the direction of $\mathbf{w}$, then systematically splitting the line into smaller and smaller regions.

The first method begins by defining a temporary hyperplane such that half of the data points lie on one side of it and half on the other side. This position is given probability $1/2$. Next, divide the data in the two regions defined by the first temporary hyperplane in half again. This introduces two more temporary hyperplanes (one for each initial region).

These positions have probability of $1/8$ each. Again, the data given each hyperplane is found. Then the data in the resulting four regions are each divided in half. The four resulting positions have probability $1/32$ each. This halving process is continued for the desired number of iterations, and sum of the probabilities is $\sum_{n=1}^{\infty} 2^{n-1}/2^{2n-1} = 1$, and thus the coding scheme is efficient.

The second method uses a simpler technique based on the position of the data points to determine offset position. In this case, a hyperplane is placed midway between each pair of data points and the distance between the points is taken. This distance is then divided by the total range of the points to form a ratio, implicitly assuming a uniform prior. The $-\log_2$ of this ratio is taken to form an additional cost called the Separation Ratio. The purpose of the Separation Ratio is to act similarly to the margin in Support Vector Machine theory - the further apart two points are the less chance there is of misclassification.

For any encoded hyperplane, the data given the hyperplane is encoded by calculating the distributions of points on each side of the hyperplane. Each point is encoded according to its given classification, y and the distribution corresponding to the side of the hyperplane it is on.

4.2   Class Distributions and Class for Each Point

'Class distributions' give the proportion of each kind of object on each side of the hyperplane. In this case, these distributions could be described by two binomials, one for each side of the hyperplane. However, in general any type of distribution, such as multinomial, Gaussian, Poisson, von Mises, etc. could be used.

In the second part of the message, the 'class for each point' is the class which each point is assigned to, encoded with respect to the class distributions. This penalises misclassified points by using a longer code word to describe the position of the point than what would be used for a correctly classified point.

These two costing procedures were implemented by forming a single cost called the 'pqCost'. The 'p' stands for the proportion of positive points on one side of the hyperplane and the 'q' the proportion of positive points on the other side of the hyperplane. So, using the MML estimate of the distributions, if there were N^+ positive points and N^- negative points above the hyperplane, then $\widehat{p} = \frac{N^+ + 1/2}{N^+ + N^- + 1}$. Similarly, if there were M^+ positive points and M^- negative points below the hyperplane, then $\widehat{q} = \frac{M^+ + 1/2}{M^+ + M^- + 1}$.

Subsequently, a weighting factor of $1/2$ is added to each point and then multiplied by the $-\log_2$ of the relevant proportion. A constant, $(1 - \log_2 12)/2$ is then added for each distribution to form the overall cost as a message length [22], [21, equation (3)]:

$$pqCost = -(N^+ + 1/2)\log_2 \widehat{p} - (N^- + 1/2)\log_2(1 - \widehat{p}) + (1 - \log_2 12)/2$$
$$-(M^+ + 1/2)\log_2 \widehat{q} - (M^- + 1/2)\log_2(1 - \widehat{q}) + (1 - \log_2 12)/2$$

In the case where no hyperplane is placed, there is only a single binomial to estimate. Hence, if $\widehat{p}$ is this estimation, the cost as a message length is:

$$pqCost = -(N^+ + 1/2)\log_2 \widehat{p} - (N^- + 1/2)\log_2(1 - \widehat{p}) + (1 - \log_2 12)/2$$

The use of the constant term comes from the MML message length formula which uses the Fisher Information to estimate the optimal precision to which to state the parameter [22], [21, page 74].

4.3   The Kullback-Leibler Distance

The data sets were read into the systems under investigation such that the success of a given system depends on how close the resulting inferred hyperplane is to the true hyperplane. To measure this, the Kullback-Leibler distance [11, 12], of the inferred distributions around the inferred line is taken from the true distributions around the true line.

The calculation involves finding the areas of the regions between the two hyperplanes. In most cases, when the hyperplanes crossed and did not coincide, four regions were present (see Figure 1). Otherwise, if the hyperplanes did not cross there were three regions.

The Kullback-Leibler formula used was:

$$A1(p_1 \ln \frac{p_1}{\widehat{p_1}} + (1 - p_1) \ln \frac{(1 - p_1)}{(1 - \widehat{p_1})}) + A2(p_1 \ln \frac{p_1}{\widehat{p_2}} + (1 - p_1) \ln \frac{(1 - p_1)}{(1 - \widehat{p_2})})$$

$$+ A3(p_2 \ln \frac{p_2}{\widehat{p_1}} + (1 - p_2) \ln \frac{(1 - p_2)}{(1 - \widehat{p_1})}) + A4(p_2 \ln \frac{p_2}{\widehat{p_2}} + (1 - p_2) \ln \frac{(1 - p_2)}{(1 - \widehat{p_2})})$$

where A1, A2, A3 and A4 are the areas of the regions between the true and inferred hyperplanes,

p_1 is the true probability associated with the distribution of positive points above the true hyperplane,

p_2 is the true probability associated with the distribution of negative points below the true hyperplane,

$\widehat{p_1}$ is the inferred probability associated with the distribution of positive points above the inferred hyperplane,

$\widehat{p_2}$ is the inferred probability associated with the distribution of positive points below the inferred hyperplane.

You may recall, however, that in the event of highly random data, the MML SVM was given the option of placing no hyperplane. In such cases, only two regions, the one above and the one below the true hyperplane, were used. The probability distributions were the proportions of positive and negative points above and below the true hyperplane as calculated from the data.

In the case of the 50% / 50% data sets where no true hyperplane was present, the distributions on either side of the inferred hyperplane were calculated and compared against the true 50% / 50% distribution.

4.4   A Real Data Set

A data set containing real world data (the Wisconsin Prognostic Breast Cancer Database, January 8, 1991) [3] was also tested. The data has 10 input attributes plus a binary class attribute. The first attribute is the sample code number, which was ignored.

Due to the fact that real data has no true hyperplane with which to calculate a Kullback-Leibler distance against, the data set was split into a training set and a test set via 10-fold cross-validation. This technique successively takes 10% of the data (randomly) as the test set and uses the remaining 90% as the training set. The 10 resulting test scores are then averaged. This was repeated 5 times and overall means and (unbiased) standard deviations of the results were taken.

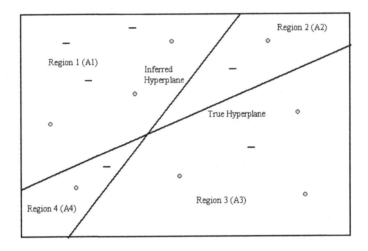

Fig. 1. The Kullback-Leibler distance between two hyperplanes

Probabilistic scoring [8,6,5,14] was used to test the generalisation ability of the inferred hyperplane. To do this, estimates of the binary distributions on either side of the inferred hyperplane were taken. Let N^+ be the number of positive points above the hyperplane in the test data, and N^- negative points above the hyperplane, and $\hat{p} = \frac{N^+ + 1}{N^+ + N^- + 2}$. Similarly, if there were M^+ positive points and M^- negative points below the hyperplane in the test data, let $\hat{q} = \frac{M^+ + 1}{M^+ + M^- + 2}$. Then the generalisation ability of the inferred hyperplane was cost via:

$$-N^+ \ln(\hat{p}) - N^- \ln(1 - \hat{p}) - M^+ \ln(\hat{q}) - M^- \ln(1 - \hat{q})$$

A second means of testing the inferred hyperplane, the "right / wrong" predictive accuracy score, was also used. It simply finds the majority class on either side of the hyperplane using the training data, then finds the number of test points which are of the majority class for each side.

These counts are summed and the sum divided by the total number of points to obtain a proportion of correctly classified points.

5   Results and Discussion

Several 'true' hyperplanes were used to test the algorithms. The one presented in this paper has the form: $y = -0.9x + 130.0$.

Various uniformly distributed data sets were generated to feed into the algorithms. Artificial sets containing 10, 50, 500 and 1000 points were generated. The distributions of the data points were relative to the pre-specified true hyperplane. The desired distributions of positive points for each side of the hyperplane were also specified. Data sets with 60% / 40% where 60% of the points were positive on one side and 40% positive on the other side were generated along with 95% / 5%, 85% / 55% and 50% / 50% data sets respectively. Note that the 50% / 50% data set is the equivalent of having no hyperplane and pure random noise.

It must be noted that on some data sets, SVM^{light} went into an infinite loop and had to be stopped before convergence to the final support vectors. The number of times this occured was recorded and is indicated in the results table.

The preliminary results indicate that are the methods improved as more data was presented and the MML methods proved to be the most effective on the large data sets, the 60%/40% and the 50% / 50% data set.

Table 1. Kullback-Leibler distances (mean ± standard deviation) between the true hyperplane $(y = -0.9x + 130.0)$ and inferred hyperplanes. The 'n' in *mean ± standard deviation* ^{*n} denotes the number of data sets on which SVM^{light} did not converge.

	N = 10	N = 50	N = 500	N = 1000
60/40				
MML_{NU}^{WT}	0.0532 ± 0.0814	0.0271 ± 0.0183	**0.0047 ± 0.0033**	**0.0035 ± 0.0027**
MML_{SR}^{WT}	**0.0163 ± 0.0030**	**0.0133 ± 0.0004**	0.0129 ± 0.0000	0.0129 ± 0.0000
SVM^{light}	0.0442 ± 0.0520	0.0174 ±0.0120 *1	0.0127 ±0.0013 *3	0.0129 ±0.0000 *1
Lagrangian	0.0755 ± 0.0753	0.0396 ± 0.0392	0.0179 ± 0.0174	0.0175 ± 0.0170
SMOBR	0.0208 ± 0.0172	0.0142 ± 0.0030	0.0129 ± 0.0000	0.0129 ± 0.0000
85/55				
MML_{NU}^{WT}	0.0825 ± 0.0716	0.0424 ± 0.0285	**0.0080 ± 0.0063**	**0.0053 ± 0.0034**
MML_{SR}^{WT}	**0.0441 ± 0.0105**	**0.0343 ± 0.0008**	0.0338 ± 0.0001	0.0337 ± 0.0001
SVM^{light}	0.0781 ± 0.0647	0.0375 ±0.0128 *2	0.0338 ±0.0001 *3	0.0337 ±0.0001 *2
Lagrangian	0.0462 ± 0.0459	0.0374 ± 0.0370	0.0272 ± 0.0267	0.0279 ± 0.0275
SMOBR	0.0527 ± 0.0239	0.0357 ± 0.0059	0.0338 ± 0.0001	0.0337 ± 0.0001
95/05				
MML_{NU}^{WT}	0.2804 ± 0.1387	0.0775 ± 0.0602	0.0348 ± 0.0189	0.0296 ± 0.0169
MML_{SR}^{WT}	0.3815 ± 0.0443	0.3475 ± 0.0109	0.3413 ± 0.0011	0.3411 ± 0.0006
SVM^{light}	0.3774 ±0.0502 *3	0.1707 ± 0.1079	0.0371 ±0.0210 *2	0.0297 ±0.0152 *1
Lagrangian	**0.0191 ± 0.0186**	**0.0141 ± 0.0136**	**0.0084 ± 0.0079**	**0.0076 ± 0.0070**
SMOBR	0.3826 ± 0.0481	0.3475 ± 0.0109	0.3414 ± 0.0010	0.3412 ± 0.0006
50/50				
MML_{NU}^{WT}	0.0376 ± 0.0653	0.0129 ± 0.0227	0.0019 ± 0.0022	0.0009 ± 0.0012
MML_{SR}^{WT}	**0.0000 ± 0.0000**	**0.0000 ± 0.0000**	**0.0000 ± 0.0000**	**0.0000 ± 0.0000**
SVM^{light}	0.0373 ± 0.0478	0.0115 ± 0.0182	0.0008 ± 0.0012	0.0005 ± 0.0005
Lagrangian	0.0412 ± 0.0408	0.0466 ± 0.0462	0.0486 ±0.0483 *2	0.0442 ±0.0438 *3
SMOBR	0.0147 ± 0.0338	0.0045 ± 0.0098	0.0006 ± 0.0014	0.0003 ± 0.0006

Table 1 shows the Kullback-Leibler distances (mean ± standard deviation) between the inferred hyperplanes and the true hyperplane $y = -0.9x + 130.0$. In the majority of cases, the mean Kullback-Leibler distance decreases as the size of the data set increases. Our preliminary MML schemes obtained the lowest distance in 12 out of the 16 trials, 8 going to the $\mathbf{MML_{SR}^{WT}}$ and 4 going to the

Table 2. Real Data Set – Wisconsin Prognostic Breast Cancer Database. Probabilistic prediction bit score error [8,6,14] results and "right/wrong" predictive accuracy results using 10-fold cross-validation (mean ± standard deviation).

	Prob. Predicition (bit score) error	Right/Wrong Accuracy
MML_{NU}^{WT}	10.035377 ± 4.689809	0.960580 ± 0.023718
MML_{SR}^{WT}	44.540905 ± 2.579899	0.655072 ± 0.059755
SVM^{light}	10.327132 ± 4.406510	0.964638 ± 0.019645
Lagrangian	12.029075 ± 6.396449	0.958261 ± 0.028850
SMOBR	44.540905 ± 2.579899	0.655072 ± 0.059755

$\textbf{MML}_{\textbf{NU}}^{\textbf{WT}}$ (the two schemes producing equal results on one of the data sets). SVM^{light} and SMOBR (for which we assumed Gaussian input) did not produce the lowest distance for any of the trials while the Lagrangian did for only 5 of the trials. It is possible, however, that SMOBR might be slightly disadvantaged by the non-Gaussian distribution of the training data.

Tests on 100 point data sets were also done [10], but omitted due to page limits. In addition to this, further tests were done on two more hyperplanes, $y = 1.6x + 10.0$ and $y = -1.7x + 80.0$. The results for the first hyperplane were similar to those in Table 1. However, for the second hyperplane the Lagrangian produced the lowest Kullback-Leibler distances for 14 out of the 20 trials. The $\textbf{MML}_{\textbf{SR}}^{\textbf{WT}}$ scheme produced the second lowest distance for these trials, and managed to produce the lowest distance for the remaining 6 trials.

In regards to the real data set, it appears that the $\textbf{MML}_{\textbf{NU}}^{\textbf{WT}}$ obtained the smallest probabilistic prediction cost [8,6,5,14] and the second largest "right/wrong" predictive accuracy score. SVM^{light} obtained the second smallest probabilistic prediction cost and the largest "right/wrong" predictive accuracy score. The Lagrangian followed closely behind whereas $\textbf{MML}_{\textbf{SR}}^{\textbf{WT}}$ and SMOBR tended to perform comparatively badly on this real data set.

The reason for the bad behaviour on the $\textbf{MML}_{\textbf{SR}}^{\textbf{WT}}$'s behalf is that it tended to choose to place no hyperplane. This, of course, would perform poorly when classifying new points because all points would be allocated to the same class.

It was also noticed that the separation ratio implementation tended to give longer message lengths for this data set than the non-uniform code implementation. In principle, the shorter MML message is favoured – as such results indeed show. Based on this idea, a new system where several MML implementations are run, but the one with the shortest message length is chosen, could be devised. This system will be investigated further.

6   Conclusion

A preliminary attempt at reformulating an SVM in a message length framework was presented in this paper. Its performance on data sets, both artificial and real-world, was compared against that of three classical SVMs via the Kullback-Leibler distance. It was found that all implementations improved as the size of the data sets increased. Of the two preliminary MML implementations, the one using the Separation Ratio search method ($\mathbf{MML^{WT}_{SR}}$) tended to perform better on artificial data than the one using the data-partitioning search method ($\mathbf{MML^{WT}_{NU}}$).

In general, for the artificial data sets it appears that the MML Separation Ratio and the Lagrangian gave the lowest Kullback-Leibler distances. Moreover, MML performed the best on the large data sets and also on the 60%/40% and the 50% / 50% data sets.

On the real data set, $\mathbf{MML^{WT}_{NU}}$ and SVM^{light} performed very well followed closely by the Lagrangian.

In light of these results we intend to develop an improved message length framework which combines the best features of several MML implementations together with the Separation Ratio search method. We expect this new framework to produce even more competitive results. Also, we plan to investigate the effect of using other distributions on either side of the hyperplane.

References

1. Barros de Almeida, Marcelo (2001).
   http://www.litc.cpdee.ufmg.br/~barros/svm/smobr/.
2. Bennett, K. P., Wu, D., & Auslender, L. (1998). On support vector decision trees for database marketing. (Research Report 98–100). Rensselaer Polytechnic Institute, Troy, NY.
3. Blake, C. L., & Merz, C. J. (1998). *UCI Repository of machine learning databases.* http://www.ics.uci.edu/~mlearn/MLRepository.html. Irvine, CA: University of California, Department of Information and Computer Science.
4. Brown, M., Grundy, W., Lin, D., Cristianini, N., Sugnet, C., Furey, T., Ares Jr, M., & Haussler, D. (2000). Knowledge-based Analysis of Microarray Gene Expression Data using Support Vector Machines. *Proceedings of the National Academy of Sciences*, 97(1), 262–267.
5. Dowe, D.L., G.E. Farr, A.J. Hurst and K.L. Lentin (1996). Information-theoretic football tipping, in N. de Mestre (ed.), Third Australian Conference on Mathematics and Computers in Sport, Bond University, Qld, 233–241, 1996.
6. Dowe, D.L, & Krusel N. (1993). A decision tree model of bushfire activity, (Technical report 93/190) Dept Computer Science, Monash University, Melbourne, pp 7, 1993
7. Fitzgibbon, L. J., Allison, L., & Dowe, D. L. (2000). Minimum message length grouping of ordered data. In H. Arimura, S. Jain & A. Sharma (Eds.) *Lecture Notes in Artificial Intelligence*, Springer-Verlag, Berlin, Germany, 1968, 56–70.
8. Good, I. J. (1965). The Estimation of Probabilities: An Essay on Modern Bayesian Methods. Research Monograph No. 30, Cambridge Massachusetts: MIT Press.
9. Joachims, T. (1998). Making Large-Scale SVM Learning Practical. In B. Scholkopf, C. J. C. Burges & A. J. Smola (Eds.), *Advances in Kernel Methods: Support Vector Learning*. MIT Press, Cambridge, USA, 1998.
   http://www.kernel-machines.org

10. Kornienko, L., Dowe, D.L. , Albrecht, D.W. (2002). Message Length Formulation of Support Vector Machines for Binary Classification. Technical Report. Monash University, Clayton, Australia.
11. Kullback, S. (1959) *Information Theory and Statistics*. John Riley and Sons, Inc.
12. Kullback, S. & Leibler, R. A. (1951). On Information and Sufficiency. *Ann. Math. Statist.*, Vol 22, pp 79–86.
13. Mangasarian, O. L., & Musicant, D. R. (2000). *Lagrangian Support Vector Machines*. (Technical Report 00-06). Data Mining Institute. http://www.kernel-machines.org
14. Needham, Scott L., & Dowe, David L. (2001). Message Length as an Effective Ockham's Razor in Decision Tree Induction. Proc. 8th International Workshop on Artificial Intelligence and Statistics (AI+STATS 2001), pp 253–260, Key West, Florida, U.S.A., Jan. 2001.
15. Osuna, E., Freund, R., & Girosi, F. (1997). Training Support Vector Machines: an Application to Face Detection. *Proceedings of CVPR'97*, Puerto Rico.
16. Platt, J. (1999). *Sequential minimal optimization: A fast algorithm for training support vector machines* in *Advances in Kernel Methods – Support Vector Learning*, Bernhard Scholkopf, Christopher J. C. Burges and Alexander J. Smola, Eds. 1999, pp. 185–208, MIT Press.
17. Vapnik, V. (1995). The Nature of Statistical Learning Theory. Springer, New York.
18. Viswanathan, M., & Wallace, C. S. (1999) A note on the comparison of polynomial selection methods. In D Heckerman and J Whittaker (eds), *Proceedings of Uncertainty 99: The Seventh International Workshop on Artificial Intelligence and Statistics*, pp 169–177. Fort Lauderdale, Florida, 3–6 January, 1999. Morgan Kaufmann Publishers, Inc., San Francisco, CA, USA.
19. Wallace, C. S., & Boulton, D.M. (1968). An information measure for classification. *Computer Journal*, 11, 185–194.
20. Wallace, C .S., & Dowe, D. L. (1999). Minimum Message Length and Kolmogorov Complexity. *Computer Journal Special Issue: Kolmogorov Complexity*. 42(4), 270–283.
21. Wallace, C.S. and D.L. Dowe (2000). MML clustering of multi-state, Poisson, von Mises circular and Gaussian distributions, Statistics and Computing, Vol. 10, No. 1, Jan. 2000, pp 73–83
22. Wallace, C. S., & Freeman, P.R. (1987). Estimation and Inference by Compact Coding, *J Royal Stat. Soc. B*. 49, 240–252.
23. Wallace, C. S., & Patrick, J. D. (1993). Coding Decision Trees. *Machine Learning*, 11, 7–22.

MML Inference of Decision Graphs with Multi-way Joins

Peter J. Tan and David L. Dowe

School of Computer Science and Software Engineering, Monash University,
Clayton, Vic 3800, Australia
{ptan, dld}@bruce.csse.monash.edu.au

Abstract. A decision tree is a comprehensible representation that has been widely used in many machine learning domains. But in the area of supervised learning, decision trees have their limitations. Two notable problems are those of replication and fragmentation. One way of solving these problems is to introduce decision graphs, a generalization of the decision tree, which address the above problems by allowing for disjunctions, or joins. While various decision graph systems are available, all of these systems impose some forms of restriction on the proposed representations, often leading to either a new redundancy or the original redundancy not being removed. In this paper, we propose an unrestricted representation called the decision graph with multi-way joins, which has improved representative power and is able to use training data efficiently. An algorithm to infer these decision graphs with multi-way joins using the Minimum Message Length (MML) principle is also introduced. On both real-world and artificial data with only discrete attributes (including at least five UCI data-sets), and in terms of both "right"/"wrong" classification accuracy and I.J. Good's logarithm of probability "bit-costing" predictive accuracy, our novel multi-way join decision graph program significantly out-performs both C4.5 and C5.0. Our program also out-performs the Oliver and Wallace binary join decision graph program on the only data-set available for comparison.

Keywords. Machine learning, decision trees, decision graphs, supervised learning, probabilistic prediction, minimum message length, MML, MDL

1 Introduction

In spite of the success of decision tree systems in supervised classification learning, the search for a confirmed improvement of decision trees has remained a continuing topic in the machine learning literature. Two well-known problems from which the decision tree representation suffers have provided incentives for such efforts. The first one is the replication problem which leads to the duplication of subtrees in disjunctive concepts. For example, a decision tree in which the term $(C \wedge D)$ requires two subtrees to be represented gives an inefficient representation of the proposition $(A \wedge B) \vee (C \wedge D)$. The effect of the replication

R.I. McKay and J. Slaney (Eds.): AI 2002, LNAI 2557, pp. 131–142, 2002.

problem is that many decision tree learning algorithms require an unnecessarily large amount of data to learn disjunctive functions.

The second problem is the fragmentation problem, which occurs when the data contains attributes with more than 2 values. When decision nodes in a tree are split on high arity attributes (say $arity \geq 10$), it will quickly fragment the data into many partitions with relatively little data.

Both of these problems increase the size of decision trees and reduce the number of instances in the individual nodes. One way of resolving these problems, particularly when the number of instances in nodes are crucial for inferring the underlying concept, is to use decision graphs to provide an elegant, generalizing solution. Decision graphs can be viewed as generalizations of decision trees and both decision trees and decision graphs have decision nodes and leaves. The feature that distinguishes decision graphs from decision trees is that they may also contain joins (or disjunctions), which are represented by two nodes having a common child. This representation specifies that two subsets have some common properties, and hence can be considered as one subset. As shown on the right hand side of Figure 1, by merging duplicated subtrees with a join operator, the repeated subtrees - from the left hand side of Figure 1 - representing the term $(C \wedge D)$ are united into one subtree.

Fig. 1. Decision tree and Decision graph representations for $(A \wedge B) \vee (C \wedge D)$

One attempt as generalizing decision trees was proposed by Mehta et al. [9]. As a refined decision tree system, it allowed multi-way joins but restricted these joins to nodes which have common parents. This improvement does, however, not help with decision tree replication problems such as that of Figure 1.

More recently, Mansour and McAllester [8] introduced a decision graph representation called the branch program. In their system, where decision trees were viewed as a form of boosting, the use of a boosting algorithm guaranteed that the training error declines as $2^{-\beta\sqrt{|T|}}$, where $|T|$ is the size of the decision tree and β is a constant determined by the weak learning hypothesis. Compared to decision trees, whose training error declines as $|T|^{-\beta}$, the branch program showed some promising theoretical results. However, the analysis of the generalization error of the branch program remained open, and thus no comparison with other systems could be made. Together with some earlier works [10,11,7,9], the branch program certainly indicated that decision graphs was a reasonable approach.

The HOODG system, introduced by Kohavi [7], used an Oblivious Read-Once Decision Graph (OODG). OODG was closely related to Order Binary Decision Diagrams(OBDDs). In the HOODG system, variables had to be strictly ordered and decision graphs were generated so that the graph would only test the variables in the specific order. But because the system insisted on a canonical representation, nodes with irrelevant attributes have to be included in the inferred graphs. Kohavi [7] reported significant improvement over decision tree algorithms such as C4.5 and ID3 [13] on artificial data sets generated from disjunctive functions, but the system achieved less success on real-world data sets. The system also did not adequately address noise in data.

Oliver and Wallace's system [10,11,12] used decision graphs that allowed joins with a pair of nodes. They also presented a MML inference coding scheme and a graph growing algorithm for the system. Our decision graph system builds on the Oliver and Wallace system but eliminates their limitation by allowing for multi-way joins. In this way, our scheme not only generalizes the Oliver-Wallace binary join decision graph but also generalizes the scheme of Mehta et al. [9], which only allowed joins of nodes which have common parents. For a detailed comparison between our multi-way join scheme and the Oliver and Wallace binary join scheme, see section 3.3.

2 Decision Graphs with Multi-way Joins

In this paper, we propose a decision graph system which allows multi-way joins. We use directed acyclic graphs in our system as in both the Oliver and Wallace system [12,11] and the Kohavi system [7]. In addition to decision nodes and leaf nodes, we introduce join nodes which are merged to have a common child. Join nodes are represented by a lozenge shape in the figures. Although we may represent a join by directly attaching arcs from decision nodes to a child, we have explicitly included them in the figures to clarify our coding scheme. The main idea behind our new decision graph representation is that a decision graph can be decomposed into a sequence of several decision trees. By doing this, we are able to re-use some well-proved decision tree inductive techniques in our system. The details of our algorithm are discussed in section 3.2. Figure 2 illustrates an example of how a decision graph can be decomposed into a sequence of decision trees.

3 MML Inference of Decision Graphs

3.1 Bayesianism and MML

The Minimum Message Length (MML) Principle [16,19,17] provides a guide for inferring the best model given a set of data. If a set of data is to be transmitted, it can either be transmitted directly (as it is); or alternatively a theory can be inferred from the data, then the set of data is transmitted with the help of the theory. Thus, the transmitted message is composed of the following two parts:
  I. the description of the theory, or hypothesis, H

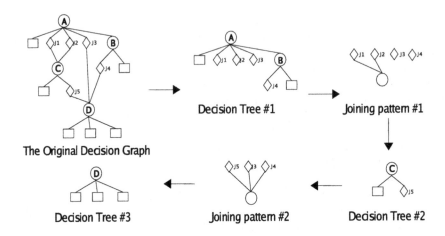

Fig. 2. Decomposing a decision graph into a sequences of decision trees

II. the data, D, explained with help of the theory

From Bayes's rule, we know that $\Pr(D)\Pr(H|D) = \Pr(H\&D) = \Pr(H)\Pr(D|H)$

So $\Pr(H|D) = \frac{\Pr(H)\Pr(D|H)}{P(D)}\ldots\ldots(1)$,

where $\Pr(H\&D)$ is joint probability of D and H, $\Pr(H)$ is the prior probability of the hypothesis H, $\Pr(D)$ is the marginal probability of the data D, $\Pr(D|H)$ is the likelihood function of D given H and $\Pr(H|D)$ is the posterior probability of H given observed data D. From (1), we get that

$-\log \Pr(H|D) = -\log \Pr(D|H) - \log \Pr(H) + \log \Pr(D)$

To maximize $\Pr(H|D)$ is equivalent to minimizing $-\log \Pr(H|D)$. Because log $\Pr(D)$ is a constant, we can ignore it and seek a minimum of $-\log P(D|H)$ $-\log P(H)$. Thus the hypothesis with the minimum two-part message length can be said to be the model of best fit for the given data. For details of the MML Principle, see [16,19,17,12]. For a comparison between MML and Minimum Description Length (MDL) [15], see, e.g., [17] and other articles in that 1999 special issue of the *Computer Journal.*

3.2   Coding Decision Graphs with Multi-way Joins

Much effort has been put into the development of tree-based classification techniques in recent years. Quinlan and Rivest [14] proposed a method for inferring decision trees using the Minimum Description Length (MDL) Principle [15]. Based on it, Wallace and Patrick [20] presented a refined coding scheme for decision trees using the Minimum Message Length Principle, MML in which they identified and corrected some errors in Quinlan and Rivest's derivation of the message. They also introduced a "Look Ahead" heuristic of arbitrarily many ply for selecting the test attribute at a node.

Oliver et al. presented an inference scheme [12,11] to construct decision graphs using MML [16,19,17]. The machine-learning technique of decision graphs was successfully applied to the inference of a theory of protein secondary structure from a particular dataset by Dowe et al. [4] (see Section 4.4). The resulting decision graphs provided both an explanation and a prediction method for the problem. However, the Oliver-Wallace coding scheme [12,11] only allows binary joins. When there are more than two nodes involving in a join, some intermediate nodes have to be created. Immediately below in Section 3.2, we present a refined coding scheme for decision graphs which allows multi-way joins to eliminate such inefficiency.

In this paper, we refine the coding scheme for decision graphs so that a join operation is no longer limited to one pair of nodes. An arbitrary number of nodes can be involved in a join operation and form a common child node. We also refer the reader to the earlier and similar coding scheme of Oliver et al., which only permitted binary joins [12]. To transmit a decision graph now allowing multi-way joins, we use following steps.

1. From the root node of the decision graph, a prefix traversal of the decision tree is performed, treating any join nodes as leaves. Any join nodes that have been transmitted are added to an open list.

2. When step 1 is finished, if this results in any join nodes in the open list, then the combination pattern of the nodes in the open list is described. A combination pattern lists those groups in the open list which combine to have a child. Any groups of nodes in the open list that are involved in a join are deleted from the open list. Add their children to a new node list, in which nodes will become roots of new traversals.

3. If there is any node in the new node list, step 1 is repeated to transmit them.

By decomposing a decision graph into a sequence of decision trees (as in Figure 2), which are transmitted in step 1, we are able to re-use the MML decision tree coding scheme proposed by Wallace and Patrick [20]. Since we treat join nodes as leaves, we implement an adaptive code to describe which leaves are actually join nodes and should be put into the open list.

In step 2 of the above process, a description of the combination pattern of join nodes from the open list needs to be communicated. Firstly, we define the nodes which were added to the open list in the current iterations of transmitting to be "new" nodes, and nodes which were added to the open list in previous iterations then become "old" nodes. We can view the open list as containing N new nodes (from the most recent iteration) and Q old nodes. It should be noted that both N and Q become common knowledge for both sender and receiver before transmission of the combination pattern.

We communicate the combination pattern of join nodes from the open list in four steps, thus four numbers (see points 1-4 below) must be transmitted in the following order.

1. The number of nodes, M, which are children of joins in this iteration. Because there are at least two leaf nodes being involved in any join and because one of these leaf nodes must be a new node, so $1 \leq M \leq min(N, \frac{N+Q}{2})$. Assuming these values to be equally likely, the message length cost of transmitting this number, M, in the message would be $log(min(N, \frac{N+Q}{2}))$.

2. The number of pending nodes, P, which are not involved in any join and the numbers of nodes $(J_1, J_2, \ldots, J_M)$ in each group of joining leaf nodes from the open list in this iteration.

The task is now equivalent to finding out the number of different solutions to the following equation.

$P + J_1 + J_2 + \ldots + J_M = N + Q$ (where $P \geq 0; J_i \geq 2; i = 1, 2, \ldots, M$)

If the number of valid answers is A and every solution is assumed a priori equally likely, the cost of transmitting those numbers in the message length would be $\log(A)$.

3. The number of "new" nodes , Y, among pending nodes and the number of new nodes, $(X_1, X_2, \ldots, X_M)$ in each group of joining leaf nodes from the open list in this iteration .

Similar to the above step and because there is at least one new node in each joining group, the task is now equivalent to finding out the number of different solutions to the following equation.

$Y + X_1 + X_2 + \ldots + X_M = N$ (where $0 \leq Y \leq P; 1 \leq X_i \leq J_i ; i = 1, 2, \ldots, M$)

If the number of valid solutions is B and every solution is assumed a priori equally likely, the cost of transmitting those numbers in the message length would be $\log(B)$.

4. The number of permutations of nodes from the open list in this iteration:

$C = \frac{N!}{Y! X_1! X_2! \ldots X_M!} \frac{Q!}{(P-Y)!(J_1-X_1)!(J_2-X_2)!\ldots(J_M-X_M)!}$

If every permutation is assumed a priori equally likely, the cost of transmitting the number in the message length would be $\log(C)$.

After finishing the transmission of the combination pattern, we use an adaptive code to encode the types (i.e., leaf or fork) of nodes in the new node list, followed by new rounds of graph traversal(s). Nodes resulting from join operations can not be join nodes, because if a join operation involving such a node were to happen in a future iteration, the nodes which combined to form this node would have been labeled as "pending" until needed for such a join.

3.3   Comparison with Oliver and Wallace's Decision Graph Program

The difference between our coding scheme and Oliver and Wallace's coding scheme for decision graphs [10,11,12] has been illustrated in Figure 3. Whenever a multi-way join is required, the Oliver-Wallace coding scheme[10,11,12] encodes it by proceeding with a series of consecutive binary joins. The result of each such binary join other than the last one is an intermediate node. These intermediate join nodes are redundant (or irrelevant), even though the Oliver-Wallace scheme insists upon encoding them and is thus inefficient. Our scheme is efficient in that it can encode multi-way joins without having to introduce any redundant intermediate nodes. As the example in Figure 3 shows, while the coding scheme with multi-way joins is able to join the four nodes in one step, Oliver and Wallace's scheme has to do it in two steps and two intermediate join nodes J5 and J6 are introduced. The message length caused by coding these intermediate nodes and various possible ways to form these joins make the scheme less inefficient. For a way of partly removing the inefficiency from the Oliver-Wallace coding scheme, see Section 3.4.

3.4   Unpublished Refinement of Oliver-Wallace Coding Scheme

The Oliver-Wallace coding scheme that we have presented so far [10,11,12] is inefficient due to the fact that a series of consecutive binary joins is encoded including the order in which those consecutive binary joins occurred, even though that order is in fact irrelevant.

This coding scheme can be rectified and made efficient by accounting for this combinatorial inefficiency. For example, as Figure 3 shows, where four nodes join into one node by three consecutive binary joins, we note that this could have been done in $C_2^4 C_2^3 C_2^2 = $ 6x3x1 $ = 18$ different ways, and that log(18) can be subtracted from the length of the corresponding (inefficient) message.

It is our understanding that, although such a rectification has not been published, that J.J. Oliver might have since modified the Oliver and Wallace source code to at least partly correct for the above combinatorial inefficiency. However, his program is unavailable.

Such a(n unpublished) correction to the Oliver-Wallace coding scheme would – if correctly implemented – give it a comparable efficiency to the multi-way join coding scheme proposed in our current paper here. The difference between the refined, corrected, Oliver-Wallace scheme (if, indeed, actually and correctly implemented) and our new scheme here would essentially be a choice of Bayesian prior.

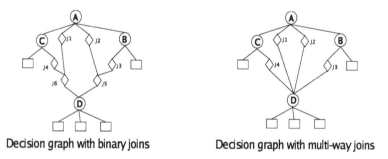

Decision graph with binary joins   Decision graph with multi-way joins

Fig. 3. Different encoding of a function by (left) decision graphs with binary joins and (right) decision graphs with multi-way joins

3.5   Growing a Decision Graph

We begin with a graph having one node, with the root being a leaf. We grow the graph by performing the following procedures iteratively until no further improvement can be achieved.

1. For each leaf L, perform tentative splits on each available attribute in the leaf, and determine the attribute A that will lead to the shortest message length when L is split on A. Record, but do not perform, the alteration (Split L on A) along with its communication saving.

2. For each leaf L, perform tentative joins with other leaves. Record, but do not perform, the alterations (join L_i and L_j; ...; join $L_i, L_j, ..., L_k$) along with its communication savings.

3. Sort the alterations from step 1 and step 2 by their communication savings. Choose the alteration (whether from step 1 or from step 2) that has greatest saving.

With help of information which we obtain from step 1, we are able to do heuristic search on potential joins rather than perform possible tentative joins exhaustively. For example, only leaves with communication savings when splitting on an identical attribute can form a join that has a possible message length saving. In the worst case, there will be $2N_a C_2^{|L|}$ tentative joins performed in each iteration, where N_a is the number of attributes available for splitting in leaves, $|L|$ is the number of leaves in the iteration, and $C_2^{|L|} = |L|(|L|-1)/2$.

4 Experiments

Six artificially generated data sets and two real-world data sets were used in the tests. Half of the artificial data sets were generated from disjunctive underlying functions. Most of them were downloaded from the UCI machine learning repository [1] and had been widely tested in other decision tree or decision graph systems [12,7,13]. All the data sets we choose have only discrete attributes without missing values. The test results were compared with the well-known classification programs C4.5 and C5 [13], although the Oliver-Wallace binary join decision graph program [10,11,12] was unavailable to us except for a past result [4] (see section 4.4). In addition to the conventional classification accuracy, a metric called probabilistic costing [6,5,2,3] was implemented for comparison. It is defined as $-\sum_{i=1}^{n} \log(p_i)$, where n is the total number of test data and p_i is the predicted probability of the true class associated with the corresponding data item [6,5,2,3]. This metric can be used to approximate the Kullback-Leibler distance between the true (test) model and the inferred model within a constant.

4.1 Testing with Artificially Generated Data

The experimental results are presented in Table 1, "accuracy" describes the classification accuracy and "pr costing" describes Good's probabilistic costing, or logarithmic 'bit costing' [6,5,2,3]. For the data sets on which 10 10-fold cross-validations were performed, the classification accuracy and probabilistic costing were presented in the form of mean ± standard deviation, $\mu \pm \sigma$ (where $\sigma^2 = \sum_{i=1}^{N} (x_i - \mu)^2 / N$).

4.2 Inferring Probabilities for a Multinomial Distribution

Given an array of occurrences of events of an m-state multinomial distribution $(c_1, c_2, ..., c_m)$, the probability of a certain event j can be estimated by (either)
$$\hat{p}_j = \frac{c_j + 0.5}{(\sum c_i) + m/2} \quad \text{[16, p187 (4), p194 (28), p186 (2)][19][18, p75]} \quad \text{or}$$

$$\hat{p}_j = \frac{c_j+1}{(\sum c_i)+m} \text{ [16, p187 (3), p189 (30)]},$$ the latter being known as the

Laplace estimate and also corresponding (with uniform prior) to both the posterior mean and the minimum expected Kullback-Leibler distance estimator. In our experiments (see Tables 1, 2 and 3), both of the formulas were used to give the probability estimates in our decision graph program while only the latter (+1) was used to give the probability estimates in C5 and C4.5. The first (+0.5) $\hat{p}_j$ estimate was used in the MML multinomial message length calculations, but both $\hat{p}_j$ estimates were used in calculating the decision graph log-prob bit cost.

Table 1. Test Results – Both 'Right'/'Wrong' and Log(Prob) – on Artificial Data-Sets

		D-Graph with M-W joins(+1)	D-Graph with M-W joins(+.5)	C5	C4.5
XD6	accuracy	89.2±1.8%	89.2±1.8%	85.2±2.5%	84.9±2.7%
	pr costing	25.2±2.4bits	27.5±2.7%	30.2±3.3bits	33.6±4.2bits
1st Monk	accuracy	100±0.0%	100±0.0%	75.2±4.3%	75.0±3.9%
	pr costing	9.8±0.0bits	5.0±0.0bits	278.4±12.1bits	285.9±11.3bits
LED-7	accuracy	72.3±3.2%	72.3±3.2%	71.2±3.5%	71.1±3.3%
	pr costing	74.5±7.4bits	72.6±6.2bits	89.7±7.9bits	89.6±7.8bits
LED-24	accuracy	68.5±4.4%	68.5±4.4%	67.8±4.7%	67.8±4.5%
	pr costing	96.4±6.2bits	95.1±6.7%	102.8±7.3bits	103.2±8.0bits
Car	accuracy	91.5±1.7%	91.5±1.7%	91.6±1.9%	91.5±2.4%
	pr costing	44.8±5.6bits	40.5±5.3bits	70.9±6.8bits	72.4±11.9bits
Scale	accuracy	79.2±3.2%	79.2±3.2%	61.9±2.8%	61.4±3.8%
	pr costing	54.6±5.9bits	55.8±6.7bits	83.4±4.7bits	83.3±6.7bits

XD6 data set: The XD6 data set [14,20,12] is an artificial set with 10 binary attributes. It was generated so that a division into two categories according to the boolean function of attributes 1 to 9

(A1 ∧ A2 ∧ A3) ∨ (A4 ∧ A5 ∧ A6) ∨ (A7 ∧ A8 ∧ A9)

with 10% noise added to the target attribute. 10 data sets, each of them containing 500 data items, were randomly generated. We then performed 10 individual 10-fold cross-validations on these data sets. Each 10-fold cross-validation consists of 10 tests. In each test, we trained on nine-tenths of the data and tested on the remaining one-tenth. This amounted to 10x10=100 tests.

1st monk's data set: The 1st monk's data set is in the UCI machine learning repository [10,1], and constructed from the noiseless function

(Jacket_Color = Red) V (Head_Shape = body_Shape)

10 independent tests were performed, with each set of training data consisting of 124 data randomly selected from full data set of size 432. We followed the UCI convention on this data set [1] of using the entire data set as test data.

LED-7 data set and LED-24 data set: The LED-7 data set [1] is an artificially generated data set in the UCI machine learning repository with 7 binary attributes and 10 output classes. Each of the attributes corresponds to one different segment in a Light Emitting Diode that displays the numbers 0 to 9. 10% noise was added to each of the seven input attributes. The only difference between LED-7 and LED-24 is that 17 irrelevant attributes with randomly generated values were deliberately added in the LED-24 data set. Again, 10 data sets, each of them containing 500 data items, were randomly generated and then an individual 10-fold cross-validation was performed on the each of the data sets - giving a total 10x10=100 tests.

Car Evaluation data set: The car evaluation data set from the UCI repository [1] was generated from an underlying decision tree model. There are 1728 instances with four output classes in the set. Each data item has 6 nominal ordered attributes, which are treated as unordered discrete attributes in our tests because data files from UCI have been set in this format. We performed 10 independent 10-fold cross-validations again on the data set.

Balance scale data set: The balance scale data set from the UCI repository [1] was generated to model psychological experimental results. There are 625 instances with 3 output classes in the set. 10 independent 10-fold cross-validations were again performed on the data set.

4.3   Discussion of Above Test Results on Artificial Data

As table 1 shows, our decision graph program achieved better or significantly better classification prediction accuracy in most of these test sets (5 out of 6), especially the data sets with a disjunctive underlying function, such as the XD6 and Scale data sets. On the fifth data set (Car), we performed only 0.1% worse. The multi-way join decision graph program also has substantially lower probabilistic bit costing than both C4.5 and C5 on all the test sets. This might best be explained by the fact that decision graphs are more expressive than decision trees and are often able to use the data more efficiently. This should give a shorter Kullback-Leibler distance from the underlying model [17].

4.4   Testing with Real World Data

UCI protein secondary structure database. The protein secondary structure database was one of the UCI molecular biology databases [1]. The data contains amino acid chains with a secondary structure specified at each point. Micro-biologists can determine the amino acid chain of a protein, but finding the secondary structures - which are "alpha-helix", "beta-sheet" and "random-coil" - is quite difficult. We constructed decision graphs that predicted the secondary structure at a point in a protein by (following [4] and) using a window of size 7 (centred at the point of interest) of the amino acid chain attributes. Each of these 7 attributes has arity 21. We tested our multi-way join decision graph program, C4.5 and C5 with the default training and test data set downloaded from the UCI repository. As shown in table 2, decision graphs with multi-way joins performed better than C4.5 and C5. In particular, the multi-way join decision graph program achieved at least 2.0% higher classification accuracy and at least 215 bits less in probabilistic costing compared to both C4.5 and C5.

Another protein data set. This protein data set was generated from a protein database [4]. We use it because we do not have access to the Oliver-Wallace program [12,11,10] and because it is the only data set for which we have the results from that program. We tested C4.5, C5 and our coding scheme by performing an 8-fold cross-validation on the data set because this was done in the original paper [4]. We also compared our test results with results achieved [4] by the Oliver-Wallace decision graph with binary joins. As shown in Table 3, decision graphs with multi-way joins performed better 6 times out of 8 than each of C4.5, C5 and the Oliver Wallace binary join decision graph program [12,11, 10]. On average, our scheme achieves 1.6%, 1.5% and 1.2% higher 'right'/'wrong' prediction accuracy respectively than C4.5, C5 and the Oliver-Wallace binary join decision graph program. Our scheme also has a lower probabilistic bit cost score than both C4.5 and C5 on all 8 test sets [4] in Table 3.

Table 2. Test Results of UCI Protein Data Set (From Section 4.4)

	D-Graph with M-W joins(+1)	D-Graph with M-W joins(+.5)	C5	C4.5
accuracy	57.6%	57.6%	55.4%	55.6%
pr costing	4715.2bits	4718.6bits	4935.1bits	4935.5bits

Table 3. Prediction accuracies on another protein data set [4] (from Section 4.4)

Test Set	D-G with Multi-Way Joins	D-G with binary Joins	C5	C4.5	D-G with Multi-Way Joins(+1)	D-G with Multi-Way Joins(+.5)	C5	C4.5
1	53.0%	54.2%	52.4%	52.4%	2296.6bits	2296.7bits	2380.7bits	2380.7bits
2	54.6%	53.3%	53.1%	53.1%	1907.7bits	1907.7bits	1975.2bits	1975.2bits
3	55.9%	51.7%	54.6%	54.6%	2185.4bits	2186.3bits	2241.7bits	2241.7bits
4	58.2%	56.4%	55.8%	55.8%	2066.2bits	2065.9bits	2252.2bits	2252.2bits
5	50.2%	46.8%	43.9%	43.9%	2227.9bits	2228.1bits	2439.2bits	2439.2bits
6	50.7%	49.0%	50.8%	51.0%	2314.8bits	2316.0bits	2362.3bits	2351.3bits
7	53.5%	52.8%	51.4%	50.5%	2218.2bits	2220.3bits	2238.1bits	2295.0bits
8	52.9%	54.6%	54.6%	54.6%	2246.3bits	2247.1bits	2281.0bits	2281.0bits
Avg	53.6%	52.4%	52.1%	52.0%	2182.9bits	2183.5bits	2271.3bits	2277.0bits

5 Conclusion

We have introduced a refined coding scheme for decision graphs which allows multi-way joins. We discussed the use of the Minimum Message Length Principle and the new coding scheme to infer (multi-way join) decision graphs. Our experimental results demonstrated that our refined coding scheme compares favourably with other decision tree inference schemes, namely C4.5, C5 and the Oliver-Wallace binary join decision graph. This pronounced favourable comparison holds both for 'right'/'wrong' prediction accuracy and I.J. Good's logarithm of probability bit costing, and both for artificially generated and real-world data. We thank Trevor Dix for useful feedback on an earlier draft of this manuscript.

References

1. C.L. Blake and C.J. Merz. UCI repository of machine learning databases, 1998. http://www.ics.uci.edu/~mlearn/MLRepository.html.

2. D.L. Dowe, G.E. Farr, A.J. Hurst, and K.L. Lentin. Information-theoretic football tipping. In N. de Mestre, editor, *Third Australian Conference on Mathematics and Computers in Sport*, pages 233–241. Bond University, Qld, Australia, 1996.

3. D.L. Dowe and N. Krusel. A decision tree model of bushfire activity. In *Proceedings of 6th Australian joint conference on Artificial intelligence*, pages 287–292, 1993.

4. D.L. Dowe, J.J. Oliver, L. Allison, C.S. Wallace, and T.I. Dix. A Decision Graph Explanation of Protein Secondary Structure Prediction. In *Proceedings of the the Hawaii International Conference on System Science (HICSS) Biotechnology Computing Track*, pages 669–678, 1993.

5. I.J. Good. Rational Decisions. *Journal of the Royal Statistical Society. Series B*, 14:107–114, 1952.

6. I.J. Good. Corroboration, Explanation, Evolving Probability, Simplicity, and a Sharpened Razor. *British Journal Philosophy of Science*, 19:123–143, 1968.

7. Ron Kohavi. Bottom-up induction of oblivious read-once decision graphs: Strengths and limitations. In *National Conference on Artificial Intelligence*, pages 613–618, 1994.

8. Yishay Mansour and David McAllester. Boosting using branching programs. In *Proc. 13th Annual Conference on Comput. Learning Theory*, pages 220–224. Morgan Kaufmann, San Francisco, 2000.

9. Manish Mehta, Jorma Rissanen, and Rakesh Agrawal. MDL-based Decision Tree Pruning. In *The First International Conference on Knowledge Discovery & Data Mining*, pages 216–221. AAAI Press, 1995.

10. J.J. Oliver. Decision Graphs – An Extension of Decision Trees. In *Proceedings of the Fourth International Workshop on Artificial Intelligence and Statistics*, pages 343–350, 1993. Extended version available as TR 173, Dept. of Computer Science, Monash University, Clayton, Victoria 3168, Australia.

11. J.J. Oliver, D.L. Dowe, and C.S. Wallace. Inferring Decision Graphs Using the Minimum Message Length Principle. In *Proceedings of the 5th Joint Conference on Artificial Intelligence*, pages 361–367. World Scientific, Singapore, 1992.

12. J.J. Oliver and C.S. Wallace. Inferring Decision Graphs. In *Workshop 8 International Join Conference on AI*, Sydney, Australia, August 1991.

13. J.R. Quinlan. *C4.5: Programs for Machine Learning*. Morgan Kaufmann, San Mateo, CA, 1992. The latest version of C5 is available from http://www.rulequest.com.

14. J.R. Quinlan and R. Rivest. Inferring Decision Trees Using the Minimum Description Length Principle. *Information and Computation*, 80:227–248, 1989.

15. J.J. Rissanen. Modeling by shortest data description. *Automatica*, 14:465–471, 1978.

16. C.S. Wallace and D.M. Boulton. An Information Measure for Classification. *Computer Journal*, 11:185–194, 1968.

17. C.S. Wallace and D.L. Dowe. Minimum Message Length and Kolmogorov Complexity. In *Computer Journal, Special Issue – Kolmogorov Complexity*, volume 42 of *No 4*, pages 270–283. Oxford University Press, 1999.

18. C.S. Wallace and D.L. Dowe. MML Clustering of multi-state, Poisson, von Mises circular and Gaussian distributions. *Statistics and Computing*, 10(1):73–83, Jan 2000.

19. C.S. Wallace and P.R. Freeman. Estimation and Inference by Compact Coding. *Journal of the Royal Statistical Society. Series B*, 49(3):240–265, 1987.

20. C.S Wallace and J.D. Patrick. Coding Decision Trees. *Machine Learning*, 11:7–22, 1993.

MML Clustering of Continuous-Valued Data Using Gaussian and t Distributions

Yudi Agusta and David L. Dowe

Computer Science & Software Eng., Monash University, Clayton, 3800 Australia
{yagusta, dld}@bruce.csse.monash.edu.au

Abstract. Clustering, also known as mixture modelling or intrinsic classification, is the problem of identifying and modelling components (or clusters, or classes) in a body of data. We consider here the application of the Minimum Message Length (MML) principle to a clustering problem of Gaussian and t distributions. Earlier work in the MML clustering was conducted in regards to the multinomial and Gaussian distributions (Wallace and Boulton, 1968) and in addition, the von Mises circular and Poisson distributions (Wallace and Dowe, 1994, 2000). Our current work extends this by applying the Gaussian distribution to the more general t distribution. Point estimation of the t distribution is performed using the MML approximation proposed by Wallace and Freeman (1987). A comparison of the MML estimations of the t distribution to those of the Maximum Likelihood (ML) method in terms of their Kullback-Leibler (KL) distances is also provided. Within each component, our application also performs a model selection on whether a particular group of data is best modelled as a Gaussian or a t distribution. The proposed modelling method is then applied to several artificially generated datasets. The modelling results are compared to the results obtained when using the MML clustering of Gaussian distributions. Our modelling method compares quite well to an alternative clustering program (EMMIX) which uses various modelling criteria such as the Akaike Information Criterion (AIC) and Schwarz's Bayesian Information Criterion (BIC).

Keywords. Clustering, Machine Learning, Knowledge Discovery and Data Mining, Unsupervised Learning, Minimum Message Length, MML, Mixture Modelling, Classification, Intrinsic Classification, Numerical Taxonomy, Information Theory, Statistical Inference.

1 Introduction

The Minimum Message Length (MML) principle [18][23][21] is an invariant Bayesian point estimation and model selection technique based on information theory. The basic idea of MML is to find an hypothesis (or theory) of a distribution or a model that minimises the total length of a two-part message encoding the hypothesis, and the data in light of that hypothesis.

Letting D be the data and H be the hypothesis, with a prior probability distribution $P(H)$, based on Bayes's theorem, the point estimation and model

R.I. McKay and J. Slaney (Eds.): AI 2002, LNAI 2557, pp. 143–154, 2002.

selection problem can be regarded as a problem of maximising the posterior probability $P(H) \cdot P(D|H)$. From the information-theoretic point of view, where an event with probability p is encoded by a message of length $l = -\log_2 p$ bits, the problem is then equivalent to minimising

$$\text{MessLen} = -\log_2(P(H)) - \log_2(P(D|H)) \qquad (1)$$

where the first term states the message length of the hypothesis and the second term states the message length of the data in light of the hypothesis.

This principle was first stated and then applied in a series of papers by Wallace and Boulton dealing with model selections and parameter estimations of multi-state and Gaussian distributions for a clustering problem [18]. A related principle has also been stated independently by Solomonoff [15]. An important special case of the MML principle observed by Chaitin [4] is that data can be regarded as random if there is no hypothesis, H, that can encode the data in a shorter message length than the null hypothesis.

Beginning with parameter estimation, this paper proposes an MML clustering which extends the clustering problem of Gaussian distributions [18][17][22] by considering the t distribution as the distribution of the continuous data investigated. Since the Gaussian distribution is a special case of the t distribution, the application also performs a more general model selection on whether the data in a particular group fits a Gaussian or a t distribution.

2 Parameter Estimation by MML

In order to apply MML to the clustering problem of Gaussian and t distributions, we need parameter estimations of the multi-state, Gaussian and t distributions.

Given the data x and parameters $\boldsymbol{\theta}$, let $h(\boldsymbol{\theta})$ be the prior probability distribution on $\boldsymbol{\theta}$, $f(x|\boldsymbol{\theta})$, the likelihood, $L = -\log f(x|\boldsymbol{\theta})$, the negative log-likelihood and

$$F(\boldsymbol{\theta}) = \det\left\{ E\left(\frac{\partial^2 L}{\partial \boldsymbol{\theta} \partial \boldsymbol{\theta}'} \right) \right\}, \qquad (2)$$

the Fisher information that is the determinant of the matrix of expected second derivatives of the negative log-likelihood. Based on equation (1), and by expanding the negative log-likelihood, L, as far as the second term of the Taylor series about the parameter $\boldsymbol{\theta}$, the message length is then calculated by [23]:

$$\text{MessLen} = -\log \frac{h(\boldsymbol{\theta})}{\sqrt{\kappa_D^D F(\boldsymbol{\theta})}} + L + \frac{D}{2} = -\log \frac{h(\boldsymbol{\theta}) f(x|\boldsymbol{\theta})}{\sqrt{F(\boldsymbol{\theta})}} + \frac{D}{2}(1 + \log \kappa_D) \quad (3)$$

where D is the number of parameters to be estimated and κ_D is a D-dimensional lattice constant [5] , with $\kappa_D \leq 1/12$. The MML estimate of $\boldsymbol{\theta}$ can be obtained by minimising equation (3).

Considering that both distributions used here are continuous, a finite coding for the message can be obtained by acknowledging that all recorded continuous data and measurements must only be stated to a finite precision, which is, in practice, made to some precision, ϵ. In this way, a constant of $N \log(1/\epsilon)$ is added to the message length expression above, where N is the number of data [22].

2.1   Multi-state Variables

For a multi-state distribution with M states (and sample size, N), the likelihood of the distribution is given by:

$$f(n_1, n_2, \cdots, n_M | p_1, p_2, \cdots, p_M) = p_1^{n_1} p_2^{n_2} \cdots p_M^{n_M}$$

where $p_1 + p_2 + \cdots + p_M = 1$, for all m: $p_m \geq 0$ and $n_1 + n_2 + \cdots + n_M = N$.

Using equation (2), it follows that the Fisher information is given by:

$$F(p_1, p_2, \cdots, p_M) = N^{(M-1)} / p_1 p_2 \cdots p_M.$$

The derivation is also shown elsewhere for $M = 2$ [22].

Assuming a uniform prior $(M - 1)!$ over the $(M - 1)$-dimensional region of hyper-volume $1/(M - 1)!$, and minimising equation (3), the MML estimate $\hat{p}_m$ is obtained by [23][22, p75][18, p187 (4), p194 (28), p186 (2)]:

$$\hat{p}_m = (n_m + 1/2)/(N + M/2) \tag{4}$$

Substituting equation (4) into the message length expression (3) provides the following total two-part message length:

$$- \log(M - 1)! + ((M - 1)/2)\big(\log(N \kappa_{M-1}) + 1 \big) - \sum_{m=1}^{M} \big(n_m + 1/2\big) \log \hat{p}_m \tag{5}$$

2.2   Gaussian Variables

For the Gaussian distribution, with a likelihood function

$$f(x | \mu, \sigma) = \frac{1}{\sqrt{2\pi}\sigma} e^{-\frac{(x-\mu)^2}{2\sigma^2}}$$

the Fisher information is given by:

$$F(\mu, \sigma) = 2N^2/\sigma^4 \quad \text{or by } [22]: \quad F(\mu, \sigma^2) = N^2/2(\sigma^2)^3$$

Assuming a uniform prior of $1/R$ on μ over a finite range of width, R, where $R = \max\{10,$ the difference between the maximum and the minimum value of the data$\}$ and a $1/\sigma$ prior on σ (which corresponds to a uniform prior on $\log \sigma$ and equivalently to a $1/\sigma^2$ prior on σ^2) over the range $[e^{-4}, e^4]$, letting $s^2 = \sum_{i=1}^{N}(x_i - \bar{x})^2$, and minimising equation (3), the MML estimates $\hat{\mu}_{\text{MML}}$ and $\hat{\sigma}_{\text{MML}}$ are then given by [22, p75]:

$$\hat{\mu}_{\text{MML}} = \bar{x} = \Big(\sum_{i=1}^{N} x_i\Big)/N, \quad \hat{\sigma}_{\text{MML}}^2 = s^2/(N - 1) \tag{6}$$

2.3 t Variables

The t distribution with mean, μ, standard deviation, σ, and degree of freedom, ν, is a continuous distribution which generalises some other distributions, such as the Gaussian ($\nu = \infty$) and Cauchy ($\nu = 1$) distributions. For large $\nu (> 100)$, the t distribution is closely approximated by a Gaussian distribution. The smaller the value of ν, the longer the tail in the t distribution. Using this property, the t distribution is often used to model data with atypical observations, such as outliers. The distribution has a likelihood function:

$$f(x|\mu,\sigma,\nu) = \frac{\Gamma(\frac{\nu+1}{2})}{\sqrt{\pi\nu}\,\Gamma(\frac{\nu}{2})}\frac{1}{\sigma}\left[1+\frac{(x-\mu)^2}{\nu\sigma^2}\right]^{-\frac{(\nu+1)}{2}} \tag{7}$$

where $\Gamma(x)$ is the Gamma function, given by (for $x>0$):

$$\Gamma(x) = \int_0^\infty t^{x-1}e^{-t}dt, \quad \text{with } \psi^{(1)}(x) = \frac{d^2\Gamma(x)}{dx^2}$$

For any positive integer x, $\Gamma(x) = (x-1)!$. For large x, the value of the Gamma function can also be approximated using the following Stirling's approximation [9]:

$$\Gamma(x) \approx e^{-x}x^{x-\frac{1}{2}}\sqrt{2\pi}(1+\frac{1}{12x}+\frac{1}{288x^2}+O|x|^{-3}) \tag{8}$$

Using equation (2), the Fisher information, F, is given by:

$$F(\mu,\sigma,\nu) = \frac{N^3}{\sigma^4}\left\{\frac{\nu(\nu+1)}{2(\nu+3)^2}\left\{\psi^{(1)}\left(\frac{\nu}{2}\right)-\psi^{(1)}\left(\frac{\nu+1}{2}\right)\right\}-\frac{1}{(\nu+1)(\nu+3)}\right\} \tag{9}$$

Assuming the same priors on μ and σ as those used for Gaussian distribution, and $2/\pi(1+\nu^2)$ prior on ν with ν being an unknown continuous parameter in $(0,\infty]$, the MML estimation of the t distribution parameters are obtained by minimising equation (3) with respect to each parameter. Since there are no sufficient statistics to estimate the parameters and each parameter is dependent on each other, the inference is performed using a binary search by setting $\partial\text{MessLen}/\partial\theta = 0$ and iterating the search process until a certain precision of estimation is obtained.

3   One-Component Univariate Model

In this section, we consider the inference of only one univariate component. We return in later sections to consider mixtures of several multivariate components.

The difference between the Maximum Likelihood (ML) and MML principles in estimating multi-state variables and Gaussian variables has been elaborated upon by Wallace and Dowe [22], and is quite pronounced for the von Mises [19] and some other distributions [21, p282]. Here, we compare the MML estimation of t variables to that of the ML method in terms of the resulting Kullback-Leibler (KL) distances. The ML estimation of t variables has been proposed in a paper by Liu and Rubin [10] in which the estimation is performed using the EM algorithm and its extensions, the ECM and ECME algorithms.

The KL distance between two continuous models $P(X)$ and $Q(X)$ is calculated by:

$$D(P||Q) = \int_{-\infty}^\infty P(x)\log\frac{P(x)}{Q(x)}dx$$

where, in this calculation, $P(X)$ is regarded as the true model and $Q(X)$ is the inferred model.

The datasets for the experiment are repeatedly generated from artificial models with $N = \{10, 100\}$, $\mu = 0.0$, $\sigma = \{1.0, 5.0\}$ and $\nu = \{1.0, 3.0, 10.0, 25.0, 50.0, 100.0\}$. Both estimators infer the datasets with ν either taking the highest value of ν, which is, in this experiment, set to 100.0 or a certain value (< 100.0). The calculation results are shown in Table 1.

Table 1. Average of KL distances of the ML and MML estimations of 100 datasets with $\mu=0.0$, $\sigma=1.0$ or 5.0 and $N=10$ or 100 (with $\pm$ standard errors).

$\sigma=1.0$ & $\nu=$		1.0	3.0	10.0	25.0	50.0	100.0
$N=10$	ML	0.655±0.89	0.419±0.70	0.170±0.21	0.169±0.25	0.172±0.19	0.173±0.26
	MML	0.292±0.48	0.205±0.45	0.118±0.17	0.140±0.20	0.131±0.12	0.134±0.17
$N=100$	ML	0.078±0.04	0.020±0.03	0.018±0.02	0.011±0.01	0.011±0.01	0.012±0.02
	MML	0.076±0.04	0.018±0.02	0.017±0.02	0.011±0.01	0.011±0.01	0.012±0.01

$\sigma=5.0$ & $\nu=$		1.0	3.0	10.0	25.0	50.0	100.0
$N=10$	ML	0.684±1.00	0.427±0.61	0.190±0.22	0.183±0.23	0.199±0.28	0.191±0.22
	MML	0.283±0.48	0.222±0.35	0.141±0.14	0.133±0.14	0.157±0.17	0.145±0.15
$N=100$	ML	0.064±0.03	0.020±0.03	0.014±0.01	0.012±0.01	0.011±0.01	0.011±0.01
	MML	0.063±0.03	0.019±0.03	0.013±0.01	0.012±0.01	0.011±0.01	0.011±0.01

As shown in Table 1, the MML estimators resulted in estimates which are closer than ML to the true model, with smaller KL distances for all cases except when $N = 100$ and ν is large (≥ 25.0). It is possible that a different choice of priors in subsection 2.3 will lead to MML outperforming ML in all cases. It is also possible that Strict MML [23][21], Dowe's MMLD or another refinement of equation (3) [23] will do likewise. The MML method performed a robust estimation with smaller standard errors of the resulting KL distances for all but one estimation (namely, $\sigma = 5.0, \nu = 50.0, N = 100$).

4   Clustering

Clustering, which is also known as mixture modelling [6][16][11][8][12], intrinsic classification [3][20], and numerical taxonomy, models a statistical distribution by a mixture (a weighted sum) of other distributions, as well as partitioning an unknown number of components (or classes or clusters) of a dataset into a finite number of components.

Such a cluster analysis will result in a description of the number of components, the relative abundances (or mixing proportions) of each component, their distribution parameters and the members that belong to them. In the latter, an issue arises as to whether each datum is assigned totally to the component or not. This issue affects the application of the MML principle to the clustering problem, and is explained further in the next section (see part 1d of the message).

In the case of the clustering problem of the t distributions, McLachlan, Peel, Basford and Adams [13] have introduced the EMMIX software for the fitting of a mixture of the Gaussian and t components. This allows datasets to be fitted as Gaussian distributions as well as t distributions. A comparison of the proposed clustering method to the application of the t distribution in the EMMIX software is provided in subsection 6.4.

5   MML Clustering

The application of MML to the problem of clustering was first introduced by Wallace and Boulton [18]. This application involved discrete multinomial and continuous Gaussian distributions. Wallace and Dowe [20][22] extended this work by adding two other distributions - Poisson and von Mises circular. An alternative MML-based approach to mixture modelling was also given very recently by Figueiredo and Jain [7].

In order to apply the MML principle to a clustering problem, a two-part message conveying the mixture model needs to be constructed. The first part of the message encodes the hypothesis, H, and the second part encodes the data in light of the hypothesis. The hypothesis comprises several concatenated message fragments, stating in turn:

1a The number of components: Assuming that all numbers are considered as equally likely up to some constant, (say, 100), this part can be encoded using a uniform distribution over the range.

1b The relative abundances (or mixing proportions) of each component: Considering the relative abundances of an M-component mixture, this is the same as the condition for an M-state multinomial distribution. The parameter estimation and the message length calculation of the multi-state distribution have been elaborated upon in subsection 2.1.

1c For each component, the distribution parameters of its attributes: In this case, an attribute of a component is inferred both as a Gaussian and a t distribution as in subsections 2.2 and 2.3, respectively. The model which results in a shorter message length is chosen.

1d For each thing, the component to which the thing is estimated to belong.

The method of assignment of things to components has changed since the MML clustering was first introduced by Wallace and Boulton [18]. The original coding scheme [18] utilised a total assignment of things to components. That scheme was inefficient because of the possible savings that can be made when two components overlap substantially [17]. The original - total assignment - scheme can also lead to inconsistent estimates, where the difference between the means of components is over-estimated and the standard deviation of components are under-estimated, as shown in Fig. 1.

Instead of assigning things totally to a component, a partial assignment was proposed [17][22]. In a partial assignment, data things are partially assigned to

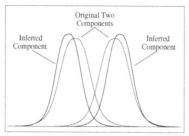

Fig. 1. Inferring two substantially overlapping components using a total assignment.

each component with a certain probability. Below, we compare the total assignment with the partial assignment in terms of their message length.

In a total assignment, let $p(j, x), j = 1, \ldots, M$, be the probability of component j generating datum x. The message length to encode x which is assigned to its best component is equal to $-\log(\max_j p(j, x))$. On the other hand, for a partial assignment, let $P(x) = \sum_{j=1}^{M} p(j, x)$, be the total probability of any component generating datum x. The datum x will then be assigned to a component j with probability $p(j, x)/P(x)$. The message length of this assignment is equal to $-\log(P(x))$, which is shorter than that of a total assignment by $\log_2(P(x)/\max_j p(j, x))$ on each datum x.

In the case where a datum x has an equal probability of being assigned to more than one component, e.g. $p(1, x) = p(2, x) = P(x)/2$, a saving of 1 bit of information can be gained by assigning x to either component 1 or component 2 at random.

Once the first part of the message is stated, the second part of the message will encode the data in light of the hypothesis stated in the first part of the message. Since the objective of the MML principle is to find the hypothesis that minimises the message length, we do not need to actually encode the message. In other words, we only need to calculate the length of the message and find the hypothesis that gives the shortest/minimum message length.

6   Experimental Evaluations

In testing the MML clustering of Gaussian and t distributions, three examples of bivariate mixture datasets were generated artificially. The data points were generated from Gaussian as well as t distributions. The procedure in generating these artificial mixture datasets is similar to that used by Baxter and Oliver [2].

Below, we compare the modelling results of our method to those obtained using the MML clustering of Gaussian distributions only. The comparison of the latter clustering method to other criteria such as AIC, BIC, PC and ICOMP can be found in [2].

At the end of this section, we also compare the modelling results of 20 datasets generated using the same parameters as the datasets mentioned above. The comparison is performed in terms of the resulting number of components and includes two other criteria such as the Akaike Information Criterion (AIC) [1] and Schwarz's Bayesian Information Criterion (BIC) [14].

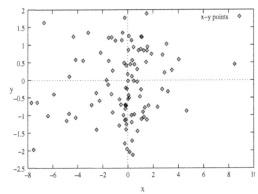

Fig. 2. One-component mixture of 100 bivariate data points generated from a combination of t and Gaussian distributions: $t_{\nu_x=1}(\mu_x = 0, \sigma_x^2 = 1) \times N(\mu_y = 0, \sigma_y^2 = 1)$.

Table 2. Comparison of two different MML modelling methods: (i) using Gaussian and t distributions, and (ii) Gaussian distributions only. (Recall that a Gaussian distribution is a special case of the t distribution with $\nu = \infty$.) 1 nit $= \log_2 e$ bits.

	MML Gaussian or t	MML All Gaussian
MessLen	754.310 nits	771.976 nits
Attribute 1	(assume measurement accuracy $\epsilon = 1.0$)	
Mean(μ)	0.101	-0.372
SD(σ)	1.199	2.609
DegOfF(ν)	**1.612**	∞
Attribute 2	(assume measurement accuracy $\epsilon = 1.0$)	
Mean(μ)	-0.134	-0.134
SD(σ)	0.968	0.968
DegOfF(ν)	∞	∞

6.1 One-Component Bivariate Mixture

Here, we extend the inference results from Section 3. The dataset used in this example (see Fig. 2) consists of 100 bivariate data points which are generated from a t distribution with three parameters: $\mu_x = 0.0$, $\sigma_x = 1.0$ and $\nu_x = 1.0$, and a Gaussian distribution with two parameters: $\mu_y = 0.0$ and $\sigma_y = 1.0$.

The modelling result (see Table 2) shows that the message length in modelling the dataset using the MML clustering of Gaussian and t distributions was shorter by roughly 18 nits than that when using Gaussian distributions only. This is an effect of the inference of the first attribute of the dataset, whereby using a combination of Gaussian and t distributions, the attribute was inferred as a t

distribution with degrees of freedom, $\nu = 1.612$. The result also shows that data from a t distribution can be inferred as coming from a Gaussian distribution with a larger standard deviation. However, since the latter inference resulted in a longer message length, the method automatically chose the t distribution as the inferred distribution.

6.2   Two-Component Bivariate Mixture

The dataset in this example, as shown in Fig. 3, is generated from a bivariate mixture with two components. The first component is a combination of a t distribution with three parameters: $\mu_{x1} = 0.0$, $\sigma_{x1} = 1.0$ and $\nu_{x1} = 1.0$ and a Gaussian distribution with two parameters: $\mu_{y1} = 0.0$ and $\sigma_{y1} = 1.0$. The data points in the second component are generated from two Gaussian distributions with two parameters, $\mu_{x2} = 2.0$ and $\sigma_{x2} = 1.0$ for the first attribute and $\mu_{y2} = 3.5$ and $\sigma_{y2} = 1.0$ for the second attribute. Both components have 50 data points.

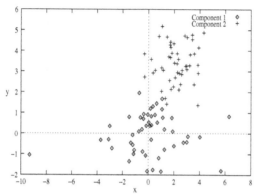

Fig. 3. Two-component mixture of 100 bivariate data points generated from a combination of t and Gaussian distributions: $0.5(t_{\nu_{x1}=1}(\mu_{x1} = 0, \sigma_{x1}^2 = 1) \times N(\mu_{y1} = 0, \sigma_{y1}^2 = 1)) + 0.5(N(\mu_{x2} = 2, \sigma_{x2}^2 = 1) \times N(\mu_{y2} = 3.5, \sigma_{y2}^2 = 1))$

Modelling the artificially generated dataset from Fig. 3, the first attribute of the first component was fitted as a t distribution with degrees of freedom, $\nu = 2.008$, instead of as a Gaussian distribution. Inferring the attribute as a t distribution resulted in a shorter message length by roughly 11 nits compared to when the attribute was inferred as Gaussian. In this result, the mixing proportions of the components for both clustering methods were almost the same with 0.527:0.473 for our MML Gaussian and t method and 0.524:0476 for the MML modelling using Gaussian distributions only.

6.3   Three-Component Bivariate Mixture

The example here (see Fig. 4) is generated from a bivariate mixture with three components. The first component is generated from two Gaussian distributions with two parameters each, $\mu_{x1} = -2.0$ and $\sigma_{x1} = 1.0$ and $\mu_{y1} = -3.5$ and $\sigma_{y1} = 1.0$, respectively. The second component is a combination of a t distribution with three parameters: $\mu_{x2} = 0.0$, $\sigma_{x2} = 1.0$ and $\nu_{x2} = 1.0$ and a Gaussian distribution with two parameters: $\mu_{y2} = 0.0$ and $\sigma_{y2} = 1.0$. The third component is from two Gaussian distributions with two parameters each: $\mu_{x3} = 2.0$ and $\sigma_{x3} = 1.0$ and $\mu_{y3} = 3.5$ and $\sigma_{y3} = 1.0$, respectively. Each component has 50 data points.

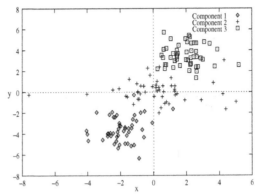

Fig. 4. Three-component mixture of 150 bivariate data points generated from a combination of t and Gaussians: $1/3(N(\mu_{x1} = -2, \sigma_{x1}^2 = 1) \times N(\mu_{y1} = -3.5, \sigma_{y1}^2 = 1)) + 1/3(t_{\nu_{x2}=1}(\mu_{x2} = 0, \sigma_{x2}^2 = 1) \times N(\mu_{y2} = 0, \sigma_{y2}^2 = 1)) + 1/3(N(\mu_{x3} = 2, \sigma_{x3}^2 = 1) \times N(\mu_{y3} = 3.5, \sigma_{y3}^2 = 1))$

Modelling the dataset illustrated in Fig. 4, the first attribute of the second component, which was generated from a t distribution, was inferred as a t distribution with degrees of freedom, $\nu = 2.225$. This inference resulted in a shorter message length by about 3 nits compared to that when the attribute was inferred as a Gaussian distribution. In this result, the mixing proportions of the components when using Gaussian and t distributions were mostly the same as those when using Gaussian distributions only.

6.4   Alternative Clustering of t Distributions: EMMIX

In 1999, McLachlan, Peel, Basford and Adams [13] introduced the EMMIX software, which allows a dataset to be modelled as either a mixture of only (correlated) Gaussian distributions or a mixture of only (correlated) t distributions. The software, which is mainly used to model datasets as a mixture of Gaussian distributions, is extended by providing an option to change the distribution of the components from Gaussian to t distributions. The parameter estimations are performed using the ML method by utilising the EM algorithm and its extensions, the ECM and ECME algorithms. The value of ν can be fixed in advance or estimated from the data for each component using the ECM algorithm.

Our MML clustering of uncorrelated Gaussian and uncorrelated t distributions allows all attributes in all components to be t or Gaussian. On the other hand, the EMMIX software permits attributes to be correlated within components (or clusters or classes) but it currently restricts either all attributes in all classes to be Gaussian or all to be t. Bearing this in mind, the empirical comparisons to follow - where all attributes are uncorrelated and some can be t and some can be Gaussian - are probably somewhat unfair in favour of our method.

Table 3. Comparison of the modelling results in terms of the resulting number of components using MML and other criteria such as AIC and BIC, based on 20 trials.

Mixture	One-Component					Two-Component					Three-Component				
Component Number	1	2	3	4	5	1	2	3	4	5	1	2	3	4	5
MML Gaussian & t	20	0	0	0	0	0	20	0	0	0	0	2	18	0	0
AIC Gaussian Only*	0	0	5	7	8	0	0	0	7	13	0	0	0	6	14
BIC Gaussian Only*	0	18	2	0	0	0	13	6	1	0	0	2	12	6	0
AIC t Only*	0	0	2	3	15	0	0	2	2	16	0	0	0	3	17
BIC t Only*	7	12	1	0	0	0	15	5	0	0	0	3	15	2	0

*Modelled using the EMMIX software [13]

6.5 Empirical Comparison: Number of Components

We consider here modelling the datasets, which are generated artificially from the same parameters as those used in subsections 6.1, 6.2 and 6.3, repeatedly 20 times. We also fed the datasets to the EMMIX software in order to see how the modelling criteria used in the software (AIC and BIC) behave toward the datasets.

As shown in Table 3, our proposed MML method showed good performance in determining the number of components in the datasets. AIC and BIC, on the other hand, rarely underfitted the datasets by inferring a smaller number of components. However, BIC showed better modelling than AIC, where for most modellings, AIC chose different numbers of components and tended to highly overfit the true number of these components. Compared to our method, BIC overfitted nearly half of the datasets investigated, especially when modelling one-component mixture datasets. See subsection 6.4 regarding the fairness of these comparisons.

7 Conclusion

In conclusion, we draw the attention of the reader to the following results from Sections 3 and 6:

1. The proposed method shows a better performance in estimating parameters of a single t distribution compared to the ML method for all settings but for large ν and large numbers of data. Smaller standard errors of the estimations proved that the proposed MML estimation is a robust method in performing parameter estimation (see Section 3).
2. The proposed method provides the flexibility for fitting an attribute of a component either as a Gaussian or a t distribution (see subsections 6.1, 6.2 and 6.3), although our attributes are currently uncorrelated.
3. The proposed method shows a good performance in determining the number of components in a dataset. MML rarely had more components than the true model (see subsection 6.5).

References

1. Akaike H.: A new look at the statistical model identification. IEEE Transactions on Automatic Control, AC-19, 6 (1974) 716–723
2. Baxter R.A. and Oliver J.J.: Finding overlapping components with MML. Statistics and Computing, 10 (2000) 5–16
3. Boulton D.M.: The information criterion for intrinsic classification. Ph.D. Thesis, Dept. Computer Science, Monash University Clayton 3800 Australia (1975)
4. Chaitin G.J.: On the length of programs for computing finite sequences. Journal of the Association for Computing Machinery, 13 (1966) 547–569
5. Conway J.H. and Sloane N.J.A.: Sphere Packings Lattices and Groups. 3rd edn. Springer-Verlag, London (1998)
6. Everitt B.S. and Hand D.J.: Finite Mixture Distributions. Chapman and Hall, London (1981)
7. Figueiredo, M.A.T. and Jain A.K.: Unsupervised Learning of Finite Mixture Models. IEEE Transactions on Pattern Analysis and Machine Intelligence, 24(3) (2002) 381–396.
8. Hunt L.A. and Jorgensen M.A.: Mixture model clustering using the multimix program. Australian and New Zealand Journal of Statistics, 41(2) (1999) 153–171.
9. Lebedev N.N.: Special functions and their applications. Prentice-Hall, NJ (1965)
10. Liu C. and Rubin D.B.: ML Estimation of t distribution using EM and its extensions, ECM and ECME. Statistica Sinica, 5 (1995) 19–39.
11. McLachlan G.J. and Basford K.E.: Mixture Models. Marcel Dekker, NY (1988)
12. McLachlan G.J. and Peel D.: Finite Mixture Models. John Wiley, NY USA (2000)
13. McLachlan G.J., Peel D., Basford K.E. and Adams P.: The EMMIX software for the fitting of mixtures of Normal and t-components. Journal of Statistical Software, 4 (1999)
14. Schwarz G.: Estimating the dimension of a model. Annals of Statistics, 6 (1978) 461–464
15. Solomonoff R.J.: A formal theory of inductive inference. Information and Control, 7 (1964) 1–22, 224–254
16. Titterington D.M., Smith A.F.M. and Makov U.E.: Statistical Analysis of Finite Mixture Distributions. John Wiley and Sons, Chichester (1985)
17. Wallace C.S. An improved program for classification. Proceedings of the Ninth Australian Computer Science Conference (ACSC-9), 8, Monash University Australia (1986) 357–366
18. Wallace C.S. and Boulton D.M.: An information measure for classification. Computer Journal, 11(2), (1968) 185–194
19. Wallace C.S. and Dowe D.L.: MML estimation of the von Mises concentration parameter. Technical Report TR 93/193, Dept. of Computer Science, Monash University Clayton 3800 Australia (1993)
20. Wallace C.S. and Dowe D.L.: Intrinsic classification by MML – the Snob program. In Zhang C. et al. (Eds.), Proc. 7th Australia Joint Conference on Artificial Intelligence. World Scientific, Singapore (1994) 37–44
21. Wallace C.S., and Dowe D.L.: Minimum Message Length and Kolmogorov Complexity. Computer Journal, 42(4) (1999) 270-283, Special issue on Kolmogorov Complexity.
22. Wallace C.S., and Dowe D.L.: MML clustering of multi-state, Poisson, von Mises circular and Gaussian distributions. Statistics and Computing, 10(1) (2000) 73–83
23. Wallace C.S. and Freeman P.R.: Estimation and Inference by Compact Coding. Journal of the Royal Statistical Society Series B, Vol. 49(3) (1987) 240–265

Optimizing Kernel-Based Nonlinear Subspace Methods Using Prototype Reduction Schemes

Sang-Woon Kim[1] and B. John Oommen[2]

[1] Div. of Computer Science and Engineering, Myongji University, Yongin, 449-728
Korea. `kimsw@mju.ac.kr`
[2] School of Computer Science, Carleton University, Ottawa, ON, K1S 5B6, Canada.
`oommen@scs.carleton.ca`

Abstract. The subspace method of pattern recognition is a classification technique in which pattern classes are specified in terms of linear subspaces spanned by their respective class-based basis vectors. To overcome the limitations of the linear methods, Kernel based Nonlinear Subspace (KNS) methods have been recently proposed in the literature. In KNS, the kernel Principal Component Analysis (kPCA) has been employed to get principal components, not in an input space, but in a high-dimensional space, where the components of the space are non-linearly related to the input variables.

In this paper, we suggest a computationally superior mechanism to solve the problem. Rather than define the matrix K with the whole data set and compute the principal components, we propose that the data be reduced into a smaller representative subset using a Prototype Reduction Scheme (PRS). Our experimental results demonstrate that the proposed mechanism *dramatically* reduces the computation time without sacrificing the classification accuracy for samples involving real-life data sets as well as artificial data sets. The results especially demonstrate the computational advantage for *large* data sets, such as those involved in data mining and text categorization applications.

Keywords. Kernel Principal Component Analysis (kPCA), Kernel based Nonlinear Subspace (KNS) Method, Prototype Reduction Schemes (PRS).

1 Introduction

The subspace method of pattern recognition is a technique in which the pattern classes are not primarily defined as bounded regions or zones in a feature space, but rather given in terms of linear subspaces defined by the basis vectors, one for each class [1]. The length of a vector projected onto a class subspace, or the distance of the vector from the class subspace, is a measure of similarity or degree of membership for that particular class, and serves as the discriminant function of these methods. More specifically, the following steps are necessary for the methods: First, we compute the covariance matrix or scatter matrix. Then, we compute its eigenvectors and normalize them by the principal components

R.I. McKay and J. Slaney (Eds.): AI 2002, LNAI 2557, pp. 155–166, 2002.
© Springer-Verlag Berlin Heidelberg 2002

analysis or the Karhuen-Loève (KL) expansion technique. Finally, we compute the projections (or distances) of a test pattern vector onto (or from) the class subspaces spanned by the subset of principal eigenvectors.

Various subspace classifiers, such as CLAFIC (CLAss Feature Compression) [1], the learning subspace method [1], and the mutual subspace method [2], have been proposed in the literature. All of the subspace classifiers have employed the Principal Components Analysis (PCA) to compute the basis vectors by which the class subspaces are spanned. The basic idea of the PCA is to represent N-dimensional data by a set of orthogonal directions - capturing most of the variance in the data. In practice, we describe the data with reduced dimensionality by extracting a few meaningful principal components, implying that we retain the most significant aspects of the structure in the data. Since the PCA is a linear algorithm, it is clearly beyond its capabilities to extract nonlinear structures from the data, which essentially limits the use of such classifiers.

To overcome the above limitation, a kernel Principal Components Analysis (kPCA) has been proposed in [3]. The kPCA provides an elegant way of dealing with nonlinear problems in an input space R^N by mapping them to linear ones in a feature space, F. That is, a dot product in space R^N corresponds to mapping the data into a possibly high-dimensional dot product space F by a nonlinear map $\Phi : R^N \to F$, and taking the dot product in the latter space.

Recently, using the kPCA, kernel-based subspace methods, such as the Subspace method in Hilbert Space (SHS) [4], Kernel based Nonlinear Subspace (KNS) method [5], Kernel Based Learning (KBL) algorithms [6], and Kernel Mutual Subspace (KMS) method [7], have been proposed. All of them utilize the *kernel trick* to obtain the kernel PCA components by solving a similar linear eigenvalue problem as explained above for the linear PCA. The only difference is that the size of the problem is decided by the *number* of data points, and not by the dimension. The above studies report that the performance of nonlinear subspace methods is better than that of linear methods possessing the same number of principal components.

On the other hand, in kPCA, to map the data set $\{x_1, x_2, \cdots, x_n\}$, (where each $x_i \in R^N$) into a feature space F, we have to define an $n \times n$ matrix, K, the so-called kernel matrix. This corresponds to the $N \times N$ covariance matrix of the linear PCA. Observe that the dimension of K is equivalent to the number of data points, n. The situation is, unfortunately, ironic. To get a good classifier with good training estimates, one typically requires a large training set. But, when a large number of observations are available, the kernel matrix has a large dimensionality. Furthermore, the same problem with a small training set yields a poorer classifier!

To solve the computational problem, a number of methods, such as the power method with deflation [3], the method of estimating K with a subset data [3], the Sparse Greedy matrix Approximation (SGA) [8] and the sparse kernel PCA method based on the probabilistic feature-space PCA concept [9], have been proposed. In [3], a method of estimating the matrix K from a subset of $n'(< n)$ data points, while still extracting principal components from all the n data points, was considered. Also, in [8], an approximation technique to construct a compressed kernel matrix K' such that the norm of the residual matrix $K - K'$ is minimized, was proposed.

We propose to solve the problem by reducing the size of the design set without sacrificing the performance. This is achieved by using a Prototype Reduction Scheme (PRS). A PRS is a way of reducing the number of training vectors while simultaneously insisting that the classifiers built on the reduced design set perform as well, or nearly as well, as the classifiers built on the original design set. The PRS has been explored for various purposes, and has resulted in the development of many algorithms [10], [11] such as the Condensed Nearest Neighbor (CNN) rule [12], the Prototypes for Nearest Neighbor (PNN) classifiers [13] (including a modified Chang's method proposed by Bezdek), the Vector Quantization (VQ) technique [15], the Learning Vector Quantization (LVQ) [17], Support Vector Machines (SVM) [16] etc[1]. Apart from the above PRS methods, the SVM can also be used as a means of selecting prototype vectors. Observe that these new vectors can be subsequently adjusted by means of an LVQ3-type algorithm. Based on this idea, a new prototype reduction method of hybridizing the SVM and the LVQ3 was introduced in [18].

In this paper we propose to utilize PRS algorithms to devise a method of reducing the computational burden of the kernel based nonlinear subspace methods. We highlight the salient contributions of the paper below.

1.1 Contributions of the Paper

PRS have typically been used as methods by which the prototypes have been selected or created in the design of pattern recognition systems. In this paper, we, first of all, show that PRS can also be used as a *tool* to achieve an intermediate goal, namely, to minimize the number of samples that are *subsequently* used in a subspace based pattern recognition system, which, *in turn* is used to design the classifier. This, in itself, is novel to the field of the applications of PRS.

The second contribution of this paper is the method by which we have reduced the computational burden of a kernel based nonlinear subspace method. Previous methods(see [3], [8], [9]), though innovative, are computationally expensive because of the associated matrix (eigenvalue/eigenvector) operations required in obtaining the basis vectors spanning the subspaces. These typically utilize particular features (for example, the sparseness) of the $n \times n$ kernel matrix, where n is the number of sample points. In this paper, we show that the burden can be reduced significantly by not considering the kernel matrix *at all*. Instead, we rather define a reduced-kernel matrix by first preprocessing the training points with a PRS scheme. Further, the PRS scheme does not necessarily have to *select* a reduced set of data points. Indeed, it can rather *create* a reduced set of prototypes from which, in turn, the reduced-kernel matrix is determined. All of these concepts are novel to the field of designing kernel-based nonlinear subspace methods.

---

[1] Bezdek *et al* [11], who have composed an excellent survey of the field, report that there are "zillions!" of methods for finding prototypes (see page 1459 of [11]).

2   Kernel Based Nonlinear Subspace (KNS) Method

In this section, we provide a *brief* overview to the kernel based nonlinear subspace method. We assume that the reader is reasonably acquainted with the principles linear subspace methods [1] (also described in some detail in [21]). Indeed, since the eigenvectors are computed linearly by the PCA, these classifiers are very effective for linear problems, but not good for non-linear feature distributions. This has naturally motivated various developments of nonlinear PCA's, including the kernel PCA.

2.1   Kernel Principal Components Analysis (kPCA)

In the previous section we explained how the eigenvalue problem was solved in the *input* space R^N. To extend this, we repeat the same computation in another space F, which is referred to as the feature space. The space F is related to the input space by a possibly nonlinear map

$$\Phi : R^N \to F, \tag{1}$$

which takes a vector $\boldsymbol{x}$ into $\Phi(\boldsymbol{x})$, where $\Phi(\boldsymbol{x})$ could have an arbitrarily large, (and possibly infinite), dimensionality. For each class, j, the Φ-based scatter matrix is estimated by $\Sigma'_j = \frac{1}{n} \sum_{i=1}^{n} \Phi(\boldsymbol{x}_i)\Phi(\boldsymbol{x}_i)^T, \Phi(\boldsymbol{x}_i) \in \omega_j$. The first $p'_j(\leq n)$ eigenvectors, $\boldsymbol{U} = \left(\boldsymbol{U}_1, \cdots, \boldsymbol{U}_{p'_j}\right)$, of the matrix Σ'_j, in the order of decreasing eigenvalues $\lambda'_1 \geq \cdots \geq \lambda'_{p'_j}$, are computed by

$$\lambda' \boldsymbol{U} = \Sigma'_j \boldsymbol{U} = \frac{1}{n} \sum_{i=1}^{n} \left(\Phi(\boldsymbol{x}_i) \cdot \boldsymbol{U}\right) \Phi(\boldsymbol{x}_i). \tag{2}$$

Here, if we do not know the function Φ explicitly, we can not compute the basis vectors directly from (2). Fortunately, however, we can compute projections of an arbitrary pattern onto the directions of the basis vectors. Since all eigenvectors with nonzero eigenvalues must be in the span of the mapped data, $\Phi(\boldsymbol{x}_i), i = 1, \cdots, n$,

$$\boldsymbol{U} = \sum_{i=1}^{n} \boldsymbol{\alpha}_i \Phi(\boldsymbol{x}_i). \tag{3}$$

By multiplying with $\Phi(\boldsymbol{x}_i)$, (2) becomes:

$$\lambda'(\Phi(\boldsymbol{x}_i) \cdot \boldsymbol{U}) = (\Phi(\boldsymbol{x}_i) \cdot \Sigma'_j \boldsymbol{U}), i = 1, \cdots, n. \tag{4}$$

Here, to compute the expansion coefficients, $\boldsymbol{\alpha}_i, i = 1, \cdots, n$, we define an $n \times n$ matrix, K, whose elements are

$$K_{ij} = (\Phi(\boldsymbol{x}_i) \cdot \Phi(\boldsymbol{x}_j)) = k(\boldsymbol{x}_i, \boldsymbol{x}_j), 1 \leq i, j \leq n. \tag{5}$$

Using this formulation, an eigenvalue problem for the $\boldsymbol{\alpha}_i$ is obtained as follows:

$$\lambda \boldsymbol{\alpha} = K \boldsymbol{\alpha}, \tag{6}$$

where the $\boldsymbol{\alpha} = (\boldsymbol{\alpha}_1 \cdots \boldsymbol{\alpha}_{p'})^T$ denotes the complete set of the first $p'(\leq n)$ eigenvectors of K which correspond to the largest p' non-zero eigenvalues, $\lambda_1 \geq \cdots \geq \lambda_{p'}$.

The solutions of $\boldsymbol{\alpha}$ further need to be normalized by imposing $(\boldsymbol{U}_k \cdot \boldsymbol{U}_k) = 1, k = 1, \cdots, p'$ in F. From (3), (5), and (6), we observe that $(\boldsymbol{U}_k \cdot \boldsymbol{U}_k) = \sum_{i,j=1}^{n} \alpha_{ki} \alpha_{kj} (\Phi(\boldsymbol{x}_i) \cdot \Phi(\boldsymbol{x}_j)) = \lambda_k (\boldsymbol{\alpha}_k \cdot \boldsymbol{\alpha}_k)$. After we perform a normalization, we see that $(\boldsymbol{U}_i \cdot \boldsymbol{U}_j)$ is δ_{ij}, the Kroneker-*delta* function, since :

$$(\boldsymbol{U}_k \cdot \boldsymbol{U}_k) = \lambda_k (\boldsymbol{\alpha}_k \cdot \boldsymbol{\alpha}_k) = \lambda_k \left(\frac{\boldsymbol{U}_k}{\sqrt{\lambda_k}} \cdot \frac{\boldsymbol{U}_k}{\sqrt{\lambda_k}} \right) = 1, \tag{7}$$

$$(\boldsymbol{U}_i \cdot \boldsymbol{U}_j) = 0, \; (whenever \; i \neq j). \tag{8}$$

Thus, to extract principle components of a new pattern $\boldsymbol{z}$ in F, we simply project the mapped pattern $\Phi(\boldsymbol{z})$ onto a direction of $\boldsymbol{U}_j$ as follows:

$$(\boldsymbol{U}_j \cdot \Phi(\boldsymbol{z})) = \sum_{i=1}^{n} \alpha_{ji} (\Phi(\boldsymbol{x}_i) \cdot \Phi(\boldsymbol{z})) = \frac{1}{\sqrt{\lambda_j}} \sum_{i=1}^{n} U_{ji} k(\boldsymbol{x}_i, \boldsymbol{z}). \tag{9}$$

Although it is nearly impossible to compute the basis vectors corresponding to the eigenvectors of (2), it is possible from (9), to compute the projections onto the directions of basis vectors. The dot product for the principal components extraction can be *implicitly* computed in F, without explicitly using the mapping Φ. Such a computational methodology is called the *"kernel trick"*, using which, nonlinear subspace classifiers can be designed.

2.2   Nonlinear Subspace Methods

The Kernel-based Nonlinear Subspace (KNS) method is a subspace classifier, where the kPCA is employed as the specific nonlinear feature extractor. Given a set of n N-dimensional data samples $X = (\boldsymbol{x}_1, \cdots, \boldsymbol{x}_n)^T \in \omega_i$ and a kernel function $k(\cdot, \cdot)$, the column matrix of the orthogonal eigenvectors, $\boldsymbol{U} = (\boldsymbol{U}_1, \cdots, \boldsymbol{U}_{p_i'})$, and the diagonal matrix of the eigenvalues, Λ, can be computed from the kernel matrix $K_{ij} = k(\boldsymbol{x}_i, \boldsymbol{x}_j), 1 \leq i, j \leq n$. Then, from (7), the length of the projection of a new test pattern $\boldsymbol{z}$ onto the principal directions of $\boldsymbol{U}$ in F is

$$\|P_i'\|^2 = \sum_{j=1}^{p_i'} \sum_{i=1}^{n} (\alpha_{ji} k(\boldsymbol{x}_i, \boldsymbol{z}))^2 = \|\frac{1}{\sqrt{\Lambda}} \boldsymbol{U}^T k(X, \boldsymbol{z})\|^2. \tag{10}$$

Thus, the analogous decision rule as that of linear subspace classifiers, classifies each $\boldsymbol{z}$ into the class on whose "class subspace" it has the longest projection as follows:

$$\forall j \neq i, \; \|P_i'\|^2 > \|P_j'\|^2 \Rightarrow \boldsymbol{z} \in \omega_i. \tag{11}$$

In KNS, the subspace dimensions, $p_i', i = 1, \cdots, C$, have a strong influence on the performance of subspace classifiers. In order to get a high classification accuracy, we have to select a large dimension. However, designing with dimensions which are too large leads to low performances due to the overlapping of the resultant subspaces. Also, since the speed of computation for the discriminant function of subspace classifiers is inversely proportional to the dimension, the latter should be kept small.

Various dimension selection methods have been reported in the literature [1], [19]. The simplest approach is to select a global dimension to be used for all the classes. A more popular method is that of selecting different dimensions for the various classes based on the cumulative proportion, α, which is defined as follow:

$$\alpha(p_i') = \sum_{i=1}^{p_i'} \lambda_i \bigg/ \sum_{i=1}^{n} \lambda_i . \tag{12}$$

In this method, the p_i' of each class for the data sets is determined by considering the cumulative proportion, $\alpha(p_i')$. For each class, the kernel matrix K is computed using the available training samples for that class. The eigenvectors and eigenvalues are computed, and the cumulative sum of the eigenvalues, normalized by the trace of K, is compared to a fixed number.

The overall procedure for kernel based nonlinear subspace classifiers is summarized as follows:

1. For every class, j, compute the kernel matrix, K, using the given training data set $\{x_i\}_{i=1}^{n}$ and the kernel function $k(\cdot, \cdot)$;
2. For every class, j, compute the normalized eigenvectors of K in F, and select the subspace dimension, p_j';
3. For all the test patterns, we compute the projections of the pattern onto the eigenvectors, and classify it by the decision rule of (11).

In the above, the computation of principal component projections for a pattern requires evaluation of the kernel function with respect to *all* the training patterns. This is unfortunate, because, in practice, the computation is excessive for large data sets. We overcome this limitation by reducing the training set using a PRS.

3   Prototype Reduction Schemes (PRS)

Various data reduction methods have been proposed in the literature - two excellent surveys are found in [10], [11]. The most pertinent ones are reviewed in [21] in two groups: the conventional methods and a newly proposed hybrid method. Among the conventional methods, the CNN and the SVM are chosen as representative schemes of *selective* methods. The former is one of first methods proposed, and the latter is more recent. As opposed to these, the PNN and VQ (or SOM) are considered to fall within the family of prototype-*creative* algorithms.

The unabridged paper [21] also describes a newly-reported hybrid scheme, the Kim_Oommen Hybridized Technique, [18], which is based on the philosophy of invoking *creating* and *adjusting* phases. First, a reduced set of initial prototypes or code-book vectors is chosen by any of the previously reported methods, and then their optimal positions are learned with an LVQ3-type algorithm, thus, minimizing the average classification error. All these methods have been used to optimize KNS.

4   Solution Proposed

The fundamental problem we encounter is that of computing the solution to the kernel subspace classifier from the set of training samples. This, in turn, involves four essential phases, namely that of computing the kernel matrix, computing *its* eigenvalues and eigenvectors, extracting the principal components of the kernel matrix from among these eigenvectors, and finally, projecting the samples to be processed onto the reduced basis vectors. We observe, first of all, that all of these phases depend on the size of the data set. In particular, the most time consuming phase involves computing the eigenvalues and eigenvectors of the kernel matrix.

There is an underlying irony in the method, in itself. For a good and effective training phase, we, typically, desire a large data set. But if the training set is large, the dimensionality of the kernel matrix is correspondingly large, making the computations extremely expensive. On the other hand, a smaller training set makes the learning less accurate, although computations are correspondingly less.

There are a few ways by which the computational burden of the kernel subspace method can be reduced. Most of the reported schemes [3], [8], [9] resort to using the specific properties of the underlying kernel matrix, for example, its sparseness. Our technique is different.

The method we propose is by reducing the size of the training set. However, we do this, by not significantly reducing the accuracy of the resultant classifier. This is achieved by resorting to a PRS. The question now is essentially one of determining which of the training points we should retain. Rather than deciding to discard or retain the training points, we permit the user the choice of either *selecting* some of the training samples using methods such as the CNN, or *creating* a smaller set of samples using the methods such as those advocated in the PNN, VQ, and HYB. This reduced set effectively represents the new "training" set. Additionally, we also permit the user to migrate the resultant set by an LVQ3-type method to further enhance the quality of the reduced samples.

The PRS serves as a preprocessor to the n N-dimensional training samples to yield a subset of n' potentially new points, where $n' << n$. The "kernel" is now computed using this reduced set of points to yield the so-called *reduced-kernel* matrix. The eigenvalues and eigenvectors of *this* matrix are now computed, and the principal components of the kernel matrix are extracted from among *these* eigenvectors of smaller dimension. Notice now that the samples to be tested are projected onto the reduced basis directions represented by *these* vectors.

To investigate the computational advantage gained by resorting to such a PRS preprocessing phase, we observe, first of all, that the time used in determining the reduced prototypes is fractional compared to the time required for the expensive matrix-related operations. Once the reduced prototypes are obtained, the eigenvalue/eigenvector computations are significantly smaller since these computations are now done for a much smaller set, and thus for an $n' \times n'$ matrix. The net result of these two reductions is reflected in the time savings we report in the next section in which we discuss the experimental results obtained for artificial and real-life data sets.

5   Experimental Results: Artificial Data Sets

5.1   Experimental Data and Results

The proposed method has been rigorously tested and compared with many conventional KNS. This was first done by performing experiments on a number of "artificial" data sets taken from the data set named "Non_normal", which has also been employed as a benchmark experimental data set [15], [21], [22]. In our experiments, three distinct data sets, "Non_normal 1,2,3", were generated with different sizes of testing and training sets of cardinality 50, 500, and 5,000 respectively. In the data sets, all of the vectors were normalized within the range $[-1, 1]$ using their standard deviations. Also, for every class j, the data set for the class was randomly split into two subsets of equal size. One of them was used for training the classifiers as explained above, and the other subset was used in the validation (or testing) of the classifiers. The roles of these sets were later interchanged. In the interest of space we merely report the result for "Non_normal 3", observing that the results for "Non_normal 1" and "Non_normal 2" are identical.

We report below the run-time characteristics of the proposed algorithm for the artificial data sets, "Non_normal" as shown in Table 1. In this table, KNS represents the method of calculating the kernel matrix with the entire data set. The KNS-Sub1 (60%) and KNS-Sub2 (14%) are methods which pertain to calculating the kernel matrix with a randomly selected subset of the data points. Here, these figures of 60% and 14% are chosen randomly, by merely considering the number of prototypes for the CNN-KNS method. However, the SGA-KNS[2], CNN-KNS, PNN-KNS, VQ-KNS, and HYB-KNS are obtained by calculating the kernel matrix using the prototypes obtained with each respective method.

The proposed methods, the CNN-KNS, PNN-KNS, VQ-KNS, and HYB-KNS can be compared with the traditional versions, such as the KNS (which utilizes the entire set), the subset KNSs, and the SGA-KNS, using two criteria, namely, the classification accuracy (%), Acc, and the processing CPU-time (in seconds), T_1. We report below a summary of the results obtained for the case when one subset was used for training and the second for testing. The results when the roles of the sets are interchanged are almost identical. In the tables, each result is the averaged value of the training and the test sets, respectively.

In KNS, the subspace dimensions have a strong influence on the performance of subspace classifiers. Therefore, the subspace dimensions, the number of prototypes employed for constructing the kernel matrix, and their extraction times in the PRSs and the SGA, should be investigated. To assist in this task, we display the results of the Acc and T_1, the subspace dimensions for the two data sets,

---

[2] In the implementation of this method, we, at first, reduced the $n \times n$ kernel matrix into a matrix of dimensions $n' \times n'$ ($n' << n$) by using the SGA technique described in [8]. Subsequently, we employed the linear subspace method to compute the eigenvectors and projections of the *latter* matrix. The program code for the SGA algorithm was graciously provided by Dr. Alex Smola, of the Australian National University. The authors are very grateful to him for his assistance in this study.

Table 1. The experimental results of the proposed method for the artificial data sets "Non_normal 3". Here, the two values, Acc and T_1, are the classification accuracy (%) and the processing CPU-time (in seconds). The values (p_1, p_2), n', and t' are subspace dimensions of each class, the number of prototypes, and their extraction times, respectively. The final column, $1nn$, is the classification result obtained by invoking a 1-nearest neighbor rule, where the reference set consists of the n' prototypes. The experimental results for the data sets "Non_normal 1" and "Non_normal 2" are identical and found in [21].

Dataset	Methods	Acc	T_1	(p_1, p_2)	n'	t'	$1nn$
	KNS (Whole Set)	94.81	12,464.00	(1,1) (1,1)	5,000	0	91.94
	KNS-Sub1 (60%)	94.78	4,099.10	(1,1) (1,1)	3,000	0	86.50
	KNS-Sub2 (14%)	94.77	546.17	(1,1) (1,1)	700	0	92.57
Non_3	SGA-KNS	92.53	7.90	(1,1) (1,1)	8	1,305.35	90.73
	CNN-KNS	94.81	360.29	(1,1) (1,1)	491	58.57	91.63
	PNN-KNS	94.76	8,534.20	(1,1) (1,1)	4,124	53,516.33	92.04
	VQ-KNS	94.51	181.21	(1,1) (1,1)	256	3.19	90.12
	HYB-KNS	94.76	488.87	(1,1) (1,1)	641	58.38	42.29

(p_{11}, p_{12}), (p_{21}, p_{22}), the number of prototypes finally utilized, $n' = \frac{1}{2}(n_1' + n_2')$, and their extraction times, $t' = \frac{1}{2}(t_1' + t_2')$.

From Table 1, we can see that the processing CPU-time of the CNN-KNS, PNN-KNS, VQ-KNS, and HYB-KNS methods can be reduced significantly by employing a PRS such as the CNN, PNN, VQ, and HYB. Indeed, this is achieved without sacrificing the accuracy so much. It should be mentioned that the reduction of processing time increased dramatically when the size of the data sets was increased. Identical comments can also be made about the PNN-KNS, VQ-KNS, and HYB-KNS schemes. The reader should observe that the computational advantage gained is significant, and the accuracy lost is marginal.

6 Experimental Results: Real-Life Data Sets

6.1 Experimental Data

In order to further investigate the advantage gained by utilizing the proposed methods, we conducted experiments on "real-life" data sets, which we refer to as the "Ionosphere", "Sonar", "Arrhythmia", and "Adult4" sets. The information about these data sets is summarized in Table 2.

The data sets "Ionosphere (in short, Ionos)", "Sonar", "Arrhythmia (in short, Arrhy)" and "Adult4", which are real benchmark data sets, are cited from the UCI Machine Learning Repository[3]. The details of these data sets is well documented [21] and omitted here. In the above data sets, all of the vectors were normalized to be within the range $[-1, 1]$ using their standard deviations, and the data set for class j was randomly split into two subsets, $T_{j,t}$ and $T_{j,V}$, of equal size,which interchangeably played the roles of the training and testing sets.

---
[3] http://www.ics.uci.edu/mlearn/MLRepository.html

Table 2. The "real-life" data sets used for experiments. The vectors are divided into two sets of equal size, and used for training and validation, alternately.

Data Set Names	# of Patterns	# of Features	# of Classes
Ionosphere	351 (176; 175)	34	2
Sonar	208 (104; 104)	60	2
Arrhythmia	452 (226; 226)	279	16
Adult4	8,336 (4,168; 4,168)	14	2

Table 3. The experimental results of the proposed method for the real-life data set "Adult4". The notation for the table is exactly the same as in Table 1. The results of the proposed method for the real-life data sets "Ionos", "Sonar" and "Arrhy" are analogous and found in [21].

Data Sets	Methods	Acc	T_1	(p_1, p_2)		n'	t'	$1nn$
	KNS (Whole Set)	85.78	15,558.00	(13,12)	(13,12)	4,168	0	93.38
	KNS-Sub1 (60%)	84.74	4,515.10	(13,12)	(13,12)	2,501	0	92.81
	KNS-Sub2 (14%)	78.33	600.00	(13,12)	(13,12)	1,084	0	92.89
$Adult4$	SGA-KNS	81.80	244.85	(27,18)	(17,19)	301	108,135.50	81.33
	CNN-KNS	90.10	536.38	(8,8)	(8,8)	755	237.69	91.56
	PNN-KNS	88.86	456.85	(9,9)	(9,8)	660	16,863.64	89.35
	VQ-KNS	54.32	13.76	(7,8)	(7,8)	16	1.31	78.21
	HYB-KNS	91.96	287.70	(11,11)	(11,11)	440	5,453.64	92.75

We report the results obtained for the data captioned *Ionos* (not included in Table 3). Processing the entire data set of 176 samples required a CPU-time of 14.32, 5.12, 2.28 and 6.61 seconds, and yielded the accuracies of 84.38, 72.73, 70.46 and 88.92 % with the KNS, KNS-Sub1, KNS-Sub2 and SGA-KNS methods. However, if the samples were pre-processed by a PRS, to yield the CNN-KNS, PNN-KNS, VQ-KNS or HYB-KNS respectively, the times taken were 2.79, 2.24, 0.34 and 2.67 seconds respectively - which represented much smaller computation times. In this case, the accuracies actually *increased* to the values of 89.20, 91.20, 79.55 and 85.80 respectively. It should be mentioned that such an increase in accuracy is an exception, rather than a rule. The accuracy typically falls marginally when the KNS is preprocessed by a PRS. It is difficult to say that which PRS is the best or most appropriate ones for a given application. However, Table 3 shows the analogous results for the data set '*Adult4*'. From all the results obtained we observe that the HYB-KNS is uniformly superior to the others in terms of the classification accuracy, Acc, while requiring a little additional prototype extraction time, t'. We thus propose that this method is the most ideal candidate of choice for enhancing a KNS using a PRS.

From Table 3, we see that the computation time of the PNN is greater than that of the others. However, in [13], it has been suggested that the time could be significantly reduced by employing an algorithm similar to the minimal spanning tree, and using a method of associating with every sample point in the data set, two distances w_i and b_i. Also, in [14], Bezdek and his co-authors proposed a modification of the PNN. Based on the results obtained from experiments conducted on the Iris data set, the authors of [14] asserted that their modified form of the PNN yielded the best consistent reduced set for designing multiple-prototype classifiers. From the table, we also see that the classification accuracy of the VQ-KNS is lower than that of the others. This result may be based on the fact that the number of prototypes of the method, 16, is too small in comparison with that of the others such as 755, 660, and 440.

7 Conclusions

Kernel based nonlinear subspace methods suffer from a major disadvantage for large data sets, namely that of the excessive computational burden encountered by processing all the data points. In this paper, we suggest a computationally superior mechanism to solve the problem. Rather than define the kernel matrix and compute the principal components using the entire data set, we propose that the size of the data be reduced into a smaller prototype subset using any Prototype Reduction Schemes (PRS). Since PRS yields a smaller subset of data points that effectively samples the entire space to yield subsets of prototypes, these prototypes can be used quite effectively for composing a "reduced-kernel" matrix, thus alleviating the computational burden significantly.

The proposed method has been tested on artificial and real-life benchmark data sets, and compared with the conventional methods. The experimental results for both large data sets demonstrate that the proposed schemes can improve the learning speed of the proposed methods by an order of magnitude, while yielding almost the same classification accuracy.

Acknowledgements. The work of the first author was done while visiting with the School of Computer Science, Carleton University, Ottawa, Canada. The work of the second author was partially supported by the Natural Sciences and Engineering Research Council of Canada.

References

1. E. Oja, *Subspace Methods of Pattern Recognition*, Research Studies Press, 1983.
2. K. Maeda and S. Watanabe, "A pattern matching method with local structure", *IEICE Trans. Information & Systems*, vol. J68-D, no. 3, pp. 345–352, Mar. 1985.
3. B. Schölkopf, A. J. Smola, and K. -R. Müller, "Nonlinear component analysis as a kernel eigenvalue problem", *Neural Comput.*, vol. 10, pp. 1299–1319, 1998.
4. K. Tsuda, "Subspace method in Hilbert space", *IEICE Trans. Information & Systems*, vol. J82-D-II, no. 4, pp. 592–599, April 1999.
5. E. Maeda and H. Murase, "Kernel based nonlinear subspace method for pattern recognition", *IEICE Trans. Information & Systems*, vol. J82-D-II, no. 4, pp. 600–612, April 1999.

6. K. R. Müller, S. Mika, G. Ratsch, K. Tsuda, and B. Schölkopf, "An introduction to kernel-based learning algorithm", *IEEE Trans. Neural Networks*, vol. 12, no. 2, pp. 181 - 201, Mar. 2001.

7. H. Sakano, N. Mukawa and T. Nakamura, "Kernel mutual subspace method and its application for object recognition", *IEICE Trans. Information & Systems*, vol. J84-D-II, no. 8, pp. 1549–1556, Aug. 2001.

8. A. J. Smola and B. Schölkopf, "Sparse greedy matrix approximation for machine learning", *Proceedings of ICML'00*, Bochum, Germany, Morgan Kaufmann, pp. 911–918, 2000.

9. M. Tipping, "Sparse kernel principal component analysis", in *Advances in Neural Information Processing Systems 13*, MIT Press, Cambridge, MA, pp. 633–639, 2001.

10. D. V. Dasarachy, *Nearest Neighbor (NN) Norms: NN Pattern Classification Techniques*, IEEE Computer Society Press, Los Alamitos, 1991.

11. J. C. Bezdek and L. I. Kuncheva, "Nearest prototype classifier designs: An experimental study", *International Journal of Intelligent Systems*, vol. 16, no. 12, pp. 1445–11473, 2001.

12. P. E. Hart, "The condensed nearest neighbor rule", *IEEE Trans. Inform. Theory*, vol. IT-14, pp. 515–516, May 1968.

13. C. L. Chang, "Finding prototypes for nearest neighbor classifiers", *IEEE Trans. Computers*, vol. C-23, no. 11, pp. 1179–1184, Nov. 1974.

14. J. C. Bezdek, T. R. Reichherzer, G. S. Lim, and Y. Attikiouzel, "Multiple-prototype classifier design", *IEEE Trans. Systems, Man, and Cybernetics - Part C*, vol. SMC-28, no. 1, pp. 67–79, Feb. 1998.

15. Q. Xie, C.A. Laszlo and R. K. Ward, "Vector quantization techniques for nonparametric classifier design", *IEEE Trans. Pattern Anal. and Machine Intell.*, vol. PAMI-15, no. 12, pp. 1326 - 1330, Dec. 1993.

16. V. N. Vapnik, *Statistical Learning Theory*, John Wiley & Sons, 1998.

17. T. Kohonen, *Self-Oganizing Maps*, Berlin, Springer-Verlag, 1995.

18. S.-W. Kim and B. J. Oommen, "Enhancing prototype reduction schemes with LVQ3-type algorithms". To appear in *Pattern Recognition*.

19. J. Laaksonen and E. Oja, "Subspace dimension selection and averaged learning subspace method in handwritten digit classification", *Proceedings of ICANN*, Bochum, Germany, pp. 227–232, 1996.

20. L. I. Kuncheva and J. C. Bezdek, "Nearest prototype classification: Clustering, genetic algorithms or random search?", *IEEE Trans. Systems, Man, and Cybernetics - Part C*, vol. SMC-28, no. 1, pp. 160–164, 1998.

21. S.-W. Kim and B. J. Oommen, On using prototype reduction schemes to optimize kernel-based nonlinear subspace methods. *Unabridged version of this paper – Submitted for publication.*

22. K. Fukunaga, *Introduction to Statistical Pattern Recognition, Second Edition*, Academic Press, San Diego, 1990.

Intention and Rationality for PRS-Like Agents

Wayne Wobcke

School of Computer Science and Engineering
University of New South Wales
Sydney NSW 2052, Australia
wobcke@cse.unsw.edu.au

Abstract. In this paper, we elaborate on our earlier work on modelling the mental states of PRS-like agents by considering the logical properties of intentions and various rationality postulates for PRS-like agents that are a consequence of this modelling, in particular Bratman's asymmetry thesis, the side effect problem for intentions and Rao and Georgeff's non-transference principles. We show that PRS-like agents do enjoy many of the accepted logical properties of intention and rationality postulates as automatic consequences of our approach, though, as we have argued before, PRS-like agents do not have intentions in the sense required by Bratman's theory.

1 Introduction

In previous work, we developed a modelling of the mental states of a class of BDI agents based on a new logic called Agent Dynamic Logic (ADL) that combines elements from Emerson and Clarke's Computation Tree Logic [4], Pratt's Propositional Dynamic Logic [8] and Rao and Georgeff's BDI Logic [9]. The motivation of that work was to develop a logical framework that is closely aligned to the operational behaviour of a range of BDI agent architectures – those based on the PRS system – which we called *PRS-like* architectures. We take the PRS-like family to include PRS itself, Georgeff and Lansky [6], Georgeff and Ingrand [5], as well as derivative architectures such as UM-PRS, C-PRS, AgentSpeak(L), JACK Intelligent Agents™ and JAM.

In Wobcke [12], we defined an abstract PRS-like architecture extending that of Rao and Georgeff [11] that aimed to capture some of the essential elements common to this family of architectures. In this paper, we focus on the logical properties of (agents and programs developed for) this architecture. We consider two aspects of agency, the logical properties of intention, and the postulates of rationality developed by Rao and Georgeff [9,10], who followed the approach of Cohen and Levesque [3] in aiming to capture formally some of the principles of rationality proposed by Bratman [1]. In particular, we examine Bratman's asymmetry thesis, the side effect problem for intentions, and Rao and Georgeff's non-transference principles. We show that PRS-like agents do enjoy many of the accepted properties of intention and rationality postulates as consequences of our approach, though, as we have argued before, PRS-like agents have only a

R.I. McKay and J. Slaney (Eds.): AI 2002, LNAI 2557, pp. 167–178, 2002.

limited notion of intention that does not fulfil the functional roles required of Bratman's theory of intention. The technical aspects of this work derive from our earlier work on Agent Dynamic Logic, Wobcke [13], for formalizing beliefs, desires and intentions, and for defining the semantics of agent programs.

The paper is organized as follows. After a summary of our previous work on Agent Dynamic Logic, we consider in Section 3 the logic of intention, and in Section 4 the rationality postulates.

2   Agent Dynamic Logic

In this section, we summarize our approach to defining the semantics of PRS-like agents' mental states; see Wobcke [13] for more explanation. Our framework is based on a new logic called Agent Dynamic Logic (ADL) that combines aspects of Computation Tree Logic (CTL), Propositional Dynamic Logic (PDL) and the BDI Logic of Rao and Georgeff (called here BDI-CTL).[1] ADL models capture the agent's beliefs, desires and intentions as viewed from a single point in time, but not the changes in the agent's mental state that may result as time progresses and the agent is forced to change beliefs, reconsider goals and possibly abandon intentions. In this respect, it is similar to other approaches to modelling BDI agents using temporal structures, e.g. Cohen and Levesque [3], Rao and Georgeff [9].

The main technical problem addressed in ADL is the interpretation of agent programs as computations over branching time structures (with emphasis on defining the meaning of special actions *achieve* γ, which correspond to subgoals in the plan language). The interpretation of an agent program is formally a set of BDI interpretations, each such BDI interpretation representing the ways a program can be executed starting from a particular situation. Following Rao and Georgeff [9], each BDI interpretation is essentially a set of worlds, where a *world* is a computation tree (each node in such a tree having an associated state), together with accessibility relations capturing the agent's beliefs, desires and intentions. It is necessary to use BDI interpretations here (rather than just computation trees) because PRS-like agent programs implicitly refer, in the tests in conditional and iterative statements, to the beliefs of the agent, so the formal modelling of the agent's actions must also include explicit reference to the beliefs of the agent.

The language ADL (Agent Dynamic Logic) is based on both BDI-CTL, which extends CTL with modal operators for modelling beliefs, desires (goals) and intentions, and PDL, which includes modal operators corresponding to program terms. Our definitions of BDI-CTL are modifications of Rao and Georgeff's, in that, though there are three modal operators, **B** (belief), **G** (goal) and **I** (intention) in the language, the operators **G** and **I** are defined in terms of other primitives. We assume there is a base propositional language $\mathcal{L}$ for expressing

---

[1] Note that Rao and Georgeff's logic was based on CTL* rather than CTL. We use CTL for simplicity.

time-independent properties of states. The language of ADL includes the formulae of BDI-CTL (which includes the CTL state formulae) plus formulae built using the PDL constructs, as defined more precisely below. We begin with a summary of the CTL definitions.

Definition 1. *The* CTL *path formulae are defined as follows. If α and β are state formulae, then $\Box\alpha$ (henceforth α holds), $\Diamond\alpha$ (eventually α holds), $\bigcirc\alpha$ (α holds in the next state) and $\alpha\mathcal{U}\beta$ (eventually β holds and α holds until β holds) are path formulae.*

Definition 2. *The* CTL *state formulae are defined as follows. First, any formula of the base propositional language $\mathcal{L}$ is a state formula. Second, if α is a path formula, then $\mathsf{A}\alpha$ (α holds on all paths) and $\mathsf{E}\alpha$ (α holds on some path) are state formulae.*

Definition 3. *A* CTL *time tree $\langle\mathcal{T},\prec\rangle$ is a nonempty set of time points $\mathcal{T}$ and a binary relation $\prec$ on $\mathcal{T}$ that is irreflexive, transitive, discrete, serial, backwards linear and rooted.*

Definition 4. *Let $\mathcal{S}$ be a nonempty set of states. A* world *w over a* CTL *time tree $\langle\mathcal{T},\prec\rangle$ based on $\mathcal{S}$ is a function on $\mathcal{T}$ giving a state $w_t \in \mathcal{S}$ for each time point $t \in \mathcal{T}$ (in the context of a particular world w, w_t is called a* situation*). For convenience, say that time points and paths in $\mathcal{T}$ are also time points and paths in w.*

The semantics of CTL state and path formulae can be given with respect to (time points and paths in) worlds using the following definitions.

Definition 5. *For any point t in a* CTL *time tree $\langle\mathcal{T},\prec\rangle$, the* subtree *of $\langle\mathcal{T},\prec\rangle$ generated from t, denoted $\langle\mathcal{T}_t,\prec_t\rangle$, is defined to be that subtree of $\langle\mathcal{T},\prec\rangle$ consisting of the set of points $\mathcal{T}_t = \{u \in \mathcal{T} : t \preceq u\}$, where $\prec_t$ is defined as $\prec$ restricted to $\mathcal{T}_t$, and $t \preceq u$ is an abbreviation for $t \prec u$ or $t = u$.*

Definition 6. *Let $\langle\mathcal{T},\prec\rangle$ be a* CTL *time tree, let p be a path in $\mathcal{T}$ and let t be a time point in p. The* successor *$s_p(t)$ of t in p is that state $u \in p$ for which $t \prec u$ but there is no $v \in p$ with $t \prec v \prec u$.*

Definition 7. *Let $\mathcal{S}$ be a set of states and let $\mathcal{L}$ be a language for expressing time-independent properties of states (we assume there is a satisfaction relation $\models$ between states and formulae of $\mathcal{L}$). Let w be a world over a* CTL *time tree $\langle\mathcal{T},\prec\rangle$ based on $\mathcal{S}$. Then w satisfies a* CTL *formula at a time point t in $\mathcal{T}$ as follows.*

$$w \models_t \alpha \qquad \text{if } w_t \models \alpha, \text{ for } \alpha \text{ a formula of } \mathcal{L}$$
$$w \models_t \mathsf{A}\alpha \qquad \text{if } w \models_p \alpha \text{ for every path } p \text{ in } \langle\mathcal{T}_t,\prec_t\rangle$$
$$w \models_t \mathsf{E}\alpha \qquad \text{if } w \models_p \alpha \text{ for some path } p \text{ in } \langle\mathcal{T}_t,\prec_t\rangle$$

$$w \models_p \Box\alpha \qquad \text{if } w \models_u \alpha \text{ for every } u \in p$$
$$w \models_p \Diamond\alpha \qquad \text{if } w \models_u \alpha \text{ for some } u \in p$$
$$w \models_p \bigcirc\alpha \qquad \text{if } w \models_{s_p(t)} \alpha$$
$$w \models_p \alpha\mathcal{U}\beta \qquad \text{if there is } u \in p \text{ with } w \models_u \beta, \text{ and } w \models_v \alpha \text{ for every } v \in p \text{ with } v \prec u$$

To enable CTL to be used for modelling rational agents, Rao and Georgeff [9] developed a logic we call BDI-CTL, which extended the language of CTL state formulae to include modal operators for modelling beliefs, desires (goals) and intentions. In our reformulation, the modal operators **B** and **G** apply to BDI-CTL state formulae, while the modal operator **I** applies to programs. Thus intentions are directed towards actions represented as programs. The basic semantic notion is a BDI interpretation, which in Rao and Georgeff's framework, is a set of worlds over the subtrees of a single time tree, where this time tree is a branching time structure as described above, and each "world" consists of an assignment of a state to each time point in the tree over which it is based. The formal definitions of BDI interpretations and of the accessibility relations rely on the notion of a subworld of a world. A subworld of a world w contains, for each time point t, a subset of the possible futures of t that w admits, according to whether or not the corresponding path is contained in the subtree from which the subworld is derived.

Definition 8. *A* BDI interpretation *is a tuple* $\langle \mathcal{T}, \prec, \mathcal{S}, \mathcal{W}, \mathcal{B}, \mathcal{I} \rangle$ *where* $\langle \mathcal{T}, \prec \rangle$ *is a time tree,* $\mathcal{S}$ *is a nonempty set of states,* $\mathcal{W}$ *is a nonempty set of worlds based on* $\mathcal{S}$ *with each world over a subtree of* $\langle \mathcal{T}, \prec \rangle$, $\mathcal{B}$ *is a subset of* $\mathcal{W} \times \mathcal{T} \times \mathcal{W}$ *defined only for tuples* (w, t, w') *for which* t *is a time point in* w *and* w', *and* $\mathcal{I}$ *is a function* $\mathcal{W} \times \mathcal{T} \to \mathcal{W}$ *mapping each time point* t *in a world* w *to a subworld of* w *containing* t.

Definition 9. *A* subworld *of a world* w *over a time tree* $\langle \mathcal{T}, \prec \rangle$ *based on a set of states* $\mathcal{S}$ *is the world* w *restricted to a subtree of* $\langle \mathcal{T}, \prec \rangle$ *whose root is the root of* w.

Any particular world $w \in \mathcal{W}$ defines a set of futures the agent considers possible starting from the initial situation in that world. Since each world is based on a branching time structure, the actions are modelled as being non-deterministic. However, since the agent has only partial information about its environment, it may be ignorant of exactly which situation it is embedded in; the agent considers only that it is embedded in a situation in which its current beliefs are true. This ignorance is captured using the relation $\mathcal{B}$. More formally, the beliefs of the agent in some situation w_t (at a time point t in a world w) are precisely those propositions holding at all epistemic alternatives w' of w at t, i.e. in those situations w'_t such that $\mathcal{B}(w, t, w')$. The relation on situations is assumed to be serial, transitive and Euclidean, and moreover, the relations $\mathcal{B}$ and $\mathcal{I}$ are assumed to satisfy the condition that $\mathcal{B}(w, t, w')$ iff $\mathcal{B}(\mathcal{I}(w, t), t, \mathcal{I}(w', t))$, i.e. the epistemic alternatives of $\mathcal{I}(w, t)$ at t are the intended subworlds of the epistemic alternatives of w at t. This simple relationship between $\mathcal{B}$ and $\mathcal{I}$ is used below to derive some basic properties of the relation between beliefs and intentions.

The intentions of the agent are those actions the agent considers that eventually it will successfully perform, according its current view of the environment, i.e. not taking into account the potential for the environment to change so as to force the agent to revise or abandon its intentions. Intentions are modelled using the function $\mathcal{I}$, which defines, for any particular world, which futures (sub-worlds) in that world are intended by the agent: in the "intended" futures, all the agent's actions are performed successfully. More formally, the intentions of an agent with respect to a world w at t are those action formulae π for which on all possible futures in $\mathcal{I}(w,t)$, the agent eventually does π, i.e. the intentions of an agent are represented by formulae of the form $\mathbf{BA}\Diamond do(\pi)$ (for the purposes of exposition, we defer the truth definition for $do(\pi)$). Finally, the goals of the agent are simply those formulae γ such that the agent intends to perform the action *achieve* γ. This is in keeping with the behaviour of the PRS-like interpreter, which has no mechanism for adopting a goal independently of a plan to achieve that goal.

Definition 10. *Let* $\langle \mathcal{T}, \prec, \mathcal{S}, \mathcal{W}, \mathcal{B}, \mathcal{I} \rangle$ *be a BDI interpretation. Then a world* $w \in \mathcal{W}$ *satisfies a* BDI-CTL *formula at a time point t in w as follows.*

$$
\begin{array}{ll}
w \models_t \mathbf{B}\alpha & \text{if } w' \models_t \alpha \text{ whenever } \mathcal{B}(w,t,w') \\
w \models_t \mathbf{I}\pi & \text{if } \mathcal{I}(w,t) \models_t \mathbf{BA}\Diamond do(\pi) \\
w \models_t \mathbf{G}\gamma & \text{if } w \models_t \mathbf{I}(achieve\ \gamma)
\end{array}
$$

We can now present the definition of Agent Dynamic Logic (ADL). Analogous to PDL, the language of ADL includes modal operators $[\pi]$ and $\langle \pi \rangle$ corresponding to each program π, and the semantics is based on computation trees, as in the approach of Harel [7]. If α is a BDI-CTL state formula, $[\pi]\alpha$ is understood to mean that α holds in all terminating situations arising from an execution of π, while $\langle \pi \rangle \alpha$, which is defined as $\neg[\pi]\neg\alpha$, is understood to mean that α holds in one terminating execution of π. In computation tree semantics, terminating situations are simply the leaf nodes of the trees (note that infinite branches correspond to programs that do not terminate). The programs are assumed to consist of a set of atomic programs that can be combined with a unary operator $*$ (iteration) and binary operators ; (sequencing) and $\cup$ (alternation), and corresponding to any formula α of the base language $\mathcal{L}$ is a test statement α? Note, however, that the test is on whether α is a belief of the agent, not whether α holds in the environment.

The semantics of ADL is based on what we call *PRS interpretations*, which provide an interpretation for each program in terms of a set of BDI interpretations. As mentioned above, the need for BDI interpretations (rather than computation trees or worlds) arises because PRS agent programs refer to the beliefs of the agent in the tests of conditional and iterative statements, so the models of the PRS programs must also include reference to the agent's beliefs. The definition of a PRS interpretation also enables us to define the satisfaction conditions for $do(\pi)$ as needed for modelling intentions.

Each program is modelled as a set of BDI interpretations that arises by varying the initial state and belief accessibility relation $\mathcal{B}$, and in which $\mathcal{I}$ is defined as the identify function (i.e. $\mathcal{I}(w,t) = w$ for all w,t). The function $\mathcal{I}$ plays no role in the interpretation of agent programs (so could be omitted), while the $\mathcal{B}$ relation is used to define the meaning of the test statements. In any BDI interpretation b modelling a program π, one distinguished world b^*

models the execution paths of π and may have *non-final* situations, situations at leaf nodes in a computation tree where execution can continue (other worlds in b represent the agent's belief states, and final situations in b^* represent paths where program execution cannot continue). Each primitive action π (except for the special action *achieve* γ – see below) is modelled by a set of worlds over a computation tree of depth 1, one world for each state $s \in S$ in which the action is executable. Each such world with root s has one child situation for each possible outcome of executing the action π in s, and each of these situations is non-final. In addition, there is a special "action" *env* that models the changes in the environment that occur over cycles in which the agent tests its beliefs.

Definition 11. *A PRS interpretation is a pair $\langle S, \mathcal{R} \rangle$, where S is a set of states and $\mathcal{R}$ is a family of sets of BDI interpretations $\mathcal{R}_\pi$ based on S, one such set of BDI interpretations for each program π.*

Definition 12. *Let $\langle S, \mathcal{R} \rangle$ be a PRS interpretation and $\langle T, \prec, S, W, B, I \rangle$ be a BDI interpretation. For a world $w \in W$ over $\langle T, \prec \rangle$ containing a point t, let w^t be the subworld of w over $\langle T_t, \prec_t \rangle$, the subtree of $\langle T, \prec \rangle$ generated from t. Then w satisfies the state formula $do(\pi)$ and $[\pi]\alpha$ at a time point t in w as follows.*

$w \models_t do(\pi)$ *if there is a BDI interpretation b in $\mathcal{R}_\pi$ such that b^* is isomorphic to a prefix of w^t*

$w \models_t [\pi]\alpha$ *if for every BDI interpretation b in $\mathcal{R}_\pi$ such that b^* is isomorphic to a prefix of w^t, $w \models_u \alpha$ for every point u in w corresponding to a leaf node of b^**

Definition 13. *A world w is a prefix of a world w' if for each end node n of w, there is a world w_n such that replacing each n in w by w_n results in w'.*

Definition 14. *A world w^1 in a BDI interpretation $\langle T_1, \prec_1, S, W_1, B_1, I_1 \rangle$ is isomorphic to a world w^2 in a BDI interpretation $\langle T_2, \prec_2, S, W_2, B_2, I_2 \rangle$ if there is a one-one correspondence f between T_1 and T_2 such that for all $t, u \in T_1$, $t \prec_1 u$ iff $f(t) \prec_2 f(u)$, and for all $t \in T_1$, w_t^1 is equivalent to $w_{f(t)}^2$.*

Definition 15. *A situation w_t in a BDI interpretation $\langle T_1, \prec_1, S, W_1, B_1, I_1 \rangle$ is equivalent to a situation $w'_{t'}$ in a BDI interpretation $\langle T_2, \prec_2, S, W_2, B_2, I_2 \rangle$ if $w_t = w'_{t'}$ (i.e. they are equal as states) and $\{u_t : B_1(w, t, u)\} = \{v_{t'} : B_2(w', t', v)\}$ (i.e. they satisfy the same basic beliefs).*

The program construction operators, sequencing, alternation and iteration, are modelled as operations on sets of BDI interpretations. The operation for sequencing is a kind of "concatenation" of worlds, denoted $\oplus$, analogous to concatenation of computation sequences. For alternation, we utilize an operation, denoted $\uplus$, that merges two worlds if they have equivalent initial situations.

Definition 16. *Let w^1 and w^2 be worlds (in BDI interpretations) over time trees $\langle T_1, \prec_1 \rangle$ and $\langle T_2, \prec_2 \rangle$. Let S be the set of end points of T_1, and let S' be the subset of elements s of S for which w_s^1 is a non-final situation and equivalent* to w_r^2, where r is the root of $\mathcal{T}_2$. For each element s of S', let $w^2(s)$ be a world isomorphic to W_2 over a time tree $\langle T_2^s, \prec_2^s \rangle$, whose accessibility relations are the same as w^2 on corresponding elements. Then the concatenation of w^1 and w^2, denoted $w^1 \oplus w^2$ is defined over a tree consisting of $\mathcal{T}_1 - S'$ and all the sets T_2^s with a precedence ordering $\prec$ extending $\prec_1$ and all the $\prec_2^s$ by also defining $t_1 \prec t_2$ if $t_1 \in \mathcal{T}_1 - S'$, $t_1 \prec_1 s$ and $t_2 \in T_2^s$. The non-final situations of $w^1 \oplus w^2$ are defined to be those of all the $w^2(s)$ (there are no non-final situations if S' is empty).

Definition 17. Let w^1 and w^2 be worlds (in BDI interpretations) over time trees $\langle \mathcal{T}_1, \prec_1 \rangle$ and $\langle \mathcal{T}_2, \prec_2 \rangle$ with roots r_1 and r_2, such that $w_{r_1}^1$ and $w_{r_2}^2$ are equivalent. Let the tree $\mathcal{T}$ be defined as the set of time points $\mathcal{T}_1 \cup \mathcal{T}_2$ in which r_1 and r_2 are identified, and with $\prec$ defined as $\prec_1 \cup \prec_2$ (so that the identified r_1 and r_2 is the root of $\mathcal{T}$, and the children of this node are the children of r_1 from $\mathcal{T}_1$ and of r_2 from $\mathcal{T}_2$). Then the merger of w^1 and w^2, denoted $w^1 \uplus w^2$, is the world defined over the tree $\langle \mathcal{T}, \prec \rangle$ that is inherited from w^1 and w^2, i.e. $(w^1 \uplus w^2)(t)$ is $w^1(t)$ if $t \in \mathcal{T}_1$ and is $w^2(t)$ if $t \in \mathcal{T}_2$. The non-final situations of $w^1 \uplus w^2$ are defined to be those of w^1 and w^2.

If b^1 and b^2 are BDI interpretations, $b^1 \oplus b^2$ is the set of all worlds formed by simultaneously concatenating, for each non-final situation w_s^1 of each world w^1 in b^1, w^1 and a world $w^2(s)$ in b^2 whose initial situation is equivalent to w_s^1 (if one exists), and $b^1 \uplus b^2$ is that set of worlds obtained by merging all pairs of worlds w^1 and w^2 in $b^1 \cup b^2$ whose initial situations are equivalent.

We can finally give the constraints on the sets of BDI interpretations $\mathcal{R}_\pi$ that ensure that each respects the operational semantics of the program construction operators.

$$\mathcal{R}_{\pi;\chi} = \mathcal{R}_\pi \oplus \mathcal{R}_\chi$$
$$\mathcal{R}_{\pi \cup \chi} = \mathcal{R}_\pi \uplus \mathcal{R}_\chi$$
$$\mathcal{R}_{\pi*} = \mathcal{R}_\pi^* \text{ (the reflexive transitive closure of } \mathcal{R}_\pi \text{ under } \oplus)$$
$$\mathcal{R}_{\alpha?} = \{b : b \in B_1, b^* \models \mathbf{B}\alpha \text{ and } b^* \text{ is isomorphic to a world in } \mathcal{R}_{env}\}$$
$$\mathcal{R}_{\neg\alpha?} = \{b : b \in B_1, b^* \not\models \mathbf{B}\alpha \text{ and } b^* \text{ is isomorphic to a world in } \mathcal{R}_{env}\}$$

Here B_1 is the set of BDI interpretations all of whose worlds are of depth 1. Note that test actions in the PRS-like architecture consume one cycle during which the environment may change. Hence the test α? $(\neg\alpha?)$ succeeds only when the agent believes (does not believe) α, but the execution context, as captured in the non-final situations in the model, are those resulting from the changes in the environment, as reflected in $\mathcal{R}_{env}$.

Definition 18. The relations $\mathcal{R}_\pi$ for the empty program Λ and for programs achieve γ corresponding to a subgoal γ are defined as follows.

$$\mathcal{R}_\Lambda = B_0$$
$$\mathcal{R}_{achieve\ \gamma} = \uplus \{\mathcal{R}_\pi \cap \{b : b^* \models pre(\pi) \wedge context(\pi)\} : \pi \in L, post(\pi) \vdash \gamma\}$$

Here B_0 is the set of BDI interpretations all of whose worlds are of depth 0, and $pre(\pi)$, $post(\pi)$ and $context(\pi)$ are the precondition, postcondition and context (respectively) of a plan π in the plan library L. The precondition and postcondition of Λ are just *true*.

Thus Λ is executable in every situation in every world, and leaves the state unchanged, while *achieve* γ is modelled as a set of BDI interpretations in which γ is achieved by the successful execution of a (hierarchical) plan built from plans in the plan library. Note that this condition is actually a set of recursive definitions of $\mathcal{R}_{achieve\ \gamma}$ for all formulae γ at once; it is recursive because the plans π may include subgoals of the form *achieve* δ (and here, of course, δ may be γ). Thus the meaning of *achieve* γ involves a least fixpoint construction.

3   Logical Properties of Intention for PRS-Like Agents

We now discuss the logic of intention implied by the above semantics for ADL. First note that, with our semantics, there are no special logical requirements for goals and intentions. The set of goals (and of intentions) can even be inconsistent, partly because of the implicit temporal aspects of our modal operators, i.e. the formulae $\mathbf{G}\gamma$ and $\mathbf{G}\neg\gamma$ are not inconsistent – they simply mean that the agent wants to achieve γ and $\neg\gamma$ at some points in the future (as determined by the current plans), though not necessarily at the same point. This differs from the presentation in Rao and Georgeff [9] in which the modal operators $\mathbf{B}$, $\mathbf{G}$ and $\mathbf{I}$ all modify propositional formulae with the temporal modality explicit, so an agent's goals γ and $\neg\gamma$ are represented using formulae $\mathbf{G}\Diamond\gamma$ and $\mathbf{G}\Diamond\neg\gamma$.

However, the language of ADL programs is more complicated than modal logic, in including program terms for conditional and iterative constructs, as in PDL. The meaning of these constructs follows the definitions from PDL, in which the *if-then-else* and *while* statements are defined in terms of the sequencing, union, iteration and test primitives as follows.

$$\mathbf{if}\ \alpha\ \mathbf{then}\ \pi\ \mathbf{else}\ \chi \;\equiv\; (\alpha?;\pi) \cup (\neg\alpha?;\chi)$$
$$\mathbf{while}\ \alpha\ \mathbf{do}\ \pi \;\equiv\; (\alpha?;\pi)^*;\neg\alpha?$$

Note, however, that the conditional and iterative constructs in PRS agent programs behave very differently: the tests in the PRS statements are tests, not on the state of the world, but on the agent's belief state (a distinction not needed for standard PDL).

We can now present some logical properties of intention that are consequences of the ADL semantics.

(I1) $\models \mathbf{I}(\pi;\chi) \Rightarrow \mathbf{I}\pi \wedge \mathbf{I}\chi$
(I2) $\not\models \mathbf{I}(\mathbf{if}\ \alpha\ \mathbf{then}\ \pi\ \mathbf{else}\ \chi) \Rightarrow (\mathbf{I}\pi \vee \mathbf{I}\chi)$
(I3) $\not\models \mathbf{I}\pi \Rightarrow \mathbf{I}(\pi \cup \chi)$
(I4) $\models \mathbf{I}(achieve\ \gamma) \Rightarrow \mathbf{I}(\pi_1 \cup \cdots \cup \pi_n)$ where the π_i are the plans whose
      postcondition logically implies γ
(I5) $\not\models \mathbf{I}(achieve\ \gamma) \wedge \mathbf{I}(achieve\ \delta) \Rightarrow \mathbf{I}(achieve\ (\gamma \wedge \delta))$

With (I1), performing the action $\pi;\chi$ requires the performance of π followed by χ, hence performing both actions. For (I2), performing an *if-then-else* statement requires that the agent perform one or other of the branches of the statement, though *which* branch is determined only by the result of a test on beliefs that may take place in the future. Hence the agent need not have a commitment (at the present time) to any particular branch. In contrast, (I3) relates to the choice(s) involved in commitment to an intention, and represents the fact that once a choice has been made, the choice no longer exists. Here $I(\pi \cup \chi)$ represents the performance of either π or χ, but $I\pi$ represents a commitment to π – the latter does not imply the former. Note, though, that the formula represents a "choice" of the agent only to the extent that which of the actions is executed is partly determined by the situation at execution time. (I4) is a consequence of the semantics for *achieve* actions, and mirrors the property defined by Cavedon and Rao [2], who obtain this property by the use of special "plan" worlds in which the only events are those actions contained in the agent's plans. Finally, (I5) is a consequence of the future directedness of intention: an agent intending to achieve γ and δ intends that γ and δ eventually hold, but not necessarily at the same time, so need not intend to achieve $\gamma \wedge \delta$.

4   Rationality Postulates for PRS-Like Agents

Rao and Georgeff [10] present a discussion of rationality for BDI agents, building on the approach of Cohen and Levesque [3]. One of their main aims is to capture formally some of the principles of rationality proposed by Bratman [1], in particular, the asymmetry thesis, side effect free principle, and what they call non-transference principles. The *asymmetry thesis* is the thesis that (i) it is inconsistent for a rational agent to both intend to perform some action and believe s/he will not do it, and (ii) it *is* consistent for a rational agent to intend to perform some action whilst not believing s/he will do it ("doing it" here means executing the action successfully, so the thesis means that the agent need not be certain that the attempt to perform the intended action will succeed, but cannot believe it will inevitably fail). The *side effect free principle* is that a rational agent need not intend the believed necessary consequences (side effects) of an intention. The *non-transference principle* for intentions states that a rational agent need not adopt an intention to achieve some condition that it believes will inevitably become true in the future.

More formally, Rao and Georgeff represent these principles using schemas of the following form, adapted to the language of ADL. The adaptation is necessary because in Rao and Georgeff's formalism, intentions are directed towards propositions (intentions that α be true), rather than towards actions (intentions to perform π).

(A1) $\models I\pi \Rightarrow \neg BA\Box \neg do(\pi)$
(A2) $\not\models I\pi \Rightarrow BA\Diamond do(\pi)$
(SE) $\not\models I(achieve\ \gamma) \wedge BA\Box(\gamma \Rightarrow \delta) \Rightarrow I(achieve\ \delta)$
(NT) $\not\models BA\Diamond\gamma \Rightarrow I(achieve\ \gamma)$

Note that there are different varieties of (SE) depending on the "strength" of belief in the connection between γ and δ (the postulate above shows the strongest connection, and hence the hardest to refute).[2]

---

[2] In ADL, the even stronger side effect free principle with $\gamma \vdash \delta$ is also invalid.

In the ADL modelling of PRS-like agents, the only intentions are those relating to actions executed by the agent, though external events are also assumed to occur. Hence (NT) is satisfied, since a condition γ that always eventually arises need not be related to a plan of the agent. Now consider the asymmetry thesis. The crucial difference between Rao and Georgeff's semantics and ADL semantics is the condition that the intended futures in some world are a subworld of that world. Hence the agent can believe there are possible futures in which its intentions are not fulfilled, but cannot believe its actions will always fail. This means that both (A1) and (A2) are satisfied automatically. For (SE), Rao and Georgeff require there to be belief-accessible worlds that are not intention worlds; thus, for example, there is an intention world in which the agent goes to the dentist to relieve a toothache and does not feel pain, even though in all belief-accessible worlds the agent feels pain in this circumstance. In contrast, our explanation for (SE) rests on the behaviour of the PRS-like interpreter in selecting actions: the agent can select a plan (and hence form an intention) to achieve δ only when the postcondition of the plan logically implies δ. Hence it is possible for an agent to intend to execute a plan whose postcondition implies γ but not δ, e.g. the goal of relieving the toothache but not the goal of feeling pain. Thus (SE) is also satisfied in ADL.

The above postulates express relationships between beliefs and intentions, following Bratman [1]; Rao and Georgeff also introduce (without justifying argument) similar postulates relating beliefs and goals, and goals and intentions. Due to the way intentions and goals are defined in ADL, postulates relating beliefs and goals follow from the above postulates, while postulates relating goals and intentions are not needed. For example, the following postulates relating beliefs and goals follow from the definition of $\mathbf{G}\gamma$ as $\mathbf{I}(achieve\ \gamma)$. Again, all are satisfied in ADL.

$$(\text{A1})\ \models \mathbf{G}\gamma \Rightarrow \neg\mathbf{BA}\square\neg do(achieve\ \gamma)$$
$$(\text{A2})\ \not\models \mathbf{G}\gamma \Rightarrow \mathbf{BA}\diamond do(achieve\ \gamma)$$
$$(\text{SE})\ \not\models \mathbf{G}\gamma \wedge \mathbf{BA}\square(\gamma \Rightarrow \delta) \Rightarrow \mathbf{G}\delta$$
$$(\text{NT})\ \not\models \mathbf{BA}\diamond\gamma \Rightarrow \mathbf{G}\gamma$$

Rao and Georgeff [9] present the following axiom schemes as the "basic system" for modelling BDI agents, reconstructed in ADL below: where our reconstruction differs significantly, the original version is also given.

$$(\text{AI1})\ \mathbf{G}\gamma \Rightarrow \mathbf{BE}\diamond do(achieve\ \gamma) \qquad \{\mathbf{G}\alpha \Rightarrow \mathbf{B}\alpha \text{ for } \alpha \text{ an O-formula}\}$$
$$(\text{AI2})\ \mathbf{I}(achieve\ \gamma) \Rightarrow \mathbf{G}\gamma \qquad\qquad\quad \{\mathbf{I}\alpha \Rightarrow \mathbf{G}\alpha\}$$
$$(\text{AI3})\ \mathbf{I}\pi \Rightarrow do(\pi) \qquad\qquad\qquad\quad\ \{\mathbf{I}do(e) \Rightarrow do(e)\}$$
$$(\text{AI4})\ \mathbf{I}\pi \Rightarrow \mathbf{BI}\pi$$
$$(\text{AI5})\ \mathbf{G}\gamma \Rightarrow \mathbf{BG}\gamma$$
$$(\text{AI6})\ \mathbf{I}\pi \Rightarrow \mathbf{GI}\pi$$
$$(\text{AI7})\ [\pi]\alpha \Rightarrow [\pi]\mathbf{B}\alpha \qquad\qquad\qquad \{done(e) \Rightarrow \mathbf{B}(done(e))\}$$
$$(\text{AI8})\ \mathbf{I}\pi \Rightarrow \mathbf{BA}\diamond\neg\mathbf{I}\pi \qquad\qquad\qquad \{\mathbf{I}\alpha \Rightarrow \mathbf{A}\diamond\neg\mathbf{I}\alpha\}$$

For (AI1), an *O-formula* is defined to be a formula with no positive occurrences of A or negative occurrence of E outside the scope of a $\mathbf{B}$, $\mathbf{G}$ or $\mathbf{I}$ operator. In (AI3) and (AI7), e denotes a primitive action.

(AI1) is meant to capture the "realism" condition, c.f. Cohen and Levesque [3], that an agent does not adopt goals it believes are unachievable. Rao and Georgeff consider the special case of (AI1) with α the O-formula $E\Diamond p$, giving the reading that if the agent has the goal of possibly eventually achieving p, then it believes that it *is* possible to eventually achieve p. In our reconstruction, the "possible future" aspect of the goal is built into the meaning of the modal operator $\mathbf{G}$, so that this special case of (AI1) follows directly from the definitions. Similarly, for (AI2), we have defined goals so that $\mathbf{I}(achieve\ \gamma) \Leftrightarrow \mathbf{G}\gamma$ is valid (there is no mechanism for a PRS-like agent to have a goal γ without a corresponding intention to achieve γ).

On Rao and Georgeff's description, (AI3) means that if the agent has an intention to do a primitive action e then the agent does e, though this does not mean that e is done successfully, only that e is attempted by the agent. Thus in the very special case where the agent has only the intention to perform one primitive action at the current time point, that intention is adopted and the action attempted. However, $\mathbf{I}\pi \Rightarrow do(\pi)$ is not valid in ADL because of the future directedness of intention built in to the definition; an agent's having an intention to perform π implies only that the agent believes it will attempt π at some future time.

The validity of (AI4) and (AI5) in ADL follow from the restriction imposed on the relations $\mathcal{B}$ and $\mathcal{I}$, the condition that $\mathcal{B}(w,t,w')$ iff $\mathcal{B}(\mathcal{I}(w,t),t,\mathcal{I}(w',t))$. Indeed the converses of (AI4) and (AI5) also follow from this condition, i.e. the agent has correct *and complete* beliefs about its goals and intentions. However, (AI6) is not well formed in ADL: on our interpretation, an intention to perform π gives rise to a goal of achieving the postcondition of π, not a goal of intending π itself. As goals are future directed, the goal to intend π (at some time in the future) is quite different from the (current) intention to perform π.

(AI7) is similar in flavour to (AI3) in that it relies on a distinction between attempted and performed actions. Rao and Georgeff's interpretation of (AI7) is that after attempting a primitive action e, the agent believes that it has attempted e. Our reconstruction preserves the idea of the agent's awareness of its own actions. However, our version of (AI7) is not intuitively valid, first because there is no way in ADL to distinguish an agent's attempted actions from the actions it performs, and second because the agent may not observe all the consequences of its actions, so not believe an action has been performed successfully even when it was performed successfully.

Finally, (AI8), which Rao and Georgeff take to mean that an agent eventually acts on an intention or else abandons that intention, does not hold for PRS-like agents. One reason for this is that this interpretation needs modification when plans can be infinite, because an intention, even though being acted on, may never be fulfilled, even in principle. A more serious reason is that it is part of the operational definition of the PRS-like interpreter that the agent always acts on a plan that has maximal value, so a low-value plan may never be activated.

In summary, (AI1), (AI2), (AI4) and (AI5) follow from the ADL definitions, while the other properties are intuitively invalid for PRS-like agents.

5 Conclusion

In this paper, we extended earlier work on modelling the mental states of PRS-like agents by considering the logical properties of intentions and various rationality postulates for PRS-like agents that are a consequence of our modelling, in particular Bratman's asymmetry thesis, the side effect problem for intentions and Rao and Georgeff's non-transference principles. We showed that PRS-like agents do enjoy many of the accepted logical properties of intention and rationality postulates as automatic consequences of our approach, even though PRS-like agents embody only a weak notion of intention.

References

1. Bratman, M.E. (1987) *Intention, Plans and Practical Reason.* Harvard University Press, Cambridge, MA.
2. Cavedon, L. & Rao, A.S. (1996) 'Bringing About Rationality: Incorporating Plans Into a BDI Agent Architecture.' in Foo, N.Y. & Goebel, R.G. (Eds) *PRICAI'96: Topics in Artificial Intelligence.* Springer-Verlag, Berlin.
3. Cohen, P.R. & Levesque, H.J. (1990) 'Intention is Choice with Commitment.' *Artificial Intelligence,* **42**, 213–261.
4. Emerson, E.A. & Clarke, E.M. (1982) 'Using Branching Time Temporal Logic to Synthesize Synchronization Skeletons.' *Science of Computer Programming,* **2**, 241–266.
5. Georgeff, M.P. & Ingrand, F.F. (1989) 'Decision-Making in an Embedded Reasoning System.' *Proceedings of the Eleventh International Joint Conference on Artificial Intelligence,* 972–978.
6. Georgeff, M.P. & Lansky, A.L. (1987) 'Reactive Reasoning and Planning.' *Proceedings of the Sixth National Conference on Artificial Intelligence (AAAI-87),* 677–682.
7. Harel, D. (1979) *First-Order Dynamic Logic.* Springer-Verlag, Berlin.
8. Pratt, V.R. (1976) 'Semantical Considerations on Floyd-Hoare Logic.' *Proceedings of the Seventeenth IEEE Symposium on Foundations of Computer Science,* 109–121.
9. Rao, A.S. & Georgeff, M.P. (1991) 'Modeling Rational Agents within a BDI-Architecture.' *Proceedings of the Second International Conference on Principles of Knowledge Representation and Reasoning (KR'91),* 473–484.
10. Rao, A.S. & Georgeff, M.P. (1991) 'Asymmetry Thesis and Side-Effect Problems in Linear-Time and Branching-Time Intention Logics.' *Proceedings of the Twelfth International Joint Conference on Artificial Intelligence,* 498–504.
11. Rao, A.S. & Georgeff, M.P. (1992) 'An Abstract Architecture for Rational Agents.' *Proceedings of the Third International Conference on Principles of Knowledge Representation and Reasoning (KR'92),* 439–449.
12. Wobcke, W.R. (2001) 'An Operational Semantics for a PRS-like Agent Architecture.' in Stumptner, M., Corbett, D. & Brooks, M. (Eds) *AI 2001: Advances in Artificial Intelligence.* Springer-Verlag, Berlin.
13. Wobcke, W.R. (2002) 'Modelling PRS-like Agents' Mental States.' in Ishizuka, M. & Sattar, A. (Eds) *PRICAI 2002: Trends in Artificial Intelligence.* Springer-Verlag, Berlin.

Modeling and Simulation for Detecting a Distributed Denial of Service Attack

Seo, Hee Suk and Cho, Tae Ho

School of Electrical and Computer Engineering Modeling & Simulation Lab,
Sungkyunkwan University Suwon, 440-746, South Korea.
{histone , taecho}@ece.skku.ac.kr

Abstract. The attackers on Internet-connected systems we are seeing today are more serious and technically complex than those in the past. So it is beyond the scope of any one system to deal with the intrusions. This paper shows a modeling and simulation of network security in which the multiple IDSes (Intrusion Detection System) and a firewall coordinate by sharing attacker's information for the effective detection of the intrusion. Another characteristic in the proposed simulation is the composition of a real intrusion by generating non-abstracted intrusion packets and, accordingly, the construction of non-abstracted version of IDS and firewall model components.

1 Introduction

As environments grow larger and more diverse, and as securing them on a host-by-host basis grows more difficult, more sites are turning to a network security model. With a network security model, we concentrate on controlling network access to your various hosts and the services they offer, rather than on securing them one by one. Network security approaches include using IDS to detect the intrusion, building fire-walls to protect your internal systems and networks, using strong authentication approaches (such as one-time passwords), and using encryption to protect particularly sensitive data as it transits the network [1].

IDS plays a vital role in network security in that it monitors system activities to identity unauthorized use, misuse or abuse of computer and network system [2], [3], [4], [5]. And a firewall [7], [8] is a way to restrict access between the Internet and internal network. For the simulation, IDS and Firewall models are constructed based on the DEVS (Discrete EVent system Specification) formalism [9], [10], [11]. With these models we can simulate whether the intrusion detection and defense, which are a core function of IDS and firewall, are effectively done under various different conditions. In this paper, we are concerned with a DoS (Denial of Service) type attack among various attacks. The DoS attack is one that's aimed entirely at preventing users from using the network services. A few DoS attacks are easier for attackers, and these are relatively poplar. However, the result of the attack can be critical [12].

The attackers on Internet-connected systems we are seeing today are more serious and more technically complex than those in the past. So it is beyond the scope of any

R.I. McKay and J. Slaney (Eds.): AI 2002, LNAI 2557, pp. 179–190, 2002.

one system to deal with the intrusions. Thus we placed multiple IDSes [13], [14], [15] in the network where the information helpful for detecting the intrusions is shared among these agents to cope effectively with attackers. Each agent coordinates through the BBA (BlackBoard Architecture) [16], [17], [18] for detecting intrusions. If an agent detects intrusions, it transfers attacker's information to Firewall model. Using this mechanism attacker's packets detected by IDS can be prevented from damaging the network.

2 Background

This section briefly describes the background related to the current research. Section 2.1 represents the DEVS formalism based on which the simulation models are defined. Section 2.2 shows the BBA of distributed artificial intelligence.

2.1 DEVS Formalism

The DEVS formalism [9], [10], [11], [12] is a theoretically well grounded means of expressing hierarchical, modular discrete-event models. In DEVS, a system has a time base, inputs, states, outputs and functions. The system function determines next states and outputs based on the current states and input. In the formalism, a basic model is defined by the structure:

$$M = < X, S, Y, \delta_{int}, \delta_{ext}, \lambda, t_a >$$

where X is an external input set, S is a sequential state set, Y is an external output set, δ_{int} is an internal transition function, δ_{ext} is an external transition function, λ is an output function and t_a is a time advance function. A coupled model is defined by the structure:

$$DN = < D, \{M_i\}, \{I_i\}, \{Z_{i \cdot j}\}, select >$$

where D is a set of component name, M_i is a component basic model, I_i is a set of influences of I, $Z_{i \cdot j}$ is an output translation, select is a tie-breaking function. Such a coupled model can itself be employed in a larger coupled model. Several basic models can be coupled to build a more complex model, called a coupled model.

2.2 BBA

The blackboard architecture, within the field of the distributed artificial intelligence, provides an approach to solving the coordination problem among distributed agents. BB (Blackboard) that is one of the components in the BBA is usually partitioned into several levels of abstraction appropriate for the problem at hand. The agents, or knowledge sources, working at a particular level of abstraction have access to the corresponding blackboard level along with the adjacent levels. In that way, data that have been synthesized at any level can be coordinated to higher levels, while higher-level goals can be filtered down to drive the expectations of lower-level agents. The simplicity with which the blackboard paradigm represents the classic problem of data driven versus goal-driven information flow is perhaps the reason why blackboard models are widely used in existing distributed artificial intelligence systems. Fig. 1 presents the structure of the blackboard architecture [16], [17], [18].

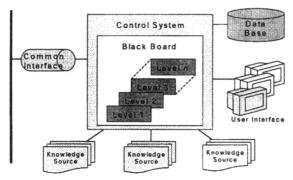

Fig. 1. Structure of the BBA

3 Target Network and Simulation Models

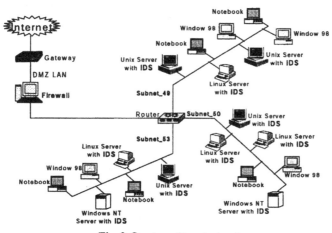

Fig. 2. Structure of target network

Fig. 2 shows the structure of the target network that has three subnets; subnet_49, subnet_50 and subnet_53. The types of component models in the network are IDS, Firewall, Router and Gateway model [19]. Each subnet has unix server, linux server, windows NT server and etc. A IDS is loaded within each host and it cooperates with other IDSes in detecting the intrusion. These models are constructed based on the

DEVS formalism. Fig. 3 shows the overall structure of the simulation models that are
based on the network described in Fig. 2. Each subnet has several ID models that is
loaded within each server.

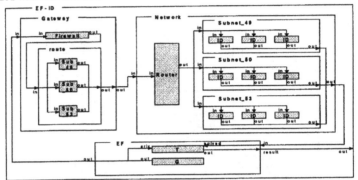

Fig. 3. Overall structure of DEVS simulation model

3.1 SES (System Entity Structure)

The SES is a knowledge representation scheme that combines the decomposition,
taxonomic, and coupling relationships. An entity may have several aspects, each
denoting a representation. An entity may also have several specializations, each representing a classification of the possible variants of the entity [9].

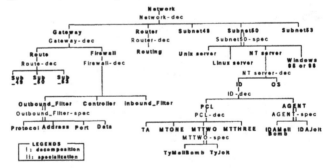

Fig. 4. SES of target network

Fig. 4 is a system entity structure for the overall network model of Fig. 2. Network
model is decomposed into five entities; Gateway, Router, Subnet49, Subnet50 and
Subnet53. Gateway model is decomposed again into two sub-entities; Route model
and Firewall model. Firewall model is further decomposed into Inbound_Filter
model, Outbound_Filter model and Controller model. Outbound_Filter model can be
specialized into several types; Protocol, Address, Port and Data model.

Subnet50 is specialized into Unix server, Linux server, NT server and Windows 95/98. Each server entity is decomposed into OS model and ID model. ID model is decomposed into PCL model and AGENT model. PCL model is decomposed again into TA, MTONE, MTTWO and MTTHREE model. MTTWO model is further specialized into TyMailBomb and TyJolt model. Finally, AGENT model is specialized into IDAMailBomb and IDAJolt model.

3.2 PCL Model

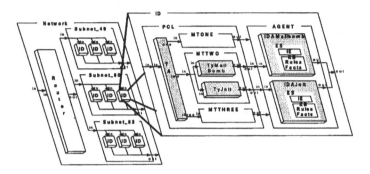

Fig. 5. Structure of ID model

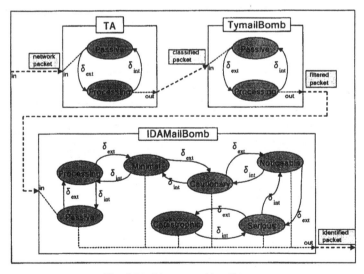

Fig. 6. Model state transition diagram

Fig. 5 shows the structure of ID model within each host, its subcomponents and their interconnections. PCL (Packet Classify Library) model in ID model receives network's packets that are generated by the intrusion generator model and classifies them according to attack type. Then it filters sorted packets to reduce processing time as the following process. For example, for the mailbomb case, TA (Task Allocator) of PCL model receives packets from the generator model and then it transmits the packets to one of the three different types of models. These are MTONE, MTTWO, MTTHREE. If the packets, send to MTTWO, are of TCP protocol and port number 25 then it transfers the packets to an agent model for further processing. Otherwise, MTTWO ignores it. Fig. 6 shows the model state transition diagram of several models in Fig. 5.

3.3 AGENT Model

AGENT model is a rule-based ES (Expert System) which plays a core component role in detecting the intrusion. It transforms the packets that are delivered by PCL model into facts to be used by ES. ES inferences according to the facts thus generated. If a new attack is to be added to ID model later on, the administrator classifies the attack and adds a proper subcomponent model to PCL model and its corresponding rules to AGENT model.

3.4 Firewall

The firewall is a way to restrict access between the Internet and the internal network. Fig. 7 shows a composition of Firewall model exploited in this simulation.

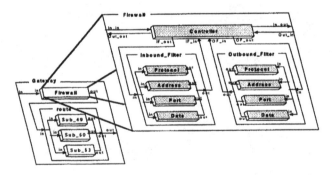

Fig. 7. Structure of Firewall model

Firewall model is composed of a controller model, a Inbound_Filter model and a Outbound_Filter model. Inbound_Filter model includes Protocol model, Address model, Port model and Data model. Controller model receives the packets from the internal network or from the Internet, and transfers the packets to Inbound_Filter model or Outbound_Filter model. Each Filter model processes the packets according to the security strategies and sends the packets to Controller model. Controller model sends the packets that are delivered by Inbound_Filter model or Outbound_Filter model to the network. For example, for the mailbomb case, Inbound_Filter model receives the packets from Controller model and examines the IP (Internet Protocol) address. If the packet contains the blacklist, it is ignored. If a e-mail contains harmful information, Data model of Inbound_Filter model filters the packet.

4 Coordination among the Security Models

This section shows how the coordination is done among the security models. First, the coordination among the ID agents is presented and then a mechanism that the attacker's packets are prevented by the coordination between the ID agents and a Firewall model is presented. Fig. 9 shows the structure of BBA of the target network. There have been large volumes of research works done for detecting intrusions within distributed environment [13], [14], [15]. This section presents a mechanism in which IDSes coordinate by BBA. BB (Black Board) in BBA is hierarchically structured shared working memory through which the agents coordinate by writing and reading the information relevant to detecting the intrusions.

4.1 Coordination among Agents of BBA

The hierarchy in BB is set according to Joseph Barrus & Neil C. Rowe [20] as shown in Fig. 8. They proposed Danger values to be divided into five different levels. The level in the BB is based on these divisions. These five BB levels are Minimal, Cautionary, Noticeable, Serious and Catastrophic.

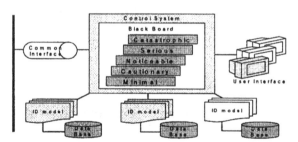

Fig. 8. Structure of blackboard within the target network

Each agent communicates by two types of messages. One is the control messages, the other is the data messages. Since the agents insert the intrusion related information to BB, each agent must request the permission to the controller for writing in order to manage consistency and contention problems. After writing is done, the agent sends the write_end message to the controller. Controller reports this event to other IDSes.

IDSes, which have received the necessary information from BB, send the read_end message to the controller. An example of transactions involved in the mailbomb intrusion case are shown in Fig. 9.

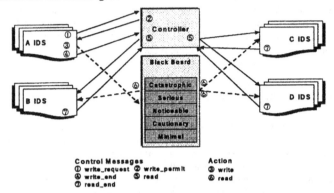

Fig. 9. Message of IDS and BBA in Mailbomb Attack

4.2 Coordination between the IDSes and a Firewall Model

The IDS and firewall system, being the major components of network security, coordinate to enhance the security level. If IDS detects the intrusion through BBA, its agent modifies the security policy of the firewall. So that the intrusion packets detected by IDS can be prevented.

In order to reduce the damage of the network to a minimum level, we have prevented attacker's packets from getting into the computer when the BB level is at beyond Serious level. When the BB level is at Serious level, the agent adds the source IP (Internet Protocol) address to the blacklist of the Firewall model, then all packets coming from these sources are blocked.

5 Simulation Result

We have executed simulations for two cases. One is the case for a single IDS to detect the intrusion, the other is the case for multiple IDSes to detect the intrusion by coordination. Mailbomb attack and jolt attack are used for the simulation in both cases.

Mailbomb attack is a type of DoS attacks. It attacks by sending a large number of mails to a mail server. For the generation of mailbomb packets, Kaboom version 3.0 is used. Jolt attack is also a type of DoS attacks. It slices a IP datagram into small pieces and then transmits the packets of these pieces to the target system. Then the CPU (Central Processing Unit) of target system that receives these packets is over loaded since the target system has to store and reassemble all these packets. As a result, the utilization of the CPU reaches close to 100 percents and can't handle any other processes. The intrusion detection time, false positive and false negative error ratio are measured for the performance indexes in the simulation.

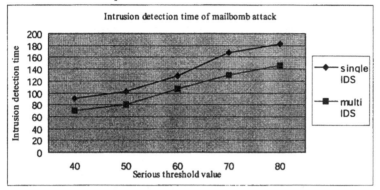

Fig. 10. Intrusion detection time of mailbomb attack

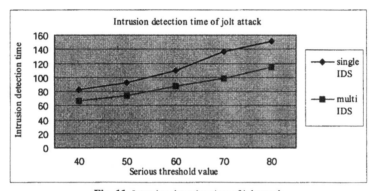

Fig. 11. Intrusion detection time of jolt attack

As shown in Fig. 10 and Fig. 11, the selected serious threshold value for the simulation are 40, 50, 60, 70 and 80. The other threshold values are changed according to the same ratio of change in the serious threshold value. The multiple IDSes detect the intrusion faster than single one does for all the threshold values. The result shows that the multiple IDS coordinate effectively through BBA for detecting the intrusion. The faster the intrusion is detected, the earlier the administrators can correspond to the intrusion. It is important that the network administrator to respond at the early stage of the intrusion for the safety of the network. When the security level is weakened by increasing the serious threshold value in our system, the difference in the intrusion detection time between multi IDSes and a single IDS cases become larger. Because the lower the security level, the stronger the sensitivity becomes due to the information sharing among IDSes. This phenomenon related to the sensitivity applies to all other cases of the simulation results.

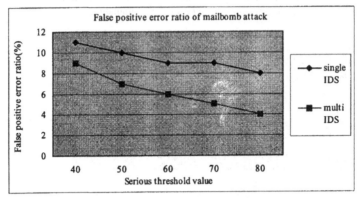

Fig. 12. False positive error ratio of mailbomb attack

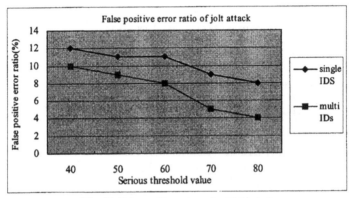

Fig. 13. False positive error ratio of jolt attack

Fig. 12 and Fig. 13 show that the false positive error ratio is increased by strengthening of the security level. This increase in the error ratio is due to the fact that the higher the security level, the more error IDSes make in both cases. That is, as the security level increases IDSes react more sensitively to the suspicious packets without referring to enough evidence of attacks.

Fig. 14 and Fig. 15 show the decrease of the false negative error ratio as the security level is strengthened. For both cases, the error ratio of multi IDSes is lower than that of single IDS since the intrusions are detected based on the shared information.

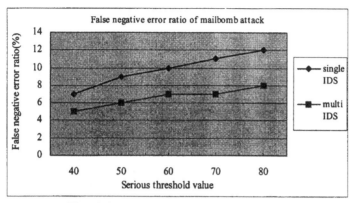

Fig. 14. False negative error ratio of mailbomb attack

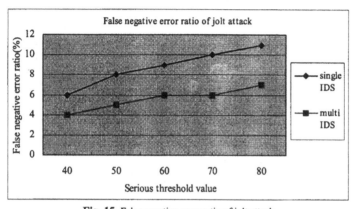

Fig. 15. False negative error ratio of jolt attack

6 Conclusion and Future Work

The attackers on Internet-connected systems we are seeing today are more serious and technically complex than those in the past. So it is beyond the scope of any one system to deal with the intrusions. If multiple agents share the intrusion related information with one another, the detection capability can be enhanced. The system which uses BBA for the information sharing can be easily expanded by adding new agents and increasing the number of BB levels. The coordination between the Firewall component and IDS will provide the added efficiency in safe guarding the network. In the future, diverse types of intrusions should be simulated and the simulation environment should also provide a proper set of threshold values according to the specific target system being modeled.

References

1. E. D. Zwicky, S. Cooper, D. B. Chapman, "Building Internet Firewalls second edition", O'reilly & Associates, 2000.
2. R. Bace, "Intrusion Detection", Macmillan Technical Publishing, 2000.
3. E. Amoroso, "Intrusion Detection - An Introduction to Internet Surveillance, Correlation, Traps, Trace Back, and Response", Intrusion.Net Books, 1999.
4. P. Neumann and D. Parker, "A Summary of computer misuse techniques", In Proceedings of the 12th National Computer Security Conference, pp. 396-407, October 1989.
5. N. Puketza, M. Chung, R. Olsson, B. Mukherjee, "A Software Platform for Testing Intrusion Detection Systems", IEEE Software, pp.43-51, October 1997.
6. F. Cohen, "Simulating Cyber Attacks, Defences, and Consequences", Computer & Security, Vol.18, pp. 479-518, 1999.
7. Duan Haixin, Wu Jianping, Li Xing, "Policy based access control framework for large networks", Proceedings of IEEE International Conference on ICON 2000, Sept. 2000.
8. Noureldien A. Noureldien, Izzeldin M. Osman, "On Firewalls Evaluation Criteria", Proceeding of TENCON 2000, pp 104-110, Sept. 2000.
9. B. P. Zeigler, "Object-Oriented Simulation with Hierarchical, Modular Models", USA:Academic Press, San Diego CA, 1990.
10. B. P. Zeigler, "Theory of Modeling and Simulation", John Wiley, NY, USA, 1976, reissued by Krieger, Malabar, FL, USA, 1985.
11. T.H. Cho, Bernard P. Zeigler, "Simulation of Intelligent Hierarchical Flexible Manufacturing: Batch Job Routing in Operation Overlapping", IEEE trans. Syst. Man, Cyber. A, Vol. 27, pp. 116-126, Jan. 1997.
12. S Mclure, J. Scambray, G. Kurtz, "Hacking Exposed: Network Security Secrets and Solutions", McGraw-Hill, 1999.
13. U. Lindqvist, P. A. Porras, "Detecting Computer and Network Misuse Through the Production-Based Expert System Toolset(P-BEST)", Proceedings of the IEEE Symposium on Security and Privacy, Oakland California, May 9-12 1999.
14. P. Porras and P. Neumann, "EMERALD: Event Monitoring Enabling Responses to anomalous live disturbances", Proceedings of the 20th National Information Systems Security Conference, National Institute of Standards an Technology, 1997.
15. M. Crosbie and G. Spafford, "Active Defence of a Computer System using Autonomous Agents", Technical Report No. 95-008, COAST Group, Dept. of Computer Science, Purdue University, Feb. 15, 1995.
16. G. Van Zeir, J. P. Kruth, J. Detand, "A Conceptual Framework for Interactive and Blackboard Based CAPP", International Journal of Production Research, Vol. 36(6), pp. 1453-1473, 1998.
17. K. Decker, A. Garvey, M. Humphrey, V. R. Lesser, "Control Heuristics for Scheduling in a Parallel Blackboard System", International Journal of pattern Recognition and Artificial Intelligence, Vol. 7, No. 2, pp. 243-264, 1993.
18. F. Klassner, V. R. Lesser, S. H. Nawab, "The IPUS Blackboard Architecture as a Framework for Computational Auditory Scene Analysis", IJCAI-95 Workshop on Computational Auditory Scene Analysis, Montreal, Canada, August 1995.
19. B. A. Forouzan, "TCP/IP Protocol Suite", McGrawHill, 2000.
20. J. Barrus, N. C. Rowe, "A Distributed Autonomous-Agent Network-Intrusion Detection and Response System", Proceedings of Command and Control Research and Technology Symposium, pp. 577-586, Monterey CA, June 1998.

Knowledge-Driven Processes Can Be Managed

John Debenham

University of Technology, Sydney
debenham@it.uts.edu.au

Abstract. Knowledge-driven processes are business processes whose execution is determined by the prior knowledge of the agents involved and by the knowledge that emerges during a process instance. They are characteristic of emergent business processes. The amount of process knowledge that is relevant to a knowledge-driven process can be enormous and may include common sense knowledge. If a process' knowledge can not be represented feasibly then that process can not be managed; although its execution may be partially supported. In an e-market domain, the majority of transactions, including requests for advice and information, are knowledge-driven processes for which the knowledge base is the Internet, and so representing the knowledge is not an issue. These processes are managed by a multiagent system that manages the extraction of knowledge from this base using a suite of data mining bots.

1   Introduction

In an experimental e-market, *transactions* [1] include: trading orders to buy and sell in an e-exchange, single-issue and multi-issue negotiations between two parties, requests for information extracted from market data *as well as* from news feeds and other Internet data. This e-market is used at UTS for research and teaching. In it *every* market transaction is managed as a business process [2]. To achieve this, suitable process management machinery has been developed. To investigate what is 'suitable' the essential features of these transactions are related to two classes of process that are at the 'high end' of process management feasibility [3]. The two classes are goal-driven processes (Sec. 2) and knowledge-driven processes (Sec. 3). The term "business process management" is generally used to refer to the simpler class of workflow processes [2], although there notable exceptions using multiagent systems [4]. Sec. 4 describes the relationship between the transactions themselves and the contextual information extracted from the Internet and from market data. Sec. 5 discusses the single-issue and multi-issue negotiation transactions. e-market transactions are typically heavily constrained—the role of constraints is described in Sec. 6.

2   Goal-Driven Processes

A *goal-driven process* has a process goal, and achievement of that goal signals the termination of the process. The process goal may have various decompositions into possibly conditional sequences of sub-goals where these sub-goals are associated with (atomic) activities and so with atomic tasks. Some of these sequences of tasks may work better than others, and there may be no way of knowing which is which [3]. A task for an activity may fail outright, or may fail to achieve its goal in time. In other

R.I. McKay and J. Slaney (Eds.): AI 2002, LNAI 2557, pp. 191–202, 2002.
© Springer-Verlag Berlin Heidelberg 2002

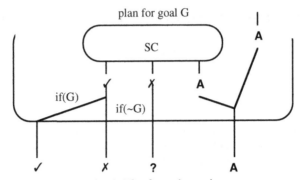

Fig. 1. The four plan exits

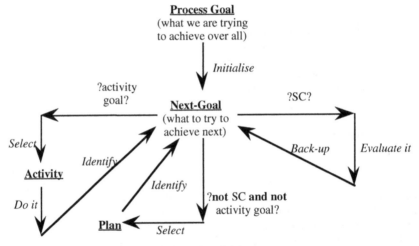

Fig. 2. A simplified view of goal-driven process management.

words, a central issue in managing goal-driven processes is the management of task failure. Hybrid multiagent architectures whose deliberative reasoning mechanism is based on "succeed/fail/abort plans" [5] are well suited to the management of goal-driven processes. Goal-driven processes are a more powerful concept than production workflows (or, called "activity-driven processes" in [6]). *Activity driven-processes* are associated with possibly conditional sequences of activities where performing that sequence is assumed to "work always".

Following [5] a plan for a goal-directed process can not necessarily be relied upon to achieve its goal even if all of the sub-goals on the chosen path through that plan have been achieved. The *success condition* (SC), described in [6], is a procedure whose goal is to determine whether a plan's goal has been achieved. The final sub-goal on *every* path through a plan is the plan's success condition. The success condition is a procedure; the execution of that procedure may succeed (✓), fail (✗) or abort (**A**). If the execution of the success condition fails then the overall success of the plan is unknown (**?**). So the four possible plan exits resulting from an attempt to execute such a plan are as shown in Fig. 1. A *plan body* is represented as a directed AND/OR graph, or state-transition diagram, in which some of the nodes are labelled with sub-goals.

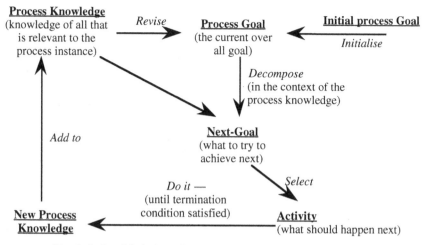

Fig. 3. A simplified view of knowledge-driven process management.

The management of goal-driven processes is shown in a simplified form in Fig. 2. There, starting with the overall process goal, repeated decomposition of plans and goals is performed until either the next goal is a success condition or is an *activity goal*—ie: a goal for which there is a hard-coded procedure. Fig. 2 is simplified because it does not show what happens if the success condition returns fail "✗", or what happens if a plan is aborted. Further it does not show the mechanism for selecting plans for goals. For goal-driven processes there is, in general, no *ex ante* 'best' choice of plan.

3   Knowledge-Driven Processes

A second class of process, whose management has received little attention, is called knowledge-driven processes. *Process knowledge* is all the knowledge that is relevant to a process instance. It includes common-sense knowledge, knowledge that was available when an instance is created, and knowledge acquired during the time that that instance exists. A *knowledge-driven process* may have a process goal, but the goal may be vague and may mutate. In so far as the process goal gives direction to goal-driven—and activity-driven—processes, the process knowledge gives direction to knowledge-driven processes. The body of process knowledge is typically large and continually growing—for example, it may include common sense knowledge—and so knowledge driven processes are seldom considered as candidates for process management. They are typically supported, rather than managed, by CSCW systems. But, even complex knowledge-driven processes are "not all bad"—they typically have goal-driven sub-processes that may be handled as described above. *Knowledge-base processes* are a special type of knowledge-driven process for which the process knowledge *can* be represented and accessed by a process management system. This proves to be a useful concept for managing e-market transactions.

The management of goal-driven and knowledge driven processes are radically different. Goal-driven processes may be managed by a goal/plan decomposition process (see Fig. 2), and knowledge-driven processes are managed by continually reviewing the growing corpus of process knowledge—this is illustrated in Fig. 3.

That Figure is deceptively simple in that the business of managing the process knowledge and of revising the process-goal and next-goal in the light of that growing body of knowledge is far from trivial in even simple examples. In general this problem will be intractable. But in some cases, including the majority of e-market transactions, smart tools may be used to do this. This is discussed in the next section.

4   E-market Transactions and Contextual Information

E-market transactions include: trading orders to buy and sell in an e-exchange (single-issue and multi-issue negotiations as described above), requests for market data *as well as* requests for information extracted from news feeds and other Internet data. In an experimental e-market, *all* e-market transactions are managed as constrained knowledge-driven processes.

Sec. 5.1 discusses single-issue one-to-one negotiation. Single-issue negotiation also takes place in exchanges, for example a 'buy' trading order to "buy a chair and a desk for less than \$100". This is represented (see Fig. 4) as a naive plan with goal $[G, c]$ = [desk and chair have been purchased, cost < 100]. This plan has sub-goal SG_1 = 'chair and desk selected', $[SG_2, c_2]$ = [chair purchased, cost < 30], $[SG_3, c_3]$ = [desk purchased, cost < 50], and $[SG_4, c_4]$ = [desk and chair delivered, cost < 20]. The management of this purchase order is represented as a plan whose goals have monetary constraints.

An example of a request for information is "find out all you can about ABC Corp within five minutes". This triggers a process to locate, extract, validate, condense and combine information from the Internet. The location and extraction tasks are achieved by data/text mining bots that are described in [7]. A handcrafted plausible inference network combines contradictory information. The use of belief nets that can be trained "off line" is very tempting and is currently being investigated [8]. The data/text mining bots produce output in the form [data, belief]—ie: some data and a measure of the belief held in the validity of that data. A request for information is first represented as a goal/constraint pair: [find_info_about('ABC Corp'): time_upper_limit = now + 5mins]. Given a goal/constraint pair, a plan (see Fig. 4) is selected for it—the mechanism for selecting a plan is described in Sec. 6. A *plan* for a goal/constraint pair is a possibly conditional state-chart of sub-goals over which constraints are distributed as described in Sec. 6. For a 'find_info_about' process, the plan uses a Dempster-Shafer network (see Fig. 5) to combine results $[D_i, b_i]$, in the form [data, belief], extracted from the Internet by a suite of data/text mining bots. The network actually does more than combine information. If the level of belief, b_R, in a result, R, derived by the network is below a set threshold then a 'reverse calculation' identifies 'inputs' whose belief levels are responsible for the low level of belief in R. Then further data/text mining is initiated in an attempt to raise this level of belief at least for future calculations if not for the present calculation.

A three-year research project commencing in 2002 at UTS, is investigating the mechanisms required to support the evolutionary process in e-markets [7]. It is presently funded by four Australian Research Council Grants; awarded variously to the author and to Dr Simeon Simoff:

http://www-staff.it.uts.edu.au/~emrktest/eMarket/

Market evolution is linked to innovation and entrepreneurship (in its technical, economic sense). Present plans for the three year project are: (1) to build an e-marketplace trader's workbench that, in principle, enables a trader to operate

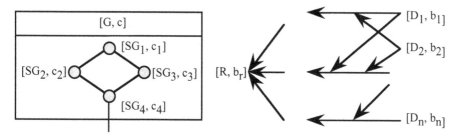

Fig. 4. A plan for goal [G, c]   **Fig. 5.** Belief network combines information

without external information, (2) to assist a trader to identify arbitrage opportunities triggered by the occurrence of rare events, (3) to assist a trader to identify innovative forms of trade, and, possibly, (4) to understand something of the evolutionary process itself.

5   Negotiation Transactions

Negotiation is a process whereby two or more agents reach an agreement on a set of issues. One-to-one negotiation, in which there are just two negotiating agents, is sometimes called *bargaining*, or informally "haggling" or "dickering". An *issue* is any good or service that one agent can provide to another, including money. The *issue set* is the range of possible issues that may be considered during a negotiation. An issue set may be *fixed*; for example, in a single-issue negotiation where the only issue on which agreement is sought is an amount of money. An *open* issue set may contain *any* issue. In a *limited* issue set, the issues that may be included in an offer is limited to those chosen from a set agreed to by the negotiating agents. An issue—for example, "period of warranty"—is normally associated with some value—for example, "two years". An *offer* consists of a particular set of issues chosen from the issue set, together with values for those issues. During a negotiation with an open or limited issue set the collection of issues in an offer may mutate although in practice it tends to be moderately stable.

A *negotiation mechanism* specifies how a negotiation may proceed; they are sometimes called "interaction protocols" in multiagent systems work [9]. Two forms of negotiation mechanism have received a considerable amount of attention in the economics literature, and in e-Markets research. First, single issue negotiation for one or more items being offered either to a set of buyers or to a set of sellers; see, for example, the extensive work on forward and reverse auction mechanisms [10, and second, one-to-one negotiation, or bargaining, mechanisms.

Management of the negotiation process in an e-Market—both for negotiation through e-exchanges and through single- and multi-issue one-to-one negotiation—includes a continual investigation of the negotiation *context* as well as the construction, evaluation and revision of offers. For example, the bone fide of the opponent may require verification, the quality of the goods should be confirmed, alternatives should be investigated, and so on. In the experiments described here this information is assumed to be available on the Internet. A good e-market negotiator should conduct these contextual investigations as an integral part of the negotiation process [11]. "Good negotiators, therefore, undertake integrated processes of knowledge acquisition combining sources of knowledge obtained at and away from the *negotiation table*. They learn in order to plan and plan in order to learn" [12]. In the management of the negotiation process described here, the information and the offers develop in tandem; they both feed off each other. The term "e-marketplace" is used here to acknowledge this duality between offers and contextual information. An *e-Marketplace* is a market in which trading can be conducted over the Internet, and for which sufficient information to trade "well" is available over the Internet. This information may be derived from on-line market data, for mining historic market data, from text-mining news feeds and so on. The Sydney Stock Exchange is an example of an e-marketplace.

5.1   Single-Issue Negotiation

Single-issue negotiation is the most common form of negotiation, in particular where the issue is price. The number of issues in any form of negotiation, including single-issue, can be increased if one of the negotiating parties offers "kick backs". For example, an offer of two free bottles of wine for every dozen bought *provided that* you have spent more than $500 with that merchant in the previous twelve months. This sort of offer changes what was initially a single-issue negotiation to a multi-issue negotiation. In this Section it is assumed that the negotiation is strictly single-issue and that both parties understand the meaning of the issue. For example, such an issue could be an amount of money. It is argued that single-issue negotiation is appropriately managed as a knowledge-driven process. From a process management perspective this is interesting because the management of "real life" knowledge-driven processes is usually unfeasible.

Two important classes of bargaining mechanisms are alternating offers mechanisms and single-round, "one-hit" mechanisms that may be used when the agents have determined private valuations in advance. For example, [13] shows that a one-hit "split the difference between bid and ask" mechanism should be preferred by both buyer and seller to *any other* mechanism *ex ante*—that is, before their private valuations are actually determined. Alternatively, an agent's valuations may be refined as the negotiation proceeds—in which case an alternating offers mechanism is which information is tabled as appropriate—this is the focus here.

The negotiation protocol used is a time-constrained, unbounded alternating offers protocol [14]. In this protocol two bargaining agents exchange offers until either one agent accepts an offer from the other agent, one agent rejects an offer and withdraws without penalty, or one agent exceeds an agreed time constraint on making an offer. So negotiation using this protocol could, in principle, proceed indefinitely—hence the description *unbounded*.

Consider a transaction to purchase something. Suppose that this transaction can be appropriately managed by: identifying a need, selecting a good to satisfy that need, choosing a supplier for that good and negotiating terms for that good from that supplier. A sequential procedure based on this would not be appropriate for purchasing all classes of goods; it could, however, be suitable for purchasing a technical book. The appropriateness of this "purchasing procedure" is not of concern here. Suppose further that we wish to select the "most appropriate" good, to choose the "best supplier" and to negotiate "acceptable" terms. In an *e-marketplace* sufficient information to trade successfully in this sense is assumed to be available on the Internet.

The use of "software bots" to assist the buying process by extracting contextual information from the Internet is commonplace. For many classes of goods, bots that

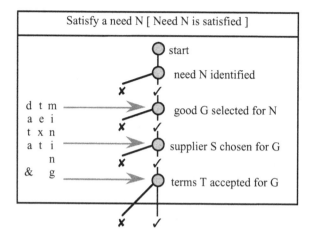

Fig. 6. A goal-driven plan to satisfy a need based on "succeed / fail" plans.

do some of this work are freely available: http://www.botspot.com/ — viz: the sections "Shopping Bots" and "Commerce Bots". The entire problem considered here lies beyond the capacity of most off-the-shelf bots that at best recommend rather than decide. Although the use of demographic data, collaborative filtering, clustering, or previously expressed user preferences can deliver reasonable performance in choosing the "most appropriate" good for the user. With current technology it could be reasonable to give the authority to a bot to select, order and pay for paper stock for photocopiers, but many would be reluctant to permit a bot to select, order and pay for a book on Bayesian Nets, for example.

In this project the contextual information from the Internet is first extracted by a range of data and text mining bots mostly written by undergraduates at UTS. Some of these bots read reviews of products in an attempt to determine the comparative inherent quality of a good as well as its basic attributes. This in general leads to a collection of contradictory evidence that is combined to give coherent advice. The approach taken to plausible inference is described in Sec. 4

A simple, double (ie: succeed / fail) branching plan to manage a "purchase something" transaction is shown in Fig. 6. That plan treats the process sequentially in that, for example, once the good is selected then its appropriateness is not reconsidered. This may be appropriate when the whole transaction can be resolved quickly, but could otherwise lead to poor decision making. That plan relies on information from data and text mining bots to support the decision making in the achievement of three of its sub-goals. [Plans for those three sub-goals are not shown here.] Despite the vital role of the bots, that plan manages the transaction as a goal-driven process. The management of the same transaction as a knowledge-driven process is described below. This is achieved by feeding the contextual information into the reactive "abort" conditions in the plans.

To simplify the following discussion the operation of the data and text mining bots is hidden in the following predicates: INeed(N) that means: "I need an N", Satisfy(N, G) that means: "good G is the most appropriate good that satisfies need N". Calculation of values to satisfy these predicates may take some time.

Fig. 7 shows one of a sequence of linked plans for the "purchase something" transaction. In that Figure "d t m" denotes information that is acquired from the

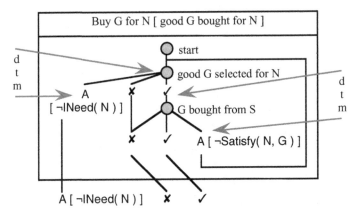

Fig. 7. Knowledge-driven plans to satisfy a need based on "succeed / fail / abort" plans.

Internet and databases by data and text mining bots and combined into coherent advice by a plausible inference network. That plan is more intricate than the previous goal-directed version. Even so this sequence is flawed in that the process may now continue indefinitely; this difficulty is addressed by constraints in Sec. 6 below. They include reactive abort triggers that redirect the course of the transaction if any prior decision ceases to be valid. The direction, and possible redirection, of this transaction is governed entirely by the contextual information received, and repeatedly reconfirmed, from the data and text mining bots. This plan is useful but is not particularly noteworthy in itself. What is of note, from a process management perspective, is that this is a fully managed knowledge driven process, despite its presentation in a goal / plan framework. It is a knowledge-base driven process where the knowledge base is the Internet and market data, the query mechanism is the bots, and the reactive 'abort' exists are used to modify the direction of the process when necessary.

5.2   Multi-issue Negotiation

The discussion in Sec. 5.1 on the management of single-issue negotiation is rather simplified in that it assumes that the single-issue in which the offers are expressed is unambiguously understandable. In practice negotiation is more complicated than this. For example, when the issue is money then an amount expressed in dollars is readily understood, but when and where the payment has to be made may not be. If the issue set contains things like an "unconditional warranty" then it would be prudent to clarify quite what this really means. So the feature of multi-issue negotiation that is explored here is the opponent as a source of information, used to clarify the meaning of an offer or otherwise.

A negotiation process with fairly minimal functionality is shown in Fig. 8. There the process is triggered by the arrival of an offer from the opponent. This is analysed to ensure that the meaning is clear—to uncover the "fine print"— and to detect any inconsistencies. Then the offer is evaluated to determine what it is "worth"—this can lead to acceptance or outright rejection, or to the development of a counter offer. Another context for the generation of the counter offer is the history of offers received in this negotiation—this enables an assessment to be made of "where are the opponent is at". Eg: "is she about to give in?" The process illustrated in Fig. 8 can

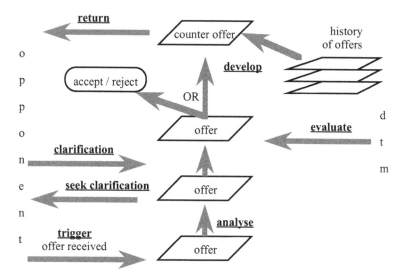

Fig. 8. High-level view of the negotiation process

seen as an attempt to satisfy the high level goal "attempt to negotiate a satisfactory outcome". But the direction that the process takes is determined by the flow of information—from the offer itself, the data and text mining bots, the opponent and from the growing history of offers. So this is a knowledge-driven process. At present the evaluation function is available from the bots as described above. At the time of writing the rest of the machinery is not yet available, but plans are to achieve this by the end of 2002. There is much to be done, for example the detection of inconsistencies in an offer is not trivial even if the terms of the offer are represented in Horn clause logic.

6   Transaction Constraints

All e-marketplace transactions are assumed to be constrained by time constraints and possibly by cost constraints or success constraints. *Time constraints* may be the maximum (or minimum) time by which a deal must be struck and/or by which the goods should be delivered. The *cost constraints* could be constraints on the cost of the transaction, the cost of the goods or a combination of the two. *Success constraints* may be constraints on the outcome of the deal; for example, "I must have a car for the weekend, get the best deal you can".

The e-marketplace transaction management system attempts manage transactions to "deliver the best it can whilst satisfying the constraints". To do this it selects plans to achieve goals on the basis of expected time and cost estimates. Further, if actual performance differs significantly from these estimates then estimates for subsequent plans are adjusted leading, possibly, to a revised plan. This will occur if network performance is unexpectedly degraded, for example. To derive time and cost estimates for each plan it gathers performance measurements on each plan and sub-system, such as an information gathering bot, and maintains running estimates of future expected performance. It then adjusts these estimates when measurements are observed outside expected limits. For example, if the network is slow when gathering data from New York, then time estimates for extracting data from London may be adjusted to some extent.

Time and cost performance measurements are made for each plan and for each atomic sub-system whenever it is used. These measurements enable the transaction management system to choose a plan for a goal (G in Fig. 4) and to determine the constraints ($\{c_1,..,c_4\}$ in Fig. 5) for each sub-goal in that plan. A plan's *performance estimate* is the expected time "t" and cost "c" to satisfy the plan's goal. These estimates will be calculated from performance estimates for each atomic sub-system. The parameters t and c are assumed to be normally distributed—this is a wild assumption—but it provides a framework for identifying measurements that abnormal. Given a parameter, p, that is assumed to be normally distributed, an estimate, μ_p, for the mean of p is revised on the basis of the i'th observation obj_i to $\mu_{pnew} = (1 - \alpha) \times obj_i + \alpha \times \mu_{pold}$ which, given a starting value $\mu_{pinitial}$, and some

constant α, $0 < \alpha < 1$, approximates the geometric mean $\dfrac{\sum\limits_{i=1}^{n} \alpha^{n-i} \times obj_i}{\sum\limits_{i=1}^{n} \alpha^{n-i}}$ of the set of

observations $\{obj_i\}$ where $i = n$ is the most recent observation. In the same way, an

estimate, σ_p, for $\sqrt{\dfrac{2}{\pi}}$ times the standard deviation of p is revised on the basis of the

i'th observation obj_i to $\sigma_{pnew} = (1 - \alpha) \times |obj_i - \mu_{pold}| + \alpha \times \sigma_{pold}$ which, given a starting value $\sigma_{pinitial}$, and some constant α, $0 < \alpha < 1$, approximates the geometric

mean $\dfrac{\sum\limits_{i=1}^{n} \alpha^{n-i} \times |obj_i - \mu_p|}{\sum\limits_{i=1}^{n} \alpha^{n-i}}$. The constant α is chosen on the basis of the stability

of the observations. For example, if $\alpha = 0.85$ then "everything more than twenty trials ago" contributes less than 5% to the weighted mean.

Given a transaction and its constraints (expressed in terms of t and s), the transaction management system makes two decisions. First it selects a feasible plan for that transaction's goal. Second it determines the constraints on each sub-goal in that plan. Then further plans are selected for those sub-goals, and so on. Each time a plan for goal G is used measurements are made of t and c for each sub-goal in that plan. Further each of those sub-goals may be invoked by other plans. So the estimates of the mean and standard deviation of t and c for those sub-goals may be expected to be more accurate than the estimates for goal G. So each time a plan is considered, the t and c estimates for its goal are re-computed from those on the estimated costliest path through the plan.

Plan A for goal [G, c] is *feasible* if $c > \mu_A + \kappa \times \sigma_A$, where c is expressed in terms of t and c, μ and σ are expressed likewise, and κ is a constant usually > 1. If $c < \mu_A - \kappa \times \sigma_A$ then the plan is not expected to achieve its goal within constraint c. This enables the constraints to be relaxed on each sub-goal so that the estimated costliest path through the plan satisfies c. If a sub-goal SG_i of plan P for goal G is not achieved within its constraint c_i then *first* another plan is sought for SG_i and for any other as-yet-unsatisfied 'down stream' sub-goals, for which an allocation of constraints in P is feasible, and *second* the whole plan P fails and another plan is sought for G with tighter constraints than c.

Given a goal G with constraints c the transaction management system first identifies a set of feasible plans for G. Then from this set the system selects a plan for a given goal G using the stochastic strategy: the probability that a plan is selected is the probability that that plan is the "best" plan. This strategy has been found to work well for managing high level processes [6]. Here *best* may mean "the most likely to satisfy the constraints on G" or some other criterion such as "the plan likely to deliver the best quality advice" as discussed below. Given two plans A and B for the same goal G, if the constraint on G is represented by a parameter p (in terms of t and c) that is assumed to be normally distributed then the probability that plan A is "better than" plan B is the probability that $(p_A - p_B) > 0$. Using elementary statistics, an estimate for this probability is given by the area under the normal distribution with:

mean = $\mu_A - \mu_B$ [where μ_A and μ_B are estimates of the means of p_A and p_B]

standard deviation = $\sqrt{\dfrac{\pi}{2} \times (\sigma_A^2 + \sigma_B^2)}$ [where σ_A and σ_B are estimates of $\sqrt{\dfrac{2}{\pi}}$ times the standard deviations of p_A and p_B]   for $x > 0$. This method may be extended to estimate the probability that one plan is better than a number of other plans.

The measurement of the quality, q, of work in any business process is seldom available to the management system except through subjective assessment. This issue complicates the "optimal" management of all business processes. In the experimental e-market some information sources may reasonably be given quality estimates. For example, subjective estimates of the mean and variance may be attached to text by a particular journalist in a news feed. If these estimates are available then the notion of "best" may be extended to include quality. However, if "best" is to mean some combination of q, c and t then these parameters may need to be measured in the same units, such as some monetary value.

The adjustment of estimates in the light of measurements that fall outside expected ranges is achieved using the geometric weighted mean method used to estimate s and t. These *multipliers* υ_{ij} mean: if measurement m_i of service i lies outside the expected range then multiply the estimate for service j by $\dfrac{m_i}{\mu_i} \times \upsilon_{ij}$.

This is crude but in a sense these multipliers are no cruder than the estimates that they are adjusting. What is known is the network topology and so too potential causal links between components' performance. The use of some form of belief net [8] is appealing in that the learning mechanism has a scientific basis, although here the nets will need to represent conditional t and c estimates rather than conditional probabilities. This is presently being investigated.

7   Conclusion

Two classes of business process are goal-driven processes and knowledge-driven processes. Goal-driven processes may be managed but they are inherently unpredictable. The management of knowledge-driven processes that involve human agents is seldom feasible due to the size of the process knowledge base. A significant class of knowledge-driven processes is e-market transactions in which the process knowledge base is the Internet. These are managed using a multiagent system that is supported by a suite of data and text mining bots whose output is combined using a belief network. The proactive component of these agents is specified by plans. For goal-driven processes the proactive 'succeed' exit leads the way, and for knowledge-driven processes the reactive 'abort' exit is used to determine the process' direction as knowledge is revealed.

References

[1]   Debenham, JK. Supporting the actors in an electronic market place. In proceedings Twenty First International Conference on Knowledge Based Systems and Applied Artificial Intelligence, ES'2001: Applications and Innovations in Expert Systems IX, Cambridge UK, December 2001, pp29-42.

[2]   Fischer, L. (Ed). Workflow Handbook 2001. Future Strategies, 2000.

[3]   van der Aalst, W. & van Hee, K. Workflow Management: Models, Methods, and Systems. MIT Press (2001).

[4]   Jennings, N.R., Faratin, P., Norman, T.J., O'Brien, P. and Odgers, B. (2000) Autonomous Agents for Business Process Management. Int. Journal of Applied Artificial Intelligence 14 (2) 145-189.

[5]   Rao, A.S. and Georgeff, M.P. "BDI Agents: From Theory to Practice", in proceedings First International Conference on Multi-Agent Systems (ICMAS-95), San Francisco, USA, pp 312—319.

[6]   Debenham, JK. Supporting knowledge-driven processes in a multiagent process management system. In proceedings Twentieth International Conference on Knowledge Based Systems and Applied Artificial Intelligence, ES'2000: Research and Development in Intelligent Systems XV, Cambridge UK, December 2000, pp273-286.

[7]   Debenham, JK and Simoff, S. Investigating the Evolution of Electronic Markets. In proceedings Sixth International Conference on Cooperative Information Systems, CoopIS 2001, Trento, Italy, September 5-7, 2001, pp344-355.

[8]   Cowell, RG, Dawid, AP, Lauritzen, SL and Spiegelhater, DJ. Probabilistic Networks and Expert Systems. Springer-Verlag, (1999)

[9]   Weiss, G. (ed) (1999). Multi-Agent Systems. The MIT Press: Cambridge, MA.

[10]   Klemperer, P. (Ed). The Economic Theory Of Auctions. Edward Elgar Publishing (2000).

[11]   Debenham, JK and Simoff, S. Designing a Curious Negotiator. In proceedings Third International Workshop on Negotiations in electronic markets - beyond price discovery - e-Negotiations 2002, September 2002, Aix-en-Provence, France.

[12]   Watkins, M. Breakthrough Business Negotiation—A Toolbox for Managers. Jossey-Bass, 2002.

[13]   Myerson, R. & Satterthwaite, M. Efficient Mechanisms for Bilateral Trading. Journal of Economic Theory, 29, 1–21, April 1983.

[14]   Kraus, S. Strategic Negotiation in Multiagent Environments. MIT Press, 2001.

Adaptive Multi-agent Decision Making Using Analytical Hierarchy Process

Juei-Nan Chen[1], Yueh-Min Huang[1], and William C. Chu[2]

[1] Department of Engineering Science, National Cheng Kung University,
Tainan, Taiwan, R.O.C.
n9890112@ccmail.ncku.edu.tw
raymond@mail.ncku.edu.tw
[2] Department of Computer Science and Information Engineering, TungHai University,
Taichung, Taiwan, R.O.C.
chu@csie.thu.edu.tw

Abstract. In multi-agent decision-making problems, we should treat all the participating agents with no partiality. In this paper, we seek to elicit the cooperation level from each agent's inner world. This benefit would be gained by the reasonable preference values to each alternative in the viewpoint of the group. Besides, we propose a methodology to adapt group's preference functions. It can make all the participating agents have the chances to pick up the most favorite choice after several rounds of decision-making process.

1 Introduction

Group decision-making is among the most important and frequently encountered processes within companies and organizations. Individual group members will have their own motivations and, hence, will be in conflict on certain issues [6]. Nevertheless, since the group members are 'supposed' to be striving for the same goal and have more in common than in conflict, it is usually best to work as a group and attempt to achieve consensus. Therefore, group decision-making becomes a critical issue when these participants have to make a decision. Agents are often used to assist in group decision-making and problem solving [3][7]. Each agent can be said to have a different perspective on the problem.

In this paper, we attempt to use Analytical Hierarchy Process (AHP), which was developed by Saaty [9], to assist each agent to evaluate a problem in the form of a hierarchy of references through a series of pair-wise comparisons of relative criteria. A group decision mechanism consists of a process for selecting one of the alternatives based upon the preferences of the individual agents composing the group. It is clear that any nondiscriminatory decision mechanism should treat all the participants in the same way; it should not use any information about the participants other than their preferences. We shall call this condition impartiality [10]. Since AHP couldn't satisfy this criterion, we can apply the multi-agent decision procedure, which was proposed by Yager [10], to benefit from the strategic manipulation of the preference function

R.I. McKay and J. Slaney (Eds.): AI 2002, LNAI 2557, pp. 203–212, 2002.

they provide to the group decision mechanism. However, what must be kept in mind is that each of the individual agent's real objective is not the maximization of the group function but the maximization of their own individual preference function.

Nevertheless, it seems that the multi-agent decision procedure engaged in the same decision maker in a long-term situation is unfair. Therefore, we proposed a mechanism to adjust the preference weights of each agent. This mechanism will adjust each agent's weight whenever a group decision is made.

The paper is set up as follows: the original concept of AHP is reviewed in Section 2. In Section 3, we introduce the multi-agent decision procedure. In Section 4, a tuning weight methodology is proposed. Then we integrate these processes and have an example illustration in Section 5 and Section 6. Finally, conclusions and recommendations are presented in Section 7.

2   Analytical Hierarchy Process

The Analytic Hierarchy Process (AHP) is a streamlined approach to cope with decision-making. The purpose of the AHP is to select the best choice from a number of alternatives, which are evaluated with respect to several criteria [8]. In this paper, we use the AHP to choose the individual agent's decision from several alternatives. Therefore, individual agents will pick the best solution out, and try their best to gain the best effort.

In the first step of the AHP, the decision maker has to construct the hierarchy structure of a goal. The simplest form used to structure a decision problem consists of three levels shown in Fig. 1. The goal of the decision is laid at the top level. The following is criterion level, which is assumed to be linear independent from one to another. The alternative is the lowest level, which will be evaluated by each criterion. Hierarchical decomposition of complex system is used by the human mind to find out the diversity from each criterion. Once the structuring is completed, the AHP is surprisingly simple to apply [8].

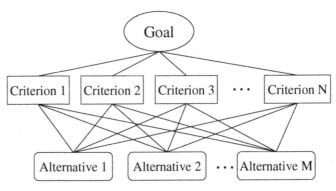

Fig. 1. A three level hierarchy

In the second step, each decision maker should subjectively accomplish the pair-wise matrices [8]; each of the matrices should pass the consistent test [5]. We can accomplish the pair-wise matrices between criterion layer and alternative layer, which is shown in Eq. (1). In the same way, the matrix among goal and criterion layer can be reckoned up.

$$
B = \begin{bmatrix} \dfrac{w_1}{w_1} & \dfrac{w_1}{w_2} & .. & \dfrac{w_1}{w_n} \\ \dfrac{w_2}{w_1} & \dfrac{w_2}{w_2} & .. & \dfrac{w_2}{w_n} \\ \vdots & \vdots & & \vdots \\ \dfrac{w_n}{w_1} & \dfrac{w_n}{w_2} & .. & \dfrac{w_n}{w_n} \end{bmatrix} = \begin{bmatrix} 1 & b_{12} & .. & b_{1n} \\ 1/b_{12} & 1 & .. & b_{2n} \\ \vdots & \vdots & & \vdots \\ 1/b_{1n} & 1/b_{2n} & .. & 1 \end{bmatrix} \tag{1}
$$

where B is the pair-wise comparison matrix (size $n \times n$); $\dfrac{w_x}{w_y}$ represents the relative importance of the x-th criterion over the y-th criterion $(x, y \in 1,2,...,n)$. In general, the value of $\dfrac{w_x}{w_y}$ is given by a decision maker subjectively. There are $n(n-1)$ judgments b required to develop the set of matrices. Reciprocals are automatically assigned in each pair-wise comparison shown in Eq. (1).

In the third step, we can get the priority vector of each matrix. The hierarchical weighting method is usually used to find the priority vector of each alternative [8]. The priority vector of each matrix can be expressed by a set of linear equations $W_1, W_2,..., W_n$. The summation of $W_1, W_2,..., W_n$ is always equal to 1, which is shown in Eq. (2).

$$
W_1 + W_2 + ... + W_n = 1 \tag{2}
$$

The other way of synthesizing is the ideal mode. In this mode, the priority vectors of the alternatives for each criterion are divided by the value of the highest rated alternative that becomes the ideal and receives a value of 1.

Table 1. Average random consistency index (RI)

Size of matrix	1	2	3	4	5	6	7	8	9	10
Random consistency	0	0	0.58	0.9	1.12	1.24	1.32	1.41	1.45	1.49

The fourth step is to calculate the consistency index, CI. as follows, $CI = (\lambda_{max} - n)/(n-1)$, where n is the matrix size and λ_{max} is the eigenvalue. We can use random index (RI) and consistency index (CI) to check if the matrix works or not, where $CR = CI/RI$ (RI is shown in Table 1). If the value of CR does not exceed 0.10, the matrix is acceptable. Otherwise, the judgment should be rechecked.

Finally, we can synthesize the priorities. There are two ways of doing that. One is the distributive mode. The other way of synthesizing is the ideal mode. The alternative becomes the ideal and receives a value of 1.

3   Group Decision Making

We use AHP to notify the individual agent the preference degree of each alternative. Because the AHP has to give different importance of each agent when we want to make the group decision. It is clear that any nondiscriminatory decision mechanism should treat all the participants in the same way; it should not use any information about the participants other than their preferences.

One of the alternatives which is from set $A = \{A_1, A_2, ...A_m\}$ must be chosen as a group decision. Let A denote a universal set. For a given fuzzy set F, the membership function $\mu_F(A)$ is usually defined as the form $\mu_F : A \rightarrow [0,1]$ where $[0,1]$ denotes the interval of real numbers from 0 to 1, inclusive.

Besides, all of the n agents must cooperate in this mechanism. Each agent will provide its preference in the way of fuzzy subset over the set A. $Agent_j$ denotes as the fuzzy subset for agent j, then $Agent_j(A_i)$ represents how satisfied $Agent_j$ is. We assume each agent assigns a value of one to its most preferred alternatives. Meanwhile, the agent is unable to know other participating agents' preference functions.

The way we combine all the individual agents is denoted as $GAgent$, also a fuzzy subset of A. As soon as we have the group preference function, the mechanism will pick the largest value in $GAgent$. Generally speaking, we know that the alternative is based upon the preference information which is provided by each of the individual participating agents.

We can model the single alternative of all the participant agents using any T-norm aggregation operator T. Let $T : [0,1] \times [0,1] \rightarrow [0,1]$, T is a T-norm, if and only if (iff) for all $a,b,c \in [0,1]$ [2] :

1) $T(a,b) = T(b,a)$ (commutativity)
2) $T(a,b) \leq T(a,c)$, if $b \leq c$ (monotonicity)
3) $T(a,T(b,c)) = T(T(a,b),c)$ (associativity)
4) $T(a,1) = a$ (boundary)

While all of the t-norm operators accomplish all the alternatives of the participant agents, we use T-conorm operator T^* to get the optimum group decision. Let $T^* : [0,1] \times [0,1] \rightarrow [0,1]$, T^* is a T-conorm, if and only if (iff) for all $a,b,c \in [0,1]$ [2]:

1) $T^*(a,b) = T^*(b,a)$

2) $T^*(a,b) \le T^*(a,c),\ if\ b \le c$

3) $T^*(a, T^*(b,c)) = T^*(T^*(a,b),c)$

4) $T^*(a,0) = a$

One example of a group collaboration imperative is to require that *all* participating agents must agree with the group choice. All the participating agents must agree upon any other group collaboration imperative. We shall call this the primal collaboration imperative. Once the participating agent doesn't like the alternative, it will dismiss the alternative automatically. It means that we can use this Min aggregation operator, $GAgent(A_i) = Min_j[Agent_j(A_i)]$ (T-norm operator), to solve this situation. Due to Min aggregation operation, we can know that for any $A_i \in A$ there exists an agent j such that $Agent_j(A_i) = 0$ then $GAgent(A_i) = 0$. That indicates any agent can single-handedly dismiss a solution. Hence, we can conclude that when all agents accept the solution, the mechanism will work perfectly without any other help.

To avoid such kind of situation, we should adjust the lower alternative value appropriately before T-norm aggregation operator. Let $S_j = \sum_i Agent_j(A_i)$, it is the sum of the scores over all alternatives by the agent j. S_j can be considered as the cooperation level of each agent tie in a group decision. The higher S_j means the higher conspiracy intent. Furthermore, let $S^* = Max_j[S_j]$ (T-conorm operation), it is the highest total score. We shall now associate with each agent a degree of importance I_j such that

$$I_j = \frac{S_j}{S^*} \tag{3}$$

We notice that $I_j \in [0,1]$ reflected the importance of *Agent_j*. The more total score he provides the more important. Furthermore, we get the divergent value $\bar{I}_j$ to be the threshold value of each alternative using Eq. (4).

$$\bar{I}_j = \frac{S^* - S_j}{S^*} \tag{4}$$

After $Max_j[\bar{I}_j, Agent_j(A)]$ in Eq. (5), the lower values are adjusted higher to be suitable value in a group. Whenever the alternative values are lower than $\bar{I}_j$, it will be seen as unreasonable condition, and the alternative should be tuned higher spontaneously. Therefore, the single-handedly condition can be solved by this method. After modifying the unreasonable condition, we use min operation to get the group decision of each alternative in Eq. (5).

$$GAgent(A_i) = Min_i \{Max_j [\bar{I}_j, Agent_j(A_i)]\} \qquad (5)$$

Finally, we can use max operation to choose the maximum alternative *GAgent* in Eq. (6). This alternative is the best group decision using this method.

$$GAgent(A) = Max_i[GAgent(A_i)] \qquad (6)$$

4 Tuning Group Decision Weight

In a group, we can not always obey the best solution and ignore the others alternative, especially in Virtual Enterprise [4] need to make the long-term decision. It is unfair in a group decision environment. So we need to modify all of the alternative values of each agent after making the decision procedure. Whenever the group decision choose the alternative A_i, the alternative A_i will be tuned down in the second round; vice versa. This variation will base on approving volition of each agent. The alternative A_i will probably be chosen, or the second priority will be picked in the second round. As a result, the opinion with fewer supports still could be chosen after several rounds of decision procedures.

If the approving volition has great majority, it means that the opinion of a group has few conflict. We will tune the weight slightly. If all of the agents approve the decision, the weight will not modify. Oppositely, if the approving volition owns less proportion, the weight will change substantially.

We use this kind of mechanism to adapt each agent's weight in a group, and it will make the group decision fairly in a long-term viewpoint. So, the following weight tuning method can be introduced:

Tuning down the alternative weight that is chosen by group (shown in Eq. (7)). To avoid the value lower than 0, we use the Max operation to choose the higher one.

$$A_i' = Max\left\{0, A_i - A_i \times C\left(1 - P/N\right)\right\} \qquad (7)$$

A_i : the alternative value provided by the agent.

A_i' : the new alternative value which is modified in the second round.

C : the tuning constant which control the variation degree. $0 \le C \le 1$

P : the number of optimal decision of the agents.

N : the total number of the agents.

Tuning up the alternative weight that is not chosen by group (shown in Eq. (8)). To avoid the value higher than 1, we use the Min operation to choose the lower one. If we have m alternatives, it means that there are m-1 alternatives not be chosen. So, the up tuning profit should be shared among these m-1 alternatives.

$$A_i' = Min\left\{ 1, A_i + A_i \times C \times \frac{1}{m-1}\left(1 - P/_N\right) \right\} \tag{8}$$

5 Group Decision Making Algorithm

In this section, we integrate the previous methodologies into an algorithm called Group Decision Making Algorithm. From step 1 to step 4 is the personal AHP decision procedure. Step 5 to step 8 is the group decision-making procedure. Finally, the step 9 is the tuning group decision weight procedure.

Algorithm 1. Group Decision Making Algorithm

Step 1: Construct the hierarchy structure of a goal.
Step 2: Subjectively accomplish the pair-wise comparison matrices between any two of layers.
Step 3: Calculate the priority vector of each matrix.
Step 4: Judgment consistency using CR. If CR > 0.1, go to step 2.
Step 5: Until all the participant agents accomplish the ideal alternative values.
Step 6: Summation all the alternatives of each agent S_j. Higher S_j means higher conspiracy intent.
Step 7: Getting $S^* = Max_j[S_j]$ to calculate I_j and $\bar{I}_j$ of each agent's conspiracy intent.
Step 8: Using Eq. (5) and (6) to compute each alternative intent of group viewpoint and choose the best one.
Step 9: Tuning the alternatives of each agent, go to step 6.

6 Illustrative Example

The main objective of a Virtual Enterprise is to allow a number of organizations to rapidly develop a common working environment; hence managing collection of resources provided by the participating organizations toward the attainment of some common goals. Because each partner brings a strength or core competence to the consortium, the success of the project depends on all cooperating as a single unit [4].

For example, there are four memberships in a Virtual Enterprise, and this Virtual Enterprise has to pick out one decision that is the best choice of viewing the situation as a whole. Hence, these four memberships have to propose the assenting level to each selective alternative. Once all of the participant members accomplish the assenting level of each selective alternative, we can use the group decision procedure to make good decision in a viewpoint of a group. Here we have three alternatives to be chosen.

Table 2 to Table 5 is the overall priority ranking of each agent. C means the criterion, and A means the alternative.

Table 2. Agent$_1$'s overall priority ranking

Agent$_1$	C$_1$(0.4)	C$_2$(0.3)	C$_3$(0.2)	C$_4$(0.1)
A$_1$	0.75	0.33	1	0.11
A$_2$	1	0.33	0.2	0
A$_3$	0.75	1	0.8	1

$Agent_1(A_1) = (0.4)(0.75) + (0.3)(0.33) + (0.2)(1) + (0.1)(0.11) = 0.61$
$Agent_1(A_2) = (0.4)(1) + (0.3)(0.33) + (0.2)(0.2) + (0.1)(0) = 0.54$
$Agent_1(A_3) = (0.4)(0.75) + (0.3)(1) + (0.2)(0.8) + (0.1)(1) = 0.86$

Table 3. Agent$_2$'s overall priority ranking

Agent$_2$	C$_1$(0.1)	C$_2$(0.1)	C$_3$(0.1)	C$_4$(0.7)
A$_1$	0.5	0.4	0	0.5
A$_2$	1	1	1	1
A$_3$	0.17	0.6	1	1

$Agent_2(A_1) = (0.1)(0.5) + (0.1)(0.4) + (0.1)(0) + (0.7)(0.5) = 0.44$
$Agent_2(A_2) = (0.1)(1) + (0.1)(1) + (0.1)(1) + (0.7)(1) = 1$
$Agent_2(A_3) = (0.1)(0.17) + (0.1)(0.6) + (0.1)(1) + (0.7)(1) = 0.88$

Table 4. Agent$_3$'s overall priority ranking

Agent$_3$	C$_1$(0)	C$_2$(0.6)	C$_3$(0)	C$_4$(0.4)
A$_1$	1	0.5	0.33	1
A$_2$	0.43	1	1	0.125
A$_3$	0	0.17	0.33	0.125

$Agent_3(A_1) = (0)(1) + (0.6)(0.5) + (0)(0.33) + (0.4)(1) = 0.7$
$Agent_3(A_2) = (0)(0.43) + (0.6)(1) + (0)(1) + (0.4)(0.125) = 0.5$
$Agent_3(A_3) = (0)(0) + (0.6)(0.17) + (0)(0.33) + (0.4)(0.125) = 0.15$

Table 5. Agent$_4$'s overall priority ranking

Agent$_4$	C$_1$(0.2)	C$_2$(0.3)	C$_3$(0.5)	C$_4$(0)
A$_1$	1	1	0.4	0
A$_2$	0.125	0	1	0
A$_3$	0.125	0.67	0.6	1

$Agent_4(A_1) = (0.2)(1) + (0.3)(1) + (0.5)(0.4) + (0)(0) = 0.7$
$Agent_4(A_2) = (0.2)(0.125) + (0.3)(0) + (0.5)(1) + (0)(0) = 0.53$
$Agent_4(A_3) = (0.2)(0.125) + (0.3)(0.67) + (0.5)(0.6) + (0)(1) = 0.53$

Then we can get their respective preferences functions are

$$Agent_1 = \left\{ \frac{0.61}{A_1}, \frac{0.54}{A_2}, \frac{0.86}{A_3} \right\}, \quad Agent_2 = \left\{ \frac{0.44}{A_1}, \frac{1}{A_2}, \frac{0.88}{A_3} \right\},$$

$$Agent_3 = \left\{ \frac{0.7}{A_1}, \frac{0.5}{A_2}, \frac{0.15}{A_3} \right\}, \quad Agent_4 = \left\{ \frac{0.7}{A_1}, \frac{0.53}{A_2}, \frac{0.53}{A_3} \right\}.$$

In this case, $S_1 = 2.01$, $S_2 = 2.32$, $S_3 = 1.35$ and $S_4 = 1.76$. Using these we get $S^* = 2.32$. Hence $I_1 = (2.01/2.32) = 0.87$, $\bar{I}_1 = (0.31/2.32) = 0.13$, $I_2 = 1$, $\bar{I}_2 = 0$, $I_3 = 0.58$, $\bar{I}_3 = 0.42$, $I_4 = 0.76$ and $\bar{I}_4 = 0.24$. Then we find the $Agent_3(A_3)$ is smaller than the threshold value $\bar{I}_3$. The original value $Agent_3(A_3)$ should be tuned to $\bar{I}_3 \vee Agent_3(A_3) = 0.42$, and it can be seem as meaningful value in a viewpoint of group.

$$Agent_1 = \left\{ \frac{0.61}{A_1}, \frac{0.54}{A_2}, \frac{0.86}{A_3} \right\}, \quad Agent_2 = \left\{ \frac{0.44}{A_1}, \frac{1}{A_2}, \frac{0.88}{A_3} \right\},$$

$$Agent_3 = \left\{ \frac{0.7}{A_1}, \frac{0.5}{A_2}, \frac{0.42}{A_3} \right\}, \quad Agent_4 = \left\{ \frac{0.7}{A_1}, \frac{0.53}{A_2}, \frac{0.53}{A_3} \right\}.$$

Taking $GAgent(A_i) = Min_i \left\{ Max_j [\bar{I}_j, Agent_j(A_i)] \right\}$ we get: $GAgent(A_1) = 0.44$, $GAgent(A_2) = 0.5$ and $GAgent(A_3) = 0.42$. Finally, taking $GAgent(A) = Max_i[GAgent(A_i)]$ we get the group decision is A_2.

After making the group decision procedure, we should tune the alternative values for second round. Taking the Eq. (7) the A_2 should be tuning down. In contrast, using the Eq. (8) the A_1 and A_3 should be tuning up. We can get the result as below.

$$Agent'_1 = \left\{ \frac{0.72}{A_1}, \frac{0.34}{A_2}, \frac{1}{A_3} \right\}, \quad Agent'_2 = \left\{ \frac{0.52}{A_1}, \frac{0.625}{A_2}, \frac{1}{A_3} \right\},$$

$$Agent'_3 = \left\{ \frac{0.83}{A_1}, \frac{0.31}{A_2}, \frac{0.5}{A_3} \right\}, \quad Agent'_4 = \left\{ \frac{0.83}{A_1}, \frac{0.33}{A_2}, \frac{0.63}{A_3} \right\}.$$

Obviously, A_2 will not be chosen in the second round, but A_1. As a result of each agent's volition has larger conflict, the group decision has greater variation in the next round.

7 Conclusions

In multi-agent decision making environment, each agent has its own concerning factors when making a choice. In this paper, we use the analytic hierarchy process (AHP) to evaluate a problem in the form of a hierarchy. Each agent can flexibly accomplish different hierarchy structure according to its situation as long as these agents have the same selective alternatives.

We have extended the group decision-making process based on fuzzy preference functions by allowing the agents to propose their favorite level of each alternative. In some cases, the participating agent might have highly preferred choice and drop the others. To avoid such kind of situation, we suggest approaches of modifying the formulation of the group decision functions to discourage strategic manipulation by the participating agents.

In long-term of viewpoint, the group decision cannot always follow the majority of the choices and ignore the rest. Hence, we should adapt the values effectively after each round of decision process. This will make it possible that the minority of the opinions being picked out after several periods of decision process.

References

1. B.A. Akash, R. Mamlook, M.S. Mohsen, "Multi-criteria selection of electric power plants using analytical hierarchy process," *Electric Power Systems Research*, Vol. 52, 1999, pp. 29–35.
2. M.M. Gupta, J. Qi, "Theory of T-norm and Fuzzy Inference Methods," *Fuzzy Sets and Systems*, 1991, pp. 431–450.
3. C.C. Hayes, "Agents in a Nutshell – A Very Brief Introduction," *IEEE Transactions on Knowledge and Data Engineering*, Vol. 11, No. 1, 1999, pp. 127–132.
4. P.K. Hye, F. Joël, "Virtual Enterprise – Information System and Networking Solution," *Computers & Industrial Engineering*, Vol. 37, Issue: 1-2, 1999, pp. 441–444.
5. L.C. Leung, D. Cao, "On Consistency and Ranking of Alternatives in Fuzzy AHP," *European Journal of Operational Research*, Vol. 24, No. 1, 2000, pp. 102–113.
6. N.F. Matsatsinis, A.P. Samaras, "MCDA and preference disaggregation in group decision support systems," *European Journal of Operational Research*, Vol. 130, 2001, pp. 414–429.
7. D.A. Roozemond, "Using intelligent agents for pro-active, real-time urban intersection control," *European Journal of Operational Research*, Vol. 131, 2001, pp. 293–301.
8. T.L. Saaty, L.G. Vargas, *Models, Methods, Concepts & Applications of the Analytic Hierarchy Process*, Kluwer Academic Publishers, 2000.
9. T.L. Saaty, *The Analytic Hierarchy Process: planning, priority setting, resource allocation*, McGraw-Hill, New York, 1980.
10. R.R. Yager, "Penalizing Strategic Preference Manipulation in Multi-Agent Decision Making," *IEEE Transactions on Fuzzy Systems*, Vol. 9, No. 3, 2001, pp. 393–403.

Autonomous Planning and Scheduling on the TechSat 21 Mission

Rob Sherwood, Steve Chien, Rebecca Castano, and Gregg Rabideau

Jet Propulsion Laboratory, California Institute of Technology
4800 Oak Grove Dr., Pasadena, CA 91109
Firstname.lastname@jpl.nasa.gov
http://ase.jpl.nasa.gov

Abstract. The Autonomous Sciencecraft Experiment (ASE) will fly onboard the Air Force TechSat 21 constellation of three spacecraft scheduled for launch in 2006. ASE uses onboard continuous planning, robust task and goal-based execution, model-based mode identification and reconfiguration, and onboard machine learning and pattern recognition to radically increase science return by enabling intelligent downlink selection and autonomous retargeting. In this paper we discuss how these AI technologies are synergistically integrated in a hybrid multi-layer control architecture to enable a *virtual spacecraft science agent*. Demonstration of these capabilities in a flight environment will open up tremendous new opportunities in planetary science, space physics, and earth science that would be unreachable without this technology.

1 Introduction

There is an increasing desire in many organizations, including NASA and the DoD, to use onboard decision-making to accomplish complex mission objectives. The Air Force Research Laboratory (AFRL) has initiated the TechSat 21 program to serve as a demonstration mission for a new paradigm for space missions. This paradigm seeks to reduce costs and increase system robustness and maintainability by using onboard autonomy to enable faster response times and improve operations efficiency.

TechSat 21 is scheduled for launch in January 2006 and will fly three satellites in a near circular orbit at an altitude of approximately 550 Km. The primary mission is one-year in length with the possibility for an extended mission of one or more additional years. During the mission lifetime the cluster of satellites will fly in various configurations with relative separation distances of approximately 100 meters to 5 Km. One of the objectives of TechSat 21 is to assess the utility of the space-based, sparse-array aperture formed by the satellite cluster. For TechSat 21, the sparse array will be used to synthesize a large radar antenna. Three modes of radar sensing are planned: synthetic aperture radar (SAR) imaging, moving target indication (MTI), and geo-location.

B. McKay and J. Slaney (Eds.): AI 2002, LNAI 2557, pp. 213–224, 2002.

The principal processor onboard each of the three TechSat 21 spacecraft is a BAE Radiation hardened 175 MIPS, 133MHz PowerPC 750 running the OSE 4.3 operating system from Enea Systems. Each satellite will have 256 Kbytes of EEPROM for boot loads and 128 Mbytes of SDRAM. Communications will be through a Compact PCI bus.

The ASE onboard flight software includes several autonomy software components:
- *Onboard science algorithms* that will analyze the image data to detect trigger conditions such as science events, "interesting" features, and changes relative to previous observations
- *Robust execution management software* using the Spacecraft Command Language (SCL) [7] package to enable event-driven processing and low-level autonomy
- The Continuous Activity Planning, Scheduling, and Replanning (CASPER) [4] *planner* that will replan activities, including downlink, based on science observations in the previous orbit cycles
- Observation Planning (OP) software will enable the satellites to predict overflights of targets to facilitate onboard retasking.

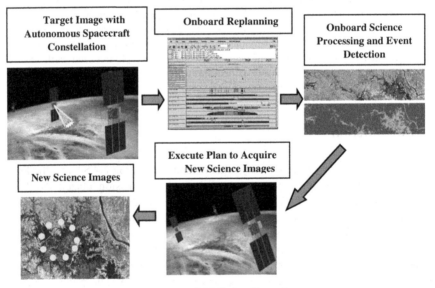

Fig. 1. ASE Mission Scenario

The onboard science algorithms will analyze the images to extract static features and detect changes relative to previous observations. Prototype software has already been demonstrated on X-band radar data (from shuttle missions) to automatically identify regions of interest including: regions of change (such as flooding, ice melt, and lava flows), and feature recognition (such as crater and volcano recognition). Such onboard science will enable retargeting and search, e.g., shifting the radar aim-point on the next orbit cycle to identify and capture the full extent of a flood. On future interplanetary space missions, onboard science analysis will enable capture of short-lived science phenomena at the finest time-scales without overwhelming on-board caching or downlink capacities. Examples include: eruption of volcanoes on Io, formation of jets on comets, and phase transitions in ring systems. Generation of de-rived science products (e.g., boundary descriptions, catalogs) and change-based trig-gering will also reduce data volumes to a manageable level for extended duration missions that study long-term phenomena such as atmospheric changes at Jupiter and flexing and cracking of the ice crust on Europa.

The onboard planner (CASPER) will generate mission operations plans from goals provided by the onboard science analysis module. The model-based planning algo-rithms will enable rapid response to a wide range of operations scenarios based on a deep model of spacecraft constraints, including faster recovery from spacecraft anomalies. The onboard planner will accept as inputs the science and engineering goals and ensure high-level goal-oriented behavior for the constellation.

The robust execution system (SCL) accepts the CASPER-derived plan as an input and expands the plan into low-level commands. SCL monitors the execution of the plan and has the flexibility and knowledge to perform event-driven commanding to enable local improvements in execution as well as local responses to anomalies.

One of the ASE demonstration scenarios involves monitoring of flooding regions in Arizona. (See Fig. 1.) Radar data have been used in ground-based analysis to study this phenomenon. The ASE concept would be applied as follows:

1. Initially, ASE has a list of science targets to monitor that have been sent as high-level goals from the ground.
2. As part of normal operations, CASPER generates a plan to monitor the targets on this list by periodically imaging them with the radar.
3. During execution of this plan, a spacecraft images a river area with its ra-dar.
4. Onboard, a reflectivity image is formed.
5. The *Onboard Science Software* compares the new image with previous image and detects that the water region has changed due to flooding. Based on this change the science software generates a goal to acquire a new high-resolution image of an area of flooding.
6. The addition of this goal to the current goal set triggers CASPER to mod-ify the current operations plan to include numerous new activities in order to enable the new science observation. During this process CASPER inter-acts with the Observation Planner to compute when the spacecraft will fly over the target and determine the required slews to acquire the target.
7. The SCL software executes this plan in conjunction with several autonomy elements. The MI-R software assists by continuously providing an up to date picture of system state and achieving configurations requested by SCL.

Based on the science priority, imagery of identified "new flood" areas are down-linked. This science priority could have been determined at the original event detec-tion or based on subsequent onboard science analysis of the new image.

As demonstrated by this scenario, many different capabilities are used synergistically to enable the spacecraft to behave as an autonomous exploration agent. In our agent architecture, ASE allocates responsibilities both based on abstraction level and domain (e.g., same level of abstraction but a specific discipline such as science or maneuver planning). Specifically, each of the software components has responsibilities as follows. First, for the areas of science decision-making and maneuvers, responsibilities are delegated based on the discipline involved. All of the processing and analysis of science data analysis is performed by the Onboard Science software. This design makes sense because the science processing we are performing is very specialized image processing and pattern recognition and requires special purpose algorithms. Because this is primarily a batch process, there is no real-time decision-making component to the Onboard Science software. However, this is a TechSat 21 specific distinction. Many other autonomous science missions might have a real-time science component, such as to rapidly detect a very short duration science event (such as a supernova) or to control a science instrument rapidly based on science analysis. The Observation Planner software is used to reason about maneuvers, determine when a target can be observed, and determine when communication with the spacecraft is possible. Again, this architecture is chosen because this decision-making capability relies on highly specialized reasoning algorithms to minimize fuel consumption and to reason geometrically about orbits and orbital dynamics. In this case there is both a plan-time and real-time execution component.

In the space operations arena, ASE uses CASPER, SCL, and MI-R to provide distinct, synergistic capabilities. Long-term mission planning, which requires search and the ability to reason about complex states and resources, is performed by CASPER. CASPER is able to respond on a several minute timescale to replan in response to anomalies and science opportunities. CASPER uses a model-based approach to represent operations knowledge. For decision-making at a lower level and requiring a more rapid response, ASE uses SCL and MI-R. SCL and MI-R are able to respond on the order of seconds, and in some cases even more quickly. SCL and MI-R are complementary in that SCL uses a procedural (script and rule based) representation while MI-R uses a declarative stochastic finite state model. These representations are complementary; in different cases one may be more appropriate. Additionally, MI-R's stochastic model is particularly adept at interpreting noisy data from sensors and achieving hardware configurations in the presence of unreliable hardware.

While the TechSat 21 mission is amenable to a multi-agent formulation with each of the three spacecraft being a separate agent, ASE operates the three spacecraft as a single agent exerting centralized control over the three spacecraft. From a mission perspective, operating three spacecraft as self-coordinating agents was viewed as being too risky. After all, ASE will already be performing revolutionary on-board decision-making.

ASE will fly on the TechSat 21 mission and the necessary software is currently being matured and brought into flight readiness. A working version of the flight software described in this paper exists operating on Sun workstations on a wide range of operational scenarios. Already, two out of five components are operational on the flight processor. The remaining three components have been ported to the flight operating system on embedded processor (completed in the Spring of 2002). Final delivery of the spacecraft and software is expected complete in late 2003. Nominal launch date is January 2006.

2   Onboard Science

There are two components of the onboard science software, the *image formation module* and the *onboard science algorithms*. The image formation module forms a reduced resolution SAR image onboard the spacecraft from the raw phase history. In the ASE mission concept, we only need to form a few images per orbit cycle (in contrast to a global mapping mission such as Magellan); hence, the necessary processing can be carried out onboard.

Once the image has been formed, the *onboard science algorithms* can then analyze the SAR image to create derived science products and detect trigger conditions, such as change relative to a previous orbit cycle. For example, the backscatter properties of a lava flow are a function of the composition of the lava; thus, new lava flows with a distinct composition from the old flow can be easily detected and localized. Likewise, water has very different backscatter characteristics than soil, enabling detection of flooding.

Fig. 2. Automatically identified lava cones in X-SAR image of Lava Beds National Monument, CA

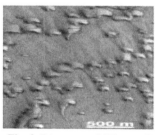

Fig. 3. Discovery of "Unusual" Visual Features

We are currently investigating demonstrating several methods of converting images into derived science products. The derived products will in effect be summarizations that are significantly more compact than the raw image (or phase history) data. Statistical pattern recognition techniques [1] [3] will be used to identify specific types of features such as volcanoes, lakes, and iceberg fragments. Fig. 2 shows results from a prototype lava cone recognition algorithm under development for ASE flight. Output from such a module could be used to downlink higher resolution data around items of interest or by downlinking a summary catalog of the interesting features. Recently developed discovery techniques [2] will also be applied to identify "interesting" regions that differ from their local background leading to a compact description of an image in terms of sub-image patches and locations. (See Fig. 3.)

In addition to calculations based on a single image, the onboard science analysis software will include change detection algorithms that compare images of the same region taken at different times. The change detection capability is particularly relevant for capture of short-term events at the finest time-scale resolutions without over-whelming onboard caching systems and for compressing long-term "monitoring" observations in which changes are infrequent.

To detect change, we will test for statistically significant differences in derived de-scriptors such as region sizes, locations, boundaries, and histograms, as well as in the raw pixel data. The latter case is complicated by the need to ensure that the two im-ages are approximately co-registered. In part, the orbit repeatability and small absolute positional uncertainty of the TechSat 21 group will help insure approximate co-registration. Also, since the magnitude of change necessary to initiate a trigger event can be specified as a parameter, some degree of robustness to image misalignment will be built in. For change detection, radar observations have the advantage that the illumination, target, and receiver geometry remains basically the same from pass to pass. (In optical imagery, irrelevant change caused by sun position complicates the change detection problem.) Fig. 3 contains successive X-SAR radar images indicating lava flow on the Kilauea volcano in Hawaii. The changes in the highlighted areas of the image are indicative of lava flow that occurred in between images. This is the type of change detection that our algorithms will perform onboard TechSat 21.

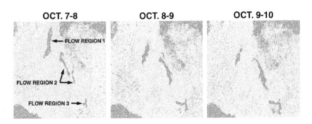

Fig. 3. Hawaii Lava Flows

Detection of the image and change-based triggers described here will enable a range of automated spacecraft reactions. On the conservative end of the spectrum, triggers can be used to prioritize data for downlink. For example, regions in which change was detected may be downlinked first. (With TechSat 21, it will take a full four days to downlink the entire onboard cache of the three spacecraft.) Early access to the "interesting data" would be especially valuable to the project scientist, poten-tially enabling a request for modification of the original observation plan.

A slightly more aggressive use of the trigger information involves actually "dis-carding data". For example, if nothing significant has changed in a region, exclude that region from the downlink. Although the scientist would never like to discard data, the realities of a finite onboard cache and constrained downlink bandwidth will some-times force a discard to satisfy the primary objective.

A third, more aggressive, but potentially extremely rewarding, use of the trigger in-formation that we will demonstrate onboard TechSat 21 is to autonomously retarget observations. For example, if an image indicates flooding in a region, subsequent orbits will employ the planner to close the loop onboard and use a modified radar aim-point in an attempt to capture the full scope of the flooding.

3   Robust Execution

TechSat 21 will fly the Spacecraft Command Language (SCL) [7] to provide robust execution. SCL is a software package that integrates procedural programming with a real-time, forward-chaining, rule-based system. A publish/subscribe software bus allows the distribution of notification and request messages to integrate SCL with other onboard software. This enables either loose or tight coupling between SCL and other flight software as appropriate. Dynamic messages are supported to allow for future growth as ever-smarter software agents are added to the constellation in different satellites.

The SCL "smart" executive supports the command and control function. Users can define scripts in an English-like manner. Compiled on the ground, those scripts can be dynamically loaded onboard and executed at an absolute or relative time. Ground-based absolute time script scheduling is equivalent to the traditional procedural approach to spacecraft operations based on time. In the ASE concept, SCL scripts will also be planned and scheduled by the CASPER onboard planner. The science processing agents, cluster management software, and SCL work in a cooperative manner to generate new goals for CASPER. These goals are sent with the messaging system.

Spacecraft telemetry from all satellites is gathered onboard and fed into the integrated expert system. Significant change in the data will trigger user-defined rules. Those rules can be used for fault detection, isolation and recovery. In that case, rules can be used to execute recovery scripts. Another application of rules is for mission constraint checking to prevent operator errors or, more simply, command pre-processing.

SCL is a mature software product, and has successfully flown on Clementine-I and ROMPS. SCL has also been used in a wide range of ground-based control and operations contexts. As such it represents a good basis for integrating the multiple ASE autonomy functions: onboard science, mode identification and reconfiguration, planning, and constellation management.

4   Onboard Mission Planning

Traditionally, the majority of planning and scheduling research has focused on a batch formulation of the problem. In this approach, when addressing an ongoing planning problem, time is divided up into a number of planning horizons, each of which lasts for a significant period of time. When one nears the end of the current horizon, one projects what the state will be at the end of the execution of the current plan. The planner is invoked with a new set of goals for the new horizon, and the expected initial state for the new horizon. The planner then generates a plan for the new horizon. For example, the Remote Agent Experiment operated using this approach [8].

This approach has a number of drawbacks. In this batch oriented mode, typically planning is considered an off-line process, which requires considerable computational effort, and there is a significant delay from the time the planner is invoked to the time that the planner produces a new plan. If a negative event occurs (e.g., a plan failure), the response time until a new plan is generated may be significant. During this period the system being controlled must be operated appropriately without planner guidance. If a positive event occurs (e.g., a fortuitous opportunity, such as activities finishing early), again the response time may be significant. If the opportunity is short lived, the system must be able to take advantage of such opportunities without a new plan (because of the delay in generating a new plan). Finally, because the planning process may need to be initiated significantly before the end of the current planning horizon, it may be difficult to project what the state will be when the current plan execution is complete. If the projection is wrong the plan may not be executable.

To achieve a higher level of responsiveness in a *dynamic planning* situation, we utilize a *continuous planning* approach and have implemented a system called CASPER (Continuous Activity Scheduling Planning Execution and Replanning) [4]. Rather than considering planning a batch process in which a planner is presented with goals and an initial state, the planner has a current goal set, a plan, a current state, and a model of the expected future state. At any time an incremental update to the goals, current state, or planning horizon (at much smaller time increments than batch planning) may update the current state of the plan and thereby invoke the planner process. For the spacecraft control domain we are envisioning an update rate on the order of tens of seconds real time. This update may be an unexpected event or simply time progressing forward. The planner is then responsible for maintaining a consistent, satisficing plan with the most current information. This current plan and projection is the planner's estimation as to what it expects to happen in the world if things go as expected. However, since things rarely go exactly as expected, the planner stands ready to continually modify the plan. From the point of view of the planner, in each cycle the following occurs:

1. Changes to the goals and the initial state first posted to the plan,
2. Effects of these changes are propagated through the current plan projections (including conflict identification)
3. Plan repair algorithms [5] are invoked to remove conflicts and make the plan appropriate for the current state and goals

This approach is shown in Fig. 4. At each step, the plan is created by using incremental replanning from:

- The portion of the old plan for the current planning horizon
- The change (Δ) in the goals relevant for the new planning horizon
- The change (Δ) in the state
- The new (extended) planning horizon

In the ASE concept, CASPER is responsible for long-term mission planning in response to both science goals derived onboard as well as anomalies. In this role, CASPER must plan and schedule activities to achieve science and engineering goals while respecting resource and other spacecraft and constellation operations constraints. For example, when change is detected in an image, CASPER plans a response. If it is appropriate to take a more detailed image of the change area, CASPER will modify the operations plan to include the necessary activities to re-image. Other required activities, such as calibration of the radar, acquisition of the image, and subsequent science processing are all planned by CASPER. Each of the planned activities is derived from the original goal to re-image the change area. This goal will have state requirements for the radar instrument to be on during the over-flight, the memory available for the new image, the resources to downlink the new image, etc.

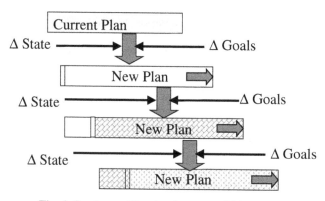

Fig. 4. Continuous Planning Incremental Plan Extension

When a new goal is placed on the schedule, conflicts occur for each of these related resources. CASPER modifies the schedule using iterative repair until no conflicts exist [15]. Operations for modifying the schedule include adding new activities, moving activities, deleting activities, changing activity parameters, etc. Each activity has a list of permissible operations for the iterative repair algorithm. The algorithm is fast, performing several hundred operations per second on a workstation, or a few operations per second on an 8 MIPS flight processor. (The typical response time for ASE is less than 10 minutes to elaborate a new complex goal.) The choice of operations can be guided with user defined scheduling heuristics [16]. The heuristics can be activity specific or generic. An example would be to try moving activities 50% of the time, adding activities 35% of the time, and deleting activities 15% of the time.

5   ASE Software Validation

Because of the significant TechSat 21 mission cost (> $100M), and that ASE will be controlling the spacecraft activities, TechSat 21 Management required significant safeguards on ASE development and operations. These safeguards include: analysis of ASE impact on the spacecraft, testing and validation requirements on ASE, and phased operations during actual flight.

First, the project conducted an independent analysis of the ways in which ASE actions could damage the spacecraft. This analysis determined approximately 30 general ways in which inappropriate commanding by ASE could adversely impact spacecraft health. For each of these ways, one or more mechanisms for detecting and preventing such commands were identified and required as part of the baseline experiment and mission design. For example, if ASE kept the radar payload on to long (e.g. did not power it down at the end of a data collect), this would overheat the payload (causing damage to the payload) as well as drain the battery. Both of these potential conditions will be monitored in both SCL and the TechSat 21 flight software. Additionally, this capability will be extensively tested before flight. Therefore the risk of ASE endangering the spacecraft via this interaction is remote. An important point is that a careful log of experiment operations will be kept and any misbehavior by ASE that results in the activation of TechSat 21 fault protection would be considered a failure of ASE.

Second, the ASE software is being extensively validated by: code, scenario, and model walkthroughs as well as testing. We are relying on years of past experience with both CASPER and SCL for basic software functionality validation. Science software can be unit validating using existing radar data with known science targets. For the TechSat 21 specific model deployments, we have developed a set of test cases. For each of the software builds, the range of cases covered is defined, designed, and reviewed by cognizant personnel. Additionally, for each build the software is tested on a wide range of test cases. For build 2, completed in June 2002, there are approximately 3000 test cases in the integrated system test suite.

Third, the experiment operations concept has a phased operation concept designed to build confidence in the system and shake out any remaining issues. In the first phases of the experiment, the ASE software will run in shadow mode, developing plans and commands but these commands will not be sent on to the spacecraft. In this phase ASE will score and evaluate science data onboard but will not be authorized to command the spacecraft based on the data analysis. In the full operational phase of the experiment, the ASE software will replan based on the science analysis and all ASE commands will be sent on to the spacecraft.

6   ASE and Multi-agent Systems

While TechSat 21 is a multi-spacecraft constellation, ASE is not a multi-agent system. In the ASE architecture, the constellation is treated as a single agent, with each of the spacecraft being a redundant subsystem. On one spacecraft, the "master" spacecraft, CASPER is running in order to perform the planning (and replanning) for the entire constellation of three spacecraft. The plans developed on the "master" spacecraft are sent on to the other two "slave" spacecraft. Because of this architecture there is no decentralized coordination problem. While there is significant interest in multi-agent coordinating spacecraft at NASA [12,13], for the TechSat 21 mission, use of a multi-agent, distributed architecture was viewed as too risky for flight at this time.

7   Related Work and Conclusions

In 1999, the Remote Agent experiment (RAX) [9] executed for a few days onboard the NASA Deep Space One mission. RAX is an example of a classic three-tiered architecture [11], as is ASE. RAX demonstrated a batch onboard planning capability (as opposed to ASE's continuous planning) and RAX did not demonstrate onboard science. RAX also included an earlier version of the Livingstone and Burton mode identification and fault recovery software. PROBA [10] is a European Space Agency (ESA) mission that will be demonstrating onboard autonomy and launches in 2001. However, ASE has more of a focus on model-based autonomy than PROBA.

More recent work from NASA Ames Research Center is focused on building the IDEA planning and execution architecture [14]. In IDEA, the planner and execution software are combined into a "reactive planner" and operate using the same domain model. A single planning and execution model can simplify validation, which is a difficult problem for autonomous systems. For ASE, the CASPER planner and SCL executive use separate models. We have designed the CASPER modeling language to be used by domain experts, thus not requiring planning experts. In ASE, SCL is running the plan and performing an independent local check of the plan. The "plan runner" in IDEA performs this function although without the validation check. The ASE science analysis software is defined as one of the "controlling systems" in IDEA. In the IDEA architecture, a communications wrapper is used to send messages between the agents, similar to the software bus in ASE. We are unaware of any deployments of the IDEA architecture, so a comparison of the performance or capabilities is not possible at this time.

The Three Corner Sat (3CS) University Nanosat mission will be using the CASPER onboard planning software integrated with the SCL ground and flight execution software [6]. The 3CS mission is scheduled for launch in late 2003. 3CS will use onboard science data validation, replanning, robust execution, and multiple model-based anomaly detection. The 3CS mission is considerably less complex than TechSat 21 but still represents an important step in the integration and flight of onboard autonomy software.

ASE will fly on the TechSat 21 mission will demonstrate an integrated autonomous mission using onboard science analysis, replanning, robust execution, model-based estimation and control, and formation flying. ASE will perform intelligent science data selection that will lead to a reduction in data downlink. In addition, the ASE experiment will increase science return through autonomous retargeting. Demonstration of these capabilities in onboard the TechSat 21 constellation mission will enable radically different missions with significant onboard decision-making leading to novel science opportunities. The paradigm shift toward highly autonomous spacecraft will enable future NASA missions to achieve significantly greater science returns with reduced risk and cost.

Acknowledgement. Portions of this work were performed at the Jet Propulsion Laboratory, California Institute of Technology, under a contract with the National Aeronautics and Space Administration.

References

1.   M.C. Burl, L. Asker, P. Smyth, U. Fayyad, P. Perona, J. Aubele, and L. Crumpler, "Learning to Recognize Volcanoes on Venus," *Machine Learning Journal,* April 1998.

224 R. Sherwood et al.

2. M.C. Burl and D. Lucchetti, "Autonomous Visual Discovery", *SPIE Aerosense Conference on Data Mining and Knowledge Discovery,* (Orlando, FL), April 2000.
3. M.C. Burl, W.J. Merline, E.B. Bierhaus, W. Colwell, C.R. Chapman, "Automated Detection of Craters and Other Geological Features *Intl Symp Artificial Intelligence Robotics & Automation in Space,* Montreal, Canada, June 2001
4. S. Chien, G. Rabideau, R. Knight, R. Sherwood, B. Engelhardt, D. Mutz, T. Estlin, B. Smith, F. Fisher, T. Barrett, G. Stebbins, D. Tran, "ASPEN - Automating Space Mission Operations using Automated Planning and Scheduling," *SpaceOps,* Toulouse, France, June 2000.
5. S. Chien, R. Knight, A. Stechert, R. Sherwood, and G. Rabideau, "Using Iterative Repair to Improve Responsiveness of Planning and Scheduling," *Proc Fifth International Conference on Artificial Intelligence Planning and Scheduling,* Breckenridge, CO, April 2000.
6. S. Chien, B. Engelhardt, R. Knight, G. Rabideau, R. Sherwood, E. Hansen, A. Ortiviz, C. Wilklow, S. Wichman " Onboard Autonomy on the Three Corner Sat Mission," *Intl Symposium on Artificial Intelligence Robotics and Automation in Space,* Montreal, Canada, June 2001
7. Interface & Control Systems, Spacecraft Command Language, http://www.sclrules.com, June 2002.
8. A. Jonsson, P. Morris, N. Muscettola, K. Rajan, and B. Smith, "Planning in Interplanetary Space: Theory and Practice," *Procs 5th Int Conference on Artificial Intelligence Planning Systems, Breckenridge,* CO, April 2000. J. Kurien and P.P. Nayak, "Back to the Future for Consistency-based Trajectory Tracking," *Proc. National Conference on Artificial Intelligence,* Austin, TX, 2000.
9. Remote Agent Experiment Home Page, http://rax.arc.nasa.gov, June 2002.
10. PROBA Onboard Autonomy Platform, http://www.estec.esa.nl/proba/, June 2002.
11. R. P. Bonasso, R. J. Firby, E. Gat, D. Kortenkamp, D. Miller, and M. Slack, Experiences with Architecture for Intelligent, Reactive Agents, Journal of Experimental and Theoretical Artificial Intelligence , Vol. 9, No. 1, 1997.
12. S. Chien, A. Barrett, T. Estlin, and G. Rabideau, A Comparison of Coordinate Planning Methods for Cooperating Rovers, Fourth International Conference on Autonomous Agents (Agents 2000), Barcelona, Spain, June 2000.
13. B. Clement, A. Barrett, E. Durfee, and G. Rabideau, "Using Abstraction to Coordinate Multiple Robotic Spacecraft," Proceedings of the 2001 Intelligent Robots and Systems Conference, Maui, HI, November 2001.
14. N. Muscettola, G. Dorais, C. Fry, R. Levinson, and C. Plaunt, "IDEA: Planning at the Core of Autonomous Reactive Agents," Proceedings of the AIPS-2002 Conference, Tolouse, France, April 2002.
15. G. Rabideau, R. Knight, S. Chien, A. Fukunaga, A. Govindjee, "Iterative Repair Planning for Spacecraft Operations in the ASPEN System," *Intl Symp on A.I. Robotics and Automation in Space,* Noordwijk, The Netherlands, June 1999.
16. R. Sherwood, G. Rabideau, S. Chien, B. Engelhardt, "ASPEN User's Guide," http://aspen.jpl.nasa.gov, August 2002.

Omni-drive Robot Motion on Curved Paths: The Fastest Path between Two Points Is Not a Straight-Line

Mark Ashmore and Nick Barnes

Department of Computer Science and Software Engineering
The University Of Melbourne, Vic, 3010, AUSTRALIA
nmb@cs.mu.oz.au

Abstract. Omni-drive systems operate by having individual wheels apply torque in one direction in the same way as a regular wheel, but are able to slide freely in another direction (often perpendicular to the torque vector). The key advantage of omni-drive systems is that translational and rotational motion are decoupled for simple motion. However, in considering the fastest possible motion this is not necessarily the case. In this paper, we review all the current popular designs of omni-drive transport systems, and compare them in terms of practical and theoretical considerations. We then present a kinematic analysis that applies to two major omni-drive robot vehicles classes, for any number of wheels. Finally, we show that for three-wheeled omni-drive transport systems and certain ranges of trajectories and starting conditions, a curved path can be traversed faster than a straight-line path, we confirm this result experimentally.

1 Introduction

Of mobile robots, wheeled drives are by far the most common means of transportation. Wheeled systems support accurate odometry over smooth flat surfaces. Within the class of wheeled systems, the majority are differential drive, where two parallel wheels execute straight-lines by moving with the same velocity, or curves with differences in velocity. Ackerman steering is common for larger vehicles, particularly road vehicles. However, omni-drive and synchro-drive vehicles have the kinematic advantage of allowing continuous translation and rotation in any direction. Synchro-drive systems have a number of wheels that are aligned in a common direction, and can be turned in any direction. This advantage is apparent for transport systems in confined spaces such as factory floor robots [2]. Also, in competitive high-speed environments, such as the RoboCup competitions, this agility has demonstrated great advantage. For example to move sideways, a differential drive robot can turn 90 degrees, move forward, and then turn back to its original direction. An omni-drive robot can execute a single sideways motion, and further can easily track a moving object while maintaining a required orientation with respect to it, such as following a ball, while maintaining the alignment of a kicking mechanism. Omni-drive robots have the particular advantage of decoupling translational and rotational motion. The kinematics of omni-drive systems are well known [2], and many designs have been published, e.g., six wheels [1], three wheels [4], and four wheels [5]. However, analysis of omni-drive motion on curved paths has been inadequate to date. Such an analysis is necessary to optimise performance of this type of robot in high-speed

R.I.. McKay and J. Slaney (Eds.): AI 2002, LNAI 2557, pp. 225–236, 2002.

competitive domains. That the robot can move in any direction with any rotational velocity is adequate for path planning if speed is not a key consideration, however we want to optimise the performance of the robot for translational paths when rotation is not constrained.

We are interested in optimising robot performance for the Robocup F180 League, a competitive environment where speed is important. Approaches such as the dynamic window [3] can be used to exploit these faster curved paths presented here. The dynamic window was developed on synchro-drive robots.

In this paper, we review omni-directional ground transport systems before examining a particular class of omni-drive vehicles, orthogonal universal wheel-based systems, in more detail. Finally, we look at the motion of omni-drive systems for curved paths. We find that, theoretically, omni-drive systems can travel between points faster for certain curved trajectories than in a straight line. We verify this result experimentally.

1.1   Omni-drive Transport Systems

The basis of the most common omni-drive transport systems is wheels that allow free motion in a direction that is not parallel to the wheel's drive direction. By combining a number of such wheels, each is able to apply a force on the centre of mass of the transport system, and as each wheel has some axis along which it can freely rotate, a velocity can be induced by the other wheels in this direction. The well-known omni-directional transport systems can be separated into two basic classes: orthogonal wheels (pairs of near-spherical wheels), and universal wheels (wheels with rollers).

1.1.1   Universal Wheels

The universal wheel (see figure 2.1.1) has a set of rollers aligned around its rim that make contact with the ground. Carlisle [2] describes two alternative wheel designs. In the standard design the rollers are aligned so that the wheel can roll freely orthogonally to its driving direction. We will refer to such wheels as orthogonal universal wheels. Platforms with three or more such wheels can produce full omni-directional motion, i.e., arbitrary translation and rotation can be performed, and are decoupled. A second wheel design has the rollers able to free wheel at a non-orthogonal angle to the driving direction of the wheel, typically 45 degrees, e.g., [2,5].

Orthogonal universal wheels are usually placed all at the same distance from the centre of the transport system with their driving direction vector aligned tangentially to the circle connecting them, and with a uniform angle between neighbouring pairs of wheels, see Figure 3.1.2. Both three [2] and four [1] wheeled configurations have been published. The three-wheeled design is mechanically simpler and maintains contact with the ground at all times on rough surfaces, provided there is adequate clearance for the chassis. For the four-wheeled version, suspension is necessary to guarantee contact by all wheels on uneven surfaces, complicating the design. However, in 2002, the Cornel University F180 Robocup team demonstrated that suspension was unnecessary for four wheeled systems if the ground surface is flat.

For transport systems using non-orthogonal universal wheels a minimum of four wheels are required. The standard configuration (e.g., [2,5]) has two rows of two wheels with all driving directions aligned. Forward motion occurs by driving all motors forwards, sideways motion occurs by setting each motor in the opposite direction to its neighbours. Rotation about the centre of mass can be induced by spinning the wheels on one side in the opposite direction of the other side. However, such platforms also require suspension to guarantee ground contact on uneven surfaces, complicating the design. Carlisle also criticises the poor efficiency of the sideways motion [2]. We do not consider this design family further in this paper.

1.1.2   Orthogonal Wheels

Pin and Killough [6] describe transport systems based on orthogonal wheels. The idea is that a pair of wide, almost spherical, wheels are placed with their axels in orthogonal directions. The wheels are able to rotate freely about their axels. A bracket holds the extremities of the wheel axel, which allows it to be driven to roll on its portion of spherical surface, while free-wheeling in the orthogonal direction. This gives the same effect as the universal wheels. With correctly aligned wheels that are close to spherical, and have synchronised motion, ground contact on one spherical surface or the other is assured at all times while leaving sufficient clearance for the bracket. Thus, an orthogonal pair can drive in one direction and slide in the orthogonal direction. Again, by combining three or more such wheel pairs it is possible to produce omni-directional motion. They present two designs: one where the wheels of a pair are aligned radially from the centre of the robot; and, a more complex design where the wheels of a pair are aligned tangentially. The latter case simplifies the robot kinematics and dynamics because the wheels can be placed such that the point of contact is always a constant distance from the centre of the robot for all wheels.

Watanabe, et. al. [8] present a dynamic model and control scheme for a restricted class of three-wheeled omni-drive robots where the centre of mass is the same distance from the contact points for all wheels. This corresponds to the tangentially aligned pairs variant of Pin and Killough's orthogonal wheel design, where the centre of mass of the robot corresponds to its physical centre (the simplest case of an omni-drive robot for dynamics).

Pin and Killough favour their orthogonal wheels design over the universal wheel-based design. The major reasons given are: the lack of continuous contact with the ground given a single set of rollers; fewer parts; and, a smaller wheel well. These advantages of the orthogonal wheel design have been reduced for builders of mobile platforms of certain sizes by the availability of mass-market universal wheels that are small and reasonably priced. Constructing a platform using pre-manufactured universal wheels (at the sizes for which they are available) is simpler than constructing an orthogonal wheel-base and the size difference when restrictions apply (such as F180 Robocup) is often not significant. Wheels with two rows of rollers, as shown in Figure 2.1.1, ensure smooth contact with the ground, but add a complication for control and odometry in that the point of contact of the wheel moves between the inner and outer row of rollers. However, if the distance between the rollers is small in comparison with the radius of the transport system, the problem remains manageable. Trade-offs like these have currently lead to the greater popularity of the orthogonal universal wheel design, as can be particularly seen in the small and medium leagues of the Robocup competition [7].

In the remainder of this paper we examine motion models that are common to the orthogonal wheels and the orthogonal universal wheel designs. Previously there has been some study of the motion of a three-wheeled omni-drive robot (e.g. [2,8]), the kinematics for body motion, and dynamics for restricted cases, have been presented. In this paper, we extend this analysis to the kinematics of n-wheeled robots. We also analyse the motion of robots on curved paths, and examine the implications for maximal speed, and experimentally verify the derived results.

2   Analysis of Omni-drive Systems

In this section, we analyse the motion of omni-drive systems. We first describe the motion of a simple two wheeled omni-wheel system. We use this to introduce the velocity augmentation factor, the motion equations, and derive the general case for an n-wheeled system. In this analysis we examine the case of orthogonal universal wheels, however, the analysis is the same for the orthogonal wheels design. This analysis does not apply to non-orthogonal universal wheel-based systems.

2.1   A Simple Omni-wheeled System

A single wheel can only propel itself in the direction of applied force. The simplest possible omni-wheel system that is capable of moving in something other than a straight-line has two wheels attached together so that their directions of driving force are not parallel, as shown in Figure 2.1.1. Due to the angling of the omni-wheels, by varying the speed at which each wheel rotates, we are able to drive the system in any direction we choose. It must be noted at this point that the system described in Figure 2.1.1 is *not* an omni-drive as it is not capable of arbitrary simultaneous translation and rotation, which requires a minimum of three wheels.

Fig. 2.1.1. Simple omni-wheeled system with angled universal wheels.

2.2   Induced Velocity

While the system described in Figure 2.1.1 may appear simple, the kinematics are non trivial. The nature of the omni-wheel means that a wheel can obtain a velocity (in its direction of sliding) without applying any driving force itself. The force comes from the motion of the other wheel. We refer to this velocity as **induced velocity**. Consider Figure 2.2.1.

In Figure 2.2.1, wheel 1 (right) is driving, while wheel 2 (left) is locked, that is cannot rotate about its axle. Assuming no slippage, only rolling in the direction perpendicular to the driving direction of wheel 2 is possible. In this case, the system will rotate about a single point that must lie along a line perpendicular to the velocity of each wheel. The centre of rotation may be found at the intersection of the lines perpendicular to V_{w1} and Vin_{w2}. Wheel 2, which provides *no* driving force, has obtained the velocity Vin_{w2}. This is the induced velocity.

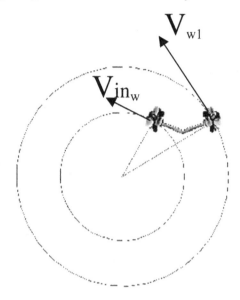

Fig. 2.2.1. Wheel 1 on the right is driving. Wheel two on the left is locked, $\mathbf{V_{w1}}$ is the velocity of driving wheel one, and $\mathbf{Vin_{w2}}$ is the induced velocity of wheel two.

2.3   Omni-wheeled System Motion

We now consider the motion of a simple omni-wheeled system, where rotation is fixed. Consider Figure 2.3.1, showing the vectors acting on one driving wheel.

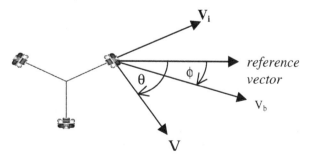

Fig. 2.3.1. Analysis of omni-wheel

where, V_w is the velocity of the wheel, θ is the reference wheel angle, V_{in} is the induced velocity on wheel, ϕ is the reference body velocity angle, and V_b is the body velocity of robot.

Now V_{in} and V_w are always orthogonal:

$$V_b^2 = V_w^2 + V_{in}^2 \tag{1}$$

Also:

$$V_{in}^2 = V_b^2 + V_w^2 - 2\,V_w\,V_b\cos(\theta - \phi)$$

$$= V_b^2 + V_w^2 - 2\,V_w\,V_b\,(\cos\theta\cos\phi + \sin\theta\sin\phi) \tag{2}$$

Substituting (2) into (1), we may obtain:

$$V_w = V_b(\cos\theta\cos\phi + \sin\theta\sin\phi) \tag{3}$$

For a given rotational velocity of the centre of mass, $\dot{\Psi}$, each wheel must apply velocity:

$$V_w = R\dot{\Psi}, \tag{4}$$

where R is the distance of the wheel from the centre of mass. Thus, for each wheel:

$$V_w = V_b(\cos\theta\cos\phi + \sin\theta\sin\phi) + R\dot{\Psi} \tag{5}$$

This is a general equation that is independent of the number of wheels. Consider a three wheeled omni-directional vehicle with wheels arranged at angles of 0°, 120° and 240°, equation (5) yields:

Wheel 1 ($\theta = 0°$): $$V_{w1} = V_b\cos\phi + R\dot{\Psi} \tag{6}$$

Wheel 2 ($\theta = 120°$): $$V_{w2} = V_b(\frac{-1}{2}\cos\phi + \frac{\sqrt{3}}{2}\sin\phi) + R\dot{\Psi} \tag{7}$$

Wheel 3 ($\theta = 240°$): $$V_{w3} = V_b(\frac{-1}{2}\cos\phi - \frac{\sqrt{3}}{2}\sin\phi) + R\dot{\Psi} \tag{8}$$

Similar equations for this three-wheeled case appear in [6]. The translational component only appears also in [2]. As pointed out by Pin and Killough [6], if we separate V_b into x and y components, where $V_{bx} = V_b\cos\phi$, and $V_{by} = V_b\sin\phi$, this becomes a linear relation. We may invert the matrix for any n-wheeled system. Consider, for example, the three-wheeled system above:

$$\begin{bmatrix} V_{bx} \\ V_{by} \\ \dot{\psi} \end{bmatrix} = \begin{bmatrix} \dfrac{-1}{\sqrt{3}} & \dfrac{-2}{3\sqrt{3}} & \dfrac{1}{\sqrt{3}} \\ \dfrac{-1}{3} & \dfrac{-4}{3} & \dfrac{-1}{3} \\ \dfrac{1}{3R} & \dfrac{1}{3R} & \dfrac{1}{3R} \end{bmatrix} \begin{bmatrix} w_1 \\ w_2 \\ w_3 \end{bmatrix} \tag{9}$$

Now, consider again the system shown in Figure 2.3.1, with initial conditions: $\theta = 60°$, $V_w = 1$, $\phi = 90°$. Substituting these values into Equation (3) gives: $Vb = 2/\sqrt{3}$

Thus, the addition of angled omni-wheels can result in a net body velocity that is greater than the maximum radial velocity of the wheel. We refer to this additional velocity as the Velocity Augmentation Factor (VAF).

Fig. 2.3.2. 3, 4 and 5 wheeled omni-drives.

Let us now apply Equation (3), in particular the VAF, to some plausible omni-drive designs, as shown in Figure 2.3.2. Figure 2.3.3 plots the theoretical VAF and average velocity obtained by varying ϕ over the range $0° - 360°$.

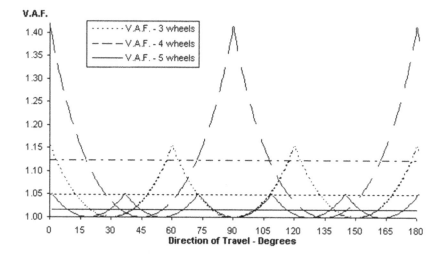

Fig. 2.3.3. Plots of VAF vs direction for 3, 4 and 5 wheeled omni-drives.

Figure 2.3.3 shows that the four-wheeled design produces the greatest VAF of $\sqrt{2}$ every $90°$. Furthermore, as the number of wheels increases above four, while the number of peaks increases, the height of the peaks will always be less than $\sqrt{2}$, as the angle of the relative angle of the wheels affects the VAF.

Consider the configurations shown in Figure 2.3.4 below. The design on the right has a smaller driving angle, that is the interior angle between drive shafts, than the design on the left and so will generate a larger VAF. In the five wheeled omni-drive in Figure 2.3.2 we see that both of these designs are in fact present on the one system. Here, a small driving angle will obtain a large VAF, however, the pair with the large driving angle will not be able to keep up. Since the system as a whole may only go as fast as the pair of wheels with the largest driving angle, any more than four wheels and the VAF is reduced.

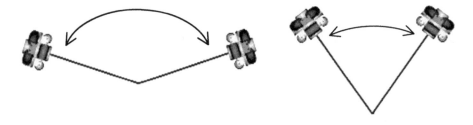

Fig. 2.3.4. Example of large (left) and small (right) driving angles.

2.4   Velocity for a Three-Wheeled Omni-drive with Rotation

Returning to Figure 2.3.2, we see that for a three-wheeled omni-drive, as used by The University of Melbourne, the maximum VAF is approximately 1.15, however this is only for travel *without* rotation. We may use Equation (9), or its equivalent for higher numbers of wheels to consider the maximum velocity when angular velocity is also allowed. We may take the two components of V_b and combine them to find the total velocity, and set this to a maximum given the maximal velocities for the wheels. We find:

$$V_b^2 = \frac{4}{9}(v_1^2 + v_2^2 + v_3^2 - v_1 v_2 - v_1 v_3 - v_2 v_3) \tag{10}$$

By maximising Equation (10) we are now able to calculate the maximum possible velocity for the transport system. By inspection, we find that the equation is maximised under the conditions given in Table 2.4.1 below. (Note: All values are in terms of a maximum wheel velocity of 1).

Table 2.4.1. Conditions for maximum body velocity.

Velocity	Case 1	Case 2	Case 3
V_1	∓ 1	± 1	± 1
V_2	± 1	∓ 1	± 1
V_3	± 1	± 1	∓ 1
Vb	4/3	4/3	4/3

This value 4/3 is greater than, in fact the square of, the maximum VAF $(2/\sqrt{3})$ found previously. We can also see from Equation (9) that there will be a net rotational velocity of the system, i.e., the system will follow a circular path.

We now examine a case where it will be faster to travel a curved path at higher velocity than to travel in a straight line. Figure 2.4.1 shows a curved path D of radius R, and the corresponding direct path d. By calculating d and D and dividing by the maximum speed of traversal, we calculate the time taken to traverse both paths, as follows:

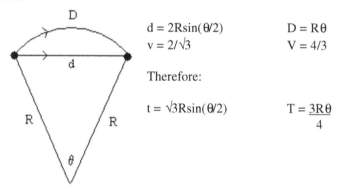

$$d = 2R\sin(\theta/2) \qquad D = R\theta$$
$$v = 2/\sqrt{3} \qquad V = 4/3$$

Therefore:

$$t = \sqrt{3}R\sin(\theta/2) \qquad T = \frac{3R\theta}{4}$$

Fig. 2.4.1. Curved vs direct paths

Using this information we plot t vs T to establish when the time taken to travel a curved path is less than the time taken to travel a direct path. This is shown in figure 2.4.2 below. As we can see, for distances under approximately $7.3r$, where r is the radius of the robot, a destination may be reached earlier by travelling a curved path rather than a direct path.

This result is for the case of pursuing maximal velocity on both the curved and the straight-line paths. Clearly different rates of curvature with lower translational velocities can also be pursued, however, we do not analyse the other cases here. Also, we have not considered system dynamics. To confirm this result, we now present several experiments.

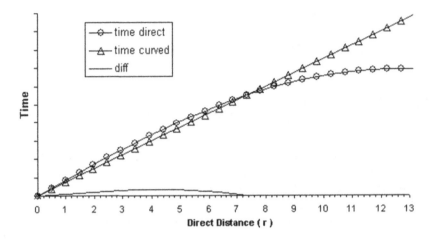

Fig. 2.4.2. Comparison of direct vs curved path travel times.

3 Experiments

3.1 Experimental Procedure

The experiment was conducted using the robots pictured in figures 3.1.1 and 3.1.2. Each of the three wheels were set to a velocity and allowed to run for a significant period of time. A calibrated overhead camera filmed the robot at a rate of 12.5 frames per second facilitating accurate measurements of the path and velocities. 12 experiments were conducted to test four states of the robot, with each state being tested using three alternate configurations of wheel velocities, as given in table 3.1.1.

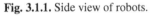

Fig. 3.1.1. Side view of robots.   **Fig. 3.1.2.** Base of robot

In state 1, Equation (9) predicts a circular path of radius $2r$, again where r is the robot radius (in this case 7.5cm), at a VAF of 2/3. States 2 and 3, will result in a straight line path with VAF of 1.00 and 1.15 respectively, while state 4 will induce a circular path of radius $4r$ at a VAF of 1.33. Table 3.2.1 shows the results. We can see that the robot was able to travel faster along a curved path than in a straight line.

Table 3.1.1. Experimental wheel velocities.

State	Wheel Velocities (cm/s)		
1	12.6	0	0
2	12.6	-6.3	-6.3
3	12.6	-12.6	0
4	12.6	12.6	-12.6

Table 3.1.2. Experiment results.

State	Theoretical VAF	Observed VAF	Error	Theoretical Path Radius (r)	Observed Path Radius (r)	Error
1	0.67	0.69	3.0%	2.00	1.73	14%
2	1.00	0.99	1.0%	∞	∞	N/A
3	1.15	1.09	5.2%	∞	∞	N/A
4	1.33	1.32	0.75%	4.00	3.71	7.3%

3.2   Experimental Errors

Errors here may be primarily attributed to the control system used to maintain the desired wheel velocity. Each wheel was under position-based control, thus, if the exact wheel velocity is not maintained, the robot will not travel required path or velocity precisely and therefore cause errors. A further irregularity occurs due to dropped frames. This results in large extremes in velocity to be calculated. Such frames generally appear as outliers, and were removed from the results.

It is difficult to precisely quantify these sources of error. However, given that the actual variation from theory across multiple trials was 2.5% on average while the VAF is 33% we view the results as being adequate to support the theory.

4   Conclusion

We reviewed omni-drive robot systems and showed the reasons for the popularity of systems based on orthogonal universal wheels. We presented a derivation of a velocity equation for an n-wheeled omni-drive robot, valid for these systems as well as systems using the orthogonal wheels design. We introduced the concept of a velocity augmentation factor, and found that the VAF is maximal with a four-wheeled omni-drive system. We also found that the fastest path between to points, less than $7.3r$ of the robot, is a curved path for a three-wheeled omni-drive system, given particular starting conditions. These results were verified experimentally.

The curved path result becomes useful when considered in the context of competitive environments such as RoboCup, where optimising paths is of great advantage, especially for points close to the robot. In the Dynamic Window approach [3], the robot searches through a set of possible trajectories to choose the best for the particular situation, given goal direction, current system state (position, orientation and velocities), and neighbouring obstacles. In such an approach we can easily consider that some curved trajectories have different associated velocities. The analysis presented in this paper shows that for certain trajectories and initial conditions curved paths should be considered as faster paths in such an approach.

References

1. H Asama, M Sato, L Bogoni, H Kaetsu, A. Matsumoto and I. Endo: Development of an Omni-Directional Mobile Robot with 3 DOF Decoupling Drive Mechanism. In IEEE Int. Conf. on Robotics and Automation (1995)
2. B Carlisle: An Omni-Direction Mobile Robot. In B. Rooks, (ed.): Developments in Robotics. IFS Publications/North-Holland Publishing Company. (1983) 79–87
3. D Fox, W Burgard and S Thrun: The Dynamic Window Approach to Collision Avoidance. In IEEE Int. Conf. on Robotics and Automation (1997)
4. K Moore and N Flann: Hierarchical Task Decomposition Approach to Path Planning and Contol for an Omni-Directional Autonomous Mobile Robot. In *IEEE* Int. Symp. on Intelligent Control/Intelligent System & Semiotics, (1999)
5. C Voo: Low Level Driving Routines for the OMNI-Directional Robot, Centre for Intelligent Information Processing Systems, Department of Electrical & Electronic Engineering, The University of Western Australia, Honours Thesis, January (2000)
6. F G Pin and S M Killough: A New Family of Omnidirectional and Holonomic Wheeled Platforms for Mobile Robots, IEEE Transactions on Robotics and Automation **10**(4), Aug (1994) 480–489
7. G A Kaminka, P U Lima, R Rojas (Eds.): RoboCup-2002: Robot Soccer World Cup VI: The 2002 RoboCup Symposium Proceedings. Fukuoka, Japan, June, Springer Verlag (2002)
8. K Watanabe, Y Shiraishi, S G Tzafestas, J Tang, and T Fukuda: Feedback Control of an Omnidirectional Autonomous Platform for Mobile Service Robots. Journ. Intelligent and Robotic Systems, **22** (1998) 315–330

Indexing of Image Databases Using Untrained 4D Holographic Memory Model

Raj P. Gopalan and Grant Lee

School of Computing, Curtin University of Technology
Kent St, Bentley, Western Australia 6102
raj@computing.edu.au
grant@primus.com.au

Abstract. An interesting application of the holographic memory model is the indexing of multi-media databases for efficient retrieval of matching patterns. Two dimensional holographic memory models have been previously investigated for indexing collections of gray scale images. In this paper, we describe the implementation of a four dimensional holographic memory model that can be used for indexing colour images and video frames. We have investigated the model using both simulations and real image data to determine the effective operational range of the 4D holograph. Our experiments show that a high level of retrieval accuracy is achieved even if fifty percent of pixels in the query image are distorted by noise. The results provide the basis for designing a robust indexing scheme for retrieving matching images from large image databases.

1 Introduction

Ever since Gabor [1] published his original paper, the fascinating phenomenon of optical holography has attracted the interest of researchers from many fields. Sutherland [8] proposed a new associated memory model based on the mathematical representation of optical holography in 1990. He represented information in the form of stimulus-response patterns as phase angle orientations on a Riemann plane. The governing equations of his method formed a non-connectionist approach in which a large number of stimulus-response associations could be enfolded onto a single memory element.

Khan [6] adapted Sutherland's approach to the indexing of large image archives. He mapped each image and its index to a stimulus-pattern association that were then encoded into an associative memory. Several such associations could be superimposed in the same memory using the analogy of optical holography. When a query image is presented, its index can be retrieved from the memory, by first mapping the image to a query stimulus pattern and then using it to retrieve the response pattern associated with a matching pattern that was previously encoded in the holographic memory. When encoding the holograph, a training process was applied to minimize the recall errors that would occur during retrieval. The training involved 10-30 iterations over the stimulus-response pattern associations such that the average recall error is below a given small value.

R.I. McKay and J. Slaney (Eds.): AI 2002, LNAI 2557, pp. 237–248, 2002.

Khan's work focused on image archives that are encoded once and retrieved many times [7]. In a typical image database, however, both additions and deletions of images may be relatively frequent. For example, an image database may be used by a security system to confirm the identity of those authorized to enter a certain area. As this security database is updated, new images may be added or existing ones deleted. Hendra et al. [4] proposed an untrained holographic model as the basis for dynamic indexing of images. The untrained model has the advantage that it can be modified without the training overhead whenever additions and deletions of images are made in the database. Their results showed that the untrained model compared well with the trained model for the effective operational range of the 2D holographic memory.

Though Khan had discussed the theoretical basis for a multidimensional memory model, his implementation and experimental evaluations involved only trained two-dimensional holographic models [7]. Hendra et al. [4] investigated the untrained two-dimensional memory model for grayscale images. Representation of colour images however, requires higher dimensional models. In this paper, we describe a four-dimensional holographic memory model for indexing images encoded in the RGB format. We have investigated the performance of the untrained 4D model using both simulated data and real images. We also studied the retrieval accuracy of the 4D model when significant levels of noise distort the query image. The experiments show that a high level of retrieval accuracy is achieved even if fifty percent of pixels in the query image are distorted by noise. The results provide the basis for designing a robust indexing scheme for retrieving matching images from large image databases.

The rest of this paper is organized as follows: Section 2 describes the mathematical background of holographic associative memory. The untrained four-dimensional holographic memory is described in Section 3. The performance characteristics of the 4D model are discussed in Section 4. Section 5 is the conclusion of the paper and also contains some pointers for further research.

2   Mathematical Background of Holographic Memory

This section describes the computational model of a holographic memory and how it is used for information encoding and retrieval. This model is adapted from Khan [7] who derived it from the earlier work by Sutherland [8].

2.1   Representation of Information

The main idea of the holographic memory model is the principle of information storage (encoding) and retrieval (decoding) using stimulus-response pattern associations. A stimulus pattern can be generally expressed as a set of elements, and is represented in the form:

$$S = (s_1, s_2, s_3, \dots, s_n). \tag{1}$$

Each element s_k represents the kth piece of information or feature. In the holographic memory model proposed by Sutherland [8], a *degree of significance* or meta-knowledge is associated with each element. The kth information element and its meta-knowledge are modelled as follows:

$$s_k = (\alpha_k, \beta_k).$$

(2)

Here, α_k corresponds to the measurement of the kth element, and β_k represents the meta-knowledge. It is transformed into a complex number representation, denoted as a vector in d-dimensional space, as follows:

$$s_k = (\alpha_k, \beta_k) \Rightarrow \lambda_k e^{\left(\sum_{j}^{d-1} i_j \theta_{j,k} \right)}$$

(3)

Each $\theta_{j,k}$ is the spherical projection or phase component of the vector along the dimension $\hat{i}_j$. The meta-knowledge, β_k, is mapped into a magnitude, λ_k, which is bounded within the unit interval [0, 1]. A stimulus pattern with n elements of information is then represented as

$$[S^\mu] = \left[\lambda_1^\mu e^{\left(\sum_{j}^{d-1} i_j \theta_{j,1}^\mu \right)}, \lambda_2^\mu e^{\left(\sum_{j}^{d-1} i_j \theta_{j,2}^\mu \right)}, \dots, \lambda_n^\mu e^{\left(\sum_{j}^{d-1} i_j \theta_{j,n}^\mu \right)} \right],$$

(4)

where μ is the pattern index, and n is the number of elements in the stimulus pattern. The magnitude, λ_k^μ, corresponds to the degree of significance of the kth element in the μth pattern. The representation of a response pattern is similar to that of the stimulus pattern:

$$[R^\mu] = \left[\gamma_1^\mu e^{\left(\sum_{j}^{d-1} i_j \phi_{j,1}^\mu \right)}, \gamma_2^\mu e^{\left(\sum_{j}^{d-1} i_j \phi_{j,2}^\mu \right)}, \dots, \gamma_m^\mu e^{\left(\sum_{j}^{d-1} i_j \phi_{j,m}^\mu \right)} \right],$$

(5)

where R^μ is the response pattern associated with stimulus pattern S^μ, and m is the number of response pattern elements. The phase component $\phi_{j,k}^\mu$ represents the measurement of a response pattern element, and the magnitude $\gamma_{j,k}^\mu$ represents the expected *confidence* (system assigned significance) on $\phi_{j,k}^\mu$.

2.2 Encoding Process

The input information is first mapped to a stimulus pattern as indicated in Section 2.1. The index of input is mapped to a response pattern using a suitable function. Each stimulus and its response pattern is associated by a correlation matrix [X], also called a stimulus-response pattern association, obtained as the inner product of the corresponding complex vectors:

$$[X^\mu] = [\overline{S}^\mu]^T [R^\mu].$$

(6)

Here, $\left[\overline{S}^{\mu}\right]^{T}$ is the conjugate transpose of $[S^{\mu}]$. Several stimulus-response pattern associations can be superimposed onto the same matrix space as follows:

$$[X]=\sum_{\mu=1}^{p}[X^{\mu}]=\sum_{\mu=1}^{p}[\overline{S}^{\mu}]^{T}[R^{\mu}], \qquad (7)$$

where p is the number of stimulus and response pattern associations (or the number of patterns for short), and $[X]$ is called the *holograph matrix*.

2.3 Decoding Process

The decoding process retrieves the response pattern associated with a given query stimulus pattern. The query stimulus pattern $[S^{q}]$ is defined in a similar way to the encoded stimulus patterns:

$$[S^{q}]=\left[\lambda_{1}^{q}e^{\left(\sum_{j}^{d-1}i_{j}\theta_{j,1}^{q}\right)},\lambda_{2}^{q}e^{\left(\sum_{j}^{d-1}i_{j}\theta_{j,2}^{q}\right)},\dots,\lambda_{n}^{q}e^{\left(\sum_{j}^{d-1}i_{j}\theta_{j,n}^{q}\right)}\right]. \qquad (8)$$

The degree of significance of each query stimulus element is indicated by its magnitude. The value of one indicates that the query element fully contributes to the decoding process. Lower values indicate lower contributions of the query element. The elements with zero magnitude contribute nothing to the decoding operations. Computing the inner product of the query stimulus pattern and the holograph matrix as follows retrieves the response pattern:

$$[R^{q}]=\frac{1}{c}[S^{q}][X], \qquad (9)$$

where c is the normalisation factor defined by:

$$c=\sum_{k=1}^{n}\lambda_{k}^{q}. \qquad (10)$$

If all elements in the query stimulus pattern $[S^{q}]$ match an existing stimulus pattern $[S']$, the retrieved response pattern $[R^{q}]$ will be close to the associated response pattern $[R']$. Here, closeness is reckoned in terms of the phase values and the magnitudes (confidence level) of each element. If the query stimulus pattern only partially matches an existing pattern, then the retrieved confidence level is expected to be lower than one. It would be very low if the query stimulus pattern does not match any existing pattern. These characteristics correspond to the capability of optical holography to reconstruct a noisy version of the reference beam from the partial wave fronts of an object.

To understand how the retrieval of a response pattern works, the right term of Equation 9 is grouped as *principal* and *crosstalk* components, by substituting $[X]$ from Equation 7 as follows:

$$[R^q] = \frac{1}{c}[S^q][\overline{S}^t]^T[R^t] + \frac{1}{c}\sum_{\substack{\mu=1 \\ \mu \neq t}}^{p}[S^q][\overline{S}^\mu]^T[R^\mu]$$

$$= [R^q_{principal}] + [R^q_{crosstalk}]. \tag{11}$$

Here, $[S^t]$ is an existing stimulus pattern, that closely matches the query stimulus pattern $[S^q]$, and $[R^t]$ is the original response pattern, associated with the stimulus pattern $[S^t]$ in the encoding process. When the query stimulus pattern fully matches the existing stimulus pattern, the principal component will be the same as the original response pattern. The crosstalk, given by the second term, is the noise or interference that comes from other stimulus-response pattern associations, because the query stimulus pattern $[S^q]$ does not match the other encoded stimulus patterns, $[S^\mu]$, where $1 \le \mu \le p$, $\mu \neq t$.

Theoretically, the number of patterns (p) that can be stored in the holographic memory for reliable retrieval never exceeds the number of stimulus pattern elements (n). This characteristic named *load factor* (L), is given as (p/n), for $p \le n$. L is in the range 0–1.0. Haykin [2] defined this concept for the basic associative memory.

3   Four-Dimensional Holographic Memory

The general holographic memory model was presented in Section 2. We use a four-dimensional model to index images encoded in the RGB format. To implement an untrained holograph, each association is encoded into the holographic matrix by a direct application of the mathematical expressions of Section 2. An image corresponds to a stimulus pattern and the intensity values of pixels to the measurements of stimulus pattern elements. The response pattern is obtained from the corresponding index number indicating the location of the image in a database. The stimulus-response pattern association is superimposed onto the holograph. To retrieve from the image archive it is necessary to find the index number of the required image or pattern. Given a query image, its index number is retrieved from the holograph by the decoding process.

3.1   Representation of Information

Each stimulus and response element is represented by a magnitude and three phase values. An element is mapped to a vector bounded by the complex, four-dimensional, unit hyper-spherical space. Elements of the stimulus and response patterns are represented as in Equation 3, where $d = 4$, $0 \le \theta_{1,k} \le 2\pi$, and $0 \le \theta_{2,k}, \theta_{3,k} \le \pi$. For the stimulus pattern, the element s_k in the equation corresponds to information of the kth pixel obtained by mapping the colors red, green and blue in RGB format.

3.2 Computational Issues

As seen in Equation 7, the encoding process involves an inner product of the stimulus and response vectors. It requires performing additions and products of the four-dimensional complex hyper-spherical vectors. For efficient manipulation, each vector in hyper-spherical coordinate form is converted to its equivalent rectilinear form.

A hyper-complex number in four dimensions is known as a *quaternion* [5], and the operations for addition and multiplication have been taken from the quaternion algebra. Consider the hyper-spherical coordinate $s = \lambda e^{\left(\hat{i}_1 \theta_1 + \hat{i}_2 \theta_2 + \hat{i}_3 \theta_3\right)}$, where $0 \le \theta_1 \le 2\pi$, and $0 \le \theta_2, \theta_3 \le \pi$. The conversion from the hyper-spherical form to the rectilinear form is given by the following set of expressions:

$$
\begin{aligned}
x_1 &= \lambda \sin \theta_3 \sin \theta_2 \sin \theta_1 \\
x_2 &= \lambda \sin \theta_3 \sin \theta_2 \cos \theta_1 \\
x_3 &= \lambda \sin \theta_3 \cos \theta_2 \\
x_4 &= \lambda \cos \theta_3
\end{aligned}
\tag{12}
$$

Conversely, to convert from the rectilinear coordinates to hyper-spherical coordinates, the following expressions are used:

$$
\begin{aligned}
\theta_1 &= \tan^{-1}\left(\frac{x_1}{x_2} \right) \\
\theta_2 &= \tan^{-1}\left(\frac{\sqrt{x_1^2 + x_2^2}}{x_3} \right) \\
\theta_3 &= \tan^{-1}\left(\frac{\sqrt{x_1^2 + x_2^2 + x_3^2}}{x_4} \right) \\
\lambda &= \sqrt{x_1^2 + x_2^2 + x_3^2 + x_4^2}
\end{aligned}
\tag{13}
$$

Initially, all stimulus and response patterns are mapped to the hyper-spherical form. They are converted to the quaternion form before the stimulus response associations are computed and superimposed onto the holograph matrix. All the intermediate computations are performed using quaternion algebra. Once a response pattern is retrieved using a query pattern, its elements are converted back to the hyper-spherical form.

3.3 Encoding Algorithm for Untrained Holograph

The algorithm for encoding an untrained holograph is shown in Fig. 1. The complex matrices of the stimulus pattern, the response pattern, the stimulus-pattern association, and the holograph are denoted by [S], [R], [X] and [H] respectively.

```
1   FOR i = 1 to p patterns DO
2   BEGIN
3     GET iᵗʰ pattern information;
4     MAP iᵗʰ pattern to Stimulus Pattern
          [S] = SPMap(pattern-i);
5     MAP iᵗʰ patt. idx. number to Response Patt.;
          [R] = RPMap(pattern-index);
6     COMPUTE iᵗʰ Stimulus-Response Patt. Assoc.
          [X] = conjugate(transpose([S])) × [R];
7     ADD the iᵗʰ stimulus-response
      patt. assoc.onto the Holograph
          [H] = [H] + [X];
8   END
9   SAVE the Holograph [H]
```

Fig. 1. Algorithm for encoding untrained holograph

The pattern information obtained in line 3 is mapped to a stimulus pattern using a suitable function (line 4). The pattern index number is mapped to a unique response pattern using an appropriate function (line 5). The stimulus response association is computed using Equation 6 (line 6), and the association is superimposed onto the holographic matrix (line 7). Lines 3 – 7 are repeated for p number of patterns. After that, the holographic memory is saved (line 9).

3.4   Mapping Stimulus Patterns

Khan [7] and Hendra [3] have investigated a number of mapping schemes for the 2D holographic model. We have used a Reverse Modulus Weight Code (RMWC) for the 4D model. The RMWC mapping function attempts to distribute the stimulus elements in a symmetrical fashion; close pixel intensities are mapped to vectors that have directions far apart. The distribution of vectors will depend on the nature of the image being mapped, but in general, RMWC mapping gives better results than a linear mapping, where close pixel intensity values are mapped to vectors with similar orientations. Due to space limitations, we do not describe the coding scheme here.

3.5   Response Pattern Mapping

Each image has a unique index number to identify it in the database. Using an appropriate function, the image index is mapped to a unique response pattern of m elements, where m is given by Equation 14 as discussed below. As mentioned in Section 2.1, each element of the response pattern can be regarded as a vector. The magnitude of the vector is set to one. Three phase values of the vector in polar form correspond to predefined intervals in the ranges of $0 - 2\pi$, $0 - \pi$, and $0 - \pi$. We have experimented by varying the number of intervals and found that the best retrieval results are obtained when there are just two intervals in each phase range, which gives a total of 8 intervals for each vector.

If q is the number of predefined intervals in the hyper-spherical space, the number of elements m needed to encode a maximum of p patterns is given by the formula:

$$m = \log_q p \tag{14}$$

For example, if $q = 8$ and $p = 512$, m would be 3. In this case, there would be 3 elements, each with 8 intervals, and each of these three elements could have 1 out of 8 possible combinations of phase values. The index number for a given pattern is mapped to one of these unique element combinations. A Reverse Modulus Weight Code (RMWC) function is used to obtain a symmetrical distribution of vectors, even when the number of encoded patterns is far less than the maximum number p.

3.6 Retrieval of Response Patterns

Hendra et al. [4] had used an error threshold method to determine correct retrievals of response patterns from the 2-dimensional holograph. We have extended this to the 4-dimensional holographic model. Equation 15 gives the error threshold for the first phase value and Equation 16 for the second and third phase values, where q is the number of positions a vector can take in that plane.

$$\phi_T^1 = (\pi / q) \tag{15}$$

$$\phi_T^{2,3} = (\pi / 2q) \tag{16}$$

In simulation experiments to determine the performance characteristics of the holograph, three phase errors are associated with each retrieved response pattern. Let ϕ_i^t be the phase value of the original response, ϕ_i^q be the phase value of the retrieved response of the tth response element, then the phase errors ϕ_i^e are calculated by Equations 17 (one for each of the three response element phases). An incorrect retrieval occurs whenever one of the phase errors is greater than the corresponding threshold value.

$$\begin{aligned}
\phi_{i,1}^e &= \min\left\{\left|\phi_{i,1}^t - \phi_{i,1}^q\right|, 2\pi - \left|\phi_{i,1}^t - \phi_{i,1}^q\right|\right\} \\
\phi_{i,2}^e &= \min\left\{\left|\phi_{i,2}^t - \phi_{i,2}^q\right|, \pi - \left|\phi_{i,2}^t - \phi_{i,2}^q\right|\right\} \\
\phi_{i,3}^e &= \min\left\{\left|\phi_{i,3}^t - \phi_{i,3}^q\right|, \pi - \left|\phi_{i,3}^t - \phi_{i,3}^q\right|\right\}
\end{aligned} \tag{17}$$

In a real application, the original response patterns of query patterns are unknown, and the only way to measure the correctness of retrieval is by using the retrieved confidence levels (or magnitudes) of the response pattern elements. The original magnitudes of the response pattern elements are set to one, and if the query pattern exists in the holograph, then the retrieved response pattern elements would have magnitudes close to one.

4 Performance Study of Untrained 4D Holograph

In this section, we present the performance results from experimental evaluation of the untrained 4D holograph. A large number of experiments were conducted using both simulated patterns and real images. Due to space limitations, only a sample of our results are included in this paper. We first define the performance measures used, before presenting the performance characteristics of the holograph. We also provide retrieval results for query images distorted by the presence of noise.

4.1 Performance Measures

Two main measures are used to quantify performance of the untrained 4D holograph. The first, *mean normalised confidence* (MNC) is given by the following expression:

$$MNC = \frac{\sum_{i}^{m} \gamma_i^{T(\mu)}}{m},$$ (18)

where m denotes the number of elements in the response pattern, and μ the pattern number. Here, $\gamma_i^{T(\mu)}$ is the magnitude of the ith element of retrieved response pattern. MNC denotes the confidence level about the existence of the query pattern [7]. A value close to one is returned when a query pattern *fully matches* an encoded pattern, and less than 0.5 for an unmatched query pattern.

The second measure is the *percentage of correct retrieval* (PCR), which is the proportion of correct retrievals to the total number of retrievals expressed as a percentage.

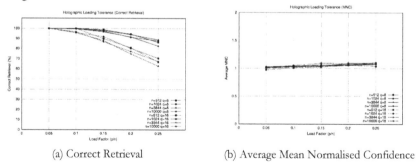

(a) Correct Retrieval   (b) Average Mean Normalised Confidence

Fig. 2. Retrieval characteristics of untrained 4D holograph

4.2 Retrieval Characteristics of Untrained 4D Holograph

We used randomly generated patterns, with various sizes in terms of number of pixels ($n = 512, 1024, 3844$ and 10000). Two separate simulations were conducted with the same stimulus patterns using two different response pattern intervals ($q=8$ and $q=16$).

The patterns were loaded into the holograph increasing the load factor in stages of 0.05, 0.1, 0.15, 0.2 and 0.25.

Fig. 2(a) shows the percentage of correct retrieval achieved. Using 8 intervals in the response pattern, almost 100% correct retrieval was obtained up to a load factor of 0.15. The correct retrieval percentage is significantly better with 8 response pattern intervals than with 16. So 8 intervals were chosen for all subsequent experiments. The MNC levels are close to one for all retrievals as shown in Fig. 2(b). It can be seen that the holograph capacity is dependent on the load factor, irrespective of the number of elements in the stimulus patterns.

4.3 Experimental Results on Real Images

A collection of 188 photographs, of size 100x75 pixels was used. The images were encoded into a holograph for a load factor of 0.025. The original images were then used as query stimulus patterns, and 185 of the 188 images were correctly recalled (98.40%).

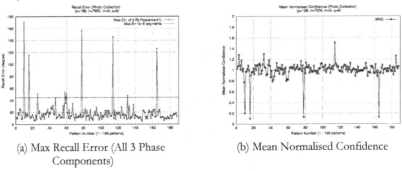

(a) Max Recall Error (All 3 Phase   (b) Mean Normalised Confidence
           Components)

Fig. 3. Recall errors and MNC values when queried with original patterns and some patterns not encoded in the holograph

If we query with patterns that do not exist in the holograph, the retrieved MNC values are very low. Different query patterns were substituted for the original patterns that were in positions 10, 16, 78, and 165. Fig. 3 shows that the recall errors of the new patterns are high and the associated MNC values are very low, indicating that they do not exist in the holograph.

4.4 Retrieval Using Distorted Query Patterns

Not all query patterns presented to the holographic memory will exactly match one of the patterns encoded into the holograph. In order to test the tolerance of the holographic memory to query patterns with distortion, random noise was added to the original set of images before using them as query patterns. Examples of an image with different levels of noise are shown in Fig. 4. A summary of the results for various noise levels is shown in Table 1. As seen, correct retrieval of 95.74% is achieved when 40% of pixels in the query pattern is distorted by noise. Even with 60%

distortion, the original patterns can be retrieved with a correct retrieval rate of 86.17%. This demonstrates the robustness of the 4D holographic memory.

Table 1. Performance characteristics of holograph when queried with noisy patterns

Percent Distortion	% Correct Retrieval	Average MNC
40%	95.74%	0.47586
50%	94.68%	0.39923
60%	86.17%	0.32208
70%	67.02%	0.25825
80%	28.72%	0.19471

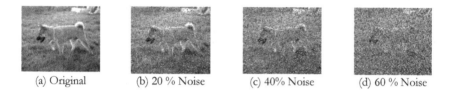

(a) Original	(b) 20 % Noise	(c) 40% Noise	(d) 60 % Noise

Fig. 4. Example of query pattern distorted with random noise

Table 2. Comparison of space requirements for the 2D and 4D holographic models

	2D Model	4D Model
Number of stimulus patterns (p)	1000	1000
Number stimulus pattern elements (n)	10000	10000
Intervals per response pattern element for best performance	2	8
Number of response patterns (m)	10	4
Bytes required for complex number representation (d)	8	16
TOTAL SPACE REQUIRED (s)	880,000 bytes	704,000 bytes

4.5   Comparison with 2D Model

The retrieval performance of the 4D holograph with color images is similar to that of 2D holograph obtained by Khan [6] and Hendra et al. [5] for gray-scale images. However, a surprising aspect of the 4D implementation is that it needs less space than the corresponding 2D scheme for an equal number of images. To illustrate, the comparison of space requirements for 1000 patterns of size 100x100 is summarized in Table 2. The total space requirement in bytes is given by the following expression:

$$s_{total} = m.d(n + p),\tag{19}$$

where there are p patterns, $n \times m$ holograph elements, each requiring d bytes of storage. The detailed analysis of time and space complexity is omitted in this paper due to space limitations.

5 Conclusions and Further Work

We have investigated the 4D holographic model for indexing image databases and evaluated the retrieval performance of the model using both simulated data and real images. The holographic model allows encoding a large number of patterns on a single memory element, and supports accurate retrieval even when the query image is distorted by significant level of noise.

The performance of the 4D model on color images is comparable to that of the 2D model for gray-scale images [5], [6]. The 4D model allows us to index the color images directly without discarding information by converting to a gray-scale representation. Interestingly, the 4D model needs less space than the corresponding 2D holograph for image collections of similar size.

An important extension of this work would be to study dynamic indexing of large image databases where additions and deletions are frequent. Another area for further work is the retrieval using query objects rather than full images. Using the holographic method to index video data is also an interesting problem because of the high level of similarity that exists among nearby video frames.

References

1. Gabor, D., "Associative holographic memories," *IBM Journal of Resarch and Development*, Vol. 3, (1969) 156–159.
2. Haykin, S., *"Neural Netoworks: A Comprehensive Foundation,"* Macmillan College (1994).
3. Hendra,Y.,*"Content-Based Retrieval of Information from Image and Video Databases Using A Holographic Memory Model,"* Masters Thesis, School of Computing, Curtin University of Technology, Perth, Western Australia (1999).
4. Hendra, Y., Gopalan, R. P., and Nair, M.G. "A method for dynamic indexing of large image databases," *Proceedings of the 1999 IEEE International Conference on Systems, Man and Cybernetics*, Tokyo, Japan, (1999) 302–307.
5. Kantor, I. L. and Solodovnikov, A. S. (1989). *Hypercomplex Numbers: An Elementary Introduction to Algebras*. Springer-Verlag: New York (1989).
6. Khan, J. I., "Characteristics of multidimensional holographic associative memory in retrieval with dynamically localizable attention," *IEEE Transactions on Neural Networks*, Vol. 9, No.3, (1998) 389–406.
7. Khan, J. I. *Attention Modulated Associative Computing and Content-Associative Search in Image Archive*, PhD. Dissertation, Department of Electrical Engineering, University of Hawaii, Hawaii, (1995).
8. Sutherland, J. G., "A holographic model of memory, learning and expression," *International Journal of Neural Systems*, Vol. 1, No. 3, (1990) .259–267.

The Flux-Oriented Control of an Induction Machine Utilizing an Online Controller Parameter Adaptation Scheme

Zaiping Chen[1,2,3], Qiang Gao[1], Chao Dong[1], Hongjin Liu[1], Peng Zhang[1], and Zhenlin Xu[2]

[1]The Department of Automation, Tianjin University of Technology
Hongqi Nan Road, Tianjin, 300191, P.R.China
ganbei@eyou.com
[2]The Department of Automation, Tianjin University
Weijing Road, Tianjin, 300070, P.R.China
zlxu@eyou.com
[3]Centre for Intelligent Systems and Complex Processes, BSEE
Swinburne University of Technology, Hawthorn,VIC.3122, Australia
zchen@groupwiseswin.edu.au

Abstract. Dynamic models of an induction motor with a synchronous reference frame and a stationary frame are introduced. According to the dynamic behaviour of ac drive system, an intelligent scheme based on self-tuning parameters has been applied to the ac drive controller so that meets the requirements of real-time behaviour in uncertainty control system. The scheme of flux-oriented control of an induction motor based on online controller parameter adaptation is proposed in this paper. When changes of command speed and the large range fluctuation of load torque occurred, a good dynamic and static performance is achieved under this parameter adaptive control scheme, which is obviously superior to the conventional control. The effectiveness of the control scheme under varying speed, load torque changes and the fluctuations of rotor resistance, is verified, and the robustness of the presented scheme is also demonstrated by simulation results.

1   Introduction

DC motors have been widely used in industrial drives because of the simple control strategies required to obtain good performance in variable speed applications. However, in comparison with induction motor drives, DC motor drives are typically more expensive and less robust because of their periodic maintenance problems due to the commutator and brushes. In spite of the superiority of induction drives over DC motor drives, they were rarely used in variable speed control in the past, because of their non-linear models and coupling variables. In a DC motor, brushes affixed to the stator and commutator on the rotor could provide the direct link between the field and armature circuits. Therefore, if the proper position of the brushes is fixed, the optimal

R.I. McKay and J. Slaney (Eds.): AI 2002, LNAI 2557, pp. 249–258, 2002.

conditions for torque production under any operating conditions are obtained. This is not the case for an induction motor, whose rotor is physically isolated from the stator. To optimise the torque production conditions in this motor, the so-called flux orientation scheme has been introduced. The flux orientation principle was originally presented by Blaschke [1]. By means of a variable transformation to a rotational frame, the two current components to produce the torque and the flux respectively can be derived. Thus, it is possible that an induction motor can be controlled like a separately excited DC motor. However the dynamic performance of induction motor flux-oriented control strongly depends on model parameter accuracy. A parameter mismatch produces an error in flux-orientation and undesirable coupling between the flux and torque controllers. Although it is possible to determine in advance the model parameters, some changes may take place during normal operation. In addition, the fluctuations of induction motor's parameters can be induced by some disturbances. As a result traditional control scheme can't achieve good performance under these conditions. A number of control schemes have been proposed to overcome the problems mentioned above in the literature [2][3][4][5][6][7][8][9], but most of these schemes involve complex computations. In this paper the novel scheme of indirect flux oriented control based on the online controller parameter adaptation is proposed, which is less computationally demanding than the other schemes. Because the parameter of controller is modified online, good dynamic performance of the flux oriented control system has been obtained. Simulation results are given to verify the robustness and real time behaviour of the proposed control scheme.

2   Induction Motor Dynamic Model

2.1 Dynamic Models Based on Synchronous Reference Frame [10]

Considering the existence of the speed emf aroused by rotation of the axes, the stator circuit equations under the synchronous reference frame d^e-q^e can be written:

$$v_{ds} = R_s i_{ds} + \frac{d}{dt}\psi_{ds} - \omega_e \psi_{ds} \tag{1}$$

$$v_{qs} = R_s i_{qs} + \frac{d}{dt}\psi_{qs} + \omega_e \psi_{qs} \tag{2}$$

Since the rotor actually moves at speed ω_r, the d-q axes fixed on the rotor move at a speed ω_e-ω_r relative to the synchronous reference frame. Therefore the rotor equation should be given as follows:

$$v_{dr} = R_r i_{dr} + \frac{d}{dt}\psi_{dr} - (\omega_e - \omega_r)\psi_{qr} \tag{3}$$

$$v_{qr} = R_r i_{qr} + \frac{d}{dt}\psi_{qr} + (\omega_e - \omega_r)\psi_{dr} \tag{4}$$

The flux linkage expressions in terms of the currents can be written:

$$\psi_{ds} = L_{ls}i_{ds} + L_m(i_{ds} + i_{dr}) \tag{5}$$

$$\psi_{qs} = L_{ls}i_{qs} + L_m(i_{qs} + i_{qr}) \tag{6}$$

$$\psi_{dr} = L_{lr}i_{dr} + L_m(i_{ds} + i_{dr}) \tag{7}$$

$$\psi_{qr} = L_{lr}i_{qr} + L_m(i_{qs} + i_{qr}) \tag{8}$$

$$\psi_{dm} = L_m(i_{ds} + i_{dr}) \tag{9}$$

$$\psi_{qm} = L_m(i_{qs} + i_{qr}) \tag{10}$$

Combining the above expressions with equations (1), (2), (3), and (4), the state equation of the current of induction motor in the synchronously rotating reference frame can be given in equation (11):

$$\frac{d}{dt}\begin{bmatrix} i_{ds} \\ i_{qs} \\ i_{dr} \\ i_{qr} \end{bmatrix} = \frac{1}{L_H} \cdot$$

$$\begin{bmatrix} R_s L_r & (\omega_e - \omega_r)L_m^2 - \omega_e L_s L_r & -R_r L_m & -\omega_r L_r L_m \\ -(\omega_e - \omega_r)L_m^2 + \omega_e L_s L_r & R_s L_r & \omega_r L_r L_m & -R_r L_m \\ -R_s L_m & \omega_r L_s L_m & R_r L_s & -(\omega_e - \omega_r)L_r L_s + \omega_e L_m^2 \\ -\omega_r L_s L_m & -R_s L_m & (\omega_e - \omega_r)L_r L_s - \omega_e L_m^2 & R_r L_s \end{bmatrix}$$

$$\cdot\begin{bmatrix} i_{ds} \\ i_{qs} \\ i_{dr} \\ i_{qr} \end{bmatrix} + \frac{1}{L_H}\begin{bmatrix} -L_r & 0 & L_m & 0 \\ 0 & -L_r & 0 & L_m \\ L_m & 0 & -L_s & 0 \\ 0 & L_m & 0 & -L_s \end{bmatrix}\begin{bmatrix} v_{ds} \\ v_{qs} \\ v_{dr} \\ v_{qr} \end{bmatrix}$$

$$\tag{11}$$

where $v_{dr} = v_{qr} = 0$, due to the cage motor investigated. The development of torque by the interaction of air gap flux and rotor mmf can be generally expressed as follow:

$$T = \frac{P}{3}L_m \operatorname{Im}(i_s i_r)$$

$$= \frac{P}{3}L_m(i_{qs}i_{dr} - i_{ds}i_{qr}) \tag{12}$$

where

R_s, R_r	stator and rotor resistance;
L_s, L_r, L_m	stator, rotor, and mutual inductance;
$L_H = L_m^2 - L_s L_r$	hybrid leakage coefficient;
ω_r	rotor angular velocity;
ω_e	synchronous angular velocity.

2.2 Dynamic Model Based on Stationary Reference Frame

It is necessary to build the model with stationary reference frame for investigating the flux-oriented control of the induction motor. This model can be easily derived by letting $\omega_e = 0$ in equation (11). The torque developed with stationary frame is the similar to equation (12) and is given as follow:

$$T = \frac{P}{3} L_m (i_{qs}^s i_{dr}^s - i_{ds}^s i_{qr}^s) \tag{13}$$

where the superscript s denotes the stationary reference frame.

3   Vector Control under the Rotor Flux Orientation

Since the natural decoupling control can be obtained through rotor flux orientation, the investigation is carried out under this condition, and the indirect or feedforward vector control method is utilized in this paper. According to equations (7) and (8), the rotor currents can be expressed in vector i_r form:

$$i_r = \frac{1}{L_r} (\psi_r - L_m i_s) \tag{14}$$

Substituting equation (14) into equation (12), the torque equation can be written as

$$T = \frac{P}{3} \frac{L_m}{L_r} (i_{qs} \psi_{dr} - i_{ds} \psi_{qr}) \tag{15}$$

For decoupling control requirement, it is desirable that

$$\psi_{qr} = 0 \tag{16}$$

then

$$T = \frac{P}{3} \frac{L_m}{L_r} \psi_{dr} i_{qs} \tag{17}$$

Hence, when equation (16) is satisfied and

$$\psi_{qr} = constant \tag{18}$$

An induction motor is similar to a linear current to torque converter as that of a DC motor.

The rotor circuit equations can be written as follows:

$$\frac{d}{dt} \psi_{dr} + \frac{R_r}{L_r} \psi_{dr} - \frac{L_m}{L_r} R_r i_{ds} - \omega_{sl} \psi_{qr} = 0 \tag{19}$$

$$\frac{d}{dt} \psi_{qr} + \frac{R_r}{L_r} \psi_{qr} - \frac{L_m}{L_r} R_r i_{qs} - \omega_{sl} \psi_{dr} = 0 \tag{20}$$

where $\omega_{sl} = \omega_e - \omega_r$

Substituting equation (16) and (18) in equation (19) and (20), and considering the relation of $\psi_r = \psi_{dr}$, yields

$$\frac{L_r}{R_r}\frac{d}{dt}\psi_r + \psi_r = L_m i_{ds} \tag{21}$$

$$\omega_{sl}\psi_{dr} - \frac{L_m}{L_r}R_r i_{qs} = 0 \tag{22}$$

Under the rotor flux orientation, the ideal model of an induction motor can be derived from equations (17), (21) and the following mechanical equation:

$$T - T_L = \frac{2J}{P}\frac{d\omega_r}{dt} \tag{23}$$

Considering equations (21), (22) and the relation of synchronous angular velocity ω_e and rotor electrical angular velocity ω_r, the indirect vector control scheme can be achieved.

4 Indirect Rotor Flux Oriented Control Based on Online Controller Parameter Adaptation

The block diagram of indirect vector control using the online controller parameter adaptation is shown in Fig. 1, in which the PID control strategy is employed in the flux and speed controllers respectively. FC is the rotor flux controller, SC is speed controller and PAU is controller parameter adaptation unit in Fig.1. Because the online controller parameter adaptation is introduced, the effects of disturbances and some parameter uncertainties can be reduced.

In the investigation of typical second order system dynamic processes, the system output is y, the desired output is y_g, error is $e=y_g-y$ and the change in the error is Δe. The dynamic processes can be divided into 4 stages, namely I, II, III and IV stage. After the system operation is analysed, the operation behaviour are given as follows:

I stage: $e>0$, $\Delta e<0$. In this stage, the change of dynamic processes trends to desired value, therefore the effect intensity of proportional and integral components should suitably weaken. The closer to the expected value, the smaller effect intensity has. Over action that leads to promote vibration and overshoot is avoided.

II stage: $e<0$, $\Delta e<0$. In this stage, the change of dynamic processes departs from the desired value, therefore, the effect intensity of proportional and integral components should suitably strengthen.

The same principle can be applied to III, IV stages. On the basis of the analysis above, the online adaptive algorithm can be built. Considering the important effect on the dynamic and static characteristics of the system by adjusting proportional component K_P, the online adaptive control can be obtained through on-line adjusting K_P. The online adaptive scheme of controller can be given in table 1:

Table 1. Online parameter adaptive algorithm

K_P \ e Δe	NB	NM	NS	ZE	PS	PM	PB
P	PM	PM	PS	PS	PS	PM	PB
ZE	PB	PM	PS	PS	PS	PS	PM
N	PB	PM	PS	PS	PS	PM	PM

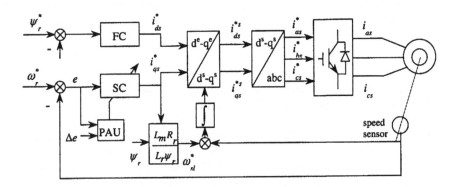

Fig. 1. The block diagram of indirect rotor vector control

5 Simulations

The speed and the developed torque waveforms of induction motor with the stationary reference frame are given in Fig. 2 and Fig. 3 respectively. When the changes of load torque take place, the variation of motor speed is shown in Fig. 2 and Fig.3, note that the revolution rate dropped to 1165rpm, and was unable to be adjusted to the original level.

The simulations [11] of dynamics of induction motor with the synchronously rotating reference frame are also carried out. The waveforms of stator current in d-q axes are shown in Fig.4 and Fig.5. From the corresponding simulation waveforms under the synchronous reference frame, the results of time-variable d.c. signals are apparent. If the stationary reference frame is adapted, the a.c. signals can be seen in the waveforms of rotor and stator current on d-q axes in Fig.6 and Fig.7. The d.c. signals with the synchronous reference frame are easier to analyse in control processes than that of a.c. signals with the stationary reference frame. The parameters of induction motor utilized in simulations are as Power=7.5kW, P=6, L_s=42.4mH, L_r=41.7mH, L_m=41mH, R_s=0.294 Ω, R_r=0.156 Ω, J=0.4kg m^2.

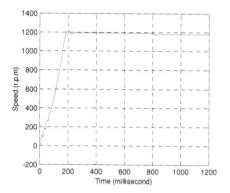

Fig. 2. The speed of induction motor with the stationary reference frame

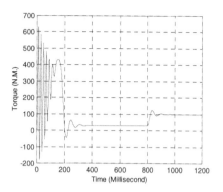

Fig. 3. The developed torque of induction motor with the stationary reference frame

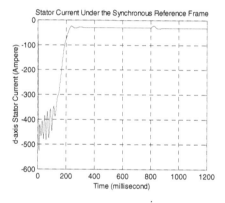

Fig. 4. The d-axis current of stator

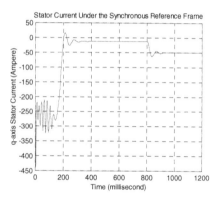

Fig.5. The q-axis current of stator

The simulations of the flux oriented control with respect to the rotor flux vector are made. Due to the decoupling characteristics of flux orientation under the rotor flux vector, the performance of speed adjustment is analogous to a DC motor drive system. The simulation of the processes of speed adjustment under the indirect rotor flux orientation with the online controller parameter adaptation is given in Fig 8. Fig. 8 shows two comparisons between conventional control and parameter adaptation control, the dash line presents conventional control responses, and the solid line presents the system responses with parameter adaptive control. When changes of command speed occurred, a good speed performance is obtained under this control scheme, which is obviously superior to the conventional control. The simulation results of system responses with the variations of load torque are given in Fig. 9 and Fig. 10 respectively. From Fig. 10 it can be seen that the variations of load torque is between 25Nm and 65Nm. In this case, the ideal performance of the system is still obtainable and is shown in Fig.9.

The simulations of system response with the online controller parameter adaptation are shown in Fig. 11 and the fluctuation of rotor resistance is given as Fig. 12. The fluctuation of rotor resistance will lead to the model variations of the plant. Thus, the good robustness can be verified by the system response that presents adjusted performance in Fig.11. The simulation results demonstrate that under the online controller parameter adaptation control, good dynamic and static characteristics are obtained whatever the changes of load torque and fluctuations of rotor resistance.

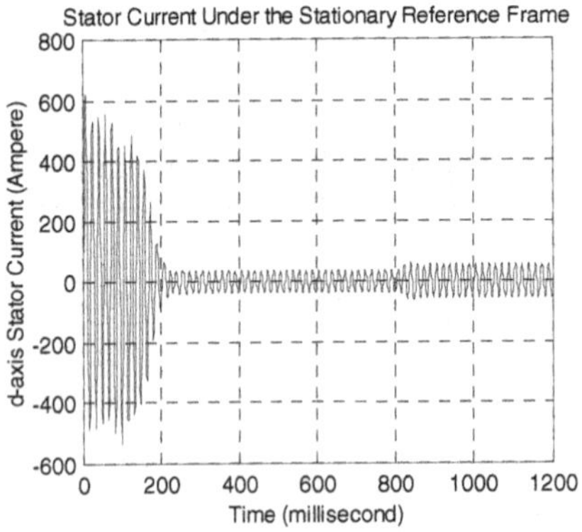

Fig. 6. d-axis stator current with stationary frame

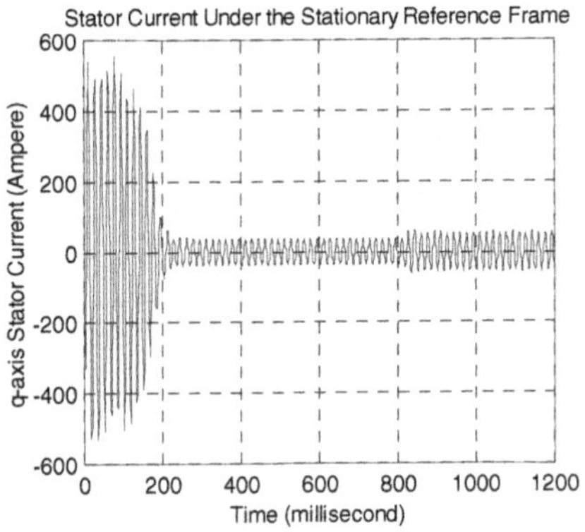

Fig. 7. q-axis stator current with stationary frame

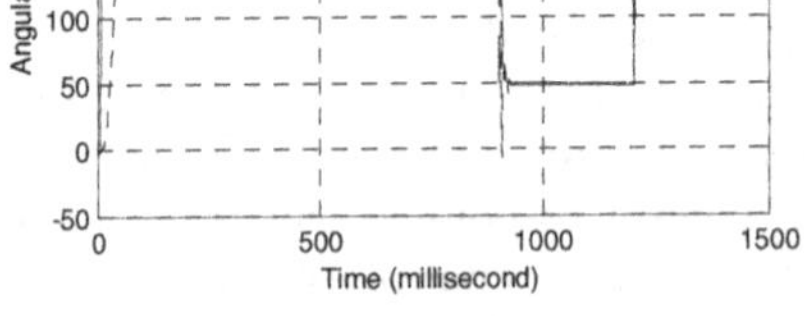

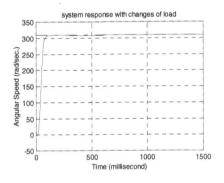

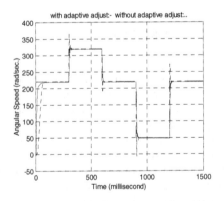

Fig. 8. The speed under the indirect rotor flux orientation control system

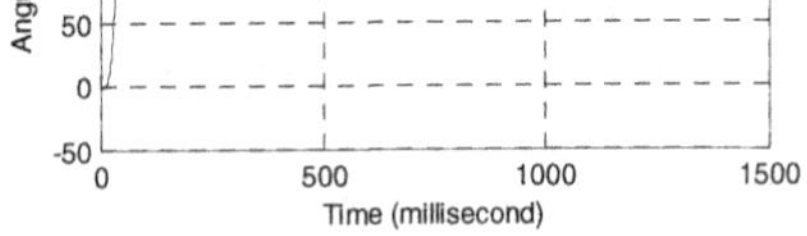

Fig. 9. The system response of indirect rotor flux control with load changes

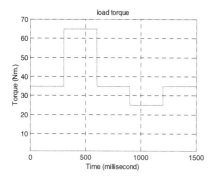

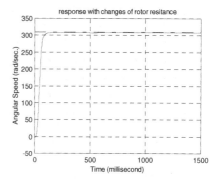

Fig. 10. The system load

Fig. 11. The system response with rotor resistance changes

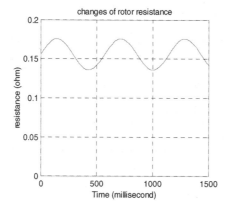

Fig. 12. The resistance of rotor

6   Conclusions

The dynamic models of an induction motor under the synchronous reference frame and stationary reference have been explained. The scheme of the flux oriented control with respective to the rotor flux vector based on the online controller parameter adaptation approach is proposed in this paper. The simulations verified that the good dynamic performances of varying speed and the better robustness under the uncertainty of parameters are obtained.

Acknowledgements. The authors acknowledge with thanks the financial support by China Scholarship Council, Tianjin Natural Science Foundation under Grant 003800811, Tianjin Education Committee Key Discipline Grant and Tianjin University of Technology. The contribution from M. Dafilis and Professor T. Hendtlass the Centre for Intelligent Systems and Complex Processes, Swinburne University of Technology, in reading and commenting on drafts of this paper is also gratefully acknowledged. The authors would also like to thank the anonymous reviewers for their helpful comments.

References

1. Blaschke, F.: The principle of field orientation as applied to the new transvector closed loop control system for rotating field machines, Siemens Review, vol.34, pp 217–220, May 1972
2. Sen, P.C.: Electric motor drives and control – past, present, and future, IEEE Transactions on Industrial Electronics, 6, pp 562–575, 1990
3. Kazmierkowski, M.P. and Sulkowski, W.: A novel vector control scheme for transistor PWM inverter fed induction motor drive, IEEE Transactions on Industrial Electronics, 1, pp.41–47, 1991
4. Xu, X. and Novotny, D.W.: Selection of the flux reference for induction machine drives in the field weakening region, IEEE Transactions on Industry Applications, 6, pp.1353–1358, 1992
5. Zinger, D.S., Profumo, F., Lipo, T.A. and Novotny, D.W.: A direct field oriented controller for induction motor using tapped stator windings, IEEE Transactions on Power Electronics, 4, pp.446–453, 1990
6. Iwasaki, M and Matsui, N.: Robust speed control of IM with torque feedforward control, IEEE Transactions on Industrial Electronics, vol.40, pp. 553–560, 1993
7. Wishart, M.T. and Harley, R.G.: Identification and control of induction machines using artificial neural networks, IEEE Transactions on Industry Applications, vol.31, pp.612–619, 1995
8. Friedland, B.: A nonlinear observer for estimating parameters in dynamic systems, Automatica, vol. 33,pp. 1525–1530, 1997
9. Lin, F., Wai, R., Lin, C. and Liu, D.: Decoupled stator-flux-oriented induction motor drive with fuzzy neural network uncertainty observer, IEEE Transactions on Industrial Electronics, vol.47, pp. 356–367, 2000
10. Bose, B.K.: Power electronics and ac drives, Prentice Hall,Englewood Cliffs, pp 45–51,1986
11. Chen Zaiping, Du Taihang, Gao Qiang, Li Lianbing, Liu Zuojun: Control System Simulations and CAD. Tianjin University Press, Tianjin(2001)

Modelling the Acquisition of Colour Words

Mike Dowman

School of Information Technologies, F09,
University of Sydney, NSW2006, Australia
Mike@it.usyd.edu.au

Abstract. How Bayesian inference might be used as the basis of a system for learning and representing the meanings of colour words in natural languages was investigated. The paper is primarily concerned with cognitive modelling, but has potential applications in natural language processing. A Bayesian cognitive model was constructed to test the hypothesis that people learn language, and in particular the meanings of colour words, using Bayesian inference. The model learned the range of colours which could be named by a particular colour word from examples of colours which could be denoted by that word, and was able to do so accurately even in the presence of large quantities of random noise in the input data. The resulting meaning representations display many of the properties of colour words in natural languages, in particular prototype properties.

1 Introduction

This paper describes a computational model which aims to account for how people learn the meanings of colour words. It takes as its input data examples of colours which can be named by a colour word, and then uses Bayesian inference to generalize from those examples to determine the full range of colours which that word can identify. The task of learning colour words is far from straightforward, because they differ substantially between languages, and they have complex prototype structures, with some colours being better examples of the word than others. Despite these factors, children appear to have little difficulty in learning colour words, despite the limited and noisy data from which they must learn.

All languages have many words that may be used to identify particular colours, but there is always a special subset of these words known as *basic colour terms* . Each of these words identifies a range of colour which is not included in the range of colour identified by any other colour word, and the words themselves usually divide up the colour space so that there is one colour term which can identify every colour. Furthermore, these words are psychologically salient, in that they come readily to mind when speakers of a language are asked to name colour words, and each basic colour term in a particular language will be known to every speaker of that language. These criteria were specified by Berlin and Kay (1969), who, by examining descriptions of a wide range of languages, determined that all languages had between two and eleven such words, a finding that remains largely unchallenged today.

R.I. McKay and J. Slaney (Eds.): AI 2002, LNAI 2557, pp. 259–271, 2002.
© Springer-Verlag Berlin Heidelberg 2002

The concept of basic colour term can probably be made clearer with some examples. English has eleven basic colour terms, 'black', 'white', 'red', 'orange', 'yellow', 'green', 'blue', 'purple', 'pink', 'brown' and 'gray', but it also has many other colour words which are not basic, such as 'crimson', 'turquoise' and 'beige'. In contrast Danian Lani, a language from Irian Jaya in Indonesia, has only two basic terms, one of which, 'laambu', names roughly white, red, yellow and very light colours, and the other, 'mili', names black, green blue and very dark colours (MacLaury, 1997). From these examples we can see that there is considerable variation between the meanings of colour words in different languages, and so children must learn the range of colours which can be denoted by each colour word in their own language.

Taylor (1989) noted that basic colour terms, in common with many other kinds of word, have prototype properties. There is usually a single colour which is the best example of the category identified by the colour term, and this is called the *prototype*. Colours gradually become less good members of the category the further they are away from this prototype, until at categories' fuzzy boundaries it becomes unclear exactly which colours are members of the category and which are not. While there is usually good agreement between speakers as to the location of the prototype, speakers tend to disagree about exactly where the category boundaries are.

The model aims to account for the acquisition of the meanings of colour words, and to explain why colour words have prototype properties, but in order to construct the model, it was first necessary to consider exactly wh at information children have available from which to learn. There is a large body of evidence which suggests that the principal way in which children learn language is through observing the speech of other people, and that explicit teaching and formal education play only a relatively marginal role in language acquisition (Bloom, 2000). In the case of learning the meaning of a colour word, it would seem that children must observe which particular colours that word was used to identify, and from a number of such examples generalize to determine the full range of colours which the word can be used to name.

In this paper, I propose that the mechanism that children use to learn the meanings of colour words is a form of Bayes' optimal classification (Mitchell, 19 97). The model calculates the probability that the meaning of a colour word corresponds to a particular range of colours, making use of all the examples of the use of that word which have been observed. By using the standard Bayesian procedure of hypothesis averaging, it is then possible to determine the overall probability that each particular part of the colour space could be named by that word. Interestingly this produces the prototype properties characteristic of colour words, because the model is most that certain colours near to the centre of a colour category can be named by the word, but it is not sure exactly where the category's boundaries are. The model is described in more detail in section 2, but first it is necessary to provide some justification for the Bayesian approach.

The primary motivation for the Bayesian approach is simply that there already exist a number of studies which have shown that Bayesian models can accurately account for data concerning human performance in other situations. These studies include the work of Griffiths and Tenenbaum (2000) who demonstrated how Bayesian inference could be applied to predicting the frequency of periodic events, and that of Tenenbaum and Xu (2000) who used Bayesian inference to explain how children could learn the denotations of concrete nouns. If people learn one aspect of language using Bayesian inference then it would seem likely that they also use Bayesian inference to learn other aspects of language.

Previous approaches to explaining colour term semantics have usually used prototype representations. Taylor (1989) suggests that prototypes play a central role in defining the full extent of colour categories, but there seem to be problems with this approach. Firstly, as is apparent from data collected by Berlin and Kay (1969), and many subsequent researchers, the size of colour categories varies between languages. So, simply knowing the location of a category's prototype is not enough to determine how far beyond this prototype the category extends. Secondly, categories vary not only in size but also in shape, sometimes extending further from the prototype in one direction through the colour space than in another. Lammens (1994) created a computer model of colour term semantics which defined categories using prototype representations. The representation of the meaning of each colour term consisted of a specification of the location of the prototype and a parameter controlling the size of the category. Lammens made a proposal a s to how a learner could determine the appropriate setting for the size parameter, but he presumed that the category prototypes must be predetermined innately. This latter assumption seems untenable, because while Berlin and Kay (1969) did find that the foci of colour categories in different languages were often the same, this is certainly not true for all categories in all languages.

Kay and McDaniel (1978) attempted to derive the meanings of colour words from the neural response functions of opponent process cells in the retina of the eye. These cells transform signals coming from light sensitive cells into signals which indicate the extent to which the light striking that part of the retina is green as opposed to red, or blue as opposed to yellow. Kay and McDaniel hypothesized that the values of these response functions would correspond to the degree of membership of colours in colour categories. In order to explain how colour categories vary between languages, they proposed that fuzzy logic could be used to combine two response functions, either fuzzy intersection to produce smaller categories, or fuzzy union to produce larger ones. However, the range of colour categories that can be produced in this way is still very limited, and does not appear to include the full range of colour categories attested throughout the world's languages. Therefore it would seem that this approach is much too inflexible to account for colour term acquisition, and so an approach which involves a much greater degree of learning is required. The Bayesian model presented here is similar to Kay and McDaniel's theory in that it also uses fuzzy sets to represent colour terms, but it is much more flexible because it derives those fuzzy sets by generalizing from observations rather than by applying the operations of fuzzy logic.

2 The Bayesian Model

The Bayesian model learns by making use of Bayes' rule, given in equation (1). This allows the probability of a hypothesis, h, to be determined based on some observed data, d . The hypotheses will correspond to possible meanings of colour words, and the data to examples of colours identified by them. However, before this equation can be applied, it is first necessary to determine exactly what form the colour examples take , and to specify the form of the hypotheses. This is described in the next two subsections, and then it is shown how the examples and hypotheses can be used to determine the probability that each colour comes within the meaning of each colour term, and so finally how fuzzy sets may be derived.

$$(1) \qquad P(h \mid d) = \frac{P(d \mid h)P(h)}{P(d)}$$

2.1 The Conceptual Colour Space

There is considerable psychological and linguistic evidence to show that people have a three dimensional conceptual colour space, structured on the dimensions of *hue, saturation* and *brightness* (Thompson, 1995, Gärdenfors, 2000). However, for reasons of simplicity, the present model is concerned only with the dimension of hue. If we consider only colours of maximum saturation and of the degree o f lightness at which maximum saturation may be achieved, then the colours will form a one dimensional colour space as shown in Figure 1. As this colour space does not include colours of zero saturation, it excludes examples of *black, white,* and *grey* . *pink* is excluded because it is a light version of *red,* and *brown* is excluded because it is essentially a dark and low saturation counterpart to some orange, red and yellow hues. This colour space is, however, sufficient to allow an account of the meanings of *red, orange, yellow, green, blue* and *purple* , and of the meanings of many other terms in other languages.

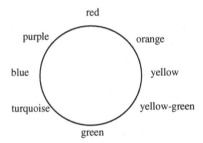

Fig. 1. The Phenomenological Colour Space

When an example of a colour which has been identified using a colour term is observed, it will be represented as a point in this colour space. For the purpose of identifying locations in the colour space an arbitrary scale from 0 to 100 will be used. This scale has its origin (location 0) at red, and increases as we move clockwise through the colour space. Location 100 will correspond to the end of the colour space, which is also the beginning, and so will be in the same place as location 0. Hence the data from which the Bayesian model learns will always consist of a list of (possibly fractional) numbers between 0 and 100, each of which corresponds to one particular example.

2.2 Hypotheses about Colour Word Meanings

The next step in the construction of the Bayesian model is to specify the possible hypotheses, and to assign a probability to each. Each hypothesis will define a continuous section of the colour space, and will correspond to the belief that all and only those colours within that section can be named by the colour word. This restricts the range of possible hypotheses to only those which correspond to words denoting continuous ranges of colour. This is consistent with typological evidence which appears to show that all colour words do in fact have this property, although that does not necessarily entail that learners will know that before they start learning. However, Gärdenfors (2000) has suggested that it is a general property of concepts used by humans that they do not denote disjoint sections of conceptual spaces, so a word which denoted, for example, green and red hues, but not yellow or blue, ones would be impossible, or at least highly unlikely. Hence this restriction on possible hypotheses seems reasonable, because even if it is not entirely accurate, it should at least lead to a good approximation to implicit assumptions made by people when they begin to learn colour word denotations.

As is shown in Figure 2, each hypothesis will have a start point, s, and an end point, e, and will include all those colours which come after the start point but before the end point. The size of the section of colour space corresponding to a hypothesis is thus given by $(e-s)$. Where a hypothesis encompasses the origin, then 100 (the size of the colour space) must be added to e, as otherwise the value of e would be less than s, resulting in a negative value for the size of the hypothesis. A hypothesis may begin and end anywhere within the colour space, and all possible start and end points are considered equally likely *a priori*. This entails that there will be a continuous space of hypotheses, with the sizes of those hypotheses ranging from not including any of the colour space at all to including the whole of the colour space. It also follows that all sizes of hypothesis will be equally likely *a priori*.

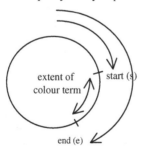

Fig. 2. A Hypothesis as to the Denotation of a Colour Term

2.3 Calculating the Probability of Observed Examples

Given a hypotheses and its *a priori*, it is possible to determine how likely it is that we would have observed the colour examples if that hypothesis was correct. Firstly it is assumed that children make no *a priori* assumptions that some colours are named by colour words more often than other colours are, and that a colour word is equally likely to be used to identify colours anywhere with the range of colours corresponding to its meaning.

Given these assumptions, we can calculate how likely we would be to have observed each individual example. As the number of examples does not vary between hypotheses we need not be concerned with considering how likely it is that we would have observed the actual number of examples which we did, but instead we can concern ourselves simply with calculating the probability that an example was observed at a particular point in the colour space. In order to calculate such values, we must divide the colour space into a finite number of sections, so that there is a non-zero probability of an example being observed in each section. We will use q to represent the number of such sections into which the colour space is divided.

If we can be sure that all the examples are accurate, then there is an equally likely probability of observing an example in any of the sections of the colour space within the range of the hypothesis[1]. This probability, P, is given by equation (2).

$$(2) \qquad\qquad P = \frac{100}{(e-s)q}$$

However, it would seem likely that some of the examples which a child observes might not be accurate, and so if learning is to proceed successfully in the presence of such examples children must have some degree of expectation that any particular example might not be accurate. If the example is not accurate, then a child would have no way of knowing whereabouts in the colour space it would be observed, and so it is assumed that such examples would be equally likely to occur anywhere in the colour space, and this probability, also represented by P, is given by equation (3). (We should note firstly that even if an example is erroneous, it could nevertheless come within the hypothesis simply by chance, and secondly that equation (3) is independent of the hypothesis under consideration.)

$$(3) \qquad\qquad P = \frac{1}{q}$$

A child will not know which examples are accurate examples of the colour word, and which are simply random, so it is necessary to introduce a parameter, p, which corresponds to the certainty with which a child believes an example to be accurate. This parameter can vary from 1, when the child will be completely certain that all examples are accurate, to 0, when the child believe that all examples are random. In the first of these situations a single erroneous example could have a catastrophic effect on learning, while in the second no learning would occur at all, as the child would not believe that the examples gave any indication of the meaning of the colour word. This paper assumes that this parameter is always set to a value between these extremes, so that the model will believe that the examples are indicative of the

---

[1] We should note here that this assumes that each hypothesis begins and ends between sections, rather than somewhere within a section, so that each section is either wholly within or wholly outside of the hypothesis. It will be shown below that the number of such sections can be made to tend to infinity, thus making the color space continuous, and so this assumption is unproblematic.

meaning of the colour word, but will still be able to learn even if some of them are misleading.

Examples which fall outside of the hypothesis must be inaccurate, and so their probability, $P(e)$, is given by multiplying together the probability that an example is not accurate, $(1-p)$, by the probability of observing an inaccurate example given in equation (3). The equation resulting from this operation is given in (4).

If a colour example comes within the range of the hypothesis, then it may be accurate, in which case the equation for its probability could be derived from equation (2), but it could also be inaccurate, in which case its probability could be derived from equation (3). However, when a child is learning they will not be able to be sure which of these two situations applies, and so must consider each possibility according to its probability as defined by the parameter p. We must derive an equation for the overall probability of an example, based on the possibilities of it being either accurate or inaccurate, with both of these possibilities being weighted in accordance with their probabilities, which are p and $(1-p)$ respectively. The total probability of such an example, also written $P(e)$, will be found by adding its probability under each of these possibilities, which produces the equation given in (5).

(4)
$$P(e) = \frac{(1-p)}{q}$$

(5)
$$P(e) = \left(\frac{100p}{(e-s)} + (1-p) \right) \frac{1}{q}$$

The equations so far are all concerned with only a single example. The probability of all the observed examples given a particular hypothesis $(P(d \mid h))$ can be found by multiplying together the probabilities of each individual example. Where there are n examples which come within the scope of the hypothesis, and m examples which come outside of the hypothesis, this probability can be calculated using equation (6).

(6)
$$P(d \mid h) = \left(\left(\frac{100p}{(e-s)} + (1-p) \right) \frac{1}{q} \right)^n \left(\frac{(1-p)}{q} \right)^m$$

We can extract q from the terms put to the power of n and the power of m, to create a new term of q to the power of n plus m. However, n plus m is always the total number of examples observed, and so this value will be constant across all hypotheses. Equation (6) is rewritten as (7) below, where r is used to represent the total number of examples.

(7)
$$P(d \mid h) = \left(\frac{100p}{(e-s)} + (1-p) \right)^n (1-p)^m \frac{1}{q^r}$$

2.4 Calculating Hypothesis Probabilities

So far we have specified how probabilities will be assigned to two of the three terms on the right hand side of Bayes' rule (equation (1)), but in order to calculate the probability of a hypothesis we must also be able to calculate the *a priori* probability of the data, *P(d)* . We can do this by taking the product of the probability of the data given a hypothesis and the *a priori* probability of the hypothesis, and finding the total of all these products for all the hypotheses.

However, ideally we do not want to divide the colour space into a number of arbitrarily sized sections, as there does not appear to be any empirical motivation to do so. Hence it would seem desirable that we increase the number of sections of the colour space, *q*, so that *q* tends to infinity, and the colour space effectively becomes continuous. *P(d)* can then be calculated using calculus, as in (8), where *H* is the set of all possible hypotheses. (We will see below that the term *q* will cancel out of the equations, and so its exact value is unimportant.)

$$(8) \qquad\qquad P(d) = \int_{h \in H} P(d \mid h)P(h)dh$$

We now have all the terms which we need in order to calculate the *a posteriori* probability of a hypothesis using Bayes' rule. Substituting equation (8) into Bayes' rule we obtain equation (9), where the hypothesis whose probability is being calculated is now labeled h_i. All hypotheses have equal *a priori* probability, so the terms $P(h_i)$ and $P(h)$ will cancel out. The terms $P(d \mid h_i)$ and $P(d \mid h)$ also both contain the constant term q^r, and so this term will also cancel, as was noted above.

$$(9) \qquad\qquad P(h_i \mid d) = \frac{P(d \mid h_i)P(h_i)}{\int_{h \in H} P(d \mid h)P(h)dh}$$

2.5 Generalizing from Examples to Other Colours

The aim of the model is not to determine the probability of any one hypothesis, but to determine how likely it is that any particular colour can be named with the colour word. We can express the probability that a particular colour, *x*, comes within the set of colours which can be named by the colour word, *C*, using the expression $P(x \in C \mid h_i)$. However this expression only applies when we are sure that h_i is correct, in which case if *x* comes within *C* this expression will evaluate to one, and otherwise it will evaluate to zero.

However, what is really needed is an expression for the probability that a colour can be named by the colour word which takes account of all the possible hypotheses. This can be achieved by using the procedure of hypothesis averaging, where the probability that a colour can be named by the colour word if a particular hypothesis is correct is multiplied by the probability of that hypothesis given all of the observed data. Equation (10) shows how the overall probability that the colour can be named by the colour word can be found by summing over these products for all the hypotheses.

$$(10) \qquad\qquad P(x \in C \mid d) = \int_{h_i \in H} P(x \in C \mid h_i)P(h_i \mid d)dh_i$$

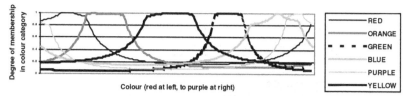

Fig. 3. Fuzzy Category Memberships Learned for English Color Words

The summation can be performed. using calculus, because the colour space is continuous. However, the number of examples which are within the hypotheses changes discretely at the locations of the colour space where the examples occur, and the value of $P(x \in C \mid h_i)$ changes discretely at the location of the colour under consideration. For these reasons, the value of the sum must be calculated separately for sections of the colour space between such points, and then these values added together. There is not sufficient space to give the full derivation of the integrals here, though this is presented in detail in (Dowman, 2001). It is worth noting however that the integration is straightforward if the binomial expansion is used to transform the first part of equation (7), although there will be special cases when there are less than three examples within the scope of a hypothesis, or when the hypotheses include either all of the colour examples or none of them.

So far the model has been described simply with respect to determining whether one particular colour can be named by a colour word. However, if we consider not just a single colour, but the full range of colours, then we can assign a probability to each. These probabilities can be interpreted as corresponding to the degree of membership in a fuzzy set, and so the Bayesian model can be seen as defining a fuzzy set representation for the meanings of colour words. This inference procedure is similar to a proposal made by Tenenbaum (1999), except that Tenenbaum's procedure did not allow for parameterization so that inference could be modelled under conditions where a learner's degree of confidence in the data varied.

3 Learning English and Berinmo Colour Words

In order to investigate the performance of the Bayesian model empirically it was trained on the six basic chromatic colour words of English. The approximate range of each colour word was determined from data published in Berlin and Kay (1969) and ten examples of each word chosen randomly from within the range of colours which the word can name were then given to the model. (The ranges can only be approximate, as even speakers of the same language disagree about the exact range of each colour word.) The model's degree of certainty that each example was correct was set at 0.8, and the probability of membership was calculated for each colour word at 200 points evenly spaced along the colour space. These values were then plotted to produce Figure 3, in which the horizontal axis corresponds to the conceptual colour space, with red at the left, then orange, yellow, green, blue and purple. As the colour space is circular, the left and right edges of the graph represent adjacent points in the colour space.

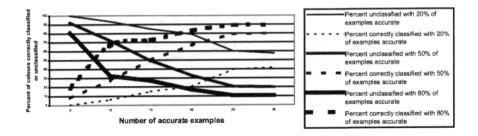

Fig. 4. Accuracy of Learning with Noisy Data

We can see from the graph that the learned meaning representations have the prototype properties characteristic of colour words. For each colour word there is a single colour which is the best example of it (that is has the greatest degree of membership in the colour category). Moving away from this prototype colour, membership in the category gradually decreases, which corresponds to colours becoming increasingly poor members of the category the further that they are from the prototype. The categories also have fuzzy boundaries, because there is no clear point at which colours stop being members of the category, so some colours may be considered marginal members, especially where their degree of membership is around 0.5.

4   Robustness of the System to Noisy Data

Having seen that the system is able to learn when presented with accurate data, it was decided to investigate to what extent the learning process would be disrupted by the addition of random noise. A target category of size 30 was created for the model to learn (the whole colour space being 100 units wide). Examples of this category were generated in the same way as for the English and Berinmo colour categories, but varying amounts of completely random examples were added to the training data to simulate noise. The parameter, p , was adjusted, so that it always accurately reflected the proportion of examples which were accurate, so that the model had advance knowledge of how reliable the data was, though it did not know which particular examples were accurate and which were not.

The model was judged to have correctly categorized a colour if the colour came within the category and was assigned a degree of membership of greater than 0.95, or if the colour came outside of the category and it was assigned a degree of membership of less than 0.05. If a colour was assigned a degree of membership between 0.05 and 0.95 then that colour would be considered not to have been classified. Examples were wrongly classified if they were assigned a degree of membership greater than 0.95, but were in fact outside of the category, or if they were assigned a degree of membership of less than 0.05 but came within the category.

The results of these experiments are given in Figure 4, which shows the proportion of colours classified accurately, and left unclassified, when the level of noise in the data varied from 20% to 80%, and the number of accurate training examples observed varied from 5 to 30. These examples would in each case be accompanied by the number of random examples needed to simulate the appropriate level of noise. The results were derived from sampling at 100 evenly spaced points in the colour space, and in each case investigating whether that colour was classified by the system as coming within the colour category, outside of the colour category, or whether the system did not classify that colour at all. If we view these experiments from the perspective the standard machine learning test data–training data paradigm, then these 100 points would correspond to a stratified sample of 100 test data items, each of which has to be classified. The results from which Figure 4 was plotted were all averages over 20 runs of the system.

We can see that, as more training examples are observed, a higher proportion of colours are correctly classified. Also, if a higher proportion of training examples are accurate, this leads to more accurate classification. However, even when 80% of the data are random, once 30 accurate training examples have been observed (by which time 120 random training examples would also have been seen), over 40% of test colours are classified accurately. When 50% percent of the data was accurate, the model achieved very good performance with 30 accurate training examples, correctly classifying over 80% of the test colours.

Of course classifying a high proportion of examples accurately would not be an impressive result if a large proportion of examples were also classified inaccurately. However, the highest proportion of test colours which were ever classified inaccurately, in any condition, was 0.8%. (This was when 80% of examples were random, and only 10 accurate examples had been observed, and 0.8% is an average, based on all 20 runs of the system in this condition.) In most cases there were even fewer colours classified inaccurately, and in many cases none at all. So we can see that learning can proceed with a very high degree of precision even in the presence of large quantities of noise. When there are very high levels of noise in the training data, or when there is only a small number of training examples available, a large proportion of test colours are left uncategorized. However, even in such conditions, very few examples are classified incorrectly.

5 Discussion

The model described in this paper has shown that a Bayesian inference procedure can learn the meanings of colour words from the same kind of evidence that is available to children when they learn the same words. Moreover, the representations it learns account well for psycholinguistic evidence concerning colour words, in particular that they have prototype properties, and so this provides additional support for the proposal that colour words may be learned using a Bayesian inference procedure, or at least some procedure which approximates Bayesian inference. However, most common nouns, and many other types of word also have prototype properties (for example we may view blackbirds or robins as prototypical birds, but penguins are very marginal members of the bird category). Hence I would suggest that it may be the case that people use Bayesian inference to learn other aspects of language.

The main limitation of the Bayesian model is that it does not account for data from the field of linguistic typology. Large surveys of the colour vocabularies of speakers of many languages have been conducted (for example Berlin and Kay, 1969 and MacLaury, 1987), and these have revealed that, while both the number of colour words and the ranges of colours which each word can name varies between languages, this variation is not completely random. In particular the location of the prototypes of the colour words is partly predictable, so, for example, if a language has three basic colour words these are always focussed on black, white and red. Experiments have been conducted to try to account for the typological data using the Bayesian model.

Firstly learning biases were add ed to the model so that it preferentially remembered examples of focal red, yellow, green and blue. Then several copies of the model were created to form a community of artificial people (agents) who then named colours to one another, usually based on the colour words they had learned up till that point, but occasionally being creative and making up a new colour word. At random intervals one of the agents would be replaced by a new one, and so the evolution of the language was simulated over several generations. This work builds on that of Belpaeme (2002), who also performed computational evolutionary simulations of the cultural evolution of colour term systems, although his agents learned using adaptive networks, not Bayesian inference. Belpaeme was able to show how coherent colour term systems could emerge in a population, but his model was not able to account for typological patterns. Preliminary results using the augmented Bayesian model show that the colour term systems which emerge in the simulations display many of the properties observed in colour term systems across languages. While the evolutionary model is not the topic of this paper, the Bayesian model's ability to account for aspects of linguistic typology helps support the proposal that people learn colour words with Bayesian inference.

Acknowledgements. I would like to thank my Ph.D. supervisor Judy Kay and all the other people who have helped me with this paper. This paper was supported by IPRS and IPA scholarships.

References

Belpaeme, Tony (2002) *Factors influencing the origins of colour categories* . Ph.D. Thesis, Artificial Intelligence Lab, Vrije Universiteit Brussel.

Berlin, B. & Kay, P. (1969). *Basic Color Terms.* University of California Press.

Bloom, P. (2000). *How Children Learn the Meanings of Words.* MIT Press.

Dowman. (2001). *A Bayesian Approach to Colour Term Semantics.* (Technical Report Number 528). Basser Department of Computer Science, University of Sydney.

Gärdenfors, P. (2000). *The Geometry of Thought.* MIT Press.

Griffiths, T. L. & Tenenbaum, J. B. (2000). Teacakes, Trains, Taxicabs and Toxins: A Bayesian Account of Predicting the Future. In L. R. Gleitman & A. K. Joshi (Eds.) *Proceedings of the Twenty-Second Annual Conference of the Cognitive Science Society.* Mahwah, NJ: LEA.

Kay and McDaniel (1978). The Linguistic Significance of the Meanings of Basic Color Terms. *Language,* Volume 54, Number 3.

Lammens, J. M. G. (1994). *A Computational Model of Color Perception and Color Naming.* Ph.D. dissertation, State University of New York at Buffalo.

MacLaury, R. E. (1997). *Color and Cognition in Mesoamerica: Construing Categories as Vantages.* Austin: University of Texas Press.

Mitchell, T. M. (1997). *Machine Learning.* New York: McGraw-Hill.

Taylor, J. R. (1989). *Linguistic Categorization: Prototypes in Linguistic Theory.* Oxford University Press.

Tenenbaum, J. B. (1999). *A Bayesian Framework for Concept Learning* . PhD Thesis, MIT.

Tenenbaum, J. B. & Xu, F. (2000). Word Learning as Bayesian Inference. In L. R. Gleitman & A. K. Joshi (Eds.) *Proceedings of the Twenty-Second Annual Conference of the Cognitive Science Society.* Mahwah, NJ: LEA.

Thompson, E. (1995). *Color Vision: A Study in Cognitive Science and the Philosophy of Perception.* New York, NY: Routledge.

Bayesian Information Reward

Lucas R. Hope and Kevin B. Korb

School of Computer Science
and Software Engineering
Monash University
Clayton, VIC 3168, Australia
{lhope,korb}@csse.monash.edu.au

Abstract. We generalize an information-based reward function, introduced by Good (1952), for use with machine learners of classification functions. We discuss the advantages of our function over predictive accuracy and the metric of Kononenko and Bratko (1991). We examine the use of information reward to evaluate popular machine learning algorithms (e.g., C5.0, Naive Bayes, CaMML) using UCI archive datasets, finding that the assessment implied by predictive accuracy is often reversed when using information reward.

Keywords: Evaluation metrics, information reward, Bayesian evaluation, evaluation of machine learners, predictive accuracy.

1 Introduction

Predictive accuracy as an evaluation metric for machine learners has a number of notable weaknesses: it fails to differentiate between the value of correct classification and incorrect classification, a problem addressed by cost-sensitive classification (cf. Turney (1995)); it also fails to take into account the uncertainty of predictions, treating a fully certain binary prediction as the same as one with probability 0.51. Given these substantial drawbacks, it is somewhat surprising how many researchers use predictive accuracy (or its converse, error rate) as their one and only metric. Perhaps it is the extreme simplicity of its application which maintains its widespread use: computing accuracy requires only a simple yes/no answer to the question, does this instance belong to this class?

We believe a cost-sensitive assessment, namely which machine learner maximizes expected reward, is clearly the best one for evaluating learning algorithms. Unfortunately, finding an appropriate cost function may be difficult or impossible. No expert may be available to provide a suitable cost function; or the algorithms being assessed may be applied across an open-ended variety of domains. An evaluation method independent of cost function which has become popular recently uses ROC curves, as in Provost and Fawcett (1997). ROC curves, however, again ignore the probabilistic aspect of prediction, as does predictive accuracy simpliciter. Here we examine a metric which specifically attends to the estimated probability of a classification, but is also independent of cost, and so

R.I. McKay and J. Slaney (Eds.): AI 2002, LNAI 2557, pp. 272–283, 2002.
© Springer-Verlag Berlin Heidelberg 2002

easier to apply than cost-sensitive metrics; in particular, we examine the *Information Reward* (*IR*) measure, its properties, requirements, and generalization. We also present some empirical results which show the surprising dominance of Naive Bayes when compared with other well known machine learning algorithms, such as C5.0 (Quinlan 1998).

We take the right model for computing reward in uncertain predictions to be that of gambling: a bettor is rewarded not just for identifying the ultimate winners and losers, but more importantly for identifying the appropriate *odds*— namely, those odds which give neither side to a bet an advantage over the other, that is *fair odds*. An agent, artificial or natural, which can consistently beat its opposition in making bets about outcomes in a domain, or across a range of domains, is clearly a superior predictor to is opposition. Predictive accuracy can never hope to assess this ability, since it is constrained to ignore probabilities and therefore odds. *IR* measures exactly this ability. *IR* reports an information-theoretic function of class predictions in comparison with their prior probabilities, rewarding domain understanding as reflected in the correctness of modal predictions, but also rewarding the *calibration* of predictions, penalizing over- and under-confidence while rewarding matches between probabilitistic predictions and the frequency with which those predictions are realized. *IR* is equivalent to the gambling reward over a series of fair bets (see Korb et al. (2001)).

2   Definitions

2.1   Original Information Reward

The original definition of *IR* was introduced by Good (1952) as *fair betting fees*, that is, the cost of buying a bet which makes the expected value of the purchase zero. Good's *IR* positively rewarded binary classifications which were informative relative to an uninformed, uniform prior. The score of a single classification is generated in terms of the generating machine learner's estimated probability *p*. *IR* is split into two cases: that where the classification is correct, indicated by a superscripted '+', and where the classification is incorrect, indicated by a superscripted '−'.

Definition 1. *The IR of a binary classification with probability p is*

$$I^+ = 1 + \log_2 p \qquad \text{(for correct classification)} \qquad (1a)$$

$$I^- = 1 + \log_2(1 - p) \quad \text{(for misclassification)} \qquad (1b)$$

IR has the range $(-\infty, 1)$. For successful classification, it increases monotonically with *p*, and thus is maximized as *p* approaches 1. For misclassification, *IR* decreases monotonically from the value 0 when $p = 0.5$.

While the constant 1 in (1a) and (1b) is unnecessary for simply ranking machine learners, it makes sense in terms of fair fees. When the learner reports a probability of 0.5, it is not communicating any *information* (given a uniform prior), and thus receives a zero reward. Ignoring the constant 1, *IR* has a clear information-theoretic basis: it reports (the negation of) the number of bits required in a message reporting an outcome of the indicated probability. Thus, a certain message requires no bits at all, whereas a certainly false message can never be communicated successfully, requiring an infinitely long message.

Kononenko and Bratko (1991), when introducing a related metric (more about which below), have expressed the intuition that when such a reward is applied to a correct prediction with probability 1 and an incorrect prediction also with probability 1, the correct and incorrect predictions ought precisely to counterbalance, resulting in a total reward of 0. This intuition, however, is at variance with the supposed information-theoretic basis for their reward: on any account in accord with Shannon's information measure, a reward for a certain prediction coming true can only be finite, while a penalty for such a *certain* prediction coming false must always be infinite. Putting these into balance guarantees there will be no proper information-theoretic interpretation of a reward function.

2.2   Generalized Bayesian Information Reward

Our search for a definition of IR that generalizes Good's began with an attempt to apply Good's measure to multiclass datasets (Korb et al., 2001). Good's measure 'hardcodes' a zero score to one where the confidence p is 0.5. So, for example, if a machine learner correctly identifies class A in a 3-class problem with confidence of 0.4, the machine learner will receive a *negative score*. Following Good's treatment of binary variables, it seems that correct classification with probability greater than $\frac{1}{3}$ should be given a positive score. So one possible generalization simply replaces the relativization to a uniform prior over two cases with a uniform prior over n cases. But what if prior information about class A in the 3-class problem indicates that without any further information, its probability is 0.8? Should the machine learner be rewarded for its correct prediction at 0.4, or should it be penalized? We believe it should be penalized for underconfidence, and hence introduce a Bayesian prior p' to the IR calculation.

The idea behind fair fees, that you should only be paid for an *informative* prediction, is simply not adequately addressed by Definition 1. Suppose an expert has diagnosed patients with a disease that is carried by 10% of some population. This particular expert is lazy and simply reports that each patient does not have the disease, with 0.9 confidence. The expected reward per patient for this strategy, under Definition 1 is

$$0.9(1 + \log_2 0.9) + 0.1(1 + \log_2 0.1) = 0.531$$

So the expert is rewarded substantially for the uninformed strategy! The expected reward per patient we should like to see is 0, which our generalization below provides. Definition 1 breaks down in its application to multinomial classification: any *successful* prediction with confidence less than 0.5 is penalized, even when the confidence is greater than the prior. Good's fair fees are actually fair only when both the prior is uniform and the task binary.

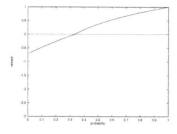 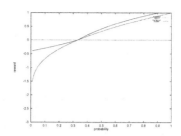

Fig. 1. Both figures show probability along the x-axis and reward along the y-axis. Left: Bayesian Information Reward. This is computed assuming three possible classes, with the x axis indicating the posterior probability given to the true class, and assuming a prior of $1/3$. Right: Generalized Bayesian information reward (BIR) together with Kononenko & Bratko's information reward (KBir). These are computed based upon three classes and a uniform prior distribution, with the probability for the true class given on the x axis.

Hence, we now define the IR of a single classification in terms of the estimated probability p and the class's prior probability p'. Henceforth, Definition 1 will be referred to as IR_G; Definition 2, immediately below, replacing it pro tem. IR is again split into two cases: that where the classification is correct, and that where the classification is incorrect.

Definition 2. *The Bayesian IR of a single classification with estimated probability p and prior probability p', is*

$$I^+ = 1 - \frac{\log p}{\log p'} \qquad \textit{(for correct classification)} \qquad (2a)$$

$$I^- = 1 - \frac{\log (1 - p)}{\log (1 - p')} \qquad \textit{(for misclassification)} \qquad (2b)$$

This IR also has the range $(-\infty, 1)$. For successful classification, it increases monotonically with p, and thus is maximized as p approaches 1, and approaches negative infinity as p approaches 0. IR is 0 precisely when $p = p'$. So, increased certainty $(p > p')$ is rewarded, while decreased certainty $(p < p')$ is punished. For misclassification, IR decreases monotonically as p increases, taking the value 0 when $p = p'$. Thus, misplaced increased certainty $(p > p')$ is punished, while a decreased certainty $(p < p')$ when misclassifying is rewarded.

The prior probability p' can be obtained any number of ways, including being set arbitrarily (or subjectively). We use frequency from the training set given to the machine learner to calculate the prior, for two reasons. First, we are obtaining the prior from a source that the machine learner has full access to, and thus there is no 'unfair' bias in the measure. Second, this means that the simplest algorithm, one which translates observed prior frequencies into posterior probabilities of future occurrence, will receive a score of zero, acting as a baseline for assessing more intelligent algorithms.

Our Definition 2 subsumes Definition 1: given a uniform prior and binary classification, IR_G and IR are identical.

There are, however, some difficulties with Definition 2 since it assesses the machine learner's probability distribution over classes only on the basis of the modal class, that is, that class which has the greatest probability according to the learner. Since the posterior distribution is only being assessed against a single class, its potential to inform us about the quality of its learning by examining *other* classes is being wasted. This also has the effect of producing the "kink" reported for information reward in Figure 1 (left): since the true class in that figure is no longer the modal class below its prior probability of $1/3$, IR is computed relative to a different class; and the penalty for that modal class changes at a different rate than the reward for the true class when it is modal. Even worse than these points is the fact that should the learner incorrectly assign probability zero to some class, and thus be potentially deserving of an infinitely negative reward (as we argued above), the learner will escape its due punishment, since that class will never be modal. These difficulties are all easily rectified by summing the reward function over all the classes:

Definition 3. *The Generalized Bayesian IR for a classification into classes $\{C_1, \ldots, C_k\}$ with estimated probabilites p_i and prior probabilities p'_i, where $i \in \{1, \ldots, k\}$, is*

$$IR = \frac{\sum_i I_i}{k} \tag{3}$$

where $I_i = I_i^+$ below for correct classes and I_i^- for incorrect classes:

$$I_i^+ = 1 - \frac{\log p_i}{\log p'_i} \qquad \textit{(for correct classification)} \tag{3a}$$

$$I_i^- = 1 - \frac{\log (1 - p_i)}{\log (1 - p'_i)} \quad \textit{(for misclassification)} \tag{3b}$$

Generalized Bayesian information reward reflects the gambling metaphor more adequately than does Definition 2. Book makers are required to take bets for and against whatever events are in their books, with their earnings depending on the spread between bets for and against particular outcomes. They are, in effect, being rated on the quality of the odds they generate for all outcomes simultaneously. Generalized IR does the same for machine learning algorithms: the odds (probabilities) they offer on all the possible classes are simultaneously assessed, extracting the maximum information from each probabilistic classification.

We illustrate generalized Bayesian information reward in Figure 1 (right), which also displays Kononenko and Bratko's measure (discussed immediately below). Some differences will be observed with Figure 1 (left), where generalized IR modifies the assessment of Definition 2 by incorporating non-modal class probabilities. This is most noticeable when the low probability accorded the true class (in the range $(0, 1/3)$) keeps it out of the assessment in Figure 1 (left). This final version of Bayesian information reward again subsumes the original one of Good: since for classification into two classes $\{C_0, C_1\}$, where C_0 is for example correct, $IR_G = 1 + \log_2 p_0$, whereas, (taking logs to base 2) $IR = \frac{2 + \log_2 p_0 + \log_2(1-p_1)}{2} = IR_G$ on the assumption of a uniform prior.

3   Kononenko and Bratko's Measure

A related measure introduced by Kononenko and Bratko (1991) also relativizes reward to prior probabilities. Furthermore, it too is nominally based upon information theory, although as we pointed out above, that interpretation is undermined by the introduction of an inappropriate symmetry in the reward for correct and incorrect classifications.

Another dubious aspect of Kononenko and Bratko's analysis is their claim that costs can be computed from prior probabilities. Thus, they assert that when $P(C_1) > P(C_2)$, "if we denote the credit for correct classification into class C with $V_c(C)$, and the penalty for misclassification with $V_m(C)$, then the following should hold: $V_c(C_1) < V_c(C_2)$ and $V_m(C_1) > V_m(C_2)$" (p. 70). Cost and probability functions are, in fact, orthogonal: any combination of high and low cost with high and low probability is possible. For example, the cost of misclassifying a disease might be very high (e.g., leading to death), even when the frequency of the disease is also very high, as might be the case for patients referred to a specialty clinic. We nevertheless agree with Kononenko and Bratko that the kind of cost-neutral reward we are attempting to identify here needs to be relativized to prior probability: otherwise there is no way to avoid rewarding a learner which slavishly mimics frequencies in a training set and no way to penalize algorithms which simply fail to learn from such frequencies.

Kononenko and Bratko specifically introduced the following reward function, which is assessed for each instance against the true class only:

$$I_{KB}^{+} = \log p - \log p' \qquad \text{(for correct classification)} \qquad (4a)$$

$$I_{KB}^{-} = -\log(1-p) + \log(1-p') \qquad \text{(for misclassification)} \qquad (4b)$$

This function is mapped for the simple three-class case with a uniform prior probability and varying probabilities for the true class in Figure 1 (right), while being compared with IR. There are two substantive differences between the two metrics, both of which are unfavorable to Kononenko and Bratko's reward. (1) Their reward function has a kink located at the true class's prior probability, as did our intermediate IR; this reflects their inappropriate concern to even out rewards and punishments, so that their reward function no longer has a suitable information-theoretic interpretation. (2) Their reward function is assessed only against the prior probability of the *true* class. This is a failing again with some analogy to that of our intermediate Definition 2: since the probabilities of false classes are not considered, an overconfident assessment of what is false will go unpunished. For these reasons we do not consider the Kononenko and Bratko function to be adequate; however, we will examine their measure empirically below.

4   Information Reward for a Test Set

Ideally, we would like to know the expected information reward for each machine learner in a domain, or across a set of domains over which we anticipate they will be used. Since we often don't know enough about the domain(s) of application, we may sample from the domain(s), obtaining a test set with which the learners can be evaluated. The cumulative reward, divided by the number of test cases, then serves as a best estimator for expected reward.

For a binary task, where one class is denoted as *Positive (+ve)* and the other as *Negative (-ve)*, there are four different types of classification that can be made: *True Positive (TP)*, where the learner correctly classifies a positive instance, *False Positive (FP)*, where the learner misclassifies an instance as positive (the instance was actually negative), *True Negative (TN)*, where the learner classifies a negative instance correctly, and *False Negative (FN)*, where the learner incorrectly classifies a positive instance as negative.

Lemma 1. *The cumulative IR for the machine learner ML on a binary classification task, where ML generates n classifications, each classification $i \in \{1 \ldots n\}$ having an associated probability p_i, is given by:*

$$I(ML) = n - \left(\frac{\log wz}{\log p'} + \frac{\log xy}{\log(1 - p')} \right) \tag{5}$$

where,

$$w = \prod_{i \in TP} p_i, x = \prod_{i \in FP} (1 - p_i), y = \prod_{i \in TN} p_i, z = \prod_{i \in FN} (1 - p_i),$$

and p' represents the prior probability of the +ve class.

Proof. The IR for an entire test set is the sum of each IR for individual classifications, thus:

$$I(ML) = n - \sum_{i \in TP} \frac{\log p_i}{\log p'} - \sum_{i \in FP} \frac{\log(1 - p_i)}{\log(1 - p')}$$

$$- \sum_{i \in TN} \frac{\log p_i}{\log(1 - p')} - \sum_{i \in FN} \frac{\log(1 - p_i)}{\log p'}$$

$$= n - \frac{\log \prod_{i \in TP} p_i}{\log p'} - \frac{\log \prod_{i \in FP}(1 - p_i)}{\log(1 - p')}$$

$$- \frac{\log \prod_{i \in TN} p_i}{\log(1 - p')} - \frac{\log \prod_{i \in FN}(1 - p_i)}{\log p'}$$

And with w, x, y and z as defined in (5),

$$= n - \left(\frac{\log wz}{\log p'} + \frac{\log xy}{\log(1 - p')} \right), \text{ as required.}$$

The uniform IR for a test set (that is, where each class has equal prior) is simplified substantially. For the binary case, this is precisely what applying Definition 1 to each case in a test set would yield.

Lemma 2. *The uniform IR on a binary task, corresponding to Definition 1, is denoted by $I_u(ML)$ and simplifies as follows:*

$$I_u(ML) = n + \frac{\log(wxyz)}{\log 2} \tag{6}$$

with w, x, y, z and n as defined in (5).

Proof. Lemma 2 is obtained from Lemma 1 by setting $p' = 1 - p'$ and applying the log laws.

5   Information Reward and Evaluation

With Lemma 1 and Lemma 2 in hand, we may now investigate the application of Bayesian IR to evaluation. We first consider whether IR can make a difference between the relative rankings of two machine learners, ML_1 and ML_2, compared to IR_G. If our generalization cannot make any difference to the relative rankings of machine learners, then it cannot represent any very important improvement upon IR_G.

Thesis 1 *There exists a binary test set, machine learners ML_1 and ML_2 and prior probability p' such that:*

$$I_u(ML_1) < I_u(ML_2) \tag{7a}$$
$$and \quad I(ML_1) > I(ML_2) \text{ for some } p' \neq 0.5. \tag{7b}$$

Proof. Substituting (6) into (7a):

$$n + \frac{\log w_1 x_1 y_1 z_1}{\log 2} < n + \frac{\log w_2 x_2 y_2 z_2}{\log 2} \tag{8}$$
$$\Longleftrightarrow \quad w_1 x_1 y_1 z_1 < w_2 x_2 y_2 z_2 \tag{9}$$

(Note that (9) implies that a ranking produced by the original IR will be the same as a maximum likelihood ranking.)

$$\Longleftrightarrow \quad \frac{w_1 z_1}{w_2 z_2} < \frac{x_2 y_2}{x_1 y_1} \tag{10}$$

Substituting (5) into (7b):

$$n - \left(\frac{\log w_1 z_1}{\log p'} + \frac{\log x_1 y_1}{\log(1 - p')} \right) > n - \left(\frac{\log w_2 z_2}{\log p'} + \frac{\log x_2 y_2}{\log(1 - p')} \right) \tag{11}$$

$$\Longleftrightarrow \frac{\log w_1 z_1}{\log p'} + \frac{\log x_1 y_1}{\log(1-p')} < \frac{\log w_2 z_2}{\log p'} + \frac{\log x_2 y_2}{\log(1-p')} \tag{12}$$

$$\Longleftrightarrow \frac{\log w_1 z_1 - \log w_2 z_2}{\log p'} < \frac{\log x_2 y_2 - \log x_1 y_1}{\log(1-p')} \tag{13}$$

$$\Longleftrightarrow \log(1-p') \log\left(\frac{w_1 z_1}{w_2 z_2}\right) < \log p' \log\left(\frac{x_2 y_2}{x_1 y_1}\right) \tag{14}$$

To finish the proof, we simply produce a set of numbers simultaneously satisfying inequalities (10) and (14). Setting $w_1 z_1 = 0.6$, $w_2 z_2 = .5$, $x_2 y_2 = .7$, $x_1 y_1 = .3$, together with a prior $p' = .8$ suffices. Thus the thesis is proven.

6   Results

For this study we tested a number of well-known machine learning algorithms, using the same datasets employed by Holte (1993) and Korb et al. (2001):

- **C5.0** (Quinlan, 1998): C5.0 is an improvement over C4.5, and comes with the option of *boosting*. C5.0 was run with both boosting enabled (cB) and disabled (c5).
- **Causal MML (ca)** (Wallace et al., 1996): This learns Bayesian Networks from data using the Minimum Message Length (MML) principle (Wallace & Boulton, 1968).
- **Naive Bayes (nb)**: These simple Bayesian net models split on class membership, with the leaves representing the different available attributes. They are "naive" because they assume that the attributes, given knowledge of class membership, are independent of each other. Observed attribute values are filled in and a simple Bayesian net propagation provides a posterior probability of class membership. We implemented the algorithm as described by Mitchell (1997).

Each of these learning algorithms allowed classification probabilities to be read.

The empirical evaluation in this study was performed using Dietterich's 5x2cv paired t test, which has been shown in his empirical work to be superior to standardly used tests (Dietterich, 1998). Briefly, this method requires 5 replications of 2-fold cross-validation and approximates a t test with 5 degrees of freedom. The method is used because it more closely approximates the t distribution by better supporting the independence assumptions required than more common tests such as the resampled paired t test and other cross-validation techniques (Dietterich, 1998).

Three different evaluation measures are shown. Predictive accuracy is calculated by giving each classification a score of 1 if the true class is given the highest probability by the machine learner, and 0 otherwise. Kononenko and Bratko's measure is calculated as in Section 3. Information reward is calculated as in Definition 3. All the measures are normalised by dividing by the number of items in the test set.

Since both IR and Kononenko and Bratko's measure can penalize wrong predictions without limit — for example, probabilities of 0 and 1 correspond to offering infinite odds, and so when wrong are penalized infinitely — we applied a cutoff to extreme probability estimates supported by MML theory (Dowe, 2000), enforcing the range $\left[\frac{0.5}{n+(0.5k)}, \frac{n+0.5}{n+(0.5k)}\right]$ where n is the sample size and k is the number of classes.[1]

The results for predictive accuracy are shown in Table 1. Notice that Naive Bayes is ranked worse than all other learners five times (those being datasets ch, hy, mu, se and vo).

Kononenko and Bratko's measure is shown in Table 2. Under this measure, Naive Bayes does even worse than on accuracy. It is deemed worse on the ir dataset, as well as those found using the accuracy measure.

Information reward is shown in Table 3. Using information reward, Naive Bayes is shown to be better than the other machine learners, contrary to both the accuracy and Kononenko and Bratko's measures. Although Naive Bayes appears to be soundly beaten by the alternatives on the ch and mu datasets, on the whole it is substantially better, with 10 statistically significant results outperforming them. For example, in the hy data set C5.0 with boosting outperforms Naive Bayes to statistical significance in both accuracy and KB reward, but this verdict is reversed with IR.

7 Discussion and Conclusion

The interpretation of IR presented in this paper has numerous advantages over that presented by Good (1952), used to evaluate football tipsters (Dowe et al., 1996) and recently machine learners (Korb et al., 2001).

The key argument for generalized IR rests on the interpretation of information. Information reduces uncertainty about the world. Thus when a machine learner correctly classifies an instance with probability p, p must be greater than the prior probability p' to inform, or reduce uncertainty. This is reflected in the definition of generalized IR; thus $p > p'$ is rewarded and $p < p'$ is penalized, given correct classification. Given misclassification, $p < p'$ is rewarded and $p > p'$ penalized. This can be interpreted as the following: the machine learner indicated that the probability p of the event was less than what you had expected (p'). That event did not occur, so the learner should be rewarded for reducing the expectation in the event, while if p was increased, the expectation was increased, and thus the learner should be penalized for its estimation.

Information reward is a good objective measure of classification performance. The constant 1 is added so that good machine learners are rewarded, that is $I(ML) > 0$, and bad ones penalized: $I(ML) < 0$. Bad machine learners are actually *misinforming*, relative to the prior! That is, they perform worse than a

---

[1] C5.0, and to a lesser extent CaMML, reported numerous classes with extreme probabilities; thus, this adjustment gave them an important advantage in estimating these reward metrics. Only Naive Bayes avoided extreme probability estimates on its own.

Table 1. Left: Predictive accuracy reported by each machine learner, for each dataset. Right: Significant differences between machine learners, using the accuracy measure. Each cell records which machine learners were judged inferior to that particular machine learner, on each particular dataset.

Dataset	c5	cB	ca	nb
bc	0.7622378	0.7622378	0.73426574	0.7692308
ch	0.99248594	0.99686915	0.95241076	0.77332497
g2	0.7160494	0.8518519	0.91358024	0.86419755
gl	0.69158876	0.69158876	0.8224299	0.6168224
hd	0.7086093	0.78807944	0.7549669	0.80794704
he	0.7922078	0.8181818	0.8051948	0.8961039
ho	0.8369565	0.8152174	0.8097826	0.8043478
hy	0.9886148	0.98987985	0.9892473	0.9550917
ir	0.94666666	0.96	0.96	0.97333336
la	0.8214286	0.8214286	0.89285713	0.8214286
ly	0.7702703	0.7027027	0.7432432	0.7702703
mu	1.0	1.0	1.0	0.9054653
se	0.97975963	0.97975963	0.97406703	0.9089184
so	1.0	1.0	1.0	1.0
v2	0.85714287	0.9078341	0.92626727	0.875576
vo	0.95852536	0.95852536	0.9447005	0.89400923

Dataset	c5	cB	ca	nb
bc				
ch		ca nb	ca nb	nb
g2		c5	c5	c5
gl			c5 cB nb	
hd		ca		c5 ca
he				
ho				
hy	nb	nb	nb	
ir				
la				
ly				
mu	nb	nb	nb	
se	ca nb	ca nb	nb	
so				
v2		c5	c5 nb	
vo	nb	nb	nb	

Table 2. Left: Kononenko and Bratko reward reported by each machine learner, for each dataset. Right: Significant differences between machine learners, using the Kononenko and Bratko reward. Each cell records which machine learners were judged inferior to that particular machine learner, on each particular dataset.

Dataset	c5	cB	ca	nb
bc	0.069981635	0.069981635	−0.0018902452	0.13689728
ch	0.6723401	0.64563507	0.5885489	0.16337916
g2	0.2591113	0.35606107	0.5546989	0.37491697
gl	0.81675977	0.86755884	1.130047	0.65977937
hd	0.2506573	0.31211603	0.3526309	0.32222697
he	0.1018493	0.13039692	0.09669634	0.23335941
ho	0.3245233	0.31426513	0.3549378	0.28417683
hy	0.1355615	0.07641858	0.13847339	−0.014177129
ir	1.0032248	0.9701727	1.0044801	0.7756945
la	0.24943754	0.24943754	0.3933418	0.3677128
ly	0.42263785	0.39556766	0.43005717	0.3594238
mu	0.69259095	0.69259095	0.69259053	0.55018294
se	0.22789803	0.22789803	0.21835881	0.049714945
so	1.3987643	1.3987643	1.4630065	1.2994881
v2	0.43209726	0.48362544	0.52688074	0.47609127
vo	0.5957392	0.5655813	0.59266555	0.5302857

Dataset	c5	cB	ca	nb
bc	ca		ca	ca
ch	ca cB nb	ca nb	nb	
g2			c5 cB nb	c5
gl		nb	c5 cB nb	
hd				
he				c5 ca
ho			nb	
hy	nb	nb	nb	
ir	nb	nb	nb	
la				
ly				
mu	nb	nb	nb	
se	nb	nb	nb	
so				
v2		c5	c5 cB nb	
vo	cB nb	nb	cB nb	

Table 3. Left: Information reward reported by each machine learner, for each dataset. Right: Significant differences between machine learners, using information reward. Each cell records which machine learners were judged inferior to that particular machine learner, on each particular dataset.

Dataset	c5	cB	ca	nb
bc	−0.23610511	−0.23610511	−0.002686911	0.2808528
ch	0.9522189	0.93266416	0.79834837	0.2326152
g2	−0.49246055	0.45041668	0.7281166	0.5455182
gl	0.07175887	0.2923216	0.5108723	0.44003078
hd	−0.22732624	0.20924993	0.22064793	0.37742698
he	−0.15546304	0.0129868025	−0.4243838	0.5606905
ho	0.18764098	0.28545344	0.20742324	0.3494705
hy	0.5477152	0.46073914	0.60719365	0.6828912
ir	0.79086244	0.82428205	0.81571364	0.64188224
la	0.2903297	0.2903297	0.3076863	0.5979209
ly	−0.40623546	0.1889826	0.17918634	0.61388963
mu	0.9998209	0.9998209	0.99982065	0.6382106
se	0.58898747	0.58898747	0.4046343	0.62509626
so	0.9015267	0.9015267	0.9772743	0.8461196
v2	0.4839226	0.5787031	0.58912724	0.35221466
vo	0.8161831	0.7789633	0.81813234	0.62418294

Dataset	c5	cB	ca	nb
bc				ca cB
ch	ca nb	ca nb	c5 cB nb	c5
g2		c5	c5 cB nb	c5
gl				cB
hd		c5	c5	c5 ca cB
he		ca		ca cB
ho				
hy				cB
ir				
la				
ly				cB
mu	nb	nb	nb	
se				
so				
v2		nb		
vo				

machine learner who just reports the modal class and its prior for each instance. The average information reward $(I(ML)/n$, where n is the test set size), also has the advantage of being bounded by 1, the value only a perfect predictor could obtain.

Where do the priors come from? In most machine learning tasks, the samples are split into two sets, a training set and a data set. A straightforward prior is to use the relative frequencies of the classes from the training set. Thus the prior is obtained from a source that is accessible by the machine learner. IR also allows us to measure machine learners against any prior standard if we wish, for example one derived from a human expert.

References

Dietterich, T. G. (1998). Approximate statistical tests for comparing supervised classification learning algorithms. *Neural Computation, 7*, 1895–1924.

Dowe, D. L. (2000). *Learning and prediction notes.* School of Computer Science and Software Engineering, Monash University.

Dowe, D. L., Farr, G. E., Hurst, A. J., & Lentin, K. L. (1996). *Information-theoretic football tipping* (Technical Report 96/297). Dept. of Computer Science, Monash University.

Good, I. J. (1952). Rational decisions. *Journal of the Royal Statistical Society. Series B (Methodological), 14*, 107–114.

Holte, R. C. (1993). Very simple classification rules perform well on most commonly used datasets. *Machine Learning, 11*, 63–91.

Kononenko, I., & Bratko, I. (1991). Information-based evaluation criterion for classifier's performance. *Machine Learning, 6*, 67–80.

Korb, K. B., Hope, L. R., & Hughes, M. J. (2001). The evaluation of predictive learners: Some theoretical and empirical results. *European Conference on Machine Learning (ECML'01)* (pp. 276–287).

Mitchell, T. (1997). *Machine learning.* McGraw-Hill.

Provost, F., & Fawcett, T. (1997). Analysis and visualization of classifier performance: Comparison under imprecise class and cost distributions. *Proceedings of the Third International Conference on Knowledge Discovery and Data Mining (KDD-97).* AAAI Press.

Quinlan, R. (1998). *Data mining tools See5 and C5.0* (Technical Report). RuleQuest Research.

Turney, P. (1995). Cost-sensitive classification: Empirical evaluation of a hybrid genetic decision tree induction algorithm. *Journal of Artificial Intelligence Research, 2*, 369–409.

Wallace, C., & Boulton, D. (1968). An information measure for classification. *The Computer Journal, 11*, 185–194.

Wallace, C. S., Korb, K. B., & Dai, H. (1996). Causal discovery via MML. *International Conference on Machine Learning (ICML'96)* (pp. 516–524). Morgan Kaufmann Publishers.

Prediction of User Preference in Recommendation System Using Associative User Clustering and Bayesian Estimated Value

Kyung-Yong Jung and Jung-Hyun Lee

Department of Computer Science & Engineering
Inha University, Inchon, Korea
dragon@nlsun.inha.ac.kr, jhlee@inha.ac.kr

Abstract. The user predicting preference method using a collaborative filtering (CF) does not only reflect any contents about items but also solve the *sparsity* and *first-rater* problem. In this paper, we suggest the method of prediction by using associative user clustering and Bayesian estimated value to complement the problems of the current collaborative filtering system. The Representative Attribute–Neighborhood is for an active user to select the nearest neighbors who have similar preference through extracting the representative attributes that most affects the preference. Associative user behavior pattern 3_UB(associative users are composed of 3-users) is clustered according to the genre through Association Rule Hypergraph Partitioning Algorithm, and new users are classified into one of these genres by Naive Bayes classifier. Besides, to get the similarity between users belonged to the classified genre and new users, this paper allows the different estimated values to items which users evaluated through Naive Bayes learning. We evaluate our method on a large CF database of user rating and it significantly outperforms the previous proposed method.

1 Introduction

In recent years, most of personalized recommender systems in electronic commerce utilize the collaborative filtering(CF) system in order to recommend more appropriate items. However, the collaborative filtering system has three shortcomings according to the followings. First, the *first-rater* problem; that is, the item cannot be recommended to the active user unless the user has rated it before. Second, the *sparsity* problem; most users do not rate most all kinds of item and hence the user-item data set is typically very sparse. Third, it could not use the information of users who are not correlated with the user. The information can be useful data for predicting the preference even if the preference between a pair of users does not correlate with each other that much[4,8]. Methods used in [3,4,20] solve only the *first-rater* problem not the *sparsity* problem. As the method of LSI [19], SVD [5] decreases the dimension of user-item data set, it solves the *sparsity* problem of the collaborative filtering. However, it does not solve the *first-rater* problem. In addition, a method used in [17], it just tried to solve both the *first-rater* problem and the *sparsity*

R.I. McKay and J. Slaney (Eds.): AI 2002, LNAI 2557, pp. 284–296, 2002.
© Springer-Verlag Berlin Heidelberg 2002

problem. In this paper, to overcome these drawbacks of the collaborative filtering, we proposed the method for predicting the user preference by using associative user clustering and Bayesian estimated value. We improved the efficiency using Representative Attribute-Neighborhood with age, gender, and zip code grouping to the collaborative filtering complementary [11,12].

2 System Overview

Fig. 1 shows system overview for prediction a user preference by using associative user clustering and Bayesian estimated value in order to complement the problem of the collaborative filtering system. To complement the shortcoming that does not regard the item attribution, we use Representative Attribute-Neighborhood(RA-Neighborhood)[12] when we select the nearest neighbors through extracting the representative attributes that most affects the preference.

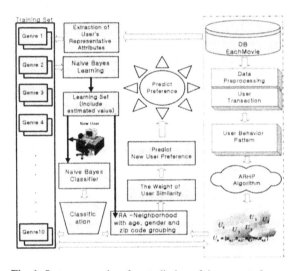

Fig. 1. System overview for prediction of the user preference

In the method suggested, in order to solve the *sparsity* problem in the collaborative filtering system, using Association Rule Hypergraph Partitioning Algorithm [9,13] reduces the dimension of user-item data. Thought applying Apriori algorithm [1,2] to user transaction, the association rule and confidence can be calculated. After that, we substitute vertices for users included in the association rule and hyperedges for frequent usersets. The weight for hypergraph partitioning is used to be confidence, and hypergraph partitioning algorithm is used to find clusters. New users are classified into one of 10 genres by Naive Bayes classifier [16]. Accordingly, it solves the *first-rater* problem by generating new users profile. In the learning set estimated the weight, this paper allows to reflect the information about the missing value granted the weight of user preference about items differently. It figures out the problem not reflecting directly the user preference about the item attribution.

3 Associative User Clustering through Data Mining

We use associative user clustering through data mining to complement the *sparsity* problem. It is also used to promote the accuracy of prediction by reducing the dimension of user-item data set.

3.1 User Representation for User Behavior

We adopt the commonly used 'bag-of-users' [18] user representation scheme, in which we ignore the structure of a user profile and the order of users in the database[6]. In this paper, we propose effective user selection method using associative user mining. We represent 'bag-of-users' as 'bag-of-associative users' that includes a few users instead of single users. The feature vectors represent associative users observed in the EachMoive datasets [15]. The associative user-list in the training set consists of all the distinct users that appear in the training samples after preprocessing the user datasets.

The UB (user behavior)_List is defined to be : UB = $\{(U_{1r}: u_{11}\&u_{12}...\&u_{1(r-1)}\rightarrow u_{1r})$, $(U_{2r}:u_{21}\&u_{22}...\&u_{2(r-1)}\rightarrow w_{2r}),..,(U_{kr}:u_{k1}\&u_{k2}..\&u_{k(r-1)}\rightarrow u_{kr}),..,(U_{pr}:u_{p1}\&u_{p2}...\&u_{p(r-1)}\rightarrow u_{pr})$ $\}$. Here, each of $\{u_{k1},u_{k2},...,u_{k(r-1)},u_{kr}\}$ in $(u_{k1}\&u_{k2}...\&u_{k(r-1)}\rightarrow u_{kr})$ represents a user for composing associative user. "p" in UB represents the number of associative users in the database. "r" in UB represents the number of users in the associative user. "&" in pairs of users means that pairs of users have high degree of semantic relatedness. "$u_{k1}\&u_{k2}...\&u_{k(r-1)}$" is an antecedent of the associative user $(u_{k1}\&u_{k2}...\&u_{k(r-1)}\rightarrow u_{kr})$ and "u_{kr}" is a consequent of the associative user $(u_{k1}\&u_{k2}...\&u_{k(r-1)}\rightarrow u_{kr})$. The user representation is used the feature selecting for associative user mining.

3.2 Feature Selecting for Associative User Mining

Apriori Algorithm [1,2] can mine association rule by using the data mining technique. Mining association rule between users consists of two stages. In the first stage, composition having transaction support in excess of min_support is found to constitute a frequent user item. In the second stage, the frequent user item is used to create association rule from the database. As for all frequent user items(L), find subset instead of all empty set of frequent user item. As for each subset(A), if ratio of support(L) against support(A) is not less than min_confidence, rule of A$\rightarrow$(L-A) type is displayed. Support of this rule is support(L).

In order to constitute the associative user, the confidence and support should be decided. Equation (1) to decide confidence can be obtained as follows. Equation (1) is the result of dividing the number of transaction that includes all items of u_1 and u_2 with the number of transaction that includes item of u_1.

$$Confidence(u_1\rightarrow u_2) = Pr(u_2|u_1) \tag{1}$$

Equation (2) to decide support represents frequency of each associative user among all user sets. Equation (2) is result of dividing the number of transaction that includes all items of u_1 and u_2 with the number of all transactions within the database.

$$Support(u_1 \rightarrow u_2) = Pr(u_2 \cup u_1) \qquad (2)$$

In order to extract the most proper associative user, confidence should be fixed at not less than 85 and support should be not more than 25[11,12]. Table 1 shows the step for extracting associative users using Apriori Algorithm. According to this method of feature selecting, we can describe user $\{U_i\}$ to be as following.

$$\{U_i\}=\{ U_{1r}, U_{2r}, U_{kr}, U_{pr} \}, \quad i=1,2,...,m$$

Table 1. The step for extracting association users using Apriori Algorithm

C_1 Candidate 1-userset	$u_{1(2)}, u_{2(3)}, u_{3(6)}, u_{4(1)}, u_{5(2)}, u_{6(1)}, u_{7(1)}, u_{8(1)}, u_{9(1)}, u_{10(1)}, u_{11(1)}, u_{12(1)}, u_{13(1)}, u_{14(1)}, u_{15(2)}, u_{16(1)}, u_{17(1)}, u_{18(1)}, u_{19(1)}, u_{20(1)}, u_{21(1)}, u_{22(1)}, u_{23(1)}, u_{24(1)}, u_{25(1)}$
L_1 Frequent 1-userset	$u_{1(2)}, u_{2(3)}, u_{3(6)}, u_{5(2)}, u_{13(3)}, u_{15(2)}$
C_2 Candidate 2-userset	$(u_1,u_2)_{(2)}, (u_1,u_3)_{(2)}, (u_1,u_5)_{(1)}, (u_1,u_{13})_{(0)}, (u_1,u_{15})_{(0)}, (u_2,u_3)_{(3)}, (u_2,u_5)_{(2)}, (u_2,u_{13})_{(0)}, (u_2,u_{15})_{(0)}, (u_3,u_5)_{(2)}, (u_3,u_{13})_{(3)}, (u_3,u_{15})_{(2)}, (u_5,u_{13})_{(0)}, (u_5,u_{15})_{(0)}, (u_{13},u_{15})_{(2)}$
L_2 Frequent 2-userset	$(u_1,u_2)_{(2)}, (u_1,u_3)_{(2)}, (u_2,u_3)_{(3)}, (u_2,u_5)_{(2)}, (u_3,u_5)_{(2)}, (u_3,u_{13})_{(3)}, (u_3,u_{15})_{(2)}, (u_{13},u_{15})_{(2)}$
C_3 Candidate 3-userset	$(u_1,u_2,u_3)_{(2)}, (u_1,u_2,u_5)_{(0)}, (u_1,u_2,u_{13})_{(0)}, (u_1,u_2,u_{15})_{(0)}, (u_1,u_3,u_5)_{(1)}, (u_1,u_3,u_{13})_{(0)}, (u_1,u_3,u_{15})_{(0)}, (u_2,u_3,u_5)_{(2)}, (u_2,u_3,u_{13})_{(0)}, (u_2,u_3,u_{15})_{(0)}, (u_2,u_5,u_{15})_{(2)}, (u_2,u_5,u_{13})_{(0)}, (u_3,u_5,u_{13})_{(0)}, (u_3,u_5,u_{15})_{(0)}, (u_3,u_{13},u_{15})_{(2)}, (u_{13},u_{15},u_1)_{(0)}, (u_{13},u_{15},u_2)_{(1)}, (u_{13},u_{15},u_3)_{(0)}, (u_{13},u_{15},u_5)_{(0)}$
L_3 Frequent 3-userset	$(u_1,u_2,u_3)_{(2)}, (u_2,u_3,u_5)_{(2)}, (u_2,u_5,u_{15})_{(2)}, (u_3,u_{13},u_{15})_{(2)}$

3.3 User Behavior Pattern Generation

The associative user pattern representation includes not only 2-associative users but also up to 5 associative users occurring in the database. At confidence 85 and support 25 in Apriori algorithm [1,2], we can capture some characteristic user combinations, in which number of users increases. The process of generating pattern is performed in n database retrieval, where n-associative users are generated in the last pass. For illustration we show in Fig. 2(a), Let UB denote associative user in generating user behavior. In Fig. 2(a), we can see that the number of associative user pattern generated using 2-UB is larger than the others (149889 for 2-UB vs. 13934 for 3-UB vs. 3804 for 4-UB vs. 102 for 5-UB). Fig. 2(b) shows the result of clustering by using new features generated. In order to evaluate the performance of clustering by using each UB(2- UB, 3-UB, 4-UB, 5-UB), we use ARHP algorithm on 20864 users. In case that ARHP algorithm using UB clusters a user behavior into the other classes except genre class, it is an incorrect clustering. The accuracy of clustering is the rate of user behavior correctly classified for 20864 users.

In Fig. 2(b), time(sec) is the response time for associative user clustering. As the graph shows, 2-UB has a very bad speedup performance. On the other hand, the accuracy of clustering using 2-UB is higher than using 4-UB but it is lower than using 3-UB. The clustering using 3-UB is much more accurate than the others. In addition, 3-UB has a good speedup comparatively. 4-UB has a very good speedup performance. However, the accuracy of clustering using 4-UB is far lower than the others. Therefore, it is relevant to use 3-associative users format at pattern selection for associative user clustering.

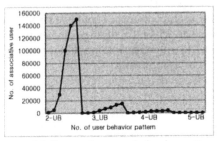 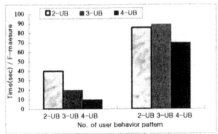

(a) Generating user behavior pattern   (b) Result of clustering

Fig. 2. The accumulated number of associative user pattern during the process of generating pattern on 20864 users and the result of clustering

3.4   Clustering of Associative Users Using ARHP Algorithm

Association Rule Hypergraph Partitioning(ARHP) Algorithm is for clustering related items by using association rules and hypergraph partitioning[9,13]. Formally, A hypergraph H={V, E} consists of a set of vertices(V) constituted with users and a set of hyperedges(E) denoted frequent usersets, where each hyperedge is a subset of the vertex set V. A hypergraph is an extension of a graph in the sense that each hypergraph can connect more than two vertices. In this paper, the vertex set corresponds to the distinct users in the EachMovie dataset[15] and the hyperedges correspond to the frequent k-usersets. The weight for Hypergraph Partitioning is used to the confidence of the association rule using Apriori algorithm[1,2]. The frequent k-usersets derived from association rules are used to group users into a hypergraph edge, and hypergraph partitioning algorithm is used to find clusters. For example, if $\{u_1, u_2, u_3\}$ is a frequent 3-userset, then the hypergraph contains a hyperegde that connects u_1, u_2, and u_3. The weight of a hypergraph is determined by functioning confidences of all the association rules involving all the users of hypergraph. We determine the cluster that the transaction belongs by calculating the score of each cluster based on the users in the transaction and users in clusters. A simple score function might be the ratio $|T \cap C_i|/|C_i|$, where T is the transaction and C_i is a cluster of users. A transaction belongs to the cluster that has the highest score with respect to the transaction.

4   RA-Neighborhood and Collaborative Filtering Using Bayesian Estimated Value

The RA-Neighborhood is to select the nearest neighbors who have similar preference to an active user through extracting the representative attributes that most affects the preference. The difference between current collaborative filtering and Representative Attribute-Neighborhood based collaborative filtering [12] is that all the neighbors are used or not. That is, pure collaborative filtering uses all other users who have similar tastes or opposite tastes to active users by the Pearson correlation coefficient [5].

These users' preferences are used in predicting the preference of a target item for active user. On the other hand, the RA-Neighborhood based collaborative filtering only applies that have similar tastes in order that have higher correlation with active users. The correlation is generally computed with Pearson correlation coefficient.

4.1 Representative Attribute-Neighborhood (RA-Neighborhood)

To complement these shortcomings that does not consider the item attribution accompanying more efficient filtering, we use Representative Attribute-Neighborhood through the extraction of user representative genre. We assume representative attributes about the movie to be genre. In general, this means that user preferences for movies are mainly affected by its genre. We define representative attributes to be a primary attribution that influences the preference about the item. The extraction of the user representative attributes uses items rating the user preference. For the purpose of extracting the representative genre, this paper sums ratings of user preference by genre of the item. The one with the maximal summation can be the representative attribute. We use RA-Neighborhood for composing the training set restricted to each representative attribute and for predicting when we find correct neighborhoods [12].

We present another collaborative filtering that uses age, gender, and zip code group to improve an accuracy of prediction. The rating of user preference depends on the user environment. Therefore, this paper groups user by age, gender, and zip code through generation gap, discrimination between male and female, and regional disparity. For each age, gender, and zip code grouping from all user profiles, active user who has a profile that is composed of the average of group preference for each Representative-Attribute Neighborhood is created. We split the users ages into 8 age groups (1-14, 15-19, 20-24, 25-29, 30-39, 40-49, 50-59, 60-69) and we divided the zip codes into 7 US regions (Mid-Atlantic, Midwest, Northeast, Rockies, South, Southeast, and West). We gain predicted preference with Representative Attribute-Neighborhood, age, gender, and zip code group together.

4.2 The User Similarity Weight Applied Naïve Bayes Algorithm

Naïve Bayes algorithm can classify items according to learning phase and classification phase [16]. The learning phase gives a probability to item from the training set which is collected data through the genre item based in the genre user's clustering after extracting user's representative genre though Representative Attribute-Neighborhood.

Equation (4) is used to give a probability to item(itm_i) within $GenreID$. In this paper, a probability of item(itm_i) within $GenreID$ is expressed as $P(itm_i|GenreID)$. In that case, n is the total number of item in the training set whose target value is $GenreID$. n_k is the frequency of itm_i in $GenreID$, and $|TIS|$ is the total items within all $GenreID$.

$$P(itm_i|GenreID) = \frac{n_k + 1}{n + |TIS|} \qquad (4)$$

Learning process is divided into the phase for accumulation and the phase for granting probability. In the phase for accumulation, the number of times is accumulated of item existent within *GenreID*. In the phase for granting probability, output of accumulation is applied to Equation (4) and probability is granted to items of the training set. Through this process, the probability is added to items in *GenreID*.

The user similarity weight differently is applied to the preference of items which users evaluated as an object to the genre estimated value. For this process, as the user applies the learning set which the estimated value granted to the item rating the preference, the genre item; $P(itm_i|GenreID)$ is multiplied by $V_{a,k}$. $V_{a,k}$ represents the preference that the user a rates about item k.

$$\beta_{a,k}=P(itm_i|GenreID)\times V_{a,k} \qquad (5)$$

Applying to Pearson correlation coefficient[6,9] Based on Equation (5), the user similarity weight between the user a and i can be defined with the Equation (6).

$$\beta(a,i) = \frac{Cov(a,i)}{\delta_a \cdot \delta_i} = \frac{\sum_k (\beta_{a,k} - \overline{\beta_a})(\beta_{i,k} - \overline{\beta_i})}{\sqrt{\sum_k (\beta_{a,k} - \overline{\beta_a})^2 \sum_k (\beta_{i,k} - \overline{\beta_i})^2}} \qquad (6)$$

$\beta_{a,k}$ means the preference granted the estimated value between the user a and the item k, β_a means the average value granted to the weight value of the item user a already has the input of the preference. k means the item the user a and i that had input of the preference in common.

4.3 Categorizing Users Using Naïve Bayes Classifier

Naïve Bayes classifier[16] classifies the new user according to the genre by Equation (7) by using the learning set with the estimated value.

$$GenreID = \underset{GenreI\in GenreTot}{\arg\max} \ p(GenreID)\prod_{i\in I} v_{a,k} P(itm_i|GenreID) \qquad (7)$$

The new user with the preference value about each item is represented as $u_{new}=\{x\in p|$ $itm_1(x), itm_2(x),.., itm_n(x)\}$. $itm_n(x)$ indicates the item which preference the user rates. The genre which itm_{new}, which is going to be categorized is represented as *GenreID*; the total genre as *GenreTot*. $P(itm_i|GenreID)$ is the probability according to Equation (6) and $P(GenreID)$ is the probability classified as *GenreID*.

The genre decision of new users is allotted to the genre of the highest probability value. The preferences are applied to the estimated value differently according to the genre. First, the learning set which the estimated value is granted is applied to items which users rate. Second, the user preference is multiplied by the genre items. As shown, we can reduce the prediction error caused by missing value. In addition, we grant to the weight user preference differently about items according to classified the genre by categorizing the items. This method grants the weight based on the statistical value only on the preference [11,12].

4.4 The Prediction for the New User Include Weight β(a, i)

The prediction for the new user applies the similarity weight between the user a and i applying the Bayesian estimated value to Pearson coefficient correlation. This method can suggest the predictive precision improving because it is based on statistical value not on the user preference. Through the weighted average of the similarity with the neighborhood distance between the preference of the neighbors selected by the RA-Neighborhood about the specific item and the preference of the mean value about each neighbors, the preference about the user's item can be predicted. Equation (8) shows the definition.

$$P_{a.k} = \overline{v_a} + \frac{\sum_{i=1}^{n}(\beta(a,i))(v_{i.k} - \overline{v_i})}{\sum_{i=1}^{n}\beta(a,i)} \tag{8}$$

$P_{a.k}$ represents the prediction of the preference that the estimated value is granted for the active user a about item k. V_a means the preference value granted the user a's weight value. n represents that the similarity between the user a and other users isn't 0 but the number of neighbors. The existent CF uses the user similarity weight between the active user and neighbor n as defined by Pearson correlation coefficient, but β(a, i) is calculated by the user similarity weight by using the Equation (6).

5 Evaluation

5.1 Evaluation Method and Result

The EachMovie [15] data is processed the experimentation about 20864 users such that user rated at least 80 movies and 1612 kinds of movie through the data integrity. This is the training set for Naïve Bayes learning. 20862 users are selected for the systematic sample in preprocessed EachMovie data. We follow the schema in the EachMovie data for genre classification according to action, animation, art-foreign, classic, comedy, drama, family, horror, romance, and thriller.

In order to cluster associative users, we first represent users as 3-associative users feature using Apriori algorithm to 20864 users. Apriori algorithm can mine associative users at confidence 85 and support 25 and 3-association rule. As the experiment result, 167729 numbers of the user behavior pattern and the confidence are created in the user transaction. In addition, 3-UB has a good speedup comparatively. It is relevant to use 3-associative users format at pattern selection for user behavior pattern. The user behavior pattern is clustered according to the genre using Association Rule Hypergraph Partitioning Algorithm.

The users decided to the representative attributes are used for making the training set. As a matter of fact, they are used for the Representative Attributes-Neighborhood with gender, age, and zip code group predicting by finding the similar neighborhood. The training set made the item denoted the preference based on the user's representative genre, the below table 2 shows the classification of items into 10 genre classes. The learning set comes from the training set through granting the estimated value using Equation (4) and Equation (5). Many users decided to the representative attributes are determined to action and drama genre because most users like both genres.

Table 2. Training Set

n : number

GenreID		Item voted the preference	User(n)	Item(n)
1	Action	Golden eye, Clueless, 12Monkeys, Star gate, Star Wars, Drop Zone, Mission, ..	9637	1502
2	Animation	Toy Story, Exit to Eden, Heavy Metal, Pocahontas, Space Jam, Robin Hood	115	163
3	Art/Foreign	Four Rooms, Birdcage, Antonia's Line, Birdcage, Stalker, Diva, Shine, ..	353	961
4	Classic	Jumanji, Balto, Happy Gilmore, Foreign Student, Alien, Amadeus Annie Hall, ..	245	1541
5	Comedy	Ace Ventura, Bronx Tale, Fatal Instinct, Four Rooms, Palookaville, Heather, ..	2107	1545
6	Drama	Sabrina, Nixon, Ace Ventura, Clerks, Get Shorty, High Noon, Cape Fear, ..	7566	1604
7	Family	Casper, Apollo13, Bad Boys, Batman Forever, Gordy, Fly Away Home, Shiloh	158	1248
8	Horror	Copycat, Screamers, Mary Reilly, Babe, Clueless, M, Braindead, Scream, ..	87	453
9	Romance	American President, Swiss Family Robinson, Beautiful Thing, Benny & Joon, ..	166	603
10	Thriller	Die Had, Taxi Driver, Crimson Tide, The Net, Breakdown, Head Above Water	428	916

The item of training set is learned to grant the estimated value through Naïve Bayes algorithm. The following table 3 presents the reflection of information about the missing value, which the weight value of the user preference about item is granted differently according to the classified genre in the learning set with the estimated value. If a new user genre is classified according to Naïve Bayes classifier, the new user is differently granted the estimated value to item in order to get the similarity between users included to the classified genre and the new user. The shaded boxes represent the predictive preference granted the Bayesian estimated value to the missing value using Equation (8).

Table 3. The preference with tha estimated value

Item	User ID in Cluster 1							
	5	6	10	127	13	18	NewUser	...
1	0.0025	0.0038	0.0098	0.0035	0.0029	0.0097	0.0084	...
19	0.0012	0.0015	0.0024	0.0018	0.0027	0.0075	0.0027	...
21	0.0020	0.0037	0.0034	0.0023	0.0020	0.0037	0.0037	...
35	0.0008	0.0013	0.0006	0.0019	0.0075	0.0026	0.0008	...
45	0.0012	0.0020	0.0017	0.0026	0.0007	0.0047	0.0007	...

▭ : The predictive preference granted the Bayesian estimated value to the missing value

5.2 Analysis & Evaluation

Through the experimentation between the method selecting the neighborhood by using threshold (T)[14] and Representative Attribute-Neighborhood, we compare with the predictive accuracy value such as MAE, Coverage, and F-measure[5,10]. MAE is used to measure the absolute prediction error $|r_a - r_p|$ where r_a is the actual rating while r_p is the predicted rating. Coverage is a measure of the percentage of items for which a recommendation system can provide predictions. A basic coverage metric is the percentage of items for which predictions are available. F-measure(F) is a weighted average of precision and recall frequency used in information retrieval, that is, F is $(2 \times Recall \times Precision)/(Recall + Precision)$.

As can be seen in Fig. 3, if we apply RA-Neighborhood with age, gender, and zip code group to current collaborative filtering system, there will be much improvement of the prediction accuracy. As the number of clusters increases, the accuracy does not rise coherently. At around 45 it begins to level off. Beyond this is the point of diminishing returns; as no matter how large the data set is, prediction accuracy improves only marginally. Therefore, the Representative Attribute-Neighborhood based collaborative filtering has better quality of prediction than current collaborative filtering using threshold(T).

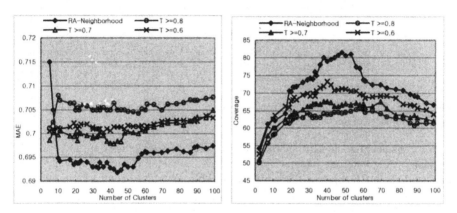

Fig. 3. Changes of MAE, Coverage based on RA-Neighborhood

We experiment the user similarity weight according to three methods that applied the Bayesian estimated value as in this paper what is suggested. The First method; (P_Corr), is that we apply only the Pearson Correlation efficient to the pure CF. The Second method; (P_Corr_N_Bayes) is reflecting the information of item which granted the weight value to the user's preference about item according to the category classified the item. The Last method; (AUC_P_Corr_N_Bayes) is applied to the second method within associative user clustering.

Fig. 4 shows that the bigger confidence the more accurate associative user become but the lower recall becomes. However recall is almost consistent and accuracy recorded high at not less than 85 of confidence. Accordingly, in order to extract the most proper associative user, confidence should be fixed at not less than 85. Curve of accuracy and recall is identical at support of 25 and at this point, the most proper associative user is extracted. However, if support is not less than 25, both accuracy and recall become lower. Accordingly, in order to extract the trustworthiest associative user, support of not more than 25 should be designated.

As shown in Fig. 4, the accuracy is improved compared with the current collaborative filtering. Even though method 1 and method 2 shows the similar accuracy in the first part, the more number of user cluster, the higher accuracy is shown. In the method 3, when we are compared with the collaborative filtering, the result of accuracy is higher, which isn't related with the number of user cluster. Because of the fact that we granted the weight value by the statistic value reflecting the information of item, the predicting accuracy is improved.

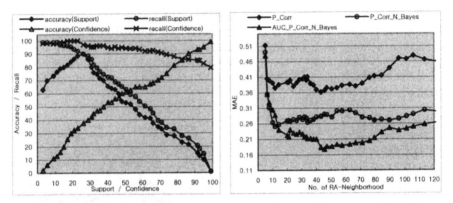

Fig. 4. The change in accuracy and recall according to change in Support and Confidence / MAE performance of Recommender System

We considered proposal method using associative user clustering and Bayesian estimated value into one integral approach and maintained that it should outperform the stand-alone CF approach. However, it is also important to compare our approach with the combination of content-based filtering and collaborative filtering approaches. Though the experimentation between the method suggested in this paper and Soboroff [19], Pazzani [17], Fab [3], we compare with the predictive accuracy value such as MAE and Rank scoring [5,10].

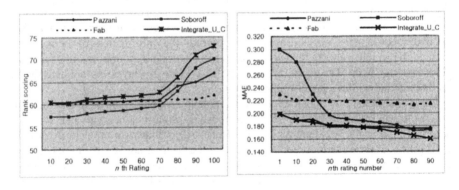

Fig. 5. Rank scoring, MAE of *n*th rating

Fig. 5 represents Rank Scoring and MAE as increasing the frequency that the user evaluates the *n*th rating number. Fig. 5 shows that Soboroff [19] which covers the problem of the First-Rater indicates lower-performance when the number of evaluation is lower. Other methods show higher-performance than Soboroff. As a result, Pazzani and Integrate_U_C that settled the *sparsity* and *first-rater* problem show the highest accuracy rate.

6 Conclusion

In this paper, we proposed the new collaborative filtering method for predicting the preference using the associative user clustering and Bayesian estimated value. We have proposed the user pattern representation that includes associative users instead of just single users. And we have shown that when associative users are composed of 3-users, performance of associative user clustering is most efficient. Representative Attribute-Neighborhood with age, gender, and zip code grouping to select the nearest neighbors who have similar preference to active user through extracting the representative attributes that most affects the preference. We grant the weight value of preference using the Bayesian estimated value differently. So reflect the information of item to the attributive value. The result compared with the CF system shows better efficiency than before. In the future, we would like to verify this method through more users and combine proposed method with memory-based method.

References

1. R. Agrawal and R. Srikant, "Fast Algorithms for Mining Association Rules," Proc. of the 20th VLDB Conference, Santiago, Chile, 1994.
2. R. Agrawal and T. Imielinski and A. Swami, "Mining association rules between sets of items in large databases," In Proc. of the 1993 ACM SIGMOD Conference, Washington DC, USA, 1993.
3. M. Balabanovic, and Y. Shoham, "Fab: Content-based, Collaborative Recommendation," Communication of the Association of Computing Machinery, pp. 66–72, 1997.
4. C. Basu, et al., "Recommendation as classification: Using social and content-based information in recommendation," In Proc. of the 15th National Conference on AI, pp. 714–720, Madison, WI, 1998.
5. D. Billsus, M. J. Pazzani, •Learning Collaborative Information Filters,• Proc. of ICML, pp. 46–53, 1998.
6. D. D. Lewis, *Representation and Learning in Information Retrieval*, PhD thesis(Technical Report pp. 91-93, Computer Science Dept., Univ. of Massachussetts at Amherst, 1992.
7. J. S. Breese, D. Heckerman, C. Kadie, "Empirical Analysis of Predictive Algorithms for Collaborative Filtering," Proc. of the 14th Conference on Uncertainty in AI, 1998.
8. M. O. Connor and J. Herlocker, "Clustering Items for Collaborative Filtering," Proceedings of the ACM SIGIR Workshop on Recommender Systems, Berkeley, CA, 1999.
9. E. H. Han, et al., "Clustering Based On Association Rule Hypergraphs," Proc. of SIGMOD Workshop on Research Issues in DMKD, May, 1997.
10. J. Herlocker, et al., •An Algorithm Framework for Performing Collaborative Filtering,• In Proc. of ACM SIGIR'99, 1999.
11. K. Y. Jung, Y. J. Park, and J. H. Lee, "Integrating User Behavior Model and Collaborative Filtering Methods in Recommender Systems," Proc. of International Conference on Computer and Information Science, Seoul, Korea, August 8–9, 2002.
12. K. Y. Jung, J. K. Ryu, and J. H. Lee, "A New Collaborative Filtering Method using Representative Attributes-Neighborhood and Bayesian Estimated Value," Proc. of International Conference on Artificial Intelligence, USA, June 24–27, 2002.
13. G. Karypis, et al., "Multilevel k-way Hypergraph Partitioning," DAC, pp. 343-348, 1999.
14. G. Karypis, "Evaluation of Item-Based Top-N Recommendation Algorithms," Technical Report CS-TR-00-46, Computer Science Dept., University of Minnesota, 2000.

15. P. McJones, EachMovie collaborative filtering dataset,
    URL:http://www.research.digital.com/SRC/eachmovie, 1997
16. T. Michael, *Maching Learning*, McGraq-Hill, pp. 154–200, 1997.
17. M. Pazzani, "A Framework for Collaborative, Content-Based and Demographic Filtering,"
    AI Review, pp. 393–408, 1999.
18. M. Pazzani, D. Billsus, *Learning and Revising User Profiles: The Identification of Interesting Web Sites*, Machine Learning 27, Kluwer Academic Publishers, pp. 313–331, 1997.
19. I. Soboroff, C. Nicholas, "Combining Content and Collaboration in Text Filtering," In Proc. of the IJCAI'99 Workshop on Machine Learning in Information filtering, pp. 86–91, 1999.
20. W. S. Lee, "Collaborative learning for recommender systems," In proc. of the Conference on Machine Learning, 1997.

Argument Interpretation Using Minimum Message Length*

Sarah George and Ingrid Zukerman

School of Computer Science and Software Engineering
Monash University, Clayton, VICTORIA 3800, AUSTRALIA
{sarahg,ingrid}@csse.monash.edu.au

Abstract. We describe an argument interpretation mechanism which receives as input a segmented argument composed of Natural Language sentences, and employs the Minimum Message Length Principle to select an interpretation among candidate options. This principle enables our mechanism to cope with noisy input in terms of wording, beliefs and argument structure. The performance of our system was evaluated by distorting automatically generated arguments, and passing them to the system for interpretation. Our evaluation showed that in most cases, the interpretations produced by the system matched precisely or almost-precisely the representation of the original arguments.

1 Introduction

Discourse interpretation consists of constructing a model from the utterances of our interlocutor. This model hopefully matches the interlocutor's mental model which was the basis for his/her utterances. However, since we cannot directly compare mental models, the best we can realistically hope for is to build a model that makes sense in our own mind and is reasonably close to the speaker's utterances. In order to build such a model we must understand the words used by our conversational partner, the propositions built with these words, and the relations between these propositions. All of these tasks are fraught with difficulty, as our vocabulary may differ from that of our interlocutor, our syntactic abilities may differ (e.g., his/her utterances may be ungrammatical), we may disagree in our domain knowledge, and we may have different inferential patterns.

In this paper, we present an approach to the interpretation of Natural Language (NL) arguments which is based on the Minimum Message Length (MML) Principle [1]. This principle provides a uniform and incremental framework for combining the uncertainty arising from different stages of the interpretation process. Our interpretation mechanism is embedded in a web-based argumentation system called BIAS (Bayesian Interactive Argumentation System). BIAS uses Bayesian Networks (BNs) [2] as its knowledge representation and reasoning formalism. Linguistic information is incorporated in our domain BN by associating each node with a canonical sentence, which is generated using a simple English generator (Section 3). BIAS is designed to be a complete argumentation system which will eventually engage in unrestricted interactions with users. However,

---

* This research was supported in part by Australian Research Council grant A49922712.

R.I. McKay and J. Slaney (Eds.): AI 2002, LNAI 2557, pp. 297–308, 2002.

298   S. George and I. Zukerman

(1*) Somebody has the keys to *the* house [**Likely**],
(2*) Mr Body's window was *smashed*
⇒ (3) Mr Body was killed from inside the window [**Likely**]
(4) Mr Green fired the found gun
⇒ (5*) Mr Green had the means *[ ]* [**ALittleLikely**]
(6) Mr Green and Mr Body were enemies,
(7) Mr Green had the means to murder Mr Body,
(8*) *At the time of death,* Mr Green was in the garden,
(9) Mr Body was killed from inside the window
⇒ (10*) *[ ]* Green murdered *[ ]* Body [**ALittleLikely**]

Fig. 1. Sample argument

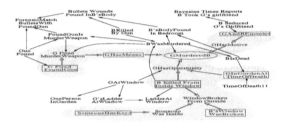

Fig. 2. Interpretation of sample argument in Bayesian subnet

currently BIAS performs two activities: it generates its own arguments (from a BN) and interprets users' arguments. In this paper we focus on the interpretation task.

The interpretations generated by BIAS take the form of a Bayesian subnet which is a subset of our 82-node domain BN. As such, BIAS' interpretations represent inference structure and beliefs, as well as linguistic information (in the form of canonical sentences). Figure 1 shows a sample argument obtained from a user through a web interface (the uncertainty values in square brackets are optional). Figure 2 shows a portion of our domain BN, with BIAS' interpretation of the sample argument drawn on a shaded background; the nodes corresponding to the user's statements are boxed, and the goal node is circled. The user's input may differ from the system's interpretation in its structure, belief values and wording. For instance, Sentences 4 and 5 in Figure 1 match the sub-argument from node GFiredFoundGun to GHasMeans in Figure 2, omitting the intermediate node GFiredMurderWeapon – a structural difference. Sentence 2 in Figure 1 corresponds to node B'sWindowWasBroken, but it differs from the canonical sentence for this node, which is "Mr Body's window was broken".[1]

---

[1] Sentences in Figure 1 which differ from the canonical sentences for the corresponding BN nodes have been asterisked (divergent text is italicized, and omissions are marked with *[ ]*).

Next, we discuss related research. We then describe our argument interpretation process, and the application of the MML criterion to argument interpretation. The results of our evaluation are discussed in Section 5, followed by concluding remarks.

2   Related Research

Our research integrates reasoning under uncertainty for plan recognition in discourse understanding with the application of the MML principle [1]. BNs in particular have been used in several such plan recognition tasks, e.g., [3,4,5]. Charniak and Goldman's system handled complex narratives, using a BN and marker passing for plan recognition. It automatically built and incrementally extended a BN from propositions read in a story, so that the BN represented hypotheses that became plausible as the story unfolded. In contrast, we use a BN to constrain our understanding of the propositions in a user's argument, and apply the MML principle to select a plausible interpretation. Both Horvitz and Paek's system and Zukerman's handled short dialogue contributions. Horvitz and Paek used BNs at different levels of an abstraction hierarchy to infer a user's goal in information-seeking interactions with a Bayesian Receptionist. They also used decision-theoretic strategies to guide the progress of the dialogue. We expect to use such strategies when our system engages in a full dialogue with the user. Zukerman used a domain and user model represented as a BN, together with linguistic and attentional information to infer a user's goal from a short-form rejoinder. However, the combination of these knowledge sources was based on heuristics.

The approach presented in this paper extends our previous work in that (1) it handles lengthy arguments, (2) it offers a principled technique for selecting between alternative interpretations of a user's discourse, and (3) it handles discrepancies between the user's input and the system's expectations at all levels (wording, beliefs and inferences). Further, this approach makes no assumptions regarding the synchronization between the user's beliefs and the system's beliefs. However, we assume that the system is a domain expert. Finally, this approach may be extended to incorporate various aspects of discourse and dialogue, such as information pertaining to the dialogue history and user modeling information.

The MML principle is a model selection technique which applies information-theoretic criteria to trade data fit against model complexity. Selected applications which use MML are listed in http://www.csse.monash.edu.au/~dld/Snob.application.papers.

3   Interpreting Arguments

The MML criterion implements Occam's Razor, which may be stated as follows: "If you have two theories which both explain the observed facts, then you should use the simplest until more evidence comes along". According to the MML criterion, we imagine sending to a receiver a message that describes a user's NL argument, and we want to send the shortest possible message.[2] This message corresponds to the simplest interpretation of

---

[2] It is worth noting that the sender and the receiver are theoretical constructs of the MML theory, which are internal to the system and are not to be confused with the system and the user. The

the user's argument. We postulate that this interpretation is likely to be a reasonable interpretation (hopefully the intended one). A message that encodes an NL argument in terms of an interpretation is composed of two parts: (1) instructions for building the interpretation (a Bayesian sub-net in our case), and (2) instructions for rebuilding the original argument from this interpretation. These two parts balance the need for a concise interpretation (Part 1) with the need for an interpretation that matches closely the user's utterances (Part 2). For instance, the message for a concise interpretation that does not match well the original argument will have a short first part but a long second part, while a more complex interpretation which better matches the original argument may yield a shorter message overall. Thus, the message describing the interpretation (BN) which best matches the user's intent will be among the messages with a short length (hopefully the shortest).

To find this interpretation, we compare the message length of the candidate interpretations, which are sub-nets of the domain BN. These sub-nets are obtained by (1) proposing nodes in the domain BN that match the user's sentences, and (2) finding different ways to connect these nodes – each variant is a candidate interpretation.

3.1   Proposing Nodes in the Domain BN

The selection of nodes that are good interpretations of the input sentences is based on the idea of mutual information. That is, a node N that constitutes a plausible interpretation of an input sentence S_{UArg} is one which shares substantial information with this sentence (and hence enables us to easily reconstruct the sentence).

In order to implement this idea, we associate each node N in the domain BN with a canonical sentence S_N produced by a simple English generator. Our language interpreter compares each input sentence S_{UArg} against each S_N in the domain BN by evaluating $ML(S_{UArg}|S_N)$ – the length of the message which conveys the operations needed to transform S_N into S_{UArg} (Section 4.3). This measure is minimal when the mutual information shared by these sentences is maximal. Hence, the node N whose S_N-to-S_{UArg} transformation is described by the shortest message is considered the best match for S_{UArg}.[3]

If one or more messages are significantly shorter than the input sentence, then we have produced a list of plausible interpretations for the sentence. Otherwise there is only a small amount of mutual information between the input sentence and the node which best-matches it. This means that there is no plausible interpretation for this sentence in the domain BN. This does not automatically invalidate the user's argument, as it may still be possible to interpret the argument as a whole, even if a particular sentence is not understood (Section 4.2).

3.2   Finding Bayesian Sub-nets which Connect the Nodes

The above process may match more than one node to each of the user's sentences. Hence, we first generate the possible sets of nodes which are consistent with the

---

concept of a receiver which is different from the sender ensures that the message constructed by the sender to represent a user's argument does not make unwarranted assumptions.

[3] Our current focus is on assessing the usefulness of MML for selecting a plausible interpretation of a sentence. More efficient search strategies that eschew inspecting all S_N-S_{UArg} pairs will be explored in the future.

user's argument. For instance, given the following argument in the context of the BN in Figure 2: "Green fired the found weapon → Green killed Body", the antecedent matches {GFiredFoundGun, GFiredMurderWeapon}, while the consequent matches {GMurderedB}. This yields two sets of nodes: {GFiredFoundGun, GMurderedB}, and {GFiredMurderWeapon, GMurderedB}.

Now, the following is done for each set of nodes. For each node in a set we perform two expansions. That is, we connect it to its neighbours in the domain BN, and then to its neighbours' neighbours. This process, which is similar to that described in [5], is carried out to enable the system to "make sense" of an argument with small inferential leaps. If upon completion of this process, some nodes are still unconnected, the system rejects this set of nodes.

Upon the successful completion of this step, the system has found a sub-net of the domain BN which connects all the nodes in a set of nodes. This Bayesian sub-net is then refined into *Spanning BNs*, where each Spanning BN contains a different subset of the arcs in the sub-net, such that all the nodes in the sub-net are still connected. This refinement, which is computationally intensive, is necessary to model cases where there is more than one path between two nodes. For example, if the user had argued Ladder-AtWindow ⇒ GHasOpportunity in the context of the BN in Figure 2, one interpretation would go through BKilledFromInsideWindow, another would go through GAtWindow, and a third interpretation would include both paths.

4   Using MML for Evaluating Interpretations

The MML criterion is derived from Bayes Theorem: $\Pr(D\&H) = \Pr(H) \times \Pr(D|H)$, where D is the data and H is a hypothesis which explains the data.

An optimal code for an event E with probability $\Pr(E)$ has message length $\mathrm{ML}(E) = -\log_2 \Pr(E)$ (measured in bits). Hence, the message length for the data and a hypothesis is:

$$\mathrm{ML}(D\&H) = \mathrm{ML}(H) + \mathrm{ML}(D|H).$$

The hypothesis for which $\mathrm{ML}(D\&H)$ is minimal is considered the best hypothesis.

Now, in our context, *UArg* contains the user's argument, and *SysInt* is a Bayesian sub-net which contains an interpretation generated by our system. Thus, we are looking for the *SysInt* which yields the shortest message length for

$$\mathrm{ML}(\mathit{UArg}\,\&\,\mathit{SysInt}) = \mathrm{ML}(\mathit{SysInt}) + \mathrm{ML}(\mathit{UArg}|\mathit{SysInt}).$$

The first part of the message describes the interpretation, and the second part describes how to reconstruct the argument from the interpretation. To calculate the second part, we rely on an intermediate representation called *Implication Graph* (*IG*). An Implication Graph is a graphical representation of an argument, which represents a basic "understanding" of the argument. It is composed of simple implications of the form *Antecedent₁ Antecedent₂ ...Antecedentₙ* ⇒ *Consequent* (where ⇒ indicates that the antecedents imply the consequent, without distinguishing between causal and evidential implications). $\mathit{IG}_{\mathit{Usr}}$ represents an understanding of the user's argument. It contains nodes from the BN, but retains the structure of the user's argument. $\mathit{IG}_{\mathit{SysInt}}$ represents an understanding of a candidate interpretation. It is directly obtained from *SysInt*. Hence, both its structure and its nodes correspond to the underlying representation. Since both

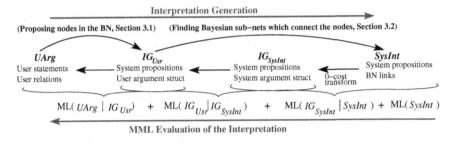

Fig. 3. Argument interpretation and MML evaluation

IG_{Usr} and IG_{SysInt} use domain propositions and have the same type of representation, they can be compared with relative ease.

Figure 3 illustrates the process for argument interpretation and message-length calculation. The interpretation process obtains IG_{Usr} from the user's input, and *SysInt* from IG_{Usr} (top of Figure 3). If a sentence in *UArg* matches more than one domain proposition, the system generates more than one IG_{Usr} from *UArg* (Section 3.2). Each IG_{Usr} may in turn yield more than one *SysInt*. This happens when the underlying BN has several ways of connecting between the nodes in IG_{Usr} (Section 3.2). The message length calculation goes from *SysInt* to *UArg* through the intermediate representations IG_{SysInt} and IG_{Usr} (center arrows in Figure 3). This calculation takes advantage of the fact that there can be only one IG_{Usr} for each *UArg*–*SysInt* combination. Hence,

$$
\begin{aligned}
\Pr(UArg \,\&\, SysInt) &= \Pr(UArg, IG_{Usr}, SysInt) \\
&= \Pr(UArg|IG_{Usr}, SysInt)\Pr(IG_{Usr}|SysInt)\Pr(SysInt) \\
&\stackrel{\text{cond. ind.}}{=} \Pr(UArg|IG_{Usr})\Pr(IG_{Usr}|SysInt)\Pr(SysInt)
\end{aligned}
$$

Thus, the length of the message required to transmit the user's argument from an interpretation is

$$
\mathrm{ML}(UArg \,\&\, SysInt) = \mathrm{ML}(UArg|IG_{Usr}) + \mathrm{ML}(IG_{Usr}|SysInt) + \mathrm{ML}(SysInt) \quad (1)
$$

That is, for each candidate interpretation, we calculate the *length* of the message which conveys:

- *SysInt* – the BN interpretation,
- $IG_{Usr}|SysInt$ – how to obtain the belief and structure of IG_{Usr} from *SysInt*,[4] and
- $UArg|IG_{Usr}$ – how to obtain the sentences in *UArg* from the nodes in IG_{Usr}.

The interpretation which yields *the shortest message* is selected. The message-length equations for each component are summarized in Table 1(a).

Throughout the remainder of this section, we describe the calculation of the components of Equation 1 and illustrate this calculation by means of the example in Figure 4 (the message length calculation for our simple example is summarized in Table 1(b)).

---

[4] We use IG_{SysInt} for this calculation, rather than *SysInt*. This does not affect the message length because the receiver can obtain IG_{SysInt} from *SysInt* by means of a 0-cost transformation.

UArg	IG_{Usr}	IG_{SysInt}	SysInt
Mr Body and Mr Green argued → Mr Green had a motive to kill Mr Body	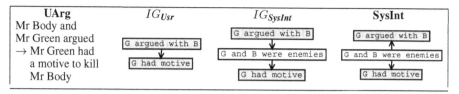		

Fig. 4. Simple argument and interpretation

4.1 Calculating ML(SysInt)

In order to transmit *SysInt*, we simply send its nodes and arcs. A standard MML assumption is that the sender and receiver share domain knowledge (recall that the receiver is not the user, but is a construct of the MML theory). Hence, one way to send *SysInt* consists of transmitting how *SysInt* is extracted from the domain BN. This involves first transmitting the number of nodes and arcs in *SysInt*, next selecting these nodes from the nodes in the domain BN, and then choosing which of the arcs incident upon the selected nodes are included in the interpretation. Thus the message length for *SysInt* is

$$\log_2(\#\_nodes(SysInt)) + \log_2(\#\_arcs(SysInt)) +$$
$$\log_2 C_{\#\_nodes(SysInt)}^{\#\_nodes(domainBN)} + \log_2 C_{\#\_arcs(SysInt)}^{\#\_incident\_arcs(SysInt)} \qquad (2)$$

For the example in Figure 4, to transmit *SysInt* we must choose 3 nodes from the 82 nodes in the BN which represents our murder scenario (the Bayesian subnet in Figure 2 is a fragment of this BN). We must then select 2 arcs from the 3 arcs that connect these nodes. This yields a message of length $\log_2 C_3^{82} + \log_2 C_2^3 = 16.4 + 1.6 = 18$ bits.

4.2 Calculating ML(IG_{Usr}|SysInt)

The message which describes IG_{Usr} in terms of *SysInt* (or rather in terms of IG_{SysInt}) conveys how IG_{Usr} differs from the system's interpretation in two respects: (1) belief, and (2) argument structure.

Belief differences. For each node N in both IG_{SysInt} and IG_{Usr}, we transmit any discrepancy between the belief stated by the user and the system's belief in this node – obtained by performing Bayesian propagation (nodes that appear in only one IG are handled by the message component which describes structural differences). The length of the message required to convey this information is

$$\sum_{N \in IG_{Usr} \cap IG_{SysInt}} ML(Bel(N, IG_{Usr}) | Bel(N, IG_{SysInt}))$$

where $Bel(N, IG_x)$ is the belief in node N in IG_x.

Assuming an optimal message encoding, we obtain

$$\sum_{N \in IG_{Usr} \cap IG_{SysInt}} - \log_2 Pr(Bel(N, IG_{Usr}) | Bel(N, IG_{SysInt})) \qquad (3)$$

which expresses discrepancies in belief as a probability that the user's argument will posit a particular belief in a node, given the belief held by the system in this node. We model this probability using a function which yields a maximum probability mass when the belief in node N according to the argument agrees with the system's belief. This probability gradually falls as the discrepancy between the belief stated in the argument and the system's belief increases, which in turn yields an increased message length.

Structural differences. The message which transmits the structural discrepancies between IG_{SysInt} and IG_{Usr} describes the structural operations required to transform IG_{SysInt} into IG_{Usr}. These operations are: node insertions and deletions, and arc insertions and deletions. A node is inserted in IG_{SysInt} when the system cannot reconcile a sentence in the user's argument with any node in its domain BN. In this case, the system proposes a special *Escape* (wild card) node. Note that the system does not presume to understand this sentence, but still hopes to achieve some understanding of the argument as a whole. Similarly, an arc is inserted when the user mentions a relationship which does not appear in IG_{SysInt}. An arc (node) is deleted when the corresponding relation (proposition) appears in IG_{SysInt}, but is omitted from IG_{Usr}. When a node is deleted, all the arcs incident upon it are rerouted to connect its antecedents directly to its consequent. This operation, which models a small inferential leap, preserves the structure of the implication around the deleted node. If the arcs so rerouted are inconsistent with IG_{Usr}, they will be deleted separately.

For each of these operations, the message announces how many times the operation was performed (e.g., how many nodes were deleted) and then provides sufficient information to enable the message receiver to identify the targets of the operation (e.g., which nodes were deleted). Thus, the length of the message which describes the structural operations required to transform IG_{SysInt} into IG_{Usr} comprises the following components:

$$\text{ML(node insertions)} + \text{ML(node deletions)} + \text{ML(arc insertions)} + \text{ML(arc deletions)} \tag{4}$$

- **Node insertions** = number of inserted nodes plus the penalty for each insertion. Since a node is inserted when no node in the domain BN matches a user's statement, we use an insertion penalty equal to the message length of the worst acceptable word-match. Thus, the message length for node insertions is

$$\log_2(\#\_nodes\_ins) + \#\_nodes\_ins \times Word\_Match\_Penalty \tag{5}$$

- **Node deletions** = number of deleted nodes plus their designations. To designate the nodes to be deleted, we select them from the nodes in *SysInt* (or IG_{SysInt}):

$$\log_2(\#\_nodes\_del) + \log_2 C_{\#\_nodes\_del}^{\#\_nodes(IG_{SysInt})} \tag{6}$$

- **Arc insertions** = number of inserted arcs plus their designations plus the direction of each arc. (This component also describes the arcs incident upon newly inserted nodes.) To designate an arc, we need a pair of nodes (head and tail). However, some nodes in IG_{SysInt} are already connected by arcs. These arcs must be subtracted from the total number of arcs that can be inserted, yielding

$$\#\_poss\_arc\_ins = C_2^{\#\_nodes(IG_{SysInt})+\#\_nodes\_ins} - \#\_arcs(IG_{SysInt})$$

We also need to send 1 extra bit per inserted arc to convey its direction. Hence, the length of the message that conveys arc insertions is:

$$\log_2(\#\_arcs\_ins) + \log_2 C_{\#\_arcs\_ins}^{\#\_poss\_arc\_ins} + \#\_arcs\_ins \tag{7}$$

– **Arc deletions** = number of deleted arcs plus their designations.

$$\log_2(\#\_arcs\_del) + \log_2 C_{\#\_arcs\_del}^{\#\_arcs(IG_{SysInt})} \tag{8}$$

For the example in Figure 4, IG_{SysInt} and IG_{Usr} differ with respect to the node [G and B were enemies] and the arcs incident upon it. To transmit that this node should be deleted from IG_{SysInt}, we must select it from the 3 nodes comprising IG_{SysInt}. This information is conveyed in a message of length $\log_2 C_1^3 = 1.6$ bits (the automatic rerouting of the arcs incident upon the deleted node yields IG_{Usr} at no extra cost).

4.3   Calculating ML(UArg|IG$_{Usr}$)

A user's argument is structurally equivalent to IG_{Usr}. Hence, in order to transmit $UArg$ in terms of IG_{Usr} we need to transmit only the instructions for reconstructing each of the user's sentences from its matching node in IG_{Usr}.

If S_{UArg} is a particular sentence in the user's argument, N is its matching node in IG_{Usr}, and S_N is the canonical sentence for that node, then the length of a message that reconstructs all the sentences in $UArg$ is

$$\sum_{S_{UArg} \in UArg} ML(S_{UArg}|S_N) \tag{9}$$

Calculating ML($S_{UArg}|S_N$). $ML(S_{UArg}|S_N)$ conveys the cost of transforming a particular node's canonical sentence (S_N) into a sentence from the user's argument (S_{UArg}).

The message length of an S_N-to-S_{UArg} transformation is calculated on the basis of the operations required to effect this transformation. For example, consider the node GArguedB in Figure 4, which has a canonical sentence "Mr Green argued with Mr Body". Transforming this sentence into the user's sentence "Mr Green and Mr Body argued" involves moving the word "argued" and rewriting "with" as "and".

The transformation operations performed by our system are: insert a word, delete a word, move a word, rewrite a word, and change a word's relation tag. Relation tags consist of SUBJ/OBJ tags as well as parts-of-speech such as NOUN or VERB (obtained using the MINIPAR parser [6]). The optimal sequence of operations is obtained using a dynamic programming algorithm.

Word insert, delete and change-relation-tag. The contribution of these operations to the length of a message describing an S_N-to-S_{UArg} transformation depends on the "importance" of the modified words to the meaning of their sentences. This importance is represented by a word's relation tag. For example, nouns are considered important, while articles are relatively unimportant. The importance of a word determines the precision with which the operations performed on that word are described. For instance, operations performed on nouns are described exactly, thereby requiring a longer message, while operations performed on articles are described only vaguely. This resembles the approach taken in "lossy" image compression algorithms.

Word move. The contribution of this operation to the length of a message describing an S_N-to-S_{UArg} transformation is obtained from the distance the word is moved and the importance of the word. The longer the distance, the higher the length of the message

Table 1. Summary of message length calculation.

(a) Equations

ML(*UArg & SysInt*)	Equation 1
ML(*SysInt*)	Equation 2
ML(*IG$_{Usr}$|SysInt*)	
belief operations	Equation 3
structural operations	Equations 4, 5, 6, 7 and 8
ML(*UArg*|*IG$_{Usr}$*)	Equation 9

(b) Simple argument

ML(*SysInt*)		18.0 bits
ML(*IG$_{Usr}$|SysInt*)		
belief operations (no beliefs stated)		0.0 bits
structural operations		1.6 bits
ML(*UArg*|*IG$_{Usr}$*)		65.6 bits
ML(*UArg & SysInt*)		85.2 bits

required to express this distance (we use a Normal distribution with a mean equal to the position of the word in S_N to convey this information). Since the movement of important words, e.g., nouns, is more significant than that of less important words, e.g., articles, the resulting message length is scaled according to the word's importance. In our example, moving the verb "argued" is a relatively costly operation.

Word rewrite. The contribution of this operation to the length of a message describing an S_N-to-S_{UArg} transformation depends on the method(s) used to rewrite a word in S_N to obtain a word in S_{UArg}. The "rewrite" methods considered by our mechanism are: (0) leave the word in S_N unchanged; (1) spell out the ASCII characters in the word in S_{UArg} (relevant only when the word is not recognized by our system); and (2) select the word in S_{UArg} from one of the following word lists: (2.1) English dictionary, (2.2) synonyms, (2.3) hypernyms and (2.4) hyponyms returned by WordNet [7], (2.5) word stems of these, and (2.6) antonyms (to support the interpretation of disbelief in a node). For example, if the user had said "Mr Green quarreled with Mr Body", the word "argued" in the canonical sentence $S_{GArguedB}$ would be rewritten to "quarreled" by selecting it from an English dictionary, and by selecting it from a list of hyponyms of "argued". In contrast, when rewriting the canonical sentence for the node GMurderedB, "Mr Green murdered Mr Body", the word "quarreled" can be selected only from the dictionary (none of the shorter word lists for the word "murdered" includes "quarreled"). After determining the various rewriting options, we use *partial assignment* [8] to combine their results. This technique adds the rewrite-probability contributed by each method to yield an overall probability of rewriting a word in S_N into a word in S_{UArg}. Rewrites with a higher probability yield a shorter message, where the probability of a rewrite is inversely proportional to the length of the list from which the target word was obtained.

For the example in Figure 4, the discrepancy between the canonical sentences for nodes GArguedB and GMurderedB and the corresponding user sentences yields a message of length 33.6 bits + 32 bits respectively (=65.6 bits).

5   Evaluation

Our evaluation consisted of an automated experiment where the system interpreted noisy versions of its own arguments. These arguments were generated from different sub-nets of its domain BN, and they were distorted at the BN level and at the NL level. At the BN level, we changed the beliefs in the nodes, and we inserted and deleted nodes and arcs. At the NL level, we distorted the wording of the sentences in the resultant arguments.

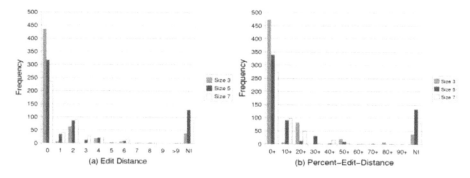

Fig. 5. Frequency of edit-distances for all noise conditions (1750 trials)

All these distortions were performed for Bayesian sub-nets of different sizes (3, 5 and 7 arcs). Our measure of performance is the edit-distance between the argument BN (the original sub-net used to generate an argument) and the BN produced as the interpretation of this argument. This is the number of operations required to convert the source BN into its interpretation.

Overall, our results were as follows. Our system produced an interpretation in 85% of the 1750 trials. In 78.5% of the 1750 cases, the generated interpretations had an edit-distance of 3 or less from the original argument BN, and in 58% of the cases, the interpretations matched perfectly the original argument BN. Figure 5(a) depicts the frequency of edit distances for the different sizes of argument BN under all noise conditions. We plotted edit-distances of $0, \ldots, 9$ and > 9, plus the category NI, which stands for "No Interpretation". As shown in Figure 5(a), the 0 edit-distance has the highest frequency, and performance deteriorates as the size of the argument BN increases. Nonetheless, the majority of the interpretations have an edit distance of 3 or less. Figure 5(b) provides a different view of these results. It displays edit-distance as a percentage of the possible changes for a BN of a particular size (the x-axis is divided into buckets of 10%). For example, if a selected interpretation differs from its source-BN by the insertion of one arc, the percent-edit-distance will be $100 \times \frac{1}{2N+1}$, where N is the number of arcs in the source-BN.[5] The results shown in Figure 5(b) are consistent with the previous results, with the vast majority of the edits being in the $[0,10)\%$ bucket. That is, most of the interpretations are within 10% of their source-BNs.

Figure 6 shows the recognition accuracy of our system (in terms of average edit distance) as a function of arc-noise and word-noise percentages for distortions between 0 and 30% (a distortion of P% for a particular noise type, e.g., word noise, means that each element of an argument, e.g., each word in a sentence, will be distorted with probability P%). The performance for the different sizes of argument BN (in arcs) is also shown. Our system's performance for node insertions and belief noise is similar to that obtained for arc noise (the graphs were not included owing to space limitations). As seen in Figure 6, recognition performance is mainly affected by word noise and by the size of the argument BN, while the average edit distance remains relatively stable for arc-noise (at less than 1.6), as well as for belief-noise and node insertions. Specifically,

---

[5] A BN of N arcs has at most $N+1$ nodes, requiring a maximum of $2N+1$ edits to create it.

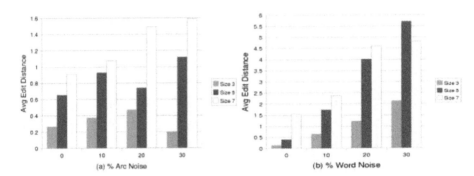

Fig. 6. Effect of arc noise and word noise on performance (450 trials)

for arc noise, belief noise and node insertions, the average edit distance was 3 or less for all noise percentages, while for word noise, the average edit distance was higher for several combinations of word-noise and size of argument-BN. Further, performance deteriorated as the percentage of word noise increased. However, it is worth noting that sentences with 30% word noise are usually unintelligible.

6   Conclusion

We have offered a mechanism which produces interpretations of segmented NL arguments. Our application of the MML principle enables our system to handle noisy conditions in terms of wording, beliefs and argument structure. The results of our automated evaluation were encouraging, with interpretations that match perfectly or almost-perfectly the source-BN being generated in 78.5% of the cases under all noise conditions. In the near future, we will test our system with real users.

References

1. Wallace, C., Boulton, D.: An information measure for classification. The Computer Journal **11** (1968) 185–194
2. Pearl, J.: Probabilistic Reasoning in Intelligent Systems. Morgan Kaufmann Publishers, San Mateo, California (1988)
3. Charniak, E., Goldman, R.P.: A Bayesian model of plan recognition. Artificial Intelligence **64** (1993) 50–56
4. Horvitz, E., Paek, T.: A computational architecture for conversation. In: UM99 – Proceedings of the Seventh International Conference on User Modeling, Banff, Canada (1999) 201–210
5. Zukerman, I.: An integrated approach for generating arguments and rebuttals and understanding rejoinders. In: UM01 – Proceedings of the Eighth International Conference on User Modeling, Sonthofen, Germany (2001) 84–94
6. Lin, D.: Dependency-based evaluation of MINIPAR. In: Workshop on the Evaluation of Parsing Systems, Granada, Spain (1998)
7. Miller, G., Beckwith, R., Fellbaum, C., Gross, D., Miller, K.: Introduction to WordNet: An on-line lexical database. Journal of Lexicography **3** (1990) 235–244
8. Wallace, C., Dowe, D.: MML clustering of multi-state, Poisson, von Mises circular and Gaussian distributions. Statistics and Computing **10** (2000) 73–83

Genetic Programming for Classification: An Analysis of Convergence Behaviour

Thomas Loveard and Vic Ciesielski

School of Computer Science
RMIT University
GPO Box 2476V, Melbourne Victoria 3001, Australia
{toml,vc}@cs.rmit.edu.au

Abstract. This paper investigates the unexpected convergence behaviour of genetic Programming (GP) for classification problems. Firstly the paper investigates the relationship between computational effort and attainable classification accuracy. Secondly we attempt to understand why GP classifiers sometimes fail to reach satisfactory levels of accuracy for certain problems regardless of computational effort. The investigation uses an artificially generated dataset for which certain properties are known in advance for the exploration of these areas.

Results from this artificial problem show that by increasing computational effort, in the form of larger population sizes and more generations, the probability of success for a run does improve, but that the computational cost far outweighs the rate of this success. Also, some runs, even with very large populations running for many generations, became stagnant and were unable to find an acceptable solution. These results are also reflected in real world classification problems.

From analysis of sub-tree components making up successful and unsuccessful programs it was noted that a small number of particular components were almost always present in successful programs, and that these components were often absent from unsuccessful programs. Also a variety of components appeared in unsuccessful programs that were never present in successful ones. Evidence from runs suggests that these components represent paths leading to optimal and sub-optimal branches in the evolutionary search space. Additionally, results suggest that if suboptimal components (which mirror the concept of deception in genetic algorithms) are relatively greater in number than the optimal components for the problem, then the chances of GP finding a successful solution are reduced.

1 Introduction

The Genetic Programming (GP) methodology of program induction has emerged as a useful and accurate method for performing classification tasks [5,8,12]. In such tasks GP programs are evolved over a number of generations to classify a given set of data examples. The accuracy of the classifier is often of very high importance. GP has emerged as a method capable of performing classification to a high degree of accuracy over a variety of different classification tasks.

R.I. McKay and J. Slaney (Eds.): AI 2002, LNAI 2557, pp. 309–320, 2002.
© Springer-Verlag Berlin Heidelberg 2002

It is common in the classification domain for certain classification algorithms to perform comparatively better in terms of accuracy than other algorithms over differing datasets. One major reason for this variation is the method of representation used for a problem. Some of the representations previously used in the classification community have been decision trees, decision rule sets, statistical functions and neural networks, with each method seeming to work particularly well for certain datasets, and comparatively poorly for others. A second major factor in the accuracy of a methodology is the means used to find a given classifier from amongst the possible candidates solutions allowed by the representation. For example, neural networks often use the back-propagation algorithm to arrive at a one network from the millions of alternate possible networks.

The representation used by GP offers an alternative methodology to conventional means as it offers solutions to a classification problem in the powerfully expressive form of a computer program. Additionally, the genetic search paradigm has been shown to be highly efficient in arriving at good solutions to problems from a massive and uneven search space of candidate solutions. Given the two factors of a highly expressive representation and powerful search algorithm used by GP systems for evolving classifiers it is of great interest to know why some GP classifiers fail to classify as accurately as other methods for certain datasets.

The aim of this research investigation is to apply GP in an attempt to better understand the dynamics of a GP run in application to a classification problem. An artificial dataset, for which problem characteristics are known, is used in an attempt to view how the GP process arrives at solutions. We aim to understand how computational effort plays a part in arriving at successful solutions. Secondly we attempt to understand reasons as to why the GP methodology sometimes fails to arrive at acceptable solutions for some datasets. This understanding is made difficult by the complexity and variability of GP runs for such classification problems and the lack of existing methodology for performing such analysis.

2   Background: The GP Search Method and Its Application to Difficult Problems

Early in the history of GP, researchers realised that the genetic programming algorithm is a form of search [1,7]. The algorithm searches the space of possible computer programs allowable by the chosen set of functions and terminals comprising the program components, with the aim of arriving at a single, and hopefully acceptable, solution for the problem at hand.

As a result of this, the sample size of programs in the overall search space (the population of programs for GP) has often been seen as a critical parameter for the successful application of GP. The larger the sample of programs, and the more recombinations these programs undergo, the greater the chance that an optimal, or near-optimal solution will be discovered. As a result of this the population size used, and the number of generations run have become critical parameters for adjustment when hard problems are encountered, and most researchers recommend that for both of these parameters in hard problems, the larger the better [3].

Some evidence has emerged to argue against the absolute reliance on very large population sizes and many generations as a solution to successfully applying GP to complex problems. In [5] evidence from GP runs on two problems showed that small population sizes of 50 programs run for a very large number of generations were capable of outperforming (in terms of both accuracy and processing time required for training) population sizes of 5000 or 10000 run for a fewer number of generations. Work in [4] in the specific domain of combinatory logic indicated that very little change (and in some case negative change) in performance is achieved through the use of successively larger populations. Evidence in [9] scrutinised the use of very large numbers of generations in problem solving, and results suggested that for some problems it is more efficient to run a number of different runs of a small number of generations, rather than run a single run of a very large number of generations. These works cast some doubt on the usefulness of both large populations and large numbers of generations. However, there are few indications given as to the causes for the underlying mechanisms that result in the success or failure of certain parameter choices.

3   The Artificial Dataset

Given the inherent difficulty of understanding GP run dynamics for real world classification problems an artificial problem was created with known characteristics. Using such a problem where optimal solutions can be predicted we can more easily investigate how GP comes to find solutions to such problems. The artificial dataset was constructed such that perfect classification accuracy could be attained.

For this dataset 3 randomly generated variables in the range [0,1] were used as the 3 attributes of the problem. 200 data examples were generated and each example was assigned one of two classes. The following equation was used to divide the two classes over the range of the three variables:

$$((NATTR3 * NATTR2) - ((0.24 * NATTR1)/(NATTR2 * NATTR2)))$$

Any data item that evaluated to $>= 0$ was given as one class, and any item < 0 was given as a second class. The absence of noise within the attributes of the problem gave for a possible perfect classification of the data.

Although artificially created, this problem shares commonality with many real world classification tasks in that some dissecting hyperplane exists within the space of the problem attributes. The task of the classification methodology being applied is to find some model which is best able to reflect this division. In GP this equates to a search through the space of possible programs for a program which can accurately divide the data elements. Of course, given the enormous variety of possible classification problems it is impossible for any one dataset to typify or characterise all possible classification problems. However, in this investigation we are more interested in the means by which GP solves the problem, and this process (the evolutionary search methodology) is one which will be common across classification problems for GP. Thus by the investigation of the GP process for this small problem with a known solution we hope to gain an understanding of how GP is able to form solutions for larger, more cluttered problems.

4   Experiments in Effort versus Solvability

Given the previous arguments raised within the GP community over the relative merit of the computational effort (in the form of parameter choices for population size and number of generations run) verses gain (in the form of acceptable solutions), we first attempted to determine how such critical parameters affected the ability of the GP method to arrive at acceptable solutions for this problem.

4.1   Experimental Configuration

We ran a series of runs over the artificial problem with varying parameters for population size and number of generations. It was of interest to see whether the adjustment of these supposedly critical parameters effected the ability of the GP system to arrive at a perfect solution for the problem. Population sizes of 50, 250, 500, 1000 and 5000 were used, each run for 20, 50, 100 and 200 generations. Of each combination of parameters 20 separate GP runs were performed, in order to give a view of the range of expected behaviours of GP runs over the given parameter choices.

In such runs we attempted to avoid problems often associated with poor performance in the GP model in the form of bloat (program tree size growing unnecessarily large) and in the loss of genetic diversity. Bloat was effectively eliminated due to the known size of necessary solutions to the artificial problem used in this investigation. A perfect GP solution with a node depth of 4 was possible, and thus all GP program trees were limited to a depth of 4 nodes. Genetic diversity was encouraged through the use of the mutation operator (10% per generation) which is capable of introducing new genetic material, and through the use of tournament selection with a tournament size of 2. With only two individuals competing in a tournament the relative chance of extinction for individuals (selection pressure) is less than in tournaments with more individuals.

The function set for all runs consists of the mathematical operator set +, -, *, % and the comparison operator If_LTE. The terminal set consisted of random constants in the range [-1,1] and the numeric attributes of the classification problem. The dynamic range selection method developed in [8] was used to evaluate the fitness of individuals.

All results into classifier accuracy in this investigation pertain to training accuracy. This is primarily because we seek to investigate the behaviour of the GP methodology in the search for an accurate classifier to match the training data. The GP search method is never applied to the test data (only the single best resulting program) and the aim of the search is to find one program tree which best matches with the training data. Of course, some classifiers which match

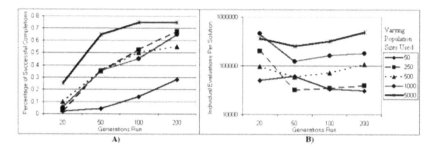

Fig. 1. A) Success Rate of Varying Sized Populations. B) Computational Effort to Success Ratio of Varying Sized Populations

well with the training dataset will perform poorly over a test set due to over-specialisation of the training data. However in a previous investigation [8] it was found when many GP runs were performed over the same dataset, runs which performed well for the training dataset almost always resulted in more accurate classification results over the test dataset. Similarly, runs which performed comparatively poorly over the training dataset consistently performed poorly over the test dataset. Any classifier which is unable to form an appropriate model for data examples with know classes cannot hope to accurately predict examples who's classes are unknown.

4.2   Results

Figure 1A) shows the percentage of perfect solutions arrived at out of the 20 runs for each of the various population sizes and generation sizes for the artificial problem. As expected the GP runs of fewer generations have less chance of being successful then those of more generations and the general trend is that the larger the population size, so too is the chance of success greater. This is not altogether uniform, as population sizes of 250 compare very well to those of 500 and 1000 over all the generational zones. However, the general trend is one in which the increasing population size does yield more solutions per the number of runs. This result is in accordance with the general GP belief that the greater the computational effort in terms of breadth of search space (in population size), and depth of search space (in terms of generations run), then the greater the overall yield.

This however is not necessarily cause to always use a large population size for many generations in an attempt to efficiently solve this classification problem using GP. It can be seen that with a population size of only 50 for 200 generations, almost 30 percent of runs are capable of finding a solution. Even with some 100 times the number of individuals, runs of 5000 are not always capable of finding a solution in this number of generations. Thus some runs of 50 individuals can be better than some runs consisting of 5000 individuals.

This account for the overall effort is highlighted in Figure 1B). Here it becomes evident that the overall number of program evaluations required per so-

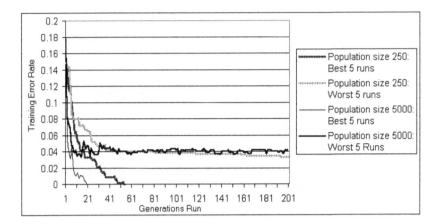

Fig. 2. Best 5 and Worst 5 Runs. Average Training Error for Populations of Size 250 and 5000

lution found is far greater for population sizes of 1000 and 5000 than is required for the smaller population sizes of 50 and 250.

Upon further analysis of runs it was seen that a vast difference existed in outcomes in all choices of parameters in the runs that succeeded and the runs that failed for each parameter choice. Runs with the same population size and number of generations could produce vastly different results for different runs. This effect can be seen in Figure 2 in which the average error rate of the best and worst 5 runs of population size 250, and the average error rate of the best and worst 5 runs of population size 5000, both allowed to run to 200 generations, are plotted. It can be seen that vast differences exist between the best and worse runs. For those runs which succeed, the population size of 5000 was advantageous to success in terms of generations required. However when the worst 5 runs are considered, there was very little difference in the overall outcome of runs from population sizes of either 5000 or 250. Both appear to stagnate at around 4% error, and are unable to improve from this point. This data shows clearly that a large population size over many generations can often perform far worse than can the better runs of a population size twenty times smaller over the same number of generations. It would appear that the additional effort introduced yields little here in terms of gain in successful solutions.

In further experiments these effects have shown to be consistent with a real world data set for which GP has previously shown poor performance against when compared with other conventional methods of classification [8]. The Image Segmentation dataset from the UCI machine learning repository [2] showed trends in which vast differences appeared in the good and bad runs of varying population sizes. When success to effort analysis was applied to runs on this dataset, again it was seen that smaller population sizes were far more efficient than larger ones, although over a different range of generations than the artificial problem used in this investigation. For the Image Segmentation dataset, the best parameters for effort to success ratio found were at 400 generations, with a population size of 250.

5   In Search of Failure

The results given above clearly demonstrate that simply pouring more computational effort into GP for solving a classification problem of this type will yield little in gain for successful solutions compared with the computational effort introduced. They also show that even with a very large population size, mutation and low selection pressure (all of which should give for a diverse and broadly encompassing selection of the search space), it is possible for runs to become stagnant to a point from which they are seemingly incapable of improving. In this section analysis of further runs on the artificial dataset are performed in an attempt to find some explanation as to why these effects may be occurring, with the interest of better improving the application of GPs to such classification problems.

Koza [7] provided an argument for the process by which GP arrives at a suitable solution in the form of a schema theorem for GP which has been significantly refined in recent years [11,10]. The schema theorem of GP indicates that the GP process works by propagating GP tree components (schemata) in varying numbers into subsequent generations based on the fitness of programs containing these schemata. It argues that certain schemata will predispose a program to a higher fitness value. Due to the higher fitness of the individual posing an evolutionary advantage in selection, the important schemata are propagated more readily and come to be represented more often in the evolving population, while schemata tending towards poor fitness will decline in number due to evolutionary disadvantage. This theory gives rise to the idea that GP programs are constructed out of the building block components of the schemata.

While the schema theorem provides an explanation for the workings of GP, it is not possible to predict and interpret, using the schema modelling equations, how the complex and diverse differences between different runs come about. As a result of this we use a different approach here in our attempt to explain such differences by searching for relevant program components (instances of schemata) in the aftermath of GP runs. Program components can be found that appear in individuals from successful runs and unsuccessful runs. If different components can be identified for successful and unsuccessful solutions for this problem it is then possible to identify how they relate to the success or failure of a given run.

From the experiments in the previous section it was seen that a population size of 250 running for 200 generations was a reasonable selection of parameters for producing solutions for the artificial problem. Using these parameters 1000 runs were performed, and the best of run individual of the most successful 250 programs (those that converged in the least number of generations) were analysed for the program components they were comprised of that might have led to this success. Also the best individual in runs from the worst 250 runs (runs that failed to produce a successful solution and suffered more misclassification errors) were also selected and analysed for program components that might have led to failure.

In this investigation the program components selected were limited to the set of sub-tree components consisting of a single terminated function (a function whose arguments all end in terminals) which we refer to as a terminated function sub-tree (TFS). An example of such a TFS might be the s-expression: (* Attrib_2 Attrib_1) which performs the simple function of multiplying two attributes together. The TFS form is certainly a restricted subset of all sub-tree types possible in GP and thus the selection of this form of program building block for analysis is somewhat restrictive. However, given that, for the artificial problem, very small solutions are required, and the GP runs are restricted to the tree depth size required for a solution (four nodes), these small, terminated function sub-trees are necessarily highly important components for any successful solution.

5.1   Further Results and Discussion

From the analysis of the numbers of TFS prevalent in the best individuals of successful and unsuccessful runs large differences were noted. For successful solutions, the 10 most prevalent TFS accounted for 82% of all TFS used in all of the successful programs. This means that effectively 8 out of every 10 TFS used in any successful program came from this very restricted set of important TFS. From this huge prevalence it becomes clearly evident that the presence of these 10 TFS is highly consistent with arriving at a successful solution. Further evidence of this exists in that many of these program components also reflected components of the initial equation that was used to divide the two classes in the artificial dataset.

When the TFS from the best programs from unsuccessful runs were analysed a number of these 10 best TFS (from the successful runs) were present in some individuals but in far fewer numbers, accounting for only 28% of all TFS over all unsuccessful programs. Additionally, in these unsuccessful solutions large numbers of other TFS that were never present in the successful solutions were often present. These TFS that never occurred in successful solutions accounted for a majority 56% of all TFS used by all unsuccessful solutions, and comprised a much broader variety of different TFS types than did the successful solutions.

It is important to note that the unsuccessful solutions analysed above represent the single best solution of their respective runs. These solutions are the result of a large amount of genetic recombination and, from the schema theorem, must contain TFS components that are genetically favoured as they give higher fitness values, resulting in these programs being the best of their respective runs. However it is clear from the above results that the TFS that form these unsuccessful (but still highly fit) solutions cannot effectively lead to successful solutions, due to their absence in any of the successful solutions. This concept is highly similar to the concept of deception in genetic algorithms [6]. Highly fit, but sub-optimal components deceive the search methodology to follow an evolutionary path that cannot yield a globally optimal solution.

Given the results shown in Figure 2 of the previous section it would follow that programs that failed to converge to the optimal 0% error rate failed because of the use of these deceptive TFS. The similarity in the error rate of the worst runs for population sizes of 250 and 5000 would provide support for the idea that similar deceptive TFS are being favoured by both small and large population sizes, leading to similar classification error rates. Through the use of these deceptive TFS a limit is effectively set as to the accuracy that can be realistically produced, regardless of computational effort. The improved success rate achieved by using large populations shown in Figure 1A) would indicate that larger populations are more likely to effectively avoid deception. However, even with a much larger population than is sensible with respect to computational effort, it is still possible for a sub-optimal path of evolution to be followed, and that once taken, no further improvement in performance can be realistically expected from this evolutionary track.

5.2   Exactness of Division Verses Solvability

One further set of experiments was performed to test the hypothesis that it was the presence and preference of deceptive sub-tree components over optimal components that led to evolutionary stagnation (and as a consequence, to the failure of a run to converge to a successful solution).

If, over the space of all possible program sub trees, the number of sub-optimal, but highly fit deceptive components was much greater than the number of optimal, highly fit components, then the selection of such deceptive components in preference of the optimal ones would be far more probable. As a consequence the GP algorithm would be more likely in this event to arrive at a sub-optimal solution (due to the use of deceptive building block components). If however, larger number of components were able to optimally represent a problem (proportional to deceptive components), then the greater would be the probability of success of the GP algorithm as more optimal components would be chosen.

To test this a set of 3 new datasets were created, all based upon the original artificial dataset. Unlike the original dataset however, where data-points were divided by their being on one side or another of a single equation over three variables, a degree of space was given between the two classes. The same equation given in Section 3 was used to divide the data points. However if data points fell very close to the dividing equation they were eliminated, with the degree of closeness data points could come to the dividing equation varying for the 3 datasets. By widening the separating boundary between the data points of the two classes it was expected that TFS that had previously been unable to optimally solve the problem would come to be able to do so at a certain degree of the widening of the division boundary and cease to be deceptive to the evolutionary search. Thus, with more TFS able to form optimal solutions it was expected that more optimal solutions would be arrived at by the GP process overall.

Results given in Table 1 show the application of the GP process for datasets of varying degrees of closeness allowed to the division boundary. It can be seen that as the data points are removed further and further from the division boundary

Table 1. GP results for datasets of varying degrees of closeness to the dividing boundary function

Closeness to Function Boundary Allowed	% of Data Points Excluded	% of runs that completed in a successful soln.	Number of TFS found in 20 or more successful solns.
0	0.0%	49%	11
0.05	6.9%	57%	14
0.1	14.9%	81%	21
0.15	28.6%	98%	31

(eliminating more and more points from the dataset) the percentage of runs arriving at a perfect training error rate increases. This is somewhat expected as it is generally the case that data points lying close to division boundaries are more problematic for classification, and are thus more often misclassified. Removing these data points is almost certain to improve training accuracy. Of greater interest however is the means through which GP is more readily able to solve the classification problem as the closeness to the boundary widens. The means by which GP is able to take advantage of this is reflected in the numbers of TFS that were used to form perfect solutions. From the analysis of TFS that could be found in more than 20 successful solutions it can be seen that as the division region widens, a greater variety of TFS are used by programs that form successful solutions. Only 11 TFS are used more than 20 times when the exact division boundary is required, but the number increases with each successive widening of the division boundary.

This data indicates that the requirement of the use of certain key components needed for solving the problem of a very close boundary region is alleviated with each widening of the separation boundary. This is also reflected in the overall use of top 10 TFS for each region of closeness. For the 0.0 closeness figure, the top 10% of TFS accounted for 82% of all TFS used by all programs. For 0.05, 0.1 and 0.15 closeness figures the top 10 TFS accounted for less and less of the overall number of TFS used (76%, 70% and 61% respectively).

These results indicate that the number of optimal components, relative to the number of deceptive components, have improved as the closeness boundary is widened, giving more possibility of using and combining them into optimal solutions.

Generally, this finding would predict that the expected success or failure of GP when applied to such a classification problem is rooted within the overall nature of the problem. This is specifically related to the prevalence of optimal (or near optimal) sub-tree components within the GP representation for the problem, relative to the numbers of sub-optimal, but highly fit deceptive components in the representation. If larger numbers of deceptive components are present then it appears that even the application of very large population sizes over many generations is computationally ineffective for the production of accurate classifiers.

6 Conclusions: Ramifications for the Application of GP to Real World Classification Problems

This investigation has shown, through the use of an artificially created dataset, that the GP process for classification will not necessarily benefit from the addition of vast amount of computational resources for ever larger populations over large numbers of generations. Performing many runs with moderate sized populations and generations can be more effective than performing fewer runs with much larger parameter choices. In the artificial problem with only 3 attributes and a small program size possible for a perfect solutions, evidence indicates that certain building block components play a very important role in determining the probable success or failure of a run. Some components with characteristics for forming optimal solutions will exist, as will some components with high fitness but which can only ever lead to sub-optimal solutions. The relative numbers of these components is of critical importance for the successful application of GP to a problem.

Real world classification problems will generally consist of a much larger attribute space and require larger programs to represent accurate classifiers than the artificial problem used in this investigation. With a greater number of attributes and large program sizes, the exponential explosion in the space of possible useful and necessary sub-tree components increases so dramatically that it subsequently becomes very difficult to analyse solutions, components and the effects of certain components over a run. There are however almost certain to be sub-tree components of varying degrees of applicability to a solution, tending to bias an individual towards higher or lower fitness values. Some such components will likely be deceptive, which can only ever lead to sub-optimal solutions, and some will be present which can possibly lead to highly fit, near optimal solutions. If relatively larger numbers of components which can form optimal (or near optimal) solutions are prevalent, then GP will be likely to arrive at very good solutions to the problem, and will likely be a suitable approach to solving such a problem. If however larger numbers of deceptive components are more so prevalent, then the GP algorithm will often lead to sub-optimal solutions. This appears to be the case regardless of the population size used and generations run. In such a case it would appear then GP would be an unsuitable approach to preforming classification and some other approach such as decision tress or neural networks would be a preferable approach to the problem.

Unfortunately the relative prevalence of any building block components can never realistically be known for large, real world problems. These results do however provide some insight into why the evolutionary process used by GP consistently arrives at poor solutions for some problems. They also indicate that when such poor solutions are consistently arrived at, the application of ever greater computational resources may well be unlikely to improve the performance of GP classifiers to any real extent, and would suggest the application of an alternative classification methodology.

References

1. Wolfgang Banzhaf, Peter Nordin, Robert E. Keller and Frank D. Francone. *Genetic Programming – An Introduction; On the Automatic Evolution of Computer Programs and its Applications.* Morgan Kaufmann, dpunkt.verlag, January 1998.
2. C.L. Blake and C.J. Merz. UCI repository of machine learning databases http://www.ics.uci.edu/~mlearn/ mlrepository.html.
3. Robert Feldt and Peter Nordin. Using factorial experiments to evaluate the effect of genetic programming parameters. In Riccardo Poli, Wolfgang Banzhaf, William B. Langdon, Julian F. Miller, Peter Nordin and Terence C. Fogarty (editors), *Genetic Programming, Proceedings of EuroGP'2000*, Volume 1802 of *LNCS*, pages 271–282, Edinburgh, 15–16 April 2000. Springer-Verlag.
4. Matthias Fuchs. Large populations are not always the best choice in genetic programming. In Wolfgang Banzhaf, Jason Daida, Agoston E. Eiben, Max H. Garzon, Vasant Honavar, Mark Jakiela and Robert E. Smith (editors), *Proceedings of the Genetic and Evolutionary Computation Conference*, Volume 2, pages 1033–1038, Orlando, Florida, USA, 13–17 July 1999. Morgan Kaufmann.
5. Chris Gathercole. *An Investigation of Supervised Learning in Genetic Programming.* Ph.D. thesis, University of Edinburgh, 1998.
6. D. Goldberg. Simple genetic algorithms and the minimal, deceptive problem. In L. Davis (editor), *Genetic Algorithms and Simulated Annealing*, pages 74–88. Morgan Kaufmann, 1987.
7. John R. Koza. *Genetic Programming: On the Programming of Computers by Means of Natural Selection.* MIT Press, 1992.
8. Thomas Loveard and Victor Ciesielski. Representing classification problems in genetic programming. In *Proceedings of the Congress on Evolutionary Computation*, Volume 2, pages 1070–1077, COEX, Seoul, Korea, 27–30 May 2001. IEEE Press.
9. Sean Luke. When short runs beat long runs. In Lee Spector, Erik D. Goodman, Annie Wu, W. B. Langdon, Hans-Michael Voigt, Mitsuo Gen, Sandip Sen, Marco Dorigo, Shahram Pezeshk, Max H. Garzon and Edmund Burke (editors), *Proceedings of the Genetic and Evolutionary Computation Conference (GECCO-2001)*, pages 74–80, San Francisco, California, USA, 7–11 July 2001. Morgan Kaufmann.
10. Riccardo Poli. General schema theory for genetic programming with subtree-swapping crossover. In Julian F. Miller, Marco Tomassini, Pier Luca Lanzi, Conor Ryan, Andrea G. B. Tettamanzi and William B. Langdon (editors), *Genetic Programming, Proceedings of EuroGP'2001*, Volume 2038 of *LNCS*, pages 143–159, Lake Como, Italy, 18–20 April 2001. Springer-Verlag.
11. Riccardo Poli and W. B. Langdon. A new schema theory for genetic programming with one-point crossover and point mutation. In John R. Koza, Kalyanmoy Deb, Marco Dorigo, David B. Fogel, Max Garzon, Hitoshi Iba and Rick L. Riolo (editors), *Genetic Programming 1997: Proceedings of the Second Annual Conference*, pages 278–285, Stanford University, CA, USA, 13–16 July 1997. Morgan Kaufmann.
12. Walter Alden Tackett. Genetic programming for feature discovery and image discrimination. In Stephanie Forrest (editor), *Proceedings of the 5th International Conference on Genetic Algorithms, ICGA-93*, pages 303–309, University of Illinois at Urbana-Champaign, 17–21 July 1993. Morgan Kaufmann.

Lineage and Induction in the Development of Evolved Genotypes for Non-uniform 2D CAs

Piet van Remortel, Tom Lenaerts, and Bernard Manderick

COMO – Dept. of Computer Science
Vrije Universiteit Brussel (VUB)
Pleinlaan 2, 1050 Brussels, Belgium
{pvremort,tlenaert,bmanderi}@vub.ac.be

Abstract. Biological development is a stunning mechanism that allows robust generation of complex structures from a linear building plan. This makes it an interesting source of inspiration for solving problems where direct manipulation of a higher-order structure is hard, and the generative building plan can be used as a substitute for indirect manipulation of the unfolded structure. In this paper we propose CA-DEV as a simple computational model for development of rules for non-uniform 2D cellular automata. While being a simplified version of more complex bio-inspired models, CA-DEV incorporates both lineage and induction, and is easily combined with artificial evolution through a binary genotype. We report a number of basic experiments in evolving genotypes for CA-DEV with different settings related to cell division and induction. These experiments show that while the power to introduce diversity is high with most settings, structural properties of developed phenotypes are of a different nature depending on the properties of the development adopted.

1 Introduction

A recurring issue in any kind of computational learning is the manipulation of ever more complex models. Whether linguistic models, environment models or electronic circuits, the overcoming of both size and complexity limitations is essential. A possible solution is indirect manipulation through a secondary representation. Given a suitable conversion mechanism, this secondary representation can be smaller, structurally simpler, or possibly both. This paper focuses on development as such a conversion algorithm inspired by the biological developmental mapping from genotype (DNA) to a phenotype (multi-cellular organism).

The problem inspiring the efforts reported here is the evolution of computational networks and electronic circuits. In combination with artificial evolution, development possible offers a number of interesting advantages. It could allow for relatively shorter genotypes, and resulting in a smaller search-space. It can possibly also lead to improved modularity of solutions and a remapping of the search-space to improve the search performance [BK99]. The goal of this paper is twofold:

R.I. McKay and J. Slaney (Eds.): AI 2002, LNAI 2557, pp. 321–332, 2002.

1. Introduce CA-DEV as a relatively simple developmental model for CAs (or simple circuits), that is easily combined with artificial evolution through a binary-encoded genotype.
2. Investigate the effect of lineage and induction in a number of basic experiments, giving first indications of the possibilities and limitations of the proposed model.

In the next section we will look into the basic mechanisms of biological development, and use these as starting point for introducing the CA-DEV computational model. In the next section we will report the experiments on lineage and induction and form a conclusion from observations. Finally we will conclude and give an overview of related and future work.

2 Development

2.1 Development in Biology

Biological development is an example of a stunning mechanism that allows robust generation of a complex multi-cellular organism from a simple (linear) building plan (the DNA). In general, development is responsible for creating a multitude of different cells, starting from the combination of a single cell and a single building plan. Apart from being structurally simple, this building plan is also generative, meaning that is describes how to build a structure, as opposed to a descriptive plan, which would describe the composition of the finished structure. For a clarifying analogy, imagine the task of describing the state of a chess board full of pieces in the middle of a chess game. A descriptive plan would list all pieces and their positions, while a generative plan would list the necessary sequence of moves that lead to that particular position on the board.

At the start of the development an initial fertilised egg holds a copy of the building plan. Like all cells that will be produced later on down the developmental track it has the following macroscopic properties: it has internal state, can communicate locally, divide, move or die.

The **internal state** consists of the total of chemical mixture within the cell wall, the most prominent of which are proteins, acting as catalysts for internal chemical reactions, building blocks for intra-cellular structures, receptors, carriers for other molecules etc.

Local **communication** between cells, or 'induction' occurs through the exchange of chemical signals. This can either occur by diffusion of a molecule to the outside of the cell, which is then picked up by the receptors of the cell at the receiving end. Two other possibilities are direct contact between two proteins at the cell surfaces, and the exchange of small molecules through a gap created between the touching cell walls of both cells. It is important to note that induction is a way for cells to change state based on the environment they are in.

Through cell **division**, new cells can be created. If the daughter cells have properties that are different from each other, the division is called asymmetric, and accounts for a way to make cells of different identity based on their 'lineage' or line of descent. This is a second mechanism by which cells of different identity can be generated. As opposed to the induction mechanism mentioned above, the identities of the resulting cells are not directly based on their environment.

Cells also have the **ability to move** or 'migrate'. This is important in the gastrulation phase of the development, during which dramatic changes in form occur. Cells also have **ability to die** based on activation of genes. This process, called 'apoptosis', is for example responsible for creating fingers or toes from a continuous sheet of tissue. Both cell migration and apoptosis will be of less importance in the context of this paper.

At the microscopic level, all these macroscopic cell behaviours are governed by activation and inhibition of the genes on the DNA. Active genes are generally translated into RNA and further on to proteins. The genes control development by producing the correct proteins at the correct moment, in this way deciding on the cell's state and behaviour. Since the building plan is shared between all cells, it is the differential expression of genes of the shared DNA that is the underlying mechanism introducing different cell types.

2.2   A Computational Model for Development

From a computational point of view, development can be seen as a construction process that builds a global complex structure consisting of smaller components. A generative plan is used, and applied to an initial starting structure. The main point of development could be summarised as producing building blocks with different identities at the correct locations.

In the previous section we have pointed out that in a broad sense the mechanisms of lineage and induction can account for the introduction of different cell types. Through lineage, or line of descent, cells can obtain identities based on the identity of the parent cell. Induction allows for cells to change identity based on the environment of neigbouring cells they are in. Two well known computational models for development each exhibit one of these mechanisms.

On the one hand, L-systems [Lin68] are based solely on lineage. L-systems are among the first models for multicellular growth, and are a system of grammar-like production rules, applied to a specified starting axiom. The axioms and variables are written in symbols chosen from a pre-defined alphabet. The best known application of L-systems is the generation of turtle-graphics of fractal growth in plants. Applications in other domains such as electronic circuits are also possible [HTvR], which would then benefit from alternative architectures for reconfigurable electronic devices [HvR01].

On the other hand, cellular automata (CAs) [von66] consist of a collection of cells in a regular lattice, each changing state based on transition rules that reference a local neighbourhood around the focal cell. The transition rule can be shared ('uniform' CAs) or different for every cell ('non-uniform' CAs). CAs change cell states using the mechanism of induction. CAs have been used in a wide range of scientific research topics such as self-replication[Lan84], dynamics of complex systems[Wol83,WL92], etc.

More complex computational models have been proposed that exhibit both lineage and interaction. An example particularly well suited in the scope of this paper are 'Cell Systems', which describe development of planar multi-cellular shapes [LF95,Fra96]. In general these models often aim at visualising the developmental outcome of a hand-crafted genome. In this way the necessary properties or genes for specific visual patterns in the organism can be identified. The use of variable shape cells and complex, variable length genes make them un-fit for purpose of artificial evolution. Moreover, the complex computations of cell shapes etc. would make fitness evaluation extremely slow.

In this paper we introduce a general framework for a simplified model for development. The main goal will be to develop the rule-set of non-uniform two-dimensional CAs, since this resembles reprogrammable electronic circuits (FPGAs) which is our main research interest. For convenience the framework introduced here will be called CA-DEV, and will be inspired by the Cell Systems mentioned above. While still incorporating the possibility for both lineage and induction, the genomes for CA-DEV are binary strings of fixed length. This makes evolutionary design of genomes technically straightforward. The use of a binary representation also opens possibilities for analysing the fitness landscape by means of classical analysis techniques, which are devised for this archetypical GA representation.

General principles. The binary genome of CA-DEV consists of three main parts : the number of developmental steps, a number of constants, and a larger block of developmental rules. These parts are encoded sequentially, as shown in Figure 1 (a). Important for understanding the way CA-DEV operates is the clear distinction between the CA itself and the developmental mechanism that programs it. For this purpose some definition of terminology is required: *cells* are the single computational units of the CA, while *areas* are groups of CA cells that are regarded as a whole from the development system's point of view. In this way the entire grid of cells can be partitioned in a smaller amount of areas. Figure 1 (b) clarifies the situation on a 5x5 CA.

CA-DEV areas will function as an abstraction of biological cells. Areas have a timestamp, indicating the relative time at which they were created during development, as well as a number of proteins in concentrations between 0 and 1. Over the amount of steps that is encoded in the genome, the encoded rules will be applied to an initial area, which covers the entire surface of the CA. By repeatedly firing rules on the available areas, this initial area will divide into smaller areas, whose protein concentrations will change to take on different states. Among the encoded rules will be some that affect the transition program in the CA cells that belong to the area that the rule is fired in. In this way the underlying CA cells will be programmed by the rules in the CA-DEV genome.

Development Rules. All rules in CA-DEV consist of the same amount of bits in the genotype. They consist of two parts: a set of two conditions and an action, all of which are defined by accessing a lookup table using the binary

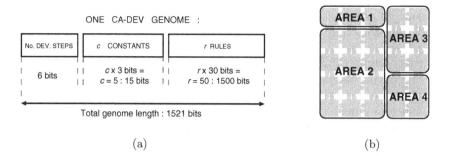

(a)   (b)

Fig. 1. (a) Global composition of a CA-DEV genome (b) 25 CA cells grouped into 4 CA-DEV areas.

encoding from the genotype as an index. General operation is straightforward : if the conditions are both valid, the action will be executed. Conditions and actions come in different kinds. A condition compares a referenced value with a fix numerical value. The referenced values can be any area parameter of the focal or neigbouring areas. In addition the encoded global constants, and the global developmental clock can be used as referenced values. Note that referencing values in neighbouring areas implements cellular induction as described in the previous section, since actions executed in the focal cell can now be triggered by conditions that reference values from the area's neighbourhood. The numerical values used as comparison value are hard-coded in the rule, using a system of fractions that designate numerical values in the interval [0,1]. The comparison predicate used can be 'less-then or equal' ($\leq$) or 'more then' ($>$). Note that all values involved in the system are always between 0 and 1, which makes comparison to a general numerical value possible. The actions of the rules can be any of three kinds:

I. **Area division rules**: These split the focal area in two new areas, either by a vertical or horizontal division. The relative size of the daughter areas is encoded in the rule. The divisions can be symmetric or asymmetric, depending on the CA-DEV settings. Symmetric divisions produce two daughter areas with smaller size, but identical protein concentrations as the parent area. Asymmetric divisions lower or raise all protein concentrations in one of the two daughter areas by a fixed value. Which of both daughter cells is affected by this change, and whether the concentrations are lowered or raised is encoded in the rule. Note that through these asymmetric divisions, CA-DEV allows for lineage to decide cell types of daughter cells. At the moment of creation the daughter areas are stamped with the current development time to indicate their 'age'.

II. **Rules affecting a protein concentration**: These rules alter the concentration of one of the area's proteins by lowering or raising it with a fixed value. As a standard value concentrations are changed by an arbitrary amount of 0.1. Which protein is affected, and whether its concentration is lowered or raised is encoded in the rule.

III. **Rules affecting underlying CA transition rules**: These rules affect the transition rule of all CA cells that are contained within the focal area. The rule encodes which of the bits encoding the CA rule is affected. As a result of applying the rule the designated bit is flipped in the cell's transition rule. In the scope of this paper the CA used the Von Neumann neighbourhood, which results in 5 cell states affecting the next state. This is equivalent with a transition rule of length $2^5 = 32$ bits.

Operational and technical details. In order to have a clear view on how CA-DEV operates, a few things need to be mentioned related to the general way of operating:

- Update order: One development time step consists of asynchronously testing the conditions of all rules on all areas. The areas are subjected to the rules ordered by their creation time. The rules are ordered according to their natural order in the genotype. This ensures deterministic development without ambiguities.
- Area boundaries: When referencing values of neighbouring areas, two situation can occur that need further explaining. When referencing a value to the outside of the collection of areas, two choices can be made. Either CA-DEV is set to perform wrap-around referencing, allowing for example the rightmost areas to reference the leftmost areas, of a standard virtual area is set to surround the operational areas. This virtual area has standard values for its parameters and can be references as if it were part of the system.
  When a large area references a value to a side where multiple smaller areas neighbour the focal area, the average of all the values of the smaller areas is calculated, and returned to the focal area as the result of the reference. In Figure 1 (b) this would for example mean that area 2 referencing a variable to its east, would receive the average of the values of that variable of areas 3 and 4.

3   Experiments

As a roundup for the introduction of the CA-DEV development model, we report a number of experiments. The experiments are aimed at gaining some indicative knowledge of the importance of the cooperation between induction and lineage. We will report 2 types of experiments:

- **Cell differentiation:** In this type of experiment the goal will be to fill a 10 by 10 non-uniform CA with as many cell types as possible. The goal is to test the power of introducing diversity in the phenotype.
- **Pattern development:** These experiments aim at producing a pattern in the cell types of a 10 by 10 non-uniform CA. The predefined pattern must be formed with identical cell types, while this same cell type must be inhibited in the background of the pattern.

All experiments used a standard GA with the following settings: population size 50, max 500 generations, 10% 1-bit-flip mutation, 20% uniform crossover, fitness-proportionate selection and power-law fitness scaling (exponent 0.25). The general settings for CA-DEV were to use 50 rules and 5 constants (resulting in a genotype of size 1521 bits), use a virtual area as boundary, and to adopt a maximum of 64 development steps. For each of the fitness cases, CA-DEV was parameterised choosing one of the four following settings:

1. **Induction only:** No area divisions are allowed in these experiments. The rule-action lookup table is re-scaled so that area divisions (rules of type I) are no longer possible, and only state-changing rules (type II and III) remain. This setup clearly inhibits the lineage effect, since no area divisions are allowed. The initial area is manually subdivided in areas containing one CA cell. All initial areas are thus identical in shape, age and protein concentrations. From that start-point CA-DEV functions very similar to a a a uniform CA, using the (non-splitting) rules in the genome to change cell states. Updating of cells is asynchronous with a fixed order, allowing for a first cell to change state based on the properties of the initial areas. This changed cell type can then start a cascade of propagating changes over the grid of areas. This type of experiment will be tagged '**IND**' for 'induction'.

2. **Induction with symmetric cell division:** As a next step towards the fully active CA-DEV, symmetric cell divisions are combined with state-changing rules. Manual subdivision of the initial area is no longer needed and is left to development. Note that changes in state can still not be achieved by lineage, since asymmetric cell divisions are not allowed. This type of experiment will be tagged '**IND+DIV**' for 'induction + division'.

3. **No induction and asymmetric cell divisions:** By switching off any referencing to neighbouring areas, induction is no longer possible in these experiments. State changes can only be achieved by asymmetric area divisions and state changing rules that reference *focal* variables, the system constants or the development clock. This type of experiment will be tagged '**LIN**' for 'lineage'.

4. **Induction and asymmetric cell division:** Here both lineage and induction can be active in changing cell states. No options are cancelled out, leaving the conditions and actions of CA-DEV at their full expressive power. This type of experiment will be tagged '**IND+LIN**' for 'induction+lineage'.

3.1 Cell Differentiation

Goal: Produce a 10×10 CA with as many different cell types as possible. Length of the produced phenotype is 100×32 bits $= 3200$ bits. Fitness is the number of different cell types developped, adding up to a maximum of 100. Position of the different cell types is irrelevant for fitness calculation.

Set of performed experiments: This experiment was performed with all 4 flavours of CA-DEV : IND, IND + DIV, LIN and IND + LIN. All results are averaged over 20 runs.

Results: The following table summarises the results of this set of experiments:

DEV-CA Setting	IND	IND+DIV	LIN	IND+LIN
Fitness (max 100)	19.8	97.6	96.1	99.4
(St. Dev.)	(7.8)	(2.5)	(6.38)	(0.98)

Observations:

1.1 IND scores are extremely low compared to the other approaches. This might be a sign that lineage is the factor needed to introduce variety. This is counterparted by the high score of IND+DIV, where the same mechanisms for state change are active as in IND, but now in combination with symmetric area divisions, scoring almost five times as high.

1.2 Both IND+DIV, LIN and IND+LIN seem to obtain an overall high score. Note however the very low standard deviation on the highest score, which is achieved by IND+LIN.

3.2   Pattern Development

Goal: Produce the patterns shown in Figure 2 on a 10×10 CA. The horizontal pattern should be possible to form using only area divisions, since grouping of information in the horizontal direction only should suffice. The diagonal pattern is specifically aimed at requiring information exchange in the diagonal direction, which against the nature of the orthogonal area division. The circle pattern is a proposition of a pattern where both orthogonal as well as diagonal information exchange is necessary. Fitness is calculated as follows: the CA cells lying on the pattern (cells coloured black on Figure 2 are scanned and the transition rule that occurs the most along the pattern is chosen as the reference rule R_{ref}. The maximum score (in this case a score of 100, indicating that all cells on the grid obey the pattern requirement), is then decreased by two penalty values:

1. the number of cells on the pattern that have other rules then R_{ref}
2. the number of cells outside the pattern that contain rule R_{ref}

In this way a correct pattern production decreases both penalties to zero and scores the maximum. The resulting fitness is a measure of the number of cells that are correctly classified by the pattern.

Set of performed experiments: This experiment was performed with IND+DIV,LIN and IND+LIN. All results are averaged over 20 runs.

Results:

DEV-CA Setting	IND+DIV	LIN	IND+LIN
Horizontal: Fitness (max 100)	87.5	89	86.4
(St. Dev.)	(7.16)	(8.8)	(7.5)
Diagonal: Fitness (max 100)	59.5	66.2	66.1
(St. Dev.)	(3.4)	(5.0)	(4.6)
Circle: Fitness (max 100)	73.3	75.3	73.1
(St. Dev.)	(2.12)	(1.87)	(2.14)

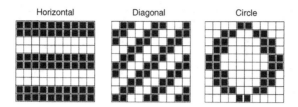

Fig. 2. Patterns to be produced by development, ranging from simple (horizontal), to more complex (circle).

Observations:

2.1 Scores are highest for the horizontal pattern, as expected. Scores for the diagonal pattern however, are lower then for the circular pattern.
2.2 For the patterns, LIN scores the highest score in all experiments.
2.3 The difference between the scores of the three CA-DEV varieties are low.
2.4 Only during the horizontal pattern experiment were scores of 100 recorded. (not visible in scores table)

3.3 Discussion of Experimental Results

During the experiments described above, variants of the development system were used. The differences are situated in the use of area division rules, either with symmetrical or asymmetrical divisions, and the use of inductive references in the rule conditions.

From the 'cell differentiation' experiments we have learned that to introduce variety in cell-types, the main mechanism responsible is abstraction of CA cells into larger CA-DEV areas. In CA-DEV this abstraction is due to the mechanism of area-division. This shows from the comparable high scores for both IND+DIV and LIN, while IND scores low with the same state-modifying rules. This was noted in observation 1.1. Based on our experiments we conclude that it seems of less importance whether the variety in cell identities is introduced by lineage or by induction. The combination of both however produced slightly higher, but certainly more reliable results, possibly indicating a higher expressiveness for this type of problem.

The pattern experiments aimed at testing the possibility to develop CAs where the position of the correct cell type is important. These positions are dependent on neighbouring cell types, in order to obtain the groups of identical cell types enforced by the pattern. The scores obtained by the different development types was comparable. This however is also function of the fitness measure. It is therefore interesting to visually inspect some of the results obtained. Figure 3 gives an overview of typical results for the circular problem.

A few recurring observations are interesting to note in the following subfigures:

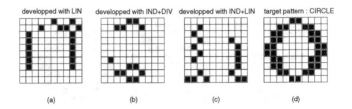

Fig. 3. Evolved patterns for the circle experiment.

(a) Developed with LIN: The high scoring parts of the evolved pattern are clearly the result of two areas on the left and right, which were the direct result of a vertical area division. These areas make out the main part of the evolved pattern. This kind of orthogonal organisation shows typical for results of non-induction development. The pattern shown scored 78 on a maximum of 100.

(b) Developed with IND+DIV: By introducing induction, cell groups tend to get less orthogonal, and circular or diagonal - like parts appear. The pattern shown scored 73.

(c) Developed with LIN+LIN: here combinations of both orthogonal grouping and more complex patterning appears. Note for example the toggle-like structure on the left, probably the result of a vertical area of identical cells, adapted to the toggle pattern by local interactions. The pattern shown scored 70.

4   Conclusions

In this paper we have presented and analysed a computational model for a development process, aimed at developping transition rules for 2D non-uniform cellular automata. The main mechanisms for introducing different cell identities in a multi-cellular organism have been pointed out based on a short overview of the principles of biological development. With this background knowledge our model CA-DEV was explained, showing that it allows for both induction and lineage to change cell types during development.

It was pointed out how the CA-DEV genotypes map to a binary string, in order to easily fit it into the framework of genetic algorithms. Such a genetic algorithm was then used to subject CA-DEV to a number of basic experiments, in view of gaining more understanding of the cooperation of lineage and induction in obtaining more complex phenotypes.

In a first step genomes were evolved that develop into a CA with a high number of different cell types. These experiments indicated that the necessary mechanism for obtaining high diversity is cell-division. Whether combined with lineage or induction as change-introducing process, average scores are comparable with the 'full-option' lineage+interaction variant, but less reliable.

In a second step genomes were evolved that develop intro CAs in which a pattern of the same cell type is formed on a background of other types. Patterns aimed at ranged from orthogonal in orientation, over diagonal, to a circle pattern. All tested variants of development scored comparably high on all patterns, but a closer look at the solutions revealed the effect of the different mechanisms that are active during the development process. Smaller scale, more detailed, patterns showed the result of development that incorporates induction, while switching off induction allows for more globally organised grouping as a direct result of cell divisions during development.

5   Future and Related Work

Related Work. The groundwork on which the system presented here is based was performed by efforts such as Kitano [Kit90], using a development process to evolve neural and other networks. Gruau devised 'cellular encoding' [Gru94], a generative grammar which now is the heart of Koza's development system for analog circuits [KDBK99], the genomes of which are evolved by genetic programming. Related efforts in the area of neural network development are described in the work of Boers [BK92,Boe95]. More biological models such as 'Cell Systems' [Fra91,LF95,Fra96] offer a more fundamental view of the mechanisms involved and are a useful source of inspiration when engineering a model from scratch. Comparable work by Eggenberger [Egg97] uses differential gene expression to develop 3D structures.

Future Work. The research reported in this paper is part of a bigger effort to investigate the general role of development in 2D networks in general, and electronic circuits in particular. An overview of open questions gives an idea of the future research plans :

- What are the properties of highly evolvable developmental genomes ? Is it possible to combine there properties with high expressiveness ?
- Is it possible to relate the mechanisms active during development, to functional behaviour of the developped network ?
- Is it possible to adopt a non-deterministic development mechanism during evolution, thereby indirectly promoting robust phenotypes able to survive the non-deterministic development step ?
- What are the properties of an implementation platform on which more robust phenotypes are more easily implemented, and thus a non-deterministic development mechanism has a better chance of working ?

References

[BK92]   Egbert Boers and Herman Kuiper. Biological methaphors and the design of modular artificial neural networks. Master's thesis, Rijksuniversiteit Leiden, 1992.

[BK99]   P. J. Bentley and S. Kumar. Three ways to grow designs: A comparison of embryogenies for an evolutionary design problem. In *Genetic and Evolutionary Computation Conference (GECCO '99)*, pages 35–43, 1999.

[Boe95]   Egbert J.W. Boers. Using L-Systems as Graph Grammar : G2L systems. Technical report, Rijksuniversiteit Leiden, 1995.

[Egg97]   Peter Eggenberger. Evolving Morphologies of Simulated 3D Organisms Based on Differential Gene Expression. In Phil Husbands and Inman Harvey, editors, *Fourth European Conference on Artificial Life*. MIT Press, 1997.

[Fra91]   F. D. Fracchia. *Visualization of the Development of Mmulticellular Structures*. PhD thesis, University of Regina, 1991.

[Fra96]   F. David Fracchia. Integrating Lineage and Interaction for the Visualization of Cellular Structures. In Janice E. Cuny, Hartmut Ehrig, Gregor Engels, and Grzegorz Rozenberg, editors, *Proc. 5th Int. Workshop on Graph Grammars and their Application to Computer Science*, volume 1073 of *LNCS*, pages 521–535. Springer-Verlag, 1996.

[Gru94]   Frédéric Gruau. *Neural Network synthesis using cellular encoding and the genetic algorithm*. PhD thesis, Ecole Normale Supérieure de Lyon, 1994.

[HTvR]   Pauline Haddow, Gunnar Tufte, and Piet van Remortel. Shrinking the genotype: L-systems for evolvable hardware. In M. Iwata, T. Higuchi, M. Yasunaga, Y. Liu, K. Tanaka, editor, *International Conference on Evolvable Systems 2001 (Tokyo) (LNCS 2210)*, Lecture Notes in Computer Science, pages 128–139. Springer Verlag.

[HvR01]   Pauline Haddow and Piet van Remortel. From here to there: Future robust EHW technologies for large digital designs. In *Proceedings of the Third NASA/DoD workshop on Evolvable Hardware 2001*, pages 232–239. IEEE Computer Society, 2001.

[KDBK99]   John R. Koza, David Andre, Forrest H Bennett III, and Martin Keane. *Genetic Programming 3: Darwinian Invention and Problem Solving*. Morgan Kaufman, April 1999.

[Kit90]   H. Kitano. Designing neural networks using genetic algorithms with graph generation system. *Complex Systems*, 4(4):461–476, August 1990.

[Lan84]   C. G. Langton. Self-reproduction in cellular automata. *Physica D*, 10(1-2):135–144, 1984.

[LF95]   M. Lantin and F. Fracchia. Generalized context-sensative cell systems. In *Proceedings of Information Processing in Cells and Tissues, University of Liverpool*, pages 42–54, 1995.

[Lin68]   Astrid Lindenmayer. Mathematical Models for Cellular Interactions in Development. *Journal of Theoretical Biology*, 1968.

[von66]   John von Neumann. *Theory of Self-Reproducing Automata*. University of Illinois Press, Urbana, IL, USA, 1966.

[WL92]   Andrew Wuensche and Mike Lesser. *The Global Dynamics of Cellular Automata*, volume Ref. Vol. 1 of *Santa Fe Institute Studies in the Sciences of Complexity*. Addison-Wesley, Reading, MA, 1992.

[Wol83]   S. Wolfram. Statistical mechanics of cellular automata. *Rev. Modern Physics*, 55:601–644, 1983.

Evolution in the Orange Box – A New Approach to the Sphere-Packing Problem in CMAC-Based Neural Networks

David Cornforth

School of Environmental and Information Science, Charles Sturt University, PO Box 789, Albury NSW 2640 AUSTRALIA, tel: 02 6051 9652, fax: 02 6051 9897
dcornforth@csu.edu.au

Abstract. The sphere-packing problem is the task of finding an arrangement to achieve the maximum density of identical spheres in a given space. This problem arises in the placement of kernel functions for uniform input space quantisation in machine learning algorithms. One example is the Cerebellar Model Articulation Controller (CMAC), where the problem arises as the placement of overlapping grids. In such situations, it is desirable to achieve a uniform placement of grid vertices in input space. This is akin to the sphere-packing problem, where the grid vertices are the centres of spheres. The nature of space quantisation inherent in such algorithms imposes constraints on the solution and usually requires a regular tessellation of spheres. The sphere-packing problem is difficult to solve analytically, especially with these constraints. The current approach in the case of CMAC-based methods is to rely on published tables of grid spacings, but this has two shortcomings. First, no analytical solution has been published for the calculation of such tables - they were arrived at by exhaustive search. Second, the tables include input spaces of only ten dimensions or less. Many data mining problems now rely upon machine learning techniques to solve problems in higher dimensional spaces. A new approach to obtaining suitable grid spacings, based on a Genetic Algorithm, is described, which is potentially faster than exhaustive search. The resulting grid spacings are very similar to the published tables, and empirical trials show that where they differ, the performance on an automated classifier problem is unchanged. The new approach is also feasible for more than ten dimensions, and tables are presented for grid spacings in higher dimensional spaces. The results are applicable to any application where a regular division of input space is required. They allow the investigation of space quantising algorithms for solving problems in high dimensional spaces.

1 Introduction

The purpose of this work is to propose a new method for calculating the placement of kernel functions in certain machine learning algorithms. This will allow such methods to be applied to higher dimensional data, and thus potentially provide new techniques for data mining. Data mining is an emerging discipline that draws on work from machine learning, and applies such methods to the discovery of patterns in large databases (Han and Kamber 2000). The kernel placement problem arises in some machine learning algorithms where a uniform division of input feature space is

R.I. McKay and J. Slaney (Eds.): AI 2002, LNAI 2557, pp. 333–343, 2002.
© Springer-Verlag Berlin Heidelberg 2002

required. This is relevant for various function modelling algorithms such as the Cerebellar Model Articulation Controller (CMAC) or Albus Perceptron (Albus, 1975), the General Memory Neural Network (Koltz and Allinson, 1995), Radial Basis Functions (Powell, 1990), and finite element modelling (Yserentant, 1986). The best example is the CMAC, as the grid placement problem has already been discussed in this context (Brown, Harris and Parks, 1993), and because it has linear time complexity (Cornforth and Newth, 2001), a highly desirable property for any data mining algorithm. That is, the time to complete training grows linearly with the number of records in the database being analysed.

The sphere-packing problem arises when an arbitrary point in the feature space, corresponding to an input vector, falls within a number of regions defined by a set of overlapping grids. In this scenario, the distance between two arbitrary points may be estimated from the number of selected regions the two points have in common. It is desirable to position these grids relative to each other such that the distance estimated in this way approximates the Euclidean distance as closely as possible. To achieve this, the volume created by the union of regions should resemble a sphere as closely as possible, and this volume should be of similar size for any point. If the vertices of the grids are visualised as the centres of identical spheres, the problem can be seen to be equivalent to the sphere-packing problem.

This problem is often visualized in three-dimensional space as the task of fitting the maximum number of oranges into a box. The sphere-packing problem is well known but analytical solutions are increasingly difficult as the number of dimensions increase. Solutions are known for regular tessellations of up to eight dimensions (Conway and Sloane, 1993; Gruber and Lekkerkerker, 1987; Hilbert and Cohn-Vossen, 1999), and the density values for dimensions up to eight is given in table 2. The problem is complicated if the space is finite, but for machine learning applications edge effects can be ignored. The particular requirements of the problem domain often impose additional constraints that make an analytical solution difficult, even for low dimension spaces. This paper examines an application of the problem in the context of determining a suitable regular quantisation of space for CMAC-based neural networks. A Genetic Algorithm approach is shown to be an effective and efficient way to produce values for relative grid placements for this application.

Section 2 introduces the Cerebellar Model Articulation Controller (CMAC), as an example of a pattern recognition device that uses a set of overlapping regular quantisations of space. Section 3 describes the grid placement problem. Section 4 describes the genetic algorithm used. Section 5 describes the experiments, section 6 describes the results, and section 7 concludes the paper.

2   The Cerebellar Model Articulation Controller

The Cerebellar Model Articulation Controller, or CMAC, is a class of sparse coarse-coded associative memory algorithms that mimic the functionality of the mammalian cerebellum (Santamaria et al. 1996). Originally, CMAC was proposed as a function modeler for robotic controllers (Albus 1975), but has been extensively used in reinforcement learning (Wiering et al., 1999) and also as a classifier system (Cornforth and Elliman, 1993; Cornforth and Newth, 2001; Geng and Shen 1997).

An input vector u of size d may be visualized as a point in d-dimensional space. The input space is quantised using a set of overlapping tiles as shown in Fig. 1. For input spaces of high dimensionality, the tiles form hyper-cubes. A query is performed by first activating all the tiles that contain a query point. The activated tiles in address memory cells, which contain stored values. These are the weights of the system (see Fig. 1). The summing of these values produces an overall output.

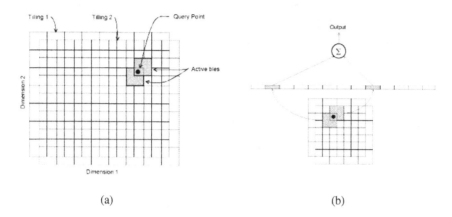

(a)   (b)

Fig. 1. (a) The CMAC quantisation is shown for two dimensions and two overlapping grids. A query point activates one tile in each quantisation. It is desirable to arrange the relative spacing of the grids so that the activated region resembles a circle as closely as possible. (b) The two active tiles activate two memory locations. These contain values that are summed to produce the output.

The relative placement of the grids controls the shape of the area of influence for a point. It is desirable to arrange the grids so that the shape of this area is the same for all points, and as close as possible to a circle in two dimensions, a sphere in three dimensions, and so on (Parks and Militzer, 1991). Two possible arrangements are shown in Fig. 2. Only one tile from each quantisation grid is shown. As the figure shows, the grid spacing proposed by Parks and Militzer (1991) is superior to that of Albus (1979), due to its more consistent coverage of the input space.

The grid spacing may be specified by a single displacement vector $s = \{s_1, s_2, \ldots s_d\}$. For example, in Fig. 2 (a), the displacement vector used by Albus (1979) is $\{1, 1\}$. The positions of the vertices of the other grids are obtained from this by arithmetic progression modulo q. In Fig. 2(b) the displacement vector proposed by Parks is $\{1,2\}$, which is expanded to specify the points $\{2,4\}$, $\{3,1\}$, and $\{4,3\}$. This arrangement is in use among almost all applications of CMAC.

The requirement for the centres to be evenly spaced means that they must be placed at integer intervals between 0 and q (the number of quantisation layers). Any other spacing arrangement would mean that the overlap of edges would not be consistent in all dimensions. Additionally, it is desirable to avoid co-linearity of edges, so the components of s must be chosen from co-primes of q (Parks and Militzer, 1991).

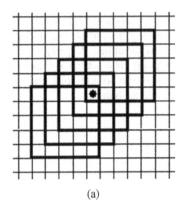 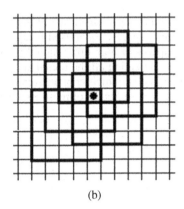

(a)   (b)

Fig. 2. The relative spacing of the overlapping grids influences the region activated by a query point, and therefore, the uniformity of distance measure. (a) Shows the original grid spacing used by Albus (1979). (b) Shows an improved grid spacing introduced by Parks and Militzer (1991).

The tables of displacement vectors published by Parks and Militzer (1991) consist of a separate table for each dimension from 2 to 10. Each table contains a row for each value of q from 2 to 50, followed by the displacement vector s. These values were obtained by exhaustive search, as analytical solutions to the sphere-packing problem are confined to real values, and to eight dimensions or less. Exhaustive search proceeds by evaluating a candidate vector by expanding to a set of q vectors, and measuring the Euclidean distance between each pair. The minimum distance is found and this is compared to the value obtained from other vectors. The vector that maximizes the minimum distance is selected. Exhaustive search through the space of possible vectors is feasible for low numbers of dimension and layers, but rapidly becomes impractical for higher numbers. For example, the number of candidate vectors for 2 dimensions and 50 layers is 9. These are the vectors {1,3}, {1,7}, {1,9}, {1,11}, {1,13}, {1,17}, {1,19}, {1,21} and {1,23}. Vectors with higher numbers than these can be excluded, as they produce mirror images of the arrangements produced by these. The number of base vectors for 10 dimensions and 50 layers is 9^9, or approximately 3.9×10^8. Generally, if the number of suitable co-primes is p, then an exhaustive search has a time complexity of $O(p^{d-1})$. Data mining seeks to apply machine learning algorithms to large databases, where the limit of 10 dimensions is very restrictive. Exhaustive search rapidly becomes infeasible, so an alternative method is required.

The sphere packing density achieved for any arrangement may be easily calculated from the minimum distance, since this distance is equal to the diameter of a sphere. In general, the packing density is the ratio of the volume occupied by the q spheres in the q^d space:

$$\delta = \frac{qv}{q^d} \qquad (1)$$

The volume of a single sphere is

$$v = \frac{\pi^{d/2} r_s^d}{\left(d/2\right)!} \qquad (2)$$

where r_s is the radius of the sphere (Kendall 1961), and

$$\left(1/2\right)! = \frac{\sqrt{\pi}}{2} \qquad (3)$$

3   The Genetic Algorithm for Grid Placement Calculation

Genetic Algorithms (Goldberg 1989; Holland 1992) are models of evolution. A population of possible solutions is used, where each candidate solution is coded as a genotype. Evolution takes place over a number of generations, in which solutions are replaced by superior ones. Each generation typically proceeds by applying operators such as mutation, crossover, and selection based on relative fitness. Genetic algorithms have proved useful in search in complex problem domains (He and Yao 2001). However, this method does not guarantee to find the best solution, but in practice will usually find a very good solution. A Genetic Algorithm requires:

- a genotype representation
- a genotype to phenotype mapping
- a fitness function
- selection mechanism
- reproduction operators

The *genotype representation* consists of *d-1* integers that are used as indexes into an array of co-primes of the number of layers. The first component of the vector is always set to one. The values that may be adopted by a gene are restricted to values from 0 to *q-1*.

The *genotype to phenotype mapping* consists of interpreting the genome as indexes into the array of co-primes. For example, the co-primes of five are 1, 2, 3, and 4. So a genome for three dimensions containing [3][1] would be interpreted as a vector {1,4,2}. For values of *d* greater than two, the vector components after the first one are sorted in ascending order to match the convention of the published tables. The example would become {1,2,4}.

The *fitness function* expands the base vector by periodic addition modulo *q* to achieve *q* vectors. The squared Euclidean distance is calculated between each pair of vectors. The minimum squared distance is used as the fitness. It is desirable to maximise this value, as this is a measure of the spread of distances, and the aim is to have a set of vectors all equally spaced from one another.

At the end of each generation, a *selection mechanism* is applied to determine which individuals are allowed to reproduce and go through to the next generation. This is based on the well-known roulette wheel strategy with elitism.

The *reproduction operators* used are point mutation and single point crossover. The mutation operator is implemented as a change in the value of each gene by plus or minus one, with a probability of 0.005 each. The crossover operator is implemented as a point chosen at random uniformly along the genotype. The crossover operator is applied to all individuals selected, except for the elite individuals, who are simply copied to the nest generation.

All experiments were performed using 10 runs of the genetic algorithm, with a population of 100, and a maximum of 100 generations. The experiment was concluded if the population converged. Convergence occurred when the genotypes of all individuals in the population were identical. The fittest individual was chosen from each run, and final vector chosen was the one with median fitness. Pseudocode for the program is shown in Fig. 4. The full program is available from the author's web site (Cornforth, 2002).

4   Experiments

In the first experiment, the genetic algorithm was used to produce displacement vectors for dimensions from 2 to 10 and number of layers from 2 to 50. These were compared with the tables published by Parks and Militzer (1991). Any disagreement was noted, and the minimum distance figure was calculated for both sets of vectors. For each displacement vector, the corresponding expanded set of vectors was produced, and the minimum distance was obtained using the Euclidean distance measure. The sphere packing density was obtained from the minimum density using equations (1) to (3).

In the second experiment, the two sets of vectors were compared by their use in an automated classification task, the parity problem. In this problem, the input space is partitioned into m regions in each dimension. If the inputs are x, and the range of input is r, then output is given by:

$$o = \left(\sum_{k=1}^{d} floor\left(\frac{mx}{r} \right) \right) \bmod m \tag{4}$$

If there are just two input variables the problem is known as Exclusive-OR (or XOR). The parity problem for three inputs and two classes is shown in Fig. 3.

Data sets were generated using randomly generated x values, and assigning a class label to each record according to equation (4) above. Seven data sets were generated, containing from 4 to 10 dimensions with 2 classes. Each database consisted of 100,000 samples, with input variables drawn from a uniform distribution. The performance of a classifier algorithm was tested by counting the number of samples correctly classified using a ten-fold cross validation method. This reduces over-fitting of the model (Weiss and Kulikowski 1991).

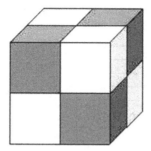

Fig. 3. A three-dimensional input space for the parity problem. Light regions represent class 0 and dark regions represent class 1.

```
Create table of co-primes of q
Generate random population
For each generation
{  For each individual
   {  Transform to list of co-primes
      Expand to set of points
      Calculate minimum distance
   }
   Copy the best individuals (elitist strategy)
   Use Roulette wheel to select for crossover
   Apply crossover and mutation
   If converged, exit
}
Display best results
```

Fig. 4. Pseudocode for the Genetic Algorithm computer program

In the third experiment, the genetic algorithm was used to produce displacement vectors for dimensions higher than 10.

5   Results

The first experiment resulted in tables of displacement vectors, produced by the GA method, that are almost identical to those previously published by Parks and Militzer (1991). Table 1 shows only the differences, which occur in 24 cases out of a total of 450. The first two columns show the number of dimensions, d and the number of quantisations, q. The third and fourth columns show the vector and the minimum squared distance published in Parks and Militzer (1991). The sixth and seventh columns show the vector and minimum squared distance produced by the GA method.

Table 1. Differences between the original grid spacings published by Parks and Militzer (1991) and the spacings obtained by a genetic algorithm.

Dims	Layers	Published Vector	Dist	Acc.	GA Vector	Dist	Acc.
5	41	1,4,10,16,18	492	8525	1,2,5,9,19	453	8483
5	47	1,2,6,10,22	551	8507	1,3,5,13,20	548	8543
6	31	1,2,4,7,10,15	363	7482	1,6,8,10,12,15	347	7443
6	37	1,6,8,10,11,14	518	7609	1,2,5,6,9,18	470	7530
6	41	1,2,6,9,13,18	615	7596	1,4,7,9,12,18	574	7588
6	43	1,2,7,11,15,20	631	7601	1,2,10,13,16,21	615	7491
7	41	1,2,3,7,11,15,20	735	6876	1,5,7,9,10,18,20	715	6838
7	43	1,2,4,8,11,16,21	903	6887	1,2,4,10,13,16,21	799	6897
7	49	1,2,3,8,12,18,24	1023	6785	1,2,6,9,13,17,22	1001	6772
8	31	1,2,3,4,8,9,13,15	539	5388	1,2,4,5,8,10,11,14	527	5435
8	37	1,2,3,6,10,12,14,18	740	5415	1,2,4,9,11,14,17,18	706	5337
8	41	1,2,4,7,10,14,16,19	900	5438	1,2,4,8,9,12,15,19	888	5419
8	43	1,2,4,8,11,15,18,20	979	5381	1,6,8,11,13,15,16,18	919	5512
8	47	1,2,4,8,13,15,18,22	1162	5384	1,4,6,11,13,14,16,22	1063	5393
8	49	1,2,4,8,13,15,18,24	1288	5363	1,2,5,8,9,12,19,23	1176	5432
9	43	1,2,4,7,8,11,13,16,21	1121	5129	1,2,8,12,13,16,17,19,21	1055	5146
9	47	1,2,4,7,10,13,15,18,23	1352	5205	1,2,5,8,12,15,17,19,21	1275	5160
9	49	1,2,5,8,9,13,17,20,23	1421	5115	1,6,8,9,13,18,20,22,24	1351	5105
10	31	1,2,3,4,6,7,8,12,14,15	743	4868	1,4,6,8,9,10,11,12,13,15	676	4982
10	37	1,1,3,5,7,9,11,13,15,18	974	5011	1,3,5,6,7,8,10,12,16,17	964	5009
10	41	1,2,4,5,8,9,10,16,18,20	1270	4898	1,2,4,5,8,10,13,14,16,20	1178	4887
10	43	1,2,3,4,8,9,11,16,18,21	1275	4930	1,2,4,8,11,13,16,17,20,21	1263	4926
10	47	1,2,3,4,8,11,13,17,18,23	1525	4930	1,3,4,6,8,12,14,16,19,21	1496	4905
10	49	1,2,3,5,9,12,13,19,20,23	1620	4917	1,2,4,5,8,10,13,17,20,23	1596	4932

The vector shown represents the median fitness out of 10 runs of the GA. These results show that the GA method did not always produce the optimum result, but this is to be expected as a trade off for increased search speed. The maximum and minimum sphere packing densities for each dimension are shown in table 2, along with the known values for these densities (Conway and Sloane, 1993). These show that the CMAC often uses grid displacements far from ideal. The minimum values show that many of the displacement vectors obtained are very poor in terms of achieving uniform space coverage.

The results of the second experiment are also shown in table 1. The fifth column shows the number of records correctly classified using the published displacement vectors, while the eighth column shows the number of records correctly classified using the displacement vectors obtained from the GA method. These results suggest a slight degradation of performance by using the GA method in those 24 cases. Note that the performance of the CMAC classifier falls as the number of dimensions increase, until it is no better than a random guess. This is due to the fact that the values of q being used are far from the ideal for this problem. Assuming that q is selected at random, the expected error arising from the use of the displacement vectors produced by the GA method can be estimated as

$$\varepsilon_E = \frac{\sum (Acc(PM) - Acc(GA))}{450 N_t} \tag{5}$$

With the number of samples $N_t = 100000$, this figure is 0.0001%, which shows that the GA method will have no appreciable affect upon classifier accuracy. Furthermore, this may be reduced, as it is possible to select the "best" displacement vector for the classifier based on the minimum distance figure.

Table 2. Table of the maximum and minimum packing densities achieved by the displacement vectors, compared with known results.

d	δ_{max}	δ_{min}	δ_{known}
2	0.890	0.262	$\pi / \sqrt{12} \approx 0.907$
3	0.680	0.076	$\pi / \sqrt{18} \approx 0.740$
4	0.617	0.023	$\pi^2 / 16 \approx 0.617$
5	0.329	0.007	$\pi^2 / (15\sqrt{2}) \approx 0.465$
6	0.183	0.002	$\pi^3 / (48\sqrt{3}) \approx 0.373$
7	0.129	0.001	$\pi^3 / 105 \approx 0.295$
8	0.067	0.000	$\pi^4 / 384 \approx 0.254$

The results from the third experiment are available on the authors' web site (Cornforth, 2002).

6   Discussion

The sphere-packing problem arises in many contexts but is difficult to solve analytically. An application of this problem such as the placement of overlapping grids for input space quantisation in machine learning algorithms imposes additional constraints, such as the placement of grid centres on integer intervals. Due to the difficulty of solving the problem analytically given the constraints of the pattern recognition device, a genetic algorithm was used to provide suitable relative placements of the grids for various values of the space dimension and number of grids required. The Genetic Algorithm approach uses standard point mutation and crossover, with roulette wheel selection, but employs a novel genotype to phenotype conversion to minimize the search space. This approach is faster than exhaustive search, and produces useable values of high quality.

I have examined the sphere-packing problem as it arises in neural networks based on the Cerebellar Model Articulation Controller (CMAC). To date, users of CMAC have relied on published tables of grid spacing, which are provided for dimensions up to 10, and number of quantising layers up to 50. These figures were arrived at by exhaustive search, as no analytical solution has been published. I have duplicated these results in a very short time, and I have shown that an approach using a genetic algorithm is capable of calculating such figures with similar accuracy. I have also provided tables for an extended range of dimensions. Tables for these values have not been previously published.

These results are applicable to other machine learning and data mining applications where multiple overlapping grids are required for quantisation of multidimensional spaces.

References

Albus, J. S. (1975). A New Approach to Manipulator Control: the Cerebellar Model Articulation Controller (CMAC). Trans. ASME, Series G. Journal of Dynamic Systems, Measurement and Control. 97, 220–233.

Albus, J.S. (1979). Mechanisms of Planning and Problem Solving in the Brain. Mathematical Biosciences, 45, 247–293.

Brown, M., Harris, C.J. and Parks, P.C. (1993). The Interpolation Capabilities of the Binary Cmac. Neural Networks 6, 3: 429–440.

Conway, J. H. and Sloane, N. J. A. Sphere Packings, Lattices, and Groups, 2nd ed. New York: Springer-Verlag, 1993.

Cornforth, D., and Elliman, D. (1993). Modelling probability density functions for classifying using a CMAC, in Techniques and Applications of Neural Networks. Taylor, M., and Lisboa, P. Ellis Horwood.

Cornforth, D. and Newth, D. (2001). The Kernel Addition Training Algorithm: Faster Training for CMAC Based Neural Networks. Proc. Conf. Artificial Neural Networks and Expert Systems, Otago.

Cornforth, D., 2002, http://life.csu.edu.au/~dcornfor/cmac.html.

Geng, Z.J., and Shen, W. (1997). Fingerprint Classification Using Fuzzy Cerebellar Model Arithmetic Computer Neural Networks. Journal of Electronic Imaging, 6(3), 311–318.

Goldberg, D.: Genetic Algorithms in Search, Optimisation and Machine Learning. Addison Wesley (1989).

Gruber, P. M. and Lekkerkerker, C. G. Geometry of Numbers. Amsterdam, Netherlands: North-Holland, 1987.

Han J. and Kamber M. (2001). Data Mining Concepts and Techniques. Morgan Kaufman.

J. He and X. Yao, (2001) Drift Analysis and Average Time Complexity of Evolutionary Algorithms,'' Artificial Intelligence, 127(1):57–85.

Hilbert, D. and Cohn-Vossen, S. Geometry and the Imagination. New York: Chelsea, p. 47, 1999.

Holland, J. (1992). Adaptation in Natural and Artificial Systems: An Introductory Analysis with Applications to Biology, Control, and Artificial Intelligence. MIT Press, second edition.

Kolcz, A. and Allinson, N.M. "The General Memory Neural Network and Its Relationship with Basis Function Architectures." Neurocomputing 29 (1999): 57–84.

Parks, P.C. and Militzer, J. (1991). Improved Allocation of Weights for Associative Memory Storage in Learning Control Systems. IFAC Design Methods of Control Systems, Zurich, Switzerland, 507–512.

Powell, M.J.D.: The Theory of Radial Basis Functions in 1990. In: Light, W.A. (ed.), Advances in Numerical Analysis Volume II: Wavelets, Subdivision Algorithms and Radial Basis Functions, Oxford University Press, 1992, pp. 105–210.

Santamaria, J. C., Sutton, R. S. and Ram A. (1996). Experiments with Reinforcement Learning In Problems with Continuous State and Actions Spaces. Technical Report UM-CS-1996-088, Department of Computer Science, University of Massachusetts, Amherst, MA.

Wiering, M, Salustowicz, R. and Schmidhuber, J. (1999). Reinforcement Learning Soccer Teams with Incomplete World Models. Autonomous Robots, 7, 77–88.

Yserentant, H.: On the Multi-level Splitting of Finite Element Spaces. Numer. Math. 49, (1986), 379–412.

Finding Worst-Case Instances of, and Lower Bounds for, Online Algorithms Using Genetic Algorithms

Andrew P. Kosoresow and Matthew P. Johnson

Department of Computer Science
Columbia University
New York, NY 10027
{kos, mpj9}@cs.columbia.edu

Abstract. This paper presents a novel application of Genetic Algorithms, as an empirical method in the analysis of algorithms. Online Algorithms are designed for the case in which the problem input does not arrive in its totality, as in Offline Algorithms, but arrives piece by piece, during the course of the computation. Generating worst-case instances for these algorithms, both for use as test cases and as lower-bound proofs, is often non-trivial. We study the use of Genetic Algorithms as a novel method for finding worst-case instances of online problems, including versions of the *Taxicab Problem*. These worst-case instances give us lower bounds on the non-competitiveness of the approximation algorithms used. In particular, our experimental results demonstrate that *6.93* is a lower bound on the competitive ratio of the hedging and optimal offline algorithms on the *Hard Planar Taxicab Problem*. This experimental result has theoretical implications for the study of the problem, i.e., further research to prove an upper bound of 7 may be warranted.

Keywords. Evolutionary algorithms, search, genetic algorithms, online algorithms, optimization algorithms

1   Introduction

In analysis of algorithms, we study the difficulty of various computational problems, seeking provably efficient algorithms for solving them. As a first approximation to finding good algorithms, we often seek to prove the cost of the algorithms we have. As a first approximation to *this*, we often seek to prove upper or, in the present case, lower bounds on the costs of our algorithms. Even this, however, can be difficult. As such, we turn to an experimental approach.

We study here the lower bounds on the competitiveness of particular Online Algorithms. The competitiveness of an algorithm is an *upper* bound on how poor the algorithm's output quality may be, relative to that of the optimal algorithm, taken over all possible problem instances (see [1]).

The analysis of algorithms is concerned with the complexity of various decision and optimization problems and with searching for provably efficient algorithms for solving such problems, under various conditions. There are many ways of partitioning

R.I. McKay and J. Slaney (Eds.): AI 2002, LNAI 2557, pp. 344–355, 2002.

problems and their attendant algorithms, including P versus NP-Complete and Offline versus Online.

Genetic Algorithms (GAs) are a form of evolutionary computation that uses the relative fitness of the members of a population of data structure instances to explore a search-space, seeking a data structure with specific features, i.e., those that are fit according to our fitness criteria. In this paper, the relevant population members will take the form of optimization problem instances (e.g. *TSP* graphs). The fitness of an instance will be the ratio of the quality of the results from the online and offline algorithms on that instance. It is this value that we will seek to maximize.

In maximizing this ratio, we are seeking worst-case instances (relative to the online algorithm used). The performance ratios of these instances provide, in turn, lower bounds on the inefficiency of the online algorithm used. Intuitively, we show that the algorithms are at least *this* bad in the worst case.

In this paper, we present work at the intersection of two areas of computer science that before now were largely unconnected. We apply our GA to several online problems. We yield empirical support of the the non-competitiveness of the greedy algorithm, and the competitiveness of the hedging algorithm, on the *Hard Planar Taxicab Problem*.

2   Previous Work

The work described in this paper should not be confused with the many applications of GAs for *solving* original hard problems. GAs have been applied to the problem of solving many *NP*-Hard problems (see, for example, [2,3,4]), but that is not what we are doing.

A recent paper by Elizabeth Johnson [5] is more closely related. In that work, the goal was to find pathological problem instances, relative to an algorithm, where "pathological" was meant in terms of computation time (or, more precisely, the number of operations executed). The purpose was to aid in the study of the empirical performance of algorithms, i.e. when run in practice.

Our work, however, differs in two key respects. First, our problem instances are worst-case in terms of an approximation algorithm, *relative to* the optimal algorithm. Second, we are studying not the running times of algorithms, but the quality of the solutions they yield. These two features are cashed out in our fitness function: the ratio of the quality of the approximation algorithm answer and that of the optimal algorithm answer. We search for problem instances on which the algorithm does badly, relative to the performance of the optimal algorithm.

This paper, then, applies GAs not to the *empirical* analysis of algorithms, but to analysis of algorithms *simpliciter*.

2.1   Analysis of Algorithms

In the analysis of (non-randomized) algorithms, conventional decision problems are divided into those termed tractable and intractable, as in the distinction between P and NP-Complete (those problems with polynomial-time algorithms and those problems computationally equivalent to SAT). For many NP-Complete decision problems there are corresponding approximation problems. The goal of optimization algorithm theory is to find tractable algorithms that provide good, if not optimal, solutions. What one wants to investigate, then, is how well a given (polynomial-time) optimization algorithm performs compared to the brute-force (often exponential-time) algorithm. This relative performance (on a problem instance) is customarily represented as the ratio between the costs of the two algorithms (on that instance). See [6,7] for surveys.

Orthogonally, another way to divide problems is to distinguish between online and offline versions of them. (See [8] for a comprehensive introduction. The seminal concepts were introduced in [1].) For many decision problems, the organization the problem instance lends itself to a natural way division. Consider, for example, the problem of routing taxicabs. Although the information describing a certain instance of the taxicab problem could, like everything else, be represented as a single number, the natural way of interpreting it is as a sequence of source-destination pairs. In the online version of a problem like this, the algorithm simulates the real-time occurrence of the instance: taxicab requests come in one at a time, and at any given time, that algorithm only knows about requests present and past. In contrast, in the offline version of the problem the entire problem instance is presented to the algorithm at once, in toto.

2.2   Genetic Algorithms

The search algorithm we use for finding worst-case instances is a Genetic Algorithm. GAs were popularized in the 1970s by John Holland [9], both as an optimization search algorithm and in order to study computationally the process of biological evolution. The core idea behind this method is that many different possible solutions to a problem compete amongst themselves, mate, mutate, are evaluated (with some testing method) and evolve (relative to the given test). As a GA's usual goal is to maximize some value, our GA maximizes *the ratio of the online algorithm's solution cost on the instance over the offline algorithm's solution cost on it.*

Several characteristics of the GA vary with the particular problem being optimized, including what constitutes a problem *solution*, the *mate operator*, the *mutate operator* and the *fitness measurement*. In a *Traveling Salesman Problem* GA, for example, a solution would take the form of a list of cities, and the fitness measurement would be the length of the cycle traced by that list (shorter being better). The mate operator might, for example, take two city lists and form a third by, for each position in the list, taking the city from the corresponding random position in either the first list or the second list. The mutate operator might, for example, switch two of the cities appearing in the list.

The basic GA functions as follows: First, a *population* of (say, 1000) solutions is created at random. This population forms Generation *0*. Then, to produce Generation *n+1* from Generation *n*, the GA (stochastically) selects pairs of fit solutions from Generation *n*, recombines them using the mate operator, and adds the (possibly mutated) result to the Generation *n*. This process continues for arbitrarily many generations, until fruitful results occur.

There are many options, of course, including carry-over (copying possibly mutated but otherwise intact population members directly from one generation to the next), creating some completely random instances each generation, and elitism (carryover of the fittest member). For a short introduction to GAs, see [10].

3   The GA

We developed ELBOWS (Evolving Lower Bounds On Worst-case Scenarios) in the Pascal-based programming environment Delphi to run GAs for finding worst-case instances of a number of optimization problems, including *Vertex Cover*, *Independent Set*, (optionally planar) *Traveling Salesman*, and (optionally planar, optionally hard) *Taxicab*. The program is available at www.cs.columbia.edu/~elbows.

Since we are searching for worst-case instances, the score will be the ratio of the cost of the online algorithm *on a given instance* over the offline cost *on that instance*. For some algorithm pairs, there is a known *optimal score* (that is, a known bound on the inefficiency of the cheap algorithm). ELBOWS displays this if it is known.

3.1   Parameters

There are a number of parameters that can be manipulated in ELBOWS to fit the problem. The *population size* is the (constant) number of members in each population of the GA. In creating subsequent generations, there are circumstances in which we want to choose fit members, and these are selected, stochastically, by tournament. In this method of selection, a subset, of size *tournament size*, is randomly chosen from the population; the fittest member of this subset is then selected.

There are several probabilities that will determine the composition of each subsequent generation. The *mutation rate* is the probability that any particular variable of a population member will be randomized. The *carry over* percentage specifies what portion of population will be copied intact from the previous generation. The *randomize* percentage specifies what portion of the population will be randomly generated. All remaining population spots will be filled with the offspring of members the previous generation. Since all algorithms analyzed thus far have been graph-theoretic, we specify the population member size parameter as *graph size*.

3.2   Genetic Operators

Likewise, as the problems we study here are graph-theoretic: each instance is a set of nodes; what varies is whether pairs of nodes share an edge and, if so, the weight of the edge. As such, the level of description on which evolution occurs is not bits but vertices and edges. Since the graphs are represented as adjacency matrices, this means that the operators modify the edge weights whole.

For recombination we use uniform crossover: in constructing the child adjacency matrix, the value in each cell is chosen at random from the corresponding values in each of the parent matrices. When a mutation occurs, a new value is chosen at random for one cell position.

4   Online Algorithms

In the theory of online algorithms, we have the following fundamental definitions:

Definition 1. The **competitive ratio of algorithm A to algorithm B**, where both algorithms solve a problem with instance space S, and where $quality(C,s)$ is the quality of the solution produced by algorithm C on instance s, is

$$\sup_{s \in S} \frac{quality(A, s)}{quality(B, s)}$$

Definition 2. An online algorithm is **c-competitive**, for a constant c, if the competitive ratio of the online algorithm to the optimal offline algorithm is c or less.

Definition 3. An online algorithm is **competitive** if there exists a constant c such that the online algorithm is c-competitive.

4.1   The k-Server Problem

The k-Server Problem is the problem of how to respond, with multiple servers, to requests from multiple locations. The problem was defined in [11], which proved the lower bound of k on the competitiveness of any online k-server algorithm, relative to the optimal offline algorithm. Our results for this problem, which are preliminary, are omitted for reasons of space.

4.2   The Taxicab Problem

The *Taxicab Problem* (TCP), first defined in [12], is a routing problem which models the problem of a taxicab agency with k taxicabs available to respond to customer requests. The goal is to accomplish this as efficiently as possible, i.e., to minimize the driving distance of the cabs. The decisions involved in computing the solution to a taxicab problem instance involve not the order in which to respond to requests—they must be tended to in order of arrival—but which taxicab to send in response to the individual requests. The k taxicabs will, in general be located in various positions and therefore be at various distances from the pick-up location of an incoming call. The simplest type of solution will therefore be of the form of an array of taxicab indices, one for each customer. More generally, however, the solution will describe how we *rearrange the taxis* in response to the calls; that is, corresponding to each request, there will be an array of new locations to which we move the taxis in response.

There are four degrees of freedom which we will consider in the definition of the taxicab problem, resulting in a total of at least 16 problem variants. First, we can consider *hard* and *soft* versions of the problem. The soft versions is as described above; the modification for the hard version is that, in totaling the cost of the problem solutions (distance traveled), the driving of passengers is ignored. The intuitive motivation for this is, of course, that the taxicabs have meters. If anything, the taxi driver will wish to extend the length of the customer's journey, although, for our purposes, we assume that the distance between any two points is fixed. The taxi driver's goal, therefore, is to minimize the distance driven without a passenger.

Second, we consider planar and non-necessarily planar problem instances—instances described by points in the plane, on the one hand, and instances described by graphs whose vertices are separated by arbitrary distances, on the other.

Third, we can vary the value of k—the number of taxicabs used. In all of our experiments, however, will use just two taxicabs.

Finally, we treat of both online and offline versions of the problem. In the offline versions, the entire array of customer requests is presented to the algorithm at the beginning and the algorithm can plan its response. The online version attempts again to model the situation of a taxi dispatcher: requests are received in real time, without warning. Each time a request is received, the dispatcher remembers the previous requests, and knows where his taxis are located, but does not know whence future requests will come.

4.3   Taxicab Algorithms

We will, in general, use greedy algorithms for the online taxicab problem, as is presumably done in practice: when a call is received, send the closest taxi. For the case of the *Hard Online Planer TCP*, however, we will also apply a hedging algorithm [13]. The intuition behind this algorithm is, when you make the decision to send one taxi for a call, to also move the other somewhat in that direction, in order to hedge the bet. The algorithm works as follows: Upon receiving a call, designate the most recently used cab as R and the other cab as O. Calculate the distance dR from the call's source point to R and the distance dO from the call's source point to O. If $dO < 3dR$, send taxi O to pick up the passenger and move taxi R a distance of $2dR$ in *the direction of the passenger's source point*; otherwise, send taxi R to pick up the passenger and leave taxi O unmoved.

For the current setting, the hedging is predicted by theory to be a better performing algorithm than the greedy algorithm. The greedy algorithm is easily shown to be non-competitive (see [11]). The hedging algorithm, however, has been conjectured to be 7-competitive and proven to be *15*-competitive by Kosorosow [13]. In our experiments we were able to generate instances on which the hedging algorithm's cost was approximately *6.93* times that of the brute force algorithm, suggesting that the upper bound of *7* is tight. This empirical result suggests that further effort towards a proof of 7-competiveness may be warrented. The *3-Hard Taxicab Problem* is currently open.

5   Results

The results of representative runs, and graphs of some runs, are listed below.

5.1   Hard Non-planar Taxicab Problem – Greedy

Problem input	A complete weighted graph $G = (V,E)$ such that V is partitioned into pairs (p_S, p_D)
Problem description	For each passenger (p_S, p_D), reposition the taxis so that some taxi is moved to the passenger's start point, such that *the total distance traveled in repositioning the taxis* is minimized.
Population size	1000
Tournament size	3
Mutation rate	2%
Carry over	1%
Randomize	20%
No. customers	5
Max. distance	100
No. generations	20

Best element details:

Greedy cost	359
Optimal cost	5
Score	71.8

We see much more dramatic results here than in the non-hard versions below, which makes intuitive sense. Although customer travel-distance is additional mutable data, it is a cost that remains constant regardless of the algorithm (as opposed to the cost of driving between customers, which varies with the order chosen by the algorithm). Note that the optimal cost reached here, 5, is the *optimal* optimal cost for this graph size. Since distances between distinct nodes are forced to be non-zero, the minimal possible cost with 5 vertices is 5. At this point, the only possible change is an increase in the greedy cost.

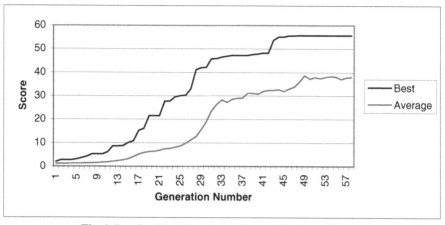

Fig. 1. Run for: Hard Non-planar Taxicab Problem - Greedy

5.2   Hard Planar Taxicab Problem – Greedy

Problem input	A complete weighted graph $G = (V,E)$ such that V is partitioned into pairs (p_s, p_D)
Problem description	For each passenger (p_s, p_D), reposition the taxis so that some taxi is moved to p_s, such that *the total distance traveled in repositioning the taxis* is minimized.
Population size	1000
Tournament size	3
Mutation rate	2%
Carry over	1%
Randomize	20%
No. customers	10
Board size	500
No. cabs	2
Online algorithm	Greedy
Score	Greedy cost / Brute-force cost
No. generations	1000

Best element details:

Greedy cost	2590.27
Brute-force cost	133.14
Score	19.46

Best element:
```
(250,250) to ( 15,166)
(147,172) to (440,401)
(249,250) to (130,479)
```

```
(440,401) to (458,423)
(130,479) to (334, 74)
(458,423) to (375,371)
(334, 74) to (317,252)
(375,371) to (467,435)
(317,252) to (  6,  2)
(467,435) to (484,106)
```

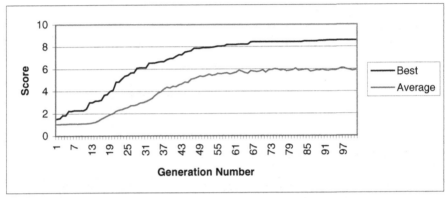

Fig. 2. Run for: Hard Planar Taxicab Problem – Greedy

5.3   Hard Planar Taxicab Problem – Hedging

Population size	1000
Tournament size	3
Mutation rate	2%
Carry over	1%
Randomize	20%
No. customers	10
Board size	500
No. cabs	2
Online algorithm	Hedging
Score	Hedging cost / Brute-force cost
No. generations	1000
Best element details:	
Hedging cost	2896.10
Brute-force cost	417.98
Score	6.93

Best element:
```
(250,250) to (456, 43)
(250,250) to ( 62,453)
(149,340) to ( 76,  9)
(456, 43) to (457,119)
(450,119) to (234,434)
(230,434) to (457,404)
(381,295) to (452, 62)
( 76,  9) to (  3,335)
(120,275) to (264,286)
(452, 62) to (341,161)
```

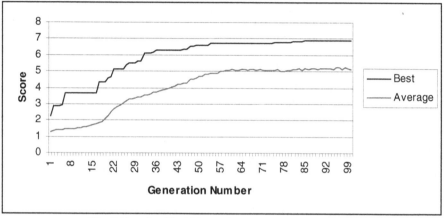

Fig. 3. Run for: Hard Planar Taxicab Problem - Hedging

As predicted, the hedging algorithm does perform better than the greedy algorithm. The hedging algorithm's score often approaches 7 on many different runs but never surpasses it. This provides evidence of its conjectured 7-competitiveness.

5.4 Summary

Although, for reasons of space, we do not provide detailed results for all possible versions of the Taxicab Problem, we provide the summary of these results as follows.

	Planar/Hedging	Planar	Non-Planar
Easy	2.82	15.60	25.33
Hard	6.93	19.46	71.82

Several generalities are apparent. First, hard versions score higher than easy versions. This is to be expected, since, in the easy case, the distance traveled with carrying passenegers is a fixed cost for either algorithm; all the algorithm has control over is the distance traveled without passengers. The passenger distance simply dulls the competitive ratio.

Second, non-planar versions score higher than planar versions. The intuition for this is that a non-planar graph has a greater degree of freedom than a planar one has, and that therefore more pathological non-planar graphs are possible ([12]).

Finally, planar/greedy versions score higher than planar/hedging versions. This is also as expected, given the known competitivenes of the hedging algorithm and the known non-competitiveness of the greedy algorithm ([12]).

6   Future Work

We plan to continue our work with the *k-Server Problem*. Further problems we intend to study in this manner include *Elevator Control* and *Job Shop Scheduling*. While we have focused here on routing problems, this approach could be broadened to many other types of optimization problems. Also, we believe this approach may be useful to the empirical study of computational complexity, as one way to study the efficiency of newly proposed algorithms whose complexity is not yet proven.

In addition, we hope to use this methodology and the ELBOWS program to attempt to solve one difficulty commonly encountered in Genetic Programming in which the evolving data structure in question is a program; see [14]. In GP, the individual member programs are tested by running them on problem instances. One subroutine in a GP system, therefore, will be to create problem instances. The fitter the member programs become, however, the more difficult it often is to obtain pessimal problem instances. If the set of problem instances is fixed, then, once the member programs master these instances, further evolutionary progress is unlikely.

We envision using ELBOWS, therefore, to create a series of increasingly hard populations on which to test the member programs in the GP system. In this way, we will create a symbiotic relationship between the set of problem instances and program instances, mirroring the relationships of co-evolving populations found in nature (see [15,16]).

7   Conclusions

We proposed a new application of genetic algorithms, i.e., to the problem of finding worst-case instances for online algorithms, relative to their offline counterparts, and we implemented several pairs of online and offline algorithms in ELBOWS, for versions of the *Taxicab Problem*.

Based on the results of our experiments, ELBOWS shows promise as a tool for experimental research in the analysis of algorithms. In particular, our experiments suggested that the lower bound of 7 on the competitiveness of the hard non-planar taxicab hedging is relatively tight with a lower bound of *6.93*; they also suggested, as expected, that the corresponding greedy algorithm is inferior. These results suggest that further research to prove an upper bound of 7 may be warranted.

Elsewhere, we have already applied ELBOWS in another context, *NP*-Complete problems and their approximation algorithms, and also got promising results (see

[17]). We plan further experimental runs and application to additional online problems.

Acknowledgments. We wish to thank Mark Weber and Holly Popowski for many useful comments.

References

1. Sleator, D., Tarjan, R.: Amortized Efficiency of List Update and Paging Rules. In: Communications of the ACM, Vol. 28(2) (1985) 202–208
2. de Jong, A., Spears, W.: Using Genetic Algorithms to Solve NP-Complete Problems. In: Proceedings 3rd International Conference on Genetic Algorithms, Morgan Kaufmann (1989) 124–132
3. Liepins, G.E., Hilliard, M.R., Richardson, J., Palmer, M.: Genetic Algorithm Applications to Set Covering and Traveling Salesman Problems. In: Brown (ed.): OR/AI: The Integration of Problem Solving Strategies (1990)
4. Hifi, M.: A Genetic Algorithm-Based Heuristic for Solving the Weighted Maximum Independent Set and Some Equivalent Problems. In: J. Oper. Res. Soc. Vol. 48 (1997) 612–622
5. Johnson, E.: Genetic Algorithms as Algorithm Adversaries. In: GECCO-2001: Proceedings of the Genetic and Evolutionary Computation Conference. Morgan Kaufmann (2001)
6. Garey, M., Johnson, D.S.: Computers and Intractability: A Guide to the Theory of NP-Completeness. W. H. Freeman & Company, New York (1979)
7. Ausiello, G. (ed.): Complexity and Approximation: Combinatorial Optimization Problems and Their Approximability Properties. Springer-Verlag, Berlin Heidelberg New York (1999)
8. Borodin, A., El-Yaniv, R.: Online Computation and Competitive Analysis. Cambridge University Press New York (1998)
9. Holland, J.: Adaptation in Natural and Artificial Systems: An Introductory Analysis with Applications to Biology, Control, and Artificial Intelligence. University of Michigan Press Ann Arbor (1975)
10. Mitchell, M.: An Introduction to Genetic Algorithms. MIT Press, Cambridge MA (1996).
11. Manasse, M., McGeogh, L., Sleator, D.: Competitive Algorithms for Server Problems. In: Journal of Algorithms, Vol. 11(2) (1990) 208–230
12. Fiat, A., Rabani, Y., Ravid, Y.: Competitive K-Server Algorithms. In: Proceedings of the Thirty-First Annual ACM Symposium on Foundations of Computer Science. The Association for Computing Machinery (1990) 454–463
13. Kosoresow, A.P.: Design and Analysis of Online Algorithms for Mobile Server Applications. University Microfilms, Publication Number 9702926 (1996)
14. Koza, J.: Genetic Programming: On the Programming of Computers by Means of Natural Selection. MIT Press, Cambridge, MA (1992)
15. Hillis, W.J.: Co-evolving Parasites Improve Simulated Evolution as an Optimization Procedure. In: Langton, C., Taylor, C., Farmer, J.D., Rasmussen, S. (eds.): Artificial Life II, SFI Studies in the Sciences of Complexity. Vol. X. Addison-Wesley, Redwood City, CA (1991) 313–324
16. Kauffman, S., Johnsen, S. Co-Evolution to the Edge of Chaos: Couple Fitness Landscapes, Poised States, and Co-Evolutionary Avalanches. In Langton, C., Taylor, C., Farmer, J.D., Rasmussen, S. (eds.): Artificial Life II, SFI Studies in the Sciences of Complexity. Vol. X. Addison-Wesley, Redwood City, CA (1991) 325–369
17. Johnson, M.J., Kosoresow, A.P. Find Worst-Case Instances and Lower Bounds for NP-Complete Problems Using Genetic Algorithms. In: 4th Asia-Pacific Conference on Simulated Evolution and Learning (2002) To appear

An Adaptive Activation Function for Higher Order Neural Networks*

Shuxiang Xu [1] and Ming Zhang [2]

[1] School of Computing, University of Tasmania, Locked Bag 1-359,
Launceston, Tasmania 7250 Australia
Phone: 61 3 6324 3416, Fax: 61 3 6324 3368
Shuxiang.Xu@utas.edu.au
[2] Department of Physics, Computer Science & Engineering,
Christopher Newport University, Newport News, VA 23606, USA
Phone: 1 757 594 7563, Fax: 1 757 594 7919
mzhang@pcs.cnu.ed

Abstract. This paper deals with higher order feed-forward neural networks with a new activation function - neuron-adaptive activation function. Experiments with function approximation and stock market movement simulation have been conducted to justify the new activation function. Experimental results have revealed that higher order feed-forward neural networks with the new neuron-adaptive activation function present several advantages over traditional neuron-fixed higher order feed-forward networks such as much reduced network size, faster learning, and more accurate financial data simulation.

Keywords. Neural network, neuron-adaptive activation function, function approx-imation, financial data simulation.

1 Introduction

Higher-Order Neural Networks (HONN's) (Lee, Doolen, *et al* [1]) are networks in which the net input to a computational neuron is a weighted sum of products of its inputs. Such neuron is called a Higher-order Processing Unit (HPU) (Lippmann, [2]). It was known that HONN's can implement invariant pattern recognition (Psaltis *et al* [3], Reid *et al* [4], Wood *et al* [5]). Giles *et al* [6] showed that HONN's have impressive computational, storage and learning capabilities. In Redding *et al* [7], HONN's were proved to be at least as powerful as any other Feed-forward Neural Network (FNN) architecture when the order of the networks are the same. Kosmatopoulos *et al* [8] studied the approximation and learning properties of one class of recurrent HONN's and applied these architectures to the identification of dynamical systems. Identification schemes based on higher order network architectures were designed and analysed. Thimm *et al* [9] proposed a suitable initialization method for HONN's and compared this method to weight initialization

* This work is supported by an IRGS (Institutional Research Grants Scheme) at University of Tasmania, Tasmania, Australia.

R.I. McKay and J. Slaney (Eds.): AI 2002, LNAI 2557, pp. 356–362, 2002.
© Springer-Verlag Berlin Heidelberg 2002

techniques for FNN's. A large number of experiments were performed which leaded to the proposal of a suitable initialization approach for HONN's.

So far there have been limited studies with emphasis on setting a few free parameters in the neuron activation function (a neuron activation function with a few free parameters is called a *neuron-adaptive activation function* in this paper). Networks with such activation function seem to provide better fitting properties than classical architectures with fixed activation function neurons. Vecci *et al* [10] studied the properties of an FNN which is able to adapt its activation function by varying the control points of a Catmull-Rom cubic spline. Their simulations confirmed that the special learning mechanism allows to use the network's free parameters in a very effective way. In Chen and Chang [11], real variables *a* (gain) and *b* (slope) in the generalised sigmoid activation function were adjusted during learning process. A comparison with classical FNN's to model static and dynamical systems was reported, showing that an adaptive sigmoid (ie, a sigmoid with free parameters) leads to an improved data modelling. In Campolucci *et al* [12], an adaptive activation function built as a piecewise approximation with suitable cubic splines had arbitrary shape and allowed to reduce the overall size of the neural networks, trading connection complexity with activation function complexity. Other authors such as Hu *et al* [13], Yamada *et al* [14] also studied the properties of neural networks with adaptive activation functions.

Nevertheless, the capabilities of HONN's with neuron-adaptive activation function to complex function approximation and financial data simulation have never been considered by anybody thus far. It is our belief that, if a traditional FNN is unable to learn a complex data set (theoretically it can), an HONN may be constructed to deal with it for faster and more efficient learning. In this paper we established such an HONN with a neuron-adaptive activation function. We proposed an empirical justification of a neuron-adaptive activation function with 6 free parameters. Following the definition of the neuron-adaptive activation function, we conducted experiments with function approximation and stock market movement simulation to exhibit the advantages of HONN's with our neuron-adaptive activation function over traditional HONN's with fixed activation functions.

2 A Neuron-Adaptive Activation Function

Definition 2.1
A *Neuron-adaptive Activation Function (NAF)* is defined as:

$$\Psi(x) = A1 \cdot \sin(B1 \cdot x) + A2 \cdot e^{-B2 \cdot x^2} + \frac{A3}{1 + e^{-B3 \cdot x}}$$

(2.1)

where

$$A1, B1, A2, B2, A3, B3$$

are real variables which will be adjusted (as well as weights) during training.

In the following experiments we used a learning algorithm that is based on steepest descent rule (Rumelhart, *et al* [15]) to adjust free parameters in (2.1) as well as connection weights between neurons. Basically our algorithm is not far from traditional back propagation algorithm, however, as parameters in (2.1) can be adjusted, it provides more flexibility and better approximation and simulation ability for HONN's.

3 Experiments to Justify NAF (2.1)

In this section we try to justify, empirically, the definition of our NAF (2.1). We show why we used a combination of the following three elementary functions as our activation function:

$$\sin x, \ e^{-x^2}, \ \frac{1}{1+e^{-x}}.$$

Our first experiment was to construct an HONN with NAF (2.1) to approximate a function of one variable:

$$f(x) = \sin x(x+1) + \cos(x^2 - 1) - 2 \quad x \in [0, 2\pi],$$

(3.1)

after training the learned NAF became:

$$\Psi(x) = 2.15 \sin(3.05x) + 0.01e^{-2.78x^2} + \frac{0.90}{1+e^{-2.45x}},$$

$$x, y \in [0, 2\pi]$$

(3.2)

$$(A1 = 2.15, B1 = 3.05, A2 = 0.01, B2 = 2.78, A3 = 0.90, B3 = 2.45)$$

Note that in the above equation, the coefficient $A2$ for the elementary function e^{-x^2} is a small real number 0.01, while the coefficients $A1$ and $A3$ for the other two elementary functions ($\sin x$ and $\frac{1}{1+e^{-x}}$) are 2.15 and 0.90, respectively. As these coefficients are *learned* during training, we inferred that, for approximating the specific function (3.1), the elementary functions $\sin x$ and $\frac{1}{1+e^{-x}}$ play more important roles than e^{-x^2}. (This is also why we call our neuron activation function *adaptive*.) We also compared our HONN with standard HONN (with sigmoid activation function), and the experimental results are displayed in Table 3.1 (RMS: Root-Mean-Squared). Table 3.1 clearly demonstrates the advantages of NAF (2.1) over traditional sigmoid function with regard to network size, training speed and simulation error.

Next, we approximated the following function of two variables:

$$f(x, y) = \sin(x + y^2) + x(y + 3) - 1, \quad x, y \in [0, 3],$$

(3.3)

Table 3.1. HONN With NAF And Standard HONN To Approximate Function (3.1) (HL: Hidden Layer)

Neural Network	No. HL	HL Nodes	Epoch	RMS
HONN with NAF	1	2	1,000	0.002658
Standard HONN	1	2	6,000	0.812069
Standard HONN	1	6	6,000	0.063508
Standard HONN	1	12	6,000	0.009869
Standard HONN	1	14	6,000	0.005623

In this example, we constructed an HONN with 2 input neurones, 1 hidden layer, and 1 output neurone. The learned NAF after training became:

$$\Psi(x) = -2.27\sin(0.99x) + 3.24e^{-1.58x^2} + \frac{0.02}{1 + e^{-5.09x}},$$
$$x, y \in [0, 3]$$

(3.4)

(A1 = -2.27, B1 = 0.99, A2 = 3.24, B2 = 1.58, A3 = 0.02, B3 = 5.09)

In this activation function (3.4), the learned coefficients A1, A2 and A3 (for the three elementary functions) are –2.27, 3.24 and 0.02, respectively. Similarly, this time we inferred that to approximate function (3.3), $\sin x$ and e^{-x^2} play more important roles than $\frac{1}{1 + e^{-x}}$. Table 3.2 demonstrates the advantages of NAF (2.1) over traditional sigmoid function with regard to network size, training speed and simulation error.

Table 3.2. HONN With NAF And Standard HONN To Approximate Function (3.3) (HL: Hidden Layer)

Neural Network	No. HL	HL Nodes	Epoch	RMS Error
HONN with NAF	1	2	1,500	0.002306
Standard HONN	1	2	6,000	0.912365
Standard HONN	1	6	6,000	0.084562
Standard HONN	1	11	6,000	0.009021
Standard HONN	1	14	6,000	0.005462

In the next experiment we used HONN with NAF to simulate the Commonwealth Bank of Australia share prices data as shown in Figure 3.1. The economic data were downloaded from the Commonwealth Bank of Australia official web site (www.commbank.com.au). For our experiments at this stage we only used 254 data points (Nov 2000 to Nov 2001, see Figure 3.2). The following NAF was obtained after training:

$$\Psi(x) = 0.04\sin(2.05x) + 10.29e^{-2.55x^2} + \frac{11.03}{1+e^{-2.03x}},$$

(3.5)

$(A1 = 0.04, B1 = 2.05, A2 = 10.29, B2 = 2.55, A3 = 11.03, B3 = 2.03)$

In this situation, we inferred that for simulating this specific financial data set, e^{-x^2} and $\dfrac{1}{1+e^{-x}}$ play more important roles than $\sin x$. The detailed comparison between our HONN and traditional standard HONN for this example is illustrated in Table 3.3, Figure 3.2, and Figure 3.3.

Table 3.3. HONN With NAF And Standard HONN To Simulate Share Prices (HL: Hidden Layer)

Neural Network	No. HL	HL Nodes	Epoch	RMS Error
HONN with NAF	1	5	6,000	0.045629
Standard HONN	1	5	12,000	0.996531
Standard HONN	1	10	12,000	0.882509
Standard HONN	1	15	12,000	0.092068
Standard HONN	1	20	12,000	0.075306

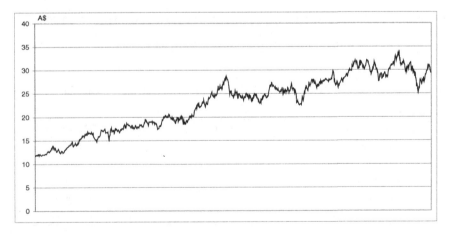

Fig. 3.1. The Commonwealth Bank Of Australia Share Prices (*Nov 1996 To Nov 2001*)

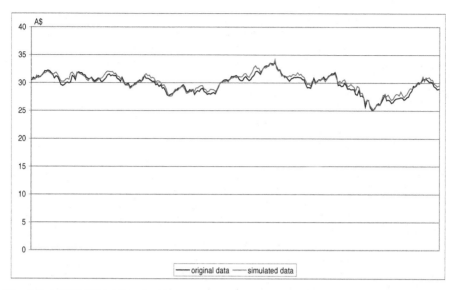

Fig. 3.2. HONN With NAF To Simulate The Commonwealth Bank Share Prices (*Nov 2000 –
Nov 2001*)

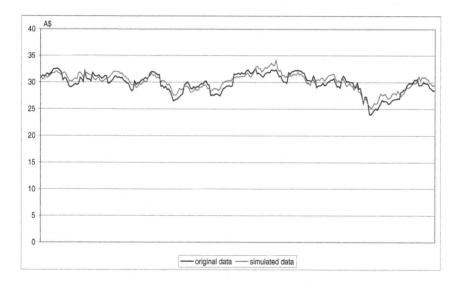

Fig. 3.3. Standard HONN To Simulate The Commonwealth Bank Share Prices (*Nov 2000 –
Nov 2001*)

4   Conclusion

In summary, by reviewing experiments in the above section and other experiments
that were not described in this paper, we have concluded that we have created a

justifiable neuron-adaptive activation function for HONN's that is superior to existing fixed activation functions. Our experiments exposed the advantages of HONN with NAF over traditional HONN such as increased training speed, much reduced network size and simulation error. Our next step will be to justify theoretically the proposed neuron-adaptive activation function for HONN's, and to explore the generalisation ability of HONN with NAF in financial forecasting.

References

[1]   Lee, Y.C., Doolen, G., Chen, H., Sun, G., Maxwell, T., Lee, H., Giles, C.L. (1986) Machine learning using a higher order correlation network, *Physica D: Nonlinear Phenomena*, 22, 276-306.

[2]   Lippman, R.P. (1989) Pattern classification using neural networks, *IEEE Commun. Mag.*, 27, 47-64.

[3]   Psaltis, D., Park, C.H., Hong, J. (1988) Higher order associative memories and their optical implementations, *Neural Networks*, 1, 149-163.

[4]   Reid, M.B., Spirkovska, L., Ochoa, E. (1989). Simultaneous position, scale, rotation invariant pattern classification using third-order neural networks, *Int. J. Neural Networks*, 1, 154-159.

[5]   Wood, J., Shawe-Taylor, J. (1996). A unifying framework for invariant pattern recognition, *Pattern Recognition Letters*, 17, 1415-1422.

[6]   Giles, C.L., Maxwell, T. (1987) Learning, invariance, and generalization in higher order neural networks, *Applied Optics*, 26(23), 4972-4978.

[7]   Redding, N.J., Kowalczyk, A., Downs, T. (1993). Constructive higher-order network algorithm that is polynomial time, *Neural Networks*, 6, 997-1010.

[8]   Kosmatopoulos, E.B., Polycarpou, M.M., Christodoulou, M.A., Ioannou, P.A. (1995). High-order neural network structures for identification of dynamical systems, *IEEE Transactions on Neural Networks*, 6(2), 422-431.

[9]   Thimm, G., Fiesler, E. (1997). High-order and multilayer perceptron initialization, *IEEE Transactions on Neural Networks*, 8(2), 349-359.

[10]   Vecci, L., Piazza, F., Uncini, A. (1998). Learning and approximation capabilities of adaptive spline activation function neural networks, *Neural Networks*, 11, 259-270.

[11]   Chen, C.T., Chang, W.D. (1996). A feedforward neural network with function shape autotuning, *Neural Networks*, 9(4), 627-641

[12]   Campolucci, P., Capparelli, F., Guarnieri, S., Piazza, F., & Uncini, A. (1996). Neural networks with adaptive spline activation function. *Proceedings of IEEE MELECON 96*, Bari, Italy, 1442-1445.

[13]   Hu, Z., Shao, H. (1992). The study of neural network adaptive control systems, *Control and Decision*, 7, 361-366.

[14]   Yamada, T., Yabuta, T. (1992). Remarks on a neural network controller which uses an auto-tuning method for nonlinear functions, *IJCNN*, 2, 775-780

[15]   Rumelhart, D.E., McClelland, J.L. (1986). *Parallel distributed computing: exploration in the microstructure of cognition*, Cambridge, MA: MIT Press.

An Adaptive Learning Algorithm Aimed at Improving RBF Network Generalization Ability

Jian Sun, Rui-Min Shen, and Fan Yang

Department of Computer Science and Engineering, Shanghai Jiao Tong University, 86-021-62933083, Shanghai, China
{sunjian, rmshen, fyang}@mail.sjtu.edu.cn

Abstract. This paper proposes a new adaptive learning algorithm of network structure aimed at improving RBF network generalization ability. The algorithm determines the initial number and center vectors of network hidden units by using forward selective clustering algorithm with decaying radius, and then adjusts them by using cluster sample transform algorithm based on impurity and variance and gets the final center vectors. The determination of widths of hidden units considers both the dispersivity of inner samples and the distance between clusters. Thus we get the final hidden structure. After determining the hidden structure, the back-propagation algorithm is used to train the weights between the hidden layer and output layer. The experiment of two spirals problem proves that our algorithm has higher generalization ability indeed.

Keywords. RBF network, generalization ability, regularization theory, statistics learning theory

1 Introduction

As a kind of single hidden layer feed-forward neural network, radial basis function (RBF) network has been successfully applied to many fields, such as pattern recognition, function approximation, signal processing, system modeling and controlling, and so on [1][11]. The extensive use of RBF network is close associated with its merits such as simple network structure, strong nonlinear approximation ability, rapid convergence speed and global convergence property [2]. At the same time, we should notice that research on network generalization ability is still an important direction. The so-called generalization ability is the ability to correctly classify the unknown samples, and it is an important index of evaluating the classification effect.

Nowadays research on improving neural network generalization ability mainly focuses on the reasonable choice of network scale, i.e, the design of network structure. Compare to parameterization learning, structure design is much more difficult because there is not yet any determinate way to follow up to now. An extensive accepted guideline (Moody rule [6]) is that the simplest network consistent with given samples is the best choice on the condition that there is no other experience knowledge. According to the viewpoint of mathematics, this is equivalent to approximate unknown nonlinear mapping using the smoothest function or the least

R.I. McKay and J. Slaney (Eds.): AI 2002, LNAI 2557, pp. 363–373, 2002.

parameter model within the error-tolerance scope. At the same time, the regularization theory [3] and the statistical learning theory [4] are increasingly mature and completed, which can play a good role in guiding the design of the network structure. On the condition that the number of hidden units is given, adopting back-propagation algorithm to train the centers and widths of hidden units, the linked weights between hidden layer and output layer is a classical RBF network learning algorithm. Because of the subjectivity of determining the number of hidden units and the effect of contaminative training data, the result of the back-propagation algorithm perhaps loses some accuracy, which can lead to the poor generalization ability of network. In contrast, SVM can also implement the training of the RBF network by taking kernel function as RBF, which can be seen as an adaptive learning algorithm of network structure, for it can automatically determine the centers and widths of basis functions and the linked weight. Many algorithms [7][8][12][13] aimed at dynamically adjusting network structure indicate that the method of dynamically determining the network structure can overcome over-fitting phenomena and improve the generalization ability of network to some extent.

Based on the foregoing research, this paper proposes a new adaptive learning algorithm of network structure aimed at improving RBF network generalization ability. The detail of the algorithm will be given in the section 2; in the section 3 we take the two-spiral problem for example to demonstrate the result of the algorithm, and compare and contrast with other algorithms. Finally a conclusion is drawn and future work is put forward.

2   RBF Network Adaptive Learning Algorithm

In essential, RBF network implements the classification function. RBF network consists of input layer, hidden layer and output layer. Through training on given sample set

$$TS = \{(\vec{x}_i, y_i)\}_{i=1}^n, \text{ where } \vec{x}_i \in R^d, \quad y_i \in \{Class_1, \cdots, Class_l\},$$

it accomplishes the following mapping: $R^d \rightarrow \{Class_1, \cdots, Class_l\}$. The mapping procedure consists of two stages: nonlinear mapping from input layer to hidden layer and linear mapping from hidden layer to output layer. In section 2.1 the **RDFSC** algorithm will be given to determine the initial values of the center vectors of the hidden units; in section 2.2 we will give the **IVCST** algorithm to modify the already formed center vectors and determine the final center vectors.; in the section 2.3 a way that can be used to determine the widths of hidden units and the linked weights between the hidden layer and the output layer is proposed. Thus we can realize the overall mapping from input layer to output layer using the methods in section 2.1, 2.2 and 2.3.

2.1   Forward Selective Clustering Algorithm with Decaying Radius (RDFSC)

Forward selective algorithm is a kind of network construction method. According to this method, network structure is empty initially, and then expanded by some certain optimum rule until some conditions are satisfied. Here forward selective clustering algorithm means that the clustering procedure proceeds in forward selective way. It is known that the choice of cluster radius could have greater effect on the network generalization ability. Too big cluster radius will lead to too many training samples included in some certain cluster(s), thus increasing the probability of higher misclassification rate of the cluster(s) and others; too small cluster radius can also produce some problems: over-fitting phenomena and poor generalization ability because of too few samples in cluster neighbor.

Considering the capacity of each cluster should shrink with the increasing of the cluster number on the condition that total capacity is given, we decide to adopt non-fixed cluster radius. On the other hand, we think decaying radius maybe achieve better efficiency by comparison to non-linear kinetic system. As is known, the nonlinear kinetic system will be possible in the stable status eventually if exposed in an environment in which the change of the conditions is gradually, which is similar to the cluster radius decaying procedure. Then we get forward selective clustering algorithm with decaying radius (**RDFSC**) which differs from forward selective clustering algorithm with fixed radius (**RDFSC**).

Firstly, we define some denotations:

$r_0 (r_{max})$: Initial (maximum) cluster radius

τ : Decaying constant of cluster radius

r_{min} : Minimum cluster radius

$\bar{x}_i \in R^d$: Input vectors, $X = \{ \bar{x}_i \mid (\bar{x}_i, y_i) \in TS \}_{i=1}^n$

C_j : The jth cluster

O_j : The center of the jth cluster

k_j : The number of samples contained in the jth cluster

k : The number of formed clusters

Then we can get the recursive forms of the cluster center and variance respectively:

$$\tilde{O}_j = O_j + \frac{1}{k_j + 1}(\bar{x}_i - O_j) \tag{1}$$

$$\tilde{S}_j^2 = S_j^2 + \frac{k_j}{k_j + 1}\left\| \bar{x}_i - O_j \right\|^2 \tag{2}$$

Forward selective clustering algorithm with decaying radius is described as follows:

Step1 Initialization: $C_1 \leftarrow \{\bar{x}_1\}, \ O_1 \leftarrow \bar{x}_1, \ S_1^2 \leftarrow 0, \ k \leftarrow 1, \ Z = \{\bar{x}_2, \bar{x}_3, \cdots, \bar{x}_n\}$

Step2 if $Z = \Phi$, then stop

Step3 Choose the first sample $\bar{x}_i$ from set Z, then look for the closest cluster center

O_j with $\bar{x}_i$, set the cluster radius as $r_i = \max\{ r_0 \tau^{i-1}, r_{min} \}$

Step4 Judge the condition $d(x_i, O_j) < r_i$ satisfied or not: if the condition is satisfied, then we join $\bar{x}_i$ to cluster C_j , i.e. $C_j = C_j \cup \{\bar{x}_i\}$, and adjust the center of cluster

$$C_j \text{ as } O_j \leftarrow O_j + \frac{1}{k_j + 1}(\bar{x}_i - O_j), S_j^2 \leftarrow S_j^2 + \frac{k_j}{k_j + 1}\left\| \bar{x}_i - O_j \right\|^2,$$

$k_j \leftarrow k_j + 1$; else create a new cluster C_n:

$k_j \leftarrow k_j + 1, C_n \leftarrow \{x_i\}, O_k \leftarrow \bar{x}_i, S_k^2 \leftarrow 0$

Step5 $Z \leftarrow Z - \{\bar{x}_i\}$, go to Step2

Step2 to step5 are the core portion of the algorithm. As for every input vector $\bar{x}_i$ ($i=2$,... ,n), we first compute the closest cluster center and the corresponding distance with $\bar{x}_i$; Then join it to existing clusters or create a new cluster according to the distance. Because it need travel each cluster center in order to compute the closest cluster center to each input vector, its costs become the most expensive part of the whole algorithm. The upper limit of the cost is $O(kn)$, where k is the number of finally formed clusters and n is the number of input vectors. So the algorithm has higher efficiency.

2.2 Cluster Sample Transfer Algorithm Based on Impurity and Variance (IVCST)

The RDFSC Algorithm belongs to the input clustering algorithm, which does not consider the classification information in the training samples. So the impurity of the formed clusters may be relatively bigger. The algorithm will combine the classification information to adjust the formed clusters and achieve the goal of reducing the impurity.

Firstly, we will expand the concept of the cluster and give the concept of the generalized cluster. The generalized cluster EC_j corresponding to the cluster C_j is defined as follow:

$$EC_j = \{(\bar{x}_i, y_i) \mid (\bar{x}_i, y) \in TS, \bar{x}_i \in C_j\}$$

and the classification set L_j corresponding to EC_j is also defined:

$$L_j = \{y_i \mid (\bar{x}_i, y_i) \in EC_j\}$$

Definition. If $|L_j| = 1$, then EC_j is called pure generalized cluster; otherwise impure generalized cluster.

Supposed that EC_j is an impurity generalized cluster, the corresponding classification set is $L_j = \{y_1, \cdots, y_s\}$, the subset typed with y_i of EC_j is $EC_j^i = \{(\bar{x}_k, y_i) \mid (\bar{x}_k, y_i) \in EC_j\}$ (the corresponding cluster subset is $C_j^i = \{\bar{x}_k \mid (\bar{x}_k, y_i) \in EC_j\}$), the ratio of EC_j^i in EC_j is $p_j^i = \frac{|EC_j^i|}{|EC_j|}$, then we can get the definition of impurity of EC_j:

$$impurity \ (EC_j) = -\sum_{i=1}^{s} p_j^i \log p_j^i \tag{3}$$

As we can see, the definition of impurity actually uses the concept of the entropy [5][9] in the information theory. Thus the concept of impurity can reflect the class distribution of the generalized cluster: the more classes there are, and the more uniform the class distribution is, the more the impurity; the less classes there are, and the less uniform the class distribution is, the less impurity. According to definition, we can conclude that $impurity$ $(EC_j) = 0$ if EC_j is a pure generalized cluster and $impurity$ $(EC_j) > 0$ if EC_j is an impure generalized cluster. Also we get the superimum of the impurity:

$$\sup\big(impurity\ (EC_j)\big) = \log s, \text{ where } s = |EC_j|$$

Following we will give the concrete steps of **IVCST** algorithm based on the impurity of the generalized cluster:

Step1 Partition EC_j, $j = 1,2,\cdots,k$ according to the output values and get the subset set $\{EC_j^i\}_{i=1}^s$ of EC_j, where $s = |L_j|$, compute p_j^i and get $impurity$ (EC_j)

Step2 Compute the impurity mean of the generalized clusters by weighted average method and get: $\overline{impurity} \leftarrow \sum_{j=1}^{k} \frac{k_j}{n} impuruty\ (EC_j)$; Computer the variance mean of the generalized clusters by weighted average method and get: $\overline{Variance} \leftarrow \sum_{j=1}^{k} \frac{k_j}{n} Variance\ (EC_j)$

Step3 Sort EC_j, $j = 1,2,\cdots,k$ by their impurities' descending order and get the following sequence: $K \equiv \{EC_{l_1}, EC_{l_2}, \cdots, EC_{l_k}\}$, where $impurity\ (EC_{l_i}) \geq impuruty\ (EC_{l_{i+1}})$.

Let $GIS \equiv \{EC_{l_1}, \cdots, EC_{l_u}\}$, $LIS \equiv \{EC_{l_k}, \cdots, EC_{l_{u+1}}\}$ where

$$u = \arg\left(\max_{impuruty\ (EC_{l_i}) > \overline{impurity}} \{impuruty\ (EC_{l_i})\}\right) \text{(if } GIS = \Phi\text{, then } u = 0\text{)}.$$

For simplification, we still denote the above sequence as $\{EC_1, EC_2, \cdots, EC_k\}$

Step4 If $GIS = \Phi$, then stop

Step5 Otherwise $\forall EC_j : EC_j \in GIS$ follows the following actions:

(1) Sort $\{EC_j^i\}_{i=1}^s$ by the ascending order of the values of $|EC_j^i|$, $i = 1,\cdots,s$, and substitute EC_j^i for its elements by above ascending order and get the sequence $S = \{(\bar{x}_{t_i}, y_{t_i})\}_{i=1}^{k_j}$. Then following actions are followed:

① $q \leftarrow 1, T \leftarrow \{(\bar{x}_{t_1}, y_{t_1})\}, S \leftarrow S - T, EC_j \leftarrow EC_j - T$,

$O_j \leftarrow O_j + \frac{1}{k_j - 1}(\bar{x}_{t_1} - O_j), S_j^2 \leftarrow S_j^2 + \frac{k_j}{k_j + 1}\|\bar{x}_{t_1} - O_j\|^2$,

$k_j \leftarrow k_j - 1$

② if $impurity(EC_j) \leq \overline{impurity}$, then go to (2)

③else $q \leftarrow q + 1, T \leftarrow T \cup \{(x_{t_q}, y_{t_q})\}, S \leftarrow S - T$,

$$EC_j \leftarrow EC_j - T \text{'} \ O_j \leftarrow O_j + \frac{1}{k_j - 1}(\bar{x}_{t_i} - O_j) \text{'}$$

$$S_j^2 \leftarrow S_j^2 + \frac{k_j}{k_j + 1}\left\|\bar{x}_{t_i} - O_j\right\|^2, k_j \leftarrow k_j - 1, \text{go to } ②$$

(2) While $(\bar{x}_{t_i}, y_{t_i}) \in T$

    ① $c \leftarrow k$

    ② If $c = u + 1$, then go to □

    ③If $imp \equiv impurity\big(EC_c \cup \{(\bar{x}_{t_i}, y_{t_i})\}\big) \leq \overline{impurity}$,

        $Var \equiv Variance\big(EC_c \cup \{(\bar{x}_{t_i}, y_{t_i})\}\big) \leq \overline{Variance}$,

        then $EC_c \leftarrow EC_c \cup \{(\bar{x}_{t_i}, y_{t_i})\}$, $impurity$ $(EC_c) \leftarrow imp$, modify the

        values of O_c, S_c^2, EC_c^i and p_j^i the same as the method in (1), $i \leftarrow i+1$,

        go to (2)

    ④ Else $c \leftarrow c - 1$, go to ②

    _ $k \leftarrow k + 1, EC_k \leftarrow \{(x_{t_i}, y_{t_i})\}$ compute the values

    of $O_c, S_c^2, EC_c^i, p_j^i$ and $impurity$ (EC_k), go to (2)

(3) $j \leftarrow j + 1$, go to Step5

By analysis the above algorithm, we can get its time complexity
is $\begin{cases} O\left(k \log k + u(m \log m + k_{max}(k - u + 2))\right) & u \neq 0 \\ O\left(k \log k + mk\right) & u = 0 \end{cases}$, where $k_{max} = \max\limits_{1 \leq j \leq k} k_j$.

So we can conclude that the algorithm has better efficiency.
For convenience, we denote the algorithm combing **RDFSC** and **IVCST** as
RDFSC+IVCST, the algorithm combing **RFFSC** and **IVCST** as **RFFSC+IVCST**.
The experiment result of these algorithms will be given in section 3.

2.3 Determining the Widths and Linked Weights of Network

The choice of the widths of the hidden units is directly associated with the
generalization ability of network. Not only should the dispersivity of the inner
samples of the cluster but also the distance between the clusters be considered. If the
dispersivity of the inner samples of the cluster or the distance between clusters is
bigger, the width σ of the kernel function should be bigger. Thus it can lead to bigger
output value in the output layer. On the contrary, σ should be smaller. Through
combing the dispersivity of the inner samples of the cluster and the distance between
the clusters, the local response ability of the RBF network can be further improved.
Following we will give the method determining the widths of the hidden units. Firstly
some definitions will be given:

    The dispersivity of the inner samples of the jth cluster: $d_j^{inner} = \sqrt{S_j^2}$

    If $d_{ji} \equiv d(O_j, O_i) = \min\limits_{1 \leq l \leq k} d(O_j, O_l)$, then C_i is the closest cluster to C_j

Supposed that C_i is the closest cluster to C_j, define the width of hidden unit corresponding the jth cluster as $\sigma_j = d_{ji} - d_i^{inner}$, the one corresponding the ith cluster as $\sigma_i = d_{ji} - d_j^{inner}$.

As for the linked weights between hidden layer and output layer, we adopt the back-propagation algorithm to train and get

$$W = (H^T H)^{-1} H^T C \equiv H^P C \qquad (4)$$

where $H^P = (H^T H)^{-1} H^T$ is referred to as pseudo inverse matrix,

$$H \equiv \varphi^T(X) = \begin{bmatrix} \varphi_1(\vec{x}_1), & \cdots, & \varphi_k(\vec{x}_1) \\ \varphi_1(\vec{x}_2), & \cdots, & \varphi_k(\vec{x}_2) \\ \vdots & \ddots & \vdots \\ \varphi_1(\vec{x}_n), & \cdots, & \varphi_k(\vec{x}_n) \end{bmatrix}, C = [c_{ij}]_{n \times m}$$ is classification matrix.

The elements of C are determined according to the following relation:

If the jth sample belongs to the ith class, then $c_{ij} = 1$, $c_{ij} = 1$ $\forall k \neq i$

3 Simulation Experiment and Result

Next we will take the two-spiral problem for example to demonstrate the result of the **RDFSC+IVCST** algorithm. The two-spiral problem [10] is a challenging benchmark problem for evaluating neural network classification ability to model complex boundaries, and also a most difficult pattern classification problem. The classification ability to two-spiral problem is usually seemed as an important index of evaluating the network generalization ability.

Two spirals consist of two intertwinded spirals, every of which is corresponding to a class. The goal of the two-spiral problem is judging input samples belong to which of the two intertwinded spirals. Because the two spirals are intertwinded, i.e, the corresponding classes are overlapped, it is of great difficulty for RBF network to correctly classify them. Following we will give the experiment result with and without the disturbance of the noise, and compare the other algorithm such as **RFFSC, IVCST** and **RFFSC+IVCST**.

The two-spiral data without the disturbance of the noise come from CMU network benchmark database. We pick up 192 samples as training data and another 192 samples as testing data. The parameter of r_0 is determined by the following formulas:

$r_0 = \dfrac{1}{2} \max\limits_{1 \leq i, j \leq n} \{d(\vec{x}_i, \vec{x}_j)\}$; The choice of the parameter of τ should follow the principle that the decaying times ($\max\{ i \mid r_0 \tau^{i-1} \geq r_{\min} \}$) should be moderate. Too much decaying times of the cluster radius could not achieve the goal of improving classification accuracy. In the table 3 and 4, the picked parameters are $r_0 = 6.5$ and $\tau = 0.9$. Detail result is listed in the table 1 to table 4.

Table 1. The result of **RFFSC** algorithm

r	Number of hidden units	Training time (s)	Training accuracy (%)	Testing accuracy (%)
4.500	5	0.09	50.00	50.00
2.500	13	0.16	50.00	50.00
1.250	40	0.39	67.19	65.63
1.125	62	0.60	81.77	81.77
1.000	92	1.92	98.44	98.44
0.875	108	2.07	99.48	99.48
0.750	122	2.47	98.96	98.96
0.500	152	2.60	100.00	100.00

Table 2. The result of **RFFSC+IVCST** algorithm

r	Number of hidden units	Training time (s)	Training accuracy (%)	Testing accuracy (%)
4.500	8	0.11	56.77	56.77
2.500	26	1.27	59.38	59.38
1.250	62	2.61	77.60	79.17
1.125	68	2.67	95.83	95.31
1.000	92	2.91	98.44	98.44
0.875	108	3.08	99.48	99.48
0.750	122	3.21	98.96	98.96
0.500	152	4.63	100.00	100.00

Table 3. The result of **RDFSC** algorithm ($r_0 = 6.5$, $\tau = 0.9$)

r_{min}	The number of hidden units	Training time (s)	Training accuracy (%)	Testing accuracy (%)
4.500	5	0.13	50.00	50.00
2.500	13	0.17	57.81	57.29
1.250	33	0.36	64.58	64.58
1.125	62	0.62	81.77	81.77
1.000	91	1.91	98.44	98.44
0.875	107	2.09	99.48	99.48
0.750	121	3.25	98.44	98.44
0.500	149	3.62	100.00	100.00

By comparing table 2 and table 1, we can conclude that adjusting the impurity of the generalized cluster could indeed improve the training accuracy and the testing accuracy, which is particular on the bigger cluster radius condition. It can also be seen

Table 4. The result of **RDFSC+IVCST** algorithm ($r_0 = 6.5$, $\tau = 0.9$)

r_{min}	The number of hidden units	Training time (s)	Training accuracy (%)	Testing accuracy (%)
4.500	8	1.12	56.71	56.77
2.500	26	1.27	59.38	59.38
1.250	62	2.62	77.60	79.17
1.125	68	2.67	95.83	95.31
1.000	92	2.95	99.48	99.48
0.875	109	3.10	100.00	99.48
0.750	122	5.24	100.00	100.00
0.500	150	5.58	100.00	100.00

that the most improving range of the training accuracy and the testing accuracy can reach 14.06% and 13.54% respectively. At the same time, the number of hidden units does not remarkably increase and the increasing range becomes smaller and smaller with the decrease of the cluster radius. By comparing table 3 and table 1, it can be concluded that using less number of hidden units, the clustering algorithm with decaying radius can achieve the same or higher training accuracy and testing accuracy as the clustering algorithm with fixed radius. By comparing table 3 and table 4, it can be verified that adjusting impurity of the generalized cluster can greatly improve the training accuracy and testing accuracy on the condition that decaying cluster radius is adopted. So we can say that in the absence from noise the **RDFSC+IVCST** algorithm is better than other algorithms in training accuracy and testing accuracy.

Due to lack of space, we only give the results of the RDFSC and RDFSC+IVCST in the presence of the noise. The term δ stands for the noise increment term.

Table 5. The result of **RDFSC** algorithm in the presence of noise ($r_0 = 6.5$, $r_{min} = 1.125$, $\tau = 0.9$)

Δ	The number of hidden units	Training accuracy (%)	Testing accuracy (%)
0.1	72	94.79	84.90
0.2	72	94.79	76.56
0.3	72	94.79	72.92
0.4	72	94.79	66.15
0.5	72	94.79	57.81
0.6	72	94.79	52.08
0.7	72	94.79	45.31
0.8	72	94.79	39.06
0.9	72	94.79	38.02
1.0	72	94.79	38.54

Table 6. The result of **RDFSC+IVCST** algorithm in the presence of noise ($r_0 = 6.5$, $r_{min} = 1.125$, $\tau = 0.9$)

Δ	The number of hidden units	Training accuracy (%)	Testing accuracy (%)
0.1	64	80.73	73.44
0.2	64	80.73	69.79
0.3	64	80.73	65.63
0.4	64	80.73	61.98
0.5	64	80.73	59.90
0.6	64	80.73	54.17
0.7	64	80.73	46.88
0.8	64	80.73	42.19
0.9	64	80.73	44.19
1.0	64	80.73	43.23

By comparing table 6 and table 5, we can conclude that above two clustering algorithm with decaying radius both have higher training accuracy in the presence of noise and can keep the training accuracy stable with the increasing of the noise increment term. In contrast, the algorithm adjusting impurity has much higher training accuracy which is higher 14.06% than that of the algorithm without adjusting impurity. It can be also seen that the testing accuracy is higher when the noise increment term is relatively less. Experiment also shows that the training accuracies of other two clustering algorithms with fixed radius are both relatively higher, which reach 89.58%; and the two algorithms have the property of keeping the training accuracy stable.

To sum, we can conclude that the clustering algorithm adjusting impurity with decaying radius presents stronger generalization ability and can achieve higher training accuracy and testing accuracy in both the presence of noise and absence from noise.

4 Conclusion

This paper proposes a new adaptive learning algorithm of network structure aimed at improving RBF network generalization ability. The algorithm determines the initial number and center vectors of network hidden units by using forward selective clustering algorithm with decaying radius, and then adjusts them by using cluster sample transform algorithm based on impurity and variance and gets the final center vectors. The determination of widths of hidden units considers both the dispersivity of inner samples and the distance between clusters. Thus we get the final hidden structure. After determining the hidden structure, the back-propagation algorithm is used to train the weights between the hidden layer and output layer. The experiment of two spirals problem proves that our algorithm has higher generalization ability indeed. Next we will focus on two points: one is realizing the adaptive selection of the parameters by introducing fuzzy technology; the other is realizing the extraction of the network rules.

References

1. Whitehead B A. Cooperative-competitive genetic evolution of radial basis function centers and widths fortime series prediction[J].IEEE Trans on Neural Networks,1996 ,7(4) :869–880 .
2. Bianchini, M., Frasconi, P., and Gori, M. (1995). Learning without local minima in radial basis function networks. IEEE Transactions on Neural Networks,1995,6(3):749–756.
3. M. J. Orr, Regularization in the selection of RBF centres, Neural Computation, vol. 7, no. 3, pp. 606–623, 1995.
4. V. Vapnik, the Nature of Statistical Learning Theory, Springer Verlag, 1995.
5. Tom Carter. An introduction to information theory and entropy. http://cogs.csustan.edu/~tom/information, June 2000
6. J. E. Moody and J. Utans. Architecture selection strategies for neural networks: Application to corporate bond rating prediction. In A. N. Refenes, editor, Neural Networks in the Capital Markets. John Wiley & Sons, 1994.
7. J.C. Platt. A resource allocating network for function interpolation. Neural Computation, 3:213--225, 1991.
8. Fritzke, B. (1994b). Growing cells structures – a self-organizing network for unsupervised and supervised learning. Neural Networks, 7(9):1441–1460.1993.
9. Y.Y. Yao, S.K.M. Wong, and C.J. Butz. On information-theoretic measures of attribute importance. In N. Zhong and L. Zhou, editors, Proceedings of the Third Pacific-Asia Conference on Knowledge Discovery and Data Mining (PAKDD'99), pages 133–137, Beijing, China, April 1999.
10. K. Lang and M. Witbrock, Learning to tell two spirals apart, in Proc.
11. L u Y W,Sundararajan N,Saratchandran P. Performance evaluation of sequential mininal radial basis function (RBF) neural network learning algorithm[J].IEEE Trans on Neural Networks,1 998,9(6) :308–317.
12. Michael R. Berthold and Jay Diamond. Boosting the Performance of RBF Networks with Dynamic Decay Adjustment. Advances in Neural information processings 7, 1995.
13. Ales Leonardis and Horst Bischof. An efficient MDL-Based construction of RBF networks. Neural Networks, 11(5):963–973, July 1998.

A Neural Network Online Training Algorithm Based on Compound Gradient Vector

Zaiping Chen[1,2,3], Jun Li[1], Youjun Yue[1], Qiang Gao[1], Hui Zhao[1], and Zhenlin Xu[2]

[1]The Department of Automation, Tianjin University of Technology
Hongqi Nan Road, Tianjin, 300191, P.R.China
{bakeryue,ganbei}@eyou.com
[2]The Department of Automation, Tianjin University
Weijing Road, Tianjin, 300070, P.R.China
zlxu@eyou.com
[3]Centre for Intelligent Systems and Complex Processes, BSEE
Swinburne University of Technology, VIC.3122, Australia
zchen@groupwiseswin.edu.au

Abstract. A new neural network online training weight update scheme based on the use of a compound gradient vector is presented in this paper. The convergent analysis indicates that because the compound gradient vector is employed during the weight update, the convergent speed of the presented algorithm is faster than the standard BP algorithm. The comprehensive parameter adaptation and the saturation compensation approaches that are introduced in the scheme enhance convergent performance. Several simulations have been conducted and the results demonstrate the satisfactory convergent performance and strong robustness obtained using the improved neural networks online learning scheme for real time control involving uncertainty parameters.

1   Introduction

The ability to learn is a most valuable property of a neural network. Feedforward neural networks (FNN) have been widely used in various areas, such as dynamic modelling, pattern recognition and system control involving uncertainty parameters. Normally the back propagation learning algorithm (BP) is used for FNN to update the neural network weight values. Several different BP algorithm improvement schemes have been presented in the literature [1],[2], – ,[12],[13]. The standard weight update formula of BP algorithms can be written as below:

$$\Delta w(k) = \nabla_w E(k) + \alpha \Delta w(k-1) = -\eta \frac{\partial E(k)}{\partial w(k)} + \alpha \Delta w(k-1) \tag{1}$$

where $\nabla_w E(k)$ is the gradient of the cost function in weight space, η is the so-called learning rate, α is the momentum factor. To speed up training and reduce convergence to local minima, several improving schemes have been investigated in

R.I. McKay and J. Slaney (Eds.): AI 2002, LNAI 2557, pp. 374–384, 2002.

[5],[8],[9],[10]. However most of these improvements are based on the use of heuristic factors to dynamically adapt the learning rate, which only leads to a slight convergence rate improvement [12]. A significant improvement is possible by using various second order approaches such as Newton, conjugate gradient, or the Levenberg-Marquardt (LM) method [7],[10],[11]. The demand for memory to operate with large Jacobians and the necessity to invert large matrices are major disadvantages of the LM algorithm [12]. The rank of matrix to be inverted is equal to the number of adjustable parameters in the system [12]. The large number of computations takes significant time and it is difficult to utilize these algorithms in real time control systems.

A novel neural network online learning scheme based on a compound gradient vector together with learning saturation compensation is presented in this paper. This overcomes the drawbacks of using heuristic factors and the large computation demands of other schemes. The convergent analysis indicates that because the compound gradient vector is employed during the weight update, the convergence speed of the algorithm presented can outperform that of the standard BP algorithm. When the improved neural network online learning scheme is utilized in real time control with uncertainty parameter, simulation results verify that satisfactory convergence performance and the strong robustness are achieved.

2   The New Weight Updating Framework

Since the choice of training rate in the BP algorithm affects the performance of the weight update and thus the convergence of BP algorithm, research about training rates has been taken as a hot spot. The standard BP weight updating formula (without momentum) can be rewritten as follow:

$$\Delta w(k) = -\eta \frac{\partial E(k)}{\partial w(k)} = \eta(-\frac{\partial E(k)}{\partial w(k)}) \tag{2}$$

The equation (2) can be written as following formation:

$$Y(k) = \eta U(k) \tag{3}$$

or

$$\frac{Y(k)}{U(k)} = \eta = D(k) \tag{4}$$

where

$$Y(k) = \Delta w(k) \tag{5}$$

$$U(k) = -\frac{\partial E(k)}{\partial w(k)} \tag{6}$$

If equation (4) is considered as the system description, $Y(k)$ and $U(k)$ represent the output and input of the system respectively, and $D(k)$ or η is the system model the control strategy is involved with. Obviously, $D(k)$ has significant effects on the response under the system input $U(k)$. Therefore, from the view of system theory, it is the reason why the training rate η in the weight updating formula needs to be paid such attention. As a result this investigation into the improvement of the weight update technique was carried out resulting in the novel online adaptive BP algorithm presented here in Fig. 1.

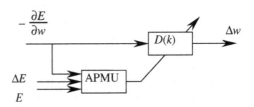

Fig. 1. Block diagram of the relationship between Δw and $-\partial E / \partial w$

Taking Δw and $-\partial E / \partial w$ to be the output and input of the system respectively, the s-domain transfer function D(s) that consists of proportional, integral and differential components can be given as follow:

$$D(s) = k_p (1 + \frac{k_i}{s} + \frac{k_d s}{1 + \frac{k_d s}{N}}) \tag{7}$$

where $\dfrac{1}{1 + \dfrac{k_d s}{N}}$ is a low-pass filter, which limits noise gain at high frequencies.

For the equivalent transform between the z-domain D(z) and s-domain D(s), the Tustin bilinear transform is used in D(s) as the below:

$$D(z) = D(s)\big|_{tustin} = k_p - \frac{\frac{1}{2} k_p k_i T(z^{-1}+1)}{z^{-1}-1} - \frac{\frac{2k_p k_d}{T}(z^{-1}-1)}{(1-\frac{2k_d}{NT})z^{-1}+(1+\frac{2k_d}{TN})} \tag{8}$$

$$D(z) = k_p - \frac{a_1(z^{-1}+1)}{z^{-1}-1} - \frac{b_1(z^{-1}-1)}{b_2 z^{-1}+1} \tag{9}$$

where

$$a_1 = \frac{1}{2} k_p k_i T \ , \quad b_1 = \frac{2k_p k_d}{T(1+\frac{2k_d}{NT})} \ , \quad b_2 = \frac{1-\frac{2k_d}{NT}}{1+\frac{2k_d}{NT}}$$

$$\frac{Y(z)}{U(z)} = k_p - \frac{a_1(z^{-1}+1)}{z^{-1}-1} - \frac{b_1(z^{-1}-1)}{b_2 z^{-1}+1} \tag{10}$$

$$Y(z) = \eta_1 U(z) + \eta_2 z^{-1} U(z) + \eta_3 z^{-2} U(z) + \alpha_1 z^{-1} Y(z) + \alpha_2 z^{-2} Y(z) \tag{11}$$

where $\eta_1 = a_1 + b_1 + k_p$, $\eta_2 = -k_p + k_p b_2 + a_1 + a_1 b_2 - 2b_1$, $\eta_3 = a_1 b_2 + b_1 - k_p b_2$, $\alpha_1 = 1 - b_2$, $\alpha_2 = b_2$. the factor of z^{-1} in the z-domain implies that the time-domain signal is delayed by one sample interval while the expression z^{-2} indicates a delay of two cycles.

Equation (11) , the z-domain model can be converted into time-based equation as the follow:

$$Y(k) = -\eta_1 U(k) - \eta_2 U(k-1) - \eta_3 U(k-2) + \alpha_1 Y(k-1) + \alpha_2 Y(k-2) \qquad (12)$$

Considering $Y(k) = \Delta w(k)$ and $U(k) = -(\partial E / \partial w)(k)$, equation (12) can be written as:

$$\Delta w(k) = \eta_1 \frac{\partial E}{\partial w}(k) + \alpha_1 \Delta w(k-1) - \eta_2 \frac{\partial E}{\partial w}(k-1) + \alpha_2 \Delta w(k-2) - \eta_3 \frac{\partial E}{\partial w}(k-2) \qquad (13)$$

The first two items on the right side of equation (13) are the weight updating formula with the momentum item of BP algorithm. The 3rd and 4th items are one order delay gradient training component. The last item in the equation (13) is the second order delay gradient training component without momentum item.

The BP algorithm approximates a local minimum of E and always converges when η is chosen to meet the relation $\sup\|Q(w)\| \leq \eta^{-1} < \infty$ in some bounded region where the relation $E(w) \leq E(w_0)$ holds[11]; $Q(w)$ denotes the Hessian matrix of E with respect to the weight vector w, and w_0 denotes the initial weight vector. The behaviour of E in the neighbourhood of a local minimum is determined by the eigensystem of the matrix Q. In the neural network implementation, the storage and computational requirements of the approximated Hessian for FNNs with several hundred weights make its use impractical. Thus, the learning rate is usually chosen according to the relation $0 < \eta < 1$ in such a way that successive steps in weight space do not overshoot the minimum of the error surface [3].

Using this restraining conditions, the training rates in this scheme can be derived. Assuming the sample interval $T=0.01s$ and $k_d=T/2$, if the relation $200 < k_i < 400$ and $k_p < 0.25$ are chosen, the condition mentioned above can be satisfied. It is important that the sample interval T is associated with the choice of training rates so that this algorithm is quite adapted to its application to practical computer based control systems.

If $|\nabla E(w_k)| < \varepsilon$ but $|E(w_k)| > \lambda$ during the search for the optimal error point, where ε and λ are both small positive values that can meet the desired requirement of error accuracy, the weight update would be stopped in the standard BP algorithm. But obviously the desired global minimum can't be obtained. In this case, two possibilities exist, one is that the search is trapped in a local minima; the other is that the search is located on a flat plateau. The adaptive parameter modification unit (APMU) is introduced in the proposed scheme to overcome the drawbacks. According to the current status of $\partial E / \partial w$, E and ΔE , the relevant parameter can be adjusted through the APMU, and thus the weight updating formulas can be adaptive to the search requirements. As interference can be expected when multiple parameters are adjusted simultaneously only the single parameter k_p, which can have a significant effect, is adjusted. To overcome the drawbacks mentioned above and the poor convergence when the desired minimum is in a flat region, a larger value of this proportional parameter is needed, leading to fluctuations so that the search climbs over the local minima and rapidly approaches the desired minimum. The strategy in the APMU is given in equation (14) and (15).

$$\tilde{k}_p = k_p + \Delta k_p \tag{14}$$

$$\Delta k_p = \Delta k_p + \beta_1 (1 - e^{-\beta_2 |E|}) \tag{15}$$

where $\beta_1 < 0.01 k_p$, and $0 < \beta_2 < 1$.

When the $|\nabla E(w_k)| < \varepsilon$ and $|E(w_k)| > \lambda$, equations (14) and (15) are utilized by the APMU control. Once $\Delta E = |E(k)| - |E(k-1)| < 0$ is satisfied for several successive iterations, the process of parameter adjustment is stopped and the original value of k_p is recovered.

3   The Learning Saturation Compensation of BP Algorithm

The derivative of the activation function must be employed in weight update formulas of BP algorithm. If the S function is chosen as the activation function $f(x)$, the factor $(1 - f(x))$ exists in the weight update item. Weight updating will cease when the outputs of hidden and/or output layer nodes trend to unity during the learning process, that is the so-called learning saturation. A new self-tuning anti-saturation strategy is proposed in order to overcome this so that weight updating can continue. Using the S function as the activation function, the output of neutrons must be less than unity even when in learning saturation. If $f(x)^p < f(x)$, $f(x) < 1$ and $p>0$, the self-tuning saturation compensation strategy in weight update formulas is given as follows[13]:

$$p = Int(\frac{1}{1 - f(x)}) \tag{16}$$

$$1 - f(x)^p \tag{17}$$

From equation (16) and (17), it can bee seen that the closer the learning procedure is to saturation, that is the closer $f(x)$ tends to unit, the larger p is and so $f(x)^p$ will not be close to unity. Obviously, the gradient term in this scheme is more effective than that of the conventional BP algorithm during the activation function saturation phases. Therefore, when factor $[1 - f(x)]$ is replaced by the $[1 - f(x)^p]$, learning saturation phenomenon will not occur and learning convergent rate will speed up.

4   Analysis of the Weight Updating Convergent Speed

In the gradient descent search method, the relationship between the two successive step gradients is given as follows [14]:

$$[-\nabla E(w_k)] \cdot [-\nabla E(w_{k-1})] = 0 \tag{18}$$

When the kth and $(k$-$1)$th time searches are carried out, w_k and w_{k-1} are the kth and $(k$-$1)$th step weight vectors. Equation (18) shows that $\nabla E(w_k)$ is always orthogonal to $\nabla E(w_{k-1})$. Obviously, the search path is always tortuous with right angles in the conventional gradient descent technique and as a result the convergent speed is affected. From the equation (12), the relation can be rewritten as below:

$$\Delta w(k) = -\eta \frac{\partial \tilde{E}}{\partial w}(k) + \alpha_1 \Delta w(k-1) + \alpha_2 \Delta w(k-2) \tag{19}$$

Where

$$\eta \frac{\partial \tilde{E}}{\partial w} = \eta_1 \frac{\partial E}{\partial w}(k) + \eta_2 \frac{\partial E}{\partial w}(k-1) + \eta_3 \frac{\partial E}{\partial w}(k-2) \tag{20}$$

In equation (20), the $\eta(\partial E/\partial w)$ term can be considered as the compound effects of the $\eta_1(\partial E/\partial w)(k)$, $\eta_2(\partial E/\partial w)(k-1)$ and $\eta_3(\partial E/\partial w)(k-2)$ three successive gradient vectors, and the $\eta(\partial E/\partial w)$ can be called a compound gradient vector. Considering the relationship between the successive step gradients, the compound gradient vector in the presented scheme is given in Fig.2.

Since the orthogonal directions between each successive step gradients, the gradient vectors $\eta_1(\partial E/\partial w)(k)$ and $\eta_2(\partial E/\partial w)(k-1)$, and vectors $\eta_2(\partial E/\partial w)(k-1)$ and $\eta_3(\partial E/\partial w)(k-2)$ respectively are vertical to each other.

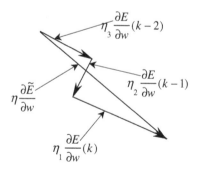

Fig. 2. Diagram of compound gradient vector

The Fig. 2 shows that, because the compound gradient $\eta \partial \tilde{E}/\partial w$ is composed of the three vectors and the known information $(\partial E/\partial w)(k-1)$, $(\partial E/\partial w)(k-2)$ using this in the update weight processes will result in the descent speed using the compound gradient of the improved algorithm normally being faster than the standard BP algorithm. Therefore the training convergence rate in the scheme could outperform that of standard BP algorithm.

5 Simulation Results

Comparisons of proposed new neural networks online training algorithm and standard BP algorithm are obtained by simulation. The simulation model of the plant is given as follow:

$$y_k = 1.9979 y_{k-1} - 0.998 y_{k-2} + 0.502 u_k + 0.0005 u_{k-1} - 0.0487 u_{k-2} \qquad (21)$$

In this model there are two poles at (-0.1001+i0.9955, -0.1001-i0.9955). When the plant model parameter 1.9979 is changed to 1.98, the poles of the controlled plant are changed from (-0.1001+i0.9955, -0.1001-i0.9955) to (-0.1001+i13.4347, -0.1001-i13.4347). Under the variations of parameter from 50th iteration to 150th iteration, the simulations with improved online training algorithm based on compound gradient vector and standard BP algorithm are given in Fig.3–Fig.10 respectively. Due to the large range changes of plant pole positions, the learning of the standard BP algorithm is not yet complete until 150th iteration about 100 time iterations lasted, which can be seen in Fig.3 and Fig.4. The learning rate utilized in the simulation is as $\eta = 0.8$. The online learning procedure of improved neural networks algorithm is shown in Fig. 5 and Fig. 6. The contrast of improved neural networks online training algorithm and standard BP algorithm, the convergent speed of improved neural networks online learning algorithm is much faster than standard BP algorithm, and the learning procedure can be finished only lasting about 50 time iterations using improved neural networks online learning algorithm with compound gradient vector.

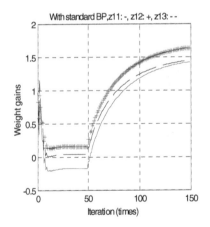

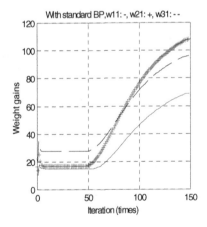

Fig. 3. Some output layer weight learning processes with standard BP algorithm

Fig. 4. Some hidden layer weight learning processes with standard BP algorithm

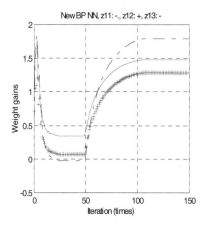

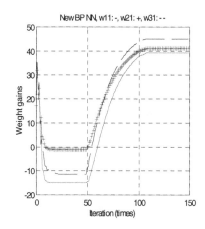

Fig. 5. Some output layer weight learning processes with compound gradient vector algorithm

Fig. 6. Some hidden layer weight learning processes with compound gradient vector algorithm

The outputs and the errors of systems with improved neural networks online learning algorithm and standard BP algorithm are shown in Fig.7, Fig.8, Fig.9 and Fig.10 respectively. From these simulation results, it can be seen that very good dynamic behaviours are obtained by utilizing presented algorithm under the variations of parameter. The system simulations with square wave command signal are given in Fig. 11 and Fig.12, in which an ideal convergent behaviour is also obtained. The parameters utilized in the compound gradient vector algorithm are as T=0.01, K_i=300, K_d =0.005, initial value of K_p=0.2, β_1 =0.01K_p, β_2 =0.6. Thus, the initial values of learning rate and momentum item in the simulations [15] are η_1 =0.6818, η_2 =0.2, η_3 =0.3, α_1 =0.01 and α_2 =0.0198 respectively.

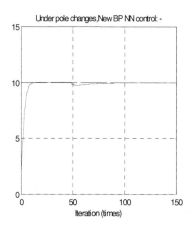

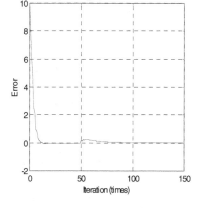

Fig. 7. The system response with compound gradient vector algorithm under pole changes

Fig. 8. The system error with compound gradient vector algorithm under pole changes

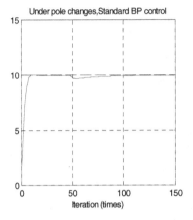

Fig. 9. The system response with standard BP

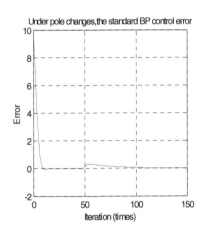

Fig. 10. The system error with standard BP algorithm under pole changes

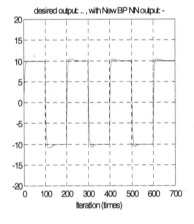

Fig. 11. The system simulation with compound gradient vector algorithm under square wave command signal

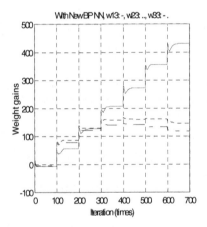

Fig. 12. Some hidden layer weight learning processes with compound gradient vector algorithm

6 Conclusion

In this paper, a new neural network online training scheme that uses a compound gradient vector and saturation compensation has been proposed. Based on the orthogonal relationship between successive gradient search vectors, a convergent analysis of the presented algorithm has been carried out and the results indicate that the convergent speed of presented algorithm is considerable faster than that of the standard BP algorithm. In addition, because the sample interval is considered in the algorithm, this scheme is quite well adapted to applications in computer based practical control systems. Various simulation results have been given and the strong robustness and ideal convergent performance obtained using the improved neural networks algorithm for real time control with uncertainty parameter system.

Acknowledgements. The authors acknowledge with thanks the financial support by China Scholarship Council, Tianjin Natural Science Foundation under Grant 003800811, Tianjin Education Committee Key Discipline Grant and Tianjin University of Technology. The authors also wish to acknowledge contributions made to this paper by Professor Tim Hendtlass, the Director of the Centre for Intelligent Systems and Complex Processes, Swinburne University of Technology. The authors would also like to thank the anonymous reviewers for their helpful comments.

References

1. Kuan Chung-Ming, Hornik Kurt: Convergence of Learning Algorithms with Constant Learning Rates. IEEE Transactions on Neural Networks, vol.2 (5, 1991) 484–489
2. Ngolediage J.E., Naguib R.N.G, Dlay S.S.: Fast Back-Propagation for Supervised Learning. Proceedings of 1993 Internatioanl Joint Conference on Neural Networks, (1993) 2591–2594
3. Maugoulas G.D., Vrahatis M.N., Androulakis G.S.: Effective Backpropagation Training with variable stepsize, Neural Networks, (1,1997) 69–82
4. Van der Smagt P.P.: Minimisation methods for Training Feedforward Neural networks, Neural Networks, (1, 1994) 1–11
5. Van Ooyen A., Nienhuis B.: Improving the convergence of the Back-Propagation Algorithm, Neural Networks, (3,1992) 465–471
6. Zhou G. Si J.: Advanced Neural Networks Training Algorithm with Reduced Complexity based on Jacobian Deficiency, IEEE Transactions on Neural Networks, (3,1998) 448–453
7. Hagan M.T., Menhaj M.B.: Training feedforward Neural Networks with the Marquardt Algorithm, IEEE Transactions on Neural Networks, (6, 1994) 989–993
8. Samad T.: Backpropagation Improvements based Heuristic Arguments, Proceedings of International joint Conference on Neural Networks, (1990) 565–568
9. Bello M. G.: Enhanced Training Algorithms, and Integrated Training/Architecture Selection for Multilayer Perceptron Networks, IEEE Transactions on Neural networks, (6,1992) 864–875
10. Shah S. Palmieri F.: MEKA-A Fast, Local Algorithm for Training Feedforward Neural Networks, Proceedings of international Joint Conference on neural Networks, (1990) 41–46
11. Parisi R., Di Claudio E. D., Orlandi G., Rao B. D.: A generalized Learning Paradigm Exploiting the Structure of Feedforward Neural Networks, IEEE Transactions on Neural networks, (6,1996) 1450–1459
12. Wilamowski Bogdan M.,Iqlikci Serdar, Kaynak Okyay, Onder Efe M.: An Algorithm for Fast Convergence in Training Neural Networks, IEEE Proceedings of International
13. Joint Conference on Neural Networks, (2001) 1778–1782

384   Z. Chen et al.

14. Zaiping Chen, Jun LI, Hui Zhao, Qiang Gao, Youjun Yue, Zhenlin Xu: Online Training of Neural Network Control for Electric Motor Drives. The Proceedings of IEEE Conference on Systems, Man and Cybernetics (to be published) 2002
15. Xu Lina: Neural Networks Control. Harbin Industrial University Press, Harbin (1999) 123–124
16. Chen Zaiping, Du Taihang, Gao Qiang, Li Lianbing, Liu Zuojun: Control System Simulations and CAD. Tianjin University Press, Tianjin(2001)

Applications of Wavelet Transform and Artificial Neural Networks to Pattern Recognition for Environmental Monitoring

Cheol-Ki Kim and Eui-Young Cha

Dept. of Computer Science, Pusan National University, Korea
{kck, eycha}@harmony.cs.pusan.ac.kr

Abstract. In this paper, using an automatic tracking system, behavior of an aquatic insect, *Chironomus sp.*(Chironomidae), was observed in semi-natural conditions in response to sub-lethal treatment of a carbamate insecticide, carbofuran. The fourth instar larvae were placed in an observation cage ($6cm \times 7cm \times 2.5cm$) at temperature of $18°C$ and the light condition of 10(light): 14(dark). The tracking system was devised to detect the instant, partial movement of the insect body. Individual movement was traced after the treatment of carbofuran ($0.1mg/l$) for four days (2 days : before treatment, 2 days: after treatment). Along with the other irregular behaviors, "ventilation activity", appearing as a shape of "compressed zig-zag", was more frequently observed after the treatment of the insecticide. The activity of the test individuals was also generally depressed after the chemical treatment. The Wavelet analysis was implemented on the data of the locomotive tracks, and the method was effective for characterizing the response behavior patterns of the organisms treated with the insecticide. This computational patterning could be an alternative tool for automatically detecting presence of insecticides in environment.

1   Introduction

The artificial neural networks have been widely applied in interpreting complex and nonlinear phenomena in machine intelligence in computer and electronics engineering [1][2]. In ecology-related fields, artificial neural networks have been implemented in data organization and classification of groups[3][4], patterning complex relationships between variables[5] – [7], and predicting population development[8]–[11]. However, not many researches have been conducted on implementation of artificial neural networks to behavioral monitoring.

Wavelet analysis and its applications have become one of the fastest growing research areas in recent years. This is in part attributed to the pioneering work by the researchers as well as practitioners in the fields of mathematics and signal processing. Wavelet theory has been employed in many fields and applications, such as signal and image

R.I. McKay and J. Slaney (Eds.): AI 2002, LNAI 2557, pp. 385–394, 2002.

processing, communication systems, biomedical imaging, radar, air acoustics, theoretical mathematics, control system, and endless other areas. However, the research on applying the wavelets to ecological analysis is still too weak. This paper focuses on this challenging research topic.

Recently, behavioral responses to sub-lethal doses of toxic chemicals have drawn attention as for developing an *in situ* bio-monitoring tool for detecting toxic chemicals in environment. Behavioral responses have been reported to be sensitive to sub-lethal exposures to various chemical pollutants[12][13]. [12] indicated that a behavioral bioassay could be more sensitive than other types of testing. In recent years, researches on the effects of sub-lethal levels of toxic substances have been rapidly accumulating for various taxa including crustaceans fish and insects. However, these studies are mostly based on observation of single or combinations of single behaviors with qualitative descriptions. Not many quantitative researches have been conducted on behavioral changes in spatial and temporal domain in response to treatments of toxic chemicals. Detailed, continuous observations of the movement tracks of small size animals have been separately initiated in the field of search behavior in chemical ecology[14][15]. In this study, we utilized the feasibility of wavelet and artificial neural networks in classification of the movement data and attempted to elucidate spatial and temporal patterning of the movement tracks with less contraction of information in feature extraction.

2   Materials and Methods

2.1   Behavioral Data

The specimens of *Chironomus flaviplumus* were collected from an urbanized stream in the Suyong river, Pusan, Korea. The stock populations were maintained in a plastic container under the light regime of LL10:DD14 at a temperature of $18\,°C\,(\pm2)$. Cabofuran was applied at the concentration of 0.1 *mg/l* directly into an aquarium in *Chironomus flaviplumus* resided. During the observational period, individual *Chironomus flaviplumus* were placed in a glass aquarium, and their vertical position was observed at 0.25 second intervals using a CCD camera (Kukjae Electronics Co. Ltd.; IVC-841®) for four days (2 days before the treatment and 2 days after the treatment). The analog data captured by the camera were digitized by using a video overlay board (Dooin Electronics Co., Ltd.; OSCARIII®), and sent to the image recognition system to locate the target organism in spatial and time domain. The software for recognition of the test individual through image processing and other mathematical analyses were conducted in our laboratory. Then center of partial body movement was detected and its two-dimensional location of was automatically recorded.

2.2 Artificial Neural Network

The artificial neural networks have been widely applied in interpreting complex and nonlinear phenomena in machine intelligence in computer and electronics engineering [1][2]. In ecology-related fields, artificial neural networks have been implemented in data organization and classification of groups, patterning complex relationships between variables, and predicting population development[8]-[11]. However, not many researches have been conducted on implementation of artificial neural networks to behavioral monitoring.

The multi-layer perceptron network with the back-propagation algorithm was used for training input and output pair in a supervised manner (Fig. 1). Training proceeds on an iterative gradient algorithm designed to minimize the mean square error between the actual output and the desired output or the target value. After parameters charactering the movement track were selected through wavelet transform, they were trained by artificial neural networks.

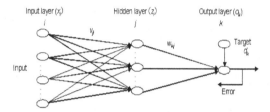

Fig. 1. The multilayer perceptron network with the back-propagation algorithm

The net input to neuron j of the hidden layer for pattern p ($NET_{p,j}$) is calculated as the summation of each input layer output ($x_{p,i}$; input value of parameter) multiplied by weight ($v_{p,ji}$). An activation function (logistic function in this case) is applied to calculate the output of neuron j of the hidden layer ($z_{p,j}$) and the output of neuron k of the output layer ($o_{p,k}$):

$$f(NET) = \frac{1}{1+\exp(-\lambda NET)} \tag{1}$$

where λ is the activation function coefficient. NET is expressed either in $z_{p,j}$ or $o_{p,k}$ as follows:

$$z_{p,j} = f(\sum_i x_{p,i} v_{p,ji}) \tag{2}$$

$$o_{p,k} = f(\sum_j z_{p,j} w_{p,kj}) \tag{3}$$

where $v_{p,ji}$ and $w_{p,kj}$ are the weight of the connection between neuron i of the input layer and neuron j of the hidden layer, and of that between neuron j of the hidden layer and neuron k of the output layer for pattern p, respectively.

The back-propagation algorithm adjusts the connection intensities (weights ($v_{p,ji}$, $w_{p,kj}$)) of the network in a way that minimizes the error. The sum of the errors in each neuron for pattern p, Err_p, is calculated as follows:

$$Err_p = \frac{1}{2}\sum_k (d_{p,k} - o_{p,k})^2 \tag{4}$$

where $d_{p,k}$ is the target value corresponding to pattern p at the neuron k. The value of activation function coefficients, λ, used in this study was 1.0, and the learning coefficient, which updates the weights in iterative calculation, was set to 0.01. The level of error tolerance was 1.0, and the threshold for determining the binary level for the activation function was 0.5. Network pruning was not required during the training process in this study.

2.3 Movement Patterns Used for Training

Through preparatory experiments the movement tracks in 60 seconds was investigated in this study. For simplicity of training, we selected two most frequently observed patterns. Pattern A generally represented the active movement spanning a wider area of the observation cage. The specimen fully used its whole body, and swam actively in a linear phase, while briefly twitching to propel its advancement. In contrast, pattern B showed a higher degree of shaking with curve-linear movements. In the preparatory experiments, pattern A was observed with a relatively low frequency after the treatments, while pattern B increased after the treatments.

Based on experience on behavior of *Chironomus flaviplumus* and suggestions in previous studies on the movement tracks [15],[16], the following parameters were selected in 60 seconds duration as input for the wavelet analysis: number of backward movements, stop duration (total time of stops; *sec*), meander (total abstract angle changes divided by the total path length; *radian/mm*), angle acceleration (*radian/sec²*) and maximum distance along short term segment (*mm*). The maximum distance was calculated as the maximum distance of five segments per window.

In total 10 specimens were observed. Considering individual variations in the movement patterns, we selected 7 individuals with similar movement patterns. Four specimens were chosen for training, while the data sets for the rest three specimens were used for evaluation. Twenty-one observations in one-minute duration were selected for each pattern A and B, and the five parameters mentioned above were measured separately for input data to the network (5 nodes in the input layer), while binary information either for pattern A or pattern B, was used for the matching output (1 node in the output layer). Four nodes were assigned to a single hidden layer.

It has been shown in preparatory experiments that sixty seconds sequence was usually suitable for characterizing the track's pattern for training with the artificial neural network. For simplicity of the modeling, we selected two typical pattern most frequently observed during the observation period. Pattern A (Fig. 2(a)) represent an active movement generally spanning a wider area over 50% of the observation cage. The specimen fully used its whole body swam actively in a linear phase. Pattern B (Fig. 2(b)) was in contrast with Pattern A in many aspects. The movements were in circular patterns, and showed a higher degree of shaking with the partial body movement. In the preparatory experiments, pattern A was observed with a relatively low frequency after treatments of carbofuran, while the frequency of pattern B increased.

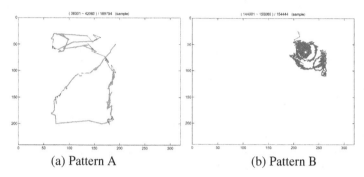

(a) Pattern A   (b) Pattern B

Fig. 2. Example of the movement tracks of *Chironomus flaviplumus*.

2.4 Training and Recognition Procedure

Fig.3, 4 shows flow-charts for implementing wavelets and artificial neural networks for pattern recognition of the movement tracks. From training (or evaluation) data, parameters mentioned above were obtained, and were subsequently given to the wavelet transform (DWT) with basic function of Daubechies'4. The Approximation coefficients at level 3 were extracted, and feature coefficients were selected to the provided as input to artificial neural networks. Multi-layer perceptron was used in this study. While the approximation coefficients were given as input to the network, the corresponding patterns were given as output in a binary format. Evaluation data were newly selected, and feature coefficients of the parameters were similarly obtained through wavelet transform. The newly obtained coefficients were in turn recognized by the trained artificial neural networks.

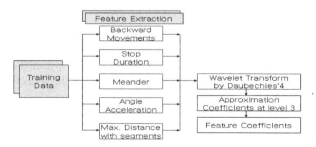

Fig. 3. Flow-chart of feature extraction using wavelet transform and artificial neural network.

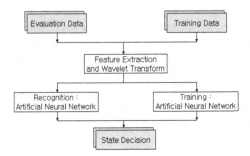

Fig. 4. Overall system flow-chart using wavelet transform and artificial neural network..

2.5 Wavelet Transform

The Wavelet Transform (Daubechies, 1988) retains the location information. There-fore, this method is used in several disciplines, like image processing, geophysics, medicine and so forth. One of the first applications in ecology can be found in [17]. The first wavelet supported model analysis was proposed by [18].

The Wavelet Transform (WT), more particularly the Discrete Wavelet Transform (DWT), has been recently implemented as a computationally efficient technique for extracting information about non-stationary signals. While, Fourier analysis is a method to find frequency characteristics of a signal over the whole period of observa-tion, the Short Time Fourier Transform (STFT) is an attempt to introduce temporal aspects to the signal analysis. Wavelet analysis is another way to discover temporal characteristics of the signal similar to STFT. The wavelet Transform has been devel-oped as an alternative to the STFT to overcome problems related to its frequency and time resolution properties[19]. The DWT provides selective resolution with different types of basic functions. The power of wavelets is their ability to increase the resolu-tion through scaling. By controlling scaling and shifting the signal can be examined at different resolutions, an ability called multi-resolution.

The DWT is defined by the following equation:

$$W(j,k) = \sum_j \sum_k x(k) 2^{-j/2} \Psi(2^{-j} n - k) \qquad (5)$$

where $\Psi(t)$ is a time function with finite energy and fast decay called the mother wavelet. The DWT analysis can be performed using a fast, pyramidal algorithm re-lated to multi-rate filter banks[20]. In our paper, we used the 4 coefficient wavelet family (Daubechies' 4) for transformation.

3 Results

The input data were effectively trained and the training rates appeared to be over 98%. New evaluation data sets for three specimens were sequentially given to the trained network as mentioned previously, and the network was capable of recognizing patterns A and B effectively. Fig. 5 shows the changes in representative behavioral patterns after the treatments of an insecticide.

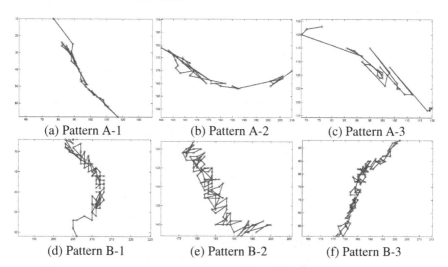

(a) Pattern A-1   (b) Pattern A-2   (c) Pattern A-3

(d) Pattern B-1   (e) Pattern B-2   (f) Pattern B-3

Fig. 5. The changes in representative behavioral patterns before and after the treatments of an insecticide.

Table 1. Comparison of recognition rates (percents) by the trained artificial neural networks for Pattern A and B in the movement tracks of *chironomids* treated with carbofuran.

Specimens	Specimen 1		Specimen 2		Specimen 3	
Patterns	A	B	A	B	A	B
Before Treatment	Mean	74.50	10.59	70.71	11.09	74.44	12.11
	SD	8.08	6.67	10.63	9.25	14.54	9.31
After Treatment	Mean	55.67	31.01	64.20	22.20	68.83	22.83
	SD	5.52	8.34	12.60	13.40	10.53	7.47

Table 1 show results of average detection rates (percents) before and after the treatments of insecticides. The values shown in the table were obtained as follows: The number of detecting pattern A or pattern B in each one-minute data segment was counted through a period of 6060 seconds (approximately 100 minutes), and the total count was expressed in percents relative to the total number of one minute observations in the period of 6060 seconds. The overlapping of one-minute window was 30 seconds. The recognition rate for the pattern ranged 70.7~74.5% before the treatment, and corresponding by decreased to 55.7~68.8% after the treatment for all the observed specimens. In contrast, the recognition rate of pattern B was low in 11.0~12.1% before the treatments; however increased consistently and distinctively to 22.2~31.0% for all the specimens after the treatment.

As mentioned before, patterns A and B were both detected in the movement tracks before and after the treatments of insecticides. This is understandable that, by considering the treatment dose is in the sub-lethal range, pattern A may also occur after the treatment if the treated specimens recover to pattern A state briefly. Appearance of the two patterns, however, changed greatly after the carbofuran treatment. Pattern A decreased significantly while pattern B correspondingly increased in a great degree after the treatment of the insecticide.

Fig. 6 shows an example of detecting changés in movement patterns in 100 minute units during the whole observation period. Initially Pattern A was abundant, however, the pattern distinctively decreased after treatments of carbofuran (Fig. 6). The reverse situation occurred with the corresponding increase in Pattern B after the treatment. Recognition of patterns A and B could be conducted even in a fine time-scale. Since one-minute data were used for training, recognition is also possible in one-minute units. Before the treatment of carbofuran, a large number of data were recognized as pattern A(symbol : ×), and in the phase of the treatment, recognition rates of pattern B(symbol : •) were increased (Fig.7). This indicated that the network and wavelet transform could be useful for detecting the response behavior on the real time basis.

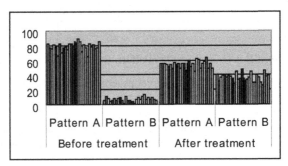

Fig. 6. Comparison of frequency before and after treatments of an insecticide.

4   Conclusion

This study demonstrated that behavioral differences of animals in response to an insecticide could be successfully detected by the trained artificial neural network. A difficulty of conducting this type of monitoring research is the necessity of handling a large amount of data. For each individual every one-minute segment was observed continuously for four days. Besides time consumption of classification, objectivity in judgments for classification is another problem. In this regard the pattern recognition by artificial neural network could be an alternative for detection the movement tracks of animals exposed to toxic chemicals in environment.

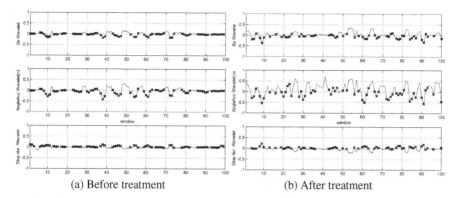

(a) Before treatment   (b) After treatment

Fig. 7. Comparison of wavelet coefficient's recognition result before and after treatments of an insecticide.

The carbofuran, an organophosphate, shows a high toxicity to organisms, especially *Chironomus flaviplumus* and aquatic invertebrates although it has relatively low toxic effects on mammals and humans.

Pattern A and B were observed at the same time before and after the treatment as mentioned before (Table 1), and this suggested that behaviors resulting from the sub-lethal treatments are not deterministic. The occurrence of behaviors appears to be probabilistic depending upon the specimens's internal and external conditions. These stochastic occurrences of patterns are effectively revealed by continuous recognition by the trained artificial neural network. However, the occurrence of Pattern A and B in the same period may also suggest that the parameters may not be effectively selected to specifically separate Pattern A or B before and after the treatments of carbofuran. The trained artificial neural network could be useful for detecting presence of toxic chemicals in environment as for an *in-situ* behavioral monitoring tool and Wavelet transform is shown that it has good time analysis ability. Further study on improving feature extraction of the movement data are needed in the future.

References

1. Zurada, J.M., 1992. Introduction to Artificial Neural Systems. West Publishing Company, New York.
2. Lippmann, R.P., 1987. An Introduction to Computing with Neural Nets. IEEE ASSP Magazine, April. pp. 4–22.
3. Chon, T.-S., Park, Y.S., Moon, K.H., Cha, E.Y., 1996. Patternizing communities by using an artificial neural network. *Journal of Ecological Modeling,* vol. 90, 69–78.
4. Levine, E.R., Kimes, D.S., Sigillito, V.G., 1996. Classifying soil structure using neural networks. *Journal of Ecological Modelling*, vol. 92(1), 101–108.
5. Lek, S., Delacoste, M., Baran, P., Dimopoulos, I., Lauga, J., Aulagnier, S., 1996. Application of Neural Networks to Modelling Nonlinear Relationships in Ecology. *Journal of Ecological Modelling*, vol. 90, 39–52.

6. Huntingford, C., Cox, P.M., 1996. Use of statistical and neural network techniques to detect how stomatal conductance responds to changes in the local environment. *Journal of Ecological Modelling*, vol. 97, 217–246.
7. Tuma, A., Haasis, H.-D., Rentz, O., 1996. A comparison of fuzzy expert systems, neural networks and neuro-fuzzy approaches controlling energy and material flows. *Journal of Ecological Modelling*, vol. 85, 93–98.
8. Elizondo, D.A., McClendon, R.W., Hoongenboom, G., 1994. Neural network models for predicting flowering and physiological maturity of soybean. *Transactions of the ASAE* 37(3), 981–988.
9. Recknagel, F., French, M., Harkonen, P., Yabunaka, K.-I., 1997. Artificial neural network approach for modelling and prediction of algal blooms. *Journal of Ecological Modelling*, vol. 96, 11–28.
10. Stankovski, V., Debeljak, M., Bratko, I., Adamic, M., 1998. Modelling the population dynamics of red deer (Cervus elaphus L.) with regard to forest development. *Journal of Ecological Modelling*, vol. 108, 143–153.
11. Tan, S.S., Smeins, F.E., 1996. Predicting grassland community changes with an artificial neural network model. *Journal of Ecological Modelling*, vol. 84, 91–97.
12. Dutta, H., Marcelino, J., Richmonds, Ch., 1992. Brain acetylcholinesterase activity and optomotor behavior in bluegills, Lepomis macrochirus exposed to different concentrations of carbofuran. Arch. Intern. Physiol. Biochim. Biophys. 100(5), 331–334.
13. Lemly, A.D., Smith, R.J., 1986. A behavioral assay for assessing effects of pollutants of fish chemoreception. *Ecotoxicology and Environmental Safety* 11(2), 210–218.
14. Bell, W.J., Tobin, R.T., 1981. Orientation to sex pheromone in the American cockroach: analysis of chemo-orientation mechanisms. *Journal of Insect Physiology* 27, 501–508.
15. Collins, R.D., Gargesh, R.N., Maltby, A.D., Roggero, R.J., Tourtellot, M.K., Bell, W.J., 1994. Innate control of local search behaviour in the house fly, Musca domestica. Physiological Entomology 19, 165–172.
16. Schal, C., Tobin, T.R., Surber, J.L., Vogel, G., Tourtellot, M.K., Leban, R.A., Sizemore, R., Bell, W.J., 1983. Search strategy of sex pheromone-stimulated male German cockroaches. *Journal of Insect Physiology* 29, 575–579
17. Gao, W & Li, B. L., Wavelet analysis of coherent structures at the atmosphere-forest interface, *Journal of Applied Meteorol*, 1993, 32, 1717–1725.
18. Thomas Clemen, The use of scale information for integrating simulation models into environmental information systems, *Journal of Ecological Modeling*, vol. 108, pp.107–113, 1998.
19. C. Sidney Burrus, Ramesh A. Gopinath, Haitao Guo, Introduction to Wavelets and Wavelet Transforms, Prentice-Hall.
20. Esa Rinta-Runsala, Drive System Monitoring; Requirements and Suggestions, Research Report, 2000.

Adapting Kernels by Variational Approach in SVM

Junbin Gao[1]⋆, Steve Gunn[2], and Jaz Kandola[3]

[1] School of Mathematics, Statistics and Computer Sciences
University of New England, Armidale, NSW 2351, Australia
jbgao@mcs.une.edu.au
[2] ISIS Group, Department of Electronics and Computer Science
University of Southampton, Southampton SO17 1BJ, UK
srg@ecs.soton.ac.uk
[3] Department of Computer Science
Royal Holloway, University of London, Egham, Surray TW20 0EX, UK
jaz@cs.rhul.ac.uk

Abstract. This paper proposed a variational Bayesian approach for the SVM regression based on the likelihood model of an infinite mixture of Gaussians. To evaluate this approach the method was applied to synthetic datasets. We compared this new approximation approach with the standard SVM algorithm as well as other well established methods such as Gaussian Process.

1 Introduction

Learning from data consists of developing a model, $\mathcal{M}$, with a particular parameterisation or function space, which best explains a set of N data-points, $\mathcal{D}$. In the case of a "learning" problem, this data consists of a set of inputs $\{\boldsymbol{x}_1, \boldsymbol{x}_2, \dots, \boldsymbol{x}_N\} \in \mathbb{R}^N$ and a set of targets $\{t_1, t_2, \dots, t_N\} \in \mathbb{R}$ which are assumed to have come from some underlying data generating distribution $y(\boldsymbol{x})$. Learning therefore consists of determining the parameters of the model through an optimisation process based on an information theoretic criteria such as the likelihood (probabilistic framework) or the functional criteria (regularization theory etc). Standard regularization theory formulates the "learning" problem as a functional variational problem of finding the function $y(\boldsymbol{x})$ that minimises a regularized empirical risk functional of the form

$$R_{\mathrm{emp}}[y(\boldsymbol{x})] = \sum_{i=1}^{N} L(t_i, y(\boldsymbol{x}_i)) + \frac{\lambda}{2}\|y(\boldsymbol{x})\|_K^2 \tag{1}$$

where $L(\cdot, \cdot)$ is a loss function and $\|\cdot\|$ is a norm in a Reproducing Kernel Hilbert Space $\mathcal{H}$ with a kernel K, see [19],[2],[14]. The solution to equation (1) has the following representation

---

⋆ Author to whom all the correspondences should be addressed.

R.I. McKay and J. Slaney (Eds.): AI 2002, LNAI 2557, pp. 395–406, 2002.
© Springer-Verlag Berlin Heidelberg 2002

$$y(\boldsymbol{x}) = \sum_{i=1}^{N} w_i K(\boldsymbol{x}, \boldsymbol{x}_i) + w_0 \qquad (2)$$

where w_0 can be assumed to be zero, for explanation, see [2].

It is well known that a variational principle of the type of equation (1) can be derived not only in the context of functional analysis [17], but also in a probabilistic framework [19],[5],[2],[16], [4] etc. Let $\mathcal{D}$ be the training dataset as defined above, and define $P[y(\boldsymbol{x})|\lambda] \propto \exp\{-\frac{\lambda}{2}\|y(\cdot)\|_K^2\}$ as the prior probability of the random field $y(\boldsymbol{x})$ and $P[\mathcal{D}|y(\cdot)] \propto \exp\{-C\sum_{i=1}^{N} L(t_i, y(\boldsymbol{x}_i))\}$ as the the conditional probability of the data given the field $y(\boldsymbol{x})$. i.e., the likelihood. Then the posterior distribution $P[y(\boldsymbol{x})|\mathcal{D}]$ can now be computed by using Bayes' rule as:

$$P[y(\boldsymbol{x})|\mathcal{D}, \lambda] = \frac{P[\mathcal{D}|y(\boldsymbol{x})]P[y(\boldsymbol{x})|\lambda]}{P[\mathcal{D}|\lambda]} \propto \exp\{-\sum_{i=1}^{N} L(t_i, y(\boldsymbol{x}_i)) - \frac{\lambda}{2}\|y(\cdot)\|_K^2\} \quad (3)$$

Hence the Maximum A Posterior (MAP) estimate of the probability distribution (3), which maximizes the a posterior probability $P[y(\boldsymbol{x})|\mathcal{D}]$, is also the minimiser of the functional (1). The MAP estimate depends on the knowledge of λ and variance of target σ_t^2.

The above framework is general enough to cover both the Gaussian Processes and the Support Vector Machines as well as classification [18], [2], i.e.,

- Standard (L_2) Regularisation Networks: $L(t, y(\boldsymbol{x})) = \frac{1}{2\sigma^2}(t - y(\boldsymbol{x}))^2$;
- Support Vector Machines Regression (SVR): $L(t, y(\boldsymbol{x})) = |t - y(\boldsymbol{x})|_\epsilon$;
- Support Vector Machines Classification (SVC): $L(t, y(\boldsymbol{x})) = \theta(1 - ty(\boldsymbol{x}))(1 - ty(\boldsymbol{x}))$
- The hard margin loss function: $L(t, y(\boldsymbol{x})) = \theta(1 - ty(\boldsymbol{x}))$;
- The misclassification loss function: $L(t, y(\boldsymbol{x})) = \theta(-ty(\boldsymbol{x}))$.

where $|\cdot|_\epsilon$ is Vapnik's ϵ-insensitive loss function, see[18], and $\theta(\cdot)$ is the Heaviside function defined as $\theta(u) = 0$ if $u \le 0$ and $\theta(u) = 1$ if $u > 0$.

The probabilistic interpretation enables Bayesian methods to be employed to determine regularisation parameters such as λ and the hyperparameters of kernel K in the framework (1) and (2). Bayesian methods have a number of virtues, particularly their uniform treatment of uncertainty at all levels of the modelling process. Recently, there has been a great deal of interests in non-parametric Bayesian approaches to regression and classification which are based on the concept of Gaussian processes [10], [20], [21], [23], [11], [22]. These ideas provide the possibility of a probabilistic interpretation and implementation of the regression and classification problems.

In this paper we first briefly review the general likelihood principle in regression learning problems and derive in more depth the variational Bayesian learning from a variational perspective based on the assumption on the likelihood of an infinite mixture of Gaussians. Then as an example we discuss the variational learning method for the SVR. Finally in section 4 we apply the approach to a synthetic dataset and compare the our approximation with the standard SVM algorithm as well as other well established methods such as Gaussian Process [21].

2 Variational Approach for the General Likelihood

2.1 The Foundation of Variational Approach

When using Bayesian theory to deal with the regression, see (3), the main difficulty is to find the normalisation constant,

$$P[\mathcal{D}|\lambda] = \frac{1}{Z^*} \int \exp\{-\sum_{i=1}^{N} L(t_i, y(\boldsymbol{x}_i)) - \frac{\lambda}{2}\|y(\cdot)\|_K^2\} dy(\boldsymbol{x})$$

$$= \frac{1}{Z^*} \int \exp\{-\sum_{i=1}^{N} L(t_i, y(\boldsymbol{x}_i)) - \frac{\lambda}{2}\boldsymbol{y}(\boldsymbol{x})^T K^{-1}\boldsymbol{y}(\boldsymbol{x})\} dy(\boldsymbol{x}) \qquad (4)$$

where $\boldsymbol{y}(\boldsymbol{x}) = [y(\boldsymbol{x}_1), \ldots, y(\boldsymbol{x}_N)]^T$ and $K = [K(\boldsymbol{x}_i, \boldsymbol{x}_j)]$ is kernel matrix. The last equality can be proven by Wahba's representer theorem [19], [14]. That is, the prior for $y(\cdot)$ can be specified by a Gaussian process:

$$P[y(\cdot)|\lambda] = P[\boldsymbol{y}(\boldsymbol{x})|\lambda] = \frac{\lambda^{N/2}}{(2\pi)^{N/2}\sqrt{|K|}} \exp\{-\frac{\lambda}{2}\boldsymbol{y}(\boldsymbol{x})^T K^{-1}\boldsymbol{y}(\boldsymbol{x})\} \qquad (5)$$

$P[\mathcal{D}|\lambda]$ is usually called the evidence of the dataset or a partition function in statistical physics. Evaluation of the evidence usually involves approximating these high dimensional integrals.

A number of approximations have been suggested, most notably Laplace approximation (local Gaussian approximation around a MAP of parameter), and integration by sampling, e.g., Markov Chain Monte Carlo (MCMC). The approach we consider in this paper is that of variational learning. The basic idea is to simultaneously approximate the distribution over both hidden states and parameters with a simpler distribution, usually by assuming that the hidden states and parameters are independent. Recently Bayesian variational method has been applied to many generative modelling problems such as the neural networks [7], non-Gaussian autoregressive models [12], Principle Component Analysis (PCA) [1] and Independent Component Analysis (ICA) [9].

In order to introduce the variational learning method, the following notation is used : $\boldsymbol{Y}$ the model hidden variables, e.g., the function process variable $y(\boldsymbol{x}_i)$ in the (3); Θ the hidden variables of some hyperparameters and θ the hyperparameters. Maximising the likelihood as a function of θ is equivalent to maximising the log likelihood:

$$\mathcal{L}(\theta) = \log P[\mathcal{D}|\theta] = \log \int_{\boldsymbol{Y}} \int_{\Theta} P[\mathcal{D}, \boldsymbol{Y}, \Theta|\theta] d\boldsymbol{Y} d\Theta$$

Using any distribution $Q[\boldsymbol{Y}, \Theta]$, called variational distribution, over the hidden variables, we can obtain a lower bound on $\mathcal{L}$:

$$
\log \int_{\boldsymbol{Y}} \int_{\Theta} P[\mathcal{D}, \boldsymbol{Y}, \Theta|\theta] d\boldsymbol{Y} d\Theta \geq \int_{\boldsymbol{Y}} \int_{\Theta} Q[\boldsymbol{Y}, \Theta] \log P[\mathcal{D}, \boldsymbol{Y}, \Theta|\theta] d\boldsymbol{Y} d\Theta
$$
$$
- \int_{\boldsymbol{Y}} \int_{\Theta} Q[\boldsymbol{Y}, \Theta] \log Q[\boldsymbol{Y}, \Theta] d\boldsymbol{Y} d\Theta \triangleq \mathcal{F}(Q[\boldsymbol{Y}, \Theta], \theta)
$$

The quantity $\mathcal{F}(Q[\boldsymbol{Y}, \Theta], \theta)$ is referred to as the negative free energy in statistical physics and can be considered to be a lower bound of $\mathcal{L}$. When $Q[\boldsymbol{Y}, \Theta]$ is equal to the joint posterior of $\boldsymbol{Y}$, and Θ given the dataset $\mathcal{D}$, viz. $P(\boldsymbol{Y}, \Theta|\mathcal{D})$,then

$$
\mathcal{F}(Q[\boldsymbol{Y}, \Theta], \theta) = \mathcal{L}(\theta).
$$

The difference between this lower bound $\mathcal{F}(Q[\boldsymbol{Y}, \Theta], \theta)$ and the log likelihood $\mathcal{L}(\theta)$ is the KL-divergence between the true and approximating posterior. The Bayesian variational algorithm alternates between maximising $\mathcal{F}$ with respect to the distribution Q and the parameters θ, respectively, holding the other fixed in a two-step procedure:

1. Step 1: Approximate E-step: With variational parameters fixed at θ update the variational distribution Q to maximise $\mathcal{F}(Q, \theta)$.
2. Step 2: M-step: With the variational distribution fixed at Q, update the variational parameters θ to maximise $\hat{F}(\theta) = \mathcal{F}(Q, \theta)$.

These steps are iterated as necessary and are analogous to the Expectation (E) and Maximization (M) steps of the EM algorithm. In general, in the approximate E-step, the parameters of the variational distribution/density or directly the variational distribution functions are updated and in the M-step the parameters of the probabilistic model are updated. The M-steps are identical, however in variational learning the exact E-step is replaced with an approximate E-step where the Kullback-Leibler divergence is *minimised*. Finally the resulting distribution $Q[\boldsymbol{Y}, \Theta]$ will be taken as an approximation to the true posterior $[\boldsymbol{Y}, \Theta|\mathcal{D}, \theta]$. A basic simple stage is to separate the dependence between the hidden variables $\boldsymbol{Y}$ and Θ, that is, to assume that $Q[\boldsymbol{Y}, \Theta] = Q[\boldsymbol{Y}]Q[\Theta]$.

2.2   The Likelihood or Noise Models

There are still several difficulties in the above Bayesian variational optimisation. Different "tricks" have been proposed for the different learning problem in the literature. For example, a variational approach for neural networks has been proposed in [8] under the assumption in which $Q[\boldsymbol{Y}]$ is a finite mixture of Gaussian distribution. In the classification problem [6] the new variational parameters were introduced to give a further lower bound over $\mathcal{L}$.

We will consider functionals of the form (1) and the Bayesian form (3) for the regression problem. In the probabilistic framework, the loss function $L(t, y(\boldsymbol{x}))$ is associated with the following likelihood (or target noise distribution)

$$
P[t|y(\boldsymbol{x}), \theta] = \frac{1}{Z} \exp\{-L(t, y(\boldsymbol{x}))\} \tag{6}
$$

where θ is the relative hyperparameters (vector) such as σ_t^2 and ϵ in the SVM and Z is a normalization constant depending on hyperparameters.

Assumptions: In our approach, the main assumption is that the likelihood defined in (6) can be considered as a superposition or mixture of Gaussian $N(u, \beta)$. That is, assume that there exist two density functions $\eta(u)$ and $\mu(\beta)$ such that

$$\frac{1}{Z}\exp\{-L(t, y(\boldsymbol{x}))\} = \int \sqrt{\frac{\beta}{2\pi}} \exp\{-\frac{\beta}{2}[t - y(\boldsymbol{x}) - u]^2\}\mu(\beta)\eta(u)d\beta du \quad (7)$$

Equation (7) means that the likelihood $P[t|y(\boldsymbol{x}), \theta]$ can be considered as the marginal distribution of $P[t, u, \beta|y(\boldsymbol{x}), \theta]$ with two hidden variables u and β which are, respectively, used to describe the Gaussian mean and variance having the prior $\eta(u)$ and $\mu(\beta)$.

Is the assumption (7) restrictive? The answer is: there are a lots of meaningful loss functions which can be gone into this function class. The simplest example is the likelihood $P[t|y(\boldsymbol{x}), \theta]$ used in the standard (L_2) regularization network with $\eta(u) = \delta(u)$ and $\mu(\beta) = \delta(\beta - 1/\sigma^2)$. Many examples can be found in [13].

The ϵ-insensitive likelihood for SVM regression can also be written in the form of (7) as follows, see [13]

$$\frac{\exp\{-|t - y(\boldsymbol{x})|_\epsilon\}}{2(\epsilon + 1)} = \int \sqrt{\frac{\beta}{2\pi}} \exp\{-\frac{\beta}{2}[t - y(\boldsymbol{x}) - u]^2\}\mu(\beta)\eta(u)d\beta du \quad (8)$$

with the following priors

$$\eta_\epsilon(u) = \frac{1}{2(\epsilon + 1)}\left[\chi_{(-\epsilon, \epsilon)}(u) + \delta(t - \epsilon) + \delta(t + \epsilon)\right]$$

$$\mu(\beta) = \frac{1}{2}\beta^{-2}\exp\{-\frac{1}{2\beta}\}$$

2.3 Optimisation Procedure

In the following discussion, we will apply the assumption (7) at each data point $(\boldsymbol{x}_i, t_i)$ in $\mathcal{D}$ and consider λ as a hidden variable. Under (5), (6) and (7) the joint distribution of dataset $\mathcal{D}$, the hidden variables $\boldsymbol{y}(\boldsymbol{x})$ and λ are given by

$$P[\mathcal{D}, \boldsymbol{y}(\boldsymbol{x}), \lambda|\theta] = \prod_{i=1}^{N} P[t_i|y(\boldsymbol{x}_i), \theta]P[\boldsymbol{y}(\boldsymbol{x})|\theta, \lambda]P[\lambda]. \quad (9)$$

where θ is a vector of hyperparameters in the likelihood model and prior of $\boldsymbol{y}$. Then the log likelihood of dataset is given by, see equation (7),

$$\mathcal{L}(\theta) = \log \int_{\boldsymbol{y}(\boldsymbol{x})} \int_\lambda \int_\beta \int_u \left[\prod_{i=1}^{N} \sqrt{\frac{\beta_i}{2\pi}} \exp\{-\frac{\beta_i}{2}[t_i - y(\boldsymbol{x}_i) - u_i]^2\}\mu(\beta_i)\eta(u_i)\right]$$

$$P[\boldsymbol{y}(\boldsymbol{x})|\theta, \lambda]P[\lambda]d\boldsymbol{y}(\boldsymbol{x})d\lambda du d\beta$$

where $\boldsymbol{\beta} = [\beta_1, \beta_2, \ldots, \beta_N]^T$ and $\boldsymbol{u} = [u_1, u_2, \ldots, u_N]^T$ are new hidden variables with the priors given by $\mu(\beta_i)$ and $\eta(u_i)$. Thus instead of considering the probabilistic generative model defined by (9) we can investigate the following generative model with more uncertain variables

$$P[\mathcal{D}, \boldsymbol{\beta}, \boldsymbol{u}, \boldsymbol{y}(\boldsymbol{x}), \lambda | \theta]$$

$$= \left[\prod_{i=1}^{N} \sqrt{\frac{\beta_i}{2\pi}} \exp\{-\frac{\beta_i}{2}[t_i - y(\boldsymbol{x}_i) - u_i]^2\} \mu(\beta_i)\eta(u_i) \right] P[\boldsymbol{y}(\boldsymbol{x})|\theta, \lambda] P[\lambda] \qquad (10)$$

In fact the model (9) is the marginal version of the model (10) over the hidden variables $\boldsymbol{\beta}$ and $\boldsymbol{u}$.

For the sake of simplicity we choose to treat the regulariser parameter λ with a Gamma prior distribution

$$P[\lambda] = \Gamma[\lambda | a_\lambda, b_\lambda] = \frac{b_\lambda^{a_\lambda}}{\Gamma(a_\lambda)} \lambda^{a_\lambda - 1} \exp\{-b_\lambda \lambda\}$$

The mean and variance of Gamma distribution is respectively, given by $\mathrm{mean}(\lambda) = a_\lambda/b_\lambda$ and $\mathrm{var}(\lambda) = a_\lambda/b_\lambda^2$. Another simplified treatment for λ is to absorb this parameter into the hyperparameter group of the prior of $\boldsymbol{y}(\boldsymbol{x})$, say into the kernel parameter in the case of Gaussian process prior.

Now the variational learning can be easily applied to the generative model (10). Under using variational Bayesian learning as described section 2.1, the learning task becomes how to find an approximation to the posterior distribution $P[\boldsymbol{y}(\boldsymbol{x}), \boldsymbol{\beta}, \boldsymbol{u}, \lambda | \mathcal{D}, \theta]$ in the density function space of separable distribution $Q[\boldsymbol{y}(\boldsymbol{x})]Q[\lambda]\prod_{i=1}^{N} Q[\beta_i]Q[u_i]$. The lower bound of $\mathcal{L}$ can then be written as (ignoring constant terms),

$$\mathcal{L}(\theta) \geq \int_{\boldsymbol{y}(\boldsymbol{x}), \boldsymbol{\beta}, \boldsymbol{u}, \lambda} Q(\boldsymbol{y}(\boldsymbol{x}))Q(\boldsymbol{\beta})Q(\boldsymbol{u})Q(\lambda) \left[-\frac{1}{2}(\boldsymbol{t} - \boldsymbol{y}(\boldsymbol{x}) - \boldsymbol{u})^T \boldsymbol{B}(\boldsymbol{t} - \boldsymbol{y}(\boldsymbol{x}) - \boldsymbol{u}) \right.$$

$$- \frac{\lambda}{2} \boldsymbol{y}(\boldsymbol{x})^T \boldsymbol{K}^{-1} \boldsymbol{y}(\boldsymbol{x}) + \log P[\lambda] + \sum_{i=1}^{N} \left(\frac{1}{2} \log \beta_i + \log \mu(\beta_i) + \log \eta(u_i) \right)$$

$$\left. + \frac{N}{2} \log \lambda - \frac{1}{2} \log |\boldsymbol{K}| \right] + \mathcal{H}(Q(\boldsymbol{y}(\boldsymbol{x}))) + \mathcal{H}(Q(\boldsymbol{\beta})) + \mathcal{H}(Q(\boldsymbol{u})) + \mathcal{H}(Q(\lambda))$$

$$+ \mathrm{const.} = \mathcal{F}(Q(\boldsymbol{y}(\boldsymbol{x})), Q(\boldsymbol{\beta}), Q(\boldsymbol{u}), Q(\lambda), \theta) \qquad (11)$$

where $\boldsymbol{B} = \mathrm{diag}(\boldsymbol{\beta})$ and $\mathcal{H}(P)$ denotes the entry of distribution P.

In order to simplify the notation in the variational algorithm, denote $\bar{u}$ and $\hat{u}$ etc the first and second moments with respect to the corresponding distribution Q, respectively.

Maximising the variational functional $\mathcal{F}$ with respect to $Q(\boldsymbol{y}(\boldsymbol{x}))$, $Q(\boldsymbol{\beta})$, $Q[\boldsymbol{u}]$ and $Q[\lambda]$ results in the following approximated distributions:

1. The best $Q[\boldsymbol{y}(\boldsymbol{x})]$ is a Gaussian given by

$$Q[\boldsymbol{y}(\boldsymbol{x})] = \mathcal{N}(\boldsymbol{y}_{MP}, \Sigma_{MP}) \qquad (12)$$

with $\boldsymbol{y}_{MP} = \Sigma_{MP}\overline{\boldsymbol{B}}(\boldsymbol{t} - \overline{\boldsymbol{u}})$ and $\Sigma_{MP} = (\overline{\boldsymbol{B}} + \langle\lambda\rangle\boldsymbol{K}^{-1})^{-1}$, where $\overline{\boldsymbol{B}} = \mathrm{diag}(\overline{\beta})$.

2. The best $Q[\beta_i]$ is given by

$$Q[\beta_i] = \frac{\sqrt{2}\exp\{\sqrt{m_i}\}}{\sqrt{\pi}}\mu(\beta_i)\sqrt{\beta_i}\exp\{-\frac{\beta_i}{2}m_i\} \tag{13}$$

where y_{MP}^i is the i-th component of $\boldsymbol{y}_{MP}$ and m_i is defined as

$$m_i = (t_i - \overline{u}_i + y_{MP}^i)^2 + [\Sigma_{MP}]_{ii} + \widehat{u}_i - \overline{u}_i^2 \tag{14}$$

3. The best $Q[u_i]$ is given by

$$Q[u_i] = \frac{1}{Z(\overline{\beta}_i, y_{MP}^i, \epsilon)}\eta(u_i)\exp\left\{-\frac{\overline{\beta}_i}{2}(t_i - u_i - y_{MP}^i)^2\right\} \tag{15}$$

where $Z(\overline{\beta}_i, y_{MP}^i, \epsilon)$ is the normalized constant.

4. The best $Q[\lambda]$ is still a Gamma distribution $\Gamma[\lambda|\widetilde{a}, \widetilde{b}]$ but with the updated parameters:

$$\begin{aligned}\widetilde{a} &= \frac{N}{2} + a_\lambda \\ \widetilde{b} &= b_\lambda + \frac{1}{2}(\boldsymbol{y}_{MP}^T\boldsymbol{K}^{-1}\boldsymbol{y}_{MP} + \mathrm{tr}[\boldsymbol{K}^{-1}\Sigma_{MP}])\end{aligned} \tag{16}$$

For the optimisation with respect to the hyperparameters θ, the lower bound $\mathcal{F}$ is a (nonlinear) function of θ given the approximated posterior Q's. Given $\mathcal{F}$ and its derivatives with respect to θ it is straightforward to feed this information into an optimisation package in order to obtain a local maximum of $\mathcal{F}$.

3   An Example: SVR Algorithm Based on the Variational Approach

In this section we consider the SVM regression problem [15] as a special example of the above discussion in which the Vapnik's ϵ-loss function is employed

$$L_\epsilon(t, y(\boldsymbol{x})) = |t - y(\boldsymbol{x})|_\epsilon.$$

where ϵ is called error factor and the prior of $y(\boldsymbol{x})$ will be described by a Gaussian Process associated with a kernel function K with some kernel parameter [4]. For this special case, the hyperparameter vector in equation (9) contains the error factor ϵ and all of other kernel parameters, for example, the RBF's kernel width and the length scale parameter etc. The best approximated posterior distribution of $y(\boldsymbol{x})$, β_i and u_i are, respectively, given by (12), (13) and (15), in which the prior distributions of u_i and β_i are

$$\eta_\epsilon(u_i) = \frac{1}{2(\epsilon + 1)}\left[\chi_{(-\epsilon,\epsilon)}(u_i) + \delta(t_i - \epsilon) + \delta(t_i + \epsilon)\right] \tag{17}$$

$$\mu(\beta_i) = \frac{1}{2}\beta_i^{-2}\exp\{-\frac{1}{2\beta_i}\} \tag{18}$$

The posterior distributions depend upon the quantities $\overline{\beta}_i$, $\overline{u}_i$ and $\widehat{u}_i$. By direct evaluation, the following formulas for these quantities can be obtained:

$$\overline{\beta}_i = \int \beta_i Q(\beta_i) d\beta_i = \frac{1}{\sqrt{m_i}} \tag{19}$$

where m_i is defined by (14). Denote

$$s_{i\pm} = t_i \pm \epsilon - y_{MP}^i \qquad r_{i\pm} = -\overline{\beta}_i s_{i\pm}^2$$

then

$$\overline{u}_i = \frac{1}{G(\overline{\beta}_i, y_{MP}^i, \epsilon)} \left[\epsilon \exp\{\frac{r_{i-}}{2}\} - \epsilon \exp\{\frac{r_{i+}}{2}\} + \frac{1}{\overline{\beta}_i} \left(\exp\{r_{i+}\} - \exp\{r_{i-}\} \right) \right.$$
$$\left. + \frac{\sqrt{\pi}}{2\sqrt{2\overline{\beta}_i}} (t_i - y_{MP}^i) \left(\text{erf}(-\sqrt{\frac{-r_{i-}}{2}})) - \text{erf}(-\sqrt{\frac{-r_{i+}}{2}})) \right) \right] \tag{20}$$

and

$$\widehat{u}_i = \frac{1}{G(\overline{\beta}_i, y_{MP}^i, \epsilon)} \left[(\epsilon^2 + \frac{s_{i-}}{\overline{\beta}_i}) \exp\{\frac{r_{i+}}{2}\} + (\epsilon^2 - \frac{s_{i+}}{\overline{\beta}_i}) \exp\{\frac{r_{i-}}{2}\} \right)$$
$$+ \frac{\sqrt{\pi}}{\sqrt{2\overline{\beta}_i}} \left((t_i - y_{MP}^i)^2 + \frac{1}{\overline{\beta}_i} \right) \left(\text{erf}(-\sqrt{\frac{-r_{i-}}{2}})) - \text{erf}(-\sqrt{\frac{-r_{i+}}{2}})) \right) \right]. \tag{21}$$

where

$$G(\cdot) = \frac{\sqrt{\pi}}{\sqrt{2\overline{\beta}_i}} \left(\text{erf}(-\sqrt{\frac{-r_{i-}}{2}})) - \text{erf}(-\sqrt{\frac{-r_{i+}}{2}})) \right) + \exp\{\frac{r_{i-}}{2}\} + \exp\{\frac{r_{i+}}{2}\}$$

If we consider ϵ to be a hyperparameter in the set of model hyperparameters θ, as soon as the approximating posterior distributions have been determined, the lower bound of the log likelihood will be

$$\mathcal{F}(\epsilon) = \sum_{i=1}^{N} \log G(\overline{\beta}_i, y_{MP}^i, \epsilon) - N \log(\epsilon + 1) + \text{const.}$$

Then maximising $\mathcal{F}$ with respect to ϵ will give the update formula for ϵ:

$$\frac{N}{\epsilon + 1} = \sum_{i=1}^{N} \frac{1}{G(\overline{\beta}_i, y_{MP}^i, \epsilon)} \frac{\partial G(\overline{\beta}_i, y_{MP}^i, \epsilon)}{\partial \epsilon} \tag{22}$$

where

$$\frac{\partial G(\overline{\beta}_i, y_{MP}^i, \epsilon)}{\partial \epsilon} = [1 + \overline{\beta}_i s_{i-}] \exp\{\frac{r_{i-}}{2}\} + [1 - \overline{\beta}_i s_{i+}] \exp\{\frac{r_{i+}}{2}\}$$

In the SVM method, an important issue is how to choose a suitable kernel. Various possible kernels in the SVM have been reviewed by Smola [15], and a frequently used kernel function which seems to work well in practice is given by [23]:

$$K(\boldsymbol{x}^{(i)}, \boldsymbol{x}^{(j)}|\theta) = v_0 \exp\{-\frac{1}{2}\sum_{l=1}^{n} \alpha_l(x_l^{(i)} - x_l^{(j)})^2\} + a_0 + \sum_{l=1}^{n} a_l x_l^{(i)} x_l^{(j)} + v_1\delta(i,j)$$

where n is input dimension and $\theta = (\log v_0, \log v_1, \log \alpha_1, \dots, \log \alpha_n, \log a_0, \log a_1, \dots, \log a_n)$ is the vector of adjustable hyperparameters. This kernel function is made up of three parts: the first term, a linear regression term and a noise term $v_1\delta(i,j)$. Given a value for θ, it is straightforward to make predictions for new test points. For simplicity here, we employ the maximum the lower bound in the Bayesian variational framework discussed above to find a θ. Similar to the procedure of maximising ϵ, we can first calculate the the lower bound of the log likelihood for the fixed posterior of all hidden variables. These calculations are facilitated by the fact that the lower bound can be calculated analytically as

$$\mathcal{F}(\theta) = -\frac{1}{2}\log\det K - \frac{1}{2}\boldsymbol{y}_{MP}^T(\overline{\boldsymbol{B}} + \langle\lambda\rangle K^{-1})\boldsymbol{y}_{MP} + \text{const.} \qquad (23)$$

$$\frac{\partial\mathcal{F}}{\partial\theta} = -\frac{1}{2}\text{tr}(K^{-1}\frac{\partial K}{\partial\theta}) + \frac{\langle\lambda\rangle}{2}[\boldsymbol{y}_{MP}^T K^{-1}\frac{\partial K}{\partial\theta}K^{-1}\boldsymbol{y}_{MP}]. \qquad (24)$$

Now the Bayesian variational method for the SVM regression problem can be arranged as an algorithm as follows:

1. Initialize $\boldsymbol{y}_{MP}$, Σ_{MP}, $\boldsymbol{\beta}$, $\overline{\boldsymbol{u}}$, $\widehat{\boldsymbol{u}}$ and $\langle\lambda\rangle$, then iterate the following step until an error precision is satisfied;
2. Compute $\boldsymbol{y}_{MP} = \Sigma_{MP}\overline{\boldsymbol{B}}(\boldsymbol{t} - \overline{\boldsymbol{u}})$ and $\Sigma_{MP} = (\overline{\boldsymbol{B}} + \langle\lambda\rangle K^{-1})^{-1}$;
3. Use (19), (20) and (21) to compute $\overline{\boldsymbol{\beta}}$, $\overline{\boldsymbol{u}}$ and $\widehat{\boldsymbol{u}}$, respectively;
4. Update $\widetilde{a}$ and $\widetilde{b}$ by (16), and compute $\langle\lambda\rangle = \widetilde{a}/\widetilde{b}$;
5. Update ϵ with (22) and, if necessarily, find the local maximum of hyperparameters in kernel function by the scaled conjugate gradient (SCG) optimization based on (23) and (24).

4 Numerical Experiment

A modelling problem proposed by Friedman [3] was used to assess the performance of the proposed approach here. In our experiment, 90% of the data was used for training and 10% of the data was used for evaluating the generalisation performance. The model is a ten input function, with five redundant inputs, given by

$$y = f(x_1, x_2, \cdots, x_{10}) = 10\sin(\pi x_1 x_2) + 20(x_3 - 0.5)^3 + 10x_4 + 5x_5 + \eta$$

where η is zero mean, unit variance, additive Gaussian noise, corresponding to approximated 20% noise, and the inputs $\boldsymbol{x} = (x_1, x_2, \cdots, x_{10})^T$ were generated

Table 1. Ranked importance of hyperparameters when using variational SVM learning

Exponential Part											Linear Bias Part										
Partition	1	2	3	4	5	6	7	8	9	10	Partition	1	2	3	4	5	6	7	8	9	10
α_1	3	3	4	3	1	3	4	5	2	3	a_1	1	4	2	1	1	2	1	4	1	2
α_2	2	1	1	1	2	1	1	1	1	1	a_2	3	1	1	2	2	3	2	2	2	1
α_3	1	2	2	2	6	2	2	2	3	2	a_3	4	3	3	5	3	1	3	1	4	3
α_4	4	-	-	-	3	4	-	-	4	-	a_4	2	6	4	4	4	5	4	6	3	5
α_5	-	-	-	4	-	-	3	4	-	-	a_5	5	2	5	6	5	6	5	5	5	6
α_6	-	4	-	-	-	-	-	-	-	4	a_6	-	-	-	-	-	-	4	-	3	-
α_7	-	-	-	-	-	-	-	3	-	-	a_7	6	-	-	3	-	-	-	-	-	-
α_8	-	-	-	-	-	-	-	-	-	-	a_8	-	-	-	-	-	-	-	-	-	4
α_9	-	-	-	-	-	-	-	-	-	-	a_9	-	-	-	-	-	-	-	-	-	-
α_{10}	-	-	3	-	-	-	-	-	-	-	a_{10}	-	-	-	-	-	-	6	-	-	-

independently and "randomly" from a uniform distribution in the hypercubes $[0, 1]^{10}$. The experiments were performed using 300 examples, 270 for training and 30 for estimating the generalisation performance.

In the experiments we set hyper-priors on λ as $a_\lambda = 1$ and $b_\lambda = 0.01$. We partitioned the dataset by ten different (random) partitions of the dataset. For each partition (training and testing) the algorithm was implemented for 100 sets of random initial values of $\boldsymbol{y}_{MP}$, Σ_{MP}, $\boldsymbol{\beta}$, $\overline{\boldsymbol{u}}$ and $\widehat{\boldsymbol{u}}$. Table 1 lists the ranked importance of input variables based on ten partitions. The final hyperparameters are determined by averaging the resulted hyperparameters from these running. Then the kernel function determined is

$$K(\boldsymbol{x}, \boldsymbol{y}) = 0.003 \exp\left\{ -\frac{1}{2} \left[0.05(x_1 - y_1)^2 + 1.64(x_2 - y_2)^2 + 0.24(x_3 - y_3)^2\right] \right\}$$
$$+ 0.15 + 0.26x_1y_1 + 0.36x_2y_2 + 0.16x_3y_3 + 0.48x_4y_4 + 0.23x_5y_5$$
$$+ 1.21 \times 10^{-6}\delta(\boldsymbol{x}, \boldsymbol{y})$$

Note that the kernel generated by the algorithm has captured the correct relevant input components. Based on this kernel, the standard SVM regression has been run again with 68% support vectors.

To compare the performance of the approach with other methods, Gaussian Process regression has been demonstrated with this example. The result is reported in Table 2.

5   Discussions

In this paper we have derive the variational Bayesian framework for the likelihood of infinite mixture of Gaussian. As an example the new SVM regression algorithm with a particular focus on variational approaches has been investigated. There are two main differences between the standard SVM regression and the variational Bayesian SVM regression: (1) the variational Bayesian SVM

Table 2. Ranked importance of input variables when using the Gaussian Process ARD kernel function.

Exponential Part											Linear Bias Part										
Partition	1	2	3	4	5	6	7	8	9	10	Partition	1	2	3	4	5	6	7	8	9	10
α_1	3	3	4	3	1	3	4	5	2	3	a_1	1	1	2	1	3	1	1	1	1	1
α_2	2	1	1	1	2	1	1	1	1	1	a_2	2	2	1	2	2	5	5	2	2	2
α_3	1	2	2	2	6	2	2	2	3	2	a_3	3	3	3	3	4	4	4	3	3	3
α_4	4	-	-	-	3	4	-	-	4	-	a_4	4	4	4	5	5	2	2	4	4	4
α_5	-	-	-	4	-	-	3	4	-	-	a_5	5	5	5	6	1	3	3	5	5	5
α_6	-	4	-	-	-	-	-	-	-	4	a_6	-	-	6	4	-	6	-	-	-	-
α_7	-	-	-	-	-	-	-	3	-	-	a_7	-	-	-	-	6	-	-	-	-	-
α_8	-	-	-	-	-	-	-	-	-	-	a_8	-	-	-	-	-	-	-	-	-	-
α_9	-	-	-	-	-	-	-	-	-	-	a_9	-	-	7	7	-	-	-	-	-	-
α_{10}	-	-	3	-	-	-	-	-	-	-	a_{10}	-	-	-	-	-	-	6	-	-	-

regression doesn't need a quadratic optimisation technique to solve the regression solution; (2) the variational Bayesian variational SVM can be used to adopt the kernel hyperparameter, whilst the standard SVM regression has to employ other techniques such as the cross validation to tune the kernel parameters, which results in a cost task which there are many kernel parameters. The examples have demonstrated that the new variational Bayesian approach for SVM is competitive with the standard SVM regression method.

References

1. C.M. Bishop. Variational principal components. In *Proceedings pf Ninth International Conference on Artificial Neural Networks, ICANN'99*, pages 509–514, 1999.
2. T. Evgeniou, M. Pontil, and T. Poggio. A unified framework for regularization networks and support vector machines. A.I. Memo 1654, AI Lab, MIT, Massachusetts, 1999.
3. J.H. Friedman. Multivariable adaptive regression splines. *The Annals of Statistics*, 19(1):1–57, 1991.
4. J.B. Gao, S.R. Gunn, C.J. Harris, and M.Q. Brown. A probabilistic framework for SVM regression and error bar estimation. *Machine Learning*, 46:71–89, 2002.
5. F. Girosi, M. Jones, and T. Poggio. Regularization theory and neural networks architectures. *Neural Computation*, 7:219–269, 1995.
6. T.S. Jaakkola and M.I. Jordan. Variational probabilistic inference and the qmr-dt database. *Journal of Artificial Intelligence Research*, 10:291–322, 1999.
7. N.D. Lawrence. *Variational inference in probabilistic models*. PhD thesis, University of Cambridge, Cambridge, UK, 2000.
8. N.D. Lawrence and M. Azzouzi. A variational Bayesian committe of neural networks. Technical report, University of Cambridge, 2000.
9. N.D. Lawrence and C.M. Bishop. Variational Bayesian independent component analysis. Technical report, University of Cambridge, 2000.
10. D.J. MacKay. Gaussian processes, A replacement for neural networks. NIPS tutorial 1997, Cambridge University, 1997.

11. R. Neal. Monte Carlo implementation of Gaussian process models for Bayesian regression and classification. Technical Report CRG-TR-97-2, Dept. of Computer Science, University of Toronto, 1997.

12. W.D. Penny and S.J. Roberts. Variational Bayes for non-Gaussian autoregressive models. Technical report, Department of Engineering Science, Oxford University, UK, 2000.

13. M. Pontil, S. Mukherjee, and F. Girosi. On the noise model of support vector machine regression. A.I. Memo 1651, AI Laboratory, MIT, 1998.

14. M. Seeger. Relationships between Gaussian processes, support vector machines and smoothing splines. Research report, Institute for Adaptive and Neural Computation, University of Edinburgh, Edinburgh, Scotland, 2000.

15. A.J. Smola. *Learning with Kernels*. PhD thesis, Technischen Universität Berlin, Berlin, Germany, 1998.

16. P. Sollich. Approximate learning curves for Gaussian processes. In *ICANN99: Ninth International Conference on Artificial Neural Networks*, pages 437–442, London, 1999. The Institution of Electrical Engineers.

17. A.N. Tikhonov and V.Y. Arsenin. *Solution of Ill-posed Problems*. W.H. Winston, Washington, D.C., 1977.

18. V.N. Vapnik. *Statistical Learning Theory*. Wiley, New York, 1998.

19. G. Wahba. *Splines Models for Observational Data*, volume 59 of *Series in Applied Mathematics*. SIAM Press, Philadelphia, 1990.

20. C.K. Williams. Computing with infinite networks. In M.C. Mozer, M.I. Jordan, and T. Petsche, editors, *Neural Information Processing Systems*, volume 9, pages 295–301. MIT Press, 1997.

21. C.K. Williams. Prediction with gaussian processes: from linear regression to linear prediction and beyond. In M.I. Jordan, editor, *Learning in Graphical Models*, pages 599–621. MIT Press, Cambridge, Massachusetts, 1998.

22. C.K. Williams and D. Barber. Bayesian classification with gaussian processes. *IEEE Trans. on Pattern Analysis and Machine Intelligence*, 20:1342–1351, 1998.

23. C.K. Williams and C.E. Rasmuseen. Gaussian processes for regression. In D.S. Touretzky, M.C. Mozer, and M.E. Hasselmo, editors, *Neural Information Processing Systems*, volume 8, pages 514–520. MIT Press, 1997.

Learning to Reach the Pareto Optimal Nash Equilibrium as a Team

Katja Verbeeck, Ann Nowé, Tom Lenaerts, and Johan Parent

Vrije Universiteit Brussel, COMO `como.vub.ac.be`,
Pleinlaan 2 1050 Brussel, Belgium
{`kaverbee|tlenaert`}`@vub.ac.be`, {`asnowe|johan`}`@info.vub.ac.be`

Abstract. Coordination is an important issue in multi-agent systems when agents want to maximize their revenue. Often coordination is achieved through communication, however communication has its price. We are interested in finding an approach where the communication between the agents is kept low, and a global optimal behavior can still be found.

In this paper we report on an efficient approach that allows independent reinforcement learning agents to reach a Pareto optimal Nash equilibrium with limited communication. The communication happens at regular time steps and is basically a signal for the agents to start an exploration phase. During each exploration phase, some agents exclude their current best action so as to give the team the opportunity to look for a possibly better Nash equilibrium. This technique of reducing the action space by exclusions was only recently introduced for finding periodical policies in games of conflicting interests. Here, we explore this technique in repeated common interest games with deterministic or stochastic outcomes.

1 Introduction

In multi-agent systems the feedback experienced by an agent is usually influenced by the actions taken by the other agents present in the same system. Therefore modeling the other agents seems the natural thing to do. This leads to what is called the joint action learning approach and in some cases this effort doesn't really payoff [1]. Moreover the joint action learning approach is very often infeasible in a multi-agent setting because it assumes that agents take actions synchronously, are informed about the payoffs other agents receive or that there is a supervisor who coordinates the learning process. On the contrary, agents may be independent learners, i.e. they only get information about their own action choice and pay-off. As such, they neglect the presence of the other agents. However this can yield a suboptimal behavior of the global system. This is for instance the case in systems where resources are limited, such as job scheduling, routing and so on, [8]. In these systems agents should make agreements on how to share the resources to obtain a global optimal behavior. Agreements are formed through communication or by rules agreed upon in advance. Since

R.I. McKay and J. Slaney (Eds.): AI 2002, LNAI 2557, pp. 407–418, 2002.

communication has its price and predefined rules are not feasible in complex and changing environments, we are interested in finding an approach where the communication between the agents is kept low, and a global optimal behavior can still be found.

In this paper we introduce a new learning algorithm that allows independent agents to reach an optimal solution in repeated common interest games with only limited amount of communication. In these games individual rationality agrees with group rationality and an optimal solution, i.e. a Pareto Optimal Nash equilibrium exists. The basic limitations of current multi-agent learning algorithms in repeated games, including common interest games, is that although they can prove convergence to a Nash equilibrium, this is not necessarily to the optimal equilibrium,[3,6]. The smaller the basin of attraction of a Nash equilibrium the harder it is for the agents to reach it, and the more important it is for the agents to behave as a team.

[7,12] reports work on coordinated exploration by independent learners for learning periodical policies[1] in games of conflicting interests. The exploration was done by letting the best performing player exclude his best action. This reduces the action space, so that another sub-area of it can be explored, leading to another Nash equilibrium which might be favored by another agent. This process is repeated so that all the agents are able to play their best Nash equilibrium in turn and pay-offs are fairly distributed. In this approach the distributed independent reinforcement learning agents are equipped with only limited means of communication. The agents send, only at certain points in time, their average pay-offs to each other. No other local state information like action values or transition probabilities are exchanged.

In the new learning algorithm we propose here, agents are also able to reduce their action space so that the team will arrive at the more interesting parts of the joint action space. Only limited communication is allowed to organize this exploration in order to reach the best possible state for the whole team.

The number of players and where the Nash equilibria are situated in the joint action space specifies the type of game. Common interest games with homogeneous players[2] and all the Nash equilibria situated on the diagonal of the joint action space are a special case. An example is a game where n players guess independently an integer between 1 and 10. When they guess the same number they win each the amount of their guess, otherwise they don't lose nor win anything. All two-player coordination games belong to this case. For those games the convergence of our algorithm is trivial even for stochastic games. In the general case convergence is shown experimentally and adaptation in stochastic environments is demonstrated.

The rest of the paper is organized as follows. In section 2 we discuss related work, amongst which joint action space learning. Section 3 discusses common

---

[1] A periodical policy switches between the different Nash equilibria of the game, so that in a game where players have conflicting interests, each player gets to play his best Nash equilibrium and the overall pay-off is equalized optimally.

[2] Meaning that all elements of the joint action space of the form $(a_1, a_2, \ldots, a_n)$ with $a_1 = a_2 = \ldots a_n$ and n the number of players, are Nash equilibria.

interest games, and when it is hard for independent agents to reach a Pareto optimal Nash equilibrium. We distinguish and formalize two classes of coordination games and introduce an exploration approach for each class in section 4. Section 5 reports some experiments. Section 6 gives some ideas for future work and section 7 concludes.

2   Related Work

For learning in a multi-agent system, two extreme approaches can be recognized. On the one hand, the presence of other agents, who are possibly influencing the effects a single agent experiences, can be completely ignored. Thus a single agent is learning in isolation as if the other agents are not around.

On the other hand, the presence of other agents can be modeled explicitly. This results in a joint action space learning approach which already received quite a lot of attention [1,2,5]. In the joint action space technique, learning happens in the product space of the set of states S, and the collections of action sets $A_1, ..., A_n$ (one set A_i for every agent i). The state transition function $T : S \times A_1 \times ... \times A_n \to P(S)$ maps a joint environment state and an action from every agent onto a probability distribution on S and each agent receives an associated reward, defined by the reward function $R_i : S \times A_1 \times ... \times A_n \to P(\Re)$. This is the underlying model for the stochastic games, also referred to as Markov games in [2,5]. The joint action space approach, is a safe technique in the sense that the influence of an agent on every other agent can be modeled. However the joint action space approach challenges the basic principles of multi-agent systems : distributed control, asynchronous actions, incomplete information, cost of communication etc. The proposed algorithms can therefore not be used for independent learners.

Furthermore, in some special cases the whole information of joint action learners is not required. For instance, any game which is dominance solvable[3] can be tackled successfully by independent distributed reinforcement learning agents. They can iteratively eliminate weakly dominated actions. For an example see Figure 1.

However in general there is no guarantee that independent learners will converge to the Pareto optimal Nash equilibrium of the game. For one-state games convergence can be proved, although not necessarily to the optimal Nash equilibrium, see [6,3]. In [4] only for deterministic games and environments the convergence to the optimal Nash equilibrium is guaranteed.

3   Independent Learning in Common Interest Games

A common interest game is a game for which at least one Pareto Optimal Nash equilibrium exists. When more than one exists, they give the same outcome for

---
[3] A strategic game is dominance solvable if all players are indifferent to all outcomes that survive the iterative procedure in which all the weakly dominated actions of each player are eliminated, see [9]

	a_1	a_2	a_3
b_1	$(9,11)$	$(5,6)$	$(1,0)$
b_2	$(5,6)$	$(5,6)$	$(5,6)$
b_3	$(1,0)$	$(5,6)$	$(1,0)$

Fig. 1. A game of common interest which is dominance solvable.

each player. An outcome of a game is said to be *Pareto optimal* if there exists no other outcome, for which all players simultaneously do better. As a consequence, in a common interest game all agents agree upon which Nash equilibrium is the best[4]. Figures 1 to 5 show some examples of common interest games.

All identical pay-off games belong to the class of common interest games. In this case, the Pareto optimal Nash equilibrium is a coordination equilibrium which gives every player his maximal possible outcome. For the sake of the argument, we will focus on this type of games in the rest of the paper, however the approach can be extended to more general common interest games.

The aim of learning for independent learners in this context is to find one of the optimal equilibria. The learner is independent in the sense that he only knows his own action choice and the pay-off this generates. Internally our agents keep a probability distribution over their action space, which they update using a reinforcement learning algorithm, such as learning automata [6] or Q-learning, [10]. A successful learning scheme in this situation is the reward-inaction learning automata scheme, where actions are selected probabilistically and actions which return high payoffs are positively reinforced. If p_i denotes the action probability of the agents i th action, the reward-inaction update for binary rewards works as follows:

$$\left. \begin{array}{l} p_i(n+1) = p_i(n) + a(1 - p_i(n)) \\ p_j(n+1) = p_j(n) - a p_j(n) \ j \neq i \end{array} \right\} \text{ if action i was chosen and successfully}$$

$$p_j(n+1) = p_j(n) \ \forall j \text{ otherwise}$$

The constant a is the reward parameter and $0 <= a <= 1$. In [6] it is concluded for general one-state games that agents converge to one of the equilibrium points, not necessarily the optimal one, with a probability arbitrarily close to one. This result, which can be translated for other reinforcement learning algorithms such as Qlearning, will be important in the development of our algorithm.

From an independent learning point of view common interest games can be very different. The game in Figure 1 is dominance solvable, the technique of eliminating dominated strategies results in the Pareto optimal Nash equilibrium, [9]. This is not the case for the game of Figure 2. Independent learners may get stuck in the suboptimal Nash equilibrium with payoff $(7,7)$. Whether the

---

[4] Of course,when more than one optimal solution exists, they have to coordinate on the same equilibrium.

agents reach the Pareto optimal Nash equilibrium with payoff $(11, 11)$ depends on the initializations when learning starts. In the state space of the agents' joint action probabilities, the Nash equilibria are attractors. In general the relative sizes of the basin of attraction of the different Nash equilibrium, determines the probability with which independent learners converge to one of the Nash equilibria, [11].

By augmenting independent learners with some minimal synchronization / communication abilities, we will show in the next sections that they are able to converge to the optimal solution in games of common interest. We will focus on a coordinated form of exploration using independent reinforcement learning agents.

	a_1	a_2	a_3
b_1	$(11, 11)$	$(-30, -30)$	$(0, 0)$
b_2	$(-30, -30)$	$(7, 7)$	$(6, 6)$
b_3	$(0, 0)$	$(0, 0)$	$(5, 5)$

	a_1		a_2	
	c_1	c_2	c_1	c_2
b_1	7	-30	0	4
b_2	0	11	4	-30

Fig. 2. Left: A common interest game from [1], Right: A common interest game with 3 players.

	a_1	a_2	a_3
b_1	$(1.0, 1.0)$	$(0.0, 0.0)$	$(0.0, 0.0)$
b_2	$(0.0, 0.0)$	$(0.5, 0.5)$	$(0.7, 0.7)$
b_3	$(0.4, 0.4)$	$(0.7, 0.7)$	$(0.8, 0.8)$

	a_1	a_2	a_3
b_1	$(1.0, 1.0)$	$(0.8, 0.8)$	$(0.0, 0.0)$
b_2	$(0.8, 0.8)$	$(0.5, 0.5)$	$(0.4, 0.4)$
b_3	$(0.4, 0.4)$	$(0.4, 0.4)$	$(0.8, 0.8)$

Fig. 3. Stochastic common interest game. The values in the matrix give the probability of success, which gives a payoff of 1 in case of success and 0 otherwise.

4   Learning to Reach the Pareto Optimal Nash Equilibrium as a Team

The identical payoff games we consider have several pure Nash equilibria, and the aim of learning is to converge to a Pareto optimal Nash equilibrium. As mentioned in section 3, from the theory of learning automata, we can make the agents converge as independent reinforcement learners to a policy which plays one of the pure Nash equilibria. Which Nash equilibrium will be played depends on the initial conditions and the basins of attraction of the Nash equilibria. The bigger the basin of attraction of some Nash equilibrium, the bigger the probability that it will be this equilibrium that will be converged to. If the agents have converged to the Pareto dominant Nash equilibrium, there is no space for improvement. If the agents have not converged to the Pareto dominant Nash equilibrium, then all agents will benefit from searching for it in the long run. Suppose for example that the agents of Figure 2 above converged to (a_2, b_2) corresponding to a payoff of 7 for both agents. Independent learners will not have the tendency to explore further to reach the better Nash equilibrium which pays off to both agents the amount of 11, this because of the high punishment of -30 which surrounds this interesting Nash equilibrium. In other words the basin of attraction of the Pareto optimal Nash equilibrium (a_1, b_1) is so small that the probability that independent learners end up in the Nash equilibrium is low. Here coordination is a solution in order not to get too much punishment before discovering that (a_1, b_1) is the best strategy. The agents should decide together to search for a better Nash equilibrium. This can be achieved by agreeing to exclude their current best action and explore the remaining subspace. This exploration can again be performed in an independent manner, and this will drive the agents towards another Nash equilibrium. In some cases, actions that are involved in inferior Nash equilibria can be excluded permanently, which results in a smaller action space to be explored. In the end the agents will converge to the best Nash equilibrium.

In the next subsection this strategy is formalized for the 2 agent case. A generalization to the n agent case is given in the following subsections.

4.1   The 2 Agent Case

The 2-player algorithm alternates between periods of independent learning and a synchronization phase. Assume the agents are using a reinforcement learning method to learn an arbitrary Nash equilibrium of the game during the periods of independent play. After a Nash equilibrium has been reached, the synchronization phase takes place, of which the pseudo-code can be found in Figure 4. During this synchronization phase every agent independently checks if this current Nash equilibrium has a lower pay-off than the best Nash equilibrium discovered up till now. Initially this cannot be the case and the agents' action associated with the current Nash equilibria is temporarily excluded. When a better Nash equilibrium was previously discovered, the action of the current Nash equilibrium is permanently excluded and the action which was involved in the best Nash equilibrium found so far, stays temporarily excluded. If the current Nash equilibrium outperforms the previous best one, the action involved in the previous best one is permanently excluded and the action involved in the current Nash equilibria becomes temporarily excluded. After synchronization, a new period of play starts in the reduced action space. This alternation is repeated until the action space has shrunk to only one action. Then the action that is part of the best Nash equilibrium is made available, and the agents keep on playing that combination.

Important here is that learning as well as making exclusions in the action space happens completely independently, only synchronization is needed so as to make the agent perform the exclusion of their actions happen at the same time. Notice that because strict inequalities are used in the synchronization phase,

```
## SYNCHRONIZATION PHASE
if (time_to_synchronize) {
if payoff(last_action) >
    payoff(temporary_excluded_action)
    { permanently_exclude(temporary_excluded_action);
    temporary_exclude(last_action);
    }
if payoff(last_action) <
    payoff(temporary_excluded_action)
    permanently_exclude(last_action);
if no_more_actions_available
    free(temporary_excluded_action);
INITIALISATION;
}
```

Fig. 4. Pseudo code of the exclusion phase for the diagonal case

agents are able to correctly coordinate on one optimal Nash equilibria, in case multiple optimal solutions exists. Furthermore since the convergence results of learning automata also hold in stochastic games, our algorithm will in turn work for games with stochastic outcomes.

4.2 The General n Agent Case

The 2-player algorithm of the previous section can straightforwardly be extended to the n-player case provided that no pair of Nash equilibria are located in the same hyper-plane. More formally, if $(a_{1_i}, a_{2_j}, \ldots, a_{n_k}) \in (A_1 \times A_2 \times \ldots \times A_n)$ is a Nash equilibrium, then the other Nash equilibria should be located in the action sub-space $(A_1 \backslash \{a_{1_i}\} \times A_2 \backslash \{a_{2_j}\} \times \ldots \times A_n \backslash \{a_{n_k}\})$

This means that the n agents can safely exclude the action involved in the current Nash equilibrium, as explained above. They can explore for alternative Nash equilibria that are located in the action sub-space, without missing any Nash equilibria. An Example is given in Figure 5. The Nash equilibria are located at the diagonal of the normal form matrix or can be put there after permutations of players and their actions.

In the remainder of this paper we call them diagonal games.

In a general identical payoff n agent game however we cannot make the assumption that all Nash equilibria are located in different hyper-planes. Or the assumption that if $(a_{1_i}, a_{2_j}, \ldots, a_{n_k})$ is a Nash equilibrium will not guarantee that $(a_{1_i} \times A_2 \times \ldots \times A_n) \cup (A_1 \times a_{2_j} \times \ldots \times A_n) \cup \ldots \cup (A_1 \times A_2 \times \ldots \times a_{n_k})$ doesn't contain any other Nash equilibrium. For the exploration this means that, it is no longer a good idea to let all the agents simultaneously exclude their action involved in the Nash equilibrium the agents converged to. On the other hand, if only one agent excludes his action, no new Nash equilibrium can be found either.

Therefore in the general n agent case the exclusion of actions is done on a probabilistic basis. Agents decide independently whether to exclude their action

	a_1				a_2				a_3		
	c_1	c_2	c_3		c_1	c_2	c_3		c_1	c_2	c_3
b_1	0.9	0.1	0.1	b_1	0.1	0.1	0.1	b_1	0.1	0.1	0.1
b_2	0.1	0.1	0.1	b_2	0.1	0.6	0.1	b_2	0.1	0.1	0.1
b_3	0.1	0.1	0.1	b_3	0.1	0.1	0.1	b_3	0.1	0.1	0.4

Fig. 5. A stochastic identical payoff guessing game with 3 players. The Nash equilibria are located on the diagonal of the normal form matrix.

or not. Their decision is based on how good the action is opposed to the best result the agent ever received during play. The pseudo-code for this decision phase can be found in Figure 6. The parameter ϵ is the probability that an agent will exclude the current played action. This parameter depends on the how good the current played Nash equilibrium is compared to best outcome the agent ever got. It also depends on the experience the agent already has. When this action was already visited often, more belief is attached to the learned value. The algorithm now alternates between 3 phases; after the learning period, their is a decision phase followed by the synchronization phase. At synchronization time, the agents communicate their decision to each other. An agent can then tell how many other agents are willing to exclude their action. Any number between 2 and n is acceptable for him. The decisions made earlier are performed, otherwise the action space is unchanged. The pseudo-code for the synchronization phase in this case can be found in Figure 6.

```
## SYNCHRONIZATION PHASE
if (time_to_synchronize) {
communicate_to_all ( explore_decision);
decisions_all := receive_from_all (explore_decision);
if more-than-two (decisions_all ) {
   if (my_explore_decision = explore)
      my_actionSet :=
      my_original_actionSet - last_action;
      INITIALIZATION ;
   }
}
## DECISION PHASE
{
visits := nr-of-visits (last_action);
alpha := (1 - (1 : (1 + visits));
epsilon := (* alpha ( Qvalue (last_action) :
                best_payoff_so_far));
my_explore_decision := generate_decision (epsilon);
}
```

Fig. 6. Pseudo code of the communication and decision phase for the general case

5   Some Experiments

In this section we report some of the experiments we conducted.

5.1   2 Agent and Diagonal Case

To test the algorithm of Figure 4, we simulated stochastic common interest games with 2 up to 6 learning automata agents. The results are reported in Figure 7. The top left figure in Figure 7 shows that 2 independent agents are indeed able to converge to the optimal Nash equilibrium in the dominance solvable game of Figure 1. No synchronization or communication is needed. For the other examples synchronization is needed. The figures show the evolution of the average pay-off the agents receive. The pay-off drops or climbs after every synchronization phase. For instance, take the simulation of the stochastic game with 2 players which is presented in Figure 3(left). The result is given in Figure 7(top, right). Synchronization happens every 800 time-steps. In the first period of play, i.e. the first 800 simulation steps, the pay-off converges to approximately 0.8, which is the pay-off associated with the first Nash equilibrium reached. This equilibrium is easily reached for the players because the basin of attraction is bigger than that of the optimal equilibrium. In the second period, the optimal Nash equilibrium is found, as the average pay-off converges to 1.0. This was now possible, because the agents excluded each one action from their action space. In the third period, the average becomes 0.4, which is no equilibrium but the first equilibrium found is already permanently excluded, while the optimal equilibrium is temporarily excluded. In the last period the non-optimal action of the previous period is also permanently excluded and the optimal one is freed again. Together with the pay-off, the action probabilities of the agents first action is shown. During the first period, these probabilities drop to zero, but become one in the second period. In the third period they are excluded nd thus zero, but in the last period they become one, as they belong to the optimal solution. Similar behavior is found for the other stochastic common interest games simulated, see Figure 7.

5.2   General n Agent Case

In this subsection we give the results for the n player algorithm of Figure 6. In Figure 8 you will find the convergence results for the guessing game of Figure 5 with 2 players and the common interest games of Figure 2(left) and (right), with 2 and 3 players respectively. For every game we did 100 runs and plotted the time of convergence. The figures show that almost every run actually did converge in the given time period. The length of the non-communication period was set to 100 time steps.

6   Discussion

As long as the agents are able to converge to a Nash equilibrium in the given time period before synchronization takes place, our algorithm given in section

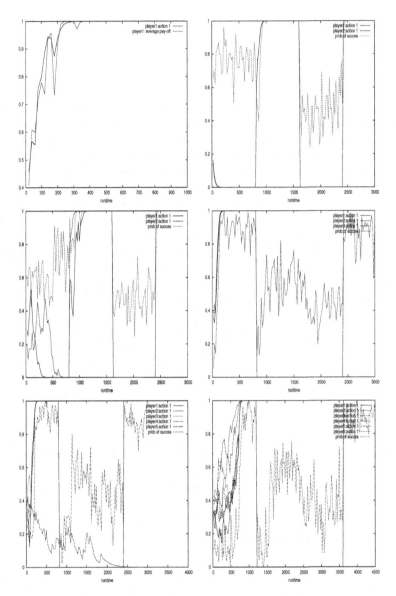

Fig. 7. Top(left) Convergence of the action probabilities in the dominance-solvable game of Figure 1. Two independent learning automata agents use a reward-inaction update scheme (a = 0.05). The other Figures show the evolution of the average pay-off received during play and the evolution of the probability of action 1 for all the participating agents in the following common interest games. Agents are learning automata players, who use the algorithm of section 4.1, see Figure 4.Synchronization happens ever 800 time steps. Top(right), Midlle(Left): Games of Figure 3 (Left) and (Right) respectively. (a = 0.05). Midlle(Right), Bottom(Left), Bottom(Right): Game of Figure 5 for respectively 3, 4 and 6 players.(a = 0.07).

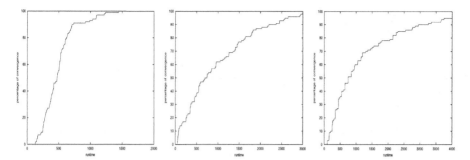

Fig. 8. Percentage of convergence for the following common interest games. Players are Q-learners using the general n player algorithm of section 4.1, see Figure 6. Synchronization and communication of the exploration decision hap[pens every 100 time steps. Left: The deterministic guessing game of Figure 5 with 2 players. Middle: The common interest games of Figure 2 (left) with 2 players. Right: The common interest game of Figure 2(right) with 3 players respectively.

4.1 converges for all 2 player and diagonal common interest games. Even for games with stochastic outcomes. The length of these time periods is thus very important. For now we arranged them manually, but it must be possible for the agents to learn when they have reached an equilibrium.

The same is true for the algorithm in section 4.2. However for convergence to appear, one must be sure to be able to reach all Nash equilibria. In the case of 2 player and diagonal games this is assured, because every action can only belong to one Nash equilibrium. The experiments reported in section 5.2 were able to converge, but only relative small joint action spaces were tested. In larger spaces we foresee to experiment with agents who are able to exclude more than one action temporarily during play. The goal is to let the joint action space shrink in the right direction. We haven't shown results on stochastic games here, due to the technical fact that the algorithm of section 4.2 keeps the best reward seen so far, which is off course not possible when rewards are binary as in the stochastic games we have used. However this problem is easy solved by keeping statistics for every action.

We reported only results on identical payoff games, however our algorithms can also be used for general common interest games. Even when this Pareto optimal solution is not a Nash equilibrium our technique is promising. For instance in the prisoners dilemma game, players will converge to the sub-optimal pure Nash equilibrium. When players agree on further exploration and exclude the actions of this equilibrium, they will find the Pareto optimal solution.

7   Conclusion

In this paper we presented an exploration strategy which drives the agents towards the Pareto optimal Nash equilibrium in repeated deterministic or stochastic common interest games. The agents are independent learners, only limited communication or synchronization is needed when the agents decide to exclude a new combination of actions. In the two agent case, and the special n-agent case which we named the "diagonal games" the convergence to a Pareto optimal Nash equilibrium is guaranteed.

References

1. Claus C., Boutilier C.: The dynamics of reinforcement learning in cooperative multi-agent systems. Proceedings of the fifteenth National Conference on Artificial Intelligence,(1998) p 746–752.
2. Hu J., Wellman M. P.: Multi Agent Reinforcement Learning. Journal of Machine Learning Research 1 (2002) p 1–32.
3. Jafari, C., Greenwald, A., Gondek, D. and Ercal, G.: On no-regret learning, fictitious play, and nash equilibrium. Proceedings of the Eighteenth International Conference on Machine Learning, (2001) p 223–226.
4. Lauer, M., Riedmiller, M.: An algorithm for distributed reinforcement learning in cooperative multi-agent systems. Proceedings of the seventeenth International Conference on Machine Learning (2000)
5. Litmann M.L.: Markov games as a framework for multi-agent reinforcement learning. Proceedings of the Eleventh International Conference on Machine Learning, (1994) p 157–163.
6. Narendra K., Thathachar M., : Learning Automata: An Introduction. Prentice-Hall (1989).
7. Nowé, A., Parent, J., Verbeeck, K.: Social agents playing a periodical poliy. Proceedings of the 12th European Conference on Machine Learning, (2001) p 382–393)
8. Nowé, A., Verbeeck, K.: Distributed Reinforcement learning, Loadbased Routing a case study. Proceedings of the Neural, Symbolic and Reinforcement Methods for sequence Learning Workshop at ijcai99.
9. Osborne J.O., Rubinstein A.: A course in game theory. Cambridge, MA: MIT Press (1994).
10. Sutton, R.S., Barto, A.G.: Reinforcement Learning: An introduction. Cambridge, MA: MIT Press (1998).
11. Samuelson, L.: Evolutionary games and equilibrium selection. Cambridge, MA:MIT Press (1997).
12. Verbeeck, K., Nowé, A., Parent, J.: Homo egualis reinforcement learning agents for load balancing. Proceedings of the first NASA Workshop on Radical Agent Concepts. (2002)

Computational Models of the Amygdala and the Orbitofrontal Cortex: A Hierarchical Reinforcement Learning System for Robotic Control

Weidong Zhou and Richard Coggins

The University of Sydney, Computer Engineering Laboratory
The School of Electrical and Information Engineering
NSW 2006, Australia
{victor, richardc}@ee.usyd.edu.au
http://www.sedal.usyd.edu.au
Tel: (02) 93512014, 93514768
Fax: (02) 93513847

Abstract. This paper presents biologically plausible computational models of brain areas involved in emotion processing and the decision-making process. In the models, the amygdala, the orbotofrontal cortex (OFC) and the basal ganglia work together as a multiple-level hierarchical reinforcement learning system. The amygdala decodes sensory cues into reward-related variables providing a reward-related abstract representation for the decision making process in the OFC, while the basal ganglia learn and execute subtask policies. Here we hypothesize how the amygdala may learn these representations. The models have been implemented in software to control a Khepera robot in a physical environment designed for comparison with animal behaviours. We show that the representation of principal emotion components in the reward function may lead to a more efficient learning algorithm than general Q learning.

1 Introduction

Recently, hierarchical reinforcement learning (HRL) has been an active branch in reinforcement learning research [1,2] which decomposes a reinforcement learning task into multiple level subtasks so that the complexity of learning may be reduced, the policies and value functions learned in subtasks can be shared (reused) for multiple parent tasks [1]. HRL still faces two difficult problems. The first of these is how to determine the invocation and termination of tasks among a group of subtask controllers to solve an overall task optimally. In existing methods, subtasks are usually defined by invocation and termination predicates. This means that transitions between subtasks are predefined and therefore are not flexible. The second problem is how to take advantage of high level features (abstract states or conditions) to produce a more efficient state space representation. In existing HRL methods, features usually used are ill-defined in terms of

R.I. McKay and J. Slaney (Eds.): AI 2002, LNAI 2557, pp. 419–430, 2002.
© Springer-Verlag Berlin Heidelberg 2002

reward and punishment, whereas we are investigating high level reward-related feature extraction learnt by the agent. Natural selection makes animals expert in efficient, flexible and adaptive coordination of a wide range of behavioural responses leading to improved fitness to their environment [3]. Emotions are thought to play an important role in these coordination processes. The decoding of stimuli into reward-related variables (through emotion and motivation processing) provides a representation for a behaviour selection mechanism that selects which subtask policy should be executed [4]. Here, in this paper we define that emotions are derived from external stimuli such as visual cues, and motivations from internal stimuli including hunger level. There are two artificial environments: internal and external as shown in Fig. 1.

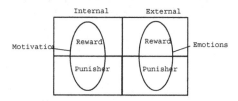

Fig. 1. Definition of emotions and motivations. From the point of view of the learning system the environment is divided into internal and external parts. Emotions are states elicited by the stimuli from the external environment, while motivations are derived from the internal stimuli.

Recently, considerable biological evidence has shown that brain areas such as the amygdala, the orbitofrontal cortex (OFC), the basal ganglia and the dopamine neurons are involved in decision-making and emotion processing for goal-directed behaviour [4,5]. In this paper we have investigated these brain areas and proposed computational models for them. Preliminary experiments have been conducted. The results are very encouraging and presented here. The paper is organized as follows. Section 2 describes biological findings that provide evidence for how the decision-making mechanism operates in an animal's brain at the neural level. Readers already familiar with or who wish want bypass the biological justifications for our models can go directly to section 3 where our computational models are presented. In section 4 the implementation of the models and experimental results are presented. Section 5 summarizes the research work.

2   Biological Background and Guidance

Brain areas including the amygdala, OFC and the basal ganglia are shown to play a critical role in emotion processing and motivational control of goal-directed and reward-oriented behaviour [5] The amygdala is a subcortical region in the anterior part of the temporal lobe, recognized to be at the center of sensory emotional associations covering fear, danger, and satisfaction, and other motivational and emotional sensations [6]. It receives highly processed information from the visual, auditory, olfactory, and taste corticies and projects the outputs to other subcortical sensorimotor areas such as the basal ganglia, cortical areas including the prefrontal cortex, and autonomic systems [4]. The amygdala is involved in stimuli-reinforcement associative learning and codes the emotional and motivational significance of cues [4,7].

The ventral part of the prefrontal area, the orbitofrontal cortex (OFC), is known for its motivation-based role and is a site of highly multisensory convergence [4]. Its inputs include gustatory, olfactory, visual, auditory, somatosensory and dopamine projections. The outputs of the OFC are projected to the striatum, and other cortical areas. The OFC has important functions in motivational behaviour such as feeding and drinking, and in social behaviour [8]. The role of the OFC in discrimination tasks is critical for guiding the selection of the appropriate behavioural responses in the context of changing task contingencies and context, provided by both internal and external signals [9].

The OFC is directly interconnected with the amygdala [4]. The amygdala and the OFC act as part of an integrated neural system guiding decision-making and adaptive response selection. The amygdala is hypothesisized to encode the emotional and motivational significance of cues and the OFC uses this information in the selection and execution of an appropriate behavioural strategy [7].

The motivational function of the OFC may involve the closely connected basal ganglia via fronto-striatal projections. The basal ganglia are parts of the brain that include several nuclei known to be critical to sensorimotor integration. The basal ganglia receive massive inputs from all parts of the neocortex and send outputs that exert both inhibitory and excitory control over parts of the cortex and brainstem. Basal ganglia are involved in reinforcement learning-based sensorimotor control [10]. Thus the basal ganglia provide one of the important information processing and behaviour execution systems in the brain concerned with emotion and motivation processing [4].

3   Framework and Computational Architectures

In spite of the known functions mentioned above, how the OFC plays its role in the use of reward-related abstract representations and the decision making process, how the amygdala assists the OFC and how the motivational behaviours selected by the OFC are evaluated and executed in the basal ganglia is poorly understood. To bridge these gaps we hypothesize that the amygdala is a primary emotion processing center that codes cue significance to predict reward. The predicted reward combined with primary reinforcement in midbrain dopamine neurons provides an error signal to the amygdala and the OFC for association learning and adaptation. The motivational value of behaviours is generated in the OFC, based on which decision-making or selection of behaviour is made. Decoding different stimuli into emotion and motivation values provides a common representation for a decision-making mechanism that takes place in the

OFC. Selection of behaviour is done with internal inhibition between neighboring neurons of the OFC. The selected behaviour is executed in the basal ganglia. Based on the aforementioned biological evidence and our hypotheses, we propose a computational architecture as shown in Fig. 2. In the models the amygdala, OFC, striatum and dopamine neurons constitute a multiple-level hierarchical reinforcement learning system. The OFC is at the top level that makes the abstract decision on choosing among component behaviour alternatives to achieve a goal. The basal ganglia are at the second level that execute the chosen behaviour. The amygdala is at the center that decodes sensory cues into reward-related variables, which we call principal emotion components (PECs). PECs provide reward-related abstract representations for the decision-making process in the OFC. Meanwhile, the amygdala provides reward/punishment predictions to the midbrain dopamine neurons that facilitate learning in the OFC and the amygdala. Using the reward and punishment predictions and primary reinforcement, the dopamine neurons provide effective reinforcement to the amygdala and OFC for associative learning. The inputs to the amygdala and OFC are highly processed abstract information from other corticies such as the inferior temporal cortex, somatosensory cortex, etc. The OFC is involved in decision-making on selection of different behavioural actions. The expected outcome for execution of the selected behaviour is represented in the OFC as state-behaviour-target pair values. Decision-making is made based on the motivational value that is expected to be received after execution of the selected behavioural action sequences.

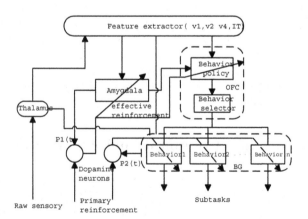

Fig. 2. Schematic diagram of proposed computational models of the amygdala, OFC, striatum and Dopamine neurons. The amygdala is an associative memory coding PECs. The OFC uses PECs and other high-level knowledge to make decisions for selection of appropriate behaviours. The basal ganglia(BG) executes the selected component behaviour. Dopamine neurons provide global reinforcement signals to facilitate the learning process.

4   Experiments

4.1   Experimental Framework

To compare with animal behaviour in the real world, a Khepera robot was utilized for a simple "feeding and drinking" task in a predetermined experimental environment. The schematic diagram of the experiment is shown in Fig. 3. The research vehicle is a sensorimotor system equipped with a color video camera. There are three alternative behaviours for the robot to select, including "feeding", "drinking" and "playing". When "food" or "water" is in the center of the field of view of the camera the robot is considered to be "feeding" or "drinking". Playing is considered to be the absence of "food" or "water". The robot is expected to make decisions to select between behaviours in order to maximize the probability of comfortable states with respect to "hunger" and "thirst" levels over time.

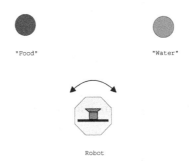

Fig. 3. The schematic diagram of the "feeding and drinking" experiment. A Khepera robot equipped with a color video camera is dedicated to select one of three alternative behaviours: "feeding", "drinking" and "playing". When "food" or "water" is in the center of the field of view of the camera the robot is considered to be "feeding" or "drinking". Playing is considered to be the absence of "food" or "water".

4.2   Architectures and Algorithms

Figure 4 shows the implementation of the proposed models. For this simple task the amygdala is simply modeled as a one-layer associator. The inputs consist of visual and taste stimuli including sight of food (SF), sight of water (SW), taste of food (TF) and taste of water (TW). (Here taste corresponds simply to centering in the visual field). The outputs are first two the PECs, Ep1 and Ep2. The amygdala parameters could be learned using a modified Hebbian learning rule as follows.

$$\Delta w = r\alpha Ain_j Aout_i \tag{1}$$

where r is reward received at next time step, α is the learning rate, Ain and $Aout$ are the corresponding input and output vectors of the amygdala respectively. Equation (1) may diverge because unconstrained growth of the weights.

Oja addresses this problem by normalizing weights during the learning process [11]. The OFC is modeled as a one-layer classifier. The inputs are hunger level signal (S_H), thirst level signal (S_T) and PECs. Its outputs are probabilities of alternative behaviours: feeding, drinking and playing. The OFC was trained using Temporal difference $Q(\lambda)$ as follows [12].

$$\delta_i(t) = r(t+1) + \gamma \max\{Q(x_{t+1}, k)\,|_{k \in behaviours}\} - Q(x_t, i) \tag{2}$$

where $\delta_i(t)$ is ith neuron's temporal difference error at time t; γ is discount factor; $Q(x_t, i)$ is ith neuron's Q value at time t; x_t is state at time t; $r(t+1)$ is the reward received at step $t+1$. For the OFC controller $r(t+1) = r_{OFC}(t+1)$, which is determined by the dominant emotion or motivation given by

$$r_{OFC} = Max(|e_1|, |e_2|, |m_1|, |m_2|) \times sign\,[max()] \tag{3}$$

The weights are updated using the delta rule with an eligibility trace given by,

$$w_{i,j} = w_{i,j} + \eta \delta_i(t) e_{i,j}(t+1) \tag{4}$$

$$e_{i,j} = (1 - \lambda) e_{i,j}(t) + \lambda in_j out_i \tag{5}$$

where w is weight matrix; in is a vector of inputs and out is a vector of outputs; η is the learning rate; λ is decay-rate parameter for the eligibility trace. $e(t)$ is the eligibility trace at time t. The interneuron inhibition between the OFC neurons is implemented by the Softmax algorithm given by,

$$Prob(b_i) = exp(b_i/T) \sum_k exp(b_k/T) \tag{6}$$

where $Prob(b_i)$ is the normalized probability for behaviour b_i; b_i is the motivational value of the behaviour, and the temperature T adjusts the exploratory aspect of behaviour selection. T is reduced as learning proceeds to reduce exploration as the policy improves.The basal ganglia are modeled as behaviour executors for three available behaviours. The executors were individually implemented as one-layer networks that associate visual position signals to motor commands of the micro robot. The basal ganglia are trained using temporal difference $TD(\lambda)$. The temporal difference error is computed as follows.

$$\delta_i(t) = r_s(t+1) + \gamma U(t+1) - U(t) \tag{7}$$

where $U(t)$ is the prediction utility at t and γ is the discount factor; $r_s(t)$ is reward received at t. When the target object is in the center of the field of view reward 1 is received. Otherwise the reward is 0. The weights are updated according to Equations (4) and (5). Exploration was implemented according to Equation (6).

4.3   Input and Output Representations

The visual features of "food" and "water" are decoded from 144x178 color images using HSI (Hue, Saturation, Intensity) color-coding, because hue value alone

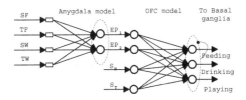

Fig. 4. Implementation of models of the amygdala, OFC and basal ganglia.

can be used to determine the color of a particular pixel, and is not affected by brightness of the pixel [13]. Visual position signals of objectives were extracted by calculating the horizontal coordinate of the center of gravity of the target objects within the visual field. The visual field is divided into 5 equally spaced rectangle regions. A region will be activated if it contains the center of gravity of the target objects. If target objects are in the field of view the corresponding sight signal is activated. When the target objects are in the center of the visual field and the robot stands for a while the corresponding taste signal is activated. In animals, food intake is mainly determined by the amount of glucose in the blood and gastric distention [4]. Thirst and drinking normally arise from a lack of water, which acts through changes in body fluid compartments to initiate drinking. According to hunger and thirst measurement experiments [4,14], hunger level and thirst level signals can be simply modeled as combinations of single time constant exponential functions. Hunger or thirst level signals exponentially decay when feeding or drinking, otherwise they exponentially increase.

$$S_H = \begin{cases} H_0 exp(-t/T_{H1}) & Feeding \\ H_0(1 - exp(-t/T_{H2})) & otherwise \end{cases} \tag{8}$$

$$S_T = \begin{cases} S_0 exp(-t/T_{T1}) & Drinking \\ S_0(1 - exp(-t/T_{T2})) & otherwise \end{cases} \tag{9}$$

where t is the time since the taste of food or water is activated; H_0 and S_0 are the initial hunger and thirst levels respectively when the taste of food or water is activated; T_{H1} or T_{T1} is feeding or drinking rates; T_{H2} or T_{T2} are consuming rates for hunger and thirst levels respectively. In our experiments, $T_{H2} = 4T_{H1}$; $T_{T2} = 4T_{T1}$, and both maximum hunger and thirst levels were set as 1. For experiment consistency, initial hunger and thirst level are set to 0.85 and 0.15 respectively.

4.4   Implementations

As a first step the amygdala representations were learnt off-line in this paper. The principal emotion components, E_{p1} and E_{p2} are replaced by hand-coded emotion variables e_1 and e_2 , which are determined according to their significance in the task and given by

$$e_1, e_2 = \begin{cases} 0.1 & taste \\ 0.05 & sight \\ 0 & otherwise \end{cases} \qquad (10)$$

Since emotion and motivation provide a common representation for evaluating OFC adaptation, emotion and motivation should have the same scale for reinforcement and punishment values. This is supposed to be achieved in the amygdala central nucleus through experience. The motivation variables m_1 and m_2 are derived from hunger and thirst level signals as follows.

$$m_1, m_2 = \begin{cases} -10(S - 0.8) & S > 0.8 \\ 10S - 2 & S < 0.2 \\ 0 & otherwise \end{cases} \qquad (11)$$

where S represents the hunger or thirst level signal. All emotions and motivations compete to be the dominant emotional or motivational state. The dominant value provides reinforcement for the OFC adaptation process. The OFC controller was trained using reinforcement learning. The learning rates are 0.1, $\lambda = 0.7$ and $\gamma = 0.9$. Temperature T is 0.05 before 300 steps, then 0.02. Behaviour actions such as feeding, drinking and playing were individually trained using reinforcement learning ($TD(\lambda)$).

To compare the performance of the proposed models, a switching controller which we denote as Q-controller was designed that was trained using conventional Q-learning [12]. The inputs of the controller are SF, SW, TF, TW, S_H and S_T. After execution of each selected subtask policy reinforcement $r_Q(t+1)$ is received. If hunger or thirst level is above 0.8 or less 0.2, the reward is -1; if both hunger and thirst level are above 0.8 or less than 0.2, the reward is -2; otherwise the reward is 0.

In order to make the training period reasonable (hours) for the real robot, the training period was set to 1000 steps. During the learning period, the following statistics including mean cumulative reinforcement, task switching rate for each action, and action switching times were recorded to assess performance. The models and associated learning implementations were implemented on a dual Pentium II 400 workstation using Visual C++. The computer communicates with the Khepera robot through a serial high-speed interface.

4.5   Results and Discussions

Learning performance for the OFC-controller and the Q-controller are shown in Fig. 5. The graphs for the OFC-controller and the Q-controller are averaged over 5 independent runs. From the learning curves we can see that the OFC controller converged by about 400 steps while the Q controller learns slowly. The averaged behavioural action switching rates of the Q-controller and OFC-controller within 1000 steps are 807 and 685 respectively. This higher frequency of changing subtask policies may cause the Q-controller to learn its tasks relatively slowly. The Q-controller changes its subtask policy so frequently that it does not have enough time to learn potential skills.

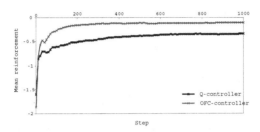

Fig. 5. Comparison of learning performance between the OFC-controller and Q-controller within 1000 learning steps. The graphs are averaged over 5 independent runs.

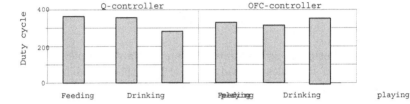

Fig. 6. Comparison of duty cycles of behavioural actions: feeding, drinking and playing during learning process of and OFC-controller Q-controller. Duty cycle denotes proportion of time for each subtask execution. The unit is epochs per 1000 epochs

Figure 6 show duty cycles of subtask policies of both controllers during learning processs. It can be seen that the OFC controlleris more able to manage time efficiently and spends less time executing the feeding and drinking subtask policies. This is because Q controller learning was frequently interrupted by subtask policy switching. Policy switching is expensive, and takes about 3 seconds to change feeding to drinking in our experiments. Figure 7 shows the time cost of switching for the feeding task. t_1 and t_2 denote the time when the feeding task commences and ends respectively; t_0 is the time when taste of food is activated. It can be seen that when the robot shifts to the feeding task from another task, it takes time $t_0 - t_1$ before "food" is actually tasted. The time when the robot consumes "food" is only $t_2 - t_0$. To avoid higher levels of "hunger" and "thirst" the robot has to spend more time feeding and drinking. Therefore, hysteresis with task switching is desirable to efficiently achieve reward. These experimental results indicate that by increasing the emotion value of a stimulus being worked for, desirable hysteresis arises in the behaviour selection mechanism. Once a subtask policy begins execution it should execute for a minimum time before termination. For example, when hungry, food is rewarding. Thus the value of feeding increases and feeding is selected. As feeding continues hunger falls. Thirst increases and may exceed hunger. However, the emotion representation allows the algorithm to learn a higher value for feeding although hunger is less than thirst.

Hence, fast switching to drinking is avoided. As thirst continues to increase, the value of drinking will be high enough for drinking to be selected.

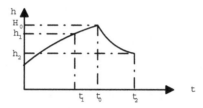

Fig. 7. Hunger level changes as feeding task being executed. t_1 and t_2 denote time when feeding task commences and end respectively; t_0 is the time when taste of food is activated. H_0, h_1 and h_2 are corresponding hunger levels

In the experiment, as a first step the amygdala was implemented using hand-coded emotion variables instead of the PECs that could be learnt online. A statistical analysis was made to investigate the PECs. The raw sensory data, SF, TF, SW,TW and reward were acquired from the Q-controller learning process. Emotion variables e_1 and e_2 were calculated using these data according to Equation 10. The reward-related correlation matrix of the sensory data is given by

$$C = 1/N \sum (X_i - \mu)^T (X_i - \mu) \qquad (12)$$

where $X_i = (rSF_i, rTF_i, rSW_i, rTW_i)$, $i = 1, \cdots N$ and $\mu = 1/N \sum X_i$. Based on the reward-related correlation matrix C and the raw data, E_{p1}, E_{p2} were determined. Future reward R was calculated from real reward with discount factor $\gamma = 0.9$. Figure 8 shows that e_1, e_2, E_{p1} and E_{p2}, and the conditional variances CV_{e1}, CV_{e2}, CV_{ep1} and CV_{ep2} of future reward given e_1, e_2, E_{p1} and E_{p2} respectively. These data correspond the interval of 500 to 600 time steps during the Q-controller learning process as shown in Fig. 5. We can see that E_{p1} and e_2, E_{p2} and e_1 have similar trends. They are related to future reward to some extent. We run the experiment with the substitution of E_{p1} and E_{p2} for e_1 and e_2 to provide state abstraction for OFC-controller. Similar learning performance as shown in Fig. 5 was achieved.

There is related research that involves improvement of switching performance among subtasks in the reinforcement learning area. Sutton et al [2] illustrated that improvement of performance can be obtained by switching flexibly between given subtask controllers. That is, subtasks can be interrupted before their termination state is reached. This method greatly depends on the programmer to predefine subtask sequences and interrupt each subtask before it reaches its termination condition to improve performance. Dietterich proposed the MAXQ decomposition [1] that has both semantics as a subroutine hierarchy – and declarative semantics – as a representation of the value function of a hierarchical policy. The MAXQ value function decomposition can represent the value function of any

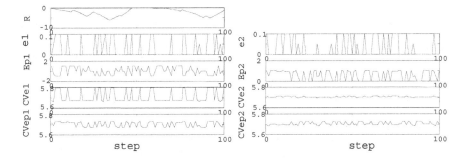

Fig. 8. Hand-wired emotion variables e_1, e_2, first two principal emotion components E_{p1} and E_{p2}. CV_{e1}, CV_{e2}, CV_{ep1} and CV_{ep2} are the conditional variances of future reward R given e1, e2, Ep1 and Ep2. The graphs correspond the interval of 500–600 time steps of Q-controller shown in Fig. 5

policy that is consistent with the given hierarchy. MAXQ also exploits state abstractions, so that individual MDPs within the hierarchy can ignore large parts of the state space. Gadanho and Hamllam [15] used an emotion-based event-detection mechanism to decide termination of behaviour. However, whether or not the emotion values trigger a corresponding behavioural action is dependent upon a threshold preset by the programmer. Whereas in our models flexible and efficient subtask policy switching was achieved by of emotion values that can be learned through experience.

5   Conclusions

Biologically inspired models of emotion processing and decision-making process have been presented. In the models, the amygdala, OFC, basal ganglia and dopamine neurons constitute a multiple-level hierarchical reinforcement learning system. The OFC is at the top level that makes abstract decisions on selecting which behavioural action to execute. The amygdala decodes sensory cues into reward-related emotion variables PECs. The amygdala provides reward-related state abstraction and reward evaluation for the OFC. The state abstraction can be learnt online. The basal ganglia are at the bottom level, which execute the chosen subtask policy. The dopamine neurons provide effective reinforcement for the amygdala and the OFC in their adaptation. Preliminary experimental results and data analysis were presented. The results show that inclusion of reward-related feature representation PECs and emotional reward evaluation leads to a more efficient learning process for the OFC.

References

1. Dietterich, T.G.: Hierarchical reinforcement learning with the MAXQ value function decomposition. J. Artificial Intelligence Research. **13** (2000) 227–303

2. Sutton, R. S., Precup, D., Singh, S.: Between MDPs and Semi-MDPs: A framework for temporal abstraction in reinforcement learning. Artificial Intelligence. **112** (1999) 181–211

3. Krebs, J.R., Davies, N.B.: Behavioural ecology: an evolutionary. 3rd ed. Oxford [England] Boston, Blackwell Scientific Publications.(1991)

4. Rolls, E.T.: The brain and emotion. Oxford University Press. (1999)

5. Schultz, W.L., Tremblay, L., Hollerman, J.R.: Reward processing in primate orbitofrontal cortex and basla ganglia. Cerebral Cortex. **10** (2000) 272–283

6. LeDoux, J.E.: Orbitofrontal cortex and basolateral amygdala encode expected outcomes during learning. Annu. Rev. Neurosci. **23** (2000) 155–184

7. Schoenbaum,G., Chiba, A. A. and Gallagher, M.: Neural Encoding in Orbitofrontal Cortex and Basolateral Amygdala during Olfactory Discrimination Learning. J. Neuroscience. **19** (2000) 1876–1884

8. Malkova, L., Gaffan, D., Murray, E.A.: Excitotoxic lesions of the amygdala fail to produce impairment in visual learning for auditory secondary reinforcement but interfere with reinforcer devaluation effects in rhesus monkeys. J. Neurosci. **17** (1997) 6011–6020

9. Bechara, A., Damasio, H., Damasio, A.R.: Emotion, decision making and the orbitofrontal cortex. Cerebral Cortex. **10**, (2000) 295-307

10. Barto. A.G.: Adaptive critics and the basal ganglia. In J.L. Davis J.C. Houk and D.G. Beiser, editors, Models of information processing in the basal ganglia. MIT Press (1995) 215–232

11. Oja, E.: A simplified neuron model as a principal component analyzer. Journal of Mathmatical Biology. **15** (1982) 267–273

12. Watkins, C., Dayan, P.: Q-Learning. Machine Learning. **8** (1992) 279–292

13. Foley, J.D., Dam, A., Feiner, S.K., Hughes, J.F.: Computer graphics: principle and practice. 2nd ed. Addison-Wesley Publishing Company. (1996)

14. Rolls, B.J., Rolls, E.T.: Thirst. Cambridge University Press. (1982)

15. Gadanho S.C., Hallam J.: Emotion-triggered learning in autonomous robot control. Cybernetics and Systems. **32** (2001) 531–559

A General Approach for Building Constraint Languages

Petra Hofstedt

Berlin University of Technology
ph@cs.tu-berlin.de

Abstract. This paper describes a general approach for the integration of arbitrary declarative languages and constraint systems. The main idea is to consider declarative programs together with the language evaluation mechanisms as constraint solvers and to integrate them into an overall system of cooperating solvers. Exemplarily, we present the integration of a logic language with a constraint system, and the extension of a functional logic language with constraints. The approach allows to build constraint languages according to current requirements and thus it enables comfortable modelling and solving of many problems.

1 Introduction

Declarative programming languages base on the idea that programs should be as close as possible to the program specification and domain. Programs of these languages usually consist of directly formulated mathematical objects, i.e. of predicates or functions in logic or functional languages, resp. In functional logic languages both are used. Our point of view is to consider *declarative programming as constraint programming*: On one hand, predicates are constraints. On the other hand, relating functional expressions with others, typically by equality relations, yields equality constraints over functional expressions. This kind of consideration opens an interesting potential: In [Hof00] a framework for cooperating constraint solvers has been introduced which allows the integration of arbitrary solvers and the handling of hybrid constraints. Considering declarative programming as constraint programming and looking at the language evaluation mechanisms as constraint solvers we are able to integrate these solvers into this framework. Within this framework it is then possible to extend the declarative languages by constraint systems and, thus, to build constraint languages customized for a given set of requirements for comfortable modeling and solving of many problems. The paper elaborates this approach.

We start with a short introduction of the framework for cooperating solvers of [Hof00] in Sect. 2. Section 3 is dedicated to the consideration of declarative languages as solvers and their integration into this system. We examine the integration of a logic language in Sect. 3.1 and we consider the approach wrt. a functional logic language in Sect. 3.2. In Sect. 4 we discuss further aspects of the approach and compare it with related work.

R.I. McKay and J. Slaney (Eds.): AI 2002, LNAI 2557, pp. 431–442, 2002.
© Springer-Verlag Berlin Heidelberg 2002

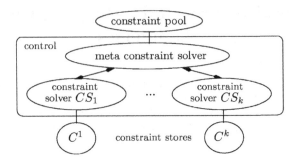

Fig. 1. General architecture for cooperating constraint solvers

2 Cooperating Solvers

In [Hof00] a framework for cooperating constraint solvers has been introduced. It allows the integration of arbitrary solvers providing typical interface functions and the handling of hybrid constraints which none of the single solvers is able to handle alone. In this section we briefly reintroduce the necessary notions.

Figure 1 shows the architecture of the system. It consists of a number of constraint solvers CS_ν, $\nu \in L^1$, with associated constraint stores C^ν, a meta constraint solver, and a constraint pool. The meta solver coordinates the work of the individual solvers. Their stores hold the constraints which have been propagated previously. The pool is a set containing the constraints which still have not been considered. Given a constraint conjunction to solve, the pool initially contains all these constraints. Step by step the constraints from the pool are propagated by the associated solvers to their stores. For information exchange between the solvers the stores are projected which may yield new information for other solvers in form of new constraints. These are put back into the pool and propagated later. This procedure continues until no more information exchange takes place. In this case, the contents of the stores and of the pool express whether the initially given constraint conjunction was unsatisfiable or not and provide restrictions of the solution space via projections of the stores, in particular cases even solutions of the initial problem. In [Hof00] the system is formally described and it is shown how to define cooperation strategies for the solvers.

Of particular interest for the generality of the approach are the requirements for the interfaces of the solvers to integrate into the system. For every solver CS_ν, first, a function $tell_\nu$ for propagating constraints from the pool to its store C^ν, and, second, a set of functions $proj_{\nu\to\mu}$, $\mu \in L$, for providing information from a store C^ν for another solver CS_μ for information exchange is required.

Constraint Propagation. The (partial) function $tell_\nu$ adds a constraint $c \in Cons_\nu$ (or part of it) to a constraint store $C^\nu \in Store_\nu$ such that the newly received store C'^ν is satisfiable in the domain $\mathcal{D}_\nu$ of CS_ν and a perhaps remaining part C''

---

[1] L denotes the set of indices of constraint solvers.

$tell_\nu: Cons_\nu \times Store_\nu \longrightarrow \{true, false\} \times Store_\nu \times \mathcal{DCCons}_\nu$ with

(1) if $tell_\nu(c, C^\nu) = (true, C'^\nu, C'')$, then

   (a) $\mathcal{D}_\nu \vDash \forall((C^\nu \wedge c) \longleftrightarrow (C'^\nu \wedge C''))$,   (b) $\mathcal{D}_\nu \vDash \forall(c \longrightarrow C'')$,

   (c) $\mathcal{D}_\nu \vDash \forall(C'^\nu \longrightarrow C^\nu)$ and   (d) $\mathcal{D}_\nu \vDash \exists C'^\nu$,

(2) if $tell_\nu(c, C^\nu) = (false, C'^\nu, C'')$, then $C'^\nu = C^\nu$, $C'' = false$, $\mathcal{D}_\nu \nvDash \exists(C^\nu \wedge c)$.

Fig. 2. Interface function $tell_\nu$ (requirements)

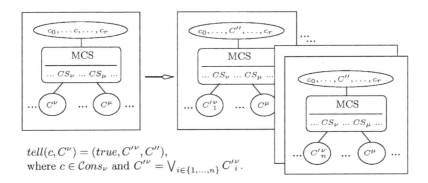

$tell(c, C^\nu) = (true, C'^\nu, C'')$,
where $c \in Cons_\nu$ and $C'^\nu = \bigvee_{i \in \{1,...,n\}} C'^\nu_i$.

Fig. 3. How the interface function $tell$ works

of c is put back into the pool. Figure 2 shows the requirements for the function $tell_\nu$.[2] The given requirements allow the integration of many existing solvers into the cooperating system and enable to take particular properties of solvers, like their incompleteness[3], into consideration.

Figure 3 visualizes the state change of the system when a solver performs a successful constraint propagation using $tell$ (Case (1)). The left side shows the system before the propagation, the right side afterwards. We propagate c to C^ν by $tell_\nu(c, C^\nu)$. Constraint c is deleted from the pool. It is propagated to store C^ν which yields C'^ν. This may be a disjunction of stores in general, i.e. $C'^\nu = \bigvee_{i \in \{1,...,n\}} C'^\nu_i$. This "splitting" of the store causes a splitting of the architecture with the different disjuncts of C'^ν as new stores of CS_ν. The third part C'' (in general a disjunction of constraint conjunctions, i.e. $C'' \in \mathcal{DCCons}_\nu$) of the result of $tell$ is put back into the pool for a later consideration.

If $tell_\nu(c, C^\nu)$ fails (Case (2)) because c and C^ν are contradictory, then $false$ is added to the constraint pool and C^ν does not change (not shown in the figure).

Example 1. The interface function $tell_\mathcal{R}$ of a solver $CS_\mathcal{R}$ for linear constraints over real numbers could work as follows:

---

[2] Originally in ([Hof00]) two forms of successful propagation are distinguished, necessary for usual solvers to ensure termination of the system. For the "language solvers", treated in the following, this can be left out.

[3] Here, it is used that $tell$ is partial.

$tell_{\mathcal{R}}((x \leq 3), C) = (true, C', true)$ with $C = true$, $C' = (x \leq 3)$, and
$tell_{\mathcal{R}}((x = 4), C') = (false, C', false)$.

Projection of Constraint Stores. Projection is used for information exchange between constraint solvers CS_ν and CS_μ, $\nu \neq \mu$. We require a function $proj_{\nu\to\mu}$: $\mathcal{P}(X_\nu \cap X_\mu) \times Store_\nu \to \mathcal{DCCons}_\mu$. At this, $proj_{\nu\to\mu}(Y, C^\nu) = C$ describes a projection of a store C^ν wrt. common variables (i.e. $Y \subseteq X_\nu \cap X_\mu$) to provide constraints C of another solver CS_μ. It provides knowledge implied by the store C^ν. To ensure that no solution is lost, $proj_{\nu\to\mu}$ must be defined in such a way that every solution of C^ν is a solution of the projection C in $\mathcal{D}_\mu$.[4]

Projecting a store at a particular stage of the system does not change the stores while the pool is enhanced by the projected constraints.

Example 2. Consider the solver $CS_\mathcal{R}$ and a finite domain solver $CS_{\mathcal{FD}}$. The projection function $proj_{\mathcal{FD}\to\mathcal{R}}$ of $CS_{\mathcal{FD}}$ could be defined on top of a function $proj_{\mathcal{FD}}$ which yields constraints of the FD solver and a conversion function $conv_{\mathcal{FD}\to\mathcal{R}}$. Let $C^{\mathcal{FD}} = ((y =_{\mathcal{FD}} 3) \wedge (x >_{\mathcal{FD}} y) \wedge (x \in_{\mathcal{FD}} \{2,3,4,5,6\}))$ hold.
$proj_{\mathcal{FD}}(\{x\}, C^{\mathcal{FD}}) = (x \in_{\mathcal{FD}} \{4,5,6\})$ and
$proj_{\mathcal{FD}\to\mathcal{R}}(\{x\}, C^{\mathcal{FD}}) = conv_{\mathcal{FD}\to\mathcal{R}}(proj_{\mathcal{FD}}(\{x\}, C^{\mathcal{FD}})) = ((x \geq 4) \wedge (x \leq 6))$.

3   Declarative Languages as Solvers

The system of cooperating solvers described in Sect. 2 allows to integrate different host languages by treating them as constraint solvers.

Our main observations at this are that the evaluation of expressions in declarative languages consists of their stepwise transformation to a normal form while particular knowledge (substitutions) is collected, and that this is similar to a stepwise propagation of constraints to a store which is at this simplified.

In the following, we consider the integration of a logic language and of a functional logic language, resp., into the system of cooperating solvers. While we extend the languages by constraints the evaluation mechanisms of the languages are nearly unchanged, they are only extended by a mechanism for collecting constraints of further integrated constraint solvers.

3.1   A Logic Language as Constraint Solver

A *logic program* P consists of a sequence of rules $Q : - L_1, \ldots, L_k$. and facts Q. and a goal $G = (R_1, \ldots, R_l)$. For a more comfortable programming and a more efficient evaluation logic programs have been extended by constraints such that in the right hand side of a rule every L_i is allowed to be not only a literal but as well a constraint of an arbitrary constraint system. This led to *constraint logic programming*. At this, the evaluation mechanism resolution of logic languages has been extended by collecting constraints and checking their satisfiability using appropriate constraint solvers ([JMMS98]).

---

[4] This required property is called *soundness*, see [Hof01].

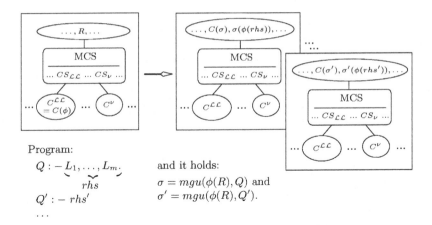

Program:

$Q : - \underbrace{L_1, \ldots, L_m.}_{rhs}$ and it holds:

$Q' : - rhs'$

$\ldots$

$\sigma = mgu(\phi(R), Q)$ and
$\sigma' = mgu(\phi(R), Q').$

Fig. 4. How the interface function $tell_{\mathcal{LL}}$ works

Substitutions and unifiers are defined as usual, see for example [Han94]. If $dom(\sigma) = \{x_1, \ldots, x_n\}$ is the domain of a substitution σ and $\sigma(x_i) = t_i$, then we write $\sigma = \{x_1/t_1, \ldots, x_n/t_n\}$. The composition of some substitutions σ and ϕ is defined by $(\sigma \circ \phi)(E) = \sigma(\phi(E))$ for every term or formula E, resp. The substitutions σ which we are handling are usually idempotent, i.e. $\sigma \circ \sigma = \sigma$. A substitution σ corresponds to a set of equations given by $\mathcal{E}(\sigma) = \{x = t \mid x/t \in \sigma\}$. Let the parallel composition $\uparrow$ of idempotent substitutions be defined as in [Pal90], i.e. $\uparrow (\sigma, \phi) = mgu(\mathcal{E}(\sigma), \mathcal{E}(\phi))$, where mgu denotes the most general unifier.

Example 3. The following constraint logic program P describes resistors of 300Ω and 600Ω and it defines the sequential and the parallel composition of resistors.

$\mathrm{rc}(\mathrm{simple}(300), 300).$ (1.1)

$\mathrm{rc}(\mathrm{simple}(600), 600).$ (1.2)

$\mathrm{rc}(\mathrm{seq}(X, Y), Z) : -\mathrm{rc}(X, XV), \mathrm{rc}(Y, YV), XV + YV =_{\mathcal{R}} Z.$ (2)

$\mathrm{rc}(\mathrm{par}(X, Y), Z) : -\mathrm{rc}(X, XV), \mathrm{rc}(Y, YV), 1/XV + 1/YV =_{\mathcal{R}} 1/Z.$ (3)

By means of the well known CLP example we will now show how to integrate a language into the system of cooperating solvers. For this, we consider the evaluation mechanism resolution as constraint solver $CS_{\mathcal{LL}}$ for constraints over the herbrand universe. Besides performing resolution steps, the solver is able to collect constraints of other domains. Thus, constraints of $CS_{\mathcal{LL}}$ are goals according to a given constraint logic program P, equality constraints $(X =_{\mathcal{LL}} t)$ between variables and terms and all constraints appearing in P.

For the integration of $CS_{\mathcal{LL}}$ into the system the interface functions $tell_{\mathcal{LL}}$ and $proj_{\mathcal{LL} \to \nu}$, $\nu \in L$, must be defined. We will use the propagation function $tell_{\mathcal{LL}}$ to emulate resolution steps and the projection functions $proj_{\mathcal{LL} \to \nu}$ to provide constraints representing the substitutions computed during resolution for other cooperating solvers for information exchange. The definitions of the

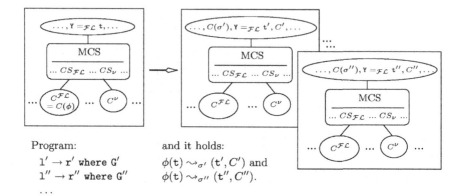

Fig. 5. How the interface function $tell_{\mathcal{FL}}$ works

interface functions are given in Fig. 6. At this, $C(\sigma) = \bigwedge_{\mathtt{X}/\mathtt{t}\in\sigma}(\mathtt{X} =_{\mathcal{LL}} \mathtt{t})^5$ denotes a constraint conjunction (resp. a store) representing a substitution σ.

Propagation: Figure 4 illustrates how the application of $tell_{\mathcal{LL}}$ is used to simulate a successful resolution step. First the constraint pool contains the constraint R (a goal), the constraint store $C^{\mathcal{LL}}$ contains a substitution ϕ, i.e. $C^{\mathcal{LL}} = C(\phi)$ holds. The successful propagation of R corresponds to a resolution step on R (Case (1a) of the $tell_{\mathcal{LL}}$ definition): For R (under ϕ) and for every rule $Q : -rhs$ with unifiable left hand side the corresponding mgu σ is built. Goal R in the pool is replaced by the right hand side of the rule under σ and ϕ, i.e. by $\sigma(\phi(rhs))$, and by a constraint conjunction $C(\sigma)$ which expresses the newly built substitution σ. If there is more than one matching rule, then we get a number of newly created constraint pools and, thus, a number of instantiations of the architecture. The remaining cases of the $tell_{\mathcal{LL}}$ definition describe the situation when there is no matching rule for a goal (Case (1b)), thus, the propagation fails (*false* is added to the pool) and they describe the propagation of an equality constraint $(\mathtt{X} =_{\mathcal{LL}} \mathtt{t})$ (Cases (2a) and (2b)). If the corresponding substitution $\{\mathtt{X}/\mathtt{t}\}$ is not contradictory wrt. the current store $C(\phi)$, it is added by parallel composition $\uparrow$ (Case (2a)). If it is contradictory (Case (2b)), then the propagation fails.

Projection: The store of $CS_{\mathcal{LL}}$ contains constraints expressing the substitution computed so far. Thus, projection for information exchange between the logic language solver $CS_{\mathcal{LL}}$ and other integrated solvers means building equality constraints implied by this substitution and adding them to the pool.

The requirements for $tell_{\mathcal{LL}}$ and $proj_{\mathcal{LL}\rightarrow\nu}$, $\nu \in L$, are fulfilled. Note in particular Case (1a) of the definition of $tell_{\mathcal{LL}}$, where $\mathcal{P}^\star, \mathcal{D}_\nu, \nu \in L \models \forall((C^{\mathcal{LL}} \wedge c) \longleftrightarrow (C'^{\mathcal{LL}} \wedge (\bigvee_{r_i\in P_R}(C(\sigma_i) \wedge \sigma_i(\phi(rhs_i))))))$ holds (see for example [JMMS98] and there in particular Lemma 5.3).

---

[5] This corresponds to $\mathcal{E}(\sigma)$, where the equality symbol is subscripted by $\mathcal{LL}$ to mark constraints of $CS_{\mathcal{LL}}$.

Example 4. Consider the cooperation of a logic language solver $CS_{\mathcal{LL}}$ based on program P of Example 3 and a solver $CS_{\mathcal{R}}$ for constraints over the reals.

The state of the cooperating system (see Fig. 1) depends on the contents of the constraint pool and of the stores. Thus, we represent it in the following by a chart, consisting of an upper part for the pool, and a lower part for the stores $C^{\mathcal{LL}}$ at the left side and $C^{\mathcal{R}}$ at the right side.

We ask for resistors R1 and R2 connected in parallel such that their overall resistor value is 200Ω, i.e. we evaluate the goal $rc(par(R1, R2), 200)$. Thus, initially the constraint pool contains the constraint $rc(par(R1, R2), 200)$ and the stores are empty, i.e. they contain $true$:

$$rc(par(R1, R2), 200)$$

true	true

Propagating the constraint of the pool means applying $tell_{\mathcal{LL}}$ which corresponds to a resolution step using Rule (3) which describes resistors in parallel:

$tell(rc(par(R1, R2), 200), C_0^{\mathcal{LL}}) = (true, C_0^{\mathcal{LL}}, X =_{\mathcal{LL}} R1 \wedge Y =_{\mathcal{LL}} R2 \wedge$
$\qquad Z =_{\mathcal{LL}} 200 \wedge rc(R1, XV) \wedge rc(R2, YV) \wedge 1/XV + 1/YV =_{\mathcal{R}} 1/200).$

This yields the following new state of our system:[6]

$$rc(R1, XV),\ rc(R2, YV),\ 1/XV + 1/YV =_{\mathcal{R}} 1/200$$

true	true

Next, we choose the goal $rc(R1, XV)$ for a resolution step using the rules of P.

$tell(rc(R1, XV), C_0^{\mathcal{LL}}) = (true, C_0^{\mathcal{LL}}, (R1 =_{\mathcal{LL}} simple(300) \wedge XV =_{\mathcal{LL}} 300) \vee$
$\qquad (R1 =_{\mathcal{LL}} simple(600) \wedge XV =_{\mathcal{LL}} 600) \vee \ldots)$

Obviously, there are four alternatives according to P. In the following, we only derive one alternative (Rule (1.1) is promising) and leave the others out.

$$R1 =_{\mathcal{LL}} simple(300),\ XV =_{\mathcal{LL}} 300,\ rc(R2, YV),\ 1/XV + 1/YV =_{\mathcal{R}} 1/200$$

true	true

Propagating the bindings, e.g., $XV =_{\mathcal{LL}} 300$, they are added to $C^{\mathcal{LL}}$ (according to Case (2a) of the $tell_{\mathcal{LL}}$ definition). As well, we propagate $1/XV + 1/YV =_{\mathcal{R}} 1/200$ as constraint over real numbers using $tell_{\mathcal{R}}$ of the solver $CS_{\mathcal{R}}$.

$$rc(R2, YV)$$

$C'^{\mathcal{LL}}$: R1 $=_{\mathcal{LL}}$ simple(300) $\wedge$ XV $=_{\mathcal{LL}}$ 300	$1/XV + 1/YV =_{\mathcal{R}} 1/200$

The current store $C'^{\mathcal{LL}}$ of $CS_{\mathcal{LL}}$ contains the computed substitution of our resolution steps. To distribute it over the full goal we project the store wrt. $CS_{\mathcal{R}}$. The result is put into the pool: $proj_{\mathcal{LL} \to \mathcal{R}}(\{XV\}, C'^{\mathcal{LL}}) = (XV =_{\mathcal{R}} 300)$.[7]

$$XV =_{\mathcal{R}} 300,\ rc(R2, YV)$$

R1 $=_{\mathcal{LL}}$ simple(300) $\wedge$ XV $=_{\mathcal{LL}}$ 300	$1/XV + 1/YV =_{\mathcal{R}} 1/200$

---

[6] We omit unnecessary parts of substitutions to shorten the trace.
[7] R1 $\notin X_{\mathcal{LL}} \cap X_{\mathcal{R}}$, thus, no projection wrt. the variable R1 takes place.

We propagate the constraint XV $=_\mathcal{R}$ 300 to the store of $CS_\mathcal{R}$. The solver proves the satisfiability of its constraints and simplifies its store:

$$\text{rc(R2,YV)}$$

R1 $=_{\mathcal{LL}}$ simple(300) $\wedge$ XV $=_{\mathcal{LL}}$ 300	XV $=_\mathcal{R}$ 300 $\wedge$ YV $=_\mathcal{R}$ 600

Unfolding the goal rc(R2, YV) would be the next step. After a number of propagations and projections of computed substitutions for information exchange, projecting the stores would finally yield redundant constraints only. Furthermore, the pool becomes empty (true). The system stops and projecting the store $C''^{\mathcal{LL}}$ of the logic language solver wrt. the variables of the initial constraint rc(par(R1, R2), 200) yields the valid bindings as answer.

$proj_{\mathcal{LL}}(\{R1\}, C''^{\mathcal{LL}}) = (R1 =_{\mathcal{LL}}$ simple(300)), and
$proj_{\mathcal{LL}}(\{R2\}, C''^{\mathcal{LL}}) = (R2 =_{\mathcal{LL}}$ simple(600)).

Thus, for R1 and R2 holds expectedly rc(par(simple(300), simple(600)), 200).

The correspondence between a CLP evaluation and a derivation using our approach of cooperating (language) solvers can be observed.

3.2   A Functional Logic Language as Constraint Solver

Let us consider now a second language: a functional logic one. In contrast to logic languages which work with predicates functional logic languages allow to work with functions which may be even arguments of functions. Let $\Sigma = (S, F; ar)$ be a signature, consisting of a set S of sorts, a set F of function symbols and an arity function $ar : F \to S^\star$. F is partitioned into a set Δ of *constructors* and a set Γ of *defined functions*. Let X be a set of variables. A *functional logic program* P over Σ is a finite set of rules of the form $f(t_1, \ldots, t_n) \to r$, where $f \in \Gamma^{s_1 \times \ldots \times s_n \to s}$, $t_i \in \mathcal{T}(\Delta, X)^{s_i}$ (i.e. t_i is constructor term over variables of X), and $r \in \mathcal{T}(F, X)^s$, $s, s_i \in S$. $f(t_1, \ldots, t_n)$ is linear, i.e. it does not contain multiple occurrences of one variable, and $var(r) \subseteq var(f(t_1, \ldots, t_n))$ holds, i.e. the right hand side of a rule does not introduce new variables. In the usual way, P induces a congruence relation $=_P$.

A typical evaluation mechanism for functional logic programs is narrowing [Han94]. We recall the necessary notions: A position p in a term t is represented by a sequence of natural numbers, $t|_p$ denotes the subterm of t at position p, and $t[r]_p$ denotes the result of replacing the subterm $t|_p$ by the term r. A *narrowing step* $t \leadsto_{l \to r, p, \sigma} t'$ is defined as follows: a term t is *narrowable* to a term t' if there is a nonvariable position p in t, i.e. $t|_p \notin X$, $l \to r$ is a new variant of a rule from P, $\sigma = mgu(t|_p, l)$, and $t' = \sigma(t[r]_p)$. We write $t \leadsto_{l \to r, \sigma} t'$ and $t \leadsto_\sigma t'$ if p and/or the rule $l \to r$ are obvious from the context.

Example 5. The following functional logic program provides rules for the addition of natural numbers which are represented by the constructors 0 and s.

add(0,X) $\to$ X   (1)
add(s(X),Y) $\to$ s(add(X,Y))   (2)

In order to solve the equation $\mathtt{add(s(A),B)} =_P \mathtt{s(s(0))}$, we apply narrowing. The chosen subterm is underlined.

$$\underline{\mathtt{add(s(A),B)}} =_P \mathtt{s(s(0))}.$$
$$\leadsto_{(2),\{\mathtt{X1/A,Y1/B}\}} \mathtt{s}(\underline{\mathtt{add(A,B)}}) =_P \mathtt{s(s(0))}$$
$$\leadsto_{(1),\{\mathtt{A/0,X2/B}\}} \mathtt{s(B)} =_P \mathtt{s(s(0))}$$

Thus, σ with $\sigma(\mathtt{A}) = 0$ and $\sigma(\mathtt{B}) = \mathtt{s(0)}$ (computed by unification of $\mathtt{s(B)}$ and $\mathtt{s(s(0))}$ after the last narrowing step) is a solution of the initial equation. That is, $\mathtt{add(s(0),s(0))} =_P \mathtt{s(s(0))}$ holds. One further solution can be computed using the rules during narrowing in a different order.

The introduction of constraints into the rules of our language yields constraint functional logic programming. A *functional logic program P with constraints over Σ* is a finite set of rules of the form $(f(t_1,\ldots,t_n) \to r \text{ where } G)$ with $f(t_1,\ldots,t_n) \to r$ as before and where G is a finite set of constraints over Σ. A *narrowing step with constraints* $t \leadsto_{s,p,\sigma} (t',C')$, where t, t' are terms and C' is a set of constraints, is defined as follows: t is *narrowable* to (t',C') if there is a nonvariable position p in t, i.e. $t|_p \notin X$, $s = (l \to r \text{ where } C)$ is a new variant of a rule from P, $\sigma = mgu(t|_p, l)$, $t' = \sigma(t[r]_p)$, and $C' = \bigwedge_{c \in C} \sigma(c)$.

Given a constraint functional logic program P, we consider the evaluation mechanism narrowing as constraint solver $CS_{\mathcal{FL}}$ for constraints over functional expressions. Besides performing narrowing steps, the solver collects constraints of other domains. Thus, the constraints of $CS_{\mathcal{FL}}$ contain the constraints appearing in P and constraints of the form $(\mathtt{W} =_{\mathcal{FL}} \mathtt{t})$, where $\mathtt{t}$ is a term and $\mathtt{W} \in X$ does not appear in $\mathtt{t}$. Constraints of the form $(\mathtt{t_1} =_{\mathcal{FL}} \mathtt{t_2})$ such that $t_1, t_2 \notin X$ are decomposed into $(\mathtt{W} =_{\mathcal{FL}} \mathtt{t_1}) \wedge (\mathtt{W} =_{\mathcal{FL}} \mathtt{t_2})$, where $\mathtt{W}$ is a new variable.

The definition of the interface function $tell_{\mathcal{FL}}$ is given in Fig. 7. The definition of $proj_{\mathcal{FL} \to \nu}, \nu \in L$, is the same as that of $proj_{\mathcal{LL} \to \nu}$ in Fig. 6 (the only difference is that every index $\mathcal{LL}$ is replaced by $\mathcal{FL}$). At this, for a substitution σ, $C(\sigma) = \bigwedge_{\mathtt{X}/t \in \sigma} (\mathtt{X} =_{\mathcal{FL}} \mathtt{t})$ holds.

Propagation: Figure 5 illustrates how the interface function $tell_{\mathcal{FL}}$ is used to simulate a narrowing step with constraints. Initially the constraint pool contains the constraint $c = (\mathtt{Y} =_{\mathcal{FL}} \mathtt{t})$ and the constraint store $C^{\mathcal{FL}}$ contains a substitution ϕ. The successful propagation of c (i.e. Case (1a) of Fig. 7) corresponds to a narrowing step with constraints on $\mathtt{t}$. For the term $\mathtt{t}$ for every matching rule a narrowing step with constraints is performed yielding the most general unifier σ' and a tuple $(\mathtt{t}', C')$. The constraint $(\mathtt{Y} =_{\mathcal{FL}} \mathtt{t})$ in the constraint pool is replaced by the constraint $(\mathtt{Y} =_{\mathcal{FL}} \mathtt{t}')$, by a constraint conjunction $C(\sigma')$ which expresses the newly built substitution σ', and by the newly built constraint conjunction C' which arose from the narrowing step.

If there is more than one matching rule, then we get a number of newly built constraint pools and, thus, a number of instantiations of the architecture.

The remaining cases of the $tell_{\mathcal{FL}}$ definition in Fig. 7 describe a failing propagation if there is no matching rule for the term to be reduced (Case (1b)), and propagations (Cases (2a) and (2b)), where the term t is already a constructor term (i.e. no narrowing takes place). A binding of Y to term t is tried to add to the constraint store $C^{\mathcal{FL}}$ by parallel composition $\uparrow$ of substitutions which may be successful (Case (2a)) or failing (Case (2b)).

Example 6. Our resistor problem of Example 3 is expressed by the following constraint functional logic program:

$$\text{rcfl(simple(300))} \rightarrow 300 \text{ where } \{\text{true}\} \tag{1.1}$$
$$\text{rcfl(simple(600))} \rightarrow 600 \text{ where } \{\text{true}\} \tag{1.2}$$
$$\text{rcfl(seq(X, Y))} \rightarrow Z \text{ where } \{XV + YV =_{\mathcal{R}} Z, XV =_{\mathcal{FL}} \text{rcfl(X)}, YV =_{\mathcal{FL}} \text{rcfl(Y)}\} \tag{2}$$
$$\text{rcfl(par(X, Y))} \rightarrow Z \text{ where} \tag{3}$$
$$\{1/XV + 1/YV =_{\mathcal{R}} 1/Z, XV =_{\mathcal{FL}} \text{rcfl(X)}, YV =_{\mathcal{FL}} \text{rcfl(Y)}\}$$

A constraint conjunction corresponding to the goal $\text{rc(par(R1, R2), 200)}$ of Example 4 is $R =_{\mathcal{FL}} \text{rcfl(par(R1, R2))} \wedge R =_{\mathcal{FL}} 200.[8]$ Initially the constraint pool contains these constraints and the stores are empty (**true**):

$$R =_{\mathcal{FL}} \text{rcfl(par(R1, R2))}, R =_{\mathcal{FL}} 200$$

true	true

Propagating the constraint $R =_{\mathcal{FL}} \text{rcfl(par(R1, R2))}$ means to apply $tell_{\mathcal{FL}}$ which corresponds to a narrowing step using the Rule (3):
$$\text{rcfl(par(R1, R2))} \rightsquigarrow_{(3),\sigma}$$
$$(Z, 1/XV + 1/YV =_{\mathcal{R}} 1/Z \wedge XV =_{\mathcal{FL}} \text{rcfl(R1)} \wedge YV =_{\mathcal{FL}} \text{rcfl(R2)}),$$
where $\sigma = \{X/R1, Y/R2\}$. Thus,
$$tell(R =_{\mathcal{FL}} \text{rcfl(par(R1, R2))}, C_0^{\mathcal{FL}}) = (true, C_0^{\mathcal{FL}}, (X =_{\mathcal{FL}} R1 \wedge Y =_{\mathcal{FL}} R2 \wedge$$
$$R =_{\mathcal{FL}} Z \wedge 1/XV + 1/YV =_{\mathcal{R}} 1/Z \wedge XV =_{\mathcal{FL}} \text{rcfl(R1)} \wedge YV =_{\mathcal{FL}} \text{rcfl(R2)})).$$
This yields the following new state of our system[9]:

$$R =_{\mathcal{FL}} Z, 1/XV + 1/YV =_{\mathcal{R}} 1/Z, XV =_{\mathcal{FL}} \text{rcfl(R1)}, YV =_{\mathcal{FL}} \text{rcfl(R2)}, R =_{\mathcal{FL}} 200$$

true	true

We propagate the constraint $1/XV + 1/YV =_{\mathcal{R}} 1/Z$ using the interface function $tell_{\mathcal{R}}$ of $CS_{\mathcal{R}}$ and the bindings $R =_{\mathcal{FL}} Z$ and $R =_{\mathcal{FL}} 200$ using Case (2a) of $tell_{\mathcal{FL}}$. The solvers simplify their stores at this:

$$XV =_{\mathcal{FL}} \text{rcfl(R1)}, YV =_{\mathcal{FL}} \text{rcfl(R2)}$$

$Z =_{\mathcal{FL}} 200 \wedge R =_{\mathcal{FL}} 200$	$1/XV + 1/YV =_{\mathcal{R}} 1/Z$

Propagating the remaining constraints of the pool means applying narrowing steps on rcfl(R1) and rcfl(R2) resp. Information exchange between the solvers can be performed using projection of computed substitutions as in Example 4.

---

[8] Remember the decomposition of constraints $t_1 =_{\mathcal{FL}} t_2$, where $t_1, t_2 \notin X$, into $(W =_{\mathcal{FL}} t_1) \wedge (W =_{\mathcal{FL}} t_2)$.

[9] We omit unnecessary parts of substitutions as before.

$tell_{\mathcal{LL}}$: Let P be a constraint logic program, let $C^{\mathcal{LL}} = C(\phi)$ be the store of $CS_{\mathcal{LL}}$.

1. Let $R = p(t_1, \ldots, t_m)$ be the constraint (goal) which is to be propagated.
    a) Let $P_R \subseteq P$ be the largest (nonempty) set of rules of P such that for every rule r_i in P_R, there is a new variant r_i' with $Q_i : -rhs_i$ s.t. no variable occurs in R and r_i', and $\sigma_i = mgu(\phi(R), Q_i)$. Then $C'^{\mathcal{LL}} = C^{\mathcal{LL}}$ and
    $tell_{\mathcal{LL}}(R, C^{\mathcal{LL}}) = (true, C'^{\mathcal{LL}}, \bigvee_{r_i \in P_R}(C(\sigma_i) \wedge \sigma_i(\phi(rhs_i))))$.
    b) If there is no rule in P for which the above item holds, then
    $tell_{\mathcal{LL}}(c, C^{\mathcal{LL}}) = (false, C^{\mathcal{LL}}, false)$.
2. Let $c = (\mathtt{X} =_{\mathcal{LL}} \mathtt{t}) = C(\sigma)$ be the constraint which is to be propagated.
    a) If $\uparrow (\sigma, \phi) \neq \emptyset$, then $tell_{\mathcal{LL}}(c, C^{\mathcal{LL}}) = (true, C'^{\mathcal{LL}}, true)$, $C'^{\mathcal{LL}} = C(\uparrow (\sigma, \phi))$.
    b) If $\uparrow (\sigma, \phi) = \emptyset$, then $tell_{\mathcal{LL}}(c, C^{\mathcal{LL}}) = (false, C^{\mathcal{LL}}, false)$.

$proj_{\mathcal{LL} \to \nu}$: The projection of a store $C^{\mathcal{LL}} = C(\phi)$ wrt. a constraint system $\nu \in L$ and a set of variables $X = X_{\mathcal{LL}} \cap X_\nu$ makes the substitutions for $\mathtt{Y} \in X$ explicit:
$$proj_{\mathcal{LL} \to \nu}(X, C(\phi)) = \begin{cases} \bigwedge_{\mathtt{Y}/t \in \phi}(\mathtt{Y} =_\nu \mathtt{t}) & \text{if } \phi \neq \emptyset \\ true & \text{otherwise.} \end{cases}$$

Fig. 6. Interface functions $tell_{\mathcal{LL}}$ and $proj_{\mathcal{LL} \to \nu}, \nu \in L$

$tell_{\mathcal{FL}}$: Let P be a functional logic program with constraints, let $C^{\mathcal{FL}} = C(\phi)$ be the current constraint store of $CS_{\mathcal{FL}}$. Let $c = (\mathtt{Y} =_{\mathcal{FL}} \mathtt{t})$ be the constraint to propagate.

1. Let $\phi(\mathtt{t})$ be unsolved, i.e. the term $\phi(\mathtt{t}) \notin \mathcal{T}(\Delta, X_{\mathcal{FL}})$ still contains symbols of functions defined in P, and let $\phi(\mathtt{t}) \notin X_{\mathcal{FL}}$ hold, i.e. $\phi(\mathtt{t})$ is not a variable.
    a) Let $P_c \subseteq P$ be the largest (nonempty) set of rules of P such that for every rule r_i in P_c, there is a new variant r_i' with $(\mathtt{l}_i \to \mathtt{r}_i \text{ where } \mathtt{C}_i)$ s.t. there exists a position p_i in $\phi(\mathtt{t})$ and a substitution σ_i with $\phi(\mathtt{t}) \rightsquigarrow_{r_i, p_i, \sigma_i} (\mathtt{t}_i', C_i')$. Then $tell_{\mathcal{FL}}(c, C^{\mathcal{FL}}) = (true, C'^{\mathcal{FL}}, \bigvee_{r_i \in P_c}(C(\sigma_i) \wedge (\mathtt{Y} =_{\mathcal{FL}} \mathtt{t}_i') \wedge C_i'))$.[a]
    The constraint store does not change, i.e. $C'^{\mathcal{FL}} = C^{\mathcal{FL}}$ holds.
    b) If there is no rule in P for which the above item holds, then
    $tell_{\mathcal{FL}}(c, C^{\mathcal{FL}}) = (false, C^{\mathcal{FL}}, false)$.
2. If $\phi(\mathtt{t})$ is solved, i.e. $\phi(\mathtt{t}) \in \mathcal{T}(\Delta, X_{\mathcal{FL}})$ or $\phi(\mathtt{t}) \in X_{\mathcal{FL}}$ holds, then:
    a) If $\uparrow (\{\mathtt{Y}/\mathtt{t}\}, \phi) \neq \emptyset$, then
    $tell_{\mathcal{FL}}(c, C^{\mathcal{FL}}) = (true, C'^{\mathcal{FL}}, true)$, where $C'^{\mathcal{FL}} = \uparrow (\{\mathtt{Y}/\mathtt{t}\}, \phi)$.
    b) If $\uparrow (\{\mathtt{Y}/\mathtt{t}\}, \phi) = \emptyset$, then $tell_{\mathcal{FL}}(c, C^{\mathcal{FL}}) = (false, C^{\mathcal{FL}}, false)$.

---

[a] Constraints $(\mathtt{t}_1 =_{\mathcal{FL}} \mathtt{t}_2)$ in C_i' are split into $(\mathtt{W} =_{\mathcal{FL}} \mathtt{t}_1) \wedge (\mathtt{W} =_{\mathcal{FL}} \mathtt{t}_2)$ if necessary.

Fig. 7. Interface function $tell_{\mathcal{FL}}$

4 Conclusion

This paper describes a general approach for the integration of arbitrary declarative languages and constraint systems. After a short reintroduction of the system of cooperating solvers of [Hof00,Hof01] we have shown how to integrate host languages into such a system by treating their evaluation mechanisms together with programs as constraint solvers and defining interface functions for them. As examples we discussed the integration of a logic language which yields CLP [JMMS98] and that of a functional logic language which yields a languages similar to [MIS99]. The integration of a functional language is left out. However, it differs from a functional logic one simply by the additional restriction that an expression for reduction must be ground. Accordingly the interface definition must be adapted. In the examples we extended the languages with constraints over real numbers. However, in general, the overall system for cooperating solvers allows the handling of hybrid constraints over different domains and, thus, as well the extension of the languages by hybrid constraints.

The aspect of strategies has been left out in the present paper. The description of particular reduction strategies for the languages is possible using the strategy definition mechanism described in [Hof00] by variation of the choice of the constraints and stores for propagation and for projection, resp.

Our approach of building constraint languages using the cooperation framework introduced in [Hof00] allows the integration of different host languages and constraint systems. This particularly distinguishes it from other existing systems of cooperating solvers (for example [Hon94,Mon96,Rue95]) that usually have one fixed host language (a logic language).

Building constraint languages customized for a given set of requirements by our approach enables comfortable modeling and solution of many problems.

References

[Han94]   M. Hanus. The Integration of Functions into Logic Programming: From Theory to Practice. *Journal of Logic Programming*, 19&20:583–628, 1994.

[Hof00]   P. Hofstedt. Better Communication for Tighter Cooperation. In *First International Conference on Computational Logic*, LNCS 1861, 2000.

[Hof01]   P. Hofstedt. *Cooperation and Coordination of Constraint Solvers*. PhD thesis, Dresden University of Technology, 2001.

[Hon94]   H. Hong. Confluency of Cooperative Constraint Solvers. Technical Report 94-08, Research Institute for Symbolic Computation, Linz, Austria, 1994.

[JMMS98]   J. Jaffar, M.J. Maher, K. Marriott, and P. Stuckey. The Semantics of Constraint Logic Programs. *Journal of Logic Programming*, 37:1–46, 1998.

[MIS99]   M. Marin, T. Ida, and W. Schreiner. A Distributed System for Solving Equational Constraints Based on Lazy Narrowing Calculi. In *JSSST Workshop on Programming and Programming Languages (PPL'99)*, 1999.

[Mon96]   E. Monfroy. *Solver Collaboration for Constraint Logic Programming*. PhD thesis, Centre de Recherche en Informatique de Nancy. INRIA, 1996.

[Pal90]   C. Palamidessi. Algebraic Properties of Idempotent Substitutions. In M.S. Paterson, editor, *Automata, Languages and Programming - ICALP*, LNCS 443, 1990.

[Rue95]   M. Rueher. An Architecture for Cooperating Constraint Solvers on Reals. In A. Podelski, editor, *Constraint Programming: Basics and Trends*, LNCS 910, 1995.

Metric SCSPs: Partial Constraint Satisfaction via Semiring CSPs Augmented with Metrics

Aditya Ghose and Peter Harvey

Decision Systems Laboratory
School of IT and Computer Science
University of Wollongong
NSW 2522 Australia

Abstract. The Semiring CSP (SCSP) framework is a popular and robust approach to solving partial constraint satisfaction problems which generalizes several other schemes such as fuzzy CSP, weighted CSP etc. We argue in this paper that it is useful to augment the SCSP framework such that each constraint specifies, in addition, a metric on the semiring values. The additional knowledge of distances between 'preference values' (the elements of the semiring) permits us to define a notion of parameterized solving of SCSPs where we can seek solutions with a preference value no worse than a given value.

1 Introduction

There has been considerable recent interest in Semiring Constraint Satisfaction Problems (SCSPs) [BMR97]. SCSPs provide an elegant generalization of CSPs where instead of specific descriptions of preference levels or preference values (for example, the interval $[0, 1]$ for fuzzy CSPs) we have an abstract notion of preference values viewed as elements of a semiring[1]. The SCSP framework supports a fine-grained representation of preferences over tuples in finite-domain constraints, which may also be viewed as local specifications of optimization criteria. This offers a rich language for modelling a variety of different applications.

The notion of distance of a candidate solution to a partial constraint satisfaction problem from a given constraint (or combined over a set of constraints) has been considered in systems such as HCLP [WB93]. The integration of such notions with the SCSP framework can open up a variety of useful possibilities. We explore such an integration in this paper, specifically by extending the notion of a constraint in the SCSP scheme to include a metric on the semiring.

One way to view the formulation of classical CSP in the SCSP scheme [BMR97] is to think of a threshold of 1 (the 'best' value in the semiring) delineating the subset of tuples in the SCSP solution that are of interest. In other words, we wish to consider only solution tuples that have a semiring value no less than 1. In general, an SCSP might not admit a solution containing tuples for which the corresponding semiring value is the 'best' value. In response, Bistarelli et al [BMR97] define the notion of an *abstract solution*,

---

[1] The semirings of interest are *c-semirings* defined later in the paper, but we shall often informally refer to these simply as semirings.

R.I. McKay and J. Slaney (Eds.): AI 2002, LNAI 2557, pp. 443–454, 2002.
© Springer-Verlag Berlin Heidelberg 2002

which is the set of those solution tuples for which tuples with a 'better' semiring value do not exist. Thus a given problem might generate an abstract solution set consisting of multiple tuples, possibly with distinct semiring values which are all incomparable under the partial order generated by the semiring. We can consider this to be using **0** (the 'worst' value in the semiring) as the threshold, finding the 'best' solutions but able to accept any.

We propose instead to generalise the notion of a threshold which determines the solution tuples of interest by allowing any arbitrary semiring value α to be specified in place of **0**. The problem thus becomes one of seeking solution tuples whose semiring values are 'no worse' than α, with a system of relaxation in the case where the threshold is not achievable. Such an approach is useful if we are interested in solutions which may potentially violate[2] some constraints, with the caveat that the degree of violation (informally speaking) is minimized. We are thus able to answer the following question: if the given problem were to be minimally changed to obtain at least one solution tuple with a semiring value no worse than α, which tuple(s) would meet this requirement? Note that by adding a parameter α, we have *not* converted the soft constraint solving problem (fundamentally an optimization problem) to a satisfaction problem. This is because we are still interested in seeking out the 'best' amongst those solutions that satisfy the threshold (should some exist), or the 'best' relaxation of the problem that enables us to satisfy the threshold.

If a given problem does in fact have solution tuples with semiring values no worse than α, the problem is easily solved. Things become difficult when there are no solution tuples which satisfy this requirement. We are then interested in identifying solution tuples which, if 'promoted' to be assigned the higher semiring value α would result in minimum deviation (in a sense similar to the intuitions use in the HCLP framework [WB93]) from the specified constraints. The SCSP formulation only offers a partial order for comparing semiring values, which is inadequate for defining a meaningful notion of minimum deviation. This motivates the extension to Metric SCSPs that we propose in this paper.

In Metric SCSPs a constraint is a triple consisting of the constraint signature, a function that maps each value in the cartesian product of the domains of the variables in the signature to a semiring value and a metric on the semiring. The ability to represent distances between semiring values permits the definition of a variety of distinct notions of what constitutes a solution to a given problem. We speculate that for many interesting instances of Metric SCSPs, it might be possible to translate the problem in polynomial time into a traditional SCSP, but observe that this is not true in general (this has to do with the our framework permitting non-binary functions for combining measures of deviation of individual constraints from candidate solutions). We also note that the polytime reduction is possible only for a fixed threshold α, whereas our motivation is to develop a system that permits exploration of the search space with alternative threshold values (we discuss later how it might be possible to define incremental resolving strategies in such settings).

---

[2] We say that an SCSP constraint is violated when we assign to a tuple a semiring value higher than that assigned by the constraint itself

Recall that a metric space consists of a set A and a function $d : A \times A \to \mathbb{R}^+$. To be seen as representing 'distance', the function d must satisfy 3 properties (a definition of a metric using only 2 properties is possible, but for clarity we use 3). These are $d(\alpha, \beta) = 0 \Leftrightarrow \alpha = \beta$, $d(\alpha, \beta) = d(\beta, \alpha)$, and $d(\alpha, \gamma) \leq d(\alpha, \beta) + d(\beta, \gamma)$.

Also recall that a c-semiring is defined as a tuple $S = \langle A, \oplus, \otimes, \mathbf{0}, \mathbf{1} \rangle$ satisfying the following properties (where $\alpha, \beta, \gamma \in A$):

- A is a set with $\mathbf{0}, \mathbf{1} \in A$
- $\oplus$ is commutative, associative, $\alpha \oplus \alpha = \alpha$, $\alpha \oplus \mathbf{1} = \mathbf{1}$ and $\alpha \oplus \mathbf{0} = \alpha$
- $\otimes$ is commutative, associative, binary, distributive ($\alpha \otimes (\beta \oplus \gamma) = (\alpha \otimes \beta) \oplus (\alpha \otimes \gamma)$), $\alpha \otimes \mathbf{1} = \alpha$ and $\alpha \otimes \mathbf{0} = \mathbf{0}$

We can derive the partial ordering $\leq_S$ from a c-semiring by $(\alpha \leq_S \beta) \Leftrightarrow (\alpha \oplus \beta = \beta)$. As a result of this definition, $\oplus$ and $\otimes$ are both monotone on $\leq_S$, $\langle A, \leq_S \rangle$ is a complete lattice and $\alpha \oplus \beta = \text{lub}(\alpha, \beta)$. For a more complete analysis of c-semirings and SCSP see [BMR97].

Augmenting the SCSP formulation with metrics is a non-trivial exercise. We begin by postulating some intuitive properties that metrics on semirings must satisfy - these properties delineate the class of metrics that are in some sense 'compatible' with a given semiring. We provide examples of useful metrics which satisfy these properties and identify some additional (and potentially useful) properties that follow from our initial axioms. We then define two alternative notions of a parameterized solution to a Metric SCSP. In the first, we seek solution tuples which, if assigned a semiring value no worse than α, would result in minimum deviation from the original set of constraints. Minimum deviation is determined via the metrics specified in each constraint and any combination function from a broad-ranging class of combination functions that we delineate. We further narrow down this set of solution tuples by seeking the equivalent of an abstract solution within them (i.e., seeking those tuples for which no tuple with a 'better' semiring value exists within the set). In the second approach, we use the metrics and the combination function to filter out from the set of possibly many abstract solution tuples those which represent minimum deviation from the original problem.

Example 1. Consider the following informal constraint satisfaction problem:
Three people wish to purchase a car together (hatchback, sedan, stationwagon, or 4-wheel drive). We wish to find the type of car which satisfies the most people, taking the approach that constraints supplied by each person will create an over-constrained problem. Each person writes down a single constraint they place on the type of car to be purchased. This constraint must reflect their opinions on the different types of cars, expressed as answers to the following questions:

1. Sufficient style
2. Sufficient passenger space
3. Sufficient luggage space

To model this problem, we use a single variable X with domain $D = \{$ hatchback, sedan, stationwagon, 4-wheel-drive $\}$, and will ask each persion to supply a single preference constraint representing their responses to the above questions. However, we must first specify a c-semiring to use such that each user can express themselves sufficiently.

One reasonable option for modelling this problem is to provide a simple linear c-semiring with the exact semantics of fuzzy constraint satisfaction. However, the result is an immediate loss of information as the answers to each of the above questions is mapped (rather arbitrarily) into a linear domain. Essentially, the relaxation strategy has been determined (by the mapping into a linear domain, specifying which trade-offs should occur first) before the constraints were written. The constraints are no longer expressions of preferences but are directives specifying a problem-specific input to the relaxation strategy.

Another reasonable option for modelling this problem is to use the c-semiring formed as the product of 3 of the above c-semirings (where the product is that described in [BMR97]). Each component c-semiring corresponds to exactly one of the above questions. In this way we do not lose any information (the answers to each question are clearly available) but two flaws present themselves. Again the relaxation strategy has become tied to the constraints themselves, evidenced by the fact that after the constraints have been written the relative 'weights' of these constraints cannot be easily adjusted. Additionally, this model provides no facilities for the types of prioritisation seen in the previous model (questions cannot be given greater priorities). This shortcoming would be present even in the case of a non-idempotent combination operator.

For both of these models there is no way an individual can express the interchangability of two properties. For example, a user cannot express that (for a specific car) they are satisfied with the *total space* available, viewing the passenger and luggage space as equivalent. A more detailed explanation of this problem is presented below in Table 3.

We will now present an alternative construction using metrics which separates the relaxation strategy from the 'constraints' themselves. To clearly demonstrate the motivation for our system we have chosen a simpler c-semiring, $S = \langle A, \oplus, \otimes, \mathbf{0}, \mathbf{1} \rangle = \langle \{0, 1\}^3, \max, \min, \langle 0, 0, 0 \rangle, \langle 1, 1, 1 \rangle \rangle$.[3] Each element of the c-semiring represents a yes or no answer to each of the above questions, with $\langle 1, 1, 1 \rangle$ being 'yes' to all questions. The operations max and min operate on each element of the tuples independently, so for example $\max(\langle 0, 0, 1 \rangle, \langle 1, 0, 0 \rangle) = \langle 1, 0, 1 \rangle$ and $\min(\langle 0, 1, 1 \rangle, \langle 1, 1, 0 \rangle) = \langle 0, 1, 0 \rangle$.

We then modify the normal definition of a constraint in SCSP by including a metric. As a result each of the three constraints $\{c_i : 1 \leq i \leq 3\}$ (one constraint per person) contains:

- A set con_i indicating the variables for this constraint (in this case $\{X\}$).
- A function $def_i : D \rightarrow A$ expressing the individuals opinion for each type of car. These are specified in Table 1.
- A metric $d_i : A \times A \rightarrow \mathbb{R}^+$ expressing their perceived difference between c-semiring values.

We can summarise each individuals preferences as follows:

def_1: Is satisfied with a small car for transporting people and luggage, and is concerned that larger cars are not stylish.

def_2: Needs a larger car for transporting luggage. A sedan would be sufficient for transporting people, but not luggage.

---

[3] To model this problem more accurately it is expected that multiple values (for example the range $[0, 1]$ as used in fuzzy CSP models) would be used per question.

Table 1. Constraint definitions

X	def_1	def_2	def_3
hatchback	$\langle 1,1,1 \rangle$	$\langle 1,0,0 \rangle$	$\langle 0,0,1 \rangle$
sedan	$\langle 1,1,1 \rangle$	$\langle 1,1,0 \rangle$	$\langle 1,1,1 \rangle$
stationwagon	$\langle 0,1,1 \rangle$	$\langle 1,1,1 \rangle$	$\langle 0,1,1 \rangle$
4-wheel-drive	$\langle 0,1,1 \rangle$	$\langle 1,1,1 \rangle$	$\langle 0,1,1 \rangle$

def_3: Considers a sedan to be the only stylish car. A hatchback has enough space for luggage, but is too small for passengers.

However, there is more information which can be revealed by having each person supply a metric over the c-semiring. We will supply two metrics which enhance the knowledge of a person's constraints, and explain the differences inferred by each.

Table 2. Metric used by first person

d_1	$\langle 0,0,0 \rangle$	$\langle 0,0,1 \rangle$	$\langle 0,1,0 \rangle$	$\langle 0,1,1 \rangle$	$\langle 1,0,0 \rangle$	$\langle 1,0,1 \rangle$	$\langle 1,1,0 \rangle$	$\langle 1,1,1 \rangle$
$\langle 0,0,0 \rangle$	0	1	3	4	3	4	6	7
$\langle 0,0,1 \rangle$	1	0	4	3	4	3	7	6
$\langle 0,1,0 \rangle$	3	4	0	1	6	7	3	4
$\langle 0,1,1 \rangle$	4	3	1	0	7	6	4	3
$\langle 1,0,0 \rangle$	3	4	6	7	0	1	3	4
$\langle 1,0,1 \rangle$	4	3	7	6	1	0	4	3
$\langle 1,1,0 \rangle$	6	7	3	4	3	4	0	1
$\langle 1,1,1 \rangle$	7	6	4	3	4	3	1	0

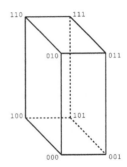

Fig. 1. Graphical representation

The metric d_1, detailed in Table 2, indicates that the person cares equally about style and passenger space, but cares little for luggage space. For example, the difference (or distance) between $\langle 0,0,0 \rangle$ (not satisfied with anything) and $\langle 0,1,0 \rangle$ (satisfied only with the passenger space) is 3. In contrast, the difference (or distance) between $\langle 0,0,0 \rangle$ (not satisfied with anything) and $\langle 0,0,1 \rangle$ (satisfied only with the luggage space) is 1, indicating that this person can see little difference between a car with insufficient luggage space and one with sufficient luggage space. This indifference may arise as the person does not carry luggage often, making the distinction between car luggage space possible but of little importance.

This particular choice of metric does not exhibit any additional information that we could not include in a SCSP formulation using a more sophisticated c-semiring. However, observe that in this metric each dimension of the c-semiring is treated as independent - the rating of a car's passenger space cannot be used to infer any rating on the luggage space. This is highlighted in Fig. 1 where the c-semiring is represented as a cube, with proportions according to the metric. This is important in light of the next metric which does not treat each dimension of the c-semiring as independent.

Table 3. Metric used by second person

d_2	$\langle 0,0,0\rangle$	$\langle 0,0,1\rangle$	$\langle 0,1,0\rangle$	$\langle 0,1,1\rangle$	$\langle 1,0,0\rangle$	$\langle 1,0,1\rangle$	$\langle 1,1,0\rangle$	$\langle 1,1,1\rangle$
$\langle 0,0,0\rangle$	0	1	1	2	1	2	2	3
$\langle 0,0,1\rangle$	1	0	1	1	2	1	2	2
$\langle 0,1,0\rangle$	1	1	0	1	2	2	1	2
$\langle 0,1,1\rangle$	2	1	1	0	3	2	2	1
$\langle 1,0,0\rangle$	1	2	2	3	0	1	1	2
$\langle 1,0,1\rangle$	2	1	2	2	1	0	1	1
$\langle 1,1,0\rangle$	2	2	1	2	1	1	0	1
$\langle 1,1,1\rangle$	3	2	2	1	2	1	1	0

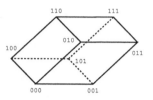

Fig. 2. Graphical representation

By the metric d_2, detailed in Table 3, the 'rating' of a vehicle with sufficient luggage space and insufficient passenger space is similar to the rating of a vehicle with sufficient passenger space but insufficient luggage space. A possible explanation is that this person can see only a small difference between luggage space and passenger space - in many cases, luggage can be placed in what is normally deemed as passenger space. The areas deemed as passenger space and luggage space overlap in the mind of this person, and so the dimensions of the c-semiring are not seen as independent.

It is extremely difficult to capture the differences between these two constraints using existing partial constraint satisfaction schemes. Although SCSP can represent c_1, it would be difficult to represent c_2 using the same c-semiring. Specifically, the preference value $\langle 0,1,1\rangle$ has a different meaning in c_1 than in c_2. The differences between the interpretation of the preference values made in each constraint become particularly important when the threshold parameter α is set to a value other than $\langle 1,1,1\rangle$.

2   Metrics for a C-Semiring

The system we propose centres on a function representing the distance of each value α in the c-semiring from each other value β. Such functions are termed metrics [Gil87]. This function is used for determining the 'size' of the differences in elements of a c-semiring. It is trivial to define such a function for a c-semiring. However, this function should meet certain goals:

- It should not be possible to define a function which could be used to map an n-dimensional c-semiring into an (n-1)-dimensional c-semiring.
- The distance between two distinct c-semiring values should not be zero. To say that the distance between two distinct c-semiring values is zero would undermine the purpose of the c-semiring.
- The function is intended to describe the difference between c-semiring values. Relationships between c-semiring values (derived from $\oplus$ and $\leq_S$) should be reflected in an intuitive way in the function, ensuring the 'meaning' of each value is kept.

We will call a function which provides the concept of 'distance' or 'difference' in a c-semiring a *c-metric*. Below we state and describe the formal properties of a c-metric $d : A \times A \to \mathbb{R}^+$:

M1: $(d(\alpha, \beta) = 0) \Leftrightarrow (\alpha = \beta)$

The differences between two c-semiring values should be zero iff the two values are the same. It may seem useful to relax this property, so as to indicate that two c-semiring values may be 'interchanged' without penalty. However, if it were relaxed an entire region of the c-semiring would become 'interchangeable' (due to properties P1 and P2 below). This region would contain its upper bound, and so the question would arise: why has the upper bound not been used in place of all other values in the region?

M2 (Symmetry): $d(\alpha, \beta) = d(\beta, \alpha)$

The function d should be defined to be the same in either 'direction'. This is obvious as d should indicate the differences between c-semiring values, which do not change if the direction of measurement is changed. Care must be taken to avoid considering the function d as a measure of 'penalty' for moving a semiring value 'upwards' in the ordering, in which case the direction of measurement would change the result.

M3 (Triangle inequality): $d(\alpha, \gamma) \leq d(\alpha, \beta) + d(\beta, \gamma)$

The shortest 'path' from a c-semiring value α to another value γ is the most direct path. By providing a geometric interpretation for d, this property helps ensure more intuitive results later.

P1 ($\leq_S$ Consistency): $(\alpha \leq_S \beta \leq_S \gamma) \Rightarrow (d(\alpha, \beta) \leq d(\alpha, \gamma))$

This property ensures that the interpretation of d as a measurement of distance is consistent with the $\leq_S$ ordering. Note that this property only guarantees that a sequence of increasing c-semiring values do not become closer to any lesser value.

P2 ($\oplus$ Consistency): $d(\alpha \oplus \gamma, \beta \oplus \gamma) \leq d(\alpha, \beta)$

This property guarantees that relationships between elements of the c-semiring (which indicate their similarity) are not discarded. To explain this property, we must discuss the purpose of $\oplus$, and how this relates it to d.

1. The $\oplus$ operation is intended to provide a projection of a constraint onto a smaller set of variables, constructing 'summary information'. This information is used in constraint propagation algorithms (and possibly other techniques such as heuristic search). To obtain 'maximum utility' from $\oplus$ the result of $\alpha \oplus \beta$ must provide the value which is most closely related to both α and β, yet which 'includes' (absorbs under addition) both.

2. Our use of metrics is based on the assumption that minimal deviation from constraints to reach a fixed level of consistency is our aim. Thus, our c-metric must be considered as a measurement of difference between two values, or decribing the total amount of 'trade-off' which occurs between two c-semiring values. This is a natural interpretation given the properties M1, M2 and M3.

Consider now the situation where $\alpha \oplus \gamma$ and $\beta \oplus \gamma$ differ more than α and β. For such a situation to arise, additional unrelated information must have been introduced by $\oplus$ when adding γ. Such additional information reduces the quality of the 'summary information' generated by $\oplus$, contrary to our assumption that $\oplus$ provides 'maximum utility'.

By this reasoning we can see that $\alpha \oplus \gamma$ and $\beta \oplus \gamma$ should differ less than α and β (the addition of γ should only increase the similarity). As our metric represents the 'difference' between elements we can conclude that $d(\alpha \oplus \gamma, \beta \oplus \gamma) \leq d(\alpha, \beta)$. Although this property may seem unusually general, it does not severely restrict the choice of metrics that we would regard as reasonable.

The first 3 properties (M1, M2 and M3) are standard properties for a metric. They ensure the function d correctly encapsulates the standard notion of a distance for a set of values (in this case, the set A). The remaining properties (P1 and P2) provide consistency with the $\leq_S$ ordering, and the $\oplus$ operation. We have considered the purpose for $\oplus$ in the construction of these last 2 properties.

Definition 1. *A function $d : A \times A \to \mathbb{R}^+$ is a c-metric for the c-semiring $\langle A, \oplus, \otimes, 0, 1 \rangle$ iff it satisfies the properties M1, M2, M3, P1, and P2.*

2.1   Examples of C-Metrics

In this part of the paper we show that the restrictions (P1 and P2) placed on c-metrics do not block the usage of common metrics.

We cannot assume any restrictions on the type of c-semiring, and so any valid c-semiring (as defined in [BMR97]) should have at least one usable c-metric. Recall that the discrete metric can be described as $d(\alpha, \beta) = 0$ if $\alpha = \beta$, $d(\alpha, \beta) = 1$ if $\alpha \neq \beta$ [Gil87]. Using this definition it is possible to prove the following result.

Theorem 1. *The discrete metric is a c-metric for any c-semiring.*

In addition to the discrete metric, other known metrics also satisfy the conditions of P1 and P2. In particular, there are the large class of metrics for $\mathbb{R}^n$ derived from the p-norm. The p-norm [Gil87] is written $\| x \|_p$, where x represents a vector $\langle x_1, x_2, \ldots, x_n \rangle \in \mathbb{R}^n$ and $1 \leq p \leq \infty$. For any such vector x, its 'length' measured according to the p-norm is $\| x \|_p = \sqrt[p]{|x_1^p| + |x_2^p| + \ldots + |x_n^p|}$. So, we can form a standard metric using the concept of 'length' between two points: $d(\alpha, \beta) = \| \alpha - \beta \|_p$. We show that a c-semiring suitable for multi-criteria optimization can use this class of metrics.

Theorem 2. *For a c-semiring $\langle [0, 1]^n, \sup, \inf, 0, 1 \rangle$, any metric $d(\alpha, \beta) = \| \alpha - \beta \|_p$ (where $1 \leq p \leq \infty$) is a c-metric.*

As d (defined using the p-norm) is a standard metric, properties M1, M2 and M3 are already proven as satisfied [Gil87]. For space considerations we have omitted the proof[4] for P1 and P2.

This theorem is useful for showing that the extra properties P1 and P2 do not exclude the usual set of metrics that could be used with such spaces. Although the theorem is stated for a Cartesian product of a fixed-size interval in $\mathbb{R}$, it applies equally for differing-sized and/or discrete intervals. This result further establishes that a range of standard c-metrics exist for multi-criteria optimization.

By Theorems 1 and 2 we have at least two possible c-metrics for the c-semiring $S = \langle [0, 1], \sup, \inf, 0, 1 \rangle$. The discrete metric represents a simple, uniform penalty for any deviation from a specified point in $[0, 1]$. In contrast, a metric based on a p-norm represents a proportional scaled penalty for any such deviation. A linear combination of these two metrics would thus represent a uniform penalty (for the fact that deviation from a specified point has occured), plus an extra penalty based on the size of the deviation. By generating additional c-metrics from existing c-metrics on the same c-semiring, we

---

[4] Note that proofs omitted from this paper are available in a longer technical version

significantly increase the possible choice of c-metrics for a given c-semiring. The most obvious (and useful) constructive methods for generating more c-metrics are the $+$, $\times$ and max of existing c-metrics.

Theorem 3. *Given any two c-metrics d_1 and d_2 for a c-semiring S, the combinations $d_1 + d_2$, $d_1 \times d_2$, and $\max(d_1, d_2)$ are also c-metrics for S.*

As d_1 and d_2 are both metrics, we know (by [Cop68]) that each of the above combinations are also metrics. Each proof that they satisfy P1 and P2 requires only a small sequence of algebraic manipulations and well-known inequalities.

In addition to constructing c-metrics from existing c-metrics defined over the same c-semiring, it is possible to construct c-metrics for the combination (Cartesian product) of two different c-semirings. We follow the method of combination of c-semirings set forth in [BMR97] and show that any weighted sum of c-metrics (valid for their respective c-semirings) forms a new c-metric for the combined c-semiring. This result allows the usual form of handling multi-criteria objectives (linear combination of numeric measures) to be simulated.

Theorem 4. *Given two c-semirings S_1 and S_2, and corresponding c-metrics d_1 and d_2, then a c-metric for the combined semiring S can be found by $d = x d_1 + y d_2$, where $x, y > 0$.*

As d_1 and d_2 are metrics it is already known that d is a metric, and so satisfies M1, M2 and M3. The proof that d satisfies P1 and P2 is based on simple linear inequality results. It is, however, too long to present here in detail and so has been omitted.

2.2 Properties of C-Metrics

We will now detail certain properties resulting from the criteria for c-metrics, which will clarify the types of metrics suitable for use on c-semirings. We assume the use of a c-semiring $S = \langle A, \oplus, \otimes, 0, 1 \rangle$ with a c-metric d. The majority of the resultant properties describe the distances between c-semiring values and higher c-semiring values.

We must define certain notation to be used; this notation is not unusual, but must be explicitly defined. In particular, Definition 3 below may appear obvious but alternative definitions can be found in other literature.

Definition 2. *If $S = \langle A, \oplus, \otimes, 0, 1 \rangle$ is a c-semiring then we define $\hat{\beta} = \{\gamma \in A : \beta \leq_S \gamma\}$, where $\beta \in A$.*

Definition 3. *The distance from α to a region $\hat{\beta}$ is written $d(\alpha, \hat{\beta})$ and is defined as $d(\alpha, \hat{\beta}) = \inf\{d(\alpha, \gamma) : \gamma \in \hat{\beta}\}$ [Cop68].*

In this paper we have asserted that the c-semiring value $\alpha \oplus \beta$ should be that value greater than both α and β and which most accurately represents each one. Also, d has been characterised as the 'difference' between any two c-semiring values. It is therefore natural that, of all the values greater than β, $\alpha \oplus \beta$ should be that one closest to α.

Lemma 1. *The smallest distance from the c-semiring value α to any value in $\hat{\beta}$ is $d(\alpha, \alpha \oplus \beta)$.*

We can now define $d(\alpha, \hat{\beta}) = d(\alpha, \alpha \oplus \beta)$. For relaxation strategies in PCSP, we expect that solution tuples assigned lower c-semiring values are not given priority over solution tuples with higher c-semiring values. Translated into c-metric terms, we would expect that given two values α and γ with $\gamma \leq_S \alpha$, α would be at least as close to $\hat{\beta}$ as γ.

Theorem 5. *Given any c-semiring values α, β and γ, if $\gamma \leq_S \alpha$ then $d(\alpha, \hat{\beta}) \leq d(\gamma, \hat{\beta})$.*

3   Metric SCSP

We now investigate the application of a c-metric to the solutions of a SCSP. First we require an additional definition for a function used to combine the distances measured by c-metrics. To allow for many different relaxation strategies, this definition places few restrictions on the function.

Definition 4. *A function $f : (\mathbb{R}^+)^m \to \mathbb{R}^+$ combines distances if $f(x_1, \ldots, x_m) = 0 \Leftrightarrow \forall i, x_i = 0$ and it is monotonic increasing in each argument.*

We can now define a Metric SCSP $P = \langle C, con, f \rangle$ where con is a set of variables, and $C = \{c_1, c_2, \ldots, c_m\}$ is a set of constraints over a predefined c-semiring S (note that we permit multiple constraints on the same signature). Each constraint is a tuple $c_i = \langle con_i, def_i, d_i \rangle$ defining the variables to be operated on, a function mapping tuples to S, and a c-metric mapping $S \times S$ to $\mathbb{R}^+$. The function $f : (\mathbb{R}^+)^m \to \mathbb{R}^+$ is used for combining the results of d_i. Our aim is to find the solution(s) such that minimal deviation is required from the SCSP $\langle C, con \rangle$ while ensuring they are assigned a c-semiring value in $\hat{\alpha}$.

We assume that we have n variables which all take values from some set D. Thus the value for a solution $t \in D^n$, as defined for SCSPs, is $def(t) = def_1(t \downarrow_{con_1}^{con}) \otimes \ldots \otimes def_m(t \downarrow_{con_m}^{con})$.[5] Normally we would select the solutions $ASol(P) \subseteq D^n$ such that there exists no $u \in D^n$ assigned a greater value. We, however, are searching for those solutions needing 'minimal deviation'. From the definition of def we can prove certain results which make finding the solutions needing 'minimal deviation' easier.

Theorem 6. $(\alpha \leq_S def(t)) \Rightarrow (\alpha \leq_S def_i(t \downarrow_{con_i}^{con}))$

This theorem comes immediately from the fact that $\otimes$ is intensive. From this theorem we know that if $\alpha \leq_S def(t)$ then $d_i(t \downarrow_{con_i}^{con}) = 0$, for all i. As we expect $\otimes$ in our modified system to be idempotent, we will prove further results with that assumption.

Theorem 7. *If $\otimes$ is idempotent,* $(\forall i, \alpha \leq_S def_i(t \downarrow_{con_i}^{con})) \Rightarrow (\alpha \leq_S def(t))$

If $\otimes$ is idempotent, then to ensure the value $def(t)$ is in $\hat{\alpha}$ we need only ensure that all $def_i(t \downarrow_{con_i}^{con})$ are also within $\hat{\alpha}$. We can thus determine a measure of the deviation from P (so that $def(t) \in \hat{\alpha}$) by measuring the distance from $def_i(t \downarrow_{con_i}^{con})$ to $\hat{\alpha}$.

Definition 5. *Define $f_\alpha(t) = f(d_1(def_1(t \downarrow_{con_1}^{con}), \hat{\alpha}), \ldots, d_m(def_m(t \downarrow_{con_m}^{con}), \hat{\alpha}))$.*

---

[5] The notation $(t \downarrow_{con_i}^{con})$ is read as 'the projection of tuple t from the set con to the set con_i'

The function f_α determines (using the function f) the size of the deviation from P required to move $def(t)$ into the region $\hat{\alpha}$. The value of $f_\alpha(t)$ can also be interpreted as the amount of *belief change* required to allow solution t to be accepted with a level of consistency α.

Definition 6. *Define $m_\alpha(P) = \min\{f_\alpha(u) : u \in D^n\}$*

Definition 7. *Define $m_\alpha^*(P) = \min\{f_\alpha(u) : u \in ASol(P)\}$*

$m_\alpha(P)$ represents the minimum deviation from the problem P required to find any solution with a c-semiring value in $\hat{\alpha}$. Alternatively, $m_\alpha^*(P)$ represents the minimum deviation from the problem P required to find any abstract solution with a c-semiring value in $\hat{\alpha}$.

Definition 8. *The set of solutions needing least deviation from P to have values in $\hat{\alpha}$ is written as $ASol_\alpha(P)$, and is defined as follows (with $t, u \in D^n$):*

$$ASol_\alpha(P) =$$
$$\{t : (f_\alpha(t) = m_\alpha(P)) \wedge (\nexists u, (def(t) <_S def(u)) \wedge (f_\alpha(u) = m_\alpha(P)))\}$$

Definition 9. *The set of abstract solutions needing least deviation from P to have values in $\hat{\alpha}$ is written as $ASol_\alpha^*(P)$, and is defined as follows (with $t, u \in ASol(P)$):*

$$ASol_\alpha^*(P) = \{t : (f_\alpha(t) = m_\alpha^*(P)) \wedge (\nexists u, (def(t) <_S def(u)) \wedge (f_\alpha(u) = m_\alpha^*))\}$$

If we require a specific level of consistency α for the problem P, then $ASol_\alpha(P)$ contains the 'best' solutions we can find for that purpose. Similarly, $ASol_\alpha^*(P)$ contains the 'best' abstract solutions we can find. To determine $ASol_\alpha^*(P)$ requires prior calculation of $ASol(P)$, reducing the complexity required to be similar to the existing SCSP framework. If $\otimes$ is idempotent we are able to utilise all of the local consistency results from [BMR97] to assist in finding $ASol(P)$. Alternatively, to determine $ASol_\alpha(P)$ we can use partial constraint satisfaction search techniques such as branch-and-bound search.

The definitions of $ASol_\alpha$ and $ASol_\alpha^*$ have been formulated to give two different methods of using c-metrics with SCSPs. However, we can still make the observation that $ASol_0^*(P) = ASol_0(P) = ASol(P)$ That is, if we can accept any level of consistency, then we should accept the standard notion of abstract solutions $ASol(P)$ as being the best solutions to our problem.

Unfortunately, due to the dependence of $ASol_\alpha$ on the parameter α we cannot possibly guarantee, for an arbitrary problem P, that $ASol_\alpha(P) \subseteq ASol(P)$. The elements of each set are determined by different methods (by the use of c-metrics, and by the direct use of the c-semiring respectively). These results simultaneously reduce the chance of applying methods for SCSPs to Metric SCSPs, and indicate that Metric SCSPs provide a facility not available otherwise.

Presume that f can be represented as repeated applications of a commutative binary operation. For example, if $f = \sum$ then it can instead be considered as repeated applications of $+$ to all it's arguments. In such a situation, and with a fixed α, a Metric SCSP reduces easily to a Valued CSP, with an additional selection scheme for the solutions with the minimal value. This result allows the use of constraint propagation techniques [Sch00] for Valued CSPs [BFM$^+$96] in the solving of a wide class of Metric SCSPs. Note that the ability to reduce to a Valued SCSP does not infer that Metric SCSPs provide no new expressive power. In the above result we made the assumption that α is fixed. If over time we wish to vary the value of α it is not easy to reduce a Metric SCSP to a Valued CSP. Herein lies the additional expressiveness and power of Metric SCSPs.

Presume that the value α represents a minimum value for multiple objective functions, where the objective functions are represented by the c-semiring. Presume also that the value α' represents a *new* minimum value which we would wish to use. Let V be the Valued CSP constructed using α and V' be the Valued CSP constructed from α'. As both are constructed using the same Metric SCSP it appears likely that incremental resolving techniques can be used to rapidly find a new solution to V' from the existing solutions to V. This can be considered similar to the modification of the objective function in linear programming where the previous solution provides a good starting position for the simplex method. Such a technique would be particularly useful in the light of the obvious practical applications of Metric SCSPs.

Metric SCSPs can be viewed as defining a class of Valued CSPs with intuitive and structured relationships between them. They allow the writing of 'constraints' in the highly expressive SCSP framework independent of the final goal or objective function. Existing CSP frameworks focus on the solution to a problem with a specific goal or objective. The Metric SCSP framework allows the variance of the goal in an intuitive fashion with sufficient restrictions to make incremental resolving techniques likely.

The application of these intuitions to parameterized notions of constraint theory maintenance in dynamic settings (e.g., parameterized constraint retraction) is being addressed in a separate paper. An implementation of a prototype Metric SCSP solver is also being planned.

References

[BFM$^+$96] S. Bistarelli, H. Fargier, U. Montanari, F. Rossi, T. Schiex, and G. Verfaillie. Semiring-based CSPs and Valued CSPs: Basic Properties and Comparison. In M. Jampel, E. Freuder, and M. Maher, editors, *Over-Constrained Systems (Selected papers from the Workshop on Over-Constrained Systems at CP'95, reprints and background papers)*, volume 1106, pages 111–150. 1996.

[BMR97] Stefano Bistarelli, Ugo Montanari, and Francesca Rossi. Semiring-based constraint satisfaction and optimization. *Journal of the ACM*, 44(2):201–236, 1997.

[Cop68] E. T. Copson. *Metric Spaces*. Cambridge University Press, 1968.

[Gil87] John R. Giles. *Introduction to the Analysis of Metric Spaces*. Number 3 in Australian Mathematical Society Lecture Series. Cambridge University Press, 1987.

[Sch00] Thomas Schiex. Arc consistency for soft constraints. In *Principles and Practice of Constraint Programming*, pages 411–424, 2000.

[WB93] Molly Wilson and Alan Borning. Hierarchical constraint logic programming. Technical Report TR-93-01-02, 1993.

A Hybrid Genetic Algorithm for School Timetabling

Peter Wilke[1], Matthias Gröbner[2], and Norbert Oster[3]

[1] Centre for Intelligent Information Processing Systems (CIIPS)
Dept. of Electrical & Electronic Engineering
The University of Western Australia
35 Stirling Highway, Crawley WA 6009, Australia
wilke@ee.uwa.edu.au

[2] Lehrstuhl für Programmiersprachen und Programmiermethodik
Universität Erlangen-Nürnberg
Martensstrasse 3, 91058 Erlangen, Germany
Phone +49-9131-85-27933, Fax +49-09131-85-28809
Groebner@informatik.uni-erlangen.de

Abstract. Hybrid Genetic Algorithms apply so called hybrid or repair operators or include problem specific knowledge about the problem domain in their mutation and crossover operators. These operators use local search to repair or avoid illegal or unsuitable assignments or just to improve the quality of the solutions already found.

Those Hybrid Genetic Algorithms have been successfully applied to different constraint satisfaction and timetabling problems such as the travelling salesman problem, scheduling problems, employee timetabling or high school timetabling.

In this paper we describe a Genetic Algorithm for solving the German school timetabling problem. The Genetic Algorithm uses direct representation of the problem and applies an adapted mutation operator as well as several specific repair operators. We redecode the computed improvements to the genotype which establishes a kind of Lamarckian evolution. One of the problems utilising these hybrid operators is how and when to apply them, i.e. how to set the parameters right to achieve the best results. Different approaches have been started to adjust these parameters in an optimal way, but in most cases these adjustments require additional computing time and consequently are quite costly. We tackled this problem by an adaptation mechanism for the repair operators which can be applied without additional computing time. These operators are switched on when the normal Genetic Algorithm does not yield any more improvements. When the Genetic Algorithm then converges again, a reconfiguration step for the operator parameters guides the search out of the local optimum.

Keywords: Applications, Constraints, Evolutionary Algorithms, Planning

R.I. McKay and J. Slaney (Eds.): AI 2002, LNAI 2557, pp. 455–464, 2002.
© Springer-Verlag Berlin Heidelberg 2002

1   Introduction

The application of standard Genetic Algorithms [7] to timetabling problems such as employee timetabling, university timetabling or high school timetabling does unfortunately not ensure the desired or required success. In most cases solutions are quite good, but too many of soft and hard constraints still remain violated [5] [8].

To solve this inconvenience, problem specific knowledge is used to construct hybrid operators [12] which are applied to reduce the number of violations for some constraints. The improved solution can be rewritten to the genotype (Lamarckism) or used as an indicator of the possible quality of the chromosome [13]. The success of the application of specific Hybrid Genetic Algorithms to school timetabling problems has been demonstrated in some implementations [1] [4] [5].

The main problem is when and how the operators should be applied. Introducing those repair operators too early to the evolution process means switching too soon to a more local search mechanism. The consequence is that the Hybrid Genetic Algorithm converges to local optima, i.e. unacceptable results.

Several approaches have been done to apply Genetic Algorithms to solve different school timetabling problems [4] [5] [6]. In this paper we present another Hybrid Genetic Algorithm that is capable of constructing a weekly school timetable [11], whereby we focus on German High Schools. In section 2 we introduce a formal description of the problem and then present the Genetic Algorithm and its hybrid operators in sections 3 and 4.

Following that we describe our attempt to introduce a meta-heuristic technique to reconfigure the parameters of the hybrid genetic algorithm during the run. By means of this method we are able to avoid premature convergence and thus improve the solution quality significantly as will be shown in section 5 of this paper.

2   The German High School Timetable Problem

The data available to us are the actual information used by a high school in Bavaria, Germany. The students attend high school up to 9 years. Here we focus on the first 7 years, because in the last two years each student can chose individual courses and thus has an individual timetable.

During the first 7 years students attend lessons as a class, i.e. the timetable is the same for all students of that class, while in the last two years they chose their subjects and lessons from the courses offered, i.e. each student has an individual timetable.

Normally teachers are in general able to give lessons with a certain subject for all classes. If they are involved in teaching grades 8-9 these time slots are blocked, i.e. the teachers involved are not available for lessons for grades 1-7 when they are assigned to lessons for grades 8-9.

Here we focus on the first seven grades of the high school where known entities have to be considered for creating a school timetable as will be described now.

2.1 Data

The data available to us consists of *classes* (with a fixed number of students), *subjects* (to be taught by a specific teacher), *teachers* (have to teach specific subjects to specific classes) and *rooms* (with a fixed capacity).

A *lesson* consists of a set of the first three items (class, subject, teacher). This triple forms a lesson and usually cannot be changed, i.e. a teacher teaches a subject for a whole school year to a class. A lesson has to be assigned to a certain time slot during the day. In addition such a lesson has to take place in a room. Of course there may be several identical lessons, even in the same room, e.g. when mathematics has to be taught several times a week.

2.2 Constraints

Several constraints have to be considered when assigning a lesson to a certain time slot. Some of the given constraints are that timetables are compact for both students and teachers and some free periods for the teachers for regeneration are granted. Lessons have to be assigned preferably to time slots in the morning. Furthermore a minimum and maximum number of mandatory basic subject lessons per day has to be taught and it has to be enforced that at least one time slot for a lunch break is free. The availabilities and working preferences for teachers have to be considered and some lessons have to be taught in dedicated rooms, i.e. laboratories.

A special challenge is are coupling lessons such as religious education for different denominations, which have to be taught at the same time. In each class there usually are students with two or three different religious denominations. For practical reasons religious education lessons for students with a certain denomination are given for all these students of the whole grade. This lesson has to take place at the same time as religious education lessons are taught to the students of the other denominations. Another example are sports lessons where boys of two or three classes are put together. These lessons have to take place at the same time as sports is taught to the girls.

Further constraints not mentioned here exist and have to be observed by the planning algorithm.

3 Implementation

3.1 Genetic Representation

The genetic representation has to use one of different views [9]. In our implementation an individual represents a school timetable that consists of a sequence of all class timetables of the school (see figure 1). This introduces an encoding from the classes point of view instead of constructing the chromosome as a sequence of teacher timetables (teacher view).

We have chosen a very high level genetic representation for our data structure. A gene represents a timetable for a single class. Such a class timetable is

constructed by a sequence of (free) timetable entries during the whole week. A
timetable entry is given by a set consisting of an assigned room and a lesson
which itself consists of an assigned teacher, class and a fixed subject.

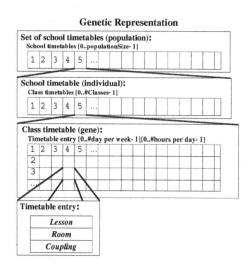

Fig. 1. Genetic representation. The figure shows the encoding of the Genetic Algorithm. A population of school timetables forms the mating pool. Each school timetable
chromosome consists of a sequence of class timetables which are the genes.

We decided to use this direct representation scheme instead of an implicit encoding even if implicit encoding has been applied successfully to school
timetabling problems [1] and the compliance with hard constraints and even soft
constraints is guaranteed from the outset. But using implicit representation has
the disadvantage that the success of the Genetic Algorithm depends strongly on
the quality of the assignment algorithm, i.e. the timetable builder. In addition
only a restricted part of the search space (limited by the assignment algorithm)
is searched [1]. This is because those timetable builders usually use deterministic
heuristics that explore the search space in a predetermined manner not allowing
to make random search steps away from the timetable builder search path.

In contrast direct encoding will lead to violation of many hard constraints
because the whole search space can be encoded. As we will see later, the consequence is that feasible solutions can hardly be computed using this representation
scheme and other mechanisms have to be applied additionally. Nevertheless, our
encoding scheme is not absolutely direct, because all lessons are assigned randomly to a time slot in the class timetable. Thus each single lesson can be assigned only once and each time slot is occupied only once. Nevertheless, multiple
assignments in teacher and room timetables are possible.

3.2   Algorithm

Initialisation of the population is done by creating chromosomes and assigning randomly all lessons of each class to a timeslot within their corresponding timetables. Thus initialisation timetables are computed completely randomly without taking into consideration possible constraint violations. This leads to a number of infeasible timetables which are improved during the evolution process.

The **fitness** of the chromosomes is proportional to the number of violations of the hard and soft constraints in the decoded representation described in section 2. Those chromosomes are fitter which have less penalty points. The penalty for the violation of hard constraints are higher than those for soft constraints reflecting their importance for the quality of the solution enforcing the algorithm to find appropriate solutions.

Penalty point for preferred lessons for the teachers e.g. are computed as follows: The preference timetable of each teacher contains a number from 1 to 6 for each time slot, whereas "3" means "indifferent", values less than 3 mean "assign to this lesson if possible" and values greater than 3 mean "do not assign to this lesson if possible". Hard constraints are penalized with more penalty points. For instance, if the number of assignments of a teacher to a lesson is more than one (clash constraint), 20 penalty points are added for each additional lesson assigned.

The complete value of the objective function is computed by adding the penalty points for all soft and hard constraint violations found. Thus, the optimization process tries to generate a feasible solution with as few soft constraint violations as possible.

For **selection** we have randomly applied two different mechanisms. The most simple and even elitist way to select two individuals for reproduction is to choose Best-Fitness-Selection, i.e. the two best chromosomes are selected. Furthermore standard Roulette-Wheel-Selection is applied.

As already mentioned we use a very **elitist strategy**. Consequently the two best individuals are retained into the next generation.

For **crossover** a variety of methods, such as One-Point-Crossover and Two-Point-Crossover is available. Here the chromosomes are cut at a certain gene (a class timetable) and merged again with the other part of the other chromosome. In addition uniform crossover was used, where each class timetable is selected randomly from one parent or the other.

To reduce the amount of lethal modifications to the chromosomes, the **mutation** operators are restricted to two different operators. The first operator swaps only two lessons or one lesson and one free slot. The second randomly changes the room assigned to a lesson.

As introduced by [5] the operator **best chromosome mutation** creates copies of the best chromosomes and only one mutation is applied to these individuals, i.e. exactly one change in one class timetable.

4   Hybrid Operators

4.1   Problem Specific Knowledge

Not surprisingly a naive approach by applying a standard Genetic Algorithm does not yield usable timetables, because too many constraints were violated. This is an effect that has been noticed in several other implementations and problem domains and led to different hybrid approaches [2] [5] [8] [4].

Because of this we implemented several hybrid operators to improve the solution quality of the individuals. These operators use problem specific knowledge about the problem domain to repair misplaced lessons.

All operators are applied to the phenotype and thus have to be re-decoded to the chromosome after application. This establishes a kind of Lamarckian evolution [10] [13].

Some of the hybrid operators are:

- Changing a room assignment randomly when a room has been assigned to two or more classes within the same time slot.
- Assigning a lesson randomly to another time slot when a teacher has been assigned twice or more to the same time slot.
- Changing a lesson assignment randomly when there exist two or more assignments of lessons with the same subject on the same day for a class.
- Changing the sequence of lessons within a day when there exist subjects that have to be taught in double lessons.
- Moving the fixed lessons to their correct time slot.
- Constructing compact daily timetables, that are timetables without free lessons. Additionally all lessons should be scheduled before lunch, if possible.

These operators are applied randomly, according to a given hybrid repair probability parameter, introduced below.

The repair operators are activated when the fitness value does not change for a certain number of generations.

4.2   Activation of the Hybrid Operators

Once the repair process has been started, we stated that further application of the hybrid operators in next generations led to an improvement of solution quality. Where the standard Genetic Algorithm converged to solutions with approximately 20,000 penalty points, the application of the hybrid operators led to solutions with approximately 17,500 penalty points for the specific circumstances as described in section 5.

On the other hand, the problem when applying problem specific knowledge to improve the quality of the population is that the search process is getting restricted to a smaller search space. This is a similar effect as search space restriction by timetable builders as described in section 3. As a consequence the Genetic Algorithm might converge in local optima and is not able to escape, because the hybrid operators prevent the Genetic Algorithm from searching a broader region in the search space [1].

To avoid premature convergence, we applied the hybrid operators only for one generation, as described above. The standard Genetic Algorithm continues again until the number of generations with no significant improvement reaches the hybridStartLevel value. And so on. This ensures that the Standard Genetic Algorithm has a chance to continue from a better place in the search space.

4.3   Reconfiguration Operator

We introduced a reconfiguration step to chose randomly new values for both the hybrid operator probabilities and the Genetic Algorithm parameters (mutation probability, which crossover operator to choose etc.).

This reconfiguration step is activated when neither the standard Genetic Algorithm nor the Hybrid Genetic Algorithm were able to create individuals with less penalty points for a certain number of generations.

This ensures a continuous adaptation of the working parameters of both standard and Hybrid Genetic Algorithm parameters. The continuous random adaptation of the parameters led to an improvement of more than further 1,500 penalty points compared with the "normal" Hybrid Genetic Algorithm.

5   Results

The program has been tested using a real world database of a German High School. The database contains 1,309 students in 46 classes, further 45 educational groups such as choir, orchestra, or theatre, 113 teachers and 100 rooms. Teachers teach 114 different subjects in 1,230 lessons.

In all tests the population size was 40 individuals, where we retained the two best individuals to the next generation as we described in section 3. All runs applied both best-fitness-selection and uniform crossover. Crossover probability was 87.5 percent and mutation probability 0.7 percent.

As shown in figure 2 the standard Genetic Algorithms converged after about 100,000 generations, i.e. a total of 4,000,000 computed school timetables. The best individuals had about 20,000 penalty points. Computing time was 10 hours on a Pentium III 600 MHz with 256 MB RAM.

The implementation has been done in Java. This programming language has been chosen because it allows a straight object-oriented implementation of the data structures. Furthermore it provides a lot of useful standard packages such as lists and containers which facilitate handling complex data as found in the school timetabling case. In addition, Java bite code can be executed on any operating system, thus platform independence is ensured.

However, one disadvantage of Java is its low running time performance compared to programming languages compiled directly to machine code, even if latest versions increased performance significantly. We accepted this quibble because advantages seemed to be greater and a commercial use — which would require shorter running times — has not been considered.

The hybrid version using the different repair operators yielded approximately 17,500 penalty points. The parameter `hybridStartLevel` was set to 40 generations, i.e. if the standard Genetic Algorithm did not yield better solutions for 40 generations, the hybrid operators were activated. The best solutions with about 16,500 penalty points were produced when applying the reconfiguration operator. The penalty point results were similar for different runs.

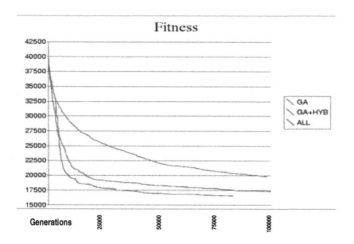

Fig. 2. Fitness graphs for runs (average over several runs) without hybrid operators (GA), with hybrid operators (GA+HYB) and both hybrid operators and reconfiguration operator (ALL).

To judge the quality of a solution with 16,500 penalty points it should be compared to the optimal schedule or the theoretical possible lowest bound. Due to the fact that teacher mark their choices with values between 1 (obligatory assignment) and 6 (not available at all) where 3 means "indifferent", the theoretical lower boundary is approximately 15.000 penalty points. Furthermore there exists a lot of contradictory constraints such as the constraint to avoid gaps in the teacher's timetable but to provide breaks after a certain number of lessons have been taught. These conflicting demands inevitably lead to a basic number of penalty points in the objective function.

Viewed in this context the solutions found in our experiments are quite acceptable. But of course there remain some other constraint violations left as shown in figure 3. These constraint violations cause additional penalty points.

Obviously the Genetic Algorithm has no problem to find solutions with only few clash constraints. One difficulty seems to be finding dense timetables for teachers and classes, i.e. timetables without gaps within a sequence of assignments. Even the hybrid operator trying to fill these gaps by changing assignments could not reduce the number of these constraint violations to zero as shown in figure 3.

Constraint violations	Standard GA (115,830 generations)	Hybrid GA with reconfig. (85,980 generations)
Fitness	19,415	16,670
Teacher / Room overlappings	65 / 31	0 / 5
Gaps in class' / teachers timetables	655 / 0	115 / 1
Double lessons not assigned successively	127	22
Max. number of basic subjects per day	11	8

Fig. 3. Number of constraints that remained violated after a Standard Genetic Algorithm run and Hybrid Genetic Algorithm run with reconfiguration operator.

Another observation is that the introduction of the so-called best chromosome mutation [5] led to significant improvements. This operator saves a certain number of the best individuals to the next generation avoiding crossover, only applying mutation. The success of this quite elitist way might be an indication that within the context of complex timetabling problems it is sufficient to evolve the population in a region of good solutions instead of searching the whole search space, even if one must take care of a too restricted search.

Nevertheless, our overall results are encouraging because the application of our hybrid operators effected that we found only few teacher or room overlappings and most hard constraints had been satisfied (see figure 3).

Even if there are some constraint violations left, a person that used to construct a timetable manually now has a good starting timetabling which needs only some slight modifications.

6   Conclusions and Outlook

In this paper we showed that Hybrid Genetic Algorithms can be successfully applied to solve the school timetabling problem. Furthermore Hybrid Genetic Algorithms can be improved significantly by applying meta-techniques which reconfigure the Hybrid Genetic Algorithm parameters.

In our implementation the parameters are reconfigured randomly. In further versions it might be reasonable to change the parameters in a more directed way, i.e. not to choose a parameter value from the broad range of possible values but to change the value in small steps only. The effect of heuristically guided hybrid parameter adaption as presented in [3] would be interesting, too.

Nevertheless, our quite simple method to adapt the parameters randomly avoids expensive and time consuming meta-algorithms like meta-Genetic Algorithms or other optimisation techniques. In addition other methods do not change the parameter values dynamically compared to our reconfiguration operator that always changes the parameter values when solution quality does not improve any more.

Furthermore it would be interesting to fit the school timetabling problem to a more general timetabling framework as proposed in [9]. Thus it would be possible to compare the suitability of standardized problem solving methods for this problem and further improvements to the algorithm might be achieved.

Acknowledgement. This work has been partly supported by a grant from the Lehrstuhl fuer Programmiersprachen und Programmiermethodik, Institut fuer Informatik, Friedrich-Alexander-Universitaet Erlangen-Nuernberg, Martensstrasse 3, 91058 Erlangen, Germany. We would like to thank them for their support.

In addition we want to thank the Adam-Kraft-Gymnasium in Schwabach, Germany, for their co-operation and support.

References

1. M. Bufé et al., "Automated Solution of a Highly Constrained School Timetabling Problem — Preliminary Results", *Proceedings of the EvoWorkshops 2001, ed. E. J. W. Boers et al.*, pp. 431–440, Springer, 2001.
2. E. Burke and D. Elliman and R. Weare, "Specialised Recombinative Operators for Timetabling Problems", in *Proceedings of the AISB (AI and Simulated Behaviour) Workshop on Evolutionary Computing*, pp. 75–85, Springer, 1995.
3. P. Cowling and G. Kendall and E. Soubeiga, "Hyperheuristics: A Tool for Rapid Prototyping in Scheduling and Optimisation", *Proceedings of the EvoWorkshops 2002, ed. St. Cagnoni et al.*, pp. 1–10, Springer, 2002.
4. C. Di Stefano and A. G. B. Tettamanzi, "An Evolutionary Algorithm for Solving the School Timetabling Problem", *Proceedings of the EvoWorkshops 2001, ed. E. J. W. Boers et al.*, pp. 452–462, Springer, 2001.
5. C. Fernandes and J. P. Caldeira and F. Melicio and A. Rosa, "High School Weekly Timetabling by Evolutionary Algorithms", in *Proceedings of 14th Annual Acm Symposium On Applied Computing*, San Antonio, Texas, 1999.
6. J. P. Caldeira and A. C. Rosa, "School Timetabling using Genetic Search", Proceedings of the Second International Conference on the Practice and Theory of Automated Timetabling, 1997.
7. D. E. Goldberg, "Genetic Algorithms in Search, Optimization and Machine Learning", Addison-Wesley, Reading, 1989.
8. M. Gröbner and P. Wilke, "Optimizing Employee Schedules by a Hybrid Genetic Algorithm", *Proceedings of the EvoWorkshops 2001, ed. E. J. W. Boers et al.*, pp. 463–472, Springer, 2001.
9. M. Gröbner and P. Wilke, "A General View on Timetabling Problems", *Proceedings of the 4th International Conference on the Practice and Theory of Automated Timetabling, ed. E. Burke and P. De Causmaecker* pp. 221–227, 2002.
10. E. Lamma and L. M. Pereira and F. Riguzzi, "Belief Revision by Lamarckian Evolution" *Proceedings of the EvoWorkshops 2001, ed. E. J. W. Boers et al.*, pp. 404–413, Springer, 2001.
11. N. Oster, "Stundenplanerstellung für Schulen mit Evolutionären Verfahren", *Thesis*, Universität Erlangen-Nürnberg, July 2001.
12. R. Weare and E. Burke and D. Elliman, "A Hybrid Genetic Algorithm for Highly Constrained Timetabling Problems", in *Proceedings of the Sixth International Conference on Genetic Algorithms, ed. L. J. Eshelman*, pp. 605–610, Pittsburg, Morgan Kaufmann, 1995.
13. D. Whitley and V. S. Gordon and K. Mathias, "Lamarckian Evolution, The Baldwin Effect and Function Optimization", in *Proceedings of the Third International Workshop on Parallel Problem Solving from Nature, ed.s H.-P. Schwefel and R. Männer*, Springer-Verlag, 1994.

Genetic Scheduling on Minimal Processing Elements in the Grid

Wensheng Yao, Baiyan Li, and Jinyuan You

Department of Computer Science and Engineering,
Shanghai Jiao Tong University, Shanghai 200030, China
{yao-ws, li-by, you-jy}@cs.sjtu.edu.cn

Abstract. This paper addresses the problem of scheduling parallel program tasks onto computational grid to minimize the execution time of the parallel program and the number of required processing elements. This task scheduling problem is known to be NP-complete. Existing scheduling algorithms either assume a fixed number of processing elements, or generate schedules that need more processing elements than necessary, which is especially obvious when using task duplication technique. To overcome the weaknesses, we propose a genetic scheduling algorithm using task duplication. The proposed algorithm can yield schedules with shorter execution time and fewer required processing elements, and without useless task duplications. The conditions under which the algorithm performs best were highlighted.

Keywords. Task scheduling, genetic algorithms, task duplication, grid

1   Introduction

Advances in commodity computers and high-speed networks have led to the emergence of *Computational Grid*, which aggregates geographically distributed resources to provide a platform for performance-sensitive applications [1]. A variety of distributed and parallel applications leverage the performance potential of computational grids to optimize their executions. In order to meet the performance need of these applications, the Grid should provide resource management and scheduling service. Hence, high-performance schedulers are a key component in the Grid environment. Enormous efforts have been given to the development of Grid schedulers [1][2][3][4][5][6][7][14].

Commonly, according to system state and application program information, schedulers effectively generate proper schedules, satisfying application performance requirements. Although the Grid is dynamic and heterogeneous, the varying performance of available resources can be monitored by the Network Weather Service (NWS) [8]. In order to describe its structure information, the program is modeled as weighted directed acyclic graph (DAG) where the nodes and edges represent the tasks and communication between the tasks, respectively. On the basis of the information, scheduling algorithms strive to seek a schedule that minimizes the execution time of the program. In addition to minimizing schedule length, minimizing the required

R.I. McKay and J. Slaney (Eds.): AI 2002, LNAI 2557, pp. 465–476, 2002.
© Springer-Verlag Berlin Heidelberg 2002

processing elements (PE) is meaningful for Grid computing. In this paper, we will present a scheduling algorithm to optimize the two performance parameters.

The scheduling problem, optimizing the two performance parameters, is known to be NP-complete [9]. The solution to the problem consists of two parts: assigning tasks onto processing elements, and determining the start time of all tasks. The communication delay between the tasks scheduled onto different PEs affects the efficiency of parallel programs. In order to shorten the execution time of parallel program, tasks are reasonably scheduled onto the same PE to eliminating communication delay. This task coalescing method is known as task clustering [10][12] or grain packing [11] in the literature. Task clustering algorithms assume an unbounded number of PEs and usually generate a large number of clusters. Another effective technique for shortening schedule length is task duplication [11], where a task may have several copies on different PEs so as to eliminate communication overhead. As an expense, these task duplications may occupy more PEs.

The scheduling problem has received considerable attention over the last few decades [13][14][15][16][17]. The existing algorithms can yield suboptimal schedules for general case and optimal schedules for special cases. Clustering algorithms usually assume that there is no limit on the number of PEs. Therefore, the size of generated schedules, i.e. the number of required PEs, is relatively large. Some task duplications in the schedules generated by the task-duplication-based algorithms are useless.

Genetic Algorithm (GA) is successfully applied to solve the scheduling problem where the number of PEs is fixed [18][23][24][26]. Most GA-based scheduling algorithms, derive from list scheduling [19] and adopt similar chromosome coding scheme, which brings difficulties to genetic operations. This coding scheme is also inflexible for task duplication and not suitable for minimizing the number of required PEs.

In this paper, we propose a GA-based algorithm for task scheduling in Grid environment, considering the number of required PEs at the same time. We assume that the upper bound of the number of required PEs is the width of task graph. Our algorithm finds a schedule that minimizes execution time of parallel program as well as the number of required PEs, and eliminates useless task duplications. The conditions under which the proposed genetic scheduling algorithm performs best will be highlighted. Our work is similar with [26], except that task duplication is used in our algorithm.

This paper is organized as follows: in section 2, we define the task scheduling problem and the principles of genetic algorithm. In section 3, we review our previous work. The proposed genetic algorithm for scheduling is described in section 4. Experimental results and comparisons are shown in section 5. We present our conclusion remarks in section 6.

2   Background

In this section, we formally define the scheduling problem and principles of genetic algorithms.

2.1 Problem Statement

In this paper, the underlying Computational Grid consists of a set of k heterogeneous PEs $P = \{p_1, p_2, ..., p_k\}$, which are connected via a network. Each processing element may be a supercomputer, cluster, or workstation. The computing capability of processing element p is represented by comp(p) and the communicating capability between p and q is represented by bandwidth(p,q). Each processing element executes only one task at one time without interrupting and task preemption is not allowed.

Fig. 1. the node weights and edge weights denote the computing capability and communication capability, respectively. comp(p1) is 2 while comp(p2) and comp(p3) are 1. Therefore, the computing capability of p1 is two times that of p2 or p3. All bandwidths between them are 1

Fig. 2. The computation cost of each task is 5. The communication delay from T1 to T3 is 2. T1 is an immediate predecessor of T3 and T3 is an immediate successor of T1. T1 is not an immediate predecessor of T4, but a predecessor of T4. T1 is an entry node and T4 is an exit node. The CCR is 4.5 and the width is 2

A parallel program is modeled as a weighted directed acyclic graph $G = (V, E, C, M)$, where each node $v \in V$ represents a task whose computation cost is $C(v)$ and each edge $(u, v) \in E$ represents the precedence relation that task u should be completed before task v can be started. In addition, at the end of its execution, u sends data to v and the communication cost is $M(u,v)$. The communication cost is zero if u and v are scheduled to the same PEs. If there is a path from u to v, then u is called a predecessor of v, while v is called a successor of u. For $(u,v) \in E$, u is an *immediate predecessor* of v, denoted by $u \in I\,\mathrm{Pr}\,ed(v)$, while v is an immediate successor of u, denoted by $v \in ISucc(u)$. A node without predecessors is called entry node and a node without successors is called exit node. The communication-to-computation-ratio (CCR) of a parallel program is defined as its average communication cost divided by its average computation cost.

The *degree of parallelism* of G, also called *width* of G, denoted by width(G), reflects the maximal number of tasks available for parallel executing. Therefore, we need at most width(G) PEs to accommodate all tasks in an optimal schedule. Computing the width of DAG is related to maximal independent set (MIS) of graph, which is beyond the scope of this paper. We assume that width(G) is available, see [21].

The *height* of node v, denoted by *height*(v), can be formally given by the following formula:

$$\begin{cases} height(v_j) = 0 & if \quad I\Pr ed(v_j) = \Phi \\ height(v_j) = \max_i \left\{ height(v_i) \mid v_i \in I\Pr ed(v_j) \right\} + 1 & otherwise \end{cases} \tag{1}$$

According to the formula (1), the heights of the tasks in Fig. 2 ({T1, T2, T3, T4}) are 0, 1, 1 and 2, respectively.

A schedule of G, denoted by $S(G)$, is a mapping of tasks onto processing elements and assigning start time to each task. For example, for task $v \in V$, it is scheduled onto $p(v) \in P$ and assigned start time $ST(v, p)$. Therefore, the finishing time of v, denoted by $FT(v, p)$, can be expressed as $FT(v, p) = ST(v, p) + \dfrac{C(v)}{comp(p)}$. A node can be mapped onto several PEs. In such a case, task duplication is used. The *makespan* of schedule S, is the maximal finishing time of all tasks, that is $makespan(S) = \max\{FT(v, p) \mid v \in V, p \in P\}$. Schedule S is optimal for G if for every other schedule S' of G, $makespan(S) \le makespan(S')$.

In order to minimize the number of required PEs, we define the PE allocation ratio in a schedule of G as:

$$AR(S(G)) = \frac{|P_a|}{width(G) + 1} \tag{2}$$

where $|P_a|$ is the number of required PEs in the schedule $S(G)$. Obviously, we have

$$0 < \frac{1}{width(G) + 1} \le AR(S(G)) \le \frac{width(G)}{width(G) + 1} < 1.$$

Our problem is that given a weighted DAG $G = (V, E, C, M)$ and networked processing elements, find an optimal schedule with minimal required PEs and without useless task duplications.

2.2 Genetic Algorithms

A Genetic Algorithm is a search algorithm, which is based on the principles of evolution and natural genetics [20]. GAs are successfully applied to solve NP-complete problems. A GA starts with a generation of *individuals*, containing feasible solutions. A certain *fitness function* is used to evaluate the fitness of every individual. Good individuals survive after *selection* according to the fitnesses of individuals. Then the survived individuals reproduce offsprings through *crossover* and *mutation* operations. This process iterates until termination condition is satisfied.

Individuals are encoded as strings known as *chromosomes*. A chromosome corresponds to a solution to the problem. Chromosome may be represented as binary vector.

An *object function* is used to characterize an individual's performance. Thereafter, a fitness function is used to evaluate the fitness of the individual.

The selection process is performed by rotating roulette wheel. Fitter chromosomes are given a proportionally higher chance to be selected. The algorithm selects good individuals until the next generation is generated.

Crossover operation cuts the parents into two parts at a random point and swaps them, producing two offsprings. Mutation operation causes partial genes of a chromosome to change. Crossover probability and mutation probability limit the number of chromosomes involved in crossover operation and mutation operation, respectively.

The GA is terminated under a given condition, for example, a certain number of iterations have been completed, a given execution time has been used out or a specific result stability has been reached.

3 Our Previous Work

In our previous work [22], we proposed a GA-based multiprocessor scheduling algorithm in homogeneous environment. Herein, we will extend our work to Computational Grid, where different processing elements have different computing capabilities, and the communicating capabilities are also different.

4 Proposed Genetic Algorithm for Task Scheduling

4.1 Coding of Solutions

Design of chromosome is crucial for devising genetic algorithms. A good coding scheme will benefit genetic operations and make object function easy to calculate. List scheduling is a fundamental heuristic algorithm. Most GAs for scheduling derive from the basic idea of list scheduling and adopt similar chromosome encoding scheme, which can naturally combine GA with various heuristics to improve the performance of algorithms. However, it is not suitable for genetic operations. Chromosomes generated by genetic operations (crossover, mutation) are usually invalid and need further adjustment operations, especially for task duplication. As for minimizing the number of required PEs, such chromosome encoding scheme is unsuitable because of adopting a fixed number of PEs as basis of chromosome encoding. In this paper, a new chromosome encoding scheme for task scheduling is proposed.

We define a chromosome as two strings $\{PE, priority\}$. Each element in PE stands for which processing elements the corresponding task is assigned. Tasks are allowed to be scheduled onto several processing elements. Processor $p_i \in P = \{p_1, p_2, ..., p_k\}, k = width(G)$ can be uniquely represented by 2^{i-1}, $i=1..k$.

The priority(v) element, varying from 1 to 512, is used to construct a priority list satisfying the precedence constraint conditions. In addition, tasks are sorted in ascending order of their heights. The priority list can be constructed by the following formula:

$$
\begin{cases}
pri(v_j) = priority(v_j) & if \quad I\Pr ed(v_j) = \Phi \\[2mm]
pri(v_j) = \max_i \left\{ pri(v_i) \mid v_i \in I\Pr ed(v_j) \right\} + priority(v_j) & otherwise
\end{cases}
\tag{3}
$$

The lower the pri value of a task is, the higher the priority of the task is. If the pri values of two tasks are same, we assume that the early-calculated task has higher priority than the later one.

For example, a chromosome c1 for task graph in Fig. 2 is shown below. Because the width of task graph is two, P1 and P2 in Fig.1 are selected for computation. The processor element corresponding to T1 in c1 is 3, so T1 is scheduled to P1 and P2. Since pri(T2) (=224) > pri(T3) (=114), T2 starts after T3 on P1.

c1:

	T1	T2	T3	T4
PE	3	1	1	1
Priority	46	178	68	326

c2:

	T1	T2	T3	T4
PE	1	3	1	1
Priority	371	23	191	128

4.2 Initialization

In this step, an initial population of chromosomes is generated. First, for every task, the PE value is generated in $[1..2^{|P|} - 1]$, where $|P| = width(G)$. Second, for every task, the priority value is randomly generated in $[1..512]$. Consequently, a chromosome is obtained. The initial population of chromosomes is generated by repeating the process as many times as the given population size.

4.3 Selection

In order to select good chromosomes, we define the fitness function as:

$$
f(i) = \left(\frac{\sum_{i=1}^{pop\_size}(makespan(i) + AR(i))}{pop\_size \times (makespan(i) + AR(i))} \right)^2
\tag{4}
$$

where chromosome i stands for a schedule. We assume that the makespan of chromosome is a positive integer. The value of AR(i) is smaller than one and larger than zero.

In order to compute makespan of chromosome, we have the following formula:

(5)

$$
FT(v_i, p) = \frac{C(v_j)}{comp(p)}, I\,Pr\,ed(v) = \Phi
$$

$$
FT(v_j, p) = \max_i \left\{ FT(v_i, q) + \frac{C(v_i)}{comp(p)} + \frac{M(v_i, v_j)}{bandwidth(p,q)}, FT(v_k, q) + \frac{C(v_k)}{comp(q)} \right\},
$$
$$
v_i, v_j, v_k \in V, v_i \in I\,Pr\,ed(v_j), p \neq q, pri(v_k) < pri(v_i)
$$

$$
FT(v_j, p) = \max_i \left\{ FT(v_i, p) + \frac{C(v_i)}{comp(p)}, FT(v_k, p) + \frac{C(v_k)}{comp(p)} \right\},
$$
$$
v_i, v_j, v_k \in V, v_i \in I\,Pr\,ed(v_j), pri(v_k) < pri(v_i)
$$

Before the above formula is applied to a schedule, we should eliminate the useless task duplication from all generated schedules. A task duplication is useless if its immediate successors receive data from other copies, which means these successors may have earlier start time. To eliminate useless task duplication, we can
1) calculate FT(v,p) for all tasks and PEs;
2) for each task (in reverse order): if 0<FT(v, q)<=FT(v, p), FT(w, p)=0, <v, w>∈ E , then delete task v on q.

time:	0 2.5 5 7.5		10		
P1		T1	T3	T2	T4
P2		T1			

Fig. 3. The makespan of the schedule corresponding to the chromosome c1 is 10. T1 in P2 is useless and should be eliminated because T2 and T3 receive data from T1 in P1 rather than from T1 in P2

Once fitness values have been evaluated for all chromosomes, we can select good chromosomes through rotating roulette wheel. The chromosomes with higher fitness values have more chance to be selected. Consequently, the same number of chromosomes as the population size are selected.

4.4 Crossover and Mutation

In this paper, we adopt the simplest form of crossover, namely single-point crossover. The crossover operation swaps portions of two chromosomes, which occurs with the crossover probability. Crossover is performed as follows: first, choose two chromosomes randomly; second, generate a random integer between 1 and |V| as crossover point; third, swap the bottom halves behind crossover point, including the gene at the crossover point. As a consequence, two new chromosomes replace the two parents.

Mutation is a basic operation, ensuring that the probability of finding the optimal solution is never zero. The mutation operation changes a gene of the chromosome, which occurs with the mutation probability. Mutation is performed as follows: for each chromosome, first, choose a task randomly with the mutation probability; and generate a new value as PE for the task, second, choose a task randomly with the mutation probability; and generate a new value as priority for the task. As a result, a new chromosome replaces the original one.

Either crossover or mutation operation needs no further adjustment.

5 Experiments

To produce the results in this section, the following parameters are adopted in our algorithm: population size = 30, crossover probability = 0.8, mutation probability = 0.12, the minimal number of generations = 500 and the maximum number of generations = 3000. Each of the tests has been performed 1000 times so as to allow a reasonable average to be calculated. At each test, the average makespan, number of used PE and running time are recorded.

The task graph representing the parallel Gaussian elimilation [25] was used in our experiments.

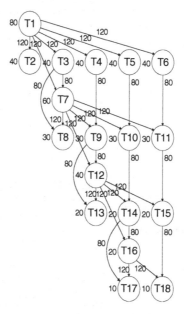

Fig. 4. task graph for the parallel Gaussian elimilation. There are 18 tasks in the program. The width of the task graph is 5 and the total computation cost is 600

5.1 Effect of Changing the Crossover Probability

In this test, ten different crossover probabilities were used to find the best point for this problem. From the results, it was found that the best value for crossover probability was 0.8, where it got better schedule with shortest makespan and less PEs (average: 2.89 PEs), and needed less execution time. Although the value of 0.4 produced near-best result, the time needed for computation was the longest of all. Thus it has to be discounted.

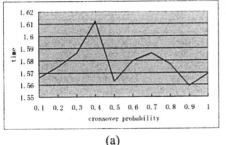
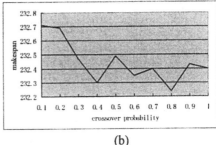

(a)   (b)

Fig. 5. (a) Computation time for different crossover probabilities; (b) makespan of schedule for different crossover probabilities

5.2 Effect of Changing the Mutation Probability

In this test, to find the best point, mutation probabilities were varied from 0.05 to 0.14. From the results, it was found that the best value for mutation probability was 0.12, where it got better schedule with shortest makespan and less PEs, and needed less execution time. The other values fail to produce better results because the larger values may have been too disruptive to the GA-based algorithm, or the smaller values not disruptive enough.

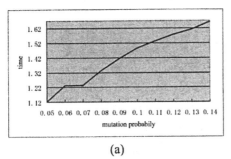
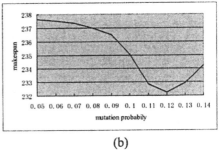

(a)   (b)

Fig. 6. (a) Computation time for different mutation probabilities; (b) makespan of schedule for different mutation probabilities

5.3 Effect of Changing the Population Size

In this test, 6 population sizes were chosen: 10, 20, 30, 40, 50 and 60. The results show that the time needed increased in a linear fashion. This is what was expected as increasing the population size gave the GA more schedules to handle. From the results, it was found that the best value for population size is 30, where it got better schedule with shorter makespan and less PEs, and needed less execution time.

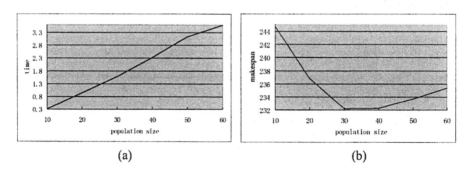

(a)   (b)

Fig. 7. (a) Computation time for different population sizes; (b) makespan of schedule for different population sized

5.4 Number of Maximal Generations

This test varied the maximal generation from 500 to 7000 and finally set no limitation on GA. From the results, the best average makespan was obtained when the maximal generation was set to 3000. After that, the average makespan could not be further optimized.

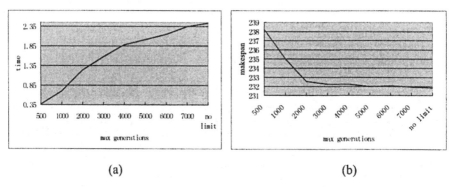

(a)   (b)

Fig. 8. (a) Computation time for different maximal generations; (b) makespan of schedule for different maximal generations

5.5 Number of Minimal Generations

This test varied the minimal generation from 0 to 1000. From the results, the better average makespan was obtained when the minimal generation was set to 500. After that, the execution time increased largely. If no limitation was set, the GA converged to a premature result.

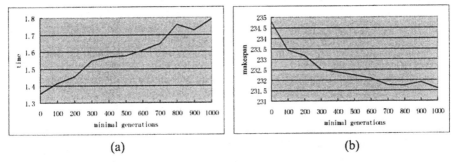

(a)   (b)

Fig. 9. (a) Computation time for different minimal generations; (b) makespan of schedule for different minimal generations

In general, the parameter set of a GA-based algorithm is very important. The results presented in this section showed different performance of the proposed algorithm with different parameter values.

6 Conclusion

In this paper, we proposed a genetic algorithm for task scheduling on Computation Grid. A new chromosome encoding scheme is used in our algorithm. The algorithm is aimed at minimizing makespan of schedule and the number of required processing elements and eliminating useless task duplications. The conditions under which the algorithm performs best were highlighted. In the future, we will integrate the algorithm into grid scheduling framework and study its performance.

References

1. I. Foster and C. Kesselman, editors. *The Grid: Blueprint for a Future Computing Infrastucture*. Morgan Kaufmann Publishers, San Francisco, Calif., 1998.
2. F. Berman and R. Wolski, "the AppLeS Project: A Status Report;" *Proceedings of the NEC Symposiumn on Metacomputing*, May 1997.
3. E. Heymann, M. A. Senar, E. Luque and M. Livny, "Adaptive Scheduling for Master-Worker Applications on the Computational Grid," *Lecture Notes in Computer Science* 1971, Springer-verlag Berlin, Berlin, pp. 214–227, 2001.
4. D. Abramson, J. Giddy, and L. Kotler, "High Performance Parametric Modeling with Nimrod/G: Killer Application for the Global Grid?", *Proceedings of IPPD/SPPD '2000*, 2000.

5. Nakada, Hidemoto, Mitsuhisa Sato, and Satoshi Sekiguchi. "Design and Implementations of Ninf: towards a Global Computing Infrastructure". *Future Generation Computer Systems, Metacomputing Issue,* 1999.
6. Takefusa, A. "Bricks: A Performance Evaluation System for Scheduling Algorithms on the Grids", *JSPS Workshop on Applied Information Technology for Science (JWAITS 2001),* January 2001.
7. I. Foster, and C. Kessleman. "Globus: A metacomputing infrastructure toolkit", *International Journal of Supercomputer Applications,* 11(2):115–128, 1997.
8. R. Wolski, N. T. Spring and J. Hayes, "The Network Weather Service: a distributed resource performance forecasting service for metacomputing," *Journal of Future Generation Computing Systems,* vol. 15, October 1999.
9. J. D. Ullman, "NP-complete scheduling problems," *Journal of Computing System Science,* vol. 10, pp. 384–393, 1975.
10. A. Gerasoulis and T. Yang, "On the granularity and clustering of directed acyclic task graphs," *IEEE Trans. Parallel and Distributed Systems,* 4(6):686–701, 1993.
11. B. Kruatrachue and T. Lewis, "Grain size determination for parallel processing," *IEEE Software,* pp. 23–32, Jan. 1988.
12. V. Sarkar, *Partitioning and Scheduling Parallel Programs for Execution on Multiprocessors,* Cambridge, Mass: MIT Press, 1989.
13. Y.K. Kwok and I. Ahmad, "Static Scheduling Algorithms for Allocating Directed Task Graphs to Multiprocessors," *ACM Computing Surveys,* 31(4):407–471, December 1999.
14. H. Casanova, "Simgrid: a Toolkit for the Simulation of Application Scheduling," *Proceedings of the First IEEE/ACM International Symposium on Cluster Computing and the Grid,* pp. 430–437, 2001.
15. R. Lepere and D. Trystram, "A New Clustering Algorithm for Scheduling Task Graphs with Large Communication Delays," Proceedings of IPDPS 2002, to appear.
16. S. Ranaweera and D. P. Agrawal, "A Task Duplication Based Scheduling Algorithm for Heterogeneous Systems," *Proceedings of 4th International Parallel and Distributed Processing Symposium,* pp. 445–450, 2000.
17. Weissman, Jon. "Scheduling Multi-component Applications in Heterogenous Wide-Area Networks." *Proceedings of the 9 th Heterogeneous Computing Workshop,* April 2000.
18. E.S.H. Hou, N. Ansari and H. Ren,"A genetic algorithm for multiprocessor scheduling," *IEEE Trans. Parallel and Distributed Systems,* 5(2):113–120, 1994.
19. Wang Q., K. H. Cheng, "List scheduling and parallel tasks," *Information Processing Letters,* 37(5):78–87, 1991.
20. D. E. Goldberg, et al, *Genetic Algorithm in search, optimization, and machine learning* (Reading, MA: Addison-Wesley, 1989).
21. P.M. Pardalos, and J. Xue, "The maximum clique problems," *Journal of Global Optimization, vol. 4,* pp. 301–328, 1994.
22. W. Yao and J. You, "Task Scheduling on Minimal Processors with Genetic Algorithms," *Proceedings of 6th Joint Conference on Information Sciences,* North Carolina: Duke University, pp.210–214, 2002.
23. T. Tsuchiya, T. Osada, and T. Kikuno, "A new heuristic algorithm based on GAs for multiprocessor scheduling with task duplication," 1997 3rd *International Conference On Algorithms and Architectures for Parallel Processing,* pp. 295–308, 1997.
24. M. Grajcar, "Genetic List Scheduling Algorithm For Scheduling and Allocation on a Loosely Coupled Heterogeneous Multiprocessors System," *Proceedings of 36th Design Automation Conference,* pp. 280–285, 1999.
25. H. El-Rewini, et al, "Scheduling parallel program tasks onto arbitrary target machines," *Journal of Parallel and Distributed Computing,* 9(2):138–153, 1990.
26. M.K. Dhodhi, I. Ahmad and R. Storer, "SHEMUS: systhesis of heterogeneous multiprocessor systems," *Microprocessors and Microsystems,* 19(6):311–319, 1995.

Protein Sequences Classification Using Modular RBF Neural Networks

Dianhui Wang[1], N.K. Lee[1], T.S. Dillon[1] and N.J. Hoogenraad[2]

[1]Department of Computer Science and Computer Engineering
La Trobe University, Melbourne, VIC 3083, Australia
Ph: +61-3-9479 3034 Fax: +61-3-9479 3060
dhwang@cs.latrobe.edu.au
[2]Department of Biochemistry
La Trobe University, Melbourne, VIC 3083, Australia

Abstract. A protein super-family consists of proteins which share amino acid sequence homology and which may therefore be functionally and structurally related. One of the benefits from this category grouping is that some hint of function may be deduced for individual members from information on other members of the family. Traditionally, two protein sequences are classified into the same class if they have high homology in terms of feature patterns extracted through sequence alignment algorithms. These algorithms compare an unseen protein sequence with all the identified protein sequences and returned the higher scored protein sequences. As the sizes of the protein sequence databases are very large, it is a very time consuming job to perform exhaustive comparison of existing protein sequence. Therefore, there is a need to build an improved classification system for effectively identifying protein sequences. This paper presents a modular neural classifier for protein sequences with improved classification criteria. The intelligent classification techniques described in this paper aims to enhance the performance of single neural classifiers based on a centralized information structure in terms of recognition rate, generalization and reliability. The architecture of the proposed model is a modular RBF neural network with a compensational combination at the transition output layer. The connection weights between the final output layer and the transition output layer are optimized by delta rule, which serve as an integrator of the local neural classifiers. To enhance the classification reliability, we present two heuristic rules to apply to decision-making. Two sets of protein sequences with ten classes of super-families downloaded from a public domain database, Protein Information Resources (PIR), are used in our simulation study. Experimental results with performance comparisons are carried out between single neural classifiers and the proposed modular neural classifier.

1 Introduction

The aim of classification is to predict target classes for given input patterns. There are many approaches available for classification tasks, such as statistical techniques, decision trees [9] and the neural networks [1]. Neural networks have been chosen as

R.I. McKay and J. Slaney (Eds.): AI 2002, LNAI 2557, pp. 477–486, 2002.

technical tools for the protein sequence classification task because: (i) the extracted features of the protein sequences are distributed in a high dimensional space with complex characteristics which is difficult to satisfactorily model using some parameterized approaches; and (ii) the decision tree techniques have no advantages in classifying patterns with continuous features especially as the number of attributes is larger.

A protein super-family consists of protein sequence members that are evolutionally related and therefore functionally and structurally relevant with each other [5]. One of the benefits from this category grouping is that some molecular analysis can be carried out within a particular super-family instead of individual protein sequence with the completion of the DNA sequencing of whole genomes it has also become apparent that the function of most genes is still unknown and classification into functionally related groups will provide valuable information on protein function. Traditionally, two protein sequences are classified into the same class if they have highly homology in terms of feature patterns extracted through sequence alignment algorithms. These algorithms, for instance, SAM[10], MEME[11], iPro-Class [8], compare an unseen protein sequence with all the identified protein sequences and provide a score based on similarity of sequences. As the sizes of the protein sequence databases are large, it is a very time consuming job to perform exhaustive comparison of existing protein sequences. Therefore, it is useful and helpful to build an intelligent classification system for effectively identifying protein sequences. Motivated by this, artificial neural networks have been applied in this area in the past and the results obtained demonstrate some merits of the methodology. Basically, there are two types of neural models applicable for protein sequences classification task, such as systems, Self Organizing Mapping (SOM) networks [2,3,12] and Multilayer Perceptrons (MLP) [13,14,15]. The SOM networks can be used to discover relationships within a set of protein sequences by clustering them into different groups. The main limitations of SOM for protein sequence classification are: (i) it is time consuming and difficult to interpret the results [11]; and (ii) the selection of the size of Kohonen layer is subjective and usually involves a trial and error procedure. The MLP based classification systems have several undesired features arising from system design, which include, for instance, (i) the determination of the neural network architecture, (ii) the lack of interpretability of the "black box"; and (iii) time needed for training as the number of inputs is over 100. Once offline training of the neural network is accomplished, the resulting neural classifier is ready to be used for future protein sequence classification and only few seconds are needed to classify a new protein sequence. This saves a lot of time as compared to the sequence alignment methods. Besides the direct protein classification, the MLP neural classifier could also been used to reduce the search scope of the sequence alignment program by only searching members of super-families [15].

Radial Basis Function (RBF) networks have received much attention due to their merits in architecture interpretability and learning efficiency [6,16]. It has been successfully applied in many real world applications. Comparative studies showed that the RBF network outperforms the MLP model in both classification performance and learning efficiency. Another reason to employ the RBF neural network to permit design of intelligent classification systems is that employ crisp or fuzzy classification rules, which are the core of knowledge-based systems. Motivated by these considerations, the RBF network is employed in this paper to design a neural protein sequence classifier. Issues within scalability and robustness of the neural protein classification systems are meaningful in coming up with a design that will allow identification of new super-families and members in existing super-families. A centralized design using a single neural network does not readily meet these requirements, leading us to explore a modular neural model to implement the protein classification task.

The remainder of the paper is organized as follows: Section 2 gives some detailed information on the design of modular RBF network classifier. Section 3 presents a heuristic approach for enhancing classification reliability. The data preprocessing including features for the extraction of protein sequences, the experimental results are reported in Section 4 and conclusions are given in the last section.

2 Design of Modular RBF Neural Classifiers

Figure 1 depicts the architecture for a fully connected RBF network. The network consists of N input features x, M hidden units with center C_i and L output units y_i. The activation functions ϕ in the hidden units are the Gauassian functions defined as:

$$\phi_j(x) = \exp(-\| x - C_j \|^2 / 2\rho_j^2) \tag{1}$$

The output is calculated by

$$y_k(x) = \sigma[\sum_{j=1}^{M} w_{kj}\phi_j(x) + w_{k0}], k = 1, 2, ..., L, \tag{2}$$

where $\sigma(s) = [1 + \exp(-s)]^{-1}$ is a sigmoid function. A supervised algorithm, APC-III [16], is adopted to determine the hidden units centers and widths.

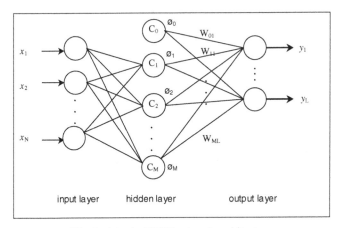

Fig. 1. A typical RBF network architecture

In this paper, we investigate the effect of learning criteria on classification performance. Two different objective functions for training neural classifiers are employed, i.e., the means squared error (MSE) cost function and the cross entropy (CE) [1] cost function:

$$MSE = \frac{1}{2}\sum_{p}\sum_{j=1}^{L}(t_i^p - y_i^p)^2 = \frac{1}{2}\sum_{p}E(p)$$ (3)

$$CE = -\sum_{p}\sum_{k=1}^{L}t_k^p \ln y_k^p = -\sum_{p}L(p)$$ (4)

where t_i^p and y_i^p are the i-th target and the network output for the p-th input pattern, respectively.

The activation function at the output layer of the RBF network using CE learning criteria is the *softmax* operation, i.e.,

$$f(z_i) = \exp(z_i)[\sum_{j=1}^{L}\exp(z_j)]^{-1}$$ (5)

where z_i is the network input to output unit i.

There have been many attempts in the past to combine the outputs of modular neural classifiers. The main purpose is to reduce the model variance of the classification systems. Two well-known methods are the bootstrap and ensembles of committee. For protein classification, a variety of features can be extracted from a protein sequence. The features combination can produce various feature subsets with different strength and characteristic. Besides the global features, the local features or motifs are also applicable to classifier design. To take advantage of the different set of features, it is desirable to improve the classification system performance by using different features as the input to the network and effectively combining the local classification results. Figure 2 shows our proposed neural classifier architecture, which consists of two RBF networks that use different input features e2 and a1, respectively.

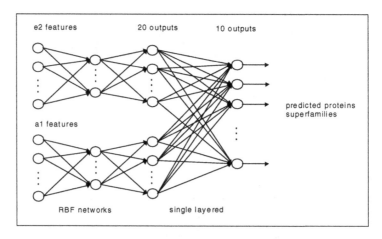

Fig. 2. Proposed modular RBF network architecture

The outputs of these two networks are applied as inputs to the third single layered network to produce the final class prediction. The two RBF networks have the exact same output classes. The single layered network can be viewed as a way to integrate the results contributed by the two local RBF neural classifiers. The advantages of this architecture are: (i) it reduces the model variance of a single classifier by assigning different weights to the networks output; (ii) it speeds up the learning process because of the use of less features for each RBF neural network; and (iii) it enhances the scalability and robustness of the intelligent classification system with respect to the weights decay. The neural network is trained by two stages, i.e., individual trainings of the RBF network classifiers followed by a training of the single layered network using delta rule. The details of the learning algorithm are omitted here.

3 Classification Criteria

The network outputs can be interpreted as the target class posterior probabilities [4]. A test pattern x is assigned to class i if $p(C_i|x) > p(C_j|x)$ for all $i \neq j$. This classification criterion suffers from several drawbacks although it is widely used in the literature. Firstly, it does not define the confidence of the output value. Suppose that two of the largest network outputs are 0.45 and 0.44, respectively. By using this criterion, the pattern will be assigned to the class with output 0.45. However, we have less confidence on the classification quality in such a situation caused by the small bias. Secondly, if the maximum output value is less than some certain threshold, for example, 0.2, it still quite difficult to assure the result has sufficient reliability. This implies that the commonly used maximum posterior probabilities classification criterion or maximum component principle will not provide a secure prediction. To overcome this shortcoming in decision-making, we suggest a heuristic approach for enhancing the classification confidence and quality. The heuristic measure can be used in decision-making with improved faith and tradeoff between the classification rate, misclassification rate and un-classification rate. Our suggested heuristic classification criterion are as follows:

Rule 1: IF ($pred(x) \geq beta$ AND $diff(x) \geq alpha$), THEN x is classified/missclassified
Rule 2: IF ($pred(x) < beta$ OR $diff(x) < alpha$), THEN x is unclassified

To apply these rules, the network prediction output values $pred(x)$ for the pattern x are sorted in decreasing order. The $diff(x)$ represents the difference between the largest output value and second largest output value of the neural classifier. The classification performance is controlled by the two parameters $alpha$ and $beta$. The $beta$ value essentially characterizes the confidence of the predicted result. Whilst the $alpha$ value controls the quality of the classification by only allowing the $diff(x)$ value to be large enough to confidently identify the protein classes. A pattern prediction is classified or misclassified if Rule 1 is activated, and the output class of the largest network output is the predicted class. Otherwise, the pattern will not be classified and a further identification will be applied. To simplify the rules above, in this paper we introduce a mathematical expression to characterize the relationship between the two parameters in the rule, that is,

$$alpha = \frac{beta}{1+beta} \qquad (6)$$

Obviously, the value of alpha is proportional to the value of beta. Figure 3 show the trade-off between classification rate, miss-classification rate and un-classification rate for difference values of *beta*. It shows that the classification rate (cls) and misclassification rate (miscls) are decreased as the value of *beta* increases. Whereas the un-classification rate (uncls) is increased as the value of *beta* increases. By setting an appropriate value of *beta*, a reliable classification performance with higher quality and confidence is attainable.

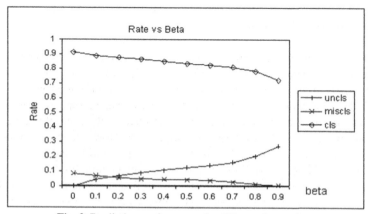

Fig. 3. Prediction performance for different *beta* values

4   Simulation Results

The protein sequences are transformed from DNA sequences using the predefined genome code. Protein sequences are more reliable than DNA sequence because of the redundancy of the genetic code [5]. Two protein sequences are believed to be functional and structurally related if they show similar sequence identity or homology. These conserved patterns are of interest for the protein classification task.

   A protein sequence is made from combinations of variable length of 20 amino acids Σ = {A, C, D, E, F, G, H, I, K, L, M, N, P, Q, R, S, T, V, W, Y} (using the ... letter code). The n-grams or k-tuples [14] features will be extracted as an input vector of the neural network classifier. The n-gram features are a pair of values (v_i, c_i), where v_i is the feature i and c_i is the counts of this feature in a protein sequence for i = 1... 20^n. In general, a feature is the number of occurrences of an animal in a protein sequence. These features are all the possible combinations of n letters from the set Σ. For example, the 2-gram (400 in total) features are (AA, AC, ..., AY, CA, CC, ..., CY,..., YA, ..., YY) . Consider a protein sequence VAAGTVAGT, the extracted 2-gram features are {(VA, 2), (AA, 1), (AG, 2), (GT, 2), (TV, 1)}. The 6-letter exchange group is another commonly used piece of information. The 6-letter group actually contains 6 combinations of the letters from the set Σ. These combinations are

A={H,R,K}, B={D,E,N,Q}, C={C}, D={S,T,P,A,G}, E={M,I,L,V} and F={F,Y,W}. For example, the protein sequence VAAGTVAGT mentioned above will be transformed using 6-letter exchange group as EDDDDEDDD and their 2-gram features are {(DE, 1), (ED, 2), (DD, 5)}. We will use e_n and a_n to represent n-gram features from a 6-letter group and 20 letters set. Each sets of n-grams features, i.e., e_n and a_n, from a protein sequence will be scaled separately to avoid skew in the counts value using equation (7) below:

$$\bar{x} = \frac{x}{L - n + 1} \tag{7}$$

where x represents the count of generic gram feature, $\bar{x}$ is the normalized x, which will be the inputs of the neural networks; L is the length of the protein sequence and n is the size of n-gram features.

In this simulation study, the protein sequences covering ten super-families (classes) were obtained from the PIR databases comprised by PIR1 and PIR2 [8]. The 949 protein sequences selected from PIR1 were used as the training data and the 533 protein sequences selected from PIR2 as the test data. The ten super-familes to be trained/classified in this study are: Cytochrome c (113/17), Cytochrome c6 (45/14), Cytochrome b (73/100), Cytochrome b5 (11/14), Triose-phosphate isomerase (14/44), Plastocyanin (42/56), Photosystem II D2 protein (30/45), Ferredoxin (65/33), Globin (548/204), and Cytochrome b6-f complex 4.2K(8/6). The 56 features were extracted and comprised by e_2 and a_1.

The parameter settings involved in the neural networks are given in Table 1. There are 71 (720 connection weights) nodes in the hidden layer of the RBF networks generated by employing the APC-III algorithm [16]. To compare the performance with MLP network classifiers, an MLP architecture 56-15-10 was selected as it has the same number of weights in the model. The NevProp [7] simulation software was applied for MLP network training, where an automatic stopping criterion to define the optimal target mean squared error and learning rate were offered.

Table 1. Parameter Settings in Neural Classifiers Training

Parameters	RBF-MSE	RBF-CE	BP-MSE/CE
Learning rate (LR)	0.015	0.02	Optimized
Stopping Criterion	Cross-validation	Cross-validation	MSE
No. Hidden units	71	71	15
LR for units centers	0.005	0.01	-
LP for units width	0.005	0.01	-
Momentum	0.9	0.9	Default

To avoid the over-fitting of training for the RBF network classifiers, we created a set of perturbed sequences made by 20-30% training data by adding small noises, and used them to check the classification performance on-line. The learning process was stopped once the recognition rate (with *beta*=0) inspected started decreasing for the noise sequences.

Table 2. Performance Comparison for Training Data Set (*beta*=0.4)

NN Classifier	Classification	Misclassification	Unclassification
BP-CE	98.63 (936)	0.32 (3)	1.05 (10)
BP-MSE	99.37 (943)	0.11 (1)	0.52 (5)
RBF-CE	95.47 (906)	1.58 (15)	2.95 (28)
RBF-MSE	99.26 (942)	0.00 (0)	0.74 (7)
MRBF-CE	98.42 (934)	0.42 (4)	1.16 (11)
MRBF-MSE	99.78 (947)	0.11 (1)	0.11 (1)

Table 3. Performance Comparison for Test Data Set (*beta*=0.4)

NN Classifier	Classification	Misclassification	Unclassification
BP-CE	84.24	3.75	12.01
BP-MSE	85.00	4.00	11.00
RBF-CE	86.00	6.00	8.00
RBF-MSE	83.5	3.60	12.90
MRBF-CE	87.00	8.00	5.00
MRBF-MSE	83.15	5.80	11.05
Average Method	79.21	4.87	15.92
Product Method	78.09	2.43	19.45

Table 2 and Table 3 show the results for training data set and test data set with *beta*=0.4. All of the neural classifiers perform well on the training data set. However, the performance for the test data set varied extremely, which demonstrates the difference in generalization capability. It has been observed that the modular RBF network classifier with MSE learning cost function performs better on the training data set, but performs worse on the test data set. The CE learning criteria results better results for both MLP and RBF networks. In Table 3, we also give the performance results obtained using average and product combination strategies [17] for the test data set. The proposed modular RBF network classifier outperforms both the average combination method and the product combination method. This suggests that the single layered network makes better decision with information fusion of the local classifiers. The classification rates obtained by C4.5 with 10 trials are 95% and 74.6% for training set and test set, respectively. It is much worse that the results obtained by neural classifiers.

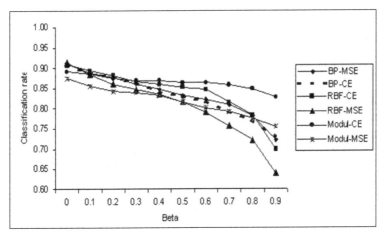

Fig. 4. Classification Rate on Test Data Set for Varying *Beta*

Figure 4 shows the classification rates from different neural classifiers versus the varying values of the *beta* for the test data set. The overall evaluation based on the experimental results demonstrate that the RBF neural networks with CE learning cost function can produce better classification performance in terms of generalization. The modular RBF network classifiers with CE learning cost function and linear fusion of different global features RBF network classifiers can further improve classification performance.

5   Conclusions

This paper considers the protein super-family classification problem using a modular RBF neural network with transition output fusion. The main investigations in this study containing: (i) the design for a modular RBF neural networks using different global features for predicting the protein patterns; (ii) a proposal for a heuristic approach for enhancing the quality and reliability in decision-making; and (iii) a comparative study using 10 classes of protein sequence for the classification problem. The experimental results demonstrate the potential of our proposed techniques, which confirm that the modular RBF network classifier with CE learning cost function and linear fusion at the transition output layer presented here is the best candidate for this domain application. Further studies on scalability and robustness of this modular neural protein classification system are in progress.

Acknowledgement. This project is financially supported by VPAC grants and FSTE small grants (#104110) at La Trobe University.

References

1. Bishop C. M., Nural Networks for Pattern Recognition, Clarendon Press, Oxford, 1995
2. H. C Wang, Dapazo J., L. G. De La Fraga, Y. P. Zhu, Carazo J. M., Self-organizing tree-growing network for the classification of protein sequences, Protein Science, (1998) 2613–2622
3. Ferran EA, Pflugfedder B, Ferrarap, Self Organized neural maps of human protein sequences, Protein Science, 3(1994) 507–521
4. S. Lawrence, I. Burns, Andrew Back, Ah Chung Tsoi, and C. Lee Giles, Neural Network Classification and Prior Class Probabilities, Neural Networks Tricks of the Trade, Lecture Notes in Computer Sciences, Springer, 1524 (1998)
5. I. Jonassen, Methods for finding motifs in sets of related biosequences, PhD Thesis, Department of Informatics, University of Bergen, (1996)
6. J. Moody and C. Darken, Faster learning in networks of locally-tuned processing units, Neural Comput., 1(1989) 281–294
7. Nevada backPropagation (NevProp), v3 http://www.scs.unr.edu/nevprop/
8. Protein Information Resources (PIR) http://pir.georgetown.edu
9. Quilan, J. R. 1994, *C4.5: programs for machine learning*, San Mateo, CA Morgan Kaufmann
10. SAM: Sequence Alignment and Modeling Software System, Baskin Center for Computer Engineering and Science, http://www.cse.ucsc.edu/researchcompbio */sam.html*
11. MEME: Multiple EM for Motif Elicitation UCSD Computer Science and Engineering *http://meme.sdsc.edu*
12. Wang H. C., Dopazo J. Fraga L. G. D. L., Zhu Y. P., Carazo J. M., Self-organizing tree-growing network for the classification of protein sequences. Protein Science, 7(1998) 2613–2622
13. Wu C. H., George Whitson, Jerry McLarty, Adisorn Ermongkonchai, Tzu Chung Change, PROCANS: Protein Classification Artificial Neural System. *Protein Science,* 1(1992), 667–677
14. Wu, C. H., Berry, M., Shivakumar, S. & McLarty, J., Neural networks for full-scale protein sequence classification: sequence encoding with singular value decomposition, *Machine Learning.* 21(1995) 177–193
15. Wu C. H., Artificial neural networks for molecular sequence analysis. *Computers Chemistry,* 21(1997) 237–256
16. Y. S. Hwang, and Y. S. Bang. An Efficient Method to Construct a Radial Basis function Neural Network Classifier, *Neural Networks,* 10(1997) 1495–1503
17. David M.J. Tax, Martijin van Breukelen, Rober P.W. Duin, and Josef Kittler,Combining multiple classifiers by averaging or by multiplying?, *Pattern Recognition* 33 (2000) 1475–1485.

Feature Extraction and Selection in Tool Condition Monitoring System

Sun Jie, G.S. Hong, M. Rahman, and Y.S. Wong

Department of Mechanical Engineering
National University of Singapore, Singapore, 119260
engp1034@nus.edu.sg

Abstract. In order to predict tool state, this paper introduces the application of feature extraction and feature selection by automatic relevance determination (ARD) to explore the optimal feature set of AE signals in tool condition monitoring system(TCMS). The experiment results confirm that this selected AE feature set is more effective and efficient to recognize tool state over various cutting conditions.

1 Introduction

With the increasing demand for the reduced production cost and improved product quality, TCMS is becoming an important component in modern manufacturing. During metal cutting, the low amplitude, high frequency stress wave generated by a rapid release of strain energy in the deformation zone is referred to as acoustic emission (AE), which is very sensitive to tool states. The merit of using AE to detect tool wear lies in its frequency range which is much higher than that of the machine vibrations and environment noises [1]. Hence, a relatively precise signal can easily be obtained by applying high-pass filter to the sensed signal. In addition, applying AE signal does not interfere with the cutting operation, and makes the continuous monitoring possible. Due to these advantages, AE signal has been widely employed to extract the useful information in TCMS.

Choi et al. [2] fused AE and cutting forces to develop a real-time TCMS for turning operations. The recorded data was analysed through a fast block-averaging algorithm for features and patterns indicative of tool fracture. Jemielniak and Otman[3] used a statistical signal-processing algorithm to identify the root mean square (RMS), skew and kurtosis of the AE signal and detect catastrophic tool failure. By selecting AE parameters recorded simultaneously with the corresponding length of flank wear land at the selected intervals, Kakade et al. [4] used AE features to predict tool wear and chip-form in a milling operation. Analysis of the results concluded that AE signals could distinguish clearly the cutting actions of a sharp, worn or broken tool. Zheng et al. [5] used an optic fiber sensor and a PZT AE sensor to conduct drilling and milling operation, and the results from the two approaches showed a reasonable agreement. Using AE features, Konig et al. [6] performed test to monitor the condition of small drills and detect fracture. They concluded that AE features were sensitive to tool

R.I. McKay and J. Slaney (Eds.): AI 2002, LNAI 2557, pp. 487–497, 2002.
© Springer-Verlag Berlin Heidelberg 2002

chipping. Moriwaki and Tobito [7] proposed a method on the basis of AE measurement and analysis for coated tool life estimation. The recorded data was used as inputs of a pattern recognition system to predict the ensuing tool life. Roget et al. [8] applied the sensed AE signals to predict the state of the cutting tool. They concluded that AE could provide sufficient warning of the ensuing changes in both tool breakage and tool wear. Dornfeld [9] found that the changes in skew, kurtosis of AE RMS signal could effectively indicate the tool wear.

However, the other researchers held a different idea. Blum and Inasaki [10] performed experiments to determine the relationship between flank wear and AE signals. With the use of AE mode, they concluded that extracting tool wear information from the AE signal was difficult.

Lister[11] believed that the reason yielding the two kinds of opinions did not lie on the sensing technology, but on the ensuing analysis. The traditional signal understanding methods are usually suffered from poor generation performance, expensive computing time and cost. Thus, choosing a suitable area to trap AE signal and selecting a suitable method to understand this signal are critical.

In order to understand the relationship between AE signal and tool state, the following techniques are needed: signal processing techniques to extract feature vectors sensitive to tool condition; feature selection technique to choose an optimal feature vector set as the inputs of neural networks; a reliable learning algorithm to predict tool state.

Based on this opinion, this paper employs some methods from neural networks(NNs) and data mining to extend the application of AE signal in TCMS.

NNs have been widely employed as the classifier to identify the tool state. Rangwala and Dornfeld[6] applied BP to classify AE and force signal for tool wear monitoring. Niu[12] used an unsupervised ART2 to perform decision-making of tool flank wear state. Xu[13] applied RBF to monitor tool wear in real time system. In this research, support vector machine(SVM) is proposed to learn the correct tool wear information in an extensive cutting conditions. Compared with other learning algorithms, the SVM possesses a firm background and excellent features, such as minimizing the system complexity, yielding a significant gain in classification accuracy.

Under the framework of SVM, Jebara and Jaakkola [14] proposed the maximum entropy discrimination for feature selection. Weston et al. [15] applied the gradient descent method to select good indicators under the given number of features. During recent years, ARD proposed by Mackay[16] and Neal [17] has become an attractive method for feature selection.

This paper employs ARD in the framework of SVM to select features from AE signal, which is sampled to monitor tool state in turning process. With the help of ARD, inputs which are irrelevant or less relevant to the tool wear will be deleted. The experimental result shows that the developed method can yield the more effective AE feature set in the tool state recognition.

Fig. 1. The scheme of intelligent feature analysis

2 Experimental Setup and Design

This experiment is carried out on an OKUMA CNC lathe. The work piece materials include ASSAB705 and ASSAB760, tool insert type is SNMN120408(uncoated, ungrooved), and insert material is A30. Experimental samples represent typical tool wear states under normal cutting conditions(speed 170-230m/min, feed: 0.2-0.4mm/r, depth of cut: 1-2mm).

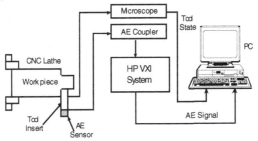

Fig. 2. Experimental setup scheme

The continuous AE signal is acquired using the signal acquisition schemes(shown in Fig. 2). The AE sensor, KISTLER 8152B, is mounted with a M6 screw onto the surface of the tool holder. This AE sensor which is widely used in monitoring processes, especially well suited for measuring AE signal above 50 kHz in the surface of machine structures. The original signals first pass through AE Piezotron Coupler 5125B (filter and amplifier), then are sampled by a HP VXI system in 2M frequency to minimize the influence of noise signals and alias errors, at last are fed to PC.

Since AE signal is sensitive to cutting parameters, and investigating all possible combinations of these parameters is not a practical choice, experiment design must be considered. The technique of defining and studying all conditions in an experiment involving multiple factors is known as the design of experiment. The parameter design of Taguchi is employed in this research. Taguchi defined a set of orthogonal arrays (OAs), each of which can be used for many experimental situations. The combination of standard experiment design and analysis methods in Taguchi approach produces consistency and reproducibility rarely found in any other statistical methods.

In this study, three levels of machining parameters(cutting speed and feed) and two level parameters(workpiece and cutting depth) are selected and shown in Table 1. The experimental layout for machining parameters using L9 orthogonal array is shown in Table 2. This array can handle two two-level and two three–level process parameters at most. Each machining parameter is assigned to a column and nine machining parameter combinations are required.

Besides, these combinations should be run in a random order to avoid the influence of experimental setup. Every combination is repeated three times, and the repetition is also planed to carry out in a random order.

Table 1. Machining Parameters and Their Levels

Machining Parameters	Level 1	Level 2	Level 3
Feed(mm/r)	0.2	0.3	0.4
Cutting Speed(m/min)	170	200	230
Depth(mm)	1	2	
Workpiece	ASSAB705	ASSAB760	

Table 2. Experimental Layout Using an L9 Orthogonal Array

No.	Feed	Cutting Speed	Depth of Cut	Work piece
1	1	1	1	1
2	1	2	2	2
3	1	3	1	1
4	2	1	2	1
5	2	2	1	1
6	2	3	1	2
7	3	1	1	2
8	3	2	1	1
9	3	3	2	1

3   Feature Extraction

Although AE might be sufficiently available on the entire machining process, the main drawback of this signal is its both sensitive to variation and noise from cutting operation. Therefore, feature extraction becomes necessary, which requires a powerful signal processing to maximize the information utilization of the sensor signals. Typically monitoring indices include time domain indices, such as mean, variance, root mean square(rms), frequency domain indices such as energy in a specific frequency band and wavelet indices.

Table 3. Commonly used features for AE signal

Index	Definition	Reference
X1	mean of bandpower (mb)	K. Jemielniak(1997), Y.M.Niu (1998), Chi L.Jiaa(1998)
X2	mean of skew (ms)	Gabriel(1995),Y.M.Niu (1998), Chi L.Jiaa(1998)
X3	mean of kurtosis (mk)	Gabriel(1995), Y.M.Niu (1998), Chi L.Jiaa(1998)
X4	standard deviation of bandpower (sb)	Y.M.Niu (1998), Chi L.Jiaa(1998)
X5	standard deviation of skew (ss)	Gabriel(1995),Y.M.Niu (1998), Chi L.Jiaa(1998)
X6	standard deviation of kurtosis (sk)	Gabriel(1995), Y.M.Niu (1998), Chi L.Jiaa(1998)
X7	Absolute deviation (ad)	R.G.Silva (1997)
X8	AE peak (peak)	R.Du (1995), J.S. Kim (1999)
X9	Mean of RMS (mrms)	R.Du (1995), Roget(1988), K. Jemielniak(1997)
X10	standard deviation of RMS (srms)	R.Du (1995), Roget(1988), K. Jemielniak(1997)
X11	ΔRMS of AE (drms)	R.Du (1995), T.W.Liao(1995)
X12	Crest-factor (cf)	R.Du (1995)
X13	cutting condition	Bernhard Sick(2001)

As shown in Table 3, the following features from AE signal in turning process are usually used. Among these features, X1 and X4 are obtained through frequency analysis(FFT), X13 comes from machining conditions, the others are achieved by statistical analysis. These features cannot be intuitively compared and decided which one is more suitable and reliable to be used as monitoring indices or as an input feature vector to NNs, since most of them fluctuate greatly in the whole machining process(as shown in Fig.3). In the following section, the effectiveness of these features will be discussed.

4 Feature Selection

The effectiveness of the extracted features are referred to as feature assessment, it has been investigated by many researchers over the last several decades.

4.1 Literature Review

The simplest methods to evaluate features is by the designer to select the features which appear to have more potential use. When problem domains is enough known, this approach is perfectly adequate. While, in most cases this approach cannot predict the existence of higher-order interactions between features. The usually used statistical-based feature selection technique consists of three major parts: a selection criterion, used to determine whether one feature subset is "better" than another; a systematic procedure whereby the space of feature subsets is searched; and a stopping criterion which indicates when the search may be terminated [18]. However this method suffers from many limitations [19], such as expensive computation and the performance of selected features. Besides, this method is only limited to assessing individual features, pays little attention to the performance of the whole feature set. Thus it could not provide an optimal feature set for real data classification.
Saliency Analysis (SA) measures the importance of features by evaluating the sensitivity of the output with respect to the weights (weight-based SA) or the feature inputs (derivative-based SA)[20]. In SVM, the weights lie in a high dimensional feature space rather than the original input space, thus the magnitude of weights is actually a reflection of the importance of the high dimensional feature inputs instead of the original inputs. Hence, the weight-based SA is not applicable to SVMs. Derivative-based SA uses a simple backward search to compute the gradient of network outputs with respect to inputs. Although this method is much easier and simpler to implement, it can not provide a desirable performance[21].

4.2 Automatic Relevance Determination (ARD)

During the last five years, automatic relevance determination (ARD) proposed by Mackay[16] and Neal [17] has attracted more attention, due to the advantage of lower

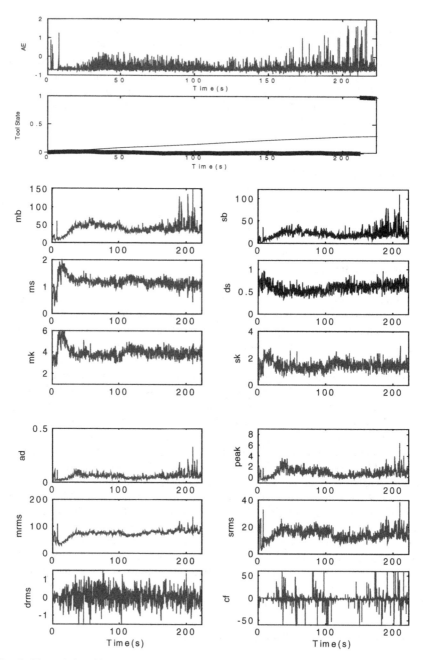

Fig. 3. The relationship between AE signal, tool state and extracted features (tool insert: SNMN12048, workpiece: ASSAB705) under cutting condition: speed=200 rev/min, feed=0.2 mm/min, depth=1mm,

computational cost and better performance. It has been found that ARD performs very well in feature selection for the multi-layer perception. This method has also been applied to SVM. In SVM, kernel functions used for the mapping from inputs to outputs in regression or classification problems are optimized using ARD. In contrast with other methods, this artificial intelligence-based method is capable to carry out classification estimation and feature selection at the same time.

In ARD method, weight vectors connected to the same input have common prior covariance, and all the covariance have common prior distribution. This allows the posterior values to adjust so that weights connected to the irrelevant input can be automatically punished in model adaptation, i.e. weights of irrelevant inputs are more efficiently driven towards zero, which reduce the influence of such weights.

In gaussian process, ARD could be embedded into the covariance function as equation (1):

$$Cov\,[f(x_i)f(x_j)] = \kappa_0 \exp[-\frac{1}{2}\sum_{l=1}^{d}\kappa_l(x_i^l - x_j^l)^2] \tag{1}$$

Here $f(x_i)$ is the outputs, κ_l determines the relevance of this input to the target. In the model adaptation rocess, if κ_l becomes large, it means that this input consists more information and less noise. On the contrary, this input has more noise rather than information. This method can force weak components of the model toward a weight of zero, thus finding the inputs that are relevant to modeling. A systematic procedure for ARD method is outlined as follows:

(1)Training SVM with the feature set which includes all candidates and getting κ_0, κ_l (l=1,...,d). (without ARD)

(2) Use κ_0 and κ_l as the initial values to retrain SVM (ARD).

(3) Using SVM algorithm to explore the maximum posterior probability $P(f/D,H_i)$ for the dataset D.

(4) In order to reach the maximum evidence $P(D/H_i)$, gradient-based optimization methods are employed to adjust $\kappa_0, \kappa_1,...\kappa_d$.

(5) At the minimum of $-\ln P(D/H_i)$, the relevance of each input dimension can be ranked by evaluating κ_i, and the corresponding $\kappa_0,...\kappa_d$ are used as the initial value for next optimization.

(6) The process is repeated from (2)-(5) until the number of evaluation equals 15, all κ_l (l=1,...,d), are ranked in a descending order as $\kappa_1^{'},...\kappa_d^{'}$, where $\kappa_1^{'} = $ max $\{\kappa_l\}$ and $\kappa_d^{'} = \min\{\kappa_l\}$.

(7) Choose a proper threshold θ, if $\kappa_l < \theta$, delete the features corresponding to these ARD parameters.

In SVM, one training run is sufficient as the solution is guaranteed to be global optimal. This is in contrast with the multi-layer preception in which multiple training runs are needed to avoid the results trapped in the local minima.

5 Decision Making through SVM

SVM is a universal constructive learning procedure based on statistical learning theory. The main idea of SVM is to construct a hyperplane as the decision surface so that the margin of the separation between the positive and negative example is maximized. Due to its high performance in solving real-life problems, its conceptual simplicity, and its basis on statistical learning theory, SVM and its related methods are becoming very popular. For clarity, the general SVM classifier problem for non-separable data is presented as follows.

For the given the training samples $\{(\mathbf{x}_i, y_i)\}|_{i=1}^{N}$, construct a decision function of the form

$$g(\mathbf{x}) = \sum_{i=1}^{N} \alpha_i y_i K(\mathbf{x}, \mathbf{x}_i) + b \tag{2}$$

by maximizing $L_D(\alpha)$

$$L_D(\alpha) = \sum_{i=1}^{N} \alpha_i - \frac{1}{2} \sum_{i=1}^{N} \sum_{j=1}^{N} \alpha_i \alpha_j y_i y_j K(\mathbf{x}_i, \mathbf{x}_j) \tag{3}$$

subject to $\sum_{i=1}^{N} \alpha_i y_i = 0$; $0 \le \alpha_i \le C$

where α_i are Lagrange multipliers at the solution of the optimization problem and b is the optimal bias.

Usually gaussian kernel, $K(\mathbf{x}, \mathbf{x}_i) = \exp(-\|\mathbf{x} - \mathbf{x}_i\|^2 / 2\sigma^2)$ is used. SVM learning algorithm, sequential minimal optimization (SMO) is applied in this research due to its fast learning speed for very large problem. It uses an analytical quadratic programming step, having heuristics for choosing which variable to optimize in the inner loop [24]. SMO always optimizes and alters two Lagrange multipliers at every step, making the problem to be solved easily and quickly.

The regularization parameter C determines the tradeoff between minimizing the training error and minimizing model complexity. δ^2 of the kernel function defines the nonlinear mapping from input space to some high dimensional feature spaces. Turning these parameters is done by k-fold cross-validation experiment which is an efficient technique for tuning SVM parameters and yields the best performance[25].

In this research, choosing optimal hyperparameter C and δ^2 of SVM is done by minimizing an estimate of generalization error. The values of and δ^2 are chosen so that the combination achieves a test error close to the highest classification rate. The relationship between the size of the training set and the performance of testing samples is also investigated.

6 Conclusion

Table 4-9 show the training and testing results of 6 samples under feature sets Y1, Y2, Y3. Among them, Y1 includes all features extracting from AE signal, Y2 and Y3 are the results from the first and second ARD procedure respectively. The training time is also illustrated in these tables, which does not include the time consumption for feature extraction.

Y1= {X1, X2, X3, X4, X5, X6, X7, X8, X9, X10, X11, X12, X13}
Y2={X1, X2, X4, X6, X7, X8, X9, X11, X12, X13}
Y3={X1, X3, X4, X6, X9, X10, X13}

From the results obtained, it can be seen that:

The feature set Y3 can yield the highest testing accuracy and need the smallest training time for the testing sample, followed by the feature set Y2. In contrast, the feature set Y1 provides the lowest accuracy and the slowest converge. This indicates that using the selected feature set can both enhance the generalization performance and reduce the time needed to learn a sufficiently accurate classification function.

Using ARD approach, the number of support vectors decreases greatly. This result shows ARD can significantly improve the performance of SVM and save the computing time in determination.

Table 4. Sample 1

Feature Set	nSV	Training Time (S)	Accuracy* (%)
Y1	4753	598	81.82
Y2	4593	556	82.28
Y3	2638	293	89.99

nSV: the number of support vectors.

Table 5. Sample 2

Feature Set	nSV	Training Time (S)	Accuracy* (%)
Y1	4350	520	81.95
Y2	4142	473	82.17
Y3	2801	271	89.98

Accuracy*: accuracy in testing samples

Table 6. Sample 3

Feature Set	nSV	Training Time (S)	Accuracy* (%)
Y1	5594	846	78.94
Y2	5141	803	81.82
Y3	4076	442	89.19

Table 7. Sample 4

Feature Set	nSV	Training Time (S)	Accuracy* (%)
Y1	5154	716	79.32
Y2	5020	670	80.74
Y3	3732	425	89.99

Table 8. Sample 5

Feature Set	nSV	Training Time (S)	Accuracy* (%)
Y1	4417	569	81.36
Y2	4241	536	83.89
Y3	2797	285	86.81

Table 9. Sample 6

Feature Set	nSV	Training Time (S)	Accuracy* (%)
Y1	5584	1341	81.83
Y2	5393	1004	82.89
Y3	4059	514	86.67

In short, the feature selection by ARD can not only improve the performance of neural networks, but also speed up the training, and reduce the complexity of NNs. As a result of this work, reliable tool wear recognition can be achieved in a wider range of machining conditions. Further work is to extend this technique to force signal.

References

1. Sata, T., Matsushima, K., Nagakura, T. and Kono: Learning and Recogintion of the Cutting States by Spectrum Analysis, Annals of CIRP, Vol. 22, 41–45, 1973.
2. Choi, D., Kwon, W.T. and Chu, C.N.: Real-time Monitoring of Tool Fracture in Turning using Sensor Fusion, International Journal of Advanced Manufacturing Technology 15 (5), 305–310, 1999
3. Jemielniak, K., Otman, O.: Tool Failure Detection Based on Analysis of Accoustic Emission Signals, Journal of Material Processing Technology 76, pp.192–197, 1998
4. Kakade, S., Vijayaraghavan, L., Krishnamurthy, R.: In-process Tool Wear and Chip-form Monitoring in Face Milling Operation Using Acoustic Emission, Journal of Material Processing Technology, 44, pp. 207–214, 1994.
5. Zheng, S.X. et al.: Intrinsic Optical Fiber Sensor for Monitoring Acoustic Emission, Sensors and Actuators, A: Physical Vol. 31, 110–114,1992.
6. Konig, W., Kutzner K., Schehl U.: Tool Monitoring of Small Drills with Acoustic Emission, International Journal of Machine Tools and Manufacture Vol. 32, No.(4,) 487–493, 1992.
7. Moriwaki, T., Tobito, M.: A New Approach to Automatic Detection of Life of Coated Tool Based on Acoustic Emission Measurement, ASME Trans. Journal of Engineering for Industry 112 (3), 212–218, 1990.
8. Roget, J., Souquet, P., Gsib, N.: Application of Acoustic Emission to The Automatic Monitoring of Tool Condition During Machining, ASNDT Materials Evaluation Vol.46, 225–229, 1988
9. Dornfeld, D.A.: Application of Acoustic Emission Techniques in Manufacturing, NDT and International Vol. 25, No. 6, 259–269,1992.
10. Blum, T., Inasaki, I.: A Study on Acoustic Emission from the Orthogonal Cutting Process, ASME Trans. Journal of Engineering for Industry 112 (3) (1990) 203–211.
11. Lister: P.M. On-line Measurement of Tool Wear. Ph.D. thesis, Manufacturing and Machine Tools Division, Department of Mechanical Engineering, UMIST, Manchester, UK, 1993.
12. Y.M.Niu et al.: An intelligent Sensor System Approach for Reliable tool flank wear recognition", Advanced Manufacturing Technology, Vol.14, (1998), pp.77–84 .
13. Xu Xin: Development On-line Tool Condition Monitoring System, Thesis for Master Degree, National University of Singapore, 2001.
14. Jebara, T. and T. Jaakkola: Feature Selection and Dualities in Maximum Entropy Discrimination, In UAI-2000: Proc. of the 16th Conference on Uncertainty in Artificial Intelligence, (2000), Stanford University, Stanford, CA, USA.
15. Weston, J., S. Mukherjee, O. Chapelle, M. Pontil, T. Poggio and V.N. Vapnik: Feature Selection for SVMs, In NIPS-13: Advances in Neural Information Processing Systems, Vol. 13, (2001), Denver, Colorado.
16. MacKay DJC: A practical Bayesian framework for back-propagation networks, Neural Computation, (1992), Vol.4, No.3, pp.448–472.
17. R.M. Neal: Bayesian Learning for Neural Networks Lecture Notes in Statistics, Springer, 1996.
18. Bishop, C.M.: Neural Networks for Pattern Recognition, Oxford University Press, 1995
19. Chenoweth, T. and Z. Obradovic: An Explicit Feature Selection Strategy for Predictive Models of the S&P 500 Index, Neurovest Journal, Vol. 3, No. 6, pp. 14–21. 1995
20. Steppe, J.M. and Jr.K.W. Bauer: Improved Feature Screening in Feed-Forward Neural Networks, Neurocomputing, Vol. 13, pp. 47–58. 1996.
21. Cao, L. J.: Support Vector Machines Based Methods for Time Series Forecasting , Thesis for PhD Degree, National University of Singapore, 2001.

22. B. Sick: Tool Wear Monitoring in Turning: A Neural Network Application, Measurement + Control; Vol. 34, No. 7, (2001), pp. 207–222, The Institute of Measurement and Control, London.
23. R. Du, M. A. Elbestawi & S. M. Wu: Automated Monitoring of Manufacturing Processes: Part 1, Monitoring Decision-Making Methods, Trans. of ASME, J. of Eng. for Industry, Vol. 117, No. 2, (1995), pp. 121–132.
24. Platt, John C. Sequential Minimal Optimization: A Fast Algorithm for Training Support Vector Machines. Technical Report MSR-TR-98-14, Microsoft Research, 1998.

A Robust Meaning Extraction Methodology Using Supervised Neural Networks

D.A. Karras[1] and B.G. Mertzios[2]

[1]Hellenic Aerospace Industry& Hellenic Open University, Rodu 2, Ano Iliupolis,
Athens 16342, Greece, dkarras@haicorp.com, dakarras@hol.gr,
dakarras@usa.net
[2]Democritus Univ. of Thrace, Dept. of Electr.and Comp. Eng., 67 100 Xanthi

Abstract. A large amount of information, stored in intranets and internet databases and accessed through the World-Wide Web, is organized in the form of full-text documents. Efficient retrieval of this information with regards to its meaning and content is an important problem in data mining systems for the creation, management and querying of very large such information bases. In this paper we deal with the main aspect of the problem of extracting meaning from documents, namely, with the problem of text categorization, outlining a novel and systematic approach to it's solution. We present a text categorization system for non-domain specific full-text documents based on the learning and generalization capabilities of neural networks. The main contribution of this paper lies on the feature extraction methodology which, first, involves word semantic categories and not raw words as other rival approaches. As a consequence of coping with the problem of dimensionality reduction, the proposed approach introduces a novel second order approach for text categorization feature extraction by considering word semantic categories cooccurrence analysis. The suggested methodology compares favorably to widely accepted, raw word frequency based techniques in a collection of documents concerning the Dewey Decimal Classification (DDC) system. In these comparisons different Multilayer Perceptrons (MLP) algorithms as well as the Support Vector Machine (SVM), the LVQ and the conventional k-NN technique are involved.

Keywords: Meaning Extraction, Supervised Neural Networks

1 Introduction

In this paper we outline a novel approach to the solution of the problem of full-text document categorization, the first step to tackle the more general problem known as text understanding, which is of great significance in the computer science field of Natural Language Processing (NLP). Classification of information with respect to its meaning is an important step in the design and implementation of improved human-machine interaction systems. Text Categorization and meaning extraction methods are highly needed in libraries, institutes, the World-Wide Web and wherever there are databases, which contain information in text format. Therefore, it is obvious that an

R.I. McKay and J. Slaney (Eds.): AI 2002, LNAI 2557, pp. 498–510, 2002.

efficient and automatic text classification method could be of great importance in data mining systems.

Numerous text categorization systems exist in the literature. They can be grouped into clustering or mapping systems where the categories are not defined by humans and into supervised text categorization systems, where the categories are predefined. Regarding the first group, several domain-specific methods have been developed, such as NLP systems for Software Libraries and Software Reuse [1], NLP architectures for collaborative computing systems solving the vocabulary problem by clustering semantically similar terms [2], through statistics and Hopfield type of neural networks, etc. Moreover, non-domain specific text categorization methods are included in this group, such as the recently proposed system for self-organization and mapping of general document collections [3], by applying a modification of the SOFM neural net algorithm.

Concerning the second group, a number of statistical classification and machine learning techniques have been applied to automatic text categorisation, including domain-specific rule learning based systems [4], regression models [5], nearest neighbour classifiers [5], decision trees [6], Bayesian classifiers [6], Support Vector Machines [7] and neural networks [8]. On the other hand, several feature extraction methodologies have already been applied to this field. The basic methodology is the frequency of word occurrence technique representing a document through the vector space model (SMART) [9]. A multitude of feature extraction methods stem from the SMART representation, like word frequency weighting schemes (Boolean, tf x idf (inverse document frequency), tfc, entropy, etc.) [10] as well as feature extraction techniques involving dimensionality reduction through feature selection schemes (document frequency thresholding, information gain, hypothesis-testing, etc.) [10] and through feature combination or transformation (For instance, Latent Semantic Indexing (LSI) related methodologies) [10]. For a recent and excellent survey of the state-of-the-art in supervised text categorization we should point out [10].

In the herein introduced approach we present a supervised text categorization system for non-specific domain full-text documents, aimed at extracting meaning according to well defined and systematically derived subject categories used by librarians. This system is based on Supervised Neural Networks of the Multilayer Perceptron (MLP) type and a novel feature extraction scheme based on semantics processing through first and second order statistical procedures. More specifically, the proposed feature extraction technique has the following attributes.

- It involves the extraction of first and second order characteristics of the input documents, based on processing individual and pairs of word semantic categories (Word semantic category Affinity - Mean distance between two word semantic categories) found in these documents.

- Both the text categorization indexing scheme and the word semantic category extraction scheme are based on widely accepted state of the art approaches. More specifically, concerning the former, the widely adopted by librarians DDC methodology [11] is considered. Concerning the latter, the use of the WorldNet [11] as a tool for processing the documents and associating semantic categories to their words has been adopted due to its high credibility and acceptance among NLP researchers. WordNet is a thesaurus that helps us to put the words we extract into a fixed number of semantic categories. These basic features will be analyzed with more detail in the next paragraphs.

To be able to measure progress in this field it is recommended to use standardized collection of documents for analysis and testing. One such data set is the Reuters-21578 collection of newswires for the year 1987 utilized by many researchers [10]. The text categories, assigned to documents included in this or other similar data sets, however, are domain specific and not scientifically derived and widely accepted by librarians as those defined by DDC. Therefore, since the final goal is to design a text categorization system for realistic applications and not for benchmarking purposes, the DDC document collection is herein exclusively involved.

In the following section 2, the suggested supervised text categorization approach is described in detail. In section 3 the experimental study is outlined. And finally, section 4 presents the conclusions and prospects of this research effort.

2   The Proposed MLP Based Text Categorization System

The suggested procedure is mainly divided into two phases. In the first phase we extract some first and second order characteristics, that is, frequency of word semantic categories appearance (extraction of keywords) and word semantic categories affinity (extraction of pairs of words semantic categories), from a set of documents collected from the Internet and labeled using DDC methodology [11]. We then use the widely accepted NLP semantics extraction program, the thesaurus called WordNet, in order to put the words we have extracted into a fixed number of semantic categories. As illustrated in the next paragraphs, the application of WordNet results in substituting a word by the vector of its semantic categories. After this stage, we use these semantic categories vectors instead of the initial words for subsequently extracting the first and second order document features of the proposed supervised text categorization system. In the second phase, employing these features, MLP Neural Networks are trained so that they can classify documents into a set of DDC text categories (note that these document categories are not related in any way with the categories of the WordNet). In the following paragraphs of this section we give a more detailed description of our novel methodology for extracting the first and second order characteristics, advancing from words to WordNet categories, creating the patterns and finally training the MLP neural networks.

The collection of documents used in this research effort, concerning the development of the proposed system, comes from the Internet site (link.bubll. ac.uk/isc2), which contains documents classified and accessed according to DDC (Dewey Decimal Classification). DDC is a document content classification system, internationally known and used in libraries and other organizations where a subject classification (catalogs) of documents is needed.

DDC defines a set of 10 main categories of documents that cover all possible subjects a document could refer to. Each one of them is divided into 10 Divisions and each division into 10 Sections. The classes of documents in DDC are defined through a systematic and objective way and not arbitrarily and subjectively. This is the reason we use DDC instead of defining our own classes of documents or following the classification schemes found in large domain-specific document collections found in the Internet, like the Reuters database. These document collections can only serve as test beds for evaluation of the preliminary design and not of the final design of text categorization real world systems. The DDC classes used in this paper are the following:

(1) Generalities,(2) Philosophy & related disciplines, (3) Religion, (4) Social sciences, (5) Language, (6) Pure sciences, (7) Technology (Applied sciences), (8) The arts, (9) Literature & rhetoric and (10 General geography, history, etc.

For each of these 10 classes a collection of 150 documents was made. The average length of these 1500 files was 256 words. Out of them, 1000 (10x100) documents (67%) comprise the training set and the rest 500 (10x50) documents (33%) comprise the test set. Following the process defined next, each document will be represented by a training (or test) pattern. So, there are 1000 training and 500 test patterns for training and testing the neural networks. We must note here that all collected documents are in English.

The first step is to remove a certain set of words, which are of less importance for meaning extraction. Specifically, it is assumed that nouns and verbs that can be found in a document are more relevant to meaning extraction, while certain adverbs, propositions and especially articles and adjectives are less relevant. This assumption is supported by the psycholinguistic theories underlying WordNet [11]. The set of such words excluded from further processing in this rsearch effort are: **"I", "you", "he", "she", "it", "us", "them", "the", "of", "end", "to", "in", "that", "is", "was", "for", "with", "as", "on", "be", "at", "by", "this", "had", "not", "are", "but", "from", "or", "have", "an", "they", "which", "there", "all", "would", "their", "we", "him", "been", "has", "when", "will", "more", "no", "if", "out", "so", "said", "what", "up", "its", "about", "into", "them", "than", "can", "only", "other", "onto"**

WordNet [11] is actually something more than a simple thesaurus. It is based on the latest psycholinguistic theories (a combination of psychological and linguistic theories) about the human lexical memory. The initial idea was to provide an aid to use in searching dictionaries conceptually, rather than merely alphabetically. In WordNet, the English nouns and verbs are organized in sets of synonyms. Each one of these sets describes a lexical concept. These sets are related in many ways to each other.

The most important of these relations between sets of word semantic categories (lexical concepts) considered in this paper, is the Hyponymy/Hyperonymy or Superset/Subset relation. A concept described by a set of synonyms $\{x,x',...\}$ is a hyponym of a concept described by another set of synonyms $\{y,y',...\}$, if people whose native language is English accept phrases such as "An x is a (kind of) y". In this way, concepts, and eventually words, are organized in a tree structure. The root (or a set of roots) of this tree describes the most general concept. For example, there is a set of 25 concepts (e.g. Process, Natural Object, Food, Communication, Knowledge and so on), which are the most general with regards to nouns.

The most important reason for using WordNet in this work is the fact that we can achieve dimensionality reduction of the space vectors representing documents and used in training the neural network subject classifiers. In particular, we use WordNet to represent each word we have extracted from the texts with a set of WordNet concepts (in our case there are 229 such concepts), or semantic categories of words. Thus, after this step, all texts are represented by space vectors with 229 dimensions of WordNet semantic categories, instead of the words extracted from them. The following list shows the 229 WordNet categories used in this work:

Table 1. The subset of WorldNet word Semantic Categories used in the proposed methodology.

Ability,Could,Kill,Prose, Abstraction,Cover,knowledge_domain,Province
Accept,Covering,land, Psychological_feature,Accomplishment,Create,language,quality
Act,Creation,leader,quantity, Activity,Creator,line,record
Affirm,currency,linguistic_relation,reject,African,decelerate,liquid,relation
Agree,decide,location,relationship,American,decoration,look,religious_ceremony
Analyze,device,lose,religious_person,Animal,differ,make,remove
Area,disease,matter,resprire,Art,displease,means,rock
Artifact,document,measure,rule,artificial_language,enter,medicine,science
Asian,entertainer,message,scientist,Athlete,entity,military_action,show
Attribute,equal,military_man,social_class,Attitude,equipment,military_unit,social_event
Attribute,european,mineral,social_group,basic_cognitive_process,event,misc,social_relation
Be,excel,money,social_science,Become,expert,motion,solid
Belief,express,move,speech,biological_group,feel,munber,speech_act
body_part,feeling,music,spiritual_being,Calculation,fight,name,spiritual_leader
Calculus,fluid,names,state,Capitalist,food,nation,statement
Care,form,native,structure,Categorize,genealogy,natural_language,succeed
Category,generality,natural_object,support,Caucasian,genitor,natural_phenomenon,surface
Cause,geological_time,natural_process,symbol,Ceremony,geology,natural_science,symptom
Change,get,nature,take,Characteristic,give,nonreligious_person,think
chemical_compound,go,number,time,chemical_element,goods,occupation,time_period
chemical_process,group,organization,time_unit,City,group_action,part,touch
Classification,grouping,permit,trait,Collection,hair,person,transfer
Color,have,phenomenon,travel,Commerce,higher_cognitive_process,physical,treat
Communicate,holy_day,physical_structure,understand,Communication,ideal,planet,undo
Communicator,imaginary_being,plant,union,Concept,imaginary_place,point,unit
Confirm,implement,possession,use,Connect,inform,power,vehicle
Content,information,print_medium,want,Continent,institution,printing,wish
Continue,interact,process,word,Control,judge,procession,work,
Convey,keep,property,worker, Writing

Another reason for using WordNet is that in this way we try to give a solution to the Vocabulary Problem [2]. The vocabulary problem refers to the problem that rises when different people, with different knowledge background, training and experience, use different sets of terms when dealing with a certain subject. By using WordNet, different words with the same meaning (synonyms) are grouped under the same concept (set of synonyms). Although WordNet is not able to classify every given word, and especially scientific terms, into one of the available concepts, it can, however, classify a large number of the words extracted and therefore, give a quite good solution to the vocabulary problem.

It has been previously mentioned that a novel and significant feature of this work is, actually, the use of pairs of word semantic categories apart from extracting keywords, that is, individual word (nouns and verbs) lexical concepts, in order to extract content information. Involving correlations of word semantic categories equals incorporating second order information in the document space vector representation.

The previous step involved the use of WordNet for passing from words and pairs of words to semantic categories of words and pairs of semantic categories. The result for each text is finally one vector of 229 elements (the number of WordNet categories) containing information about the frequency of occurrence of WordNet semantic categories in the text, instead of words occurrence frequency as in the simple word frequency weighting indexing [10] method. In addition, two matrices of 229x229 elements are derived, each containing information about the pairs of semantic categories cooccurrence. We then use cooccurrence matrices analysis, involved in texture processing of images, to transform each of the two matrices into a vector of six elements. All this methodology is described in more detail in the following.

It should be pointed out that in the proposed methodology, after preprocessing, each document could be represented (using a program in C language) in a tree structure. Each node of this tree stores information for each new word found, comprised of,

- The word itself, The number of appearances of this word in the certain text, A list with the positions of the word in the text, The DDC class in which the document belongs

It must be mentioned here that the following characters are the ones considered as separators between two words in a text:

- Line feed (\n), Tab (\t), One or more spaces (SPACE), (\r), Page feed (\f)

Having this information we create at first a vector containing each different word and the frequency of its appearance in the text. This completes the second step in the proposed feature extraction technique (words selection is the first step).

The third step in the suggested feature extraction methodology is the creation of the first out of the two matrices mentioned above, the Full Affinity Matrix. This matrix contains information about word affinity, and more specifically information about the mean distance between any pair of words found in a certain text. The number stored in position [i,j] of this matrix is the mean distance of the words i and j in the text.

The mean distance between two words i and j is calculated as follows:

1. SUM[i,j] is the total sum of distances between the two words i and j for all the possible pairs (i,j) of these two words in the text.
2. N[i,j] is the number of all the possible pairs (i,j) of the words i and j found in the text.
3. $AVN[i,j] = \dfrac{SUM[i, j]}{N[i, j]}$ is the mean distance between the two words in the text.

The next step is to create the second of the matrices, called Adjoining Affinity Matrix. This matrix also contains information about word affinity in texts, that is, about mean distance between words as in the previous case of the full affinity matrix. The difference, however, is that not all possible pairs of words are examined as before. This matrix contains information about neighboring or adjoining words in text. The following example is quite explanatory:

"Time slips by like grains of sand"

In the above phrase, adjoining words are

Time (position 1) with slips (position 2), Slips (position 2) with like (position 4), Like (position 4) with grains (position 5), Grains (position 5) with sand (position 7)

Whereas, in creating the full affinity matrix we would also consider the pairs (time, grains), (like, time), (time, like), and so on.

Note that the words "by" and "of" are not used in creating the adjoining affinity matrix because they belong to the list with the excluded words.

After creating the word frequency of occurrence vector and the two affinity matrices, the fourth step is to involve WordNet in use. The idea, as shown before, is to associate each word with a vector of semantic categories by giving the word as input to

WordNet. For example, giving "car" as input to WordNet, the result is (after automatic processing of the output) the following set:
(vehicle, artifact, entity, area, structure)

WORD	WORDNET CATEGORIES
Like	judge, think
Time	event, measure, abstraction, time, property, attribute, information, knowledge, psychological_feature

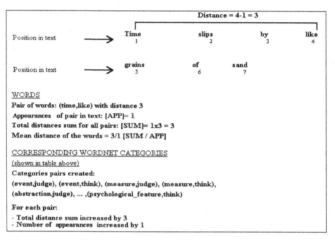

Fig. 1. An explanatory example on WorldNet use for document initial processing

The total number of word semantic categories is 229. Therefore each word frequency vector is transformed into word semantic categories frequency vector of 229 elements, while each word affinity matrix (full or adjoining) is transformed into a 229x229 matrix of word semantic categories affinity matrix. The process for these transformations is easy to understand.

First, in the case of the frequency vectors, each word is taken and its corresponding set of n semantic categories is found, word_i = (semantic_word_i_1, semantic_ word_i_2, ... semantic_word_i_n). The element in position [i] of the semantic categories frequency vector is increased by one if the semantic category in position [i] of that vector is found in the set of semantic categories associated to that particular word and produced by WordNet. Otherwise the element remains as before. Finally, each element of the semantic categories vector shows how many times the corresponding category is found in the text (by counting the matching semantic categories in the whole set of words extracted from the text).

Second, in the case of the two affinity matrices, each pair of words [i,j] encountered in the text is considered, along with the corresponding information about their associated total sum of distances (SUM[i,j]) and the number of their pairs (N[i,j]) occurred in the document. The set of semantic categories for both words is then found. The element [k,l] of the semantic categories affinity matrix is changed if category k is found in the categories set of word i and category l is found in the categories set of word j. More specifically, the corresponding total sum in the semantic categories affinity matrix is increased by SUM[i,j] and the number of pairs is increased by N[i,j].

A simple but explanatory example is presented in the table of fig. 1, which shows the words and their WordNet semantic categories, how the affinity matrices are created and how WordNet is used.

Thus, after finishing the fourth step, each text is represented by:

- A 229-element WordNet categories frequency vector
- A 229x229-element semantic categories affinity matrix (Full Affinity Matrix)
- A 229x229-element semantic categories affinity matrix (Adjoining Affinity Matrix) – semantic categories pairs frequencies.

The fifth step in the proposed feature extraction approach is to transform the above described affinity matrices into vectors of 6 elements by applying Cooccurrence Matrices Analysis to each one of them. The final result is that each text is represented by a vector of 229+6+6=241 elements by joining the semantic categories frequency vector and the two vectors obtained by applying the cooccurrence matrices analysis measures (of 6 dimensions each) to each of the two affinity matrices.

In this fifth step, concerning the feature extraction approach herein adopted, some ideas taken from Texture Analysis are utilized. Texture analysis as a process is part of what is known as Image Processing. The purpose of texture analysis in image processing is to find relations between the pixel intensities that create an image. Such a relation is for example the mean and the variance of the intensity of the pixels. A common tool for texture analysis is the Cooccurrence Matrix [12]. The purpose of the cooccurrence matrix is to describe the relation between the current pixel intensity and the intensity (gray level) of the neighboring pixels. The creation of the cooccurrence matrix is the first step of the texture analysis process. The second step is to extract a number of statistical measures from the matrix.

After cooccurrence matrices formation in image texture analysis, several measures are extracted from these cooccurrence matrices in order to best describe the texture of the source image in terms of classification accuracy. The following 6 measures in table 2 are an example of texture measures [12]. Cooccurrence matrices analysis in texture processing could be associated with word cooccurrence matrices for text understanding, in a straightforward way, where, each semantic word category (from 1 to 229) is associated with a pixel intensity. The rationale underlying such an association is explained below. It is clear that similar measures could be extracted for both word affinity matrices. Thus, the six measures shown in table 2 are, also, the ones used in this work. In every equation, f(r,c) represents the position [r,c] of the associated matrix. Therefore, texture analysis process ends up with a small set of numbers describing an image area in terms of texture information, which results in information compression. Instead of the source image (a matrix of pixels) there is a set of numbers (the results of applying the texture measures) that represent textural information in a condensed way. This is the reason why it is herein attempted to associate texture analysis and text understanding analysis, namely, dimensionality reduction of the input vectors produced in text processing. The same ideas emerging from texture analysis in image processing are applied to the document text categorization problem.

Table 2. The cooccurrence matrices analysis associated measures.

1.	**Energy:**	$M_1 = $ Sum Sum $f(r,c)^2$
2.	**Entropy:**	$M_2 = $ Sum Sum $\log(f(r,c) * f(r,c)$
3.	**Contrast:**	$M_3 = $ Sum Sum $(r-c)^2 * f(r,c)$
4.	**Homogeneity:**	$M_4 = $ Sum Sum $f(r,c)/(1+|r-c|)$
5.	**Correlation:**	$M_5 = $ Sum Sum $\{(r*c) f(r,c) - m_r m_c\}/s_r s_c$

where, m_i is the mean value and s_i is the variance of line (column) i.

6. **Inverse Difference Moment:** $M_6 = $ Sum Sum $f(r,c)/((1+(r-c))$

where, the double summation symbol {Sum Sum} ranges for all rows and columns respectively.

While cooccurrence matrices in texture analysis contain information about the correlation of neighboring pixel intensities in an image, the proposed affinity matrices contain information about the correlations of WordNet semantic categories associated with a text. Autocorrelation matrices are involved in both definitions and therefore, both processes bear some similarities. Thus, the measures defined in table 2 are applied to the word affinity matrices too. After the application of cooccurrence based matrices analysis, there will be a total of 1500 vectors of 241 elements each. The next thing to discuss is how MLP neural networks are trained by utilizing these vectors so as to correctly classify documents in the 10 DDC classes.

An important aspect concerning neural networks training is the normalization of their input vectors. Normalization of the set of features presented in this paper is achieved by substituting each feature value x with $\frac{x - \text{Min}}{\text{Max} - \text{Min}}$ where Max and Min are the maximum and the minimum values of the set where this feature value belongs in, respectively. Actually, thirteen such sets of values exist for the document space vectors under processing. Namely, one for the word semantic categories frequencies, six for the cooccurrence analysis measures with respect to the full affinity matrix and six for the cooccurrence analysis measures with respect to the adjoining affinity matrix. This normalization procedure constitutes the sixth and final step of the feature extraction stage of the proposed text categorization methodology.

There are several reasons for involving MLP neural networks instead of traditional statistical classifiers:

- Their capability to learn difficult tasks and their satisfactory generalization even in the case of classification problems with multiple input features and classes [13].
- Their capability to generalize well even with noisy data and missing information [13].
- They are universal approximators whose generalization capabilities are not affected, at least to the first order, from the curse of dimensionality [13].
- MLP training is supervised.

3 Experimental Study and Results

In order to evaluate the proposed text categorization methodology an extensive experimental study has been conducted and herein is presented. Two different sets of experiments have been organized. The first one involves the collection of documents based on the DDC classification approach and the herein proposed feature extraction methodology, while the second one involves the DDC collection again but different, proposed in the literature and well established, feature extraction techniques [10]. In the first set of experiments the proposed methodology involves the document space vectors completely defined in section 2 and illustrated in the following table.

Position in Space Vector	Feature	Position in Space Vector	Feature
1	Energy	7	Energy
2	Entropy	8	Entropy
3	Contrast	9	Contrast
4	Homogeneity	10	Homogeneity
5	Correlation	11	Correlation
6	Inv. Diff. Moment	12	Inv. Diff. Moment
	(=>1-6: Full Affinity Matrix measures)		(=>7-12: Adjoining Affinity Matrix measures)
13 – 241	WordNet word Semantic Categories Frequencies		

In the second set of experiments, in order to validate our approach, we have applied a standard feature extraction method as the **tf x idf** word frequency weighting scheme [10] to the DDC collection of 1500 documents. Therefore, a set of 1500 document space vectors, different from the ones of the first set, has been obtained. The total number of different words encountered in all the 1500 documents, after removing the words specified in section 2.2 (words selection procedure), are 6533. Therefore, all the word frequencies based document space vectors used in this set of experiments are of 6533 dimensions.

In both sets of experiments the classifiers reported in the next paragraphs define the second stage of the text categorization system. While, in the first set they are applied to the proposed document space vectors, analyzed in section 2, in the second set of experiments they have been applied to the document space vectors derived using the **tf x idf** technique.

Concerning both sets of experiments, a cross-validation methodology [13] has been applied to all the text categorization methods herein involved, in order to ensure statistical validity of the results, due to the relatively not large number of documents included in this DDC collection. As mentioned above, the 1500 document space vectors constructed from the DDC collection are divided in the training set of patterns (1000 of them) and in the test set of patterns (500 of them). In order to apply the cross-validation methodology [13], 500 different pairs of such training and test sets have been created from the set of 1500 document space vectors by randomly assigning each of them to a training or test set.

A variety of MLP training models has been applied to both sets of experiments, including standard on-line Backpropagation, RPROP and SCG (Scaled Conjugate Gradients). Several architectures have been investigated of the types 241-x-10 and 6533-x-10 (input neurons- hidden layer neurons- output neurons). Only the best of these MLP model architectures and training parameters, out of the many ones investigated, are reported in tables 4 and 5, outlining the outcomes of this study. The MLP simulation environment is the SNNS (Stuttgart Neural Network) Simulator [14]. All training parameters shown for the Pattern Classifier training algorithms used are defined in [14]. The desired output vectors for all MLP/SVM classification models are defined in table 3.

Table 3. The DDC categories and their association to desired MLP/SVM outputs.

DDC Category of the document space vector	MLP/SVM Classifier desired output vector
The Arts	1 0 0 0 0 0 0 0 0 0
Generalities	0 1 0 0 0 0 0 0 0 0
General Geography	0 0 1 0 0 0 0 0 0 0
Language	0 0 0 1 0 0 0 0 0 0
Literature & Rhetoric	0 0 0 0 1 0 0 0 0 0
Philosophy	0 0 0 0 0 1 0 0 0 0
Religion	0 0 0 0 0 0 1 0 0 0
Pure Sciences	0 0 0 0 0 0 0 1 0 0
Social Sciences	0 0 0 0 0 0 0 0 1 0
Technology	0 0 0 0 0 0 0 0 0 1

For comparison reasons the LVQ and the k-NN classifier, which is reported to be one of the best algorithms for text categorization [10] are, also, involved in this experimental study. Especially in the case of the **tf x idf** technique, the Support Vector Machine (SVM) approach has been, also, included in the comparisons, due to its very good performance in very large dimensionality spaces [10].

Concerning the performance measures utilized in this study, mean, variance, maximum and minimum of the classification accuracy obtained by each text classifier involved are reported in tables 4 and 5. To this end, if one classifier results in $G_1\%$, $G_2\%$, $G_3\%$, ..., $G_{500}\%$ over all the 10 classes classification accuracies with respect to each one of the 500 different testing sets of patterns associated with the cross-validation procedure, then,

- Mean Accuracy $= (G_1\%+G_2\%+G_3\%+ ....+ G_{500}\%)/500$
- Accuracy Variance $= \text{VARIANCE} (G_1\%, G_2\%, G_3\%, ..., G_{500}\%)$
- Max Accuracy $= \text{MAX} (G_1\%, G_2\%, G_3\%, ..., G_{500}\%)$
- Min Accuracy $= \text{MIN} (G_1\%, G_2\%, G_3\%, ..., G_{500}\%)$

where, each Gi% refers to the over all categories classification accuracy (number of correctly classified patterns/ total number of patterns) for the patterns encountered in the ith test set and not to each category classification accuracy separately. These performance measures are the usually involved statistical measures in cross-validation experiments [13]. The following tables 4 and 5 show the results obtained by conducting the above defined experimental study. Table 4 illustrates the results obtained by applying the proposed feature extraction methodology, while table 5 presents the results obtained by applying the **tf x idf** technique. These favorable text classification performance results show the validity of our approach concerning the document space vector extraction and the feasibility of the proposed solution in the real word data-mining problem under consideration.

Table 4. Text Categorization accuracy obtained involving the proposed, in section 2, document space vectors extraction methodology. The statistics obtained after 500 runs of all algorithms

Performance Measures / Text Classifier	Mean Accuracy (%)	Accuracy Variance (%)	Max Accuracy (%)	Min Accuracy (%)
LVQ, 40 code book vectors	69.8	2.4	70.6	66.4
LVQ, 28 code book vectors	70.6	2.5	71.5	67.3
Vanilla BP, 241-12-10, (0.6, 0.2)	60.8	2.8	63.9	58.2
RPROP, 241-12-10, (1,100,10)	75.5	3.5	80.1	72.4
RPROP, 241-12-10, (0.1,50,4)	74.1	3.1	76.7	71.2
RPROP, 241-14-10, (0.1,50,4)	62.3	2.7	64.8	58.1
SCG, 241-15-10, (0,0,0,0)	63.4	1.8	64.9	59.8
Vanilla BP, 241-18-10, (0.6,0.2)	61.5	1.1	62.8	60.1
RPROP, 241-18-10, (1,100,10)	72.2	0.8	72.9	71.1
Vanilla BP, 241-24-10, (0.4,0.1)	69.6	3.0	72.1	66.2
K-NN (nearest neighbor)-(K= 30)	69.2	2.6	70.1	64.3

Table 5. Text Categorization accuracy obtained involving the tf x idf word frequency based document space vectors extraction methodology. The statistics obtained after 500 runs of all the algorithms.

Performance Measures / Text Classifier	Mean Accuracy (%)	Accuracy Variance (%)	Max Accuracy (%)	Min Accuracy (%)
Support Vector Machine (RBF with 60 code-book vectors)	69.1	2.4	69.8	65.2
LVQ, 28 code book vectors	67.7	2.2	69.1	64.9
Vanilla BP (On-line BP), 6533-320-10, (0.4,0.5)	57.3	4.1	62.4	55.6
RPROP, 6533-320-10, (1,100,10)	68.4	5.2	72.3	61.6
SCG, 6533-320-10, (0,0,0,0)	61.7	2.3	64.5	60.5
K-NN (nearest neighbor)-(K= 30)	67.6	2.1	68.9	64.7

4 Conclusions and Prospects

This paper outlines a feasible solution to the problem of text categorization and its closely related meaning extraction analysis of full-text non-domain specific document collections. The collection of documents and their content categorization is based on a widely accepted and systematic methodology, namely, the DDC system. The techniques suggested involve MLP neural networks and novel feature extraction methods based on first and second order characteristics of word concept frequencies and affinities estimated by application of a widely accepted NLP thesaurus tool, namely, the WordNet and statistical techniques stemmed from Texture processing in image analysis. The promising results obtained are favorably compared to other well established text categorization document space vectors formation techniques. A comparative study with the best in the literature reported techniques is under the way by the authors, although the current DDC Web document collection (formed by the authors) should be augmented in order to avoid the time consuming but statistically valid cross-validation based comparison. Future aspects of our work include, also, the designing of a complete system based on Computational Intelligence and Artificial Intelligence Techniques for dealing with the full DDC text categorization problem, involving 1000 human understandable categories.

References

[1]   Merkl D., "Text Classification with Self-Organizing Maps: Some lessons learned", Neurocomputing, vol. 21, pp. 61–77, 1998.
[2]   Chen H., et al, "Information Visualization for Collaborative Computing", IEEE Computer, pp. 75–82, Aug. 1998
[3]   Kohonen T., et al, "Self-Organization of a Massive Document Collection", IEEE Trans. Neural Networks, vol. 11, no 3, pp. 574–585, 2000.
[4]   Cohen W. J. and Singer Y.,"Context-sensitive learning methods for text categorization", In SIGIR'96: Proc. 19th Annual Int. ACM SIGIR Conf. on Research and Development in Information Retrieval, pp. 307–315, 1996.
[5]   Yang Y. and Pedersen J. P, "Feature selection in statistical learning of text categorization", In the 14th Int. Conf. on Machine Learning, pp. 412–420, 1997.
[6]   Lewis D. and Ringuette M., "A comparison of two learning algorithms for text classification", 3rd Annual Symposium on Document Analysis and Information Retrieval, pp. 81–93, 1994.
[7]   Joachims T., "Text categorization with support vector machines: Learning with many relevant features", In Proc. 10th European Conference on Machine Learning (ECML), Springer Verlag, 1998.
[8]   Wiener E., Pedersen J. O., and Weigend A. S., "A neural network approach to topic spotting", 4th annual symposium on document analysis and Information retrieval, pp. 22–34, 1993.
[9]   Salton G. and McGill M. J., "An Introduction to Modern Information Retrieval", McGraw-Hill, 1983.
[10]   Aas K. and Eikvil L., "Text Categorisation: A Survey", Technical Report, Norwegian Computing Center, P.B. 114 Blindern, N-0314 Oslo, Norway, 1999
[11]   Chan, Mai L., Comaromi J. P. and Satija M. P., 1994. "Dewey Decimal Classification: a practical guide". Albany, N.Y.: Forest Press.
[12]   Haralick, R. M., Shanmugam, K. and Dinstein, I. "Textural Features for Image Classification", IEEE Trans. Syst., Man and Cybern., Vol. SMC-3, 6, pp. 610–621, 1973.
[13]   Haykin S., "Neural Networks. A comprehensive foundation", Prentice Hall, 1999.
[14]   Zell A., Mamier G., Vogt M., et al. , "SNNS Stuttgart Neural Network Simulator, User Manual Version 4.1", Report No 6/95, University of Stuttgart, http://www-ra.informatik.uni-tuebingen.de/SNNS/UserManual/UserManual.html

Solving Regression Problems Using Competitive Ensemble Models

Yakov Frayman, Bernard F. Rolfe, and Geoffrey I. Webb

School of Information Technology
Deakin University
Geelong, VIC, Australia
{yfraym,brolfe,webb}@deakin.edu.au

Abstract. The use of ensemble models in many problem domains has increased significantly in the last few years. The ensemble modeling, in particularly boosting, has shown a great promise in improving predictive performance of a model. Combining the ensemble members is normally done in a co–operative fashion where each of the ensemble members performs the same task and their predictions are aggregated to obtain the improved performance. However, it is also possible to combine the ensemble members in a competitive fashion where the best prediction of a relevant ensemble member is selected for a particular input. This option has been previously somewhat overlooked. The aim of this article is to investigate and compare the competitive and co–operative approaches to combining the models in the ensemble. A comparison is made between a competitive ensemble model and that of MARS with bagging, mixture of experts, hierarchical mixture of experts and a neural network ensemble over several public domain regression problems that have a high degree of nonlinearity and noise. The empirical results show a substantial advantage of competitive learning versus the co–operative learning for all the regression problems investigated. The requirements for creating the efficient ensembles and the available guidelines are also discussed.

1 Introduction

The main motivation for combining models in ensembles is to improve their generalization ability. The idea of combining models in order to achieve a better prediction has a long history, and has emerged independently in a number of different areas. For example, in econometrics, better forecasting results can be achieved by combining forecasts (model mixing) than by choosing the best model [2]. In machine learning this can be traced back to evidence combination [1].

Recently there was a resurgence of interest in model aggregation particularly in machine learning and data mining. One of the aggregation methods, bagging, is aimed at reducing the variance of predictive models [5]. Another one, stacking [24], attempted to decrease prediction bias in addition to variance. But the most popular ensemble method is boosting [20], aimed on transforming a collection of weak models into one strong model. The recently developed AdaBoost algorithm [11] sequentially fits weak models to different weighting of the observations in a data set. The observations that are predicted poorly receive greater weighting on the next iteration. The resulting AdaBoost model is

R.I. McKay and J. Slaney (Eds.): AI 2002, LNAI 2557, pp. 511–522, 2002.
© Springer-Verlag Berlin Heidelberg 2002

a weighted average of all the weak predictors. The AdaBoost is shown to be effective for reducing bias and variance in a wide range of classification problems [3]. However, the recent work on boosting [13] have shown that AdaBoost algorithm is an optimization method for finding a model that minimizes a particular exponential loss function, namely the Bernoulli likelihood. Recent investigations of the boosting algorithm from the statistical viewpoint [18] have found that while boosting algorithm appears complex on surface, it is similar to the ways linear models are fitted in statistics. This opens the possibility to unite seemingly different, but essentially similar approaches to ensemble modeling from machine learning and statistical and engineering viewpoints.

The current trend in boosting with major developments in boosted regression [9] is going in a direction similar to the statistical approach to model mixing. The boosted regression approach follows the spirit of AdaBoost algorithm by repeatedly performing weighted tree regression followed by increasing weighting of the poorly predicted observations and decreasing the weighting of the better predicted samples. The work on Gradient Boosting Machine [14] uses the connection between boosting and optimization more explicitly. At each iteration the algorithm determines the direction, the gradient, in which it needs to improve the fit to the data and selects a particular model from the available class of functions that is most in agreement with the direction. While this is a significant improvement on the approach of AdaBoost, the Gradient Boosting Machine algorithm is, however, increasingly similar to other non–parametric regression models such as neural networks. As such the Gradient Boosting Machine still does not provide a reliably guidance to selection of ensemble members and effective means of combining such ensemble members. This leads us to analysis of the available methods for creation of ensemble members and their combination for efficient ensembles.

2   Ensemble Modeling

The effectiveness of an ensemble can be measured by the extent to which the members are error–independent (show different patterns of generalization) [19]. The ideal would be a set of models where each of the models generalize well, and when they do make errors on new data, these errors are not shared with any other models [19].

2.1   Creating Ensemble Members

In order to create efficient ensembles we need to consider the relative merits of methods of creating ensemble members, and to choose and apply one that is likely to result in models that generalize differently. There are several possible ways to achieve this objective that include the following:

Sampling data: A set of models for an ensemble is commonly created by using some form of sampling, such that each model in the ensemble is trained on a different sub–sample of the training data. Re-sampling methods which have been used for this purpose include cross-validation, and bootstrapping [5]. In bagging [5], a training set containing N cases is perturbed by sampling with replacement (bootstrap) N times from the training set. The perturbed data set may contain repeats. This procedure can be repeated several times to create a number of different, although overlapping, data sets. A method similar to the sampling is the use of disjoint training sets, that is sampling without replacement. There is then no overlap between the data used to train different models.

However, the presence of correlation between the errors of the ensemble members could reduce the effectiveness of the ensemble [15]. While sampling the data might be an effective way of producing models that generalize differently, this will not necessarily result in low error correlations as it requires a representative training set where a function being inferred is similar to that which generated the test set [8]. However, two representative training sets could lead to very similar functions being inferred, so their pattern of errors on the new data would be very similar.

On the other hand, if ensemble members are trained using unrepresentative training sets, the resulting generalization performance would be poor. Each member might show different patterns of generalization, but as the amount of errors increases so does the probability that their errors will overlap.

Boosting and adaptive resampling: In boosting, as discussed previously, a series of weak learners could be converted to a strong learner as a result of training the members of an ensemble on patterns that have been filtered by previously trained members [20], [23]. AdaBoost algorithm [11] has training sets adaptively resampled, such that the weights in the resampling are increased for those cases which are most often predicted incorrectly.

Varying the learning method employed: The learning method used to train the models could be varied while holding the data constant when creating ensemble members. An ensemble might be constructed from models generated by a combination of learning techniques such as various statistical methods, linear regression, neural networks, k–nearest neighbors, decision trees, and Markov chains [7].

While this approach is not commonly used, in our opinion, it is a very promising approach to ensemble learning, as the use of different learning methods for ensemble members is more likely to result in different patterns of generalization than sampling the data. Furthermore, there is a possibility to combine varying both the learning method and the data, for example, with adaptive re–sampling of the data.

In this paper we will investigate the approach of varying the learning method for creation of ensemble members and compare it with approaches that use sampling the data.

2.2 Combining Ensemble Members

The next step in ensemble learning is to find an effective way of combining model outputs. While there exists several possible ways of combining models in an ensemble, the co–operative combination is the most dominant one. In co–operative combination it is assumed that all of the ensemble members will make some contribution to the ensemble decision, even though this contribution may be weighted in some way.

Methods of combining the models in co–operative fashion include the following:

Averaging and weighted averaging: Linear combination of the outputs of the ensemble members are one of the most popular aggregation methods. A single output can be created from a set of model outputs via simple averaging, or by means of a weighted average that takes account of the relative accuracy of the models to be combined.

Stacked generalization: Stacked generalization [24] uses an additional model that learns how to combine the models with weights that vary over the feature space. The outputs from a set of level 0 generalizers are used as the input to a level 1 generalizer, which is trained to produce the appropriate output. It is also possible to view other methods of combining, such as averaging, as instances of stacking with a simple level 1 generalizer.

In competitive combination, on the other hand, it is assumed that for each input only the most appropriate ensemble member will be selected based on either the inputs or outputs of the models [21].

The two main methods for a competitive combination (selection) are:

Gating: Under the divide and conquer approach employed by mixtures-of-experts [16] and hierarchical mixtures-of-experts [17] the complex problem is decomposed into a set of simpler problems. The data is partitioned into regions and the simple surfaces are fitted to the data into each region. The regions have soft boundaries where data points may lie simultaneously in multiple regions. Such decomposition ensures that the errors made by the expert models will not be correlated as they deal with different data points. A gating model is used to output a set of scalar coefficients that weights the contributions of the various inputs.

Rule–based switching: In this case, the switching between the models can be triggered on the basis of the input or the output of one of the models. For example, in the study on the diagnosis of myocardial infarction (heart attack), two models were optimized separately by varying the proportion of high risk and low risk patients in the training sets. The first model was trained to make as few positive errors as possible, and the second model was trained to make as few negative errors as possible [4]. The output of the first model was used unless it exceeds a threshold in which case the output of the second model was used.

There exists other examples of rule–based switching, for example, switching of control to the most appropriate model depending on the current situation as it is exploited in behavior–based robotics [6].

Our empirical observation [10] has been that the better results can be obtained through the use of a more explicit rule–based switching between models.

3   Computational Experiments

3.1   Experimental Set Up

To evaluate the performance of a competitive ensemble model, several public domain regression data sets were selected from DELVE (Data for Evaluating Learning in Valid Experiments) (see http://www.cs.toronto.edu/~delve/). DELVE is a standardized environment designed to evaluate the performance of methods that learn relationships based primarily on empirical data. DELVE makes it possible for users to compare their learning methods with other methods on many data sets. The DELVE learning methods and evaluation procedures are well documented, such that meaningful comparisons can be made. Since our approach involves ensembles, we compared the performance of our competitive ensemble model to that of multivariable adaptive regression splines (MARS) with bagging, mixture of experts, hierarchical mixture of experts, neural network ensemble and also with a standard linear regression as a baseline method. The competitive ensemble model was used in accordance with DELVE guidelines. The performance of other methods are available from DELVE. The splitting of data sets into training and testing was done using a DELVE software environment, which allows to manipulate data sets and do statistical analysis of method's performance.

We have selected from DELVE environment all the regression data sets where there are results available of the MARS with bagging, the mixture of experts, the hierarchical mixture of experts, the neural network ensemble and the linear regression as follows:

a) *Boston Housing data-set.* The Boston Housing data-set is a small but widely used data-set derived from information collected by the U.S. Census Service concerning housing in the Boston, Massachusetts area. It has been used extensively throughout the literature to benchmark algorithms. The task is to predict the median value of a home (price).

b) *Pumadyn family of data sets.* The Pumadyn family of data sets is a realistic simulation of the dynamics of a Puma 560 robot arm. The task is to predict angular acceleration of one of the robot arm's links. The inputs include angular positions, velocities and torques of the robot arm. The family has been specifically generated for the DELVE environment and so the individual data sets span the corners of a cube whose dimensions represent: (a) number of inputs (8 or 32), (b) degree of non-linearity (fairly linear or non-linear), (c) amount of noise in the output (moderate or high).

c) *Kin family of data sets.* The Kin family of data sets is a realistic simulation of the forward dynamics of an 8 link all–revolute robot arm. The task is to predict the distance of the end–effector from a target. The inputs are factors like joint positions and twist angles. The family has been also specifically generated for the DELVE environment and has the same dimensions as Pumadyn family of data sets.

We have considered both dimensionalities of the input (8 or 32) and have chosen high amount of noise and a large amount of non–linearity to make the tasks similar to other real–world tasks we have investigated. In addition, we have only considered the larger size of training and testing sets (1024 for pumadyn and kin, and 128 for boston housing) out of that available in the DELVE environment. Training and testing sets were generated randomly from the respective data sets using a DELVE software environments. Thus, there are 2 different training and testing sets for Boston Housing data set, and 4 for all the Pumadyn and Kin data sets. Table 1 summarizes the data characteristics.

Table 1. Data Characteristics.

Name	Size	Train	Test	Inputs	Noise	Non-Linearity
Boston Housing	506	128	128	13	–	–
Pumadyn-8nh	8192	1024	1024	8	high	non–linear
Pumadyn-32nh	8192	1024	1024	32	high	non–linear
Kin-8nh	8192	1024	1024	8	high	non–linear
Kin-32nh	8192	1024	1024	32	high	non–linear

3.2   Regression Methods Used

The competitive (selection) model used in this paper was created following the guidelines discussed previously.

A non–linear model (neural network) was trained to select the appropriate output of the ensemble members as a final output of the ensemble model based on the performance of ensemble members on a particular data tuple. The aim here is basically to create a global model (ensemble model) where each of the ensemble members is acting as a local predictor in the area of its best performance. In such a rule–based switching [22], the control is switched between the ensemble members depending on the output of one of the members.

For the ensemble members (level 0 generalizers) we have selected a linear method (linear regression), an efficient nonlinear method (multilayer perceptron (MLP) with two hidden layers with 20 nodes each), a logistic regression (MLP with a single hidden node) and a clustering algorithm (KNN) with k equal 10. The reasons for selecting these learning methods for creation of the ensemble members are that these methods are very different in nature and as such have different learning biases. In our experience, these learning methods have a different pattern of generalization and as such can produce an efficient ensemble.

As a level 1 generalizer (selector model) another MLP consisting of 2 hidden layers of 20 hidden nodes each was used. All MLPs were fully connected with hyperbolic tangent hidden units and linear output units. All ensemble members were trained using the back–propagation learning algorithm with early stopping to avoiding over–fitting. The pattern (on–line) learning was used. The learning rate of 0.05 and momentum of 0.99 were used for all MLPs to avoid local minima. The structure and the parameters of both MLPs and the KNN were selected based on our experience with other data sets and no attempt was made to optimize the level 0 models to the data sets considered.

The structure of the competitive model is in Fig 1. In this case all the available inputs in a training set were supplied to the level 0 models and the selection model. Selection model also receives the output of the level 0 models. In the learning phase a binary value is assigned to the output of the selection model that represents the best model or otherwise for a particular data tuple. The selection model is solving a classification problem which is to choose the appropriate output of the one of the level 0 models as the final output of the ensemble. Supplying the input data to the selection model is not strictly necessary as the MLP with 2 hidden layers is a very efficient classifier, but may help the selection model to distinguish between the level 0 models in some cases.

For comparison with our selection model we have used several popular regression methods: multivariable adaptive regression splines with bagging, mixture–of–experts, hierarchical mixture–of–experts and ensemble of neural networks. We have already discussed mixture–of–experts and hierarchical mixture–of–experts methods. In the following, we will briefly describe the rest of the methods.

Multivariable adaptive regression splines (MARS) [12] were created to provide the advantages of tree based regression methods without the disadvantages of the response being discontinuous along the boundaries. Here each step basis function in the predictor space is replaced by a pair of linear basis functions. The new splits are not required to

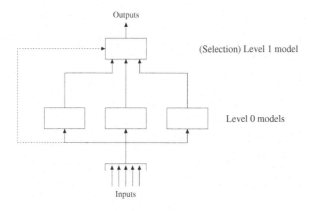

Fig. 1. Selection Model.

depend on the previous splits. The final solution is made smooth by replacing the linear functions with cubic functions after backward deletion of unnecessary basic functions.

Table 2. Results from Boston data-set.

Method	Standardized estimated expected loss	Standard error for difference estimate	Significance of difference (F-test)
Selection ensemble	0.05663	–	–
Linear regression	0.28123	0.02920	< 0.05
HME (ensemble learning)	0.16204	0.01416	< 0.05
HME (early stopping)	0.17312	0.02075	< 0.05
HME (growing and early stopping)	0.17623	0.02063	< 0.05
MARS version 3.6 with Bagging	0.15713	0.02104	< 0.05
ME (ensemble learning)	0.15937	0.02431	< 0.05
ME (early stopping)	0.16006	0.01464	< 0.05
MLP (early stopping)	0.21014	0.01697	< 0.05

MARS was used in conjunction with the bagging procedure [5]. Using this method one trains MARS on a number of bootstrap samples of the training set and averages the resulting predictions. The bootstrap samples are generated by sampling the original training set with replacement. Samples of the same size as the original training set are used.

The ensemble of neural networks from DELVE repository trains ensembles of MLPs using early stopping to avoiding over–fitting. The networks all have identical architecture: fully connected with a single hidden layer of hyperbolic tangent units and linear output units. The minimization algorithm is based on conjugate gradients.

A fraction of the training examples are held out for validation, and performance on this set is monitored while the iterative learning procedure is applied. The learning is stopped as soon as minimum in validation error is achieved.

The number of hidden units is chosen to be the smallest such that the number of weights is at least as large as the total number of training cases after removal of the validation cases. One third of the training examples were used for validation and the rest for training.

Table 3. Results from Kin-8nh and Kin-32nh data sets.

Kin-8nh			
Method	Standarized estimated expected loss	Standard error for difference estimate	Significance of difference (T-test)
Selection ensemble	0.22896	–	–
Linear regression	0.62930	0.00929	0.00002
HME (ensemble learning)	0.52120	0.00987	0.00008
HME (early stopping)	0.50874	0.01167	0.00016
HME (growing and early stopping)	0.54611	0.01005	0.00007
MARS version 3.6 with Bagging	0.57910	0.00827	0.00003
ME (ensemble learning)	0.45127	0.01050	0.00023
ME (early stopping)	0.46433	0.01149	0.00025
MLP (early stopping)	0.40543	0.00701	0.00013
Kin-32nh			
Method	Standarized estimated expected loss	Standard error for difference estimate	Significance of difference (T-test)
Selection ensemble	0.57230	–	–
Linear regression	0.81556	0.00948	0.00013
HME (ensemble learning)	0.79264	0.00750	0.00003
HME (early stopping)	0.78321	0.01413	0.00065
HME (growing and early stopping)	0.79076	0.01591	0.00084
MARS version 3.6 with Bagging	0.84432	0.01551	0.00040
ME (ensemble learning)	0.80461	0.00894	0.00002
ME (early stopping)	0.78322	0.01413	0.00065
MLP (early stopping)	0.79613	0.01170	0.00031

3.3   Experimental Results and Discussion

For each of the data sets the attribute variables were normalized to a median of zero and an average absolute deviation from the median of one. This enabled each level 0 model to learn from the same set of data as certain models have limits on the input and output data ranges.

A standard squared loss function between the target output value and the predicted value was used to calculate the error for each ensemble member. The predicted values were then un–normalised before they were compared to the target values.

We have only run the competitive model once over each training and testing sets using the same parameters for the ensemble members, in accordance with DELVE guidelines. All the results obtained are thus the averages of these runs.

DELVE uses an ANOVA (ANalysis Of VAriance) model to estimate the statistics in evaluating the performance of different models. Tables 2–6 contain the resulting statistical values from the competitive (selection) ensemble model and other ensemble models on the five data sets considered. Each table includes the standardized estimated squared error loss that is calculated against a simple baseline method within DELVE. The second statistic is the standard error of the estimated expected difference. This gives an indication of the variability of the estimated expected difference between the two methods. The final statistic is either F–test or T–test value which is a probability that the null–hypothesis (no difference between the expected loss of the two methods) is true. This means that high values of the F–test or of the T–test would indicate the two methods are probably similar, and low values of the tests indicate that the difference between the performances of different methods are statistically significant.

Table 4. Results from Pumadyn-8nh and Pumadyn-32nh data sets.

Pumadyn-8nh			
Method	Standardized estimated expected loss	Standard error for difference estimate	Significance of difference (F-test)
Selection ensemble	0.21343	–	–
Linear regression	0.63146	0.01172	0.00005
HME (ensemble learning)	0.36389	0.01085	0.00081
HME (early stopping)	0.44881	0.01749	0.00089
HME (growing and early stopping)	0.51206	0.02107	0.00076
MARS version 3.6 with Bagging	0.33650	0.00705	0.00041
ME (ensemble learning)	0.36034	0.00950	0.00059
ME (early stopping)	0.40625	0.01084	0.00039
MLP (early stopping)	0.34271	0.01358	0.00246
Pumadyn-32nh			
Method	Standarized estimated expected loss	Standard error for difference estimate	Significance of difference (T-test)
Selection ensemble	0.26010	–	–
Linear regression	0.86604	0.01413	0.00002
HME (ensemble learning)	0.88020	0.01460	0.000002
HME (early stopping)	0.87137	0.01600	0.00004
HME (growing and early stopping)	0.85896	0.01397	0.00002
MARS version 3.6 with Bagging	0.34236	0.00711	0.00139
ME (ensemble learning)	0.88173	0.01489	0.000002
ME (early stopping)	0.86792	0.01426	0.00003
MLP (early stopping)	0.70891	0.02542	0.00040

In Tables 2–6, HME (ensemble learning) is a Hierarchical mixture of experts trained using Bayesian methods, HME (early stopping) is a Hierarchical mixtures of experts trained using early stopping, HME (growing and early stopping) is a Hierarchical mixtures of experts trained using growing and early stopping, ME (ensemble learning) is a Mixtures of experts trained using Bayesian methods, ME (early stopping) is a Mix-

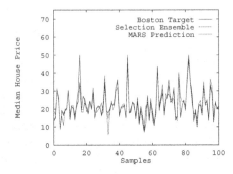

Fig. 2. First 100 samples of the Boston data, plot of the selection ensemble model and the MARS model version 3.6 with bagging versus the actual target.

tures of experts trained using early stopping and MLP (early stopping) is a Multilayer perceptron ensembles trained with early stopping.

The actual predictions of a competitive model and the best of the comparison models are shown in Figs 2–4. For clarity only the first 100 samples of testing set are shown for respective data sets.

Tables 2–6 show that the competitive (selection) model is significantly better, to a confidence of 95% ($p = 0.05$), than any of the other methods. This demonstrates that the competitive (selection) combination in conjunction with varying the learning method approach for creating ensemble members is working better than the co–operative combination in conjunction with sampling the data approach for creating ensemble members.

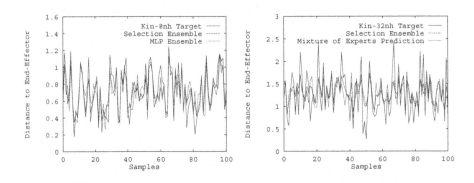

Fig. 3. First 100 samples of the (a) Kin-8nh data, plot of the selection ensemble model and the MLP ensemble model with early stopping versus the actual target (b) the Kin-32nh data, plot of the selection ensemble model and the mixture-of-experts model with early stopping versus the actual target.

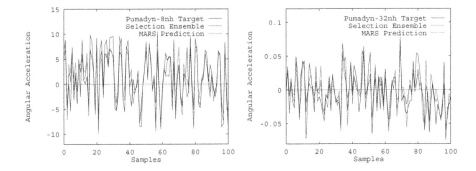

Fig. 4. First 100 samples of the (a) Pumadyn-8nh data, plot of the selection ensemble model and the MARS model version 3.6 with bagging versus the actual target, (b) the Pumadyn-32nh data, plot of the selection ensemble model and the MARS model version 3.6 with bagging versus the actual target.

However, while the competitive model is much better than the other models, there is still much room for improvement considering the actual prediction accuracy. The prediction of the competitive (selection) model for Boston Housing data set can be considered good, as seen in Fig. 2, even though there are some predictions that are not quite accurate. In case of Figs. 3 and 4, the results of the selection model are not as good, especially in case of Fig. 3(b), even though the selection model out–performs the other ensemble models.

We obviously need to keep in mind that we explicitly selected the most difficult data sets of that available in DELVE. However, based on our experience with real data sets [10] the selected regression problems are no more difficult than the many real non–linear problems with a high degree of noise. This just shows that the ultimate goal of the prediction is not just to achieve better results than the competing methods, but to achieve the best possible prediction.

References

1. Barnett, J. A. "Computational methods for a mathematical theory of evidence", *Proceedings of IJCAI*, pp. 868–875, 1981.
2. Bates, J. M. and C. W. J. Granger. "The combination of forecasts". *Operations Research Quaterly*, 20:451–468, 1969.
3. Bauer, E. and Kohavi, R. "An empirical comparison of voting classification algorithms: bagging, boosting and variants". *Machine Learning*, 36(1,2), 105–139, 1999.
4. Baxt, W. G. "Improving the accuracy of an artificial neural network using multiple differently trained networks". *Neural Computation*, 4:772–780, 1992.
5. Breiman, L. "Bagging predictors". *Machine Learning*, 26(2):123–140, 1996.
6. Brooks, R. A. "A robust layered control system for a mobile robot". *IEEE Journal of Robotics and Automation*, 2:14–23, 1986.
7. Catfolis, T. and Meert, K. "Hybridization and specialization of real–time recurrent learning-based neural networks", *Connectionist Science*, 9(1):51–70, 1997.

8. Denker, J., Schwartz, D., Wittner, B., Solla, S., Howard, R., Jackel, L. and Hopfield, J. "Large automatic learning, rule extraction and generalisation". *Complex Systems*, 1:877–922, 1987.
9. Drucker, H. "Improving regressors using boosting techniques". *Proceedings of the 14th International Conference on Machine Learning*, pp. 107–115, 1997.
10. Frayman, Y., Rolfe B. F., Hodgson, P. D. and Webb G. I. "Predicting the rolling force in hot steel rolling mill using an ensemble model". *Proceedings of the IASTED International Conference on Artificial Intelligence and Applications (AIA 2002)*, 2002. (in press).
11. Freund, Y. and R.Schapire. "A decision–theoretic generalization of on–line learning and an application to boosting". *Journal of Computer and System Sciences*, 55(1):119–139, 1997.
12. Friedman J. "Multivariate adaptive regression splines (with discussion)". *Annals of Statistics*, 19(1), 1–82, 1991.
13. Friedman, J., Hastie, T., and Tibshirani, R. "Additive logistic regression: a statistical view of boosting (with discussion)", *Annals of Statistics*, 28(2), 337–374, 2000.
14. Friedman, J. "Greedy function approximation: a gradient boosting machine". *Annals of Statistics*, 29(4). 2001.
15. Hashem, S. "Optimal linear combinations of neural networks". *Neural Networks*, 10(4):599–614, 1997.
16. Jacobs, R. A, Jordan, M. I., Nowlan, S. J., and Hinton, G. E. "Adaptive mixtures of local experts". *Neural Computation*, 3:79–97, 1991.
17. Jordan, M. I. and Jacobs R. A. "Hierarchical mixtures of experts and the em algorithm". *Neural Computation*, 6(2):181–214, 1994.
18. Ridgeway, G. "The state of boosting". *Computing Science and Statistics*, 31:172–7181, 1999.
19. Rogova, G. "Combining the results of several neural network classifiers". *Neural Networks*, 7(5):777–781, 1994.
20. Schapire, R. E. "The strength of weak learnability". *Machine Learning*, 5:197–227, 1990.
21. Sharkey, A.J.C. (Ed.) *Combining artificial neural nets: ensemble and modular multi-net systems,* Springer-Verlag, 1999.
22. Ting, K. M. "The characterisation of predictive accuracy and decision combination". *Proceedings of the 13th International Conference on Machine Learning*, pp. 498–506, 1996.
23. Webb, G. "MultiBoosting: a technique for combining boosting and wagging". *Machine Learning*, 40(2): 159–196, 2000.
24. Wolpert, D.H. "Stacked generalization". *Neural Networks*, 5:241–259, 1992.

Learning of Finite Unions of Tree Patterns with Internal Structured Variables from Queries

Satoshi Matsumoto[1], Takayoshi Shoudai[2], Tetsuhiro Miyahara[3], and Tomoyuki Uchida[3]

[1] Department of Mathematical Sciences, Tokai University, Hiratsuka 259-1292, Japan
matumoto@ss.u-tokai.ac.jp
[2] Department of Informatics, Kyushu University, Kasuga 816-8580, Japan
shoudai@i.kyushu-u.ac.jp
[3] Faculty of Information Sciences,
Hiroshima City University, Hiroshima 731-3194, Japan
{miyahara@its,uchida@cs}.hiroshima-cu.ac.jp

Abstract. We consider the polynomial time learnability of finite unions of ordered tree patterns with internal structured variables, in the query learning model of Angluin (1988). An ordered tree pattern with internal structured variables, called a term tree, is a rooted tree pattern which consists of tree structures with ordered children and internal structured variables. A term tree is suited for representing structural features in semistructured or tree structured data such as HTML/XML files. The language $L(t)$ of a term tree t is the set of all trees which are obtained from t by substituting arbitrary trees for all variables in t. Moreover, for a finite set H of term trees, $L(H) = \bigcup_{t \in H} L(t)$. Let H_*, which is a target of learning, be a finite set of term trees. An oracle for restricted subset queries answers "yes" for an input set H if $L(H) \subseteq L(H_*)$, and answers "no", otherwise. An oracle for equivalence queries returns "yes" for an input set H if $L(H) = L(H_*)$, and returns a counterexample in $L(H) \cup L(H_*) - L(H) \cap L(H_*)$, otherwise. We show that any finite union of languages defined by m term trees is exactly identifiable in polynomial time using at most $2mn^2$ restricted subset queries and at most $m + 1$ equivalence queries, where n is the maximum size of counterexamples.

1 Introduction

Large amount of Web documents such as HTML/XML files are available. Such documents are called semistructured data and considered tree structured data, which are represented by rooted trees with ordered children and edge labels [1]. As an example of a representation of tree structured data, we give a rooted tree T in Fig. 1. We give a polynomial time learning algorithm of finite unions of ordered tree patterns with internal structured variables, in the query learning model of Angluin [5]. This work is motivated from data mining of tree structured patterns from semistructured data. As a representation of a tree structured pattern in tree structured data such as HTML/XML files, we use an ordered tree pattern with internal structured variables, called a *term tree*. A term tree is a

R.I. McKay and J. Slaney (Eds.): AI 2002, LNAI 2557, pp. 523–534, 2002.
© Springer-Verlag Berlin Heidelberg 2002

rooted tree pattern which consists of tree structures with ordered children and internal structured variables. A variable in a term tree is a list of vertices and it can be substituted by an arbitrary tree. A term tree is more powerful than or incomparable to other representations of tree structured patterns, which were proposed in computational learning theory, such as ordered tree patterns [2] and ordered gapped tree patterns [7]. For example, in Fig. 1, the tree pattern $f(b, x, g(a, z), y)$ can be represented by the term tree s, but the term tree t cannot be represented by any standard tree pattern because of the existence of internal structured variables represented by x_2 and x_3 in t. This example shows that a term tree is more powerful than a standard tree pattern, which is also called a first order term in formal logic, in computational learning theory [2].

For a set of edge labels Λ, the *term tree language* $L_\Lambda(t)$ of a term tree t with Λ, which denotes the representing power of t, is the set of all labeled trees which are obtained from t by substituting arbitrary labeled trees for all variables in t. The subtrees which are obtained from t by removing the variables in t represent the common subtree structures in the trees in $L_\Lambda(t)$. A term tree t is said to be *regular* if all variable labels in t are mutually distinct. By $\mathcal{OTT}_\Lambda^{1,*}$ we denote the set of all regular term trees t with Λ as a set of edge labels such that each variable in t consists of its parent and one child.

In order to give a learning algorithm of tree structured patterns from semistructured data in multiple or heterogeneous sources of Web pages, we deal with finite unions of languages of term trees. That is, our target class of learning is the class $\mathcal{OTF}_\Lambda^{1,*}$ of all finite sets of term trees in $\mathcal{OTT}_\Lambda^{1,*}$. The language represented by a finite set of term trees $H = \{t_1, t_2, \ldots, t_k\}$ is the finite union of k term tree languages $L_\Lambda(H) = L_\Lambda(t_1) \cup L_\Lambda(t_2) \cup \ldots \cup L_\Lambda(t_k)$. Such a union of term tree languages represents multiple or heterogeneous sources of Web pages.

In query learning model, a learning algorithm accesses to oracles, which answer specific kinds of queries, and collect information about a target. Let H_* and H be finite sets of term trees, and H_* be a target of learning. An oracle for restricted subset queries answers "yes" for an input set H if $L(H) \subseteq L(H_*)$, and answers "no", otherwise. An oracle for equivalence queries returns "yes" for an input set H if $L(H) = L(H_*)$, and returns a counterexample in $L(H) \cup L(H_*) - L(H) \cap L(H_*)$, otherwise. In this model, a learning algorithm is said to *exactly learn* a target set of term trees H_* if it outputs a set H of term trees such that $L_\Lambda(H) = L_\Lambda(H_*)$ and halts, after it uses some queries and additional information. Since an edge label in tree structured data such as HTML/XML files is a word, we assume that the set of edge labels attached to edges of input trees are infinite. We show that any finite union of languages defined by m term trees is exactly identifiable in polynomial time using at most $2mn^2$ restricted subset queries and at most $m+1$ equivalence queries, where n is the the maximum size of counterexamples and the set of edge labels is infinite.

As previous work[10], we showed that string patterns are exactly learnable using queries and a positive example. In [11], we showed that unions of string subsequences are exactly learnable using queries. In [9], we studied the learnability of graph structured patterns in the framework of polynomial time inductive inference from positive data. Also our work [14] showed the class $\mathcal{OTT}_\Lambda^{1,*}$ is polynomial time inductively inferable from positive data. As an application [13], we proposed a tag tree pattern, which is an extension of a term tree, as a tree structured pattern in semistructured data and gave a data mining method from semistructured data, using a learning algorithm for term trees based on another learning model [4]. As other related works, the works [6,2,3,7] show the learnability of tree structured pattern in query learning models. The tree structured patterns and learning models of this work are incomparable to those of all these works.

This paper is organized as follows. In Section 2, we explain term trees as tree structured patterns. In Section 3, we give our query learning model. In Section 4, we show that any finite union of languages defined by term trees is exactly identifiable in polynomial time using restricted subset queries and equivalence queries.

2   Preliminaries

Let $T = (V_T, E_T)$ be an ordered tree with a vertex set V_T and an edge set E_T. A list $h = [u_0, u_1, \ldots, u_\ell]$ of vertices in V_T is called a *variable* of T if $u_1, \ldots, u_\ell$ is a sequence of consecutive children of u_0, i.e., u_0 is the parent of $u_1, \ldots, u_\ell$ and u_{j+1} is the next sibling of u_j for j with any $1 \leq j < \ell$. We call u_0 the *parent port* of the variable h and $u_1, \ldots, u_\ell$ the *child ports* of h. Two variables $h = [u_0, u_1, \ldots, u_\ell]$ and $h' = [u_0', u_1', \ldots, u_{\ell'}']$ are said to be *disjoint* if $\{u_1, \ldots, u_\ell\} \cap \{u_1', \ldots, u_{\ell'}'\} = \emptyset$.

Definition 1. Let $T = (V_T, E_T)$ be an ordered tree and H_T a set of pairwise disjoint variables of T. An *ordered term tree obtained from T and H_T* is a triplet $t = (V_t, E_t, H_t)$, where $V_t = V_T$, $E_t = E_T - \bigcup_{h=[u_0,u_1,\ldots,u_\ell]\in H_T}\{\{u_0, u_i\} \in E_T \mid 1 \leq i \leq \ell\}$, and $H_t = H_T$. For two vertices $u, u' \in V_t$, we say that u is the *parent* of u' in t if u is the parent of u' in T. Similarly we say that u' is a *child* of u in t if u' is a child of u in T. In particular, for a vertex $u \in V_t$ with no child, we call u a *leaf* of t. We define the order of the children of each vertex u in t as the order of the children of u in T. We often omit the description of the ordered tree T and variable set H_T because we can find them from the triplet $t = (V_t, E_t, H_t)$. We define the number of vertices in t as the size of t and denote it by $|t|$.

For example, the ordered term tree t in Fig. 1 is obtained from the tree $T = (V_T, E_T)$ and the set of variables H_T defined as follows. $V_T = \{v_1, \ldots, v_{11}\}$, $E_T = \{\{v_1, v_2\}, \{v_2, v_3\}, \{v_1, v_4\}, \{v_4, v_5\}, \{v_1, v_6\}, \{v_6, v_7\}, \{v_7, v_8\}, \{v_6, v_9\}, \{v_1, v_{10}\}, \{v_{10}, v_{11}\}\}$ with the root v_1 and the sibling relation displayed in Fig. 1. $H_T = \{[v_4, v_5], [v_1, v_6], [v_6, v_7, v_9]\}$.

For any ordered term tree t, a vertex u of t, and two children u' and u'' of u, we write $u' <_u^t u''$ if u' is smaller than u'' in the order of the children of u. We assume that every edge and variable of an ordered term tree is labeled with some words from specified languages. A label of a variable is called a *variable label*. Λ and X denote a set of edge labels and a set of variable labels, respectively, where

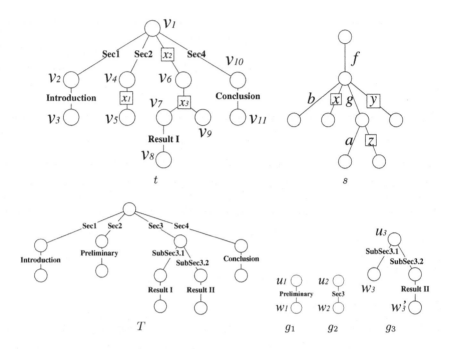

Fig. 1. A term tree t explaining a tree T. A term tree s represents the tree pattern $f(b, x, g(a, z), y)$. A variable is represented by a box with lines to its elements. The label of a box is the variable label of the variable.

$\Lambda \cap X = \phi$. An ordered term tree $t = (V_t, E_t, H_t)$ is called *regular* if all variables in H_t have mutually distinct variable labels in X.

Note. In this paper, we treat only regular ordered term trees, and then we call a regular ordered term tree a *term tree*, simply. In particular, an ordered term tree with no variable is called a *ground term tree* and considered to be a tree with ordered children.

For a term tree t and its vertices v_1 and v_i, a *path* from v_1 to v_i is a sequence $v_1, v_2, \ldots, v_i$ of distinct vertices of t such that for any j with any $1 \le j < i$, v_j is the parent of v_{j+1}. $\mathcal{OT}_\Lambda$ denotes the set of all ground term trees with Λ as a set of edge labels. Let $L \ge 1$ and $K \ge 1$ be integers. Let $\mathcal{OTT}_\Lambda^{L,K}$ be the set of all term trees t with Λ as a set of edge labels such that each variable in t has at most L child ports and any path from the root to a leaf in t has at most K variables. Let $\mathcal{OTT}_\Lambda^{L,*} = \bigcup_{K \ge 1} \mathcal{OTT}_\Lambda^{L,K}$ and $\mathcal{OTT}_\Lambda^{*,*} = \bigcup_{L \ge 1} \bigcup_{K \ge 1} \mathcal{OTT}_\Lambda^{L,K}$.

Let $f = (V_f, E_f, H_f)$ and $g = (V_g, E_g, H_g)$ be term trees. We say that f and g are *isomorphic*, denoted by $f \equiv g$, if there is a bijection φ from V_f to V_g such that (i) the root of f is mapped to the root of g by φ, (ii) $\{u, u'\} \in E_f$ if and only if $\{\varphi(u), \varphi(u')\} \in E_g$ and the two edges have the same edge label, (iii) $[u_0, u_1, \ldots, u_\ell] \in H_f$ if and only if $[\varphi(u_0), \varphi(u_1), \ldots, \varphi(u_\ell)] \in H_g$, and (iv) for

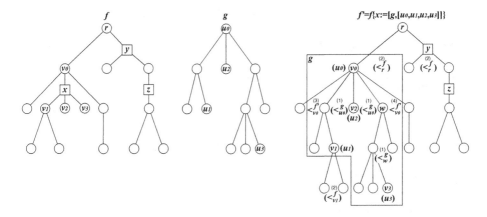

Fig. 2. The new ordering on vertices in the term tree $f' = f\{x := [g, [u_0, u_1, u_2, u_3]]\}$.

any vertex u in f which has more than one child, and for any two children u' and u'' of u, $u' <^f_u u''$ if and only if $\varphi(u') <^g_{\varphi(u)} \varphi(u'')$.

Let f and g be term trees with at least two vertices. Let $h = [v_0, v_1, \ldots, v_\ell]$ be a variable in f with the variable label x and $\sigma = [u_0, u_1, \ldots, u_\ell]$ a list of $\ell + 1$ distinct vertices in g where u_0 is the root of g and $u_1, \ldots, u_\ell$ are leaves of g. The form $x := [g, \sigma]$ is called a *binding* for x. A new term tree $f' = f\{x := [g, \sigma]\}$ is obtained by applying the binding $x := [g, \sigma]$ to f in the following way. For the variable $h = [v_0, v_1, \ldots, v_\ell]$, we attach g to f by removing the variable h from H_f and by identifying the vertices $v_0, v_1, \ldots, v_\ell$ with the vertices $u_0, u_1, \ldots, u_\ell$ of g in this order. We define a new ordering $<^{f'}_v$ on every vertex v in f' in the following natural way. Suppose that v has more than one child and let v' and v'' be two children of v in f'. We note that $v_i = u_i$ for any $0 \le i \le \ell$. (1) If $v, v', v'' \in V_g$ and $v' <^g_v v''$, then $v' <^{f'}_v v''$. (2) If $v, v', v'' \in V_f$ and $v' <^f_v v''$, then $v' <^{f'}_v v''$. (3) If $v = v_0(= u_0)$, $v' \in V_f - \{v_1, \ldots, v_\ell\}$, $v'' \in V_g$, and $v' <^f_v v_1$, then $v' <^{f'}_v v''$. (4) If $v = v_0(= u_0)$, $v' \in V_f - \{v_1, \ldots, v_\ell\}$, $v'' \in V_g$, and $v_\ell <^f_v v'$, then $v'' <^{f'}_v v'$. In Fig. 2, we give an example of the new ordering on vertices in a term tree.

A *substitution* θ is a finite collection of bindings $\{x_1 := [g_1, \sigma_1], \cdots, x_n := [g_n, \sigma_n]\}$, where x_i's are mutually distinct variable labels in X. The term tree $f\theta$, called the *instance* of f by θ, is obtained by applying the all bindings $x_i := [g_i, \sigma_i]$ on f. We define the root of the resulting term tree $f\theta$ as the root of f. Consider the examples in Fig. 1. An example of a term tree t is given. Let $\theta = \{x_1 := [g_1, [u_1, w_1]], x_2 := [g_2, [u_2, w_2]], x_3 := [g_3, [u_3, w_3, w'_3]]\}$ be a substitution, where g_1, g_2, and g_3 are trees. Then the instance $t\theta$ of the term tree t by θ is the tree T.

Let t and t' be term trees. We write $t \preceq t'$ if there exists a substitution θ such that $t \equiv t'\theta$. For a set of edge labels Λ, the *term tree language* $L_\Lambda(t)$ of a term tree $t \in \mathcal{OTT}^{*,*}_\Lambda$ is defined as $\{s \in \mathcal{OT}_\Lambda \mid s \preceq t\}$. Moreover, for a set H

of term trees, we define $L_\Lambda(H) = \bigcup_{t \in H} L_\Lambda(t)$ and call it the *term tree language defined by* H. In particular, we assume that $L_\Lambda(\phi) = \phi$. For a set S, we denote by $|S|$ the cardinality of S.

3 Learning Model

We define $\mathcal{OTF}_\Lambda^{1,*} = \{S \subseteq \mathcal{OTT}_\Lambda^{1,*} \mid |S| \text{ is finite.}\}$. When it is clear from the context, the notion $\mathcal{OTF}_\Lambda^{1,*}$ is abused to stand for the class of languages $\{L_\Lambda(H) \mid H \in \mathcal{OTF}_\Lambda^{1,*}\}$. In what follows, let $H_* \in \mathcal{OTF}_\Lambda^{1,*}$ to be identified, and we say that the set H_* is a *target*. A ground term tree t is called a *positive example* of $L_\Lambda(H_*)$ if $t \in L_\Lambda(H_*)$. First we introduce the exact learning model via queries due to Angluin [5]. In this model, learning algorithms can access to *oracles* that will answer queries about the target set $L_\Lambda(H_*)$. We consider the following oracles.

1. *Restricted subset oracle* $rSub_{H_*}$: The input is a set H in $\mathcal{OTF}_\Lambda^{1,*}$. The output is *yes* if $L_\Lambda(H) \subseteq L_\Lambda(H_*)$, and *no* otherwise. The query is called a *restricted subset query*.
2. *Equivalence oracle* $Equiv_{H_*}$: The input is a set H in $\mathcal{OTF}_\Lambda^{1,*}$. If $L_\Lambda(H) = L_\Lambda(H_*)$, then the output is *yes*. Otherwise, it returns a *counterexample* $t \in L_\Lambda(H) \cup L_\Lambda(H_*) - L_\Lambda(H) \cap L_\Lambda(H_*)$. The query is called an *equivalence query*.

A learning algorithm $\mathcal{A}$ collects information about H_* by using equivalence and restricted subset queries. We say that a learning algorithm $\mathcal{A}$ *exactly identifies* a target H_* in polynomial time if $\mathcal{A}$ halts in polynomial time and outputs a set $H \in \mathcal{OTF}_\Lambda^{1,*}$ such that $L_\Lambda(H) = L_\Lambda(H_*)$.

4 Learning Finite Unions of Term Tree Languages

In this section, we show that finite unions of term tree languages are learnable exactly by queries. The following Lemma 1 is an important property in the learning of unions of languages. This property is called *compactness*, which was proposed in [7,8]. Below we assume that $|\Lambda|$ is infinite.

Lemma 1. *Let t be a term tree in $\mathcal{OTT}_\Lambda^{1,*}$ and H a set in $\mathcal{OTF}_\Lambda^{1,*}$. Then, $t \preceq h$ for some $h \in H$ if and only if $L_\Lambda(t) \subseteq L_\Lambda(H)$.*

Proof. Only if part is obvious. Then, we only prove if part. Let c be an edge label which does not appear in any term tree in H. Let w_t be a ground term tree obtained from t by substituting all the variables in t with edges labeled with c. Since $w_t \in L_\Lambda(t)$ and $L_\Lambda(t) \subseteq L_\Lambda(H)$, there exists a term tree $t' \in H$ such that $w_t \in L_\Lambda(t')$. Since the edge label c does not appear in H, we have $t \preceq t'$ by inverting the substitutions. □

Let $t = (V_t, E_t, H_t) \in \mathcal{OTT}_\Lambda^{1,*}$ and $e \in E_t$. We denote by $t/\{e\}$ the term tree obtained by replacing the edge e with a new variable, that is, $t/\{e\} =$

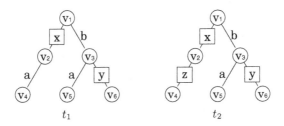

Fig. 3. A term tree $t_2 = t_1/\{e\}$ is obtained from t_1 by replacing the edge $e = \{v_2, v_4\}$ with a new variable. Then, $t_1 \preceq t_2$.

$(V_t, E_t - \{e\}, H_t \cup \{[u, v]\})$, where $e = \{u, v\}$ and u is the parent of v. For example, in Fig. 3, a term tree t_2 is obtained from t_1 by replacing the edge $e = \{v_2, v_4\}$ with a new variable. We have $t_1 \preceq t_2$. Therefore, we have the following lemma.

Lemma 2. Let $t = (V_t, E_t, H_t) \in \mathcal{OTT}_\Lambda^{1,*}$ and $e \in E_t$. Then $t \preceq t/\{e\}$.

Lemma 3. Let $t = (V_t, E_t, H_t) \in \mathcal{OTT}_\Lambda^{1,*}$ and $H \in \mathcal{OTF}_\Lambda^{1,*}$. If $L_\Lambda(t) \subseteq L_\Lambda(H)$ and $L_\Lambda(t/\{e\}) \not\subseteq L_\Lambda(H)$ for any $e \in E_t$, then there exists a term tree $t' = (V_{t'}, E_{t'}, H_{t'}) \in H$ such that $t \preceq t'$ and $|E_t| = |E_{t'}|$.

Proof. Since $L_\Lambda(t) \subseteq L_\Lambda(H)$, there exists a term tree $t' = (V_{t'}, E_{t'}, H_{t'}) \in H$ such that $t \preceq t'$ by Lemma 1. Since $t \preceq t'$, we have $|E_{t'}| \leq |E_t|$. We assume $|E_{t'}| < |E_t|$. There exists an edge $e \in E_t$ such that $t/\{e\} \preceq t'$. This implies $L_\Lambda(t/\{e\}) \subseteq L_\Lambda(H)$. This is a contradiction. Therefore, we have $|E_t| = |E_{t'}|$. □

We introduce operations reducing variables in a term tree.

Definition 2. Let $t = (V_t, E_t, H_t)$ be a term tree and $u_1, u_2, u_3 \in V_t$. We define three contractions as the following operations:

1. If $[u_1, u_2], [u_2, u_3] \in H_t$ and u_2 has exactly one child, then $V_t = V_t - \{u_2\}$ and $H_t = H_t \cup \{[u_1, u_3]\} - \{[u_1, u_2], [u_2, u_3]\}$.
2. Let u_3 be the next sibling of u_2. If $[u_1, u_2], [u_1, u_3] \in H_t$ and u_2 is a leaf, then $V_t = V_t - \{u_2\}$ and $H_t = H_t - \{[u_1, u_2]\}$.
3. Let u_3 be the next sibling of u_2. If $[u_1, u_2], [u_1, u_3] \in H_t$ and u_3 is a leaf, then $V_t = V_t - \{u_3\}$ and $H_t = H_t - \{[u_1, u_3]\}$.

Let $t = (V_t, E_t, H_t)$ be a term tree in $\mathcal{OTT}_\Lambda^{1,*}$ and t' a term tree obtained from t by applying one contraction. Then we write $t \vdash_S t'$, where S is a set of variables in H_t which are removed by the contraction. If S is clear from the context, we may write $\vdash$ instead of $\vdash_S$. For example, in Fig. 4, $T_1 \vdash_{\{[u_1, u_2], [u_2, u_3]\}} T_2$, $T_3 \vdash_{\{[u_1, u_2]\}} T_4$ and $T_5 \vdash_{\{[u_1, u_3]\}} T_6$.

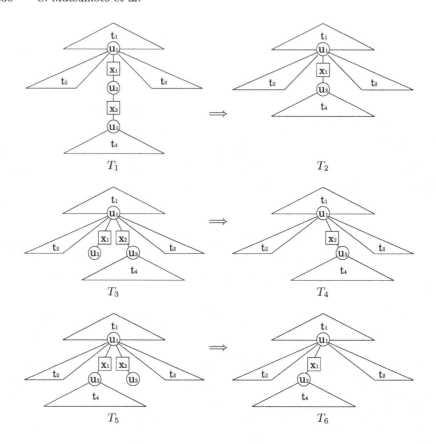

Fig. 4. Term trees T_2, T_4, T_6 are obtained by contractions from T_1, T_3, T_5 respectively, that is, $T_1 \vdash_{\{[u_1,u_2],[u_2,u_3]\}} T_2$, $T_3 \vdash_{\{[u_1,u_2]\}} T_4$ and $T_5 \vdash_{\{[u_1,u_3]\}} T_6$.

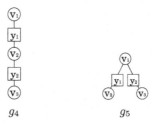

Fig. 5. Term trees g_4 and g_5.

Conversely, we can construct a substitution θ such that $t \equiv t'\theta$. For example, let $\theta_1 = \{x_1 := [g_4, [v_1, v_3]]\}$, $\theta_2 = \{x_2 := [g_5, [v_1, v_3]]\}$ and $\theta_3 = \{x_1 :=$

$[g_5, [v_1, v_2]]\}$. (Term trees g_4 and g_5 are described in Fig. 5.) We have $T_1 \equiv T_2\theta_1$, $T_3 \equiv T_4\theta_2$ and $T_5 \equiv T_6\theta_3$. Therefore, we have $T_1 \preceq T_2$, $T_3 \preceq T_4$ and $T_5 \preceq T_6$. Thus, we have the following lemma.

Lemma 4. *Let t and t' be term trees in $\mathcal{OTT}_\Lambda^{1,*}$. If $t \vdash t'$, then $t \preceq t'$.*

Lemma 5. *Let $t = (V_t, E_t, H_t)$ be a term tree in $\mathcal{OTT}_\Lambda^{1,*}$ and H a set in $\mathcal{OTF}_\Lambda^{1,*}$ such that there exists a term tree $t' = (V_{t'}, E_{t'}, H_{t'}) \in H$ with $t \preceq t'$ and $|E_t| = |E_{t'}|$. If $L_\Lambda(t'') \not\subseteq L_\Lambda(H)$ for any $t'' \in \mathcal{OTT}_\Lambda^{1,*}$ with $t \vdash t''$, then $t \equiv t'$.*

Proof. Since $t \preceq t'$, we have $|t| \geq |t'|$. We assume $|t| > |t'|$. Since $t \preceq t'$, there exists a substitution $\theta = \{x_1 := [g_1, \sigma_1], \ldots, x_n := [g_n, \sigma_n]\}$ such that $t \equiv t'\theta$. Since $|E_t| = |E_{t'}|$, we have $|H_t| > |H_{t'}|$ by the assumption. This implies that there exists a binding $x_l := [g_l, \sigma_l]$ in θ such that $|g_l| \geq 3$ and $E_{g_l} = \phi$, where $g_l = (V_{g_l}, E_{g_l}, H_{g_l})$. We can construct a new substitution θ' such that $t \vdash t'\theta'$ and $t'\theta' \in \mathcal{OTT}_\Lambda^{1,*}$. By Lemma 4, we have $L_\Lambda(t) \subseteq L_\Lambda(t'\theta') \subseteq L_\Lambda(t') \subseteq L_\Lambda(H)$. This is a contradiction. Thus, $|t| = |t'|$. Since $|E_t| = |E_{t'}|$ and $|t| = |t'|$, we have $|H_t| = |H_{t'}|$. Therefore, $t \equiv t'$. $\qquad\square$

Let $H_0, H_1, \ldots, H_i, \ldots$ and $t_1, t_2, \ldots, t_i, \ldots$ ($i \geq 0$) be the sequence of hypotheses asked in the equivalence queries by *LEARN_UNION* and the sequence of counterexamples returned by the queries respectively. Let H_0 be the initial hypothesis ϕ. And we suppose that at each stage $i \geq 1$, *LEARN_UNION* makes an equivalence query $Equiv_{H_*}(H_{i-1})$, and receives a counterexample t_i to the query.

Let $P, Q \in \mathcal{OTF}_\Lambda^{1,*}$. If there exists a term tree $q \in Q$ such that $p \equiv q$ for any $p \in P$, we write $P \sqsubseteq Q$. If $P \sqsubseteq Q$ and $P \not\sqsupseteq Q$, then we write $P \sqsubset Q$.

Lemma 6. *For each $i \geq 0$, $t_i \in L_\Lambda(H_*)$ and $H_i \sqsubseteq H_*$.*

Proof. The proof is by the induction on the number of iterations $i \geq 0$ of the main loop. If $i = 0$, then it is clear.

We assume inductively that the result holds for any number of iterations of the main loop less than i. By the inductive hypothesis, we have $H_{i-1} \sqsubseteq H_*$. If $L_\Lambda(H_{i-1}) \neq L_\Lambda(H_*)$, t_i is obtained. Since $H_{i-1} \sqsubseteq H_*$, we have $L_\Lambda(H_{i-1}) \subseteq L_\Lambda(H_*)$. Thus, $t_i \in L_\Lambda(H_*)$.

Let $t_i' = (V_{t_i'}, E_{t_i'}, H_{t_i'})$ be a term tree obtained by executing the first repeat-loop from t_i. By Lemma 1 and Lemma 3, there exists a term tree $t_*' \in H_*$ such that $|E_{t_i'}| = |E_{t_*'}|$ and $t_i' \preceq t_*'$. Let t_i'' be a term tree obtained by executing the second repeat-loop from t_i'. By Lemma 1 and Lemma 5, there exists a term tree $t_*'' \in H_*$ such that $t_i'' \equiv t_*''$. By the inductive hypothesis, we know $H_{i-1} \sqsubseteq H_*$. Therefore, we have $H_i = H_{i-1} \cup \{t_i''\} \sqsubseteq H_*$. $\qquad\square$

Lemma 7. *For each $i \geq 1$, $H_{i-1} \sqsubset H_i$.*

Algorithm *LEARN_UNION*
Given: Oracles $Equiv_{H_*}$ and $rSub_{H_*}$ for the target $H_* \in \mathcal{OTF}_\Lambda^{1,*}$;
Output: A set $H \in \mathcal{OTF}_\Lambda^{1,*}$ with $L_\Lambda(H) = L_\Lambda(H_*)$.
begin
1    $H := \phi$;
2   **while** $Equiv_{H_*}(H) \neq yes$ **do**
3   **begin**
4   Let w be a counterexample;
5   **repeat**
6   **foreach** edge e in w **do**
7   **begin**
8   Let $w' := w/\{e\}$;
9   **if** $rSub_{H_*}(\{w'\}) = yes$ **then**
10   **begin** $w := w'$; **break; end**;
11   **end**
12   **until** w does not change;
13   **repeat**
14   **foreach** $S \in C(w)$ **do**
15   **begin**
16   Let w' be a term tree with $w \vdash_S w'$;
17   **if** $rSub_{H_*}(\{w'\}) = yes$ **then**
18   **begin** $w := w'$; **break; end**;
19   **end**
20   **until** w does not change;
21            $H := H \cup \{w\}$;
22   **end**
23 **output** H;
end

Fig. 6.   For a term tree $t = (V_t, E_t, H_t)$, we define $C(t)$ as $\{S \subseteq H_t \mid$ there exists a term tree $t' \in \mathcal{OTT}_\Lambda^{1,*}$ such that $t \vdash_S t'\}$. Note that $|C(t)| < |t|$.

Proof. For each $i \geq 1$, it is clear that $H_{i-1} \sqsubseteq H_i$. We assume that $H_{i-1} \sqsupseteq H_i$ for some $i \geq 1$. Let t_* be a term tree which is added to H_{i-1} at the i-th stage, that is, $H_i = H_{i-1} \cup \{t_*\}$. Since $H_{i-1} \sqsupseteq H_i$, there exists a term tree $t'_* \in H_{i-1}$ such that $t_* \equiv t'_*$. By Lemma 2 and Lemma 4, we have $t_i \preceq t_* \equiv t'_*$. This implies $t_i \in L_\Lambda(t_*) = L_\Lambda(t'_*) \subseteq L_\Lambda(H_{i-1})$. Since t_i is an output counterexample by $Equiv_{H_*}(H_{i-1})$, we have $t_i \notin L_\Lambda(H_{i-1})$. This is a contradiction.   □

Theorem 1. *The algorithm LEARN_UNION of Fig. 6 exactly identifies any set $H_* \in \mathcal{OTF}_\Lambda^{1,*}$ in polynomial time using at most $m + 1$ equivalence queries and at most $2mn^2$ restricted subset queries, where $m = |H_*|$ and n is the maximum size of counterexamples.*

Proof. By the construction of the algorithm *LEARN_UNION*, Lemma 6 and Lemma 7, we know that the algorithm terminates and outputs H such that $L_\Lambda(H) = L_\Lambda(H_*)$.

At the i-th stage of the while-loop, we receive a counterexample t_i. The loop of lines 6–11 uses at most $|t_i|$ restricted subset queries. Since the loop of lines 5–12 is repeated at most $|t_i|$ times, the loop uses at most $|t_i|^2$ restricted subset queries. We can show that the loop of lines 13–20 uses at most $|t_i|^2$ restricted subset queries in a similar way. Note that $|H_*| = m$ and n is the maximum size of counterexamples. By Lemma 6 and Lemma 7, since the while-loop is repeated at most m times. Therefore, *LEARN_UNION* uses at most $2mn^2$ restricted subset queries and at most $m + 1$ equivalence queries. $\qquad\square$

Table 1. Our results and future works

	$\mathcal{OTT}_\Lambda^{1,*}$	$\mathcal{OTT}_\Lambda^{*,*}$	$\mathcal{OTF}_\Lambda^{1,*}$	$\mathcal{OTF}_\Lambda^{L,*}$ $(L \geq 2)$
Exact learning	Yes [12] membership & a positive example $\|\Lambda\| \geq 2$	Open	Yes [this work] equivalence & restricted subset $\|\Lambda\|$ is infinite	Open
Inductive inference from positive data	Yes [14] polynomial time $\|\Lambda\| \geq 1$	Yes [15] polynomial time $\|\Lambda\| \geq 1$	Open	Open

5 Conclusion

We have discussed the learnability of $\mathcal{OTF}_\Lambda^{1,*}$ in the exact learning model. In Section 4, we have shown that any finite set H_* of term trees is exactly identifiable using at most $2mn^2$ restricted subset queries and at most $m + 1$ equivalence queries, where $m = |H_*|$, n is the the maximum size of counterexamples and $|\Lambda|$ is infinite. As future works, we investigate the learnability of $\mathcal{OTF}_\Lambda^{L,*}$ using queries for a fixed integer $L \geq 2$. For $L \geq 2$, the corresponding statement to Lemma 1 is as follows: Let $t \in \mathcal{OTT}_\Lambda^{L,*}$, $H \in \mathcal{OTF}_\Lambda^{L,*}$ and $|\Lambda|$ infinite. Then, $t \preceq h$ for some $h \in H$ if and only if $L_\Lambda(t) \subseteq L_\Lambda(H)$. We know that the statement does not hold for $L \geq 2$. Thus, we must find a new approach to solve the future work. Moreover, we will study the learnability of $\mathcal{OTT}_\Lambda^{*,*}$ in the exact learning. Suzuki et al. [15] have shown the learnability of $\mathcal{OTT}_\Lambda^{*,*}$ in the framework of polynomial time inductive inference from positive data [4], where $|\Lambda| \geq 1$. Thus, we will study the learnability of $\mathcal{OTF}_\Lambda^{1,*}$ in the same framework. We summarize our results and future works in Table 1.

References

1. S. Abiteboul, P. Buneman, and D. Suciu. *Data on the Web: From Relations to Semistructured Data and XML*. Morgan Kaufmann, 2000.
2. T. R. Amoth, P. Cull, and P. Tadepalli. Exact learning of tree patterns from queries and counterexamples. *Proc. COLT-98, ACM Press*, pages 175–186, 1998.
3. T. R. Amoth, P. Cull, and P. Tadepalli. Exact learning of unordered tree patterns from queries. *Proc. COLT-99, ACM Press*, pages 323–332, 1999.
4. D. Angluin. Finding pattern common to a set of strings. *Journal of Computer and System Sciences*, 21:46–62, 1980.
5. D. Angluin. Queries and concept learning. *Machine Learning*, 2:319–342, 1988.
6. H. Arimura, H. Ishizaka, and T. Shinohara. Learning unions of tree patterns using queries. *Proc. ALT-95, Springer-Verlag, LNAI 997*, pages 66–79, 1995.
7. H. Arimura, H. Sakamoto, and S. Arikawa. Efficient learning of semi-structured data from queries. *Proc. ALT-2001, Springer-Verlag, LNAI 2225*, pages 315–331, 2001.
8. H. Arimura, T. Shinohara, and S. Otsuki. Polynomial time algorithm for finding finite unions of tree pattern languages. *Proc. NIL-91, Springer-Verlag, LNAI 659*, pages 118–131, 1993.
9. S. Matsumoto, Y. Hayashi, and T. Shoudai. Polynomial time inductive inference of regular term tree languages from positive data. *Proc. ALT-97, Springer-Verlag, LNAI 1316*, pages 212–227, 1997.
10. S. Matsumoto and A. Shinohara. Learning pattern languages using queries. *Proc. EuroCOLT-97, Springer-Verlag, LNAI 1208*, pages 185–197, 1997.
11. S. Matsumoto, A. Shinohara, H. Arimura, and T. Shinohara. Learning subsequence languages. In *Information Modelling and Knowledge Bases VIII*, pages 335–344. IOS Press, 1997.
12. S. Matsumoto, T. Shoudai, T. Miyahara, and T. Uchida. Learning unions of term tree languages using queries. *Proceedings of LA Summer Symposium, July 2002*, pages 21-1 – 21-10, 2002.
13. T. Miyahara, Y. Suzuki, T. Shoudai, T. Uchida, K. Takahashi, and H. Ueda. Discovery of frequent tag tree patterns in semistructured web documents. *Proc. PAKDD-2002, Springer-Verlag, LNAI 2336*, pages 341–355, 2002.
14. Y. Suzuki, R. Akanuma, T. Shoudai, T. Miyahara, and T. Uchida. Polynomial time inductive inference of ordered tree patterns with internal structured variables from positive data. *Proc. COLT-2002, Springer-Verlag, LNAI 2375*, pages 169–184, 2002.
15. Y. Suzuki, T. Shoudai, T. Miyahara, and T. Uchida. Ordered term tree languages which are polynomial time inductively inferable from positive data. *Proc. ALT-2002, Springer-Verlag, LNAI (to appear)*, 2002.

TreeITL-Mine: Mining Frequent Itemsets Using Pattern Growth, Tid Intersection, and Prefix Tree

Raj P. Gopalan and Yudho Giri Sucahyo

School of Computing, Curtin University of Technology
Kent St, Bentley
Western Australia 6102
{raj, sucahyoy}@computing.edu.au

Abstract. An important problem in data mining is the discovery of association rules that identify relationships among sets of items. Finding frequent itemsets is computationally the most expensive step in association rules mining, and so most of the research attention has been focused on it. In this paper, we present a more efficient algorithm for mining frequent itemsets. In designing our algorithm, we have combined the ideas of pattern-growth, tid-intersection and prefix trees, with significant modifications. We present performance comparisons of our algorithm against the fastest Apriori algorithm, and the recently developed H-Mine algorithm. We have tested all the algorithms using several widely used test datasets. The performance results indicate that our algorithm significantly reduces the processing time for mining frequent itemsets in dense data sets that contain relatively long patterns.

1 Introduction

In Data Mining, the topic of Association Rules has received the most attention from researchers so far. Association rule mining searches for interesting patterns among items of a given data set. The discovery of associations in business transactions can help in decision making such as catalog design, cross marketing, and loss-leader analysis. Since its introduction in [1], a large number of efficient algorithms to mine association rules have been developed [2], [3], [4], [5], [6], [7], [8].

The process of mining association rules consists of two main steps: 1) Find the frequent itemsets or large itemsets with a minimum support; 2) Use the large itemsets to generate association rules that meet a confidence threshold. Step 1 is the most expensive of the two since the number of itemsets grows exponentially with the number of items. The strategies developed to speed up the process of finding frequent itemsets fall into two categories. The first is based on the candidate generation-and-test approach. The Apriori algorithm and its several variations belong to this category. They use the anti-monotone (also known as Apriori) property that any subset of a frequent itemset must be a frequent itemset. In this approach, a set of candidate itemsets of length $n + 1$ is generated from frequent itemsets of length n and then each candidate itemset is checked to see if it meets the specified *support threshold*. The second approach of pattern-growth has been proposed more recently. It also uses the Apriori property, but instead of generating candidate itemsets, it recursively mines

R.I. McKay and J. Slaney (Eds.): AI 2002, LNAI 2557, pp. 535–546, 2002.

patterns in the database while at the same time counting the support for each pattern. Algorithms in this category include TreeProjection [5], FP-Growth [3], and H-Mine [4].

The Apriori algorithm suffers from poor performance when mining dense datasets at low support, since it has to traverse the database many times to test the support of candidate itemsets. This problem is partly overcome by the pattern growth approach. H-Mine is a recently developed pattern growth algorithm that has improved performance of frequent itemset mining by reducing the number of scans of the transaction database. In this paper, we present further improvements to the pattern-growth approach by reducing the number of transactions held in memory and the number of traversals of each transaction. The number of transactions in memory is reduced by grouping the transactions that have the same item sets. The item traversals in transactions are reduced using a modified transaction-id intersection method we name as tid-count intersection. Based on these ideas, we have designed a new algorithm for mining frequent itemsets called TreeITL-Mine.

In this paper, we present the TreeITL-Mine algorithm and compare its performance with other significant algorithms. Our algorithm uses a data structure called Item-Trans Link (ITL) that will be described briefly in the next section. We use a modified prefix tree to compress the transactions before storing them in ITL. The transactions that contain the same set of frequent items (or 1-frequent itemsets) are grouped together using the prefix tree. Each group of transactions is then replaced by a single transaction and a count of the number of transactions in the group. This can significantly reduce the traversal of items in the mining process for many typical data sets at commonly used support thresholds. Unlike the FP-Growth [3] algorithm, we do not selectively project the prefix tree for mining, but only use it to compress transactions before storing them in the ITL data structure. The subsequent mining process only uses ITL and not the tree.

The tid-count intersection method we use in our algorithm is different from previous tid intersection implementations [6], [7], [8]. A tid in our algorithm represents a group of transactions with a count of the transactions in the group, instead of only a single transaction. Therefore, our tid-count lists are actually compressed tid lists that allow faster intersection operations.

We have compared the performance of TreeITL-mine with Apriori and H-Mine. To show the cost-performance trade-offs in compressing transactions using a prefix tree, we also compare the performance of TreeITL-Mine with ITL-Mine, which is a variant of our algorithm that does not use the prefix tree. H-mine was chosen for performance comparisons because it is an improvement over FP-Growth and TreeProjection algorithms [4]. We implemented the H-mine algorithm based on its description in [4] since the program is not available from its authors. We used the Apriori program from [10] which is generally acknowledged as the fastest Apriori implementation available. The results of our experiments show that both TreeITL-Mine and ITL-Mine perform better than Apriori and H-Mine on a number of typical test datasets. TreeITL-Mine outperforms ITL-Mine for several data sets and support levels, but in a few cases, ITL-Mine performs better. All these interesting results will be discussed later in this paper.

The structure of the rest of this paper is as follows: In Section 2, we define relevant terms and describe our data structure. In Section 3, we present the TreeITL-Mine algorithm and provide an example. The experimental results on various datasets are presented in Section 4. A discussion of the results is given in Section 5. Section 6 contains conclusion and pointers for further work.

2 Preliminaries

In this section, we define the terms used for describing association rule mining, and discuss the binary representation of transactions that formed the conceptual basis for designing our data structure. Then we describe the data structure of our algorithm and the prefix tree used for grouping transactions.

2.1 Definition of Terms

We give the basic terms needed for describing association rules using the formalism of [1]. Let $I=\{i_1, i_2, \ldots, i_n\}$ be a set of items, and D be a set of transactions, where a transaction T is a subset of I ($T \subseteq I$). Each transaction is identified by a *TID*. An association rule is an expression of the form $X \Rightarrow Y$, where $X \subset I$, $Y \subset I$ and $X \cap Y = \varnothing$. Note that each of X and Y is a set of one or more items and the quantity of each item is not considered. X is referred to as the *body* of the rule and Y as the *head*. An example of association rule is the statement that 80% of transactions that purchase A also purchase B and 10% of all transactions contain both of them. Here, 10% is the *support* of the itemset {A, B} and 80% is the *confidence* of the rule $A \Rightarrow B$. An itemset is called a *large itemset* or *frequent itemset* if its *support* is greater than or equal a *support threshold* specified by the user, otherwise the itemset is *small* or *not frequent*. An association with the *confidence* greater than or equal a *confidence threshold* is considered as a valid association rule.

2.2 Binary Representation of Transactions

As mentioned in [1], the transactions in the database could be represented by a binary table as shown in Fig. 1. Counting the support for an item can be considered as counting the number of 1s for that item in all the transactions. In practice, the number of items in each transaction is much smaller than the total number of items, and therefore we need to use a more efficient representation scheme.

Tid	Items		1	2	3	4	5	6	7	8	9	10	11	12	13
1	3 4 5 6 7 9		0	0	1	1	1	1	1	0	1	0	0	0	0
2	1 3 4 5 13	⟹	1	0	1	1	1	0	0	0	0	0	0	0	1
3	1 2 4 5 7 11		1	1	0	1	1	0	1	0	0	0	1	0	0
4	1 3 4 8		1	0	1	1	0	0	0	1	0	0	0	0	0
5	1 3 4 10		1	0	1	1	0	0	0	0	0	1	0	0	0

Fig. 1. The transaction database

2.3 Item-Trans Link (ITL) Data Structure

Researchers have proposed various data representation schemes for association rule mining. These schemes can be broadly classified by their data layout as horizontal, vertical, or a combination of the two. Most candidate generation-and test algorithms (e.g. Apriori) use the horizontal layout and most pattern-growth algorithms like FP-Growth and H-Mine use a combination of vertical and horizontal layouts.

We propose a data structure called Item-Trans Link (ITL) that combines the vertical and horizontal data layouts (see Fig. 2). The data representation in ITL is based on the following observations: 1) Item identifiers can be mapped to a range of integers; 2) Transaction identifiers can be ignored provided the items of each transaction are linked together.

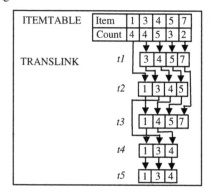

Fig. 2. The Item-Trans Link (ITL) Data Structure

ITL consists of an item table (named ItemTable) and the transactions linked to it (TransLink) as described below.
1. ItemTable: It contains all individually frequent items. In the example of Fig. 2, we consider items with a minimum support of 2, in the database of Fig. 1 as frequent. Each item is stored with its support count and a link to the first occurrence of that item in TransLink.
2. TransLink: It represents each transaction of the database that contains items of ItemTable. The items of a transaction are arranged in sorted order. For each item in a transaction, there is a link to the next occurrence of that item in another transaction. In other words, this link connects all the 1s in the binary representation of an item so that item support can be counted quickly. For example, in Fig. 2, to check the occurrences of item 7, we can go to the cell of 7 in t1 in the TransLink and then directly to the next occurrence of 7 in t3 without traversing t2.

This is the basic ITL data structure. TreeITL-Mine uses an ITL with an extra field to record the count of transactions that contain the same set of items (see Fig 4b). Since ITL has features of both horizontal and vertical data layouts, it can support algorithms that need horizontal, vertical or combined data layouts. ITL also makes it possible to adapt ideas for efficient mining that are based on different layouts.

ITL is similar to H-struct proposed in [4], except for the vertical links between occurrences of each item in the transactions. In H-struct, the links always point to the first item of a transaction, and therefore to get a certain item we need to traverse the transaction from the beginning. The occurrences of an item in ITL can be traversed faster because of the vertical link.

2.4 Transaction Tree

Often several transactions in a database contain the same set of items. Even when two transactions are originally different, early pruning of infrequent items from them could make their remaining set of items identical. These observations led us to compress the TransLink using a modified prefix tree so that transactions containing the same items can be combined. Fig. 3 shows a full prefix tree for items 1-5. All siblings are lexicographically ordered from left to right. Each node represents a set consisting of the node element and all the elements on nodes in the path (prefix) from the root. It can be seen that the set of paths from the root to the different nodes of the tree represent all possible subsets of items that could be present in any transaction. We modify this prefix tree by adding a count to each node (as shown in Fig. 4a). The count at a node indicates the number of all transactions in the database that contain the set of items in the path from the root to that node. We call this a transaction tree. In practice, the transaction tree is unlikely to have the full set of nodes as in Fig. 3, that are possible for a given set of items. Fig. 4a shows the transaction tree for the sample database of Fig. 1.

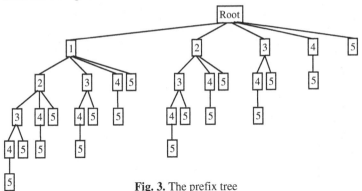

Fig. 3. The prefix tree

3 TreeITL-Mine Algorithm

In this section, we describe the TreeITL-Mine algorithm, and provide a running example. There are four steps in the algorithm as follows:
1. Identify the 1-frequent itemsets and initialize the ItemTable: In this step, we scan the transaction database once to get the 1-freq itemsets.
2. Construct the transaction tree: Using the output of the first step, based on the Apriori or anti-monotone principle, the infrequent items can be pruned or deleted since infrequent items will not be part of any frequent set. In this step, we construct the transaction tree taking only the frequent items from the transaction database. The tree will contain only 1-freq items and each node will have a count indicating

the number of transactions that contain the set of items in the path from the root to that node as shown in Fig. 4a.

3. Construct TransLink and attach to ItemTable: In this step, we traverse the transaction tree to construct TransLink and attach it to ItemTable.

4. Mine Frequent Itemsets: All the frequent itemsets of two or more items are mined in this step using a recursive function described further in this section.

The TreeITL-Mine algorithm is illustrated by the following example.

Example 1. Let the table in Fig. 1 be the transaction database and suppose the user wants to get the Frequent Itemsets with a minimum support of 2 transactions.

In Step 1, all transactions in the database are read to identify the frequent items. For each item in a transaction, the existence of the item in the ItemTable is checked. If the item is not present in the ItemTable, it is entered with an initial count of 1, otherwise the count of the item is incremented. On completing the database scan, the 1-frequent itemsets can be identified in the ItemTable as {1, 3, 4, 5, 7}.

In Step 2, we construct the transaction tree as shown in Fig. 4a. Notice that each node has a count that indicates the number of transactions where the item and its prefix appear. The tree is constructed by reading the transaction database. Items that have support below the minimum in the ItemTable are skipped.

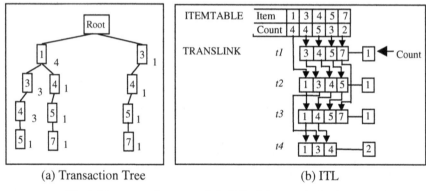

(a) Transaction Tree   (b) ITL

Fig. 4. The transaction tree and the ITL of the sample database

In Step 3, the TransLink attached to the ItemTable is constructed by traversing the tree using the depth first search algorithm. Conceptually, each path from the root to a leaf is mapped as an entry in the TransLink. The count of every node along the path is then reduced by the count of the leaf. Nodes with a zero count are pruned. The result of this step is shown in Fig. 4b.

In the last Step, each item in the ItemTable is used as a starting point to mine all longer frequent itemsets for which it is a prefix. For example, starting with item 1, we follow the link to get all other items that occur together with item 1. These items are registered in a simple table called TempList together with their support count and an associated list of {tid, count}. As seen in the sample TempList of Fig. 5, for prefix 1, we have items {3, 4, 5} that are frequent (with count ≥ 2). Generating the frequent patterns for this step involves simply concatenating the prefix with each frequent-item. For example, the frequent itemsets for this step are 1 3 (3), 1 4 (4) and 1 5 (2), where the support of each pattern is given in parenthesis. After generating the 2-

frequent-itemsets for prefix 1, since we have the tid-count list (not shown in Fig. 5) of each item in the TempList, we can recursively use the tid-count intersection scheme to generate the subsequent frequent itemsets. Every time we find a matching tid, we note the count of the tid and add it to the current count. For example, we can use the tid list of 3 and intersect with tid list of 5 to generate frequent itemsets 1 3 5. At the end of recursive calls with prefix item 1, all the frequent itemsets that contains item 1 will be generated: 1 (4), 1 3 (3), 1 4 (4), 1 5 (2), 1 3 4 (3), 1 4 5 (2). In the next sequence, item 3 will be used to generate all frequent itemsets that contain item 3 but does not contain item 1. Then item 5 will be used to generate all frequent itemsets that contain item 5 but does not contain items 1 and 3. The algorithm of TreeITL-Mine is shown in Fig. 6.

Prefix	TempList (count)	Freq-Itemset (count)
1	3 (3), 4 (4), 5 (2), 7 (1)	1 (4), 1 3 (3), 1 4 (4), 1 5 (2)
1 3	4 (3), 5 (1)	1 3 4 (3)
1 4	5 (2), 7 (1)	1 4 5 (2)
3	4 (4), 5 (2), 7 (1)	3 (4), 3 4 (4), 3 5 (2)
3 4	5 (2), 7 (1)	3 4 5 (2)
4	5 (3), 7 (2)	4 (5), 4 5 (3), 4 7 (2)
4 5	7 (2)	4 5 7 (2)
5	7 (2)	5 (3), 5 7 (2)
7	None	7 (2)

Fig. 5. Mining Frequent Itemsets Recursively (support of the pattern shown in brackets)

4 Performance Study

In this section, the performance evaluation of TreeITL-Mine is presented. The running time of our algorithm is compared with those of Apriori and H-mine on widely used test data sets. The program available from [10] and generally acknowledged as the fastest implementation of Apriori is used as a representative of the candidate generation-and-test approach in our comparisons. As already mentioned, H-mine is chosen for comparing performance since it has been the best performing algorithm based on the pattern growth approach so far. In addition, we also compare the performance of TreeITL-Mine with ITL-Mine, which is a variant of our algorithm not using transaction trees. All programs are written in Microsoft Visual C++ 6.0. All the testing was performed on an 866MHz Pentium III PC, 128 MB RAM, 30 GB HD running Microsoft Windows 2000. In this paper, the runtime includes both CPU time and I/O time.

Several datasets were used to test the performance including Mushroom, Chess, Connect-4, Pumsb* and BMS-Web-View1. The Mushroom dataset describes thecharacteristics of various species of mushrooms. The Chess dataset is derived from the steps of Chess games. In Connect-4, each transaction contains 8-ply positions in the game of connect-4 where no player has won yet and the next move is not forced. Mushroom, Chess, and Connect-4 are dense datasets since they produce many long

```
/* Input : database      Output: 1-freq itemsets */
Procedure GetOneFreq
For all transactions in the DB
   For all items in transaction
      If item in ItemTable
         Increment count of item
      Else
         Insert item with count = 1
      End If
   End For
End For

/* Input : database      Output: transaction tree */
Procedure Construct_Tree
For all transactions in the DB
   For all items in transaction
      Get the count of the item in ItemTable
      If item is frequent item
         Insert the item into the tree
      End If
   End For
End For

/* Input : transaction tree      Output: ITL */
Procedure Construct_ITL
For each path in the tree traversed by depth first search
   Map the path as an entry in TransLink
   Reduce the count of every node along the path
         by the count of its leaf
   Establish links in TransLink to previous occurrences
   Prune nodes with count = 0
End For

/* Input : ITL      Output: Frequent Itemsets */
Procedure MineFI
For all x∈ItemTable where count(x) ≥ min_sup
   Add x to the set of Frequent Itemsets
   Prepare and fill tempList for x
   For all y∈tempList where count(y) ≥ min_sup
      Add xy to the set of Frequent Itemsets
      For all z∈tempList after y where count(z) ≥ min_sup
         RecMine(xy,z)
      EndFor
   End For
End For

Procedure RecMine(prefix, testItem)
tlp:= tid-count-list of prefix
tli:= tid-count-list of testItem
tl_current:= Intersect(tlp,tli)
If size(tl_current) ≥ min_sup
   new_prefix:= prefix + testItem
   Add new_prefix to the set of Frequent Itemsets
   For all z∈tempList after testItem where count(z) ≥ min_sup
      RecMine(new_prefix, z)
   End For
End If
```

Fig. 6. TreeITL-Mine Algorithm

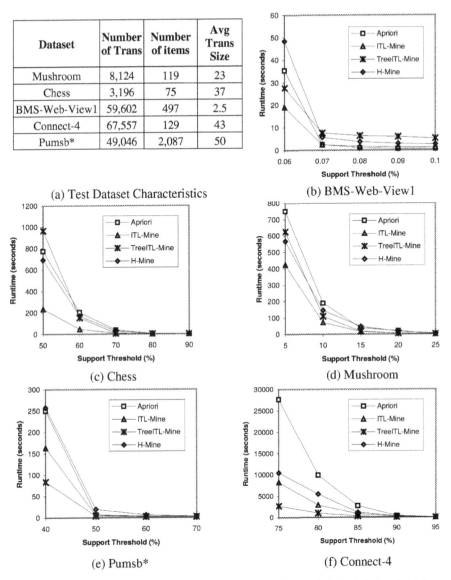

(a) Test Dataset Characteristics

(b) BMS-Web-View1

(c) Chess

(d) Mushroom

(e) Pumsb*

(f) Connect-4

Fig. 7. Test Dataset Characteristics and performance comparisons of TreeITL-Mine, ITL-Mine, Apriori and H-Mine on BMS-Web-View1, Chess, Mushroom, Pumsb* and Connect-4

patterns of frequent itemsets for very high values of support. All of them were downloaded from Irvine Machine Learning Database Repository: http://www.ics. uci.edu/~mlearn/MLRepository.html. Pumsb* contains census data from PUMS (Public Use Microdata Samples). Each transaction represents the answers to a census questionaire, including the age, tax-filing status, marital status, income, sex, veteran status, and location of residence of the respondent. In Pumsb* all items with 80% or more support in the original PUMS data set are deleted. This dataset can be downloaded from http://augustus.csscr.washington.edu/census/. BMS-Web-View1 representing a real life dataset comes from a small dot-com company called Gazelle.com, a legwear and legcare retailer, which no longer exists. It contains several months worth of clickstream data from an e-commerce web site. This dataset is available from http://www.ecn.purdue.edu/KDDCUP. Fig. 7a lists the characteristics of each dataset.

Performance comparisons of TreeITL-Mine, ITL-Mine, Apriori and H-Mine on Chess, Mushroom, Connect-4, Pumsb* and BMS-Web-View1 are shown in Fig. 7. We make the following observations about the experimental results:

1. TreeITL-Mine outperforms other algorithms on Pumsb*, Connect-4, Chess (support 70-90) and Mushroom (support 15-25). In these datasets, the number of duplicate transactions resulting from the pruning of 1-infrequent items is more than enough to overcome the additional cost of constructing the transaction tree and the cost of adding the count of each group of transactions during tid-count intersection. When the count is more than one for a tid, the cost of transaction traversal is reduced, but if the count is only one than we incur the extra cost of writing the count and using the count of that transaction during mining. When the support level gets lower, the number of frequent items increases and the occurrence of same item sets in different transactions become lower, and consequently the performance of TreeITL-Mine suffers (e.g Chess 50-60 and Mushroom 5-10).

2. In BMS-Web-View1, a sparse dataset with average transaction size of only 2.5, the gain of using the tree to compress the transactions does not outweigh the additional cost of constructing the tree at higher support levels. The time taken for mining frequent itemsets by TreeITL-Mine is not much different from other algorithms at these levels. But TreeITL-Mine spent 80% of the total time for tree construction. However, at support of 0.06, TreeITL-Mine outperformed Apriori and H-Mine.

5   Discussion

In this section, we discuss the similarities and differences between our algorithm and other well known algorithms. We also discuss the extension of our algorithm for very large databases and the support for interactive mining.

5.1   Comparisons with Other Algorithms

At a glance, our algorithm may appear to simply combine several ideas that already exist. However, in the following we discuss the significant differences between our algorithm and others:

FP-Growth. FP-Growth algorithm in [3] builds an FP-Tree based on the prefix tree concept and uses it during the entire mining process. We use a modified prefix tree for grouping transactions because it is faster than sorting the transactions by comparing their items lexicographically. The tree is mapped to ITL data structure in order to reduce the number of column traversals (in the conceptual binary table of Section 2). The cost of mapping the tree to ITL is justified by the performance gain obtained in the last step of mining frequent itemsets.

Eclat. Tid-intersection used by Zaki in [7] creates a tid-list of all transactions in which an item occurs. In our algorithm, each tid in the tid-list represents a group of transactions and we need to note the count of each group. The tid and count are used together in tid-count intersection. The tid-count lists are shorter because of transaction grouping and therefore intersections can be performed faster.

H-Mine. In the mining of frequent itemsets after constructing the ITL, our algorithm may appear similar to H-Mine but there are significant differences between our algorithm and H-Mine as given below:

1. After the ITL data structure is constructed, it remains unchanged while mining all of the frequent patterns. In H-Mine, the pointers in the H-struct need to be continually re-adjusted during the extraction of frequent patterns and so needs additional computation.
2. TreeITL-Mine uses a simple temporary table called TempList during the recursive extraction of frequent patterns. TreeITL-Mine need to store in the TempList only the information for the current recursive call which will be deleted from the memory if the recursive call backtracks to the upper level. H-Mine builds a series of header tables linked to the H-struct and it needs to change pointers to create or re-arrange queues for each recursive call. The additional memory space and the computation required by H-mine to extract the frequent itemsets from H-struct are significantly more than for TreeITL-mine.
3. H-Mine needs to traverse from the beginning of each transaction to check whether a pattern exists in it. We use tid-count-intersection, which is a merge-sort algorithm, for extending frequent patterns. Thus, we mostly avoid the expensive horizontal traversals of transactions.
4. Depending on the characteristics of the dataset, using a prefix tree to compress the number of transactions can make the number of ITL entries to be traversed by TreeITL-Mine much smaller than for H-Mine.

5.2 Mining Large Databases

Using the transaction tree, mining can be done efficiently even for relatively large databases since we need to maintain only transactions containing distinct sets of 1-frequent items in memory. However, we cannot assume that the size of the tree will always fit in memory for very large databases even with significant compression. The extension of this algorithm based on partitioning the transaction tree is currently in progress.

5.3 Interactive Mining

Our algorithm supports efficient interactive mining, where the user may experiment with different values of minimum support levels. Using the constructed ItemTable and TransLink in memory, if the user wants to change the value of support threshold (as long as the support level is higher than the previous value), there is no need to read the transaction database again.

6 Conclusion

In this paper, we have presented a new algorithm called TreeITL-Mine for discovering frequent itemsets. We described the Item-Trans Link (ITL) data structure used by our algorithm that combines the features of both horizontal and vertical data layouts for frequent pattern mining. We have compared the performance of TreeITL-Mine against ITL-Mine, Apriori and H-Mine on various datasets and the results show that for a number of typical datasets and common support levels used in mining, TreeITL-Mine outperforms others. We discussed the results in detail and pointed out the strengths and weaknesses of our algorithm.

We have assumed in this paper that ItemTable, TransLink and the Transaction Tree will fit into main memory. However, this assumption will not apply for huge databases. To extend this algorithm for huge databases, we plan to compress the tree further by looking at the frequency of each item as well as partition the tree to fit in available memory. This work is currently in progress.

Several researchers have investigated the use of constraints to reduce the size of frequent itemsets and to allow greater user focus in the mining process. The constraints are classified as monotone, anti-monotone, succinct, strongly convertible, inconvertible, etc [9]. To make the mining process more efficient, the main idea is to push the constraints deep inside the algorithm. We plan to integrate the processing of constraints into TreeITL-mine in the near future.

References

1. Agrawal, R., Imielinski, T., Swami, A.: Mining Association Rules between Sets of Items in Large Databases. Proc. of ACM SIGMOD, Washington DC (1993)
2. Agrawal, R., Srikant, R.: Fast Algorithms for Mining Association Rules. Proc. of the 20th Int. Conf. on VLDB, Santiago, Chile (1994)
3. Han, J., Pei, J., Yin, Y.: Mining Frequent Patterns without Candidate Generation. Proc. of ACM-SIGMOD, Dallas, TX (2000)
4. Pei, J., Han, J., Lu, H., Nishio, S., Tang, S., Yang, D.: H-Mine: Hyper-Structure Mining of Frequent Patterns in Large Databases. Proc. of the 2001 IEEE ICDM, San Jose, California (2001)
5. Agarwal, R., Aggarwal, C., Prasad, V.V.V.: A Tree Projection Algorithm for Generation of Frequent Itemsets. Journal of Parallel and Distributed Computing (Special Issue on High Performance Data Mining) (2000)
6. Shenoy, P., et al. Turbo-charging Vertical Mining of Large Databases. Proc. of ACM-SIGMOD, Dallas, TX USA (2000).
7. Zaki, M.J., Scalable Algorithms for Association Mining. IEEE Transactions on Knowledge and Data Engineering. 12(3) (May/June 2000) 372–390.
8. Zaki, M.J. Gouda, K., Fast Vertical Mining Using Diffsets. RPI Technical Report 01-1. Rensselaer Polytechnic Institute, Troy, NY 12180 USA: New York (2001)
9. Pei, J., Han, J., Lakshmanan, L.V.S.: Mining Frequent Itemsets with Convertible Constraints. Proc. of 17th ICDE, Heidelberg, Germany (2001)
10. Apriori version 4.01, available at http://fuzzy.cs.uni-magdeburg.de/~borgelt/

Convergency of Learning Process

Dongmo Zhang[1] and Norman Foo[2]

[1] School of Computing and Information Technology
University of Western Sydney, Australia
dongmo@cit.uws.edu.au
[2] School of Computer Science and Engineering
The University of New South Wales, Australia
norman@cse.uws.edu.au

Abstract. This paper presents a learning process analysis on stability of learning in light of iterated belief revision. We view a learning process as a sequential belief change procedure. A learning policy is sought to guarantee every learning process leads to a complete knowledge about the world if the newly accepted information is the true fact on the world. The policy allows an agent to abandon the knowledge it has learned but requires a relatively moderate attitude to new information. It is shown that if new information is not always accepted in an extremely skeptical attitude and the changes of belief degrees follow the criterion of minimal change, any learning process for learning truth will converge to a complete knowledge state.

Keywords: Belief revision, iterated belief change, learning process

1 Introduction

Theories of belief change address the problem of how an agent revises its beliefs when it learns new information about the world. Such theories have been received considerable concern in both philosophy and artificial intelligence partially because they provide formal mechanisms for modelling the evolution of knowledge of human being and the one of knowledge bases. The work on iterated belief change has even reinforced such mechanisms with considering belief and knowledge evolution as a continuous learning process[1]. Almost every aspect of the specification of iterated belief change, including axiomatization, semantic models and computational models, has been investigated in the literature. ([Spohn 1988][Boutilier 1993][Nayak 1994][Lehmann 1995][Williams 1995][Zhang 1995][Darwiche and Pearl 1997][Kelly 1998]). However, it is largely unexplored in either belief revision or learning theory literature that when the processes of sequential belief change is reliable and guaranteed to stabilize to true.

Formally, let Γ be the initial belief state of an agent and $\{A_i\}_{i=1}^{\infty}$ a sequence of pieces of information received by the agent. A learning process over Γ_0 and $\{A_i\}_{i=1}^{\infty}$ can then be specified by the sequence $\{\Gamma_i\}_{i=0}^{\infty}$, which is defined recursively as follows:

---

[1] In this sense, the meaning of learning process here is not exactly the same as in Learning Theory where learning is a process of generalization. We view learning as a procedure of knowledge evolution

R.I. McKay and J. Slaney (Eds.): AI 2002, LNAI 2557, pp. 547–556, 2002.

$$\Gamma_0 = \Gamma$$
$$\Gamma_i = \Gamma_{i-1} * A_i$$

where $*$ is an iterated belief revision operator.

The main question before us is what kind of learning policy a rational agent should hold to guarantee the reliability and stability of learning processes. Some investigations towards the problem have been done in the literature. [Zhang *el al* 1997] [Zhang and Foo 2001] explored the convergency of belief states in the settings when the newly received information comes from an infinite set of propositions. An assumption, called Limit Postulate, has been made to guarantee that the sequence of belief change by the finite subsets of an infinite set of propositions converges to the belief change by the infinite set. [Kelly 1998] contributed a more profound analysis on the learning powers of some concrete iterated belief revision mothods proposed by [Spohn 1988] [Boutilier 1993] [Nayak 1994] [Goldszmidt and Pearl 1994] and [Darwiche and Pearl 1997]. Some interesting results have been obtained through the analysis that different learning policies (minimal change) induced by different belief revision methods fall to different hierarchies of learning power, an objective measure of reliability of learning process.

This paper focus on the analysis of stability of learning process based on a flexible minimal change policy. We shall assume that every belief change is reliable in the sense that each piece of new information received by an agent is a true fact about the world. We are interested in the question that what kind of learning policy should be held by a rational agent to guarantee its belief state to lead to a complete knowledge state about the world. In other words, if all pieces of the newly received information are the truth of the world, whether a learning process converges to a complete knowledge state of the world. We prove that if an agent is not extremely stubborn on its old beliefs, and updates of epistemic state follow a rational procedure of minimal changes, the process of learning the truth will converge to the set of all the truth.

Throughout this paper, we consider the first-order language $\mathcal{L}$ as the object language. L is the set of all sentences in $\mathcal{L}$. We denote individual sentences by A, B, or C, and denote sets of sentences by Γ, Δ etc. We shall assume that the underlying logic includes the classical first-order logic with the standard interpretation. The notation $\vdash$ means the classical first-order derivability and Cn the corresponding closure operator, i.e.,

$$A \in Cn(\Gamma) \text{ if and only if } \Gamma \vdash A$$

2   Minimal Change Policies of Iterated Belief Revision

AGM theory specifies the change of belief state by a rational agent when the agent received a piece of new information. However, it has been pointed out by several authors that the AGM theory is not sufficient to specify a sequential process of belief change due to it ignored the change of agent's epistemic state after each change of belief state([Spohn 1988][Boutilier 1993][Nayak 1994] [Goldszmidt and Pearl 1994][Lehmann 1995][Williams 1995][Zhang 1995][Darwiche and Pearl 1997]). It is true that such a update of epistemic state is mainly determined by the agent's subjective estimation on its new belief state. However, some assumptions can still be made to demonstrate how a rational agent would change its epistemic state. A common assumption in the light is that the ordering information, such as epistemic entrenchment or strength of belief, which guide the revision operation of agent, should be preserved as much as possible. Such an assumption is called *minimal change of belief degrees* in light of information economics.

[Boutilier 1993] proposed a *natural* method of epistemic state modification based on the idea that new information is always accepted in the lowest degree of epistemic entrenchment while preserves the entrenchment ordering as much as possible. On the assumption, it was shown that

$$((K * A_1) * \cdots) * A_n = K * A_1 \wedge \cdots \wedge A_k \wedge A_n$$

where A_k $(k < n)$ is the most recent formula such that $((K * A_1) * \cdots) * A_k$ is consistent with A_n. [Nayak 1994] and [Zhang 1995], however, took the opposite assumption that the newly arrived information always takes priority over the existing beliefs. Based on the assumption, it can be shown that $((K * A_1) * \cdots) * A_n = K * (A_1 \wedge \cdots \wedge A_n)$ if $\{A_1, \cdots, A_n\}$ is consistent; otherwise, $((K * A_1) * \cdots) * A_n = Cn(A_k \wedge \cdots \wedge A_n)$ where k is the minimum such that $\{A_k, \cdots, A_n\}$ is consistent.

It is not difficult to find some counterintuitive examples in both systems(see [Darwiche and Pearl 1997]). This is because that the former takes an extremely skeptical view of new information, while the latter holds the other extreme. More deliberate approaches have proposed also to take account of agent's subjective estimation on its new beliefs (insert the new beliefs into the ordering of belief state and adjust the ordering in order to satisfy the criteria of epistemic entrenchment[Williams 1995]). It could be expected that a flexible minimal change policy over belief revision procedures, which imposes only loose constraints on the change of epistemic state, would be able to guarantee convergency of learning processes even we are lack of subjective estimation on newly arrived information from the epistemic agent.

Let us consider the situation when all the information an agent received is always true facts about the world. Does the agent's belief state approach eventually to a true understanding on the world? In other words, if τ denotes all pieces of the truth about the world, and the agent learns them step by step, does the agent will have all the truth? It is easy to see that this is true for Nayak's approach, but may be failed with Boutilier's assumption because in his system when a new piece of information happens to be inconsistent with all previous belief states of the agent (say the agent is extremely stubborn on some totally wrong ideas), the agent would give up the facts which contradict the wrong ideas even though they could have been reluctantly accepted in previous revision steps. Therefore, the road to truth needs a moderate attitude of new information. In fact, we will prove that if the new information is not always accepted in an extremely skeptical attitude and changes of belief degrees follow the criterion of minimal changes, the process of learning the truth will converge to the set of all the truth.

3   Total-Ordered Partitions and Belief Revision Operators

A belief revision occurs when a new piece of information that is inconsistent with the present belief state of an agent is added to the state. In this process, some old beliefs will be abandoned and others retained. Such selection is generally assumed under the guidance of some ordering information, typically Spohn's plausibility on possible worlds and

AGM's epistemic entrenchment on sentences (see [Gärdenfors 1988]). For the purpose of this paper, we will exploit a kind of ordering structure, called total-ordered partition, introduced in [Zhang and Foo 2001], which is similar to but weaker than the epistemic entrenchment ordering. The underlying intuition is that an agent could organize all its beliefs into several groups in terms of the degrees in which it believes them. Sentences in the same group are of nearly equal degree of belief. All the groups are then arranged in a total ordering or a well ordering.

Definition 1. [Zhang and Foo 2001] Let Γ be a set of sentences, $\mathcal{P}$ a partition of Γ, and $<$ a total ordering relation on $\mathcal{P}$. The triple $\Sigma = (\Gamma, \mathcal{P}, <)$ is called *a total-ordered partition(TOP) of Γ*. If $<$ is a well ordering on $\mathcal{P}$, Σ is called *a well-ordered partition (WOP) of Γ*.

For any $P \in \mathcal{P}$ and $A \in P$, P is called the rank of A, denoted by $r(A)$. Sentence in lower rank is considered with higher degree of belief. It is easy to see that the rank gives a complete pre-order on Γ, so in a sense a total-ordered partition is equivalent to the degree of epistemic relevance in [Nebel 1992].

When $\Delta \subseteq \Gamma$, we denote $\Delta_P =_{def} \Delta \cap P$.

Following [Nebel 1992], we define a notation $\Downarrow$ as follows: for any set Γ of sentences and any sentence A, $\Delta \in \Gamma \Downarrow A$ if and only if

$$\Delta \text{ is a subset of } \Gamma \text{ and } \Delta = \bigcup_{P \in \mathcal{P}} \Delta_P,$$

where for any $P \in \mathcal{P}$, Δ_P is a maximal subset of P such that $(\bigcup_{Q \leq P} \Delta_Q) \cup \{\neg A\}$ is consistent.

In fact, $\Gamma \Downarrow A$ is just a specialization of the maximal consistent subset family $\Gamma \perp A$ (see [Gärdenfor 1988]). The lower the rank of a sentence, the more priority it is chosen.

With this notation, we could define the following revision operators. Let Γ be a set of sentences and Σ a total-ordered partition of Γ.

- *Belief revision* of Γ by A:
  $\Gamma *_1 A = \bigcap(\Gamma \Downarrow \neg A) + A$;
- *Belief base revision* of Γ by A:
  $\Gamma *_2 A = \bigcap_{\Delta \in \Gamma \Downarrow \neg A} Cn(\Delta) + A$;
- *Reconstruction* of Γ by A: $\Gamma *_3 A = $
  $(\bigcap(\Gamma \Downarrow \neg A)) \cup (\{A\} \setminus Cn(\bigcap(\Gamma \Downarrow \neg A)))$.

The operator $*_1$ comes from [Zhang and Foo 2001][2]. It has been proved that if Γ is deductively closed and Σ is a nice-ordered partition of Γ [3], $*_1$ satisfies all the AGM's postulates for revision.

---

[2] It is easy to show that if Σ is a well-ordered partition, this revision operator is equivalent to the one in [Williams 1995].

[3] Σ is a nice-ordered partition of Γ if Σ is a total-ordered partition of Γ and satisfies:
If $A_1, \cdots, A_n \vdash B$, $\sup\{r(A_1), \cdots, r(A_n)\} \leq r(B)$ (See [Zhang and Foo 2001])

The operator $*_2$ comes from [Nebel 1992]. If Γ is deductively closed, it has been proved that $*_2$ satisfies all the AGM's postulates for revision but $(K * 8)$.

The operator $*_3$ comes form [Zhang and Li 1998][4]. The differences between $*_2$ and $*_3$ are:

1. $\Gamma *_3 A$ need not to be deductively closed;
2. $A \in \Gamma *_3 A$ need not to be true.

In this paper, we refer the revision operator $*$ instead of in particular to some special one but to any revision function which can be determined by a total-ordering partition[5] and satisfies the following properties:

(A1) $A \in Cn(\Gamma * A)$;
(A2) $\Gamma * A \in Cn(\Gamma \cup \{A\})$;
(A3) $\Gamma * A$ is consistent iff $\nvdash \neg A$;
(A4) $A \dashv\vdash B$ implies $Cn(\Gamma * A) = Cn(\Gamma * B)$.

where Γ and $\Gamma * A$ could be non-closed set of sentences. $A \dashv\vdash B$ means that $A \vdash B$ and $B \dashv A$. It is obvious that $*_1, *_2, *_3$ satisfy (A1)-(A4) and any AGM revision operator belongs to this category.

4 Minimal Change of Belief Degree and Learning Process

In the process of belief revision of an agent, beliefs change not only in numbers but also in degrees of belief. In general, an epistemic agent would have an estimation of belief degrees for its beliefs. Such estimation in each revision will influence the result of the next revision. Although belief degree may be the agent's subjective evaluation, a rational assumption seems to be that change of belief degree should be minimal in the case of absence of subjective information from the epistemic agent. In other words, the ordering on the original belief state should be preserved as much as possible. As we have mentioned, such a principle is called *minimal change of belief degree*, which can be specified by the following definition:

Definition 2. Let $\Sigma = (\Gamma, \mathcal{P}, <)$ be a well-ordered partition (WOP) of Γ, η be the order-type of $\mathcal{P}$. For any sentence A and an ordinal α, define a WOP $\Sigma_A^\Gamma(\alpha) = (\Gamma * A, \mathcal{P}_A^\Gamma, <_A^\Gamma)$ of $\Gamma * A$ as follows:
For any $\beta < \max\{\alpha + 1, \eta\}$, let
$$P_\beta' = \begin{cases} (P_\beta \cup \{A\}) \cap (\Gamma * A), & \text{if } \beta = \alpha; \\ P_\beta \cap (\Gamma * A), & \text{otherwise.} \end{cases}$$
$$P_\beta'' = (Cn(P_\beta') \cap (\Gamma * A)) \setminus \bigcup_{\gamma < \beta} P_\gamma''$$
Let $\mathcal{P}_A^\Gamma = \{P_\beta'' : \beta < \max\{\alpha + 1, \eta\}\}$. For any $P_\beta, P_\gamma \in \mathcal{P}_A^\Gamma$, define that

$$P_\beta <_A^\Gamma P_\gamma \qquad \text{if and only if} \qquad \beta < \gamma$$

---

[4] In the other form, if $\Gamma \vdash A$, then $\Gamma *_3 A = \Gamma$; if $\Gamma \nvdash A$ and $\Gamma \nvdash \neg A$, then $\Gamma *_3 A = \Gamma \cup \{A\}$; if $\Gamma \vdash \neg A$, then $\Gamma *_3 A = (\bigcap(\Gamma \Downarrow \neg A)) \cup \{A\}$. For more details, see [Zhang and Li 1998]

[5] So the outcomes in sequent sections is suitable at least for these three kinds of revision operation.

$\Sigma_A^\Gamma(\alpha)$ is called *the minimal change of belief degrees for Σ w.r.t. A and α.*[6]

It is not difficult to see that $\Sigma_A^\Gamma(\alpha)$ specifies such a well-ordered partition that the new piece of information A is accepted in the degree α and the old beliefs preserve the original ordering.

Now let's consider a learning process of an epistemic agent. Suppose Γ_0 is the initial belief state of the agent and Σ_0 is a WOP of Γ_0. Whenever the agent learns a piece of new information, its belief state will evolve into a new one. We call such evolutionary process of belief state a learning process of the agent. More precisely, we have the following definition.

Definition 3. Let Γ_0 be a set of sentences with a WOP Σ_0. Let $\{A_i\}_{i=1}^n$ be a sequence of sentences, $\{\alpha_i\}_{i=1}^n$ a sequence of ordinal numbers. Define recursively a sequence of sets $\{\Gamma_i\}_{i=1}^n$ and a sequence of well-ordered partitions $\{\Sigma_i\}_{i=1}^n$ as follows:

i). $\Gamma_i = \Gamma_{i-1} * A_i$, where the revision operation is based on the well-ordered partition Σ_{i-1} of Γ_{i-1};

ii). Σ_i is the minimal change of belief degree for Σ_{i-1} w.r.t. A_i and α_i.

$\{\Gamma_i\}_{i=0}^n$ is called *the learning process w.r.t. $\{A_i\}_{i=1}^n$ and $\{\alpha_i\}_{i=1}^n$ started from Γ_0.*

5   Convergency of Learning Process

Suppose a learning process started from a consistent belief state. In stead of arbitrary import of information, we suppose that all the information the agent learned are the truth or knowledge about the world. It is obvious that an agent is unlikely to keep all the learned truth in its belief states forever even though new information is always let in when it is being learnt and all the new information is consistent. However, we do not intend to impose a radical policy on it to enforce it holding all the learned things. We will allow an agent to abandon some truths it ever learned, but expect that it does not take an extremely skeptical view of new information so that every piece of the truth could be accepted. What we are interested in is whether such a moderate learning policy could promise a learning process converges. To this end, let us see a general result on the convergency of learning process.

Theorem 1. *Let M be a model of $\mathcal{L}$. $\tau_M = \{A \in L : M \models A\}$. Γ_0 is a set of sentences with a WOP Σ_0. For any sequence of ordinals $\{\alpha_i\}_{i=1}^\infty$ and an enumeration $\{A_i\}_{i=1}^\infty$ of τ_M. If $\{\Gamma_i\}_{i=1}^\infty$ is a learning process w.r.t. $\{A_i\}_{i=1}^\infty$ and $\{\alpha_i\}_{i=1}^\infty$ started from Γ_0, then*

$$\varliminf_{n\to\infty} Cn(\Gamma_n) \subseteq \tau_M \subseteq \varlimsup_{n\to\infty} Cn(\Gamma_n) \tag{1}$$

specially, if $\Gamma_0 \setminus \tau_M$ is finite, then

$$\lim_{n\to\infty} Cn(\Gamma_n) = \tau_M \tag{2}$$

---

[6] We do not consider the case that $A \in \Gamma$. In this case, a rational restriction is the ordering keeps unchanged.

Proof: First it is easy to see that for any $i > 0$, Γ_i is consistent because A_i is consistent.

(a). Suppose that $A \in \tau_M$. For there are infinite sentences in τ_M being equivalent to A, let these sentences form a subsequence $\{A_{k_j}\}_{j=1}^{\infty}$ of $\{A_i\}_{i=1}^{\infty}$. By the construction of learning process, for any $j \geq 1$, we have $A_{k_j} \in Cn(\Gamma_{k_j})$, or $A \in Cn(\Gamma_{k_j})$, which means $A \in \varlimsup_{n \to \infty} Cn(\Gamma_n)$. Thus $\tau_M \subseteq \varlimsup_{n \to \infty} Cn(\Gamma_n)$.

(b). Suppose that $A \in \varliminf_{n \to \infty} Cn(\Gamma_n)$. Then there is a number n_0 such that $A \in Cn(\Gamma_n)$ for any $n \geq n_0$. If $A \notin \tau_M$, then $\neg A \in \tau_M$. By the proof of (a), there is a subsequence $\{A_{k_j}\}_{j=1}^{\infty}$ of $\{A_i\}_{i=1}^{\infty}$ such that $A_{k_j} \vdash \neg A$ and $A_{k_j} \in Cn(\Gamma_{k_j})$ for any $j \geq 1$. Thus there exists $k_{j_0} \geq n_0$ such that $\neg A \in Cn(\Gamma_{k_{j_0}})$. But $A \in Cn(\Gamma_{k_{j_0}})$, which contradicts to the consistency of $\Gamma_{k_{j_0}}$. Thus $A \in \tau_M$, that is, $\varliminf_{n \to \infty} Cn(\Gamma_n) \subseteq \tau_M$.

(c). If $\Gamma_0 \setminus \tau_M$ is finite. Let $\Gamma_0 \setminus \tau_M = \{B_0, \cdots, B_m\}$. Then $\{\neg B_0, \cdots, \neg B_m\} \subseteq \tau_M$. Therefore there exists n_0 such that $A_{n_0} \vdash \neg B_0 \wedge \cdots \wedge \neg B_m$. By the properties of belief revision and the definition of learning process, $A_{n_0} \in Cn(\Gamma_{n_0})$. Because $\Gamma_{n_0} \subseteq \Gamma_0 \cup \tau_M$ and Γ_{n_0} is consistent, we have $\Gamma_{n_0} \subseteq \tau_M$. Then, by the definitions of learning process and revision, we conclude that $\{\Gamma_n\}_{n=n_0}^{\infty}$ is a monotonic increasing sequence, which means $\{Cn(\Gamma_n)\}_{n=0}^{\infty}$ converges. Therefore, equation (1) implies (2). □

In this theorem, M acts as an ideal model in which every satisfied statement is truth. This theorem then shows that any learning process started from a finite set will converge no matter how new information is accepted. This result, however, can not be generalized to the case that the starting point is an infinite set. In fact, a learning process would diverge even though new information is always contained in the new belief state, and all the new information is consistent.

We consider that the following additional assumption is rational:

1. The new information is not always accepted with the extremely skeptical attitude and any new information has opportunity to be accepted with relative high degrees of belief.

2. When a piece of information is accepted several times, its relative belief degrees in the learning process should not decrease.

Under this consideration, we give the following definition of rational learning processes:

Definition 4. Suppose the definitions of M, τ_M and Γ_0 as Theorem 1. $\{A_i\}_{i=1}$ numerates the set τ_M and $\{\alpha_i\}_{i=1}^{\infty}$ is a sequence of natural numbers. $\{\Gamma_i\}_{i=1}^{\infty}$ is a learning process w.r.t. $\{A_i\}_{i=1}^{\infty}$ and $\{\alpha_i\}_{i=1}^{\infty}$ started from Γ_0 and $\{\Sigma_i\}_{i=0}^{\infty}$ is a WOP of $\{\Gamma_i\}_{i=0}^{\infty}$. If the following conditions hold:

i). For any $A \in \tau_M$, there exists number n_0 such that $A_{n_0} \vdash A$ and $\{B \in \Gamma_{n_0} \setminus Cn(\phi) : r^{\Sigma_{n_0}}(B) \leq r^{\Sigma_{n_0}}(A_{n_0})\}$ is a finite set[7];

ii). For any $i, j \geq 1$, if $i < j$ and $A_i \vdash A_j$,

$$\forall B \in \Gamma_i \cap \Gamma_j (r^{\Sigma_j}(B) \leq r^{\Sigma_j}(A_j) \to r^{\Sigma_i}(B) \leq r^{\Sigma_i}(A_j))$$

---

[7] $r^{\Sigma}(A)$ denotes the rank of A under the partition Σ.

Then $\{\Gamma_i\}_{i=1}^{\infty}$ is called *a rational learning process* w.r.t. $\{A_i\}_{i=1}^{\infty}$ and $\{\alpha_i\}_{i=1}^{\infty}$ started from Γ_0.

Condition i) means any new information has opportunity to be accepted in a relatively high belief degree (the number of sentences which are not a tautology and their degrees of belief are not lower than this piece of information is finite). Condition ii) shows that when a piece of information is learned more than once, the relative belief degree in which it is accepted should not be lower than those at last times. Then we have

Theorem 2. *Any rational learning process converges and*

$$\lim_{n \to \infty} Cn(\Gamma_n) = \tau_M$$

Proof: We split the proof into the following three steps:

(a). We prove that for any $A \in \tau_M$, there is a natural number N such that $A_N \vdash A$ and $\{B \in \Gamma_N \backslash Cn(\phi) : r^{\Sigma_N}(B) \leq r^{\Sigma_N}(A_N)\} \subseteq \tau_M$.

In fact, the condition i) implies that there exists n_0 such that $A_{n_0} \vdash A$ and $\Delta = \{B \in \Gamma_{n_0} \backslash Cn(\phi) : r^{\Sigma_{n_0}}(B) \leq r^{\Sigma_{n_0}}(A_{n_0})\}$ is finite. If $\Delta \backslash \tau_M$ is empty, or $\Delta \subseteq \tau_M$, the proof is ready provided let $N = n_0$. For the case that $\Delta \backslash \tau_M$ is nonempty, let $\Delta \backslash \tau_M = \{C_1, \cdots, C_m\}$, then $\neg C_1 \wedge \cdots \wedge \neg C_m \in \tau_M$, thus there is a number $n_1 \geq n_0$ such that $A_{n_1} \vdash \neg C_1 \wedge \cdots \wedge \neg C_m$. According to the construction of learning process, $A_{n_1} \in Cn(\Gamma_{n_1})$. Since Γ_{n_1} is consistent, $(\Delta \backslash \tau_M) \cap \Gamma_{n_1} = \phi$. On the other hand, again by the construction of learning process, the sequence $\{\Gamma_n \backslash \tau_M\}_{n=0}^{\infty}$ decreases monotonically, therefore,

$$\forall n \geq n_1 ((\Delta \backslash \tau_M) \cap \Gamma_n = \phi) \tag{3}$$

Since there are infinite sentences in τ_M which are logically equivalent to A, there exists a number $N \geq n_1$ such that $A_N \vdash A$. Let $\Delta' = \{B \in \Gamma_N \backslash Cn(\phi) : r^{\Gamma_N}(B) \leq r^{\Gamma_N}(A_N)\}$. With the condition ii) of the rational learning process, we obtain that

$$\Delta' \backslash \tau_M \subseteq \Delta \backslash \tau_M$$

By the expression (3), we have $(\Delta \backslash \tau_M) \cap \Gamma_N = \phi$, thus $(\Delta' \backslash \tau_M) \cap \Gamma_N = \phi$. Note that $\Delta' \subseteq \Gamma_N$, so $\Delta' \backslash \tau_M = \phi$, that is, $\Delta' \subseteq \tau_M$.

(b). Assume that $A \in \tau_M$. By (a), there exists a natural number N such that $A_N \vdash A$ and $\Delta = \{B \in \Gamma_N \backslash Cn(\phi) : r^{\Sigma_N}(B) \leq r^{\Sigma_N}(A_N)\} \subseteq \tau_M$. Hence $\Delta \cup \{A_n\}$ is consistent for any $n \geq N$. According to the construction of learning process, $\Delta \subseteq \Gamma_n$. Specially, $A_N \in \Gamma_n$, or $A \in Cn(\Gamma_n)$. Thus $A \in \lim_{n \to \infty} Cn(\Gamma_n)$. So we have $\tau_M \subseteq \lim_{n \to \infty} Cn(\Gamma_n)$.

(c). Suppose that $A \in \overline{\lim_{n \to \infty}} Cn(\Gamma_n)$. If $A \notin \tau_M$, $\neg A \in \tau_M$. By (b), $\neg A \in \lim_{n \to \infty} Cn(\Gamma_n)$. Thus there is a number n_0 such that $A \wedge \neg A \in Cn(\Gamma_{n_0})$, which contradicts to the consistency of Γ_{n_0}. Therefore, $\overline{\lim_{n \to \infty}} Cn(\Gamma_n) \subseteq \tau_M$. $\square$

This theorem says that if all the information an agent accepted is the truth about the world, its belief state will converge to the set of all pieces of the truth provided its learning process is rational. Note that the criterion of minimal changes of belief degree and the rationality of learning processes are sufficient but not necessary for the convergency of learning processes. It is not difficult to entail some more loose conditions of the convergency from the proof of the theorem.

6 Conclusion

We have investigated a learning policy to accept new information for a rational epistemic agent. Such a policy allows an agent to abandon the knowledge it has learned but requires a relatively moderate attitude to new information. We have proved that if the new information is not always accepted in an extremely skeptical attitude and changes of belief degrees follow the criterion of minimal changes, the process of learning the truth converges to the set of all the truth.

There have been several works on the analysis of learning process by applying belief revision methods. [Eric Martin and Osherson 2000] offered a model of inductive inquiry on the basis of belief revision operation. [Kelly 1998] presented an approach to analyze the reliability of learning process based on the existing iterated belief revision operators. Different from Kelly's, our analysis on learning process does not depend on any particular iterated belief change operator. In fact, our assumption on the change of epistemic state is the loosest one among the assumptions of the existing iterated belief revision operations. However, our assumption is not a necessary condition to guarantee the convergency of learning process. It is left open how to find a sufficient and necessary condition for the convergency of learning process.

References

1. C. E. Alchourrón, P. Gärdenfors and D. Makinson, On the logic of theory change: partial meet contraction and revision functions, *The Journal of Symbolic Logic* 50(2), 510–530, 1985.
2. C. Boutilier, Revision sequences and nested conditionals, in *Proc. 13th Int. Joint Conf. on Artificial Intelligence (IJCAI'93)*, 519-525, 1993.
3. C. Boutilier,Iterated revision and minimal change of conditional beliefs, *Journal of Philosophical Logic*, 1996(25), 262–305.
4. A. Darwiche and J. Pearl, On the logic of iterated belief revision, *Artificial Intelligence*, 89:1–29, 1997.
5. E. Martin and D. Osherson, Scientific discovery on positive data via belief revision, *Journal of Philosophical Logic*, 29(5), 483-506, 2000.
6. P. Gärdenfors, *Knowledge in Flux: Modeling the Dynamics of Epistemic States,* (The MIT Press), 1988.
7. P. Gärdenfors, Belief revision: an introduction, in: P. Gärdenfors ed., *Belief Revision* (Cambridge University Press, Cambridge), 1–28, 1992.
8. M. Goldszmidt and J. Pearl, Qualitative probabilities for default reasoning, belief revision, and causal modeling, *Artificial Intelligence*, 84:57–112, 1994.
9. K. Kelly, Iterated Belief Revision, Reliability, and Inductive Amnesia," *Erkenntnis*, 50:11–58, 1998.
10. K. Kelly, The Learning Power of Iterated Belief Revision, in: *Proceedings of the Seventh TARK Conference*,111–125, 1998.

11. D. Lehmann, Belief revision, revised, In *Proc. 14th Int. Joint Conf. on Artificial Intelligence* (IJCAI'95), 1534–1540, 1995.
12. W. Li , A logical framework for evolution of specification. in *Programming Language and Systems*, (ESOP'94), LNCS 788, Springer-Verlag, 394-408, 1994.
13. E. Martin and D. Osherson, *Elements of Scientific Inquiry*, MIT Press, 1998.
14. A. Nayak, Iterated belief change based on epistemic entrenchment, *Erkentnis* 41, 353–390,1994.
15. B. Nebel, Syntax based approaches to belief revision, in: P. Gärdenfors ed., *Belief Revision* (Cambridge University Press, cambridge, 1992) 52–88.
16. W. Spohn, Ordinal conditional functions: a dynamic theory of epistemic states, in: W. Harper and B. Skyrms eds, Causation in Decision, Belief Change, and Statistics II, Kluwer Academic Publishers, 105–134, 1988.
17. M. A. Williams, Iterated theory base change: a computational model, In *Proc. 14th Int. Joint Conf. on Artificial Intelligence (IJCAI'95)*, 1541–1547, 1995.
18. D. Zhang, A general framework for belief revision, in: *Proc. 4th Int. Conf. for Young Computer Scientists* (Peking University Press), 574–581, 1995.
19. D. Zhang, Belief revision by sets of sentences, *Journal of Computer Science and Technology*, 1996, 11(2), 108–125.
20. D. Zhang, S. Chen, W. Zhu, Z. Chen, Representation theorems for multiple belief changes, in:*Proc. 15th Int. Joint Conf. on Artificial Intelligence (IJCAI'97)*, 89–94, 1997.
21. D. Zhang and W. Li, Open logic based on total ordered partition model, Science in China(Series E), 41(6), 1998.
22. D. Zhang and N. Foo, Infinitary belief revision, *Journal of Philosophical Logic*, 6(30), 525–574, 2001.

Structured Features from Concept Lattices for Unsupervised Learning and Classification

Michael Bain

School of Computer Science and Engineering,
University of New South Wales,
Sydney, Australia 2052
mike@cse.unsw.edu.au

Abstract. We present a method for identifying potentially interesting and useful concepts in a concept lattice and revising the underlying formal context and the lattice it generates to invent new descriptors and extract their definitions. This allows the re-use of concepts in an incremental way. The approach is developed using formal concept analysis and inverse resolution operators for both a theory and its lattice. A consequence of using the concept lattice to represent the concept space is that both unsupervised and supervised approaches are enabled by using different concept evaluation measures. Results are given from experiments in two standard domains with a system called Conduce which implements the method.

1 Introduction

Concept lattices have been used as a tool for examining the structure of common patterns within data sets in Machine Learning (e.g. [2]), Data Mining (e.g. [4]) and Knowledge Discovery (e.g. [5]). Underlying these approaches is the idea that making explicit the embedded formal conceptual structures in data or rules is a useful method of analysis. In this paper we extend these approaches by investigating a method for defining new features based on the sets of conditions which make up the intensional part of formal concepts. These features, or Boolean attributes, can then be used either directly as part of a structured theory or supplied to another learning system to enable a change of representation in a domain. In particular, our method can introduce structured features, that is, features which can include other non-primitive features in their definition.

1.1 Background

One approach to identifying structure present in domains is taken in formal concept analysis. Introduced by Wille [3], formal concept analysis is based on a complete lattice of all concepts in a domain. A concept in this formalism is an ordered pair of sets, one a set of attributes or descriptors of the concept, the other a set of object indices denoting all instances of the concept in the

R.I. McKay and J. Slaney (Eds.): AI 2002, LNAI 2557, pp. 557–568, 2002.

domain. The set of descriptors of a concept is the maximal set common to all
the instances of the concept. These concepts form a partial order from which
a lattice is constructed. There is a large body of theoretical work underlying
formal concept analysis. More details are in section 2.

The term "structured induction" was introduced by A. Shapiro [10]. His
work was on the construction of rule-based systems by induction in complex
domains such as chess. Based on structured programming, structured induction
is a knowledge acquisition technique whereby a domain specialist and knowledge
engineer cooperate in the design of a hierarchical set of decision tree classifiers
for the domain.

In the Duce system developed by Muggleton [7], as an approach for the partial
automation of Shapiro's structured induction, operators based on inverting the
resolution rule of deductive inference were used. A key aspect of structured induction and inverse resolution is the introduction of *theoretical* terms, additional
to the *observational* terms given a priori for the domain. These theoretical terms
are combined with observational terms to enable the construction of hierarchical
concept definitions.

1.2   Overview

We assume a standard machine learning framework where data and theories, such
as rule sets, decision trees, etc. are described in the same formalism. Examples
or rules consist of conjunctions of descriptor variables (or attributes) mapping
to a single predictor variable (or class). This representation is equivalent to a set
of propositional definite clauses, i.e. a theory. A method to find common subsets
of descriptors could be valuable in detecting conceptual structures hidden in
such theories. Given this representation we might build a concept lattice which
reflects the structure of the theory. Such a concept lattice could be scanned to
detect sub-concepts of the theory which were in some sense significant. Once
discovered, how would such structure be employed ? One answer would be to
revise the rule set and produce a new, more structured, set of rules. Recall that
this outcome was the aim of structured induction. However, this also requires
revising the concept lattice to reflect the revised set of rules.

In this scenario we have a dual requirement for revision. First, a database
or rulebase must be revised to incorporate structure. Second, the associated
concept lattice must be revised. And because the processes may be incremental,
the revisions must be iterative. In this work we adopt the revision operators
of inverse resolution for structuring rulebases. Our main contribution in this
paper is to develop methods for the revision of concept lattices based on the
operators for inverse resolution in propositional logic. The remainder of the paper
is organised as follows. In section 2 we review the basic framework of formal
concept analysis. In sections 3 and 4 we review the operators of inverse resolution
as theory revision operators and in relation to formal concept analysis. Then
in section 5 we present the methods of revising the basic relation of concept
lattices using inverse resolution. An algorithm called Conduce which implements
the revision method is presented in section 6, followed by some examples of its

application and discussion in section 7. Some directions for further work and conclusions are in section 8.

2 Formal Concept Analysis

Detailed coverage of Formal Concept Analysis (FCA) is in [3]. In this section we follow the treatments of [4,2] since they are more oriented towards machine learning. However, some naming and other conventions have been changed.

Definition 1. Formal context *A formal context is a triple* $\langle \mathcal{D}, \mathcal{O}, \mathcal{R} \rangle$. $\mathcal{D}$ *is a set of descriptors,* $\mathcal{O}$ *is a set of objects and* $\mathcal{R}$ *is a binary relation such that* $\mathcal{R} \subseteq \mathcal{D} \times \mathcal{O}$.

The notation $\langle x, y \rangle \in \mathcal{R}$ or alternatively $x\mathcal{R}y$ is used to express the fact that a descriptor $x \in \mathcal{D}$ is a property of an object $y \in \mathcal{O}$.

Definition 2. Formal concept *A formal concept is an ordered pair of sets, written* $\langle X, Y \rangle$, *where* $X \subseteq \mathcal{D}$ *and* $Y \subseteq \mathcal{O}$. *Each pair must be complete with respect to* $\mathcal{R}$, *which means that* $X' = Y$ *and* $Y' = X$, *where* $X' = \{y \in \mathcal{O} | \forall x \in X, x\mathcal{R}y\}$ *and* $Y' = \{x \in \mathcal{D} | \forall y \in Y, x\mathcal{R}y\}$.

The set of descriptors of a formal concept is called its intent, while the set of objects of a formal concept is called its extent. For a set of descriptors $X \subseteq \mathcal{D}$, X is the intent of a formal concept if and only if $X'' = X$. A dual condition holds for the extent of a formal concept. This means that any formal concept can be uniquely identified by either its intent or its extent alone. Intuitively, the intent corresponds to a kind of maximally specific description of all the objects in the extent.

The correspondence between intent and extent of complete concepts is a Galois connection between the power set $\mathcal{P}(\mathcal{D})$ of the set of descriptors and the power set $\mathcal{P}(\mathcal{O})$ of the set of objects. The Galois lattice $\mathcal{L}$ for the binary relation is the set of all complete pairs of intents and extents, with the following partial order. Given two concepts $N_1 = \langle X_1, Y_1 \rangle$ and $N_2 = \langle X_2, Y_2 \rangle$, $N_1 \leq N_2 \leftrightarrow X_1 \supseteq X_2$. The dual nature of the Galois connection means we have the equivalent relationship $N_1 \leq N_2 \leftrightarrow Y_1 \subseteq Y_2$.

The formal context $\langle \mathcal{D}, \mathcal{O}, \mathcal{R} \rangle$ together with $\leq$ define an ordered set which gives rise to a complete lattice. The following version of a theorem from [4] is the basic characterization of concept lattices.

Theorem 1. Fundamental theorem on concept lattices [4] *Let* $\langle \mathcal{D}, \mathcal{O}, \mathcal{R} \rangle$ *be a formal context. Then* $\langle \mathcal{L}; \leq \rangle$ *is a complete lattice* [1] *for which the least upper bound (Sup) and greatest lower bound (Inf) are given by*

$$Sup_{j \in J}(X_j, Y_j) = \langle \bigcap_{j \in J} X_j, (\bigcup_{j \in J} Y_j)'' \rangle$$
$$Inf_{j \in J}(X_j, Y_j) = \langle (\bigcup_{j \in J} X_j)'', \bigcap_{j \in J} Y_j \rangle$$

---

[1] Given a non-empty ordered set P, if for all $S \subset P$ there exists a least upper bound and a greatest lower bound then P is a complete lattice.

Since we are concerned with concepts formed from sets of descriptors, the partial order as well as *Sup* and *Inf* definitions are given so as to relate to lattices in machine learning rather than that which is typical in formal concept analysis. That is, the supremum *Sup* of all nodes in the lattice in the "most general" or top ($\top$) node and the infimum *Inf* is the "most specific" or bottom ($\bot$).

To illustrate the method of formal concept analysis we give an example, due to Ganter, in Figure 1. This is a theory about the natural numbers from 1 to 9 described in terms of five properties. The resulting concept lattice shows the grouping of these numbers according to their common properties. Our representation is described in more detail in the next section.

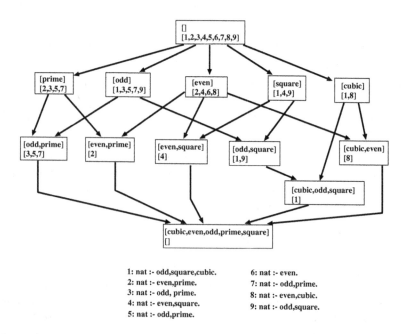

Fig. 1. Concept lattice for the first nine natural numbers using an indexed propositional definite clause for each number. $\mathcal{D} = \{\text{even}, \text{odd}, \text{prime}, \text{square}, \text{cubic}\}$ and $\mathcal{O} = \{1, \ldots, 9\}$. The relation $\mathcal{R}$ is implicit given the clause indices and conjunctions of descriptors in the clause bodies.

3   Inverse Resolution

The logical approach to machine learning is exemplified by the discipline of Inductive Logic Programming (ILP). Within ILP data (or examples), existing theories and hypotheses to be conjectured are all formalised as logic programs. Several of the early approaches to ILP were developed in the framework of inverse resolution. On this view the single deductive operator of resolution is variously transformed to give multiple operators, each of which may be described as inverting resolution.

In this paper we have chosen the Duce system [7] to provide theory revision operators based on inverse resolution. Since the formal contexts underlying concept lattices are typically defined to be zeroth-order the propositional framework of Duce is adequate. More importantly, since Duce contains operators for generalisation and predicate invention it is appropriate for a system for which a key goal is the construction of structured rule sets.

The resolution principle introduced by Robinson [9] may be viewed as a binary operator with two operands in clausal form which derives a new clause, the resolvent. We will refer to the operands as *implicants* and the resolvent as an *implicate*. Inverse resolution (IR) was introduced by Muggleton (see the review in [8]) as a set of operators for inductive inference on clausal theories. Inversion of a single resolution step may be viewed as an operator taking two clauses, treating one as an implicant and the other as an implicate, and returning a third as the conjectured "missing" implicant. Given the two implicants the implicate is now logically redundant. Replacing this implicate by the conjectured implicant in a theory results in a removal of redundancy or *structuring* of the modified theory. Also, this removal of implicates gives a *compression* of the theory without losing generality. This provides the basis of operator evaluation in revision of theories.

Since a resolution derivation is usually represented graphically as binary tree, a single resolution step can be drawn as a V-shape. For this reason single-step inverse resolutions are known as V-operators. If two resolution steps sharing a complementary pair of literals are carried out concurrently this can be depicted as two combined V-shapes, i.e. a W-shape. Therefore such double-step inverse resolutions are known as W-operators. The key aspect of W-operators is that the shared literal must be conjectured in order to fully generate the missing implicates. This step is known in ILP as *predicate invention*.

Inverse resolution for propositional clausal theories was implemented in the Duce system. The four operators used by Duce are shown in Table 1. The representation we adopt differs from Duce only in that the propositional clauses have prepended an index $k \in \mathcal{O}$. This index is currently used only for construction and revision of the concept lattice. When used as a rule base, for example to classify previously unseen instances, the indices are ignored. Clauses in a theory $\mathcal{T}$ are all definite, i.e. have exactly one positive literal, the clause head. The body of a clause is a (negated) conjunction of literals. All clause literals are elements of the set of descriptors $\mathcal{D}$.

4   Revision of $\mathcal{T}$

We are concerned with incremental theory revision. An existing theory which is to be revised is denoted $\mathcal{T}_{t-1}$. The revised theory is denoted $\mathcal{T}_t$. Therefore the inverse resolution operators in Table 1 are written to indicate a state change from time $t-1$ on the left of the vertical bar to time t on the right. Every

Table 1. Revising $\mathcal{C}_{t-1}$ to $\mathcal{C}_t$ using the four inverse resolution operators of Duce.

Description	Same Head		Different Head	
Generalisation (V-operators)	**Identification** $D_i = p \leftarrow A, B_i$ $C^- = p \leftarrow A, q$	$C_i^+ = q \leftarrow B_i$ $C^- = p \leftarrow A, q$	**Absorption** $D_i = p \leftarrow A, B_i$ $C^+ = q \leftarrow A$	$C_i^- = p \leftarrow q, B_i$ $C^+ = q \leftarrow A$
Predicate Invention (W-operators)	**Intra-construction** $D_i = p \leftarrow A, B_i$ $D_j = p \leftarrow A, B_j$	$C_i^+ = w \leftarrow B_i$ $C_j^+ = w \leftarrow B_j$ $C^- = p \leftarrow A, w$	**Inter-construction** $D_i = p \leftarrow A, B_i$ $D_j = q \leftarrow A, B_j$	$C_i^- = p \leftarrow w, B_i$ $C_j^- = q \leftarrow w, B_j$ $C^+ = w \leftarrow A$

The letters to the left of the '=' characterise the role of the clauses on the right of the '=' in resolution. The D are implicates and the C implicants. The superscript '-' denotes an implicant in which the literal of the complementary pair is negated, and '+' the opposite. In clauses upper-case letters represent conjunctions of literals while lower-case letters represent single literals. The operators are presented as sets of preconditions (to the left of the vertical line) and postconditions (to the right). Read left to right, the changes to operand clauses for each operator are apparent.

operator takes as operands a set of clauses $\mathcal{C}_{t-1} \subseteq \mathcal{T}_{t-1}$ with a common subset of literals A in each clause body.

In sections 4 to 5 we concentrate mainly on a single operator, identification or abduction, in order to simplify the exposition. This is because identification embodies all the key aspects of revising the concept lattice whilst being the operator with the fewest details involved in such updates.

4.1   Definitions for Identification

Definition 3 (Indexed clause). *An indexed clause C is a triple $\langle K, H, B \rangle$ where $K \in \mathcal{O}$ and $H, B \subseteq \mathcal{D}$. K is referred to as the clause index. H is the set of positive literals in C. If H is a unit set then C is an indexed definite clause and H is referred to as the clause head. B is the set of negative literals in the clause, referred to as the clause body.*

Definition 4 (Indexed theory). *An indexed theory $\mathcal{T}$ is a (possibly empty) set of indexed clauses.*

An indexed theory may be referred to simply as a theory.

Definition 5 (Clause index). *The function $id(C)$ returns the index K of the indexed clause C.*

Definition 6 (Clause head). *The function $hd(C)$ returns the head H of the indexed definite clause C.*

Definition 7 (Clause body). *The function $bd(C)$ returns the body B of the indexed clause C.*

Definition 8 (Clause for index). *The function $cl(K)$ returns the indexed clause C corresponding to the index K, or undefined if there is no such clause.*

In the remainder of this work "clause" will be used to mean a propositional indexed definite clause.

Definition 9. Unique clauses *Let C_1 and C_2 be clauses in theory $\mathcal{T}$. If $bd(C_1) = bd(C_2)$ then $C_1 = C_2$.*

Definition 10 (Identification). *The inverse resolution operator $ident_{\mathcal{T}}$ on indexed theories is a mapping from a set C_{t-1} of clauses and a set of literals $A \subseteq bd(C)$ for every $C \in C_{t-1}$ to a revised set of clauses C_t with the following properties. For each clause $C \in C_{t-1}$ $hd(C)$ is identical. There exists a clause $C^- \in C_{t-1}$ such that $bd(C^-) \backslash A$ is a unit set, the sole element of which is referred to as q. This clause is called the retained implicant for identification. Every other clause D_i in the set $C_{t-1} \setminus C^-$ is called an implicate for identification. The set C_t comprises the retained implicate together with the set of clauses obtained by revising each implicate D_i to C_i^+, as follows. $C_i^+ = \langle id(D_i), q, bd(D_i) \setminus A \rangle$.*

4.2   Inverse Resolution and Formal Concept Analysis

It is evident that a node in a concept lattice is a candidate source of operands for an inverse resolution operator. Let n be a node in a concept lattice $\mathcal{L}$ and let $I(n)$ denote its intent and $E(n)$ denote its extent. Then $I(n)$ provides the set of literals common to the body of every clause whose index is in $E(n)$. We follow a standard machine learning approach and view the lattice of intents as a lattice of conjunctive descriptions [6]. On this view our formalism of indexed definite clauses can be used as a common framework for formal concept analysis and machine learning to represent examples and theories.

Definition 11 (Instance). *An instance is a conjunction of literals or descriptors from the set $\mathcal{D}$, represented by the body of an indexed clause.*

Definition 12 (Example). *An example is an instance labelled with a class value (a literal or descriptor from the set $\mathcal{D}$), represented by the head and body of an indexed clause.*

Definition 13 (Object). *An object from the set $\mathcal{O}$ is represented by the index of an indexed clause.*

5   Revision of $\mathcal{R}$

Recall that the relation $\mathcal{R}$ between the set of descriptors $\mathcal{D}$ and the set of objects $\mathcal{O}$ defines a formal context from which the set of all formal concepts can be derived. Suppose we are given an indexed theory $\mathcal{T}$. Then $\mathcal{T}$ defines an implicit formal context $\langle \mathcal{D}, \mathcal{O}, \mathcal{R} \rangle$, as follows. $\mathcal{D} = \bigcup_{\forall C \in \mathcal{T}} bd(C)$. $\mathcal{O} = \bigcup_{\forall C \in \mathcal{T}} id(C)$. $\mathcal{R} = \bigcup_{\forall C \in \mathcal{T}} (\bigcup_{\forall x \in bd(C)} \langle x, id(C) \rangle)$. This is expressed procedurally as Algorithm 1.

Algorithm 1 Formal context for theory $\mathcal{T}$

Begin
 Let $D = O = R = \emptyset$;
 For each C in $\mathcal{T}$ do
  $y = id(C)$;
  $O := \{y\} \cup O$;
  For each literal x in $bd(C)$ do
   $D := \{x\} \cup D$;
   $R := \{\langle x, y \rangle\} \cup R$;
  endFor
 endFor
 Return $\langle D, O, R \rangle$;
End.

We note the following regarding the way in which $\mathcal{R}$ is defined for a theory $\mathcal{T}$:

- only body literals form the set of descriptors $\mathcal{D}$;
- since clause bodies are conjunctions of literals, and the intents of formal concepts are conjunctions of literals, this allows a common representation for clauses and concept lattices which is equivalent to the general-to-specific ordering of hypotheses used in machine learning [6];
- viewing concept lattices as a representation for machine learning, this approach allows for unsupervised or supervised modes, depending on whether information on clause heads is also used;

Let $\mathcal{T}_{t-1}$ be a theory for which $\mathcal{R}_{t-1}$ defines the relation between descriptors and objects and $\mathcal{L}_{t-1}$ is the corresponding concept lattice. Let g_{t-1} be a node chosen from $\mathcal{L}_{t-1}$ such that the intent $I(g_{t-1})$ is non-empty and the cardinality of extent $E(g_{t-1})$ is 2 or more and the set of clauses in $\mathcal{T}_{t-1}$ denoted by g_{t-1} satisfies the preconditions for identification. Let j be the index of the retained implicant clause C^- and q the sole literal in the body of the retained implicant which is not an element of $I(g_{t-1})$. If $\mathcal{T}_{t-1}$ is updated by the identification operator as in Definition 10 then the required update to $\mathcal{R}_{t-1}$ is as follows.

Definition 14. $ident_\mathcal{R}(\mathcal{R}_{t-1})$: Revising $\mathcal{R}_{t-1}$ using identification

$$\mathcal{R}_t = \mathcal{R}_{t-1} \setminus \{\langle x, y \rangle | x \in I(g_{t-1}), y \neq j, y \in E(g_{t-1})\}$$

Lemma 2. Completeness and correctness of $ident_\mathcal{R}(\mathcal{R}_{t-1})$ *The revision operator $ident_\mathcal{R}(\mathcal{R}_{t-1})$ generates $\mathcal{R}_t$ which is complete and correct w.r.t. the theory revision operator $ident_\mathcal{T}(\mathcal{T}_{t-1})$.*
Proof. *To see that all necessary changes to $\mathcal{R}_{t-1}$ are made consider all elements having a clause index in $E(g_{t-1})$ apart from the index j of the retained implicant C^-. This is the set of implicates in Definition 10. For each implicate D the operator $ident_\mathcal{R}$ first subtracts every element containing a literal in $I(g_{t-1})$. This is equivalent to the set A in Definition 10 which is subtracted from the body of each implicate clause D. Finally all elements containing the head literal p and*

a clause index in $E(g_{t-1})$ except for j have p replaced by q. Therefore $ident_{\mathcal{R}}$ is complete. No other elements of $\mathcal{R}_{t-1}$ are changed. Therefore the operator is correct.

6 Conduce

Owing to lack of space we omit the definition of the analogous operator for revision of lattice nodes, $ident_{\mathcal{L}}(\mathcal{L}_{t-1})$ However, the node revision operators defined in this operator are incorporated into the following algorithm.

Algorithm 3 Conduce

Input: theory $\mathcal{T}_{t-1}$, concept lattice $\mathcal{L}_{t-1}$
Output: theory $\mathcal{T}_t$, concept lattice $\mathcal{L}_t$

Begin
$\qquad g_{t-1} =$ *most compressive node* $n_{t-1} \in \mathcal{L}_{t-1}$*;*
$\qquad$ *op is chosen based on pre-conditions satisfied by* n_{t-1}*;*
$\qquad \mathcal{T}_t := op_{\mathcal{T}}(\mathcal{T}_{t-1})$*;*
$\qquad \mathcal{L}_t := op_{\mathcal{L}}(\mathcal{L}_{t-1})$*;*
End

Some notes regarding our implementation of Conduce:

– lattice construction and re-linking of the revised nodes is done using an incremental algorithm based on that of [4];
– the Duce operators have a preference order, essentially giving lower compression as their pre-conditions are weakened.

In our system we apply the same operator pre-conditions as Duce but calculate compression based on the complexity of the node intent in bits rather than its cardinality:

$$\text{complexity}(n) = - \left(\sum_{d \in I(n)} \log_2 P(d) \right) |E(n)|$$

where $P(d)$ is the relative frequency of occurrence of descriptor d in $\mathcal{T}$.

7 Two Case Studies

We present results from two case studies on standard datasets from the UCI repository [1]. In both cases the task was for Conduce to find interesting concepts and generate definitions of them. The system was therefore restricted to the use of the single revision operator inter-construction. This approach, referred to as forced inter-construction, was chosen since (a) it implements predicate invention, (b) inter-construction has the weakest pre-conditions of any operator and (c) it constructs a (conjunctive) definition as a single definite clause.

In a first experiment we applied Conduce to a task of unsupervised learning. The "zoo" data set contains 101 instances. Each is described using 17 attributes and a unique name, such as aardvark, ostrich, seasnake, wasp, etc. It is an artificial data set and is not supposed to be taxonomically correct. Seven classes are also given, into which the the instances are partitioned. Conduce was given the task of reconstructing these classes given only the attributes. In Table 2 we summarise the results. Notice that the invented feature we have named "flying bird" is a structured feature, since it is defined using one primitive attribute (airborne) and one previously invented feature ("bird").

Table 2. Concepts found by Conduce in the zoo data set.

	Original		Reconstructed
class	definition	class	definition
mammal	{backbone,breathes,milk}	4-legged mammal	{backbone,breathes,hair, milk,tail,toothed,legs(4)}
bird	{backbone,breathes,eggs, feathers,tail,legs(2)}	bird	{backbone,breathes,eggs, feathers,tail,legs(2)}
reptile	{backbone,tail}	fish	{aquatic,backbone,eggs, fins,tail,toothed,legs(0)}
fish	{aquatic,backbone,eggs, fins,tail,toothed,legs(0)}	hairy mammal	{backbone,breathes,hair, milk,toothed}
amphibian	{aquatic,backbone, breathes,eggs, toothed,legs(4)}	toothed predator	{backbone,breathes, predator,toothed}
insect	{breathes,eggs,legs(6)}	large predator	{large,predator}
other	{}	flying insect	{airborne,breathes,eggs,legs(6)}
		flying bird	{airborne,bird}

The left columns show the known classes in descending order as they appear in the data set description file. The right columns show the new concepts and their definitions in descending order as they were discovered by Conduce. The names were applied afterwards by the author. Two of the original classes, reptile and other, do not have meaningful definitions. Of the remaining five, two (bird, fish) were recovered exactly by Conduce, one (mammal) was recovered as two more specialised concepts and one (insect) was recovered in specialised form. Note the re-use of the bird concept in the later definition named flying bird.

Although unsupervised learning tasks are very important for problems such as conceptual clustering or ontology learning when class information is not available, machine learning applications more typically involve classification. Rather than develop a new classification algorithm from scratch we have investigated Conduce as a method for constructing new features for supervised learning.

It is relatively costly to incrementally build and revise a lattice. However it is much faster to run a decision tree learning algorithm such as C4.5 (used in this experiment) on the complete training set, even when it is augmented with new features. Therefore in this experiment a random sample is taken from the complete training set and used to build a concept lattice. We assume that most of the important concepts will be present in a sufficently large sample of the training set and will appear in the lattice. Structured features are then constructed from this lattice and supplied to a supervised learning algorithm in the form of an augmented training set. Any useful features which give the classifier learning system improved predictive accuracy will be selected in tree construction.

As a first test of this approach we used a standard data set for problems of constructive induction (e.g. [11]), the tic-tac-toe data set from the UCI repository. The problem is to predict whether each of 958 legal endgame boards for tic-tac-toe is won for 'x'. The results are shown in Table 3.

Table 3. Tic-tac-toe classification with new features.

	Accuracy (%)	Tree size	Attributes
Primitives only	86.8	118	9
Features (Compression)	77.7	92	78
Features (Compression+Entropy)	97.2	54	62
Features (Posonly+Compression+Entropy)	100.0	24	48

Four experimental conditions were tested. In each, the data set (958 examples) was split 70:30 into a training (671) and test (287) set. "Primitives only" means C4.5 was run on the data using only the primitive data, nine attributes indicating the contents of each of the squares on the 3×3 board. In the three remaining conditions, a random sample of size 100 was selected from the training set and used in lattice construction by Conduce. "Features (Compression)" denotes running Conduce to generate features using the Duce evaluation measures which were then used to augment the set of primitive attributes. "Features (Compression+Entropy)" indicates the same method except that class entropy was measured as well as compression in concept evaluation within Conduce. "Features (Posonly+Compression+Entropy)" means that the same concept evaluation method was used, but that the sample used to construct the lattice contained only positive examples.

The calculation of the measure of "Compression+Entropy" in Table 3 is essentially $(1 - H(\text{Class distn. of concept } n)) \times \text{complexity}(n)$, where H is the entropy, and concept complexity is as calculated above. Note that most of the gains in accuracy are obtained by discovery of the new features corresponding to the concepts "three-in-a-row for x". The target concept can be compactly expressed as a disjunction of eight such non-primitive features. Using feature construction from the positive data only gives a classifier containing seven out of these eight features, since the eighth feature was not selected from the lattice by Conduce (although a specialisation of it was).

8 Conclusions and Further Work

We have developed and tested a method for identifying potentially interesting and useful concepts in a concept lattice and revising the underlying formal context and the lattice it generates to extract new descriptors and their definitions. This allows the re-use of concepts in an incremental way. Experiments in two standard domains with the system Conduce which implements these methods have shown promising results.

There are many directions for continuing this work. The operator selection method is very important in determining the quality of new features. We have found in a number of domains that the current evaluation method is biased towards selection of over-specific concepts. This is probably a consequence of the exact fit of concepts to data in the lattice. One property of the lattice that may be useful is to search upwards from selected concepts (i.e. make a generalisation) for concepts which preserve classification accuracy while increasing coverage. We plan to evaluate the methods more extensively on real world domains.

Acknowledgement. Research supported by the Australian Research Council.

References

1. C.L. Blake and C.J. Merz. UCI repository of machine learning databases, 1998.
2. C. Carpineto and G. Romano. GALOIS: An order-theoretic approach to conceptual clustering. In *Proc. 10th Intl. Conf. on Machine Learning*, pages 33–40, Los Altos, CA, 1993. Morgan Kaufmann.
3. B. Ganter and R. Wille. *Formal Concept Analysis: Mathematical Foundations.* Springer, Berlin, 1999.
4. R. Godin and R. Missaoui. An incremental concept formation approach for learning from databases. *Theoretical Computer Science*, 133:387–419, 1994.
5. J. Hereth, G. Stumme, R. Wille, and U. Wille. Conceptual Knowledge Discovery and Data Analysis. In B. Ganter and G. Mineau, editors, *ICCS 2000: Proc. of the Eighth Intl. Conference on Conceptual Structures*, volume LNCS 1867, pages 421–437, Berlin, 2000. Springer.
6. T. Mitchell. *Machine Learning.* McGraw-Hill, New York, 1997.
7. S. Muggleton. Duce, an oracle-based approach to constructive induction. In *IJCAI-87*, pages 287–292. Kaufmann, 1987.
8. S. Muggleton. Inverse Entailment and Progol. *New Generation Computing*, 13:245–286, 1995.
9. J. A. Robinson. A machine-oriented logic based on the resolution principle. *JACM*, 12(1):23–41, January 1965.
10. A. D. Shapiro. *Structured Induction in Expert Systems.* Turing Institute Press with Addison Wesley, Wokingham, UK, 1987.
11. Z. Zheng. *Constructing New Attributes for Decision Tree Learning.* PhD thesis, University of Sydney, Sydney, Australia, 1996.

Towards Fewer Parameters for SAT Clause Weighting Algorithms

John Thornton, Wayne Pullan, and Justin Terry

School of Information Technology,
Griffith University Gold Coast,
Qld, 4215, Australia
{j.thornton, w.pullan,j.terry}@mailbox.gu.edu.au

Abstract. Considerable progress has recently been made in using clause weighting algorithms such as DLM and SDF to solve SAT benchmark problems. While these algorithms have outperformed earlier stochastic techniques on many larger problems, this improvement has been bought at the cost of extra parameters and the complexity of fine tuning these parameters to obtain optimal run-time performance. This paper examines the use of parameters, specifically in relation to DLM, to identify underlying features in clause weighting that can be used to eliminate or predict workable parameter settings. To this end we propose and empirically evaluate a simplified clause weighting algorithm that replaces the tabu list and flat moves parameter used in DLM. From this we show that our simplified clause weighting algorithm is competitive with DLM on the four categories of SAT problem for which DLM has already been optimised.

Keywords: Constraints, Search

1 Introduction

One of the basic aims of artificial intelligence research is to replace tasks requiring human expertise with automated or algorithmic solutions. For instance, the constraint satisfaction problem (CSP) formalism and the development of general purpose constraint solving technologies is intended to replace the task of writing specific algorithms to solve specific problems. However, human input is still required to model problems, select appropriate constraint solving techniques and to fine tune parameters that in turn optimise performance in particular problem domains. Typically, this tuning process requires a significant period of trial and error (especially for stochastic search techniques). Further, the complexity of parameter setting grows exponentially rather than linearly as the number of parameters increases. For these reasons we can conclude that, given an algorithm with a set of n parameters, removal of a subset k of these parameters without significant impact on the sensitivities and range of the remaining $n - k$ parameters generates a more effective and usable algorithm.

In this paper we look at parameter elimination for clause weighting algorithms in the satisfiability (SAT) problem domain. We have chosen SAT due to the significant and ongoing improvement in the performance of SAT algorithms that has occurred in the last decade. In particular, we are interested in clause weighting, because current

R.I. McKay and J. Slaney (Eds.): AI 2002, LNAI 2557, pp. 569–578, 2002.

techniques such as the Discrete Langrangian Method (DLM) [10], Smooth Descent and Flood (SDF) [6] and the Exponentiated Subgradient algorithm (ESG) [7] represent state-of-the-art performance on the widely used SATLIB and DIMACS benchmark problems. DLM offers the further advantage that it is a general purpose technique applicable to the broader domain of CSPs.

Specifically, the paper examines three important DLM parameters described in [10] that (i) control the number of zero cost moves taken in the weighted cost space (ii) set the length of the tabu list and (iii) control the frequency with which weights are reduced. We propose a simplified clause weighting algorithm that removes parameters (i) and (ii) and compare the performance of this algorithm with DLM in the four problem domains for which DLM was originally optimised (namely the SATLIB and DIMACS random 3-SAT, parity function learning, graph colouring and blocks world planning benchmarks). These results show that simplified clause weighting is competitive with DLM and suggest future directions for a self-tuning, general purpose clause weighting heuristic.

2   Clause Weighting

2.1   A Brief History

The clause weighting algorithm for SAT was simultaneously proposed in [5] and [8] in 1993. Developed to improve on GSAT [8], clause weighting is an incomplete local search method that escapes traps or minima by adding weight to currently false clauses. This changes the *weighted* cost surface of a problem, allowing further cost reducing moves by partially "filling in" [5] each minimum. As weights build up during the search, flip selection is biased towards moves that satisfy more heavily weighted clauses. This is analogous to a human problem solver fixing the most difficult parts of a problem first, and then moving around the less constrained resources until a solution is found.

Various enhancements to clause weighting were proposed in the mid-90s, most notably Jeremy Frank's work on multiplicative weighting and weight decay [1]. Frank anticipated much of the later work on clause weighting, particularly in controlling weight growth so that the relative clause weight magnitudes remain fairly constant during the search. However, it was not until the development of DLM that these insights were translated into significant performance improvements.

2.2   DLM

DLM was first proposed as a general purpose optimisation technique rather than as a special purpose SAT algorithm [9]. However, it has been widely recognised as the state-of-the-art for solving the larger SAT benchmark problems [6] and subsequent versions have introduced SAT specific heuristics [11]. In addition to achieving performance gains over other SAT techniques, DLM provides a mathematical foundation to clause weighting, extending the theory of Lagrangian multipliers from continuous to discrete space problem solving. When applied to SAT, DLM can be considered as a clause weighting algorithm, with the discrete Lagrangian multipliers representing the clause weights.

The main differences between DLM and earlier clause weighting techniques are in the use of a tabu list [3] to guide the search over plateau areas, and in the use of a weight reduction heuristic that periodically reduces clause weights. While tabu lists had previously been used in SAT [4] and similar weight reduction schemes had already been suggested [1], the success of DLM hinges on the careful *combination* of these heuristics within a clause weighting algorithm. This is illustrated in the pseudocode for *DLM-SAT* (in Figure 1) which is derived from *DLM-98-BASIC-SAT*, *DLM-99-SAT* [10] and the *DLM-2000-SAT* source code [11]. It represents the key features of DLM without the later *DISTANCE-PENALTY* and *SPECIAL-INCREASE* heuristics (designed to solve the harder parity, graph and hanoi problems). We present *DLM-SAT* in some detail as this algorithm acts as the base for our further development and also to isolate the three main parameters used to tune DLM to particular problem domains, namely the tabu list length (TABU), the maximum number of flat moves allowed (FLAT) and the number of weight increases before a weight decrease occurs (DECREASE).

Weight Reduction in DLM and SDF. *DLM-SAT* extends clause weighting by using a weight reduction scheme controlled by the DECREASE parameter shown in Figure 1. This scheme reduces the weights on all *weighted* clauses by a standard decrement (usually one) after the search has added weight DECREASE times. Weight increases are also of a simple additive nature. Other weighting schemes, most notably SDF [6], have used multiplicative weighting and a continuous normalisation of relative weights after each increase. While SDF has produced some improvement over DLM in terms of the flip count on smaller sized problems, there is a significant run-time overhead in maintaining SDF's real valued weights. This is caused by having to recalculate the weights on *all* clauses each time weight is added. In contrast, DLM only updates false clause weights during an increase (generally less than 5% of the total clauses) and then only updates *weighted* clauses during a reduction (with reductions occurring after each DECREASE number of weight increases). As the run-times in [6] show, SDF is up to 4 times slower than DLM, a result largely explained by the different operation of the weight control schemes.

   While multiplicative weighting and weight smoothing offer a less ad-hoc approach to weight control, DLM's additive reduction scheme works well in practice, is more efficient and is controlled by a single parameter (rather than the two required for SDF). For these reasons we decided to continue with a DLM type scheme in our own simplified clause weighting scheme described in Section 2.3.

Tabu Lists and Short-Term Memory. The second of DLM's extensions to clause weighting is the use of a tabu list to control the selection of non-cost improving moves. Earlier SAT heuristics, such as HSAT [2], used a similar approach to break ties between equal cost moves based on when a variable was last flipped. DLM's tabu list differs from these strategies by storing the most recently flipped variables in a list, the length of which is set by the TABU parameter (see Figure 1). Any variable on the list is then *tabu* and cannot be flipped unless it produces a cost improvement. The rationale behind a tabu list is to avoid cycles of repeated moves and assist the search to escape from a local minimum [3]. In DLM's case, clause weighting already acts as a minima escaping

procedure *DLM-SAT*
begin
    Generate a random starting point
    $bestWeightedCost \leftarrow$ number of false clauses
    Initialise counters and clause weights to zero
    while solution not found and $flips <$ maxFlips **do**
        $B \leftarrow$ set of best weighted cost single flip moves
        if no improving $x \in B$ **then**
            Remove all $x \in B$ with $flips - tabuAge(x) <$ TABU
        if weighted cost $< bestWeightedCost$ **then**
            $bestWeightedCost \leftarrow$ weighted cost
            $flatMoves \leftarrow 0$
        else if $++flatMoves >$ FLAT and no improving $x \in B$ **then**
            $B \leftarrow \emptyset$
            $flatMoves \leftarrow 0$
        end if
        if $B \neq \emptyset$ **then**
            Randomly pick and flip $x \in B$
            $flips \leftarrow flips + 1$
            if $flips - tabuAge(x) >$ TABU **then**
                $tabuAge(x) \leftarrow flips$
        else
            Increase weight on all false clauses
            if $++increases \%$ DECREASE $= 0$ **then**
                Decrease weight on all weighted clauses
                $bestWeightedCost \leftarrow$ weighted cost
            end if
        end if
    end while
end

Fig. 1. The basic DLM algorithm

mechanism, so the tabu list is used primarily to navigate over plateaus (i.e. areas in the search space where there are no cost improving moves). Simple clause weighting algorithms generally deal with plateaus by immediately adding weight [5] whereas the tabu list in DLM delays the weight increase in order to explore a plateau more thoroughly. Given that clause weighting when combined with a weight reduction scheme is itself a form of short-term memory [1], the question arises why DLM requires a *another* short-term memory heuristic (namely a tabu list) to search plateaus.

2.3 Simplified Clause Weighting

Eliminating the Tabu List. Our aim in this study is to produce a simplified clause weighting algorithm, and particularly to reduce the number of parameters required to tune an algorithm to different problem domains. From our analysis of clause weighting, and DLM in particular, we identified two basic choices that define the effectiveness of a search:

- When and by how much to *increase* clause weights
- When and by how much to *reduce* clause weights

DLM uses both the TABU and FLAT parameters to decide on weight increases, i.e. either weights are increased because the maximum number of flat moves has been exceeded or because all plateau moves have become tabu. Similarly, the DECREASE parameter is used to decide when to reduce weights. On the basis of our discussion in Section 2.2 we decided to eliminate the TABU and FLAT parameters from *DLM-SAT* by removing the tabu list, and so to look for a simpler approach to increase weights and control plateau searches. Early clause weighting algorithms avoided plateau search by adding weight as soon as a plateau is encountered [5]. However, we found such techniques do not scale well to larger problems (even if a weight reduction scheme is included). We therefore decided to randomise the choice between adding weight or taking a plateau move (see Figure 2). While this creates another potential parameter, we found the best plateau move selection probability P remains fairly constant across different problem domains (see Section 3). In addition P replaces replaces *both* the TABU and FLAT parameters from *DLM-SAT*.

The Maximum Age Heuristic. An analysis of the TABU parameter settings for DLM shows an unusually long list length is required to solve the larger DIMACS random 3-SAT problems [9]. Our randomised plateau move selection heuristic assumes sufficient information is stored in the clause weights alone to guide the search trajectory. However, the longer tabu list for 3-SAT suggests a longer term-memory is sometimes useful (as pointed out in [1], clause weight reduction schemes provide only *short-term* memory). We therefore developed a maximum age (*MAX-AGE*) heuristic to exploit longer-term information about when a variable was last flipped. As with a tabu list, *MAX-AGE* stores the number of flips since a variable was last flipped (this is a variable's age). However, instead of using a list, the age of each plateau flip is compared to a *maximum age* value, where *maximum age = total flips - maximum age counter* and *maximum age counter* is incremented each time *MAX-AGE* causes a plateau move to be accepted. If the age of a plateau move equals or exceeds *maximum age* then it is accepted, otherwise we use our randomised selection heuristic described above. In this way the search is biased towards flipping rarely used variables and is encouraged to occasionally take steps into previously unexplored regions (the complete *MAX-AGE* algorithm is shown in Figure 2).

3   Empirical Analysis

As our work is based on the original DLM algorithms, we decided to evaluate *MAX-AGE* in comparison with the most recent publicly available version of DLM, namely *DLM-2000-SAT* (or *DLM2K*). *DLM2K* contains the *SPECIAL-INCREASE* heuristic described in [10] and developed to solve the harder DIMACS parity learning, Towers of Hanoi and graph colouring problems. Secondly, for a more direct comparison, we generated

procedure *MAX-AGE*
begin
    Generate a random starting point
    Initialise counters and clause weights to zero
    while solution not found and $flips <$ maxFlips **do**
        $B \leftarrow$ set of best weighted cost single flip moves
        if no improving $x \in B$ **then**
            if oldest $x \in B$ has $age(x) \geq maxAge$ **then**
                $B \leftarrow x$
                $maxAge \leftarrow maxAge + 1$
            else if $random(p) \leq P$ **then**
                $B \leftarrow \emptyset$
            end if
        end if
        if $B \neq \emptyset$ **then**
            Randomly pick and flip $x \in B$
            $age(x) \leftarrow ++flips$
        else
            Increase weight on all false clauses
            if $++increases$ % DECREASE = 0 **then**
                Decrease weight on all weighted clauses
        end if
        end if
    end while
end

Fig. 2. The MAX-AGE Algorithm

results for the *DLM-SAT* algorithm shown in Figure 1. *DLM-SAT* is our own cut-down version of DLM that uses only the TABU, FLAT and DECREASE parameters, but is otherwise is derived from *DLM2K*. Finally, we generated results for the *MAX-AGE* algorithm from Figure 2, which alters *DLM-SAT* by replacing the tabu list and the TABU and FLAT parameters with the heuristics described previously in Section 2.3 (for further comparison of DLM with other leading SAT algorithms see [9], [10] and [6]).

3.1   Problem Domains

For our problem set we chose the four problem domains for which existing DLM parameters have already been developed (namely random 3-SAT, parity learning, graph colouring and blocks world). Using the DIMACS benchmarks we selected *f400* to *f3200* for random 3-SAT, *par16-1-c* to *par16-5-c* for parity learning, all the *g* graph colouring problems and the SATLIB *bw-large-a* to *bw-large-d* for blocks world. Due to the length of run-times, we did not produce a full set of results for the more difficult unsimplified *par16*, *par32* and *hanoi* problems. However we did confirm that *DLM2K* has the superior performance for these problems (due to the operation of the *SPECIAL-INCREASE* heuristic). We expect the addition of an equivalent heuristic to *MAX-AGE* would produce a similar performance improvement, but did not explore this option as it adds a further parameter to the problem.

3.2 Parameter Setting

One of the main advantages of *MAX-AGE* is that it eliminates the task of setting the TABU and FLAT parameters. We were therefore able to quickly tune *MAX-AGE* by selecting a single problem from each domain and varying the value of DECREASE until an optimum point was found. The probability P of taking a plateau move in *MAX-AGE* was treated as a constant and set at 0.85, although we did examine the effects of varying P on several example problems (see Section 3.3). For *DLM-SAT* we took the published values of FLAT and TABU for each domain, but again experimented with varying DECREASE to see if the optimum DECREASE for *DLM-SAT* was equivalent to *MAX-AGE* (the final DECREASE values for each method are shown in the D column of Table 1). Finally the *DLM2K* parameters were read directly from the *dlmparam* files supplied for each problem domain with the *DLM2K* source code.

3.3 Results

The average flips over 100 runs on the complete problem set, allowing 100 million flips per run, are shown in Table 1. In Table 2 we present the median flips (to provide an idea of the shorter-term behaviour of *DLM-SAT* and *MAX-AGE*) and the CPU time usage for each method and problem.

The average flip data in Table 1 shows *MAX-AGE* performs competitively with *DLM-SAT* and that both *MAX-AGE* and *DLM-SAT* can equal or exceed *DLM2K* on all four problem domains. In particular, *MAX-AGE* achieves above average performance on the *par16* problems and equals *DLM2K* on the harder graph colouring *g* problems. The graph colouring results are interesting because *DLM-SAT* performs considerably worse on these problems, implying that the *SPECIAL-INCREASE* heuristic in *DLM2K* is playing an important role which *MAX-AGE* is able to replace. However, on the larger *par* and *hanoi* problems (not reported here) *SPECIAL-INCREASE* still provides a decisive advantage.

The median flips data in Table 2 shows a similar pattern to the average flips data, indicating neither *MAX-AGE* or *DLM-SAT* would gain an advantage from a random restarts strategy (this was confirmed by further estimates of expected flips, based on the work in [6]). However the CPU time usage does highlight an additional overhead of 10-20% for *MAX-AGE* in comparison to *DLM-SAT*. This is caused by *MAX-AGE* only accepting 15% of plateau flips and otherwise increasing weight. Weight increases create overhead in terms of updating the flip cost of each affected variable. Both *DLM* techniques avoid a proportion of this cost by searching plateaus more extensively under the control of the tabu list. However *MAX-AGE*'s overhead is not as significant as that imposed by the alternative multiplicate weighting schemes of SDF and ESG, and on several problems *MAX-AGE*'s performance increase outweighs the time penalty.

Finally, we examined the effects of varying the value of P from 0.6 to 0.95 in *MAX-AGE* across the whole problem set. These experiments showed that P does affect performance, but no clear pattern emerged. For instance, on the 3-SAT *f* problems a P value of 0.85 is consistently better whereas on the *par* problems the optimum value ranges from 0.8 to 0.95 and on the larger *g* problems a value of 0.8 works better. Given this variation, treating P as a constant at 0.85 appears the best compromise, although meeting another problem domain where a significantly different value P is required

Table 1. Average flips and DECREASE parameter (D)

Average Flips over 100 runs						
Problem	D	DLM2K	D	DLM-SAT	D	MAX-AGE
f400	12	11,853	10	8,265	9	6,787
f600	12	66,846	10	33,947	9	30,745
f800	12	463,173	10	150,826	9	154,048
f1000	12	303,784	10	136,140	9	157,357
f1600	12	5,597,990	10	1,990,000	9	3,134,047
f2000	12	678,294	10	1,140,000	9	1,014,339
f3200	12	6,268,780	10	4,458,820	9	7,319,200
g125.17	7	813,463	6	1,693,360	4	729,628
g125.18	7	8,876	6	23,645	4	13,171
g250.15	7	2,309	6	2,272	4	2,212
g250.29	7	342,935	6	744,337	4	374,155
par16-1-c	46	3,917,350	40	2,771,220	40	1,958,802
par16-2-c	46	8,018,580	40	5,818,140	40	4,272,580
par16-3-c	46	6,920,230	40	5,672,240	40	3,941,307
par16-4-c	46	6,413,150	40	3,969,650	40	2,579,460
par16-5-c	46	6,150,910	40	5,236,300	40	4,269,350
bw-large.a	5	4,911	4	4,786	5	4,596
bw-large.b	5	51,203	4	54,480	5	76,968
bw-large.c	5	2,608,970	4	1,305,650	5	1,146,401
bw-large.d	5	6,992,680	4	2,082,610	5	1,746,582

would change our conclusions. Overall the results indicate that the tabu list and it's associated parameters in DLM can be replaced by simpler clause weighting approach without loss of performance. Although DLM's tabu list has some run-time advantage over using weights to escape plateaus (by adding weight less often), *MAX-AGE* balances this by showing more robust performance over the problem set, especially in outperforming *DLM-SAT* on the *par16* problems and matching the performance of *DLM2K* on the larger graph colouring problems (without using *SPECIAL-INCREASE*). Additionally, *MAX-AGE* has the advantage of not having to tune the length of the tabu list to each problem domain, or to decide on the optimum number of flat moves before adding weight.

4 Conclusions

The aim of this study was to produce a simplified clause weighting algorithm with comparable performance to the state-of-the-art SAT techniques. To this end we have developed the single parameter *MAX-AGE* algorithm and shown it to have comparable and, in some cases, superior performance with the latest versions of *DLM*. In terms of the future development of clause weighting algorithms *MAX-AGE* has highlighted two points:

Table 2. Median flips and CPU usage

Problem	DLM-SAT			MAX-AGE		
	Median Flips	CPU Time	Flips/ Sec.	Median Flips	CPU Time	Flips/ Sec.
f400	5,411	0.08	103,313	5,545	0.07	102,209
f600	27,875	0.35	96,991	22,533	0.34	90,507
f800	94,173	1.85	81,528	102,000	2.18	70,671
f1000	95,373	1.74	78,241	106,717	2.32	67,718
f1600	1,395,129	29.24	68,049	1,990,812	57.69	54,328
f2000	705,188	17.55	64,959	554,880	17.97	56,616
f3200	10,441,781	90.94	49,028	2,682,022	134.25	54,521
g125.17	1,148,187	100.49	16,851	607,922	53.31	13,687
g125.18	15,638	1.47	15,997	10,187	2.92	4,514
g250.15	2,257	17.34	131	2,199	18.15	122
g250.29	490,777	196.24	3,793	315,791	144.02	2,598
par16-1-c	1,901,390	21.94	126,284	1,383,090	17.72	110,549
par16-2-c	4,296,443	46.48	125,175	3,505,468	38.74	110,278
par16-3-c	3,805,261	44.45	127,617	2,849,531	34.61	113,882
par16-4-c	2,604,387	31.39	126,452	1,859,387	22.75	113,374
par16-5-c	3,474,445	40.65	128,799	3,168,043	37.56	113,657
bw-large.a	3,412	0.01	59,825	3,697	0.08	56,191
bw-large.b	36,111	1.14	47,789	62,840	1.56	49,209
bw-large.c	718,075	37.23	35,072	719,077	37.26	30,768
bw-large.d	1,364,447	118.80	17,531	1,023,887	96.91	18,023

- the use of a tabu list and its associated parameters is not a necessary feature of an efficient clause weighting technique.
- additive weighting schemes can be simply controlled by a single parameter and can be more efficiently implemented than alternative multiplicative schemes.

We consider *MAX-AGE* as a step towards developing more intelligent constraint solving technologies that do not rely on a manual fine-tuning of parameters. In future work we will look further into predicting the best value of the remaining DECREASE parameter via an analysis of various run-time measures and incorporate this within a self-tuning algorithm. Also for further research is the incorporation of parameter-free versions of *DLM*'s *SPECIAL-INCREASE* and/or *DISTANCE-PENALTY* into *MAX-AGE* to improve performance on the more difficult DIMACS benchmark problems.

References

1. J. Frank. Learning short term weights for GSAT. In "Proceedings *of the Fourteenth National Conference on Artificial Intelligence (AAAI-97)*, pages 384–389, 1997.

2. I. Gent and T. Walsh. Towards an understanding of hill-climbing procedures for SAT. In *Proceedings of the Eleventh National Conference on Artificial Intelligence (AAAI-93)*, pages 28–33, 1993.
3. F. Glover. Tabu search: Part 1. *ORSA Journal on Computing*, 1(3):190–206, 1989.
4. B. Mazure, S. Lakhdar, and E. Gregoire. Tabu search for SAT. In *Proceedings of the Fourteenth National Conference on Artificial Intelligence (AAAI-97)*, pages 281–285, 1997.
5. P. Morris. The Breakout method for escaping local minima. In *Proceedings of the Eleventh National Conference on Artificial Intelligence (AAAI-93)*, pages 40–45, 1993.
6. D. Schuurmans and F. Southey. Local search characteristics of incomplete SAT procedures. In *Proceedings of the Seventeenth National Conference on Artificial Intelligence (AAAI-00)*, pages 297–302, 2000.
7. D. Schuurmans, F. Southey, and R. Holte. The exponentiated subgradient algorithm for heuristic Boolean programming. In *Proceedings of the Seventeenth International Joint Conference on Artificial Intelligence (IJCAI-01)*, pages 334–341, 2001.
8. B. Selman and H. Kautz. Domain-independent extensions to GSAT: Solving large structured satisfiability problems. In *Proceedings of the Thirteenth International Joint Conference on Artificial Intelligence (IJCAI-93)*, pages 290–295, 1993.
9. Y. Shang and B. Wah. A discrete Lagrangian-based global search method for solving satisfiability problems. *J. Global Optimization*, 12:61–99, 1998.
10. Z. Wu and B. Wah. Trap escaping strategies in discrete Lagrangian methods for solving hard satisfiability and maximum satisfiability problems. In *Proceedings of the Sixteenth National Conference on Artificial Intelligence (AAAI-99)*, pages 673–678, 1999.
11. Z. Wu and B. Wah. An efficient global-search strategy in discrete Lagrangian methods for solving hard satisfiability problems. In *Proceedings of the Seventeenth National Conference on Artificial Intelligence (AAAI-00)*, pages 310–315, 2000.

An Investigation of Variable Relationships in 3-SAT Problems

Olena Kravchuk, Wayne Pullan, John Thornton, and Abdul Sattar

School of Information Technology,
Griffith University Gold Coast,
Qld, 4215, Australia
{o.kravchuk, w.pullan, j.thornton, a.sattar}@mailbox.gu.edu.au

Abstract. To date, several types of structure for finite Constraint Satisfaction Problems have been investigated with the goal of either improving the performance of problem solvers or allowing efficient problem solvers to be identified. Our aim is to extend the work in this area by performing a structural analysis in terms of variable connectivity for 3-SAT problems. Initially structure is defined in terms of the compactness of variable connectivity for a problem. Using an easily calculable statistic developed to measure this compactness, a test was then created for identifying 3-SAT problems as either compact, loose or unstructured (or uniform). A problem generator was constructed for generating 3-SAT problems with varying degrees of structure. Using problems from this problem generator and existing problems from SATLIB, we investigated the effects of this type of structure on satisfiability and solvability of 3-SAT problems. For the same problem length, it is demonstrated that satisfiability and solvability are different for structured and uniform problems generated by the problem generator.

Keywords: Constraints, Search

1 Introduction

Non-randomness in Constraint Satisfaction Problems (CSPs) has generated considerable interest in the CSP community [1]. This has resulted in a number of alternative models for generating CSPs with more realistic structures than using random models [2]. However it is still not possible to provide conclusions other than straight-forward ones such as: sometimes structured problems differ from non-structured in their characteristics. Partially such uncertainty is explained by the lack of a clear definition of structure. Although there has been some work on statistically classifying problem structure using symmetry [3], the level of interchangeability [4], clustering coefficient [5] and backbone size ([6], [7]) and approximate entropy [8], generally a problem is called structured if it is not uniformly random. As a consequence, research in the field has produced polar conclusions: in [4] it was noted that real-world structured problems have greater simplicity than randomly generated problems, while in [6] it was suggested that harder problems can be constructed by perturbations of regular problems. In [9] it was demonstrated that structure affects algorithm performance, while in [10] no noticeable effects were reported. It is important to note here that in this previous work, no statistical tests of specific structure have been proposed. Therefore, conclusions on structured

R.I. McKay and J. Slaney (Eds.): AI 2002, LNAI 2557, pp. 579–590, 2002.

problems were generally conclusions on the properties of generators, as problems were not tested independently for the structure investigated ([3], [4], [6]).

This study focusses on the k-SAT problem which is a special class of the Conjunctive Normal Form (CNF) problem with precisely k variables per clause, and has become a popular test-class for the properties of random problems ([11],[12]). Many important characteristics of k-SAT problems such as cross-over points, phase transition regions and satisfiability points have been studied experimentally and analytical [13].

A simple uniform binary model allows one to analyse some phenomena of k-SAT problems. The uniform binary model is a composition of two processes, one which randomly builds or selects clauses and a second which randomly negates the variables [11]. Therefore it is possible to induce a structure, in the sense of non-uniformity, for either the first or the second processes. In this paper we develop a test of non-uniformity in selecting clauses, and investigate the influence of such a structure on the satisfiability and solvability of 3-SAT problems. Satisfiability is the generic property of a problem to have at least one solution, while solvability is solver specific and is the property that the problem is able to be solved by that solver within a certain number of steps.

The remainder of this paper is structured as follows: Section 2 discusses uniform and non-uniform models for random 3-SAT problems and shows that a problem can be considered as a realization of a certain random process. Section 3 introduces a test-statistic for uniformity and investigates the distribution of the statistic for a uniformly generated 3-SAT problem, which is treated as a realization of a non-decreasing, transient discrete Markov chain. We then show examples of applications of the test to groups of problems taken from the SATLIB library [14]. Section 4 presents a structured 3-SAT problem generator using the random process developed in Section 3, introduces parameters into the problem generator and derives testable ranges for these parameters. Section 5 discusses the results obtained for two groups of tests: firstly, a test for differences in satisfiability for uniform and structured problems generated by the problem generator and, secondly, a test on differences in solvability (i.e. effort required to find a solution by a particular solver) for uniform and non-uniform problems. In Section 6 we discuss the effects of structure, in terms of variable connectivity, on the satisfiability and solvability of problems and outline the most important characteristics of the test-statistic and problem generator. Finally some directions for future research are presented.

2   Uniform and Non-uniform Binary Models for 3-SAT Problems

2.1   A Uniform Binary Model as a Two-Step Model

A 3-SAT problem is a constraint formula in conjunctive normal form with 3 variables (literals) per clause. We denote the number of clauses in a 3-SAT problem by M and the number of variables by N. The uniform binary model (often referred to as the uniform random model [15], or as the exact 1-SAT model [10], or as the uniform model [14]) uniformly selects M clauses from N3 possible combinations of variables, and then uniformly negates variables in each selected clause. The uniform binary model can be considered as a realization of two random processes: one governs adjacency of variables and another the negation of variables. By utilising non-uniform rules for how to group or negate variables, we can induce structure in either or both of the processes. In this paper we focus only on the induction of structure into the process of grouping of variables (i.e. the selecting of clauses).

2.2 Definition of a Non-uniform Binary Model

In the uniform binary model, all clauses are selected uniformly. That is, there is no underlying reason why any particular group of clauses will be selected in preference to any other group of clauses. Consequently we can define a non-uniform problem as a problem in which **there are underlying reasons that cause the condition of uniformity for selecting clauses to be violated**. We will categorise non-uniform problems as either *loose* or *compact*. A problem is loose if there is a tendency for any two clauses to share at most one variable. A problem is compact if there is a tendency that any two clauses share at least two variables. These definitions of structure can be formalized as follows. Let us denote by $n(c_i \cap c_j)$ the number of common elements in two clauses $c_i, c_j, \forall i, \forall j, i \neq j$. In a compact problem, the probability $P(\cdot)$ that any two clauses intersect in more than one variable, is greater than the same probability under the uniform model $\bar{P}(\cdot)$. In a loose problem, the probability that any two clauses intersect in no less than two variables is greater than the same probability for the uniform binary model. Fig. 1 illustrates both loose and compact problems according to this definition.

$$\text{compact: } P(n(c_i \cap c_j) > 1) > \bar{P}(n(c_i \cap c_j) > 1), \tag{1}$$

$$\text{loose: } P(n(c_i \cap c_j) < 2) < \bar{P}(n(c_i \cap c_j) < 2). \tag{2}$$

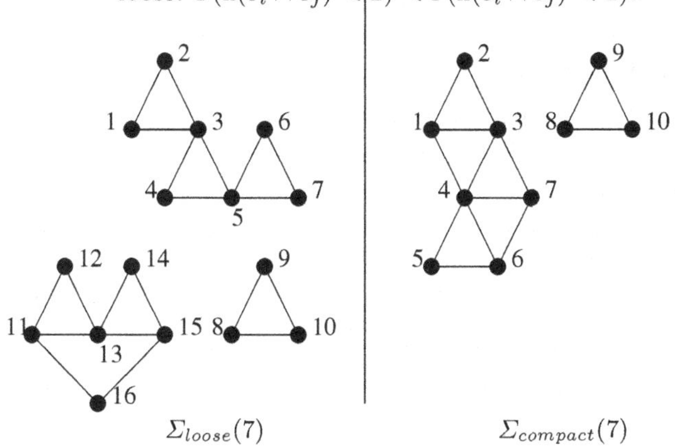

$$\Sigma_{loose}(7) \qquad\qquad \Sigma_{compact}(7)$$

Fig. 1. Planar representation of both loose and compact problems where $M = 7$ ($\Sigma_{loose} = (\neg 1 \vee 2 \vee 3) \wedge (3 \vee \neg 4 \vee 5) \wedge (5 \vee 6 \vee \neg 7) \wedge (\neg 8 \vee 9 \vee \neg 10) \wedge (11 \vee \neg 12 \vee 13) \wedge (\neg 13 \vee 14 \vee 15) \wedge (\neg 11 \vee \neg 15 \vee \neg 16)$, $N_0(7) = 21$) ($\Sigma_{compact} = (1 \vee 2 \vee 3) \wedge (\neg 1 \vee 2 \vee \neg 3) \wedge (1 \vee \neg 3 \vee 4) \wedge (3 \vee \neg 7 \vee 4) \wedge (4 \vee 7 \vee \neg 6) \wedge (\neg 4 \vee 5 \vee 6) \wedge (8 \vee 9 \vee \neg 10)$, $N_0(7) = 14$)

The definitions in (1)–(2) can be used to develop a non-uniform model. In the non-uniform model, to construct a compact problem containing M clauses, starting from the ith clause ($i > 2$, $i \ll M$), in the formula, we will, with high probability, add a clause to the formula if it intersects with at least one already selected clause in no less than two variables. Similarly, for the loose problem of size M, starting from the ith clause, $(i > 2,\ i \ll M)$, we will, with high probability, add a clause to the formula if it intersects with any selected clause in no more than one variable.

In the following section we develop a test on uniformity of 3-SAT problems which detects structure of the type defined by (1) - (2).

3   Testing for Uniformity

In Section 2, we have defined non-uniformity in random problems. To detect the structure defined by (1) - (2) requires a test which classifies a problem as either compact, loose or uniform. Therefore, for the test of uniformity, we have the following set of hypotheses:

Null hypothesis: The problem is uniformly randomly generated.
Compact alternative: The problem is not uniform but rather possesses a structure as defined by the compact model (1).
Loose alternative: The problem is not uniform but rather possesses a structure as defined by the loose model (2).

Note that, as for any statistical test, we are looking for some specific type of non-uniformity. If there is another reason for a problem to be non-uniform, our test may not detect this.

3.1   Zero Step Related Variable Pairs as a Test Statistic

Definition of Step Related Variable Pairs. To carry out the proposed test of uniformity, we require a statistic that is independent of the order of clauses. In this study we have used the number of zero step related variable pairs, $N_0(M)$, as the test statistic which is simply the count of the number of pairs of variables that appear at least once in the same clause in the problem. That is, $N_0(M)$ is the number of edges, counted without repetitions, which appear in the adjacency graph for the problem. The expected value for $N_0(M)$ for a uniform binary 3-SAT problem is given by the recurrence relation shown in Eq. (3) (where $N_0(0) = 0$) and is illustrated by Fig. 2. $N_0(M)$ is the first in a family of statistics $N_k(M)$ which could be used to classify problems in terms of the step relationships between variables. For example, in Fig. 1, $\Sigma_{loose}(7)$, variables 1 and 2 are zero step related, 2 and 4 are one step related while 2 and 6 are two step related. The general recurrence relation for $N_k(M)$, $\forall k \geq 1$ is given by (4) and shown in Fig. 2 for $N_1(M)$, $N_2(M)$ and $N_3(M)$.

$$E[N_0(i+1)] = N_0(i) + 3 - \frac{3N_0(i)}{N(N-1)/2}\ i \geq 0 \tag{3}$$

$$E[N_k(i+1)] = N_k(i) + 9 \times 2^{k+1} \frac{i}{N}\left(1 - \frac{2}{N(N-1)}\sum_{j=0}^{k} N_j(i)\right)\ \forall k \geq 1, i \geq 0 \tag{4}$$

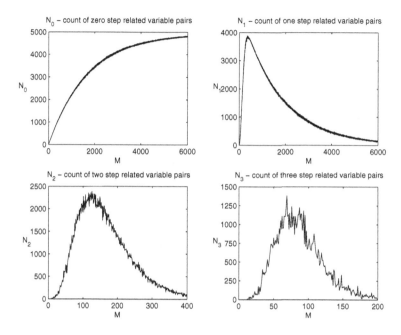

Fig. 2. Counts of step related variable pairs for uniform binary model for $N_0(M)$, $N_1(M)$, $N_2(M)$ and $N_3(M)$ where $N = 100$

$N_0(M)$ is the most suitable statistic from the $N_k(M)$ family to be used as a test statistic because $N_2(M)$ and $N_3(M)$ quickly diminish and would require sampling techniques if used for moderate size problems.

For a problem of size M, we consider how $N_0(M)$ is distributed under the null hypothesis that the problem is uniformly generated. Knowing this null-distribution we can reject or accept the hypothesis of uniformity with a certain level of confidence, measured by the probability to have the given value for $N_0(M)$ from the uniform model.

Null-distribution of $N_0(M)$. We consider a uniform problem as a realization of a non-decreasing transient discrete Markov chain, so that when uniformly selecting a clause, we can add to the collection of zero step related pairs k ($k \in \{0, 1, 2, 3\}$) new pairs from $K = \binom{N}{2}$ pairs. Then the distribution of $N_0(M)$ is completely determined by the matrix of transient probabilities on the chain. By the nature of $N_0(M)$, the larger the problem, the less the distinction between non-structured and structured problems. In the limit, when all pairs of variables are selected, $N_0(M)$ converges to K, regardless of how the problem was generated. However when $N > 10$ and $1 \ll M \ll \binom{N}{3}$, the transient probability p_{ik} to move from state i, $i \in [3, K]$, to state $i + k$ at the $(n+1)^{th}$, $n \in [2, M)$, added clause is:

$$p_{ik} = P(N_0(n+1) = i + k | N_0(n) = i) = \binom{3}{k} \left(\frac{i}{K}\right)^{3-k} \left(1 - \frac{i}{K}\right)^k \quad (5)$$

For a reasonable problem size, the probability to have at least i zero-related pairs in a problem of size M, $\bar{P}(N_0(M) \leq i)$ can be calculated by enumeration, and we use this method for calculations in this study.

The cumulative probability of $N_0(430)$, shown in Fig. 3, demonstrates the symmetry of the distribution that makes $N_0(M)$ appropriate for many statistical tests.

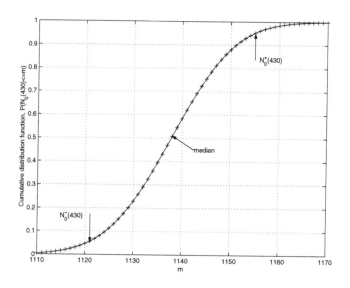

Fig. 3. Cumulative probability of $N_0(430)$ where m is zero step related pairs. The median is at 1138 pairs, the critical region is $N_0^-(430) = 1121$, $N_0^+(430) = 1153$.

For the purpose of our test, we first determine a critical region for $N_0(M)$. This is the domain of values of $N_0(M)$ where the probability of occurring under the null distribution is less than some value α. For our classification of problems as loose and compact, we denote $N_0^+(M)$ and $N_0^-(M)$ as the boundaries (loose and compact) of this critical region, and define the boundaries as follows:

$$\begin{aligned} \bar{P}(N_0(M) \leq N_0^-(M)) &\approx \alpha, \\ \bar{P}(N_0(M) > N_0^+(M)) &\approx \alpha, \end{aligned} \quad (6)$$

where α is a given confidence level that determines the error we allow for our conclusions. In all experiments reported in this study we use the approximate 5%-confidence level for both alternative hypotheses. The boundaries of the critical region for $M = 430$ and a confidence level of 5% are shown in Fig. 3 where $N_0^+(430) = 1153$ and $N_0^-(430) = 1121$.

Uniformity test procedure. For a given problem, the test is performed as follows:

1. Determine the number of variables (N) and the number of clauses (M) in the problem;
2. For the pair(N, M), calculate the critical region for the chosen confidence level α;
3. Determine the number of zero related pairs $N_0(M)$ in the given problem;
4. Reject the hypothesis of uniformity if $N_0(M)$ is in the critical region, otherwise, accept the uniformity.

At this point, we have only discussed the test in application to a problem in determining whether the problem is uniformly generated or compact/loose. However, $N_0(M)$ could also be utilised for the more general question of problem classification of 3-SAT problems. That is, is a proposed classification of 3-SAT problems justifiable (rather than just a random grouping of problems).

Test of Randomness Procedure. As we know the distribution of $N_0(M)$, we know the median of the distribution (Fig. 3). Having a group of problems of the same size from the same number of variables, we can test whether the group is a random selection by applying the standard test of randomness [16]. For every problem in the group, the probability to have $N_0(M)$ greater or less than the median is equal to 0.5. Therefore, if in the group we have an unusually large or small number of problems having $N_0(M)$ above (or below) the median, we can conclude that the group is not a random selection but has been selected using some criteria related to our definition of problem structure.

3.2   Tests on Problems from SATLIB

Uniform 3-SAT problems. This test was performed using 3-SAT problems taken from SATLIB (Uniform Random 3-SAT, phase transition region, unforced filtered). From the description given in SATLIB of the model generator for this set of problems, we would expect no regularity in the problems so the test should not conclude any evidence that a problem is non-uniformly generated. In other words, if there is any difference in the behaviour of problem solvers, such a difference cannot be explained by problem structure (1) - (2). As shown in Fig. 3, the critical region for uniform problems where $M = 430$ and $N = 100$ is $N_0^-(430) = 1121$, $N_0^+(430) = 1155$ that corresponds to the 5% confidence level. The median of $N_0(430)$ is 1138. Table 1 shows that a sample from the library (uf100-430) is in a very good agreement with our expectations: no structure is demonstrated, and the random sample is indeed random (i.e. there are approximately the same number of problems above and below the median).

Random 3-SAT models with controlled backbone size. We tested 3-SAT models taken from the SATLIB library with Controlled Backbone Size (CBS) where the backbone of a problem is basically the intersection of all solutions of the problem [7]. It is stated in SATLIB that every CBS problem was uniformly generated. Therefore, similar to what has been discussed for uniform random problems from the SATLIB, we do not expect any detection of structure under the test for any particular CBS problem. However, if we

Table 1. $N_0(430)$ for a random sample from Uniform Random 3-SAT from SATLIB, the uf100-430 series, format uf100-0###.cnf; and acceptance (A) or rejection (R) of the null-hypothesis under the critical region: $N_0^-(430) = 1121$ or $N_0^+(430) = 1155$; and the sign test on randomness.

###	107	108	119	122	125	132	146	151	170	180	187	216	224	225	228
N_0	1147	1139	1140	1149	1147	1136	1132	1133	1130	1117	1139	1153	1135	1139	1138
H_0	A	A	A	A	A	A	A	A	A	R	A	A	A	A	A
Sign	+	+	+	+	+	-	-	-	-	-	+	+	-	+	0

believe that the size of backbone is an informative statistic which is somehow connected to problem structure, we would expect that the group of CBS problems is not a random selection from uniformly generated problems. Table 2 shows that it is unlikely for the group of CBS problems to be a randomly selected group from uniformly generated problems, and therefore, with high confidence ($\alpha < 0.5\%$), it can be concluded that a backbone size is a valid criteria for the problems' classification.

Table 2. $N_0(429)$ for a random sample from problems with controlled backbones for the CBS_k3_n100_m429_b90_###.cnf series from SATLIB; acceptance (A) or rejection (R) of the null-hypothesis of uniformity under the critical region: $N_0^-(429) = 1119$ or $N_0^+(429) = 1153$; and the sign test on randomness of the sample from uniformly generated problems (the median of $N_0(429)$ is 1136).

###	107	108	119	122	125	132	146	151	170	180	187	216	224	225	228
N_0	1123	1135	1141	1130	1129	1125	1123	1137	1133	1132	1107	1121	1124	1120	1125
H_0	A	A	A	A	A	A	A	A	A	A	R	A	A	A	A
Sign	-	-	+	-	-	-	-	+	-	-	-	-	-	-	-

4   Problem Generator with Prescribed Non-uniformity

4.1   Markov Chain Underlying the Problem Generator

The uniform model can be considered as a realization of a random process of adding pairs into zero step relationships for every new clause selected. The process is a non-decreasing discrete Markov chain with finitely many states. Starting from some group of selected clauses, the chain can be considered as homogeneous, with transition probabilities given by (5).

4.2   Problem Generator

Problem Generator Algorithm. The problem generator performs the following steps to generate a problem of M clauses from N variables:

1. Uniformly selects a clause from all possible clauses.
2. Uniformly negates variables in the clause.
3. If the clause has not already been added, with some probability p (see below) add the clause.
4. Repeats Steps 1 - 4 until M clauses have been selected.

Problem Generator Parameters. The problem generator is a random generator with six parameters $G(N, M, \Pi)$, where N is the number of variables, M is the number of clauses, and $\Pi = (p_0, p_1, p_2, p_3)$ are probabilities to add a clause if it, correspondingly, adds 0, 1, 2, 3 new zero step related pairs ($G(N, M, (1, 1, 1, 1))$) generates a uniform binary problem). By using appropriate probabilities $p_i, i \in [0, 3]$, the problem generator will either produce a loose or compact problem. The generated problem is then evaluated using the test discussed in Section 3 to check that the problem is indeed structured. From a sensitivity analysis performed on the generator, we have determined that when $p_i \in (0.0 - 0.5)$, $i \in [0, 3]$, the generated problems are structured.

5   Tests on Properties of Uniform and Non-uniform 3-SAT Problems

In this section we analyze satisfiability and solvability of structured and uniform problems. For two classes of problems, we say that class A is more satisfiable than class B if the probability for a randomly selected problem in class A to be satisfiable is greater than the same probability for a randomly selected problem in class B. Similarly, we say that class A has higher solvability under problem solver C than class B if the probability for a randomly selected problem from class A to be solved in a fixed number of steps by problem solver C is higher than the same probability for a randomly selected problem from class B.

5.1   Test on Similarity of Satisfiability of Uniform and Non-uniform Problems from the Generator

We aim to test whether the structure as defined in (1) - (2) affects the satisfiability of problems. For two samples A and B, we will test the hypothesis that there is no difference in satisfiability of problems from A and B against the hypothesis that the probability that an arbitrary unsatisfiable problem from the joined sample, $A + B$, belongs to A does not equal 1/2. We will apply the one-sided U-test with tied ranks [16], on experimental data gathered in Table 3. This test allows one to reject the hypothesis if sample As distribution is shifted either left or right with respect to sample Bs distribution. That is, we reject the hypothesis of similarity because sample A is from more (less) satisfiable class than sample B.

In other studies, for example [15], it has been noted that problem satisfiability changes in the so-called transition region $(M/N \approx 4.3)$. To avoid this effect, our experiments are for $M = 400$ and $N = 100$. Five groups of problems were generated using the parameters defined in Section 4 and all problems were tested for uniformity. The problems were uniform $G(100, 400, (1, 1, 1, 1))$, compact $G(100, 400, (0, 1, 1, 0.1))$ and loose $G(100, 400, (0, 0, 1, 1))$ for which no trivial insolvability was allowed. To demonstrate that the difference, if any, is not because of $p_0 = 0$, additional compact $G(100, 400, (1, 1, 0, 0.1))$ and loose $G(100, 400, (1, 1, 0, 1))$ groups of problems were used. The test was performed on random samples from the generated groups. Table 3 shows the counts of unsatisfiable problems, in groups of 10 problems generated with different parameters of the generator. In Table 3, problems are classified loose, compact and uniform for the critical region $N_0^-(400) = 1052$, $N_0^+(400) = 1084$. With $\alpha = 5\%$,

Table 3. Number of unsatisfiable problems in series of 20 random samples in 10 problems of 400 clauses from 100 variables for different degrees of structure ($N_0^+(400) = 1084$, $N_0^-(400) = 1052$); and the rejection of the hypothesis of similarity because of lower (L) satisfiability.

Π	No unsatisfiable problems	min N_0	max N_0	class	test
1-1-1-1	0 1 0 1 2 3 0 1 0 1 0 0 0 0 0 1 1 4 0	1052	1081	uniform	-
0-1-1-0.1	4 6 7 4 4 4 6 5 4 3 7 6 4 5 5 9 6 6 4 2	868	904	compact	L
0-0-1-1	0 1 1 1 2 0 0 1 0 0 0 1 1 1 0 0 0 0 0 1	1084	1100	loose	-
1-1-0-0.1	1 2 2 1 1 2 3 3 4 2 3 4 1 1 3 1 3 0 4 2	914	951	compact	L
1-1-0-1	0 0 0 1 1 0 0 0 1 0 2 0 0 0 0 0 0 0 1 1	1120	1161	loose	-

the test cannot reject the hypothesis of similarity between uniform and loose problems. However, we would not expect unsatisfiability for problems of 400 clauses from both the classes. At this size, it is more interesting to compare the compact class with loose and uniform as well. With $\alpha = 5\%$, the test rejected the hypothesis on similarity between compact and uniform problems and between compact and loose problems. Therefore, we can say that our experimental data confirms that, for the same problem size, loose and uniform problems have greater satisfiability than compact problems.

5.2 Test on Similarity in Solvability for Uniform and Non-uniform Problems

Our goal is to determine if problem structure, as defined by (1) - (2), affects problem solvability. For two samples A and B from two classes of problems, we test the hypothesis that there is no difference in solvability of these problem classes against the hypothesis that either of the problem classes is more difficult, i.e. the probability that a problem from sample A is harder than an arbitrary problem from sample B does not equal 0.5. By applying the one-sided U-test, [16], on experimental data gathered in Table 4 we will be able to state that the hypothesis of similarity can be rejected because sample A is from a more difficult (easier) class than sample B.

For the reasons given in the test on similarity in satisfiability, we tested this hypotheses on five groups of problems: $G(100, 400, (1, 1, 1, 1))$, $G(100, 400, (0, 1, 1, 0.1))$, $G(100, 400, (0, 0, 1, 1))$, $G(100, 400, (1, 1, 0, 0.1))$, and $G(100, 400, (1, 1, 0, 1))$, testing uniform problems against compact and loose problems, and compact problems against loose problems.

Table 4 shows the average number of flips performed by MaxAge, a local search algorithm introduced in [17], for the five groups of problems. Even at 10% confidence, the test cannot reject the hypothesis of similarity between uniform and loose problems. However, the test concludes, with 5%-confidence, that there is a difference between compact and uniform and also between compact and loose problems. We can say that our experimental data rejects the hypothesis of similarity in solvability between compact and loose or uniform problems because compact problems are more difficult to solve.

Table 4. Average number of flips for MaxAge [17] in random samples of 15 problems of 400 clauses from 100 variables for different degrees of structure ($N_0^+(400) = 1084$, $N_0^-(400) = 1052$); and the rejection of the hypothesis of similarity because of lower (L) solvability.

Π	Average No of flips															class	test
1-1-1-1	276	500	569	1794	269	485	1800	305	152	158	315	2437	174	1260	327	uniform	-
0-1-1-0.1	312	617	256	271	257	110	231	413	321	99	324	2149	415	156	1077	compact	L
0-0-1-1	172	306	71	130	715	476	307	114	227	241	155	433	199	524	455	loose	-
1-1-0-0.1	67	1441	3511	355	369	168	584	337	479	93	364	168	727	557	156	compact	L
1-1-0-1	558	624	278	1380	798	443	1614	129	1031	93	717	100	318	912	408	loose	-

6   Discussion and Conclusions

In this paper we have started to address the question of the effects of structure on the properties of SAT problems. A classification of k-SAT problems as either uniform or compact or loose on the basis of variables connectivity has been introduced and justified. This classification method has been developed as a test on problem uniformity based on a simple statistic, the count of the number of zero step related variable pairs. With this test, for problems of moderate size, we have shown that compact problems have low satisfiability and they are more difficult to solve than uniform or loose problems for a local search algorithm. Also, there is no significant difference in solvability and satisfiability between loose and uniform problems. It has been discussed that the same statistic may be used to justify different classifiers. In particular, we have shown that, in terms of variable connectivity, the size of a backbone is a proper classifier for SAT problems.

Non-uniformity in a SAT problem can be induced either through connections between variables or through restrictions on values in the variable domain. We have introduced possible candidates for classifying structures that are of a higher order than the one used in this paper and feel that more sensitive structural analysis could be built using such classifiers in a manner similar to that used in this paper. Addressing structure within the domain of variables would also seem to be a logical extension for the structural analysis of SAT problems.

Another goal is to be able to identify problem structure that consists of a combination of both loose and compact substructures. Such structure should allow the application of more generic problem solvers, such as Genetic Algorithms, which should be able to identify and utilise substructures within a SAT problem.

References

1. Gent I.P., MacIntyre E., Prosser P., Smith B.M., and Walsh T. Random Constraints Satisfaction: flaws and structure. *Constraints* 2001, Vol.6: 345–372.
2. Walsh T. Search on High Degree Graphs. *Proceedings of the 17th International Joint Conference on Artificial Intelligence (IJCAI'01)* 2001; 266–274.
3. Aloul F.A., Ramani A., Markov I.L., Sakallah K.A. Solving difficult SAT instances in the presence of symmetry.*Proceedings of Design Automation Conference*, University of Michigan, 2002.
4. Beckwith A.B., Choueiry B.Y., H. Zou. How the level of interchangeability embedded in a finite constraint satisfaction problem affects the perfomance of search. *Proceedings of the 14th Australian Joint Conference on Artificial Intelligence (AI 2001)* 2001; 50–61.
5. Walsh T. Search in a small world. *Proceedings of the 16th International Joint Conference on Artificial Intelligence* 1999; 1172–1176.
6. Kautz H., Ruan Y., Achlioptas D., Gomes C., Selman B., Stickel M. Balance and filtering in structured satisfiable problems. *Proceedings of the 17th International Joint Conference on Artificial Intelligence* 2001; 351–358.
7. Parkles A.J. Clustering at the phase transition. Proceedings of the 14th National Conference on Artificial Intelligence 1997; 340–345.
8. Hogg T. Which Search Problems Are Random? *Proceedings of AAAI98*; 1998; 438–443.
9. Gomes C.P., Selman B. Problem structure in the presence of perturbations. *Proceedings of AAAI/IAAI* 1997; 221–226.
10. Gu J. Global optimization for Satisfiability (SAT) problem. *IEEE Trans. on Data and Knowledge Engineering* 1994; Vol.6: 361–381.
11. Achlioptas D., Molloy M.S.O., Kirousis L.M., Stamatiou Y.C., Kranakis E., Krizanc D. Random Constraint Satisfaction: a more accurate picture. *Constraints* 2001; Vol.6: 329–344.
12. Cook S.A., Mitchell D.G. Finding hard instances of the satisfiability problem: a survey. In: Du, Gu, Pardalos (eds.): *Satisfiability Problems: Theory and Applications*, Vol.5. Americam Mathematical Society, 1997; 1–17.
13. S.Kirkpatrick, G. Gyorgyi, N. Tishby, and L. Troyansky, The Statistical Mechanics of k-satisfaction, *Proceeedings of Advances in Neural Information Processing Systems* 1994; 439–446.
14. SATLIB – satisfiability library, main site, http://www.satlib.org
15. Crawford J.M., Auton L.D. Experimental results on the crossover point in satisfiability problems. *Proceedings of the 11th National Conference on Artificial Intelligence* 1993; 21–27.
16. Sachs L. Applied Statistics: a Handbook of Techniques, 2nd Edition, Springer-Verlag, NY, 1984.
17. Thornton J., Pullan W., Terry J. Towards fewer parameters for SAT clause weighting algorithms. *Research Report INT-02-02, Griffith University*, 2002.

Modelling More Realistic SAT Problems

Andrew Slater

Computer Sciences Laboratory, Australian National University, 0200, Canberra
andrew.slater@cslab.anu.edu.au

Abstract. The satisfiability problem is widely used in research on combinatorial search and for industrial applications such as verification and planning. Real world search problem benchmarks are not plentiful, yet understanding search algorithm behaviour in the real world domain is highly important. This work justifies and investigates a randomised satisfiability problem model with modular properties akin to those observed in real world search problem domains. The proposed problem model provides a reliable benchmark which highlights pitfalls and advantages with various satisfiability search algorithms.

1 Introduction

The truth value of a formula of classical propositional logic is totally determined by the truth assignments to the propositional variables from which it is built. A formula is satisfiable if at least one truth assignment to its propositional variables makes the whole formula true. Given a formula using a set of propositional variables of size n, deciding whether the formula is satisfiable is known to be NP-complete [1]. For this reason propositional satisfiability is a prototypical search problem commonly used to analyse search behaviour and problem hardness in combinatorial search. The advanced state of research in satisfiability has made it attractive for many real world problem domains such as planning and verification. Real world problems all have some kind of structure; they differ from random problems in that they have non-uniform distributions and that certain parts of the problem (or inferences from that part) are integral units to the problem as a whole. Real world problems model various interactions with real world objects. Consider the problem of verification of hardware or software, where we would at least expect a modular structure in terms of subroutines or logical integrated circuit components.

Our investigation focuses on identifying generic properties of real world search problems. We are motivated by the desire for a better understanding of search and search problems in the real world, and the limited availability of real world benchmarks. It is evident that, on the whole, real world problems do have exploitable properties which are independent of any particular classification of problem that we want to solve. This is shown by the performance of particular advanced search techniques that are successful on sets of real world benchmarks[2]. This work investigates modelling modular structure to emulate

R.I. McKay and J. Slaney (Eds.): AI 2002, LNAI 2557, pp. 591–602, 2002.

real world problem structure. Section 2 reviews other approaches for generating realistic satisfiability search problems. Section 3 investigates the justification for using modelling modularity in pseudo-real search problems. Our proposed problem model is presented in Section 4, and experimental analysis appears in Section 5 and 6. Section 7 discusses our observations with respect to related work.

2   Structured Problem Generators

There are two obvious approaches to modelling real world structure in problems. The first is to extend the description of a real world problem domain in order to gain further generalisation, but hopefully retain the structural properties of that problem type. The second is to attempt to construct a parameterised problem model by introducing some structural constraints in the problem definition.

There are many approaches based on generating problems using a given problem domain structure. Quasigroup completion problems encoded as constraint satisfaction were proposed by Gomes and Selman [3]; a partial definition of a quasigroup is provided, and must be completed to be solved. Generating satisfiable problem instances within the quasigroup domain is further investigated in [4]. Other approaches include problem generation by encoding the parity problem (see [5]) and the domain of cryptography [6]. A more general approach called *morphing* was devised by Gent *et al.* [7]. Their work categorises some approaches of "morphing", each of which defines a translation from given problem definitions to a new problem via the introduction of noise. The morphing technique can be a very powerful tool for generating a variety of similar problem instances.

The alternative approach is to define a model that incorporates some structural content in a problem and allows the problems to be randomly generated based upon that model. This is the approach taken in this work. We have argued that modularity is a good generic structural property of many real world domains and model this by combining instances of random 3-SAT problems as modules or *clusters*. Our model will be discussed in detail in Section 4. There are similar approaches which are briefly reviewed here.

Two methods for random generation of problems with possible real world similarity were proposed by Rish and Dechter [8]. The first model is similar to our model in that its modular components are random 3-SAT problems, which they call sub-theories. The main difference is in [8] the sub-theories are connected in a chain by joining neighbouring clusters using a single binary clause. Their observations are discussed in Section 7. Their second model, the $(k, m) - tree$, generates a randomly conglomerated set of "cliques" for which a number of clauses is defined. This model has a graph theory analogy but the details and implications for satisfiability problems are unclear. Finally we note that there are other problem generators based around pattern construction and repetition for other related problem domains (e.g. graph colouring, network topology)[9, 10,11].

3   Justifying Modularity

The observation of modular structure in search problems has been investigated by Walsh [12], motivated by the observations of "small world" phenomena observed by Watts and Strogatz [11]. The "small world" model describes a relational system which is somewhere between a completely structured object and a completely random object. Several small groups are highly related, but relations between some members of different groups also exist. Our work finds justification in Walsh's observations of small world phenomena in search problems.

In order to capture the notion of the small world topology, Watts and Strogatz combine quantified structural properties of a graph. A graph topology may be characterised by computing the *characteristic path length* and *the clustering coefficient*. The characteristic path length L specifies the average shortest distance between any two vertices in the graph. The clustering coefficient C is defined as the average fraction of the fully connected graph that any given vertex may be a member of. C may be computed as the average C_v for all vertices v, where C_v is defined as follows. A vertex v with k_v neighbours can have have at most $k_v(k_v - 1)/2$ edges between them (the fully connected graph K_{k_v}). C_v is the ratio of the actual number of edges between any of v or its neighbours to the total number of possible edges. These parameters are used to look at a range of graphs from the completely regular, or structured, to the completely random.

A graph defining a ring lattice, where each vertex is joined to k nearest neighbours, has a high clustering coefficient. We construct a random graph of the same size by randomly assigning the edge connections. Random graphs tend to have smaller characteristic path lengths and much smaller clustering coefficients relative to their regular counterparts. With appropriate bounds guaranteeing graph connectivity these two topologies are used to find the small world phenomena.

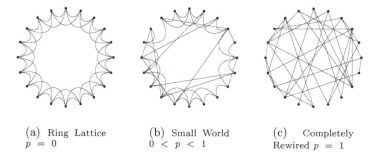

(a) Ring Lattice
$p = 0$

(b) Small World
$0 < p < 1$

(c)   Completely
Rewired $p = 1$

Fig. 1. Examples of "connectedness" with a graph of 20 vertices: (a) shows a ring lattice where each vertex is connected to the four closest neighbours, (b) shows a partially rewired ring lattice where each edge is rewired with probability p, (c) shows the graph where every edge has been rewired.

Table 1. Analysis of real networks: Film Actors – from a database of collaborations between actors in feature films; Power Grid – the electrical power grid for the western United States; *C. elegans* – the neural network from a nematode worm. The values shown are the characteristic path length, the characteristic path length for a random graph of the same size, the clustering coefficient, the clustering coefficient for a random graph of the same size, and the proximity ratio μ (see text). Note that $L \gtrsim L_{rand}$ and $C \gg C_{rand}$ which also corresponds to the small world characterisation from the Watts and Strogatz rewiring experiments. From [Walsh, 1999].

	L	L_{rand}	C	C_{rand}	μ
Film Actors	3.65	2.99	0.79	0.00027	2396
Power Grid	18.7	12.4	0.08	0.005	10.61
C. elegans	2.25	2.25	0.28	0.05	4.755

A small world graph will have a relatively high clustering coefficient and a small characteristic path length. Watts and Strogatz use a "rewiring" concept, whereby an edge is rewired to a new destination with probability p. The details of the rewiring process are less important – different approaches appear in [7]. At $p = 0$ the graph is completely regular, and at $p = 1$ the graph is completely random. Watts and Strogatz find small world graphs do exist in the interval $[0, 1]$ for p. Their analysis shows a small world network is one where $L \gtrsim L_{rand}$ and $C \gg C_{rand}$, where C_{rand} and L_{rand} are the characteristic path length and clustering coefficient from a random graph with the same number of vertices and edges. Figure 1 shows an example of the ring lattice, the partially rewired small world graph, and the random graph for visual comparison.

Watts and Strogatz apply the small world topological analysis to some examples of networked relationships and find that the small world network characterisation according to their model is apparent. Table 1 shows values for their results. Walsh extends the small world analysis of Watts and Strogatz by including the *proximity ratio*. It is defined as a normalised relationship between the characteristic path length and the clustering coefficient of a graph:

$$\mu = \frac{C}{L} \frac{L_{rand}}{C_{rand}}$$

where C_{rand} and L_{rand} are the characteristic path length and clustering coefficient from a random graph with the same number of vertices and edges. This measure allows the "small world" characterisation of one graph to be compared against another. Note that a random graph will have a proximity ratio of 1 and lattices will have small proximity ratios. For small world graphs $\mu \gg 1$.

Walsh demonstrates that several existing benchmark problems for graph colouring have high proximity ratios. Furthermore he shows that high proximity ratios can be calculated for timetabling benchmarks and quasigroup problems. In a search cost study for graph colouring Walsh also shows topological features in search problems can have a large impact on search cost [12].

Graph colouring problems have an obvious translation for network topology analysis. In the case of satisfiability, other notions defining the relations between variables, such as co-occurrence in clauses, can be used to determine the proximity ratio, and studies show high proximity ratios for a topological interpretation of some satisfiability problem benchmarks [7]. The concept of the clustering coefficient requires that the modularity be exposed at an atomic level. This means that a sub-problem or module is only identifiable when the clustering coefficient in a sub-problem is high. For variable co-occurrence this means that a "cluster" would be very small, and in practice we should not expect this. Further development of small world topological analysis may yield better formal characterisations for satisfiability problems, however the studies of small world properties in real world search problems produces a strong argument that modular structure exists and appears to be a strong feature of real world problems.

4   A Problem Model for Clustering

In order to capture modularity in a parameterisable problem set we propose a problem model based on the random generation of fixed size modules or clusters. The model uses a set of individual random 3-SAT problems which are "connected" by a small set of extra clauses.

Formally we define the random clustered problem model as follows. A clustered problem instance has n variables, m clauses, c clusters and p percent links. We may use the clause to variable ratio r, a common parameterisation in random 3-SAT experiments to indicate the 'hardness' of each cluster – each cluster has n/c variables, and $(1 - p/100)m$ clauses (ignoring remainders). As p increases, the structure of the individual clusters decay, and eventually the problem will become a regular random 3-SAT problem. To generate the problems each cluster is generated as a separate random 3-SAT problem. The remainders of clauses and variables can be distributed as evenly as possible e.g. cluster i $(0 \leq i < c)$ has n/c variables $+1$ if $i < (n \bmod c)$. The fraction of clauses that act as links are randomly generated using the entire set of variables. We wish to investigate the effects of structural changes such as this. Furthermore we want to define some level of difficulty within the individual clusters so that they appear to be a separate sub-problem to the search algorithm. We also want the link clauses to make the problem appear in some sense as a whole.

The aim of this problem model is to capture structure through some arbitrary modularity. It does not necessarily have the quantifiable properties of a "small world" problem, since the size of each individual cluster can be varied. A random cluster problem will probably only have a small world characterisation when the cluster sizes are very small since the measurement of the proximity ratio requires relationships at the atomic level. For small clusters, the clustering coefficient will be larger, and overall the characteristic path length should be shorter between most variables. On a meta-level, however, we emulate the small world situation by modelling the local interactions by clusters, and the global interactions by the links. This small world concept is relatively independent of the cluster size.

We shouldn't expect the problems to be particularly difficult if the cluster problems are not difficult. The problems should measure the ability of a search algorithm to "concentrate" on a particular problem, or at least identify which parts of the search space are relevant to the current search state. Consider why some large real world problems are not as difficult as a hard random 3-SAT problem. A good search algorithm will be able to identify, through some means, an appropriate ordering of the search so that each cluster is solved individually – a divide and conquer style approach.

5   Experimenting with the Model

Experiments were performed to measure search cost for various parameterisations of the proposed random cluster model. The experimentation reveals that the theory behind the model can predict search algorithm behaviour. There were some interesting exceptions in initial experiments which are discussed below.

The satisfiability search system `satz` [13] was chosen for performing preliminary experiments. It uses a Davis-Putnam-Logemann-Loveland (**DPLL**)[14] based search algorithm with a powerful choice heuristic. It is an efficient and reliable implementation, and furthermore is very capable in solving large random 3-SAT problems. This allows testing on larger problem sizes and the use of large sample sets. It is posited that the use of a state of the art system is a reasonable approach in testing the proposed benchmark problems. Additionally, the use of large cluster sizes allows greater potential for "isomorphic richness" in individual clusters. Very small random 3-SAT clusters is not representative. Experiments were done using a Sun UltraSPARC II (248MHz) processor.

To generate the random clustered problems, a problem generator that takes the problem set parameters and produces the set of problems was implemented. Clauses which contain a duplicate variable are not included, and problems that are unconnected are not produced; i.e. if the set of links does not join each cluster through co-occurrence then the links are regenerated.

Clustered problem sets for a range of number of clusters, and a variety of different percentage links, were generated for initial experiments. Each problem had 200 variables and 840 clauses. Surprisingly, at around 5 clusters the problems became significantly harder to solve. For low values of percentage links, a number of the problems could not be solved within the 5 minute CPU time limit set for each problem. This contrasts severely with the CPU time taken to solve a single cluster problem (the regular random 3-SAT problem) of the same size. For a set of single cluster problems a median time of 0.56 seconds was measured, where 69 percent of the instances were satisfiable. Figure 2 shows the results computed for the cluster problems using 15 percent of the clauses as links. The drop in satisfiability is consistent with predictions, but the performances are not. As the percentage of links increases, the level of difficulty drops. The most difficult problems are the ones with 5, 6 or 7 clusters. Increasing the percentage links values causes the difficulty to subside.

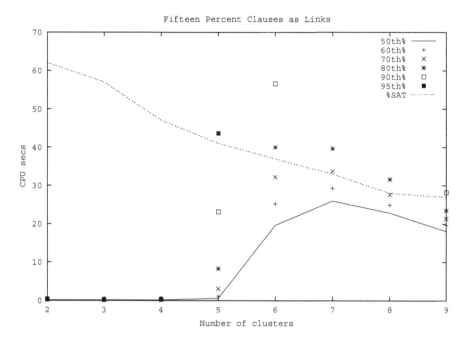

Fig. 2. Time taken for clustered problems of 200 variables and 840 clauses. The number of clusters ranges from 2 to 9. The number of clauses that are used as links is 15 percent of the total number of clauses. 200 problems were tested for each cluster size. The median values are shown by the solid curve, and various percentile points are plotted. The percentage of problems that are satisfiable is also plotted as a dashed curve. Note that for a single cluster the time taken is less than 1 second.

It appears that in the initial experiments the difficulty is a function of the percentage of links as well as the number of clusters. The source of the difficulty is not within the **DPLL** search part of satz, but in a resolution based preprocessing technique it uses. It is claimed by the authors of satz that this technique reduces the search cost by about 10 percent for hard random 3-SAT, and a variety of speed-ups is seen for benchmark problem classes [15]. The fine details of this procedure are not important - the key issue is that a weakly controlled resolution process occurs before any **DPLL** style search is performed. Although resolvent sizes are limited this does not bound the process strongly enough to cope with the situations presented in some of the random cluster problems. For the apparently difficult random cluster problems generated, satz created far too many resolvents for the preprocessing technique to cope with. The probability of co-occurrence of variables is high for small random problems, thus the potential number of small resolvents in each cluster will also be high. The small world qualities of these cluster problems is likely to be higher merely due to their size, and it is the "cliqueishness" of each cluster that causes the breakdown of the preprocessing technique. It is highly likely that a fuller version of resolution could

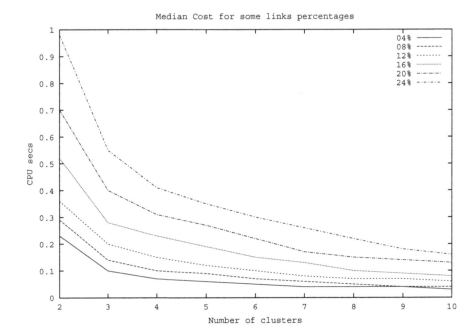

Fig. 3. Median time taken for clustered problems of 250 variables and 1061 clauses (a global clause to variable ratio of about 4.24) for a variety of percentage links. The key indicates the percentage of the clauses that are used as links for particular curves. The number of clusters ranges from 2 to 10. 1000 problems were used for each cluster size. Note that for a single cluster problem (a random 3-SAT problem of 250 variables and 1061 clauses) the median time taken for 1000 problems is around 4.2 seconds.

actually solve the individual cluster problems as in [8], which shall be discussed in further detail in Section 7. A further set of experiments was performed with the satz resolution actions disabled on problems with 250 variables and 1061 clauses, using from 2 to 10 clusters, for a variety of percentage links values. For these experiments 1000 problems were tested for each combination of parameters used. Figure 3 shows the median search cost in CPU time for a variety of percentage links, against the number of clusters in the problems. As expected, the cost decreases as the number of clusters increase since the individual sub-problems are easier to solve. For higher values of percentage links the problems are more like the single cluster, or basic random 3-SAT, and are harder to solve than the problems with well defined clustering. This may be because there is less information about where the search algorithm should concentrate as more links will direct the branching heuristics to a different sub-problem. Also note that the percentage of satisfiable problems decreases with cluster size. This is due to the compounding of the individual probability of any cluster being unsatisfiable. A problem with a higher number of clusters is easier when an unsatisfiable sub-problem is identified early, as search is terminated.

6 Measuring a System's "Concentration"

Earlier it was hypothesised that the random cluster model could be used to measure how well a satisfiability search system could "concentrate" on a problem. By this we mean how well it can search and solve a sub-problem before moving onto some other part of the problem. A variety of state of the art systems were tested with the random cluster model. In order to get an idea of how well they coped, their ability was compared to the basic random 3-SAT problems by ranking the performance results for both problem types. Those that rank highly in the random cluster problems should have a good ability to "concentrate". By comparing the rankings to those for the random 3-SAT problems we should see the relative difference when modularity is introduced. The systems used were:

satz [15] The initial system used for our experimentation which relies solely on its ability to make the best choices in the search tree. This system is renowned for its performance on random 3-SAT problems, so the individual cluster problems should not be difficult for it.

posit [16] A somewhat earlier system which uses a combination of methods to select good variable choices and prune search space. Freeman's thesis demonstrates that it is successful in solving a wide variety of benchmark problems as well as random SAT problems [16].

relsat [2] An advanced system that utilises a version of dynamic backtracking and learning techniques. Its ability to reason about relevancy in search space should make it an ideal candidate for modular problems, and it is generally very successful on real world benchmark problems.

OKSolver [17] A system which uses a variety of pruning techniques and branch ordering heuristics which seems to be motivated by complexity analysis.

sato [18] This system utilises an alternative data structure for search reasoning and has proven very successful on quasi-group problems, having solved open problems in this domain.

The results are ranked in order of smallest median score. Both sets of problems contained 1000 samples. The random 3-SAT problems had 200 variables and a clause to variable ratio of 4.25. The random cluster problems had 450 variables and a clause to variable ratio of 4.25 with 9 clusters and 20 percent of the clauses acting as links. We stress that the two sets of results are produced to gain a ranking only, as we cannot directly compare the performances on these potentially very different problem sets. Table 2 a) shows statistical data gathered from the random 3-SAT experiment. Both satz and posit outperform the other systems, and the other median scores are several times greater than the two top systems. The results shown in Table 2 b) show quite a different trend. Notably relsat copes far better with the random cluster problems. The bottom three systems again have median costs several times greater than the best, with sato and posit being slower by more than an order of magnitude. The rankings of a selection of different systems show that the search method is important

Table 2. These tables show an ordering of run-time statistics for a selection of state-of-the-art systems. Each table is ordered by increasing median value. Note that the ordering of the other statistics is similar but does not always agree. Table a) shows results and ranking for regular random 3-SAT problems. Table b) shows results and ranking for the clustered problems. The difference in the ordering of the two tables indicates how the different methods cope with the random cluster model.

System	Average	Median	Maximum	Minimum	Std Dev.
posit	0.345	0.34	1.29	0.03	0.198
satz	0.355	0.36	0.99	0.04	0.195
OKSolver	1.123	1.13	4.54	0.05	0.819
relsat	1.792	1.69	7.72	0.07	1.360
sato	3.891	3.02	28.85	0.00	3.745

a) Ranked Results for One Cluster Problems

System	Average	Median	Maximum	Minimum	Std Dev.
satz	10.806	5.68	151.57	0.19	15.140
relsat	13.051	8.56	137.30	0.29	14.452
OKSolver	28.754	19.58	277.38	0.18	31.722
sato	167.571	58.30	3852.26	0.08	333.333
posit	151.737	65.69	3392.30	0.19	266.545

b) Ranked Results for Nine Clusters Problems

for solving this kind of modular structure. Since the individual problems are random 3-SAT problems, we would normally expect that a system that solves these well will cope with random clusters. This was not the case with posit whose search technique was not powerful enough to detect the sub-problems as well as the best ranked systems. relsat, known for an ability to deal with real world domain problems fared much better in the rankings for the random cluster model problems than with the random 3-SAT problem. This is evidence that the modular structure is apparent to its search method, and furthermore suggests that the random cluster model is a far better model of the real world domain than the random 3-SAT model.

7 Related Work

We previously noted the work of Rish and Dechter [8] who independently created a structured problem model they call random 3-CNF chains. In a series of experiments that appears to show Directional Resolution (DR) is more capable than DPLL algorithms, they find anomalously hard problems for their implementation of DPLL. The search times differ by orders of magnitude. We found no anomalous hardness spikes in any of our experiments using DPLL style algorithms, bar the resolution based preprocessing problems. The difference in observations is most likely to be due to the fact that our clusters are not chained – the path length from any cluster to another is very short. Rish and Dechter pose that when a sub-problem at the end of the chain is unsatisfiable then the entire problem must be re-solved. This would infer that their algorithm chose a particularly unfortunate ordering, and it seems that such a situation would be reasonably rare. In our experiments we sampled tens of thousands of large problems with different parameterisations. It is conceivable that the same unfortunate ordering could occur when the last cluster to be solved was unsatisfiable. However we did not notice any problems that were as extremely hard as those observed in [8]. We suspect that a combination of the heuristics used and the scale of the model used by Rish and Dechter is also responsible for large search costs. In fact, for the number of variables in the problems, some of the worst search costs suggest that the supposedly advanced choice ordering has failed badly. Since this ordering is based on `tableaux` [19], we suspect that the empirically derived choice mechanism is over-fitted to random 3-SAT problems and will prefer to work on binary links rather than sub-problems. We also believe that the size of the sub-problems Rish and Dechter use is a significant factor. The probability of co-occurrence for any pair of variables is extremely high. In this situation a resolution based approach is bound for success. Larger sized chain components will eliminate this advantage. By adding back-jumping to their DPLL implementation Rish and Dechter are able to avoid most difficult problems, but they do suggest a possible phase transition phenomenon in chain problems. This seems false in view of the other experiments.

8   Conclusions

Modularity has been identified as an important structural concept based on intuitive reasoning and the work of Walsh [12]. The proposed problem model based on clusters of random 3-SAT problems gives a simple framework to generate modular problems that can be manipulated via the parameter set that defines them. This problem model generally behaves as the theory predicts when used in experimentation. However, our experimentation revealed possible problems with search methods that integrate resolution style techniques. This is because the nature of small connected sub-problems can yield an exponential explosion in the number of resolvents. The success of Rish and Dechter's DR algorithm indicates that more advanced implementations of resolution algorithms to perform the search are far less likely to succumb to the problems we observed. Our observations reveal further explanations for the performance results observed in [8] for a related problem model and highlight the fact that choice heuristics derived from 3-SAT experimentation may not translate to other problem domains.

A reasonable search algorithm is one which is able to "concentrate" on a problem by tackling sub-problems. We observed this behaviour with some state of the art systems using the random cluster model. These results indicate that the proposed model has much better real world similarity than basic random models. That problem difficulty is likely to be only as hard as the contained sub-problems is reinforced by recent work in modularity detection [20]. The proposed model yields a simple framework for generating large sets of test cases with real world properties for satisfiability search algorithms.

References

1. S.A. Cook. The complexity of theorem proving procedures. In *Proceedings of the 3rd Annual ACM Symposium on Theory of Computing*, 1971.
2. Roberto J. Bayardo, Jr. and Robert C. Schrag. Using CSP look-back techniques to solve real-world SAT instances. In *AAAI-97*, 1997.
3. C. Gomes and B. Selman. Problem structure in presence of perturbations. In *AAAI-97*, 1997.
4. D. Achlioptas, C. Gomes, H. Kautz, and B. Selman. Generating satisfiable problem instances. In *AAAI-2000*, 2000.
5. David S. Johnson and Michael A. Trick, editors. *Cliques, Coloring, and Satisfiability: the Second DIMACS Implementation Challenge*, volume 26. American Mathematical Society, 1993.
6. F. Massacci. Using walk-sat and rel-sat for cryptographic key search. In *IJCAI-99*, 1999.
7. I.P Gent, H.H. Hoos, P. Prosser, and T. Walsh. Morphing: Combining structure and randomness. In *AAAI-99*, 1999.
8. Irina Rish and Rina Dechter. Resolution versus Search: Two strategies for SAT. *Journal of Automated Reasoning*, 25(1-2):225–275, 2000.
9. Tadd Hogg. Refining the phase transition in combinatorial search. *Artificial Intelligence*, 81, 1996.
10. S. Grant and B.M. Smith. Where the exceptionally hard problems are. In *Proceedings of the CP-95 workshop on Really Hard Problems*, 1995.
11. D.J. Watts and S.H. Strogatz. Collective dynamics of 'small world' networks. *Nature*, 393:440–442, 1998.
12. Toby Walsh. Search in a small world. In *IJCAI-99*, 1999.
13. Chu Min Li and Anbulagan. Heuristics based on unit propagation for satisfiability problems. In *AAAI-97*, 1997.
14. Martin Davis, George Logemann, and Donald Loveland. A machine program for theorem-proving. *Communications of the ACM*, 5(7):394–397, July 1962.
15. Chu Min Li and Anbulagan. Look-ahead versus look-back for satisfiability problems. In *CP-97*, 1997.
16. Jon W. Freeman. *Improvements to Propositional Satisfiability Search Algorithms*. PhD thesis, University of Pennsylvania, 1995.
17. Oliver Kullman. Heuristics for sat algorithms: Searching for some foundations. Technical report, Dept. Computer Science, University of Toronto, 1999.
18. H. Zhang. SATO: An efficient propositional prover. In *CADE-14*, 1997.
19. J. M. Crawford and L. D. Auton. Experimental results on the crossover point in random 3-SAT. *Artificial Intelligence*, 81:31–57, 1996.
20. E. Amir and S. McIlraith. Partition-based logical reasoning. In *KR-2000*, 2000.

A Two Level Local Search for MAX-SAT Problems with Hard and Soft Constraints*

John Thornton, Stuart Bain, Abdul Sattar, and Duc Nghia Pham

School of Information Technology,
Griffith University Gold Coast, Southport, Qld, Australia, 4215
{j.thornton,s.bain,a.sattar,duc.pham}@mailbox.gu.edu.au

Abstract. Local search techniques have attracted considerable interest in the AI community since the development of GSAT for solving large propositional SAT problems. Newer SAT techniques, such as the Discrete Lagrangian Method (DLM), have further improved on GSAT and can also be applied to general constraint satisfaction and optimisation. However, little work has applied local search to MAX-SAT problems with hard and soft constraints. As many real-world problems are best represented by hard (mandatory) and soft (desirable) constraints, the development of effective local search heuristics for this domain is of significant practical importance.

This paper extends previous work on dynamic constraint weighting by introducing a two-level heuristic that switches search strategy according to whether a current solution contains unsatisfied hard constraints. Using constraint weighting techniques derived from DLM to satisfy hard constraints, we apply a Tabu search to optimise the soft constraint violations. These two heuristics are further combined with a dynamic hard constraint multiplier that changes the relative importance of the hard constraints during the search. We empirically evaluate this new algorithm using a set of randomly generated 3-SAT problems of various sizes and difficulty, and in comparison with various state-of-the-art SAT techniques. The results indicate that our dynamic, two-level heuristic offers significant performance benefits over the standard SAT approaches.

1 Introduction

Problems containing hard and soft constraints are very common in real world situations. For example, a typical university timetabling problem contains hard constraints specifying that only one class can be scheduled in a particular room at a particular time, with additional soft constraints expressing preferences for class times (e.g. a lecturer may prefer not to teach on Fridays). The addition of soft constraints changes the standard formulation of a Constraint Satisfaction Problem (CSP) into an over-constrained optimisation problem, where the objective is to satisfy all hard constraints and maximise the level of satisfaction of the soft constraints (according to some predefined metric).

* The authors gratefully acknowledge the financial support of the Australian Research Council, grant A00000118, in the conduct of this research

R.I. McKay and J. Slaney (Eds.): AI 2002, LNAI 2557, pp. 603–614, 2002.
© Springer-Verlag Berlin Heidelberg 2002

1.1   Representing and Solving Over-Constrained Problems

Various approaches have been proposed to represent over-constrained problems within the constraint satisfaction literature, including Freuder and Wallace's seminal paper on partial constraint satisfaction [5]. Here the objective is to maximise the total number of satisfied constraints (rather than to satisfy the hard constraints and then maximise the number of satisfied soft constraints). In [2] the idea of a two-level distinction between hard and soft constraints is extended to a multiple level constraint hierarchy, where constraints are classified into separate levels, such that the constraints of each succeeding level are strictly less important than any one constraint of the previous level. More recently, [1] proposed the more general semiring framework for representing over-constrained problems, which is capable of modelling traditional CSPs, constraint hierarchies, fuzzy CSPs and probabilistic CSPs.

Although these formalisms for representing over-constrained problems are independent of the algorithms used to solve these problems, most of the work in the area has concentrated on the use of complete techniques. For example, in [5] the standard backtracking approach for CSPs is extended to solve over-constrained problems using branch-and-bound and in both [1] and [2] arc-consistency techniques are developed, with [1] introducing extensions to the Davis-Putnam algorithm for use with semirings, and [2] detailing linear programming methods for use with constraint hierarchies. However, more recent work [7] has successfully applied local search to hierarchical constraint satisfaction.

1.2   Local Search with Hard and Soft Constraints

In this paper we are interested in applying local search techniques to over-constrained problems with hard and soft constraints. While local search can be trivially applied to the problem of maximising the total number of satisfied constraints, little work has been done in extending local search to over-constrained problems with hard and soft constraints. A start in this direction was made in [9] where the well known WalkSAT local search technique was applied to the weighted MAX-SAT problem. In this paper, the hard constraints were represented by making the weighted cost of each hard constraint exceed the sum of the weighted cost of all soft constraints. In this way the search always prefers a solution that satisfies all hard constraints regardless of the level of soft constraint violation. In [3] this work was taken further by recognising that the larger the weight differential between hard and soft constraints, the slower the search. This insight was factored into a constraint weighting algorithm by setting the hard constraint weight differential to a hand-tuned optimal level (generally slightly exceeding the average count of soft constraint violations during the search). Parallel work on Tabu search [14] looked at dynamically adjusting the weight on constraint subclasses according to whether all constraints in the subclass are satisfied (so reducing weight) or unsatisfied (so increasing weight) during a fixed period of iterations. This work was combined in [18], which introduced a dynamic constraint weighting technique capable of both adding weights to frequently violated constraints and maintaining a dynamic weight differential between the hard and soft constraints.

1.3   Recent Applications of Local Search to MAX-SAT

More recently, state-of-the-art local search SAT techniques, such as the Discrete Lagrangian Method (DLM) [16] and Guided Local Search (GLS) [12] have been successfully applied to the DIMACS benchmark over-constrained *jnh* MAX-SAT problems. The *jnh* problems are (mostly) over-constrained, with each constraint having a weight between 1 and 1000, and the search objective being to find a minimum weighted cost solution. Both DLM and GLS are *constraint weighting* techniques that add weight to unsatisfied constraints while simultaneously keeping track of original *jnh* problem weights. In the reported studies, GLS marginally outperformed DLM on the *jnh* problems but was unable to match DLM on the larger DIMACS challenge problems [11].

The motivation of this study is to advance the state-of-the-art in solving large hard and soft constraint problems. Given that constraint weighting heuristics (such as DLM and GLS) represent the state-of-the-art for SAT and weighted MAX-SAT problems [19], we decided to use a weighting heuristic as the basis for a new approach. As existing work in the area indicates that the simple fixed hard constraint multiplier used by DLM and GLS (on the weighted MAX-SAT problems) is not the best way to deal with hard constraints, we further decided to incorporate the dynamic hard constraint multiplier proposed in [18] into our new approach.

In the remainder of the paper we explain in more detail the principles underlying constraint weighting and introduce a modified constraint weighting algorithm based on DLM. We then explain and combine the dynamic constraint weighting heuristic from [18] into the modified algorithm. As a result of empirical testing of this technique on a range of randomly generated MAX-SAT problems with hard and soft constraints, we further introduce a second level Tabu search heuristic [6] that controls the search in areas where only soft constraints are violated. Finally, this two level dynamic constraint weighting heuristic is evaluated against the original one-level heuristic, a pure Tabu search and the well known NOVELTY+ SAT algorithm.

2   Constraint Weighting Local Search

The basic idea of constraint weighting is to change the cost of the solution space by adding weights to frequently violated constraints. In the SAT domain, a constraint weighting algorithm (such as [13]) will start with a complete random instantiation of variables and proceed to take local cost improving moves (i.e. flipping or changing the variable that causes the greatest decrease in the number of false clauses) until a *local minimum* is reached where no more cost improving moves are available. The algorithm will then add weight to all currently false constraints (i.e. clauses) and continue the search. In this way the local minimum is "filled in" [13] and the search can progress to new areas. Constraint weighting continues visiting local minima and adding weights until either a global minimum is reached (with cost zero) or the algorithm is timed out.

2.1   Weight Reduction Heuristics

Although simple constraint weighting techniques met with success on smaller SAT problems, other non-weighting local search techniques (such as RNOV-ELTY [10]) proved superior on larger and more difficult problems. It was reasoned that the deterioration of weighting techniques on these problems was due an excessive build up of weights, making the addition of weight in the later stages of the search less and less effective [4]. Therefore various weight reduction or normalisation schemes were proposed, most notably DLM [16] and later GLSSAT [11] and Smoothed Descent and Flood (SDF) [15]. Of these, SDF opted for a continuous normalisation of weights after each weight increase and adopted a multiplicative weight increment scheme, whereas both DLM and GLSSAT used an additive scheme with periodic weight reduction. On the basis of the published empirical results for these techniques, SDF proved promising on smaller problems but due to the large overhead of continuous weight adjustments was unable to match the overall performance of DLM. Similarly GLSSAT proved competitive on small problems, but not on the larger DIMACS instances (for instance compare the *par* problem results in [11] with [19]). On this basis we decided to use DLM as the starting point for our own work.

2.2   Simplifying DLM

There have been several versions of DLM, mainly developed to solve the larger and more challenging DIMACS *par* and *hanoi* problems. In this study we decided to remove the specialised heuristics from DLM and concentrate on the core effectiveness of the technique. We therefore retained the DLM weight reduction scheme but removed the Tabu list and Flat Moves parameters that are used to help DLM explore plateau areas[1]. This resulted in the development of the *MAX-AGE* heuristic [17], which uses a simple random probability of taking a zero cost move on a plateau (otherwise weight is added) and also has a bias to accept infrequently used zero cost moves. In this way, the difficult to tune Tabu list length and Flat Moves parameters from DLM are replaced by a fairly robust zero cost move probability (set at 15% in the current study). Our empirical studies have already shown *MAX-AGE* to be comparable to DLM on a range of the larger DIMACS problems, trading slightly fewer moves for the slightly increased overhead of adding and reducing weight more often [17] (an adapted *MAX-AGE* algorithm for solving hard and soft constraint problems is shown in Figure 1).

---

[1] A plateau is an area where only equal or deteriorating cost moves are available.

```
procedure MAX-AGE
begin
    Generate a random starting point
    bestSolutionCost ← unweighted solution cost
    hardMultiplier ← 1
    Initialise counters and clause weights to zero
    while bestSolutionCost < objective and flips < maxFlips do
        B ← set of best weighted cost single flip moves
        if no improving x ∈ B then
            if oldest x ∈ B has age(x) ≥ maxAge then
                B ← x
                maxAge ← maxAge + 1
            else if random(p) ≤ P then
                B ← ∅
            end if
        end if
        if B ≠ ∅ then
            Randomly pick and flip x ∈ B
            age(x) ← ++flips
            if unweighted solution cost < bestSolutionCost then
                bestSolutionCost ← unweighted solution cost
        else
            Increase weight on all false clauses
            if false hard clauses exist then ++hardMultiplier
            else if hardMultiplier > 1 then − − hardMultiplier
            if ++increases % DECREASE = 0 then
                Decrease weight on all weighted clauses
        end if
    end while
end
```

Fig. 1. The *MAX-AGE* Algorithm for Hard and Soft Constraints

2.3   Dynamic Hard and Soft Constraint Weighting

The *MAX-AGE* algorithm was initially developed for solving *satisfiable* problems. However, it is a trivial exercise to adapt local search for over-constrained problems, as it already searches in the space of inconsistent assignments. Hence *MAX-AGE* also keeps track of the unweighted cost of each solution point visited in the search, in order to recognise when a new best cost solution has been found[2] (this is done using *bestSolutionCost* in Figure 1). As previously discussed (in Section 1.2), hard and soft constraints can be represented by giving a weight penalty to the hard constraints. This can be incorporated into a constraint weighting algorithm by considering the hard constraint weight to be a *hard constraint multiplier*, such that the weighted cost of a particular hard constraint is the product of the hard constraint multiplier and the actual weight currently added to the constraint. In effect, using a hard constraint multiplier with a value n is equivalent to solving a problem where each hard constraint is repeated n times [3].

In [18] it was further demonstrated that performance gains could be obtained by dynamically adjusting the value of the hard constraint multiplier during the search. This idea is incorporated into Figure 1 using *hardMultiplier*. Here *MAX-AGE* continuously increases *hardMultiplier* at each local minimum (from the

---

[2] In practice a copy of the current best solution found would also be kept.

initial value of one) until a solution is found that satisfies all hard constraints. In this way, the relative importance of the hard constraints is raised until they are all satisfied. Then, in hard constraint satisfying local minima, the value of *hardMultiplier* is decremented to bring the search back to the point where the summed cost of the currently false soft constraints just balances the cost of making a hard constraint false.

The use of a dynamic hard constraint multiplier also changes the problem of measuring *bestSolutionCost*. In a system where each hard constraint is more important than the sum of all soft constraints, a solution that satisfies all hard constraints will always be preferred over a solution that does not. However allowing the hard constraint multiplier to vary destroys this property. Hence, when calculating the unweighted solution cost in Figure 1, we must reintroduce the property that each hard constraint violation costs $ns + 1$ where n is the number of soft constraints and s is the cost of violating a soft constraint.

3   A Two-Level Heuristic for Hard and Soft Constraints

In order to evaluate the hard and soft constraint version of *MAX-AGE* we developed two non-weighting local search algorithms using *NOVELTY+* [8] and an augmented Tabu search (*TABU*) based on the SAT source code developed in [15]. Starting with this code, we incorporated the hard constraint multiplier (described in the previous section) into both algorithms and additionally incorporated a random move feature and aspiration condition [6] into *TABU*. Our original SAT Tabu heuristic disallowed the undoing of a move during the search until t subsequent moves have been made (i.e. simulating a Tabu list of length t). To this we added an aspiration condition that always allows cost improving moves and moves that improve on the best cost yet achieved for a given variable value (otherwise tabu moves are disallowed). Then, in a situation where all moves are tabu, we randomly select a move from those variables that are involved in constraint violations.

Initial tests on *TABU* showed that it is relatively poor at finding hard constraint satisfying instantiations on problems where this task was *in itself* difficult. However, on problems where the hard constraint problem is relatively easy, *TABU* proved very effective at optimising the level of soft constraint violations. These observations lead us to develop a two-level heuristic using constraint weighting to satisfy the hard constraints and a Tabu search to satisfy the soft constraints (shown in Figure 2). This *TWO-LEVEL* move selection heuristic replaces the *MAX-AGE* heuristic that populates B in Figure 1. In *MAX-AGE*, moves are selected according to the minimum cost given by the function:

$$solutionCost = \alpha \sum_{i=1}^{n} w(h_i) + \sum_{j=1}^{m} w(s_j)$$

where α = the current value of *hardMultiplier*, n = the total number of hard constraints, m = the total number of soft constraints, h_i is hard constraint i, s_j

is soft constraint j and $w(x_i)$ returns the weighted cost of constraint x_i if x_i is false, zero otherwise. In the *TWO-LEVEL* cost function, the $\sum_{j=1}^{m} w(s_j)$ term is replaced by $\sum_{j=1}^{m} c(s_j)$ where $c(s_j)$ returns one (rather than the weighted cost) if soft constraint s_j is false, zero otherwise.

```
function TWO-LEVEL MOVE SELECTION
begin
    bestChange ← 0
    hCount ← total false hard constraints in current solution
    for each false constraint f_i do
        for each variable v_j ∈ f_i do
            hChange ← change in weighted hard constraint cost from flipping v_j
            sChange ← change in unweighted soft constraint cost from flipping v_j
            costChange ← (hardMultiplier × hChange) + sChange
            if costChange ≤ bestChange then
                age ← number of flips since v_j was last flipped
                sCount ← total false soft constraints resulting from flipping v_j
                if age ≤ hardTabu then tabu ← true
                else if hCount ≤ hChange and age ≤ sCount then tabu ← true
                else tabu ← false
                hBest ← least count of false hard constraints yet achieved by v_j
                sBest ← least count of false soft constraints yet achieved by v_j
                if hCount − hChange < hBest or
                    (hCount = 0 and sCount < sBest) then aspired ← true
                else aspired ← false
                if not tabu or aspired then
                    if costChange < bestChange then
                        B ← ∅
                        bestChange ← costChange
                    end if
                    B ← v_j
                end if
            end if
        end for
    end for
    if B = ∅ and hCount = 0 then
        B ← randomly selected v_j from randomly selected f_i
    return B
end
```

Fig. 2. The *TWO-LEVEL* move selection heuristic

The main principle of the *TWO-LEVEL* heuristic is that weight is only considered on violated *hard* constraints. For this reason a random move is required in the Tabu heuristic to escape local minima in regions where all hard constraints are satisfied (as adding weight in these areas will have no effect). Additionally, a hardTabu constant (= 3) is used to avoid immediately undoing the random move. As a major aim in developing *MAX-AGE* was to reduce the complexity of the parameters used in DLM (see Section 2.2) the length of the soft Tabu list in *TWO-LEVEL* was set equal to the current number of unsatisfied soft constraints in the search (rather than introduce another Tabu list length parameter). This decision was based on empirical observations rather than a strong theoretical justification, and may therefore have to be revised in the light of further evidence.

Finally the *DECREASE* parameter from Figure 1 was augmented in *TWO-LEVEL* so that the frequency of constraint weight decreases depends on the proportion of time the search spends on satisfying soft constraints, according to the following scheme:

$$AugmentedDecrease = DECREASE + \frac{softMoves \times 100}{softMoves + hardMoves}$$

where *DECREASE* has a constant value of 10 (taken from [19]), $softMoves =$ the number of moves taken with all hard constraints satisfied and $hardMoves$ = the number of moves taken with at least one hard constraint violated. The *AugmentedDecrease* feature therefore slows the rate of decrease of the hard constraint weights when the search remains in areas where all hard constraints are satisfied.

4   Experimental Study

4.1   Problem Generation

In order to evaluate the *TWO-LEVEL* algorithm we decided to look at four problem dimensions: problem size, overall problem difficulty, the hard constraint problem difficulty and the ratio of hard to soft constraints. As we were unable to find benchmark problems that vary in all these dimensions, we decided to sample the space of randomly generated 3-SAT problems. While random problems do not measure the effect of structure on algorithm performance they enable us to control average problem difficulty by varying the clause to variable ratio. In addition, using 3-SAT problems we can arbitrarily divide clauses into hard and soft constraints and still have a measure of the relative difficulty of the hard constraint sub-problem.

We based our empirical study on three sets of randomly generated 3-SAT problems all sampled from the phase transition region (i.e. with a clause to variable ratio of 4.3). To make the problems relatively challenging (in terms of size) we generated 10 problems with 400 variables, 10 with 800 variables and 10 with 1600 variables, plus we used one f-series problem at each size from the DIMACS SAT benchmark library. Then, for each problem, we randomly generated and added a extra clause for each clause in the original problem (e.g. for a 400 variable 1720 clause problem we added another 1720 clauses), resulting in a second problem set with a clause to variable ratio of 8.6. This problem set was further multiplied by dividing up the hard and soft constraints into three ratios: 50%, 75% and 100%, where an $n\%$ ratio means the first $n\%$ of the clauses in the original problem are defined as hard constraints (e.g. in a 400 variable 3440 clause problem, if $n = 50$, the first 50% of the 1720 clauses which made up original problem are defined as hard). Using these problem generation procedures we constructed 4 problem classes at each of the 3 problem sizes, making a total of 12 data sets, each containing 11 individual problems. The data sets are identified using the format h*x*hn*s, where *x* specifies the number

Table 1. Experimental Results

Problem	Method	Solved % of 110	Soft Cost Mean	Max	Min	Number of Flips Mean	Median	Std Dev	Time Mean
h400h50s	TABU	100.00	105.66	118	98	385499	358115	278057	9.98
	NOVELTY+	100.00	167.55	181	156	483528	455726	289826	7.04
	MAX-AGE	100.00	135.08	146	123	412152	395993	344137	18.16
	TWO-LEVEL	100.00	104.15	114	98	218261	111305	236683	8.53
h400h75s	TABU	100.00	123.17	144	108	487509	463778	281986	13.48
	NOVELTY+	100.00	168.71	182	148	519810	520912	283110	7.01
	MAX-AGE	100.00	148.19	158	131	355046	289414	291971	19.14
	TWO-LEVEL	100.00	119.10	129	108	314484	264277	285989	10.07
h400h100s	TABU	0.00	n/a	n/a	n/a	n/a	n/a	n/a	n/a
	NOVELTY+	99.09	180.59	200	152	423190	385968	268140	3.56
	MAX-AGE	46.36	180.51	200	156	453510	394879	279855	17.87
	TWO-LEVEL	73.64	175.33	198	151	299752	162736	299894	8.36
orig400	TABU	98.18	0.00	0	0	95725	41601	135638	0.42
	NOVELTY+	100.00	0.00	0	0	97280	33417	144974	0.35
	MAX-AGE	100.00	0.00	0	0	29682	14164	41978	0.16
	TWO-LEVEL	100.00	0.00	0	0	41638	13217	92212	0.22
h800h50s	TABU	9.09	245.00	259	214	524697	512840	235755	26.78
	NOVELTY+	100.00	359.32	377	330	451359	424782	270922	10.43
	MAX-AGE	100.00	289.63	313	257	181927	1993	306001	16.75
	TWO-LEVEL	100.00	201.45	212	193	391025	334046	258612	35.61
h800h75s	TABU	0.00	n/a	n/a	n/a	n/a	n/a	n/a	n/a
	NOVELTY+	100.00	371.39	391	347	503110	501893	277671	11.52
	MAX-AGE	100.00	318.11	337	295	361073	352352	271479	39.10
	TWO-LEVEL	100.00	241.75	258	228	398243	399929	303827	26.83
h800h100s	TABU	0.00	n/a	n/a	n/a	n/a	n/a	n/a	n/a
	NOVELTY+	90.91	369.62	412	339	505453	468170	287641	6.82
	MAX-AGE	0.91	329.00	329	329	816356	816356	0.00	70.35
	TWO-LEVEL	46.36	343.78	381	313	490876	514804	268261	30.98
orig800	TABU	41.82	0.00	0	0	361592	281072	247563	2.23
	NOVELTY+	90.00	0.00	0	0	225248	118765	226833	1.10
	MAX-AGE	100.00	0.00	0	0	108463	68454	136127	0.69
	TWO-LEVEL	100.00	0.00	0	0	87370	49610	108346	0.63
h1600h50s	TABU	0.00	n/a	n/a	n/a	n/a	n/a	n/a	n/a
	NOVELTY+	100.00	788.71	822	740	470748	402339	297055	19.52
	MAX-AGE	100.00	634.36	676	570	101848	4019	240074	28.39
	TWO-LEVEL	100.00	410.84	427	393	571933	584322	252455	161.00
h1600h75s	TABU	0.00	n/a	n/a	n/a	n/a	n/a	n/a	n/a
	NOVELTY+	100.00	790.4	832	740	515291	553617	288798	21.28
	MAX-AGE	100.00	681.71	715	642	396506	353132	289177	118.33
	TWO-LEVEL	100.00	484.73	503	452	384046	350721	265745	78.59
h1600h100s	TABU	0.00	n/a	n/a	n/a	n/a	n/a	n/a	n/a
	NOVELTY+	9.09	745.90	804	708	450650	399261	304313	10.76
	MAX-AGE	0.00	n/a	n/a	n/a	n/a	n/a	n/a	n/a
	TWO-LEVEL	2.73	674.33	693	637	523352	372545	289618	100.02
orig1600	TABU	0.00	n/a	n/a	n/a	n/a	n/a	n/a	n/a
	NOVELTY+	6.36	0.00	0	0	411237	264014	292473	3.21
	MAX-AGE	35.45	0.00	0	0	398464	374962	253588	3.89
	TWO-LEVEL	85.45	0.00	0	0	244216	180327	203094	2.53

of variables and n specifies the ratio of hard constraints. In addition, the orig$x$ problems represent the original 3-SAT problems with the 4.3 clause to variable ratio.

The data sets are designed to test the effects of problem size and difficulty by varying the number of variables and constraints, and the effects of the proportion of hard constraints and the relative difficulty of the hard constraint problem by varying the proportion of hard constraints. For example, an h800h100s problem represents a difficult hard constraint problem as all the clauses in the original phase transition problem are defined hard, whereas in the corresponding h800h50s problem the hard constraint problem will be easier, as 50% of the clauses in the original phase transition problem have now become soft.

4.2 Experimental Analysis

The results in Table 1 compare the performance of *TWO-LEVEL* with the three control algorithms introduced in Section 3 (*MAX-AGE, TABU* and *NOV-ELTY+*), giving averages of 10 runs on each problem (i.e. 110 runs per data set) with each run timed out after 1,000,000 flips. As *TABU* and *NOVELTY+* both perform flips in significantly less time than the clause weighting algorithms, we performed further experiments allowing *TABU* and *NOVELTY+* extra time to see if further cost reductions were possible. These CPU time results are summarised in the two graphs of Figures 3 and 4 showing anytime curves for each algorithm on the h400h75s and h1600h75s data sets respectively.

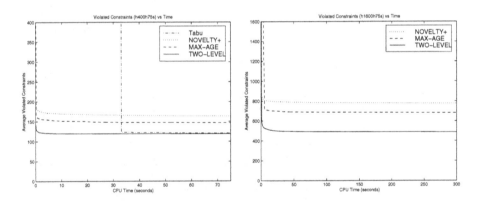

Fig. 3. h400h75s Results   **Fig. 4.** h1600h75s Results

Overall the results in Table 1 confirmed our expectations that *TWO-LEVEL* would outperform both the *MAX-AGE* and *TABU* heuristics on which it is based. While *TABU* performed well on the smallest problems with the easiest hard constraint sub-problem (h400h50s), it was uncompetitive on the larger and harder problems, timing out completely on the h1600 problems. Conversely, *MAX-AGE* showed a fairly consistent ability to find solutions across all data sets (only falling back somewhat on the larger, hardest problems h800h100s and h1600h100s). Also, as expected, *MAX-AGE* performed well on the original under-constrained data sets (orig400-1600), although *TWO-LEVEL* proved better on the larger orig800 and orig1600 problems. This suggests that *TWO-LEVEL*'s use of a hard Tabu list (see Figure 2) is also beneficial on larger under-constrained problems. Overall, however, *MAX-AGE* was consistently outperformed by *TWO-LEVEL* both in terms of average soft cost and in terms of average flip count and average CPU time.

The results for *NOVELTY+* in comparison to *TWO-LEVEL* present a more interesting case. While *TWO-LEVEL* consistently finds better soft cost solutions on the over-constrained problem sets, *NOVELTY+* is considerably more reliable in finding solutions to the hardest over-constrained problems (h400h100s, h800h100s and h1600h100s). Also, as *NOVELTY+* is significantly faster than *TWO-LEVEL* in terms of flips per second, the question arises whether *NOVELTY+* could find better solutions given an equal amount of time. To this end, we re-ran *NOVELTY+* and *TABU* on the hnh75s data sets, allowing the same time cut-off that was granted to the weighting algorithms. The graphs in Figures 3 and 4 show that these increased run-times do not alter the relative performance of the algorithms, with *TWO-LEVEL* consistently achieving the lowest soft cost, independently of the time cut-off point. Therefore, we can conclude that *TWO-LEVEL* has the better average performance on all problems except those where the problem of satisfying the hard constraints is itself difficult (i.e. the hn100s problems). In these cases *NOVELTY+* is preferred, as it shows a superior ability to find a hard constraint satisfying solution in the presence of soft constraints.

5   Conclusion

The paper has presented a new *TWO-LEVEL* algorithm for solving problems with hard and soft constraints, based on an amalgamation of a constraint weighting heuristic for satisfying hard constraints and a Tabu list with aspiration for optimising soft constraints. Our empirical study has demonstrated the usefulness of the *TWO-LEVEL* algorithm for solving a range of randomly generated MAX-SAT problems with hard and soft constraints and has shown the overall superiority of *TWO-LEVEL* on these problems in comparison to three control algorithms.

Of the three control algorithms, *NOVELTY+* proved of greatest interest, as it was able to achieve better results than *TWO-LEVEL* on those instances where the problem of satisfying the hard constraints is itself difficult (i.e. the ratio of hard clauses to variables = 4.3). This result suggests *NOVELTY+* is the better heuristic for satisfying hard constraints when soft constraints are also present. Consequently, in our future work, we intend to investigate the combination of *NOVELTY+* and *TABU* into an alternative two-level heuristic.

References

1. U. Bistarelli, S. Montanari and F. Rossi. Semiring-based constraint solving and optimization. *Journal of ACM*, 44(2):201–236, 1997.

2. A. Borning, B. Freeman-Benson, and M. Wilson. Constraint hierarchies. *Lisp and Symbolic Computation*, 5(3):223–270, 1992.

3. B. Cha, K. Iwama, Y. Kambayashi, and S. Miyazaki. Local search algorithms for partial MAX-SAT. In *Proceedings of the Fourteenth National Conference on Artificial Intelligence (AAAI-97)*, pages 332–337, 1997.

4. J. Frank. Learning short term weights for GSAT. In *Proceedings of the Fourteenth National Conference on Artificial Intelligence (AAAI-97)*, pages 384–389, 1997.

5. E. Freuder and R. Wallace. Partial constraint satisfaction. *Artificial Intelligence*, 58(1):21–70, 1992.

6. F. Glover. Tabu search: Part 1. *ORSA Journal on Computing*, 1(3):190–206, 1989.

7. M. Heinz, L. Fong, L. Chong, S. Ping, J. Walser, and R. Yap. Solving hierarchical constraints over finite domains. In *Proceedings of the Sixth International Symposium on Artificial Intelligence and Mathematics*, 2000.

8. H. Hoos. On the run-time behavior of stochastic local search algorithms for SAT. In *Proceedings of the Sixteenth National Conference on Artificial Intelligence (AAAI-99)*, pages 661–666, 1999.

9. H. Jiang, Y. Kautz and B. Selman. Solving problems with hard and soft constraints using a stochastic algorithm for MAX-SAT. In *First International Joint Workshop on Artificial Intelligence and Operations Research*, 1995.

10. D. McAllester, B. Selman, and H. Kautz. Evidence for invariance in local search. In *Proceedings of the Fourteenth National Conference on Artificial Intelligence (AAAI-97)*, pages 321–326, 1997.

11. P. Mills and E. Tsang. Guided local search applied to the satisfiability (SAT) problem. In *Proceedings of the 15th National Conference of the Australian Society for Operations Research (ASOR'99)*, pages 872–883, 1999.

12. P. Mills and E. Tsang. Guided local search for solving SAT and weighted MAX-SAT problems. *Journal of Automated Reasoning*, 24:205–223, 2000.

13. P. Morris. The Breakout method for escaping local minima. In *Proceedings of the Eleventh National Conference on Artificial Intelligence (AAAI-93)*, pages 40–45, 1993.

14. A. Schaerf. Tabu search for large high school timetabling problems. In *Proceedings of the Thirteenth National Conference on Artificial Intelligence (AAAI-96)*, pages 363–368, 1996.

15. D. Schuurmans and F. Southey. Local search characteristics of incomplete SAT procedures. In *Proceedings of the Seventeenth National Conference on Artificial Intelligence (AAAI-00)*, pages 297–302, 2000.

16. Y. Shang and B. Wah. A discrete Lagrangian-based global search method for solving satisfiability problems. *J. Global Optimization*, 12:61–99, 1998.

17. J. Thornton, W. Pullan, and J. Terry. Towards fewer parameters for SAT clause weighting algorithms. In *Proceedings of the Fifteenth Australian Joint Conference on Artificial Intelligence (AI'2002)*, To appear, 2002.

18. J. Thornton and A. Sattar. Dynamic constraint weighting for over-constrained problems. In *Proceedings of the Fifth Pacific Rim Conference on Artificial Intelligence (PRICAI-98)*, pages 377–388, 1998.

19. Wu Z. *The Theory and Applications of Discrete Constrained Optimization using Lagrange Multipliers*. PhD thesis, Department of Computer Science, University of Illinois, 2000.

Strong Pseudorandom Bit Sequence Generators Using Neural Network Techniques and Their Evaluation for Secure Communications

D.A. Karras[1] and V. Zorkadis[2]

[1]Hellenic Aerospace Industry& Hellenic Open University, Rodu 2, Ano Iliupolis, Athens 16342, Greece, dkarras@haicorp.com, dkarras@hol.gr, dakarras@usa.net

[2]Data Protection Authority, Omirou 8, 10564 Athens, Greece, zorkadis@dpa.gr

Abstract. Random components play an especially important role in secure electronic commerce and multimedia communications. For this reason, the existence of strong pseudo random number generators is highly required. This paper presents novel techniques, which rely on artificial neural network architectures, to strengthen traditional generators such as ANSI X.9 based on DES and IDEA. Additionally, this paper proposes a test method for evaluating the required non-predictability property, which also relies on neural networks. This non-predictability test method along with commonly used statistical and non-linearity tests are suggested as methodology for the evaluation of strong pseudo random number generators. By means of this methodology, traditional and proposed generators are evaluated. The results show that the proposed generators behave significantly better than the traditional, in particular, in terms of non-predictability.

Keywords. Secure Communications, Stream Ciphers, Pseudo Random Number Generators, Feed-forward Neural Networks, Hopfield Neural Networks

1 Introduction

Cryptographic protocols for electronic payment systems, authentication, integrity, confidentiality, non-repudiation or key management may have random components, which require methods to obtaining numbers that are random in some sense. For instance, authentication mechanisms in electronic commerce applications may use nonces, i.e., random numbers to protect against replay attacks [1] like the corresponding mechanisms in ITU X.509 [2]. Symmetric and asymmetric cryptographic systems like DES [3], IDEA, RSA [4] that are employed for confidentiality purposes and as basic element of other security protocols in electronic commerce require random cryptographic keys, should the cryptoanalysis remain a hard problem. Furthermore, integrity mechanisms such as ISO 8731-2 [5] or cryptographic key exchange mechanisms such as the Diffie-Hellman Protocol [6] or the construction of digital signatures like the ElGamal or Digital Signature Scheme (DSS) [4] need the generation and use of random numbers. In addition, random numbers are used for the generation of pseudonyms and of traffic and message padding, in order to protect against traffic analysis attacks and for the computation of strong and efficient stream ciphers [4].

R.I. McKay and J. Slaney (Eds.): AI 2002, LNAI 2557, pp. 615–626, 2002.

Random bit sequences of good quality, i.e., of good behavior in statistical and non-predictability terms, are desired. Otherwise it would be possible for a cryptoanalyst, given a segment of this bit sequence and reasonable computer resources, to calculate the next bits or more about them [7]. In the last two decades considerable work has been made in the design and analysis of pseudo random number or bit generators [7,8, 9]. In this paper, we briefly survey some of these generators, propose a methodology to strengthen them and to evaluate their behavior and strength.

The level of randomness of a sequence can be defined in terms of statistical tests, which emulate computations encountered in practice, and check that the related properties of the sequence under investigation agree with those predicted if every bit (or number) was drawn from a uniform probability distribution [12]. The generators we consider in this paper are those used by the system-theoretic approach to the construction of stream ciphers. Secure keystream generators have to satisfy design criteria, such as long period, ideal k-tuple distributions, large linear complexity, confusion, diffusion and nonlinearity criteria [9]. Most of them are contained in the proposed evaluation methodology.

In section 2, we shortly describe traditional pseudorandom number generators and introduce our novel method to strengthen these generators by means of neural network based mechanisms. The third section is dedicated to the proposed evaluation methodology for random number generators, namely to the non-predictability test and to the appropriate statistical and non-linearity tests. In section 4, we present evaluation results obtained by applying the proposed methodology on various traditional and strengthened generators. Finally, we conclude our paper and outline future work on this subject.

2   A Novel Methodology for Improving Strong Pseudorandom Number Generators by Means of Neural Networks

The great majority of random number generators used for traditional applications such as simulations are linear congruential generators, which behave statistically very well, except in terms of non-predictability, since there exists a linear functional relation connecting the numbers of the sequence. A sequence of random numbers produced by these generators is defined as follows: $Z_i = (aZ_{i-1} + c)(\mod m)$, where m, a and c are the coefficients, i.e., the modulus, the multiplier and the increment, correspondingly. z_0 is the seed or initialization value. All are nonnegative integers. Each random number can be expressed, as mentioned above, as a function of another random number or of its predecessors or of the seed and the coefficients: $Z_i = \left\lceil \dfrac{a^i + ca^{i-1}}{a-1} \right\rceil (\mod m)$

So, if the coefficients and the seed or any random number belonging in the sequence is known, then all numbers of the sequence can be inferred. Such generators are inappropriate for security mechanisms, since the disclosure of one of them could very easily lead to the computation of the others.

In random components of secure electronic commerce systems like electronic payment systems, authentication and key generation and exchange the primary concern of the used pseudorandom bit sequences is that they are unpredictable, while being uniformly distributed comes as requirement next. True random numbers are independent from each other and therefore unpredictable but they are rarely employed, since it is difficult to obtain and they are not reproducible. It is more common that numbers that behave like random numbers are obtained by means of an algorithm, i.e., a pseudorandom number generator.

Based on the OFB of symmetric cryptosystems, like DES, cryptographically strong pseudorandom number generators are some of the most commonly employed in security mechanisms of electronic commerce systems. For instance, in [9] a procedure is suggested to generate session keys from a master key. Each pseudorandom bit string, i.e., the session key, is obtained from the cipher of a counter value encrypted under the control of a master key. The counter has a period of N and its value is incremented by one after a session key generation. $S_i = C_i = E_{k_m}(C)$. As a pseudorandom number generator the output feedback operation mode of symmetric cryptosystems is employed. It can be used for session key generation and the implementation of stream cipher computation. According to this method the encryption function of the symmetric cryptosystem is, at first, applied to an initialization variable under the control of a cryptographic key. The resulting cipher is the pseudorandom bit string or number. Subsequently, the output of the encryption function, i.e., the cipher is the new input to the encryption function E_k, $R_1 = E_k(I)$, $R_2 = E_k(R_1) \cdots R_n = E_k(R_{n-1})$.

In this paper, we describe an approach for constructing robust random number generators to be used in security mechanisms of electronic commerce applications, which are based on feed-forward Artificial Neural Network (ANN) techniques. It is well known that ANNs possess very interesting function approximation capabilities making them a very powerful tool in many scientific disciplines. For instance, feed-forward ANNs of the MultiLayer Perceptron (MLP) type have the theoretical ability to approximate arbitrary nonlinear mappings as well as their differentials [10]; there is also the possibility that such an ANN approximation is more parsimonious, i.e., it requires less parameters, than other competitive techniques such as orthogonal polynomials, splines, or Fourier series. Also, since ANNs are parallel and distributed processing devices they can be implemented in parallel hardware and, consequently, they can be used for real-time applications.

Their most important and intriguing property that makes them useful for applications is their generalization capabilities, that is their ability to produce reasonable outputs when they are fed with inputs not previously encountered. To be more specific, ANNs generalize when they compute or recall full patterns from partial or noisy input patterns, when they recognize or classify objects not previously trained on, or when they predict new outcomes from past facts. The ability to classify objects, which have not been previously learned can be characterized as a form of interpolation between trained patterns [10]. The ability to predict from past data might be characterized as a form of extrapolation [10], but what really happens is that ANNs predict well only if their present input vectors are similar to past behavior vectors. It could be in general said that by generalization, the ANN ability to respond with similar outputs for similar inputs is considered. There exists no other constraint for the position in the problem space the unknown input vectors should lie, in order to achieve good generalization performance by ANNs, apart from their short distance from training set vectors. It is irrelevant whether, they are inside or outside of the topological space occupied by the learning vectors. Therefore, ANN generalization capability cannot actually be characterized as an interpolation or extrapolation property but as a characteristic based on the topological similarities of their training and test sets. The multitude of real world applications of ANNs and especially MLPs, ranging from pattern classification to time series prediction and systems control, exist exactly due to their unique generalization performance.

The above desired abilities, however, are acquired in MLPs by training them well with known input vectors provided overfitting has not occurred [10]. In the case of overfitting it is well known [10] that the network, on the one hand, learns very well the training samples but, on the other hand, it is unable to generalize when fed with unknown input patterns. This happens, because the network draws the fitting surface of the training samples in a much more complex way, that is its fitting surface is of much higher degree, than needed to map the actual pattern population distribution. In such a case MLP response is not predictable since there is no analytic formula for describing the previously mentioned complex fitting surface. Even for unknown data with small distances from the training samples (similar inputs) network outputs will be very different from the ones obtained with the corresponding training data. Although in pattern recognition/control/prediction applications such a situation is highly undesirable, it could be exploited, however, in the case of random number generation. We demonstrate, in this paper, that overfitting in MLPs could be exploited as a mechanism for the generation of strong pseudorandom bit sequences as follows

1. Train an MLP of topology e.g 4-6-6-1 in the parity-4 problem so as to learn it more than it is required, i.e., for instance for 2500 epochs even when 500 epochs are enough. The goal is that overfitting should occur in this MLP training process. Of course other binary such benchmarks as well as much more complex MLP topologies could have been involved.

2. Test the already trained MLP using test input vectors with components produced by a traditional (pseudo)random number generator, like the ones involved in the experimental section of the paper, whose values are in the interval [0,1].

3. Form a complex function of the internal representations of such an MLP and compute its value when a test input vector as previously defined is presented to the network.

In this way a sequence of (pseudo)random numbers is produced whose quality is quantitatively evaluated by utilizing the statistical tests presented in the next section. The complex function of MLP internal representations used in the present paper has the following analytic formula.

$$Y = \mod f (1000* \text{Sum} (|O_k - O_{k+1}|/|O_{k+1} - O_{k+2}|))$$

where y is the random number obtained and O_k, O_{k+1}, O_{k+2} are the activations of the processing elements of the MLP layer preceding its output one. **modf** is a Unix-function that extracts the fractional part of a real number.

The previous discussion determines all the steps of the approach adopted here for designing strong (pseudo)random bit sequences generators employing the overfitting MLP recall properties.

Apart from MLPs we consider how Hopfield type neural networks could produce strong pseudo-random numbers for electronic commerce systems. The methodology for transforming Hopfield type recurrent ANNs into strong (pseudo)random number generators is herein depicted by exploiting their properties to minimize a cost function involving their weights and neuron activations under certain conditions concerning their weight matrix [10]. More specifically, a Hopfield network possesses the following important characteristics [10], which are next summarized.

a) If the weight matrix of a Hopfield recurrent ANN is symmetric with zero valued diagonals and furthermore, only one neuron is activated per iteration of the recurrent recall scheme then, there exists a Liapunov type cost function involving its weights and neuron activations, which decreases after each iteration until a local optimum of this objective function is found.

b) The final output vector of the Hopfield network, after the convergence of the above mentioned recurrent recall scheme, has minimum distance or is exactly equal to one prototype stored in the network during its weight matrix definition (learning phase) provided that the prototypes stored are orthogonal to one another and their number M <= 0.15 N, where N is the number of neurons in the network.

c) If the prototypes stored in the Hopfield ANN are not orthogonal or their number M > 0.15 N then, the recurrent recall scheme converges to a linear combination of the prototypes stored when it is fed with a variation of one of these prototype vectors, provided that the weight matrix has the properties discussed in (a) above.

d) Hopfield net outputs are given by the following formula, which is precisely the update formula for the single neuron activated during the iterations of the recurrent recall scheme mentioned in (a) above.

$$O_k = g(\text{Sum} (W_{ki} O_i))$$

A sigmoidal nonlinearity is considered for g, in the following.

These properties lead us intuitively to the principles of the proposed random number generation methodology involving such recurrent ANNs, summarized as follows.

1) If we impose a perturbation to the recurrent network weight matrix so that its symmetry is broken and its diagonal units obtain large positive values then, the convergence property of the recurrent recall scheme will be lost. This can be achieved, for instance, by adding a positive parameter δ to every unit in the upper triangle of the matrix, including diagonal units, and subtracting the negative quantity $-\delta$ from every unit in the lower triangle of the matrix

2) Moreover, if we let a large number of neurons (in our experiments N/2 neurons) update their activations by following the formula of (d) above, then, the recurrent

recall scheme will loose its convergence property to a local optimum of the suitable Liapunov function associated to the network.

3) If the recurrent recall scheme is not guaranteed to converge to a network output that corresponds to the local optima of a cost function then, the behavior of the network becomes unpredictable.

4) If the network is large and the patterns stored in it are orthogonal and thus, uncorrelated (that is, they have maximum distances from one another) then, the possibility of obtaining predictable outputs after several iterations of the recurrent recall scheme is minimum compared to the one associated with storing non-orthogonal prototypes, which are correlated to one another. In our experiments we use binary valued orthogonal patterns.

5) If the history of the network outputs during its recall phase is considered for T iterations of the recurrent recall scheme then, predicting the sequence of these output vectors is much harder than trying to predict a single output vector.

The above principles lead us to use the following function of network outputs over T iterations of the recurrent recall scheme as a pseudorandom number generator. To obtain better quality pseudorandom numbers, we have considered the Unix-function **modf**, which outcomes the non-integral part of a real number, as the required mechanism for aiding Hopfield net output to acquire the desired properties, since the first digits of its decimal part are predictable, due to the fact that the sigmoidal nonlinearity g is a mapping on the (0,1) interval. Consequently, the formula of the Hopfield recurrent ANN proposed random number generator is as follows.

$$O = \text{mod f} \; (1000*(1/TN) \; \text{Sum Sum} \; (g(\; \text{Sum} \; (W_{ki} \; O_i(t))))^2)$$

The previous discussion determines all the steps of the approach adopted here for designing strong (pseudo)random bit sequences generators employing the recurrent recall scheme of Hopfield networks.

Additionally, the above two presented neural network based methodologies for constructing strong pseudo-random bit sequences could be involved in strengthening traditional generators as follows. The initial weights of MLP are drawn from the traditional random number generator produced bit sequence and then, the MLP is employed as previously described as a random number generator mechanism. Thus, a two-stage generator is created, which, as illustrated in section 4 enhances the quality characteristics of the corresponding traditional one. On the other hand, Hopfield recurrent ANN initial input values are drawn in the same way from the traditional random number generator produced bit sequence and then, this Hopfield net is involved as a random bit generator. Thus, again, a two-stage generator with enhanced properties is produced, which is evaluated in section 4.

3   An Evaluation Methodology for Random Number Generators in Communication Systems Involving a Novel Non-predictability Test Based on ANN

Two criteria are used for the evaluation of the quality of random numbers obtained by using some generator in traditional applications such as simulation studies: uniform distribution and independence. The most important requirement imposed on random number generators is their capability to produce random numbers uniformly distributed in [0,1]; otherwise the application's results may be completely invalid. The independence requires that the numbers should not exhibit any correlation with each other. Additionally, random number generators should possess further properties: to be fast in computing the random numbers, to have the possibility to reproduce a given sequence of random numbers and to be able of producing several separate sequences of random numbers. However, for random number generators involved in the implementation of security mechanisms such as authentication, key generation and exchange in electronic commerce systems the most important property might be to produce unpredictable numbers. True random numbers possess this property. It is well known that pseudorandom number generators, that are used for simulations such as the linear congruential generators have not this property since each number they produce can be expressed as a function of the initialization value or of its predecessor value and the coefficients of the generator.

In addition to these traditional tests we introduce a predictability test for random bit sequences based on the MLP capabilities to approximate functions without any kind of assumption about their model, either linear or nonlinear [10]. To this end, if we consider a random bit sequence as a time series, then, by scanning it with a sliding window of length M we could form from it a series of patterns suitable for defining a training task for an MLP. Thus, M such samples comprise its inputs while their corresponding next one comprises its desired output. The training task for such an MLP is to perfectly learn these predictability patterns. If the random bit sequence has N samples then, there exist N-M such patterns. The rationale underlying the suggested test is that if such a task is learnable then, obviously, there exists great possibility that future numbers of the sequence under consideration can be inferred from their present and past values in the sequence. Therefore, by applying the above discussed learning task to an MLP and estimating the corresponding Minimum Average Sum of Squared Errors (SSE) per pattern we could have a view of how difficult is to predict the given random bit sequence. This SSE based measure of non-predictability, however, provides a hint for the average performance of the generator only. There might exist portions of the sequence that could be more predictable than others. A measure, suitable to account for such a fact, is the Maximum Approximation Probability (MAP), which counts the maximum number of correctly predicted patterns, with respect to a predefined approximation error ε per pattern, within the total number of patterns. It is obtained during the above specified MLP training session. Therefore,

MAP = max [predicted patterns (with SSE < ε)] / [total number of patterns (=N-M)] during the whole MLP training session. In our simulations the quantities above described take on the values ε = 0.001, N=5000 and M=2 respectively.

Statistical tests are applied to examine whether the pseudorandom number sequences are sufficiently random [9,11,12]. In the following we shortly discuss the empirical tests we use to evaluate the quality of the pseudorandom numbers obtained by the generators involved in this paper, i.e., how well they resemble true random numbers.

The first empirical test we apply is the most basic technique in the suite of the methods used for evaluating pseudorandom numbers quality, namely, the chi-square test (x^2 test). According to this method the interval $[0,1)$ is divided into k subintervals of equal length. The k should be at least 100, and $\frac{n}{k}$ should be at least 5, where n is the length of the sequence [12]. In our examples $n = 5000$ and $k = 101$. We build $X^2 = k/n*SUM_{i=1..k}\{(f_i-n/k)^2\}$, where f_i is the number of random quantities that fall in the jth subinterval. For large n, X^2 will have an approximate chi-square distribution with $k-1$ df (degrees of freedom) under the null hypothesis that the obtained pseudorandom numbers are identically, independently and uniformly distributed in the interval $[0,1)$ [11, 12]. We reject this hypothesis at level of confidence $1-a$ if $x^2 > x^2_{k-1,1-a}$, where $x^2_{k-1,1-a}$, is the upper $1-a$ critical point of the chi-square distribution with $k-1$ df [11,12]. In this paper, we make use of an approximate value of the

$$x^2_{k-1,1-a} \approx (k-1)\left\{1-\frac{2}{9(k-1)}+z_{1-a}\sqrt{2/[9(k-1)]}\right\}^3 \quad \text{suggested in [11,12], where}$$

z_{1-a} is the upper $1-a$ critical point of the $N(0,1)$ distribution.

The second empirical test we use is the run test. The run tests look for independence and therefore, as discussed in the introduction of this work, are the most important tests for electronic commerce applications. With these tests we examine the length of monotone (increasing) portions of the pseudorandom number sequence. The test statistic is $V= 1/N*SUM_{i=1..k} SUM_{j=1..k} A_{ij}(R_i-NB_i)(R_j-NB_j)$, where N is the sequence length, R_i is the number of monotone portions of length i with $i < 6$ and R_6 is the number of the rest portions of length > 5. The matrices of coefficients A_{ij} and B_i are approximate values taken from [11]. The statistic V should have the chi-square distribution with six degrees of freedom, when N is large, i.e., greater than 4000. If V is greater than the critical point of the x^2 distribution with 6 df at confidence level $1-a$ we reject the hypothesis of independence.

Finally, concerning the classical empirical tests, the sample means and variances of the pseudorandom number sequences obtained by the generators herein employed have been computed and compared with their expected values associated to the uniform distribution in the range [0,1), i.e. 0.5 and (1/12), respectively.

4   Evaluation and Discussion

An experimental study has been carried out in order to demonstrate the efficiency of the suggested, in section 2, procedures for designing pseudorandom number generators. The following experiments have been conducted by applying the empirical tests depicted in section 2, on

1. A random sequence produced by the DES algorithm.
2. A random sequence produced by the Hopfield recurrent ANN using the methodology described in section 2.
3. A random sequence produced by an overfitting MLP based pseudorandom number generator, whose initial weights and all its inputs have been computed from a random sequence resulted by running a linear congruential number generator.
4. Two two-stage generators involving in their second stage an MLP generator while, at their first stage, this MLP's weights are initialized from: (a) the DES sequence of (1) above, (b) the MD5 sequence of (2) above

The Hopfield ANN herein employed has $N = 100$ neurons connected following the conventional feedback architecture. All the sequences herein produced and compared have 5000 points. All the results obtained from the above specified experiments concerning the statistical and the non-predictability tests are presented in Tables 1 and 2, respectively. theoretical (2-D, 3-D spectral tests) From these tables we can derive the following:

1. Indeed, it is possible to obtain strong pseudorandom numbers using the complex recurrent recall scheme of Hopfield type ANNs.
2. It is possible to obtain strong pseudorandom numbers using the complex mapping properties of overfitting feedforward ANN of the MLP type to respond unpredictably in unknown input vectors even when they are similar to the training patterns.
3. Additionally, the proposed pseudo-RNG can enhance the quality of random numbers obtained by traditional generators when they are involved in a two stage procedure.
4. These pseudorandom numbers are of good quality, passing several critical evaluation tests.
5. Although it has been demonstrated that there exists at least one function of MLP weights, or Hopfield network parameters, which can be designed to have the required properties, it is not obvious how to construct it. Building such functions relies on intuition and experimentation.
6. The proposed nonlinear non-predictability test can reveal hints when analyzing a given pseudorandom number sequence. To be more specific, it can provide indications about average and maximum predictability properties of such a series.

Table 1. The classical empirical test results

Generator	χ^2 test (max = 118.499)	Run test (max=10.645)	Sample mean	Sample Variance
DES	109.2	2.464	0.503	0.0836
MD5	68.87	24.861	0.500	0.0828
Hopfield-recurrent ANN	79.84	3.745	0.498	0.0835
MLP(4-20-20-1) Off-line BP	57.874	0.268	0.500	0.0832
MLP (4-6-6-1) Off-line BP, parity-4, (n=1.0)	80.098	4.323	0.498	0.0819
DES-MLP (4-6-6-1), Off-line BP, parity-4 (n=0.4)	102.68	2.351	0.506	0.0830
MD5-MLP (4-6-6-1), Off-line BP, parity-4 (n=1.0)	93.026	1.078	0.503	0.0833

5 Conclusions

We have studied the use of recurrent ANN of the Hopfield type and the use of Over-fitting MLP neural network training properties as generators of pseudorandom numbers and as strengthening elements of traditional generators to be integrated in the protocols of multimedia communications. The former ANN method relies on their ability to perform complex mappings between their inputs and outputs during their recurrent recall phase, which are unpredictable when a suitable perturbation of the weight matrix is involved. The second ANN technique is exploiting the fact that they respond unpredictably to unknown inputs even when they are similar to the ones employed in their training set, provided overfitting has occurred in network training.

The same characteristics of the neural network architectures are exploited by their role as strengthening elements of traditional generators. The proposed non-predictability test, which is based on the time series forecasting properties of MLP, along with empirical and theoretical tests comprise an evaluation methodology of pseudorandom number generators.

Table 2. Non-predictability test results. SSEs are considered on all the N-M patterns of each random sequence, where N=5000 is the sequence length and M=2 is the sliding window length.

Generator	Minimum SSE per pattern (= total Min SSE/ number of patterns=4998) in a 2-35-35-1 MLP, On-line BP (n=0.2, a=0.3)	MAP (ε =0.001)
DES	421.81/4998	68.03%0
MD5	418.54/4998	54.02%0
Hopfield-recurrent ANN	416.48/4998	53.04%0
MLP (4-20-20-1) Off-line BP	413.54/4998	52.08%0
MLP (4-6-6-1) Off-line_BP, parity-4(n=1.0)	412.50/4998	52.00%0
DES-MLP, (4-6-6-1) Off-line_BP, parity-4(n=0.4)	418.58/4998	50.02%0
MD5-MLP(4-6-6-1) Off-line_BP, parity-4(n=1.0)	420.31/4998	44.02%0

The neural-network-based and the strengthened generators have been shown to behave better than the traditional ones in terms of statistical and non-predictability tests. Future work aims to extent the role of further neural network architectures as generators or as strengthening elements of generators. The evaluation of often used generators by means of the proposed methodology is, also, a pursuit of our current work. But the most practical aspect of our work is to integrate such algorithms in the protocols of multimedia communications for secure transactions in the delivery of multimedia content, which is under way and will be presented in the near future.

References

[1]   D.Gollmann, T. Beth, F. Damm, *"Authentication Services in Distributed Systems"*, J. Computers & Security, 12 (1993), pp. 753–745.

[2]   ITU-T X.509 Authentication Framework

[3]   DES77, Data Encryption Standard, Federal Information Processing Standards Publication 46, NBS, January 1977.

[4]   Schneier B.,*"Applied Cryptography"*, J. Willey & Sons, second edition, 1996

[5]   ISO 8731-2, *"Approved Algorithms for Message Authentication, Part 2: Message Authenticator Algorithm (MAA)"*.

[6]   W. Diffie, M.E. Hellman: *"New Directions in Cryptography"*, IEEE Transactions on Information Theory, Vol. 22, No 6, 1976, pp. 644–654.

[7]   K. Zeng, C-H Yang, D.-Y. Wei, and T.R.N Rao, "Pseudo random Bit Generators in Stream Cipher Cryptography", IEEE Computer, 8–17, 1991.

[8]   A. Shamir, "On the Generation of Cryptographically Strong Pseudorandom Sequences", J. ACM Transactions on Computer Systems, Vol. 1, No. 1, February 1983, pp. 38–44.

[9]   C. P. Schnorr, "On the Construction of Random Number Generators and Random Function Generators", Proc. Advances in Cryptology – EUROCRYPT '88, Springer-Verlag, 1988, pp. 225–232.

[10] Patterson D. W., "Artificial Neural Networks. Theory and Applications", Prentice Hall, 1996.

[11] A. M. Law, W. D. Kelton. Simulation Modeling and Analysis, MacGraw-Hill, 1991.

[12] Knuth, D. The Art of Computer Programming, Volume2: Seminumerical Algorithms. Reading, MA: Addison-Wesley, 3rd ed., 1998.

Surface Feature Recognition of Wear Debris

Mohammad Shakeel Laghari

Department of Electrical Engineering,
United Arab Emirates University,
P.O. Box: 17555,
Al-Ain, U.A.E.
mslaghari@uaeu.ac.ae

Abstract. Microscopic wear debris is produced in all machines containing moving parts in contact. The debris (particles), transported by a lubricant from wear sites; carry important information relating to the condition of the machinery. This information is classified by compositional and six morphological attributes of particle size, shape, edge details, color, thickness ratio, and surface texture. The paper describes an automated system for surface features recognition of wear particles by using artificial neural networks. The aim is to classify these particles according to their morphological attributes and by using the information obtained, to predict wear failure modes in engines and other machinery. This approach will enable the manufacturing industry to improve quality, productivity and economy. The procedure reported in this paper is based on gray level cooccurrence matrices, that are used to train a feed-forward neural network classifier in order to distinguish among seven different patterns of wear particles. The patterns are: *smooth, rough, striations, holes, pitted, cracked,* and *serrated.* An accuracy classification rate of 94.6% has been achieved and is shown by a confusion matrix.

1 Introduction

Computer vision is a process to locate and recognize objects in digital images. It is a relatively new and fast growing field and involves techniques from image processing, pattern recognition and artificial intelligence. Image segmentation is an important function of computer vision and image processing. Segmentation is concerned with splitting an image up into segments or regions such that each holds some property distinct from its neighbors. It is a basic requirement for the identification and classification of objects in a scene. Segmentation can be approached from two points of view; by identifying edges and shapes that run through an image, or by identifying regions such as texture [1], [2].

Computer vision has been used in diverse areas of applications. One of the important areas is in the field of automation of visual inspection systems, which enables the manufacturing industry to improve quality, productivity and economy of operation. These inspection systems include applications where information is obtained by using microscopes.

One such application is the analysis of microscopic wear particles that are produced in all machines with moving mechanical parts. During the initial run period of a machine, large amount of wear debris is produced due to the contact between new mechanical parts. Later, a steady state condition exists which produces relatively less amounts of wear debris. Any change in the steady state operation of the machine, creates a change in the normal wear mechanism. The associated changes in the microscopic wear particles, transported by a lubricant from wear sites, carry important information relating to the

B. McKay and J. Slaney (Eds.): AI 2002, LNAI 2557, pp. 627–637, 2002.
© Springer-Verlag Berlin Heidelberg 2002

condition of engines and other machinery. Experts in the field extract this information to diagnose occurring wear modes and thus attempt to predict wear failures in machines.

Monitoring of wear debris is very specific in aircrafts especially helicopter engines. Increase in typical wears may increase in the risk of fatal accidents. As these machines have to be airborne, on-line as well as off-line monitoring is performed on routine basis.

The aim of the current work is to identify particles according to their surface textural features by using artificial neural networks. A visual comparison between cooccurrence matrices representing seven different texture classes is described. Based on these comparisons, matrices of reduced sizes are utilized to train a feed-forward neural network classifier with a single hidden layer in order to distinguish between the various texture classes. Experiments are performed by varying the number of nodes in the hidden layer. A classification accuracy of 94.6% is achieved and is shown by a confusion matrix.

2   Wear Particle Definition

The term *Wear Particle* or *Wear Debris* is associated with the field of "Tribology" which is the study of wear, friction and lubrication [3].

An image-processing computer may effectively perform the identification and analysis of these particles with the ability to make 'human-like' diagnosis. One such computer based automated system could release an expert from this task and produce quantitative data not revealed by the human eye. Using the proposed techniques for monitoring at an early stage, expensive equipment failure and the loss of valuable production time can be avoided.

2.1   Particle Viewing and Separation

Using techniques such as X-rays and Ultrasound monitors machine wear. Particles contained in the lubricating oil can be separated for examination and analysis using several methods. An analytical method, developed in 1971, permits particles to be deposited on a glass slide, and identified by using a microscope. Different size filters are used in machines to separate particles from the lubricant [4].

Ferrography is another technique in which wear particles are separated from the lubricant and arranged according to size on a transparent substrate for analysis, thereby allowing further observation of the particles. The particle size range is typically between 1 to 100 μm [5].

The MCD *(Magnetic Chip Detectors)* or *Magnetic Plugs*, is yet another method used for extracting particles. Magnetic plugs are small removable units fitted with a powerful permanent magnet and situated in convenient positions in the machine. Due to magnetism, particles stick to the plug and later; the plug is wiped on a substrate or slide. The particle size in this case is typically greater than 100 μm [6].

2.2   Examples of Wear Particle

Particles generated by different wear mechanisms have characteristics, which can be identified with the specific wear mechanism. The following are a few examples of wear particles [4].

Rubbing wear or normal wear particles are generated as the result of normal sliding wear in a machine. The wear producing this particle is of benign nature and has a characteristic of normal rubbing wear. These are found in the lubricant of most machines in the form of platelets, typically ranging in size from 0.5 to 15 µm. Rubbing wear particles usually have a smooth surface texture.

Cutting wear or abrasive wear particles are generated as result of one surface penetrating another. It takes the form of spirals, loops, and long bent wires similar to the lathe-machining swath. The typical sizes of a cutting wear particle ranges from 2-5 µm wide to 25-100 µm long. Concentrations in such particles indicate severe wear mode and imminent machine failure. These particles do not have a particular surface texture, except that the spirals are very smooth and glossy.

Severe sliding wear particles are generated when the wear surface stresses become excessive due to poor lubrication, load and/or speed. These wear particles range in size from 15 µm up. Particles generated from severe sliding have very distinct surface features of striation marks. Again, concentration of such particles, and also with more prominent striation marks, indicate severe wear mode.

Laminar particles are associated with rolling bearing fatigue. These are very thin free metal particles between 20 and 50 µm, and are generated by the passage of wear particles through a rolling contact, possibly after adhering to a rolling element. Its surface features are recognized by frequent occurrence of holes in the particle.

Research in the field has suggested 29 different types of wear Particles [7].

2.3 Wear Particle Characteristics

The relationship between the wear particle properties and the condition under which they are formed enables particles to be classified in terms of a number of types. Each particle type gives a different clue about the machine condition and performance.

Particle features could be divided in terms of their *size, quantity, morphology* and *composition.* From these four features, tribologists know that quantity of the particles give the severity and rate at which they are generated, composition indicates the source of the generated particles, morphology indicates the source, type and rate of generation, and likewise particle size gives the rate, type and severity [8].

2.4 Wear Particles Classification

Particles can be classified in terms of their *compositional* and *morphological* attributes. The compositional attributes represent whether the particles obtained are metallic or non-metallic, if metallic, then ferrous (magnetic)or non-ferrous metals, etc. Fig. 1 shows the compositional attributes.

Morphological analysis is an off-line procedure carried out by using a microscope. Experts in the field characterize the particles in terms of their morphological attributes and relate them to known wear modes. The analysis yields specific information about the condition of the moving surfaces of the machine elements from which they were produced, the mechanism of their formation, and the mode of wear [9].

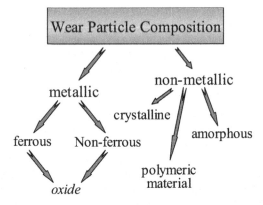

Fig. 1. Wear particle compositional attributes

Fig. 2 shows six morphological attributes of shape, size, edge detail, color, texture, and thickness ratio. Few examples of the shape, edge detail, and textures (cracked, smooth, pitted, and striations) are also shown in the Figure.   These attributes, if correctly diagnosed, can assist in predicting wear failure modes. The diagnosis part is very much related with an overall assessment of a particle with respect to all the six attributes.

A typical particle is viewed for its shape; such as regular, irregular, elongated, etc, its edge details; such as curved, straight, rough, etc, its size; usually increase in benign size is an indication of abnormal wears, its color; gives an indication of the source of particle generation, its thickness ratio; indication of some abnormalities in relation to size. Particle is carefully examined for its textural attribute. Specific texture patterns are clues for known wear modes. As mentioned earlier that the particle types such as laminar and severe sliding have holes and striation marks, respectively. Particles generated due to general fatigue typically results in a surface texture of pitting marks, which is another example of the importance of the texture attribute.

3   System Hardware and Software

The system hardware consists of an optical microscope with facility for viewing in transmission and/or incident light. . Images of the deposited particles are transmitted from the field of view in the microscope via a CCD color camera to an IBM compatible computer. The computer contains a Transtech motherboard with space to plug in up to 10 transputer modules (TRAM's). The motherboard is equipped with a fully programmable frame-grabber with one Mbyte of frame-store and four Mbytes of program memory. A graphics processor TRAM displays the image captured by the frame-grabber. The system is capable of processing 25 frames of 512 by 512 pixels (picture elements) per second [10].

The language used for programming the transputer system is `Parallel C' from the Company 3L. 3L's Parallel C can be used to write conventional sequential programs or use the full support for concurrency offered by transputers. The treatment of parallel processing in transputer systems is based on the idea of communicating sequential processes. In this model, a computing system is a collection of concurrently active sequential processes, which can only communicate with each other by channels. Although, use of parallel processing does not bare much significance for texture recognition only, but will be quiet essential when particles are recognized by using all the six morphological attributes.

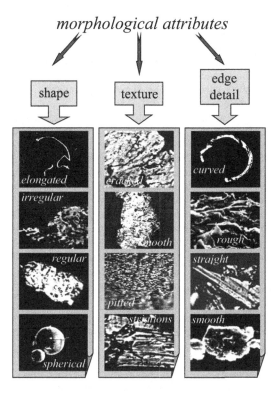

Fig. 2. Wear particle morphological attributes with examples

4   Analysis

Procedures are developed to provide a set of data to represent the morphological attributes of shape, edge detail, size and texture. Two types of analysis are carried out; one deals with the classification of particle profile attributes of size, shape and edge detail. The other is *Texture Analysis*, which is to classify the particles in terms of their surface texture.

4.1   Profile Analysis

The profile analysis is carried out on the perimeter or profile data and produces data in the form of particle size, major and minor dimensions, size averages, aspect ratio, roundness factor, and edge details analysis [11], [12], [13].

4.2 Texture Analysis

Texture analysis procedure is designed to execute within a devised "Wear Particle Texture Analysis" *(WPTA)* package. It is a multiple window, hierarchical interactive graphics interface that controls the software environment.

In a texture classification problem, a specific texture sample is assigned to one of a specified number of *k* possible classes. The decision is taken by a classifier, which is normally fed by data based on measurements made over the entire sample.

A statistical approach is used to describe the texture. It is based on cooccurrence matrices, which describe second-order statistics of the texture, and is usually used for the computation of features, which capture some characteristics of textures such as homogeneity, coarseness and periodicity [14], [15], [16].

The problem associated with the use of cooccurrence matrices is the handling of large amounts of data by the classifier. This is because the number of elements in a matrix is equal to the square of the number of distinct gray levels in the image. Therefore, the original number of gray levels (256) in the image is reduced in order to make the cooccurrence matrix smaller and hence reduces the amount of mathematical calculations involved. Dividing the gray levels into a small number of bands having equal widths performs this. Three different band numbers of *4*, *5*, and *6* have been used.

Since the number of elements in a matrix is equal to the square of the number of gray levels in the image, therefore the resulting matrices associated with these bands are '4 × 4', '5 × 5', and '6 × 6', respectively. The number of the bands used for current work is 6, which results in an image having new gray levels ranging from 0 to 5 and hence a matrix of 6 × 6 is computed. Therefore, a total of from 0 to 255 gray levels are reduced to from 0 to 5 by a method called *gray scale reduction* [17].

Cooccurrence Matrix. The cooccurrence matrix is related to the estimation of the second-order probability density function:

$$f\,(i, j,\, dist,\, ang)$$

It is defined as the probability of joint occurrence of two gray levels, '*i*' and '*j*' in a digital image, such that the distance between the two corresponding pixels is '*dist*' and at a direction defined by the angle '*ang*'. Therefore, a matrix can be computed by counting the number of times a pair of gray levels occurring at a separation of *dist* pixels and in a direction specified by *ang* degrees.

Fig. 3 shows an example of a digital image and its corresponding cooccurrence matrix for 6 bands. The matrix has been computed for horizontal adjacent gray level pairs, where the distance between pairs is *dist* = 1(adjacent) and at an angle of *ang* = 0 (horizontal in both directions). The Figure also shows how the cooccurrence matrix coordinates of (1, 2) computes the value of 7 from the digital image. The generated matrix is symmetric about the main diagonal. The data extracted from the matrix is used directly to feed the neural network classifier [18].

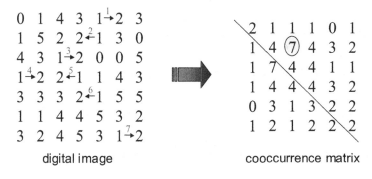

Fig. 3. Digital image gray level values and its corresponding six-band cooccurrence matrix

The Neural Network Classifier. A feed-forward neural network with a single hidden layer is used as the classifier in which a supervised scheme using the backpropagation algorithm is implemented. The algorithm requires several iterations in order to train the network. The input database consists of a set of input vectors included with the corresponding classifications. Each input training vector consists of a number of components, which is equal to the number of utilized features, plus the number of target texture classes. A trained network is designed to classify new unseen vectors and assign each one to a specific texture class [19].

The classifier consists of three layers: input, hidden, and an output layer. The input layer consists of a number of nodes, which is equal to the number of elements in the input vector. The hidden layer consists of a chosen variable number of nodes. The output layer consists of seven nodes, which represent the proposed wear particle texture classes. All connections between pairs of nodes in adjacent layers carry a weight, which keeps changing until the training phase is completed. Once this is achieved, the network is ready for use as a classifier.

5 WPTA Experiments

Texture analysis is carried out on the stored images for seven texture types of smooth, rough, striation, holes, pitted, cracked, and serrated.

Gray scale images of size 512×512 are captured from wear particle slides and displayed on the screen. The cursor is used in a *manual selection* procedure to select a sub-image of size 64×64 pixels on the particle image. Therefore, each particle image gives a choice of 64 ($512 \times 512 \div 64 \times 64$) sub-images. For the texture analysis experiment, a total of 48 sub-images per texture class are extracted from a reasonable number of particle images, which are in relation to the size of the particle and the region of interest in that particle. The extracted sub-images for each texture class are then divided equally at random for training and testing purposes in such a way that each of the training and test file consisted of 168 vectors (24×7).

For each texture sample, not one but four cooccurrence matrices are computed. Each matrix   corresponds   to   one   of   the   four   main   directions

($ang = 0°$, $45°$, $90°$, $135°$) between a pair of adjacent pixels. The respective elements in these four matrices are averaged in order to produce a rotation invariant matrix. The input to the classifier is based directly on this rotation invariant matrix.

As the matrix is symmetric along the main diagonal, this further reduces the input vectors of the classifier such that only 21 values of one end of the diagonal are fed instead of all 36 values. A texture classification system using cooccurrence matrices is shown in Fig. 4.

For the experiment, the classifier uses small to medium size of node numbers for the hidden layer. This is due to the limited number of input and output (7) vectors. Consequently, experiments are performed with the hidden layers of 4, 8, 12, 16 and 20 nodes. Fig. 5 shows a typical output generated by the WPTA classification package. The package identifies the particle texture as well as displays the particle sub-image. The shown example is classified as pitted with some concentration of roughness, holes & serration.

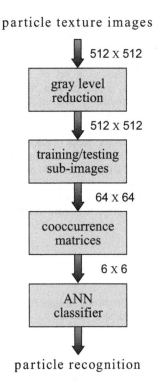

Fig. 4. The structure of WPTA system using cooccurrence matrices

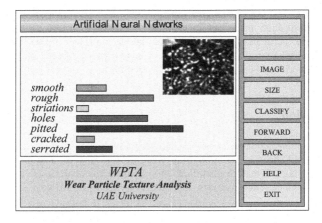

Fig. 5. A typical output screen of WPTA package with a particle sub-image

In the testing phase, the network with four hidden nodes achieved a maximum classification rate of 93%. All the other four networks achieved a maximum rate of 94.6%. This rate corresponds to a correct classification of 159 out of a total of 168 unseen test samples. Fig. 6 shows a confusion matrix, which illustrates the sample classification.

It is evident from the Figure that because of similarity of many textural features, for example, between serrated and striation; two serrated samples are misclassified as striation. Similarly, other misclassifications are; a cracked particle image as rough, two pitted classes as rough, a particle image of holes as pitted, and a serrated is misclassified as striations. It is suggested that the reason for this could be the slight variations in the surface texture between different particles, or even different areas in the same particle.

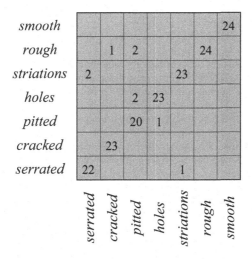

	serrated	cracked	pitted	holes	striations	rough	smooth
smooth							24
rough		1	2			24	
striations	2				23		
holes			2	23			
pitted			20	1			
cracked		23					
serrated	22				1		

Fig. 6. Confusion matrix showing the classification performance

As indicated, texture is an important attribute for the recognition of wear particles. The particle with striation marks as an example is produced due to *severe sliding* under pressure. These particles are generated when the wear surface stresses become excessive due to poor lubrication, load and/or speed. A concentration of such particles indicates a severe wear mode and hence needs immediate attention.

6 Conclusion

Computer vision and image processing techniques are used to collect important quantitative and other information from wear particle images. The paper describes an important attribute of texture identification system for the analysis of microscopic wear particles. A cooccurrence matrices approach is used to prepare data from an 64×64 image to a matrix of size 6×6. This reduced image is fed to a classifier based on an artificial neural network with a single hidden layer. Experiments performed indicated that by varying the number of nodes in the hidden layer, a classification rate of 94.6% is achieved.

Future work will concentrate on the procedures of WPTA package for automatic selection of sub-image windows for the wear particle texture classification. The particle image of 512×512 will be automatically scanned as a whole to select all the 64 sub-images for test purpose.

References

1. Shapiro, L.G., Stockman, G.C.: Computer Vision. Prentice Hall, New Jersey, 2001
2. Umbaugh, S.E.: Computer Vision and Image Processing – Using A Practical Approach. Prentice Hall, Europe, 1998
3. Jost, H.P.: Tribology - Origin and Future. Int. J. Wear. Vol. 136 (1990) 1-17
4. Anderson, D.P.: Wear Particle Atlas. (Revised), 4th print, prepared for the Naval Air Engineering Center, Lakehurst, NJ (1991)
5. Bowen E.R., Scott, D., Seifert, W., Westcott, V.C.: Ferrography. Int. J. Tribology. (1976) 109-115
6. Cumming, A.C.: Condition monitoring today and tomorrow - an airline perspective. In: 1st Int. Conf. COMADEN 89, Birmingham, U.K., September (1989)
7. Albidewi, I.A.: The application of Computer Vision to the Classification of Wear Particles in Oil. Ph.D Thesis, University of Wales, Swansea, U.K. (1993)
8. Roylance, B.J.: Wear debris analysis for condition monitoring. Int. J. INSIGHT. Vol. 36. (1994) 606-610
9. Laghari, M.S., Albidewi, I.A., Luxmoore, A.R., Roylance, B.J., Davies, T., Deravi, F.: Computer Vision System for the Recognition of Wear Particles. In: 2nd Int. Conf. Automation, Robotics and Computer Vision (ICARCV'92), Singapore, September (1992) CV-13.6.1 - CV-13.6.5
10. Laghari M.S.: Processor Scheduling for Transputer Networks. Ph.D. Thesis. University of Wales, Swansea, U.K. (1993)
11. Laghari, M.S., Albidewi, I.A., Luxmoore, A.R., Roylance, B.J., Davies, T., Deravi, F.: Knowledge based computer vision system for the classification of wear particles. In: Int. Symp. Comp. and Infor. Sciences VII, Antalya, Turkey (1992) 635-638

12. Laghari, M.S., Boujarwah, A.: Wear particle identification using image processing techniques. In: ISCA 5th Int. Conf. Intelligent Systems, Reno, U.S.A., June (1996) 26-30
13. Khuwaja, G.A., Laghari, M.S.: Computer vision techniques for wear debris Analysis. Int. J. Comp. App. in Tech. Vol. 15. No. 1/2/3 (2002) 70-78
14. Gool, L.V., Dewafele, P., Costerlink, A.: Texture analysis ann 1983. Int. J. Computer Vision, Graphics and Image Processing. Vol. 29 (1983) 336-358
15. Haralick, R.M., Shanmugan, K., Dinstein, J.: Textual features for image classification. IEEE Trans. Syst. Man. Cybern. SMC-3 (1973) 610-621
16. Garcia-Consuegra, J., Cisneros, G.: Integration of gabor functions with cooccurrence matrices: Application to woody crop location in remote sensing. In: IEEE Int. Conf. on Image Processing, vol II, Kobe, October (1999) 330-333
17. Muhamad, A.K., Deravi, F.: Neural networks for texture classification. In: IEE 4th Int. Conf. on Image Processing and its Applications - IPA'92, Maastricht, The Netherlands. (1992) 201-204
18. Davis, L.S., Clearman, M., Aggarwal, J.K.: An empirical evaluation of generalized cooccurrence matrices. IEEE Trans. Pat. Analysis and Machine Intelligence PAMI-3 (1981) 214-221
19. Muhamad, A.K.: Texture Classification Using Artificial Neural Networks. PhD Thesis, University of Wales, Swansea, U.K. (1998)

Improved Defect Detection Using Novel Wavelet Feature Extraction Involving Principal Component Analysis and Neural Network Techniques.

D.A. Karras[1] and B.G. Mertzios[2]

[1]Hellenic Aerospace Industry& Hellenic Open University, Rodu 2, Ano Iliupolis,
Athens 16342, Greece, dkarras@haicorp.com, dakarras@hol.gr,
dakarras@usa.net
[2]Democritus Univ. of Thrace, Dept. of Electr.and Comp. Eng., 67 100 Xanthi

Abstract. This paper aims at investigating a novel solution to the problem of defect detection from images, that can find applications in the design of robust quality control systems for the production of furniture, textile, integrated circuits, etc. The suggested solution focuses on detecting defects from their wavelet transformation and vector quantization related properties of the associated wavelet coefficients. More specifically, a novel methodology is investigated for discriminating defects by applying a supervised neural classification technique, employing a Multilayer Perceptron (MLP) trained with the conjugate gradients algorithm, to innovative multidimensional wavelet based feature vectors. These vectors are extracted from the K-Level 2-D DWT (Discrete Wavelet Transform) transformed original image using Vector Quantization techniques and a Principal Component Analysis (PCA) applied to these wavelet domain quantization vectors. The results of the proposed methodology are illustrated in defective textile images where the defective areas are recognized with higher accuracy than the one obtained by applying two rival feature extraction methodologies. The first one of them uses all the wavelet coefficients derived from the k-Level 2-D DWT, while the second one uses only image intensities characteristics. Both rival methods involve the same classification stage as the proposed feature extraction approach. The promising results herein obtained outline the importance of judicious selection and processing of 2-D DWT wavelet coefficients for industrial pattern recognition applications.

Keywords. Defect detection, Neural Networks, Wavelets

1 Introduction

Defect recognition from images is becoming increasingly significant in a variety of applications since quality control plays a prominent role in contemporary manufacturing of virtually every product. Despite the lot of interest, little work has been done in this field since this classification problem presents many difficulties. However, the resurgence of interest for neural network research has revealed the existence of powerful classifiers. In addition, the emergence of the 2-D wavelet transform [1],[2] as a popular tool in image processing offers the ability of robust feature extraction in im-

R.I. McKay and J. Slaney (Eds.): AI 2002, LNAI 2557, pp. 638–647, 2002.

ages. Combinations of both techniques have been used with success in various applications [3]. Therefore, it is worth attempting to investigate whether they can jointly offer a viable solution to the defect recognition problem. To this end, we propose a novel methodology in detecting defective areas in images by examining the discrimination abilities of their K-level wavelet coefficients based features. Besides neural network classifiers and the K-Level 2-D wavelet transform, the tools utilized in such an analysis are vector quantization and Principal Component related analysis [4] of the vectors quantizing the K-Level wavelet domain of an image window.

The problem at hand can be clearly viewed as image segmentation one, where the image should be segmented in defective and non-defective areas only unlike its conventional consideration. Concerning the classical segmentation problem, that is dividing an image into homogeneous regions, the discovery of a generally effective scheme remains a challenge. To this end, many interesting techniques have been suggested so far including spatial frequency techniques [5] and relevant ones like texture clustering in the wavelet domain [5]. Most of these methodologies use very simple features like the energy of the wavelet channels [5] or the variance of the wavelet coefficients [6].

Our approach stems from this line of research related to the wavelet domain judicious processing. However, there is need for much more sophisticated wavelet feature extraction methods if one wants to solve the segmentation problem in its defect recognition incarnation, taking into account the high accuracy required. Following this reasoning we propose to incorporate in the research efforts multidimensional wavelet features, unlike the previously presented scalar feature extraction methodologies in the wavelet domain [6,5]. These multidimensional features, coming from the application of the K-Level 2-D DWT, are, in the sequel, processed using vector quantization and PCA methodology, which offer the accurate tools for describing transformed image characteristics and especially complex second order ones [4]. More specifically, PCA of the autocorrelation matrices analysis is well known to provide second order information about pixel intensities, while Vector Quantization algorithms provide the means for efficient vector space encoding. Two are the main stages of the suggested system. Namely, efficient multidimensional feature selection in the wavelet domain and neural network based classification. The viability of the concepts and methods employed in the proposed approach is illustrated in the experimental section of the paper, where it is shown that our methodology is very promising for use in the quality control field, by comparing its performance in defective areas classification accuracy with the one obtained by two rival feature extraction techniques.

2   Stage A: Efficient Multidimensional Feature Extraction in the K-Level Wavelet Domain

The problem of defect discrimination, aiming at segmenting the defective areas in images, is considered in the wavelet domain, since it has been demonstrated that discrete wavelet transform (DWT) can in general lead to better image modeling, as for instance to better encoding (wavelet image compression [7,8] is one of the best compression methodologies) and to better texture modeling [7]. Also, in this way, we can better exploit the known local information extraction properties of wavelet signal decomposition as well as the known features of wavelet de-noising procedures [9]. We use the popular 2-D discrete wavelet transform scheme ([1],[2] etc.) in order to obtain the wavelet analysis of the original image data containing defects. It is expected that the images considered in the wavelet domain should be smooth but due to the known time-frequency localization properties of the wavelet transform, the defective areas – whose statistics vary from the ones of the image background – should more or less clearly emerge from the background. We have experimented with the standard 2-D Wavelet transform using nearly all the well known wavelet bases like Haar, Daubechies, Coiflet, Symmlet etc. as well as with Meyer's and Kolaczyk's 2-D Wavelet transforms [2]. However, Daubechies and Haar wavelets have exhibited similar and the most accurate results and we employ them in the experimental section of the paper.

The proposed methodology involving multidimensional wavelet features obtained from the K-Level 2-D DWT, with application to defect detection, can be outlined in the following steps.

1) The N X N image is raster scanned by M X M sliding windows

2) Each such window is transformed into the wavelet domain using the K-Level 2-D DWT. As a result, the wavelet coefficients organized in $3 * K + 1$ channels (or bands) are obtained. (See Figure 1)

3) Starting from the channel LL_K (the upper left window in Figure 1, which represents the Low Pass filtered image), the multidimensional vectors V_j are formed from the wavelet coefficients, having as components $3 * K + 1$ windows (each one associated with one channel) of $2^{(K- MAX\_ LEVEL\_INDICATED\_IN\_QMF)} * 2^{(K - MAX\_ LEVEL\_INDICATED\_IN\_QMF)}$ points. These points comprise a sub-window of wavelet coefficients belonging in the corresponding channel, and the position of this sub-window, as defined by its upper left point, is exactly the point in the QMF window under consideration associated with the LL_K channel point comprising the first component of vector V_i. For instance, concerning the three-level DWT of figure 1, each V_j is comprised of 10 main components, which are windows of wavelet coefficients. Each such window includes $2^{(3 - MAX\_ LEVEL\_INDICATED\_IN\_QMF)} * 2^{(3 - MAX\_ LEVEL\_INDICATED\_IN\_QMF)}$ of wavelet coefficients. For the LL_3, HL_3, LH_3, HH_3 QMFs we have MAX_ LEVEL_INDICATED_IN_QMF = 3 and, thus, 1 DWT coefficient is considered. For the HL_2 , HH_2, LH_2 QMFs we have MAX_ LEVEL_INDICATED_IN_QMF = 2 and, thus, 2 * 2 DWT coefficients are considered. Finally, for the HL_1, HH_1, LH_1 QMFs we have MAX_ LEVEL_INDICATED_IN_QMF = 1 and, thus, 4 * 4 DWT coefficients are considered. Therefore, a total of 4 * 1 + 3 * 4 + 3 * 16 = 64 wavelet coefficients comprise each multidimensional wavelet vector V_j, in the case depicted in figure 1. The above mentioned sub-windows are illustrated in figure 1.

4) Obviously, the K-Level 2-D DWT space is spanned by the vectors V_i. In the sequel, the K-Level 2-D DWT domain is quantized using the vector quantization method of Kohonen Self Organizing Feature Map (SOFM) [4], which produces topology preserving codebook vectors [4]. These codebook vectors encode the topological space of the DWT domain by preserving input vectors probability distribution and are estimated as the associated with the SO map weight vectors [4]. Let's Cb1, Cb2,.... Cbn stand for these codebook vectors, where n<<r, if r is the multitude of Vi input vectors, that span K-Level 2-D DWT domain.

5) For each such Cbi we formulate its corresponding autocorrelation matrix $Cbi*Cbi^T$ and by applying the well known PCA techniques the associated ratio (Lmin / Lmax)i is calculated for the minimum and maximum eigenvalues of this autocorrelation matrix. Such a ratio plays a significant role in expressing the properties of these autocorrelation matrices and thus, to quantify the properties of the codebook vectors [4].

6) All the above calculated (Lmin / Lmax)i for every Cbi, form the input vectors for the neural classifiers of the subsequent stage B.

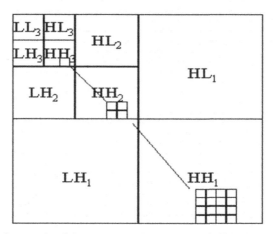

Fig. 1. Illustration of a sample of the corresponding wavelet coefficients sub-windows taking place in the formation of vectors Vi that span K-Level Wavelet domain. Three such windows are shown out of a total of 10 (one for each QMF channel).

The practical aspects of the above proposed feature extraction approach, are next presented.

a) We have experimented with 256 x 256 images and we have found that M=32 is a good size for a sliding window raster scanning them and capable of locating defective areas (step 1).

b) A two-level 2-D DWT wavelet decomposition of these sliding windows associated images has been performed for each such window, resulting in seven main wavelet channels (step 2).

c) Step 3 above leads to vectors Vi having 4*1 + 3*4 = 16 wavelet coefficients as components. There are 64 (since LL_2 channel includes 8*8 coefficients) such vectors Vi that span the 2-Level wavelet domain. A total of 1024 wavelet coefficients comprise this domain, which is a large number of features to be employed in the classification stage of the proposed defect detection approach, since the curse of dimensionality obviously arises [4]. A judicious compression of this 64 vector space is therefore, required.

d) This is achieved through applying step 4 depicted above. To this end, a Kohonen SOM neural network involving 16 component (the wavelet coefficients) input vectors Vi as inputs and a 4 X 4 map of 16 output neurons compresses this vector space. The associated codebook vectors compressing the input space of 64 vectors are the 16 corresponding SOM weight vectors.

e)   The autocorrelation matrices of these codebook vectors are of 16 X 16 dimensions. In step 5 above their 16 eigenvalues are calculated along with their min and max values. Therefore, for each Kohonen's SOM weight vector i the corresponding (Lmin / Lmax)i is estimated as indicated in step 5.

f)   The input vectors of the neural based classification stage that follows, constructed by the suggested feature extraction technique, therefore, comprise 16 elements like (Lmin / Lmax)i, one for each codebook vector.

Thus, using the above in detail outlined feature extraction procedure, we have obtained 16 feature input vectors efficiently describing spatial distribution in the wavelet domain of each 32 x 32 sliding window raster scanning the images. These 16 features uniquely characterize such sliding windows and the corresponding feature vectors feed the neural classifier of the subsequent stage of the suggested methodology, next defined.

3   Stage B: Neural Network Based Segmentation of Defective Areas

After obtaining the wavelet domain based characteristics of each M X M sliding window raster scanning the N X N image, involving the above defined methodology, we employ a supervised neural network architecture of the multilayer feedforward type (MLPs), trained with the conjugate gradients algorithm (Polak-Ribiere variation) [4], having as goal to decide whether such a sliding window covers a defective area or not. The inputs to the network are the 16 components of the feature vectors extracted from each such sliding window as previously defined. The best network architecture that has been tested in our experiments is the 16-8-8-1. The desired outputs during training are determined by the corresponding sliding window location. More specifically, if a sliding window belongs to a defective area the desired output of the network is one, otherwise, it is zero. We have defined, during MLP training phase, that a sliding window belongs to a defective area if the majority of the pixels in the 4 x 4 central window inside the original 32 X 32 corresponding sliding window belongs to the defect. The reasoning underlying this definition is that the decision about whether a window belongs to a defective area or not should come from a large neighborhood information, thus preserving the 2-D structure of the problem and not from information associated with only one pixel (e.g the central pixel). In addition and probably more significantly, by defining the two classes in such a way, we can obtain many more training patterns for the class corresponding to the defective area, since defects, normally, cover only a small area of the original image. It is important for the effective neural network classifier learning to have enough training patterns for each one of the two classes but, on the other hand, to preserve as much as possible the a priori probability distribution of the problem. We have experimentally found that a proportion of 1:3 for the training patterns belonging to defective and non-defective areas respectively is very good for achieving both goals.

4   Results and Discussion

The efficiency of our approach in recognizing defects in automated inspection images, based on utilizing wavelet domain information, is illustrated by applying it to the textile images shown in fig. 2,3,4 which contain various types of defective areas. Two other rival feature extraction methodologies are applied to these images too. The former of them uses all the 32 X 32 (=1024) wavelet coefficients obtained by the 2-D DWT transformation of each 32 X 32 sliding window without any further processing, while the latter uses the 32 X 32 (=1024) image intensities corresponding to the same sliding window. Therefore, the first feature extraction procedure used in this experimental study is the suggested novel one outlined in section II, which involves 16 components feature vectors. The second and the third feature extraction procedures as mentioned above, involve 1024 components feature vectors. The three images shown in figures 2,3,4 are of 256 x 256 dimensions and their associated 2-Level 2-D DWT are shown in figures 2, 3, and 4 respectively. The QMF channels shown in these figures have been obtained through applying the 2-D DWT with Daubechies wavelet bases to the original images. Obviously, the defective areas are preserved and enhanced in the corresponding wavelet domains and this explains the selection of the 2-D DWT as the baseline for the herein presented feature extraction methodology. There exist 50625 sliding windows of 32 x 32 size for each original image. The three rival feature extraction procedures used in this study are applied to every such sliding window, yielding the corresponding feature vectors. Therefore, for each image a set of 50625 training and test patterns is derived.

The neural networks corresponding to the classification stage (stage B) of the three defect detection systems under comparison are of the MLP type trained with the conjugate gradients algorithm (Polak-Ribiere variation). The best architectures found and compared are 16-8-8-1, 1024-64-32-1, 1024-64-32-1. For an image involved in the study, each MLP has been trained with its corresponding training set containing 1500 patterns extracted from the associated sliding windows as described above. On average (for the three images) 480 out of these 1500 patterns belong to the defective areas, while the rest belong to the class of non-defective areas. Each MLP has been tested on all 50625 patterns from which its training set comes from. The results obtained by involving our methodology are shown in fig. 5, 6 and 7 and clearly are very favorably compared, in terms of defect classification performance, to the two other feature extraction methodologies.

5   Conclusions

A novel methodology is developed for defect detection employing a new feature extraction approach applied to the k-Level wavelet domain and also, employing neural classifiers of the MLP type. This feature extraction approach considers multidimensional vectors of wavelet coefficients having as components suitably selected windows of these coefficients from their associated QMF channels. The K-Level wavelet domain is, therefore, composed as the space of all these vectors by using the suggested methodology. A vector quantization algorithm is subsequently applied to this

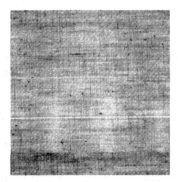 

Fig. 2. First original textile image containing a defect and the 2-Level 2-D Wavelet transformation of this image

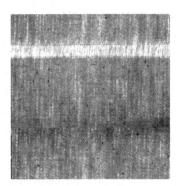 

Fig. 3. Second original textile image containing a defect and the 2-Level 2-D Wavelet transformation of this image

 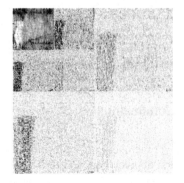

Fig. 4. Third original textile image containing a defect and the 2-Level 2-D Wavelet transformation of this image

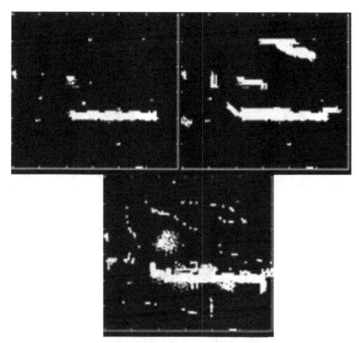

Fig. 5. Defect Detection results for the first textile image. From left to right the results obtained using the proposed feature extraction method, the 32 X 32 wavelet coefficients and the 32 X 32 pixel intensities as described in section 4

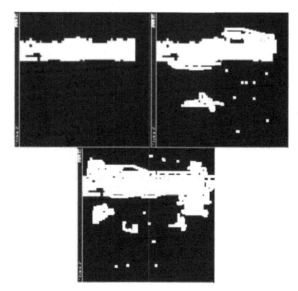

Fig. 6. Defect Detection results for the second textile image. From left to right the results obtained using the proposed feature extraction method, the 32 X 32 wavelet coefficients and the 32 X 32 pixel intensities as described in section IV

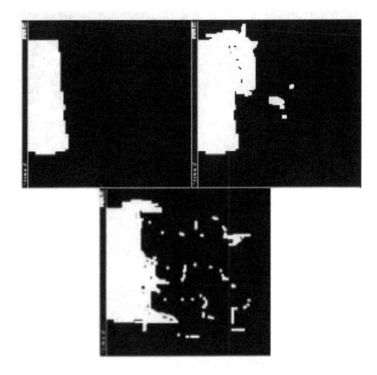

Fig. 7. Defect Detection results for the third textile image. From left to right the results obtained using the proposed feature extraction method, the 32 X 32 wavelet coefficients and the 32 X 32 pixel intensities as described in section IV

new vector space and the associated codebook vectors are extracted. The vector quantization algorithm used is the Kohonen topology preservation map (SOM) and the resulting codebook vectors are the corresponding SOM weight vectors. A PCA analysis of the autocorrelation matrices associated with these codebook vectors provides the components of the feature vectors, which feed the supervised MLP architectures of the classification stage of the proposed defect detection system. The proposed defect detection system is favorably compared with one involving as feature vectors the image intensities and another one having as feature vectors the 2-D DWT wavelet coefficients only. Both rival systems use the same MLP based classification technique as the herein proposed system. The promising results herein obtained set the baseline for the future work of the authors, which is currently focused on building a real world defect detection system for the textile industry instead of the prototype investigated in this paper.

References

[1] Meyer, Y. "Wavelets: Algorithms and Applications", Philadelphia: SIAM, 1993

[2] Kolaczyk, E. "WVD Solution of Inverse Problems", Doctoral Dissertation, Stanford University, Dept. of Statistics, 1994

[3] Lee, C. S., et. al, "Feature Extraction Algorithm based on Adaptive Wavelet Packet for Surface Defect Classification", to be presented in ICIP 96, 16-19 Sept. 1996, Lausanne, Switzerland.

[4] Haykin, S. "Neural Networks, A comprehensive foundation", Prentice Hall, Second edition, 1999.

[5] Porter, R. and Canagarajah, N. "A Robust Automatic Clustering Scheme foe Image Segmentation Using Wavelets", IEEE Trans. on Image Processing, April 1996, Vol. 5, No. 4, pp.662 - 665.

[6] Unser, M. "Texture Classification and Segmentation Using Wavelet Frames", IEEE trans. Image Processing, Vol. 4, No. 11, pp.1549-1560, 1995

[7] Ryan, T. W., Sanders, D., Fisher, H. D. and Iverson, A. E. "Image Compression by Texture Modeling in the Wavelet Domain", IEEE trans. Image Processing, Vol. 5, No. 1, pp. 26-36, 1996.

[8] Antonini, M., Barlaud, M., Mathieu, P. and Daubechies, I. "Image Coding Using Wavelet Transform", IEEE trans. Image Processing, Vol.1, pp. 205-220, 1992.

[9] Donoho, D. L. and Johnstone, I. M. "Ideal Time-Frequency Denoising." Technical Report, Dept. of Statistics, Stanford University.

Effectiveness for Machine Translation Method Using Inductive Learning on Number Representation

Masafumi Matsuhara[1], Kenji Araki[1], and Koji Tochinai[2]

[1] Graduate School of Engineering, Hokkaido University,
Kita 13 Nishi 8, Kita-ku, Sapporo, 060-8628 Japan.
{matuhara, araki}@media.eng.hokudai.ac.jp
[2] Graduate School of Business Administration, Hokkai-Gakuen University,
Asahimachi 4-1-40, Toyohira-ku, Sapporo, 062-8605 Japan.
tochinai@econ.hokkai-s-u.ac.jp

Abstract. On our proposed method, source language is translated into target language via Number Representation. A text in the source language is translated into a number representation text. The number representation text is the number string corresponding to the original source language text. The number representation text is translated into a number representation text for the target language. The number representation text is translated into a text in the target language. The text is the translation result finally. A number representation text is more abstract than the original text because the number representation text corresponds to several texts. The system based on our proposed method is able to acquire more translation rules on number representation than that on the original text by Inductive Learning. Moreover, the system disambiguates number representation by its own adaptability. In the experiment, the correct translation rate for our proposed method is higher than that for the method without number representation. Thus, it is proved that our proposed method is more effective for machine translation.

1 Introduction

Opportunities and needs are increasing to communicate with people in other countries because of the rapid expansion of the computer networks. However, the language problem disturbs smooth communication. The machine translation system is very effective to solve this problem.

The main method of machine translation systems is the Rule-based method. A system based on the Rule-based method is able to increase its correct translation rate when a large dictionary is given for the translation. However, it is impossible to implement the large dictionary dealing with complete linguistic phenomena to the system. Therefore, its correct translation rate is still low and the quality is poor. The Example-based and the Statistical machine translation[1][2] have been proposed to resolve this problem. A system based on these methods

R.I. McKay and J. Slaney (Eds.): AI 2002, LNAI 2557, pp. 648–659, 2002.
© Springer-Verlag Berlin Heidelberg 2002

is able to increase its correct translation rate as the learning data increases. The system needs large data for the high quality translation. It is difficult that the system enables translation for various languages because there are languages without adequate corpora.

K. Araki and H. Echizen-ya et al. have proposed the machine translation method using Inductive Learning with genetic algorithms[3][4]. The system based on this method is able to learn the translation rules from the only appearance of written characters on data by Inductive Learning and generate new translation examples through crossover and mutation in genetic algorithms automatically. However, many erroneous rules have been acquired in spite of selection ability of genetic algorithms.

Our proposed method uses number representation for Inductive Learning. The system based on our proposed method acquires common and different parts as the translation rules from the inputted text by Inductive Learning on number representation. The common part is the same characters between two sentences. The different part is the sentence without the common part. The system is not able to acquire the rules from the text which does not have the common parts because the system uses the only appearance of written characters. A number representation text is more abstract than the original text because the number representation text corresponds to several texts. There are more common parts on number representation than that on the original text. Therefore, the system based on our proposed method is able to acquire more translation rules on number representation than that on the original text. Some translation rules include different texts with same meaning. These rules are effective for the translation. The system needs number representation in order to acquire these translation rules. Moreover, we have proved that the number representation text is able to be translated into the correct text[5][6]. Then, the system is able to disambiguate the number representation text by its own adaptability. Thus, the system based on our proposed method is able to learn more rules which are effective for the translation by number representation and translate into the correct text.

This paper describes our proposed method "Machine Translation Method Using Inductive Learning on Number Representation" and the results of the evaluation experiment for English-Japanese translation in our proposed method.

2   Outline of Our Proposed Method

First of all, a user inputs a source language text into the system based on our proposed method. The text is translated into a number representation text. The number representation text is the number string assigned to the original text. The number representation text for the source language is translated into a number representation text for the target language. Last of all, the number representation text for the target language is translated into a text in the target language. Thus, a source language text is translated into a target language text via number representation on our proposed method. A number representation text is more abstract than the original text because the number representa-

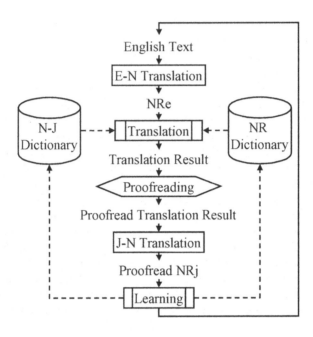

Fig. 1. Procedure

tion text corresponds to several texts. Then, the system based on our proposed method is able to acquire more translation rules on number representation than that on the original text by Inductive Learning. A translation rule is able to include different texts with same meaning when the different texts correspond to the same number representation text. The system selects the translation rules which are fit for the inputted data and translates into the target language text. Thus, the system based on our proposed method is able to efficiently learn and translate by the abstraction of the number representation.

3   Processes

Figure 1 shows the procedure for our proposed method applied to English-Japanese translation. The procedure consists of E-N Translation, Translation, Proofreading, J-N Translation and Learning Process in this order. The E-N translation process is for the translation of English into NRe. The NRe expresses number representation for English. The J-N translation process is for the translation of proofread translation result into Proofread NRj. The NRj expresses number representation for Japanese.

Table 1. Correspondence of Number to Alphabet

1:.?-'	2:ABC	3:DEF
4:GHI	5:JKL	6:MNO
7:PQRS	8:TUV	9:WXYZ
*:	0:	#:space

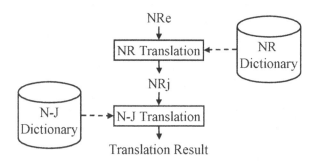

Fig. 2. Translation Process

3.1 E-N Translation Process

An English text inputted by a user is translated into the NRe in this process. Table 1 shows how to translate English characters into the number characters. For example, any of the characters "p", "q", "r" and "s" are translated into "7". The translation is able to apply to any language because this is the normal assignment for mobile phones. When the user inputs "I enjoy baseball.", this English text is translated into "4#36569#227322551".

An NRe is able to correspond to some texts and is abstract. For example, "home" is translated into "4663" and the "4663" is able to also correspond to "good" and so on. However, the system based on our proposed method disambiguates the number representation by its own adaptability. Thus, The system is able to efficiently learn and translate by the abstraction of number representation.

3.2 Translation Process

The NRe is translated into a Japanese text in this process. This process consists of NR Translation and N-J Translation Process. Figure 2 shows it. The NR translation process is for the translation of NRe into NRj. The N-J translation process is for the translation of NRj into Japanese.

NR Translation Process. The NRe is translated into an NRj by the number representation dictionary in this process. The dictionary is expressed as NR

Table 2. Translation Example

English Text	I enjoy baseball.
E-N Translation Process	
NRe	4#36569#227322551
NR Dictionary	
(English	: Japanese)
4#36569# @a 1	: @b 0324*##
2273225	: 8281
NR Translation Process	
NRj	82810324*##
N-J Dictionary	
8281:*yakiyuu* 0:*wo* 3:*su*	
24*:*kida* ##:.	
N-J Translation Process	
Translation Result	*yakiyuuwosukida.*
Proofreading Process	
Proofread Translation Result	*yakiyuuwotanosimu.*
J-N Translation Process	
Proofread NRj	828104537##

Dictionary in Figure 2. The NR dictionary has rules to translate NRe into NRj. The rules in the NR dictionary are acquired in the learning process. When there are some candidates for the translation, their credibility is evaluated by the credibility evaluation function(CEF). The function is defined as :

$$CEF = AF + \alpha \times CF - \beta \times EF \tag{1}$$

where α and β are coefficients. AF is the appearance frequency in text. CF is the correct translation frequency. EF is the erroneous translation frequency. CF and EF are based on the NR dictionary and are updated in the NR feedback process. The credibility for the translation is higher when AF is higher, CF is higher and EF is lower.

Table 2 shows an example of the translation. In Table 2, the NR dictionary has two rules "4#36569# @a 1 : @b 0324*##" and "22732255 : 8281". "@x" in the rule expresses a variable and is able to be replaced with another rule. Then, "@a" and "@b" are replaced with "2273225" and "8281" in Table 2. Therefore, the NRe is translated into "82810324*##".

N-J Translation Process. The NRj is translated by N-J Dictionary in this process. The N-J dictionary has rules to translate NRj into Japanese. When there are some candidates for the translation, their credibility is evaluated by the function which is similar to the equation (1). We show the detail of the

Table 3. Correspondence of Number to *Kana*

1:*a,i,u,e,o*	2:*ka,ki,ku,ke,ko*	3:*sa,si,su,se,so*
4:*ta,ti,tu,te,to*	5:*na,ni,nu,ne,no*	6:*ha,hi,hu,he,ho*
7:*ma,mi,mu,me,mo*	8:*ya,yu,yo*	9:*ra,ri,ru,re,ro*
*:Voiced Sound, P-Sound	0:*wa,wo,n*	#:Punctuation Marks

function in [6]. The ideal translation result is the Japanese text intended by the user.

Table 2 shows an example of the N-J translation. In Table 2, the N-J dictionary has five rules "8281:*yakiyuu*"[1], "0:*wo*", "3:*su*", "24*:*kida*" and "## :.". Then, the NRj "82810324*##" is translated into "*yakiyuuwosukida.*".

3.3   Proofreading Process

When the translation result has errors, the user proofreads the only appearance of written characters for them. Therefore, the proofread translation result is the Japanese text intended by the user.

In Table 2, the translation result has errors. The user replaces "*sukida*" with "*tanosimu*" to proofread the errors. The proofread translation result "*yakiyuuwotanosimu.*" is the sentence intended by the user.

3.4   J-N Translation Process

The proofread translation result is translated into the proofread NRj in this process. The proofread NRj is used in the learning process. Table 3 shows how to translate Japanese *Kana* characters into the number characters. For example, any of the *Kana* characters "*ma*", "*mi*", "*mu*", "*me*" and "*mo*" are translated into "7". This is the normal assignment for Japanese mobile phones. When the proofread translation result is "*yakiyuuwotanosimu.*", this Japanese text is translated into "828104537##". The proofread NRj is as abstract as the NRe.

3.5   Learning Process

The translation rules are acquired and registered into the NR dictionary and the N-J dictionary in this process. This process consists of NR Feedback, Re-N-J Translation and N-J Feedback Process. Figure 3 shows it. In the NR feedback process, the NR dictionary is updated. In the Re-N-J translation process, proofread NRj is again translated into Japanese. In the N-J feedback process, the N-J dictionary is updated.

---

[1] Japanese characters are written in *italics*. "*yakiyuu*" is generally expressed as "*yakyuu*" in Japanese. However, "*kyu*" is translated into "28" and the "28" also corresponds to "kiyu" in the system. Therefore, "*yakyuu*" is expressed as "*yakiyuu*" in this paper.

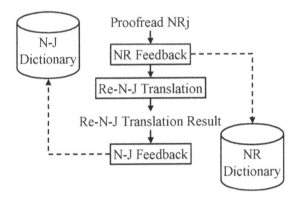

Fig. 3. Learning Process

NR Feedback Process. The NR dictionary is updated based on the NRe, the NRj and the proofread NRj in this process.

Learning for NR Dictionary.   The translation rules are acquired from the NRe and the proofread NRj, and registered into the NR dictionary. The pair "NRe:Proofread NRj" is compared to the translation rules in the NR dictionary. When there are common parts between the pair and the translation rule in the NR dictionary, the common and different parts are registered as new translation rules into the NR dictionary.

Table 4 shows an example of the learning. The pair "NRe:Proofread NRj" and the translation rule in the NR dictionary are as follows:

"4#36569#22732255̲1:828104537##"

"4#36569#8366471̲:45304537##"

The common parts between the pair and the translation rule are underlined. The acquired NR translation rules are shown in Table 4. "@x" in the rule expresses a variable and is able to be replaced with another rule in the translation process.

Updating for NR Dictionary.   CF and EF for the translation rules are updated based on the NRj and the proofread NRj. If the proofread NRj includes a translation rule of the NRj, the translation rule is correct. Then, the system adds 1 to the value of CF for the translation rule. If the proofread NRj does not include a translation rule of the NRj, the translation rule is erroneous. Then, the system adds 1 to the value of EF for the translation rule. Thus, credibility of the translation rules is updated in the NR dictionary.

In Table 4, the proofread NRj includes "8281" of the NRj and does not include "0324*##" of the NRj. Then, the system increases CF of the translation rule "22732255:8281" and increases EF of the translation rule "4#36569# @a 1:@b 0324*##". Thus, the credibility of "22732255:8281" increases and that of "4#36569# @a 1:@b 0324*##" decreases.

Table 4. Learning Example

NRe	4#36569#227322551
Proofread NRj	828104537##
NR Dictionary	
(English :	Japanese)
4#36569#8366471 :	45304537##
Acquired NR Translation Rules	
4#36569#8366471 :	45304537##
4#36569# @a 1 :	@b 04537##
22732255 :	8281
836647 :	453
NRj	82810324*##
Re-N-J Translation Process	
Re-N-J Translation Result	*yakiyuuwo* 4 *nasu* 7.
Proofread Translation Result	*yakiyuuwotanosimu.*
Acquired N-J Translation Rules	
8281:*yakiyuu* 0:*wo* 45:*tano*	
37:*simu* ##:.	

Re-N-J Translation Process. The proofread NRj is again translated in order to evaluate only the N-J translation process because the Translation Result in Figure 2 may include errors by the NR translation process. The translation result in this process is expressed as Re-N-J Translation Result in Figure 3.

In Table 4, the proofread NRj is translated into "*yakiyuuwo* 4 *nasu* 7.". "4" and "7" in the Re-N-J translation result have not been translated.

N-J Feedback Process. The N-J dictionary is updated based on the proofread translation result, the proofread NRj and the Re-N-J translation result in this process.

Learning for N-J Dictionary.   The translation rules are acquired from the proofread translation result and the proofread NRj, and registered into the N-J dictionary. The proofread translation result is compared to the proofread NRj. When there are common parts between the proofread translation result and the proofread NRj, the common and different parts are registered as new translation rules into the N-J dictionary.

In Table 4, the proofread translation result and the proofread NRj are as follows:

yakiyuuwotanosimu.

828104537##

The underlined segments are common parts because "*wo*" and "*simu*" of the proofread translation result are expressed as *Kana* characters which are Japanese

Table 5. Data of Experiment

Scene	Sentence Number	Character Number for Input	Word Number for Input	Character Number for Proofread
On the Plane	300	7,975	1,562	3,965
At the Airport	550	15,855	2,987	6,927
On the Check-in	400	11,891	2,277	5,366
On the Telephone	250	7,487	1,360	3,328
Total	1,500	43,208	8,186	19,586
Average		28.8	5.5	13.1

phonograms. The segments excluding them are different parts because *"yakiyuu"* and *"tano"* of the proofread translation result are expressed as *Kanji* characters which are Chinese ideographs. The acquired N-J translation rules are shown in Table 4.

Updating for N-J Dictionary.   CF and EF for the translation rules are updated based on the Re-N-J translation result and the proofread translation result. If the proofread translation result includes a translation rule of the Re-N-J translation result, the translation rule is correct. Then, the system adds 1 to the value of CF for the translation rule. If the proofread translation result does not include a translation rule of the Re-N-J translation result, the translation rule is erroneous. Then, the system adds 1 to the value of EF for the translation rule. Thus, credibility of the translation rules is updated in the N-J dictionary.

In Table 4, the proofread translation result includes *"yakiyuu"* and *"wo"* of the Re-N-J translation result and does not include "nasu" of the Re-N-J translation result. Then, the system increases CF of the translation rule "8281:*yakiyuu*" and "0:*wo*", and increases EF of the translation rule "53:*nasu*". Thus, the credibility of "8281:*yakiyuu*" and "0:*wo*" increases and that of "53:*nasu*" decreases.

The next translation is performed by the NR dictionary and N-J dictionary which have been updated in the learning process when the user inputs a next English text. Thus, the system based on our proposed method acquires the translation rules and improves because of the repetition of these processes gradually.

4   Evaluation Experiment

The system based on our proposed method has been developed for the experiment. The system translates English into Japanese.

4.1   Data and Procedure

The data for the experiment has four scenes and is shown in Table 5. This data was taken from 10 English travel books for Japanese[7]-[16]. Every English

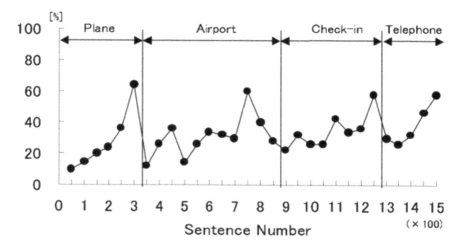

Fig. 4. Change in Correct Translation Rate

text of the data is inputted into the system step by step. If the translation result has errors, they are proofread based on the Japanese text of the data. The initial dictionaries are empty because of evaluation of adaptability of our proposed method. The system is able to improve its own translation performance by Inductive Learning.

We evaluate the correct translation rate per 50 sentences. The correct translation rate is proportion of the number of correct translation sentences to the number of sentences. The translation result was judged by the first author of this paper. The translation result is correct when the meaning of the translation result is identical with that of the Japanese text in the data. In this experiment, the values of the coefficients in equation (1) are $\alpha = 0.1$ and $\beta = 0.5$. It is based on [5][6].

4.2   Results and Considerations

Figure 4 shows the change in the correct translation rate. In Figure 4, the rate of the correct translation increases as the input data increases. When the scene of input data changes, the correct translation rate decreases. The reason is that there are the rules not registered into the NR dictionary and N-J dictionary. However, the correct translation rate increases again because the system acquires the translation rules for the new scene. The last rate of the correct translation is about 60[%] whereas the number of rules in the NR dictionary is only 5,155 and that in the N-J dictionary is only 764. We have also evaluated the translation performance for our proposed method without number representation. The mean of the correct translation rate for this method is lower than that for our proposed method by 4.6[%].

Table 6. Example of NR Rule

NR Dictionary
(English : Japanese)
26853#968# @a #63# @b #8447# @c 1 : 25 @d 40 @e 4144*2732##
8355, 469#86#3455#46, 2273 : 214*5222, 131
English Text
Could you tell me how to fill in this card?
NRe
26853#968#8355#63#469#86#3455#46#8447#22731
NRj
25214*522240131414*2732##
Translation Result
konokaadonokakikatawoosieteitadakemasuka?

The system is able to translate English text into Japanese one which is fit for the scene because of its own adaptability. The translation result for "Beef, please." is "*giyuunikunoriyouriwoonegaisimasu.*" in the scene "on the plane". The translation result is strongly fit for the scene "on the plane".

Since the system acquires NR translation rules which are special for the system, the segmentation of the rules is different from the general one. The translation is performed by the special rules for the system. The example of the rule which is used for the translation is shown in Table 6. In Table 6, the segmentation of the rules in the NR dictionary is different from the general one. However, the NRj is generated by these NR rules. The NRj is able to be translated into the translation result in Table 6. The translation result is correct.

5   Conclusion

In this paper, we evaluated the translation performance in the system based on our proposed method. English is translated into Japanese via number representation on our proposed method. A number representation text is more abstract than the original text because the number representation text corresponds to several texts. Then, the system based on our proposed method is able to acquire more translation rules on number representation than that on the original text by Inductive Learning. Some translation rules include different texts with same meaning. These rules are effective for the translation. The system needs number representation in order to acquire these translation rules. Moreover, the system is able to disambiguate number representation by its own adaptability. Thus, the system translates English into Japanese via number representation. In the evaluation experiment, the last rate of the correct translation is about 60[%] because the system is able to learn the translation rules which are fit for the inputted data and adapt to the present field. The mean of the correct translation rate for our proposed method is higher than that for the method without the number representation by 4.6[%]. Therefore, it is proved that our proposed method is more effective for machine translation.

A future problem is to tune up the correspondence of number characters with English characters and that with *Kana* characters in order to more improve the translation performance.

References

1. S. Sato.: MBT2: a method for combining fragments of examples in example-based translation. In *Artificial Intelligence*, volume 75, pages 31–49, May 1995.
2. P. F. Brown et al.: A Statistical Approach to Machine Translation. In *Computational Linguistics*, volume 16, number 2, pages 79–85, June 1990.
3. K. Araki, H. Echizen-ya and K. Tochinai.: Performance Evaluation in Travel English for GA-ILMT. In *Proceedings of the IASTED International Conference Artificial Intelligence and Soft Computing*, pages 117–120, Banff, Canada, July 1997.
4. H. Echizen-ya, K. Araki, Y. Momouchi and K. Tochinai.: A Study of Performance Evaluation for GA-ILMT Using Travel English. In *Proceedings of the 13th Pacific Asia Conference on Language, Information and Computation*, pages 285–292, Taipei, Taiwan, February 1999.
5. M. Matsuhara, K. Araki, Y. Momouchi and K. Tochinai.: Evaluation of Number-Kanji Translation Method of Non-Segmented Japanese Sentences Using Inductive Learning with Degenerated Input. In *N. Foo (Ed.): Advanced Topics in Artificial Intelligence(AI'99), Lecture Note in Artificial Intelligence 1747*, pages 474–475, December 1999.
6. M. Matsuhara, K. Araki, Y. Momouchi and K. Tochinai.: Evaluation of Number-Kanji Translation Method Using Inductive Learning on E-mail. In *Proceedings of the IASTED International Conference Artificial Intelligence and Soft Computing*, pages 487–493, Banff, Canada, July 2000.
7. Y. Araki and J. Lee.: *Travel English pocket book. Nihon Bungei Sha*, (Tokyo), 1995.
8. Ryokou Kaiwa Kenkyuukai.: *Kaigai Ryokou Eikaiwa. Jitugyou no Nihon Sha*, (Tokyo), 1980.
9. K. Gilbert.: *Kent no Travel Eikaiwa. Jitugyou no Nihon Sha*, (Tokyo), 1995.
10. Y. Ishikawa and Travel Communication Kenkyuukai.: *A Timely Handbook for Single Travelers Travel English. Jitugyou no Nihon Sha*, (Tokyo), 1995.
11. Y. Maekawa.: *America wo Jiyuu ni Aruku Tabi no Beikaiwa. Ikeda Shoten*, (Tokyo), 1994.
12. Tikyuu no Arukikata Hensyuusitu.: *Tabi no Kaiwasyuu 2 Beigo/Eigo. Diamond Sha*, (Tokyo), 1993.
13. Book Maker.: *Kaigai Ryokou Kantan Eikaiwa Hand Book. Ikeda Shoten*, (Tokyo), 1996.
14. Junko Kai.: *Hitori Aruki no Eigo Jiyuujizai. Nihonn Koutuu Kousha Shuppan Jigyou Kyouku*, (Tokyo), 1991.
15. W. Read.: *Komatta Toki no Travel Eikaiwa Nyuumon. Nihon Bungei Sha*, (Tokyo), 1995.
16. A. Saito.: *Rokkakokugo Kaiwa I pocket interpreter. Nihon Koutuu Kousha Shuppan Jigyou Kyoku*, (Tokyo), 1960.

Estimating Episodes of Care Using Linked Medical Claims Data

Graham Williams[1], Rohan Baxter[1], Chris Kelman[2], Chris Rainsford[1],
Hongxing He[1], Lifang Gu[1], Deanne Vickers[1], and Simon Hawkins[1]

[1] Enterprise Data Mining
CSIRO Mathematical and Information Sciences
GPO Box 664, Canberra, ACT 2601, Australia
Firstname.Lastname@csiro.au
http://datamining.csiro.au
[2] Commonwealth Department of Health and Ageing
Firstname.Lastname@health.gov.au

Abstract. Australia has extensive administrative health data collected
by Commonwealth and state agencies. Using a unique cleaned and linked
administrative health dataset we address the problem of empirically
defining episodes of care. An episode of care is a time interval containing
medical services relating to a particular medical situation. In this paper
the medical situation is a hospital admission. The medical services
of interest are pathology tests, diagnostic imaging and non-invasive
investigative procedures performed before or after the hospital admission, but 'associated' with the hospital admission. The task can
be viewed as detecting a signal in a time series relating to a hospital
admission, distinct from the background noise of on-going medical
care. Our approach uses an ensemble (panel of experts) paradigm
where we implement multiple agents (alternative predictive models) to
separately estimate intervals and then choose a robust interval estimate
using a voting scheme. The results have been used in a study for the
Commonwealth Department of Health and Ageing.

Keywords: Applications, knowledge discovery and data mining, machine learning, record linkage, administrative data, health services.

1 Introduction

In collaboration with the Commonwealth Department of Health and Ageing
and Queensland Health, CSIRO Data Mining has created a unique cleaned and
linked administrative health dataset bringing together State hospital morbidity
data and Commonwealth Medicare Benefits Scheme (MBS) and Pharmaceutical
Benefits Scheme (PBS) data. The Queensland Linked Data Set (QLDS) links de-
identified, administrative, unit-level data, allowing de-identified patients to be
tracked through episodes of care as evidenced by their MBS, PBS and Hospital
records [1]. This dataset provides a unique view of service utilisation and cost

R.I. McKay and J. Slaney (Eds.): AI 2002, LNAI 2557, pp. 660–671, 2002.
© Springer-Verlag Berlin Heidelberg 2002

trends and patterns in the overall delivery of Commonwealth and State funded health care.

An ongoing central issue in health services research is how to identify the groups of services and costs relating to a particular episode of care [2,3,4,5]. Episodes of care are defined as: *A block of one or more medical services, received by an individual during a period of relatively continuous contact with one or more providers of service, in relation to a particular medical problem or situation* [2]. One example of the application of episodes of care is their use in measuring the costs and services for a particular disease or condition of interest, such as diabetes, asthma or depression.

In our application, the particular medical problem is a hospital admission and the block of related medical services are pathology tests, diagnostic imaging and non-invasive investigative procedures. *A priori* these medical services are likely to be associated with a hospital admission rather than ongoing ambulatory health care. These medical services are not complete, but they contain the most expensive items in pre-admission preparation for a hospital admission and post-discharge care.

We anchor our episode of care around a particular hospital admission. The episode of care begins x days prior to the admission and ends y days after discharge from hospital. All related medical services received in these two intervals are included in the episode of care. For our purposes services rendered whilst in hospital are ignored.

Previous work using episodes of care has concentrated on one or two narrow clinical areas. This meant that the model for estimating an appropriate episode of care interval could be hand-crafted and clinically assessed. In contrast, our application required episodes of care to be estimated for 666 Diagnostic Related Groups (DRGs) covering the full range of hospital admission types.

In a previous study we assumed fixed intervals of a 90-day pre-admission interval and a 90-day post-discharge interval for each of the DRGs. These fixed interval assumptions are clearly not clinically valid. For example, the DRG for a broken femur should have a 0-day pre-admission interval (since broken legs are not planned for) and a 40 day post-discharge interval (the average recovery time). A delivery admission DRG for a birth will have a six-month pre-admission time (as women typically obtain pathology tests and diagnostic imaging six-months prior to a birth).

Time and resources do not allow for individual assessment of each of the 666 DRGs. Our solution is a robust and automatic means, based on machine learning techniques, to estimate the intervals for the 666 episodes of care.

Others have explored the problem of identifying cut-points (change-points or segmentation). The problem arises in many applications in data mining, artificial intelligence and statistics, including segmenting time series [6], decision tree algorithms and image processing. A range of criteria have been proposed in the literature for determining if some time series data should be segmented into two or more regions [7]. [8] describe the segmentation of categorical time series data using a voting experts approach to combine evidence for segmentation boundaries.

This paper presents our solution using data driven estimates for the DRG episodes of care resulting from an ensemble of alternative estimation models (or panel of experts) being combined through a voting scheme [9]. We perform sensitivity analysis to assess the accuracy of the episodes of care estimates. We have also obtained a preliminary clinical assessment of the episode of care estimates for five of the 666 DRGs.

In Section 2 we review the data from which we determine the episodes of care. Section 3 presents our methodology for a data driven approach to estimating appropriate pre/post intervals for each DRG while Section 4 presents the results and describes how they can be used by the Commonwealth Department of Health and Ageing.

2   Experimental Design

The data used for this study were extracted from the QLDS [1]. Hospital separations (data associated with an episode in hospital) have been used to identify admission and discharge information. For each separation all of that patient's relevant MBS services have been extracted and these form the basis of the service counts and aggregated cost used in this study.

The QLDS hospital data was filtered to remove hospital separations corresponding to changes in admission status that do not reflect end of episode. These records include statistical admissions and discharges as well as hospital transfers[1].

The data were also filtered to remove MBS items provided in hospital, corresponding to MBS item sub-groups with hospital flag set to 'h'.

Only MBS items in the following categories are considered:

- *diagnostic imaging*: MBS items from 55028 to 63946, inclusive;
- *pathology*: MBS items from 65060 to 73811, inclusive;
- *non-invasive investigative procedures*: MBS items from 11000 to 12533, inclusive.

Our dataset includes 70% of the total Queensland hospital admissions. We assume that the missing 30% do not affect the estimates of the episodes of care. This assumption is reasonable because it is not expected that the missing episodes of care will differ from the 70% in the dataset.

3   Ensemble Methodology

We have developed a data driven technique to time-frame-adjust DRG intervals of workup (pre-admission) and followup (post-discharge), motivated by [10]. The

---

[1] These records are identified by *admission source* codes 4, 6, and 11 and *separation modes* 2, 6, 10, and 11.

approach employs a *multiple experts* or *ensemble* paradigm [9] where several change-point estimators are employed and an averaged majority voting scheme is used to determine the final change-points, which then define the pre/post intervals.

A number of alternative estimators were investigated and four were chosen to form the *ensemble*: mean and variance optimisation; regression tree; multivariate adaptive regression splines; and multi point splines.

For each DRG a table containing a count of all pre-admission (and separately post-discharge) MBS services in diagnostic imaging, pathology, and non-invasive investigative procedures was constructed. Services were counted on a daily basis over all separations for the particular DRG. These were counted up to 180 days (6 months) pre-admission (and separately 180 days post-discharge). The daily counts were then normalised by dividing by the number of hospital admissions for that DRG.

The choice of 180 days pre/post was made to allow for a background pattern of servicing to be identified and then any intervals of increased servicing could be identified as being associated with the hospital separation.

We describe each of the four methods and then describe how the *ensemble* voting method is employed to determine the final set of pre/post intervals.

3.1   Mean and Variance Optimisation

The approach here is to search for a cut point t_c between T_1 and T_{180} ($T_1 < t_c < T_{180}$) that partitions the 180 day period (pre or post) into two parts $[T_1, t_c]$ and $[t_c, T_{180}]$. The search finds the value of t_c which maximises the difference between the mean of the two partitions and minimises the variance in each partition.

The original service count data are smoothed using a moving average of 3 days prior and 3 days post and then normalised to values between 0 and 1. Suppose then that μ_1 is the normalised mean of $[T_1, t_c]$ and σ_1 is the standard deviation of this interval. Similarly μ_2 and σ_2 for $[t_c, T_{180}]$. The t_c chosen is that which minimises:

$$\frac{1}{|\mu_1 - \mu_2|} + \beta(std_1 + std_2) \tag{1}$$

The parameter β allows fine tuning of the importance of the variance with respect to the mean. By experimentation β was set to 20.

3.2   Regression Tree

Regression trees [11] recursively partition data to build a regression model for separate parts of the data. *Rpart*, the regression tree routine provided by R [12], was used, fitting a constant model to the leaves of the tree. The splitting criterion is based on ANOVA (performing an analysis of the variance on the data) whereby the cut-point maximising the reduction in the squared error fit to the actual data is chosen.

Other parameters chosen for the modelling are:

- *Maximum number of splits*: 3. This was chosen to limit the choice of cut-points. Other settings could be investigated but have not been for this study.
- *Minimum number of data points in a leaf node*: 6. This is the default setting for *Rpart*. A consequence of this choice is that it is not possible for a cut-point to be less than 6 days from the boundaries [181, 0].

3.3   Multivariate Adaptive Regression Splines

Multivariate adaptive regression splines (MARS) is a spline fitting regression approach where splines are fitted to distinct intervals of the data [13]. The cut points (called knots in MARS) are searched for through an exhaustive approach, optimising a so called loss of fit criterion. The R package [12] *mda* provides the implementation of the function *mars* used for this analysis.

The primary parameter chosen was:

- *Maximum number of terms*: $nk = 3$. By limiting the number of models to 3 (and thus the knots or cut point candidates to 2) the choice of cut-points is made easier.

3.4   Multi Point Splines

A series of natural splines were fitted to the data points using the R *spline* function with the *mean* function to approximate the background level of activity before the workup to admission from the first 100 (of 180) days of the data.

Once the splines have been fitted a search from the day of admission finds the first spline knot (cut point) that falls below the mean value (ignoring the knot at day 0).

The parameters chosen for the spline are:

- *Number of splines*: $n = 51$. Thus, the 360 days (pre and post interval for each DRG) is effectively split into 51 segments of approximately one week each.

3.5   Ensemble

Each of the methods discussed in the previous four sections identifies a pre and post interval for each of the 666 DRGs. A successful approach in statistical modelling and machine learning has been to combine multiple predictive models through a voting mechanism. This approach is adopted here to combine the proposed pre and post cut points from each of the four "experts" into single pre and post cut points for each DRG.

The method selects from the four proposed cut points the three having the least *variance*. The final cut point is chosen to be the *mean* value of these three.

4 Experimental Results

4.1 Example DRGs

We present here a small sample of DRGs to illustrate the resulting pre/post intervals. The first example is perhaps the 'most typical' of the patterns found. However there is a wide diversity of patterns that is not reflected in these example DRGs.

Each figure plots data for 180 days prior to a hospital admission for the specified DRG and 180 after discharge. The data plotted is the daily count of MBS items in diagnostic imaging, pathology, and non-invasive investigative procedures received by all patients, divided by the number of separations for the DRG.

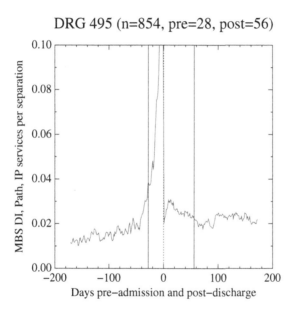

Fig. 1. DRG 495: Major procedures for malignant breast conditions. The estimated pre-admission and post-discharged intervals are shown as the solid vertical lines around the dotted central line at day 0 (day 0 essentially represents a period of time in hospital, collapsed to a single point in the plots). The plot title indicates the DRG population as 854 hospital separations, and the *ensemble* methodology estimating a pre-admission interval of 28 days and a post-discharge interval of 56 days.

In Figure 1 the pre-admission interval illustrates a marked increase in MBS activity 28 days prior to admission. The post-discharge interval of 56 days illustrates some activity after the episode in hospital. The post-discharge activity then stabilises to a new, but apparently increased, base line of activity.

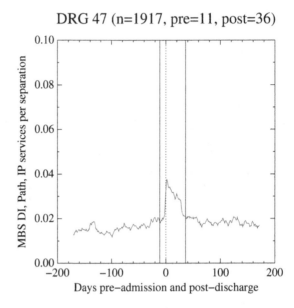

Fig. 2. DRG 47: Seizure, age < 65 without complication and/or comorbidity DRG.

Figure 2 illustrates what may be an emergency admission where there is very little or no pre-admission MBS workup but there is an interval of post-discharge MBS followup activity. The *ensemble* methodology has identified reasonable estimates in this case.

Figure 3 shows quite a different and unusual pattern, if not unexpected for this DRG (renal dialysis). In such cases the ensemble approach has essentially identified no particular pre-admission or post-discharge interval and has instead used, approximately, a 90 day pre/post interval. Results for this DRG are then similar to those produced in the previous study where 90 days was used for all DRGs. This DRG is an example of where expert advice might estimate the best pre/post interval to be 0, in which case the methodology could be refined to automatically identify these situations.

Figure 4 shows another class of patterns with a long lead up time before hospitalisation (for birth). There is clearly a lot of activity about 5 months prior to birth, then again about 3 months prior to birth. The methodology has identified 100 days for the pre-admission interval. Post-discharge identifies increased activity about 1 month after discharge.

4.2 Sensitivity Analysis

We tested the sensitivity of our episode of care estimation method as follows. We applied the method to each of the four years of data. Figure 5 summarises the resulting overall spread of the pre-admission and post-discharge interval

DRG 572 (n=58269, pre=87, post=113)

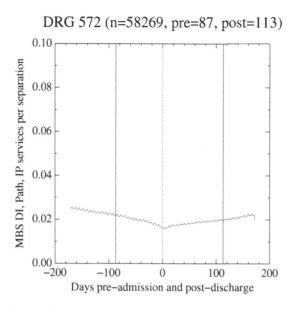

Fig. 3. DRG 572: Hospital admission for renal dialysis.

DRG 670 (n=5084, pre=100, post=34)

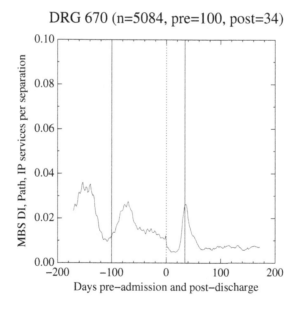

Fig. 4. DRG 670: Cesarean delivery without complicating diagnosis.

identified. Table 1 identifies, for each method, the average interval identified over the four years. The variance of the resulting estimates are shown in Figure 6.

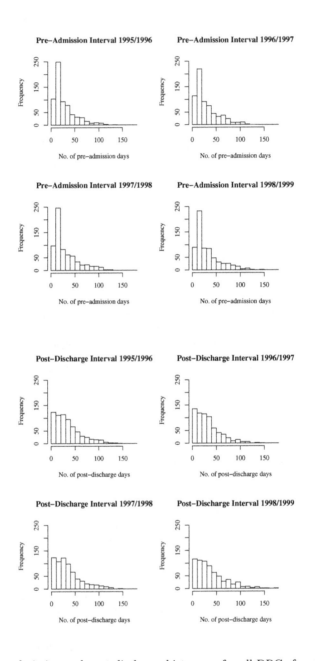

Fig. 5. Pre-admission and post-discharge histogram for all DRGs for all 4 years.

4.3   Application

Pathology tests, diagnostic investigations and doctor visits are health services that occur both before and after a hospital admission. Prior to the current study

Table 1. Mean and standard deviation of the mean variation of different methods' estimates across all DRGs and all years. A lower mean variation suggests that the method is more robust to noise (changes from year to year). The combined method, *vote* has the lowest mean variation. This is an advantage of an ensemble prediction method like *vote*.

Method	Mean	StdDev
dev	20.5	21.50
tree	18.17	20.06
mars	15.14	18.73
spline	14.60	9.34
vote	13.00	12.21

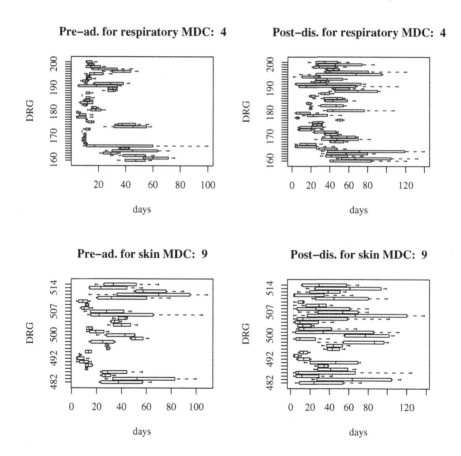

Fig. 6. Two example MDCs and ranges of estimates for pre-admission and post-discharge intervals over 4 years.

very little information was available on the number of services, and their costs, provided out-of-hospital in connection with an admission. The current linked data, combined with the ensemble methodology for interval estimation, allows the measurement of pre-admission and post-discharge service utilisation and costs.

Understanding utilisation and cost is important in decision-making for policy initiatives for improved service delivery and resource allocation. The utilisation and cost can be broken down by public and private patients, and public and private hospitals in order to understand the mix of out-of-hospital services and in-hospital services.

5   Discussion and Conclusions

We have introduced an AI-based method for determining intervals of care relevant to hospitalisation. The approach begins with aggregating counts of all patient services prior to and after episodes in hospital. The resulting data is effectively a time series where we are searching for a significant change in the trends. An ensemble approach applies multiple "experts" to solve the problem in different ways and to then combine the results using an averaged voting method. This approach has been found to be quite effective in estimating relevant periods of pre-admission and post-discharge services.

A key assumption underlying this research is that a single pre-admission interval and a single post-admission interval is adequate for capturing individual DRG episodes of care. The implication is that all patients in a particular DRG have similar medical service utilisation patterns. This is more likely to be true for patients from similar age-gender mixes and with similar co-morbidities. For some DRGs patients do have similar characteristics. An obvious example is the DRG covering births where the patients are women of child-bearing age. For other DRGs though there is considerable diversity among the patients. Investigating different intervals of episodes of care within a single DRG was considered outside the scope of this application. It is an interesting area for future work.

Further validation of this approach, particularly by having the intervals automatically discovered reviewed by panels of relevant clinicians, is under way.

References

1. Williams, G., Vickers, D., Baxter, R., Hawkins, S., Kelman, C. Solon, R., He, H., Gu, L. Queensland linked data set. Technical Report CMIS 02/21, CSIRO Mathematical and Information Sciences, Canberra, 2002. Report on the development, structure and content of the Queensland Linked Data Set, in collaboration with the Commonwealth Department of Health and Ageing and Queensland Health.
2. Solon, J.A., Feeney, S.H., Jones, S.H., Rigg, R.D., Sheps, C.G. Delineating episodes of medical care. American Journal of Public Health, **57** (1967) 401–408
3. Wingert, T.D., Kralewski, J.E., Lindquist, T.E., Knutson, D.J. Constructing episodes of care from encounter and claims data: some methodological issues. Inquiry, **32** (1995) 162–170

4. Lestina, D., Miller, T., Smith, G. Creating injury episodes using medical claims data. The Journal of Trauma **45** (1998) 565–569
5. Schulman, K.A., Yabroff, K.R., Kong, J., Gold, K.F., Rubenstein, L.E., Epstein, A.J., Glick, H.. A claims data approach to defining an episode of care. Pharmacoepidemilogy and Drug Safety **10** (2001) 417–427
6. Tong, H. Non-Linear Time Series: A Dynamical System Approach. Oxford University Press, New York (1990)
7. Oliver, J.J., Baxter, R.A., Wallace, C.S.. Minimum message length segmentation. In: Research and Development in Knowledge Discovery and Data Mining: Lecture Notes in Artificial Intelligence, Springer (1998) 223–233
8. Cohen, P., Adams, N. An algorithm for segmenting categorical time series into meaningful episodes. In: Proceedings of the Fourth International Symposium on Intelligent Data Analysis, Lisbon Portugal (2001)
9. Dietterich, T.G.. Ensemble methods in machine learning. In Kittker, J., Roli, F., eds.: Proceedings of the First International Workshop on Multiple Classifier Systems (MCS00): Lecture Notes in Computer Science. Volume 1857, Cagliari, Italy, Spinger (2000) `citeseer.nj.nec.com/dietterich00ensemble.html`.
10. Kelman, C. Monitoring health care using national administrative data collections. PhD thesis, National Centre for Epidemiology and Population Health, Australian National University, Canberra (2000)
11. Breiman, L., Friedman, J.H., Olshen, R.A., Stone, C.J.. Classification and Regression Trees. Wadsworth, Belmont, CA (1984)
12. Venables, W.N., Smith, D.N., The R Development Team: An Introduction to R. 1.5.0 edn. (2002)
13. Friedman, J.. Multivariate adaptive regression splines. The Annals of Statistics **(19)** (1991) 1–141

Adaptation of a Mamdani Fuzzy Inference System Using Neuro-genetic Approach for Tactical Air Combat Decision Support System

Cong Tran[1], Ajith Abraham[2], and Lakhmi Jain[1]

[1] School of Electrical and Information Engineering
University of South Australia, Adelaide, Australia
tramcm001@students.unisa.edu.au, L.Jain@unisa.edu.au

[2] Department of Computer Science, Oklahoma State University (Tulsa)
700 N Greenwood Avenue, Tulsa, OK 74106-0700, USA
ajith.abraham@ieee.org

Abstract. Normally a decision support system is build to solve problems where multi-criteria decisions are involved. The knowledge base is the vital part of the decision support system containing the information or data that is used in decision-making process. This is the field where engineers and scientists have applied several intelligent techniques and heuristics to obtain optimal decisions from imprecise information. In this paper, we present a hybrid neuro-genetic learning approach for the adaptation of a Mamdani fuzzy inference system for the Tactical Air Combat Decision Support System (TACDSS). Some simulation results demonstrating the different learning techniques are also provided.

1 Introduction

Several decision support systems have been applied mostly in the fields of medical diagnosis, business management, control system, command and control of defence and air traffic control and so on. For most Decision Support Systems (DSS), people normally make use of their experience or expert knowledge. The problem becomes very interesting when no prior knowledge is available. Recently researchers have started using expert systems, fuzzy logic, rough sets and neural network learning methods to develop DSS. For a detailed review of different techniques, please refer to [2]. Our approach is based on the development of different adaptive fuzzy inference systems using several learning techniques [2] [3]. Fuzzy logic provides a computational framework to capture the uncertainties associated with human cognitive process such as thinking and reasoning [8]. The disadvantage of fuzzy inference system is the requirement of expert knowledge to set up the fuzzy rules, membership function parameters, fuzzy operators etc. Neural network learning methods [1] and evolutionary computation [2] could be used to adapt the fuzzy inference system.

In Section 2, we present the complexity of the tactical air combat environment problem followed by the modeling of the TACDSS using an adaptive Mamdani fuzzy

R.I. McKay and J. Slaney (Eds.): AI 2002, LNAI 2557, pp. 672–680, 2002.

inference system in Section 3. Section 4 deals with experimentation setup / results and some conclusions are also provided towards the end.

2   Decision Making in Tactical Air Combat

The air operation division of Defence Science and Technology Organisation (DSTO) and our research team has a collaborative project to develop the TACDSS for a pilot or mission commander in tactical air combat. In Figure 1 a typical scenario of air combat tactical environment is presented. The Airborne Early Warning and Control (AEW&C) is performing surveillance in a particular area of operation. It has two hornets (F/A-18s) under its control at the ground base as shown "+" in the left corner of Figure 1. An air-to-air fuel tanker (KB707) "□" is on station and the location and status are known to the AEW&C. Two of the hornets are on patrol in the area of Combat Air Patrol (CAP). Sometime later, the AEW&C on-board sensors detects 4 hostile aircrafts (Mig-29) shown as "O". When the hostile aircrafts enter the surveillance region (shown as dashed circle) the mission system software is able to identify the enemy aircraft and its distance from the Hornets in the ground base or in the CAP.

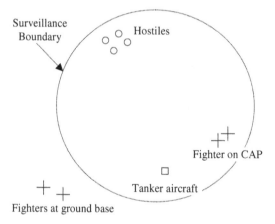

Fig. 1. A simple scenario of the air combat

The mission operator has few options to make a decision on the allocation of hornets to intercept the enemy aircraft.

- Send the Hornet directly to the spotted area and intercept,
- Call the Hornet in the area back to ground base and send another Hornet from the ground base,
- Call the Hornet in the area to refuel before intercepting the enemy aircraft

The mission operator will base his decisions on a number of decision factors, such as:

- Fuel used and weapon status of hornet in the area,

- Interrupt time of Hornet in the ground base and the Hornet at the CAP to stop the hostile,
- The speed of the enemy fighter aircraft and the type of weapons it posses,
- The information of enemy aircraft with type of aircraft, weapon, number of aircraft.

From the above simple scenario, it is evident that there are several important decision factors of the tactical environment that might directly affect the air combat decision. We made use of the fuzzy neural network framework [5] to develop the TACDSS. In the simple tactical air combat, the four decision factors that could affect the decision options of the Hornet in the CAP or the Hornet at the ground base are the following:

- '*fuel status*' – quantity of fuel available to perform the intercept,
- '*weapon possession status*' – quantity of weapons available in the Hornet,
- '*interrupt time*' – time required by the hornet to interrupt the hostile and
- '*danger situation*' – information of the Hornet and the hostile in the battlefield.

Each factors has difference range of unit such as the *fuel status* (0 to 1000 litres), *interrupt time* (0 to 60 minutes), *weapon status* (0 to 100 %) and *danger situation* (0 to 10 points). We used the following two expert rules for developing the fuzzy inference system.

- The decision selection will have small value if the *fuel status* is too low, the *interrupt time* is too long, the hornet has low *weapon status*, and the *danger situation* is high.
- The decision selection will have high value if the *fuel status* is full, the *interrupt time* is fast enough, the hornet has high *weapon status* and the *danger situation* is low.

In the air combat environment, decision-making is always based on all states of decision factors. But sometimes, a mission operator or commander could make a decision based on an important factor, such as the fuel used is too low, the enemy has more powerful weapons and the quality and quantity of enemy aircrafts. Table 1 shows some typical scores (decision selection point) taking into account of the various tactical air combat decision factors.

Table 1. Decision factors for the tactical air combat

Fuel used	Time Intercept	Weapon Status	Danger Situation	Evaluation Plan
Full	Fast	Sufficient	Very Dangerous	Good
Half	Normal	Enough	Danger	Acceptable
Low	Slow	Insufficient	Endanger	Bad

3   Modeling TACDSS Using Adaptive Fuzzy Inference System

We made use of the Fuzzy Neural Network (FuNN) framework [5] for learning the Mamdani inference method. A functional block diagram of the FuNN model is depicted in Figure 2 and it consists of two phases of learning processes. The first phase is the structure-learning (*if-then* rules) phase using the knowledge acquisition module. The second phase is the parameter-learning phase for tuning membership functions to achieve a desired level of performance. FuNN uses a gradient descent-learning algorithm to fine-tune the parameters of the fuzzy membership functions. In the connectionist structure, the input and output nodes represent the input states and output control-decision signals, respectively, and in the hidden layers, there are nodes functioning as quantification of membership functions (MFs) and *if-then* rules. Please refer to [5] for more details regarding architecture and function of the various layers.

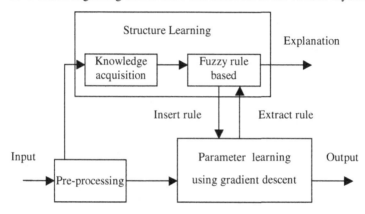

Fig. 2. A general schematic diagram of the hybrid fuzzy neural network

We used a simple and straightforward method proposed by Wang and Mendel [6] for generating fuzzy rules from numerical input-output training data. The task here is to generate a set of fuzzy rules from the desired input-output pairs and then use these fuzzy rules to determine the complete structure of the TACDSS.

Suppose we are given the following sets of desired input $-(x_1, x_2)$ output (y) data pairs (x_1, x_2, y): (0.6, 0.2; 0.2) and (0.4, 0.3; 0.4). Input variable *fuel used* has a degree of 0.8 in *half*, a degree of 0.2 in *full* and input variable *time intercept* has degree of 0.6 in *empty* and of 0.3 in *normal*. Next, assign x_1^i, x_2^i, and y^i to a region that has maximum degree. Finally, obtain rules from desired input-output data as follows:

$$(x_1^1, x_2^1, y^1) \Rightarrow [x_1^1(0.8 \text{ in } half), x_2^1(0.2 \text{ in } fast), y^1 (0.6 \text{ in } acceptable)], \qquad (1)$$
- R_1: if x_1 is *half* and x_2 is *fast*, then y is *acceptable*;

$$(x_1^2, x_2^2, y^2), \Rightarrow [x_1(0.8 \text{ in } half), x_2 (0.6 \text{ in } normal), y^2(0.8 \text{ in } acceptable)], \qquad (2)$$
- R_2: if x_1 is *half* and x_2 is *normal*, then y is *acceptable*.

By assigning a degree to each rule we could also solve a conflict problem, i.e. rules having the same antecedent but with different consequent. This will also help to reduce the number of rules. We assign a degree to each rule generated from data pairs and accept only the rule from a conflict group that has a maximum degree. In other words, this step is performed to delete redundant rules, and to obtain a concise fuzzy rule base. The following product strategy is used to assign a degree to each rule. The degree of the rule denoted by

$$Ri : \text{if } x_1 \text{ is } A \text{ and } x_2 \text{ is } B, \text{ then } y \text{ is } C(w_i), \tag{3}$$

The rule weight is defined as

$$w_i = \mu_A(x_1)\mu_B(x_2)\mu_c(y) . \tag{4}$$

For example, R_1 has a degree of

$$W_1 = \mu_{half}(x_1) \, \mu_{fast} (x_2) \, \mu_{acceptable} (y) = 0.8 \times 0.2 \times 0.6 = 0.096, \tag{5}$$

and R_2 has a degree of

$$W2 = \mu_{half}(x_1) \, \mu_{normal}(x_2) \, \mu_{acceptable} (y) = 0.8 \times 0.6 \times 0.8 = 0.384. \tag{6}$$

Note, that if two or more generated fuzzy rules have the same preconditions and consequents, then the rule that has maximum degree is used. In this way, assigning the degree to each rule, the fuzzy rule base can be adapted or updated by the relative weighting strategy: the more task related the rule becomes, the more weight degree the rule gains. As a result, not only is the conflict problem is resolved, but also the number of rules are reduced significantly. After the structure-learning phase (*if-then* rules), the whole network structure is established, and the network enters the second learning phase to optimally adjust the parameters of the membership functions using a gradient descent-learning algorithm to minimize the error function

$$E = \frac{1}{2}\sum_x \sum_{l=1}^{q}(d_1 - y_l)^2 . \tag{7}$$

where d and y, are the target and actual outputs for an input x. We also explored Genetic Algorithms (GA) to optimize the membership function parameters. Given that the optimisation of fuzzy membership functions may involve many changes to many different functions, and that a change to one function may effect others, the large possible solution space for this problem is a natural candidate for a GA based approach. The GA module for adapting the membership function parameters acts as a stand-alone system that already have the *if-then* rules. GA optimises the antecedent and consequent membership functions. The GA used in the system is, in essence, the same as simple genetic algorithm, with the important exception that the chromosomes are represented as strings of floating point numbers, rather than strings of bits. Figure 3 depicts the chromosome architecture representing the centre of input and output MFs. One point crossover was used for the reproduction of chromosomes.

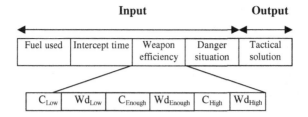

Fig. 3. The chromosome of the centres of inputs and output MFs of TACDSS

4 Experimentations Results

The fuzzy inference system was created using the FuNN framework [7]. The TACDSS has four inputs and one output variable. We used triangular membership functions and each input variable were assigned three MFs. 16 fuzzy rules were created using the methodology mentioned in Section 3. With the momentum at 0.8 (decided after a trail and error approach), we varied the learning rates to evaluate the performance. For 10 epochs, we obtained a RMSE of 0.5775 (learning rate 0.1) and RMSE of 0.2889 (learning rate 0.3) respectively. Figure 6 shows the 16 fuzzy *if-then* rules of the developed TACDSS.

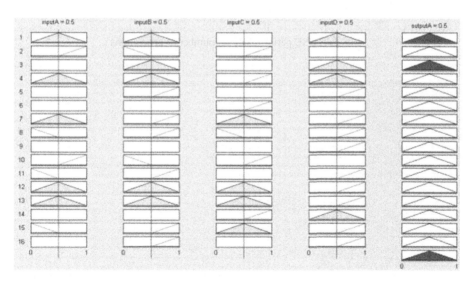

Fig. 4. Developed Mamdani fuzzy inference system for TACDSS

We also explored the fine-tuning of membership functions using evolutionary algorithms. We started with a population size 10, tournament selection strategy, mutation rate 0.01 and implemented a one point crossover operator. After a trial and error approach (please refer to Figures 5 and 6) by increasing the population size and the number of iterations (generations), we finalized the population size and number of iterations as 100. To improve the accuracy we extracted 52 fuzzy *if-then* rules to describe the TACDSS. We obtained an RMSE of 0.0324 after 100 generations of evolutionary learning with a population size of 100. Figure 7 demonstrates the effect of parameter tuning of membership functions (before and after evolutionary learning) for the input variable *'fuel used'*.

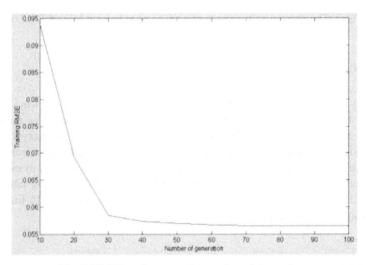

Fig. 5. RMSE performance for number of generations

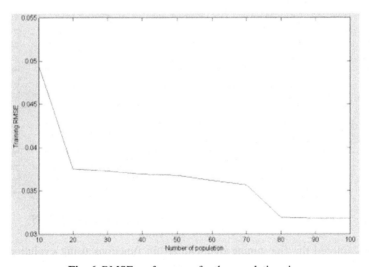

Fig. 6. RMSE performance for the population size

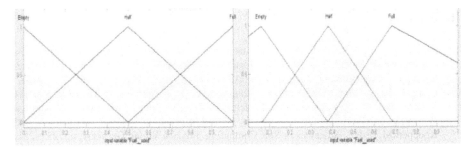

Fig. 7. The MFs of input variable *'fuel used'* before and after GA learning

The developed TACDSS for a worst and good situation is depicted as follows.

Bad situation: When the *fuel used* is 0.05, *time intercept* is 0.95, *weapon status* is 0.05 and *danger situation* is 0.95 then *tactical decision score* is 0.416

Good situation: When the *fuel used* is 0.95, *time intercept* is 0.05, *weapon status* is 0.95 and *dangerous situation* is 0.05 then *tactical decision score* is 0.503

For the test set *fuel used* 0.938, *time intercept* 0.05167, *weapon status* 0.975, *danger situation* 0.124 the expected *tactical decision* is 0.939 and the developed TACDSS decision score was 0.668 (approximately 28.9% less than the required value).

5   Conclusion and Future Research

In this paper, we have explained a hybrid fuzzy inference model for developing a tactical air combat decision support system. Our case study of the simple scenario of the air tactical environment demonstrates the difficulties to implement the human decision-making. We have explored two learning techniques using backpropagation and evolutionary learning to fine-tune the membership function parameters. Empirical results reveal that evolutionary approach performed better in terms of low RMSE with a trade off in computational cost.

This work is an extension of our previous research work wherein we have used a Takagi-Sugeno fuzzy inference model for developing the TACDSS. Empirical results on test data indicate that the Takagi-Sugeno version of TACDSS performed better than the current Mamdani version. Our future work includes development of decision trees and adaptive reinforcement learning systems that can update the knowledge base from data when no expert knowledge is available.

References

1. Abraham, A., Neuro-Fuzzy Systems: State-of-the-Art Modeling Techniques, Connectionist Models of Neurons, Learning Processes, and Artificial Intelligence, Springer-Verlag Germany, Jose Mira and Alberto Prieto (Eds), Spain, pp. 269–276, 2001.
2. Cong T., Jain, L. and Abraham, A., Adaptive Database Learning in Decision Support System Using Evolutionary Fuzzy Systems: A Generic Framework, First international Workshop on Hybrid Intelligent Systems, Hybrid Information Systems, Abraham A. and Koeppen M. (Eds.), Advances in Soft Computing, Physica Verlag Germany, pp. 237–251, 2002.
3. Cong T., Jain, L. and Abraham, A., TACDSS: Adaptation of a Takagi–Sugeno Hybrid Neuro-Fuzzy System, Seventh Online World Conference on Soft Computing in Industrial Applications, Springer Verlag, Germany, September 2002 (forth coming)
4. Kasabov, N., Learning Fuzzy Rules and Approximate Reasoning in Fuzzy Neural Networks and Hybrid Systems, Fuzzy Sets and Systems, Vol.82, pp. 135–149, 1996.
5. Kasabov, N., Kim, J. S. and Gray, A. R., FUNN – A Fuzzy Neural Network Architecture for Adaptive Learning and Knowledge Acquisition, Information Sciences, Vol. 101, Issue 3, pp. 155–175, 1996.
6. Wang, L. X. and Mendel, J. M., Generating Fuzzy Rules by Learning from Examples, IEEE Transcation on System, Man and Cybernetics, Vol. 22, Issue 6, pp. 1414–1427, 1992.
7. Watts, M., Woodford, B. and Kasabov, N., FuzzyCOPE: A Software Environment for Building Intelligent Systems – The Past, The Present and the Future, In Proceedings of ICONIP'99 Workshop, New Zealand, pp. 188–192, 1999.
8. Zadeh, L. A., Fuzzy Sets, Information Control, Vol. 1 pp. 338–353, 1965.

Optimization of Recurrent NN by GA with Variable Length Genotype

Dragos Arotaritei[1] and Mircea G. Negoita[2]

[1] Aalborg University Esbjerg, Niels Bohrs Vej 8,
6700 Esbjerg, Denmark
dragos@cs.aue.auc.dk
[2] Wellington Institute of Technology (WELTEC), Private Bag 39803, The Puni Mail Center
Buick Street, Petone,
Wellington, New Zealand
mircea.negoita@weltec.ac.nz

Abstract. The gradient based learning algorithms for complex hybrid neuro-fuzzy architectures have a lot of local minima and a seriously time consumption complexity is involved as a consequence. **G**enetic **A**lgorithms *with variable length genotypes* are successfully used in getting better performances for systems with complex structure or, at the same performances, a less complex structure of the system. We propose a sophisticated algorithm that solves simultaneously the optimization objectives of learning algorithms in fuzzy recurrent neural networks: both regarding the fuzzy **NN** performances (by its fuzzy weights matrix) and regarding the architecture (number of fully connected neurons). In this paper we developed a genetic algorithm with variable length genotypes that offers *a systematic way of getting a minimal neuro-fuzzy structure satisfying* the above mentioned *requested performance*. This advantage is not to be neglected when a complex hybrid intelligent architecture must be designed without any previous details regarding it requested architecture.

1 Introduction

Various fuzzification approaches of neural networks (**NN**) have been proposed by using fuzzy numbers [6]. A special class of intelligent hybrid (neuro-fuzzy) systems, based on **NN**s and fuzzy algebraic systems is taken into account, for different **NN** topologies (multilayer perceptron, **R**adial **B**asis **F**unction [5] and fuzzy recurrent **NN** [1]). The usage of fuzzy **NN** is very large, from prediction of time series to modeling of complex chaotic systems. Most of the times, the results are significant better than those obtained in case of crisp inputs, that justifying the increasing interest of researchers to develop more efficient (learning) algorithms for this types of intelligent hybrid structures.

The general learning methods are based on gradient techniques, developed for working with fuzzy numbers. The well-known typical problems to the gradient learn-

R.I. McKay and J. Slaney (Eds.): AI 2002, LNAI 2557, pp. 681–692, 2002.
© Springer-Verlag Berlin Heidelberg 2002

ing techniques (many local minima, learning factor determined experimentally, e.g.) are naturally present in these structures too, but their effect is more amplified due to constraint problems with regard to definition of the membership function of fuzzy numbers.

A recently proposed **NN** structure is a recurrent artificial neural network with fuzzy numbers (**RAFNN**) in [1]. The recurrent topology is a fully connected one that uses symmetric triangular fuzzy numbers in the fuzzy algebraic framework. A computational expansive gradient-based algorithm is proposed in order to compute the matrix of fuzzy weights, but the structure (number of neurons) is supposed to be known, or discovered by simple incremental trials starting from minimal number of neurons set to two. *This can be very costly (excessive time consumption) in case of modelling complex systems that could require large number de neurons.*

The methodological background and terminology of genetic algorithms (**GA**) (as well as of all other evolutionary algorithms - **EA**) are rooted in the so called neo-Darwinian paradigm, whose elements were taken from Darwin's evolutionary theory, genetics and population genetics. The fundamental principles of this paradigms reflects the fact that natural organisms have evolved from simple to ever more complex ones with associated increase of genotype length. Some features of traditional **GA** are leading to a recombination operator having a simple implementation: they use genotypes of predetermined length, that is homologues features are coded for on homologous positions within the genotype.

Complex organisms in nature present a kind of *gene's specialization: structural genes* (**qualitative**) and *adjusting genes* (**quantitative**). The adjusting genes affect globally the structural genes [8]. Another interesting evolution aspect is that a correspondence for a recombination operator that involves individuals with significant different genotypes is not possible to be found at any level of beings in natural environment. These two last aspects of evolution in nature made possible implementation of optimisation methods in form of **GA** *with variable length genotypes*, where: absolute position of the symbols usually do not provide information about the related feature, the recombination operator should be implemented in a different manner and, most implementations are application-dependent.

GA *with variable length genotypes* are successfully used in getting better performances for systems with complex structure or, at the same performances, a less complex structure of the system [3]. The work in this paper has the aim of a simultaneously **RAFNN** optimization, namely both the structure (number of neurons) and **NN** parameters (the weight matrix). A **GA** *with variable length genotypes* is developed to do it.

A **GA** with variable length genotypes has a suitable structure and properties for design and optimisation of complex systems. Such a **GA** was implemented and used for learning simultaneously optimisation of both the structure and parameters of a complex system, a fuzzy inference system namely [1].

The rest of the paper is organized as follow. In section two we present the structure elements of our proposed **RAFNN** to be used by us in our simulations, along with its basic operation and performance measures. The **GA** learning algorithm for fuzzy weighs and recurrent structure (number of neurons) is described in section three. The experimental results using simulations are presented in the next section. The summary of conclusions and further remarks are presented in the last section.

2 The Hybrid Structure of RAFNN (Recurrent Algebraic Fuzzy Neural Network)

We denote the Triangular Fuzzy Numbers (**TFN**) by $\tilde{X} = (x^L, x^C, x^R)$. A non-standard algebraic operation between two **TFN** is defined by:

$$\tilde{C} = \tilde{A} \tilde{*} \tilde{B} = (c^L, c^C, c^R) = (min(SP), a^C * b^C, max(SP)) \tag{1}$$

$$SP = \{a^L * b^L, a^L * b^R, a^R * b^L, a^R * b^R\} \tag{2}$$

All above operations are in classic arithmetic, $* \in \{+, -, \bullet\}$, and $\tilde{*} \in \{\tilde{+}, \tilde{-}, \tilde{\bullet}\}$ are the corresponding modified operations in fuzzy arithmetic, defined according to (1). The algebraic fuzzy neuron (Fig. 1) is based on the operations defined above. The values $f(s^L, s^C, s^R)$ are computed, using the modified extension principle and (1):

$$\tilde{s} = \tilde{x}_1 \tilde{*} \tilde{w}_1 \tilde{+} \tilde{x}_2 \tilde{*} \tilde{w}_2 \tilde{+} \ldots \tilde{+} \tilde{x}_n \tilde{*} \tilde{w}_n \tilde{+} \tilde{\theta} \tag{3}$$

$$\tilde{y} = f(\tilde{s}) = (f(s^L), f(s^C), f(s^R)) \tag{4}$$

Let the Recurrent Neural Network (**RNN**) have n units and m inputs [7]. Each bias allocation will be seeing as an input line whose value is always $(1, 1,1)$. The architecture of **RAFNN** is similar to a crisp one (Fig. 2).

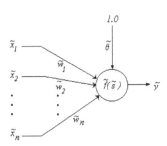

Fig. 1. The algebraic fuzzy neuron.

We denote the set of indices for input units, output units and target units by (I, U, T). Let $\tilde{x}(t)$, $\tilde{y}(t)$ and $\tilde{d}(t)$ denote the inputs, the outputs and the targets (if exists) of the units in **RNN** at time t, respectively. We denote a generalized $\tilde{z}(t)$ similar to [7] as follows:

$$\tilde{z}_k = \begin{cases} \tilde{x}_k(t) & if \ k \in I \\ \tilde{y}_k(t) & if \ k \in U - T(t) \end{cases} \tag{5}$$

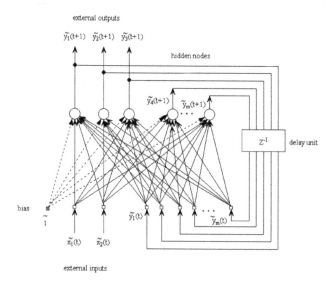

external outputs

$\tilde{y}_1(t+1)$ $\tilde{y}_2(t+1)$ $\tilde{y}_3(t+1)$

hidden nodes

$\tilde{y}_4(t+1)$ $\tilde{y}_m(t+1)$

z^{-1} delay unit

bias

$\tilde{1}$

$\tilde{y}_1(t)$ $\tilde{y}_m(t)$

$\tilde{x}_1(t)$ $\tilde{x}_2(t)$

external inputs

Fig. 2. The recurrent neural network structure.

The basic algebraic fuzzy neuron (Fig. 1) is based on the operations defined in (1). The activation value of each neuron $f(s^L, s^C, s^R)$ is computed by:

$$\tilde{s}_k(t) = \sum_{r \in U \cup I} \tilde{w}_{kr} \cdot \tilde{z}_r(t) = \tilde{w}_{k1} \cdot \tilde{z}_1(t) \mp \ldots \mp \tilde{w}_{k,m+n} \cdot \tilde{z}_{m+n}(t) \mp \tilde{b} \tag{6}$$

$$\tilde{y}_k(t+1) = \tilde{f}_k(\tilde{s}_k(t)) = f_k(s_k^L, s_k^C, s_k^R) \tag{7}$$

$$f_k(x) = 1/(1 + \exp(-x)) \tag{8}$$

The **NN** performance measure is defined by:

$$e_k^{L,C,R}(t) = \begin{cases} d_k^{L,C,R}(t) - y_k^{L,C,R}(t) & if \ k \in T(t) \\ 0 & otherwise \end{cases} \tag{9}$$

$$J^C(t) = -1/2 \cdot \sum_{k \in U} \left[e_k^C(t) \right]^2 \tag{10}$$

$$J^{L,R}(t) = \sum_{O=L,R} J^{L,R} = -\frac{1}{2} \cdot \left[\sum_{k \in U} \left[\left(e_k^L(t)\right)^2 + \left(e_k^R(t)\right)^2 \right]^2 \right] \tag{11}$$

$$J_{total}(t) = J^C + J^{L,R} \tag{12}$$

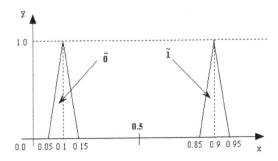

Fig. 3. The **TFN** with $\tilde{0}$ and $\tilde{1}$ values

We extended **XOR** problem in the frame of fuzzy numbers as in [1]. The crisp values "0" and "1" are extended to triangular fuzzy number (**TFN**) values: $\tilde{0} = (0.05, 0.1, 0.15)$ and $\tilde{1} = (0.85, 0.9, 0.95)$, as in Fig. 3.

The aim was to demonstrate that a recurrent neural network could learn to do an *XOR* in the frame of the fuzzy numbers continuously with two simultaneously changing inputs. In each update cycle, the teacher is delayed by $q=2$ cycles relative to the input that is used for *XOR* [7]. *A major disadvantage of the algorithm is that the structure is supposed to be known* **apriori,** *or the structure is discovered by incrementally search that means a costly computational operation.*

3   The Genetic-Based Learning Method

The task of our method is to *simultaneously learn the structure and parameters* of a **RAFNN**, that means (**GA**) *optimisation of the number of neurons and its weight matrix.*

The first design step of our method was to adopt a suitable chromosomes code structure to the application (see Fig. 4). But such a   chromosomes structure is the key element that leads to code length of different (variable) sizes, the length of genotypes being subject to change during the algorithm. Therefore, the genetic operators and the strategy of evolution were adapted to this special application request (see Fig. 5).

STRUCTURAL GENES	ADJUSTING GENES
(a)	
n gene (for *number of neurons*)	n(m+n) genes (the *weight matrix*)
(b)	

Fig. 4. The chromosome code structure (a) for any **GA** *with variable length genotype*; b) for **RAFNN** optimization)

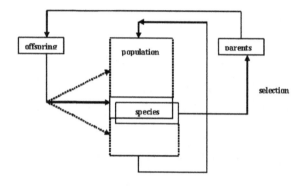

Fig. 5. The flow chart of the **GA** *with variable length chromosomes*

The flow-chart procedure of our **GA** *with variable-length genotype* is similar to that one in [3]:

STEP1 – *Generate initial population* individual by individual
   (two fields for each of the individuals : *structural genes* generation followed
   by *adjustable genes* generation);
STEP2 – *Group* the individuals *in species*
STEP3 – *Evaluate* the initial population
STEP4 – repeat
  for each *species*
    advance *(selection, crossover , mutation)*
  end
STEP5 – global selection on the whole population
STEP6 – until *STOP conditions*

3.1 STEP1

The initial population is randomly generated in two steps for each of the individuals, as follows:

- first, the *structural genes* (representing **n** - the number of neurons) are generated
- these are random generated numbers , in a mapping format of 15 binary bits (*0* or *1*) corresponding to a number of neurons in a range **n** $\in$ [*2 , 15*]
- second, the *adjusting gene* is generated in form of a matrix with **n x (m+n)** elements
- **m** is the number of **NN** inputs, incremented by **1** – the bias input (**m** = *2* in case of an XOR problem)
- the **n x (m+n)** matrix is a linear representation of fuzzy symmetric triangular numbers (see Fig. 3)
- The **Wc** matrix of weights are randomly generated **Wc** $\in$ [*-0.5 , +0.5*], followed by a linear *15* bit mapping and the correspondent desired neuronal outputs - **d** - are next generated in *d* $\in$ [*0.05 , 0.45*], followed by a linear *15* bit mapping too.

3.2 STEP2

The individuals are grouped in *species* taking into account the genotype - **n** - of the structural field in each chromosome, following an ascending order from the lowest to largest number **n** . A *species* means all the chromosomes with the *same length* (really, in a larger meaning: the *same length* and the *same structure*). This means more than the same length, because different individuals in **GA** *with variable length chromosomes* may usually have the same length despite of having different structures. But *no special precautions are to be made with regard to this aspect in this application because of the suitable coding structure. This is another advantage of particularly using a* **GA** *with variable length chromosome in this application*

3.3 STEP3

Each individual of each species is evaluated during this step. The fitness function is defined in order to combine two different optimization problems, i.e. a minimal **NN** error related to a set of desired outputs and a minimal **NN** structure. The formula of fitness function g(*chromosome*) is as follows:

$$g(cromosome) = \lambda \cdot E_1 + \delta \cdot E_2 \qquad (13)$$

$$E_1 = |1.0 - J_{total}| \qquad (14)$$

$$E_2 = 1/(1+n) \qquad (15)$$

The parameters λ and δ are determined experimentally. The value J_{total} is given by (11). The value of these parameters shows criteria weights in our composed fitness function. E_1 is the most important parameter and is given by total error during the *k*-

steps of tests (k is usually 1000). A penalty function [2] is included in the fitness formula above.

The complex structure is penalized after p steps if the error J_{total} has not a decreasing with a threshold σ.

$$\sigma = \sigma(k, \rho(J_{total}), generation) \tag{16}$$

3.4 STEP4

Each species contains structures of the same complexity (see **STEP2**) and advance independently under common **GA** operators (selection, crossover, mutation) as **GA** are running in parallel. For species containing just one individual, only mutation is applied. The resulted offspring is appended to the species if it is better than the worst fitted chromosome in the whole species. In this manner each species grows as far as it produces well fitted offspring.

New species can be created when a mutation occurs in the structural field, the chromosome lengths are modified, the individual goes to another species or another species is created .The number of species is subject to change during the algorithm.

3.5 STEP 5

After a predetermined number of iterations, *global selection operator* – **GSO** – is applied, doesn't matter for it the species. The number of fittest chromosomes is fixed no matter what species they belong to.

GSO frequency is by choice (application-dependent), not necessarily at each iteration: species with short chromosomes are favoured by a high frequency of **GSO**, species with long chromosomes are favoured by a low frequency of **GSO**. A *Boltzmann selection* was applied in this case with a probability as follows:

$$p = e^{-\frac{E_i(t)}{kT}} \tag{17}$$

where T depends on iteration number *iter* and k on chromosome length, $E_i(t)$

$$k = 1/(1 + l_{chrom}) \tag{18}$$

$$T(iter + 1) = 0.9 \cdot T(iter), \quad T(0) = T_0 \text{ if } iter \text{ is multiple of predefined } k_{gen} \tag{19}$$

$$E_i(t) = -J_{total} \tag{20}$$

In our experiments, $T_0 = 17.5$. Only the fittest chromosomes survive when **GSO** is applied: some species may then grow, others disappear; the evolution is similar with the natural environment where different competitive species share the limited resources

4 Experimental Results

We started with a population of *200* **NNs**, being split in *14* species; the number of members in each species is between *5* and *20*. The label of one species is given by – **n** - the number of neurons in the **RAFNN** and it belongs to integer numbers between *2* and *15*. The population is randomly generated by using a flip coin probability.

The structural gene is represented by 15 allele belonging to {2, 3,...,15} and each adjusting gene by successive pairs of (w_{ij}^{C}, d_{ij}) where w_{ij}^{C} is the central value of the weight and d_{ij} is the corresponding distance between left and right value of symmetric triangular fuzzy numbers (see Fig 3).

A particular case of **TFN**, a symmetric **TFN** was used for this stage of experiments. A first evolution aspect – the fitness function - of **GA** *with variable length genotype* during the learning algorithm was illustrated in Fig. 6:

- g (chromosome) = $\lambda E_1 + \delta E_2$ is represented on *y* axis;
- a normalized number of generation, *gen/250* – the number of generation divided by 250 is represented on x – axis ; this means any (x,y) point is represented after *250* generations
- the total number of represented generation is 5×10^{4}

The zoomed graphic illustrates the fitness of best individual between generation *250×130* and generation *250×170*. One of the optimal **RAFNN** was of *5* output neurons, with *2* active inputs and *1* bias input, where bias was set up to the fuzzy crisp (degenerated) value of *(1,1,1)*.

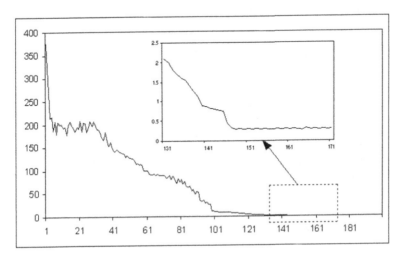

Fig. 6. The evolution of learning algorithm for variable length genotype.

A second evolution aspect – the output error – of **GA** *with variable length genotype* during the learning algorithm was illustrated in Fig. 7 (just for the first *100* iterations). In order to better prove the capability of **GA** *with variable length genotype*, the **test conditions were set up a little more restrictively**, apart from crisp case, where a value below *0.5* is considered to be *0.0* and a value greater than *0.5* is considered to be *1.0*.

The maximal error $E_{max} = max\{E^L, E^C, E^R\}$), where E^L, E^C and E^R are defined in Fig. 7. A very good error for an *XOR problem extended to fuzzy triangular numbers* $E_{max} < 0.23$ was got just after *4* iterations; this means the **RAFNN** dynamics was already stabilized. And this stabilization is kept during the whole test, *1000* iterations namely. In the figure only the first 100 steps are presented for the sake of clearness.

In the **GA** case, the optimal solution appeared after a magnitude order of 10^2 meanwhile in case of gradient method used in [1], the solution appeared after around 5×10^4 iterations. The improvement by more than one order of magnitude proved that our **GA** solution is significant better than gradient solution used in [1].

Usual, the test stage is considered successful as in [7] if the output of selected neuron (in our case he last neuron of the **RAFNN**) produces a correct extended **XOR** delayed during a sufficient large number of steps. In our case, the number of steps is *1000* and the delay is set to 2 steps.

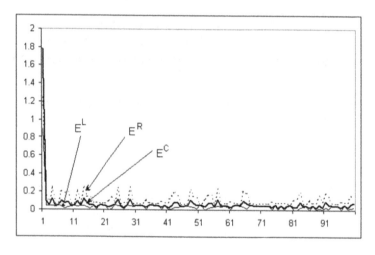

Fig. 7. Output Error for test stage during test period in the extended *XOR* problem; $E^\gamma = |d^\gamma - y^\gamma|$ with $\gamma \in \{L, C, R\}$ and d – the target output.

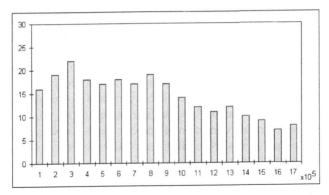

Fig. 8. The number of species evolution during the learning algorithm. On the X is represented the number of iterations and on the Y axe is represented the number of species.

The evolution of population along the training period of time is presented in Fig. 8. We can observe that our algorithm moderates the pressure over variety of individuals in order to avoid excessive elitism in species.

5 Concluding Remarks

We proposed a new type of **GA** as a solution for solving a problem that simultaneously finds the structure and the weights for **RAFNN**.

The work in this paper has the aim of **RAFNN** optimization, namely both the structure (number of neurons) and **NN** parameters (the weight matrix). A **GA** *with variable length genotypes* is developed to do it. This algorithm is performing satisfactory and its application area can be extended.

This **GA** uses species that evolve independently; the number of species and the population size are subject to change during the algorithm. There are two kind of intrinsic competition: between individuals within each of the species and between species (simulated by the global selection operator - **GSO**). The genotype lengths do not increase unlimitedly during the algorithm, due to **GSO** and due to a penalty introduced by the fitness function.

Experimental optimization results show a slow **NN** evolution to a point of maximum: a relative high number required iterations (approx. 105) comparative with the crisp case, but a real advantage in case of fuzzy number weights. *A sensible less number of iterations is required by this kind of* **GA** *than by adapting gradient algorithm.* The capability of a **GA** *with variable length genotype* is illustrated by the fact that its performances were got in conditions of weight solutions in a form of (short) fuzzy numbers, but not crisp numbers. **NN** structures are usually determined experimentally, *but our* **GA** *offers a systematic way of getting a minimal* **NN** *structure satisfying the requested performance.* And this advantage is not to be neglected when a complex hybrid intelligent architecture must be designed without any previous details regarding its requested architecture (number of neurons and weight values in case of a **NN**).

Our work is different from [4] that consider chromosomes of variable length but the number of members of population is constant and the crossover is applied for members of the species indifferent of the lengths of chromosomes.

In the further research we will extend the algorithm to other architectures using non-symmetric triangular fuzzy number (three values coded for each fuzzy parameter). Another possible further extension of our proposed **GA** could be made to other architectures that use crisp number but also fuzzy numbers (i.e. multiplayer perceptron and **RBF**). The structure of connection of neurons can be considered as a matrix of 1 and 0 values. The further research will include this parameter as third element in the space of solutions (the first two are the weights and the number of neurons).

A more promising further research direction seems to be the applicability of this **GA** to a *class of specific to data mining problems*, with regard to "which are the sequences that determine the behavior of the time series according to a defined objective?" Actually the response is known for a given length of mined sequence only, but we plan to apply our method to simultaneously discover the length of sequence too.

References

1. Arotaritei, D.: Dynamic Adapted Gradient Algorithm for Hybrid Recurrent Structure. Word Multiconference on Systemics, Cybernetics and Informatics ISAS/SCI 2001, Orlando, Florida, USA (2001) 568–571
2. Coello, C.A.: A Survey of Constraint Handling Techniques used with Evolutionary Algorithms. Lania-RI-99-04, Laboratorio Nacional de Informática Avanzada (1999)
3. Fagarasan, F., Negoita, Gh. M.: Genetic Based Method for Learning the Parameters of a Fuzzy Inference System, Proceedings of ANNES'95, Dunedin, Otago, New Zealand (1995) 223–226
4. Harvey, I.: Species Adaptation Genetic Algorithms: a basis for a continuing SAGA, Proceedings of the First European Conference on Artificial Life. Toward a Practice of Autonomous Systems, MIT Press, Cambridge, York (1991) 346–354
5. Kandel, A., Teodorescu, H.N., Arotaritei, D.: Analytic Fuzzy RBF Neural Network. Proceedings of the 17th Annual Meeting of the North American Fuzzy Information Processing Society NAFIPS'98, Pensacola Beach, Florida, USA (1998)
6. Teodorescu, H.N.: Non-Linear Systems, Fuzzy Systems, and Neural Networks. Proc. 3rd Int. Conference on Fuzzy Logic, Neural Nets and Soft Comp. (1994) 17–28
7. Williams, R.J., Zipser, D.: Experimental Analysis of the Real-time Recurrent Learning Algorithm. Connection Science, Vol. 1, No. 1 (1989) 87–111
8. Zimmerman, H.-J., Negoita, Gh. M, Dascalu, D., (Eds): Real World Application of Intelligent Technologies, Editura Academiei Romane (1996)

Theoretical Foundation for Nonlinear Edge-Preserving Regularized Learning Image Restoration

Dianhui Wang and Tharam S. Dillon

Department of Computer Science and Computer Engineering
La Trobe University, Melbourne, VIC 3083, Australia
dhwang@cs.latrobe.edu.au

Abstract. Image restoration is an important issue in image processing, which helps recovering of degraded images caused by various factors in different circumstances. Neural networks models have been successfully applied in handling image restoration problems and some progress and promising results have been reported in the past. A popular neural networks model for image restoration is the Hopfield network due to its ability on dealing with optimization problems. A degraded image may have multiple corresponding solutions, i.e., the restored images, and the obtained solution can be sub-optimal which is related to a local minimum point in the weight space of the Hopfield network. This paper gives an algebraic characterization on images and shows that images with lower complexity can be restored uniquely from their degraded images and edge information. The obtained result in this paper establishes a mathematical basis for employing the mapping neural networks to realize a learning based image restoration scheme. The linear image restoration model is firstly generalized to a nonlinear one to broaden the scope of application. Secondly, we view the image restoration task as a set of approximation problems in a high dimensional space, and a mapping relationship between the degraded images with edge information and the source images is then built using feed-forward neural networks and the well trained neural network can be used to restore the degraded images in real-time. Computer simulations demonstrate the effectiveness of the learning image restoration techniques proposed in this paper.

1 Introduction

A degraded image may be caused by various factors such as atmospheric turbulence, distortions in the optical imaging system, lack of focus, sensor or transmission noise injection, coding techniques, and object or camera motion [1]. The task of image restoration is to remove these degradations to enhance the quality of the image for further use in domain applications. Image restoration can be defined as a problem of estimating a source image from its degraded version. In the past, to solve this fundamental and important issue for image processing, considerable studies have been carried out using various approaches [3],[8]. The techniques involving an iterative method to minimize a degradation measure attracted many researchers and recently

R.I. McKay and J. Slaney (Eds.): AI 2002, LNAI 2557, pp. 693–703, 2002.
© Springer-Verlag Berlin Heidelberg 2002

different models and approaches were developed such as constrained least square error [2], [4], [5], and adaptive regularization techniques [6],[7]. To implement the minimization tasks for image restoration, however, we should take into account several practical factors, such as real-time requirement, or even many of the numerical optimization techniques can be used.

Neural networks can be defined as a massively parallel and distributed processor that has a natural propensity for storing and recalling experiential knowledge [15]. As potential tools, neural networks have been successfully applied in image processing mainly due to the ability to generate and recall an internal data representation through pattern samples learning. Some encouraging results on image restoration using neural networks have been reported in literature [6],[7],[9],[10],[11]. So far, almost all of the related works use a Hopfield network to find an equilibrium of the network as the solution for a constrained least square error measure with a regularization term [9],[10], which plays an important role in controlling the quality of the restored image. If the regularization term is weighted too weakly in the error measure, the resultant restored image will contain noise artifacts. On the other hand, if the regularization measure is weighted too strongly in the error measure, the resultant restored image will be bluffed [3]. Several approaches have been developed to adaptively vary the regularization parameter to achieve the optimal balance between removing edge ringing effects and suppressing noise amplification [6],[7],[9]. Recently, we presented a pattern learning based image restoration technique using neural networks to enhance the quality of transformed coding images, where *a priori* knowledge of the image dependent edge information was incorporated into the regularized error measure to improve the upper bound estimation of the high frequency content [11]. A multilayer perceptron model with a single hidden layer architecture was employed for modeling and an image similarity measure was used as the cost function for training. Experimental results reported in our previous study demonstrate the potential of the proposed learning image restoration technique.

This paper discusses solution characterization and approximation issues for the learning based image restoration scheme. A generic nonlinear image restoration model is considered in this paper. The edge information as *a priori* knowledge about the source image to recover the details is introduced in the regularization cost function to enhance the restoration performance both objectively and subjectively. An image subset characterized by using the second derivative information is established. Furthermore, it has been shown that the restored image in the defined subset is unique and it can be well approximated by mapping neural networks providing that the training samples are rich enough. Some aspects associated with the implementation are also discussed. The remainder of the paper is organized as follows. Section 2 develops a generic image restoration model for general degradation processes and formulates the well-known regularization cost function with the inclusion of edge information. In Section 3, we first generate the local implicit mapping theorem to a global version, and apply the obtained result to characterize algebraically the image space, where a class of degraded images can be surely and uniquely restored. Section 4 presents a set of computer simulations to demonstrate the effectiveness of the proposed techniques. Concluding remarks are given in the last section.

2 Nonlinear Regularized Restoration Model

Usually, the relationship between a degraded image g and its original image f can be expressed by

$$g = L(f) + n \qquad (1)$$

where L is a matrix operator, i.e., a linear mapping, and n is an additive noise, respectively.

The objective of image restoration can be formulated as " to get an estimated image $\hat{f}$ from some class of images such that it will minimize the noise function n ". One popular approach for implementing this is to minimize the following objective function [3]:

$$J_0 = \lambda \, \| S(\hat{f}) \|^2 + \| g - L(\hat{f}) \|^2 \qquad (2)$$

where S is a regularizing operator of a appropriate dimension, which is generally a high-pass filter used to reduce the amount of noise in the restored image, $\|x\|$ denotes the Euclidean norm of x, λ is a constraint factor which controls the degree of smoothness of the restored image.

The linearity assumption on mapping L is not necessary although the model in (1) characterizes some image restoration problems [8]. In this paper, we generalize the image restoration model (1) by replacing the linear mapping L with an nonlinear operator P, which may represent any distortion operation or process, for example, it can be a coding algorithm, spatial shift or an additive noise from a sensor. To obtain a better upper bound in estimating the high frequency content, we also introduce $a\ priori$ knowledge of the image dependent edge information in the objective function. The modified objective function is given by

$$J_1 = \lambda \, \| S(f - \hat{f}) \|^2 + \| g - P(\hat{f}) \|^2 \qquad (3)$$

As can be seen any numerical optimization technique will lose their power in solving (3) due to the presence of the unknown nonlinear mapping P.

The nonlinear operator P in (3) can be expressed by $P = I + \Psi$, where I is the identity mapping and Ψ is a smooth unknown nonlinear mapping with a small norm bound. It is important to realize that the nonlinear mapping Ψ in (3) represents a process comprising some operations, also it may be time-varying and usually unknown. This implies that we have no easy way to restore an image through directly minimizing the regularization cost function (3). On the other hand, the solution arg $min(J_1)$ of (3) can be multiple for some pair of degraded image g and the edge information. Naturally, it will be interesting to see what kinds of images can be restored successfully by using the learning image restoration approach. For a specific Ψ, which corresponds to some certain process, the quality of the restored image will depend upon the "distance" between the degraded image and the source image, and also it is closely related to the nature of the image being restored. In the next section, we characterize a subset of images where a function can be well defined.

3 Solutions Existence and Characterization

The following mathematical preliminaries are needed.

Suppose that $F : R^{m+n} \mapsto R^n$ is continuously differential in a neighborhood of (a, b) and $h : U \mapsto R^n$, where $U \subset R^m$ and $F(x, y) = 0$ at the point (a,b). The components of the vector equation $F(x, y) = 0$ can be written as

$$F_1(x_1,...,x_m, y_1,...y_n) = 0$$
$$\vdots \tag{4}$$
$$F_n(x_1,...,x_m, y_1,...y_n) = 0$$

Denoted by $D_2 F(a,b)$ the last n columns of the derivative $F'(a,b)$. We will say that $y = h(x)$ solves the equation $F(x, y) = 0$ in a neighborhood W of (a,b) if the graph of h agrees in W with the zero set of F, that is, if $(x, y) \in W$ and $x \in U$, then

$$F(x, y) = 0 \text{ if and only if } y = h(x) \tag{5}$$

Theorem 1. (Local Implicit Mapping Theorem) Let the mapping $F : R^{m+n} \mapsto R^n$ be continuously differential in a neighborhood of the point (a, b) where $F(a,b) = 0$. If the partial derivative matrix $D_2 F(a,b)$ is nonsingular, then there exists a neighborhood U of a in R^m, a neighborhood W of (a, b) in R^{m+n}, and a continuously differential mapping $h : U \mapsto R^n$, such that $\mathbf{y} = h(\mathbf{x})$ solves the equation $F(x, y) = 0$ in W.

In particular, the implicitly defined mapping h is the limit of the sequence of successive approximations defined inductively by

$$h_0(x) = b, h_{k+1}(x) = h_k(x) - D_2 F(a,b)^{-1} F(x, h_k(x)) \tag{6}$$

for $x \in U$.

Proof: See [12, pp.190–192].

Theorem 2. (Global Implicit Mapping Theorem) Let the mapping $F : R^{m+n} \mapsto R^n$ be continuously differential in an open set $\Omega = \Omega_x \times \Omega_y \subseteq R^m \times R^n$, $\Omega^0 = \Omega_x^0 \times \Omega_y^0 \subset \Omega$ a closed set and, $F(x, y) = 0, \det D_2 F(x, y) \neq 0$ for any $(x, y) \in \Omega$. Then, there exists a continuously differential function $h : \Omega_x^0 \mapsto R^n$ such that $y = h(x)$ solves the equation $F(x, y) = 0$ in Ω^0.

Proof: By Theorem 1, for each $x \in \Omega_x^0$, there is an open set $B_x \subset \Omega_x$ containing x, and there is a unique differentiable function $h_x : B_x \mapsto \Omega_y$ such that $\mathbf{y} = h_x(\mathbf{x})$ solves equation $F(x, y) = 0$ locally, that is, $F(x, h_x(x)) = 0$ for $x \in B_x$.

Let $\Im = \{B_x : x \in \Omega_x^0\}$. Then, $\Im$ is an open cover of the compact set Ω_x^0. By Borel-Lebesgue covering theorem [13], there must be a finite sub-cover of $\Im$, namely $\Im_F = \{B_{x1}, B_{x2},..., B_{xp}\}$, that is,

$$\Omega_x^0 \subset \bigcup_{i=1}^{p} B_{xi} . \tag{7}$$

According to the uniqueness of the local implicit function (see Theorem 1), we have

$$h_{xi}(x) = h_{xj}(x), i \neq j \quad \text{for} \quad x \in B_{xi} \cap B_{xj}, \tag{8}$$

if $B_{xi} \cap B_{xj} \neq \phi$ (empty set). Hence, a continuously differentiable function can

be well defined on the closed set Ω_x^0 in a piece-wise fashion, that is,

$$h(x) = \begin{cases} h_{x1}(x), x \in B_{x1;} \\ \quad\vdots \\ h_{xp}(x), x \in B_{xp}. \end{cases} \tag{9}$$

This solves the equation $F(x, y) = 0$ in Ω^0, that is,

$$F(x, h(x)) = 0 \quad \text{for all} \quad x \in \Omega_x^0 . \tag{10}$$

This completes the proof.

Minimizing J_1 with respect to $\hat{f}$ leads to the following normal equation:

$$G(\hat{f}, g, S^t S f) = \lambda S^t S(\hat{f} - f) + \nabla P^t(\hat{f})[P(\hat{f}) - g] = 0 \tag{11}$$

where M^t denotes the transpose of matrix M, $\nabla P(\hat{f})$ is the Jacobian of the nonlinear mapping P with respect to variable $\hat{f}$. The term $S^t S f$ in (11) is simply an edge extraction of the source images as S is taken as a Laplacian mask. For any given pair $p = \{ g, S^t S f \}$, the corresponding solution of (11) offers a restored image. To proceed with our work, the following basic assumption is necessary and reasonable:

Assumption. The unknown mapping Ψ in P is an uniformly bounded, that is, there exists a real positive constant δ such that for all $\hat{f}$

$$\| \Psi(\hat{f}) \| \leq \delta \tag{12}$$

Also, let $c > 0$ be the uniform bound of the difference between the degraded image g and the restored one $\hat{f}$, that is,

$$\| \hat{f} - g \| \leq c \tag{13}$$

The following result is important and forms the basis of our proposed learning image restoration (LIR) techniques, which characterizes an image subset in which the restored image for any given pair $p = \{ g, S^t S f \}$ is uniquely determined.

Theorem 3. Let $\rho(M), \det(M)$ and $\| M \|_E$ be the smallest singular value, determinant and the 2-norm of a matrix M, respectively. Denote that

$$\Re = \{x : \| \frac{\partial \nabla \Psi^t(x)}{\partial x} \|_E < \frac{\lambda \rho(S'S)}{c + \delta} \} \tag{14}$$

Then, for any $\hat{f} \in \Re$ and $q = (\hat{f}, g, S'Sf)$ satisfying (11), we have

$$\det(\frac{\partial G(q)}{\partial \hat{f}}) \neq 0 \tag{15}$$

Proof: From functional analysis, it is easy to know that (14) defines an open set in N^2-dimensional Euclidean space. To show the inequality (15), we calculate

$$\frac{\partial G}{\partial \hat{f}} = \lambda S'S + \nabla P'(\hat{f}) \nabla P(\hat{f}) + \frac{\partial \nabla \Psi^t(\hat{f})}{\partial \hat{f}} [P(\hat{f}) - g] \tag{16}$$

Note that the operator S is a nonsingular matrix, so the term $\lambda S'S + \nabla P'(\hat{f}) \nabla P(\hat{f})$ is a positive matrix, and the following holds for any $\lambda > 0$ and all $\hat{f}$, that is

$$\rho[(\lambda S'S)^{-1}] \geq \rho[(\lambda S'S + \nabla P'(\hat{f}) \nabla P(\hat{f}))^{-1}] \tag{17}$$

Hence, for any $\hat{f} \in \Re$ and $q = (\hat{f}, g, S'Sf)$ satisfying (11), we have

$$\| \frac{\partial \nabla \Psi^t(\hat{f})}{\partial \hat{f}} [P(\hat{f}) - g] \|_E \leq (c + \delta) \| \frac{\partial \nabla \Psi^t(\hat{f})}{\partial \hat{f}} \|_E \tag{18}$$

$$< \lambda \rho(S'S) \leq \rho[\lambda S'S + \nabla P'(\hat{f}) \nabla P(\hat{f})],$$

which ensures the inequality (15). This completes the proof.

From Theorem 3, we know that the solution, if any, of equation (11) for given pairs p is unique in $\Re$. This implies that for certain classes of images the normal equation (11) may be explicitly rewritten as

$$\hat{f} = F_*(g, S'Sf) \tag{19}$$

where F_* is a nonlinear continuously differentiable function defined in $\Re$.

If the mapping F_* is available, the restored image will be calculated directly for any given pair $p = \{ g, S'Sf \}$. The goal of the LIR scheme is to build a good approximation of this unknown nonlinear mapping through pattern learning.

A simple calculation gives that

$$\| \frac{\partial \nabla \Psi^t(x)}{\partial x} \|_E = \sqrt{\sum_{k,i,j} \left(\frac{\partial^2 \Psi_k}{\partial x_i \partial x_j} \right)^2} \tag{20}$$

where Ψ_k is the k-th component of the mapping Ψ.

Like other regularization model based image restoration techniques, the regularizing factor λ in (3) plays an important role. From (14) and (20), for fixed c and δ, the larger the value of λ takes, the larger the domain of the $\Re$ will be. This implies that some images with higher complexity (or more edges) measured by (20) will be included. This is consistent with the implication expressed by regularization model, where a larger regularizing factor implies a heavier weight on the edge information. We have realized that the choice of the regularizing factor is significant and meaningful. It is necessary and important to properly express, control and use the edge information in our LIR scheme. An adaptive version of the proposed LIR scheme is being expected.

4 Computer Simulation

In this simulation study, a subband coding based gray image compression problem is considered. The proposed LIR algorithm is applied as a component of post processing. Five images of resolution 256×256 pixels with eight bits per pixel (bpp) are used to generate the training data. The image *Lenna* (outside the training set) is employed as the test image for stopping the neural network training process. A block size of 4x4 is adopted, with a total number of 40960 training patterns, in our computer simulations. These training patterns were derived from the images *Barbara, Airplane, Sailboat, Cameraman, Bridge, Building*. The test images are used as *Baboon, Goldhill, Germany, Lenna,* and *Peppers*. A multilayer perceptron (MLP) with architecture *32-30-16* is employed to restore images blocks by blocks. A 3×3 *Laplacian* filter is used as the regularization operator S. SPIHT [16], which is one of the outstanding wavelet based codes, was used to code the image. As can be seen there exists a rate budget between the amount of transformed image data and the *a priori* edge knowledge. A GFA-based edge bit-planes coding scheme is used to compromise the amount of information carried by the image data and the corresponding edges and to ensure an adaptive image-independent encoding of the edge image [17]. Extensive experiments on the robustness of the image restoration with respect to the amount of edge data were conducted. It showed when the amount of the edge data is at about 30 percent of the total rate, the restored image would achieve the best perceptual quality and the best PSNR results. The amount of edge data could be controlled by varying the threshold parameter in the edge-coding scheme. An arithmetic coder was used as the entropy coder throughout the experiment.

The mean square error (MSE) was used as a measure of the performance for the training procedure. The MSE is decreased at the beginning of the training phase for both the training set and the test set. However, at a certain point in the training, it begins to increase slightly for the test image although it may continue to decrease for the training data. Such a point is termed as the *saturation point* (SP). If the training work is continued after this point, the MSE performance on the test image becomes worse, which implies a decrease of the peak signal-to-noise ratio (PSNR). Therefore, the cross-validation scheme is employed in the training procedure to prevent overfitting and terminate the training process when the *SP* is reached. Upon completing the training phase, the trained neural network can be applied to restore images.

Table 1 below shows the performance comparison of the proposed approach along with SPIHT on several images selected from both inside and outside the training images, where the images marked * are from inside the training data and others are completely outside the training data. Although these test images may have quite different statistics from the training data, the neural network still works well on them.

Table 1. Objective Performance Evaluation and Comparison

Images	PSNR(dB) for bit-rate at 0.25 bpp		PSNR(dB) for bit-rate at 0.5 bpp	
	SPIHT	LIR	SPIHT	LIR
Barbara*	23.83	24.67	26.57	26.96
Airplane*	26.29	25.91	29.88	30.07
Sailboat*	25.12	25.00	27.65	28.13
Cameraman*	26.95	26.60	30.46	30.61
Bridge*	24.09	23.88	26.04	26.19
Goldhill	26.85	27.00	29.17	29.26
Germany	30.78	30.72	33.25	33.20
Lenna	28.55	28.58	32.41	32.66
Baboon	20.84	21.52	22.54	23.41
Peppers	27.98	27.88	31.49	31.37

To evaluate the usefulness of the edge information used in (3), we investigated the following aspects: edges representation via weights in the neural network, function and the effect on the PSNR performance. Firstly, let the content input vector be null (i.e., zero component). The corresponding output images then can be observed as in Figure 1(b) for *Barbara*. Clearly, the edge information has been well stored and represented internally by neural network. Secondly, we ignore the edge information (i.e., take the edge information as null vector in training patterns) and re-train the neural network by using the degraded image alone. A visual comparison of the results on *Barbara* at 0.25 bpp was shown in Figure 1(c) and 1(d). As can be seen in Figure 1 the function of edge information used in our approach is obvious, that is, it made the edges sharper in the reconstructed images.

It is also important to study the robustness of this LIR algorithm with respect to the effect of input noise, weight changes and hidden nodes damage. This is because it is directly related to transmittal noise and hardware implementation issues. The image *Baboon* was employed here for this investigation. We first added a white noise with unit variance into the input vectors. The restored image was shown in Figure 2(a). Although the performances were logically affected by the additive noise, they were still acceptable both subjectively and visually. Next, we tested the robustness of the neural network with respect to weight changes. A certain percentage of the trained weights were selected at random, and the values were changed within some specified tolerance ranges. As expected, the changed weights in neural model yielded lower PSNR performance. The images in Figure 2(b) and 2(c) shown the visual difference between the actual system output and the output obtained by altering all of the weights within a 10% tolerance range. In order to study the robustness of the system with respect to the network architecture, a number of hidden nodes were removed after training and the performances were calculated for some images. It was observed that the fidelity of the reconstructed image is greatly degraded as some hidden nodes are discarded. As can be seen in Figure 2(d), the image is still recognizable even up to a 20% removal of hidden nodes.

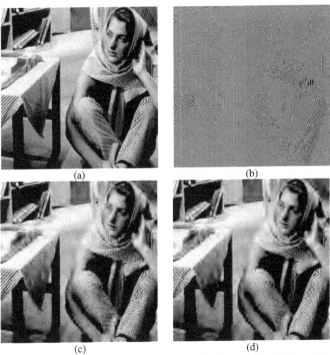

(a)

(b)

(c)

(d)

Fig. 1. (a) Original image "Barbara", (b) Reproduced edge image from NN model, (c) Restored image with CR=0.5 bpp, PSNR=26.96, (d) Restored image with CR=0.5 bpp and without using edge information, PSNR=23.94.

5 Conclusions

This paper investigates the image restoration problem using feed-forward neural networks. A pattern learning based image restoration scheme proposed by the authors was further explored from a mathematical perspective. The learning image restoration (LIR) scheme incorporates *a priori* knowledge on edge information of the source images in reconstructing a higher quality image by means of minimizing a regulariza-

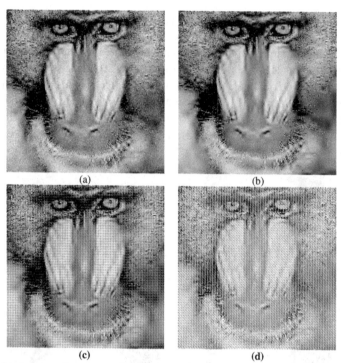

(a)   (b)

(c)   (d)

Fig. 2. Robustness performance of the proposed approach for test image "Baboon" with CR=0.25bpp. (a) Restored image with input noises, PSNR=21.03, (b) Restored image without any perturbations, PSNR=21.52, (c) Reconstructed image with all weights perturbation within 10% tolerance range, PSNR= 19.67, (d) Restored image with deleted 6 hidden nodes, PSNR=15.28.

tion model. The edge information used in practice will be extracted from the degraded image instead of the source images if the source images are not available in some circumstances. This will somehow weaken the performance of the LIR system.

The established theoretical foundation for the LIR scheme is important to the further development of the learning image restoration technique. On a subset of images, the degraded images can be uniquely and effectively restored using an estimated mapping implemented by neural networks. The mapping approximation task can be viewed as a function approximation problem where the patterns from the images are viewed as points in a high dimensional space. It has been realized that the MLP outputs would converge to *a posteriori* probability as the training data is sufficiently large. A further study on the functionality and control of the regularizing factor is being expected. The learning image restoration scheme has good potential in real-time applications and time-varying environments.

Acknowledgement. This project is financially supported by VPAC grants and FSTE small grants (No.104110) at La Trobe University.

References

1. H. Andrew and B. Hunt, Digital Image Restoration, Englewood Cliff, NJ: Prentice Hall (1977)
2. R. L. Lagendijk, J. Biemond, and D. E. Boekee, Regularized iterative image restoration with ringing reduction, IEEE Transactions on Acoust. Speech, Signal Processing, 12(1988) 1874–1888
3. M. G. Kang and A. K. Katsaggelos, General choice of the regularization functional in regularized image restoration, IEEE Transactions on Image Processing, 4(1995) 594-602
4. B. R. Hunt, The application of constrained least squares estimation to image restoration by digital computers, IEEE Transactions on Computer, 22(1973) 805–812
5. A. K. Katsaggelos and R. M. Mersereau, A regularized iterative image restoration algorithm, IEEE Transactions on Signal Processing, 4(1991) 914–929
6. S. Perry and L. Guan, Weight assignment of neural networks in adaptive image restoration, IEEE Trans. on Neural Networks, 1(2000) 156–170
7. H. S. Wong and L. Guan, A neural learning approach for adaptive image restoration using a fuzzy model-based network architecture, IEEE Trans. on Neural Networks, 3(2001) 516–531.
8. J. F. Abramatic and L. M. Silverman, Nonlinear restoration of noisy images, IEEE Transactions on Pattern Analysis and Machine Intelligence, 4(1982) 141–149
9. Y. Zhou, R. Chellappa, A. vaid and B. Jenkins, Image restoration using neural network, IEEE Transactions on Acoust., Speech, Sig. Proc., 7(1988) 1141–1151
10. J. Paik and A. Katsaggelos, Image restoration using a modified Hopfield network, IEEE Transactions on Image Processing,1(1992) 49–63
11. D. H. Wang, T. S. Dillon and E. Chang, Pattern learning based image restoration using neural nets, Proceedings of 2002 International Joint Conference on Neural Networks, Hilton Hawaiian Village, Honolulu, USA, May 12-17 (2002) 1481–1486
12. C. H. Edwards, Jr., Advanced Calculus of Several Variables, Academic Press, New York (1973)
13. Nicolas Bourbaki. Elements de Mathematique, volume Topologie Generale. HERMANN, troisieme edition (1960)
14. K. I. Funahashi, On the approximate realization of continuous mappings by neural Networks, Neural Networks, 2(1989) 183–192
15. S. Haykin, Neural Networks-A Comprehensive Foundation, 2nd Edition, Prentice Hall (1999)
16. A. Said and W. A. Pearlman, A new, fast, and efficient image codec based on set partitioning in hierarchical trees, *IEEE Transactions on Circuits and Systems for Video Technology,* 3(1996) 243–250
17. K. Culik II and V. Valenta, "Finite Automata Based Compression of Bi-level Images", The *Proceedings of Data Compression Conference*, (1996) 280–289

The Application of Case Based Reasoning on Q&A System

Peng Han, Rui-Min Shen, Fan Yang, and Qiang Yang

Dept. of Computer Science and Engineering, Shanghai Jiao tong Univ., Shanghai, China
{phan, rmshen, fyang } @mail.sjtu.edu.cn

Abstract. Q&A (Question and Answer) system is an important aiding tool for people to obtain knowledge and information from the Internet. In this paper, we introduce CBR (Case Based Reasoning) into traditional Q&A system to increase the efficiency and accuracy of retrieving the solution. We put forward an interactive and introspective Q&A engine which uses keywords of the question to trigger the case and sorts the results by the relationship. The engine can also modify the weights of the keywords dynamically based on the feedbacks of the user. Inside the engine, we use a feature-weight maintenance algorithm to increase the accuracy. We also extend the 2-layer architecture of CBR to a 3-layer structure to make the system more scalable and maintainable.

1 Introduction

Question and Answer (Q&A) System is one of the most important components in E-Learning environment which aims at answering the questions asked by the student during their study processes. Accuracy and efficiency are the main two criteria used to evaluate the Q&A systems. Many Q&A systems have already developed based on email-solution, keyword-matching or word-segmentation techniques [12, 13, 14, 15]. With the growth of the number of users and questions, the process time of these systems will become longer and the matching accuracy will become lower due to different presentations of the question and variable interests of the user.

In order to overcome the above disadvantages, we introduce CBR (Case Based Reasoning) into traditional Q&A system. CBR, representing a new generation of expert system technology, has enjoy tremendous success as a technology for solving problems related to knowledge reuse. In this paper, we put forward an interactive Q&A engine based on CBR. This engine uses keywords of the question to trigger case and sorts the results by the relationship and can modify the weights of the keywords dynamically depending on the feedbacks from the user. We also present a new feature-weight maintenance algorithm to increase the accuracy. At last we extend the 2-layer architecture of CBR to a 3-layer structure to make the system more scalable and maintainable.

In next section we present the architecture of the introspective Q&A system based on CBR technique. Section 3 introduces the Case Authoring Module in the architecture and the construction of Case Base in details. We also discuss the definition of question-answer case and the construction of 3-layer Case Base structure

R.I. McKay and J. Slaney (Eds.): AI 2002, LNAI 2557, pp. 704–713, 2002.

there. We still introduce the related feature-weight maintenance algorithm. In Section 4 we discuss the experiment results for evaluating the performance of our system. We give our conclusion in Section 5, where we will also explore our future work.

2   Architecture of the Auto Q&A System

Our Q&A system is based on the CBR technology. The whole system is divided into two separate modules, with the first one called Case Authoring Module and the second one introspective Q&A Engine.

The Case Authoring Module is to represent the unstructured field knowledge structurally based on empirical expert knowledge and application background. All these structural representations can be transferred into question-answer instances and stored in the system case base. The introspective Q&A Engine is the kernel of our system. It is triggered by the keywords or description of the problems and returns the similar problems related to the description ranked by the score. So the user can select the most similar problems and get the answer. Furthermore, the system provides a feedback module to adjust the weights of keywords according to the user's score. The architecture of the Q&A system is shown as Figure 1:

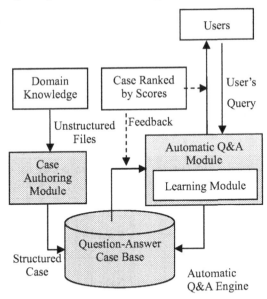

Fig. 1. Architecture of the Q&A System

The system has been used in the professional e-learning site of Shanghai Jiao Tong University (www.nec.sjtu.edu.cn). So all the questions, answers and the relativity between them are accessed through the standard web interfaces. The users, especially the students, produced a great number of questions and potential answers during the learning process. All the questions and answers are assembled in log files.

So we can train the index architecture of the relationship between questions and answers based on the log files. This process is running during the life cycle of the system, which makes the Q&A system become a closed-loop system.

3   Case Authoring Module and Case Base Construction

3.1   Definition of the Question-Answer Case

The description and definition of case is the foundation of a CBR system, and there isn't a uniform standard for it so far since it has strong domain characteristic [7, 8]. In the Case Authoring Module, we define our case-description based on the e-Learning domain characteristics and organize the unstructured domain knowledge in a structural way. The cases in the Q&A system are the description of question and answer. The representation of a case is as follows:

Keywords: short description of the case, which can be used in fuzzy string matching with the user's initial free-form text input.

Attributes: the features that present the main content and characteristics of the question.

Question Description: This is a more detailed textual description of the question's object or content used to confirm the general problem area.

Answer: The answer provides a solution to the case in either textual format or any multimedia format.

Table 1 and Table 2 give an example of the case representation for the Q&A system. The cases in Table 1 are fairly refined, down to the detailed features and their values, while the cases in Table 2 have only two major parts: problem description and answer.

Table 1. Case Representation with Detailed Features (Attributes are not shown due to lack of space)

Type	Keyword1	Keyword2	Answer
Concept & Difference	Switcher	Router	Describe the concepts and difference of Switcher and Router.

Table 2. Case Representation with Natural Language Description

No.	Problem Description	Answer
1	What's the difference between the Switcher and Router?	The function of switcher is quite different from the router ...... (Just present the difference between them)
2	What are the concepts of Switcher and Router?	Switcher is the ...... Router is the ...... (Just list the concepts of them)

3.2   The 3-Layer Architecture of the Question-Answer Case Base

After the description of the case has been defined, the next essential task is to construct the case base and feature index. Each case is associated with a set of feature-value pairs. These pairs are combinations of important descriptors of a case, which distinguish it from other cases. So a case base could naturally be viewed as 2-layer architecture comprised of the feature-value layer and case layer. Using the weights assigned to the connections between the feature-value pairs and the case, a CBR system determines the most relevant cases ranked by the feature information submitted by the user and then returned the results to the user for considerations.

However, in practical implementations we find that the definition of the 2-Layer structure sometimes does not work well since when the number of cases becomes too large the efficiency and scalability of the system will decrease dramatically. So we expand the 2-layer architecture into a 3-layer by dividing the case layer into question layer and answer layer. Additionally, we introduce a second set of weights, which attaches to the connections between questions and their possible answers. This second set of weights represents how important an answer is to a particular question.

In order to describe the situation of user's query, we extend the traditional 2-level case base architecture into a 3-level network structure and take the 2-layer structure as a special case. Consider each case as presented as a triple <F, P, S>, where F corresponds to the feature values, P are the problem description and S are the answers. We can split this representation into three levels: a feature level corresponding to feature values F, a problem description level corresponding to P and an answer level corresponding to S. With this model, when a user enters the feature-values at the first level, the system ranks problem descriptions for users' consideration at the middle layer. The user then selects one intended problem description and the system provide the possible answers which is also ranked according to the second set of weights. New system architecture is shown in Figure 2.

An important motivation for this separation in a case is to reduce the redundancy. Given N cases and M solutions, a case base of size N × M is now reduced to the one of size N + M, which eases the scale-up problem and helps make the case base maintenance task easier. A solution can now be shared by several cases and will only need to be revised once if needed.

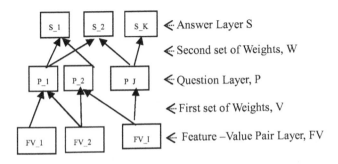

Fig. 2. Tree-layer Architecture of a Question-Answer Case Base

4 The Rank Computation and Maintenance Algorithm

There are two sets of weights, which is similar to the weights in a 3-layer back-propagation neural network. Suppose that there are N features. For each feature F_i, there are m_i values, where i=1, 2... N. The case base contains J problems and K answers. For the architecture shown in Figure 2, there is a total of $I= \sum_{i=1}^{N} m_i$ feature-value pairs, that is to say, there are I nodes in the feature-value layer. We label these feature-value pairs as FV_i, i=1,2,...,I. In the problem layer, we use P_j to represent each problem, where j=1,2,..,J. In the answer layer, we use S_k to represent each answer, where k=1,2,...,K.

The first set of weights $V_{j,i}$ is attached to the connection between a problem P_j and a feature-value pair FV_i if there is an association between them. The second set of weights $W_{k,j}$ is attached to the connection between a answer S_k and a problem P_j if S_k is an answer to P_j.

Given the feature-value pairs selected by a user, the corresponding nodes at the feature-value layer are turned on. A problem's score is computed base on those selected feature-value pairs. For each problem P_j, its score is computed using the following formula:

$$S_{P_j} = \frac{2}{1+e^{-\lambda * \sum_{i=1}^{I}(V_{j,i}*X_i)}} - 1 \qquad (1)$$

where $j = 1,2,\cdots,J$, S_{Pj} is the score of the problem P_j, and X_i is 1 if there is a connection between problem P_j and feature-value pair FV_i, then FV_i is selected. Otherwise X_i is 0.

After the problem scores are computed, the problems and their scores will be presented to the user for selection and confirmation. For the current *selected confirmed* problem, the computation of an answer's score is also similar to the computation of an output in a back-propagation neural network:

$$S_{S_k} = \frac{2}{1+e^{-\lambda * \sum_{i=1}^{I}(W_{k,j}*S_{P_j}*\alpha)}} - 1 \qquad (2)$$

where S_{Sk} is the score of answer S_k, and S_{Pj} is the score of problem P_j. If there is no connection between answer S_k and P_j, then we do not include it in $\sum_{j=1}^{J}(W_{k,j}*S_{P_j}*\alpha)$.

Since the user should first decide which problem at the problem layer is the most desired one based on his or her current preference and this information needs to be reflected in the subsequent computation of the solution score, we introduce a new parameter α into our learning network and call it the *bias factor*. We expected the selected problem to have a higher bias factor than the unselected ones so as to contribute more in the final answer scores. Thus the answers of the selected problems might have relatively higher scores.

The computation of the learning delta value is first done at the answer layer [16, 17]. We only compute the delta values for the answers associated with the current *selected and confirmed* problem. The following formula is employed:

$$\delta_{S_k} = \frac{1}{2} * (D_{S_k} - S_{S_k}) * (1 - S_{S_k}^2) \tag{3}$$

where δ_{Sk} is the learning delta value for answer S_k, and D_{Sk} is the desired score for S_k.

The learning delta values are then propagated back to the problem layer. The computation of the delta value at this layer is done using the following formula:

$$\delta_{P_j} = \frac{1}{2} * (1 - S_{P_j}^2) * \sum_{k=1}^{K} (\delta_{S_k} * W_{k,j}) \tag{4}$$

where δ_{pj} is the learning delta value of problem P_j. If there is no connection between answer S_k and problem P_j, we do not include it in $\sum_{k=1}^{K} (\delta_{S_k} * W_{k,j})$.

After computing S_{Pj}, S_{Sk}, δ_{Pj}, δ_{Sk}, we need to adjust the weights of the connections between the answer layer and the problem layer, and then connections between the problem layer and the feature-value pair layer. We will adjust the weights attached to the answers which are associated with the current *selected and confirmed* problem. The formula for this adjustment is:

$$W_{k,j}^{new} = W_{k,j}^{old} + \eta * \delta_{S_k} * S_{Pj} \tag{5}$$

where $W_{k,j}^{new}$ is the old weight to be computed, and $W_{k,j}^{old}$ is the new weight attached to the connection between answer S_k and P_j.

The weights attached to connections between the problems and the feature-value pairs will be adjusted next using the learning delta values as follows:

$$V_{j,i}^{new} = V_{j,i}^{old} + \eta * \delta_{P_j} * X_i \tag{6}$$

where $V_{j,i}^{new}$ is the new weight to be computed, $V_{j,i}^{old}$ is the old weight attached to the connection between problem P_j and feature-value pair FV_i. X_i is 1 if there is a connection between them and FV_i is selected by the user. Otherwise X_i is 0.

In addition to scaling-up and redundancy advantages, an added advantage of this architecture is that we can now represent a context sensitive case base. In this way, the second layer, which consists of problem descriptions, can be used to represent both the problem and the context layers, the latter representing different contexts in which problems occur. Under such conceptual representation, the third layer now contains the actual cases. A user can enter a problem's description in the form of feature value pairs and then select the desired context in which to solve the problem. The second set weights in turn can help rank the right case for solving the problem. A set of features can simultaneously influence the contexts and the cases at the same time.

5 Case Study and Experiment

We have implemented the introspective Q&A system based on our professional distance learning web sites. Figure 3 to Figure 5 show an example of the process to solve a problem (since it is a system for Chinese users, so even the English version still has some Chinese information). As can be seen in Figure 3, user can first enter a problem description to identify the context under which the problem is solved. User can describe the problem with any natural description language as he wishes.

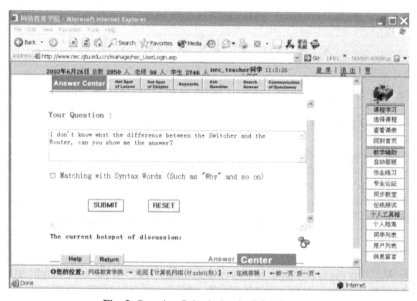

Fig. 3. Question Submission in Q&A System

After submitting the question, a collection of initial cases which match the partial description are retrieved and returned to the user. These cases serve as the candidate answers for subsequent problem solving. Questions that are associated with the candidate cases are then presented to the user (as shown in Figure 4).

The system will return the questions ranked by the average score. Then user can select any similar question to see the answer. If they think the ranking and the score of the question is not fit for him, he can adjust the score in the answer showing column. And the system will then adjust the corresponding weights based on the score given by the user and use the new weights to calculate score next time (As shown in Figure 5).

In order to evaluate the efficiency and validity of our algorithm, we give the test results based on the Network Course database from the NEC Question/Answer Repository. The Network Course database contains 300 instances and 28 attributes. We divide the main case base into several incremental sub-case base, containing 50, 100, 150, 200, 250 instances respectively.

In our experiment, we first convert these databases into the case bases that our algorithm can handle by converting all rows into cases and all columns into features

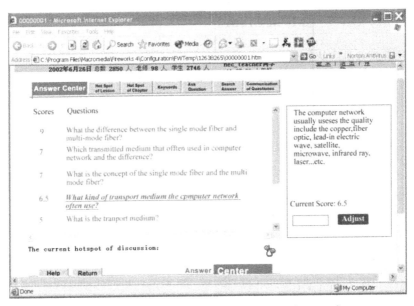

Fig. 4. The Returned Similar Question Lists Ranked by Average Scores

In these tests, the score of a case or an answer is between 0.0 and 1.0; meanwhile, suppose the initial values of the weight are 0.5.

Based on the 3-layer architecture, we perform ten training based on the sub-case bases. Finally, we can get the mean-errors convergence plot (As shown in Figure 6).

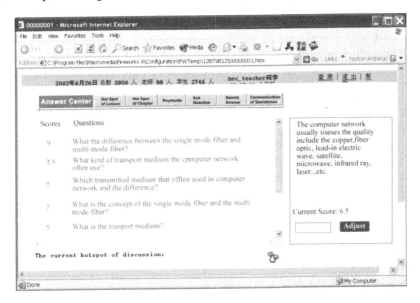

Fig. 5. The Adjusted Question List Based On the Learning Network

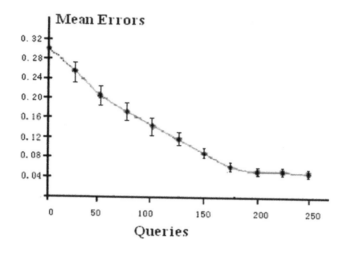

Fig. 6. Plot of the mean errors convergence and 95% confidence interval along the CBR process

In this figure, the 95% confidence interval is also shown on each datum point, where the size of the interval indicates the fluctuation around the mean values, and the average processing time is approximately 1.8 seconds.

6 Conclusion and Future Work

Our work aims at achieving the goal of implementing a Question and Answer system with high efficiency and accuracy to help the users in E-Learning get the professional direction in time. The 3-layer Q&A system based on Case Based Reasoning technique can improve the scaling-up and redundancy of the Q&A system. Furthermore, the context sensitive case base due to the 3-layer architecture can also make the ranking more accuracy. The test based on the real professional site database also proves the performance of our algorithm.

The system has a number of areas to be improved. With the continual growth of the user and the expert fields, the number of cases may become very large, and as a result, the problem will become more complex and the number of returned similar cases will become extra large. In our future work, we will try to find an effective cluster method to merge the similar cases together. And find a way to reduce the number of returned similar cases.

References

1. D. B. Leake. CBR in context: The present and future. In David B. Leake, editor, Case-Based Reasoning, Experinces, Lessons & Future Directons, page 1–30. AAAI Press/ The MIT Press, Menlo Park CA, USA, 1996.

2. I. Watson. Appling Case-Based Reasoning: Techniques for Enterprise System. Morgan Kaufmann Publishers, Inc.,1997.
3. Costas Tsatsoulis, Qing Cheng, Hsin-Yen Wei . Integrating Case-Based Reasoning and Decision Theory. IEEE Transactions on Intelligent Systems, Vol. 12, No. 4, pp. 46–55, 1997.
4. D. B. Leake, A. Kinley, and D.Wilson. Learning to improve case adaptation by introspective reasoning and CBR. In Proceedings of the First International conference on Case-Based Reasoning, pages 229–240, Sesimbra, Portugal, 1995. ISO Publishers.
5. Masaaki Takahashi, Jun-ichi Oono, Kazuyuki Saitoh, Shunji Matsumoto. Reusing Makes It Easier: Manufacturing Process Design by CBR with KnowledgeWare, IEEE Transactions on Intelligent Systems, Vol. 10, No. 6, pp. 74–80, 1995.
6. Ivo Vollrath, Wolfgang Wilke, Ralph Bergmann. Case-Based Reasoning Support for Online Catalog Sales, IEEE Transactions on Internet Computing. Vol. 2, No. 4, pp. 47–54, 1998.
7. K.Racine and Q.Yang. Maintaining Unstructured case bases. In proceedings of the Second International Conference on Case-Based Reasoning, ICCBR-97, pages 553–564, Providence RI, USA, 1997.
8. Barry Smyth, Mark T. Keane, Pádraig Cunningham. Hierarchical Case-Based Reasoning Integrating Case-Based and Decompositional Problem-Solving Techniques for Plant-Control Software Design. IEEE Transactions on Knowledge and Data Engineering. Vol. 13, No. 5, pp. 793–812, 2001.
9. V. Ganti, J. Gehrke, R. Ramakrishnan. Mining very large databases. COMPUTER, 32(8):38–45, 1999.
10. Zhong Zhang and Qiang Yang. Feature Weight Maintenance in Case Bases Using Introspective Learning. Journal of Intelligent Information Systems, Kluwer Academic Publishers, 16, Pages 95–116, 2001. The Netherlands.
11. Qiang Yang and Jing Wu. Enhancing the Effectiveness of Interactive Case-Based Reasoning with Clustering and Decision Forests. In Applied Intelligence Journal; Special Issue on Interactive CBR (Editors: David Aha and Hector Munoz-Avil). Jan/Feb 2001. Vol 14, No. 1. Pages 49–64. Kluwer Academic Pubslishers.
12. http://www.ejiajia.com
13. http://www.sijiehe.com
14. http://www.ibm.com/FAQs
15. http://www.mit.ed
16. D.E.Rumelhart and J.L.McClelland, editors. Parallel Distributed Processing, MIT Press, Cambridge, Massachusetts, 1986.
17. G. Hinton and J.Anderson. Parallel Models of Associative Memory. Lawrence Erlbaum, Potomac, Maryland, 1981.

Development of an Intelligent Tutoring System on Design of Liquid Retaining Structures

K.W. Chau[1], F. Albermani[2], and S.L. Chan[1]

[1]Department of Civil & Structural Engineering, Hong Kong Polytechnic University, Hunghom, Kowloon, Hong Kong
[2]Department of Civil Engineering, University of Queensland, Australia
cekwchau@polyu.edu.hk

Abstract. Liquid retaining structures, which are mainly used to retain domestic water, sewage, or industrial waste, are usually constructed with reinforced concrete in Hong Kong. During the design, novice engineers often encounter problems including decision-making based on rules of thumb, judgment, previous experience, heuristics, and code of practice. A computer-aided tool that incorporates engineering judgment along with algorithmic tools is highly desirable. This paper presents an intelligent tutoring system, with hybrid knowledge representation techniques including production rule system and object-oriented approach, which provides expert advice on design of liquid retaining structures. Intelligent tutoring system is a type of knowledge-based expert system with the particular purpose of teaching. It can serve the purpose for one-to-one tutoring, which is generally acknowledged to be the most effective teaching method, yet requiring high ratio of resources. This system is based on British Standards Code of Practice BS8007: 1987: Design of concrete structures for retaining aqueous liquids. Training exercises, learner model as well as tailored explanations on real design practice are furnished to help inexperienced designers or civil engineering students to learn how to design liquid retaining structures. Nowadays, with the popularity of personal computer, civil engineering students as well as novice engineers can glean hand-on knowledge on design of liquid retaining structures more effectively through this system. An evaluation of the developed system and investigation of the effectiveness to learn the domain design knowledge are undertaken.

References

1. Chau, K.W.: An Expert System for the Design of Gravity-Type Vertical Seawalls. Engineering Applications of Artificial Intelligence **5(4)** (1992) 363–367
2. Chau, K.W., Albermani, F.: Expert System Application on Preliminary Design of Liquid Retaining Structures. Expert Systems with Applications **22(2)** (2002) 169–178
3. Chau, K.W., Chen, W.: An Example of Expert System on Numerical Modelling System in Coastal Processes. Advances in Engineering Software **32(9)** (2001) 695–703
4. Chau, K.W., Lee, S.T.: Computer Aided Design Package `RCTANK' for Analysis and Design of Reinforced Concrete Tanks. Computers and Structures **41(4)** (1991) 789–799
5. Chau, K.W,. Ng, Vitus: A Knowledge-Based Expert System for Design of Thrust Blocks for Water Pipelines in Hong Kong. Water Supply Research and Technology **45(2)** (1996) 96–99

R.I. McKay and J. Slaney (Eds.): AI 2002, LNAI 2557, p. 714, 2002.
© Springer-Verlag Berlin Heidelberg 2002

Real-Time Prediction of Water Stage with Artificial Neural Network Approach

K.W. Chau and C.T. Cheng

Department of Civil & Structural Engineering, Hong Kong Polytechnic University,
Hunghom, Kowloon, Hong Kong
cekwchau@polyu.edu.hk

Abstract. An accurate water stage prediction allows the pertinent authority to issue a forewarning of the impending flood and to implement early evacuation measures when required. Existing methods including rainfall-runoff modeling or statistical techniques entail exogenous input together with a number of assumptions. In this paper, neural networks are used to predict real-time water levels in Shing Mun River of Hong Kong with different lead times on the basis of the upstream gauging stations or stage/time history at the specific station. The network is trained by using two different algorithms. It is demonstrated that the artificial neural network approach, which is able to provide model-free estimates in deducing the output from the input, is an appropriate forewarning tool. It is shown from the training and verification simulation that the water stage prediction results are highly accurate and are obtained in very short computational time. Both these two factors are important in water resources management. Besides, sensitivity analysis is carried out to evaluate the most suitable network characteristics including number of input neurons, number of hidden layers, number of neurons in hidden layer, number of output neurons, learning rate, momentum factor, activation function, number of training epoch, termination criterion, etc. under this specific circumstance. The findings lead to the reduction of any redundant data collection as well as the accomplishment of cost-effectiveness.

Acknowledgement. This research was supported by the University Research Grants of Hong Kong Polytechnic University (G-T592).

References

1. Chau, K.W., Lee, J.H.W.: Mathematical Modelling of Shing Mun River Network. Advances in Water Resources **14(3)** (1991) 106–112
2. Chau, K.W., Chen, W.: A Fifth Generation Numerical Modelling System in Coastal Zone. Applied Mathematical Modelling **25(10)** (2001) 887–900
3. Chau, K.W., Jiang, Y.W.: 3D Numerical Model for Pearl River Estuary. Journal of Hydraulic Engineering ASCE **127(1)** (2001) 72–82

On the Design of Mathematical Concepts

Manfred Kerber[1] and Martin Pollet[1,2]

[1] School of Computer Science, The University of Birmingham, England
http://www.cs.bham.ac.uk/~mmk
[2] Fachbereich Informatik, Universität des Saarlandes, Saarbrücken, Germany
http://www.ags.uni-sb.de/~pollet

It is one of the deep mathematical insights that foundational systems like first-order logic or set theory can be used to construct large parts of existing mathematics and formal reasoning. Unfortunately this insight has been used in the field of automated theorem proving as an argument to disregard the need for a diverse variety of representations. While design issues play a major rôle in the formation of mathematical concepts, the theorem proving community has largely neglected them. We argue that this leads not only to problems at the human computer interaction end, but that it causes severe problems at the core of the systems, namely at their representation and reasoning capabilities. In order to improve applicability, theorem proving systems need to take care about the representations used by mathematicians.

Donald Norman gives a fascinating introduction into "The Design of Everyday Things." His insights are of a very general nature and we argue that the principles for good design hold in mathematics as well. The design of concepts in mathematics takes a lot of the burden on getting things right from the human user and puts it into an appropriate representation. The different representations are used to keep information together, hide unimportant details and allow to concentrate on the important parts. Sometimes the right representation is the key step in the process of problem solving. If one were to use a foundational system directly, however, everything would have to be expressed explicitly in a uniform representation, which offers no or only little structural support.

To exemplify this, we will take a closer look at multiplication tables. The information accessible from the table is that it is a binary operation, it is discrete and defined on a finite domain. Domain and range are directly given. The table has its own notion of well-formedness, that is, all d_i have to occur and have to be different, the table must be fully filled. In the design we find

$$
\begin{array}{c|ccc}
\circ & d_1 & \cdots & d_n \\
\hline
d_1 & c_{11} & \cdots & c_{1n} \\
\vdots & \vdots & \ddots & \vdots \\
d_n & c_{n1} & \cdots & c_{nn}
\end{array}
$$

natural and cultural constraints. Multiplication tables are designed in a way that their structure puts "information in the world" that makes it difficult to violate well-formedness. An under-specification would leave a hole in the structure, it is impossible to enter more than one entry per field. Furthermore, although the order of the d_i in the columns and rows could in principle be different, cultural conventions prevent that. This in turn makes particular reasoning methods possible which are connected to the representation. For instance, the commutativity of $\circ$ is checked by verifying that the table is symmetric with respect to the diagonal. For more details, see the full technical report of this contribution at ftp://ftp.cs.bham.ac.uk/pub/authors/M.Kerber/TR/CSRP-02-06.pdf or .ps.gz.

R.I. McKay and J. Slaney (Eds.): AI 2002, LNAI 2557, p. 716, 2002.
© Springer-Verlag Berlin Heidelberg 2002

Consistency of Trust Theories

Chuchang Liu and Maris A. Ozols

Information Networks Division
Defence Science and Technology Organisation
PO Box 1500, Edinburgh, SA 5111, Australia
{Chuchang.Liu,Maris.Ozols}@dsto.defence.gov.au

Liu [1] proposed a logic called TML (Typed Modal Logic), which extends first-order logic with typed variables and modal operators to express agent beliefs. Based on TML, a *trust theory* for a specific secure system can be established. In our approach, the assumptions regarded as a basis that agents place their trust in a given system are encapsulated in the notion of trust and represented by a set of rules, called trust axioms of the system, and the logic together with the set of trust axioms forms a trust theory for the given system. Formally, let AX be the axiom system of TML and $TA^{(\tau)}$ be a set of trust axioms chosen for a given system τ, which captures the initial beliefs and trust relationships of the agents within the system τ, then $AX \cup TA^{(\tau)}$ is called a *trust theory* for the system τ.

Such a trust theory provides a foundation for reasoning about trust in the system. Our previous work has shown how the general techniques for finding trust theories apply to models for agent beliefs. However, to ensure correct reasoning about trust, the soundness of the trust theory must be guaranteed. In [1], we claimed that the logic TML is sound and complete, but gives no proof of this claim. Moreover, we ignored the critical problem how to obtain the soundness of a theory, such that the correct reasoning can be guaranteed.

In this paper, focusing on the possible-worlds approach to modelling trust and belief, we discuss the soundness of trust theories. We first revise TML to be a variant of the modal logic **KD** of beliefs, so that it is more standard, and can easily be extended with additional modal axioms if required. Then we show that the axiom system of the logic TML is sound and complete with respect the semantics scheme for TML. Finally, we obtain the following theorem:

Theorem 1. *Let τ be a given system and $TA^{(\tau)}$ be a set of proper axioms related to trust involved in the system. If $TA^{(\tau)}$ is consistent to TML, then $AX \cup TA^{(\tau)}$ is a sound theory, denoted by $\mathbf{Th}^{(\tau)}$. Thus, a sound trust theory, $\mathbf{Th}^{(\tau)}$, is established for the system τ.*

References

1. C. Liu. Logical foundations for reasoning about trust in secure digital communication. In *AI2001: Advances in Artificial Intelligence*, Lecture Notes in Artificial Intelligence, Vol. 2256, pages 333–344. Springer-Verlag, 2001.

R.I. McKay and J. Slaney (Eds.): AI 2002, LNAI 2557, p. 717, 2002.
© Springer-Verlag Berlin Heidelberg 2002

An Artificially Intelligent Sports Tipper

Alan McCabe

School of Information Technology
James Cook University
alan@cs.jcu.edu.au

This paper presents a description of an artificially intelligent model for predicting the outcome of particular sporting contests. Sports prediction (or "tipping") contests are a common pastime among sports fans worldwide. Many participants in these contests have developed their own systems (computerised or otherwise) with which they select winners. The major problems with these systems however is that the user is often swayed by emotion, misguided intuition, or they do not capture enough meaningful information about the competing teams. The work described here is an attempt to extract insightful information from sporting contests in an effort to make objective predictions about likely winners. It is not meant as an aid to gambling, but rather an interesting case study of using neural networks for predicting probabilistic events in a sporting scenario.

Several model structures and learning algorithms were examined during the experimentation phase, with the most successful model found to be a three-layer perceptron learning via the back-propagation algorithm. Experimentation was also done with differing numbers of layers and hidden units and an arrangement consisting of nineteen input units (one unit for each feature), ten hidden units and a single output unit was found to be the most robust. The features used consisted of those which were thought to be highly indicative of a teams current level of performance (or "form") and included details such as points scored, points against, position on league ladder, home ground advantage, winning percentage etc. The prediction process consisted of firstly training the network (one network for each team) using previous matches as input, and secondly computing an output value normalized to be between zero and one. The output values (analogous to a "confidence of success") for each team were calculated and the team with the highest confidence value was taken as the "tip" for a given match.

The system has undergone a public "live" testing under the name of "Mc-Cabe's Artificially Intelligent Tipper" (MAIT) using data from the National Rugby League competition. The live testing environment involved predictions for each week being made several days in advance and advertised in local print media as well as on a website[1]. The system performed quite favourably, easily outperforming naive heuristics (for example, always picking the home team), outperforming most human "experts" as well as other computerised systems. Results also included a study of which features were most useful, along with an investigation (for interests sake and as an alternative measure of performance) of different betting strategies and the amount of money this system would have potentially won if it was placing bets at a sports betting outlet during the season.

---

[1] http://www.mymait.com

R.I. McKay and J. Slaney (Eds.): AI 2002, LNAI 2557, p. 718, 2002.
© Springer-Verlag Berlin Heidelberg 2002

Selecting Semantics for Use with Semantic Pruning of Linear Deductions

Marianne Brown

School of Information Technology
James Cook University
marianne@cs.jcu.edu.au

The main problem with using semantics to guide automated theorem proving systems is the overhead involved in performing the semantic checks. When the semantics provide effective guidance, the overhead is more than offset by the reduction in the search space. This leads to the question: "What are good semantics and how can the *best* semantics be selected from a range of choices?". This paper proposes one solution based on the semantic guidance system used in the PTTP+GLiDeS theorem prover.

PTTP+GLiDeS is a model elimination (ME) based prover which uses semantic pruning to guide its search. It uses PTTP [4] as the theorem prover and MACE [3] as the model generator. The pruning is based on a strategy that can be applied to linear-input deductions (see [1], [2] for more information. A model is generated for a subset of the clauses and is used to prune the search space such that in a completed linear refutation, all centre clause literals that have resolved against input clause literals are required to be FALSE in the given model.

It is usually possible to generate a number of possible models. During experimentation, it was noted that different models sometimes produced very different results. The system requires a way of determining which model, from a set of models, would be the best choice for using with GLiDeS.

A clause set is called *semantic Horn* for a given model if when the clauses are instantiated with the model's domain elements and evaluated in that model, there is at most one TRUE literal in each clause. It can be shown that if a model of the model clauses produces a *semantic Horn set* of ground clauses for a given input clause set then PTTP+GLiDeS is refutation complete. It is suspected that PTTP+GLiDeS is incomplete otherwise. It is hypothesized that the model which produces a ground clause set closest to semantic Horn will be the better choice for using with GLiDeS.

A measure of how far from semantically Horn a set of clauses are has been developed and tested. Experiments were carried out on non-Horn problems for the TPTP Library v2.3.0 [5]. In the majority of cases where more than one model is generated, it seems to make little difference which model is used. If one model finds a solution, the rest will usually perform similarly. However in some cases, the choice of model has a dramatic effect on the end result. In these cases, the model selection criteria of selecting the model which produces a ground clause set closest to semantic Horn seems to be effective. As the evaluation of models takes little time it seems to be a worth-while exercise.

R.I. McKay and J. Slaney (Eds.): AI 2002, LNAI 2557, p. 719, 2002.
© Springer-Verlag Berlin Heidelberg 2002

Calibration of Flow and Water Quality Modeling Using Genetic Algorithm

Kwokwing Chau

Department of Civil & Structural Engineering, Hong Kong Polytechnic University,
Hunghom, Kowloon, Hong Kong
cekwchau@polyu.edu.hk

Abstract. In mathematical simulation for flow prediction and water quality management, the inappropriate use of any model parameters, which cannot be directly acquired from measurements, may introduce large errors or result in numerical instability. In this paper, the use of a genetic algorithm for determining an appropriate combination of parameter values in flow and water quality modeling is presented. The percentage error of peak value, peak time, and total volume of flow and water quality constituents are important performance measures for model prediction. The parameter calibration is based on field data of tidal as well as water quality constituents collected over five year span from 1991 to 1995 in Pearl River. Another two-year records from 1996 to 1997 are utilized to verify these parameters. Sensitivity analysis on crossover probability, mutation probability, population size, and maximum number of generations is also performed to determine the most befitting algorithm parameters. The results demonstrate that the application of genetic algorithm is able to mimic the key features of the flow and water quality process and that the calibration of models is efficient and robust.

Acknowledgement. This research was supported by the University Research Grants of Hong Kong Polytechnic University (G-T592).

References

1. Chau, K.W., Chen, W.: A Fifth Generation Numerical Modelling System in Coastal Zone. Applied Mathematical Modelling **25(10)** (2001) 887–900
2. Chau, K.W., Jiang, Y.W.: 3D Numerical Model for Pearl River Estuary. Journal of Hydraulic Engineering, ASCE **127(1)** (2001) 72–82
3. Chau, K.W., Jiang, Y.W.: Three-Dimensional Pollutant Transport Model for the Pearl River Estuary. Water Research **36(8)** (2002) 2029–2039
4. Chau, K.W., Jin, H.S.: Eutrophication Model for a Coastal Bay in Hong Kong. Journal of Environmental Engineering ASCE **124(7)** (1998) 628–638
5. Chau, K.W., Jin, H.S., Sin, Y.S.: A Finite Difference Model of Two-Dimensional Tidal Flow in Tolo Harbor, Hong Kong. Applied Mathematical Modelling **20(4)** (1996) 321–328

A Comparison of Machine Learning Approaches for the Automated Classification of Dementia

Herbert Jelinek[1], David Cornforth[1], Patricia Waley[2], Eduardo Fernandez[3] and Wayne Robinson[1].

[1] Charles Sturt University, PO Box 789, Albury NSW 2640 AUSTRALIA, tel: 02 6051 9652, fax: 02 6051 9897
{hjelinek, dcornforth, wrobinson}@csu.edu.au

[2] Centre for Education and Research on Ageing (C25)Concord Hospital, Concord NSW 2139, tel: 02 9767 6586, fax: 02 9767 8069
patw@med.usyd.edu.au

[3] Instituto de Bioingenieria, Universidad Miguel Hernández, Elche, Spain, tel: 96 5919427, fax: 965 91943
e.fernandez@umh.es

Abstract. Like many diseases, dementia is associated with a changed physical structure of diseased tissue. This study is a preliminary attempt to show that these changes are detectable using image processing, and could facilitate the automated classification of dementia subtypes. The identification of a link between different pathologies and the physical structure of tissue is potentially of great benefit to our understanding of this group of diseases. We have shown the existence of such a link by applying machine learning techniques to features derived using fractal analysis, as well as classical shape parameters.

Automated classification is a common goal of machine learning, and consists of assigning a class label to a set of measurements. Classification of unlabelled samples is preceded by a learning phase, where labeled samples are presented, and the relationship between measurements and class label is determined. A variety of statistical and machine learning methods are applicable to this kind of problem, but rely on the availability of a suitable set of measurements comprising a feature vector.

Dementia is a group of diseases of which Alzheimer's Disease (AD) is the most common, followed by Small Vessel Disease (SVD). Changes to the structure of small blood vessels in the brain have been demonstrated in both AD and SVD dementia. However, these differences are not readily apparent when viewing images obtained from these regions.

Grayscale images were obtained from prepared medical samples, comprising 18 images from the parietal (side) region, 20 images from the frontal region and 12 from the occipital (rear) region. Each image was labeled according to its pathology, i.e. Normal, AD, SVD or both AD and SVD. The branching structure of blood vessels lends itself to fractal analysis, so we calculated the. Correlation Dimension and Lacunarity for each image. These measures have not previously been applied to dementia classification.

In our first experiment, a fully crossed two fixed factor Analysis of Variance (ANOVA) was performed to test for differences between pathologies. The results of these tests found no evidence that the presence of different pathologies influenced the measures we used. One of difficulties of this type of

R.I. McKay and J. Slaney (Eds.): AI 2002, LNAI 2557, pp. 721–722, 2002.
© Springer-Verlag Berlin Heidelberg 2002

study is the scarcity of suitable images of diseased brain tissue. A larger sample size may increase the power for the ANOVAs allowing a better chance of statistically detecting an effect.

In our second experiment, automated classification was attempted using five machine learning algorithms (Nearest Neighbour, Naive Bayes, Decision Tree Induction, CMAC, and Decision Table). The classification accuracy on cross validation tests was compared to that achieved using a default classifier. These results indicate that dementia subtypes can be distinguished in samples from the parietal and frontal regions. A test to indicate only the presence or absence of disease, by grouping AD, AVD and both diseases into one class, showed increased accuracy, suggesting that such differences are feasible for these measurements.

Our results suggest that dementia subtypes can be distinguished from images of cortical tissue, as long as suitable measurements are used. We also found evidence of a difference between the structure of small blood vessels from different regions of the cortex. This has implications for understanding of the causes, pathology and treatment of these diseases. Our findings demonstrate the utility of multi-fractal analysis combined with machine learning techniques in dementia research. This has implications for the understanding of this group of diseases, as well as for the analysis of cortical images in other contexts.

A Defeasible Logic of Policy-Based Intention (Extended Abstract)

Guido Governatori[2], Vineet Padmanabhan[1], and Abdul Sattar[1]

[1] Knowledge Representation & Reasoning Unit (KRRU)
School of Information Technology
Griffith University, Gold-Coast Campus, Queensland, Australia.
{vineet,sattar}@cit.gu.edu.au
[2] School of Information Technology and Electronic Engineering
The University of Queensland, Queensland, Australia
guido@itee.uq.edu.au

Most of the theories on formalising intention interpret it as a unary modal operator in Kripkean semantics, which gives it a monotonic look. Moreover they model such an operator as a normal modal operator (i.e., it admits the necessitation rule: $\vdash A / \vdash \Box A$). This means that such intention formalisations are affected by the logical omniscience problem, which requires an agent to intend all consequences of a given intention. Logical omniscience is a well-known problem with many facets, one of them being that the epistemic state of an agent must be closed under logical theories in the classical sense. That is, it contains an infinite set of formulas, which implies that the agent must have infinite computational power.

In this paper we argue that policy-based intentions [3] exhibit non-monotonic behaviour which cannot be fully captured by monotonic modal logics. Accordingly we have to identify a non-monotonic logic appropriate to model policy-based intentions.

We believe that Defeasible Logic [2] is the right logic for this task. Many variants have been devised to capture different and incompatible aspects of non-monotonic reasoning [1]; it works on finite knowledge bases and the set of all consequences of a given knowledge base (or policy), which is finite, and can be computed in linear time [4].

Intentions are captured by means of a modal operator and the inference rules of defeasible logic are modified to deal with it. The proposed technique alleviates most of the problems related to logical omniscience.

References

1. Antoniou G., D. Billington, G. Governatori, and M.J. Maher. A flexible framework for defeasible logics. In *(AAAI-2000)*, pages 401–405. AAAI/MIT Press, 2000.
2. Antoniou G., D. Billington, G. Governatori, and M.J. Maher. Representation results for defeasible logic. *ACM Transactions on Computational Logic*, 2(2):255–287, 2001.
3. Bratman M. E. *Intentions, Plans and Practical Reason.* Harvard University Press, Cambridge, MA, 1987.
4. Michael J. Maher. Propositional defeasible logic has linear complexity. *Theory and Practice of Logic Programming*, 1(6):691–711, 2001.

R.I. McKay and J. Slaney (Eds.): AI 2002, LNAI 2557, p. 723, 2002.

A Self-Organizing Territorial Approach to Multi-robot Search and Surveillance

Toby J. Richer and Dan R. Corbett

Advanced Computing Research Centre, University of South Australia
{richer,corbett}@cs.unisa.edu.au

1 Introduction

This paper presents a control strategy for multi-robot search and surveillance. Each robot develops and maintains its own territory in searching the space. Territories are defined by a pheremone-marking system based on ant colony optimization [1].

2 Control Strategy

The search space is represented using a grid. Each grid square is marked with the ID of the robot that last marked that square, and a steadily decaying pheremone.

The robots start by marking the grid square corresponding to their initial position. The square's ID is set to the robot's ID, and the pheremone value is set to the maximum.

The robots extend their territory by wandering randomly. Each time they enter a square of their own territory, the pheremone is set to the maximum. When they enter a square that is not in their territory, the pheremone strength in that square is compared to the minimum strength in the robot's own territory. If the pheremone in that square is below the pheremone in all squares the robot has recently visited, it is marked. Whether it is marked or not, the robot turns around and selects a new direction to wander in.

3 Implementation

The system was implemented using the TeamBots simulator [2]. The behaviour of the system described in Sect. 2 was compared with a random wander. Using this control strategy, the robots built up large contiguous blocks of territory. The average time between visits of a square was lower than for random wander. This shows the robots cover the territory more evenly, and are thus better suited to surveillance tasks.

References

1. Dorigo, M., G. Di Caro, et al. (1999). "Ant algorithms for discrete optimization." Artificial Life 5(2): 137-72.
2. Balch, T. 2000 TeamBots 2.0. www.teambots.org.

R.I. McKay and J. Slaney (Eds.): AI 2002, LNAI 2557, p. 724, 2002.
© Springer-Verlag Berlin Heidelberg 2002

Knowledge-Based Techniques for Constraints Satisfaction in Resource Allocation Problems

K.A. Mohamed, A. Datta, and R. Kozera

Department of Computer Science & Software Engineering
The University of Western Australia
35 Stirling Highway,
Crawley, W.A. 6009
khaireel@graduate.uwa.edu.au, {datta, ryszard}@csse.uwa.edu.au
http://www.csse.uwa.edu.au/~datta

1 Introduction

Knowledge-based techniques are as effective as mathematical techniques for satisfying constraints in manpower resource allocation (MRA) problems. Our knowledge-based techniques allow direct implementation for logical reasoning, reduce efforts in setting up and interpreting rules of constraints, fair well in giving correct solutions, and are adaptable to human rules. This class of problems arises in the management of manpower for organisations that provide round-the-clock services, requiring special expertise and experience to ensure that resultant rosters optimally match the skills of the available manpower resources to the various conditions and requisites of the deployment posts.

2 Structuring Constraints for Interpretation

We can define the MRA problem with a given set of manpower resources R, each of whom has zero or more skills, and is identified by their distinctive ranks of seniority. Let u denote a set of skills, and v a set of ranks. Let $R[u \cup v]$ represent the set of resources with skills u and rank v. There is also a set of deployment posts $P[s \cup v]$, each of which has one distinct requirement s, and a range of possible ranks for accommodation v. Here, both R and P are represented as unique binary strains, as information placements for use in the algorithm.

3 The MRA Algorithm Approach

The entire approach is based on the principles of the *Dynamic Allocation* (DA) algorithm, where matrices are defined to have the rows and columns information, R and P, to coincide with the positioning of the binary strain information described above. The DA algorithm performs the necessary feasibility checks, solves the rostering constraints, and generates a feasible solution. The incorporation of the binary strains expedites the process by naturally describing the rostering constraints, and allowing local and global improvement procedures to be made via additional methods applied into the DA algorithm. Using this approach, all our experimental simulations ended with all candidate resources allocated a post, taking fewer than 20 iterations to complete.

R.I. McKay and J. Slaney (Eds.): AI 2002, LNAI 2557, p. 725, 2002.

Effective SAT Planning by Speculative Computation*

Hidetomo Nabeshima[1], Koji Iwanuma[1], and Katsumi Inoue[2]

[1] Yamanashi University, 4-3-11 Takeda, Kofu-shi 400-8511, Japan
{nabesima,iwanuma}@iw.media.yamanashi.ac.jp
[2] Kobe University, Rokkodai-cho, Nada-ku, Kobe 657-8501, Japan
inoue@eedept.kobe-u.ac.jp

In recent years, *SAT planning* has been studied actively. In this paper, we propose a new method, called *speculative computation*, for accelerating the SAT planning. A SAT planner firstly translates a planning problem into the boolean satisfiability (SAT) problem, and secondly solves it by a general-purpose SAT solver. Blackbox [1], which is one of the fastest planning systems in the world, is based on this approach. Given a planning problem, Blackbox performs the following; (i) assumes that the plan length is i (initially, $i = 1$), (ii) translates the planning problem into a SAT problem P_i, and (iii) solves P_i. If P_i is found to be satisfiable, the Blackbox extracts a plan of length i from the truth assignment satisfying P_i. When P_i is unsatisfiable, the planner increases the plan length to be $i + 1$, and returns to (i).

Blackbox consecutively generates $P_1, P_2, P_3, \cdots$, and halts when it encounters a satisfiable problem P_k. Notice that each P_i can be constructed independently, regardless of the satisfiability of others P_j. The new method, called *speculative computation*, uses this individuality, and performs a parallel/concurrent computation. More concretely speaking, given n different processors (or threads), the proposed method starts to simultaneously solve the first n problems $P_1, \cdots, P_n$ in a parallel/concurrent manner. Every time a certain problem P_i is found to be unsatisfiable, then the planner selects a remaining unsolved problem P_j in a successive manner, and invokes a new process/thread of solving P_j. When a certain problem P_h is found to be satisfiable, we halt all SAT solvers and outputs a plan obtained from P_h. If P_h contains the shortest plan, then the immediate predecessor P_{h-1} must be unsatisfiable. Moreover, in general, P_{h-1} is often the most difficult task, among $P_1, \ldots P_h$, for checking its satisfiability. Since the predecessor P_{i-1} should be invoked in advance, we should save a huge amount of computation time if we abandon such a difficult task P_{i-1} halfway. Conversely speaking, the speculative computation can produce at least a semi-optimal plan, i.e., an almost shortest plan, in most cases.

The experimental results of 14 benchmark problems show that a speculative SAT planner using parallel computation with two processors is 181% faster than the one with single processor. Moreover the speculative planner using two con-

---

* This research is partially supported by Grant-in-Aid from The Ministry of Education, Science and Culture of Japan.

R.I. McKay and J. Slaney (Eds.): AI 2002, LNAI 2557, pp. 726–727, 2002.
© Springer-Verlag Berlin Heidelberg 2002

current threads in a single processor still achieves 123% faster computation as the average. Furthermore, the super-linear speedup often appears.

References

[1] Kautz, H., Selman, B.: BLACKBOX: A new approach to the application of theorem proving to problem solving. In: AIPS98 Workshop on Planning as Combinatorial Search. (1998) 58–60

Author Index

Lecture Notes in Artificial Intelligence (LNAI)

Lecture Notes in Computer Science